Government and Politics in the Lone Star State

Twelfth Edition

L. Tucker Gibson, Jr.
Professor Emeritus, Trinity University

Clay Robison
Houston Chronicle, Retired

Joanne Connor Green
Professor of Political Science, Texas Christian University

Content Management: Pam Chirls
Content Production: Tina Gagliostro, Heather Pagano, Rob DeGeorge
Product Management: Amy Wetzel
Product Marketing: Rachele Strober
Rights and Permissions: Ben Ferrini

Please contact https://support.pearson.com/getsupport/s/ with any queries on this content

Cover image by Anton Balazh/Shutterstock

Copyright © 2022, 2020, 2018 by Pearson Education, Inc. or its affiliates, 221 River Street, Hoboken, NJ 07030. All Rights Reserved. Manufactured in the United States of America. This publication is protected by copyright, and permission should be obtained from the publisher prior to any prohibited reproduction, storage in a retrieval system, or transmission in any form or by any means, electronic, mechanical, photocopying, recording, or otherwise. For information regarding permissions, request forms, and the appropriate contacts within the Pearson Education Global Rights and Permissions department, please visit www.pearsoned.com/permissions/.

Acknowledgments of third-party content appear on the appropriate pages within the text, which constitute an extension of this copyright page.

PEARSON, ALWAYS LEARNING, and REVEL are exclusive trademarks owned by Pearson Education, Inc. or its affiliates in the U.S. and/or other countries.

Unless otherwise indicated herein, any third-party trademarks, logos, or icons that may appear in this work are the property of their respective owners, and any references to third-party trademarks, logos, icons, or other trade dress are for demonstrative or descriptive purposes only. Such references are not intended to imply any sponsorship, endorsement, authorization, or promotion of Pearson's products by the owners of such marks, or any relationship between the owner and Pearson Education, Inc., or its affiliates, authors, licensees, or distributors.

Library of Congress Cataloging-in-Publication Data

Names: Gibson, L. Tucker, author. | Robison, Clay, author. |
  Green, Joanne Connor, author.
Title: Government and politics in the Lone Star state /
  L. Tucker Gibson, Clay Robison, Joanne Connor Green.
Description: Twelfth edition. | New York, NY: Pearson, 2022. |
  Includes bibliographical references and index.
Identifiers: LCCN 2020054887 (print) | LCCN 2020054888 (ebook) |
  ISBN 9780136902249 (Paper) | ISBN 9780136902461 (epub)
Subjects: LCSH: Texas—Politics and government—1951-
Classification: LCC JK4816 .G53 2022 (print) | LCC JK4816 (ebook) | DDC 320.4764—dc23
  LC record available at https://lccn.loc.gov/2020054887
  LC ebook record available at https://lccn.loc.gov/2020054888

2 2022

Access Code Card:
ISBN-10:   0-13-690202-2
ISBN-13: 978-0-13-690202-7

Rental:
ISBN-10:   0-13-690224-3
ISBN-13: 978-0-13-690224-9

Brief Contents

1	The Social and Economic Environment of Texas Politics	1
2	The Texas Constitution	33
3	Texas Government and Politics in the Federal System	58
4	Local Government in Texas	98
5	The Texas Legislature	136
6	The Texas Executive	177
7	The Texas Bureaucracy and Policy Implementation	216
8	The Judicial System in Texas	237
9	Political Socialization, Political Behavior, and Public Opinion	271
10	The Party System in Texas	307
11	Elections, Campaigns, and Voting in Texas	338
12	The Mass Media in Texas Politics	378
13	Interest Groups and Political Power in Texas	412
14	Contemporary Public Policy Issues in Texas	440

Contents

Preface ... x
About Your Authors ... xx

1 The Social and Economic Environment of Texas Politics ... 1

Challenges of the Twenty-First Century ... 4
The Myths of Texas's Political Culture ... 6
    The Sources of Texas's Political Myths ... 6
    Changing Political Myths ... 7
The Political Culture of Texas ... 8
    The Individualistic Subculture ... 9
    The Moralistic Subculture ... 10
    The Traditionalistic Subculture ... 10
The People of Texas ... 10
    Native Americans ... 10
    Hispanics ... 11
    African Americans ... 13
    Anglos ... 13
    Asian Americans ... 15
    Politics, Race, and Ethnicity ... 15
Growth and Changing Demographics ... 17
    Population Growth ... 17
    The Aging Population ... 19
    Urban Texas ... 19
    Wealth and Income Distribution ... 22
    Education and Literacy ... 23
    The Size and Geographic Diversity of Texas ... 24
    The Economy of Texas ... 25
    Economic Regions of Texas ... 27
        HIGH PLAINS REGION 28 • SOUTH TEXAS BORDER REGION 29 • UPPER EAST TEXAS REGION 29
Conclusion ... **30**
    Review the Chapter 31 • Learn the Terms 32

2 The Texas Constitution ... 33

Constitutionalism ... 35
The Constitutional Legacy ... 38
    The Constitution of *Coahuila y Tejas* (1827) ... 38
    The Constitution of the Republic of Texas (1836) ... 39
    The Constitution of 1845 ... 40
    The Civil War Constitution (1861) ... 41
    The Constitution of 1866 ... 41
    The Constitution of Reconstruction (1869) ... 42
The Constitution of 1876 ... 43
    General Principles of the Texas Constitution ... 45
    The Three Branches of Texas Government ... 45
        LEGISLATIVE BRANCH 45 • EXECUTIVE BRANCH 46 • JUDICIAL BRANCH 47
    Weaknesses and Criticisms of the Current Constitution ... 47
        PUBLIC EDUCATION 47 • BUDGETING AND FINANCES 47 • INDIVIDUAL RIGHTS 47 • EXCESSIVE DETAILS 48 • THE AMENDMENT PROCESS 48
Constitutional Change and Adaptation ... 49
    Amendments ... 49
    Constitutional Convention ... 50
    The Constitutional Reform Efforts of 1971 to 1975 ... 50
    Further Piecemeal Reforms ... 52
    Constitutional Provisions, Interest Groups, and Elites ... 52
Conclusion ... **54**
    Review the Chapter 56 • Learn the Terms 57

3 Texas Government and Politics in the Federal System ... 58

Structuring Regional and National Interests ... 61
    Federal-State Relationships in a Comparative Context ... 62
    Defining Federalism in the United States ... 63
    Federal-State Relationships from a Constitutional Perspective ... 64
    Relationships among the States ... 65
Changing Patterns in Federal Relationships ... 67
    Metaphors for Federalism ... 67
    State-Centered and Dual Federalism ... 68
    Cooperative Federalism ... 69
    Centralized Federalism ... 71
    The Multiple Phases of New Federalism ... 71
        REPUBLICAN OPPOSITION (PRESIDENTS NIXON, REAGAN, AND H.W. BUSH) 72 • THE CLINTON YEARS (1993–2001) 73 • THE BUSH II YEARS (2001–2009) 74 • THE OBAMA YEARS (2009–2017) 75 • THE TRUMP YEARS (2017–2021) 76
    The Role of the U.S. Supreme Court in Defining Federalism ... 78
The Impact of Federalism on State Finances ... 80
    Changing Sources of State Budgets and Federal Grants ... 81
    Reactions to the Expanded Role of the Federal Government ... 82
    Mandates Meet State Agencies and Local Communities ... 82
Transnational Regionalism ... 83
    Maquiladoras ... 84
    The United States–Mexico–Canada Agreement ... 85
        CONCERNS ABOUT NAFTA 86 • CHANGES UNDER USMCA 86 • TRADE PATTERNS BETWEEN TEXAS AND MEXICO 86

Immigration	87
FEDERAL GOVERNMENT LAWS AND POLICIES 87 • STATE ACTIONS 92	
Border Drug Violence	93
Common Borders, Common Problems	94
Conclusion	**95**
Review the Chapter 96 • Learn the Terms 97	

4 Local Government in Texas — 98

Urban Texas	100
Cities in the State's Formative Period	101
General Features of Contemporary Texas Cities	101
The Legal and Constitutional Framework for Texas Cities	103
General Law and Home Rule Cities	104
Forms of City Government	105
MAYOR-COUNCIL 105 • CITY COMMISSION 106 • COUNCIL-MANAGER 107	
Municipal Election Systems	110
NONPARTISAN CITY ELECTIONS 111 • AT-LARGE ELECTIONS 111 • SINGLE-MEMBER DISTRICTS 111 • LEGAL ATTACKS ON AT-LARGE ELECTIONS 112	
City Revenues and Expenditures	112
Urban Problems	114
GRAYING OF TEXAS CITIES 114 • "WHITE FLIGHT" AND GENTRIFICATION 114 • DECLINING INFRASTRUCTURES 115 • CRIME AND URBAN VIOLENCE 115 • STATE- AND FEDERAL-MANDATED PROGRAMS 116 • ENVIRONMENTAL ISSUES 116 • PUBLIC EMPLOYMENT 116	
County Government in Texas	117
The Diversity of Counties	117
The Structure of County Government	117
COMMISSIONERS COURT AND COUNTY JUDGE 117 • COUNTY CLERK 120 • DISTRICT CLERK 121 • COUNTY AND DISTRICT ATTORNEYS 121 • TAX ASSESSOR–COLLECTOR 121 • COUNTY LAW ENFORCEMENT 121 • COUNTY AUDITOR 122 • COUNTY TREASURER 122	
Criticisms of County Government	122
Special Districts in Texas	123
Functions and Structures of Special Districts	124
Consequences of Special-Purpose Districts	125
Independent School Districts	125
Inequities in the Public Education System	126
Differences among School Districts	126
Local School Governance	128
Solutions to the Problems of Local Government	128
Privatization of Functions	129
Annexation and Extraterritorial Jurisdiction	129
Modernization of County Government	130
Economic Development	130
Interlocal Contracting	131
Metro Government and Consolidation	131
Public Improvement Districts	132
Conclusion	**132**
Review the Chapter 133 • Learn the Terms 135	

5 The Texas Legislature — 136

Legislative Functions	137
Enacting Laws	139
Budgeting and Taxes	139
Overseeing State Agencies	139
Educating the Public	139
Representing the Public	139
Organization of the Texas Legislature and Characteristics of Members	139
Legislative Sessions	140
Terms of Office and Qualifications	141
Pay and Compensation	141
Legislative Meeting Facilities	142
Membership	143
Legislative Careers	144
Legislative Turnover	144
Representation and Redistricting	144
Federal Courts Order Equality in Redistricting	146
Contemporary Redistricting Battles	147
Legislative Leaders and Committees	149
Legislative Leadership	149
HOUSE LEADERSHIP 149 • SENATE LEADERSHIP 151	
Control over the Legislative Process	156
The Committee System	156
STANDING COMMITTEES 158 • CONFERENCE COMMITTEES 159 • SELECT COMMITTEES 159	
Legislative Staff	160
Rules and the Lawmaking Process	160
The Lawmaking Process	160
Procedural Obstacles to Legislation	162
Shortcuts and Confusion	163
Legislative Norms	164
The Emerging Party System	166
The Growth of Partisanship	166
Republicans Take Control	167
Other Legislative Caucuses	168
Legislative Behavior	168
Legislators and Their Constituents	168
Legislative Decision Making	169
Legislative Styles	171
Legislative Ethics and Reform	171
THE SHARPSTOWN SCANDAL 171 • SENATORS GET CHECKS; SPEAKER GETS INDICTED 172 • THE TEXAS ETHICS COMMISSION IS BORN 173 • ETHICS IN THE CONTEMPORARY ERA 173	
Conclusion	**174**
Review the Chapter 175 • Learn the Terms 176	

6 The Texas Executive — 177

A Historical Perspective on the Executive Function in Texas	180
The Constitutional Framework for the Plural Executive	181
The Potential for Conflict in the Plural Executive	182

Historical Overview of the Men and Women Who Have Served as Governor	183
Qualifications and Backgrounds of Texas Governors	184
Impeachment and Incapacitation	186
The Salary and "Perks" of the Governor's Office	186
The Powers of the Governor	186
Legislative Powers	188
Budgetary Powers	190
Appointive Powers	190
Judicial Powers	192
Military Powers	192
Informal Resources of the Governor	192
The Governor's Staff	193
The Governor and the Mass Media	195
The Governor and the Political Party	195
The Governor and Interest Groups	196
Leadership Styles of Recent Texas Governors	196
Ann Richards (1991–1995)	197
George W. Bush (1995–2000)	198
Rick Perry (2000–2015)	200
Greg Abbott (2015–)	203
Other Offices of the Plural Executive	205
Lieutenant Governor	206
Attorney General	206
Comptroller of Public Accounts	208
Commissioner of the General Land Office	209
Commissioner of Agriculture	209
Secretary of State	210
Elected Boards and Commissions	210
TEXAS RAILROAD COMMISSION 210 • STATE BOARD OF EDUCATION 212	
Conclusion	**212**
Review the Chapter 214 • Learn the Terms 215	

7 The Texas Bureaucracy and Policy Implementation — 216

Bureaucratic Systems in Texas	218
The Characteristics of the Texas Bureaucracy	218
Replacing an Aging Workforce	220
An Expanding Government Workforce	220
Privatization of Public Services	222
Bureaucrats and Public Policy	223
Policy Implementation	223
Obstacles to Policy Implementation	224
State Regulatory Functions	224
Appointment to State Agencies	225
Legislative Control of the Bureaucracy	227
Legislative Budgetary Control	227
Performance Reviews	227
Sunset Legislation	228
The Revolving Door	229
Whistle-Blower Provisions	229
Texas Citizens and the Bureaucracy	231
Merit Systems and Professional Management	232
Conclusion	**234**
Review the Chapter 235 • Learn the Terms 236	

8 The Judicial System in Texas — 237

The Structure of the Texas Court System	239
Texas in the Federal Court System	239
Criminal and Civil Procedure	239
Five Levels of Courts	240
MUNICIPAL AND JUSTICE OF THE PEACE COURTS 242 • COUNTY-LEVEL COURTS 242 • DISTRICT COURTS 243 • COURTS OF APPEALS 244 • SUPREME COURT AND COURT OF CRIMINAL APPEALS 245	
Participants and Procedures in the Judicial System	246
Texas Judges	246
Prosecuting Attorneys and Clerks	246
The Jury Systems	247
THE GRAND JURY 247 • THE PETIT JURY 247	
Judicial Procedures and Decision Making	247
TRIAL COURTS 248 • APPELLATE COURTS 249	
Changing the Face of the Judiciary	249
Minorities	250
Women	252
Judicial Controversies and the Search for Solutions	253
Judicial Activism	253
Campaign Contributions and Republican Gains	254
Legislative Reaction to Judicial Activism	255
Winners and Losers—A New Era of Judicial Activism?	256
Searching for Solutions	258
Crime and Punishment	259
Rights of Suspects	259
Punishment of Criminals	260
The Politics of Criminal Justice	261
Slamming the Courthouse Door on a Last-Gasp Appeal	262
Criminal Injustices	263
Increased Policy Role of the State Courts	264
The Courts and Education	265
The Courts and Environmental Policies	266
WATER RIGHTS 266 • OPEN BEACHES 266 • PLASTIC BAGS 267	
The Courts and Abortion Rights	267
The Courts and Voting	267
Conclusion	**268**
Review the Chapter 269 • Learn the Terms 270	

9 Political Socialization, Political Behavior, and Public Opinion — 271

Opinion and Core Values	273
Role of Public Opinion in Democratic Governments and Societies	273
Stability of Key Values	274
Formation of Political Values and Opinions	276

Political Ideology	276
Political Socialization	278
Agents of Socialization	278
FAMILY 279 • SCHOOLS 280 • PEERS AND COMMUNITY 281 • MEDIA 282 • RELIGION 282 • EVENTS 283	
Group Membership and Public Opinion	283
Political Party and Public Opinion	284
Gender and Public Opinion	285
Race, Ethnicity, and Public Opinion	286
Education and Public Opinion	288
Religion and Public Opinion	288
Age and Public Opinion	290
Political Participation	290
Voting Patterns	292
NONVOTING 296	
How Texans Voted in Recent Elections	297
VOTING BY KEY DEMOGRAPHICS 298 • THE LOOMING HISPANIC VOTE 298	
Public Opinion Polling	299
Survey Research	300
Controversies Surrounding Polls	302
Conclusion	**304**
Review the Chapter 305 • Learn the Terms 306	

10 The Party System in Texas — 307

Political Parties and a Democratic Society	308
What Are Political Parties?	309
Parties versus Interest Groups	309
Two-Party System	310
Third Parties in Texas	311
The Functions of Political Parties	313
Recruit and Nominate Candidates	313
Contest Elections and Mobilize Voters	314
Organize and Manage the Government	314
Mediate the Effects of Separation of Powers	315
Provide Accountability	316
Manage Conflict and Find Common Interests	316
Set the Policy Agenda	316
The Party in the Electorate	317
One-Party Democratic Politics	317
Factionalism in the Democratic Party	318
Modified One-Party Democratic Politics	319
Two-Party Politics in Texas	322
Republican Dominance	324
Changing Party Identification	325
Differences between Traditional Republicans, Tea Party Republicans, and Democrats	327
Party Realignment, Dealignment, or Revitalization?	328
The Party Organization	330
The Permanent Organizations	330
PRECINCT CHAIR 330 • COUNTY EXECUTIVE COMMITTEE AND COUNTY CHAIR 330 • STATE EXECUTIVE COMMITTEE, CHAIR, AND VICE CHAIR 331	
The Temporary Organizations: The Party Conventions	331
THE PRECINCT, COUNTY, AND SENATORIAL CONVENTIONS 331 • STATE CONVENTIONS 332	
The Party Activists	333
The Party in Government	334
Conclusion	**335**
Review the Chapter 336 • Learn the Terms 337	

11 Elections, Campaigns, and Voting in Texas — 338

The Functions of Elections	340
State and Local Elections	341
Election Cycles	341
Primary Elections	342
General Elections	346
City, School Board, and Single-Purpose Districts	346
Special Elections	347
Extended Absentee Balloting	347
Straight-Ticket Voting	349
Ballot Security	350
Political Suffrage in Texas: A Struggle for Mass Suffrage	350
The Poll Tax	351
The White Primary	352
Restrictive Registration Law	352
Property Ownership and the Right to Vote	352
Women and the Right to Vote	353
Extension of the Vote to Those 18 Years of Age and Older	353
Other Discriminatory Aspects of Election Systems	353
The Voting Rights Act	354
Motor Voter Registration	355
Facilitating Voter Participation	355
Contemporary Restrictions on Voting	356
Political Gains by Minorities and Women	357
HISPANICS 358 • AFRICAN AMERICANS 358 • WOMEN 359	
Campaign Technology	360
Social Media and Public Opinion Polling	361
Segmentation and Targeting of the Electorate	364
Grassroots	365
Media and Advertising	366
Controlled Media	366
Uncontrolled Media	368
Direct Mail and Online Fund-Raising	369
Money and Campaigns	369
Campaign Costs and Fund-Raising	370
PACs, Fat Cats, and the Really Big Money	372
Why People Contribute to Campaigns	374
Attempts at Reform	374
Conclusion	**375**
Review the Chapter 376 • Learn the Terms 377	

12 The Mass Media in Texas Politics — 378

The Mass Media and the Policy Agenda	380
Media Influence on Public Opinion and Policy	382
Guardians of Open Government	383

News Media and the Electoral Process 384
   Covering the "Horse Race" 385
   Television and Digital Advertising 385
   Media Coverage of Recent Statewide Races in Texas 386
      2014: STRONG DIFFERENCES 387 • 2010: PERRY IS UNTOUCHABLE 388 • 2002: CAMPAIGNING IN THE MUD 388
   The 2012 and 2018 U.S. Senate Races: Grass Roots and "Betomania" 389
The Early Development of the Media in Texas 390
   Frontier Newspapers 390
   Newspapers and "The Establishment" 391
   The Evolution of Texas Newspapers 391
Current News Media Trends 393
   Modern Newspapers, Modern Problems 394
   Electronic Media 395
   Growing Media Conglomerates 396
   The Capitol Press Corps 399
   Governmental Public Relations 400
   Twitter Nation: The Role of Social Media and "Citizen Journalism" 401
   Fake News and the Abuse of Social Media 403
How Well Informed Are Texas Citizens? 405
   Media Literacy: Becoming an Informed Consumer 405
   Public Confidence and Media Bias 407
Conclusion **410**
   Review the Chapter 410 • Learn the Terms 411

13 Interest Groups and Political Power in Texas 412

What Are Interest Groups? 414
   Roles and Functions of Interest Groups 415
   Role in Democracies 416
   Who Joins Political Groups? 416
   Why Do People Join Interest Groups? 417
Interest Group Theory 418
   Pluralism and Democratic Theory 418
   The Elitist Alternative 420
   Hyperpluralism, Policy Subsystems, and Single-Issue Interest Groups 421
Interest Groups and the Policymaking Process 423
   Direct Lobbying 424
      DRAFTING LEGISLATION 424 • PLANNING AND IMPLEMENTING A LEGISLATIVE STRATEGY 424 • PERSONAL CONTACTS AND COMMUNICATIONS 424 • TESTIFYING AT HEARINGS 425 • PUBLIC OPINION OF LOBBYING 426
   Indirect Lobbying 427
      ELECTORAL ACTIVITIES 427 • PUBLIC OPINION 428 • PROTESTS AND MARCHES 430
Dominant Interest Groups in Texas 430
   Business 431
   Professional Groups 431
   Labor 431
   Public Interest Groups 432
   Education 432
   Minorities 432
   Agricultural Groups 433
   Religious Groups 434
   Local Governments 434
Resources and Power of Interest Groups 435
   Who Are the Lobbyists? 436
Conclusion **437**
   Review the Chapter 438 • Learn the Terms 439

14 Contemporary Public Policy Issues in Texas 440

The Policy Process 441
   The Elements of Public Policy 441
   The Stages of the Policy Process 442
      IDENTIFICATION AND FORMATION OF AN ISSUE 443 • ACCESS AND REPRESENTATION 443 • FORMULATION 443 • ADOPTION OR LEGITIMATION 444 • IMPLEMENTATION 444 • EVALUATION 445
   Iron Triangles and Issue Networks 445
The State Budget 446
   Two-Year Budgets 447
   Dedicated Funds 448
State Taxes 449
   A Regressive Tax System 449
      SALES TAX 449 • FRANCHISE, OR MARGINS, TAX 450 • PROPERTY TAX 450 • SEVERANCE TAX 450 • OTHER TAXES AND FEES 450
   Gambling on New Revenue 451
   Bonds: Build Now, Pay More Later 452
   The Income Tax: An Unpopular Alternative to a Regressive Tax System 452
Educational Policies and Politics 453
   Public Education: A Struggle for Equity and Quality 454
   Persistence of Funding Problems 455
   Other Issues Affecting the Public Schools 457
      TEACHER PAY, WORKING CONDITIONS, AND MORALE 457 • STUDENT TESTING AND "ACCOUNTABILITY" 457 • SPECIAL EDUCATION 458 • CHARTER SCHOOLS 458 • PRIVATE SCHOOL VOUCHERS 458
   Higher Education: Another Quest for Excellence and Equity 459
   A Struggle over Affirmative Action in Higher Education 460
   Tuition Issues 462
   Guns on Campus 463
   Keeping Campuses Safe 464
Criminal Justice 465
   Reforms Prompted by Crowded Prisons 465
   The Death Penalty in Texas: Popular and Controversial 466
      RISK OF EXECUTING THE INNOCENT 467 • INTELLECTUALLY DISABLED CONVICTS 467

Health and Human Services	468
The Struggle of Many Texans for Health Care	468
Controversy over Abortion and Women's Health Care	470
CONTROVERSY OVER PLANNED PARENTHOOD 470 • NEW ABORTION RESTRICTIONS 471	
Environmental Problems and Policies	472
Dirty Air	472
Global Warming	473
An Endangered Water Supply	475
WATER DEVELOPMENT AND CONSERVATION 475 • SUBSIDENCE 475	
Oil Field Pollution Risks	476
Transportation in Texas	476
Texas Traffic Exhausting Tax Revenue	478
Building Highways and Toll Roads with Plastic	478
Mass Transit Offers Limited Relief	480
Conclusion	**480**
Review the Chapter 481 • Learn the Terms 483	
Appendices	484
Glossary	498
Notes	506
Index	536

Preface

In this twelfth edition of *Government and Politics in the Lone Star State*, we discuss the impact of the COVID-19 pandemic on Texas citizens and institutions and the state's response, cover the 2020 election results, and provide extensive updates on major policy issues. As in previous editions, we continue to emphasize the institutions and decision-making processes of state and local governments and how they reflect the values and interests of Texas citizens. We try to explain why citizens and officeholders pursue specific policy priorities and why they choose certain options over others. We also continue to describe and analyze Texas government and politics from multiple perspectives – that of political scientists who have taught a variety of courses in national, state, and local politics; that of a journalist who has covered state Capitol politics for almost forty years; and that of a consultant who has worked with local governments in redrawing political boundaries for elected officials.

We incorporate general theories of political science into each chapter to provide a conceptual framework for the reader. For example, the chapter on political parties draws from research on party realignment and explains how Texas politics have been transformed from one-party Democratic control to the current period of Republican dominance. The issues raised by this theory continue to be relevant to the much-discussed prospects of changing demographics eventually contributing to a resurgence of the Democratic Party. Democrats hold most of the state judgeships and other elected offices in several of the state's urban counties. But a major Democratic push in 2020 to regain the party's first majority in the Texas House of Representatives in almost twenty years failed, and state government remains solidly in Republican control. The chapter on the legislature draws from the concept of institutionalization, addressing changes that occurred as the legislature adapted to a more complex political environment. Although the theoretical aspects of the narrative's analysis are critical building blocks, we also use anecdotes to focus on how the theory plays out in current political events and policy decisions.

Tucker Gibson and Clay Robison have collaborated since 1991 on some thirty texts on Texas government and politics, including previous editions of this book. They were joined in 2013 by Joanne Connor Green of the Department of Political Science at Texas Christian University. She has contributed to an expanded treatment of the mass media in Texas, political socialization, public opinion, political behavior, gender politics, and federalism. In addition to her teaching and research interests in several subfields of political science, Dr. Green has given considerable attention to effective teaching and has collaborated on a publication about how "teaching matters."

In this twelfth edition, we once again attempt to guide readers through the historical, economic, demographic, and political environment that has made Texas government and political culture what it is. We also explain Texas's governmental institutions, their functions, the players who influence them, and how these factors compare to governmental institutions and politics in other states. Our updates in major policy areas reflect political and policy priorities that will continue to evolve as Texas's demographic and political cultures continue to change. Our goal is to help readers learn how to navigate their government and political system, to be informed voters, to learn about the core values underlying the contemporary political debate, and, if they wish, to become active participants in the dynamic policymaking process.

We are passionately committed to democracy and, although we may sound skeptical at times, have not lost faith in Texas citizens. Some argue that the core values of democracy are under attack in this country as well as around the world. A rigorous assessment of these purported threats is required of each generation to "secure the blessings of liberty." Democracy is predicated not only on the right but also on the obligation of citizens to participate in a wide range of political activities. Our passion for democracy leads us to call for open, transparent government; public access to information about the actions of public officials; informed and civil discourse that recognizes intense differences of political opinions; renewed interest and commitment to the Bill of Rights; and the accountability of public officeholders.

The twelfth edition of *Government and Politics in the Lone Star State* includes the same pedagogical features students currently enjoy in traditional American Government textbooks. Students who have completed the 2305 course will find this material extending their learning experience seamlessly into 2306. In addition to revisions that cover recent changes in the political landscape and public policy, demographic data and other factual information have been updated throughout the book.

This new edition includes the authors' efforts to present the impact of the COVID-19 pandemic on the state, its people, and its institutions. We do not presume to have a complete understanding of the pandemic's long-term implications, but in several chapters we have included information about the health emergency that we consider relevant to state government and its leaders as well as public opinion and political behavior. Economic losses and inequities, and access to health care are among long-term issues that seem to have been exacerbated by the pandemic.

Although systemic racism and economic inequality have long been part of this book's narrative on our state's political culture, we give it more emphasis in this edition, focusing on the protests and other reactions that followed the death of George Floyd, an unarmed African American man and former Houston resident, in police custody in Minneapolis.

In previous editions, we have discussed party realignment in Texas, when the state shifted from a one-party Democratic state to Republican domination. In this new edition, we discuss evidence of changing party affiliations that signal another potential realignment, although, judging from the 2020 election results, not likely in the immediate future. We discuss the 2020 election returns and also address the increasing partisanship in Texas, including sharp differences over policy between Democratic leaders in major Texas cities and Republican officials in the state Capitol.

The new edition discusses changes in public opinion, political ideology, policy preferences, party identification, and political participation, drawing on survey research conducted by a number of well-respected research groups.

We wrote several new chapter opening stories and updated others to reflect recent public events and changing patterns in public policy.

Features

We are committed to helping readers move beyond learning about government and politics to "doing politics." We believe in civic education and political participation. We also recognize that most students who read this text will not become political scientists or elected officeholders. Nevertheless, we firmly believe that informed citizenship is the only way individuals can exercise some control or influence over those who make political or policy decisions.

Therefore, this book is written to help students navigate their way through the political process—from dealing with bureaucrats at City Hall, to carrying out their responsibilities as jurors, to weighing their choices when voting for elected officials up and down the ballot. We provide a historical perspective to help readers understand the evolving heritage that has shaped contemporary political issues and help them anticipate and influence future changes that will occur in their lifetimes.

To provide greater focus and direct the reader to think about the core themes of each chapter, we have structured our analysis around learning objectives, and then structured the chapter summaries and conclusions around these learning objectives. Thus, the structure of the text includes:

- **Learning objectives** tied to the major headings in every chapter that identify the key concepts students should know and understand with respect to Texas politics and government, and which also structure the end-of-chapter summaries.
- **"Review the Chapter"** sections organized around the learning objectives that summarize and highlight the most important concepts covered in each chapter.
- A **running marginal glossary** that clearly defines bolded key terms for students at the points in the chapters where the terms are discussed.
- A **fully updated art and photo program** that provides a friendly and accessible reading experience, whether in print or online.

Here is a summary of the content covered in each chapter of this twelfth edition:

- **Chapter 1** focuses on the political culture of Texas. It draws, in part, from the formative ideas of Alexis de Tocqueville and the scholarship of Daniel Elazar. It attempts to explain the conservative patterns in Texas politics and what some scholars refer to as "Texas exceptionalism." Early migration and settlement patterns shaped the state's political culture, and throughout Texas history, race and ethnicity have played a major role in state politics. Drawing on recent U.S. censuses and *American Community Surveys*, this chapter describes the economic and social attributes of the main ethnic and racial groups living in Texas and links these demographic factors to contemporary politics and public policy discussions that follow in later chapters. In the twelfth edition, we have a new opening story to emphasize the social and economic impact of the COVID-19 pandemic and loss of food security for thousands of Texans. We also take a closer look at systemic racism in Texas, focusing on reactions to the death of George Floyd, a former Texan, while in police custody in Minneapolis. And we take a closer look at the violent and racist history of the iconic Texas Rangers.

- **Chapter 2** presents a brief summary of the state's constitutional history and discusses how Texas's earlier constitutions influenced the current document, the Constitution of 1876. Texas functioned under a Mexican constitution prior to independence, but its later constitutions drew primarily from the general tradition of American constitutionalism. The chapter outlines the main provisions of the Constitution of 1876 and the restrictions it imposes on state government. It also discusses similarities and differences among state constitutions and the U.S. Constitution. This edition has a new opening story about the adoption of a new constitutional amendment to strengthen the ban against a state income tax, illustrating the basic fiscal conservatism of Texas, and we update the total number of amendments to the Texas Constitution.

- **Chapter 3** places the government and politics of Texas within the nation's federal framework. This chapter explores the state's changing relationship with the national government, its dependency on federal funds, and elements of interstate relationships, as well as the unitary relationship between state and local governments. It also discusses Texas's relationship and interdependency with Mexico and implications on the Texas economy of any potential changes in trade relations with Mexico. This edition has a new opening story and is updated with the impact of President Trump's policies on federalism, including a discussion of the pandemic and urban unrest. We also include updated information on the Supreme Court's decisions on federalism. We update immigration policy under Trump, including the effect on the Deferred Action for Childhood Arrivals (DACA) program, and we have a new section on the United States-Mexico-Canada Agreement.

- **Chapter 4** focuses on local governments, including counties, cities, and special districts. The state creates local governments and defines most of their powers and functions, and some recent legislation has placed additional constraints on local governments. In many respects, local governments have developed without a statewide or comprehensive perspective on how they should interact or coordinate public services in urban and suburban areas. There is no one state agency that has oversight of the actions of local governments. Consequently, some local governments have overlapping or possibly competing jurisdictions. In other instances, special districts have been created to serve narrowly defined objectives when no other government was available. This twelfth edition updates the demographic characteristics of Texas's ten largest cities and updates the expanding efforts of Republican state leaders to restrict the policy autonomy of local governments.

- **Chapter 5** covers the Texas Legislature, a part-time institution that meets regularly for only five months every two years and has the primary responsibility of enacting public policy and appropriating the billions of dollars that go into each biennial budget. The chapter describes a more complex institution than that which existed forty years ago. Although now using computer-age technology, the legislature still operates within the restrictions that were written into the state constitution in the nineteenth century. And, while many other industrialized states developed complex party structures within their legislatures, voting alignments in the Texas legislature historically were based more on ideology than on party affiliation. Political parties, however, are beginning to exercise more influence on selected legislative issues, reflecting the increased political polarization in Texas and throughout the country. This edition has a new opening story updating the partisan makeup of the legislature resulting from the 2020 election. It also includes the new apparent speaker of the Texas House and recounts the successes of one-term Speaker Dennis Bonnen and the political scandal resulting in his downfall.

- **Chapter 6** describes the plural executive, which is part of the reason that, historically, the governor of Texas has been ranked, from an institutional standpoint, as one of the weaker governors in the United States. Although the powers of the office are institutionally weak, some governors, such as Rick Perry, have developed a strong role in state policymaking, using informal and personal resources. This chapter focuses primarily on the governor, but the analysis also includes the other offices of the plural executive and their responsibilities in the administrative structure of state government. This edition has a new opening story discussing Governor Greg Abbott's emergency response to the COVID-19 pandemic and the criticism he received from both Democratic detractors and conservative members of his own Republican Party. We also update the section on Governor Abbott's leadership style to show how he, like Governor Rick Perry before him, is trying to strengthen the governor's role, despite constitutional limitations. The chapter also includes an update on Attorney General Ken Paxton's conservative priorities and his latest legal controversy.

- **Chapter 7** focuses on how policy is developed and carried out by the 1.5 million public employees who work for state and local governments in Texas. The implementation of public policy is a governmental responsibility assigned to thousands of state and local agencies. Despite the anti-bureaucracy sentiment rooted in the state's conservative political culture, governments grow as population increases and new or expanded programs are implemented. Bureaucrats do much more than shuffle paper. They are involved in every stage of the policymaking process. Texans expect that public services—roads, water treatment, trash collection, and education, to name a few—will be provided effectively and efficiently. In this new edition, the authors update employment numbers for state and local governments and anticipate how future employment trends may be impacted by the pandemic.

- **Chapter 8** discusses the Texas judicial system, which is structured around five levels of courts with overlapping jurisdiction among some courts. Except for municipal judges, Texas judges are elected in partisan elections. Most other states use appointments—some with retention elections—or nonpartisan elections. Many Texans, including some judges, dislike the high cost of judicial campaigns and the implication that campaign contributions influence judicial decisions. However, the legislature has refused to change the partisan election system. This chapter also discusses the criminal justice system and the effect of politics on criminal justice. In this edition, we discuss additional gains by Democrats and women in races for state district and appellate court seats in urban counties and add a new section on the Texas Supreme Court's decision against expanding mail-in voting during the COVID-19 pandemic.

- **Chapter 9** focuses on the political behavior of Texans, public opinion and core political values, and the processes by which citizens obtain their political beliefs and learn to engage in political processes. In addition to general election results, this chapter relies heavily on surveys conducted with Texas voters. The techniques of polling are also discussed. The twelfth edition includes updated data on changing patterns of ideology in Texas, including opinions on race and Black Lives Matter. It also includes voting patterns and demographic changes in Texas and has a new section on intersectionality (different identities, such as race and sex, which interact to impact life experiences).

- **Chapter 10** is structured, in part, around theories of party realignment, detailing the transformation of the state from one-party Democratic control to Republican domination. The current discussion of the state's potential to move from "red" to "purple" status is essentially a discussion of the potential for another party realignment in Texas in the future. This chapter draws from V. O. Key's three-part concept of the political party in the electorate, as an organization, and in government. In this edition, the chapter has a new opening story on Donald Trump carrying Texas in the 2020 election to extend the Republican string of presidential victories in Texas, while losing nationally to Joe Biden. We also discuss the growing conflict over policy in Texas between Democrats and Republicans.

- **Chapter 11** examines elections and campaigns with the purpose of explaining differences in the ways Texans engage in the political process. The chapter discusses issues such as changing campaign technology and increasing campaign costs, changing electoral laws as well as the individuals and interest groups who contribute large sums of money to political candidates and the questions raised by their contributions. This edition includes 2020 election outcomes, including primary returns; updates the diversity of candidates and officeholders and money in elections; has an expanded section on absentee ballots in the pandemic; and has a new section on campaigning in the pandemic.

- **Chapter 12** focuses on the mass media in Texas, which continue to undergo major changes. The media link citizens to those in office. What the public knows about politics and the actions of officeholders comes, directly or indirectly, through the media, either the traditional media or, increasingly, social media. The media have traditionally played a major role in shaping public policy, although that role continues to evolve. This edition updates the opening story to illustrate the continued blurring of lines between objective news reporting and political advocacy. The chapter also updates the growing distrust of traditional news media and cites polling showing marked differences between how Democrats and Republicans view the media, another indication of political polarization. It also updates the role of advertising and social media in 2020 political campaigns, continues the discussion of "fake news" and media literacy and updates ownership trends in Texas newspapers.

- **Chapter 13** discusses both the criticisms frequently directed at interest groups and the positive role of these groups in bringing like-minded people together in pursuit of collective action and political participation. A number of theoretical issues are raised in this chapter regarding interest groups and democracy, including questions of political power and influence that are nested in the "elitist-pluralist" debate. Inequities exist in the resources, power, and influence of Texas interest groups, but the chapter emphasizes that no group has a monopoly on power and the actions of governments, and that there are occasions when marginal groups are effectively mobilized to shape public policy according to their interests. Public policy can be understood in terms of the roles that groups play at every stage of its development. This new edition has a new chapter opening on the Black Lives Matter movement and includes a section on protests and marches and new data on lobbyists and lobbying.

- **Chapter 14** provides theoretical perspectives on the policymaking process and then applies these concepts to state finances, the budgeting process, educational policies, the criminal justice system, health and human services, environmental policies, and transportation. This chapter is updated extensively in this edition with recent developments affecting all these issues. These updates include the impact of the COVID-19 pandemic on the state budget, public schools and higher education.

Here is a summary of how students can interact with multiple types of media and assessments integrated directly within the authors' narrative:

- Chapter-opening **Current Events Bulletins** titled *Contemporary Texas: Government in Action* feature chapter-related news articles (refreshed twice yearly).
- *What's Happening Now in Texas?* are **current event bulletins** placed in every chapter and feature weekly article updates from *The Texas Tribune*.
- Chapter-specific **videos** can be found in-line in all Revel chapters. Video excerpts from *The Texas Tribune*, as well as existing videos featuring Texas politicians, judges, lobbyists, political activists, bureaucrats, and journalists, introduce students to current issues and larger debates that address key topics found in each chapter.
- **Pearson Originals for Political Science** are compelling videos about contemporary issues. These short-form documentaries contextualize the complex social and political issues impacting the world today.
- **Texplainer videos** walk students through more difficult concepts—such as "Can the Government Keep Schools Safe?," "Texas Tax Dollars: Where Do They Go?," and "What's Really Behind Political Polls?"—in a clear, interesting way. These include compelling discussions with *Texas Tribune* founders Ross Ramsey and Evan Smith, as well as many of their reporters. Through the visual storytelling approach, Texplainer videos cater to visual and audio learners and hit a high level of engagement in students who can see the concepts come to life.
- Pearson Originals for Political Science and Texplainer videos are incorporated into the chapters and can also be easily accessed from the instructor's Resources folder within Revel.
- **Shared Media activities** allow instructors to assign and grade both pre-written and their own prompts that incorporate video, weblinks, and visuals and ask students to respond in a variety of formats, in writing or by uploading their own video or audio responses. Pre-written assignments around the Pearson Originals for Political Science and Texplainer videos are available.
- **Interactive maps, figures, and tables** featuring Social Explorer technology allow updates to the latest data, toggles to illustrate movement over time, and clickable hot spots with pop-ups of images and captions. "Think About" questions that feature hide/reveal answers also accompany some figures and tables so students can further explore important chapter illustrations.
- **Social Explorer surveys** featured in Chapter 9, Political Socialization, Political Behavior, and Public Opinion, allow students to compare what they think about important public policy issues to what Texans think, based on statewide surveys of citizens conducted by the University of Texas and *The Texas Tribune*.
- **Interactive scenarios** in some chapters allow students to explore critical issues and challenges facing elected officials, bureaucrats, political activists, voters, and educators in Texas, and apply key chapter concepts in realistic situations.

- Chapter review can be found in interactive **Review the Chapter** summaries that utilize Learning Objectives and flashcards featuring key terms and definitions.
- **Assessments** tied to primary chapter sections, as well as full chapter exams, allow instructors and students to track progress and get immediate feedback.
- **Texas State Learning Outcomes** are aligned with module assessments, chapter exams, and test files.
- **Integrated Writing Opportunities** help students reason and write more clearly; each chapter offers two varieties of writing prompts:
- **Journal prompts,** related to chapter videos featuring interviews with notable Texans, ask students to consider critical issues that relate to topics at the module level.
- *Think About* journal prompts are aligned with some Social Explorer interactive activities in most chapters to encourage data literacy.
- **Shared writing prompts,** related to specific *Texas Tribune* articles found at the end of every chapter, encourage students to address multiple sides of an issue by sharing their own views and responding to each other's viewpoints, encouraging all to interpret current events in Texas communities.
- **Essay prompts** enable instructors to assign both automatically graded and instructor-graded prompts.

Supplements

Make more time for your students with instructor resources that offer effective learning assessments and classroom engagement. Pearson's partnership with educators does not end with the delivery of course materials; Pearson is there with you on the first day of class and beyond. A dedicated team of local Pearson representatives will work with you to not only choose course materials but also integrate them into your class and assess their effectiveness. Our goal is your goal—to improve instruction with each semester.

Pearson is pleased to offer the following resources to qualified adopters of *Government and Politics in the Lone Star State*. Several of these supplements are available to instantly download on the Instructor Resource Center (IRC); please visit the IRC at **www.pearsonhighered.com/irc** to register for access.

TEST BANK. Evaluate learning at every level. Reviewed for clarity and accuracy, the Test Bank measures this book's learning objectives with multiple choice and essay questions. You can easily customize the assessment to work in any major learning management system and to match what is covered in your course. Word, Blackboard, and PDF versions are available on the IRC, and Respondus versions are available upon request from **www.respondus.com**.

PEARSON MYTEST. This powerful assessment generation program includes all of the questions in the Test Bank. Quizzes and exams can be easily authored and saved online and then printed for classroom use, giving you ultimate flexibility to manage assessments anytime and anywhere. To learn more, visit **www.pearsonhighered.com/mytest**.

INSTRUCTOR'S RESOURCE MANUAL. Create a comprehensive roadmap for teaching classroom, online, or hybrid courses. Designed for new and experienced instructors, the Instructor's Manual includes learning objectives, lecture and discussion suggestions, activities for in or out of class, research activities, participation activities, and suggested readings, series, and films as well as a Revel features section. Available within Revel and on the IRC.

LECTURE POWERPOINTS. Make lectures more enriching for students. The accessible PowerPoint presentations include full lecture outlines and photos and figures from the book. Available within Revel and on the IRC.

Acknowledgments

We run the risk of overlooking individuals who have provided assistance in our research and writing, but in this edition we want to start by acknowledging the editorial support we have received from our colleagues at Pearson. In addition to providing technical support and instruction, it was their job to keep us on schedule, coordinate the activities of the three authors, provide suggestions for improving our work product, and help with new photos and features.

We are pleased with the interviews interspersed throughout the online Revel edition of this book conducted by the authors with elected public officials and others engaged in contemporary public affairs in Texas. A note of thanks goes to Joshua Johnson for a job well done with the videography and editing. We also are very grateful, of course, to the interviewees: Gary Bledsoe, Eva DeLuna Castro, Tony Garza, Gina Hinojosa, Donna Howard, Wallace Jefferson, Jenny LaCoste-Caputo, Ed Martin, Rick Perry, Evan Smith, Kathie Tovo, Arlene Wohlgemuth, and Nelson Wolff. We also are grateful to *The Texas Tribune* for the use of some of their videos and other materials.

Many other individuals are part of the editorial and production staff of Pearson. Although they remain anonymous to us, we have a keen appreciation for their craft and their abilities to transform material into a comprehensible finished product.

We also wish to thank the many professors who gave their time to provide invaluable input during the following reviews, conferences and Pearson events:

10th Edition Reviewers: David Smith, Texas A&M University–Corpus Christi; John Osterman, San Jacinto Community College; Robert Michael McAvoy, Hill College; Alan Lehmann, Blinn College; Jalal Nejad, Northwest Vista College; Ahad Hayaud-Din, Brookhaven College; and Karl Clark, Coastal Bend College

Spring 2018 Revel Editorial Workshops: Christopher Hallenbrook, Bloomsburg University; Ben Christ, Harrisburg Area Community College; Laci Hubbard-Mattix, Spokane Falls Community College–Pullman; Shobana Jayaraman, Savannah State University; Jeneen Hobby, Cleveland State University; John Arnold, Midland College; Reed Welch, West Texas A&M; Amanda Friesen, IUPUI; Thomas Ambrosio, North Dakota State; Ted Vaggalis, Drury University; Coyle Neal, Southwest Baptist University; Hanna Samir Kassab, Northern Michigan University; Julie Keil, Saginaw Valley State University; Henry Esparza, University of Texas at San Antonio; Sierra Powell, Mount San Antonio College; Edgar Bravo, Broward College; Alicia Andreatta, Angelina College; Robert Sterken, The University of Texas at Tyler; Jessica Anderson, University of Louisiana Monroe; Pat Frost, San Diego Miramar College; Scott Robinson, Houston Baptist University; Cessna Winslow, Tarleton State; Carrie Currier, Texas Christian University; Paul Jorgensen, University of Texas Rio Grande Valley; Steve Lem, Kutztown University; Meng Lu, Sinclair Community College; James Pearn, Southern State Community College; Blake Farrar, Texas State University; Carlin Barmada, NVCC; Michael Chan, California State University, Long Beach; Mehwish, SUNY Buffalo State; Daniel Tirone, Louisiana State University; Richard Haesly, California State University, Long Beach; Hyung Park, El Paso Community College; Jesse Kapenga, UTEP; Stephanie A. Slocum-Schaffer, Shepherd University; Augustine Hammond, Augusta University; Shawn Easley, Cuyahoga Community College; Darius Smith, Community College of Aurora; Robert Glover, University of Maine; Carolyn Cocca, State University of NY, College at Old Westbury; Benjamin Arah, Bowie State University; Ahmet Turker, Pima Community College; Eric Loepp, UW–Whitewater; Holly Lindamod, University of North Georgia; Denise Robles, San Antonio College; Asslan Khaligh, Alamo–San Antonio College; Brandy Martinez, San Antonio College; Andrew Sanders, Texas A&M University, San Antonio; Mohsen Omar, Northeast Lakeview College; Heather Frederick, Slippery Rock University; Heather Rice, Slippery Rock University; Leslie Baker, Mississippi State University; Jamie Warner, Marshall University; Will Jennings,

University of Tennessee; Arjun Banerjee, University of Tennessee, Knoxville; Jonathan Honig, University of Tennessee; Rachel Fuentes, University of Tennessee, Knoxville; Andrew Straight, University of Tennessee, Knoxville; Margaret Choka, Pellissippi State Community College; Christopher Lawrence, Middle Georgia State University; LaTasha Chaffin, College of Charleston; Jeff Worsham, West Virginia University; Cigdem Sirin-Villalobos, University of Texas at El Paso; Lyle Wind, Suffolk Community College; Marcus Holmes, College of William & Mary; Kurt Guenther, Palm Beach State College; Kevin Wagner, Florida Atlantic University; Eric Sands, Berry College; Shari MacLachlan, Palm Beach State College; Sharon Manna, North Lake College; Tamir Sukkary, American River College; Willie Hamilton, Mt. San Jacinto College; Linda Trautman, Ohio University–Lancaster; Dr. William H, Kraus, Motlow State Community College; Kim Winford, Blinn College; Lana Obradovic, University of Nebraska at Omaha; Doug Schorling, College of the Sequoias; Sarah Lischer, Wake Forest University; Ted Clayton, Central Michigan University; Steven Greene, North Carolina State University; Sharon Navarro, University of Texas at San Antonio; Curtis Ogland, San Antonio College; Henry Esparza, UT San Antonio; Mario Salas, UTSA; Robert Porter, Ventura College; Will Jennings, University of Tennessee; Haroon Khan, Henderson State University; Brenda Riddick, Houston Community College; Julie Lantrip, Tarrant County College; Kyle C. Kopko, Elizabethtown College; Kristine Mohajer, Austin Community College (ACC); Dovie D. Dawson, Central Texas College; Joycelyn Caesar, Cedar Valley College; Daniel Ponder, Drury University

APSA 2017: Jooeun Kim, Georgetown; Leonard L. Lira, San José State University; Abigail Post, University of Virginia; Jamilya Ukudeeva, Chabot College; Shannon Jenkins, University of Massachusetts–Dartmouth; Matthew Platt, Morehouse College; Sara Angevine, Whittier College; Andy Aoki, Augsburg University; Stephen Meinhold, University of North Carolina–Wilmington; Manoutchehr Eskandari-Qajar, Santa Barbara City College; Clayton Thyne, University of Kentucky; Alice Jackson, Morgan State University; Mark Rom, Georgetown University; Krista Wiegand, University of Tennessee; Geoffrey Wallace, University of Washington; Precious Hall, Truckee Meadows Community College; Patrick Larue, University of Texas at Dallas; Margot Morgan, Indiana University Southeast; Patrick Wohlfarth, University of Maryland; Christian Grose, University of Southern California; Clinton Jenkins, George Washington University; Jeffrey W. Koch, US Air Force Academy and SUNY Geneseo; Albert Ponce, Diablo Valley College; Justin Vaughn, Boise State University; Joe Weinberg, University of Southern Mississippi; Cindy Stavrianos, Gonzaga University; Kevan M. Yenerall, Clarion University; Katherine Barbieri, University of South Carolina; Elsa Dias, Metropolitan State University of Denver; Maria Gabryszewska, Florida International University; Erich Saphir, Pima Community College; Mzilikazi Kone, College of the Desert; Mary McHugh, Merrimack College; Joel Lieske, Cleveland State University; Joseph W. Roberts, Roger Williams University; Eugen L. Nagy, Central Washington University; Henry B. Sirgo, McNeese State University; Brian Newman, Pepperdine University; Bruce Stinebrickner, DePauw University; Amanda Friesen, IUPUI; LaTasha Chaffin, College of Charleston; Richard Waterman, University of Kentucky

MPSA 2018: Adam Bilinski, Pittsburg State University; Daniel Chand, Kent State University; Agber Dimah, Chicago State University; Yu Ouyang, Purdue University Northwest; Steven Sylvester, Utah Valley University; Ben Bierly, Joliet Junior College; Mahalley Allen, California State University, Chico; Christian Goergen, College of DuPage; Patrick Stewart, University of Arkansas, Fayettville; Richard Barrett, Mount Mercy University; Daniel Hawes, Kent State University; Niki Kalaf-Hughes, Bowling Green State University; Gregg R. Murray, Augusta University; Ryan Reed, Bradley University; Kimberly Turner, College of DuPage; Peter Wielhouwer, Western Michigan University; Leena Thacker Kumar, University of Houston/DTN; Debra Leiter, University of Missouri Kansas City; Michael Makara, University of Central Missouri; Ola Adeoye,

University of Illinois–Chicago; Russell Brooker, Alverno College; Dr. Royal G. Cravens, Bowling Green State University; Vincent T. Gawronski, Birmingham-Southern College; Benjamin I. Gross, Jacksonville State University; Matthew Hitt, University of Northern Colorado; Megan Osterbur, New England College; Pamela Schaal, Ball State University; Edward Clayton, Central Michigan University; Ali Masood, California State University, Fresno; Joel Lieske, Cleveland State University; Patrick Wohlfarth, University of Maryland; Steven Greene, NC State; Will Jennings, University of Tennessee; Haroon Khan, Henderson State University; Kyle Kopko, Elizabethtown College; Hyung Lae Park, El Paso Community College; Linda Trautman, Ohio University–Lancaster

We are grateful to the **Test Bank Advisory Board members** who provided feedback used to improve our assessment questions: Debra Cardona, Northwest Vista College; Glen Hunt, Austin Community College; Elizabeth Rexford, Wharton County Junior College; Claudia D. Stravato, West Texas A&M University; Ronald Vardy, Wharton County Community College; Mathis Theron Waddell, Galveston College.

We have read and reread this material and checked and rechecked the data. If there are errors, the fault is ours.

About Your Authors

Tucker Gibson taught for forty-three years at Trinity University, focusing on state and local government, political parties and interest groups, public policy, and religion and politics. He has assisted governments in Central Texas in redistricting, owned a market research firm, and consulted with political candidates and businesses. In addition to multiple editions of this book, he has coauthored the Texas chapters in numerous national and Texas government textbooks published by Pearson.

Clay Robison covered state government and politics in Texas for almost forty years as a journalist, including twenty-six years as Austin Bureau Chief for the *Houston Chronicle*, before retiring in 2009. He now is a public affairs and communications specialist for the Texas State Teachers Association, based in Austin. He is coauthor of *Politics in America: Texas Edition*.

Joanne Connor Green is Professor of Political Science at Texas Christian University. Green studies the role of gender in American politics. She and her colleagues are examining how the presence of women and non-Caucasian representatives in state legislatures affect public policies, specifically as they pertain to elders, the disabled, and children. Joanne Connor Green, who is also interested in promoting civic engagement, regularly speaks to community groups regarding campaigns and elections as well as gender in American politics.

The Social and Economic Environment of Texas Politics

THE LINES WERE LONG. THE NEED WAS GREAT.
Thousands of cars waited in line at a food bank distribution center in San Antonio as the coronavirus pandemic began to take hold during the spring of 2020, forcing emergency closures of many businesses and restaurants and the loss of thousands of jobs.

LEARNING OBJECTIVES

1.1 Assess major challenges facing Texas in the twenty-first century, p. 4.

1.2 Describe the political myths used to define and interpret the political culture of Texas, p. 6.

1.3 Compare and contrast the political subcultures of Texas, p. 8.

1.4 Describe the history and characteristics of the major population groups in Texas, p. 10.

1.5 Assess the impact of demographic and economic changes on the political system of Texas, p. 17.

At first glance, the aerial photo looked as if it might have been shot above a shopping mall parking lot on a busy weekend afternoon. It was a huge flea market, but no shoppers were there. It was early spring 2020, and the market was closed because of the coronavirus pandemic, which had begun to erupt in Texas. The flea market had been temporarily converted into a distribution center for the San Antonio Food Bank, and thousands of cars were lined up for hours as groceries were handed out to families whose breadwinners had unexpectedly lost their jobs. When a *San Antonio Express-News* photographer took the photo in early

April, the food bank was feeding 120,000 people a week, more than twice its normal load, from 16 counties, and at the time there was no end in sight. The food bank CEO, Eric Cooper, feared the organization could use up its inventory of food in less than a month.

Responding to the emergency, private citizens had increased their monetary donations, and several food-distribution companies had made large donations of groceries. With unemployment worsening, the food bank needed more and, with the assistance of state legislators from the area, appealed to Governor Greg Abbott for emergency government aid.[1] Over the next several weeks, the organization received several million dollars from the state. Long lines at food banks, meanwhile, were repeated in other Texas cities during the health and economic crisis.

Texas, dating back to the nineteenth century frontier era, has a long history of volunteerism and self-help. In the modern era, nonprofits, such as food banks and other charitable organizations, are formed by people independently of government to address public needs that state and local governments don't have the resources, the political will, or the public support to adequately address. In major emergencies and disasters, when unmet needs can be overwhelming, charitable organizations often are forced to turn to elected officials for help, and much of that assistance is provided with emergency funding from the federal government.

State government's assistance to the San Antonio Food Bank was applauded. But as we shall note in Chapter 6 Texas's overall response to the coronavirus outbreak was not without controversy. Looking forward, the pandemic also posed questions about what the short-term and long-term future of Texas may look like, economically and in terms of the delivery and quality of public services. Millions of Texans lost jobs, at least temporarily, and state and local governments lost billions of dollars in tax revenue as many restaurants and other businesses were closed for weeks to slow the spread of the virus.

Even before the pandemic, Texas, like many other states, was struggling with a host of twenty-first-century problems. Many are growth-related. Roads and highways in urban and suburban areas are clogged, and air pollution is an ever-present problem for many communities. State policymakers must weigh the electricity needs of a growing population—and the potential for rolling blackouts during 100-degree Texas summers—with the environmental risks posed by power plants. Texas also must figure out how to ensure an adequate water supply for an ever-increasing demand, a necessity stamped with a special sense of urgency following a record drought in 2011.

Rooted in a conservative political culture of individualism and self-help, Texas policymakers, Republicans and Democrats alike, have historically supported a low-tax, low-regulatory climate favoring business interests. State leaders also have used public financial resources to stimulate economic development and subsidize the private sector. This has made Texas a national leader in job creation, attracting people from other states as well as other countries. Some of the wealthiest men and women in the world call Texas home. Some have struck it rich in the oil and natural gas industry, which remains a signficant part of the state economy. But that economy has diversified, and Texas now has many high-tech and telecommunications companies and an assortment of manufacturing, shipping, service, and transportation industries. Agriculture also remains an important industry in some parts of the state. But the legendary frontier image of cowboys and wide-open spaces has been replaced by the reality that almost 90 percent of the state's population now lives in cities and ever-expanding suburbs. Three of the nation's ten largest cities—Houston, San Antonio, and Dallas—are in Texas and are among the fastest-growing cities in the country, and Texas, with 29 million residents, is the nation's second most-populous state.

Despite the wealth that can be found in Texas, millions of residents live below the poverty line. Texas has some of the poorest counties in the nation. But the state's conservative political values have produced policies that consistently rank Texas near the bottom of the states in spending on education, welfare, and health care for the poor, issues that are becoming more critical with the state's population growth.

The face of Texas has changed dramatically over the past generation and will continue to change. The non-Hispanic white population that dominated the state for more than a century is being overtaken by the Hispanic population, which, aided by immigration, soon will constitute a majority of Texas's residents. The Asian American population also is growing rapidly in Texas. These changes are creating new cultural and political challenges—and offering new cultural and political opportunities. According to U.S. Census Bureau surveys, some 145 languages are spoken regularly in homes in the nine-county Houston metropolitan area, and 156 languages are spoken in the Dallas-Fort Worth area. Spanish is the most common language other than English, but tens of thousands of residents speak Vietnamese or one of the Chinese languages, the next most common. African languages, Hindi, Arabic, Korean, Nepali and various European languages also are represented.[2]

According to the 2018 *American Community Survey*, approximately five million or 17 percent of Texas residents 5 years old or older were born in countries other than the United States. Only 38 percent of these foreign-born residents are U.S. citizens. Many others have complied with federal laws and are residing in the state legally. Others are classified as unauthorized residents, with estimates of their numbers in Texas ranging from 1.5 to 1.7 million.[3]

Amid all these changes, government officials are making decisions that affect your daily lives. You may not be conscious of most of these decisions, but occasionally something happens, such as an increase in college tuition, higher taxes, or the shutdown of college campuses because of a pandemic, which you notice and may dislike. However, if you don't know who made the decision and why, you won't have a chance to do anything about it. It takes a conscious effort to be informed about your government and political leaders, but it is worth the effort because knowledge is potential power.

Our democratic system doesn't force a citizen to participate in the political life of a community, the state, or the nation. You may be indifferent toward government and politics, believe you are too busy to pay much attention, or believe your input won't have any effect. But active and engaged citizen participation is essential to the health of our political system. And active participation in public life and the political process is most likely to be effective when it is based on "self-interest rightly understood," and those self-interests are tied to the interests of the community or society as a whole.[4]

This book's authors are committed to active citizen participation in politics and public affairs, and in our teaching and writing we try to help readers and students understand the structure and operations of the political system and how politics, government processes, and policies can change as population characteristics, the economy, and other conditions change.

We also try to help people navigate state and local politics in Texas because we want our readers to know how to "do politics." To get started, we introduce in this chapter the environment, or milieu, in which the 5,000 or so governmental institutions in Texas function. This will include discussions of the state's people, including many of those who shaped the state's governmental institutions and its political system; the historical development of the state's political traditions and culture; and the state's changing economy. Subsequent chapters will focus on the state's constitution, its governmental institutions, the political process, forces that affect the political process, and the historical development of major policy decisions. Along the way, we will compare Texas's institutions, policies, and political climate with those of other states, so you can view Texas from a national perspective and decide for yourself if your government is on track or needs to do some things differently.

Above all, we hope that this book will help convince you that your involvement—your ability to navigate your government—is important to your own self-interests as well as the vitality of the Texas political system.

Challenges of the Twenty-First Century

1.1 Assess major challenges facing Texas in the twenty-first century.

The issues cited at the beginning of this chapter are just some of the challenges of contemporary Texas politics. They reflect the fundamental conflicts between competing interests and the way Texans decide "who gets what, when, and how."[5] Government and politics are the systems that we have developed to structure conflict; develop an orderly and stable process by which competing interests can be expressed; and, finally, decide who will benefit and who will pay the bill.

As we begin our analysis of Texas government and politics, we ask why Texans and their public officials make the political choices they do. Why, for example, do per-student expenditures for public education in Texas rank low in comparison to most other states? How do we account for Texas's **regressive tax** system, which requires low-income and middle-income citizens to pay a higher proportion of their income in state and local taxes than do the wealthy? Why do Texans let their state rank near the bottom (49th in 2018) of all the states in per capita expenditures for public services?[6]

These policy issues are directly linked to a variety of other questions about government and the political system. Why are Texans content to live under a state constitution that most scholars regard as obsolete? Why, until recently, was Texas a one-party Democratic state? Why do Republicans now dominate state politics? And what difference, if any, does this make in public policies? Does a small group of powerful individuals determine the primary policy decisions for the state, or are there various competitive centers of power? Do Texans believe they are paying more but getting less for their tax dollars? Are Texans increasingly disenchanted with government?

For many Texans, state and local governments work just fine. Until the emergency restrictions imposed during the coronavirus pandemic, there was minimal governmental intrusion into their lives, or, at least, little intrusion of which they were aware. Many Texans appreciate the absence of a personal income tax, and if they own a business, their profits may benefit from Texas's relatively low regulatory climate, allowing them to hire more employees and make more money. These factors help spur Texas's population growth at one of the highest rates in the country.

For better or worse, political choices affect Texans personally. They pay the costs, even though they may not receive the benefits of every policy decision. The actions or inactions of governmental leaders can have an immediate and direct effect on people's lives, and, from time to time, those holding positions of power have made—or neglected to make—decisions of critical importance to millions of Texans. Water, for example, has been a perennial issue for state and local leaders, but only piecemeal progress had been made to develop sufficient water resources for population growth and economic expansion before a devastating drought struck Texas in 2011 and persisted in some areas of the state until the spring of 2015. A few small communities even ran out of water or came dangerously close, and some larger cities began worrying about their future water supplies. The heightened crisis prompted the legislature and Texas voters to approve a new $2 billion water fund for new reservoirs and other water projects in 2013, but even more preparation needs to be done. Cuts in education, health care, and other public services—or increases in tuition at state-supported universities—often result when the Texas legislature refuses to increase taxes.

Each generation has to address fundamental questions about the role of government, the relationship of the people to that government, and what can be done to make government more responsive and responsible. When one hears or reads of

---

regressive tax
A tax that imposes a disproportionately heavier burden on low-income people than on the more affluent.

ONE OF THE NATION'S BUSIEST PORTS

The Port of Houston comprises 25 miles of facilities along the 52-mile Houston Ship Channel. For a number of years, the port has been ranked first in the United States in "foreign waterborne tonnage," and more than 200 million tons of cargo move through the port annually.

many of the contemporary policy debates or policy failures, there is a real sense of déjà vu—we have seen these problems and issues before. Funding of public education, a major problem now, also was an issue during the Texas revolution of 1836, the Reconstruction era after the Civil War, and throughout much of the state's history. There also are new issues, such as the legalization or decriminalization of marijuana, same-sex marriage, and climate change. But many of today's issues are enduring issues of government and politics.

The fundamental changes in the social, economic, and political structure of the state require new solutions. Funding public education in the days of the one-room schoolhouse was one thing. Funding today's educational system in a way that provides equity among the state's 1,100 school districts is much more complex.

The demographics, or population characteristics, of the state have changed dramatically since the 1940s, when Texas was still predominantly rural. Texas is now an urban state with urban problems. With more than 29 million residents, Texas is second only to California in population. Its ethnic and racial composition has changed, and it is now home to a large number of individuals who were born and reared in other parts of the United States or outside the country—people who have a limited sense of Texas history and politics. Although oil and natural gas are still important to the state's economy, business leaders, government officials, and economists promote **economic diversification** as the dominant theme. Change places heavy demands on the state's governmental institutions, and Texans will need to give increased attention to modernizing and adapting their government to new realities.

In this chapter, we introduce you to the people of Texas, the views they have of themselves, the state's political subcultures, and its economy. We refer to these factors generally as the "political environment," a concept developed by political scientist David Easton to refer to the milieu, or context, in which political institutions function.[7] To understand the government and politics of Texas, one must have a keen sense of its people, the similarities and differences in their respective histories, and the population and economic changes that have occurred since independence and statehood. Although much of our discussion focuses on broad patterns or characteristics of the political environment, individual and collective behavior of groups will determine ultimately how our governments respond to changing conditions.

economic diversification
The development of new and varied business activities. New businesses were encouraged to relocate to or expand in Texas after the oil and gas industry, which had been the base of the state's economy, suffered a major recession in the 1980s.

The Myths of Texas's Political Culture

1.2 Describe the political myths used to define and interpret the political culture of Texas.

Although most Texans have only a cursory knowledge of their state's governmental institutions, political history, and contemporary public policy, they do have views—often ill defined—of the state, its people, and its culture. Key elements of these views, shared by millions of Texans, are described by some scholars as **political myths**.

In recent years, serious scholarship has focused on myths as a way to assess the views people have of their common historical and cultural experiences. A myth can be regarded as a "mode of truth that codifies and preserves moral and spiritual values" for a particular culture or society.[8] Myths are stories or narratives that are used to describe past events, explain the significance of those events to successive generations, and provide an interpretive overview and understanding of a society and its culture.[9] Myths provide a world picture or, in our case, a picture of the state of Texas. Myths serve, in part, to affirm the values, customs, and beliefs of Texans.[10] The relevance of a myth depends, in part, on the degree to which it approximates the events it describes and its pervasiveness in the literature, symbols, rituals, and popular culture of the state. The daily lives of many Texans are so infused with elements of these myths that some people scarcely recognize that their attitudes, views, or behavior have been shaped by these narratives. Even newcomers to the state can be easily assimilated into the political culture built on these myths.

1.2.1 The Sources of Texas's Political Myths

Texas has produced its own myth of origin, which continues to be a powerful statement about the political system and the social order on which it is based. For many Texans, the battle of the Alamo clearly serves to identify the common experiences of independence and the creation of a separate, unique political order.[11] No other state was a **republic** prior to joining the Union, and several scholars argue that independence and "going at it alone" from 1836 to 1845 resulted in a cultural experience that distinguishes the Texas political system from that of other states.[12] The state's nickname—the Lone Star State—is a constant reminder of this unique history. A set of heroes came out of the formative period of Texas history, including many who fought and died at the Alamo or secured Texas independence on the San Jacinto battlefield. Texas schoolchildren are introduced to these heroes at a very early age with field trips, or "pilgrimages," to the Alamo in San Antonio and visits to the San Jacinto monument in Houston.

The Texas mythology also includes the Texas Ranger and the cowboy. There is considerable lore about the invincible, enduring ranger defeating overwhelming odds on the wild Texas frontier. Newspapers and dime novels in the nineteenth century introduced readers throughout the United States to the cowboy, who was often portrayed as an honest, hardworking individual wrestling with the harsh Texas environment.

The cowboy's rugged **individualism**, with strong connotations of self-help and independence, symbolizes a political culture in Texas that does not like to look to government as a solution to many of its problems.[13] It is the kind of individualism that continues to be exploited by political candidates in campaign ads and by the state legislature in limited appropriations for welfare, health care, and other public-assistance programs. This legacy of individualism and risk taking is further reinforced by stories of wildcatters who made and lost fortunes in the early days of oil exploration in the state.

The frontier to which the Texas Ranger and the cowboy belong is part of a cultural myth of limited government and unlimited personal opportunity. The Texas frontier

---

political myths
Generally held views rooted in the political culture that are used to explain common historical and cultural experiences.

republic
A political system in which sovereign power resides in the citizenry and is exercised by representatives elected by and responsible to them.

individualism
An attitude, rooted in classical liberal theory and reinforced by the frontier tradition, that citizens are capable of taking care of themselves with minimal governmental assistance.

TEXAS RANGER STATUE REMOVED
Workers remove a Texas Ranger statue from Love Field in Dallas. The statue had been at the airport for many years but was ordered removed following renewed attention to the controversial history of the elite law enforcement organization.

experience also perpetuates the myth of "land as wilderness and land as garden."[14] The hostile Chihuahuan Desert of the far southwestern part of the state eventually gives way to the more Edenic green of the Piney Woods of East Texas. Descriptions of space, distance, and size are pervasive in a great deal of the literature on the state. Literally thousands of books written about Texas provide varied perspectives on the geography and topography of the land. One might argue that the "wide-open spaces" of the frontier shaped Texans' views of their autonomy, independence, and vulnerability. They have clearly shaped attitudes toward land and the legal rights to use land as one sees fit.

1.2.2 Changing Political Myths

The Texas myths, however, have been primarily the myths of the white (Anglo) population and have limited relevance to the cultural and historical experiences of many African American, Hispanic, or Asian Texans, including newly arrived immigrants. From the 1840s to the mid-1960s, these latter groups were excluded from full participation in Texas politics and the state's economic and social life. To many Hispanics, for example, the Texas Ranger is not a hero, but a symbol of ruthless suppression.

The modern Texas Rangers are considered by many Texans to be an elite, crime-solving state police force, and a book by author Doug J. Swanson, published in 2020, acknowledges the role the Texas Rangers played in fighting frontier crime and protecting the early American settlers in what was then the Mexican territory of Texas. But the book, *Cult of Glory: The Bold and Brutal History of the Texas Rangers,* also exposes an underside of the legendary group. Swanson said rangers of old often "functioned as executioners" whose "job was to seize and hold Texas for the white man." As recently as the early twentieth century, Swanson said, they "executed hundreds, perhaps thousands, of Mexicans and Mexican Americans," many along the Texas-Mexico border. Some of their targets were bandits, he said, but many victims were simply living on land that white ranchers wanted.[15] Partly in reaction to the book, local officials in 2020 removed a statue of a Texas Ranger that had been in the Love Field airport in Dallas since 1963. The model for the statue was a captain who in 1956 commanded a Ranger detachment ordered by then-Governor Allan Shivers to keep African American students from integrating a high school in Mansfield, near Dallas. He later was sent to prevent integration of Texarkana Junior College. The statue's removal took place as protesters demonstrated in Texas and throughout the country over the death of George Floyd, an unarmed African American man, in police custody in Minneapolis.

Since the 1970s, African Americans, Hispanics, and Asian Americans have made significant political and economic gains. Their share of the population also has been increasing, and these three groups combined now constitute a majority of the state's population. As their numbers increase, their historical experiences are likely to be incorporated into the mythology of the state, and components of the white-based mythology will continue to be challenged and redefined. Recent research, for example, contradicts some of the traditional beliefs about what actually took place during the battle of the Alamo. Several scholars have concluded that some of the Alamo's defenders surrendered to Mexican soldiers and were executed, rather than fighting to the death, as generations of Texans were led to believe. There also has been increasing attention to the role that Hispanics played during the revolutionary period.[16]

In 1991, after several years of trying, African Americans in Texas were successful in convincing the state legislature to make Martin Luther King Jr.'s birthday a state holiday. June 19, the day enslaved people in Texas learned of their emancipation in 1865, also has significant meaning for the state's African Americans and is celebrated as the Juneteenth holiday. For Hispanics, the Cinco de Mayo and Diez y Seis celebrations speak to common cultural and historical experiences with Mexico. In recent years, the State Board of Education has approved new high school elective courses in Mexican American and African American studies, recognizing, although belatedly, the contributions of those groups to the state's history and culture and their growing influence. The Black Lives Matter movement has risen to raise public awareness of and demand changes in a culture in which African American men are disproportionately the victims of violence at the hands of some white police officers and individuals who embrace extreme racial hostility and violence.

The Political Culture of Texas

1.3 Compare and contrast the political subcultures of Texas.

Texas shares the common constitutional, institutional, and legal arrangements that have developed in all fifty states, including a commitment to personal liberties, equality, justice, the rule of law, and popular sovereignty with its limitations on government. But there are cultural differences among the states and even among regions within individual states. Texas is a highly diverse state, with racial and ethnic differences from one region to another and divergences in political attitudes and behavior that are reflected in the state's politics and public policies.

The concept of **political culture** helps us compare some of these differences. Political culture has been defined as the "set of attitudes, beliefs, and sentiments which give order and meaning to a political process and which provide the underlying assumptions and rules that govern behavior in the political system."[17] The political culture of the state includes fundamental beliefs about the proper role of government, the relationship of the government to its citizens, and who should govern.[18] These complex attitudes and behaviors are rooted in the historical experience of the nation, shaped by the groups that immigrated to the United States, and carried across the continent to Texas.

One authority on American political culture, Daniel Elazar, notes that three political subcultures have emerged over time in the United States: the individualistic, the moralistic, and the traditionalistic. All three draw from the common historical legacy of the nation, but they produced regional political differences. Sometimes they complement one another; at other times, they produce conflict.[19]

political culture
A widely shared set of views, attitudes, beliefs, and customs of a people as to how their government should be organized and run.

The historical origins of these three subcultures can be explained, in part, by the early settlement patterns of the United States and by the cultural differences among the groups of people who initially settled the eastern seaboard. In very general terms, the New England colonists, influenced by Puritan and congregational religious groups, spawned the moralistic subculture. Settlers with entrepreneurial concerns and individualistic attitudes tended to locate in the Mid-Atlantic states, whereas traditionalistic elites who aspired, in part, to recreate a semifeudal society, dominated the initial settlement of the South.

Expansion toward the western frontiers progressed in identifiable migration patterns from the initial three settlement regions. Texas was settled primarily by people holding the individualistic and traditionalistic views of a political system. The blending of these two views, along with the historical experience of the Republic and frontier, contributed to the distinct characteristics of Texas's political culture.[20]

These two political subcultures have merged to shape Texans' general views of what government should do, who should govern, and what constitutes good public policy. Given the characteristics of these two traditions, one might well conclude, as have many scholars, that the Texas political culture is conservative. Politics in Texas tends to minimize the role of government, is hostile toward taxes—especially those that are allocated toward social services—and is often manipulated by the few for their narrow advantages at the expense of the general population. During much of its history, Texas was one of the least democratic states, with restrictions on voting rights, limited party competition, and low rates of voter participation.[21] Some restrictions on voting rights have been eased by federal civil rights laws, but voting issues continue to spark fights between the major political parties over laws and rules regulating voter registration, early voting, and mail-in voting.

Some scholars have reservations about the concept of political subcultures because the theory is difficult to test. Although these reservations are legitimate, we know of no other single theory that presents such a rich historical perspective on the relationship of settlement patterns in the state and the evolution of political attitudes and behavior. These attitudes and behaviors are likely to continue evolving as the population mix of Texas continues to change, just as the political myths described earlier are evolving.

1.3.1 The Individualistic Subculture

The political view of the **individualistic subculture** holds that politics and government function as a marketplace. Government does not have to be concerned with creating a good or moral society but exists for strictly "utilitarian reasons, to handle those functions demanded by the people it is created to serve."[22] Government should be limited, and its intervention in the private activities of its citizens should be kept to a minimum. The primary function of government is to ensure the stability of a society so that individuals can pursue their own interests.

In this view, politics is not a high calling or noble pursuit but is like any other business venture in which skill and talent prevail and the individual can expect economic and social benefits. Politics is often perceived by the general public to be a dirty business that should be left to those willing to soil their hands in the political arena. This tradition may well contribute to political corruption, and members of the electorate who share this view may not be concerned when government corruption is revealed. New policies are more likely to be initiated by interest groups or private individuals than by public officials, and it is assumed that those elected to public office will pursue their own self-interests or support policies advocated by interest groups whose political support they enjoy.[23]

individualistic subculture
A view that government should interfere as little as possible in the private activities of its citizens while ensuring that adequate public facilities and a favorable business climate are available to permit individuals to pursue their self-interests.

1.3.2 The Moralistic Subculture

moralistic subculture
A view that government's primary responsibility is to promote the public welfare and that government should actively use its authority and power to improve the social and economic well-being of its citizens.

The **moralistic subculture** regards politics as one of the "great activities of man in his search for the good society."[24] Politics, it maintains, is the pursuit of the common good. Unlike the attitude expressed in the individualistic subculture that governments are to be limited, the moralistic subculture considers government a positive instrument with a responsibility to promote the general welfare.[25] Politics, therefore, is not to be left to the few but is a responsibility of every individual. Politics is a duty and possibly a high calling. This cultural tradition has a strong sense of service. It requires a high standard for those holding public office, which is not to be used for personal gain. Politics may be organized around political parties, but this tradition produced nonpartisanship whereby party labels and organizations play a reduced role.[26] The moralistic subculture produces a large number of "amateur" or "nonprofessional" political activists and officeholders and has little toleration for political corruption. From the moralistic perspective, governments should actively intervene to enhance the social and economic interests of their citizens. Public policy initiatives can come from officeholders as well as from those outside the formal governmental structure.[27]

1.3.3 The Traditionalistic Subculture

traditionalistic subculture
A view that political power should be concentrated in the hands of a few elite citizens who belong to established families or influential social groups. Public policy basically serves the interests of this small group.

The **traditionalistic subculture** holds the view that there is a hierarchical arrangement to the political order. This hierarchy serves to limit the power and influence of the general public, while allocating authority to a few individuals who comprise self-perpetuating elites. The elites may enact policies that benefit the general public, but that is secondary to their own interests and objectives. Public policy reflects the interests of those who exercise influence and control, and the benefits of public policy go disproportionately to the elites.

Family, social, and economic relationships, not mass political participation, form the basis for maintaining this elite structure. In fact, in many regions of the country where traditionalistic patterns existed, there were systematic efforts to reduce or eliminate the participation of the general public. Although political parties may exist in such a subculture, they have only minimal importance that is often subject to manipulation or control by elites. Many of the states characterized by the traditionalistic subculture were southern states in which factionalism within the Democratic Party replaced two-party politics.[28]

The People of Texas

1.4 Describe the history and characteristics of the major population groups in Texas.

The politics and government of Texas can be understood, in part, from the perspective of the people living in the state. What follows is an assessment of a select number of demographic, or population, characteristics of Texans. In subsequent chapters, we examine the relationship of race, ethnicity, and other demographic characteristics to partisan behavior, public opinion, institutional power, and public policy.

1.4.1 Native Americans

Only three small Native American groups (Alabama-Coushatta, Tigua, and Kickapoo) live on reservations in Texas, and the Native American population is approximately 1 percent of the state's total population. Unlike Native Americans in Oklahoma, New Mexico, and Arizona, those in Texas have little influence, as a group, on governmental institutions, politics, or public policy.

In the early nineteenth century, at least twenty-three Native American groups resided in Texas. During the period of the Republic (1836–1845), President Sam

GAMBLING AND ECONOMIC DEVELOPMENT

The small Kickapoo tribe, located in Eagle Pass, has staked its economic development on a limited gambling casino on its reservation. Two other small tribes—the Tigua in El Paso and the Alabama-Coushatta in Livingston—had been thwarted by state law and litigation in their efforts to develop gambling, until a ruling by two federal agencies in 2015.

Houston attempted to follow a policy of "peace and friendship" with the Native Americans, but he was followed by President Mirabeau B. Lamar, who set out to "expel, defeat, or exterminate" them. Statehood did not improve the Native Americans' conditions, and the period between annexation in 1845 and the Civil War (1861–1865) was "one of devastation, decimation, and dislocation" for many of the state's tribes.[29] As Anglo settlers expanded to lands traditionally claimed by various Native American tribes, conflict ensued, and most of the Native American population was eventually eliminated or displaced to other states.

In recent years, Native American tribes have cooperated with officials in many states to establish gambling casinos on tribal reservations. Such casinos are allowed under federal law, but most forms of casino gambling are barred by Texas law. The Kickapoos operate a limited casino outside of Eagle Pass, but until a ruling by two federal agencies in 2015, the Tiguas and Alabama-Coushattas were denied the right to run casinos on their reservations. Some Native American leaders consider casinos a major potential source of revenue, jobs, and economic development for their people, but recent efforts to change Texas law have been unsuccessful.

1.4.2 Hispanics

In the eighteenth and nineteenth centuries, neither Spain nor Mexico was successful in convincing Hispanics to settle in Tejas or the northern territory of Mexico. Part of the reason was a lack of security; there was only a limited presence of Mexican troops to protect settlers continually threatened by indigenous tribal groups. The Spanish regarded Tejas as a border province of relatively little value, except as a strategic buffer between Spanish colonies and those held by the British and the French. By the time Mexico declared its independence from Spain in 1821, the total Texas population under Spanish control was estimated to be approximately 5,000 people. With the rapid expansion of Anglo-American immigration to Texas in the 1820s and 1830s, Hispanics became a small minority of the population.[30]

Some Hispanics were part of the Texas independence movement from Mexico. After independence in 1836, men such as Jose Antonio Navarro and Juan Seguin were part of the Republic's political establishment. But the Anglo migration rapidly overwhelmed the Hispanic population and greatly reduced its political and economic power. There was even an effort at the Constitutional Convention of 1845 to strip

TEJANO PATRIOT JOSE ANTONIO NAVARRO

Jose Antonio Navarro, born into a prominent San Antonio family, was one of the most influential Tejano leaders in the first half of the nineteenth century. He was a leader in Texas's independence movement, represented San Antonio at the Constitutional Convention of 1836, was one of the document's signers, served in the Texas Congress, participated as the only Tejano in the Constitutional Convention of 1845, and championed the rights of Tejanos as Texas and U.S. citizens.

Hispanics of the right to vote. The attempt failed, but it was an early indication of Anglo hostility toward the Hispanic population.[31]

By 1887, the Hispanic population had declined to approximately 4 percent of the state's population. In 1930, it was 12 percent and was concentrated in the border counties from Brownsville to El Paso (see Figure 1–1). Modest increases in the Hispanic population continued until it reached 18 percent of the state's population in 1970, after which it grew at a more rapid rate. By 1990, it had reached 25 percent, spurred by immigration from Mexico and other Latin American countries, as well as by higher birth rates among Hispanic women. These growth patterns continued in the next two decades, and by 2018 Hispanics comprised 39.6 percent of the state's population.[32] In addition to their traditional concentrations in the Rio Grande Valley and South-Central Texas, large Hispanic populations are found in most metropolitan areas. Except for the Asian American population, which is considerably smaller, the Hispanic population has grown at a significantly higher rate than other populations in Texas.

Hispanics will probably continue to increase at a higher rate than most other populations. By 2022, Hispanics are likely to surpass Anglos as the largest population group in the state.[33] This growth is steadily increasing the political power and influence of this group. Eight Hispanics have been elected to statewide office. After successful redistricting and legal challenges to city, county, school board, and state legislative districts, which will be discussed in later chapters, Hispanics held 2,739 elected positions in Texas in 2019, the highest number of any state.[34]

The regions of the state where Hispanics concentrated (South Texas and along the Mexican border) before their more widespread migration to cities were areas heavily influenced by the traditionalistic subculture. Extreme poverty, low levels of education, and local economies based on agriculture contributed to the development of political systems dominated by a few Anglos, who often considered Hispanics to be second-class citizens. Hispanics' increasing political clout, however, has produced major political and governmental changes in those regions.

FIGURE 1-1 ETHNIC AND RACIAL COMPOSITION OF TEXAS, 1860–2018

The composition of the state's population has changed significantly since the 1960s, with large increases in the Hispanic and Asian American populations.

SOURCES: Terry G. Jordan with John L. Bean, Jr., and William M. Holmes, Texas: A Geography (Boulder: Westview, 1984), pp. 81–83; U.S. Census Bureau, U.S Censuses, 1860–2010; and U.S. Census Bureau, *2018* American Community Survey.

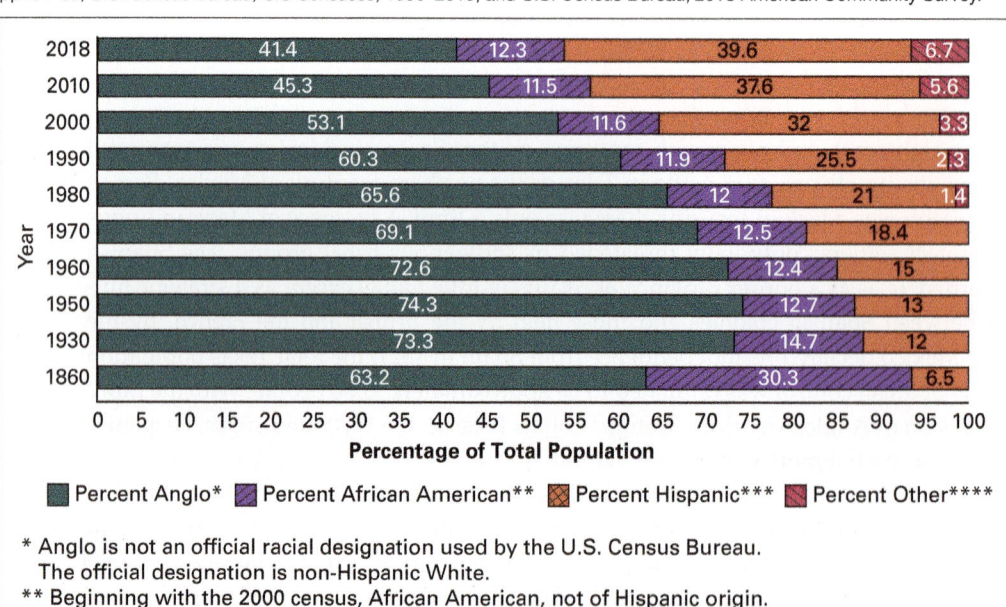

* Anglo is not an official racial designation used by the U.S. Census Bureau. The official designation is non-Hispanic White.
** Beginning with the 2000 census, African American, not of Hispanic origin.
*** Spanish total for 1970 based on "Persons of Spanish language or surname."
**** Data for Asian and other populations not tabulated by the Bureau of the Census prior to 1980.

1.4.3 African Americans

Relatively few African Americans lived in Texas during the colonization period, and the story of African American settlement did not begin until after Texas independence in 1836. When Texas was part of Mexico, Mexican law restricted slavery within the territory. During the period of the Republic and early statehood prior to the U.S. Civil War, the African American population increased significantly as Anglo-Americans settling in Texas brought cotton cultivation and the slavery system with them. At the time of the Civil War, 30 percent of the state's residents were African American, but that percentage declined after the war. By 1960, it had leveled off at 12 percent, about the same level counted in the 2010 census. African Americans are expected to represent between 11 percent and 12 percent of the state's population through the 2020 census.

Large concentrations of African Americans are in East Texas, where white southerners and the people they enslaved originally settled. African Americans also settled in large numbers in the urban areas of Dallas, Fort Worth, Houston, and Austin. Relatively few African Americans live in the western counties or in the counties along the Mexican border. The increased number of African American state legislators, city council members, county commissioners, and school board trustees representing urban communities indicates the political power of the African American population in selected areas.

The whites who enslaved people migrated to Texas from the lower southern states brought with them the dominant values of the traditionalistic political subculture. Although enslaved people were freed after the Civil War, continued political and economic discrimination against African Americans was commonplace in the eastern part of Texas into the 1960s. As in South Texas, the politics of East Texas served the interests of the white elites by reducing or eliminating African American participation in the political process through restrictive election laws and outright physical intimidation.

1.4.4 Anglos

In the vernacular of Texas politics, the white population is referred to as "Anglos," although there is no census designation by that name. The term includes Jews, the Irish, Germans, Poles, and just about any other individual that the Bureau of the Census designates as "non-Hispanic white." Scholars have identified two distinct early patterns of Anglo migration into Texas from other states. These patterns, as well as population movements through much of the late nineteenth and early twentieth centuries, largely explain the regional locations of the state's two dominant political subcultures.

In the early nineteenth century, the first Anglos moving to Texas came from the upper South—Tennessee, Kentucky, Arkansas, and North Carolina—a region significantly influenced by the individualistic subculture that emphasized limited government. The earliest settlements were primarily in what is now northeastern Texas, in the Red River Valley. After Mexican independence from Spain, a second wave of immigration came from the upper South and also generally settled in northeastern Texas.[35] Few of these early colonists were people who enslaved people on plantations in the lower South.

After Texas gained its independence and legalized slavery, settlers from the lower South began arriving. By the outbreak of the Civil War, Anglos who had moved to Texas from the lower South were roughly equal in number to those from the upper South. Newcomers from the lower South where slavery was legal initially settled in southeastern Texas, near Louisiana, but soon they began to move northward and westward.

A line drawn from Texarkana to San Antonio in effect divides Texas subcultures. Most of those Anglos who settled north and west of this line were from the upper South and were heavily influenced by the individualistic subculture. Anglos who settled south and east of the line were by and large from the lower South and were

SLAVERY AND THE TRADITIONALISTIC SUBCULTURE

Minerva and Edgar Bendy, both born in slavery, lived most of their lives in Woodville, Texas, near the Red River in Tyler County. They were interviewed and photographed in 1937 as part of the Portraits of African Americans in the Ex-Slave Narratives conducted by the Works Progress Administration. At the time of this photo, Minerva and Edgar, who had been married for fifty-nine years, related their memories of plantation life and the abrupt impact of emancipation after the Civil War.

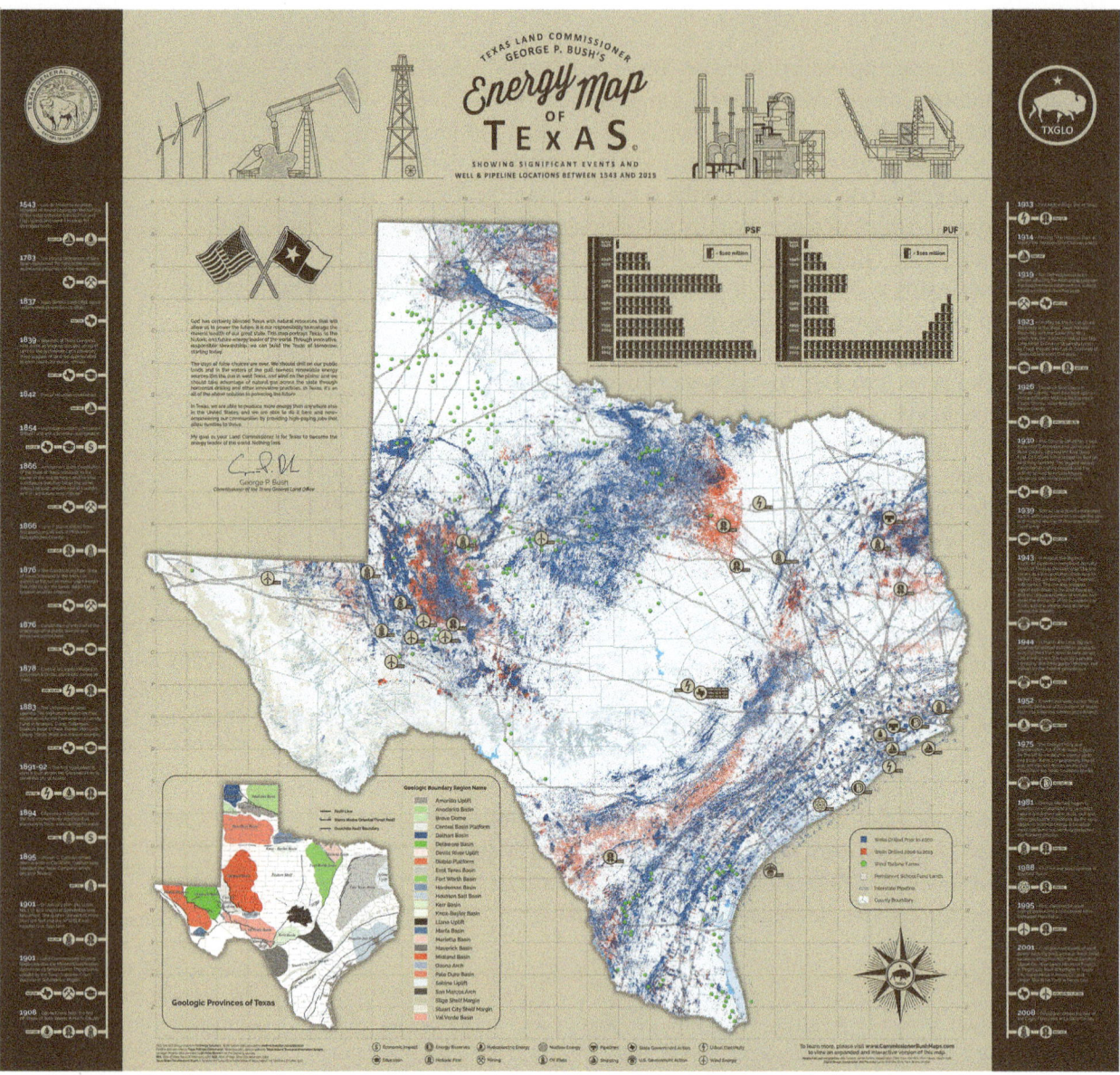

MAPPING THE DIVERSITY OF TEXAS

To navigate the complexities of Texas politics, a keen understanding of the state's geography, regional economic resources, and demographic diversity is essential. Oil and natural gas production, for example, is concentrated in sparsely populated rural counties, but approximately 90 percent of Texans live in widely diverse urban areas.

shaped by the traditionalistic subculture. Although the characteristics of these two subcultures were somewhat different, they merged to create a conservative political system that limited the scope of government and often served the interests of elites.

This pattern of immigration and settlement continued after the Civil War. Primarily, the populations from the upper South pushed westward to the Panhandle and West Texas. This expansion introduced into the western part of the state the individualistic cultural experience of those who resisted the notion that government existed to solve all of society's ills. To this day, West Texas is still one of the most politically conservative areas of the state.[36]

In 1860, Anglos constituted approximately 63 percent of Texas's population. The Anglo population increased until it reached 74 percent in 1950. But by 1990, the stabilization of the African American population and the increase in the Hispanic population had reduced the Anglo share to 60 percent. Anglos accounted for only 53 percent of Texas's population by the year 2000 and 41.4 percent in 2018. Although the absolute number of Anglos will continue to increase with Texas's projected growth, their share of the total population will continue to decrease.

The Anglo population is diverse, as exhibits in the Institute of Texan Cultures in San Antonio remind us. Towns throughout Texas are identified by immigrants of national origin other than Anglo-Saxon, and these national groups brought with them a rich heritage. Castroville, for example, is identified with the Alsatians; New Braunfels and Fredericksburg, the Germans; Panna Maria, the Poles; and West and Halletsville, the Czechs.

1.4.5 Asian Americans

In 1980, Asian Americans accounted for 0.8 percent of Texas's population. By 2018 this group had grown to 5 percent and is expected to continue to increase. This rapid increase parallels national trends. Changes in immigration policy and the dislocation of Asians because of war and political persecution have resulted in larger numbers of Asian immigrants entering the United States and Texas since the 1970s. Moreover, the Asian population is increasingly diverse and includes individuals from India, Vietnam, China, Iraq, Iran, Pakistan, South Korea, and a number of other countries.

The largest concentration of Asian Americans in Texas is in Houston, where several Asian Americans have been elected to major public offices. Among them, community activist Martha Wong was elected to the Houston City Council in 1993 and then to the Texas House of Representatives in 2002. Wong, who was defeated in her reelection bid in 2006, was the second Asian American to serve in the Texas House. Tom Lee of San Antonio, who served in the 1960s, was believed to be the first. Another Houstonian, Democrat Hubert Vo, a Vietnamese American, was elected to the Texas House in 2004 and was reelected to a ninth term in 2020. Angie Chen Button (R-Richardson) was elected to the House in 2008 and reelected to a seventh term in 2020. And Gene Wu (D-Houston) was elected to the House in 2012 and reelected to a fifth term in 2020. Asian Americans also hold or have held local offices in several other Texas cities.

1.4.6 Politics, Race, and Ethnicity

Today, unlike during earlier periods of the state's history, few Texans run around wearing Ku Klux Klan robes, burning crosses, or marching in support of white supremacy. But there still is racial violence, cruelty, and abuse, including the murder of James Byrd Jr. in 1998 and the abusive arrest and subsequent death of Sandra Bland in 2015. Both were African Americans. Byrd was dragged to death behind a pickup truck by three white men near Jasper in East Texas. Two of his murderers were executed, and

INCREASED DIVERSITY IN PUBLIC LIFE

Representative Gene Wu, a Houston Democrat, was first elected in 2012 to the Texas House of Representatives, joining other Asian American public officials. Wu, born in Odessa, is a lawyer who previously worked for the Texas Workforce Commission and the House Higher Education Committee. He has a reputation for community service and a commitment to public education.

the third sentenced to life in prison. The tragedy prompted the legislature to enact a hate crimes law that bears Byrd's name. Bland, a 28-year-old woman from the Chicago area who was in Texas to begin a job at Prairie View A&M University, was pulled over by a white state trooper for the minor traffic offense of failing to signal a lane change. The traffic stop in Waller County quickly became confrontational with the trooper pulling a stun gun and threatening to "light up" the young woman. Bland was arrested and jailed, and three days later her body was found hanging in her jail cell. Her death was officially ruled a suicide. The case attracted international attention and rallied the Black Lives Matter movement as well as other people concerned with how white police officers interact with people of color, often with deadly consequences. After an investigation, the arresting officer was indicted for perjury for claiming that he removed Bland from her car to more safely conduct a traffic investigation. But the charge was dropped in exchange for the officer's promise never to work in law enforcement again.

There are still instances of political insensitivity to racial issues and concerns. When George Floyd, an unarmed African American man, died in police custody in Minneapolis in 2020, Texans of all races and ethnicities joined in protests that lasted for days in cities throughout the state. Most of the protests in Texas and throughout the country were peaceful, but some were disrupted by violence. As the protests continued, several Republican Party county chairs in Texas, apparently concerned that the demonstrations were hurting President Donald Trump's reelection prospects, pushed back by spreading false reports on social media that Floyd's death had been staged and protesters paid to start a race war to undermine Trump's support among African Americans. State Agriculture Commissioner Sid Miller joined in, claiming that the protesters were being paid by billionaire George Soros, a longtime financial supporter of liberal and pro-democracy causes and frequent target of political conservatives. The Republican chair-elect in Harris County, home to Houston, where Floyd had grown up, posted a picture of a banana, a longtime racist trope, to accompany the Martin Luther King Jr. quote, "Injustice anywhere is a threat to justice everywhere." That individual resigned from the party leadership after the mainstream media reported his post. And Governor Greg Abbott and other Texas Republican leaders condemned the racist-tinged social media activity.[37]

So, progress has been made in Texas toward creating a more equitable society, but inequities and more challenges remain. A state law barring African Americans from voting in party primaries was declared unconstitutional in the 1940s, and other laws that reduced the political participation of African Americans and Hispanics have been eliminated. The federal Voting Rights Act, which was enacted in 1965 and extended to Texas in 1975, helped minority political candidates win election to more state and local offices, but the effectiveness of that law has since been weakened by a U.S. Supreme Court ruling in a voting rights case from Alabama, which will be discussed in more detail later in this book. Meanwhile, legal battles continue over changes in political districts to help increase Hispanic and African American representation on city councils and school boards and in the legislature and Congress. There is still evidence of employment and housing discrimination, but restrictive codes prohibiting a specific group of people from buying residential property have been declared unconstitutional, and federal and state laws have given minorities greater access to jobs.

Disproportionately high poverty rates among minority residents often influence political and policy discussions about public services. Many minority legislators are particularly outspoken about the need for funding increases for education and health and human services programs. Throughout an ongoing debate over improving equity in the state's school finance system, school districts usually are identified as "rich" or "poor." For the most part, these are alternative terms for predominantly white and predominantly minority school systems. Race and ethnicity also emerge as factors in

PROTESTING AGAINST INJUSTICE
Demonstrators march in Houston, protesting the death of former Houston resident George Floyd, an unarmed African American man who died in police custody in Minneapolis, Minn., in 2020.

jury selection, employment patterns, and contracts with state and local governments. Higher education admissions policies have produced a series of legal disputes over affirmative action.

More than seventy years ago, V. O. Key, a Texan scholar of American politics, concluded that Texas politics was moving from issues of race to issues of class and economics. He argued that voters in Texas "divide along class lines in accord with their class interests as related to liberal and conservative candidates."[38] In part, he was correct that unabashed racial bigotry and public demagoguery are no longer acceptable; however, he was much too optimistic. If the state divides on economic issues, this division often puts the majority of Anglos on one side and the majority of Hispanics and African Americans on the other.[39]

Growth and Changing Demographics

1.5 Assess the impact of demographic and economic changes on the political system of Texas.

As noted earlier, Texas's population has grown at a significant rate for many years. That growth will continue, and the more the state grows, the more its population will change.

1.5.1 Population Growth

Over the past fifty years, the population of Texas has increased much faster than the national average. According to the 2010 census, the state's population was 25,145,561, an increase of approximately 4.3 million people in ten years. This growth rate of 20.6 percent was significantly higher than the national growth rate of 9.7 percent.[40] By 2019, the state's population had increased by another 3.85 million and stood at 28,995,881. Texas is the second most populous state, second only to California.[41]

High birth rates explain part of the population increase; migration from other states and from Mexico also has been a significant factor. In recent decades, demographers (those who study populations) have described a nationwide shift in population from the Northeast and Midwest to the South and West. For each census from 1940 to 1970, in-migration from other areas accounted for less than 10 percent of Texas's growth. But in-migration jumped to 58.5 percent of the total growth between 1970 and 1980, the period in which demographers identified massive shifts of population from the "Frostbelt" to the "Sunbelt." Between 1980 and 1990, it contributed 34.4 percent to the state's growth.[42] In-migration slowed down somewhat between 1990 and 2000, but it has been a significant component of the state's growth during the past two decades. In 2018, approximately 28 percent of American-born residents reported other states as their place of birth.[43]

Although it is expected to become less significant in the future, this influx of residents from other states contributed to the restructuring of Texas's traditional one-party, Democratic political system into a Republican-dominated one. Many new residents came from states with strong Republican Party traditions and brought their party affiliation with them.

Texas also attracts people from other countries. The state was home to approximately 21 million people in 2000. Of this number, some 2.4 million, or 11.4 percent, were identified as foreign born.[44] By 2018, the foreign-born component had increased to 4.9 million, or 17 percent of all Texas residents. Some 1.86 million of those foreign-born were U.S. citizens, and approximately 3 million were not. Approximately 11 percent of all Texas residents in 2018 were non-citizens, a fact that has several implications.[45]

Citizenship is directly related to political participation; noncitizens, although counted in the census for reapportionment of congressional and legislative seats, cannot vote. The overwhelming majority of noncitizens are Hispanic, thus reducing the number of eligible Hispanic voters in relation to their population. Under current federal policy, noncitizens have been denied access to some public social services that are funded in whole or in part by the national government. Needy immigrants are especially affected by such policies; in some instances, the state has found it necessary to use its own funds to provide services.

Approximately one-third, or some 9.5 million Texans older than age 5, speak languages other than English at home, and some 3.7 million people report that they do not speak English well.[46] Some states have adopted English as their official language, but there has not been a significant English language movement in Texas. Nonetheless, language is a policy issue for Texas in terms of bilingual education, official documents and publications, translators for court proceedings, and a host of related issues in the workplace.

The increase in population places demands on all levels of government, and many local governments throughout Texas are hard pressed to provide adequate services. Many Texas cities, for example, are running out of landfill space. Environmental laws make it difficult to obtain new licenses for garbage and waste disposal. Without additional dumpsites, new population growth cannot be served. The increased population also has raised questions about the adequacy of water supplies throughout the state with cities, regions, and industries competing intensely for the resources now available. These water battles will intensify in the future.

Streets and highways in urban and suburban areas are clogged with traffic. Driving and subsequent congestion dropped during the recession of 2008, but by 2014 travel had rebounded at levels that exceeded those of 2008.[47] Congestion and delays mean additional gasoline consumption, pollution, and costs in time.[48] Additionally, congestion increases potential health hazards. Building new roads is one solution, but it is impossible to build enough new roads to keep up with the increasing population demand. Other possible solutions include managing road systems more efficiently, restructuring demand, relieving choke points, diversifying patterns for new housing developments, and increasing use of public transportation.[49]

1.5.2 The Aging Population

According to the 2018 American Community Survey, the state with the youngest population was Utah. Texas ranked forty-eighth among the states in median age, largely as a result of the high birth rates of a growing Hispanic population. In 2018, the median age in Texas was 34.9 years, compared to 38.2 years for the entire country.[50] Approximately 12.5 percent of the state's population was older than 65 in 2018, and that group was expected to increase to 18.7 percent by 2042.[51] This aging population will place unprecedented demands on the public and private sectors for goods and services, including expanded health care and long-term care. In recent years, increasing state expenditures under the Medicaid program for long-term nursing care have strained the state's budget, resulting in shifts of some funding from other public programs.

Younger Texans will be asked to pay higher taxes to support the needs of the projected aging population. These intergenerational obligations, critical to a stable political system, often are overlooked in debates over funding public services. Younger Texans with children need older voters to support public education through their tax dollars, and older voters need younger Texans to support health care services. If push were to come to shove and civility and respect were to disappear, the older population would have significantly more political clout than younger voters, who are generally less informed about politics and usually vote at rates much lower than older people.

1.5.3 Urban Texas

Although Texas was a rural state during the first 100 years of its history, 89 percent of the state's population in 2019 lived in areas classified by the Bureau of the Census as urban (see Figure 1–2).[52]

Urbanization and suburban sprawl now characterize Texas's settlement patterns, and many urban corridors and suburban areas cross county boundaries, often making it difficult for local governments to address growth problems. More than 75 percent of Texans live in 66 counties (58,000 square miles)—the so-called Texas Urban Triangle—anchored by the metropolitan areas of Dallas–Fort Worth, Houston, and San Antonio. For the foreseeable future, three-fourths of the state's population growth will occur in this area (see Figure 1–3, Texas Urban Triangle).

urbanization
The process by which a predominantly rural society or area becomes urban.

The dramatic growth of Texas's largest cities is shown in Figure 1–4. Plano, north of Dallas, was a small city of fewer than 5,000 residents until 1960, but by 1980 it was a mid-size city of 72,000. From 1990 through 2018, Plano grew from 128,713 to 287,765, an increase of 124 percent. Austin's population more than doubled between 1990 and 2018. Houston's population grew by 44 percent; San Antonio, 64 percent; and Dallas, 34 percent in this period. Between 2010 and 2019, the 15 fastest growing cities of 50,000 or more in the United States were in the South and the West. Six of these cities are in Texas. Houston, San Antonio, Austin, Fort Worth, and Dallas combined increased by almost 933,600 people in this decade.[53]

Three of the ten largest cities in the United States—Houston, San Antonio, and Dallas—are in Texas, and, like urban areas throughout the country, Texas's largest cities increasingly are home to minority and lower-income residents. This trend results from higher birth rates among minority populations, urban migration patterns, and what is often referred to as "white flight" from the cities to suburban areas. Minority groups now account for the majority of the populations in nine of Texas's ten largest cities (Plano has a non-Hispanic white or "Anglo" population of 54 percent). These minority residents include Hispanics, African Americans, and Asian Americans—groups that do not always constitute cohesive interest blocs. As minority growth continues, there will be areas of potential competition or political conflict among these groups.

FIGURE 1-2 URBAN-RURAL POPULATION OF TEXAS, 1850–2019

Texas's population has become increasingly urban, as this graph dramatically illustrates. Almost 90 percent of Texans now live in urban areas.

SOURCES: U.S. Census Bureau, U.S. Censuses, 1850–2000; United States Department of Agriculture; Economic Research Service, "State Fact Sheets: Texas," data updated May 23, 2020.

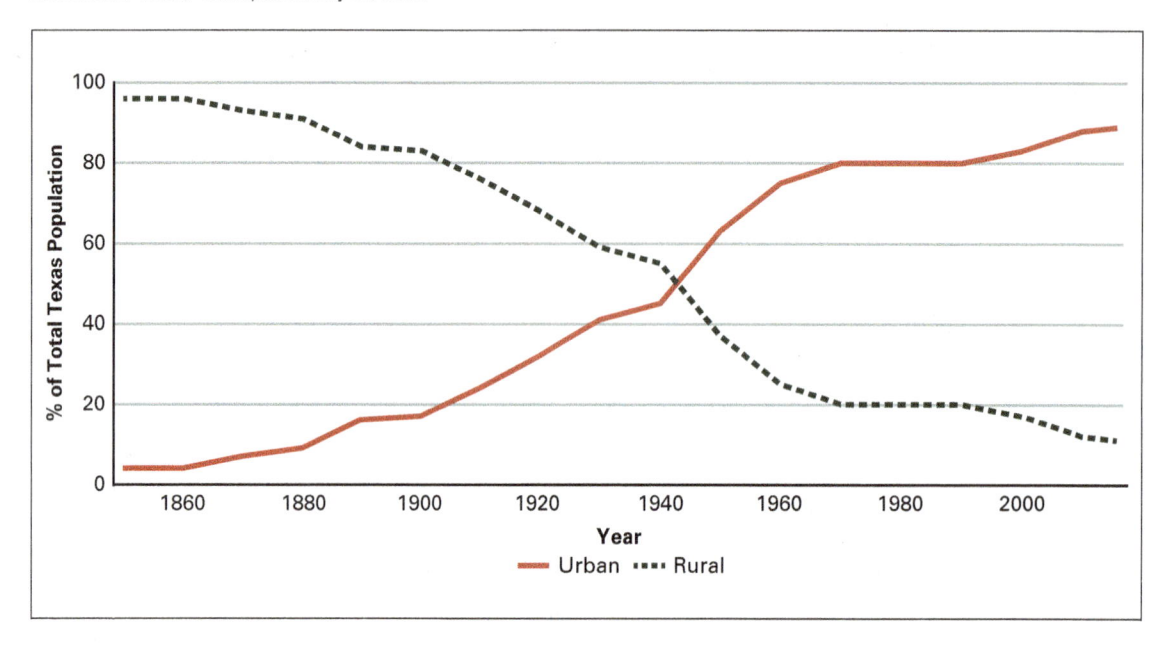

FIGURE 1-3 TEXAS URBAN TRIANGLE

Three-fourths of Texans live within or near the Texas Urban Triangle, the shaded area shown here. Based on current population estimates, most of the state's future population growth will occur in this area.

SOURCE: U.S. Census Bureau, "Annual Estimates of the Resident Population for Counties in Texas: April 1, 2010 to July 1, 2019."

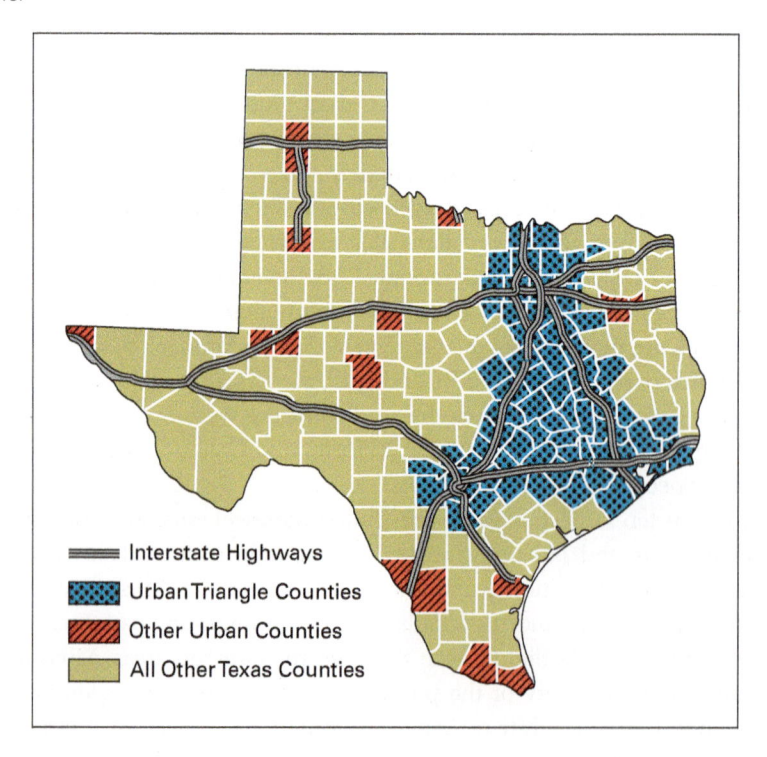

FIGURE 1-4 TEN LARGEST TEXAS CITIES, 1920–2016

A strong indication of the urbanization of Texas is the growth of its ten largest cities. Three of the ten largest cities in the United States—Houston, San Antonio, and Dallas—are in Texas.

NOTE: Population of Plano and Arlington not shown for early years: Plano was under 4,000 in 1920, 1940, and 1960; Arlington was under 5,000 in 1920 and 1940.

SOURCES: U.S. Census Bureau, U.S. Censuses, 1920–2010; U.S. Census Bureau, 2016 American Community Survey. Available at https://factfinder.census.gov/faces/tableservices/jsf/pages/productview.xhtml?pid=ACS_16_1YR_S0101&prodType=table.

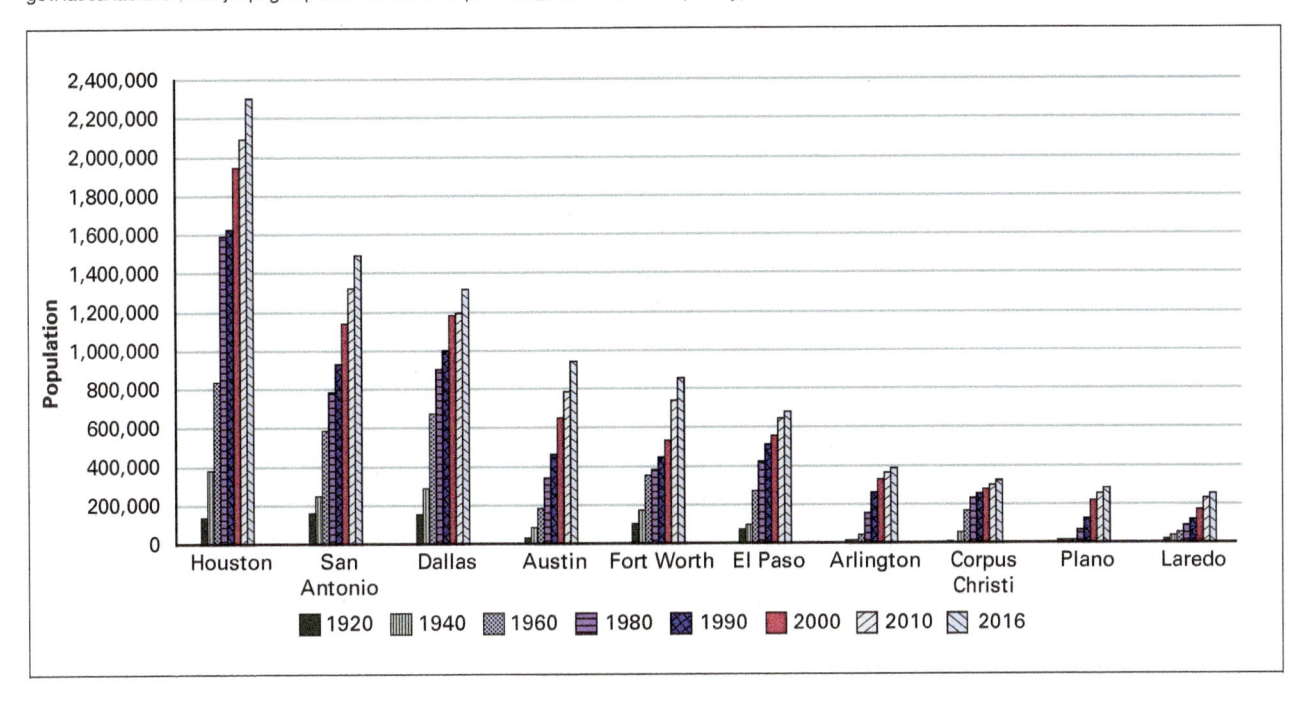

Urban populations continue to shift and resettle, and in recent years a pattern of gentrification has begun to occur as higher-income, Anglo residents have started moving back to the central cities. Cities have focused on urban redevelopment, and some Texans who work downtown are looking for alternatives to the long drives to the suburbs. As higher-income groups return to the central city, they are encroaching on minority residential areas and displacing lower-cost housing with housing that is often unaffordable for low-income minorities. This trend has generated conflict in San Antonio and other Texas cities, with significant political implications centering on zoning and land use.

Population density refers to the number of people per square mile in a political jurisdiction, and it provides another measure of urbanization. As people crowd into smaller areas, living in closer proximity to one another, problems are inevitable. Noise, land use, property maintenance, traffic patterns, and numerous other issues must be addressed.

Marked differences exist among the population densities of Texas's 254 counties. Loving County in West Texas, the least populated county in the nation, has a population of about 169 living in an area of 669 square miles. The most populous county is Harris County (Houston), with more than 4.71 million people living within 1,703 square miles.[54] Clearly, the problems and issues that Loving County faces are significantly different from those that Harris County faces, but both counties have to function with the same form of government created by the state's constitution of 1876.

Texas politics frequently have divided along urban-rural lines, creating conflict, a trend compounded by suburban areas taking on more importance. Redistricting battles and a host of other public policy issues are evidence of that. Until relatively recently, the Texas legislature was dominated by rural lawmakers, many of whom often were insensitive to urban needs. Now, suburban legislators with a different constituency base and interests sometimes pursue policies in conflict with both central city and rural legislators. Moreover, many of urban Texas's problems are aggravated by constitutional restrictions written when Texas was still a rural state.

population density
Number of persons residing within a square mile.

1.5.4 Wealth and Income Distribution

In 2018, the median household income in Texas was $60,629, approximately $1,300 below the national median household income (see Table 1–1). Approximately 20 percent of Texas households reported incomes less than $25,000 per year. By contrast, 41 percent of Texas households reported incomes in excess of $75,000.[55] But there are wide disparities in the distribution of income and wealth among racial and ethnic groups, and in recent years some of these disparities have become more pronounced. The median household income for Collin County, north of Dallas and heavily Anglo, was $94,142 in 2018, and the per capita income exceeded $43,000. Only 6 percent of the population fell below the poverty line. In sharp contrast, the median household income for Hidalgo County on the border with Mexico was $38,398 with 30 percent of the population, which is predominantly Hispanic, falling below the poverty level.[56]

On all measures of income, Hispanics and African Americans fall significantly below Anglo and Asian American residents in Texas. Approximately 27 percent of Texas's Hispanic and some 32 percent of African American households reported incomes in 2016 below $25,000, compared to 17 percent of Anglo households and a similar proportion of Asian American households. By contrast, 34 percent of Anglo households and 42 percent of Asian American households, but less than 15 percent of Hispanic and African American households, reported incomes of more than $100,000.[57]

Many Texans live in severe poverty. Some of the nation's poorest counties are in Texas. These are border counties (Cameron, Hidalgo, Maverick, Starr, Webb, Willacy, Zapata, and Zavala) with large Hispanic populations and unemployment rates that are frequently more than twice the state average.[58] The per capita income (total state income divided by the population) for Texas was $30,641 in 2018. For the Anglo population it was significantly higher, $42,931; for African Americans the figure was $24,061, and for Hispanics, $19,091. The per capita income for Asian Americans was $37,849, but household income for the Asian American population was markedly higher than for any other ethnic or racial group.

In 2018, the poverty level guidelines used in Texas to establish eligibility for many federal and state assistance programs were $25,465 for a family of four (two adults and two children) and $13,064 for one person younger than 65 years.[59] According to the U.S. Bureau of the Census, 14.9 percent of the state's population, or 4.2 million people, fell below the poverty level. Nationally, 13.1 percent, or 42 million persons, fell below the poverty level in 2018.[60] The impact of poverty disproportionately affects children, particularly those living in a one-parent household, and those who are Hispanic or African American. In the eight border counties mentioned earlier, poverty levels for all residents ranged from 26 percent to 35 percent in 2018. Poverty levels for children in these counties ranged from 36 percent to 62 percent.[61] Many of these families do not have adequate housing or health care and depend on food stamps,

TABLE 1-1   U.S. AND TEXAS INCOME FIGURES, 2018

	United States	Texas				
	All Persons	All Persons	Anglos	Hispanics	African Americans	Asian Americans
Median Income for Households	$61,937	$60,629	$74,589	$48,175	$45,545	$87,120
Per Capita Income	33,831	30,641	42,931	19,091	24,061	37,849
Percentage of Persons below Poverty Level	13.1%	14.9%	8.5%	20.9%	19.6%	10.8%
Percentage of Children Below Poverty Level	18.0%	21.1%	9.0%	36.3%	27.3%	10%

SOURCE: U.S Census Bureau, *2018 American Community Survey.*

now called the Supplemental Nutrition Assistance Program (SNAP), or charities for food. Prior to the Affordable Care Act enacted under the Obama administration, some 25 percent of Texans did not have health insurance, and that percentage was even higher in many counties throughout the state. With the implementation of the law, the number of uninsured Texans is estimated to have fallen below 20 percent, but the state still leads the nation in the percentage of uninsured residents.[62]

At the top of the economic scale, a relatively small number of Texans are super-wealthy, including some on the annual (*Forbes* 400) list of the richest Americans. Forty Texans made the list in 2019, with a reported net worth ranging from $2.2 billion to $51 billion apiece.[63] The vast majority of Texans, however, have incomes or assets that are nowhere near those of this select group.

Although the state's economic growth over the past decade has reduced poverty somewhat, scholars who study demographic trends fear that poverty is likely to worsen in Texas if several policy issues are not addressed. Without significant changes in educational levels and expanded economic opportunities, it is possible that approximately 20 percent of the state's households will fall below the poverty level by 2030, and income disparity will be especially problematic for minorities.[64]

Financial resources can be translated into political power and influence through campaign contributions; funding one's own campaign for public office; access to the mass media; and active support for policy think tanks, interest groups, and lobbying activity. Wealth is not the only dimension of political power, but some Texans obviously have the potential for much greater clout than do others.

1.5.5 Education and Literacy

Public education has been a dominant issue in state politics for many years. Lawsuits have forced the legislature to struggle with changes in the funding of public schools, and education will be a primary factor in determining whether Texas can continue to compete in the global economy.

Over the next decade, a large proportion of the new jobs created in Texas will be in service industries. Most of these jobs will require increased reading, writing, and math skills, and high school dropouts will find fewer and fewer opportunities for decent-paying jobs. Across the nation, millions of low-skilled jobs have been outsourced to other countries, and most of the higher-paying jobs now require a college education. Texas faces a crisis in public education, largely because it has not been adequately and equitably funded, and the state's ability to resolve it will directly affect the future financial security of many Texans.

According to the *2018* American Community Survey, 84 percent of Texans ages 25 and older had completed high school, and 30 percent had completed college (see Table 1–2). Educational attainment has improved since 1990 for all racial and ethnic groups in the state.[65] However, wide disparities among the four major groups still exist.

TABLE 1-2 EDUCATIONAL ATTAINMENT IN THE UNITED STATES AND TEXAS BY RACE AND ETHNICITY, 2018 (PERSONS 25 YEARS OF AGE AND OLDER)

	United States		Texas	
	High School Diploma	College Degree	High School Diploma	College Degree
Anglo*	93.1%	36.3%	94.3%	39.3%
Hispanic	69.7	17.0	67.0	15.2
African American	86.5	22.0	90.0	25.0
Asian	87.6	55.0	87.9	59.9
All Persons	88.3	32.6	84.0	30.3

*White, not of Hispanic origin.
SOURCE: U.S. Census Bureau, *2018* American Community Survey.

In 2018, some 94 percent of the state's Anglo population reported that they had completed high school, and approximately 40 percent reported college degrees. By contrast, some 67 percent of the Hispanic population had high school diplomas, and only 15 percent reported having college degrees. Some 90 percent of African Americans graduated from high school, with approximately 25 percent indicating they had college degrees. Particularly noteworthy is the Asian American population, which reported that approximately 60 percent of those ages 25 and older had college degrees. Education not only helps determine a person's employment and income potential, but it also affects his or her participation in politics. Individuals with high educational levels are much more likely to believe they can be informed about politics, participate in the political process, and influence the actions of policymakers.

1.5.6 The Size and Geographic Diversity of Texas

Texas is a big state. Covering more than 260,000 square miles, it is second only to Alaska in landmass. Although Texans appear to have adjusted to long distances—they do not seem to mind driving fifty miles for a night out—visitors from out of state often are overwhelmed by Texas's size and diversity. The distance from Texarkana in northeastern Texas to El Paso in far West Texas is about 800 miles, which makes a person living in Texarkana closer to Chicago than to El Paso. Brownsville in South Texas is closer to Mexico City than it is to Texline in the Texas Panhandle.[66]

Many would contend that perceptions of the state's size have helped shape political attitudes and concepts, and size obviously has affected state policy. Roads and highways, for example, historically have received a significant—some would argue, disproportionate—share of the state's budget. Economic development in such a large and diverse state required a commitment to highway construction because roads were regarded as essential to the development of an integrated economy. Size also contributes to the economic diversity of the state. Some parts of the state may experience economic growth while other areas may experience economic downturns.

One scholar has argued that the great distances in Texas are politically important because they make it difficult for a politician to develop a statewide following, such as can be cultivated in many southern states. Size works against the organizational strategies and continued negotiations necessary to sustain a statewide political machine similar to those that developed in Virginia and Louisiana in the 1920s and 1930s. Although there have been regional or local political machines, such as the now-defunct Parr machine that controlled politics for many years in parts of South Texas, none of these was extended statewide.[67]

Size also contributes to the high costs of political campaigns. Candidates in statewide campaigns spend millions of dollars to communicate with and mobilize Texas voters. Candidates in the 2002 gubernatorial race spent more than $100 million, and the figure for gubernatorial candidates in 2010 exceeded $82 million. Texas has about twenty separate media markets, and the cost of communicating with voters statewide continues to increase despite new technologies.

If Texas were still an independent nation, it would be the thirty-seventh largest in geographic area. The state has one-twelfth of the total coastline of the United States. It has 23 million acres of forest and more than 4,790 square miles of lakes and streams. A traveler driving across Texas is struck by the diversity in topography, climate, and vegetation. The state's "landforms range from offshore bars and barrier beaches to formidable mountains, from rugged canyons, gorges, and badlands to totally flat plains."[68] The western part of the state is dry and semiarid, whereas the eastern section is humid and covered with vegetation. South Texas often enjoys a semitropical winter, whereas North Texas experiences cold winters with snowfall.[69] The growing season in the South is virtually year-round; that in the North is approximately 180 days.

Geography shaped historical migration and land use in Texas. Although we can partially compensate for climate and geography through modern technology, geography continues to shape the economy and population patterns of the state.

1.5.7 The Economy of Texas

Politics, government, and economics are inextricably linked. An economy that is robust and expanding provides far more options to government policymakers than an economy in recession. A healthy tax base is dependent on an expanding economy. When the economy goes through periods of recession, state and local governments confront the harsh reality of increasing taxes or cutting back on public services, usually at a time when more people are in need of governmental assistance.

Historically, the health of the Texas economy was linked to oil and natural gas, but by the last decade of the twentieth century, the state's economy had experienced significant diversification. In 1981, before diversification, 27 percent of the state's economy was tied to energy-related industries. The decade started with rapid increases in the world price of oil, and an economic boom occurred throughout the financial, construction, and manufacturing sectors of the state's economy.[70] But changes in international fuel markets, particularly a big drop in oil prices in the 1980s, staggered the Texas petroleum industry. Natural gas prices also fell. Thousands of energy-related jobs were lost, and many exploration and drilling companies went out of business. Cheaper foreign oil replaced the demand for Texas oil, and a decline in recoverable reserves further reduced the importance of fossil fuels to the state's commerce. Within two decades, oil- and gas-related industries were contributing only 10 percent to the Texas economy; in 2019, the figure was approximately 14 percent.[71]

The drop in oil prices was not the only factor that put the Texas economy into a tailspin in the 1980s. Mexico's peso also experienced a precipitous decline, which had a negative impact on the economies of border cities and counties. In 1983, a harsh freeze in South Texas and a severe drought in West Texas had serious adverse effects on the agricultural sector. There also was a worldwide slump in the electronics industry. These events hurt the construction and real estate sectors of the economy and, in

WELLS THROUGHOUT THE CITY

For much of the twentieth century, oil played a dominant role in the Texas economy, as the derricks in this photo of the city of Kilgore in the 1930s reflect. But with increased U.S. reliance on imported oil and the subsequent decline in Texas oil exploration and production, the Texas economy diversified, reducing the state's reliance on oil and natural gas.

turn, manufacturing and retail trade. For sixteen straight months in 1986 and 1987, the state's employment rate dropped, with a loss of an estimated 233,000 jobs.[72]

These reversals had disastrous effects on Texas's banks and savings and loan institutions. "In 1987 and 1988, more Texas financial institutions failed than at any other time since the Great Depression," the state comptroller's office reported.[73] The pattern of bank failures continued through 1990. The federal government developed a plan to bail out institutions that were covered by the federal deposit insurance program, and the state's banking system ultimately was restructured. But as the magnitude of the problem became clearer, there was a bitter debate over its causes, including the deregulation of the savings and loan and banking industries, inadequate government scrutiny of banking practices, a frenzy of speculation with questionable or unsecured loans, and outright fraud and malfeasance.[74]

State and local governments consequently suffered significant declines in revenue. The legislature convened a special session in 1986 to pass an $875 million tax bill and cut the state budget by about $580 million in an attempt to "patch up" the widening holes in projected state revenues. In 1987, the legislature, mandated by the constitution to a "pay as you go" system of government and denied the option of deficit financing, enacted a $5.6 billion tax bill, including an increase in the sales tax.[75]

Following this experience, state leaders began to take steps to diversify the state's economy by encouraging other industries to relocate to or expand in Texas. These included high-tech companies producing semiconductors, microprocessors, computer hardware, software, telecommunications devices, fiber optics, aerospace guidance systems, and medical instruments.[76] High-tech additions also included biotechnology industries producing new medicines and vaccines and performing genetic engineering of plants and animals. State and local governments developed aggressive recruitment programs, including tax breaks, for many of these companies.

Diversification transformed the Texas economy and put the state in a much stronger position to minimize the impact of economic downturns. When one sector of the economy or region of the state may be suffering a recession, others can be experiencing growth. Oil and natural gas production, for example, has made a significant comeback in recent years in three fields—the Barnet Shale formation, the Eagle Ford Shale, and the Permian Basin.[77] But were oil and gas prices to drop again, as they began to do in 2015, the state's overall economy would be better protected through the strength of other industries. That, at least, is the goal of diversification, and so far it has proven mostly successful. The Texas economy, except for a few years, outpaced the overall national economy from 1990 to 2013, including during the Great Recession, which broke across the nation in the summer of 2008 and arrived in Texas in early 2009.[78]

This worldwide crisis in financial and credit markets was linked to subprime lending, accounting scandals, overextended credit to consumers, dramatic declines in manufacturing and trade, and a loss of confidence on the part of the consumer. With massive federal intervention—Texas received approximately $26.5 billion in federal stimulus money—a concerted effort was made to stop the slide, and by the first quarter of 2010, Texas's economy had begun to recover.[79] The recession cost thousands of Texas jobs and was partly to blame for billions of dollars in state budget cuts in 2011, but employment and state revenue soon began rebounding, and the recession was shorter-lived and unemployment consistently lower than in the rest of the country.

For several years, oil and gas production in Texas had been strong, thanks in part to the wide use of a drilling technique, hydraulic fracturing, or fracking, which allowed the tapping of reserves that previously had been too difficult or too expensive to reach. At the height of this boom, oil was selling at or near $100 a barrel, oilfield jobs in Texas were plentiful, and oil and natural gas production taxes were boosting the state treasury. But a worldwide glut, or oversupply, of oil caused energy prices to start falling in 2015, and drilling in Texas began slowing down. Some companies shut down operations or went out of business, many oilfield workers lost jobs, and oil and gas tax revenue declined. By January 2016, oil prices had dropped as low as $30 a barrel, but by early summer of 2018, the price of a barrel of oil exceeded $70 with signs of recovery and expansion.[80]

In 2019, Texas had a gross state product of $1.9 trillion, compared to $21.3 trillion for the United States.[81] During the period of 2000 through 2019, the average annual growth rate in the state's gross product was 3.5 percent, while the nation's gross domestic product grew at an average annual rate of 2.07 percent. The Texas economy was the second largest among the states, surpassed only by California. If Texas were a nation, its economy would rank tenth in the world.[82] But the Texas economy, like the economies of most other states, was hammered by the COVID-19 pandemic in 2020. Many businesses were shut down for weeks, and thousands of Texans lost their jobs. Oil production suffered a double whammy as demand for oil dropped during the health crisis and an international dispute over oil prices also helped produce an oversupply of oil. For a while, oil prices plummeted. State and local governments lost billions of dollars in tax revenue, and as the pandemic persisted through the end of 2020, it remained to be seen what the final economic toll would be.

Texas's restructured economy is heavily oriented toward exports, with approximately 910,000 jobs in 2016 supported by exports from the state.[83] More than 40,000 companies exported goods from their Texas locations in 2015, and some 585,000 Texans worked for foreign owned or controlled companies.[84] Just as we can speak of the **globalization of the economy** nationally, a similar pattern has developed in Texas. In 1999, Texas exported some $83 billion in merchandise to other countries. By 2019, exports to other countries totaled $330 billion, with approximately 33 percent ($108 billion) going to Mexico.[85] The North American Free Trade Agreement (NAFTA) among the United States, Mexico, and Canada was signed in 1994. It produced changes in the economic relationships and increased economic interdependence among these countries. But President Trump's attacks on Canada and Mexico, his call for increased tariffs on products shipped by both countries to the United States, and his demands for changes in some of NAFTA's provisions created considerable uncertainty for the future of this economic bloc.[86] Some of that uncertainty was eased when the three countries agreed on a new treaty, the U.S.-Mexico-Canada Agreement (USMCA), to replace NAFTA. The new agreement included some significant changes, but early assessments concluded there were more similarities than differences between the two agreements. The new trade agreement as well as the maquiladora program, a cooperative manufacturing program between the United States and Mexico, have linked much of the Texas economy to the Mexican economy and will be discussed in more detail in Chapter 3.[87]

globalization of the economy
Increased interdependence in trade, manufacturing, and commerce between the United States and other countries.

1.5.8 Economic Regions of Texas

The economic diversity of Texas can be described in terms of twelve distinct economic regions (see Figure 1–5).[88] One region may be undergoing rapid economic growth, whereas another may be experiencing stagnation. Regions vary in population, economic infrastructure, economic performance, and rates of growth. One region's economy may be heavily dependent on only two or three industries. If one or two of those industries suffer an economic downturn, that region may have a more severe recession than the state overall. There also are marked differences in personal income, poverty levels, and geography among the areas. All regions, though, share in one economic sector—significant levels of government employment.

The economic factors at play in a region help shape the priorities of local governments and the priorities of state legislators elected from that area. The following descriptions of three of the twelve regions offer a sampling of the economic differences encountered throughout Texas.

PRESSURES ON THE BORDER INFRASTRUCTURE

Population growth and economic development on the border between the United States and Mexico have taxed the current capabilities of the infrastructure of this region. Millions of annual border crossings have contributed to long delays, increased air pollution, and economic costs in terms of time, wages, and costs of fuel. The future growth of the region will require expensive investments in new roads and other facilities.

HIGH PLAINS REGION The High Plains Region is made up of forty-one counties and includes Amarillo, Lubbock, the XIT Ranch, and Palo Duro Canyon. Agricultural production, whose major source of water is the Ogallala Aquifer, is a dominant industry. The Ogallala, which underlies 174,000 square miles in eight states, is being rapidly depleted. This makes the future of agriculture in this region dependent on conservation and securing alternative water sources. Related businesses include agricultural services; food processing; and the manufacturing of feed, fertilizers, and farm

FIGURE 1-5   ECONOMIC REGIONS OF TEXAS

The office of the Texas Comptroller of Public Accounts has divided the state into twelve economic regions, which vary markedly in terms of population, economic infrastructure, economic performance, and rates of growth.

SOURCE: Texas Comptroller of Public Accounts.

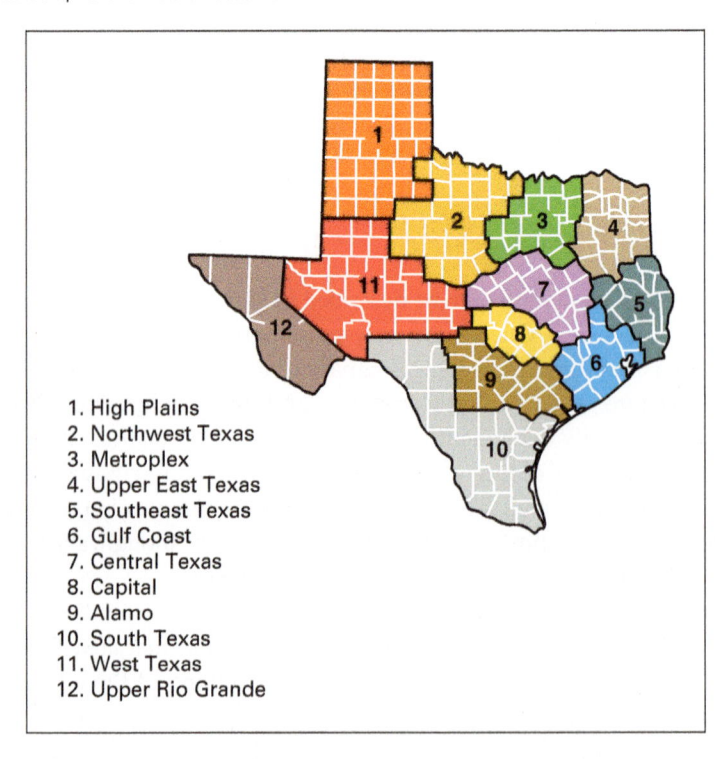

1. High Plains
2. Northwest Texas
3. Metroplex
4. Upper East Texas
5. Southeast Texas
6. Gulf Coast
7. Central Texas
8. Capital
9. Alamo
10. South Texas
11. West Texas
12. Upper Rio Grande

machinery and equipment. Lubbock is home to the largest health care center between Phoenix and Dallas, employing 17,000 people with a payroll that exceeds $543 million a year. But future access to health care is a serious issue in this region because eleven of the forty-one counties have no doctors. Oil and gas production are still an important part of the region's economy, but employment in the energy industry is predicted to decline. Approximately three percent of the state's population lives in this area but is growing at a lower rate than the state recently. Wages and household income are below statewide averages. More than half of the population is identified as Anglo, with African Americans comprising 5 percent and Hispanics, 38 percent.[89]

SOUTH TEXAS BORDER REGION The *South Texas Border Region* encompasses twenty-eight counties, including the cities of Corpus Christi, Brownsville, Laredo, Del Rio, McAllen, Eagle Pass, and Harlingen. Eight of its counties share borders with Mexico, and a significant amount of commerce flows through border crossings within these counties. The region has five seaports, including the Port of Corpus Christi, one of the nation's largest ports in total cargo tonnage. This area is identified with agriculture, including cattle, cotton, sugarcane, citrus, table produce, and food processing. Oil and natural gas production and processing also are key parts of the area's economy. With the discovery of new, recoverable oil and gas reserves and new drilling with the fracking technique, eight counties in this region experienced boom-like growth in jobs, commercial and residential construction, and tax revenue, beginning in 2008. The rapid influx of new people also challenged the capabilities of local governments to provide enough roads, water and sanitation systems, schools, and other public services.[90] The boom appeared to have run its course by 2015 due to a number of factors, including a worldwide surplus of oil and plummeting oil prices. By early 2018, with oil prices above $60 a barrel, industry analysts were cautiously predicting a new round of exploration and production in Texas.[91] The COVID-19 pandemic and dropping oil prices in the spring of 2020 raised significant questions about the future direction of the petroleum industry.

In recent years, this area has received a significant boost from the construction of manufacturing plants in Mexico and increased trade prompted by NAFTA. Although the region was impacted by the Great Recession, economic recovery has since occurred on both sides of the border. Border crossings of all types continue to increase, although violence associated with drug trafficking raises concerns about safety when traveling to and from Mexico. Some improvements have been made in the colonias (an estimated 1,200 residential slums along the border), but poor housing conditions continue to be a significant problem for many people. Health care has been a growth industry in this area. More than 80 percent of the population is Hispanic. The region's population growth has been slightly lower than the state's rate of growth, and its residents' educational attainment and income are below the state average.[92]

UPPER EAST TEXAS REGION The Upper East Texas Region, which includes twenty-three counties, is located in the northeast corner of the state. It includes the cities of Longview, Texarkana, and Tyler (the "City of Roses"). Since 2000, its growth rate has been significantly lower than the statewide average. The average population of this region is older than the state's average, putting pressure on the workforce and the tax base of many local governments, and is predominately Anglo. In recent years, the rate of population growth has been approximately one-third of the state's rate.[93] Agriculture—including horticulture, timber, and the dairy industry—is a key component of the region's economy, as are food processing and food distribution. Transportation-related industries—including the manufacture of railroad rolling stock and motor vehicle bodies—have a strong presence. So do distribution, warehousing, and storage. Oil and gas production also can be found in this region.[94] Wages and household income in this region are significantly lower than those in other regions of the state.

CONCLUSION

Politics often is referred to as a game. Before you can play a game or even appreciate watching it, you have to learn how the game is played, where it is played, and something about the people who are playing it. In this book, we want to help you develop the ability to play the political game in Texas, to navigate the political process, and to understand state and local governmental institutions. Your civic competency begins with knowledge of the environment, or milieu, of the state's political system and how its characteristics shape governments and participants in the political process.

In this chapter, you have learned something about the historical, cultural, political, demographic, and economic environment in which state and local governments in Texas operate and how it has an impact on decisions made by those governments. Returning to our game metaphor, you have learned something about the political playing field and the players. This introduction, we believe, is essential to understanding the rules and practices of political players and institutions in Texas and how governments and politics in Texas compare with other states, subjects that will be discussed throughout this book.

The general characteristics of the state's political culture were framed during the nineteenth century, the formative period when Texas was settled, broke from Mexico, formed a Republic, and then became a state. Many of the attributes still associated with Texas—including a strong, underlying political conservatism—were established during this period. But Texas also has undergone significant demographic, cultural, economic, and political changes during its transformation from a rural, frontier colony to a modern state of 29 million people.

Information about both history and current events is important in understanding and operating in the political environment of the state. We have provided you with a lot of information about the state's historic and political roots that, even as the playing field and the players continue to change, will remain essential to successfully navigating Texas's political system, either as an active participant in the political process or simply as an informed citizen and voter.

CELEBRATING A STRONG LEGACY

The San Jacinto Monument, east of Houston, is a reminder of the historic battle that won Texas's independence from Mexico in 1836. It also is a symbol of the state's independent spirit.

REVIEW THE CHAPTER

Challenges of the Twenty-First Century

1.1 Assess major challenges facing Texas in the twenty-first century, p. 4.

With an ever-increasing population that is now highly urban, Texas confronts a range of economic, social, and political issues that directly shape the state's political system and political leadership. Some of these major issues include transportation, waste disposal, sewerage and sanitation, pollution, water resources, education, health care, and an outdated and regressive tax system.

The Myths of Texas's Political Culture

1.2 Describe the political myths used to define and interpret the political culture of Texas, p. 6.

Political myths are common views that people have of their historical experiences, and Texans have a distinguishable myth tradition rooted in their state's period of independence, its large landmass, and its rugged frontier experience. Some of these myths, including the cowboy and the Texas Ranger, continue to be popular reminders of the state's independence and rugged individualism. The prevailing Texas myths were rooted in the earlier Anglo history of the state, however, and some critics argue they neglect the contributions of Native Americans, African Americans, and Hispanics. Only time will tell if these myths are redefined in terms of the increasing minority populations of the state.

The Political Culture of Texas

1.3 Compare and contrast the political subcultures of Texas, p. 8.

Texas was a vast, mostly unpopulated land prior to independence and statehood. The distinct settlement patterns of different populations provide insight into the development of the regional patterns of the state's political culture. Anglo immigrants who arrived from the United States brought with them the individualistic and traditionalistic subcultures, and the Spanish subculture was traditionalistic. As settlers spread out over the state, they carried with them the core values of their political cultures, producing a mosaic of local variations that have blended into a dominant conservative political culture. The conservative politics of Texas are rooted in its individualistic and traditionalistic subcultures. The moralistic subculture has had limited impact on Texans' value system. The beliefs Texans hold about the role of governments, what they should do or not do, who should govern, expectations of leaders, and what constitutes good public policy are rooted in these cultural patterns that vary across the state.

The People of Texas

1.4 Describe the history and characteristics of the major population groups in Texas, p. 10.

Demographic patterns serve to provide an understanding of the development of the state's contemporary political culture. Native Americans, who now comprise a very small part of the state's population, were the prevailing population prior to the period of European conquest of Texas, but their influence on Texas contemporary politics is negligible. African Americans arrived in Texas enslaved; although slavery ended with the Civil War, they experienced a long history of political and economic discrimination. In the post–Civil Rights era, African Americans have played a significant role in state politics and in regions of the state where they reside in greatest numbers. Hispanics were part of Texas's population at independence but were marginalized through most of the nineteenth and twentieth centuries. With the dramatic increase of the Hispanic population, however, they have played an ever-increasing role in the state's politics over the past four decades. Throughout the formative period and through the modern era, Texas was dominated by highly diverse Anglo national origin groups. With expanded immigration from other states and European countries, distinguishable patterns of settlement spread across the state. Politics and public policy were shaped primarily by these conservative populations. Asian Americans, another highly diverse group, arrived late as a significant component of the state's population. They tend to locate in urban areas, where they are showing some evidence of political influence.

Growth and Changing Demographics

1.5 Assess the impact of demographic and economic changes on the political system of Texas, p. 17.

The dominant demographic themes that run through the state's modern history center on population growth, urbanization, inequities in wealth and income, disparities in education and literacy, and geographical diversity. The state's population now exceeds 29 million and is projected to continue to increase at a fast clip. The state is now about 90 percent urban with more than 70 percent of the population concentrated in the 66 counties designated as the Texas Urban Triangle.

Despite the size of the state's economy and the impressive gains in personal income and wealth for many, there are significant disparities among ethnic and racial groups. African Americans and Hispanics are more likely to have lower incomes than Anglos or Asian Americans. And Asian Americans are among the most educated of the state's residents. The disparities in education have spawned an extensive debate about the state's educational system and its ability to sustain future economic growth that is dependent on a highly educated population.

The gross domestic product of Texas exceeds one trillion dollars. With some exceptions during recessionary periods, the state's economy has outstripped the national economy and the economies of most other states in its rate of growth. No longer heavily reliant on oil and gas, the state's economy is highly diversified, and a substantial part of its growth is based on exports to other countries.

LEARN THE TERMS

regressive tax, p. 4
economic diversification, p. 5
political myths, p. 6
republic, p. 6
individualism, p. 6
political culture, p. 8
individualistic subculture, p. 9
moralistic subculture, p. 10
traditionalistic subculture, p. 10
urbanization, p. 19
population density, p. 21
globalization of the economy, p. 27

The Texas Constitution

2

SLAMMING THE DOOR ON A STATE INCOME TAX

Governor Greg Abbott and Lieutenant Governor Dan Patrick led a successful effort to put an almost insurmountable barrier to a state income tax in the Texas Constitution. Opponents said the proposal was short-sighted, but the overwhelming majority of Texas voters agreed with the two state leaders and approved the constitutional amendment.

Eric Gay/Associated Press

LEARNING OBJECTIVES

2.1 Identify the functions of a constitution and place the Texas Constitution in a national comparative context, p. 35.

2.2 Describe the historical influences, similarities, and differences among Texas's first six constitutions, p. 38.

2.3 Discuss the origins of the Constitution of 1876, its general principles, and the weaknesses and restrictions it still imposes on state government today, p. 43.

2.4 Contrast the relative ease and frequency of the constitutional amendment process with the difficulty of enacting more fundamental change through the constitutional convention process, p. 49.

Texas is one of only seven states without a personal income tax, and any idea of enacting one had been a non-issue since 1993, when Texas voters overwhelmingly approved a constitutional amendment to prohibit the legislature from ever enacting an income tax without voter approval. This was a pretty high bar for a state where opposition to an income tax traditionally has been high among Republicans, Democrats, and independent voters alike. But opposition to any kind of a tax is particularly strong among Republican voters, and in 2019 Republican Governor Greg Abbott and Republican legislative leaders dusted off the income tax issue and proposed a constitutional amendment that would make it even more difficult to enact an income tax in Texas. The legislature passed the proposal, and it was put on the ballot for the November 2019 election.

There were two key differences between the 1993 amendment and the proposed 2019 amendment, which would replace it. The first was a higher vote requirement for the legislature. Under the 1993 amendment, a future legislature could have put an income tax on the ballot on simple majority votes in the House and the Senate. The new amendment would require more-difficult two-thirds votes of the House and the Senate to put an income tax before voters. The other key difference was a provision in the 1993 amendment, engineered by the late Lieutenant Governor Bob Bullock, a Democrat, which dedicated at least two-thirds of the revenue from a future income tax to reducing school property taxes and the remainder to funding for education. This latter provision would be repealed by the new amendment.

This loss of a potential rich source of school funding prompted the Texas State Teachers Association and other education advocates to oppose the 2019 amendment. Other opponents called the new amendment politically motivated to enhance the conservative credentials of state leaders. They said the proposal was short sighted and warned it would make it more difficult for future governors and legislatures to adequately pay for increasingly expensive public services in a growing state. Who could predict, they asked, what Texas's needs would be 20, 50, or 100 years in the future? But there was little doubt that Texas voters, given the chance to erect another hurdle against a state income tax, would approve the amendment, and they did, by a margin of almost three to one.

The income tax proposal was one of ten amendments on the 2019 constitutional amendments ballot, and all but one were approved by voters, adding more restrictions to a state constitution that was designed to put strong restraints on government. Written by frontier Texans at the close of the Reconstruction period following the Civil War, the Texas Constitution was adopted in 1876 and has been amended many times since. It is so restrictive that many scholars and politicians believe it is counterproductive to effective, modern governance. They believe the document, bogged down with statutory detail, is a textbook example of what a constitution should not be. State government functions despite its constitutional shackles: an institutionally weak chief executive; an outdated, part-time legislature; a poorly organized judiciary; and dedicated funds that limit the state's budgetary options. But a total rewrite of the constitution has been elusive, thanks to opposition from numerous special interests that find security in the present document, those who hold obsolete public offices, and those who benefit from dedicated funds. Public ignorance and indifference to the problems created by the restrictive constitutional provisions also thwart an overhaul of the document.

It is our position, shared by others who study state governments, that one cannot develop a clear understanding of Texas government or navigate one's way through its political system without some familiarity with the Texas Constitution, its historic development, and knowledge of how it compares with the U.S Constitution and constitutions of other states.[1] Constitutions are more than the formal frameworks that define the structure, authority, and responsibilities of governmental institutions. They also reflect fundamental political, economic, and power relationships as determined by the culture, values, and interests of the people who create them and the events of the period in which they were written.[2] The addition of a restrictive anti-income tax amendment to the constitution in 2019 reflected the conservative attitude toward government spending that many modern Texans shared with their nineteenth-century ancestors.

Learning what the constitution does and doesn't allow is helpful, if not essential, for anyone in Texas who aspires to start a business, run for political office, or simply be a productive citizen and informed voter. You already have learned something about the state's history and political and demographic culture. The constitution, which reflects that history and culture, is the next step on the road to figuring out what Texas government is all about.

Constitutionalism

2.1 Identify the functions of a constitution and place the Texas Constitution in a national comparative context.

A **constitution** defines the principles of a society and states or suggests the political objectives that society is attempting to achieve. It outlines the specific institutions that the people will use to achieve their objectives, and it defines who can participate in collective decisions and who can hold public office. It also defines the relationship between the people who govern and those who are governed and sets limits on what each group can and cannot do. Because of the stability of the American political system and a general commitment to the rule of law, we often overlook the fact that a constitution also reflects the way a society structures conflict through its institutional arrangements.[3]

The Texas Constitution is not easy to read, and many of its details may make little sense to casual readers. But a careful study of the document can provide insight into the distribution of power among competing groups and regions within the state. The constitution outlines the powers of and defines the limits imposed on state and local governments. From the perspective of political economy, the constitution also speaks to "the relation of the state to economic activity, including both the extent of direct governmental support for enterprise and the appropriate balance between promotion and regulation of economic development."[4]

Some twenty-nine states, including Texas, have had multiple constitutions. Louisiana has had the most, eleven, since it was admitted to the Union in 1812. Texas has had seven constitutions; understanding that legacy is critical to understanding contemporary Texas politics and public policy (see Table 2–1). The first constitution was adopted in 1827, when the state was still part of Mexico. The second was drafted when Texas declared its independence from Mexico in 1836 and became a republic. The third was adopted in 1845 when the state joined the Union. The fourth constitution was written when Texas joined the Confederacy in 1861, and the fifth was adopted when the state rejoined the Union in 1866. The sixth constitution was adopted in 1869 to satisfy the Radical Reconstructionists' opposition to the 1866 constitution, and the seventh was adopted in 1876 after the termination of Reconstruction policies. The seventh constitution, amended 507 times through 2019, remains in effect today.

> **constitution**
> A document that provides for the legal and institutional structure of a political system. It establishes government bodies and defines their powers.

TABLE 2-1 THE SEVEN TEXAS CONSTITUTIONS

1827: Constitution of *Coahuila y Tejas*

Adopted in 1827 while Texas was still part of Mexico, this constitution recognized Texas as a Mexican state with Coahuila.

1836: Constitution of the Republic

The constitution of March 16, 1836, declared independence from Mexico and constituted Texas as an independent republic.

1845: Constitution of 1845

Texas was admitted to the Union under this constitution.

1861: Civil War Constitution

After the state seceded from the Union and joined the Confederacy in 1861, Texans adopted this constitution.

1866: Constitution of 1866

This was a short-lived constitution under which Texas sought to be readmitted to the Union after the Civil War and before the Radical Reconstructionists took control of the U.S. Congress.

1869: Reconstruction Constitution

Power was centralized in the state government, and local governments were significantly weakened under this constitution, which reflected the sentiments of Radical Reconstructionists, not of most Texans.

1876: Texas Constitution

Adopted at the end of Reconstruction and amended more than 500 times since, this is the constitution under which Texas currently functions. Highly restrictive and antigovernment, this constitution places strict limitations on the powers of the governor, the legislature, and other state officials.

statutory law
A law enacted by a legislative body. Unlike constitutional law, it does not require voter approval.

The formal, legal language of a constitution can obscure the general objectives of the document and its relevance to contemporary issues of political power and public policy. Scholars believe, first, that constitutions should be brief and should include general principles rather than specific legislative provisions. In other words, constitutions should provide a basic framework for government and leave the details to be defined in **statutory law** by a legislative body. Second, experts say, constitutions should grant authority to specific institutions, so as to increase the responsiveness and the accountability of individuals elected or appointed to public office. Scholars also believe that constitutions should provide for orderly change but should not be written in such a restrictive fashion that they require continual modifications to meet contemporary needs.[5]

Amended only twenty-seven times since its adoption in 1789, the U.S. Constitution is a concise, 7,000-word document that outlines broad, basic principles of authority and governance. No one would argue that the government of the twenty-first century is comparable to that of the 1790s, yet the flexibility of the U.S. Constitution makes it as relevant now as it was in the eighteenth century. It is often spoken of as "a living constitution" that does not have to be continually amended to meet society's ever-changing needs and conditions. Its reinterpretations by the courts, the Congress, and the president have produced an expansion of powers and responsibilities within the framework of the original language of the document.

By contrast, the Texas Constitution—like those of many other states—is an unwieldy, restrictive document. Now numbering approximately 90,000 words, it has been on a life-support system (the piecemeal amendment process) for most of its lifetime. It is less a set of basic governmental principles than it is a compilation of detailed statutory language, often referred to as "constitutional legislation," reflecting the distrust of government that was widespread in Texas when it was written and the fact that the national Constitution says so very little about state government.[6] In effect, the Texas Constitution attempts to diffuse political power among many different institutions. As the 1876 document was drafted, it also included restrictions on elections and civil rights that later were invalidated by the U.S. Supreme Court. Those early provisions were efforts to limit the power of minority groups to participate fully in state government.[7]

The historical constitutional experiences of Texas parallel those of many southern states that have had multiple constitutions in the post-Civil War era. The former Confederate states, Texas included, are the only states whose constitutions formally acknowledge the supremacy of the U.S. Constitution, a provision required for readmission to the Union.

General comparisons between the Texas Constitution and the U.S. Constitution are fairly straightforward, as presented in Table 2–2. One noticeable difference between the U.S. Constitution and the Texas Constitution (and the constitutions of other states as well) is how individual rights are enumerated. Every state has a bill of rights at the beginning of its constitution. These bills were not added as amendments, which is how the Bill of Rights was added to the U.S. Constitution. Individual rights provisions—such as freedom of speech, freedom of religion, and other personal liberties—in some state constitutions are much longer and more detailed than those in the U.S. Constitution. The Texas Constitution, for example, has four sections pertaining to religious freedom, but the section of the First Amendment to the U.S. Constitution that guarantees religious freedom and prohibits an established church has only sixteen words.

For much of the twentieth century, federal courts applied provisions of the federal Bill of Rights to states in a process that constitutional scholars call the "nationalization of the Bill of Rights." On a case-by-case basis, provisions of the federal Bill of Rights were applied selectively to the states through the due process language of the Fourteenth Amendment to the U.S. Constitution. In effect, this process limited

TABLE 2-2 COMPARISON OF THE TEXAS CONSTITUTION AND THE U.S. CONSTITUTION

	U.S. Constitution	Texas Constitution
General principles	Popular sovereignty	Popular sovereignty
	Limited government	Limited government
	Representative government	Representative government
	Social contract theory	Social contract theory
	Separation of powers	Separation of powers
Context of adoption	Reaction to weakness of Articles of Confederation—strengthened national powers significantly	Post-Reconstruction—designed to limit powers of government
Style	General principles stated in broad terms	Detailed provisions
Length	7,000 words	90,000 words
Date of implementation	1789	1876
Amendments	27	507
Amendment process	Difficult	Relatively easy
Adaptation to change	Moderately easy through interpretation	Difficult; often requires constitutional amendments
Bill of rights	Amendments to the Constitution—adopted in 1791	Article 1 of the Constitution of 1876
Structure of government	Separation of powers (with a unified executive) based on provisions of Articles I, II, III	Separation of powers (with plural executive) defined by Article 2
Legislature	Bicameral	Bicameral
Executive	Single or unified president	Plural executive
Judiciary	Creation of one Supreme Court and other courts to be created by the Congress	Detailed provisions creating two appellate courts of last resort and other state courts
Distribution of powers	Federal	Unitary
Public policy	Little reference to policy	Detailed policy provisions

or preempted actions of state governments under the individual rights provisions of their own constitutions. In cases where individual rights guaranteed by a state constitution differed from those in the federal Bill of Rights, the federal provisions prevailed, and state courts were obliged to follow the decisions of federal courts with little or no reference to their own state constitutions. When a more conservative U.S. Supreme Court under the leadership of chief justices Warren E. Burger (1969) and William Rehnquist (1972) began to render more constrained decisions on individual rights, state courts began to render more expansive protections under their own bills of rights. This more active role on the part of state courts was soon termed the "new judicial federalism." Moreover, states are not precluded from protecting individuals in areas in which there are no federal protections. We will discuss the Texas bill of rights in more detail later in this chapter.

The U.S. Constitution, it is generally accepted, provides no national guarantee of a person's right to a public education. But some state constitutions, including Texas's, do have such a guarantee, and some state judges have ruled that state legislators have a responsibility to fund public education equitably. On another issue that raised the question of equal treatment, some states, including Texas, amended their constitutions to prohibit same-sex marriages while others did not, forcing the federal courts to step in and address the controversy. The issue was resolved when the U.S. Supreme Court, in a landmark decision in 2015, upheld same-sex marriages. That ruling invalidated the prohibition in the Texas Constitution.

The U.S. Constitution ignores the subject of local governments, which falls under the constitutional authority of the states. The Texas Constitution has two articles covering local governments, with very detailed provisions governing their structure, jurisdiction, and authority.

We will discuss further differences between federal and state constitutional authority and how authority in these areas is determined in Chapter 3.

The Texas Constitution created a state government that shares features with most other states, but there are differences. Texas and most states, for example, have an executive branch headed by an elected governor who shares executive authority with several other independently elected officeholders. This plural executive arrangement contrasts sharply with the president of the United States' appointed cabinet administration. As in every other state except Nebraska, lawmaking authority in Texas is vested in a bicameral (two-chamber) legislature. Nebraska has a unicameral (one-chamber) legislature. But Texas is one of only four states and by far the most populous state whose legislature doesn't meet in regular session every year. And Texas is one of only two states that have two state appellate courts of last resort. Every other state has only one supreme court. These institutional differences will be discussed in more detail later in this chapter and in Chapters 5, 6, and 8.

The Constitutional Legacy

2.2 Describe the historical influences, similarities, and differences among Texas's first six constitutions.

Each of Texas's constitutions was written in a distinct historical setting, and there are significant differences as well as similarities among these documents. All of these different constitutions have contributed to the state and local governments that exist today.

2.2.1 The Constitution of *Coahuila y Tejas* (1827)

Texas was part of Mexico when Mexico secured its independence from Spain in 1821, about the time that Stephen F. Austin began to bring Anglo colonists to the sparsely populated Texas region. In 1824, the new Republic of Mexico adopted a constitution for a federal system of government that recognized Texas (Tejas) as a single state with Coahuila, which adjoined Texas across the Rio Grande. Saltillo, Mexico, was the state capital.

The constitution of *Coahuila y Tejas*, completed in 1827, provided for a **unicameral** congress of twelve deputies, including two from Texas, elected by the people. Most of the members of congress were from the more populous and Spanish-speaking Coahuila, and the state's laws were published in Spanish, which few Anglo colonists in Texas understood. The executive department included a governor and a vice governor. The governor enforced the law, led the state militia, and granted pardons. Catholicism was the state religion, but that provision was not enforced among Texas's Anglo settlers. Anglo Texans also were not subject to military service, taxes, or custom duties. Texas primarily served as a buffer between Mexico and various Native American tribes—and the United States.

But as Anglo immigration increased, Mexico began to fear the possibility of U.S. expansion and soon started trying to exercise more control over Texas. Many Anglo settlers from the United States also felt more allegiance to the U.S. than they did to the Mexican government. These developments reinforced cultural differences and soon led to revolution by Anglo Texans.[8]

This formative period produced contributions to the Texas constitutional tradition that still exist, including some property and land laws, water laws and water rights, and community property laws. One justification for the Texas revolution of 1836 was the Mexican government's failure to sufficiently fund public education. Even though there were expectations of funding by the central government, a "concept of local control over school development was firmly established" during that era.[9] Issues of local control and adequate funding of public schools persist today.

unicameral
A single-body legislature.

2.2.2 The Constitution of the Republic of Texas (1836)

During the late 1820s and the early 1830s, increased immigration into Texas from the United States heightened tensions between the Anglo settlers and the Mexican government. Mexico's efforts to enforce its laws within Texas produced conflicts between cultures, legal traditions, and economic interests that sparked open rebellion by the colonists.

At the same time, Mexico was embroiled in its own internal dissension, which resulted in the seizure of power by the popular general Antonio López de Santa Anna Pérez de Lebrón. Santa Anna began to suspend the powers of the Mexican Congress and local governments, and in October 1835, the national Constitution of 1824 was voided. Mexico adopted a new constitution providing for a **unitary system** with power centralized in the national congress and the presidency, and local governments having only those powers granted to them by the central government. It repealed the principle of **federalism**, which had divided power between the national government and the Mexican states and had given states considerable autonomy within their areas of responsibility. This major change intensified conflicts between the national government and the states; although Texas was eventually successful in establishing its autonomy, several other Mexican states were subjected to harsh military retaliation.

As the new Mexican government tried to enforce control over Texas, colonists who initially supported the national government and others who were ambivalent began to support the independence movement. Stephen F. Austin, for example, had initially supported the position that Texas was a Mexican state, and he represented a large part of the Texas Anglo population. But when Mexican troops marched into Texas in the fall of 1835, Austin called for resistance.

Fifty-nine male colonists convened in the small Texas settlement of Washington-on-the-Brazos to declare Texas's independence from Mexico on March 2, 1836, and to adopt a constitution for the new republic two weeks later. They had two overriding interests: the preservation of their fledgling nation and the preservation of their own lives. By the time they had finished their work, the Alamo, only 150 miles away, had fallen to a large Mexican army under Santa Anna, and a second Mexican force had crossed the Rio Grande into Texas. So, the frontier constitution writers wasted little time.

Consequently, the Constitution of the Republic, adopted on March 16, 1836, was not cluttered with the details that weaken the present Texas Constitution. It drew heavily from the U.S. Constitution and from the constitutions of several southern states, from which most of the delegates had immigrated to Texas. The new constitution created an elected **bicameral** congress and provided for an elected president. There was no official, state-preferred religion, and members of the clergy were prohibited from serving as president or in congress. Slavery was legal under the new document, but it prohibited the importation of enslaved people from any country other than the United States.

On April 21, 1836, approximately six weeks after the Texans' defeat at the Alamo, the Texas army, under the command of Sam Houston, defeated Santa Anna's army at the Battle of San Jacinto. The war for independence was relatively short and had limited casualties, but the problems of creating a new, stable political system in the sparsely populated, wilderness republic were seemingly formidable. There was no viable government in place, no money to pay for a government, and no party system.[10] In addition, although defeated, Mexico did not relinquish its claims to Texas and remained a threat to try to regain its lost territory. Nevertheless, the "transition from colony to constitutional republic was accomplished quickly and with a minimum of disorganization."[11]

The experience of national autonomy from 1836 to 1845 has contributed significantly to the development of a sense of historical uniqueness among Texans.

unitary system
A system in which ultimate power is vested in a central or national government and local governments have only those powers granted to them by the central government. This principle also describes the relationship between the state and local governments in Texas.

federalism
A system that balances the power and sovereignty of state governments with that of the national government. Both the states and the national government derive their authority directly from the people, and the states have considerable autonomy within their areas of responsibility.

bicameral
A lawmaking body, such as the Texas legislature, that includes two chambers.

Although the effects on the state's political psyche may be difficult to measure, the "Lone Star" experience has been kept alive through school history texts, the celebration of key events, and the development of a mythology of the independence period.

2.2.3 The Constitution of 1845

During the independence movement and immediately thereafter, some Texans made overtures to the United States for annexation. That possibility initially was blocked by the slavery issue and its relationship to economic and regional influence in U.S. politics. But increased immigration to Texas in the late 1830s and early 1840s, more interest among Texans in joining the Union, and expansionist policies of the U.S. government stepped up the pressure for annexation. It was a major issue in the U.S. presidential campaign of 1844, and James K. Polk's election to the White House accelerated Texas's admission to the United States in 1845 because he campaigned for it.

The annexation treaty approved by the U.S. Congress included a compromise that allowed slavery to continue in Texas.[12] Racial issues that emerged in this period continue to affect politics and public policy in the state. Texas still struggles with voting rights issues, inequities in education funding, and unequal distribution of economic resources, affecting the quality of life of many minority group members today.

The state constitution drafted to allow Texas's annexation was about twice as long as the Constitution of 1836. It borrowed from its predecessor and from the constitutions of other southern states, particularly Louisiana.

The Constitution of 1845 created an elected legislature that included a House of Representatives and a Senate, which met biennially. It provided for an elected governor and an elected lieutenant governor, and it empowered the governor to appoint a secretary of state, attorney general, and state judges, subject to Senate confirmation. The legislature appointed a comptroller, treasurer, and land commissioner. In 1850, however, Texas voters amended the constitution to make most state offices elective, following a national pattern of fragmenting the powers of the executive branch of state government. Texas still has a **plural executive** under which practically all statewide officeholders are elected independently of the governor, a system that contrasts sharply with the appointive cabinet system of executive government headed by the president of the United States.

plural executive
A fragmented system of authority under which most statewide, executive officeholders are elected independently of the governor. This arrangement, which is used in Texas, places severe limitations on the governor's power.

CAMPAIGNING FOR TEXAS STATEHOOD

An 1844 political cartoon depicted presidential candidate James K. Polk (upper right, holding American flag) welcoming Texas leaders Stephen F. Austin and Sam Houston (crossing bridge) to the United States. Polk was elected to the White House that year after campaigning for Texas's admission to the Union, and Texas became the twenty-eighth state in 1845. Several prominent American opponents of Texas statehood are depicted at the bottom of the cartoon.

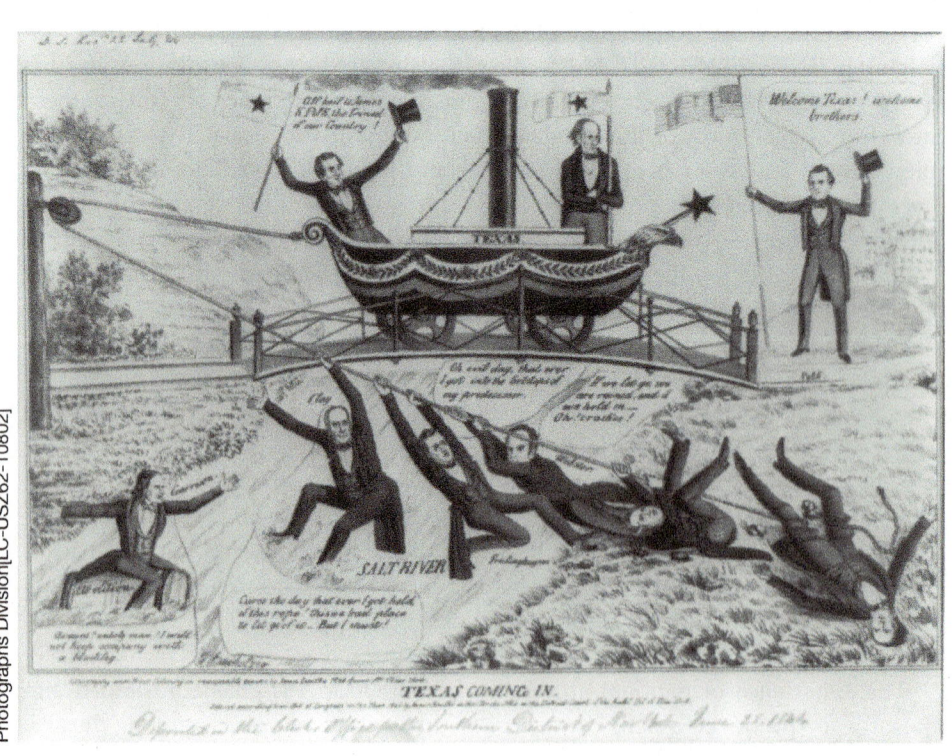

The 1845 constitution established a permanent fund for the support of public schools, protected homesteads from foreclosure, and guaranteed separate property rights for married women—provisions found in the present constitution. The 1845 document also recognized slavery, prohibited state-chartered banks, and barred anyone who had ever participated in a duel from holding public office. This constitution "worked so well that after several intervening constitutions, the people of Texas recopied it almost *in toto* as the Constitution of 1876."[13]

2.2.4 The Civil War Constitution (1861)

When Texas seceded from the Union in 1861, just before the outbreak of the Civil War, the state constitution was again revised. Most of the provisions of the 1845 document were retained, but significant changes were made in line with Texas's new membership in the Confederacy. The constitution required public officials to pledge their support of the Confederate constitution, gave greater protection to slavery, and prohibited the freeing of enslaved people. Governor Sam Houston, the hero of San Jacinto, opposed secession and refused to pledge his loyalty to the Confederacy. This prompted the delegates to the secession convention to declare the office of governor vacant and replace Houston with Lieutenant Governor Edward Clark. His political career ended, Houston retired to his home in Huntsville, where he died in 1863.

Slavery and secession destroyed any semblance of a two-party system in Texas. Personalities, factions, and war-related issues dominated state politics. Factionalism within the Democratic Party persisted for more than 100 years, until the emergence of a two-party system in the 1980s.

The Civil War era also contributed to a protracted, post-war dispute between southern state leaders and the federal government over so-called "states' rights," which persisted well into the next century and sparked an extended struggle for desegregation. Fighting to preserve slavery, the southern states contended that the national government was a **confederacy**, from which a state could withdraw, or secede. Although the northern victory dispelled this interpretation, Texas and other southern states found ways to thwart national policy—including a series of discriminatory laws and practices, as well as violence, against African Americans—through the 1960s. The southern efforts were based, in part, on the continued arguments for "states' rights."

SAM HOUSTON
The early Texas hero opposed secession and was replaced as governor when Texas joined the Confederacy in 1861. He died two years later.

confederacy
A view of the national government taken by eleven southern states, including Texas, that a state could withdraw, or secede, from the Union. Upon secession that began in 1860, the Confederate States of America was formed, leading to the Civil War.

2.2.5 The Constitution of 1866

After the Civil War, Texas government returned to national control, first through a military government and then through a provisional government headed by A. J. Hamilton, a former U.S. congressman who had remained loyal to the Union. Those were dark days for Texans. Although relatively few battles had been fought in Texas and the state had not suffered from the scorched-earth tactics used by Union generals elsewhere, the economy was in disarray. Many Texas families had lost loved ones, and many surviving Confederate veterans had been wounded physically or psychologically. New policies adopted by the federal government to assist newly freed enslaved people were never fully funded and were only halfheartedly, and often dishonestly, carried out. The presence of an occupation army also heightened tensions and shaped subsequent political attitudes.

The Reconstruction plan initiated by President Abraham Lincoln but never fully carried out envisioned a rapid return to civilian government for the southern states and their quick reintegration as equals into the U.S. political system. Requirements were few: the abolition of slavery, the repudiation of the Secession Ordinance of 1861, and the repudiation of all debts and obligations incurred under the Confederacy.[14]

Texas voters revived the Constitution of 1845 and amended it to include the new Union requirements. The new constitution formally eliminated slavery and gave formerly enslaved people the right to own property and legal rights before a jury. But African Americans were prohibited from testifying in court against whites and denied the right to vote.[15] The new constitution was adopted in June 1866; a new government was elected, and on August 20, 1866, President Andrew Johnson, who had become president after Lincoln's assassination, "declared the rebellion in Texas at an end."[16]

Very soon, however, **Radical Reconstructionists**, who had captured control of the U.S. Congress in 1866, replaced Johnson's mild Reconstruction policies with more severe ones. The new Congress invalidated the new Texas Constitution. It also passed, over the president's veto, the Reconstruction Acts, which established military governments throughout the South. The civilian government initiated by the state's Constitution of 1866 was short lived, and Texas functioned for two years under a reinstituted military government.

This period had an enduring impact on Texas constitutional law and politics. It prolonged the full reintegration of Texas into the national political system, and it transformed Texas's constitutional tradition into one of hostility and suspicion toward government.

Radical Reconstructionists
The group of Republicans who took control of Congress in 1866 and imposed military governments on the former Confederate states after the Civil War.

MEMBERS OF THE 1875 CONVENTION
Ninety delegates, including six recently emancipated African Americans, were elected to the Constitutional Convention of 1875.

2.2.6 The Constitution of Reconstruction (1869)

The Reconstruction Acts required a Texas Constitution that would grant African Americans the right to vote and include other provisions acceptable to Congress. A Republican Party slate of delegates to a new constitutional convention drafted a new charter in 1869. It did not reflect the majority of Texans' sentiments of the time, but it conformed to Republican wishes. Centralizing more powers in state government while weakening local government, the charter gave the governor a four-year term and the power to appoint other top state officials, including members of the judiciary. It gave African Americans the right to vote; provided for annual legislative sessions; and, for the first time in Texas, established a centralized, statewide system of public schools. Texans were unhappy with their new constitution and outraged by the widespread abuses that followed under the administration of Radical Republican Governor Edmund J. Davis.

In the 1869 election, the first under the new constitution, large numbers of formerly enslaved people voted, whereas white Texans who had fought for the Confederacy were not allowed to cast ballots as retribution for taking up arms against the United States. Radical supporters of Davis, a former Union Army officer, supervised the election process. The military governor certified that Davis beat Conservative Republican A. J. Hamilton by 39,901 to 39,092 votes, despite widespread flagrant incidents of voter fraud, which also were ignored by President Ulysses S. Grant and Congress. Davis, who had moved to Texas from his native Florida as a young man, opposed the Confederacy and fled Texas after secession before joining the Union Army. During Reconstruction, his promotion of civil rights programs for the recently freed enslaved African Americans put him at odds with many white, secessionist Texans. And other actions of his administration angered many of his constituents even more. A radical majority in the new Texas legislature approved a series of authoritarian—and, in some cases, unconstitutional—laws proposed by Davis. They gave the governor the power to declare martial law and suspend the laws in any county and created a state police force under the governor's control that could deprive citizens of constitutional protections. The governor was empowered to appoint mayors, district attorneys, and hundreds of other local officials. Another law designating newspapers as official printers of state documents in effect put much of the press under government control.

Texans soon struck back. In 1872, they elected a Democratic majority to the legislature, which abolished the state police and repealed other Davis-backed laws. Then, in 1873, they elected a Confederate veteran, Democrat Richard Coke, governor by more than a two-to-one margin over Davis. Like the Radical Republicans in the previous gubernatorial election, however, the Democrats abused the democratic process. Voting fraud again was widespread. "Democrat politicos bluntly indicated that power would be won depending on who outfrauded whom. No practice was ignored. There were terror, intimidation, and some murders on both sides," wrote historian T. R. Fehrenbach.[17]

Davis initially refused to leave office as his term was ending in January 1874, and armed supporters and opponents of the governor began to gather in and around the capitol, threatening an eruption of violence. Davis sent a telegram to President Grant, asking for federal troops to help keep order. Grant refused. Davis then yielded and left the capitol, preventing additional bloodshed. Reconstruction was ending, and the Constitution of 1869 was doomed.

The Constitution of 1876

2.3 Discuss the origins of the Constitution of 1876, its general principles, and the weaknesses and restrictions it still imposes on state government today.

The restored Democratic majority promptly took steps to assemble a new constitutional convention, which convened in Austin on September 6, 1875. The delegates were all men. Most were products of a rural and frontier South and, still smarting from Reconstruction, they considered government a necessary evil that had to be heavily restricted. Many, however, had previous governmental experience. Initially, seventy-five Democrats and fifteen Republicans were elected delegates, but one Republican resigned after only limited service and was replaced by a Democrat.[18]

The vast majority of the delegates were white, and some disagreement remains over how many African Americans served in the convention. Some historians say there were six. According to one account, however, six African Americans were elected but one resigned after only one day of service and was replaced in a special election by a white delegate. All of the African American delegates were Republicans.[19]

Only four of the delegates were native Texans. Most had immigrated to Texas from other southern states, including nineteen—the largest single group—from Tennessee. Their average age was 45. The oldest was 68; the youngest was 23.[20] Eleven of the delegates had been members of previous constitutional conventions in Texas, but there is disagreement over whether any had participated in drafting the Reconstruction Constitution of 1869. In any event, the 1869 constitution was considered a negative influence, not a positive one, by most delegates.

At least thirty delegates had served in the Texas legislature, two had served in the Tennessee and Mississippi legislatures, two had represented Texas in the U.S. Congress, and two had represented Texas in the Confederate Congress. Delegates also included a former Texas attorney general, a former lieutenant governor, and a former secretary of state of Texas; at least eight of the delegates had been judges. Many had been high-ranking Confederate military officers. One, John H. Reagan, had been postmaster general of the Confederacy.[21] Reagan later would become a U.S. senator from Texas and the first chairman of the Texas Railroad Commission.

Another delegate who epitomized the independent, frontier spirit of the time was John S. "Rip" Ford, a native of South Carolina who had come to Texas in 1836 as a physician. He later became a lawyer, journalist, state senator, mayor of Austin, and Texas Ranger captain. In 1874, he had been among those marching on the capitol to force Edmund J. Davis to relinquish the governor's office to his elected successor. Ford had been a secessionist delegate to the 1861 convention and, during the Civil War, had commanded a makeshift cavalry regiment that fought Union soldiers along the Texas–Mexico border.[22]

According to one account, delegates to the 1875 convention included thirty-three lawyers, twenty-eight farmers, three physicians, three merchants, two teachers, two editors, and one minister. At least eleven other delegates were part-time farmers who also pursued other occupations.[23] Other historians have suggested slightly different breakdowns, but all agree that agricultural interests substantially influenced the writing of the new Texas charter.

About half the delegates were members of the Society of the Patrons of Husbandry, or the **Grange**, an organization formed to improve the lot of farmers. The Grange became politically active in the wake of national scandals involving abuses by big business and government. It started organizing in Texas in 1873, and it influenced constitutional provisions that limited taxes and governmental expenditures and restricted banks, railroads, and other corporations.

The delegates did not try to produce a document that would be lauded as a model of constitutional perfection or mistaken for a literary classic. They faced the reality of addressing serious, pressing problems—an immediate crisis that did not encourage debate over the finer points of academic or political theory or produce any prophetic visions of the twenty-first century.

The Civil War and Reconstruction had ruined the state economically and driven state government deeply into debt, even though Texas citizens, particularly property owners, had been heavily taxed. Land prices had plummeted, a disaster for what was then an agricultural state. Pervasive governmental corruption and Governor Davis's administration had left deep scars and resentments among Texans.

In an effort to restore economic stability and governmental control to the people, the framers of the Texas Constitution of 1876 drafted what was essentially an antigovernment charter. They replaced centralization with more local control; strictly limited taxation; and put short leashes on the legislature, the courts, and the governor.[24] Agricultural interests, which had been called upon to finance industrial development and new public services during Reconstruction, were again protected from excessive governmental intrusion and taxation.

The changes in the new constitution would later hamper the state's commercial and economic development. But the post-Reconstruction Texans liked all the restrictions placed on government. They ratified the new constitution in February 1876 by a vote of 136,606 to 56,052.

Grange
An organization formed in the late nineteenth century to improve the lot of farmers. Its influence in Texas after Reconstruction was felt in constitutional provisions limiting taxes and government spending and restricting banks, railroads, and other big businesses.

THE CONSTITUTION OF 1876
The seventh constitution, amended more than 500 times, remains in effect today.

2.3.1 General Principles of the Texas Constitution

The underlying principle of the Texas Constitution of 1876 is expressed in a relatively short preamble and the first two sections of a bill of rights (see Table 2–2). It is a social compact, formed by free men (no women participated in its drafting), in which "all political power is inherent in the people . . . founded on their authority, and instituted for their benefit."[25] These sections are based on the principles of **popular sovereignty** and **social contract** theory, both part of a legacy of constitutional law in the United States. But the declarations of a free and just society were limited in scope and application. Women and minorities were initially denied full citizenship rights. Women would not gain the right to vote until 1920, and it would take much longer for African Americans and Hispanics to receive full constitutional protections.

Other major principles of the Texas Constitution are **limited government** and **representative government**. The bill of rights and other provisions throughout the constitution place limits on governmental power and spell out traditional citizens' rights. The constitution also provides for elected officials to represent the people's interest in making laws and other governmental decisions.

The Texas bill of rights (Article 1) includes thirty-three sections covering such issues as freedom of worship, freedom of speech and press, protection from unreasonable searches and seizures, the right of assembly, and the right to bear arms. It also includes lengthy, detailed provisions on the due process rights of criminal defendants and the rights of victims, including the right to restitution. Section 32 of the bill of rights article, added as an amendment in 2005, banned same-sex marriages in Texas until it was invalidated by the U.S. Supreme Court in 2015, as noted earlier in this chapter. The most recent addition to the bill of rights, Section 33, adopted as an amendment in 2009, gave constitutional status to something Texans have enjoyed for generations, free access to state beaches. Only a few years later, however, the Texas Supreme Court issued a decision that, some experts believe, may undermine that right (see Chapter 8).

The principle of **separation of powers** also is part of the state constitution. Unlike the U.S. Constitution, in which this principle emerges through powers defined in the three articles related to Congress, the president, and the judiciary, Article 2 of the Texas Constitution specifically provides for a separation of powers.

popular sovereignty
The constitutional principle of self-government; the belief that the people control their government and governments are subject to limitations and constraints.

social contract
The view that governments originate from the general agreement among and consent of members of the public to address common interests and needs.

limited government
The constitutional principle restricting governmental authority and spelling out personal rights.

representative government
The constitutional principle that people elect representatives to make laws and other governmental decisions on their behalf.

separation of powers
The division of authority among three distinct branches of government—the legislative, the executive, and the judicial—that allows the branches to serve as checks and balances on one another's power.

2.3.2 The Three Branches of Texas Government

The Constitution of 1876 created three branches of government—legislative, executive, and judicial—and provided for a system of checks and balances to ensure that no branch would dominate the others. This principle originated with the U.S. Constitution, whose drafters were concerned about the so-called mischief of factions.[26] They feared that special interest groups would be able to capture control of governmental institutions and pursue policies harmful to the national interest. To guard against that potential problem, they fragmented institutional power. In some respects, this was an issue of even greater concern to the framers of the Texas Constitution, reacting, as they were, to the highly centralized authority and controversies of the Davis administration.

LEGISLATIVE BRANCH Lawmaking authority in Texas is assigned to an elected legislature that includes a 150-member House of Representatives and a 31-member Senate. It meets in regular sessions in odd-numbered years and in special sessions of limited scope and duration when called by the governor. The sixty-five sections of Article 3 spell out in detail the powers granted to and the restrictions imposed on the legislature.

The constitution created a low-paid, part-time legislature to ensure the election of citizen–lawmakers who would be sensitive to the needs of their constituents, not the election of professional politicians who would live off the taxpayers. Unwittingly, however, the constitution writers also produced a lawmaking body easily influenced by special interest groups. And the strict limitations placed on the legislature's operations and powers slow its ability to meet the increasingly complex needs of a growing, modern Texas.

In 1972, voters approved a constitutional amendment to lengthen the terms of the governor and most other executive officeholders from two to four years. This change gave the governor more time to develop public policies with the prospect of seeing them implemented. But voters repeatedly have rejected proposals to provide for annual legislative sessions, and legislative pay remains among the lowest in the country.

EXECUTIVE BRANCH An elected governor shares authority over the executive branch with several other independently elected, statewide officeholders. The governor can veto bills approved by the legislature, and a veto can be overridden only by a two-thirds vote of the House and the Senate.

Many experts believe that the Texas Constitution excessively fragments governmental authority and responsibility, particularly in the executive branch. Although the public may expect the governor to establish policy priorities, the governor does not have control over other elected state executives but, instead, shares both authority and responsibility for policy with them. This restriction can create problems. Governor Bill Clements, for example, was the only Republican in the executive branch when he first took office in 1979 and had to share executive responsibilities with Democrats who sharply disagreed with his priorities. Even when the governor and other elected officials are of the same party, differences in personality, political philosophy, and policy objectives can produce tension and sometimes deadlock. This divisiveness became particularly strident in 2006, when Comptroller Carole Keeton Strayhorn, a Republican, repeatedly questioned Republican Governor Rick Perry's policies and then became an independent candidate to challenge his reelection unsuccessfully.

The governor's power has been further diffused by the creation over the years of numerous boards and commissions that set policy for executive agencies not headed by elected officials. Although the governor appoints most of these board members, they serve staggered six-year terms that are longer than a governor's term. And a newly elected governor—who cannot fire a predecessor's appointees—usually has to wait through most of his or her first term to gain a majority of appointees to most boards.

ON THE SAME POLITICAL PAGE
Governor Greg Abbott campaigns with Comptroller Glenn Hegar (left) and Lieutenant Governor Dan Patrick. All three officeholders are Republicans and share many governmental priorities.

Fragmented authority also is a characteristic of county governments, which the constitution created as administrative agencies of the state. Various elected county officials often clash over public policy, producing inefficiencies or failing to meet public needs. And just as voters have to fill out a long ballot for statewide offices, they also must choose among a long, often confusing list of county officers. A long ballot discourages many people from voting, and this obstacle reduces public accountability, an end result that the framers of the Constitution of 1876 certainly never intended.

JUDICIAL BRANCH Also elected are members of the judiciary—from justices of the peace, with limited jurisdiction at the county level, to those on the highest statewide appellate courts. This provision reflects the strong sentiment of post-Reconstruction Texans for an independent judiciary and is a major difference from the federal government, in which the president appoints judges to lifetime terms. Also, unlike the federal system, in which the U.S. Supreme Court is the court of last resort in both civil and criminal appeals, Texas has two courts of last resort. The Texas Supreme Court has jurisdiction over civil matters, and the Texas Court of Criminal Appeals has final review of criminal cases.

2.3.3 Weaknesses and Criticisms of the Current Constitution

In addition to the structural weaknesses in the three branches of government already discussed, the Texas Constitution of 1876 has been criticized for other inherent weaknesses built into the document. Experts have identified these as an inequitable public education system, budgeting and finances that cannot be easily altered to meet changing state needs, past restrictions on individual rights for African Americans and other groups, an unnecessary level of confusing statutory detail, and an amendment process that requires excessive amendments to enable state government to adapt to changes.

PUBLIC EDUCATION Like the executive branch of state government, the public school system is decentralized. The centralized school system authorized under the Constitution of 1869 was abolished, and local officials were given the primary responsibility of supervising public education. The concept of "local control" over their schools is important to many Texans, but decentralization and wide disparities in local tax bases have produced an inequitable public education system.

BUDGETING AND FINANCES The Texas Constitution, including amendments adopted after 1876, requires a balanced state budget. It also dedicates large amounts of revenue to specific purposes, making it increasingly difficult for lawmakers to address changing state needs. Voters increased the amount of dedicated revenue in 2015 when they approved an amendment setting aside a portion of sales tax revenue for highway construction to supplement the gasoline tax revenue already dedicated to highways.

INDIVIDUAL RIGHTS Although declaring a general commitment to democracy and individual rights, the constitution was used for many years to slow democratic development in Texas.[27] Like many other southern states, Texas had restrictive laws on voter participation. It levied a poll tax, which reduced voting by minorities and poor whites until 1966, when an amendment to the U.S. Constitution and a U.S. Supreme Court decision outlawed poll taxes. Federal courts also struck down a Texas election system that excluded African Americans from voting in the Democratic primary, which decided elections when Texas was a one-party Democratic state. The elimination of significant numbers of people, especially minorities, from participating in elections helped perpetuate the one-party political system for approximately 100 years.[28] It also severely limited the number of African Americans and Hispanics elected to office in Texas during that period.

EXCESSIVE DETAILS The Texas Constitution is burdened with excessive detail. Although few individuals have read the entire 90,000-word document, a person casually perusing it can find language, for example, governing the operation of hospital districts in specific counties. Another provision deals with expenditures for relocating or replacing sanitation sewer lines on private property. And if one rural county wants to abolish an outdated constitutional office, the legislature and voters throughout the state have to approve the necessary constitutional amendment. Whereas the 7,000-word U.S. Constitution leaves the details for implementation to congressional legislation, the Texas Constitution often spells out the authority and power of a governmental agency in specific detail. Most experts would argue that many constitutional articles are of a legislative nature and have no business being in a constitution.[29] The excessive detail limits the adaptability of the constitution in the face of changing circumstances and places undue restrictions on state and local governments.

Consequently, obsolete and contradictory provisions in the constitution create confusion in interpretation and application. Constitutional amendments have been periodically approved to "clean up" such deadwood, but the problem persists.[30]

THE AMENDMENT PROCESS Another important criticism of the Texas Constitution focuses on amendments and the amendment process. Alabama has had more constitutional amendments (946) than any other state (see Figure 2–1), but Texas ranked fourth, behind Alabama, California, and South Carolina with 507 amendments through 2019. In contrast, the U.S. Constitution has been amended only twenty-seven times since 1789, and ten of those amendments were adopted as the Bill of Rights

FIGURE 2–1 TEXAS CONSTITUTION COMPARED WITH OTHER STATE CONSTITUTIONS (2019)

This map shows when each state's current constitution was adopted and the number of amendments that have been added since then. Texas is one of only eight states that have amended their constitutions more than 200 times.

SOURCE: Based on data found in *The Book of the States*, 2019 Edition, Table 1.3 (Lexington, KY: The Council of State Governments, 2019) accessed at http://knowledgecenter.csg.org/kc/content/book-states-2019-chapter-1-state-constitutions.

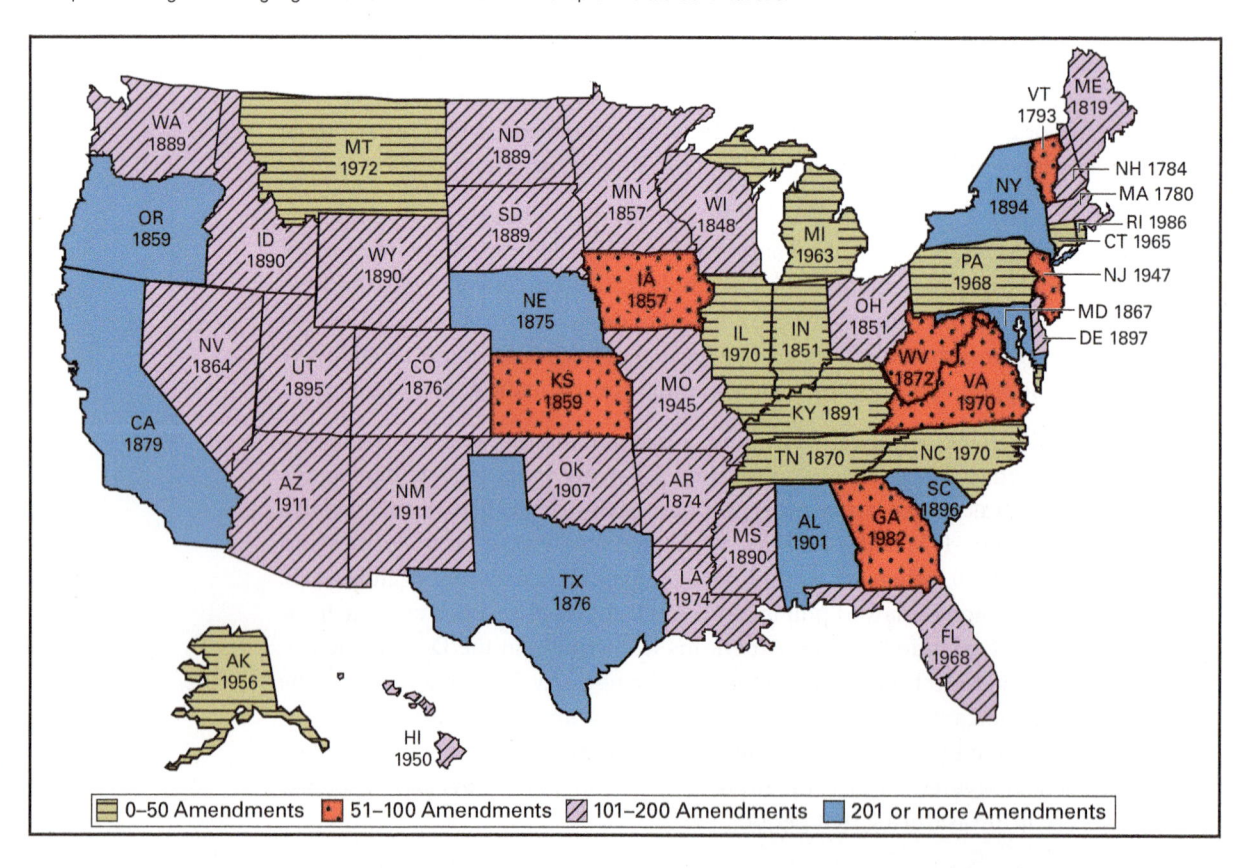

immediately after the government organized. The numerous restrictions and prohibitions in the Texas Constitution require excessive amendments to enable state government to adapt to social, economic, and political changes.

Constitutional Change and Adaptation

2.4 Contrast the relative ease and frequency of the constitutional amendment process with the difficulty of enacting more fundamental change through the constitutional convention process.

Although they loaded the constitution with numerous restrictive provisions, the nineteenth-century drafters also provided a relatively easy method of amending it. Over the years, this piecemeal amendment process has enabled state government to meet some changing needs, but it also has added thousands of words to the document.

2.4.1 Amendments

Proposed constitutional amendments can be submitted to Texas voters only by the legislature. Approval by two-thirds of the House and the Senate puts them on the ballot; adoption requires a majority vote. Although voters had approved 507 amendments through 2019, they had rejected 180 others. The first amendment was adopted on September 2, 1879. Each regular legislative session normally approves several amendments for the voters to approve or reject. A record twenty-five amendments were placed on the November 3, 1987, ballot. Seventeen were adopted, and eight were defeated. Twenty-two amendments were on a September 13, 2003, special election ballot, and all were approved. Most of the amendments have been adopted since 1971, as continued population growth and the complexities of modern urbanization have required or prompted an increasing number of constitutional changes (see Table 2–3).

Some amendments are of major statewide importance, but many affect only a single county or a handful of counties or have been offered simply to rid the constitution of obsolete language. One amendment adopted in 1993 affected only about 140 families, two church congregations, and one school district in two counties. It cleared up a property title defect. Numerous amendments, it can be argued, are offered to benefit influential special interest groups or specific communities. Voters in 2001 approved an amendment to allow a property tax exemption for raw coffee beans and cocoa imported through the Port of Houston. The amendment was promoted by businesspeople seeking to increase imports of those commodities through Houston.

Unlike voters in many other states, Texas citizens cannot force the placement of constitutional amendments or binding statewide referenda on the ballot because Texas does not have an **initiative** or **referendum** system on a statewide level. Adopting that process would require still another constitutional amendment, and the legislature historically has opposed giving such a significant policy prerogative to the electorate.

initiative
A petition and election process whereby voters propose laws or constitutional amendments for adoption by a popular vote.

referendum
An election, usually initiated by a petition of voters, whereby an action of a legislative body is submitted for approval or rejection by the voters.

TABLE 2–3 A MORE POPULOUS AND MORE URBAN TEXAS REQUIRES MORE AMENDMENTS

Period	State's Characteristics	Amendments Adopted
1876–1900	Overwhelmingly rural, population reaching 3 million	16
1901–1950	Gradually changing from rural to urban, population rising to 7.7 million	90
1951–1970	Urban population increasing to 80 percent, population climbing to 11 million	94
1971–2019	Urban population heading toward 90 percent, population passing 28 million	307

A RIGHT TO A CUP OF COFFEE?
The Texas Constitution may not go that far, but it does include a provision granting a tax break on coffee beans imported through the Port of Houston.

Sometimes, however, the legislature has sought political cover by selectively letting voters decide particularly controversial issues, such as a binding referendum in 1987 to legalize pari-mutuel betting on horse and dog racing.

2.4.2 Constitutional Convention

The constitution also provides for revision by constitutional convention, which the legislature can call with the approval of the voters. Delegates to such a convention have to be elected, and proposed changes adopted by a constitutional convention also must be approved by voters. Voters overwhelmingly rejected a proposal for a constitutional convention in 1919.[31] Subsequent efforts, including an attempt by Governor John Connally in 1967, to hold conventions also were defeated.[32] Connally's efforts, however, resulted in adoption of a "cleanup" amendment in 1969 that removed many obsolete provisions from the constitution and laid the groundwork for a constitutional convention in 1974.

2.4.3 The Constitutional Reform Efforts of 1971 to 1975

The **Constitutional Convention of 1974** has been the only one ever held under the present constitution, and it ended in failure. Its delegates were the 181 members of the legislature. The idea originated in 1971, when state Representative Nelson Wolff of San Antonio and several other first-term legislators won the leadership's backing for a full-scale revision effort, and the legislature submitted a constitutional amendment for a convention to the voters. In 1972, voters approved the amendment, which provided that the delegates would be the state senators and house members elected that year.

In 1973, the legislature created a thirty-seven-member Constitutional Revision Commission to hold public hearings throughout the state and make recommendations to the convention. The constitutional convention, or "con-con," as it came to be called by legislators and members of the media, convened on January 8, 1974. House Speaker Price Daniel, Jr., was elected president, and Lieutenant Governor Bill Hobby, in an address to delegates, offered a prophetic warning: "The special interests of today will be replaced by new and different special interests tomorrow, and any attempt to draft a constitution to serve such interests would be futile and also dishonorable."[33]

Hobby's warning was ignored. Special interests dominated the convention, which adjourned in failure on July 30, failing by three votes to get the two-thirds vote necessary to send a new constitution to Texas voters for ratification.

The crucial fight was over a business-backed attempt to lock the state's **right-to-work law** into the constitution. The right-to-work law prohibits union membership as a condition of employment, so organized labor bitterly fought the effort. Then as now, business was politically stronger than labor in Texas, but the two-thirds vote necessary to put a new constitution on the ballot was too great an obstacle.

Governor Dolph Briscoe's refusal to exercise leadership for a new constitution also hurt the revision effort. Except for opposing proposals that he thought would further weaken the governor's authority, Briscoe provided little input to the convention. Louisiana voters approved a new state constitution the next year, and Governor Edwin Edwards's strong support was considered instrumental. Gubernatorial leadership in other states also appears to have been critical to successful constitutional conventions.

Constitutional Convention of 1974
The last major attempt to write a new Texas Constitution. Members of the legislature served as delegates and failed to overcome political differences and the influence of special interests.

right-to-work law
Law prohibiting the requirement of union membership in order to get or hold a job.

Another major obstacle was the convention's makeup. The 181 members of the legislature were the delegates; soon after the convention began its work, many of them faced reelection campaigns in the party primaries, which diverted their attention and, in some cases, affected their willingness to vote for significant constitutional changes.

Additionally, a minority of legislators—dubbed "cockroaches" by convention President Daniel—did not want a new constitution and attempted to delay or obstruct the convention's work at every opportunity. Most legislators, even those who wanted a new constitution, were susceptible to the influence of special interests, far more susceptible than most private-citizen delegates likely would have been, and special interests were legion at the convention. In addition to various business and professional groups and organized labor, many county officeholders whose jobs—protected by the Constitution of 1876—were suddenly in jeopardy put pressure on the delegates.

During its next regular session in 1975, the legislature tried to resurrect the constitutional revision effort. Lawmakers voted to present to Texans—as eight separate constitutional amendments—the basic document that the convention had barely rejected the previous summer. The first three articles dealing with the separation of powers and the legislative and executive branches were combined into one ballot proposition. Each of the remaining seven propositions was a separate article, each to be independently approved or rejected by the voters. The most controversial issues that the 1974 convention had debated, such as right-to-work, were excluded. The streamlined amendments would have shortened the constitution considerably and provided major changes, including annual legislative sessions, a unified judicial system, and more flexibility in county government. Voters rejected all eight propositions on November 4, 1975, some by margins of more than two to one. A stock fraud scandal in the legislature in 1971 and the Watergate scandal that forced the resignation of President Richard Nixon in 1974 had raised Texans' distrust of government, and the proposed new constitution had been drafted by state officials, not by private citizens.

FINAL DAYS OF THE 1974 CONVENTION

After much preparation and deliberation, the proposed constitution of 1974 failed by three votes in the final hectic session of the constitutional convention, when the gallery was filled with interested onlookers, including many representatives of labor and other interest groups.

Nelson Wolff, who years later would be elected mayor of San Antonio and then county judge of Bexar County, also noted a general lack of citizen interest in the work of the constitutional convention. In his book, *Challenge of Change*, he wrote:

> The constitutional revision effort in Texas had attempted to use every means known to get citizen participation in the process. A toll-free telephone had been set up for the convention. Committees of the convention met at night and on weekends to provide working people an opportunity to testify. We provided to the best of our ability optimum conditions for testimony. Yet many people avoided participation in the revision process.[34]

Most people know little about the details of constitutions and constitutional revision, and many voters distrust governmental institutions.[35] Voter distrust and apathy played into the hands of numerous special interests that did not want a new constitution because they did not want to give up the protections that the old constitution afforded them.

The comprehensive constitutional amendments were thwarted, again, by Governor Dolph Briscoe. Although he had never taken an active role in the revision effort, three weeks before the 1975 election, he openly opposed the eight propositions and suggested that the existing constitution had served the state well and would continue to be adequate for the future.[36]

2.4.4 Further Piecemeal Reforms

The legislature then returned to its pattern of piecemeal constitutional changes. Between 1976 and 2019, Texas voters approved 285 amendments and rejected 47. Some amendments were designed to improve government operations; others were driven by political ideology. Significant amendments adopted during this period included the creation of the state lottery in 1991, two erecting obstacles to a state income tax in 1993 and 2019, and a series of propositions authorizing $3 billion in tax-backed bonds for a huge prison expansion program in the 1990s. In 1985, voters approved an amendment to give the governor and legislative leaders limited authority to deal with budgetary emergencies between legislative sessions, and in 1995, they approved an amendment to abolish the state treasurer's office and transfer its duties to the comptroller. In 2003, in a major dispute between doctors and trial lawyers, voters narrowly approved a constitutional amendment to ratify limits on monetary damages in medical malpractice lawsuits. In 2013, they approved a $2 billion fund for water development and conservation.

In 1999, the legislature rejected another proposal to rewrite the constitution but approved an amendment, which voters also approved, to remove more obsolete language from the document.

2.4.5 Constitutional Provisions, Interest Groups, and Elites

Only a small percentage of the voting-age population—often less than 10 percent—participates in elections when constitutional amendments are the only issues on the ballot (Figure 2–2). Turnout is higher when the legislature submits amendments to voters in gubernatorial or presidential election years. In many instances, though, a relative handful of Texans decides on fundamental changes in government, and often they are heavily influenced by one special interest group or another.

Interest groups, which historically have been strong in Texas, work to get provisions into the constitution that would benefit them or to keep provisions out that they fear would hurt them. Because most amendments do not involve partisan issues, a well-financed public relations campaign is likely to produce public support for an amendment.[37]

FIGURE 2-2   AVERAGE PERCENTAGE OF VOTER TURNOUT FOR CONSTITUTIONAL AMENDMENT, GUBERNATORIAL, AND PRESIDENTIAL ELECTIONS IN TEXAS, 1974–2017

Most constitutional amendment elections do not attract many voters. This graph shows the significant differences in voter turnout for constitutional amendment elections, compared to presidential and gubernatorial elections.

SOURCE: Texas Secretary of State, Elections Division.

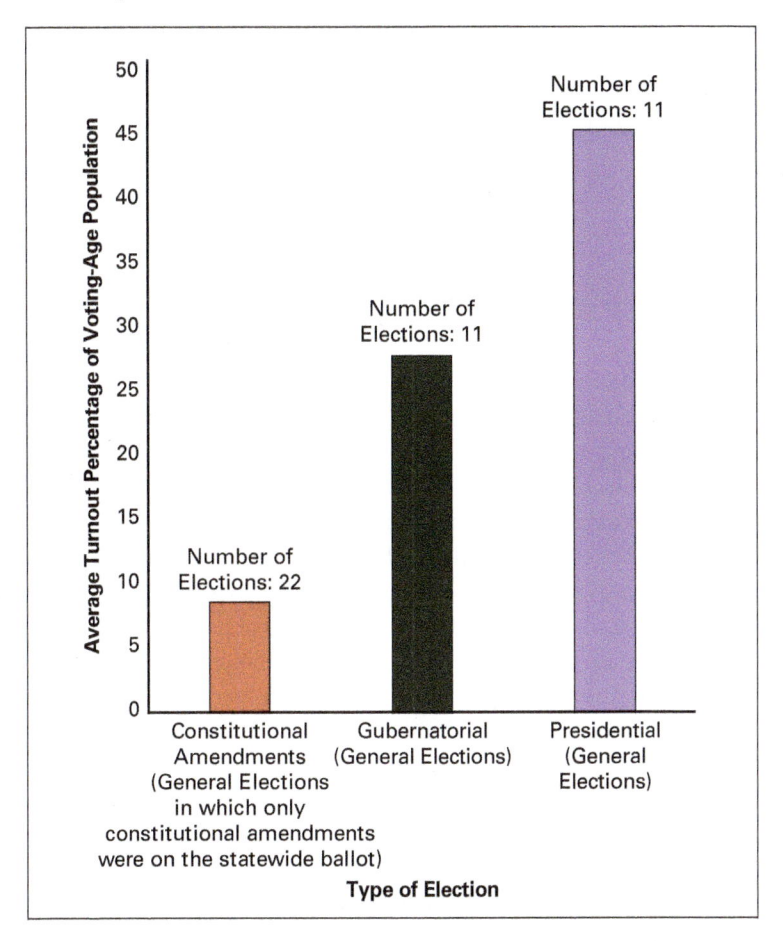

   Interest groups often play defense to maintain their status quo and are able to kill many proposed constitutional changes in the legislature, where the two-thirds vote requirement works to their advantage. Only a small fraction of constitutional amendments proposed by legislators get put on the ballot, and one or more interest groups usually support those amendments and finance publicity campaigns to promote the propositions to the voters. Relatively few amendments attract organized opposition after being put on the ballot, but there have been notable exceptions. One occurred in 2003, when doctors, insurance companies, and business interests heavily promoted Proposition 12, the ratification of new medical malpractice limits. They were successful, despite a media campaign against the amendment financed primarily by plaintiffs' lawyers. The amendment to ban same-sex marriage also attracted strong opposition in 2005, but it was approved by a wide margin. Voter turnout in these elections was above average for recent amendment elections, but still low.

   Many recent constitutional changes have reflected a pro-industry and economic development point of view contrasting sharply with the antibusiness sentiment of the original constitutional framers. However, one notable exception occurred in 2011 when voters, in a low-turnout election, rejected a proposed amendment that would have permitted counties to issue bonds for economic development. The amendment—one of ten on the ballot that year—received little publicity, and voters

VOTING CAN BE LONELY

A woman votes during a recent election in Tarrant County. Constitutional amendment elections consistently attract the lowest voter turnout.

may have been influenced by the fact that Texas and the country were emerging from a recession that had hit both household and government budgets hard.

Other recent amendments have helped build up a public-bonded indebtedness that the nineteenth-century constitution writers would have been unable to comprehend. Texas was rural then. It is now largely urban and the second most populous state, following California. As the state works to diversify and expand its economy and provide the infrastructure to support continued population growth, business has repeatedly turned to state government for tax breaks and other economic incentives and has found receptive ears in the legislature and the governor's office.

It has been argued that the Texas Constitution serves the interests of a small number of elites—individuals who control businesses and other dominant institutions in the state. According to this argument, the constraints built into the constitution limit the policy options of state government and historically have thwarted efforts to restructure or improve the tax system, education, social services, health care, and other policies that would benefit low- and middle-income people. Power is so fragmented that public interest advocates have repeatedly had to turn to the courts to force change. This same argument also has been made often about the U.S. Constitution.

If this interpretation is accurate, it is ironic that the original writers of the Texas Constitution of 1876 directed much of their wrath against railroads, banks, and other institutions that are today considered elitist. The tumultuous last quarter of the nineteenth century witnessed much class and economic conflict with the emergence of the Greenback and Populist political parties, which promoted the interests of lower-income people. But moneyed business interests eventually used the state constitution and subsequent legislation to reestablish their dominance over Texas government. Although the elite structure of the state has changed since 1876, some scholars argue that there has been a gradual transfer of power and control to new elites, who continue to exercise enormous influence over public policy.

CONCLUSION

Here you are, a twenty-first-century Texan, stuck with a nineteenth-century state constitution that has been dusted off, patched, and spliced so many times that a legion of lawyers could spend their entire careers trying to interpret all of it. Although that statement is admittedly an exaggeration, if you are like most Texans, you would rather ignore the constitution and let the lawyers worry about it. Even if you ignore it, however, it isn't going away. As long as you live in Texas, the constitution will have a significant impact on your life, whether or not you realize it. Both directly and indirectly, the Texas Constitution will help determine what kind of taxes—and how much—you will pay throughout your life, the quality of the public schools your children may someday attend, and even how much you can claim in damages if you are injured on the operating table by a careless surgeon. In the future, you might encounter an important neighborhood emergency that the legislature needs to address, only to discover that the legislature won't be meeting for another year because the Texas Constitution, unlike the constitutions of most other states, allows the legislature to meet in regular session only every other year.

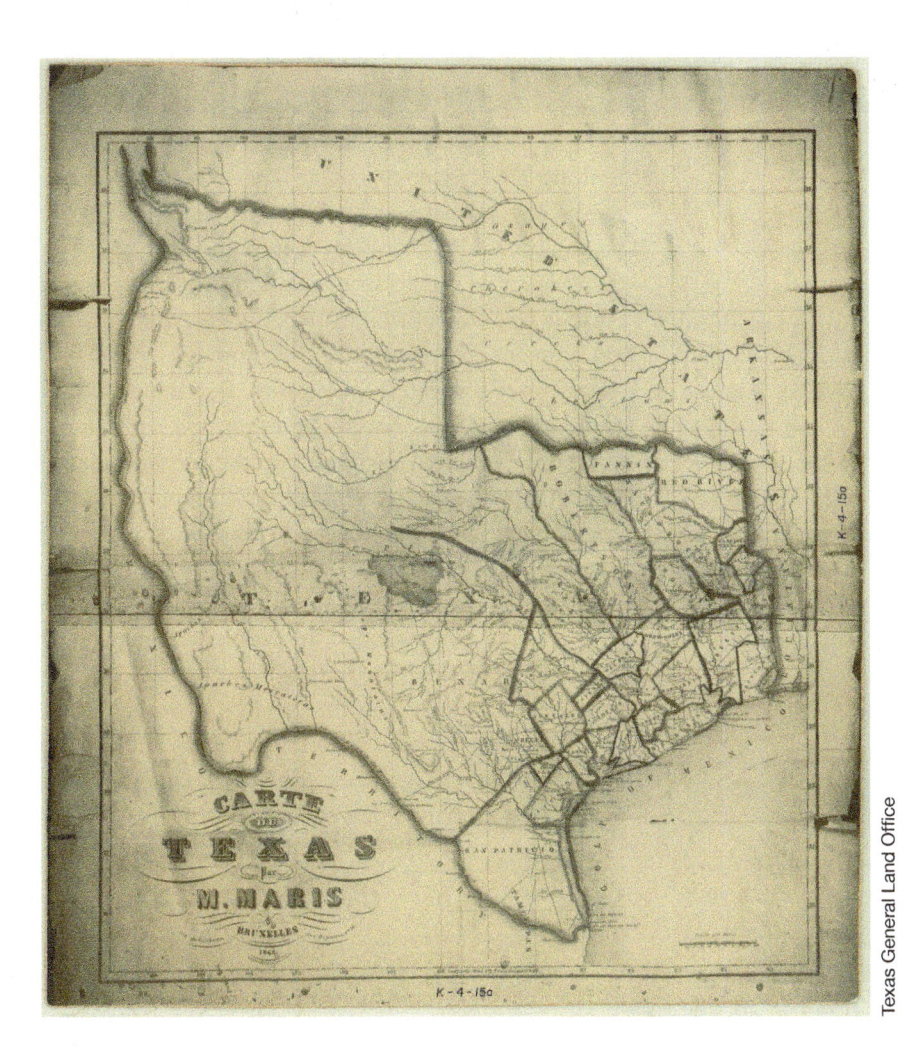

TEXAS DURING EARLY STATEHOOD
Texas has been trimmed down a bit since 1846, when this map of the state was produced.

For generations, many Texans have been suspicious of government, but most have made little effort to learn how government functions and why. Most Texans know little about the constitution and how it affects their lives. They are concerned about governmental abuses and excesses but care little about the mechanics of government, beginning with the state constitution. In the popular vernacular, "If it ain't broke, don't fix it." And the average layperson, if he or she thinks much about the state constitution at all, does not consider it to be "broke." Meanwhile, special interests, including some business groups, and people elected to obsolete public offices, which benefit from the existing constitution, will continue to resist efforts to change it, unless they see a chance to promote another self-serving amendment.

After reading this chapter, you have a better understanding of both the document and its historical development, and you know how it compares with constitutions in other states. The Texas Constitution is a basic map to the many highways, detours, and dead ends of state and local government in Texas. Many people think Texas needs a better, more modern map. But before that can happen, people like you need to better understand and know how to navigate with the current one.

REVIEW THE CHAPTER

Constitutionalism

2.1 Identify the functions of a constitution and place the Texas Constitution in a national comparative context, p. 35.

In addition to defining the formal institutional structure of governments, constitutions reflect the primary values and political objectives of a state. A constitution defines the relationships between those who govern and the general population and ultimately structures political power. A constitution limits the power and authority of government and provides basic protection for citizens from excesses and abuses of those who hold power. Whereas the U.S. Constitution is a concise, 7,000-word document that outlines broad, basic principles of authority and governance, the Texas Constitution, with its approximately 90,000 words, is (like the constitutions of many other states) an unwieldy and restrictive document.

The Constitutional Legacy

2.2 Describe the historical influences, similarities, and differences among Texas's first six constitutions, p. 38.

As have many other states, Texas has functioned under a series of constitutions: the Constitution of *Coahuila y Tejas* (1827), the Constitution of the Republic of Texas (1836), the Constitution of 1845, the Civil War Constitution (1861), the Constitution of 1866, the Constitution of Reconstruction (1869), and the Constitution of 1876. Each is appropriately understood from the perspective of the period in which it was adopted. These constitutions share some general similarities, but they also reveal a progression of changes over the state's history. Some changes improved the institutions of state government. Others served to constrain both state and local governments. Many contributions from the earlier documents can be found in the current constitution, the Constitution of 1876. But the Constitution of Reconstruction (1869) differed markedly from the current document.

The Constitution of 1876

2.3 Discuss the origins of the Constitution of 1876, its general principles, and the weaknesses and restrictions it still imposes on state government today, p. 43.

Texas currently operates under a constitution—its seventh—that was adopted following the Civil War and the Reconstruction era. Events of that period left a legacy of suspicion of government that still exists in Texas today, and that legacy is reflected in constitutional provisions limiting governmental power. The 1876 constitution was predicated on the theory that governmental excesses could be minimized by carefully defining what governments could or could not do. The major guiding principles of the current Texas Constitution are popular sovereignty, limited government, representative government, social contract theory, and separation of powers. But the constitution's detailed limitations on the governor, the legislature, and other governmental institutions and its decentralization of governmental authority limit the ability of state and local governments to adapt effectively to economic and demographic changes. Restrictions that the nineteenth-century constitution writers viewed as solutions to the problems of their era have compounded the problems of state and local governments today. The writers were unable to anticipate that the limitations they imposed on government would ultimately allow major economic interests and other elites within the state to dominate the policymaking process, often to the detriment of lower socioeconomic groups.

Constitutional Change and Adaptation

2.4 Contrast the relative ease and frequency of the constitutional amendment process with the difficulty of enacting more fundamental change through the constitutional convention process, p. 49.

Efforts to overhaul the Texas Constitution have failed. Consequently, the state has continually amended the document on a piecemeal basis to address specific needs or political priorities. This process has had some success in modernizing the charter, but some structural problems of state government require major changes that could be better accomplished through comprehensive constitutional reform.

Over the years, numerous groups have attempted to protect their interests through constitutional amendments. The same groups usually oppose any proposed changes that threaten their influence, power, or benefits. Because voter turnout for most constitutional amendment elections is low, the interests of small segments of the state's population often have a disproportionate influence over the amendment process.

In many ways, the Texas Constitution reflects the values of the state's conservative political culture, which continues to be suspicious of far-reaching constitutional changes. Moreover, constitutions and debates about them are complex, and most people pay little attention to these issues. Consequently, it is much easier to mobilize public opinion against rather than for major change.

LEARN THE TERMS

constitution, p. 35
statutory law, p. 36
unicameral, p. 38
unitary system, p. 39
federalism, p. 39
bicameral, p. 39
plural executive, p. 40
confederacy, p. 41
Radical Reconstructionists, p. 42
Grange, p. 44
popular sovereignty, p. 45
social contract, p. 45
limited government, p. 45
representative government, p. 45
separation of powers, p. 45
initiative, p. 49
referendum, p. 49
Constitutional Convention of 1974, p. 50
right-to-work law, p. 50

Texas Government and Politics in the Federal System

3

WHO WILL HELP?
Who will help? The pandemic has caused significant challenges for governments across the nation. As the country struggles to address the physical and economic tolls of the pandemic, individuals turned to government to provide leadership and relief.

LEARNING OBJECTIVES

3.1 Explain three ways in which nations structure relationships among national, regional, and local levels of government and how the Constitution of the United States is used to navigate federal-state relations, p. 61.

3.2 Outline the changing patterns in the relationship between the U.S. national government and the states, p. 67.

3.3 Assess the impact of federalism on state finances, p. 80.

3.4 Describe the increased interdependency between the United States and Mexico, p. 83.

Under our federal system of government, the national government and state governments have distinct powers and responsibilities. As you will see in this chapter, the nature of our federal system has evolved throughout time, but at its core is the fact that the federal and state governments share power and authority. The events surrounding the COVID-19 pandemic, the summer 2020 protests regarding the death of George Floyd, the call for racial justice, and the controversies surrounding the 2020 presidential elections in the United States have laid bare many challenges facing our federal system of government. The question of how much authority and responsibility the federal government ought to have has been the subject of much controversy in each of these areas. Just looking at governmental response to the pandemic illustrates these questions—to whom should Americans turn to address their concerns over health, safety and economic challenges? Should we turn to our president, our governors, our mayors to provide leadership?

Citizens and state officials initially turned to the federal government to guide the response to the pandemic. We looked to the Center for Disease Control (CDC) for testing and safety guidelines. We turned to the federal government for much-needed supplies like respirators, testing kits, and personal protective gear and other medical equipment for health care professionals. It seems reasonable for us to expect the federal government to provide leadership and to direct responses to national emergencies. For example, a number of federal agencies—from the American Red Cross to the Federal Emergency Management Agency (FEMA) to the National Domestic Preparedness Office—are created with the very purpose of helping our country prepare for and respond to crises. The National Defense Production Act was passed in 1950 to give the president a broad array of powers to help during a national crisis. The law, which requires continued renewal by Congress (the most recent iteration was the John S. McCain National Defense Authorization Act of 2019 [expires in 2025]), empowers the president to "allocate materials, services, and facilities" for national defense purposes. Modeled after the War Powers Acts of 1941 and 1942, the law allows the president to help procure necessary and strategic materials to help the country respond to national crises. President Trump, while initially hesitant to invoke the law to respond to the COVID-19 pandemic, used the law to order General Motors to produce ventilators and 3M to produce N95 masks. We also have a Strategic National Stockpile to ensure that our country has sufficient medical materials to respond to disasters. In 1998, Congress passed the Consolidated Appropriations Act, which allocated $51 million for the CDC to stockpile vaccines and other pharmaceuticals. In 2002, the Public Health Security and Bioterrorism Preparedness Response Act was passed to establish that the Secretary of Health and Human Services is responsible for the inventory and security of the stockpile.[1] Allocations of federal tax dollars are authorized by Congress to purchase materials for the national stockpile.

However, President Trump repeatedly asserted that testing and other responses were the responsibility of the state governments. Such assertions can be seen as reasonable as states also have a variety of agencies that are tasked with responding to emergencies and protecting the health and welfare of its residents. For example, the Texas Civil Protection Act of 1951 created the state's emergency management organization, the Disaster Relief Council (which later became the Texas Division of Emergency Management, TDEM), and the state's first emergency management plan. The law was replaced by the Texas Disaster Act of 1975, which enhanced the coordination between local and state emergency management response efforts. TDEM has been a division of the Department of Public Safety (DPS) since 2005. In addition to TDEM, which is charged with providing comprehensive all-hazard emergency management for the state, other agencies tasked with public safety include the Texas Division of Emergency Management, the Department of Public Safety, the Department of State Health Services and the Texas Health and Human Services Commission. Moreover, in 1996 Congress authorized the creation of the Emergency Management Assistance Compact (EMAC). The EMAC is a mutual aid agreement among states and territories to share resources (including supplies, equipment, and personnel) to respond effectively to disasters (natural and human-made, such as terrorism). For example, after Hurricane Harvey, 36 states, through EMAC, sent assistance of some sort to the state. There will be more on compacts later in the chapter.

However, when President Trump asserted that the states needed to bear the responsibility for testing to reopen the economy, governors were very frustrated. When disasters or crises strike a state, the initial response ought to be theirs. If the demand for assistance is larger than their capacity allows, other states often help (for example, through arrangements made through EMAC). However, when capacity is still not met, the federal government is expected to provide backup assistance. With a crisis that extends beyond one state's border, like a global pandemic, many governors and other leaders assert that the country needs a federal response. During COVID-19, many governors claimed insufficient resources and an inability to compel private corporations to render assistance. They noted that, unlike the president, governors do not have the power to require private companies to produce necessary testing and medical equipment. Moreover, many states do not have the budgets needed to do mass testing. Governors claimed that a national crisis needed a national response.

The question remains—who should be responsible to provide leadership through this global pandemic? Which level of government should be responsible, for example, for testing for COVID-19 and for antibody testing? In May, 2020 (following the first wave of the pandemic), the vast majority of Americans, 61 percent, thought COVID-19 testing should be the responsibility of the federal government, but views varied considerably depending upon partisanship. Seventy-eight percent of Democrats believed that the responsibility fell primarily with the federal government, while only 42 percent of Republicans felt similarly.[2] There can also be tension between localities and state officials when addressing crises like a pandemic. Consider, for example, Dallas County Judge Clay Jenkins, the first Texas official to issue stay-at-home orders in the state, and Governor Greg Abbott's differing perspectives on the role of state and local officials. Jenkins issued his order a week prior to Abbott's statewide directive but later found his order superseded by the governor's order to reopen Texas businesses (despite the fact that infection rates in Dallas were still on the rise). Under normal circumstances, the state has a rather decentralized public health system that allows local officials to respond with a good deal of flexibility to local public health needs. Such was the case in 2014 when Jenkins helped Dallas navigate an Ebola outbreak (three individuals were diagnosed with Ebola in Dallas county). Unlike 2014, the governor has approached the management of COVID-19 in a more centralized manner, causing some challenges and confusion for localities with higher infection rates. Likewise, tension has escalated between the mayors of some of the largest cities in the state and state officials. The governor's orders to reopen businesses and places of worship supersedes the desires of local officials to keep local social distancing requirements in place longer while local cases of COVID-19 are still on the rise. Likewise, a number of county Republican officials were upset with Governor Abbott's statewide mask mandate (issued on July 2, 2020 for counties with 20 or more positive cases of COVID-19). They believed that the mandate infringed upon the ability of localities to set policies, interfered unduly with free enterprise and infringed upon personal responsibility. In July, six county Republican party organizations voted to censure Governor Abbott largely over his statewide mask order, a remarkable step given the governor was easily reelected in 2018 and had been widely popular.[3]

When faced with a medical and economic crisis like COVID-19, frightened individuals turn to the "government" for solutions. But, to which governmental entity should they turn? Understanding the nature of our federal system, whereby federal, state, and local governing authorities share power and responsibilities, is of fundamental importance. Comprehending the evolution of federalism through time is especially consequential if you are to fully understand the diversity of current opinions regarding the proper role and scope of federal and state governments. Moreover, in order to become an active participant, you need to understand which level of government most directly impacts specific areas of public policy, and hence your life. As you'll see, states tend to approach problem solving differently, and even within our state, localities vary considerably. Understanding the complexity of the layers of government is a necessary first step to empower you to be politically active.

Structuring Regional and National Interests

3.1 Explain three ways in which nations structure relationships among national, regional, and local levels of government and how the Constitution of the United States is used to navigate federal-state relations.

Finding the proper balance of power between central governments and regional subunits is a challenge with which all governments struggle. Moreover, no method forever resolves the struggle to balance power throughout time. Hence, maintaining the appropriate distribution of power is a perennial struggle for all governments.

Many governments, beyond the obvious federal and state governments, have authority in one fashion or another over Texas residents. If you live in a large metropolitan area, you may be under the jurisdiction of as many as ten or more different governments or taxing authorities. A person living within the corporate limits of San Antonio, for example, is subject to the laws, regulations, and taxes of the federal government, the state of Texas, Bexar County, the city of San Antonio, the Alamo Community College District, one of sixteen independent school districts, the Edwards Aquifer Authority, the San Antonio River Authority, the Bexar County Hospital District, and a public transportation authority.

There are more than 90,000 governmental units in the United States, with approximately 500,000 persons serving on their governing bodies. According to a 2017 census of governments (the most current data available), Texas's individual governments included

FIGURE 3-1 GOVERNMENTS IN TEXAS, ILLINOIS, FLORIDA, AND MASSACHUSETTS, 2017

People typically think of "the government" in terms of one or two levels, but as you can see, it is far more complex than that. The government of Texas is actually composed of more than 5,340 governmental units, each with different tasks to perform. Moreover, states approach local governance differently. Some states, like Texas and Illinois, have a large number of local governments, while other states, like Massachusetts and Florida, have fewer local governments even though they also have large populations. Understanding which governmental entity does what task in each setting is an important part of becoming an informed participant.

NOTE: The U.S. Census Bureau conducts a Census of Governments of all state and local governmental organization units every five years, for years ending in 2 and 7.

SOURCE: U.S. Department of Commerce, Bureau of the Census, *2017 Census of Governments, Government Organizations*, vol. 1, Table 2.

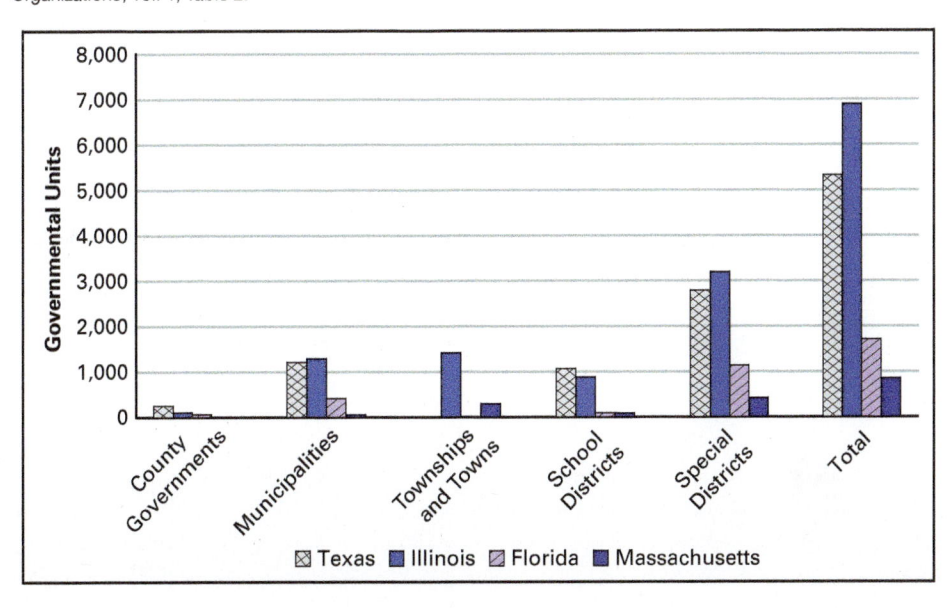

254 counties, 1,218 municipalities, and 3,871 school districts and other special districts. (See Figure 3–1) What's more, the total number of governments in Texas increased by nearly 1,900 between 1967 and 2017. Most of those added are special districts.

The jurisdictional structure of governments in the United States is complex and confusing, and people often are frustrated when they try to identify the government that has the authority or responsibility to address a specific need or concern. Governments in the United States and in Texas share many responsibilities, and it is quite possible for individuals to find themselves enmeshed in jurisdictional disputes between agencies of different governments.

From our country's very beginnings, Americans have been leery of highly centralized government.[4] These diverse and complex jurisdictional arrangements, therefore, were created to limit government, especially the federal government. Moreover, the enormous size of the country and the great distances between settlements during the nation's formative period made it extremely difficult for a centralized government at either the national or state level to serve and control political subdivisions. This contributed to the proliferation of smaller governmental units. Regional differences in religion, economics, and political cultures also encouraged decentralization and the development of local governments.

3.1.1 Federal-State Relationships in a Comparative Context

Governments around the world have struggled to find ways to coordinate local and regional interests with national interests. Countries in the former Soviet bloc, for example, have struggled, sometimes violently, with political systems for diverse racial, cultural, and ethnic groups. Canada, which has a stable political system, still seeks political and institutional solutions to the controversy surrounding the movement for French separatism. The effort to rebuild Iraq has been compounded by debate over the geographical distribution of power among the Sunnis, Shiites, Arabs, and Kurds. Many similar issues confronted the framers of the U.S. Constitution during the formative period of the United States.

Three fundamental systems—unitary, confederal, and federal—are used in structuring the relationship of a central government and its constituent parts. Over the history of our nation, all three organizational principles have been used at one time or the other.

WHO IS RESPONSIBLE FOR IMMIGRATION ENFORCEMENT?

Border Patrol agents question undocumented immigrants from Central America after a van holding twenty-six crashed on a Texas highway.

In some countries, democratic as well as authoritarian, ultimate power is vested in a national or central government. Under such a **unitary system**, local or regional governments are created by the national government, have only the power and authority granted to them by the national government, and serve "only to implement policies established by the national government."[5] In the United States, the unitary principle has been used only to define relationships between state and local governments.

A **confederation** is based on the principle that each component government is sovereign in its own right, and the powers of the national government are limited to those powers delegated to it by the member governments. The United States experimented with a confederal system prior to the adoption of the present Constitution in 1789, and the southern states used the confederal principle during the Civil War. Such a system has inherent weaknesses, including the ability of member governments to nullify the acts of the national government and withdraw from the relationship. Citizenship in and loyalty to the component governments take precedence over citizenship in and loyalty to the central government.

Delegates to the U.S. Constitutional Convention of 1787 rejected the confederal principle in favor of **federalism**, which balances the power and sovereignty of the state governments with those of the national government. Both the states and the national government derive their authority directly from the people, and the states have considerable latitude and autonomy within their areas of defined power and responsibility. In many respects, federalism is a middle ground between a confederal system and a unitary system of government. In Federalist 10, one of a series of essays written in support of the adoption of the U.S. Constitution, James Madison stated that "the federal Constitution forms a happy combination . . . the great and aggregate interests being referred to the national, the local and particular to the State legislatures."[6] Our system of federalism allows for diversity in governing and stability with an increasingly diverse and geographically dispersed population.

The unitary principle, however, is the basis for the relationship between state and local governments under the Texas Constitution and state laws. Counties, cities, and special districts have only those powers granted to them by the state. Sovereignty of local government does not exist in Texas. Local governments are primarily administrative subdivisions of the state. The prevailing constitutional theory regarding local governments in the United States, which has been incorporated into Texas law, was articulated in the **Dillon rule**, which held that if a state could create local governments, it also could destroy or eliminate them.[7] Political and practical considerations, however, usually preclude the elimination of local governments.

unitary system
A system in which ultimate power is vested in a central or national government and local governments have only those powers granted to them by the central government. This principle describes the relationship between the state and local governments in Texas.

confederation
A system in which each member government is considered sovereign, and the national government is limited to powers delegated to it by its member governments.

federalism
A system that balances the power and sovereignty of state governments with those of the national government. Both the states and the national government derive their authority directly from the people, and the states have considerable autonomy within their areas of responsibility.

Dillon rule
A principle holding that local governments are creations of state government and their powers and responsibilities are defined by the state.

3.1.2 Defining Federalism in the United States

Although the U.S. Constitution outlines federalism in broad terms, it does not clearly specify the governmental relationships that should be established. For more than 200 years, scholars, politicians, judges, and bureaucrats have not only been debating the complexities of the federal system, but they have also been trying to figure out how to define *federalism*.[8] One scholar has identified 267 definitions and concepts relating to the term.[9] The problem is compounded by the fact that the relationships among federal, state, and local governments have changed over the past two centuries, and they continue to change.

If scholars cannot agree on a definition of federalism and the current elements of these complex governmental relationships, how can you, as a student, understand contemporary federalism? It is important to assess federalism over time in order to understand the complexity of the balance of power so that contemporary challenges are placed into context. In some periods of our political history, the pendulum of power shifted from the states to the national government, while at other points a decentralizing tendency in federal-state relationships occurred. Our discussion attempts to provide a broad overview of these historical patterns.

An assessment of broad historical periods leads to a tendency to overgeneralize and oversimplify. In any given period, the three branches of the federal government do not speak with a unified voice on federal issues. Congress and the president may pursue policies that centralize power in Washington; the federal judiciary may pursue a different course of action through its decisions in cases involving federal issues. Moreover, different subunits within the executive and congressional branches of the national government may pursue different objectives in federal–state relationships.

Additionally, the policy process relating to federalism is so complex with so many different actors that often it is difficult to measure the exact impact of the national government's actions on the states. These complex "policy networks," discussed later, involve many participants, including elected officials, administrators, political parties, interest groups, and private organizations. Some policy arenas show a tendency for centralization of public goods and services. In others, participants favor decentralization.[10]

3.1.3 Federal–State Relationships from a Constitutional Perspective

We tend to think of federalism as a division of power between the states and the national government, and we look to the U.S. Constitution to specify the powers and responsibilities of each. However, the Constitution is vague on these points, and "all efforts to define the distribution of authority among governments have been unsuccessful."[11] The structure and operation of our federal system of government confuse many individuals. It is a system of numerous shared functions and responsibilities that often make it difficult to identify a single person or institution as having the ultimate responsibility for addressing a specific issue or problem.

Ambiguous constitutional provisions have produced jurisdictional conflicts throughout the nation's history. We even fought a war among ourselves to determine the powers and authority of the states and national government. Although the Civil War resolved the issue that a state could not withdraw from the federal Union, many other questions have continued to be debated. The ambiguities and changes in political and economic conditions make the relationships among governments subject to further change in the future. Over the past several decades, much debate at all levels of government over **devolution**, or the return of power to the states, has occurred.

The enumerated or **delegated powers** of the national government are outlined primarily in Article I, Section 8, of the U.S. Constitution. They include the powers to tax, to borrow and coin money, to declare war, and to regulate interstate and foreign commerce. The first seventeen paragraphs of Section 8 are rather specific, in part because the framers of the Constitution, apprehensive about potential abuses, intended to limit the powers of the national government. They did not, however, close the door to unforeseen events. In paragraph 18 of Section 8, they further provided that Congress shall have the power "to make all Laws which shall be necessary and proper for carrying into Execution the foregoing Powers."[12] This provision is the **implied powers** clause, which has been used to justify the subsequent expansion of the federal government's powers.

To further compound the jurisdictional question, Article VI states that the U.S. Constitution and the laws made in pursuance "shall be the supreme Law of the Land."[13] This **supremacy clause** suggests that when a conflict develops between the powers of the states and the national government, the federal law prevails.

Although the Constitution does not spell out the authority of the states and their subdivisions in detail, the states have assumed a formidable array of powers and responsibilities in domestic affairs. State or local governments take most actions affecting our daily lives as they relate to police, regulatory, and taxing powers, and most litigation in the country takes place in state or local courts, not in federal courts.

devolution
Return of powers assumed by the federal government to the states.

delegated powers
Powers specifically assigned to the national, or federal, government by the U.S. Constitution, including powers to tax, borrow and coin money, declare war, and regulate interstate and foreign commerce.

implied powers
Although not specifically defined by the U.S. Constitution, these are powers assumed by the national government as necessary in carrying out its responsibilities.

supremacy clause
A provision of the U.S. Constitution that says federal law prevails in conflicts between the powers of the states and the national government.

The absence of specific constitutional language spelling out many powers of the state concerned many state governments. The Tenth Amendment, with its **reserved powers** clause, was adopted to address these concerns. Today, conservatives in Texas and other states cite it to argue for more limits on federal power, although their interpretation is far from universal.

In addition to the Tenth Amendment's reserved powers for the states, there are **concurrent powers** held by the states and the national government. Both have the power to raise taxes, develop and implement public policies, spend money, borrow money, and establish their own court systems.

There are certain constitutional guarantees to the states. Texas is assured a republican form of government, protection against invasion and domestic violence, and the power to maintain a militia. If a person is accused of a federal crime in Texas, the trial is to be held in a federal court in Texas. Texas cannot be divided into another state without its permission and is assured two members in the U.S. Senate and membership in the U.S. House of Representatives based on its population in relation to the other states. After the 2010 census, Texas had 36 members in the U.S. House (second only to California's 53 members). Following the 2020 census and reapportionment, Texas is expected to gain additional representation in the House. The state also has a role in ratifying amendments to the U.S. Constitution and controls many aspects of federal elections.[14]

Reflecting its drafters' concerns about governmental excesses, the Constitution limits the powers of both the states and the national government. These prohibitions or **denied powers** are interspersed throughout the document and are enumerated, in particular, in the first ten amendments—the Bill of Rights. The original intent of the Bill of Rights was to limit the powers of the national government. Since the Civil War, however, the federal courts have gradually incorporated the Bill of Rights into the Fourteenth Amendment, which was intended to restrict the powers of the state governments. Some have described this expansion as the nationalization of the Bill of Rights.

The broad and often ambiguous language of the U.S. Constitution lends itself to controversy and interpretation. Over the years, Congress, the states, and the courts have attempted to resolve conflicts about powers and jurisdiction. In many instances, the Supreme Court has played an instrumental role in redefining the relationship between the states and the federal government.

3.1.4 Relationships among the States

The federal system is not limited to the relationship between the states and the national government (vertical federalism). It also includes the relationship of the states to one another (horizontal federalism). Many of these constitutional–legal obligations were included in the Articles of Confederation, which established the first system of national government in the United States. Conflict as well as cooperation among the states during that period provided the rationale for defining the obligations and responsibilities of the states to one another.

The Constitution states, "Full Faith and Credit shall be given in each State to the public Acts, Records, and judicial Proceedings of every other state."[15] To eliminate chaos and to stimulate cooperation, this **full faith and credit clause** ensures that official governmental actions of one state are accepted by other states. Business contracts in Texas are recognized as legal in other states, as are driver's licenses and marriages. For a period of time, homosexual marriages legally performed in one state were not recognized in many states. The 1996 federal Defense of Marriage Act, which denied federal recognition of same-sex marriages or civil unions, enabled states to refuse to recognize marriages or civil unions of same-sex couples performed in other states. The Obama administration announced in 2011 that it considered the Defense of Marriage

---

reserved powers
Powers given to state governments by the Tenth Amendment. These are powers not delegated to the national government nor otherwise prohibited to the states by the Constitution.

concurrent powers
Powers shared by both the national and state governments.

denied powers
Powers that are denied to both the states and national government. The best-known restrictions are listed in the Bill of Rights.

full faith and credit clause
A provision in the U.S. Constitution (Article IV, Section 1) that requires states to recognize civil judgments and official documents rendered by the courts of other states.

Act unconstitutional and would no longer defend it against legal challenges. In 2013, the Supreme Court declared Section 3 of the act to be unconstitutional. As a result of this ruling, same-sex couples who were legally married were eligible to receive federal marriage benefits.

By November 2014, Texas was one of only eighteen states to prohibit same-sex marriages, either by state statute or a provision in the state constitution (states had begun legalizing same-sex unions since Massachusetts first began in 2004). On June 26, 2015, the Supreme Court ruled in *Obergefell* v. *Hodges* that marriage was a fundamental right of citizenship and was to be guaranteed to same-sex couples by the due process and equal protection clauses of the Fourteenth Amendment. The Court required all states to issue marriage licenses to same-sex couples and to recognize marriages performed in other jurisdictions. Prior to the ruling, thirty-six states, as well as the District of Columbia, Guam, and several Native American tribunal jurisdictions, had legalized same-sex marriages.

Another area that has recently caused friction between states centers around marijuana. According to federal law, marijuana is considered a Schedule 1 drug (meaning it is illegal as it has no medical value, like cocaine and heroin). However, as of January 2021, thirty-five states and the District of Columbia have laws that allow some use of marijuana as legal. The vast majority of states only allow marijuana to be used for medical purposes, but fifteen states and the District of Columbia have passed laws allowing for the recreational use of marijuana. In 2015, Texas passed a law allowing for the use of low-THC, high-CBD products for medical purposes (meaning cannabis oil, which has very low psychoactive components and high levels of a noneuphoric component known as CBD oil that treats epilepsy and other chronic medical conditions). The prescription oil is very difficult to obtain and has very strict restrictions. The Compassionate Use Program, allowing the sale of low-THC medical cannabis, began in Texas in early 2018, but very few patients qualify for the program. The 2018 Farm Bill legalized the commercial production of hemp in the United States. States were encouraged to submit plans to allow hemp programs; in 2019, Governor Abbott signed into law House Bill 1325, which authorized the production, manufacture, and sale of hemp crops and products in Texas. This law has allowed for the sale of low-THC, high-cannabidiol (CBD) products produced from hemp, although marijuana remains illegal. The distinction between legal hemp and illegal marijuana has complicated drug enforcement policy in the state as crime laboratories were not given adequate time and resources to develop proper tests to distinguish the two.

Unlike the Obama administration, the Trump administration was far more critical of marijuana and threatened to crack down on marijuana-related offenses. Having the drug legal in some states and illegal in other states complicates law enforcement for some. For example, a person could purchase the drug legally in one state, then travel to another state with the legally purchased drug and get arrested for possession of a controlled substance. When legally purchased marijuana is transported illegally into another state, that state's resources can become taxed as the number of arrests for illegal possession and distribution can increase. Like the issue of same-sex marriage, marijuana is a challenging issue in our federal system.

As a person travels from one state to another, the Constitution entitles that person to the **privileges and immunities** of the states where he or she goes. A person can acquire property in another state, establish residency and eventually citizenship, and be assured of access to the legal system of that state. But exceptions have been established by court interpretation. States, for example, can charge nonresidents higher college tuition or higher fees for hunting and fishing licenses.

The Constitution also provides for the return of a person accused of a crime. If a person who has been charged with a crime in Texas attempts to avoid trial by fleeing to another state, he or she can be returned to Texas by a process called **extradition**. States routinely handle hundreds of these cases each year. Once the

privileges and immunities
The right of a resident of one state to be protected by the laws and afforded the legal opportunities in any other state he or she visits. Certain exceptions, however, have been allowed by the courts, including the right of states to charge nonresidents higher college tuition or higher hunting and fishing license fees.

extradition
A process by which a person in one state can be returned to another state to face criminal charges.

accused has been located, the state seeking the individual will request that the second state arrest and return him or her. The governor is responsible for granting extradition requests.

Until fairly recently, governors used an 1861 court decision to maintain that they had the discretion to refuse another state's extradition request.[16] This was the prevailing view for 125 years, until Puerto Rico challenged the discretionary powers of the governor in a 1987 case.[17] The Supreme Court held that the "duty to extradite is mandatory, and the federal courts are available to enforce that duty."[18]

The U.S. Constitution also anticipated the need for structuring more formal, long-term, cooperative relationships among the states. Article I, Section 10, allows the states, with the approval of Congress, to enter into **interstate compacts**. There are more than 200 of these, some affecting only two states, whereas others include all fifty states. On the average, states belong to thirty interstate compacts, which include border, advisory, and regulatory compacts. Texas now belongs to thirty-two interstate compacts, including the Interstate Compact to Conserve Oil and Gas, the Interstate Compact on Adoption and Medical Assistance, the Emergency Management Assistance Compact, the Red River Compact, and Nurse Licensure Compact.[19]

Although cooperation is desired, states often find themselves involved in disagreements that only lawsuits can resolve. Boundary disputes, control or use of water resources, and licensing fees that affect interstate shipping are among issues that are litigated in the federal judiciary, where the Supreme Court has original jurisdiction in all "controversies between two or more states."[20]

interstate compact
A formal, long-term cooperative agreement among the states dealing with common problems or issues and subject to approval of the U.S. Congress.

Changing Patterns in Federal Relationships

3.2 Outline the changing patterns in the relationship between the U.S. national government and the states.

Federal relationships have changed over the nation's history, generating some of the confusion in reaching conclusive descriptions and definitions of federalism. We can assess broad patterns of federal–state relationships by historical periods, although relationship patterns do not start or stop in specific years but can continue over multiple eras. Various scholars have developed different classifications of federalism, but centralization and federal authority have generally increased over the years.

3.2.1 Metaphors for Federalism

The constitutional–legal descriptions of federalism outlined earlier can leave one with the idea that the federal, state, and local levels of government are autonomous and function independently with distinct and separate spheres of responsibility, a view often linked to **dual federalism** or a "layer-cake" theory of intergovernmental relations. Morton Grodzins, an authority on federalism, has argued that this perspective is now inaccurate and suggests that intergovernmental relations can be symbolized more accurately by the metaphor of a "marble cake." Rather than possessing distinct and separate powers and responsibilities, governments have shared responsibilities. In describing federalism, Grodzins writes:

dual federalism
Nineteenth-century concept of federalism in which the powers or functions of the national and state governments were sharply differentiated with limited overlapping responsibilities.

> Whenever you slice through it [marble cake] you reveal an inseparable mixture of differently colored ingredients. There is no neat horizontal stratification. Vertical and diagonal lines almost obliterate the horizontal ones, and in some places there are unexpected whirls and imperceptible merging of colors, so that it is difficult to tell where one ends and the other begins. So it is with federal, state, and local responsibilities in the chaotic marble cake of American Government.[21]

cooperative federalism
Policies emphasizing cooperative efforts among the federal, state, and local governments to address common problems and provide public services to citizens.

Public functions are not neatly divided among the different levels of government. In virtually every area of public policy, governments coordinate, collaborate, and cooperate to meet shared goals and objectives. This view reflects, in large measure, governmental relationships associated with **cooperative federalism**, which we discuss later in this chapter.

Another metaphor, the "picket-fence" theory of federalism, builds on Grodzins's notions of shared powers and responsibilities but focuses on specific policy arenas that cut across each level of government. This metaphor suggests that we look at a specific policy arena (e.g., highways, education, or welfare), identify the primary participants at each level of government, and map out their patterns of interaction. Although the concept is an oversimplification, it does suggest complex institutional and political relationships that cut across all levels of government.[22]

As might be expected, the complexity of federalism has generated much discussion about how to best describe and assess the relationships among governments. The problem is compounded by the fact that governmental relationships are shaped by changes in the political parties, presidents, the composition of Congress, the courts, prevailing economic and social conditions, and the public's expectations of their governments.

3.2.2 State-Centered and Dual Federalism

In both theory and practice, federal relationships from 1790 to the 1930s usually are defined in terms of dual federalism. During the early decades of our political history, the primary responsibility for domestic policy fell to the states and local governments with very little involvement or intervention by the federal government. Yet there were domestic policies that generated conflict, and both the national and state governments continually engaged in legal and policy issues that attempted to define the lines of demarcation between their respective powers.[23] Conflicts usually were resolved through court cases and statutory laws, but the federal–state issues centering on slavery erupted into the Civil War. The dual federalism of this era was marked by adversarial, if not antagonistic, relationships at various levels of government.

The U.S. Supreme Court first addressed the issue of state–federal relationships in 1819 in the case of *McCulloch* v. *Maryland*.[24] The state of Maryland had levied a tax on the Baltimore branch of the Bank of the United States. McCulloch, the bank's cashier, refused to pay the tax, thus precipitating a lawsuit. The case raised a fundamental issue regarding federalism. Did the national government have the power to create a bank that, in fact, would compete with state banks? The Supreme Court, then headed by Chief Justice John Marshall, an advocate of central power, ruled that the implied powers clause of the Constitution, linked to the delegated or enumerated powers, gave the federal government this authority.

A second issue was whether a state could tax the branch bank, an institution of the national government. The Court again ruled in favor of the U.S. government. It held that the states do not have the power to tax the national government because, if this were to be permitted, the states could destroy national institutions, and federal laws would become subordinate to those of the states, thus undermining the supremacy clause of the Constitution.

Hundreds of federal-state issues have been litigated in the federal courts since *McCulloch*, and those cases making it to the Supreme Court demonstrate the role of the Court in arbitrating disputes between state and federal authority.[25] Along with political and economic changes, these cases have been central to redefining federal–state relationships over the past 200 years, although the principles outlined in *McCulloch* remain intact.

3.2.3 Cooperative Federalism

The economic hardships produced by the Great Depression of the 1930s resulted in demands for a greater role of the federal government in domestic policy. States and cities simply were unable to provide many basic services or address the personal needs of large numbers of people who were unemployed. The states did not have the economic resources to deal with problems that extended beyond their borders, and many lacked the political or institutional will to implement new policies. Moreover, the increased economic interdependency of the states and the national scope of economic problems provided compelling arguments for federal intervention. Although there were precedents for greater federal–state cooperation prior to the 1930s, the New Deal expanded dramatically the role of the federal government in relation to state and local governments.[26]

V. O. Key, who wrote extensively on state government, summarized the extent of these changes:

> The federal government underwent a radical transformation after . . . 1932. It had been a remote authority with a limited range of activity. It operated the postal system, improved rivers and harbors, maintained armed forces on a scale fearsome only to banana republics, and performed other functions of which the average citizen was hardly aware. Within a brief time, it became an institution that affected intimately the lives and fortunes of most, if not all, citizens.[27]

Those supporting the development of cooperative federalism rejected the notion of dual federalism, whereby each level of government had virtual or exclusive authority in select areas of domestic policy. The commerce and supremacy clauses of the Constitution were used to support an expanded role of the federal government. Many of the new programs engaged local, state, and federal policymakers in cooperative efforts—from program development to program implementation. Cooperative federalism ensures that all three levels of government share the responsibility for domestic programs "by making the larger governments primarily responsible for raising revenues and setting standards and the smaller ones primarily responsible for administering the programs."[28]

Throughout the nation's history, the federal government has used various devices to shape and implement domestic policies through cash assistance programs known as "federal grant programs" or "federal domestic assistance programs." Of the 2,100-plus federal

CHALLENGES FACING VETERANS
Hundreds of homeless veterans wait in line to receive free basic necessities like food, clothing and shelter from the National Veterans Outreach Program. Addressing the complex challenges of the veteran population involves cooperation between state and national governments as well as nonprofit organizations to ensure that the men and women who have served our country are provided help when needed.

categorical grant-in-aid
A grant of federal money that can be spent only for specific programs or purposes. This is the source of most federal assistance to state and local governments.

project grant
A federal grant for a defined project.

formula grant
A federal grant based on specific criteria, such as income levels or population.

matching funds
Money that states or local governments have to provide to qualify for certain federal grants.

domestic programs authorized by Congress, some 1,700 are federal grant programs. There are 225 formula grant programs and approximately 1,500 project grant programs. Federal outlays to state and local governments in the 2017 fiscal year were nearly $675 billion. A lion's share of these federal expenditures is in the form of **categorical grants-in-aid**. Money allocated as a categorical grant-in-aid can be spent only for its designated purpose. Federal laws also include specific standards or requirements that recipients must meet, such as prohibitions against racial or sex discrimination or prohibitions against nonunion pay scales.[29]

There are two types of categorical grants. The first is the **project grant**, which requires a state or local government to apply for a grant to the appropriate federal agency and compete against other state or local governments for the funds. The money is awarded on the merits of an application. There are hundreds of these grant programs ranging from airport construction to youth programs. The second type of categorical grant is the **formula grant**. As the name implies, federal funds are allocated to states and local governments on the basis of a prescribed formula. These formulas vary from program to program but might include a state's population or income or the poverty level of its residents. Congress determines the formulas for specific programs such as Medicaid, highway construction, and family assistance, to name a few, and the federal dollars then are distributed on the basis of the statutory criteria. Many of these federal grants require **matching funds** from the governments that receive the money. The percentage of costs borne by the federal government varies from program to program, with the state or local governments picking up the balance. One reason for requiring such matches is to encourage state and local governments to have a strong commitment to the funded program and its policy objectives.

The amounts of the grants vary throughout time, as does the dependency of states and localities on federal outlays. For example, in 1960, federal grants to state and local governments totaled $54.8 billion (to show growth over time, all figures are in constant fiscal year [FY] 2012 dollars).[30] In 1970, federal grants to state and local governments increased to $151.7 billion. Subsequent decades saw steady increases (with only one period of slight decline in the 1980s), reaching $389.1 billion in 2000. Since 2000, however, we've witnessed remarkable increases reaching $556.9 billion in 2014 (down from a record high of $637.6 billion in 2010). If we look at real dollars (rather than 2012 dollars), it is estimated that the federal government will outlay $790 billion to state and local governments in 2020 (an increase of 9.7 percent from 2019), representing 3.6 percent of our gross domestic product (GDP) and 16.5 percent of total federal outlays. Nationally, prior to the Great Recession of 2009, federal spending accounted for nearly 28 percent of state revenue (in fiscal year 2008); that percentage increased to

TAXES IN ACTION
Pictured here is construction on a highway in Dallas. Many construction projects are undertaken with matching funds. Next time you are sitting in traffic, or enjoying a newly repaved road, remember that you are seeing your tax dollars at work!

35.5 percent in fiscal year 2010.[31] The most current data prior to COVID-19 indicates that the percent of state revenue that came from the federal government was 32.4 percent (in fiscal year 2017). Texas is more dependent than most states; during the height of the Great Recession, (FY 2008), 40 percent of state revenue came from federal funds. By FY 2018, the percent of state revenue Texas received from the federal government nearly equaled that of the national average (33) percent.[32] For the entire century, Texas has received a larger percent of its revenue from the federal government than the national average of all states. By comparison, during the same time period, the percent of state revenue from federal funds in California has been below the national average. It is too soon to see how the COVID-19 pandemic will impact these trends. Based upon past times of economic recession, these percentages are likely to increase substantially.

3.2.4 Centralized Federalism

The nature of federalism continued to evolve throughout the twentieth century. The domestic initiatives introduced by President John F. Kennedy (1961–1963) and expanded by President Lyndon B. Johnson (1963–1969) in the Great Society programs resulted in a dramatic expansion of the federal government's role to virtually every area of domestic policy. The number of federal grant programs and funding increased significantly during those years, as did the federal share of state and local budgets. Many programs targeted specific populations for assistance and were intended to redistribute resources primarily to lower-income groups. Several federal programs bypassed state governments and went directly to local governments, thus eroding the legal relationship of local governments to the states.[33] Some scholars suggest that this massive extension of federal initiatives in domestic policy transformed cooperative federalism into coercive federalism or regulatory federalism, a relationship in which state power is subordinate to federal power in a wide range of policy areas.[34]

3.2.5 The Multiple Phases of New Federalism

Conservative opposition to cooperative federalism began in the 1930s. This opposition became more intense against the centralized federal programs of the Kennedy and Johnson administrations, and the Republican Party began to stake out what has become a rather consistent rhetorical theme of decentralization and devolution, or return of more authority to the states.

Opposition to the increased role of the national government in domestic policy is based on many factors. Some have argued that the Constitution never provided for the expanded powers claimed by the national government. The new programs, many of which were required, placed a heavy financial burden on state and local governments. Moreover, these policies often encouraged state and local governments to pursue federal dollars even when the funded programs were not their most pressing needs. The new programs, even though some were inefficient or mismanaged, also helped swell the federal bureaucracy. Finally, federal programs placed restrictions on how monies could be spent, and it was argued that federal requirements did not always meet local conditions or needs.

The expanded federal role has created new political issues. As grant programs evolved, various groups and individuals—that is, stakeholders—developed vested interests in maintaining them. Members of Congress viewed many of the programs as "pork" for the folks back home, and administrators at all levels of government justified their jobs and their agencies' existence on the basis of these programs. Many of the constituencies that benefited from federal grants traditionally supported the Democratic Party. If the Republican Party wanted to become the majority party, it would have to break up the implicit alliances built on federal funding of state and local programs.

new federalism
A term used to describe recent changes in federal–state relationships. Used primarily by conservative presidents, it suggests a devolution or return of power to the states and a decreased role of the federal government in domestic policy.

block grant
A federal grant of money to states and local governments for broad programs or services rather than narrowly defined programs. A block grant gives state and local governments more discretion over the use of the funds than other types of grants do.

revenue sharing
A program begun under President Nixon and later repealed in which state and local governments received federal aid that could be used for virtually any purpose the recipient government wanted.

mandate
A federal law or regulation that requires state or local governments to take certain actions, often at costs that the federal government does not reimburse. The state government also imposes mandates on local governments.

preemption
A federal law that limits the authority or powers of state and local governments.

REPUBLICAN OPPOSITION (PRESIDENTS NIXON, REAGAN, AND H. W. BUSH)

Republicans, beginning with President Richard Nixon (1969–1974), defined their views of federal–state relationships with the term **new federalism**. Although there have been several versions of "new federalism," reflecting the philosophical differences among Republican presidents, the general objective has been to return responsibilities for many domestic policies to state and local governments. This effort has included attempts to reduce federal spending for many domestic programs and reduce the federal budget, a policy widely supported by Republican constituents.

Nixon said his new federalism was designed to "rationalize the intergovernmental system by restructuring the roles and responsibilities of governments at all levels."[35] Nixon wanted to reduce the role of the federal government and largely decentralize federal programs. He proposed changes to expedite the grant application process and consolidate many categorical grants into a few large **block grants**, which would give state and local governments greater discretion over how to spend federal money. He also proposed the replacement of many categorical grants with **revenue sharing** dollars, which could be used by recipient governments for virtually any purpose—with "no strings attached." In addition, Nixon unsuccessfully proposed a plan to restructure the nation's welfare system.[36]

After almost six years of supposedly trying to increase state and local powers, Nixon's administration produced results that appeared to be just the opposite. Many believe that Nixon actually left behind "a more centralized federal system than the one he inherited."[37] Federal expenditures for many domestic programs had increased dramatically, and the regulatory powers of the federal government had been expanded.

President Ronald Reagan (1981–1989), a Republican who often is given credit for initiating what some call the "Reagan Revolution," also expressed a commitment to reducing federal programs—especially welfare programs—and revitalizing the powers of state and local governments. In 1981, Reagan "convinced Congress to consolidate seventy-six categorical grant-in-aid programs and a block grant program into nine new or reconstituted block grants."[38] He also attempted to consolidate additional grant programs during subsequent congressional sessions but had little success because of Democratic legislative opposition.

Reagan opposed revenue sharing, the program initiated under President Nixon, and the federal government ended it in 1986. Reagan attacked the program for contributing to the federal budget deficit, funding governments that did not need the money, funding programs of questionable merit, and producing a reliance on revenue sharing dollars for the operating budgets of many state and local governments.

Despite Reagan's announced goals, little was done during his administration and that of his successor, President George H. W. Bush (1989–1993), to reduce federal power and return more authority to the states. Although some efforts were made, primarily through executive orders and administrative initiatives, to increase the discretionary powers of the states, **mandates** and **preemptions** enacted by Congress, as well as court decisions affecting federal relations during this period, had the opposite effect. Moreover, some argue that Reagan's new federalism supported a smaller role for the national government but not a correspondingly larger role for state and local governments.[39]

Congress first began enacting laws preempting state or local authority in 1789, but the number of these preemptions increased significantly after 1965. Many preemptions adopted with Reagan's approval appear to reflect his commitment to marketplace economics and a reduced role for all government.[40] They certainly did little to restore governmental authority to the states.

The federal government can require states or local governments "to undertake a specific activity or provide a service meeting minimum national standards."[41] Throughout the 1980s, although decentralization and return of power to the states were major themes of the Reagan and first Bush administrations, Congress enacted numerous laws and mandates that imposed additional requirements on the states.[42] The numerous mandates and preemptions have imposed billions of dollars in costs on state and local governments and have forced them to "divert funds from many worthy projects to finance the national policies."[43] According to data from the Congressional Budget Office, federal regulations adopted between 1983 and 1990 imposed cumulative estimated costs of between $8.9 billion and $12.7 billion on states and localities, depending on how mandates were defined. These costs increased at a pace faster than overall federal aid.[44] In 1994, the Texas Legislative Budget Board reported that increases in mandates and other federal programs had accounted for $13 billion, or 65 percent, of a $20 billion increase in the Texas budget since 1990–1991.[45]

THE CLINTON YEARS (1993–2001) Democrat Bill Clinton became president in 1993 after serving six terms as governor of Arkansas, and many expected him to be more responsive to the impact of mandates and other issues facing the states. But, like his predecessor, Clinton failed to provide a coherent theory of federalism in the wide range of proposals he initially submitted to Congress. Under the leadership of Vice President Al Gore, Clinton's emphasis on "reinventing government" led to the elimination of some 400,000 positions in the federal bureaucracy and a similar reduction in the military, along with a considerable increase in governmental contracting with private firms for services previously provided by government employees or the military. Clinton's policies reduced the size of the federal bureaucracy, but with the exception of welfare reforms, no significant devolution of powers to the states occurred.[46]

Committed to deficit reduction, Clinton and Congress left little leeway to provide financial relief or expand funding to states and local governments. The Motor Voter Bill (i.e., National Voter Registration Act) enacted in 1993 encouraged the registration of more voters but also expanded federal authority over state elections. Congress passed the Goals 2000: Educate America Act in 1994, which expanded the federal role in public education through the development of national curriculum content and student performance standards.

Many of the Republicans who took control of both houses of Congress in 1994 were committed to restricting the powers of the national government. In response to state demands, Congress enacted the Unfunded Mandates Reform Act (1995). Any legislation that would impose $50 million or more in costs to state and local governments would be subject to a parliamentary procedure requiring members of Congress to go on record that they were voting to impose more costs on the state and local governments. The act did nothing to remedy mandates that were already on the books, and since its enactment, it has had very little effect on reducing costs to the other governments in the federal system.[47]

During this time, Congress enacted a welfare overhaul bill in 1996 that eliminated the entitlements under the 61-year-old Aid to Families with Dependent Children program. That program was replaced with a new program, Temporary Assistance for Needy Families, which is funded by block grants to the states and gives the states a wide range of options for establishing their own welfare programs.[48] In 1998, Congress enacted a $216 billion public works program, which was designed to help states and local governments build roads, bridges, and mass transit systems.[49] Despite the Unfunded Mandates Act of 1995, Congress enacted additional requirements and preemptions in health care, telecommunications, immigration reform, securities reform, and minimum wages in 1997.[50]

Some experts have argued that the "devolution revolution" of 1996 transformed the federal system into a "new federal order," in which the "federal government intrudes less into the affairs of states and also offers less financial assistance."[51] Others have concluded that congressional action gave states and local governments greater "flexibility" in carrying out federally funded programs because of waivers included in several pieces of legislation. But there have been skeptics. John Kincaid, a specialist in federalism, has

GEORGE W. BUSH

George W. Bush, when elected in 2000, was the third Texan to be elected president. The only other Texans elected to the White House have been Lyndon B. Johnson and George H. W. Bush. Only 18 of the 50 states have elected one of their residents to the presidency. Pictured here is then-Governor Bush campaigning with his running mate, Dick Cheney.

argued that "devolution [was] plodding along at a turtle's pace while centralization [was] still racing ahead at a rabbit's pace."[52] Despite symbolic rhetoric about greater state and local responsibility, a closer assessment suggests that there were minimal changes in federal relationships. There also was some evidence of the national government actually increasing its influence in select policy areas such as the National Voter Registration Act of 1993.[53]

THE BUSH II YEARS (2001–2009) In the initial months of his administration, President George W. Bush gave few clues as to how his domestic policy objectives would affect federal–state relationships. He established an Interagency Working Group on Federalism in February 2001, but there is no evidence that it met.[54] Some government watchers expected him to outline and pursue policies similar to his Republican predecessors, but the September 11, 2001, terrorist attacks sidetracked the development of any initiatives that he may have been considering. Homeland security took priority.

Historically, the federal government had played a limited role in police functions and domestic security. America has never had a national police force because that responsibility was—and still is—allocated to the states and local governments. But the magnitude of the terrorist threat to domestic security prompted President Bush to call for the creation of a new national agency charged with coordinating the security programs of federal, state, and local agencies. The Department of Homeland Security, created by Congress in November 2002, represented a comprehensive realignment of federal agencies with functions relating to security, including everything from commercial air travel to patrols along U.S. borders. The new department also developed collaborative programs with state and local governments. With greater emphasis on domestic security, it was argued, these initiatives tipped "the federal system—in matters of politics, police functions, and the law—towards Washington to an unprecedented degree."[55]

As more and more of the states' National Guard troops were federalized to fight the wars in Iraq and Afghanistan, states began to resist, and the issue came to a head when Louisiana Governor Kathleen Blanco "refused to accede to the president's request that Guard troops be placed under federal command in the immediate response to Hurricane Katrina."[56] Congress passed legislation in 2006 that increased "the president's ability to federalize Guard troops without gubernatorial consent."[57]

In addition to the Bush administration's antiterrorism legislation, another significant piece of legislation that passed was the No Child Left Behind (NCLB) Act of 2002. As governor of Texas, Bush had boasted of his record on education, which was intended to bring accountability into the public schools while expanding state support for local school districts. Education reform was a cornerstone of his presidential campaign and his legislative agenda. His education initiatives as president were significant to state–federal relationships because, historically, education had been primarily a function of state and local governments. Federal aid to public education had been limited and often targeted toward specific groups of students, such as the disabled or those from low-income families. The impact of NCLB was enormous because it included new federal mandates for reading and math proficiency. Test scores were to be used to evaluate the progress of a school or a school district. If schools failed to meet specified standards, they would suffer repercussions, including loss of funding and loss of students, who would be allowed to transfer to better-performing schools.[58]

Experts across the political spectrum agreed that the power of the states was diminished during the second Bush administration. Bush said relatively little about federalism; neither did he develop an explicit federalism agenda.[59] As noted, however, his homeland security and education policies expanded the presence of the federal government in domestic programs. Preemptions, mandates, and other "centralizing statutes" continued at a significant rate; tax policy, especially tax cuts and the phasing out of the federal estate tax, hurt state finances; and federal rule making, with limited waivers, constrained state discretion.[60]

It is ironic that conservative Republicans, who have long decried centralization, helped lead the country in that direction. As far as we know, Bush never used the term "new federalism," but if his administration inspired a new term for federalism, it would be "big government conservatism" in which the powers of the "federal government and the executive branch were expanded" to achieve a social and economic policy agenda.[61]

As details of the Bush administration's policies became clear, states began a counteroffensive against the increased centralization and conservative economic and social objectives. Through effective lobbying and political maneuvering, states successfully secured some relief from "burdensome federal directives regarding the National Guard, homeland security, education, and welfare policy."[62] Several state legislatures passed measures vowing they would not cooperate with the federal government and demanding the repeal of a variety of federal directives. Some federal officials became more cooperative with state governments, producing a number of significant waivers in federal programs. States also were at the center of debates about immigration, climate change, universal health care, election reform, property rights, social policy, capital punishment, and water allocation.[63]

THE OBAMA YEARS (2009–2017) President Obama entered office with the clear intention of working in partnership with states (even throwing a gala for governors shortly after taking office); however, he left office with what could be fairly characterized as a very tense relationship between the federal and state governments. He came into office in the middle of an economic crisis, and much of his initial focus was on economic recovery. Obama won congressional approval in 2009 of a $787 billion stimulus package with $280 billion to be administered by states and local governments. He obtained additional stimulus legislation in 2010 with a tax cut and an unemployment extension agreement,[64] but the president failed to win congressional approval of two subsequent stimulus proposals.

Despite Governor Rick Perry's criticisms of Washington and government centralization, Texas accepted at least $14.4 billion in stimulus funds to help balance the state budget drafted by the legislature for fiscal years 2009, 2010, and 2011. Accepting the stimulus money allowed the state to balance its fiscal shortfall without tapping into its Rainy Day Fund. Five state agencies accounted for 93 percent of these appropriations: Texas Education Agency, Health and Human Services Commission, Texas Department of Transportation, Texas Department of Housing and Community Affairs, and the Texas Workforce Commission.[65] Money also was spent on military bases and was sent directly to local governments. The only money that Perry rejected was about $500 million in extra unemployment compensation funds. Approximately 70 percent of the money that Texas accepted was used to help fund education, transportation, and health and human services programs.[66] Some figures estimate that Texas received as much as $17.4 billion in federal stimulus money in all.[67]

Aware of long-standing state complaints about federal mandates and preemptions, the White House issued a memorandum shortly after Obama took office that attempted to address this issue. The memo declared that, as a general policy, the Obama administration would preempt state laws "only with full consideration of the legitimate prerogatives of the States and with a sufficient legal basis for preemption."[68] The memo was interpreted as a clear move to appease frustrated states and to help build partnerships. He appointed many former and current governors to key cabinet positions and named many state officials to key bureaucratic positions. However, the relationship between the administration and states soured and became increasingly combative, beginning with the 2010 midterm elections with large Republican wins in Congress, state legislatures, and governorships. His Justice Department sued states over voting rights and immigration law. The state of Texas sued the federal government forty-eight times while Obama was president. The state sued over such things as Obama's executive order to establish DAPA (Deferred Action for Parents of Americans and Lawful Permanent Residents), the resettlement of Syrian refugees in the state, directives on bathroom use in public schools, and environmental policy. Between 2008 and 2017, the state spent nearly $8.1 million suing the federal government; the state spent $1.98 million defending voter identification laws, nearly $930,000 defending redistricting plans, and $817,000 fighting DAPA/DACA.[69]

By 2014, the most significant domestic achievement of the Obama administration was the Patient Protection and Affordable Care Act of 2010 (commonly called Obamacare or the Affordable Care Act), a major reform of health insurance that was attacked by twenty-six states, including Texas. In a lawsuit heard before the U.S. Supreme Court, the states objected to, among other things, provisions expanding Medicaid coverage and requiring virtually every American to have health insurance. To help carry out the latter provision, the law required that states create health exchanges to assist individuals in shopping for insurance coverage. The states argued that the law was an onerous, unconstitutional intrusion into state authority. But the Supreme Court, in a 5–4 decision issued in June 2012, said the individual health insurance mandate and most other provisions of the law were constitutional; however, the Court struck down the provision requiring states to expand Medicaid eligibility (allowing Texas to opt not to expand coverage). For states who opted in for expanded Medicaid funds, the federal government had a far larger say in how money was spent than it previously did. In 2015, the Supreme Court provided a second key victory for the Obama administration when it upheld the tax credit language of the law in *King* v. *Burwell*. These legal victories helped shape the role the federal government played in providing health care to a large percentage of the population.

Often frustrated by congressional inaction and Republican governors and state legislatures, President Obama increasingly turned to executive orders and working with cities (to bypass Republican legislatures and governors). For example, he worked with Salt Lake City, Phoenix, and New Orleans to help end homelessness among veterans and praised cities who increased their minimum wage laws and improved family leave policies.[70] He used executive orders to push his agenda on the environment and immigration. For example, in 2015 he issued an executive order to require federal agencies to reduce their use of fossil fuels (to help with greenhouse gases), designated 548 million acres of habitat to be under federal protection (to promote land preservation and climate change initiatives), and used an executive order to protect minors brought into the country without legal permission as children (DACA). Many of these orders were highly criticized by Donald Trump when he ran for office. Once elected, he immediately began issuing executive orders meant to reverse many Obama policies.

THE TRUMP YEARS (2017–2021) President Trump campaigned on many issues that directly impact federalism—from repealing Obamacare to building a wall on our southern border to regulating many environmental issues. Under President Trump, the matter of the proper division of power and responsibilities between the states and the federal government has grown in importance, surrounding issues such as criminal justice reform, the environment, marijuana, sanctuary cities, immigration, sports gambling, and the response to COVID-19. While many of these issues do not directly impact Texas, they do impact federal–state interactions and are important to understand in any discussion of federalism.

In June 2017, President Trump declared that the United States was withdrawing from the Paris Climate Agreement (negotiated under the Obama administration). He stated he believed the agreement would harm our ability to create jobs (especially in the energy sector) and would burden economic growth with growing regulation. Almost immediately, states and localities (as well as citizens) began to protest the move. In addition to withdrawing from the Paris Climate Agreement, the Trump administration dismantled many of the Obama administration's environmental regulations and land preservation initiatives. For example, President Trump reduced two of Utah's national monuments (established by Presidents Obama and Clinton). He reduced Bears Ears National Monument by 85 percent and cut 1.88 million acres (nearly half) of the Grand Staircase Escalante National Monument (designated by President Clinton in 1996). President Trump argued that these reductions were necessary to allow the state greater access to natural resources, but environmentalists, outdoor tourism advocates, and Democrats are very troubled by the potential environmental impact these changes will have. Added to this concern was his administration's edicts to open new mineral, oil, and gas leasing in protected lands, ease oil drilling regulation, and reduce protections for endangered species.[71] By January 2021, the Trump administration reversed 100 environmental rules, including carbon dioxide emissions from power plants, cars, and trucks and many regulations governing clean air, water, and toxic chemicals.[72] He believed the excessive rules unnecessarily stymie the fossil fuel industry and harm economic growth.[73]

President Trump threatened to take away federal money from "sanctuary cities" (cities that refuse to deport undocumented immigrants), but few if any federal grants are predicated upon cooperation with federal immigration policy. He renewed his threats to withhold federal funds to "sanctuary cities" during the pandemic (in April, 2020). In February 2020, acting secretary of Homeland Security, Chad Wolf, announced that residents of New York could no longer enroll in certain Trusted Traveler Programs, including Global Entry, because the administration objected to provisions in the state's "Green Light Law," which allows undocumented immigrants the ability to apply for state driver's licenses while protecting this information from immigration enforcement agencies.

California and the Trump administration seemed to be in open warfare over a variety of issues—most notably the environment and immigration. In 2018, President Trump targeted then-Governor Brown on Twitter several times, for instance after the governor pardoned five ex-convicts facing deportation so they could remain in the country (part of a wider action that pardoned fifty-six people who had completed their sentences years ago). The five subjected to deportation have lived crime-free lives for years. The California Values Act, which took effect on January 1, 2018, strictly limits state and local agencies from sharing information with federal officials about suspects unless they have been convicted of a serious crime (part of the attempt to protect sanctuary cities in California). In March 2018, the Trump administration announced it was suing California over the law. The state and several local governments have set up legal defense funds to help immigrants facing deportation.[74] After then, former President Trump openly clashed with Governor Newsom. The Bureau of Land Management announced in October 2019 that it was beginning to allow the selling of oil and gas drilling leases on public lands on California's central coast after a five-year moratorium. In addition to increasingly harsh rhetoric on both sides, litigation from both abounded. By the end of 2020, California had sued the Trump administration more than one hundred times, and the Trump administration had sued California numerous times in its short tenure. However, relations seemed to have improved a bit at times during the pandemic, as Governor Newsom, a liberal Democrat, thanked President Trump in April 2020 for assistance. In what was quite a reversal, both men praised one another.[75] This cooperative approach was once again seen in September as California battled horrific wildfires. The two worked together in a very collaborative manner to address the disaster.[76]

Interestingly, many of the arguments that conservatives made against Obama were used by liberals against President Trump. Liberals argued that state and local governments could refuse to help enforce federal law (as conservatives argued during the Obama years), citing cases such as *Printz* v. *U.S.* (1997), *New York* v. *U.S.* (1992) and *Murphy* v. *National Collegiate Athletic Association* (2018), in which the Supreme Court ruled that the Tenth Amendment prohibits federal "commandeering" of state governments to help enforce federal law.[77] The anti-commandeering doctrine is also at the center of the fight over sanctuary cities and state marijuana laws.[78]

The COVID-19 pandemic, the protests stemming from the killing of George Floyd, and the battle over the certification of the 2020 presidential election have demonstrated the complex relationship President Trump has with the states. Traditionally, conservatives strongly emphasize the rights of state governments, seeing them as important actors in our federal system of government. President Trump appeared to be making this argument when he asserts that the states are best suited to be responsible for the critical task of virus testing. However, he also asserted that he had the "absolute authority" to order states to reopen their businesses to stimulate the economic recovery devastating the country because of the pandemic. Moreover, he openly encouraged people to violate state stay-at-home orders instituted to advance public safety, thereby undermining the authority of governors. He not only offered federal troops to governors who would request them (none did) to respond to protestors, he openly discussed evoking the Insurrection Act. This law, from 1807, gives the president the extraordinary power to send U.S. military troops into American cities to end domestic unrest. In an address from the Rose Garden on June 1, 2020, he said that if a state or city refused to take the necessary actions to defend the life and property of residents he would deploy the military to "quickly solve the problem for them." In challenging the 2020 election results, President Trump directly challenged the ability of state officials to certify the results of state-run elections and discharge their constitutional duties.[79]

As part of his focus on criminal justice, President Trump helped pass the bipartisan First Step Act (Formerly Incarcerated Reenter Society Transformed Safely Transition Every Person Act) in 2018. The law, the most significant criminal justice reform in years, is designed to give nonviolent offenders the chance to reenter society to become contributing members with a better chance for redemption. The law only applies to the federal criminal system but it does ease punitive prison sentences for over 180,000 people and could cut prison sentences for more in the future. Since a fair percentage of federal inmates are housed in Texas, this reform has immediate impact on Texans and some champion it as a blueprint for reform in states who have yet to implement such reform actions.[80]

Given that the last two presidents, one a Democrat the other a Republican, have had wide levels of conflict with state governmental leaders, it seems likely that the same will occur with the Biden administration. However, only time will tell if this level of hostility will become the "new normal" or if this is a temporary situation reflective of broader polarization in American politics. This polarized federalism may become normalized in a way that largely signals an end of our more cooperative model which dominated much of the 20th Century.

3.2.6 The Role of the U.S. Supreme Court in Defining Federalism

The federal courts have played a central role in defining power, authority, and jurisdiction in the federal system. In looking to the courts to provide the definitive theory of federalism, we might expect a conservative Supreme Court to be most concerned with states' rights and to reconsider the doctrines underlying mandates and preemptions, but this has not always been the case.

In a 1985 Texas case, *Garcia v. San Antonio Metropolitan Transit Authority*, the U.S. Supreme Court held 5 to 4 that states could not claim immunity from federal regulation over functions that have been defined as "integral" or "traditional."[81] This case, which involved municipal employees and their coverage by the Fair Labor Standards Act, had far-reaching implications for federal–state relationships.[82] In the extreme, the case suggested that Congress, not the courts interpreting the Constitution, would define federalism. The case also suggested that there are no "discrete limitations on the objects of federal authority" other than those provisions of the Constitution that give the states a role in the selection of the president and members of Congress.[83]

By 1995, the Court, under the leadership of Chief Justice William Rehnquist, had become much more concerned with the expansion of federal powers and reasserted itself in cases that involved federal issues. The Court ruled 5 to 4 in the case of *United States v. Lopez* that "the Congress had overreached its constitutional power to regulate interstate commerce when it passed the Gun-Free School Zones Act of 1990."[84] In *Bush v. Vera*, the Court struck down a Texas political redistricting plan, suggesting that it was less likely to support redistricting that was designed primarily to benefit minority groups. Other cases soon followed that challenged race and ethnicity as criteria for redistricting, and the Court's position was clarified somewhat in a 2001 decision (*Easley v. Cromartie*) in which it held that race is not an unconstitutional consideration in redistricting as long as it is not the "dominant and controlling" factor.[85] In another case, the Court held that federal laws did not preempt state laws that penalized negligent manufacturers.[86]

A Texas case, *City of Boerne, Texas v. Flores* (1997), also demonstrated the Supreme Court's disposition to place limits on congressional powers.[87] In this case, the high Court ruled that the Religious Freedom Restoration Act of 1993 was unconstitutional because it was too broad in its protection of religious freedom. The Court held that provisions of the act infringed on state powers and also threatened "the authority of the court to determine the constitutionality of federal and state laws."[88] The ruling was handed down after a Roman Catholic parish in Boerne used the law to challenge the city's decision to deny it a permit to enlarge a church in a historic district. In addition, the Court struck down provisions of the Brady Handgun Violence Prevention Act, which required background checks on gun purchasers, in *Printz v. United States*.[89]

The Court has not been single-minded in its efforts to restrain the powers of the national government.[90] In 1996, the Court handed down several civil-rights decisions that imposed limits on state powers. It also struck down a 1992 Colorado constitutional amendment that prohibited governments from defining homosexuals as a protected class. In another case, Virginia, on the basis of the Fourteenth Amendment, was required to permit women to attend the Virginia Military Institute, which had been an all-male school.[91] In the *Seminole Tribe v. Florida* case, the Supreme Court concluded that Congress had virtually all "authority to legislate in the area of Indian affairs and states had none."[92]

Although the Rehnquist Court handed down a number of notable decisions that advanced the conservatives' new federalism agenda, it is not clear how the current U.S. Supreme Court under Chief Justice Roberts will deal with the balance of state and federal power. So far, it has been "fairly quiet in this area."[93] However, there have been some indications that the Roberts Court is receptive to federal powers. It has "decided more preemption cases in favor of the federal government at a higher rate" than previous courts, "separately and combined."[94] In *United States v. Comstock*, it upheld the authority of federal judges to issue civil commitment orders for sex offenders after they had completed their criminal sentences on a broad interpretation of the necessary and proper clause of the U.S. Constitution.[95]

In addition, the Roberts Court upheld state sovereignty in *Sossamon v. Texas*, a case in which a Texas inmate sued the state for monetary damages, arguing that he was denied access to the prison's chapel in violation of the Religious Land Use and Institutionalized

Persons Act (RLUIPA). The Court ruled that Texas, even though it accepted federal funds, did not waive its right to sovereign immunity from private suits for monetary damages.[96]

In early spring 2012, the U.S. Supreme Court heard a challenge by twenty-six states, including Texas, to President Obama's health care law, as discussed earlier in this chapter, and later upheld most of the law. In a more recent test of state sovereignty, *Whole Woman's Health* v. *Hellerstedt* (2016), the Supreme Court overturned a number of key provisions in a 2013 Texas abortion law (notably the requirements that doctors who perform abortions have admitting privileges at a local hospital and that abortion clinics meet the costly standards for ambulatory surgical centers) as these regulations placed an undue burden on women seeking to terminate a pregnancy. Recent research by political scientist John Dinan found that the Supreme Court has continued the trend of limiting the power of the federal government established by Court rulings beginning in the late twentieth century.[97] In 2018, the Supreme Court once again sided with the power of the states in *Murphy* v. *National Collegiate Athletic Association* (the case was previously filed under *Christie* v. *NCAA*, but Christie was dropped as a named participant when he was no longer the governor of New Jersey, with Governor Murphy replacing him in the lawsuit). In this case, New Jerseyans passed a 2011 referendum to legalize sports betting. The following year, the state legislature enacted a law legalizing sports wagering at casinos and racetracks. The law was opposed by the major sports leagues and the National Collegiate Athletic Association (NCAA) as a violation of the Professional and Amateur Sports Protection Act (PASPA) passed by Congress in 1992. The law forbids states from passing laws to authorize legalized sports betting. The Supreme Court ruled that the law unconstitutionally commandeered state officials in violation of the Tenth Amendment.

The Impact of Federalism on State Finances

3.3 Assess the impact of federalism on state finances.

Federal taxes paid into the national treasury from Texas in 2017 (the most recent data available to allow a comparative examination) totaled approximately $133.4 billion. Only California and New York paid larger amounts (though Texas is not even in the top ten in federal taxes paid per capita). The District of Columbia paid the highest federal taxes per capita ($10,500) with Connecticut being a close second ($10,400). A study by the Rockefeller Institute of Government (a public policy research institute affiliated with the State University of New York, Albany) examined the differences between what taxpayers in each state pay in federal income taxes and what the states receive back in federal expenditures, which includes direct federal funding of programs (such as Medicaid), as well as federal grants, contracts, and income earned by federal employees in each state. The study was published in 2019 and examined data from FY 2016; an earlier study examined data from FY 2015. Certainly, one would expect that many states receive more from the federal government than their taxpayers contribute, but the numbers might surprise you. Thirty-nine states, including Texas, receive more from the federal government than is paid by their residents in taxes. Ten states receive less from the federal government than they pay in taxes; California receives approximately the same in expenditures as what is paid in taxes.[98] In the earlier study, Texans paid more than they received.[99] In the most recent study, Texans received approximately $36.2 billion more in federal expenditures than they paid in federal taxes, amounting to an advantage of $1,280 per capita. The state with the worst balance in expenditures-receipts was Connecticut; the imbalance in this state amounted to negative $1,240 per capita. Looking at it another way, for every $1 of federal income taxes residents of Connecticut paid, they received just $.74 in federal expenditures. West Virginia received the most back in relationship to what its residents paid in taxes. The per capita net between federal taxes and federal expenditures in West Virginia is nearly $8,000.[100]

3.3.1 Changing Sources of State Budgets and Federal Grants

For years, state officials have complained about the disparity between federal taxes collected in Texas and the distribution of federal funds in the state. The state has long attempted through its congressional delegation and the Office of State–Federal Relations to obtain more equitable formulas as Congress amends or reauthorizes grant programs.

Federal funds accounted for approximately $74.9 billion, or about 33 percent, of the approximately $224 billion state budget for the 2018–2019 biennium (a decrease of 3.8 percent from the last budget cycle) (see Figure 3–2). The overall state budget is .9 percent more than fiscal year (FY) 2016–2017 levels.[101]

With more federal funds flowing into the state, officials slightly increased the budgets of several governmental agencies. For example, the agencies of the Health and Human Services Commission, which includes a wide range of social services for millions of low-income Texans and accounts for over 31.6 percent of all funds spent by the state, received nearly $1.1 billion more in 2018–2019 than it did in 2016–2017. In the 2014–2015 budget, the agencies of education lost $1.6 billion in allocations (while the agencies lost $3.5 billion in the previous budget cycle). The 2016–2017 budget cycle saw a significant increase (though not funding the agency to levels previously seen), and the 2018–2019 budget cycle saw another slight increase. The Agencies of Education–Public Education received $656 million more in 2018–2019 than it did in 2016–2017 (1.2 percent more). The Agencies of Education–Higher Education received $154 million more (representing a .9 percent increase, while in 2014–2015 the spending on higher education decreased by $5.4 billion—a 23.3 percent decrease).[102]

The state government, through the Office of State–Federal Relations, and many of the larger cities in Texas have full-time staffers working to obtain additional federal dollars. Like other states, Texas lobbies the federal government for additional programs,

FIGURE 3–2 SOURCES OF REVENUE FOR TEXAS 2018–2019 VERSUS 2016–2017

As indicated by this chart, Texas government receives a large share of its funding from the federal government.

NOTE: Numbers may total to more than 100 percent due to rounding.

SOURCE: Texas Legislative Budget Board, *Legislative Budget Board Fiscal Size-Up: 2016–2017 Biennium*, May 2016, Figure 29, p. 33, http://www.lbb.state.tx.us/Documents/Publications/Fiscal_SizeUp/2939_Fiscal_Size-Up_2016-17.pdf; Texas Legislative Budget Board, *Legislative Budget Board Fiscal Size-Up: 2018-2019 Biennium*, September 2018, Figure 28, p. 33, https://www.lbb.state.tx.us/Documents/Publications/Fiscal_SizeUp/Fiscal_SizeUp.pdf

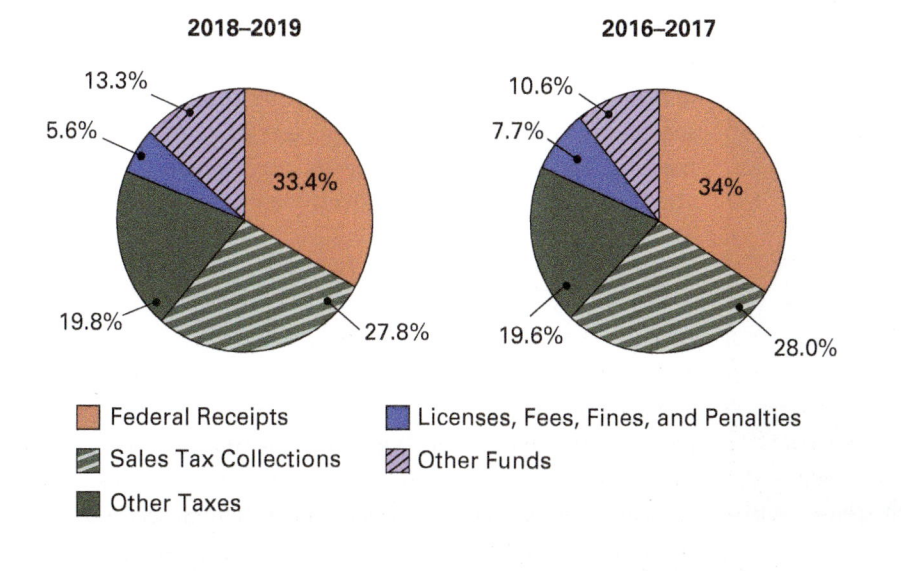

2018–2019
- Federal Receipts: 33.4%
- Sales Tax Collections: 27.8%
- Other Taxes: 19.8%
- Licenses, Fees, Fines, and Penalties: 5.6%
- Other Funds: 13.3%

2016–2017
- Federal Receipts: 34%
- Sales Tax Collections: 28.0%
- Other Taxes: 19.6%
- Licenses, Fees, Fines, and Penalties: 7.7%
- Other Funds: 10.6%

changes in existing programs, relief from mandates and preemptions, and adjustments in funding formulas that adversely affect the state.

Many of the grants that come to Texas are formula grants, based on population, levels of poverty, or some other criteria. Others are competitive and must be sought out by Texas governments. Some state agencies and local governments are aggressive and often successful in obtaining competitive grants, but others are not. Governments with limited staff often find it difficult to reallocate employees' time to the complex grant application process. Available programs must be identified through publications such as the *Federal Register*, and applications must be submitted in a timely manner. Some assistance is available to local governments through their regional councils of governments, and some consultants provide grant-writing services. Local governments may choose to not apply for grants, due to disinterest, political opposition, or other reasons.

State agencies are required to pursue relevant federal grants for their programs. The governor's office has a State Grants Team that works to increase Texas's access to available federal money. This group helps identify grant programs, informs other state and local agencies of available grants, and helps write grant applications.[103]

WHY NO NATIONAL DRINKING AGE?

Although the federal government often acknowledges the right of the states to set policies in a variety of areas, it can exert influence by providing financial incentives to states. The federal government, for example, did not pass a national drinking age that required change, but rather passed a law that required states with drinking ages of less than 21 to forgo 10 percent of their federal highway budgets. Many are concerned that the power of the federal government can continue to grow as long as states and localities need financial support. As the old saying goes, "Whoever pays the piper, calls the tune."

3.3.2 Reactions to the Expanded Role of the Federal Government

Many citizens argue that economic, environmental, and social issues are national in scope and cannot be adequately addressed at the state or local level. These problems, they believe, require a coordinated national effort with common standards and objectives. Not all governments have the financial resources to deal with many of these problems, and without federal assistance, some significant segments of our society would suffer. The COVID-19 pandemic demonstrated many of these concerns as well as concerns people have regarding what was perceived as a too aggressive and too powerful federal response.

Many governments, it also has been argued, would not address such issues if they were not required to do so by federal mandates. People note the long history of discrimination in the United States and argue that changes promoting civil rights and equality would not have occurred if the federal government had not taken the lead through legislation and public policy.

Government centralization, however, has been a dominant fear throughout our country's history since its founding. In the eighteenth-century debates over ratifying the U.S. Constitution, the Anti-Federalists made many of the arguments against a strong national government that are heard today. In addition to a fear of tyranny, corruption, and abuses was a concern that people in one area of the country could impose their will on others. Was it possible for officials in Washington to understand local issues and problems facing citizens across the country? Many believe that state governments are more successful in understanding and meeting the needs of citizens, and consequently are leery of a strong and powerful federal government.

3.3.3 Mandates Meet State Agencies and Local Communities

Today, the large number of federal mandates and preemptions restrict the policy options of state and local governments and often increase their costs. When the federal government provides money, it usually has strings attached. State agencies and local communities sometimes resist taking federal dollars because they do not want these restrictions to force them to rearrange their local priorities. Most public officeholders, though, find it difficult to refuse available federal dollars.

Some federal grant programs have provisions that link different policy areas together. For example, the Texas legislature, after lowering the legal drinking age to 18 for a few years, restored it to 21 in 1986. Although many Texans had lobbied for the restoration of the older drinking age, another major impetus for the change came from a federal law linking a state's drinking age to federal grants for road construction. Texas could have refused to adopt the higher age, but it would have lost 10 percent of its federal highway dollars after 1988.

Many federal assistance programs were designed to redistribute resources from wealthier Americans to those with lower incomes, a policy that some people oppose. Moreover, this redistribution is linked in Texas to issues of race and ethnicity because minority groups constitute a disproportionate part of the state's low-income population. Some political leaders have resisted federal grant programs for fear that funding projects would enhance the political position of minority groups. Other opposition is fiscally driven, as state residents generally contributed more to the federal treasury than was received in direct assistance for social welfare programs. Consequently, some are opposed to allowing officials in Washington to distribute their tax dollars to citizens in others states or for programs they do not support.

Moreover, Texans are proud of their abilities to address the needs of the state's residents and feel that the federal government could learn more efficiency from following our lead. For example, our unemployment level is typically lower than national averages. We largely escaped the extreme situation created by the housing crisis and have had many years of steady economic growth. We fear that federal dominance undermines the creative capacity of states and local governments to deal with many local and regional problems.

Likewise, many Texans would argue that the states are now much more innovative than the federal government in policy initiatives and administrative streamlining. Some suggest that the increased use of fiscal federalism (federal grants linked to preemptions and mandates) has produced a mindset that the federal government should assume more responsibility for domestic programs, in terms of both program development and funding.[104] One should not, therefore, be surprised when Texans resist federal intervention.

Transnational Regionalism

3.4 Describe the increased interdependency between the United States and Mexico.

Texas shares a 1,200-mile border with Mexico, and common problems and interests that bond the two neighbors, referred to as **transnational regionalism**, have taken on increased importance since the mid-1980s. Historically, relations between the United States and Mexico often were strained. The United States fought a war against Mexico from 1846 to 1848, and on subsequent occasions, American troops entered Mexican territory, ostensibly to protect U.S. economic and national security interests. Apprehension about U.S. objectives resulted in Mexican policies on trade, commerce, and foreign ownership of property that were designed to insulate the country from excessive foreign influence and domination. Nevertheless, the interests of the two countries have long been bound by geopolitical factors, economics, and demographics. One Mexican author has compared the interdependence of the two countries to Siamese twins, warning that "if one becomes gangrenous, the other twin will also be afflicted."[105]

Donald Trump's election to the presidency in 2016 signaled the opening of a new chapter in U.S.–Mexico relations. Trump campaigned on pledges to build a wall along the Mexican border, take other steps to clamp down on undocumented

transnational regionalism
The expanding economic and social interdependence of South Texas and Mexico.

immigration, and remove the United States from the North American Free Trade Agreement (NAFTA), an agreement approved in the 1990s to improve trade among the United States, Mexico, and Canada. His harsh rhetoric drew criticism at home and abroad. When Mexico's then-President Enrique Peña Nieto hosted then-candidate Trump, Nieto received strong, vocal opposition from his constituents, many of whom were very disappointed that their leader hosted a presidential candidate who habitually spoke about their country and its people in less than flattering ways (and routinely pledged that Mexico would pay for the border wall). Perhaps the most vocal opponent of President Trump was former Mexican President Vincente Fox, who repeatedly and strongly criticized President Trump for his stance toward his country. In January 2017, President Trump signed an executive agreement to renegotiate NAFTA. Officials from Mexico, Canada, and the United States met at least seven times during 2017 and 2018 prior to announcing an amenable new agreement to replace NAFTA on September 30, 2018. The new treaty was ratified by Mexico in June 2019, by the United States House in December 2019, by the Senate in January 2020, and by the Canadian parliament two months later. The United States–Mexico–Canada Agreement (USMCA) was the result of lengthy negotiations and is widely seen as creating modest changes to the historic NAFTA agreement.[106] But it did include some strengthened provisions, including key labor provisions that won the support of the AFL-CIO, which had opposed NAFTA.

3.4.1 Maquiladoras

Changes in the economic relationship between Mexico and the United States began with the **maquiladora program**, an initiative under Mexico's 1964 Border Industrialization Program to boost employment, foreign exchange, and industrial development. It was designed also to transfer technology to Mexico, help train workers, and develop managerial skills among Mexican nationals.[107]

maquiladora program
Economic program initiated by Mexico to increase manufacturing and the assembly of goods.

The concept was to develop twin plants, one in the United States and one in Mexico, under a single management. The plant in the United States would manufacture parts, and its Mexican counterpart would assemble them into a product, which would be sent back to the United States for further processing or shipping to customers.[108] Parts shipped into Mexico would not be subject to the normal tariffs, and the tax imposed on the assembled product would be minimal. In 1984, Mexico permitted the United States and other countries to establish these relationships throughout Mexico, rather than just on the border, and allowed 100 percent foreign ownership of the assembly plants in Mexico. The latter step was a radical departure from previous Mexican law, which prohibited such foreign ownership.[109]

The maquiladora program has not resulted in the construction of a significant number of manufacturing plants on the Texas side of the border because American companies have used existing plants throughout the United States to produce parts to be assembled in Mexico. Nevertheless, Texas's border counties have benefited from the creation of thousands of support jobs in transportation, warehousing, and services.[110] Statistics are difficult to verify, but the most reliable and current source, the government-run National Institute for Statistics and Geography (INEGI), states that the program employed close to 2 million Mexican workers at more than 6,000 plants by April 2016.[111]

The maquiladora program continues to play a major role in transnational economic development but also remains controversial. American organized labor opposes the program, arguing that the maquiladoras drain jobs from the United States. But the program provides a source of inexpensive labor for American businesses, which have complained for years that they cannot compete against low foreign labor costs. The living and working conditions of workers, however, many of whom are single women, are very difficult and in some cities with high population

PROMISING NEW BORDER POLICIES

President Donald Trump, shown speaking at an event in Dallas, campaigned on pledges to crack down on immigration and change trade policies with Mexico.

density, highly exploitive and dangerous. One such city, Juarez, has had hundreds of homicides of women (femicide) since 1990, with more than 300 in 2010 alone. No accurate estimates exist about the number of women killed or kidnapped in Juárez, but gender-based violence in the city is common. In 2019, the Mexican government indicated that 31 women were killed in Chihuahua state (the home of Juárez), with 1,006 nationwide (representing a 137 percent increase since 2014).[112] These numbers only account for the bodies of the women found; mothers and other loved ones have mobilized nationwide to find information about the many thousands who are missing. Large protests spread across the country in 2019 and 2020 demanding change to reduce gender-based violence.

3.4.2 The United States–Mexico–Canada Agreement

Negotiations on a free-trade agreement in 1991 marked another significant change in the relationship between Mexico and the United States. The negotiations were precipitated, in part, by world economics and the emergence of regional trading zones. The administration of Mexican President Carlos Salinas de Gortari also reacted to the failure of Mexico's economic policies of the 1980s and a fear of economic isolation. The end of the Cold War, a reduction in Central American conflicts, and internal population pressures were other factors.[113]

The convergence of interests of the United States, Mexico, and Canada produced the North American Free Trade Agreement (NAFTA) to reduce tariffs and increase trade among the three countries. It created one of the world's largest trading blocs, which had a combined population of approximately 494.5 million in 2018 and combined gross domestic product (GDP) of more than $21.2 trillion in 2016.[114] Between 1992 and 2018, U.S. trade with Mexico increased by nearly 500 percent (by contrast, U.S. trade with Canada increased by approximately 175 percent in the same time period).[115] Other regions of the world have recognized the value of creating large trading blocs, and the European Union, now composed of twenty-seven nations, is estimated to have a combined population of 446 million and a combined GDP of $15.9 trillion in 2018 (compared to $25.5 trillion for the United States and $13.8 trillion for China).[116]

Approved by the U.S. Congress in late 1993, NAFTA has increased trade among the three countries, strengthened previous economic ties, and created new ones. Texas has experienced significant economic changes from these new relationships, but the benefits have not been distributed uniformly throughout the state. Also, NAFTA was plagued by controversy.

CONCERNS ABOUT NAFTA Some people on both sides of the U.S.–Mexico border believed that NAFTA, despite its overall trade and economic benefits, harmed their respective countries. Labor unions in the United States were particularly concerned that low labor costs in Mexico moved jobs from the United States. There was some concern in Mexico, at least initially, that American corporations would dominate and reduce Mexico's control over its own economy because approximately 80 percent of Mexico's exports were going to the United States. Human rights advocates expressed concerns about working conditions, workers' benefits, and the broader social impact of manufacturing plants on the lives of hundreds of thousands of Mexican citizens, especially women. Environmentalists argued that increased manufacturing and commerce worsened air, water, and waste pollution problems in the border area. Both countries have environmental laws, and the treaty called for collaboration on environmental issues, but there were allegations that U.S. manufacturers shipped their dirty plants to Mexico, which, as an emerging country, was less inclined or able to crack down on polluters.[117]

There has been strong opposition in Texas and throughout the United States to a provision of the treaty allowing Mexican trucks to deliver products between destinations in Mexico and the U.S. interior. Many residents and government officials in the United States have feared that the Mexican trucks would increase safety problems on American highways and American truckers and labor unions have opposed the competition from lower-paid Mexican drivers. After years of controversy and negotiations, some Mexican trucking companies were given authority to haul freight on U.S. highways between the border and U.S. destinations but were prohibited from hauling freight between two points within the United States. Similar provisions were included in the new **United States–Mexico–Canada Agreement (USMCA)**, which won the approval of the American Trucking Associations. Under the new agreement, the number of Mexican trucking companies allowed to operate in the U.S. is capped.[118]

United States-Mexico-Canada Agreement (USMCA)
Treaty signed in 2018 to lower trade barriers among the United States, Mexico, and Canada and to continue the common economic market created two decades earlier by the North American Free Trade Agreement, or NAFTA, which it replaced.

CHANGES UNDER USMCA The USMCA strengthens provisions important to organized labor and won the AFL-CIO's endorsement of a trade agreement for the first time in 18 years. Those provisions were designed to make it easier to identify and prevent labor violations, especially in Mexico. The new agreement has updated guidelines for food safety in all three countries, e-commerce, and the use of online data. Additionally, the new pact includes new anticorruption provisions and sets higher thresholds for what percentage of an automobile must be manufactured in North America to avoid tariffs. USMCA, which won bipartisan approval in both the U.S. House and the Senate, also is credited with strengthening some environmental protections. But some Democrats who voted against the agreement said they did so because the pact does little, if anything, to address climate change. "When it comes to climate change, the agreement still contains many of the same flaws of the original NAFTA, which I voted against," said Senator Chuck Schumer of New York, the Senate minority leader, who also voted against USMCA.[119]

TRADE PATTERNS BETWEEN TEXAS AND MEXICO The United States and Texas do a lot of business with Mexico. Exports from the United States to Mexico increased from $41.6 billion in 1993 to approximately $256 billion in 2019 (an increase of over 515 percent).[120] Texas exports to Mexico totaled less than $24.1 billion in 1993 but rose to $109.7 billion in 2018 and fell to $108.6 billion in 2019 (see Figure 3-3). Texas exported over $330 billion worth of goods worldwide and accounted for over 20 percent of total U.S. exports in 2019.[121] Imports from Mexico, now the third-largest

FIGURE 3-3   TEXAS AND U.S. EXPORTS TO MEXICO, 1993–2019

This chart depicts the dramatic increase in exports from Texas and the United States to Mexico since the passage of NAFTA in 1993.

SOURCE: Massachusetts Institute of Social and Economic Research and the U.S. Census Bureau (based on "origin of movement to port" state-level data series); Texas Department of Economic Development, April 2000; and International Trade Administration, *Trade Stats* program, 2012–2017; "State Exports from Texas," United States Census Bureau, https://www.census.gov/foreign-trade/statistics/state/data/tx.html; "Trade in Goods with Mexico," https://www.census.gov/foreign-trade/balance/c2010.html.

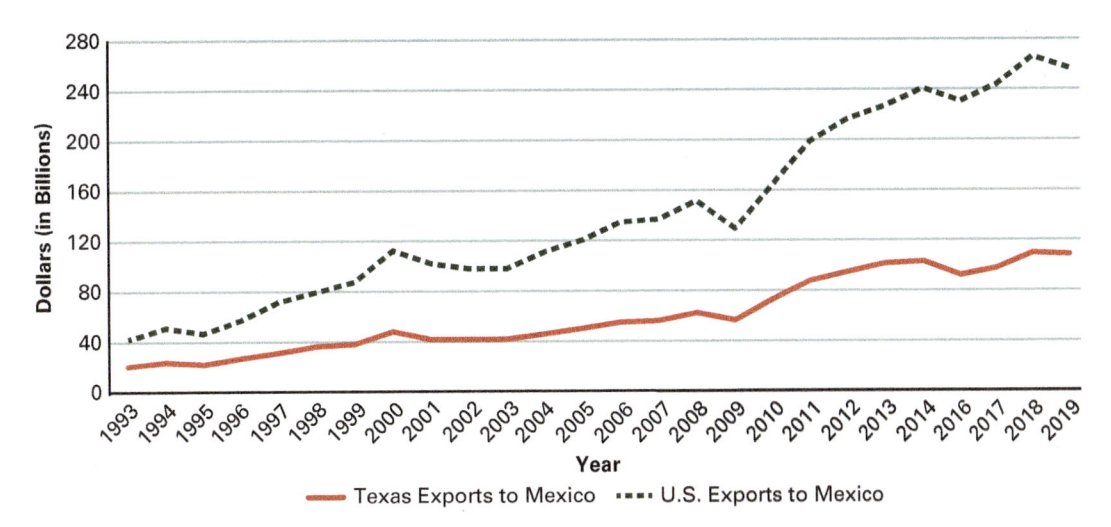

trading partner of the United States, increased from $39.9 billion in 1993 to $358.1 billion in 2019 (an increase of 797 percent). Mexico accounted for 14.3 percent of all goods imported into the United States in 2019 and 15.6 percent of U.S. exports.[122]

The sheer volume of goods, services, and people being moved is obvious on the highways leading into Mexico and from the long lines of people on foot and in autos and trucks at border crossings in Brownsville, Laredo, and El Paso. There were over 127 million border crossings at points of entry between Texas and Mexico in 2019, including approximately 32.2 million personal vehicle crossings, 19.9 million pedestrian crossings, 1.7 million bus passengers and 4.5 million truck crossings. On average, approximately 20,900 pedestrians crossed the border at El Paso each day, and nearly 6,500 trucks crossed the border each day at Laredo, the nation's largest inland port.[123] Billions of dollars are required to upgrade and expand the roads, highways, bridges, water and sanitation systems, and other facilities on both sides of the border. Both countries have taken some initiative, but many of these facilities will not be completed for years, contributing to delays and gridlock in both countries at border crossings. The North American Development Bank was created to help address these needs.

3.4.3 Immigration

Population growth in Texas always has been affected by migration from other states and foreign countries. But the proximity of Texas to Mexico has put the state at the center of a long-running dispute over the undocumented immigration of large numbers of Mexicans and other Latin Americans. That dispute heated up with the election of President Donald Trump. After taking office, President Trump's views on immigration hardened. In the summer of 2018, President Trump declared a "crisis" of illegal immigration and implemented strict guidelines for border control agents. These policies drew swift and strong protests by a large proportion of Americans. As we will see, the issue of immigration is complex and multifaceted.

FEDERAL GOVERNMENT LAWS AND POLICIES The federal government, not the states, has the authority to determine immigration laws and policies; however, states are intimately and directly impacted by the federal government's actions (or inactions).[124] Congress enacted the Nationalization Act of 1790, which limited naturalization to "free white persons" of "good moral character" and established residency requirements for citizenship. The Chinese Exclusion Act (1882) was the first major law restricting immigration into the United States. It limited Chinese immigration and denied this population naturalization rights. Quotas based on national origin were central to the national immigration policy until 1965 and gave preference to immigrants from northern European countries. Piecemeal legislation dealing with immigration was consolidated in the Immigration and Nationality Act of 1952, which maintained the quota system, established preferences for skilled labor and relatives of U.S. citizens, and enhanced screening and security procedures.

The quota system discriminated against Asians, eastern Europeans, African Americans, and Latin Americans. During World War II, when the United States faced a labor shortage, the *bracero program* was negotiated with Mexico, which made it possible for temporary workers from Mexico to enter the United States. This program, however, was terminated in 1964.

The Immigration and Nationality Act of 1965 eliminated national quotas but set limits on the number of immigrants from different regions of the world. The law produced a dramatic shift in immigration patterns, with large numbers of Asians now entering the country. As war and political instability affected developing countries, additional immigrants began entering the United States, creating a huge backlog in applications for documented immigrant status. Consequently, a massive influx of undocumented immigration began. If arrested, undocumented immigrants were deported, but until 1986, it was not illegal for American employers to hire them.[125] Moreover, large portions of the Texas and American economies were built on the availability of cheap, low-skilled foreign labor, and businesses and individuals were willing to ignore the undocumented status of millions of immigrants, particularly from Mexico and other Latin American countries.[126]

As the scale of the problem became more evident, the U.S. Congress enacted the Immigration Reform and Control Act in 1986. That law imposed fines on employers who hired undocumented immigrants and provided jail sentences for flagrant violators. Potential employees had to provide documentation, and employers had to verify their employees' citizenship. Because there was no practical way to deport millions of undocumented immigrants, the law also provided a means for giving legal status, or amnesty, to undocumented immigrants who had moved to the United States before January 1, 1982. In addition, it provided temporary status for agricultural workers who could satisfy specific residency requirements.[127]

But undocumented immigration continued, and public pressure mounted for more rigorous action. Additional legislation was passed in 1996 to increase funds for border guards and inspectors, to increase penalties for smuggling people into the United States and for using fraudulent documents, to construct fences along the border, and to make it easier to detain and deport undocumented immigrants.[128] The U.S. Congress also passed major changes in welfare laws in 1996, cutting off most public assistance, except for emergency medical care, to both documented and undocumented immigrants in the United States.

Critics of the previous welfare system had argued that the accessibility of public funds and services was a strong attraction to immigrants, many of whom were poverty stricken. They argued that American taxpayers had no obligation to support anyone who entered the country as undocumented or even to help documented immigrants who could not support themselves. Undocumented workers increase demands on public health care and welfare programs.[129] Some citizens, particularly unskilled workers, viewed the undocumented arrivals as a threat to their jobs and standard of living.

Several years after the 1996 public assistance restrictions were enacted, however, there was considerable evidence that the restrictions were not deterring undocumented immigration or reducing immigrants' use of public services.[130] For one thing, children of undocumented immigrants represented a heavy financial burden for many school districts and taxpayers throughout the country; but the U.S. Supreme Court, in a case from Texas, ruled years ago that public school districts were required to educate immigrant children who sought enrollment.

Immigration reform was a centerpiece of President George W. Bush's domestic program, but border security became a greater concern after the terrorist attacks of September 11, 2001. The creation of the Department of Homeland Security in 2002 combined and realigned a number of existing agencies in order to increase control on the borders. Meanwhile, political debate intensified over the competition for jobs between U.S. citizens and undocumented immigrants, along with a host of other immigration-related issues.

In late 2005, the U.S. House approved a bill to improve border security and make undocumented immigrants criminals, ignoring a proposal by President Bush to provide undocumented immigrants already in the country a way to become citizens. The U.S. Senate rejected the House bill and approved legislation providing a so-called "pathway" to citizenship for undocumented immigrants who paid fines, learned to speak English, and met certain other requirements. The controversy played out in peaceful but noisy demonstrations in many American cities, including Dallas, Houston, and San Antonio, and in numerous political campaigns. Thousands of immigrants, their descendants, and supporters took to the streets to wave American and Mexican flags for their cause.

Although immigration reform legislation failed, Congress in 2005 authorized a border wall or fence along the U.S.–Mexico border by attaching it as a rider to the REAL ID Act, a law requiring states to develop a standard driver's license for use as identification. When details of the fence became public in 2007, another round of intense political controversy on both sides of the border followed. More fuel was added to the political fire in 2008, when the Department of Homeland Security announced it would pursue construction despite potential conflicts with some thirty-four existing laws. Given the physical barrier that the Rio Grande presents to vehicles, most fences built on the Texas border are designed to prevent illegal crossings by pedestrians.[131]

President Bush also ordered several thousand National Guard troops to the border to help the Border Patrol in 2006. It was widely believed the president took this additional step to "secure" the border in order to boost support for his proposal to allow immigrants already in the country illegally to earn citizenship and to help members of his party in the 2006 congressional elections.

Border security remained an issue during President Barack Obama's administration. As drug-related violence increased on the border, President Obama ordered 1,200 National Guard troops to help contain the violence.[132] President Obama also sought comprehensive immigration-law changes, including a way for undocumented but law-abiding immigrants who already were in the country to become citizens. Obama actively lobbied for the so-called Development, Relief and Education for Alien Minors (DREAM) Act, a measure that was initially proposed several years before he took office. It would have allowed children who were brought to the country illegally to eventually receive legal, permanent residency if they went to college or signed up for the military. Despite Obama's efforts, a filibuster by Senate Republicans blocked the bill in a showdown vote in late 2010. Opponents contended the bill would offer amnesty to as many as 2 million undocumented immigrants and would increase the federal deficit. Although Senator Orrin Hatch, a Republican from Utah, initially offered the DREAM Act in 2001 with bipartisan support, Republicans began to abandon it as conservatives took more control of their party.[133] With Congress still refusing to act on immigration reform, Obama in 2012 used his executive authority to offer renewable two-year work permits to several hundred thousand undocumented immigrants who had come to the

United States before their sixteenth birthday and before June 2007 (a program known as DACA—Deferred Action for Childhood Arrivals). The policy did not grant legal status to those who qualified, but it did allow them to avoid deportation.

Following the 2014 midterm elections, President Obama issued a series of administrative changes in rules and refocused enforcement of existing immigration law. The Department of Homeland Security (through its Immigration and Customs Enforcement (ICE) branch) was to focus on deporting undocumented immigrants who were recent arrivals or who had criminal convictions, especially those who presented threats through gang membership, terrorist links, or other criminal behavior. Additionally, the president moved to allow undocumented immigrants who entered the country illegally but were the parents of U.S. citizens or permanent residents to stay if they lived in the U.S. longer than five years, registered, passed a criminal background check, and paid taxes (the program is called Deferred Action for Parents of Americans or DAPA). The final key component of Obama's executive action involved a program expansion of DACA to include a broader age group. Twenty-six states, led by Texas, sought an injunction to prevent the executive orders from being enforced. On November 10, 2015, the U.S. Fifth Circuit Court of Appeals upheld a lower court injunction against DAPA and DACA. Texas asserted that these executive actions would force the state to change existing laws to provide the immigrants "state-subsidized driver's licenses," unemployment insurance, and other state services. The president argued that the orders were within the executive branch's discretionary power to enforce existing immigration laws (notably the Immigration and Naturalization Act), but conservatives argued that the actions were an unconstitutional usurpation of Congress's power to write immigration law. In June 2016, a deadlocked Supreme Court left in place the appeals court ruling blocking the plan to allow millions of undocumented immigrants to remain and work legally in the country. President Obama and millions of supporters were profoundly disappointed with the lack of action by the Court. In 2017, President Trump attempted to terminate the DACA program (which protects approximately 700,000 young adults brought to the United States undocumented as children) by executive order. His order gave Congress six months to pass legislation to address the issue. People protected under DACA must register every two years, providing them with work permits but not a path to citizenship. There are strict rules that regulate eligibility, and to remain eligible, participants must not be convicted of a felony or three misdemeanors. A federal District Judge in California blocked the plan to end the program; the U.S. Court of Appeals upheld the injunction leading the Trump administration to appeal the ruling to the Supreme Court. While the case was being appealed, participants continued to register as dictated by the program. Seemingly in reaction to the federal injunctions, on May 1, 2018, Texas Attorney General Ken Paxton led six other states to sue the federal government to end DACA (which protects more than 120,000 young people in Texas). The Mexican American Legislative Caucus (MALC) denounced the lawsuit, alleging the case could dramatically harm families in the state and cost billions of dollars in GDP losses.[134] On June 18, 2020, the Supreme Court ruled that the Trump administration could not immediately end the program. Surprising many, as it seemed that a majority of justices were inclined to let Trump end the program during the oral arguments in late-2019, Chief Justice Roberts sided with the court's four liberal justices in upholding President Obama's executive order creating the program. The decision did not rule that DACA could never be rescinded by executive action, but rather that the process followed by the Trump administration was insufficient to do so. The rationale used by the administration to end the program was "arbitrary and capricious." Hence, if better-developed arguments were put forward, the program could still be rescinded. This ruling only provided temporary protection for these hundreds of thousands of young people, frequently called Dreamers. About 27,000 of the young immigrants protected from deportation work in health care, and many were on the front lines treating coronavirus victims.[135] In his first week in office, President Biden issued an executive order directing the secretary of homeland security to take actions to "preserve and fortify" DACA and is prioritizing immigration reform.

The Obama administration deported a record number of immigrants, including many who had been convicted of crimes in this country. According to U.S. Immigration and Customs Enforcement (ICE), the number of deportations of undocumented immigrants has increased at a rapid rate. In 1999, only 175,000 people were deported. Beginning in 2008, the number of deportations increased so that by the 2012 a record 432,228 people were deported. The figure has decreased since the 2013.[136] In the 2011, a total of 390,423 people were deported (51.4 percent of whom were noncriminal immigration violators); in 2013, 432,228 people were removed (54.1 percent of whom were noncriminal violators). The numbers were reduced dramatically in 2015 with only 325,328 individuals being deported (63 percent of whom were noncriminal violators). The numbers increased slightly in 2016 to 331,717 (65.2 percent were noncriminal violators) but decreased again in 2017 to 287,093 (61.8 percent were noncriminal violators). In the 2018, 328,093 people were deported (54.9 percent were noncriminal violators); in 2019 the number increased again to 359,885 (56.7 percent were noncriminal violators).[137]

The most current data from the U.S. Department of Homeland Security, January 2015, estimates that 12 million people were in the United States and undocumented, a slight increase from the 11.5 million estimated in 2014 (yearly reports were typically issued by the department but have not been published since 2015). The number had been decreasing for a number of years.[138] The Department of Homeland Security has attributed the small drop to unemployment problems in the United States, improved economic conditions in Mexico, and increased border enforcement. According to the Pew Research Center, 4.9 million unauthorized Mexicans were living in the United States in 2017 (down from 6.9 million in 2007), representing less than half, about 47 percent, of undocumented immigrants.[139] Non-Mexican undocumented immigrants grew from 5.3 million in 2007 to 5.5 million in 2017. Furthermore, 57 percent of all undocumented immigrants live in six states (California, Texas, Florida, New York, New Jersey, and Illinois).[140] A report issued in June 2020 by the American Immigration Council indicates that nearly one-sixth (4.9 million) of the state's total population were immigrants in 2018; another one-sixth of the population is made up of citizens with at least one immigrant parent.[141] Undocumented immigrants represented six percent of the state's total population (1.6 million) in 2016, and 1.4 million citizens lived with at least one undocumented family member between 2010 and 2014.[142] These immigrants are vital to the state's economy, especially in construction and extraction, manufacturing, health care and social assistance, building and grounds cleaning and maintenance, transportation, food services, sales, and retail. Immigrant-led households in Texas paid $26.3 billion in federal taxes and $12.3 billion in state and local taxes in 2018; undocumented immigrants paid an estimated $2.6 billion in federal taxes and $1.6 billion in Texas state and local taxes in 2018.[143] Immigrant-led households in Texas had $112.8 billion in spending power, after-tax income, in 2018; with immigrant business owners accounting for $10.8 billion in business income. In 2018, over half of businesses in Houston/Baytown/Sugar Land were owned by immigrants.[144]

Early in his administration, President Trump issued executive orders to bar immigration from several majority-Muslim countries and to deny federal funding to so-called "sanctuary cities" that refused to cooperate in the enforcement of federal immigration laws. Those orders were blocked temporarily by federal courts that questioned the legality of the president's directives. The Trump administration also ordered immigration enforcement officers to begin rounding up undocumented immigrants with criminal records. A number of undocumented immigrants without criminal records, including some who had been in the United States for years and were raising families in this country, were detained and deported in those operations. In February 2017, the first full month after Trump took office, the number of apprehensions of undocumented immigrants along the U.S. border with Mexico dropped by 40 percent.[145] Illegal crossings increased steadily during the 1970s and 1980s. During the 1990s they increased dramatically as individuals, mostly Mexicans, crossed the border to fill jobs during the economic boom. Since 2000, though, apprehensions of individuals illegally crossing the southern border have been decreasing, while the number of border control agents has been increasing (apprehensions are one of the most commonly used measures of illegal border crossings).[146] Despite these trends, President Trump continued to harden his rhetoric surrounding immigration, with his administration instituting a zero-tolerance policy to prosecute all individuals attempting to cross the border without permission (many previous administrations deported individuals after a court hearing but did not pursue criminal prosecutions of all individuals). For the first illegal entry into the country, a person can be charged with a misdemeanor under the federal penal code. This policy resulted in the separation of several thousand children from their families and drew widespread protests across the country. The family separation practice was officially ended on June 20, 2018, but the zero-tolerance policy was still in effect (families were to be detained together). Many children were soon reunited with their parents. But months later, immigrant advocates were still trying to complete an accounting of all children and families. And even after the separation practice had been officially ended, immigration officials were still separating some children from parents at the border if parents had a criminal history or gang affiliations or officials believed separation was necessary to protect the children. But immigrant advocates said some border agents were relying on unreliable criminal data or overreacting to minor offenses, such as traffic citations. In late 2019, The Associated Press reported that more than 5,400 immigrant children had been separated from their families at the border during the Trump administration. Altogether, the AP reported, an unprecedented 69,550 migrant children were held in U.S. government custody at one time or another—and for varying lengths of time—in fiscal 2019, despite being put "at risk of long-term physical and emotional damage." These included children separated from their parents at the border and children who crossed the border alone. Some 90 percent of the children were fleeing violence and poverty in Central America, the news organization said.[147] In October 2020, lawyers appointed by a federal judge were unable to locate the parents of 545 children; it is estimated that two-thirds were deported to Central American without their children. Representatives from the Trump administration asserted many of the parents voluntarily surrendered custody so the children could remain in the country; attorneys appointed by the court disputed this characterization as unverified.[148]

On October 29, 2018, President Trump announced he was sending 5,200 active duty troops to secure the southern border to prevent illegal crossing by members of a caravan of Central American refugees traveling to the United States. It was initially thought that the troops would be temporary, but nearly two years later, the troop buildup remained. In fact, additional troops were sent. In July 2019, 2,100 troops were sent to the border, including up to 1,000 soldiers from the Texas National Guard. In March 2020, 160 additional troops were sent to the border, approximately eighty to El Paso. In April 2020, Defense Secretary Mark Esper indicated 540 additional troops joined the approximate 5,200 service members—about 2,500 National Guard and 2,700 active-duty troops—deployed at the U.S.–Mexico border to assist Border Patrol agents.[149] Congress is under great pressure to resolve many ongoing immigration issues with many pushing for comprehensive immigration reform, but passage is unlikely.

STATE ACTIONS The federal government's failure to address the immigration problem has prompted many states and local communities to enact their own remedies, including restrictions on driver's and occupational licenses, penalties for companies that hire undocumented immigrants, and limitations on immigrants' access to higher education and public services.[150] The Obama administration sued to block key provisions of a strict law enacted in Arizona, contending it conflicts with federal laws and policies. On June 26, 2012, the Supreme Court rejected key components of the Arizona law, but let stand one highly controversial provision. With the decision, the Supreme Court upheld the authority of the federal government to set immigration law and public policy; however, the Court acknowledged the frustration states are feeling from problems caused by undocumented immigration. The Arizona law requires state law enforcement officers to determine the immigration status of anyone they stop or arrest if they suspect the person may be an undocumented immigrant. The law attempted to make it a state crime for immigrants to fail to register and for undocumented immigrants to work or seek jobs. The statute also attempted to allow police to arrest people without warrants if they had probable cause to believe the individuals were deportable under federal law.[151] The U.S. Supreme Court upheld the requirement that police verify the documented status of people they arrest, leading many to worry that use of racial profiling will grow, but struck down much of the rest of the law.

After much debate, the Texas Legislature in 2017 enacted a "sanctuary cities" law (Senate Bill 4) to assess monetary penalties against local governments, including public universities, that refused to cooperate with federal immigration officials. The penalties also included criminal sanctions against local law enforcement officers who didn't cooperate. Supporters of the law said it was necessary to crack down on immigrants who were violent criminals. But the law allowed police to ask the immigration status of any person they detained, not just of people arrested for alleged crimes. One opponent, Senator Sylvia Garcia, a Democrat from Houston, argued the law would allow police to stop and question people for "walking while brown." The measure, for which Governor Greg Abbott advocated, sparked impassioned legislative debate and public demonstrations and was passed along partisan lines, with most Republicans in support and Democrats opposed.[152] On September 25, 2019, President Trump issued an executive order declaring that state governments and municipalities must provide written consent before refugees can be resettled. On January 10, 2020, Governor Abbott announced that Texas would be the first state to reject refugees' resettlements under this new rule. He noted that since 2009, Texas has accepted approximately 10 percent of all refugees resettled in the United States and that the state deals with an excessively large migration problem since the federal immigration system is broken.[153] His actions were opposed by a wide array of entities, including faith leaders, immigration advocacy groups and agribusiness. The executive order was blocked by a federal judge in January 2020.

3.4.4 Border Drug Violence

No one knows for sure how many people have died in the wars between Mexico and its drug cartels and among the competing cartels themselves. The Mexican government has reported that between 2007 and 2018, approximately 220,000 people were victims of homicide in the war on cartels; over 33,000 murders in 2018 were related to drug violence, the highest since the government started to count these types of homicides in 1997.[154] Thousands of the killings have occurred along the border with Texas, including in the Mexican city of Ciudad Juarez, directly across the border from El Paso. Much of the worst violence has occurred in the Mexican state of Tamaulipas, which runs across the southernmost border of Texas, covering the American cities of Brownsville, McAllen, and Laredo.[155] Many Americans do not want to take any responsibility for this violence, but much of the criminality can be tied to the demand for illicit drugs in the United States. Although the federal government is supposed to secure our borders, its actions (or inaction) have an immediate effect on residents of border states in dramatic ways.

Bodies have been found dangling from freeway overpasses, and human heads have been discovered in public places, as the competing drug gangs have carried out vengeance killings and sought to intimidate rivals, local officials, and journalists.

Many of the victims have been suspected drug gang members, and others have been Mexican police and security forces. Still others have been journalists, targeted by drug gangs for what they had been reporting, and innocent bystanders.

Many Texans fear that the violence could spread across the border, and it is a popular subject for political figures advocating tougher border security. Governor Abbott, like his predecessor, frequently makes border security an issue, and Presidents Obama and Trump have both ordered National Guard troops to the border. As noted above, there has been a significant militarization of our southern border in the last decade. Obviously, there is a lot of drug trafficking across the Rio Grande, since residents of the United States are the drug dealers' biggest customer base (and guns made in the United States largely arm the cartels). Residents along the Texas side of the border sometimes hear gunfire on the other side of the river, and occasionally a stray bullet flies across the international boundary. Examining the tale of two cities—one on each side of the border—illuminates the complexity of the current balance. Ciudad Juarez, a Mexican city of approximately 1.5 million people, sits directly across the border from El Paso (the sixth largest city in Texas). Downtown El Paso is a stone's throw—or short rifle shot—from the crowded areas of Juarez; but in one important respect, it may as well be miles away.

Ciudad Juarez has been at the center of much of the drug cartel violence afflicting Mexico. Thousands of people have been killed in the city over the past five years (many of them young women), and media accounts have even referred to Juarez as the "Murder Capital of the World." The violence in the city calmed between 2012 and 2016 (from 3,158 in 2010, the deadliest year), but spiked in 2017 with more than 770 homicides. Since that time, the homicide rate has continued to rise, going up to 1,247 in 2018 and 1,499 in 2019 (the fourth deadliest year on record).[156] El Paso, by contrast, has been cited as having among the lowest crime rates for a city its size in the United States with crime rates below the national average every year since 2005 except for three years.[157] In fact, El Paso has ranked among the top ten American cities with the lowest crime rates since 1997. Although little violence has spilled over into Texas, for those people who cross the border almost every day for work or to visit relatives, the threat of violence is very real.

3.4.5 Common Borders, Common Problems

To anyone living on the border, the economic interdependence of the United States and Mexico is evident every day. Tens of thousands of pedestrians, cars, and trucks move across the international bridges, to and from the commercial centers on both sides of the Rio Grande. When the Mexican economy suffered a precipitous decline in 1982, the peso devaluation severely disrupted the Texas border economy, causing unemployment to skyrocket and a considerable number of U.S. businesses to fail.

Much of the effort toward improving relations between the United States and Mexico has focused on potential economic benefits, but other complex problems confronting both countries merit attention. One is health care. On both sides of the border, many children have not been immunized against basic childhood diseases. On the Texas side are hundreds of *colonias*—rural, unincorporated slums that have substandard housing, roads, and drainage and, in many cases, lack water and sewage systems. These conditions have contributed to severe health problems, including hepatitis, dysentery, and tuberculosis. Higher-than-normal numbers of both Texan and Mexican children along the border have been born with serious birth defects. Public health officials in Texas report that Mexican women come across the border to give birth to their children in American facilities. This practice, which has the effect of creating binational families, increases the burden on public hospitals—and taxpayers—in Texas. Children born in the United States are U.S. citizens and are entitled to various public services.[158]

Industrial development and population growth along the border also increase environmental problems. Antipollution laws in the United States have been more stringent than those in Mexico, but air and water pollution generated in Mexico does not stop at the border. A component of USMCA (like NAFTA before it) provides a basic framework for addressing environmental problems, but some have argued that a country such as Mexico, under enormous pressure to industrialize rapidly, is less likely to be concerned with environmental issues. In addition, U.S. efforts to impose its environmental standards on Mexico could be interpreted as another American effort to dominate the country.[159] In June 1994, several maquiladora plants in Matamoros, across the border from Brownsville, settled lawsuits alleging that pollution caused rare birth defects in children born in Texas. Even with greater attention placed on these environmental concerns, a good deal of air and water pollution still presents challenges to residents in the areas around these plants.

Regional interdependence, though perhaps not recognized by most people on both sides of the border, has taken on greater importance in the press and in academic, business, and labor communities in the United States. Transnational public policies are emerging, creating legal issues in product liability, insurance, copyrights, and patents that still must be resolved.

CONCLUSION

As we saw with challenges facing the country stemming from the COVID-19 pandemic and the issue of legalization of marijuana, the relationship among the federal, state, and local governments is complex, changing, and increasingly tense. The situation is unlikely to become less difficult or dynamic in the future. Texans are unique in their duality of loyalties and sense of community. On the one hand, Texans are fiercely patriotic, with a strong sense of national pride and responsibility. According to the Department of Defense, Texans are strongly represented in the Active Duty military personnel as well as Selected Reservists populations (second only behind California in each category).[160] Simply traveling around the state demonstrates the profound commitment Texans have to the country, and yet it also demonstrates the competing sentiment of our unofficial slogan: "Don't Mess with Texas." This duality—of being proud to be an American coupled with a strong isolationist sentiment and independent

DON'T MESS WITH TEXAS

For more than thirty-five years, the state of Texas Department of Transportation has run a highway beautification program, urging people to clean up after themselves and "Don't Mess with Texas." The slogan captures a broader political culture that epitomizes state pride.

streak—characterizes the state unlike any other. We pride ourselves on having a strong economy and a tough "do-anything" frontier mentality, which complicates the important relationship we have with our federal government as well as with our fellow states.

Comprehending the relationship among the federal, state, and local governments is fundamentally important for those who desire to influence politics. When most people think about politics, they envision national institutions or individuals. On most issues, however, the actions of state and local officials have a more primary impact on daily lives. Examining how the levels of government interact, from the national to the state to the locality, is vital. Moreover, examining who pays for what and how levels of interdependency between Washington and the state are changing is also essential. Learning to appreciate transnational relations between state governments and Mexico will become increasingly important in the future. The shifting landscape of power and influence represents an excellent opportunity for those who are informed and engaged to bring about change.

REVIEW THE CHAPTER

Structuring Regional and National Interests

3.1 Explain three ways in which nations structure relationships among national, regional, and local levels of government and how the Constitution of the United States is used to navigate federal-state relations, p. 61.

Countries around the world have used three forms of government to structure relationships among national, regional (or state), and local governments. All three of these forms—federal systems, confederations, and unitary systems—have been used in the United States at different points in time. The U.S. Constitution provides for a federal system, which divides powers between the national and state governments, according to extensive constitutional provisions. In a confederation, the individual states retain extensive powers, and the authority of the central government is limited. The confederation principle was used twice in the nation's history—prior to the Constitution of 1789 and by the southern states during the Civil War. The unitary system gives central governments the authority to create local governments and impose restrictions on them. Some democratic and authoritarian governments structure national and regional powers on the unitary principle. It defines the relationship between state and local governments in Texas.

Changing Patterns in Federal Relationships

3.2 Outline the changing patterns in the relationship between the U.S. national government and the states, p. 67.

Scholars have advanced various definitions of federalism, in part because of the ongoing changes that occur in federal relationships. In its simplest terms, federalism is the manner of division of power between the states and the national government and is defined in the U.S. Constitution. The national government has delegated powers specifically spelled out in Article I, as well as implied powers. States have reserved powers under the Tenth Amendment. The supremacy clause of the Constitution provides that the national government prevails when there are jurisdictional conflicts between the national government and the states. Finally, there are powers denied to both national and state governments and constitutional limits on what governments can do.

Federalism also applies to the states. States must recognize most actions taken by other states, including contracts and driver's licenses. States also must extend the same protections to individuals from other states they do to their own citizens. In the nation's formative period, state and local governments were much more prominent and played a much greater role in the lives of Americans than did the national government. Over the constitution's 230-year history, because of changing economic, social, demographic, and political conditions, as well as the expanded role of the national government in domestic affairs, federalism has changed.

During the era of dual federalism from 1790 to the 1930s, state and local governments took the lead in domestic policy. But states were unable to address the economic hardships caused by the Great Depression in the 1930s, and the federal government assumed a more dominant domestic role through the enactment of New Deal policies, such as Social Security. This era of cooperative federalism dramatically expanded the role of the federal government, an expansion that was continued during the Kennedy and Johnson administrations. In more recent years, the increased role of the national government has produced a countermovement with a series of presidents arguing for new federalism. They argued that the powers of the federal government had been extended too far and much authority should be returned to the states, a process called devolution. Those efforts, although prompting much debate, have done nothing to curb Washington's power. In fact, Washington assumed even more power under President George W. Bush's administration, with the creation of the Department of Homeland Security, following the terrorist attacks of September 11, 2001, and an expanded role of the federal government in setting public education accountability requirements. This expanded role continues today.

The Impact of Federalism on State Finances

3.3 Assess the impact of federalism on state finances, p. 80.

State and local governments depend on a massive infusion of federal funds to help support public health care, public housing, transportation, and other programs. Although often critical of the "strings," or policy conditions, usually attached to federal funds, state and local officials readily accept the money and often lobby for more. More than 30 percent of the Texas budget is funded by federal dollars.

Federalism was a core issue at the Constitutional Convention in 1787, and it remains a core issue today. Supporters of the federal government's role note that the federal government has more resources than many states and local governments for funding important services. They also argue that many environmental and civil rights initiatives ordered by the federal government might never have been enacted if left up to state and local governments.

Other people argue that federal policies can be administered in a heavy-handed fashion. The availability of federal grants may prompt state and local governments to distort their priorities and pursue programs that their residents do not need. It also has been argued that excessive dependency on the federal government stifles innovation by state and local governments. Finally, some observers believe that the mandates and preemptions imposed by the federal government limit the policy options of state and local governments.

Transnational Regionalism

3.4 Describe the increased interdependency between the United States and Mexico, p. 83.

The politics, economy, and social system of Texas are inextricably linked to those of Mexico. Transnational regionalism can be used to explain and assess the complex interdependency between the two neighbors. Mexico and Texas are major trading partners, a role that was enhanced by the ratification of the United States–Mexico–Canada Agreement (USMCA), a renegotiation of the North American Free Trade Agreement (NAFTA) from 1993. Texas, as a border state and home to approximately 5 million immigrants, an estimated 1.6 million of which are undocumented, is at the center of the prolonged political dispute over Washington's failure to enact a workable immigration policy. Immigrants, both documented and undocumented, have a huge impact on education, health care, and other social services in Texas. Although the war between illegal drug cartels, which has killed thousands of people in Mexico, has not yet spilled over into Texas, political figures use the threat of drug violence to advocate for stronger security along the Texas–Mexico border. Many are growing increasingly concerned with the heightened militarization of our border. The increased industrialization along the border has worsened environmental problems affecting both countries, an additional source for concern.

LEARN THE TERMS

unitary system, p. 63
confederation, p. 63
federalism, p. 63
Dillon rule, p. 63
devolution, p. 64
delegated powers, p. 64
implied powers, p. 64
supremacy clause, p. 64
reserved powers, p. 65
concurrent powers, p. 65

denied powers, p. 65
full faith and credit clause, p. 65
privileges and immunities, p. 66
extradition, p. 66
interstate compact, p. 67
dual federalism, p. 67
cooperative federalism, p. 68
categorical grant-in-aid, p. 70
project grant, p. 70
formula grant, p. 70

matching funds, p. 70
new federalism, p. 72
block grant, p. 72
revenue sharing, p. 72
mandate, p. 72
preemption, p. 72
transnational regionalism, p. 83
maquiladora program, p. 84
The United States–Mexico–Canada Agreement(USMCA), p. 86

Local Government in Texas

4

A LOCAL FIGHT AGAINST FRACKING
Denton residents urge support of a local ordinance, or law, against fracking, a form of drilling for oil and natural gas, in their city's limits because of concerns over noise and pollution. The ordinance passed but later was overturned by the legislature and the governor, as have a number of other local laws.

LEARNING OBJECTIVES

4.1 Trace the transition of Texas from an agrarian to an urban state, p. 100.

4.2 Compare and contrast the governments of Texas cities, p. 103.

4.3 Describe the structure of county government in Texas, p. 117.

4.4 Describe the functions and challenges of special-purpose districts in Texas, p. 123.

4.5 Describe the structure of independent school districts in Texas, p. 125.

4.6 Assess proposed solutions to the problems of local government in Texas, p. 128.

Cities, counties, and other local governments are administrative subdivisions of state government, which has the power to tell locally elected officials what they can and cannot do. Historically, Texas has had a strong tradition of local control, and the legislature has given cities and, to a lesser extent, counties the latitude to govern themselves. But in recent years, Governor Greg Abbott and a Republican-dominated legislature have enacted significant state laws to overturn or restrict local policies that conflicted with their own political priorities. In so doing, Republican state leaders have flexed their political powers over Democrats who recently regained control of elected offices in some of the state's urban areas. The conflict was particularly pronounced during the 2015, 2017, and 2019 legislative sessions, the first three sessions after Abbott was elected governor and Republican Dan Patrick was elected lieutenant governor, and is likely to continue during the 2021 session. The legislature meets in regular session every other year.

In 2015, the legislature enacted a law, which Abbott signed, overturning an ordinance that had been approved by local voters in the north Texas city of Denton to prohibit oil and gas producers from using hydraulic fracturing, or fracking, within the Denton city limits. Fracking is a drilling method that involves the high-pressure injection of large amounts of water and chemicals into underground rock formations to release previously untapped oil and natural gas reserves. Denton residents complained about noise and toxic fumes spewing from wells near their houses. But Abbott said the state law overriding the ordinance was necessary to protect private property rights and remove local regulations that threatened oil and gas production, which contributes many millions of tax dollars a year to the state treasury. He also complained about a "patchwork quilt of [local] bans and rules and regulations that is eroding the Texas model," which, at the state level, has traditionally avoided overregulating most businesses, not just the oil and gas industry.[1]

The state-versus-local war resumed in 2017, during the regular and a subsequent special session, over several bills advocated by Abbott, Patrick, and their legislative allies. The legislature enacted a so-called sanctuary cities law to force local governments to take a harder line against undocumented immigrants. Over the objections of some Democratic officeholders, it required local law-enforcement officers to be more active in enforcing immigration laws and cooperating with federal immigration officials. Lawmakers also enacted a law requiring some cities to gain consent from property owners before annexing their property and another law setting statewide regulations for ride-sharing companies, such as Uber and Lyft. The rideshare law invalidated a more restrictive ordinance adopted by the Austin city council.

But a so-called "bathroom bill" advocated by Patrick and Abbott failed to pass. It would have required transgender individuals to use public restrooms corresponding to the gender identities on their birth certificates and would have prohibited cities from adopting local ordinances that conflicted with the state restrictions. Although Abbott and Patrick argued the proposed bathroom law was a matter of public safety, especially for women and children, many business leaders and some moderate Republicans, including then-House Speaker Joe Straus, considered it discriminatory and a threat to economic development. They feared that businesses, conventions, and high-profile athletic events would have boycotted Texas had it become law. The state Senate, over which Patrick presided, approved the bill, but it died in the House.

In 2019, Abbott, Patrick, and their legislative supporters won the enactment of another priority, a bill to make it more difficult for cities, counties and other local governments to raise property tax revenue. They prevailed over strong opposition from local officials, who argued that the limitations would curtail their ability to raise sufficient revenue to pay for police and fire protection and other important public services. The governor and other advocates of the new law insisted that Texas homeowners and other property taxpayers were overtaxed, primarily because of rising property values. Under the new law, cities, counties, and most special districts were prohibited from increasing the revenue they raised from property taxes by more than 3.5 percent a year without voter approval. The limit for school districts was 2.5 percent a year. These limits were sharp reductions from the previous 8 percent annual limit, although the new limit excluded taxes levied on new construction.

The Texas Municipal League, which lobbies the legislature on behalf of city governments, said the bills restricting local governments amounted to an "all-out assault" on the ability of local voters to fashion the "character of their communities." The incursion of "an all-powerful, overreaching state government is a recipe for disaster," the group said in a statement.[2]

Less than a year after the legislature had enacted the new property tax limits, a health and economic disaster struck in the form of the coronavirus pandemic in 2020. It cost local governments in Texas millions of dollars in lost sales and hotel tax revenue following weeks of restaurant and other business closures and sharply reduced economic activity. City and county officials believed they should be exempted from the new property tax limits as they attempted to recover from the disaster and provide satisfactory levels of public services, but Governor Abbott said local governments should honor the new tax caps.

The governor initially let local governments take the lead in addressing the coronavirus outbreak with their own emergency orders for business closures and other restrictions to slow the spread of the virus. Abbott soon issued statewide emergency orders, but his critics were quick to point out his delay and what they considered an inconsistency in the governor's view of local control (see Chapter 6).

In recent years, similar battles between state and local governments have been fought over regulatory issues in a number of other states. These so-called preemption laws have banned cities in some states from raising the minimum wage, regulating landlords, or regulating e-cigarettes. Some of these efforts have been driven by industries that find it easier to lobby legislators and governors than to try to influence thousands of city councils and other local governing boards across the country. According to an article in *The New York Times*, Republicans who control statehouses in other states use preemption laws to block or overturn regulations passed by more liberal city officials.[3]

Texas has more than 5,300 local governments of all sizes, many with overlapping jurisdictions. Some operate with a handful of employees and budgets of $100,000 or $200,000 a year; others have tens of thousands of employees with billion dollar–plus budgets. Some special districts perform one basic function, whereas cities perform any number of services that are limited only by budgetary and legal restraints. Loving County in remote West Texas has fewer than 200 residents; on the other side of the state, Harris County, the state's largest, has approximately 4.7 million residents. One school district, Divide ISD in the rural Texas Hill Country in Kerr County, had only 24 students in the 2019–2020 school year; the Houston Independent School District had more than 200,000. Three of the ten largest cities in the United States are in Texas, but many cities across the state have fewer than 1,000 residents.

To get a complete picture of government in Texas and learn how to effectively make your way around or navigate the state's political system, you must learn something about local governments—the governments, as has often been said, that are closest to the people. The first step toward understanding local governments in Texas is understanding what responsibilities the Texas Constitution and statutory law have assigned to them. Texas ranks second (more than 5,300) behind the state of Illinois (more than 6,900) in the number of local governments, but comparatively, other states have more governments per capita than does Texas. There are some forms of government used in other states that are not found in Texas. For example, many northeastern states and states that were part of the Northwest Territory make extensive use of the township, while Texas does not.

Once the institutional structures and functions of local governments have been studied, we will turn our attention to the role these institutions play in urban politics. Finally, we will look at a number of core problems confronting local governments and their political capacities to address these issues. Two questions underlie this analysis: What changes can make local governments more effective, and is it possible or desirable to reduce the fragmentation in local governments?

Urban Texas

4.1 Trace the transition of Texas from an agrarian to an urban state.

Despite popular images of wide-open ranges dotted with cattle and oil wells, Texas is an urban state. Some areas, particularly in West Texas, still offer much room to roam, but about 90 percent of Texans live in cities or urban areas. First-time visitors to the state often express surprise at the size and diversity of Houston and Dallas and the more relaxed charm of San Antonio, whose River Walk reminds many tourists of some European cities. Austin, the seat of state government and location of a world-class university, is highly attractive to young professionals and high-technology businesses. From a historical perspective, urbanization has been a central feature of the state's population growth and the transformation of its economy.

4.1.1 Cities in the State's Formative Period

When the Texas Constitution was adopted in 1876, the state was rural and agrarian. Less than 10 percent of the population lived in cities. According to the 1880 Census, there were 73 towns and cities in Texas. Galveston was the largest city with a population of 22,248, followed by San Antonio with 20,550. Dallas, a relatively new settlement, had 10,358 residents, and Houston, 16,513. Galveston and San Antonio placed with the 100 largest U.S. cities, ranking 82nd and 96th, respectively, but New York's population was 1.2 million and New Orleans, the 10th largest city, had a population of 216,090.[4]

For most of the period from 1880 to 1920, San Antonio was Texas's largest city, but since the 1930 census, Houston has held that distinction.[5] Many other states became urban earlier than Texas. By the 1920 census, a majority (51 percent) of Americans were identified as living in urban areas. Twenty years later, in 1940, only 45 percent of Texans lived in urban areas, but by 1950, some 60 percent of the population resided in cities. By 1970, the urban share of the Texas population had reached 80 percent.[6] Now, about 90 percent of the state's population is urban.

A DISTINCTIVE ARCHITECTURAL STYLE THAT DRAWS ATTENTION
San Antonio's City Hall, located in the center of Military Plaza (Plaza de Armas), follows an Italian Renaissance Revival style and was completed in 1891.

4.1.2 General Features of Contemporary Texas Cities

Houston, San Antonio, and Dallas are among the ten largest cities in the United States. According to the *2018 American Community Survey*, Houston had a population of 2,325,502; San Antonio, 1,532,233; and Dallas, 1,345,047. New York City topped the list with 8.4 million residents, and San Jose, California, ranked tenth with a little more than one million persons.

Seven additional Texas cities—El Paso, Fort Worth, Austin, Corpus Christi, Arlington, Plano, and Laredo—each had more than 250,000 residents. Austin had almost one million residents and Fort Worth, about 900,000. Growth rates, however, have varied widely from city to city, thanks to differences in economic expansion, annexation policies, in-migration from other areas, and fertility and mortality rates. In some instances, the growth rate for the central city has been relatively modest, whereas growth in surrounding suburban areas has been quite high, reflecting continued urban sprawl.

Compared with many other parts of the country, Texas cities have a relatively low ratio of population to their legal or incorporated boundaries. Texas cities are relatively young and had a lot of inexpensive land available to them during their early development. So, unlike older cities in other states, they tended to expand outward rather than upward. Texas cities also have used liberal annexation powers granted by the legislature to block the development of nearby, small municipalities that would curb their expansion. Houston covers approximately 600 square miles, the largest landmass of any city in the state, and has a **population density** of approximately 3,500 persons per square mile. Population density affects policy and budgetary issues relating to virtually every public service provided by the city. As more people are squeezed into a limited geographical area, more attention must be directed toward governmental issues such as land use, zoning laws, police and fire protection, the location of libraries and parks, and the development of water and sanitation systems.

population density
Number of persons residing within a square mile.

GOVERNMENT IN A HIGHLY URBAN STATE

The Harris County Courthouse, located in downtown Houston, houses some of the many functions of a county that serves approximately 4.7 million residents.

The racial and ethnic composition of Texas cities also is a major factor in urban diversity. Plano, located north of Dallas, reported in the *2018 American Community Survey* a combined minority population of approximately 47 percent, including an Asian population of 20 percent (see Table 4–1). By contrast, Hispanics comprised more than 95 percent of the population of Laredo. Other cities along the Texas–Mexico border also showed very high numbers of Hispanics. Brownsville was 94 percent Hispanic; Harlingen, 81 percent; McAllen, 85 percent; and El Paso, 81 percent. In 2018, the African American population in Dallas was approximately 24 percent. Houston's African American population was 23 percent, and Fort Worth's was 19 percent. In contrast, the African American population in El Paso was approximately 4 percent; Corpus Christi, 4 percent; and San Antonio, 7 percent.[7]

The 1,200-plus incorporated towns and cities in Texas are diverse, as urban life, politics, and government have developed different styles across the state. Statutory and constitutional laws define the basic forms of city government, but cities vary in their demographic makeup, their economies, the historical experiences that shaped their development, and their quality of life.[8]

TABLE 4–1 SELECT CHARACTERISTICS FOR THE TEN LARGEST CITIES IN TEXAS, 2018

City	Total Population in 2018	Median Age	Percentage African American*	Percentage Hispanic**	Percentage Asian*	Median Household Income 2018	Percentage of All Persons Below Poverty Level 2018
Houston	2,325,502	33.1	22.5	44.8%	6.9%	$51,140	20.6%
San Antonio	1,532,233	33.7	6.9%	64.2%	2.8%	$50,980	18.6%
Dallas	1,345,047	33.3	24.3%	41.7%	3.4%	$50,100	20.5%
Austin	964,254	33.6	7.8%	34.3%	7.3%	$67,462	14.5%
Fort Worth	895,008	33.2	19.0%	35.0%	4.2%	$59,255	16.0%
El Paso	682,669	33.1	3.8%	80.9%	1.4%	$45,656	20.0%
Arlington	398,112	33.1	22.5%	29.2%	6.9%	$58,502	15.7%
Corpus Christi	326,554	35.3	4.1%	62.9%	2.2%	$55,709	15.8%
Plano	288,061	38.3	8.4%	15.2%	20.4%	$92,121	6.8%
Laredo	261,639	29.3	0.4%	95.4%	0.5%	$43,351	29.1%
State Totals	28,701,845	34.9	12.8%	39.6%	5.2%	$59,570	14.9%

* Race alone or in combination with one or more other races
** Hispanic or Latino of any race
SOURCE: U.S. Census Bureau, *American Community Survey,* 2018.

The Legal and Constitutional Framework for Texas Cities

4.2 Compare and contrast the governments of Texas cities.

Since the nation's founding, Americans have expressed a strong belief in the right to local self-government.[9] In many areas of the young country, local governments existed long before there was a viable state or federal government. Early communities had to fend for themselves and had limited expectations of services or protections to be provided by state or federal governments. Early Tejanos had similar experiences, largely depending on their own resources and initiative rather than those of any central government under the Spanish or Mexican governments.

This history of local government rooted in self-help has led to the popular notion that local governments have fundamental rights based on the concept of local sovereignty, or ultimate power. Thomas Jefferson, for example, developed a theory of local government, designed in part to strengthen the powers of the states, in which local sovereignty was rooted in the sovereignty of the individual. Local governments, which he termed "wards," would have a wide range of responsibilities, including education, police, roads, caring for the poor, conducting elections, some minor judicial functions, and a semblance of a militia to maintain local defenses.[10]

In light of the expanded role of state and federal governments, we might find Jefferson's view outdated and naive. Nonetheless, the concept has permeated American attitudes toward government and continues to shape citizen responses to government initiatives. Some people suggest that this cultural legacy persists in grassroots politics, large numbers of elected local officials, the flight to suburbia, the creation of neighborhood organizations and gated communities, and the persistence of distrust of the national and state governments. It still is common to hear the argument that local government is closest to the people and best represents their interests and desires.[11]

The state has granted cities—unlike counties and special districts—a wide range of discretionary power over organizational structure and local public policy. Historically, Texas ranked high among the states in that regard, but cities still are strongly affected by state laws and policies, and as noted at the beginning of this chapter, the legislature in recent years has enacted several laws attempting to preempt some city regulations. Cities, therefore, actively lobby the legislature and other state officials on numerous issues. Member cities support the Texas Municipal League (TML), which maintains a full-time staff in Austin to monitor the activities of the legislature and state agencies. Many of the larger cities also designate staff members to serve as legislative liaisons, or they retain professional lobbyists. Larger cities usually work with community leaders and civic organizations to establish legislative agendas. Thirty-seven metropolitan counties, comprising more than 80 percent of the state's population, also collaborate on shared policy concerns through the Texas Conference of Urban Counties.[12] But the lobbying efforts of local governments also have come under attack from some legislators in Austin, and efforts have been made to prohibit any expenditure of tax dollars for lobbying purposes. So far, those efforts have been unsuccessful, but they are expected to continue.

Texas, like most other states, assigns the primary responsibility for public education to local school districts while retaining the primary responsibility for highways, public welfare, and public health at the state level. Police and fire protection, water and sanitation services, parks, recreation, and libraries are the primary responsibility of city governments. Public hospitals are a shared function of the state, counties, and special districts.[13] Texas counties share with the state a primary responsibility for the courts and criminal justice system. It takes considerable knowledge to sort through the roster of local governments and develop an understanding of the varied responsibilities assigned to each. But this knowledge is important for people who are confronted with public service problems that they need someone in government to address.

4.2.1 General Law and Home Rule Cities

The prevailing constitutional theory on the relationship of local governments to the state is the unitary system, which holds that local governments are the creations of the state. The state government grants or delegates to local governments their powers, functions, and responsibilities, and no local government has sovereign powers. Numerous court cases have spelled out this principle, referred to as the **Dillon rule**, but the best summary is from an Iowa case in which a court held the following:

> The true view is this: Municipal corporations owe their origin to, and derive their powers and rights wholly from, the legislature. It breathes into them the breath of life, without which they cannot exist. As it creates, so it may destroy. If it may destroy, it may abridge and control. Unless there is some constitutional limitation on the right, the legislature might by a single act, if we can suppose it capable of so great a folly and so great a wrong, sweep from its existence all of the municipal corporations in the State, and the corporations could not prevent it. We know of no limitation on this right so far as the corporations are concerned. They are so to phrase it, the mere tenants at will of the legislature.[14]

The Dillon rule applies to local governments in Texas. Local governments are administrative subdivisions of the state and have no rights except those granted to them by the state. Moreover, as the state has grown, the state and federal governments have ordered, or mandated, significant improvements in environmental, educational, health, and other services while requiring cities, counties, school districts, and special districts to bear much of the cost. Local school districts, for example, are at the mercy of the legislature, which in recent years has ordered expensive educational programs and raised classroom standards without fully paying for them. Local governments have to shoulder much of the responsibility—and often take much of the public outrage—for policy decisions made in Austin and Washington.

Although the Dillon rule subordinates local governments to the state, there are practical and political limitations on what the state can do with local governments.[15] More importantly, the state relies on local governments to carry out many of its responsibilities. The Texas Constitution provides for two general categories of cities: general law and home rule. **General law cities** have fewer than 5,000 residents and face restrictions in organizing their governments, setting taxes, and annexing territory. They are allowed only those powers specifically granted to them by the legislature. Most Texas cities—approximately 850—are general law cities.[16] Texas enacted legislation in 1912 that granted eligible cities home rule authority. **Home rule cities**, which include all of the state's major and medium-sized cities, have considerable authority and discretion over their own local policies, but within limits set by state law.

Under home rule, a city with more than 5,000 inhabitants can adopt any form of government its residents choose, provided it does not conflict with the state constitution (Article 11, Sections 4, 5) or statutes. This option is formalized through the voters' adoption of a **city charter**, which is the fundamental document—something like a constitution—under which a city operates. A charter establishes a city's governing body; the organization of its administrative agencies and municipal courts; its taxing authority; and procedures for conducting elections, annexing additional territory, and revising the charter. As of early 2018, there were 375 home rule cities in Texas.[17]

City charter elections, much like elections for amendments to the Texas Constitution, are frequently decided by only a handful of voters. In Boerne, a small home rule city just northwest of San Antonio, a charter amendment was proposed to raise the limit on the value of city purchases that could be approved without competitive bids. The proposed change would have brought the city's purchasing procedures in line with state law. In an election in which only 57 of 4,836 registered voters participated, the charter amendment was defeated, 29–28. There were no offices or other issues on the ballot to attract more voters, and the charter issue had not received much

---

Dillon rule
A principle holding that local governments are creations of state government and their powers and responsibilities are defined by the state.

general law city
A Texas city with fewer than 5,000 residents. Such cities are allowed to exercise only those powers specifically granted to them by the legislature. Most cities in Texas are classified as general law cities.

home rule city
A Texas city with more than 5,000 residents. Such cities can adopt any form of government residents choose, provided it does not conflict with the state constitution or statutes. Home rule powers are formalized through local voters' adoption of a city charter spelling out how the city is to be governed.

city charter
A document, defined or authorized by state law, under which a city operates. In Texas home rule cities, local voters may choose among several forms of city government.

attention.[18] Low rates of participation are not limited to small towns or cities. San Antonio held a charter amendment and general election in May 2015, and only 12 percent of the city's registered voters participated.[19]

These are not unusual, isolated examples of voter disinterest in city charter elections. Except for issues such as term limits or pay raises for city council members, most proposed changes to city charters generate little public interest. Basic changes in a city's governmental structure, which must be approved by home rule voters, can polarize a community.

Most Texas cities have functioned under various forms of government, which will be described in the following section, during their histories. Changes in local governmental structures often follow population changes, periods of crises, intense political conflict, or an inability of those in government to address long-term problems.

4.2.2 Forms of City Government

Many of the larger cities in Texas have gone through a succession of different forms of governments, and there are local histories behind these changes, particularly in the three largest cities. However, citizens, elected officials, and those who study local governments continue to raise the question of whether the form of city government affects how a city is run, how responsive it is to its citizens, how able it is to address current issues and anticipate future issues, and how efficient and effective its government is.

According to the Texas Municipal League, there were more than 1,200 municipal, or city, governments in Texas in 2018.[20] Some 900 cities operated with some variation of the mayor–council form of government, approximately 300 used some form of council–manager or commission–manager government, and a handful used the commission form of government.[21]

MAYOR–COUNCIL The mayor–council form, the most common type of municipal government in Texas, derived from the English model of city government. The legislative function of the city is vested in the city council, and the executive function is assigned to the mayor. This type of government is based on the separation of powers principle, which also characterizes the state and federal governments. In terms of power, however, the two distinguishable forms of mayor are the weak mayor and the strong mayor—and in most Texas cities, the mayor is weak.

The city charter determines a mayor's strength. The **weak mayor** has little control over policy initiatives or implementation. The mayor's power may be constrained by one or more of the following: limited or no appointment or removal power over city offices, limited budgetary authority, and the election of other city administrators independently of the mayor (see Figure 4–1). Under these circumstances, the mayor shares power with the city council over city administration and policy implementation and "is the chief executive in name only."[22] These restrictions limit both the political and administrative leadership of the mayor. Although it is possible for a mayor to use personal or political resources to influence the city council and other administrators and to provide energetic leadership, formidable obstacles need to be overcome.[23]

A **strong mayor** has real power and authority, including appointive and removal powers over city agency heads. Such appointments often require city council approval, but the appointees are responsible to the mayor and serve at mayoral discretion. The mayor has control over budget preparation and exercises some veto authority over city council actions. This form of city government clearly distinguishes between executive and legislative functions.

The strong mayor form of government is found in many larger American cities, but it now is used by only one major city in Texas—Houston (see Figure 4–2). El Paso functioned under this form of government until 2004, when the city changed to the council–manager government. The strong mayor form may be unpopular in the state because it often was associated with urban political machines, ward politics, and

weak mayor
A form of city government in which the mayor shares authority with the city council and other elected officials but has little independent control over city policy or city administration.

strong mayor
A form of city government that gives the mayor considerable power, including budgetary control and appointment and removal authority over city department heads.

FIGURE 4-1 THE WEAK MAYOR FORM OF GOVERNMENT: ORGANIZATIONAL CHART OF THE CITY OF CASTROVILLE, TEXAS

The vast majority of general law cities with populations fewer than 5,000 are organized in the weak mayor–council form of government in which there are significant limits on the powers of the mayor and a sharing of some administrative and appointive functions with the city council.

SOURCE: City of Castroville, *FY 2018 Proposed Annual Operating and Capital Budget*, http://www.castrovilletx.gov/DocumentCenter/View/1083/Proposed-FY2018-Annual-Operating-Capital-Budget.

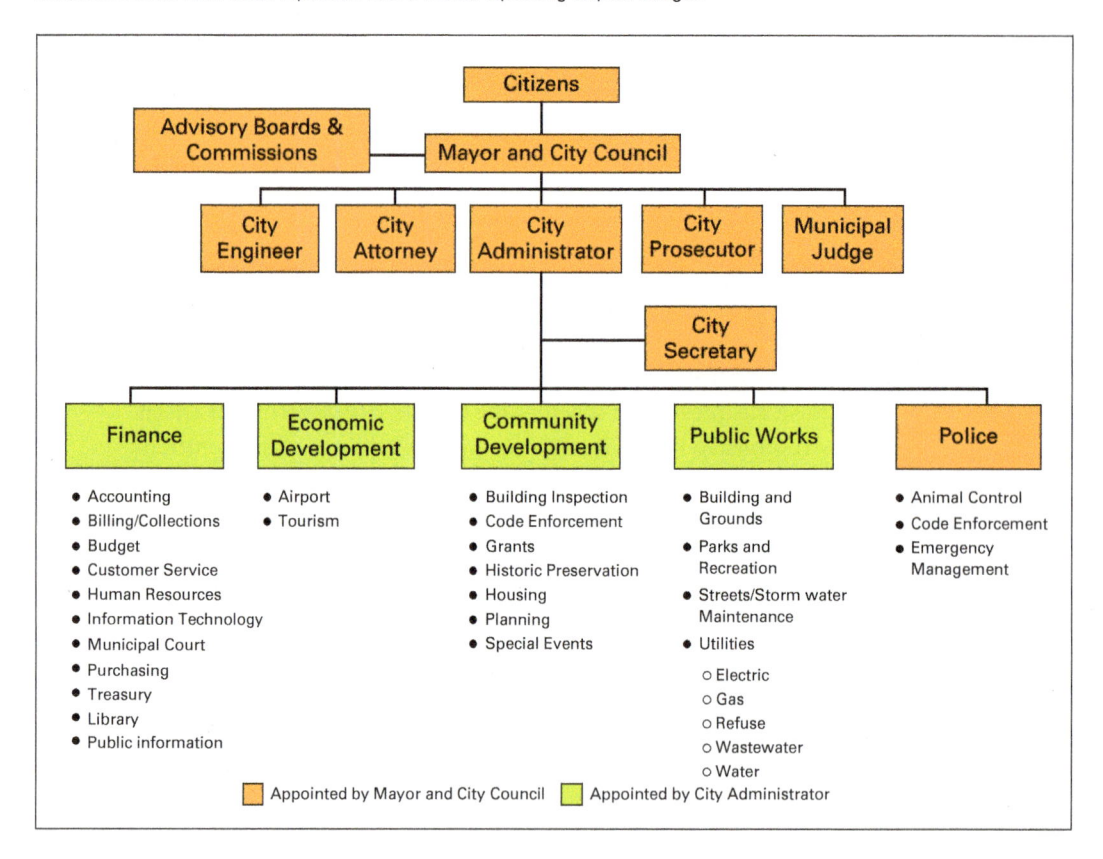

```
                              Citizens
                                 |
    Advisory Boards &    Mayor and City Council
    Commissions
                                 |
   City        City          City         City        Municipal
  Engineer   Attorney   Administrator   Prosecutor     Judge
                                 |
                             City
                           Secretary
                                 |
   Finance    Economic     Community    Public Works   Police
              Development  Development
```

- Finance: Accounting, Billing/Collections, Budget, Customer Service, Human Resources, Information Technology, Municipal Court, Purchasing, Treasury, Library, Public information
- Economic Development: Airport, Tourism
- Community Development: Building Inspection, Code Enforcement, Grants, Historic Preservation, Housing, Planning, Special Events
- Public Works: Building and Grounds, Parks and Recreation, Streets/Storm water Maintenance, Utilities (Electric, Gas, Refuse, Wastewater, Water)
- Police: Animal Control, Code Enforcement, Emergency Management

☐ Appointed by Mayor and City Council ☐ Appointed by City Administrator

---

political corruption. A strong mayor also is at odds with the fragmentation of authority and responsibility that marks most local governments and the state government in Texas. This fragmentation stems from a historic distrust of government, a lingering legacy of the Reconstruction era discussed in Chapter 2. Finally, the state's individualistic and traditionalistic political subcultures reinforce hostile attitudes toward governmental institutions, such as a strong mayor government, which are potentially more responsive to lower socioeconomic groups.

As might be expected, the salaries of the mayor and council members in a strong mayor city are generally higher than in cities with other forms of city government. In many cities, mayors and council members receive little or no pay or only modest reimbursements for services. But the mayor of Houston earned $236,189 in 2019, and each council member earned $62,983.[24]

CITY COMMISSION The commission and council–manager forms of government are products of the twentieth century. Both reflect, in part, efforts to reform city governments through administrative efficiency, the reduction of partisan conflict, and the adaptation of a businesslike approach to running city government.

The origin of the **city commission** usually is traced to the Texas island city of Galveston. After a hurricane and subsequent flooding devastated most of the city in 1900, the government then in office proved incompetent and incapable of responding. The crisis prompted a group of citizens to win the legislature's approval of a new form of government designed to be more responsive by combining the city's legislative and administrative functions in the offices of five city commissioners. City commissions

---

city commission
A form of city government in which elected commissioners collectively serve as a city's policymaking body and individually serve as administrative heads of different city departments. Often referred to as the Galveston Plan, this form of government, which was part of the city reform movement, does not appear to be used in any Texas city today. Although some cities still refer to their legislative bodies as commissions, these cities function much like council–manager cities.

FIGURE 4-2 THE STRONG MAYOR FORM OF GOVERNMENT: ORGANIZATIONAL CHART OF THE CITY OF HOUSTON

Houston is the only large Texas city that uses the strong mayor form of government in which the mayor has major day-to-day administrative responsibilities.

SOURCE: City of Houston, *Fiscal Year 2016*, http://www.houstontx.gov/budget/16budadopt/index.html.

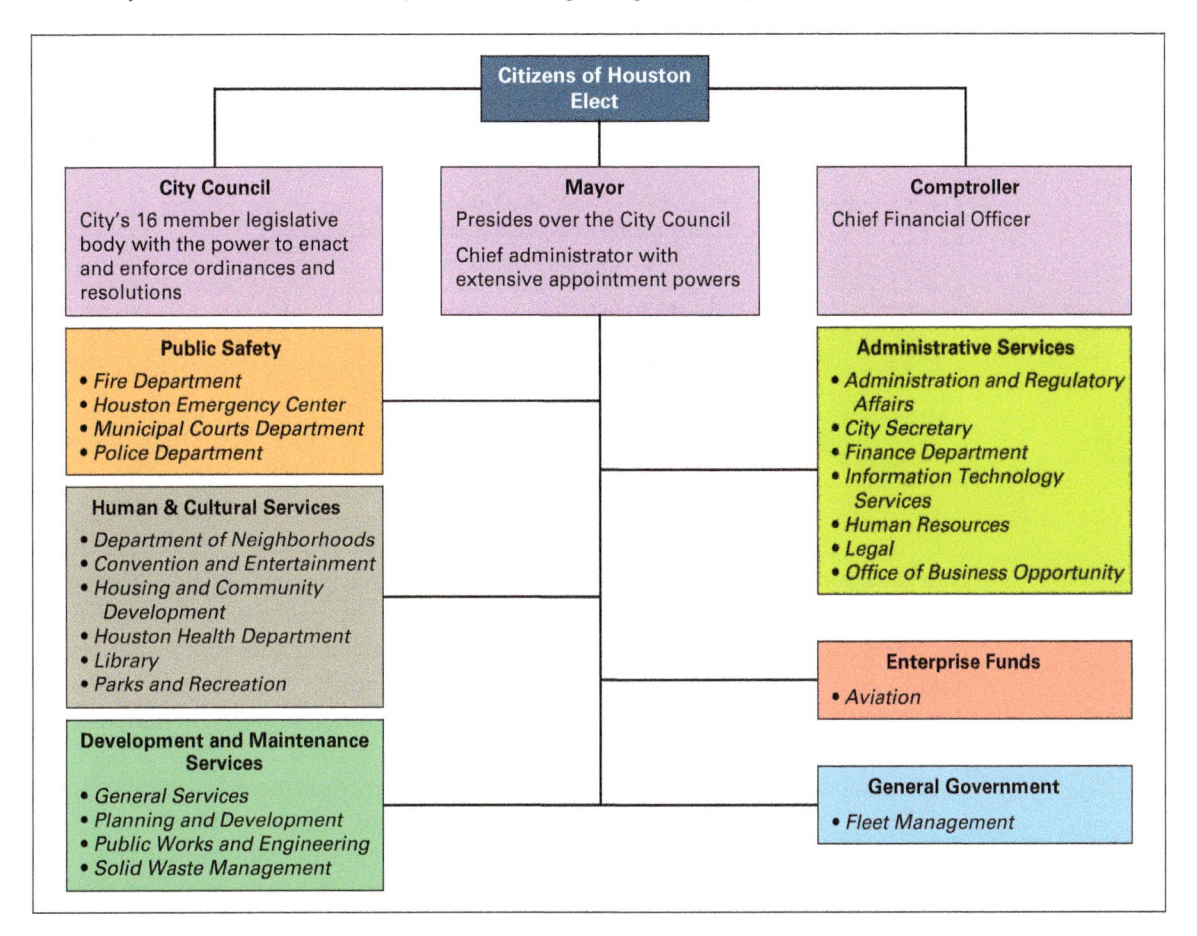

```
                    Citizens of Houston
                          Elect
         ┌────────────────┼────────────────┐
   City Council         Mayor          Comptroller
  City's 16 member   Presides over     Chief Financial
  legislative body   the City Council     Officer
  with the power     Chief administrator
  to enact and       with extensive
  enforce ordinances appointment powers
  and resolutions

   Public Safety                      Administrative Services
   • Fire Department                  • Administration and Regulatory
   • Houston Emergency Center           Affairs
   • Municipal Courts Department      • City Secretary
   • Police Department                • Finance Department
                                      • Information Technology
   Human & Cultural Services            Services
   • Department of Neighborhoods      • Human Resources
   • Convention and Entertainment     • Legal
   • Housing and Community            • Office of Business Opportunity
     Development
   • Houston Health Department        Enterprise Funds
   • Library                          • Aviation
   • Parks and Recreation

   Development and Maintenance        General Government
   Services                           • Fleet Management
   • General Services
   • Planning and Development
   • Public Works and Engineering
   • Solid Waste Management
```

soon were adopted by other major Texas cities, including Dallas, Houston, and San Antonio. Following the subsequent development of council–manager government as an alternative, a marked decline in the city commission's popularity occurred. All major Texas cities have replaced the city commission with other forms of government. Nationally, Portland, Oregon, is the last remaining large city to use the commission form of government.[25] Some thirty Texas cities refer to their city councils as commissions, but these institutions are not based on the original commission form of government, often known as the Galveston Plan. They more closely resemble the council–manager form of government.[26]

Initially, the commission was supported as a businesslike approach to running city government. By eliminating partisan elections and combining the executive, administrative, and legislative functions, it was argued, cities could provide services more efficiently. However, critics have identified several problems. The commission minimizes the potential for effective political leadership because no single individual can be identified as the person in charge. Moreover, oversight and review of policies and budgets are minimal. Commissioners are elected primarily as policymakers, not administrators, and there are downsides to electing amateurs to administer increasingly technical and complex city programs (see Figure 4–3).

COUNCIL–MANAGER After enthusiasm for the city commission waned, urban reformers, both in Texas and nationally, looked to the **council–manager** form of government (see Figure 4–4). Its specific origins are disputed, but the commission form influenced it. The first cities in Texas to use council–manager government were

council–manager government
A form of city government in which policy is set by an elected city council, which hires a professional city manager to head the daily administration of city government. With the exception of Houston, larger cities in Texas are organized under this form of government.

FIGURE 4-3 CITY COMMISSION FORM OF GOVERNMENT

Commissioners combine policy and administrative functions under the commission form of government, developed in Galveston after the 1900 hurricane. The original form of commission government does not appear to be used today by any Texas city, although some thirty cities still refer to their city councils as commissions, and many have added a manager.

SOURCE: Charles A. Beard, ed., *A Loose Leaf Digest of Short Ballot Charters* (New York: The Short Ballot Organization, 1911), p. 36001.

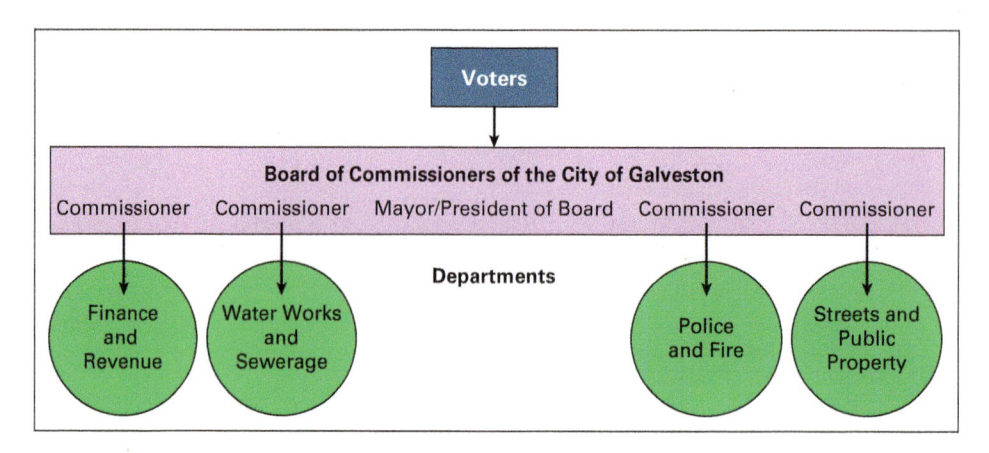

```
                          Voters
                            │
                            ▼
        Board of Commissioners of the City of Galveston
  Commissioner  Commissioner  Mayor/President of Board  Commissioner  Commissioner

                          Departments

   Finance      Water Works                          Police      Streets and
   and          and                                  and Fire    Public
   Revenue      Sewerage                                         Property
```

Amarillo and Terrell in 1913, and it soon became popular among home rule cities. Nine of the state's ten largest cities now function under council–manager government. Its principal characteristics are a professional city management, nonpartisan city elections, and a clear distinction between policymaking and administration. In recent years, however, the increased role of mayors and city council members in the day-to-day operations of city government has modified the policy–administration distinction.

In some council–manager cities, the city council chooses the mayor from among its membership to preside over council meetings and fulfill a primarily symbolic role. In other cities, the mayor is elected citywide, an arrangement that enhances the political position of the office without necessarily giving it formal legal authority. The mayor is usually a voting member of the city council but has few other institutional powers. The mayor does, however, have the opportunity to become a visible spokesperson for the city and has a forum from which to promote ideas and programs.

In the not-too-distant past, the salaries of mayors and council members serving in council–manager cities were very low, but a trend in recent years has increased salaries in response to the expanded workload. Annual salaries of the mayor and city council members in Austin were set for the 2017–2018 fiscal year at $82,387 and $74,235, respectively.[27] Until 2001, the mayor and council members in Dallas received $50 per meeting, but voters approved a charter amendment that year to raise the mayor's pay to $60,000 a year and council members' pay to $37,500.[28] In another charter amendment election in 2014, Dallas voters increased the mayor's salary to $80,000 and council members to $60,000.[29] From 1951, when San Antonio's city charter was adopted, until 2015, San Antonio's council members and mayor earned $20 per meeting and the mayor an additional $3,000 per year.[30] After years of public debate over these low salaries, the city charter was amended in 2015 to provide the mayor with a salary of $61,725 and the council members, $45,722.[31]

The city council is primarily responsible for developing public policy. It creates, organizes, and restructures city departments; approves the city budget; establishes the tax rate; authorizes the issuance of bonds (subject to voter approval); enacts local laws (ordinances); and conducts inquiries and investigations into the operations and functions of city agencies.[32]

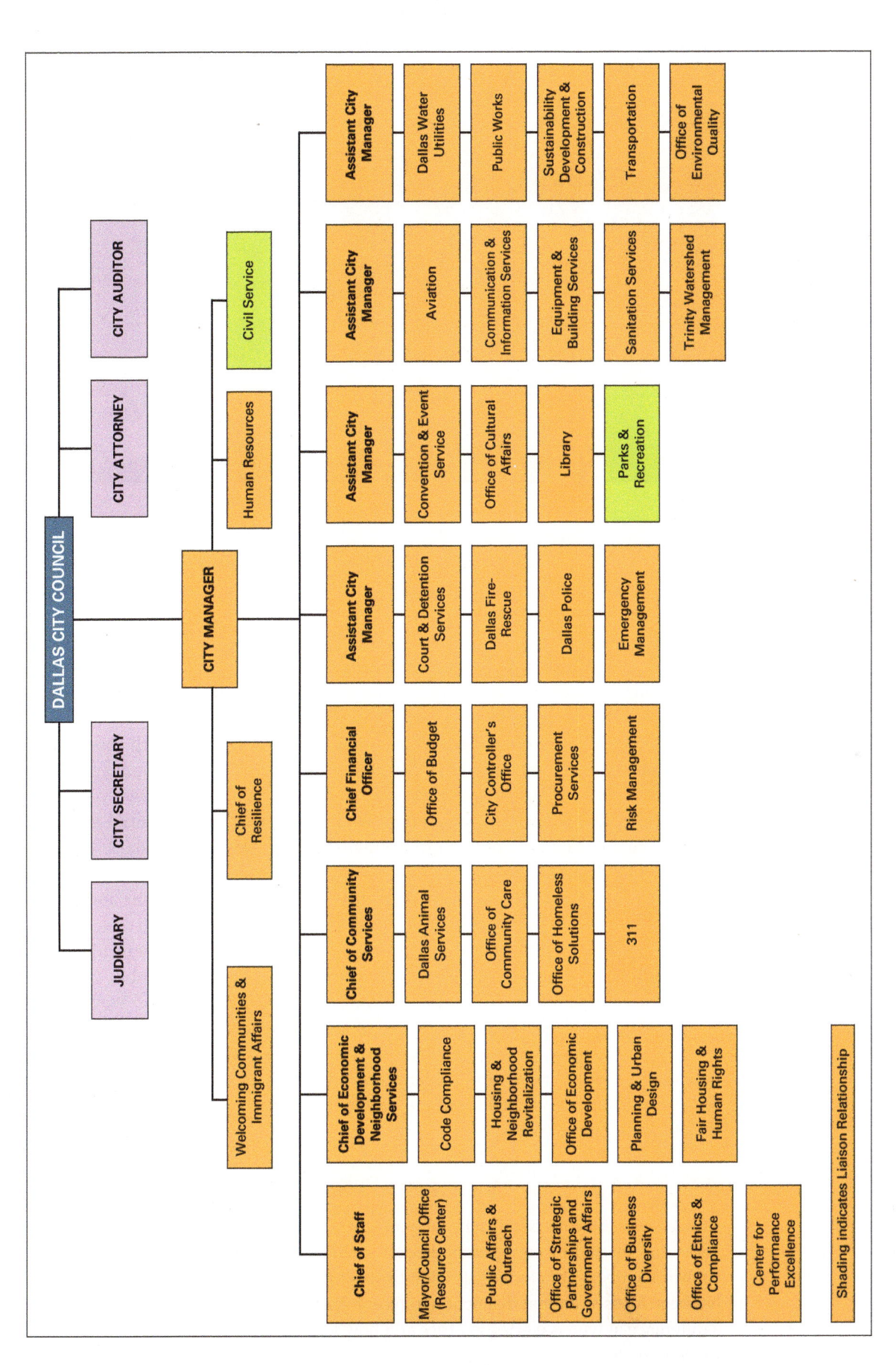

FIGURE 4–4 COUNCIL-MANAGER FORM OF GOVERNMENT: ORGANIZATIONAL CHART FOR THE CITY OF DALLAS

With the exception of Houston, all major Texas cities use the council–manager form of government in which the mayor and council set policy, and the administrative responsibilities are assigned to a manager chosen by the council.

NOTE: Agencies shaded green have a liaison relationship with the city manager.

SOURCE: City of Dallas, *Annual Budget for Fiscal Year 2017–2018*, http://dallascityhall.com/departments/budget/financialtransparency/AnnualBudget/12-Appendices.pdf.

109

FROM SIMPLE AND INFORMAL TO ORNATE AND HISTORICAL

City council meeting rooms of the state's 1,200-plus cities range from the very simple and informal to the ornate and historical. Seen here are the chambers of the San Antonio City Council, which meets in the renovated lobby of a historical bank located one block from city hall in the central business district.

The council hires a full-time city manager, who is responsible for administering city government on a day-to-day basis. The manager hires and fires assistants and department heads, supervises their activities, and translates the policy directives of the city council into concrete action by city employees. The city manager also is responsible for developing a city budget for council approval and then supervising its implementation. Professionalism is one of the key attributes of the council–manager form of government. Initially, many city managers were engineers, but in recent years managers have tended to be generalists with expertise in public finance. City managers are fairly well paid. In 2018, the city manager of San Antonio was paid $450,000 and a bonus of $100,000.[33] The city manager of Austin earned $309,000. Even city managers of small cities receive substantial compensation. The city manager of Seguin (population of approximately 28,000 in 2017) received $243,658 in 2018.[34]

A delicate line exists between policymaking and administration, and a city manager is, in principle, supposed to be politically neutral. The overall effectiveness of city managers depends on three main factors: their relationships with their city councils, their ability to develop support for their recommendations within the council and the community at large without appearing to have gone beyond the scope of their authority, and the overall perception of their financial and managerial skills. In the real world of municipal government, city managers play a central role in setting policy as well as carrying it out. Managers' adroit use of their resources and their sensitivity to political factions and the personal agendas of elected officials are keys to determining their success.

4.2.3 Municipal Election Systems

Unlike state and county officials, who are elected on partisan ballots, city officials in Texas are selected in nonpartisan elections. Cities differ, however, on whether their council members are elected citywide or in single-member districts. Much attention has been focused on that distinction in recent years because in some cities it can make a difference in who is elected to office and how well the interests of minority residents are represented.

NONPARTISAN CITY ELECTIONS Virtually every city in Texas elects its council members in **nonpartisan elections**. Claiming that there was "no Democratic or Republican way to pave a street," city reformers who were part of the nonpartisan movement (1920s to 1950s) expressed a strong aversion to political parties and particularly to urban political machines. To enforce separation of city elections from party politics, many municipal elections are held at times other than the party primaries or the general election.

The nonpartisan ballot—combined with at-large, citywide elections—has historically benefited higher social and economic groups. Parties and party labels normally serve as cues for voters. When city elections eliminate these cues, voters are forced to find alternative sources of information about candidates. Many local newspapers, which endorsed candidates and decided how much coverage to give them, had ties to the dominant urban elites. Candidates from lower socioeconomic groups had few contacts with the influential civic and business organizations that recruited, supported, and endorsed candidates. Although no longer in existence, San Antonio's Good Government League and Dallas's Citizens Charter Association controlled the recruitment and election of candidates in those two cities for several decades. Both organizations drew members from the Democratic and the Republican parties, but they reflected and pursued the interests of higher socioeconomic groups, often to the detriment of lower-income and minority populations.

Despite the nonpartisan ballots, partisanship can play a role in city elections. Mayors and members of city councils are often identified by their party affiliations through news stories, endorsements by party organizations, and campaign advertisements. In many recent city elections, party affiliations of major candidates have been widely known, and national party committees have contributed money to some of the campaigns. Areas of cities that are Republican in partisan orientation are likely to support individuals with Republican attributes, and, conversely, areas that vote Democratic in general elections are likely to support candidates with Democratic leanings. These developments clearly challenge the nonpartisan traditions of many cities throughout Texas. In 2020, the mayors of several of the state's larger cities were Democrats, as were many of the council members, a factor that has contributed to policy disputes with Republican leaders at the state Capitol, as discussed at the beginning of this chapter.

AT-LARGE ELECTIONS Another notable feature of city politics in Texas is the general use of citywide or **at-large elections**. Most Texas cities use this method. In an at-large election, all of a city's voters participate in the selection of all the members of the city council. In a pure at-large system, every candidate runs against every other candidate. If eight candidates are running for five positions on the city council, the candidates with the five highest vote totals are the winners.

A variation of the at-large system is the place system. Candidates file for a specific council seat and run citywide for places, or positions. Cities using the place system may require that the winning candidate receive a simple plurality of votes (more votes than any other candidate running for the same position) or an absolute majority of votes (more than half of the votes cast). If a city requires the latter and more than two persons are in a race, **runoff elections** between the two highest vote-getters are often required.

SINGLE-MEMBER DISTRICTS An alternative to at-large elections is the **single-member district**, or ward. Under this system, a city is divided into separate geographic districts, each represented by a different council member. A candidate must live in and run for election from a specific district, and voters can cast a ballot only in the race for the council seat that represents their district. A person elected from a single-member district can, depending on the city's charter, be elected by a plurality or an absolute majority of votes.

nonpartisan election
A local election in which candidates file for place, position, or district with no political party label attached to their names.

at-large election
A system under which city council members or other officeholders are elected by voters in the entire city, school district, or single-purpose district. Many of these election systems have been struck down by the federal courts or by the U.S. Justice Department under the Voting Rights Act as discriminatory against minorities.

runoff election
A required election if no candidate receives an absolute majority of the votes cast in a primary race or in many nonpartisan elections. The runoff is between the top two vote-getters.

single-member district
A system in which a legislator, city council member, or other public official is elected from a specific geographic area.

LEGAL ATTACKS ON AT-LARGE ELECTIONS Election systems are not politically neutral. At-large systems have historically benefited the white, higher-income areas of a city, whereas single-member districts tend to be more inclusive of all groups and areas. Minority candidates unable to get elected in citywide, at-large elections dominated by Anglo voters often have won elections running from districts with larger proportions of minority voters.

Hispanics and African Americans, through various advocacy groups such as the National Association for the Advancement of Colored People, the Mexican American Legal Defense and Educational Fund, Texas Rural Legal Aid, the G.I. Forum, and the Southwest Voter Registration and Education Project, have challenged in federal courts the election systems used by numerous Texas cities. From the small East Texas town of Jefferson to El Paso, Houston, Dallas, San Antonio, and most other larger cities in Texas, minority groups have, with considerable success, proved the inequities of at-large elections and forced city governments to adopt electoral plans with single-member districts that give minorities a better chance of electing candidates to city councils. As a result, the ethnic and racial composition of city councils has changed dramatically since the mid-1970s, with a marked increase in the numbers of Hispanics and African Americans elected to these governing bodies. Voters in Austin approved a referendum converting that city's council to single-member districts in 2015. Unlike in other Texas cities, though, the change did not result from a lawsuit.

The minority gains were aided by the Voting Rights Act, a federal law that helped minorities in Texas and certain other states with a history of racial discrimination in elections win fairer election procedures, such as single-member districts. In a 2013 lawsuit, the U.S. Supreme Court invalidated a key provision of that act, but other court decisions and laws were still relevant to voting procedures and, some experts believe, could continue to have an impact on city election systems.

4.2.4 City Revenues and Expenditures

Despite a growing number of expenses, Texas cities have limited financial options. Unlike counties and school districts, they receive no state appropriations. City governments are heavily dependent on **regressive taxes**, such as property taxes and a sales tax (up to 2 percent) (see Figure 4–5), which fall disproportionately more heavily on lower-income residents. Other revenue sources include franchise fees, court fines, hotel occupancy taxes, taxes on amusements, fees for various permits, and revenue generated by city-owned utilities.[35]

regressive tax
A tax that imposes a disproportionately heavier burden on low-income people than on the more affluent.

City revenues tend to track the state's economy. When the economy is robust and expanding, city revenues usually grow. Revenue from property taxes increases with the construction of new homes and businesses. Rising property values also result in higher tax appraisals and increased revenue. Sales tax revenue increases as retailers sell more products. When the economy weakens, however, cities are forced to raise property tax rates, increase fees, lay off city workers, freeze the hiring of new employees, reduce services, or postpone capital expenditures.[36]

Texas cities are often threatened by proposals from state lawmakers to place caps or other restrictions on their taxing authority. As noted at the beginning of this chapter, cities lost a tax-limitation fight in 2019 when the legislature enacted a law to cap their ability to increase property tax revenue at 3.5 percent a year, excluding taxes on new construction, without voter approval in a rollback election. Unhappiness with local property taxes was driven, in part, by increasing property values. An individual's or business's property tax bill is determined by the assessed value of a piece of property and the rate at which that property is taxed, usually so many cents or dollars per $100 of valuation. So, in many cities, property tax bills—and the cities' revenue from them—were increasing even though local governments had not raised tax rates.

FIGURE 4–5 WHERE DO TEXAS CITIES GET THEIR MONEY?

Texas cities collect two-thirds of their local revenues from property and sales taxes, both of which are classified as regressive taxes. Other revenues come from franchise fees, court fines, hotel occupancy taxes, permit fees, and funds transferred from locally owned utilities.

SOURCE: *Texas Town and City*, 102 (January 2015), p. 16.

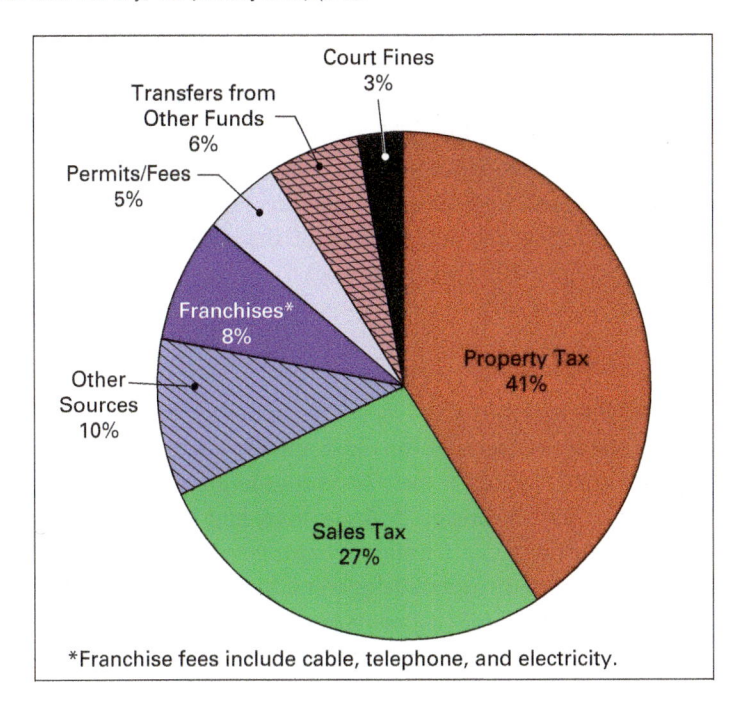

- Court Fines: 3%
- Transfers from Other Funds: 6%
- Permits/Fees: 5%
- Franchises*: 8%
- Other Sources: 10%
- Property Tax: 41%
- Sales Tax: 27%

*Franchise fees include cable, telephone, and electricity.

The previous limit on property tax increases for cities and other local governments had been 8 percent, and voters could petition for a **rollback election** if a government exceeded that limit. The 2019 law not only lowered the limit to 3.5 percent, but it also made the requirement for a rollback election automatic if a property tax revenue increase exceeded that limit. This is a much stronger rollback provision because under the old law, citizens often did not petition for a rollback election when local officials exceeded the 8 percent limit.

The new restrictions on property taxes, a major source of local revenue, could prove particularly difficult for cities and other local governments in the wake of the coronavirus pandemic that struck Texas in 2020. Cities lost millions of dollars in sales tax revenue—their other major tax funding source—following the ordered, temporary closures of thousands of businesses to help stem the spread of the virus. "Sales taxes are typically 29 percent to 30 percent of an average city's revenue. And sales taxes are just going to be way off for the foreseeable future," said Bennett Sandlin, executive director of the Texas Municipal League.[37]

Many cities also suffered from severe drops in tourist-related revenue—including hotel taxes and revenue from convention centers—after travel dried up during the pandemic. Despite receiving some emergency federal aid, cities and other local governments faced the prospects of reduced public services, hiring freezes, employee layoffs and other cost-cutting steps. The Texas Municipal League believed the governor's declaration of a disaster during the coronavirus crisis exempted local governments from the new property tax limit, but Governor Greg Abbott disagreed.

Although cities are required by law to balance their operating budgets, many municipal construction projects are financed by loans through the issuance of **general obligation bonds**, which are subject to voter approval. These bonds are secured by the city's taxing power. The city pledges its full faith and credit to the lender and, over a number of years, repays the bonds with tax revenue. Cities also fund various projects

rollback election
An election in which local voters can nullify a property tax increase that exceeds 3.5 percent in a given year.

general obligation bond
A method of borrowing money to pay for new construction projects such as streets and drainage systems. Interest on such bonds, which require voter approval, is paid with tax revenue.

revenue bond
A bond sold by a government that is repaid from the revenues generated from income-producing facilities.

through **revenue bonds** that are payable solely from the revenues derived from an income-producing facility, such as a city-owned parking garage.[38]

Cities and towns share responsibilities for providing services with other local governments, so it is difficult to calculate total expenditures for all city services. But police and fire protection, primary functions of city governments, account for more than 55 percent of city expenditures. Other major city expenditures include streets and roads, solid waste management, sewer treatment and drainage, water supply, parks and recreation, public transportation, and libraries. Some Texas cities provide electricity and natural gas service, but private utilities provide those services in other communities. Cities often contract out services, such as garbage collection, to private companies, but the legal authority for such functions remains with the city. In some cases, special districts, which are independent of the cities, have been established within city boundaries to provide specific services.[39]

4.2.5 Urban Problems

During the 1970s and through the early 1980s, Texas cities participated in the dramatic economic growth of the state. Many of the older cities of the country—particularly in the East and the Midwest—"looked at their Texas counterparts and envied their capacity to attract population and business."[40] Texas cities had low taxes, a pro-business tradition, an abundant workforce, proximity to natural resources, and governing bodies that favored economic growth and development. In large measure, Texas continues to provide an attractive model for investments and economic opportunities, but as the state entered the third decade of the twenty-first century, many Texas cities were confronting some of the problems associated with the older urban areas outside Texas.[41]

GRAYING OF TEXAS CITIES The Texas population is aging, or graying, but at rates lower than that of other areas of the country. In fact, the average age of the state's population (34.5 years) was the third lowest in the nation, partly because of the large number of children born to the growing Hispanic population. Across the nation, Americans are living longer, and older age groups are among the fastest-growing segments of the population. Approximately 12 percent of Texans—some 3.3 million people—were age 65 or older in 2016. The state's population is projected to grow to some 32.7 million people by 2030, and 17 percent—5.5 million people—are likely to be 65 or older.[42]

An aging population places additional pressures on city governments and the state for public services. The local property tax, a major source of revenue for city governments, is stretched almost to its limits. Moreover, in addition to the standard **homestead exemption**, many Texas cities have granted additional property tax exemptions for individuals older than age 65. Exemptions are special breaks that lower the amount of property taxes a person pays. As more and more people become old enough to claim these exemptions, younger taxpayers may be called upon to shoulder the burden through higher tax rates. It also is possible that older citizens on fixed incomes will be much more reluctant to support bond issues if they result in significant property tax increases.

homestead exemption
Legal provision that permits a person who owns a home and is living in it to obtain a reduction in property taxes on the house.

"WHITE FLIGHT" AND GENTRIFICATION The population characteristics of Texas cities have changed since the 1960s. Major metropolitan areas experienced "white flight" to the suburbs, a dramatic increase in the growth rate of minority populations, and small growth rates among Anglos in the central cities.[43] Nine of the state's ten largest cities have combined majorities of Hispanics, African Americans, and Asian Americans. With the exception of Asian Americans, income levels for most minority Texans have always been lower than those of Anglos, and a larger proportion of the minority population falls below the poverty level. The increased concentration of lower-income people in the central cities increases pressure for more public services, while a declining proportion of affluent property owners weakens the local tax structures that pay for the services.

In recent years—particularly in Fort Worth, Dallas, Austin, San Antonio, and Houston—gentrification is replacing the white flight of old. Gentrification is the migration of upwardly mobile younger people, particularly whites, to the inner cities, where older, more affordable housing is being replaced with expensive condominiums and other housing that appeal to the more affluent. Consequently, low-income people, including many minority Texans, are being displaced from the central cities because they can no longer afford to live there. Many are moving to the suburbs or to communities some distance from the central city.

Significant numbers of higher-income Hispanics, Asian Americans, and African Americans also have moved from the central core of cities to the surrounding suburbs, but for different reasons than have lower-income people.[44] They apparently moved to the suburbs to be nearer other higher income and better educated people, a change from patterns of clustering or locating by racial and ethnic groups.[45]

DECLINING INFRASTRUCTURES There has been much concern across Texas and the United States about the declining infrastructures within local governments. In its 2017 "Report Card for America's Infrastructure," the American Society of Civil Engineers gave Texas a mediocre score of C-.[46] This survey mirrored a number of federal agency studies of the states' infrastructure problems. The message seems clear. Public facilities must be constantly maintained or expanded to support a growing population. Governments at all levels must plan for growth, allocate funds, and build facilities as this growth occurs, and many local governments will look to the state and federal governments for financial assistance. When capital improvements are neglected, infrastructure problems worsen, and the costs of improvements can begin to exceed the capacity of governments to pay for them. With the population growth projected for the state, an estimated $63 billion will be required in the next fifty years to maintain and expand Texas's 6,900 public water systems.[47] Many Texas cities already are out of compliance with federal standards for treating water and sewage and disposing of solid waste and are risking fines. Costs for these upgrades over the past decade alone were estimated at $25 billion.[48]

Some capital improvements are paid for out of current operating budgets, but a more common practice is for cities to borrow money to improve roads, streets, water systems, and the like. Property taxes are used to repay these bonds. When property values decline, cities are restrained—by the state constitution and statutes—in how much indebtedness they can incur to support needed improvements. A construction boom that began in the 1990s and continued through much of the first decade of the twenty-first century added a significant new tax base, but by 2011 construction declined, as did housing values in many areas of the state. Within two years, construction rebounded.[49] Nevertheless, a growing population has increased the demand for roads, utilities, water and wastewater systems, and an array of other capital needs; cities are having trouble keeping up.

CRIME AND URBAN VIOLENCE Crime, both violent and property crimes, has generally been decreasing in Texas for the past 30 years, following a peak of 8,017 crimes per 100,000 Texas residents in 1988. There were 2,778 crimes per 100,000 Texas residents in 2018.[50] But crime nevertheless remains a critical issue for victims and their families and for many others who fear becoming victims. The number of criminal incidents also varies significantly among cities and neighborhoods within a city, and crime remains an economic drain on public resources. Consequently, crime is an important issue for cities, for city leaders, and for candidates running for public offices. Texas has a historical tradition of political candidates campaigning on law-and-order platforms, which will be discussed more fully in Chapter 14. Political candidates and elected officials often propose expansion of law enforcement, but many city budgets cannot absorb the costs.

mandate
A federal law or regulation that requires state or local governments to take certain actions, often at costs that the federal government does not reimburse. The state government also imposes mandates on local governments.

STATE- AND FEDERAL-MANDATED PROGRAMS Both federal and state governments have increasingly used mandates in recent years to implement public policy. A **mandate** is a law or regulation enacted by a higher level of government that compels a lower level of government to carry out a specific action. In simpler terms, it can be a form of "passing the buck" or "cost shifting." Federal mandates cover a wide range of governmental functions, including transportation, education for the disabled, water and air quality, and voter registration. States, meanwhile, have shifted much of the cost of public education to local governments.

Despite a decrease since the 1980s in federal funding for many programs addressing urban problems, federal mandates on the states, counties, and cities have increased, as have state mandates on local governments, often with no financial support. In some cases, the state simply passes the responsibility for—and the costs of—carrying out federal mandates to local governments. Congress enacted a law in 1995 to restrict unfunded mandates, but the law applied only to future, not existing, mandates. Such restrictions still can be circumvented if Congress chooses.

Although this practice may seem unfair and illogical, it is politically attractive to federal policymakers because they can "appease a large and vocal interest group that demands an extensive program without incurring the wrath of their constituents." They get the credit for such programs, but they do not get the blame for their costs.[51] Cities and other local governments across Texas claim that these unfunded requirements are excessively expensive, force them to rearrange their priorities, and limit local initiatives dealing with their most pressing issues. "Texas is now the only state that denies state financial assistance to its cities even as the legislature imposes greater responsibilities on its cities."[52] If local governments do not comply with mandates, they can be subject to litigation and face the prospects of losing federal or state funds. If they comply with mandates, they then are likely to reduce other services or seek alternative sources of funding now denied them.

ENVIRONMENTAL ISSUES Texas is one of the most polluted states in the nation. Petrochemical industries generate a large amount of pollutants as by-products in processing fossil fuels or manufacturing chemicals. The indiscriminate disposal of much of this waste in years past has produced toxic waste dumps in many cities, often in low-income, minority neighborhoods. Heavy automobile traffic and coal-burning power plants spew tons of pollutants into the air, and fertilizers and herbicides threaten local water supplies. Cities are frequently on "ozone alert" days, which could trigger additional federal and state requirements to contain the problems.

Some cities address these issues through "smart growth" programs and, more recently, "sustainability" and "green city" programs. After the administration of President George W. Bush made little effort to deal with the problem of climate change, many Texas cities joined other local governments with a wide array of environmental initiatives, including efforts to reduce traffic congestion and air pollution, increase reliance on renewable energy, and reduce urban temperatures through extensive urban forestry, to name a few. As noted at the beginning of this chapter, voters in Denton approved a local ordinance to ban the hydraulic fracturing, or fracking, method of drilling for oil and gas in their city. But that ordinance was overturned by the Texas legislature.

PUBLIC EMPLOYMENT As the baby boom generation continues to retire, governmental agencies will face an increasing problem of replacing highly trained public employees. Since the late 1970s, bureaucrat bashing by political candidates, legislators, think tanks, and the media has helped increase public hostility toward government. This, in turn, has discouraged many highly skilled young people from seeking careers in public service. Retiring public employees also have accumulated expensive pensions, including health care benefits, which many cities may have trouble paying. Local governments often made commitments to provide retirement benefits without allocating sufficient funds to ensure that all benefits would be paid.

County Government in Texas

4.3 Describe the structure of county government in Texas.

Prior to Texas's independence from Mexico, local government was organized under both Spanish and Mexican law around the municipality. This unit consisted of large land areas with "presidios for military protection, missions established by the Catholic Church, and settlements established by various colonists and impresarios."[53] Twenty-three such municipalities existed at the time of independence, and they became the first twenty-three counties organized under the Texas Constitution of 1836.

Texas now has 254 counties, more than any other state. The state constitution gives the legislature the power to create, abolish, or alter counties. It also prescribes certain requirements for a new county, including its size and the proximity of its boundaries to the county seat of the county from which it is created. The last county created was Kenedy in 1921.[54]

Counties are administrative subunits of the state that were developed initially to serve a predominantly rural population and to administer state law. They possess powers delegated to them by the state, but they have relatively few implied powers.[55] Unlike home rule cities, counties lack the basic legislative power of enacting ordinances. They can carry out only those administrative functions granted them by the state. Counties administer and collect some state taxes and enforce a variety of state laws and regulations. They also build roads and bridges, administer local welfare programs, aid in fire protection, and perform other functions primarily local in nature.[56] All Texas counties function under the same constitutional restrictions and basic organizational structure, despite wide variations in population, local characteristics, and public needs.

4.3.1 The Diversity of Counties

According to the *2018 American Community Survey*, Loving County, the state's least populous county, had only 169 residents, compared to 4.7 million residents in Harris County, the most populous (see Table 4–2). Rockwall County, the smallest county in Texas, includes only 127 square miles; Brewster County covers 6,184 square miles and is the largest Texas county in terms of geography. About 60 percent of the state's population lives in the ten most populous counties.[57]

Foard County, with a population of 1,155 in 2019, had a 2018 budget of $2.7 million and paid its county judge $33,090 a year and each of its commissioners $27,370. Dallas County had an $860 million budget and paid its county judge $171,367 and each commissioner $158,829. Harris County's 2018 budget was $4.6 billion. Its county judge was paid $190,891 and each of its commissioners received $182,562.[58] Although there is an obvious relationship between the population of a county and salaries paid to its officials, the county's tax base also is a significant factor. For example, Loving County, the smallest county in the state, had a $9 million budget in 2018, and paid its county judge $79,582 and its commissioners $40,538.[59]

4.3.2 The Structure of County Government

The organizational structure of county government is highly fragmented, reflecting the principles of Jacksonian democracy and the reaction of late-nineteenth-century Texans to Radical Reconstruction. The governing body of a county is the **commissioners court**, but it shares administrative functions with other independently elected officials (see Figure 4–6). Moreover, the name "commissioners court" is somewhat misleading because that body has no judicial functions.

COMMISSIONERS COURT AND COUNTY JUDGE The commissioners court includes a **county judge**, who is elected countywide, and four county commissioners, who are elected from a county's four commissioners precincts. Like other elected

---

commissioners court
The principal policymaking body for county government. It includes four commissioners and the county judge, all elected offices. It sets the county tax rate and supervises expenditures.

county judge
The presiding officer of a county commissioners court. This office also has some judicial authority, which is assumed by separate county courts-at-law in most urban counties.

TABLE 4-2 TEN LARGEST AND TEN SMALLEST TEXAS COUNTIES, 1980–2018

	1980 Population	1990 Population	2000 Population	2010 Population	2018 Population
State Total	14,229,191	16,986,510	20,318,262	25,145,561	28,995,881
Ten Largest Texas Counties					
Harris County	2,409,547	2,818,199	3,400,578	4,092,459	4,713,325
Dallas County	1,556,390	1,852,810	2,218,899	2,368,139	2,635,516
Tarrant County	860,880	1,170,103	1,446,219	1,809,034	2,102,515
Bexar County	988,800	1,185,394	1,392,391	1,714,773	2,003,554
Travis County	419,573	576,407	812,280	1,024,266	1,273,954
Collin County	144,576	264,036	491,675	782,341	1,034,730
Denton County	143,126	273,525	432,976	662,614	887,207
Hidalgo County	283,229	383,545	569,463	774,769	868,707
El Paso County	479,899	591,610	679,622	800,647	839,238
Fort Bend County	130,846	225,421	354,452	585,375	811,688
Ten County Total	7,416,866	9,341,050	11,798,555	14,614,417	17,170,434
Ten Smallest Texas Counties					
Motley County	1,950	1,532	1,426	1,210	1,200
Foard County	2,158	1,794	1,622	1,336	1,155
Roberts County	1,187	1,025	887	929	854
Terrell County	1,595	1,410	1,081	984	776
Kent County	1,145	1,010	859	808	762
McMullen County	789	817	851	707	743
Borden County	859	799	729	641	654
Kenedy County	543	460	414	416	404
King County	425	354	356	286	272
Loving County	91	107	67	82	169
Ten County Total	10,742	9,308	8,292	7,399	6,989

SOURCES: U.S Census Bureau, *U.S. Censuses, 1980, 1990, 2000, 2010*; and July 1, 2019, state and county population estimates from the U.S. Census Bureau, *2018 American Community Survey*.

county officials, the judge and the commissioners serve four-year terms and are elected in partisan elections.

Until the 1960s, there were gross inequities in the population distributions among commissioners precincts in most counties. This issue of malapportionment came to a head in the 1968 case of *Avery v. Midland County*. Ninety-seven percent of the county's population, which lived in the city of Midland, elected only one commissioner, and the remaining 3 percent of the county's residents elected the other three. Similar inequities were prevalent all over the state, but the U.S. Supreme Court applied the "one person, one vote" principle to the counties and required that districts be equally apportioned.[60] Subsequently, Congress placed Texas under the Voting Rights Act in 1975, and counties were required to consider the interests of minority populations in drawing the boundaries for commissioners precincts. African Americans and Hispanics across the state challenged county electoral systems and increased minority representation on county commissioners courts.

The county judge presides over the commissioners court, participates in the court's deliberations, and votes on issues before it. If there is a vacancy among the commissioners, the county judge appoints a replacement. If the county judge vacates his or her office, the commissioners choose a replacement.

The Texas Constitution also gives the county judge some judicial responsibilities but does not require the officeholder to be a lawyer. Most urban counties have county courts-at-law that relieve the county judge of judicial duties. A county judge in most urban counties takes on active administrative roles and is generally perceived as a county's chief executive officer.[61] County judges in some rural counties perform a judicial as well as an executive role, combining two sets of duties in one office.

FIGURE 4-6 COUNTY GOVERNMENT: ORGANIZATIONAL CHART FOR BEXAR COUNTY

Whereas urban counties such as Bexar County function with many employees and provide a wide array of services, all counties in Texas function under a similar structure, which provides for the election of many officials and fragments authority among them.

SOURCE: Bexar County, *Adopted Annual Budget, Fiscal Year 2017–2018*, p. 27, https://www.bexar.org/DocumentCenter/View/14100/Complete-Budget-FY-2017-18-28-MB.

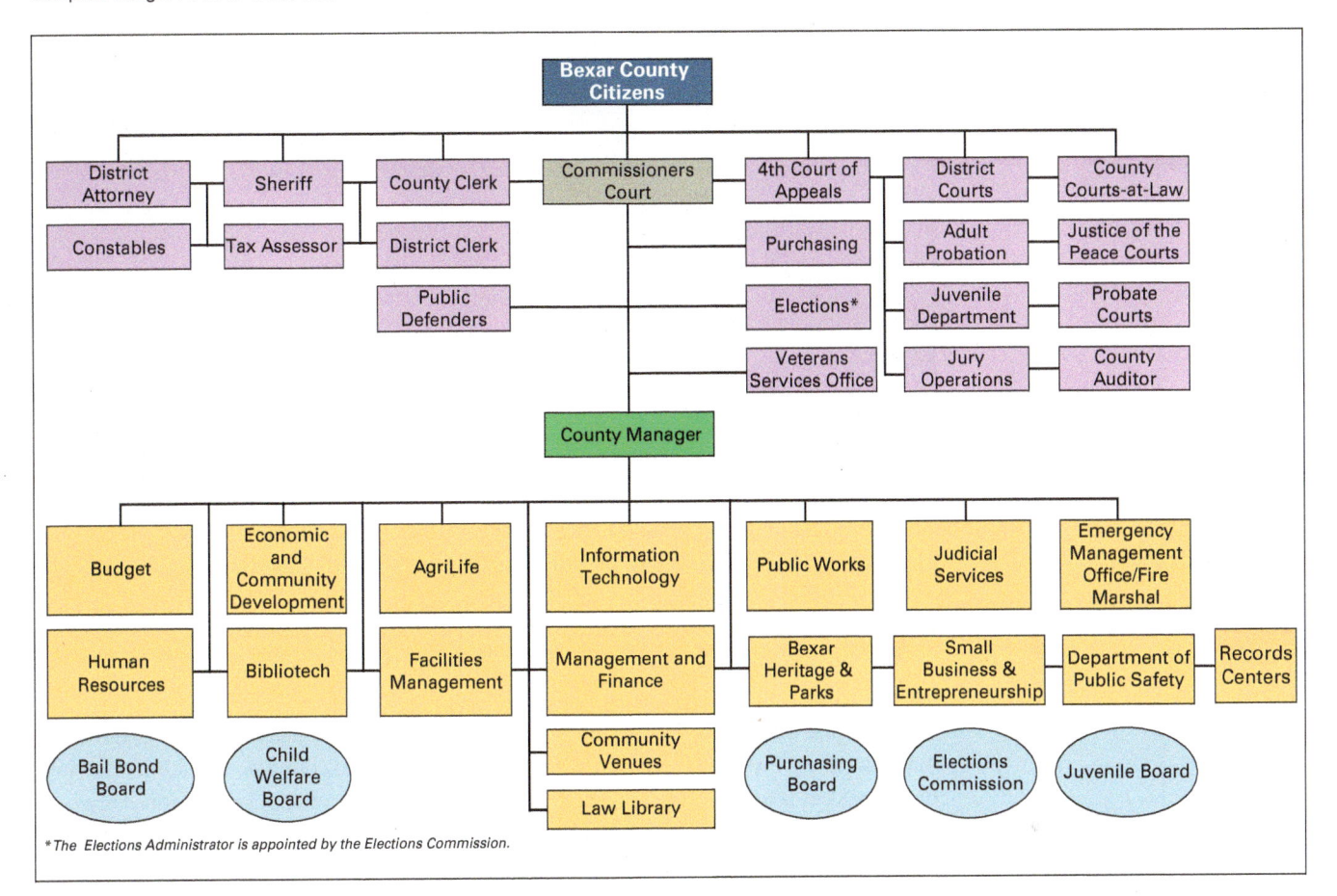

*The Elections Administrator is appointed by the Elections Commission.

When the coronavirus pandemic began to strike Texas in 2020, Dallas County Judge Clay Jenkins was one of the first local leaders in the country to use his emergency powers to try to protect his constituents' health and safety. Jenkins issued a local disaster declaration and emergency orders shutting down non-essential businesses and restricting the movements of residents to slow the spread of the virus. Other local officials, including Harris County Judge Lina Hidalgo, issued similar orders before Governor Greg Abbott issued statewide orders outlining restrictions.

Hidalgo had gained national attention two years earlier when, as a 27-year-old immigrant, she had narrowly unseated a Republican incumbent for the top elected post in Texas's most populous county. As a teenager, Hidalgo had fled drug-war violence in her native Colombia with her family before settling in the United States. She became a U.S. citizen in 2013, the same year she earned a degree in political science from Stanford University. Her election as Harris County judge in 2018 was her first race for elected office.

The commissioners court fills midterm vacancies in other county offices (see Table 4–3). It also has authority over the county budget, which permits the court to exercise some influence, if not control, over other elected officeholders.[62] The court sets the annual tax rate, which is limited by the Texas Constitution; approves the tax roll; and supervises all expenditures of county money. Other county officials must obtain the court's authorization for personnel positions, salaries, and office expenses. Consequently, the budgetary process often sparks political disputes and other conflicts.

A LOCAL LEADER

Harris County Judge Lina Hidalgo, an immigrant, received a lot of attention when she was elected county judge of Harris County in 2018. Two years later, she was in the middle of the fight to protect her constituents against the COVID-19 pandemic, receiving both praise and criticism.

Historically, county road construction and maintenance were primary functions of commissioners courts. The Optional Road Law of 1947 gave counties the authority to create a consolidated road system under the supervision of a county engineer, who relieved commissioners of road maintenance and construction headaches. But the importance of roads to the commissioners and their constituents still can generate political disputes.

Over the past three decades, more and more responsibilities have been assigned to the counties by the state legislature. In many respects, urban counties are taking on many of the tasks of large cities and providing a wider array of services. Comparisons between the functions of urban counties and those of cities show fewer and fewer differences.

county clerk
The chief record-keeping officer of a county.

COUNTY CLERK The constitution provides for an elected **county clerk**, one officeholder to serve as the clerk of the commissioners court, the clerk of the county courts, and, in the smaller counties, the clerk of the district court. Over the years, the legislature has enacted hundreds of statutory provisions defining specific responsibilities of the office, prompting one writer to describe the office as the "dumping ground for miscellaneous functions" of the county.[63] The office is the depository of a county's vital statistics, such as birth and death records and documents related to real estate transactions. It issues marriage licenses and various other licenses required by state

TABLE 4-3   MAJOR DUTIES OF THE COMMISSIONERS COURT

1. Set tax rate and adopt county budget.
2. Appoint county officials authorized under statutory law and hire personnel.
3. Fill county elective and appointive vacancies.
4. Administer elections, including the establishment of voting precincts, the appointment of an election administrator, the appointment of precinct judges, the calling of county bond elections, and the certification of election returns.
5. Award contracts and authorize payment of all county bills.
6. Build and maintain county roads and bridges.
7. Build, maintain, and improve county facilities, including jails.
8. Provide for libraries, hospitals, and medical care for the indigent.
9. Provide for emergency relief and civil disaster assistance.
10. Provide for fire protection and sanitation.

SOURCE: Texas Commission on Intergovernmental Relations, *An Introduction to County Government* (Austin, TX, 1985), p. 9.

law.[64] The county clerk also serves as a county's chief elections administrator if the commissioners court has not created a separate elections administrator's office.[65]

DISTRICT CLERK The district clerk, also elected countywide, assists a county's district court or courts by maintaining custody of court documents and records.[66] In small counties, the county clerk is authorized to double as the district clerk, and sixty-two counties combined these two offices in 2018.[67]

COUNTY AND DISTRICT ATTORNEYS The state's legal interests in both civil and criminal matters are represented at the local level by one of three officers—the **county attorney**, the **district attorney**, or the criminal district attorney. The legislature has enacted numerous provisions for legal departments that vary from county to county. Some counties have no county attorney but have a criminal district attorney. Under state law, other counties are authorized to have both a county attorney and a district attorney. Inconsistencies exist in the specific functions and responsibilities of the offices from county to county.[68] District attorneys prosecute the more serious cases, usually felonies, in the district courts, whereas the county attorneys prosecute lesser offenses, primarily misdemeanors, in the county courts.[69]

These officers also can provide legal advice and opinions to other county officials and give legal counsel to public officials or employees who have been sued for acts committed in carrying out their official duties. Upon request of the commissioners court, the district attorney or county attorney may initiate lawsuits on behalf of the county. Various other laws charge these attorneys with protecting the public health, assisting the attorney general in cases involving deceptive trade practices, enforcing the state's election laws, collecting delinquent taxes, and even enforcing the Texas Communist Control Act of 1951.[70]

TAX ASSESSOR–COLLECTOR The property tax is the primary source of revenue for counties. Although the commissioners court sets property tax rates, the **county tax assessor–collector**, another elected officer, has the task of ascertaining who owns what property and how much tax is owed on that property and then collecting the tax. In counties with fewer than 10,000 people, these responsibilities are assigned to the sheriff, unless voters decide to create a separate tax assessor–collector office. At least ten counties, mainly those with fewer than 5,000 in population, continue to let the sheriff handle the job.[71]

Prior to reforms enacted in the 1970s, the tax assessor–collector also was responsible for appraising property or determining its value. This process often was steeped in politics because the higher the value of a piece of property, the more taxes its owner has to pay. Lowering property values for selected friends or supporters gave those holding this office considerable power, which often was abused. In an effort to move toward greater consistency across the state and to enhance the professionalism of tax appraisals, the legislature now requires each county to create an **appraisal district** that is separate from the tax office.[72] The appraisal district, whose members represent other local governmental units, now determines the value of all property in the county. The district also certifies the tax rolls, and other governmental units are required by law to use its appraisals.[73]

COUNTY LAW ENFORCEMENT **Sheriffs** and **constables**, a county's law enforcement officers, are part of an old tradition under the Anglo-Saxon legal system. Each county has one sheriff with countywide jurisdiction, but the number of constables can vary. In counties with fewer than 18,000 residents, the commissioners court can designate the entire county as a single justice of the peace precinct or can create as many as four precincts, each assigned one constable. In the large counties, as many as eight justice of the peace precincts can be created with a constable assigned to each.[74]

In a small rural county, the sheriff is the primary law enforcement officer. In urban counties, city police departments generally assume exclusive jurisdiction in the

county attorney
An elected official who is the chief legal officer of some counties. He or she also prosecutes lesser criminal offenses, primarily misdemeanors, in county courts.

district attorney
An elected official who prosecutes the more serious criminal offenses, usually felonies, in state district courts.

county tax assessor–collector
An elected official who determines how much property tax is owed on the different pieces of property within a county and then collects the tax. This officeholder acts on the basis of property values determined by the county appraisal district and a tax rate set by the county commissioners court.

appraisal district
Countywide tax office that appraises the value of property and certifies the tax rolls used by every taxing authority in the county.

sheriff
An elected official who is the chief law enforcement officer of a county. In urban areas, his or her jurisdiction usually is limited to the unincorporated areas of a county, while local police departments have jurisdiction over incorporated cities.

constable
An elected law enforcement officer assigned as an administrative officer in a justice of the peace precinct. He or she is responsible primarily for executing court judgments, serving subpoenas, and delivering other legal documents. Constables also are authorized to patrol their precincts, make arrests, and conduct criminal investigations.

incorporated municipal areas, leaving the sheriff jurisdiction over the unincorporated areas. Most sheriffs have considerable discretion in the hiring, promotion, and firing of deputies and other employees, although some counties have adopted a merit employment system for the sheriff's office. The sheriff also serves as the administrative officer for the district and county courts.

Constables are authorized to patrol their precincts, make arrests, and conduct criminal investigations, but their primary function is to serve as administrative officers of the justice of the peace courts. They are responsible for serving subpoenas, executing judgments of the court, and delivering other legal documents.[75]

County governments are responsible for constructing and staffing county jails, which are managed in most counties by the sheriff and in some counties by a jail administrator. During the late 1980s and early 1990s, counties across the state pursued an aggressive policy of jail construction in response to court decisions, increased crime rates, and a shortage of prison space. Jail construction was a "growth" industry during this period, but by the mid-1990s, some counties found that they had overextended their finances to construct these jails. They also were left with excess jail capacity after the state built new prisons. To compensate for these problems, several counties contracted with other states to house prisoners in Texas jails.

All counties are authorized to create an office of the medical examiner. The commissioners court appoints this individual, who determines the cause of death of murder victims or others who die under suspicious or unusual circumstances. In counties that do not have a medical examiner, the justice of the peace must conduct an inquest to determine if there are conditions to merit an autopsy.

Counties, either individually or as part of multicounty judicial districts, must provide facilities for a criminal probation office. The state sets probation standards, and district judges choose the chief adult probation officer.

COUNTY AUDITOR All counties with populations of 10,000 or more are required to have a county auditor, and smaller counties may have one if the commissioners court so chooses. Two counties with fewer than 25,000 residents may jointly agree to hire an auditor to serve both counties. The **county auditor** is appointed by the district judges of the county for a two-year term. He or she is primarily responsible for reviewing every bill and expenditure of a county to ensure its correctness and legality. Such oversight can, in effect, impose budgetary restrictions on commissioners courts and produce political conflict with other county officers.

The role of the auditor varies from county to county. In counties with more than 225,000 people, the auditor prepares the county budget for submission to the commissioners court unless an alternative has been authorized by the legislature.[76] In smaller counties, the commissioners court prepares the budget, based on estimates provided by the auditor.

COUNTY TREASURER The **county treasurer** is responsible for receiving and disbursing county funds. This office has existed since 1846, but its primary functions are now carried out by the county auditor, and constitutional amendments have eliminated this office in several counties.

4.3.3 Criticisms of County Government

The structure of county government in Texas, designed for a rural state, has inhibited efforts of urban counties to respond to growing needs for public services. The state has experimented with county home rule, but the provisions were so poorly written, confusing, and contradictory that local home rule at the county level was never given a real chance. Efforts were made in the 1997 and 1999 sessions of the legislature to amend the constitution to once again allow counties to adopt home rule, but statewide support was limited, and the efforts failed.

---

county auditor
An officer appointed by the district judges of the county. This person is primarily responsible for reviewing every bill and expenditure of a county to ensure that it is correct and legal. In counties with more than 225,000 people, the auditor also is the budget officer who prepares the county budget for consideration by the commissioners court.

county treasurer
An elected officer who is responsible for receiving and disbursing county funds. The office's primary functions are now carried out by the county auditor, and the office has been eliminated in a number of counties.

Even though the county functions primarily as an extension, or administrative subdivision, of state government, there is little supervision of the counties by the state and wide disparity in the way counties interpret and administer their functions. Some counties do a good job; others have a dismal record. The fragmentation represented by several independently elected officers always poses the potential for jurisdictional conflict, administrative inefficiency, and even government deadlock.

Like other local governments in Texas, counties rely heavily on the property tax for revenue but cannot exceed tax rate limits set by the state constitution and limits on annual increases in property tax revenue set by the legislature. The 3.5 percent annual revenue limit that applies to cities applies to counties. These limits further restrict the ability of counties to provide services.

Historically, county courthouses were associated with political patronage and the **spoils system**. Victorious candidates claimed the right to appoint personal and political friends to work for them, and state courts held that elected county officials had wide discretion in the selection of their employees. Reformers advocated a **civil service system** for county employees based on merit and competitive examinations and offering job security from one election to the next. A 1971 law allows counties with more than 200,000 in population to create a civil service system, but it excludes several county offices, including the district attorney. An elected public official retains considerable control over the initial hiring of employees through a probationary period of six months.[77]

spoils system
Practice, usually identified with machine politics, of awarding public jobs to one's political friends or supporters with little regard to abilities or skills.

civil service system
A personnel system under which public employees are selected for government jobs through competitive examinations and the systematic evaluation of job performance.

Special Districts in Texas

4.4 Describe the functions and challenges of special-purpose districts in Texas.

Every day, Texans use the services of municipal utility districts (MUDs), water conservation and improvement districts (WCIDs), hospital districts, and a host of other local governments such as drainage districts, navigation districts, freshwater supply districts, river authorities, underground water districts, sanitation districts, housing authorities, and soil conservation districts, to name a few. **Special districts** or special-purpose districts have been deemed by some as the "invisible governments of the state," and practically every year additional units are created.[78] At last count, there were more than 3,350 of these special districts, including more than 1,000 independent school districts.[79]

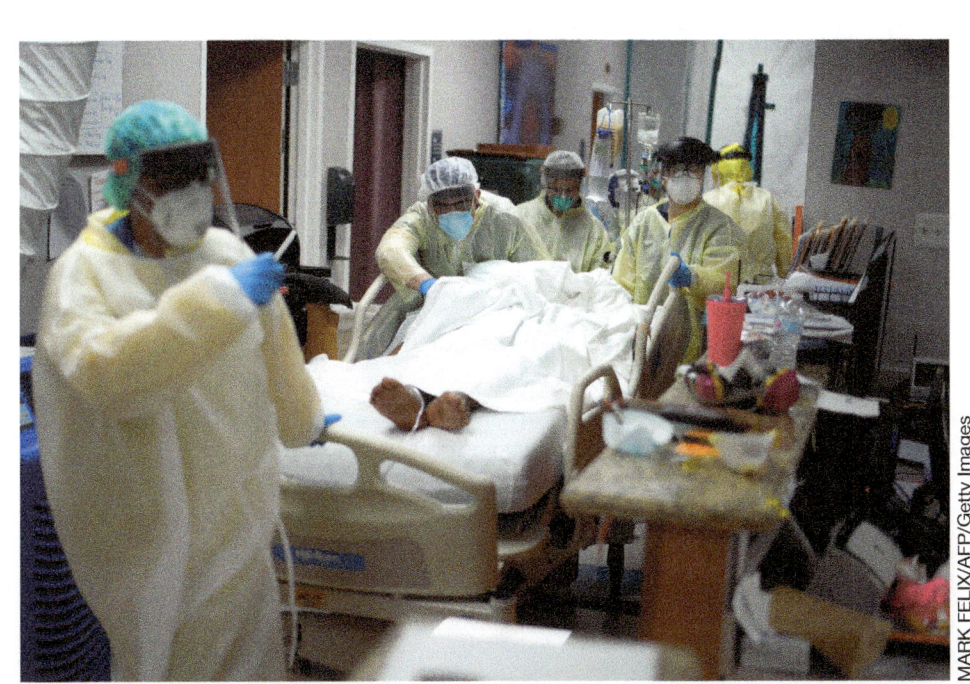

special district
A unit of local government created by the state to perform a specific function or functions not met by cities or counties, including the provision of public services to unincorporated areas.

ON THE FRONT LINE IN A HEALTH EMERGENCY

Health care workers tend to a COVID-19 patient in an emergency room in Houston as the pandemic threatened to overwhelm hospitals in Texas's most populous city during the summer of 2020.

4.4.1 Functions and Structures of Special Districts

Special districts are units of local government created by the state to perform specific functions. Wide variations in their functions, taxing and borrowing authority, governance, and performance limit generalizations about them. Most special districts are authorized to perform a single function and are designated single-purpose districts. Others, such as some municipal utility districts (MUDs), are multipurpose districts because the laws creating them permit them to provide more than one service to constituents. For example, in addition to providing water to people in their service areas, MUDs may assume responsibility for drainage, solid waste collection, firefighting, and parks and other recreational facilities.[80] Some districts, such as hospital districts, normally cover an entire county. Others, such as MUDs, cover part of one county; still others, such as river authorities, cover a number of counties.

A board, either appointed by other governmental units or elected in nonpartisan elections, governs a special district. County commissioners courts appoint the board members of hospital districts, and mayors or city councils appoint city housing authority boards. Many of these districts have taxing and borrowing authority, but others have no taxing powers and are supported by user fees or funds dedicated to them by other governmental agencies. Many special districts are eligible for federal grants-in-aid.

Special districts exist for a variety of reasons. Independent school districts were created, in part, to depoliticize education and remove the responsibility for it from county and city governments. Reformers in the late nineteenth and early twentieth centuries argued that the governance of schools had to be autonomous and insulated from partisan politics. That goal could be accomplished only by the creation of districts that had their own governing bodies and tax bases. Similar arguments have been made about other specialized governmental functions.[81]

In some cases, existing governments are unwilling or unable—because of state restrictions on their tax, debt, or jurisdictional authority—to provide essential services to developing communities. Counties are particularly limited by state law and the constitution and do not have the authority to provide many of the services now demanded by their citizens. Therefore, special districts were created to fill the gap. Because many districts can be created by statute, it has been far easier to create an additional layer of government than to change the authority or powers of existing governments by constitutional amendment.[82]

The cost of providing a particular governmental service is another reason for the growth of special districts. By creating a special district that includes a number of governmental units and a larger population and tax base, the costs can be spread over a wider area.

Individuals, groups, or corporations often promote special districts for personal economic gains. Builders, for example, sometimes develop plans for large tracts of land in the unincorporated areas of a county and then ask local governments or the legislature to create municipal utility or water districts to provide water and sewer services.[83]

It is not unusual to find that a small handful of people who purportedly live in an area have voted to incorporate a special district in a special election. With little public attention, a few influential people may have convinced the legislature to establish the election and give the new district extensive powers, including eminent domain, as well as the authority to levy taxes, borrow money, and issue bonds. In a November 2013 bond election, held at the same time as a statewide constitutional amendments election, the one registered voter of the North Oak Cliff Municipal Management District, a special district covering 400 acres, voted to authorize the sale of $97 million in bonds to finance infrastructure construction for a $700 million development in southwest Dallas.[84]

Some special districts have been designed to serve specific geographical areas. River basins that extend for thousands of square miles and cover ten or twenty counties present a particular problem. Because no existing governments had jurisdiction over the use of water resources in these basins, the legislature created river authorities with multicounty jurisdictions.[85]

4.4.2 Consequences of Special-Purpose Districts

From one perspective, special districts compensate for the fragmentation and limited authority of local governments that exist throughout Texas. But ironically, these districts also contribute to further fragmentation and delay the more difficult development of comprehensive, multipurpose governmental units that could more efficiently provide public services.

A special district has been called a "halfway house between cityhood and noncityhood, between incorporation and nonincorporation."[86] Residents of a developing community or subdivision may not want to create a new city or become part of a nearby existing city, but they need certain basic services, such as water, electricity, and fire protection, some of which can be provided through the creation of special districts.

Many special districts are small operations with limited financial resources and few employees. Salaries often are low, and some districts have difficulty retaining the licensed technical people required to perform daily operations. In some cases, record keeping and management operations are shoddy and amateurish, and the costs of providing services by many of these operations may actually be higher than the costs of similar services in larger governmental systems. Special districts also may use outside legal and professional assistance, which can be very costly, and many districts lack the expertise to maximize their investments or borrowing potential.[87]

Some special districts expand their functions beyond the original purpose for which they were created. The metropolitan transit authority in San Antonio, for example, authorized under state law to impose a 1 percent sales tax for public transportation, became involved in building the Alamodome, a multipurpose convention and sports facility. As governments expand their functions, the potential for intergovernmental rivalry, conflict, deadlock, and duplication of costs increases.

Except for the 1,000-plus independent school districts and a small number of other highly visible districts such as river authorities and hospital districts, most special districts operate in anonymity. The public has only limited knowledge of their jurisdiction, management, operations, and performance. Many taxpayers may not be aware that they pay taxes to some of these entities, nor do they have any concept of the districts' indebtedness. Their work gets little media coverage, few individuals attend their board meetings, and turnout for their elections is extremely low. In the case of the governing boards appointed by other governmental agencies, a small number of individuals or groups often dominate the appointment process and the activities of the special districts.

Independent School Districts

4.5 Describe the structure of independent school districts in Texas.

The recurring controversy over educational quality and equity in Texas has roots in the early organization and governance of the public schools. Education was an issue in the Texas independence movement, but the Reconstruction period set the stage for many of the long-term issues of school finance and governance. During Reconstruction, the Radical Republicans attempted to centralize the education system at the state level. With the end of Republican control prior to the Constitutional Convention of 1875, the centralized system was eliminated, and the control and financing of public education were transferred to the counties.

Instead of an orderly, comprehensive system that ensured public education to every child, community schools were created. They could be formed by any group of parents petitioning the county judge, who had considerable influence and control over the schools. County judges could appoint trustees nominated by the organizing parents and distribute money from the state's Available School Fund, earnings from mineral rights and other uses of state lands, to the organized schools within their respective counties. This produced marked differences in the availability, funding, and quality of public education across the state. Community schools also were self-selective. People who initiated the creation of a school could decide which children attended. As a result, racial and economic segregation occurred, and the children of Texans with limited political clout were denied access to an adequate public education. These characteristics dominated public education in Texas at the end of the nineteenth century, and vestiges remained until 1909.

The **independent school district**, currently the basic organizational structure for public education in Texas, had its origins in the Constitution of 1876. Cities and towns were allowed to create independent school districts and to impose a tax to support them. Initially, the city government served as the school board, but in 1879, a school district was permitted to organize independently of the city or town, elect its own board of trustees, and impose its own school tax. However, residents of rural areas, where most nineteenth-century Texans lived, were denied these powers and had only the option of forming community schools. So, in effect, Texas operated under a dual school system, with the majority of students subject to the discretionary and often arbitrary powers of county governments.

independent school district
A specific form of special district that administers the public schools in a designated area. It is governed by an elected board of trustees empowered to levy local property taxes, establish local school policies, and employ a school superintendent as its chief administrator.

4.5.1 Inequities in the Public Education System

From the very beginning, the inequities in such a school system were clear to many parents, elected officials, and educators, and early efforts were initiated to reform and modernize public schools. Most were linked to national education reform movements funded by northern philanthropists after the Civil War to promote public education in the South. George Peabody of Massachusetts created the Peabody Education Fund in 1867 and was followed by others, including John D. Rockefeller, who established the General Education Board. These organizations provided financial aid and technical support to leaders of state reform movements during the early part of the twentieth century.

Education reform efforts in Texas have been an ongoing saga. Early initiatives focused on the accessibility of schools to children in rural areas, compulsory school attendance, funding, recruitment of teachers, and teacher training. Schools were segregated, and school revenues were tied to local property taxes. Subsequent reforms were directed at the structure and governance of local school districts. The diverse and fragmented structure of Texas schools has been modified over the years through consolidation, greater uniformity in the organization of school districts, the extension of the independent school district to virtually every community in the state, and the expansion of the authority of the Texas Education Agency.

Texas now has more than 5 million children in public schools and a host of new issues, including bilingual and special education, graduation rates, student performance, and mandated testing for progress and accountability.

4.5.2 Differences among School Districts

Although regulation and coordination are provided on a statewide level through the State Board of Education (SBOE) and the Texas Education Agency (TEA), public education now is administered through 1,023 local independent school districts and

177 charter school districts, which served approximately 5.4 million students in the 2017–2018 school year. The largest, the Houston Independent School District, enrolled more than 210,000 students. In marked contrast, the Divide Independent School District in Kerr County enrolled 17 students.

The 20 largest districts—with more than 50,000 students each—enrolled approximately 1.6 million or 30 percent of the pre-kindergarten through grade 12 students in the state's public schools. By contrast, 391 primarily rural districts, serving fewer than 500 students each, enrolled 101,128 students. Students from minority ethnic or racial groups constituted approximately 72 percent of the public school enrollment in Texas in 2017–2018, and their numbers are projected to increase. Almost 60 percent of all students were economically disadvantaged.[88] As might be expected, school districts vary in financial resources, facilities, graduation rates, and other performance measures.

Revenue for public schools in Texas now exceeds $60 billion a year. The federal government provides about 10 percent, and the remainder is provided by the state and local school districts. In recent years, school districts have provided a greater share than the state, raising the money through local property taxes. In 2017, school district property taxes totaled $32.1 billion, or 59 percent of all property taxes collected in the state.[89]

School districts were expected to suffer significant budgetary losses in the economic recession brought on by the coronavirus pandemic of 2020. Those losses may be compounded by the new state law, enacted in 2019, to prohibit districts from increasing their property tax revenue by more than 2.5 percent a year. Property taxes are the only source of local revenue that school districts have.

Like other governments in Texas, school districts cannot borrow money for operating expenses. But they are permitted to borrow money for capital improvements and the purchase of equipment such as buses and technology. They do so by issuing tax-backed bonds that have to be approved by district voters. At the end of fiscal 2019, the total indebtedness for all school districts in Texas was approximately $88 billion, or almost 37 percent of all the debts of local governments.[90]

ONE OF THE SMALLEST SCHOOL DISTRICTS IN TEXAS

The Divide Independent School District is located west of the unincorporated community of Mountain Home some 40 miles from Kerrville. The district seldom enrolls more than a dozen or so students each year. Classes for students in the first to eighth grades are held in one room of a building constructed in 1936. The district's superintendent is also the principal and a teacher.

school board
The governing body of a public school district.

4.5.3 Local School Governance

School boards, ranging in size from three to nine members, govern school districts; most boards have seven members. Trustees are elected in nonpartisan elections for terms that vary from two to six years, with most serving three-year terms. By 2018, some 160 of the 1,000-plus independent school districts elected their boards from single-member districts.[91] School districts with significant minority populations have shifted from at-large elections to single-member districting, primarily as a consequence of lawsuits or the threats of lawsuits by minority plaintiffs under the Voting Rights Act.

Many school board elections are held on the first Saturday in May, the same day most cities hold their elections. In recent years, though, some school districts as well as cities have begun holding their elections in November, although on separate ballots from partisan races for federal, state, and county offices. School board election turnouts are low, usually less than 10 percent of registered voters. But turnout increases when there are highly visible issues, such as the firing of a superintendent or an unpopular increase in taxes.

Recruiting qualified candidates for school boards often is difficult, and many elections are uncontested. The superintendent, other members of the board, or key community leaders often ask individuals to run. People frequently have little knowledge of what school board members do, and because many trustees serve for only one term, some boards have high turnover rates. Moreover, a potential trustee cannot anticipate the amount of time it will take for briefings by the superintendent and staff, preparing for and participating in board meetings, and taking phone calls from parents and taxpayers. A board member also must deal with the political aspect of the job, including attendance at community functions and major school programs and meetings with teachers and taxpayer groups. Board members are unpaid but are reimbursed for travel related to board business.

school superintendent
Chief administrator of a school district who is hired by the school board.

The most important decision that a school board makes is the hiring of a **school superintendent**. In organization and management structure, the school district is similar to the council–manager form of government used by many cities. The board hires a superintendent, who is in charge of the district's day-to-day operations. Although the board has the primary policymaking responsibility for a district, boards often defer to the superintendent and the superintendent's staff, who have the expertise to interpret technical information and can control its flow to the board.

School trustees and superintendents tend to talk about "keeping politics out of education," and superintendents often attempt to convey the impression that they serve simply to carry out the will of their boards. In most instances, however, the superintendent establishes a school board's agenda, and the board members depend on the superintendent and other professional staff members for information and policy recommendations. Very few board members have much time to give to the district, and most have only limited knowledge of the many laws affecting education. State law, in fact, restricts the intrusion of board members into the daily management and administration of a district. An excessively politicized school board that becomes involved in day-to-day administration can be called to task by the Texas Education Agency. In an extreme case, the TEA can even take over the management of a school district. (Recent educational policies and issues will be discussed in Chapter 14.)

Solutions to the Problems of Local Government

4.6 Assess proposed solutions to the problems of local government in Texas.

Finding solutions to their various challenges and problems is a never-ending task for many local governments, and what works for one city or county may not work for another. What follows are some solutions that governments have tried, with varying degrees of success.

4.6.1 Privatization of Functions

As local governments have juggled their financial problems with increased demands for public services, they have resorted to contracting out some services to private companies. Many governments believe **privatization** can reduce costs through businesslike efficiency, and they consider it an attractive alternative in the face of voter hostility toward higher taxes. Cities, for example, contract for garbage pickup, waste disposal, towing, food services, security, and a variety of other services. Privatization also provides a way for local governments that have reached their limit on bonded indebtedness to make new capital improvements by leasing a facility from a private contractor. A civic center or a school facility can be constructed by a private contractor and leased back to the government for an extended period.

privatization
Government contracting with private companies to provide some public services.

4.6.2 Annexation and Extraterritorial Jurisdiction

Population growth in the areas surrounding most large Texas cities has forced municipalities and counties to wrestle with urban sprawl. El Paso, for example, included 26 square miles in 1950 but had expanded to 255 square miles by 2010. Houston grew from 160 square miles in 1950 to 600 square miles in 2010, with its extraterritorial jurisdiction encompassing more than 1,300 square miles, excluding the other cities that lie within this area.[92]

The ability of cities to expand their boundaries beyond suburban development derives from their **annexation** powers and their **extraterritorial jurisdiction** over neighboring areas. Faced with the prospect that areas surrounding them will eventually be annexed, cities do not want to be saddled with new communities when there has been limited or no planning and substandard buildings, roads, and infrastructure. With the Municipal Annexation Act of 1963, the legislature granted cities considerable discretionary authority over nearby unincorporated areas. Specific annexation powers and extraterritorial jurisdiction vary with the size of a city and the charter under which it functions. Generally, cities have extraterritorial jurisdiction over unincorporated areas within one-half mile to five miles of the city limits, making development in those areas subject to the city's building codes, zoning and land-use restrictions, utility easement requirements, and road and street specifications. This authority restricts the use of unincorporated land and requires those building outside the city to build according to at least minimal standards. Later, when those areas are annexed by the city, they are less likely to quickly degenerate into suburban slums that will require a high infusion of city dollars for basic services.

annexation
The authority of cities to add territory, subject to restrictions set by state law.

extraterritorial jurisdiction
The power of an incorporated city to control development within nearby unincorporated areas.

Residents and businesses outside of a city's corporate limits also benefit from access to public and private facilities and services in the city. City residents argue that those living or doing business outside the city should "share the tax burden associated with constructing and maintaining those facilities and services."[93]

Cities can annex areas equivalent to 10 percent of their existing territory in a given year, and if this authority is not exercised in one year, it can be carried over to subsequent years. Except for large cities affected by a 2017 law, annexation usually does not require a vote of those people who are to be incorporated into the city. However, within two and a half years, a city is required to provide annexed areas with services comparable to those provided in its older neighborhoods. Otherwise, individuals living in these newly annexed areas can exercise an option to be de-annexed, a situation that rarely occurs.

Cities even have annexed thin strips of land, miles from urban development, along major roads and arteries leading into them. Because a city's extraterritorial jurisdiction extends as far as five miles on either side of the strip that is annexed, this practice enables a city to control future development over a large area. In San Antonio, these annexation policies often have been referred to as "spoke annexation," and it has taken more than thirty years for much of the territory brought under the city's jurisdiction to be developed and annexed by the city.[94]

The aggressive use of annexation has permitted many large cities in Texas to expand geographically with population growth. Texas cities have been able to share in the benefits of growth in the areas surrounding them and limit the development of small suburban towns that would potentially halt future expansion.[95]

For more than thirty years after passing the Municipal Annexation Act, the state legislature did little to restrict the annexation powers of cities. However, since the late 1990s, many lawmakers have demonstrated, along with their constituents, an anticity sentiment with proposals that would have eroded municipal authority, reduced municipal revenues, and imposed costly new mandates. Of particular concern to cities were attacks on annexation powers. The Seventy-Fifth Legislature in 1999 enacted a major overhaul of annexation authority, including a provision that requires cities to outline their annexation plans three years in advance. But city officials believed that they were able to obtain, through their lobbying efforts, a relatively "well-balanced" law.[96] The legislature in 2001 continued to reflect growing suburban-rural hostility toward the central cities. It enacted a law that modified the extraterritorial jurisdiction of cities by requiring city–county agreements on the regulation of subdivisions. In effect, this law placed more limits on the powers of Texas cities.[97]

A major change in the annexation powers of some large Texas cities was enacted in a special session of the 2017 legislature. This law now requires annexations by these cities to be approved by landowners or voters in the affected areas. Proponents of these changes argued that it was the "democratic" thing to do to provide citizens with a voice on whether they wished to be incorporated into a city. But city advocates argued that people living in the areas near cities benefited from the use of city roads, attractions, and other economic improvements but did not have to pay for them if they weren't annexed.[98]

4.6.3 Modernization of County Government

City governments provide most basic public services in urban areas, and as cities expand to county boundaries and beyond, overlapping jurisdictions of county and city governments increase along with a reduction of county services in the annexed areas. Counties, nevertheless, still play an important role in Texas. Rural Texans, in particular, continue to rely on counties to provide a number of services, and demands on counties will increase. Recommendations to modernize county government include another attempt at county home rule; granting counties some legislative or ordinance-making authority; modernizing county information and communications systems; and creating an office of county administrator, appointed by a commissioners court, to run the departments now assigned to commissioners. Another recommendation is to extend the civil service system to smaller counties and to all county employees.[99]

4.6.4 Economic Development

Historically, cities have collaborated with the private sector to stimulate local economies. Private sector initiatives have come from chambers of commerce or economic development foundations, corporations, other groups, or individuals, and city governments have participated. Cities also are using a variety of new financing techniques to assist in economic development, including development impact taxes and fees, user charges, creation of special district assessments, tax increment financing, and privatization of governmental functions.[100] A state law, enacted in 1989, permits cities, with the approval of local voters, to impose a 0.5 percent sales tax for local economic development.[101] Voters in several hundred cities have approved this tax option.

Texas cities, as well as some counties, aggressively court American and foreign companies to relocate to or develop new plants or operations in their communities. Cities and local chambers of commerce sponsor public relations campaigns touting local benefits and attractions. Local governments offer **tax abatements**—exemptions from property taxes on a business for a specified period—to encourage a company to locate or expand in particular Texas cities. Other financial incentives to companies being courted include lowered utility bills and assistance in obtaining housing for employees. Many cities have established relationships with "sister cities" in foreign countries, and state government has assisted cities by establishing trade and commerce offices in a few key foreign cities. The city of San Antonio aggressively wooed Toyota to locate a new manufacturing plant in South Texas, and the coordinated efforts of the city, the state, and the private sector resulted in a decision in 2003 to bring the new plant to the city. State and local officials predicted the facility would be a major economic generator and help transform the city's economy. Toyota invested more than $2 billion in the facility, which now employs more than 2,200 workers and produces full-size and compact pickup trucks.

tax abatement
A device used by governments to attract new businesses through the reduction or elimination of property taxes for a specific period of time.

The legislature permits counties to form industrial development corporations or enterprise zones and to relax state regulatory policies to encourage the redevelopment of depressed areas. Portions of a county may be designated as reinvestment zones, in which tax abatements can be offered to attract new businesses. Counties also can create county boards of development, civic centers, foreign trade zones, and research and development authorities.[102]

A wide range of federal programs for local economic development also are available. Most depend on local initiatives in the planning and application processes and require a political commitment by elected officials and a demonstrated rationale for the receipt of federal dollars.

4.6.5 Interlocal Contracting

Because many small governments have limited tax bases and staffs, they enter into contracts with larger governments for various public services. In 1971, the legislature, following a constitutional amendment, enacted the Interlocal Cooperation Act, which gave cities, counties, and other political subdivisions rather broad authority for such contracts.[103] The law has been amended several times to expand the scope of these agreements, and local governments now contract with one another for services in at least twenty-five functional areas, ranging from aviation to water and wastewater management.[104] Contracting is not an alternative to consolidation of local governments, but it does hold some promise for improving the quality of local services and reducing their costs.

4.6.6 Metro Government and Consolidation

In the metropolitan areas of the state's ten largest counties, more than 1,100 cities, school districts, and special districts provide public services. Harris County (Houston) alone has 503 separate governmental units (see Table 4–4). Legislators, scholars, and reform groups have studied the duplication and other problems produced by such proliferation and fragmentation and have made numerous recommendations over the years. Various proposals have been designed to eliminate duplication and overlap, including city–county consolidation and various forms of **metro government**. However, efforts in the late 1990s by counties to obtain constitutional authority to propose city–county consolidation to voters in the counties failed. Without such authority, city–county collaboration is more likely to take the form of increased intergovernmental contracting and the informal cooperation that local governments develop out of necessity and mutual self-interest.[105]

metro government
Consolidation of city and county governments to avoid duplication of public services. This approach has been tried in several other parts of the country but so far has attracted little interest in Texas.

TABLE 4-4 LOCAL GOVERNMENTS IN THE TEN LARGEST AND TEN SMALLEST TEXAS COUNTIES, 2018

	Population (2018)	Total Governments	County Governments	Municipal Governments	School Districts	Special Districts
State	**28,995,881**	**5,343**	**254**	**1,218**	**1,073**	**2,798**
Ten Largest Texas Counties						
Harris	4,713,325	534	1	28	23	482
Dallas	2,635,516	60	1	25	15	19
Tarrant	2,102,515	69	1	34	17	17
Bexar	2,003,554	66	1	24	16	25
Travis	1,273,954	122	1	18	8	95
Collin	1,034,730	59	1	23	15	20
Denton	887,207	101	1	33	11	56
Hidalgo	868,707	81	1	22	16	42
El Paso	839,238	42	1	7	10	24
Fort Bend	811,688	199	1	17	4	177
Ten Smallest Texas Counties						
Motley	1,200	7	1	2	1	3
Foard	1,155	7	1	1	1	4
Roberts	854	5	1	1	1	2
Terrell	776	4	1		1	2
Kent	762	4	1	1	1	1
McMullen	743	6	1		1	4
Borden	654	2	1		1	
Kenedy	404	4	1		1	2
King	272	3	1		1	1
Loving	169	2	1			1

SOURCE: U.S. Census Bureau, *Census of Governments, 2017, Government Organization*; U.S. Census Bureau, *2018 American Community Survey*.

4.6.7 Public Improvement Districts

public improvement district (PID)
Specific area of a city in which property owners pay special taxes in return for improvements to streets and other public facilities in their neighborhood.

Under one state law, property owners in a specific area of a city or its extraterritorial jurisdiction can petition the city to create a special **public improvement district (PID)**. These districts can undertake a wide range of improvements—landscaping, lighting, signs, sidewalks, streets, pedestrian malls, libraries, parking, water, wastewater, and drainage facilities. Public improvement districts do not have the same autonomy as other special districts. They are created solely through the discretionary powers of the city and are funded by assessments on property within their boundaries.[106] Although their budgets and assessments must be approved by the city, they can be operated and managed by private management companies or by the citizens themselves. Fort Worth created a public improvement district for its downtown area in 1986 and now has ten additional functioning districts.[107] Other cities, including Dallas, Houston, and San Antonio, also have created PIDs.

CONCLUSION

After learning about the different structures of local governments and some of the issues and restraints they face, do you think these governments can be responsive to the concerns of everyday citizens like you? Sometimes, yes, and sometimes, no, you may say. It may depend on the issue, the governmental body involved, and the individuals holding elected offices in your community. As we pointed out in this

MANUAL RECORD KEEPING

For much of the state's history, local governments relied on personnel to hand enter records in large ledgers. The process was tedious, indexing information was often complex, and loss of files through fires, floods, or oversight was always a problem. Here, a stenographer in the county clerk's office in San Augustine County is manually transcribing records from a ledger.

chapter, Texas cities, counties, and other local governments have many differences—of function, size, geography, and the demographic and political characteristics of their residents. The San Antonio City Council may consider it very important to regulate payday lenders because hundreds of its citizens are in a never-ending cycle of growing debt. But the governing body of a city in another part of the state may have its hands full with a different local problem of its own. All local governments, nevertheless, share some common characteristics and concerns. They all operate under the Texas Constitution and state laws. They all, to one extent or another, have to provide services ordered but not always fully funded by the state. And they all are an important part of Texas's system of governance. Consequently, you can't fully learn how to find your way through Texas's political structure without understanding the basic differences and similarities among the local units of government and how they operate.

REVIEW THE CHAPTER

Urban Texas

4.1 Trace the transition of Texas from an agrarian to an urban state, p. 100.

From Texas's formative period, local governments, which are created by and subordinate to the state, have played a central role in the state's development. What was once an overwhelmingly rural state has been transformed into a highly urban one with about 90 percent of the population living in urban areas. Of the ten largest cities in the nation, three—Houston, San Antonio, and Dallas—are located in Texas. Nine of the state's ten largest cities have more than 50 percent minority populations, contributing to a long-standing controversy over urban electoral systems.

The Legal and Constitutional Framework for Texas Cities

4.2 Compare and contrast the governments of Texas cities, p. 103.

Texans use four forms of city government—the strong mayor–council, the weak mayor–council, the city commission, and the council–manager. For cities with populations of fewer than 5,000, the state limits the forms of government that can be used. But for cities with more than 5,000 residents, the legislature permits home rule, which allows a city to choose the form of government it wishes, provided that it does not conflict with the state constitution or state law. The form of government a city chooses reflects complex political dynamics; as social, economic, and political environments change, cities often change their form of government. At one point in the state's history, for example, the city commission was perceived to be the ideal form of effective government. It was subsequently replaced as a reform system by the council-manager.

A notable feature of city politics in Texas is the widespread use of nonpartisan, at-large elections. In homogeneous communities, these election systems appear to work quite well. In communities with highly diverse racial, economic, and social groups—in which voting is polarized—at-large elections adversely affect key segments of the population. Prompted by legal attacks on at-large elections under the Voting Rights Act, many cities, as well as special-purpose districts, have adopted single-member districts, thus increasing minority representation on local governing bodies.

Cities receive no state appropriations, have limited financial options, and are disproportionately dependent on regressive taxes, fees, or transfers of funds from locally owned utilities, if they have them.

County Government in Texas

4.3 Describe the structure of county government in Texas, p. 117.

County governments, initially created to serve a rural population, function primarily as the administrative subdivisions of the state. In urban counties, significant populations now reside outside the boundaries of any municipalities. In effect, urban counties are called on to provide more and more services, but still function with the structure and authority prescribed by the constitution more than 140 years ago. Much like state government, county government is highly fragmented, with administrative powers shared by a variety of elected officials: the county judge, the four commissioners, the district and county clerks, the tax assessor-collector, the sheriff, and constables. Although budgetary and policy factors often prompt cooperation among these officials, the fragmentation also creates the potential for personal or partisan conflicts over policy.

Special Districts in Texas

4.4 Describe the functions and challenges of special-purpose districts in Texas, p. 123.

Thousands of special-purpose districts have been created across the state to provide public services that county and city governments cannot or do not provide, and this number increases every year. Some were created to serve a geographical area extending over many counties or to provide a single public service at a reduced cost. The services and facilities they provide include water service, solid waste management, firefighting, parks, public housing, and recreational facilities. Some districts cover multiple counties; others, a single county; and still others, a very small part of a county. Special districts have their own governing bodies, which can be elected or appointed. These special districts have added to the fragmentation of governments. Most people know little about them or their taxing authority, and few people participate in their board elections. Most of the funding for infrastructure development in special districts is derived from bonds that are linked ultimately to property taxes. These property taxes will eventually be paid by those who locate in the areas served by the special district.

Independent School Districts

4.5 Describe the structure of independent school districts in Texas, p. 125.

In addition to 177 charter school districts reported by the Texas Education Agency in its 2017-2018 report, Texas had 1,023 independent school districts, ranging in size from the largest, the Houston Independent School District, with more than 200,000 students, to rural districts with only a few dozen students each. School boards elected in nonpartisan elections govern all districts. The board hires a superintendent to perform the daily administration of the district.

Students from minority racial and ethnic groups now account for 72 percent of the public school enrollment in Texas, and about 60 percent of all students are economically disadvantaged. School districts are funded by a combination of state revenue and local property taxes with a small percentage of federal funding.

Solutions to the Problems of Local Government

4.6 Assess proposed solutions to the problems of local government in Texas, p. 128.

Increased population, urban sprawl, white flight, an increase in low-income residents, mandated programs from the state and federal governments, limited revenue options, and inadequate and declining infrastructure are among the problems confronting local governments in Texas. Local governments use a variety of strategies to deal with their problems. Cities have used their annexation powers and extraterritorial jurisdiction to expand their tax bases and exercise limited control over development in adjacent areas. Cities also use public improvement districts to permit targeted areas to impose additional taxes for needed services. Both counties and cities privatize some governmental functions to decrease costs and increase efficiency. Interlocal contracting permits governments to provide services to one another on a contractual basis, and many counties and cities engage in aggressive economic development programs. Some people advocate consolidation of local governments, but support is limited for this alternative in Texas.

LEARN THE TERMS

population density, p. 101
Dillon rule, p. 104
general law city, p. 104
home rule city, p. 104
city charter, p. 104
weak mayor, p. 105
strong mayor, p. 105
city commission, p. 106
council–manager government, p. 107
nonpartisan election, p. 111
at-large election, p. 111
runoff election, p. 111
single-member district, p. 111
regressive tax, p. 112

rollback election, p. 113
general obligation bond, p. 113
revenue bond, p. 114
homestead exemption, p. 114
mandate, p. 116
commissioners court, p. 117
county judge, p. 117
county clerk, p. 120
county attorney, p. 121
district attorney, p. 121
county tax assessor–collector, p. 121
appraisal district, p. 121
sheriff, p. 121
constable, p. 121

county auditor, p. 122
county treasurer, p. 122
spoils system, p. 123
civil service system, p. 123
special district, p. 123
independent school district, p. 126
school board, p. 128
school superintendent, p. 128
privatization, p. 129
annexation, p. 129
extraterritorial jurisdiction, p. 129
tax abatement, p. 131
metro government, p. 131
public improvement district (PID), p. 132

The Texas Legislature

5

THE VIEW FROM THE GALLERY
Lobbyists and visitors in the third-floor gallery in the west wing of the state Capitol watch the Texas House of Representatives at work during a recent legislative session.

Eric Gay/Associated Press

LEARNING OBJECTIVES

5.1 List five functions of the Texas legislature, p. 137.

5.2 Explain the organizational structure of the Texas legislature and the characteristics of its members, p. 139.

5.3 Explain redistricting and its impact on the composition of the Texas legislature, p. 144.

5.4 Contrast the leadership and committee structure of the Texas House with that of the Texas Senate, p. 149.

5.5 Outline how a bill becomes a law and the obstacles in the lawmaking process in Texas, p. 160.

5.6 Outline the changes in partisanship in the Texas legislature, p. 166.

5.7 Assess the influences on the decision making of Texas lawmakers, p. 168.

Preparing for the 2021 legislative session, members of the Texas House of Representatives faced the task of selecting a new speaker to help lead the state's recovery from the most challenging crisis of their lifetimes, the societal and economic trauma spawned by the coronavirus pandemic, which had struck in 2020. Even an emergency of this magnitude, though, didn't remove the partisan fighting over legislative seats. Going into the 2020 elections, when all 150 House seats were on the ballot, Republicans held an 83-67 partsian edge. Democrats made a strong effort to recapture a House majority they had not held in almost twenty years and elect a Democrat as the new House leader, but they failed to make a dent in the

Republican majority. The day after the November election, Representative Dade Phelan, a Republican from Beaumont, announced that he had secured pledges of support from enough House members, including some Democrats, to be elected speaker when the new session convened in January. He would succeed Republican Dennis Bonnen of Angleton, whose speakership and political career had ended in scandal.

Bonnen was the first speaker of either party in more than forty years to not preside over multiple legislative sessions, even though he had enjoyed a largely successful session as the House's presiding officer in 2019, including the enactment of a major bipartisan funding bill for public education. Bonnen's troubles began a few weeks after the session ended, when he and Representative Dustin Burrows of Lubbock, chair of the House Republican Caucus, met privately at the state Capitol with Michael Quinn Sullivan, a hardline conservative activist who was unhappy that the legislature hadn't enacted a number of conservative priorities. Sullivan was president and CEO of Empower Texans, a group that has made large financial contributions to help right-wing Republican candidates win election to the legislature. Soon after the meeting, Sullivan alleged that Bonnen and Burrows had given him a list of ten incumbent House members and suggested that Empower Texans target them for defeat in the 2020 Republican primary. Sullivan said Bonnen also indicated that in return Empower Texans, although not a traditional media organization, would be given media access to the House chamber during the next session. Sullivan also accused Bonnen of making ugly personal remarks about some Democratic legislators.

Bonnen initially denied the allegations. But Sullivan had secretly recorded their meeting, and a few months later he released the recording, which largely confirmed his accusations. Most Republican House members then made it clear to the speaker that he needed to step down, and Bonnen announced he would not seek reelection to the House, ending a legislative career that had begun more than twenty years before with Bonnen's first election to the legislature. Burrows remained in the House but resigned as Republican Caucus chair.

The legislature is the state's main policymaking body, and elections for the legislature, as well as elections for its leadership positions, are crucial to determining what policies are adopted and what policies are rejected. Although the House speaker is elected by members of the House, the Senate's presiding office, the lieutenant governor, is elected by voters statewide. Unfortunately, many Texans, particularly in urban areas, don't even know who their state senators and state representatives are and don't know much about the presiding officers. If you want to have an impact on public policy, or at least understand why some policies and laws are enacted and others aren't, you first must learn about the legislature: how it is structured, how it operates, and who represents you. Then you will know something about navigating the policymaking process should you have an issue of your own that you want your state senator or state representative to address.

In this chapter, you not only will learn about the Texas legislature and the historical origins of its structure and operations, you also will learn something about how it has changed politically, demographically, and institutionally over the years and how it compares to legislatures in other states in terms of size, membership, and frequency of sessions.

Legislative Functions

5.1 List five functions of the Texas legislature.

Although lawmakers still have to operate under some outdated constitutional restrictions, including strict limits on when they can meet, which were written for a rural state in a bygone era, the Texas legislature has undergone significant changes over the past 140 years. Some changes have resulted from external factors, such as the transformation of Texas into an urban state, the development of a two-party system, changes in the interest group system, changes in the racial and ethnic characteristics of the population, and

institutionalization

The complex process of institutional change and adaptation in the organization and operations of the legislature.

changes in the Texas economy. Other changes have been internal, including increases in the number of years many legislators remain in office, changing career and leadership patterns, expanded workload, the development and enforcement of complex rules and procedures, the evolution of professional staffs, and the emergence of partisan divisions. Political scientists describe these developments as **institutionalization**.[1]

Institutionalization varies throughout the fifty states. Some state legislatures are highly professional, whereas others are not.[2] In some states, salaries are high, turnover is limited, and legislators think in terms of legislative careers. Similarly, some legislatures have developed sophisticated staff and support services. In other legislatures, members are poorly paid, turnover is high, legislative service is regarded as part time, and support services are limited. The Texas legislature falls somewhere between those legislatures that can be classified as highly professional and those that can be classified as amateurish or citizen–lawmaker bodies (see Figure 5–1). The institutionalization process has produced a more professional legislature in Texas, although it remains a part-time institution.

The Texas legislature, whose members are elected from districts throughout Texas, is the chief policymaking branch of state government. Its basic role is similar to that of the U.S. Congress at the federal level, although there are major differences between the two institutions. The Texas legislature performs a variety of functions, but its primary task is to decide how conflicts between competing groups and interests are to be resolved through the lawmaking process. Although often taken for granted, this orderly, institutionalized process of conflict management and resolution is critical to a stable political system.[3]

FIGURE 5-1 PROFESSIONALISM IN THE LEGISLATURE

State lawmaking bodies around the country have significant differences in salaries, lengths of sessions, and how often they meet.

SOURCE: National Conference of State Legislatures, "Full- and Part-Time Legislatures," June 14, 2017, at http://www.ncsl.org/research/about-state-legislatures/full-and-part-time-legislatures.aspx; and National Conference of State Legislatures, "The Term-Limited States," March 13, 2015, at http://www.ncsl.org/research/about-state-legislatures/chart-of-term-limits-states.aspx.

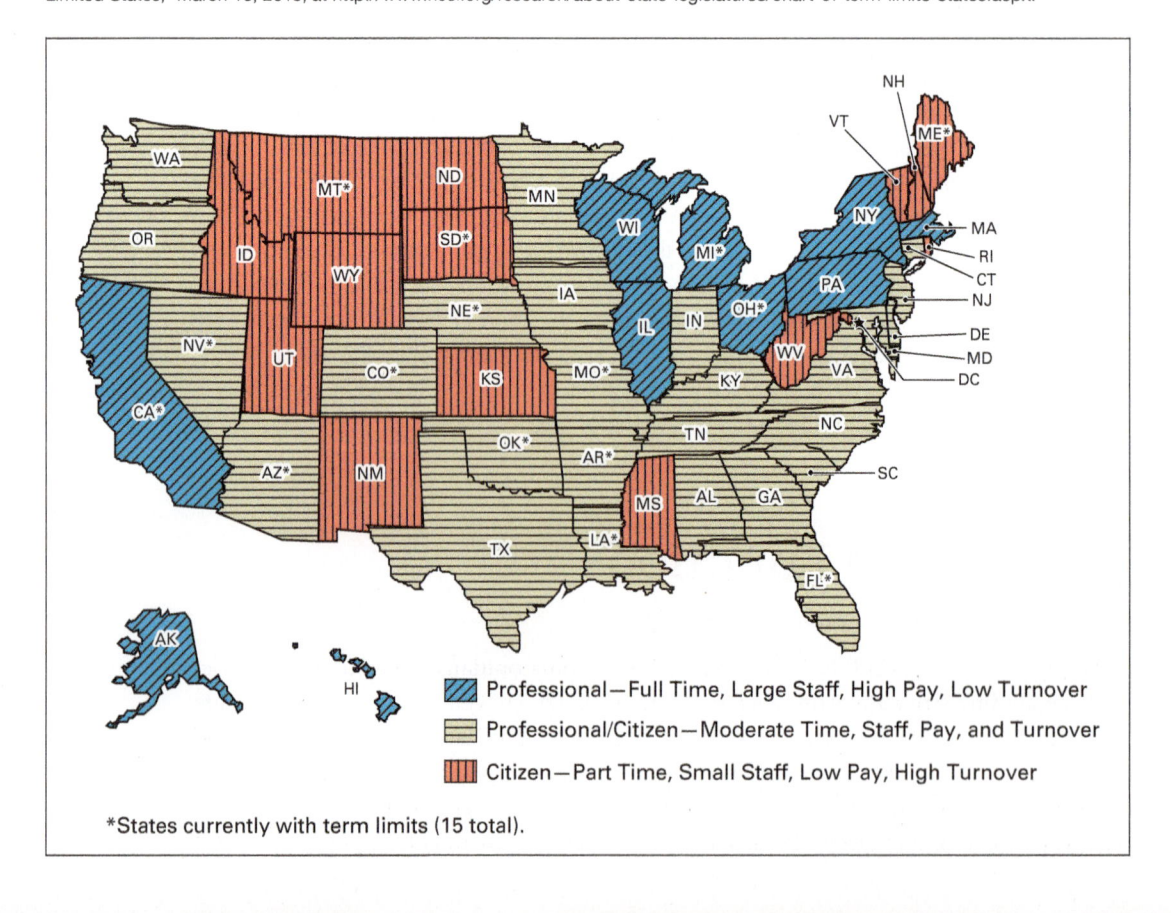

- Professional—Full Time, Large Staff, High Pay, Low Turnover
- Professional/Citizen—Moderate Time, Staff, Pay, and Turnover
- Citizen—Part Time, Small Staff, Low Pay, High Turnover

*States currently with term limits (15 total).

5.1.1 Enacting Laws

Every two years, the legislature enacts several hundred laws governing Texans' behavior; allocating resources, benefits, and costs; and defining the duties of those institutions and bureaucrats responsible for putting these laws into effect. From local legislation affecting one city or county to general statewide policies and proposals for constitutional amendments, thousands of ideas are proposed for new laws every legislative session. The legislative arena includes a wide range of players in addition to legislators, and lawmaking requires compromise and accommodation of competing ideas and interests.

5.1.2 Budgeting and Taxes

The legislature establishes programs providing a variety of public services and sets priorities through the budgetary process. It sets the budgets for the governor, the bureaucracy, and the state courts. It decides whether state taxes should be increased or reduced and, if so, by how much and how the tax burden should be distributed. Its actions affect local tax rates as well.

5.1.3 Overseeing State Agencies

The legislature assigns specific state agencies and local governments the responsibility for carrying out hundreds of new laws enacted each session. It is ultimately the legislature's responsibility to make sure agencies are doing what they are charged with by law, and this review, or "oversight," process is achieved through legislative budget hearings, other committee investigations, and program audits. The Senate further influences policy by confirming or rejecting the governor's appointees to hundreds of state boards and commissions that administer public programs.

5.1.4 Educating the Public

The 181 members of the Texas legislature represent a variety of political viewpoints. But individual lawmakers try to inform the public about their own actions and the collective actions of the lawmaking body. They use speeches, letters to constituents, news releases, newsletters, websites, emails, social media, and other techniques to explain the legislative process and substantive policy issues.

5.1.5 Representing the Public

The legislature is a representative body whose members are chosen in free elections. This process provides legitimacy to legislative actions and decisions. People may disagree over how "representative" the legislature is in terms of race, ethnicity, gender, or class, and many Texans may be indifferent toward or ignorant about public policy. But successful lawmakers must demonstrate concern for the attitudes and demands of their constituents. Legislators use many methods to learn what their constituents think, including public opinion polls, questionnaires, phone calls, town hall meetings, and personal visits.

Organization of the Texas Legislature and Characteristics of Members

5.2 Explain the organizational structure of the Texas legislature and the characteristics of its members.

Following the aggressive efforts of Governor Edmund J. Davis and the Radical Reconstructionists to centralize power and authority in Texas after the Civil War, the rural delegates who dominated the Constitutional Convention in 1875 were distrustful, even fearful, of the excesses and abuses of big government. They created a part-time,

bicameral legislature
A lawmaking body, such as the Texas legislature, that includes two chambers.

bicameral legislature that included a 31-member Senate and a 150-member House of Representatives. All other states have bicameral legislatures, except Nebraska, which has a unicameral system with only one lawmaking body of 49 members. The sizes of other state Senates range from 20 in Alaska to 67 in Minnesota. Houses of representatives vary in size from 40 in Alaska to 400 in New Hampshire.[4] There also are major differences in legislative salaries, lengths of sessions, and other characteristics of legislatures among the states.

5.2.1 Legislative Sessions

regular legislative session
The 140-day period in odd-numbered years in which the legislature meets and can consider laws on any issue or subject.

special session
A legislative session called by the governor at any time other than the regular legislative session. Special sessions are limited to thirty days and can consider only subjects or issues designated by the governor.

To curb lawmakers' power, the Texas constitutional framers limited the **regular legislative session** to a maximum of 140 days every two years but gave the governor the authority to call special sessions when necessary. Lawmakers convene in regular session on the second Tuesday of January in odd-numbered years and can consider any issue they wish during that period. **Special sessions** are limited to thirty days each and to subjects submitted by the governor, who can call an unlimited number of special sessions.

There have been periods of frequent special sessions. The seventy-eighth legislature had three special sessions in the summer and early fall of 2003 in a protracted, partisan fight over the drawing of congressional districts. Governor Rick Perry called one special session in the spring of 2004 and two more in the summer of 2005 to try to lower school property taxes and change the educational funding system, but all three were unsuccessful. The legislature finally met those goals in still another special session in the spring of 2006, but only after the Texas Supreme Court had declared the school finance system unconstitutional and given lawmakers a deadline. Governor Perry called three special sessions in the summer of 2013 to deal with redistricting and transportation funding and to win enactment of a law restricting abortions, a priority of the governor and the Republican legislative majority.

Some state officials and government experts believe the Texas legislature should have annual regular sessions, at least for budgetary purposes. As of 2020, Texas was one of only four states whose legislatures didn't meet every year. The others were Montana, Nevada, and North Dakota.[5] Annual sessions in Texas would require an amendment to the state constitution.

THE TEXAS STATE CAPITOL
Completed in 1888 and now surrounded by state office buildings, this historic building is a prominent landmark in downtown Austin. The part-time, bicameral legislature meets here in odd-numbered years.

5.2.2 Terms of Office and Qualifications

Article 3 of the Texas Constitution establishes the structure, membership, and selection of the Texas legislature. Representatives serve two-year terms; senators are elected to four-year, staggered terms. That means sixteen senators are up for election in one election cycle, and the other fifteen senators run for election two years later in the next election cycle. A senator has to be a qualified voter, at least 26 years old, a resident of Texas for five years preceding his or her election, and a resident of the district from which elected for at least one year. A representative must be a qualified voter, at least 21 years old, a Texas resident for two years, and a resident of the district represented for one year.[6] There is no limit on the number of terms an individual can serve in the legislature.

5.2.3 Pay and Compensation

Members of both the House and the Senate and their presiding officers have a base pay of $7,200 per year. This figure is set by the state constitution and can be raised only with voter approval. This is one of the lowest legislative pay levels in the country and was last increased in 1975 by a constitutional amendment that also set lawmakers' per diem, or allowance for rent and other personal living expenses, at $30 a day while the legislature was in session.

The last time the legislature tried to win a pay increase was in 1989, when it proposed a constitutional amendment to increase legislative salaries to more than $20,000 a year. Voters rejected the proposal by a two-to-one margin. In 1991, Texas voters approved a constitutional amendment creating a state Ethics Commission that could recommend legislative pay raises to the voters and change per diem on its own. The commission has never recommended a legislative pay raise, but it periodically adjusts the session per diem for lawmakers. The commission set per diem at $221 per day for the 2019 legislative session. That amounted to almost $31,000 for the 140-day session, an expense allowance that was more than four times larger than legislators' annual pay.

By 2011, only Alabama, Texas, New Hampshire, and Rhode Island had limits on legislative pay that could be changed only by constitutional amendment. Compensation commissions now recommend legislative pay levels in some states, and legislatures in other states set their own salaries, often with the approval of the voters. In 2019, legislative pay ranged from a high of $110,549 in California, where lawmakers set their own salaries and are considered members of a full-time legislature, to a low of $100 a year in New Hampshire, which has annual sessions but a constitutional limit on salaries.[7]

Advocates of higher legislative pay in Texas say raising the salary is necessary because legislative service has become much more than a part-time job for many lawmakers, particularly during periods of frequent special sessions. They argue that the present low compensation level restricts legislative service to wealthy individuals, retirees, or people who have law practices or own businesses in which partners or employees can help take up the slack while they are in Austin. They believe higher pay would broaden the potential pool from which legislators are drawn—and make the legislature more representative of the public—by encouraging more salaried working people to run for legislative office. A wider pool of candidates also could broaden the perspectives from which policy issues are viewed and addressed.

The outside personal income of many legislators obviously does suffer while the legislators are in office, but legislative service also can enhance business and professional connections. Critics of higher legislative pay also note that candidates, many of whom spend thousands of dollars to get elected to the legislature, know the pay level before they run for office. In addition, Texas lawmakers have provided themselves one of the best legislative retirement plans in the country, and they can increase their retirement benefits without voter approval. Retirement benefits are computed on the basis of state district judges' salaries, which legislators raise periodically, thereby increasing their own retirement benefits as well. Many former legislators receive pensions that are much larger than their paychecks were while they were in office.

5.2.4 Legislative Meeting Facilities

The House chamber and representatives' offices traditionally have been located in the west wing of the Texas State Capitol, and the Senate chamber and senators' offices are in the east wing (see Figure 5–2). The pink granite building was completed in 1888, but the growth of state government and periodic renovations created a hodgepodge of cramped legislative offices. After one visitor died in a fire behind the Senate chamber in 1983, it became obvious that the building was unsafe. So, the state launched a $187 million Capitol building restoration and expansion project that included a four-story underground addition to the building. Legislative committee hearing rooms and many lawmakers' offices were relocated from the main building to the underground extension, and offices in the historic Capitol were restored to their original, larger sizes.

When the legislature is in session, access to the floor of each chamber on the second floor of the Capitol building is restricted to lawmakers, certain other state officials, some staff members, and accredited media representatives. The galleries, to which the public is admitted, overlook the chambers from the third floor of the Capitol. In both the House and Senate chambers, members' desks face the presiding officer's podium, which is flanked by desks of the clerical staff. Unlike the U.S. Congress, where seating is arranged by party affiliation, seats are assigned to state legislators by seniority.

FIGURE 5–2 THE IMPORTANT SECOND FLOOR OF THE TEXAS CAPITOL

The second floor of the Texas Capitol, shown here, houses the Senate and House chambers, the Legislative Reference Library, the Governor's Reception Room, and the governor's private office.

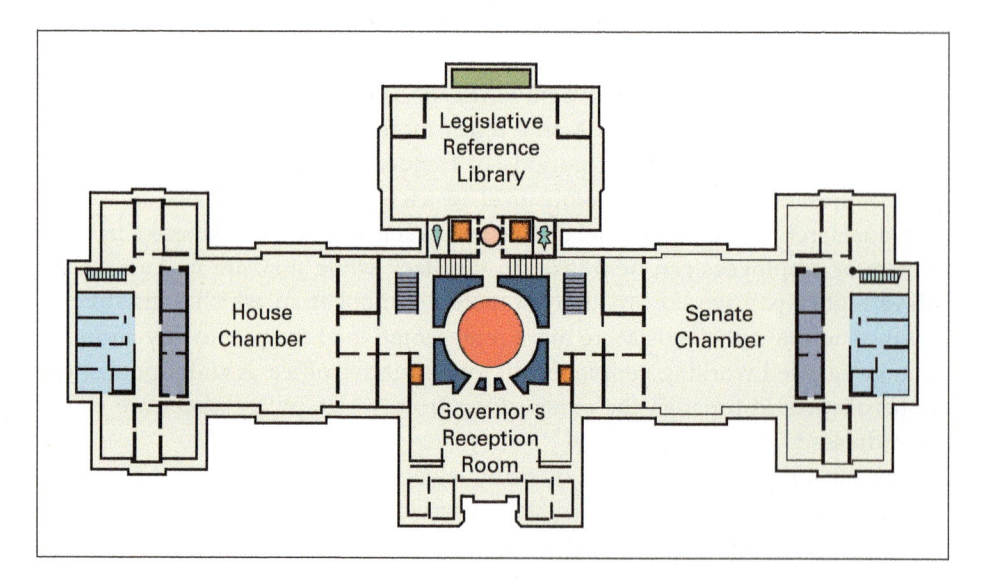

5.2.5 Membership

In 1971, the Texas legislature was overwhelmingly white, male, and Democratic. Two African Americans served in the 150-member House and one in the 31-member Senate. The one African American senator, Barbara Jordan of Houston, was the only woman in the Senate. (Two years later, she began a distinguished career in the U.S. Congress.) Frances Farenthold of Corpus Christi was the only woman in the House. A reform-minded lawmaker, she often was referred to as the "Den Mother of the Dirty Thirty," a coalition of liberal Democrats and conservative Republicans who challenged the power of House Speaker Gus Mutscher during a major stock fraud scandal involving the speaker. In 1972, Farenthold ran a strong race for governor in the Democratic primary but lost a runoff election to Uvalde rancher Dolph Briscoe. In 1971, there were only twelve Hispanic legislators—one served in the Senate and eleven served in the House—and only twelve legislators were Republican—two in the Senate and ten in the House.

By 2019, changing demographics, political patterns and attitudes, redrawn political boundaries, and court-ordered single-member districts for urban House members had significantly altered the composition of the legislature (see Table 5–1). That year, Republicans had a 19-to-12 majority in the Senate. The Senate also had two African American members, seven Hispanics, and nine women. The House in 2019 had an 83-to-67 Republican majority, a decrease from the 101-to-49 majority the party had in 2011, which was the largest Republican majority of modern times. The 150 House members in 2019 included 34 women, 38 Hispanics, 17 African Americans, and three Asian Americans. Representation from the urban and suburban areas of the state also had grown, reflecting the population shifts accommodated by redistricting.

Nevertheless, some observers still questioned whether the legislature was truly representative of the state's population because growth in the number of minority legislators had not kept pace with population changes, and women historically have been underrepresented in the House and the Senate and still are. At the beginning of the 2019 session, *The Texas Tribune* wrote: "Once again, the disparities between the makeup of the Legislature and the people they are elected to represent are stark: In a state where people of color are in the majority, almost two out of every three lawmakers are white. And not even a quarter of them are women."[8] This issue of representation and its relation to redistricting will be discussed in more detail later in this chapter.

In recent years, business and law have been the dominant occupations of legislators. The low legislative pay and increasing demands on legislators' time, even when they are not formally in session, preclude many salaried people from serving. Consequently, many legislators are business owners, who have employees and partners back home to look out for their business interests while they are in Austin. Recent legislators also have included several physicians and veterinarians, a paramedic, several farmers and ranchers, a children's book author, and a former National Football League player.

TABLE 5–1 COMPARATIVE PROFILE OF TEXAS LEGISLATORS, 1971–2019

	House				Senate			
	1971	1981	2001	2019	1971	1981	2001	2019
Democrats	140	112	78	67	29	24	15	12
Republicans	10	38	72	83	2	7	16	19
Males	149	139	120	116	30	30	27	22
Females	1	11	30	34	1	1	4	9
Hispanics	11	17	28	38	1	4	7	7
African Americans	2	13	14	17	1	0	2	2
Asian Americans	0	0	0	3	0	0	0	0
Anglos	137	120	108	92	29	27	22	22

SOURCE: Texas House and Senate rosters, 1971, 1981, 2001, and 2019.

5.2.6 Legislative Careers

Various career patterns lead to election to the Texas legislature.[9] Lawmakers include former members of city councils and school boards, former prosecutors, former judges, former legislative aides, and Democratic and Republican Party activists. Almost half of the thirty-one senators in 2019 had previously served in the House. Many first-term legislators, however, arrive in Austin with relatively little political experience. During the 2013 session, the last session with readily available age data, two members of the House were younger than 30, and three were 70 or older. More than half of the representatives were between 40 and 59. All thirty-one state senators that year were between 40 and 69.

5.2.7 Legislative Turnover

Compared to other states, turnover in the Texas legislature is generally low during most election cycles.[10] Six of the thirty-one senators and thirty of the 150 House members in 2019 were serving their first terms.[11] Yet few individuals who serve can be considered career legislators. In 2011, the most recent data available, the average tenure of incumbents was 14.7 years in the Senate (combining Senate and House experience) and 8 years in the House.[12]

In addition to the effects of redistricting of legislative seats after every U.S. census, turnover is due to the low pay and the personal costs involved in running for public office. While in session, many legislators lose income from their regular sources of employment. Political ambition also is a factor. Many lawmakers who want to move up the political ladder serve only a few terms in the Texas House before running for the Texas Senate, the U.S. Congress, or other state or local offices. Other legislators quit after a few sessions to become lobbyists.

Representation and Redistricting

5.3 Explain redistricting and its impact on the composition of the Texas legislature.

Many European legislatures use a system of proportional representation, in which legislative seats are allocated on the basis of each party's vote. In effect, the number of legislative seats held by a party reflects the proportion of votes cast for the party by voters. By contrast, the Texas legislature and most other American legislatures allocate seats geographically on the basis of single-member districts, and the candidate with the most general election votes in each district wins, a process often referred to as "winner take all." The long legal and political battles over the allocation of legislative seats address some of the fundamental questions of who should be represented and how they should be represented.

The Texas Constitution requires the legislature to redraw state representative and senatorial districts every ten years, "at its first session after the publication of each United States decennial census," to reflect changing population patterns (see Figure 5–3). At the same time, the legislature redraws districts for the members of the U.S. House who represent Texas in Washington and for the State Board of Education. This is a process known as **redistricting**. Members of earlier rural-dominated legislatures ignored the constitutional requirement to apportion the legislative seats equitably to reflect the increased urbanization of the state. Since there were no legal mechanisms to force compliance at the time, inequities grew. In 1948, Texas voters approved a constitutional amendment creating the Legislative Redistricting Board to carry out redistricting responsibilities if the legislature failed to do so during the required session. The board includes the lieutenant governor, the speaker of the House, the attorney general, the comptroller, and the commissioner of the General Land Office.

---

redistricting

The process of redrawing legislative and other political district boundaries to reflect changing population patterns. Districts for the Texas House, state Senate, State Board of Education, and U.S. Congress are redrawn every ten years by the legislature.

FIGURE 5-3 STATE SENATE DISTRICTS

These were the thirty-one districts from which state senators were elected in 2014, 2016, 2018, and 2020. The districts were approved on an interim basis by a federal court presiding over a redistricting lawsuit. They also were approved by the legislature in 2013 and later upheld by the U.S. Supreme Court.

SOURCE: Texas Legislative Council, http://gis1.tlc.state.tx.us/?PlanHeader=PLANS172.

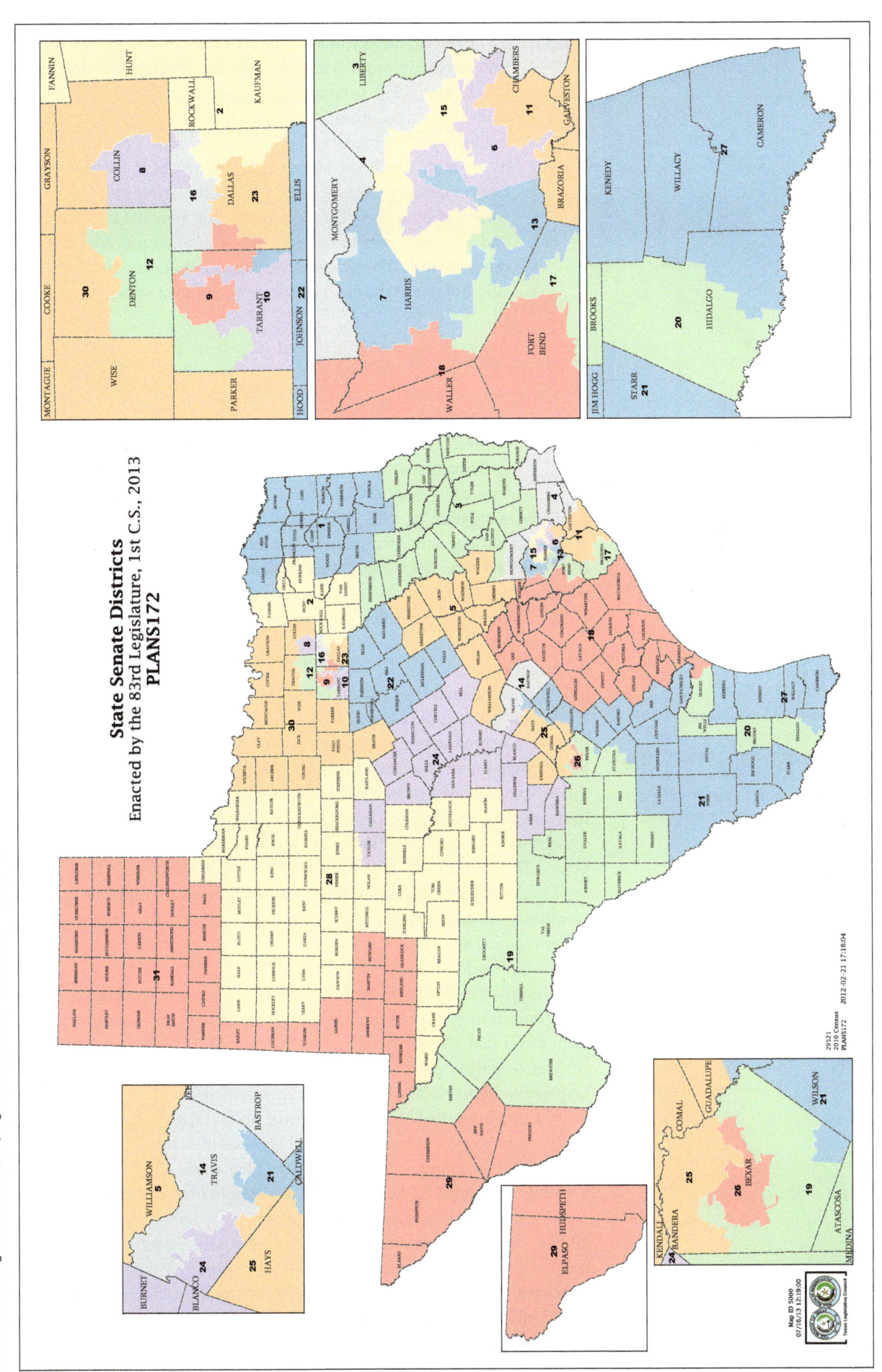

145

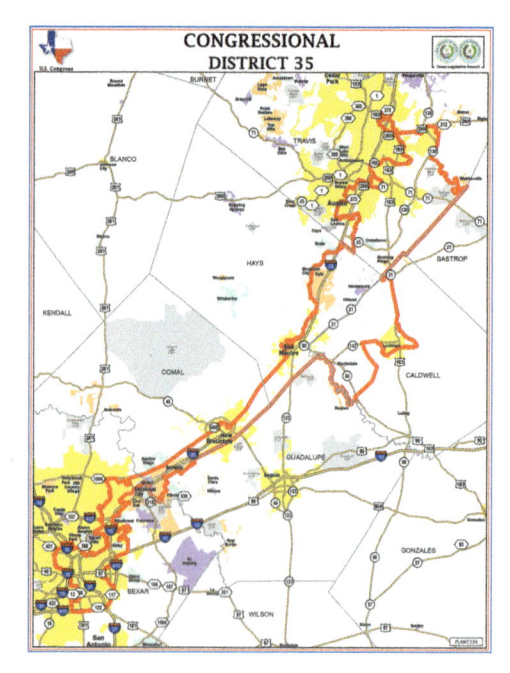

A SALAMANDER OR A GERRYMANDER?

Use your imagination to figure out what this looks like. In reality, it is U.S. House District 35 in Texas, which stretches down Interstate 35 from Austin to San Antonio. Democrats said it was gerrymandered by Republicans in the Texas legislature in 2011 to try to defeat Democratic congressman Lloyd Doggett of Austin. After a federal court made some changes in the district, Doggett was reelected anyway. But the district remained a subject of legal and political dispute for several more years.

gerrymandering
Drawing of political district lines in such a way that they favor a particular political party or racial group.

Even so, the urban areas of the state were denied equality in representation for many more years. In 1960, the House districts ranged in size from 23,602 to 155,393 persons, and Senate districts from 131,970 to 1,243,155.[13] With those disparities in population, it was possible for rural voters, who made up approximately 33 percent of the state's population, to elect a majority of both the Texas House and the Senate.[14] Rural legislators tended to neglect urban problems. Although such glaring inequalities have since been corrected by federal courts, redistricting remains a highly political exercise, and anyone trying to navigate the legislative process needs to know something about it. The redistricting process can be extremely technical and legalistic, but it is at the heart of our representative system of government.

5.3.1 Federal Courts Order Equality in Redistricting

In 1962, the federal courts finally ordered equality in redistricting. The U.S. Supreme Court, in *Baker* v. *Carr*, applied the principle of equality to congressional redistricting. Then, in *Reynolds* v. *Sims*, the court held that state legislative districts had to be apportioned on the "one person, one vote" principle. Litigation in 1965 (*Kilgarlin* v. *Martin*) extended this ruling to Texas, and the "reapportionment revolution" soon began to produce dramatic changes in the composition of the Texas legislature.[15] To a large degree, the increased representation of minorities and Republicans in Texas's lawmaking body was a result of legal and political redistricting battles. But issues such as **gerrymandering**—the drawing of political district lines to favor a particular political party or racial group—continue to be fought today.

The Texas Senate has always been elected by single-member districts, and after the 1970 Census, the application of the equality principle to the Senate resulted in districts that were comparable in size. Rural members of the Texas House also were elected from single-member districts, but elections were held in multimember districts in the urban counties that had been allocated more than one representative. Candidates in those races had to run countywide, which put ethnic and political minorities at a disadvantage because the dominant Anglo and Democratic voters outnumbered their voters. The Democratic Party dominated Texas politics then.

A federal court ruled in 1972 that multimember districts in Dallas and Bexar counties were unconstitutional because they diluted the voting strength of African Americans in Dallas and Hispanics in Bexar. Coincidentally, they also diluted the voting strength of Republicans in both counties.

Despite the fact that 50 percent of Bexar County's population was Hispanic at that time, under the countywide, or at-large, election system, only one Hispanic from Bexar had served in the Texas House in 1971. Dallas County, which had a large African American population, had only one African American House member. The Legislative Redistricting Board had drawn single-member districts in Harris County in 1971, and after the U.S. Supreme Court upheld the lower court's decision regarding Dallas and Bexar counties, multimember legislative districts were soon eliminated in all other urban counties. The numbers of Hispanics, African Americans, women, and Republicans elected to the Texas House began to increase significantly.

After 1975, Congress put Texas under the federal Voting Rights Act, which prohibited the dilution of minority voting strength. Texas was placed under the law because it had a history of discriminatory practices in voting. The law required preclearance, or approval, of redistricting plans by the U.S. Department of Justice or the U.S. District Court in Washington, D.C., and it gave African Americans and Hispanics a strong weapon to use in challenging a redistricting plan in court.

Based on 2010 Census data, the average Texas House district included 167,637 residents, and the average state Senate district included 811,147 residents. But those numbers are constantly changing, which is why redistricting is required every ten years to redistribute the population changes among the districts.

5.3.2 Contemporary Redistricting Battles

At the beginning of the twenty-first century, however, minorities believed that their fight for equal representation was still far from over because the Voting Rights Act was under attack by conservatives. Some conservatives also wanted to replace the total population figures on which redistricting historically has been based with the number of eligible voters, a change that many Democrats said would dramatically reduce the potential representation of minorities in legislative bodies. Many Hispanics in Texas, for example, are too young to vote, and many others are noncitizens. Also, the U.S. Supreme Court, the final decider of constitutional issues and redistricting cases, had become more conservative following key appointments by President George W. Bush and, later, President Donald Trump.

Texas Republicans scored huge redistricting victories in 2001 after the legislature—with Democrats in control of the House and Republicans in control of the Senate—failed to redraw its own districts during that year's session. The task then fell to the five statewide elected officials, four Republicans and one Democrat, on the Legislative Redistricting Board. The board drew new legislative maps for the 2002 elections that helped increase Republican majority strength in the 31-member Senate to 19 senators. It also enabled Republicans to capture their first majority of modern times in the 150-member Texas House.

In the 2002 elections, the GOP increased its strength in the House from 72 to 88 seats, a net gain of 16 seats that cleared the way for state Representative Tom Craddick of Midland, a Republican, to be elected speaker after the regular session convened in 2003. The GOP takeover of the Texas House also allowed Republicans to significantly redraw the lines for Texas's congressional districts later that year. They prevailed after a bitter partisan fight that included two walkouts by Democratic legislators, which attracted national media attention.

In a well-organized, furtive break from Austin, more than fifty Democratic members of the House fled to Ardmore, Oklahoma, near the end of the regular legislative session to break a quorum and prevent House Republicans from acting on the redistricting plan. Although Democrats were in the minority, their unusual tactic worked because two-thirds of the House or Senate members have to be present to establish a quorum and conduct business. They left the state in order to avoid being rounded up by Texas state troopers and ordered to return to Austin at the direction of the Republican House speaker. Similarly, eleven Democratic senators flew to Albuquerque, New Mexico, to break a quorum in the Senate after Governor Rick Perry had called the legislature back into special session that summer to complete the redistricting work. The Democrats remained in Albuquerque for several weeks before they finally returned to Austin during a third special session that fall, allowing Republicans to finally pass a new congressional redistricting plan.

The new congressional map gave Republicans a 21-to-11 majority among members of the U.S. Congress elected from Texas in 2004 and ended the congressional careers of several veteran Democratic incumbents. The U.S. Supreme Court later upheld most of the plan but ordered the redrawing of some district lines in South Texas to protect minority voting rights.

By 2011, the next redistricting year, Republicans had increased their margin in the state's congressional delegation to 23 to 9. According to the 2010 U.S. Census, Texas's population had grown during the previous decade from 21 million people to approximately 25 million, and most of the growth occurred among Hispanics. As a result, Texas was awarded four additional congressional seats to give the state a total of thirty-six, and Hispanic leaders believed most of the new districts should be drawn to give Hispanics the opportunity to elect the new congressional members. But the Republican-dominated legislature drew maps that retained strong Republican majorities in the legislature and the congressional delegation. Anglos also dominated the new districts. In 2011, Democrats and minority groups filed a lawsuit in federal court in San Antonio to overturn the redistricting plans, contending they violated the Voting Rights Act. The U.S. Department of Justice and the federal district court in Washington, D.C., delayed action on preclearing the legislature's maps, and both sides prepared for a lengthy redistricting fight.

The federal court in San Antonio issued interim redistricting plans under which races for the Texas legislature and Congress were held in 2012. The plans slightly reduced the number of Republican districts approved by the legislature but failed to give Democratic plaintiffs as many districts favoring Democratic and minority candidates as they wanted.[16]

In the 2012 elections, Republicans and Democrats split the four new congressional seats under the court's interim redistricting plan. The new Democratic congressmen included one Hispanic and one African American.

In 2013, the legislature made minor changes to the court-drawn redistricting plan for the Texas House and kept the interim Senate and congressional maps unchanged for the 2014 elections (see Figure 5-3). The state and the Democratic plaintiffs agreed on the new state Senate districts, but litigation over final redistricting plans for the Texas House and Congress was not resolved until 2018.

In August 2017, a three-judge federal court panel in San Antonio ruled that two of the congressional districts and nine districts for the Texas House had been drawn to reduce the influence of minority voters, particularly Hispanics, in violation of the U.S. Constitution and the Voting Rights Act. But in 2018, the U.S. Supreme Court overruled the appellate panel, concluding that the legislative majority had not intentionally discriminated against minority voters. The high Court upheld all of the disputed districts except one, a Texas House district in Fort Worth.

Acting in 2013 in an unrelated case from Alabama, *Shelby County v. Holder*, the U.S. Supreme Court issued a ruling that experts believe will cripple the Voting Rights Act as a tool for minority plaintiffs in future redistricting cases. The high Court ruled that the formulas used to determine which states are subject to the law's strict preclearance requirements were unconstitutional because they were based on old data. That decision will make it more difficult for minority groups to prove discrimination in redistricting cases, unless Congress amends the Voting Rights Act to correct the problem.[17]

In December 2015, the U.S. Supreme Court heard legal arguments in still another case, *Evenwel v. Abbott,* in which two Texas residents sued the state over the traditional apportionment of legislative districts by total population. Plaintiffs Sue Evenwel of rural Mount Pleasant and Edward Pfenninger of suburban Montgomery County, near Houston, said basing districts on total population caused a "gross malapportionment" of the value of their votes because there weren't an equal number of eligible voters in their districts. Pfenninger's suburban district had more noncitizens, who were ineligible to vote but were counted for redistricting purposes. The disparity could be resolved, the plaintiffs said, by apportioning districts on the basis of eligible voters. The conservative Cato Institute sided with the plaintiffs, and in an unusual alliance conservative Republican Governor Greg Abbott sided with Democrats opposing the proposed change. The Democrats argued that nonvoters are entitled to equal representation and government services. Then-state Senator Rodney Ellis, a Democrat from Houston, said the change in apportionment standards would produce "lopsided, overcrowded urban districts packed with non-voters" and "much smaller districts in rural areas where people are older and there are far fewer non-citizens." He said the overall effect would be "grossly unequal access to legislators, resources, and services." Rural voters in Texas also are more likely to vote for Republican candidates. The high Court with an 8-0 vote in 2016 ruled against the plaintiffs and upheld the apportionment of legislative districts by population.[18]

The next redistricting session for the Legislature was 2021, which added to the importance of the 2020 elections and the House's need to elect a new presiding officer, described at the beginning of this chapter. With a Republican governor and a Senate that was all but certain to retain its Republican majority, Democrats were determined to recapture a majority of the House or, at least, tighten the Republican margin, so as to increase Democratic influence over the redistricting process and the partisan composition of the legislature and the Texas congressional delegation for the next ten years. But Republicans kept their House majority, despite a major Democratic campaign effort.

Legislative Leaders and Committees

5.4 Contrast the leadership and committee structure of the Texas House with that of the Texas Senate.

The basic leadership structure of the Texas legislature has remained unchanged since the current state constitution was adopted in 1876. The House leader, the speaker, is selected by members of the House, and the Senate's presiding officer, the lieutenant governor, is elected by Texas voters. Each is in a position to exert significant influence over the lawmaking process, but the amount of influence is determined to a large extent by each leader's personality and leadership capabilities. Committees in each chamber are created under legislative rules and have remained largely unchanged in recent years. But the committee lineup can be altered from session to session to accommodate changing state needs and political interests. Learning the powers of the legislative leaders and committees is another major step on the road to understanding how laws are made.

5.4.1 Legislative Leadership

The highly institutionalized leadership structure found in the U.S. Congress is beginning to emerge in the Texas legislature, but only to a limited extent. The Texas legislature is a part-time institution that, until about forty years ago, was dominated by conservative, primarily rural Democratic lawmakers. With no significant party opposition or minority representation until recent years, legislative leadership remained highly personal and dependent on the political relationships between the presiding officers and key legislators. Republican growth in the statehouse, however, has been forcing changes.

HOUSE LEADERSHIP The presiding officer of the House of Representatives is the **speaker**, who is elected by the House from among its membership. Two of the speaker's most important formal powers are appointing House committees and assigning legislation, or proposed laws, to the committees for initial review in the lawmaking process. Until the 1950s, it was unusual for a speaker to serve more than one two-year term. The position traditionally was circulated among a small group of Democratic legislators who dominated the House. But multiple terms have been the norm for more recent speakers. Gib Lewis and James E. "Pete" Laney, the last two speakers during the era of Democratic dominance, are tied with Republican Joe Straus for the longevity record with five terms each. Unlike most of their predecessors, recent speakers have devoted long hours to the job and kept large staffs.

Laney, a farmer-businessman from Hale Center, a small town in West Texas, became speaker in 1993. During his five terms, the state completed a multibillion-dollar expansion of its prison system, overhauled criminal justice laws, and enacted a school finance law

speaker
The presiding officer of the House of Representatives.

A ONE-TERM SPEAKER
Unlike most recent speakers, Dennis Bonnen served only one term as the House's presiding officer. He was speaker during the 2019 session but retired from the House after provoking a controversy during a meeting with a conservative activist.

to provide more equity in education spending among school districts. In a bipartisan endeavor, Laney actively supported many of Republican Governor George W. Bush's priorities. He also won significant changes in House rules that produced, in the view of many House members, a more democratic lawmaking process than under some of his predecessors.

After winning a House majority in the 2002 elections, Republicans elected state Representative Tom Craddick, a Republican from Midland, to succeed Laney in 2003. A House member since 1969, Craddick became the first Republican speaker of modern times. Unlike Laney, he exercised an iron-fisted leadership style. As did his predecessors, Craddick gave his key supporters, Republicans and Democrats, choice leadership positions when he made his committee assignments. Backed by a Republican majority, Craddick insisted on spending cuts in many state programs to help bridge a $10 billion revenue shortfall in 2003. He opposed raising state taxes, but he insisted the legislature enact a law allowing university governing boards to raise college tuition. Craddick also played a key role in the enactment of the redistricting bill, discussed earlier in this chapter, to increase the number of Republicans elected to Congress from Texas.

By 2007, Craddick's speakership had come under attack from some Republicans as well as Democrats. Many blamed his authoritarian style for the defeat of several incumbent Republican House members in 2006. Critics accused the speaker of forcing the lawmakers to vote against the best interests of their districts on such important issues as education, thus making them vulnerable to challengers. Craddick was elected to a third term as presiding officer at the beginning of the 2007 session, but in the closing days of the session he faced an open rebellion on the House floor.

Craddick's speakership was all but over when Democrats won additional House seats in the 2008 elections, trimming the Republican majority to 76 to 74. Several weeks later, eleven anti-Craddick Republicans met behind closed doors and selected moderate Republican Joe Straus of San Antonio as their choice for speaker. Straus then won the endorsement of sixty-four Democratic House members to easily win the speakership when the 2009 session convened.

Straus, then 41, faced two major obstacles. Beginning only his third term in the House, he was the most inexperienced speaker in recent Texas history, and he was a Republican who owed his election primarily to Democrats. The new speaker appointed Democrats to leadership positions but named Republicans to chair most of the major committees. Straus had a more relaxed leadership style than Craddick and, outmaneuvered by Democrats in a late-session parliamentary fight in 2009, failed to win House approval of the Republicans' top legislative priority, a bill to require voters to show photo identification cards.

Straus nevertheless was well liked personally by his House colleagues, both Democrats and Republicans, and received generally favorable marks when the session ended.[19] Straus believed he had restored civility to the House. "There may be a few voices out there who want to rewind the clock," he said. "They miss the point that leadership by encouragement can be more successful than leadership by full frontal force."[20]

Strong Republican gains during the 2010 election cycle, including the unseating of several moderate Republicans by more-conservative candidates in the Republican primary, prompted a move to replace Straus with a more-conservative Republican at the beginning of the 2011 session. The effort failed, but Straus, presiding over an overwhelming 101-to-49 Republican majority, subscribed to the conservative Republican agenda. The House joined the Senate in making deep cuts to the state budget to bridge a huge revenue shortfall without raising taxes, passed a law requiring doctors to perform sonograms before conducting abortions, and passed a law requiring photo identification for voting, the same proposal that House Democrats had killed two years earlier.

Straus was elected to third, fourth, and fifth terms as speaker in 2013, 2015, and 2017 and presided over the enactment of other conservative priorities, including tax cuts and a new law imposing more restrictions on abortion. Ultraconservative Republicans, including many influenced by the Tea Party movement, kept trying to topple him by supporting challengers in Republican primary races against House members who were friendly to Straus. Several of Straus's supporters in the House lost Republican primary races in 2014 and 2016 to more-conservative challengers, and others retired from the legislature. Straus faced two reelection opponents of his own in the 2016 Republican primary in his home district in San Antonio but defeated them.

During the regular and special legislative sessions in 2017, ideological and philosophical differences over policy widened between Straus and the other two top Republican state leaders, Governor Greg Abbott and Lieutenant Governor Dan Patrick. By the time the special session adjourned that summer, their working relationship had become particularly contentious. Straus soon announced that he would not seek reelection to his House seat, and jockeying for the 2019 speaker's race began almost immediately. After early, unsuccessful efforts by other speaker candidates, Republican Dennis Bonnen of Angleton was elected to succeed Straus at the beginning of the 2019 session. Bonnen, a veteran House member, was more receptive than Straus had been to some of Abbott's and Patrick's priorities, particularly their drive to put tighter limits on local property taxes, and the new speaker enjoyed a largely successful session. In addition to lowering limits on property tax revenue for local governments (see Chapter 4), Bonnen joined the governor and the lieutenant governor to win legislative enactment of a significant increase in public education funding. But as noted at the beginning of this chapter, Bonnen did not seek reelection to the House after he was caught on tape making controversial statements to a political activist. Republican Dade Phelan claimed to have enough support to succeed Bonnen.

The speaker appoints a speaker pro tempore, or assistant presiding officer. In 1981, Speaker Bill Clayton named the first African American, Representative Craig Washington of Houston, to the post. Clayton was a rural conservative and Washington was an urban liberal, but Washington proved to be a critical member of the speaker's team. He also exercised considerable influence on numerous issues of importance to minorities. Ten years later, Gib Lewis named another African American, Representative Wilhelmina Delco of Austin, as the first woman speaker pro tempore. Joe Straus, who owed his election in 2009 to the key support of Democrats, appointed Democratic Representative Craig Eiland of Galveston to the post that year. But he appointed Republicans to the post during his subsequent four terms as speaker. Dennis Bonnen appointed a Democrat, Representative Joe Moody of El Paso, to the job in 2019.

The membership of most House committees is determined in part by seniority. The speaker has total discretion, however, in naming committee chairs and vice chairs and in appointing all the members of procedural committees, including the influential Calendars Committee, which will be described in more detail later in this chapter.

SENATE LEADERSHIP The presiding officer of the Senate is the **lieutenant governor**, who is elected statewide to a four-year term. Unlike the vice president of the United States—the office's counterpart in the federal government, who has only limited legislative functions—the lieutenant governor has traditionally been the Senate's legislative leader. This office, elected independently of the governor, often has been called the most powerful office in state government because it offers the opportunity to use a statewide electoral base to develop a dominant legislative role.[21] Lieutenant governors, however, get most of their power from rules set by the senators, not from the constitution.

lieutenant governor
The presiding officer of the Senate. This officeholder becomes governor if the governor dies, resigns, becomes incapacitated, or is removed from office.

The lieutenant governor's power is based, in part, on the same coalitions that the speaker uses through committee assignments and relationships with interest groups. But the lieutenant governor has more direct control over the Senate's agenda than the speaker has over the House's. Under long-standing Senate rules, the lieutenant governor determines when—and if—a committee-approved bill will be brought up for a vote by the full Senate. In the House, the Calendars Committee determines the order of floor debate.

The lieutenant governor also has more formal control over the membership of Senate committees than the speaker has over House panels. The Senate's rules allow the lieutenant governor to appoint members of all standing committees without regard to seniority or other restrictions.

The Senate has a president pro tempore, or assistant presiding officer, who is chosen by senators from among their membership on a seniority basis. The president pro tempore is third in line of succession to the governorship. Traditionally, the governor and the lieutenant governor both allegedly "leave" the state on the same day so that the president pro tempore can serve as "governor for a day" at one point during his or her limited term.

Bill Hobby, a quiet-spoken media executive, served a record eighteen years as lieutenant governor before voluntarily leaving the office in January 1991. A Democrat, he patiently sought consensus among senators on most major issues and rarely took the lead in promoting specific legislative proposals. One notable exception occurred in 1979, when Hobby tried to win Senate approval of a presidential primary bill opposed by most Democratic senators. After Hobby announced that he would change the Senate's traditional operating procedure to give the bill special consideration, twelve Democratic senators, dubbed the "Killer Bees," hid out for several days away from the Capitol to break a quorum and keep the Senate from conducting business. They succeeded in killing the bill and reminding Hobby that the senators set the rules.

Hobby's successor, Bob Bullock, had demonstrated strong leadership and a mercurial personality during sixteen years as state comptroller. On taking office as lieutenant governor, he had major policy changes in mind and was ready to see them enacted. Bullock took the lead in making proposals and then actively lobbying for them. During his first session in 1991, he reportedly had shouting matches with some lawmakers behind closed doors and one day abruptly adjourned the Senate when not enough members were present for a quorum at the scheduled starting time. Even so, his experience and knowledge of state government and his tireless work habits won the respect of most senators and their support for most of his proposals.

Bullock, a Democrat, strengthened his leadership role during the 1993 and 1995 sessions, despite growth in the number of Republican senators. He engineered closed-door compromises on several major issues, including some long sought by business interests. His strong-willed approach defused partisanship, but it also prompted remarks that the Senate had abandoned democracy. There were so many unanimous or near-unanimous votes in the Senate in 1993 that some House members joked that those senators who wanted to show dissent voted "aye" with their eyes closed.[22]

Bullock helped Republican Governor George W. Bush enact some of his key proposals in 1995, but he played a less active role during the 1997 session, after Republicans had won a Senate majority for the first time since Reconstruction. He supported some legislation, including a statewide water conservation and management plan, but he did little to promote a property tax relief effort that Governor Bush had made his highest priority for the session.

A few days after the 1997 session ended, Bullock announced that he would not seek reelection in 1998. Bullock, who had a history of health problems, was later diagnosed with lung cancer, and he died in June 1999.

After defeating Democrat John Sharp in a hard-fought race in 1998, former Agriculture Commissioner Rick Perry became Texas's first Republican lieutenant

MARKING TEXAS HISTORY

Former Lieutenant Governor Bob Bullock, left, leans on a shovel handle at a ceremony in April 1999 marking construction of a state history museum that now bears his name in Austin. Bullock died two months later. Then-Governor George W. Bush is at right.

Harry Cabluck/Associated Press

governor of modern times in 1999. Although Perry had to follow in Bullock's legendary footsteps, he had the advantage of entering the 1999 session with a $6 billion state budgetary surplus and a rare absence of emergencies. Perry was lower key than Bullock, perhaps choosing to learn more about the Senate before plunging into potential controversies. Nevertheless, he was credited with helping Republican and Democratic lawmakers negotiate a compromise on one of the key legislative packages of the session—a series of tax cuts, teacher pay raises, and other increased education spending.

Perry was elected to a lieutenant governor's term set to expire in January 2003. But after George W. Bush resigned the governorship in December 2000 to become president, Perry was promoted to governor and vacated the lieutenant governor's office. Acting under a constitutional amendment adopted in 1999 in anticipation of such an eventuality, senators elected state Senator Bill Ratliff, a Republican from Mount Pleasant, to serve as lieutenant governor during the 2001 session.

Ratliff, a former chair of both the Senate Education and Finance Committees, was businesslike in his role as presiding officer, and he received favorable reviews. He appointed the first African American, state Senator Rodney Ellis, a Democrat from Houston, to chair the budget-writing Finance Committee. He also opposed most Republican senators and supported Ellis's bill to strengthen a state law against hate crimes, including crimes motivated by prejudice against homosexuals, which passed that session. Ratliff declined to seek election to a full term as lieutenant governor and won reelection to his Senate seat instead in 2002. After serving in the regular and special sessions in 2003, Ratliff resigned in early 2004, expressing weariness after fifteen years in the legislative arena.

Republican David Dewhurst won the 2002 lieutenant governor's race over Democrat John Sharp, who had narrowly lost to Rick Perry in 1998. A wealthy businessman, Dewhurst had no legislative experience. His only time in elected office had been his four previous years as state land commissioner, but he moved quickly to establish credibility as the Senate's new leader. He appointed respected legislative insiders to key staff positions and spent hours studying issues and meeting with individual senators. Although Republicans held a 19-to-12 Senate majority, he continued the tradition of appointing both Republicans and Democrats as committee chairs.

Dewhurst's leadership was severely challenged, however, during the bitter partisan fight over congressional redistricting that took three special sessions in the summer and fall of 2003 to resolve. As noted earlier in this chapter, eleven Democratic senators flew to Albuquerque, New Mexico, to break a quorum and delay a vote on the redistricting bill for several weeks. They did so after Dewhurst served notice that he would break with a long-time Senate tradition and allow the redistricting bill to be advanced on a simple majority, rather than the traditional two-thirds vote. (The so-called two-thirds rule will be discussed in more detail later in this chapter.) The boycotting senators eventually returned to Austin, and the legislature approved the Republicans' redistricting bill. This fight was only the first in which Dewhurst, over the next several legislative sessions, would anger Democrats as partisan tensions increased in the Senate.

Dewhurst was instrumental in the accomplishment of a number of legislative goals in subsequent sessions, including a 2006 special session in which he helped win Senate approval of changes in the school finance law to comply with a Texas Supreme Court order. In 2011, Dewhurst and Republican senators again bypassed the two-thirds rule to pass two major Republican priorities, a bill to require Texas voters to have photo identification cards before voting and a state budget that made deep cuts in education and other state programs to bridge a multibillion-dollar revenue shortfall without raising state taxes. Although in the minority, the twelve Democratic senators would have had enough votes to block both measures had Dewhurst not bypassed the traditional two-thirds vote requirement. Republicans argued the voter ID bill was necessary to guard against fraudulent voting, but Democrats said it was designed to discourage voting by minority voters, who usually supported Democrats (see Chapter 11).

Dewhurst's actions in changing the Senate's operating procedures in order to advance conservative priorities were widely viewed as efforts to appeal to the growing influence of the Tea Party movement and ultraconservative voters in the Texas Republican primary. And, soon after the legislature adjourned in 2011, Dewhurst announced he would run in 2012 for the U.S. Senate seat of retiring U.S. Senator Kay Bailey Hutchison. Despite being the early favorite, Dewhurst lost the race to Ted Cruz, an ultraconservative who waged a tireless, antiestablishment campaign in the Republican primary and became a Tea Party favorite.

Dewhurst remained lieutenant governor because he was in the middle of a four-year term and, a few months after losing to Cruz, resumed his job presiding over the Texas Senate during the 2013 legislative session. But many of his Republican colleagues viewed him as politically wounded, and would-be opponents in his own party began circling, shark-like, in anticipation of the 2014 lieutenant governor's race. On the last night of a summer special session in 2013, Dewhurst was in the middle of another partisan drama, a fight over an abortion regulation bill. Several hundred abortion rights protesters, upset when Republicans ended a filibuster against the bill by Democratic Senator Wendy Davis, made enough noise in the Senate gallery to drown out Dewhurst's efforts to pass the measure before a midnight deadline. Dewhurst blamed the bill's failure on an "unruly screaming mob" and vowed that the fight was "far from over."[23] Governor Rick Perry called another special session, and the bill finally was passed. But opponents blamed Dewhurst for the bill's initial failure, and he drew three prominent opponents in the 2014 Republican primary. Senator Dan Patrick, who was chairman of the Senate Education Committee under Dewhurst, unseated him in a primary runoff and then defeated Democratic Senator Leticia Van de Putte of San Antonio in the general election.

Patrick had developed a political base as a conservative radio talk show host in Houston before winning his first elective office as a state senator from Houston in 2006. Within a few years after taking office,

WIELDING THE GAVEL

Lieutenant Governor Dan Patrick, a Republican, presides over the Senate. The former state senator from Houston has used his position to win Senate approval of several conservative priorities.

Patrick had successfully tapped into the rising Tea Party movement with an appeal, often delivered with evangelical fervor, for limited government, low taxes, abortion restrictions, gun rights, and stronger border security. At the January 2015 inauguration ceremony he shared with Governor Greg Abbott on the state Capitol steps, he emphasized his Christian faith, repeated his goals and vowed to take conservatism "to the next level." To the surprise and amusement of many in the inaugural audience, he also turned his back on the crowd to snap several "selfies" from various angles with his cell phone.[24]

Patrick had a very conservative Senate with which to work. One Democratic and three moderate Republican senators had been replaced by more-conservative Republicans in the 2014 elections. Republicans outnumbered Democrats twenty to eleven, and after engineering a change in the Senate's two-thirds rule to keep the eleven Democratic senators from being able to block his priorities, Patrick saw several successes during his first session as the Senate's presiding officer. The legislature appropriated millions of additional dollars for border security, cut property and business taxes by $3.8 billion, left a multibillion-dollar balance in the state treasury, and enacted two controversial gun laws. One allowed adults with state licenses to openly carry handguns in public, and the other allowed licensees to take their pistols, in a concealed manner, onto state-supported college campuses. Texas had had a concealed-carry law for several years, but the old law prohibited guns from being carried in open view and banned guns from college campuses. The two-thirds rule change was critical in achieving Senate approval and eventual enactment of the two new gun laws. But Patrick failed to win approval of two other major priorities—a bill to repeal a state law allowing some students in the country illegally to pay in-state college tuition and a bill to spend state tax dollars on vouchers for private school tuition. Patrick and other state leaders also angered many advocates who believed they had underfunded public education and health care, an issue made more sensitive by the fact that billions of tax dollars were left unspent to meet conservative, limited-government priorities.

At the beginning of the 2015 session, Patrick appointed a grassroots advisory board of Tea Party activists, a step that may have provided political benefits for the lieutenant governor. But it also led to a highly publicized dispute with Governor Abbott when, during the session, Patrick's group publicly criticized one of Abbott's priorities—a bill promoting pre-kindergarten education. After the bill had been approved by the House, Patrick's advisory board issued a letter saying the governor's proposal would take children out of religious pre-schools and put them into a "Godless environment." Patrick denied having anything to do with the letter, but he took heat over it from both the governor and Speaker Joe Straus. The confrontation over the letter and other legislative issues broke out during one of the private, weekly breakfast meetings the three leaders held during the session, and word of it was quickly leaked to the media. At one point during the meeting, Patrick reportedly declared that he was tired of Abbott and Straus "picking on me."[25] Abbott's pre-kindergarten priority became law, and several weeks after the session ended, Patrick disbanded his grassroots advisory board.

Patrick had virtually the same conservative Senate with which to work during a regular and a special session in 2017, and he had the support of Governor Greg Abbott for much of his legislative program. He won Senate and House approval of one of his top priorities, a "sanctuary cities" law to require local law-enforcement officers to cooperate with federal officials in the enforcement of laws against undocumented immigrants. He and the Senate majority defeated attempts by then-Speaker Joe Straus and the House to increase state funding for public schools. The Senate also approved Patrick's priorities to spend tax dollars on private school vouchers, to impose stricter limits on city and county governments' authority to increase property taxes, and to restrict which public restrooms could be used by transgender persons. But the House killed all three of those measures.

Patrick handily won the Republican nomination for another term in 2018 and defeated Democrat Mike Collier, a Houston area accountant, in the general election.

But he modified his agenda, at least temporarily, for the 2019 session, following the loss of two Republican Senate allies and 12 Republican House members to Democratic challengers in the 2018 elections. Instead of making a top priority of tax-paid vouchers to send students to private schools, he called for a pay raise for public school teachers and joined Governor Greg Abbott and Dennis Bonnen, the new House speaker, to win enactment of a major increase in public education funding. Patrick also abandoned in that session any effort to pass a so-called "bathroom bill," the measure to regulate the use of public restrooms by transgender individuals that had sparked major controversy before failing to become law in 2017. But the lieutenant governor maintained his zeal to place tighter limits on local property taxes and, with Abbott's and Bonnen's help, was successful in 2019. Patrick also won Senate approval of a bill to prohibit local governments from using public money to lobby the legislature, but that measure was killed in the House. Patrick was a leader of President Donald Trump's election campaigns in Texas in 2016 and 2020.

5.4.2 Control over the Legislative Process

In the Senate, the lieutenant governor can vote only to break a tie. The speaker can vote on any issue in the House but normally abstains from voting except to break a tie or to send a signal to encourage reluctant or wavering House members to vote a particular way on an issue. The speaker and the lieutenant governor derive tremendous influence over the lawmaking process from their power to appoint and assign legislation to committees and their application of legislative rules, including those set in the state constitution and those adopted by the House and the Senate. A parliamentarian advises each presiding officer on procedures.

The speaker and the lieutenant governor do not participate in House or Senate debates on bills and, except when their own political priorities are at stake, usually attempt to present an image of neutral presiding officers. That image of neutrality obviously was compromised during the Senate fight in 2013 over the abortion regulation bill and in the public disputes between Lieutenant Governor Dan Patrick and Speaker Joe Straus over the transgender "bathroom bill," amongst other issues, in 2017. The presiding officers' formal powers are strengthened by their relationships with their committee leaders and interest groups. With the notable exceptions of the separate walkouts by House and Senate Democrats during the 2003 redistricting battle, a late-session House uprising against Speaker Tom Craddick in 2007, and the chaotic Senate episode over the abortion regulation bill in 2013, the presiding officers rarely lose control of the process.

Traditionally, and unlike the U.S. Congress and some other state legislatures, there has been no formal division along party lines or a formal system of choosing floor leaders in the Texas House or the Senate. The committee chairs constitute the speaker's and lieutenant governor's teams and usually act as their unofficial floor leaders in developing and building support for the leadership's legislative priorities. Most chairs are philosophically, if not always politically, aligned with the presiding officers.

5.4.3 The Committee System

The backbone of the legislative process is the committee system, molded by the lieutenant governor and the speaker.[26] It is a screening process that decides the fate of most legislation. Technical errors and oversights in bills can be corrected in committees, and compromise can begin there for those bills that eventually do become law. Typically, no more than about one-fourth of the bills, or proposed laws, introduced during a regular session win final legislative approval. In 2019, the approval rate was lower than that, with 1,439 of the 7,541 bills and constitutional amendments filed

HEARING LEGISLATION
Witnesses and spectators listen to testimony in a Senate committee hearing room in the Capitol extension during a recent session. The committee members are seated on the raised platform at the front of the room.

during the regular session winning final legislative approval; fifty-six of those bills were vetoed by Governor Greg Abbott. Most bills that do not make it die in a Senate or a House committee, many without ever being heard (see Figure 5–4). A committee occasionally may kill a bill on an outright vote, but there are other, less obvious ways to scuttle legislation. A bill can be gutted or so drastically amended or weakened that its sponsor may abandon it, or a bill simply can be ignored.

FIGURE 5–4 PASSAGE RATE OF LEGISLATION

The number of bills and constitutional amendments proposed by Texas legislators during each regular session has increased significantly over the past half-century. But the percentage of bills passed has leveled off at about 24 percent, noticeably lower than the percentage in 1963. The success rate was even lower in 2015, 2017, and 2019. The 140-day limit and other restrictions on regular sessions serve to put a practical, as well as political, limit on how many laws can be passed.

SOURCE: Texas Legislative Reference Library, "Session: Bill Statistics."

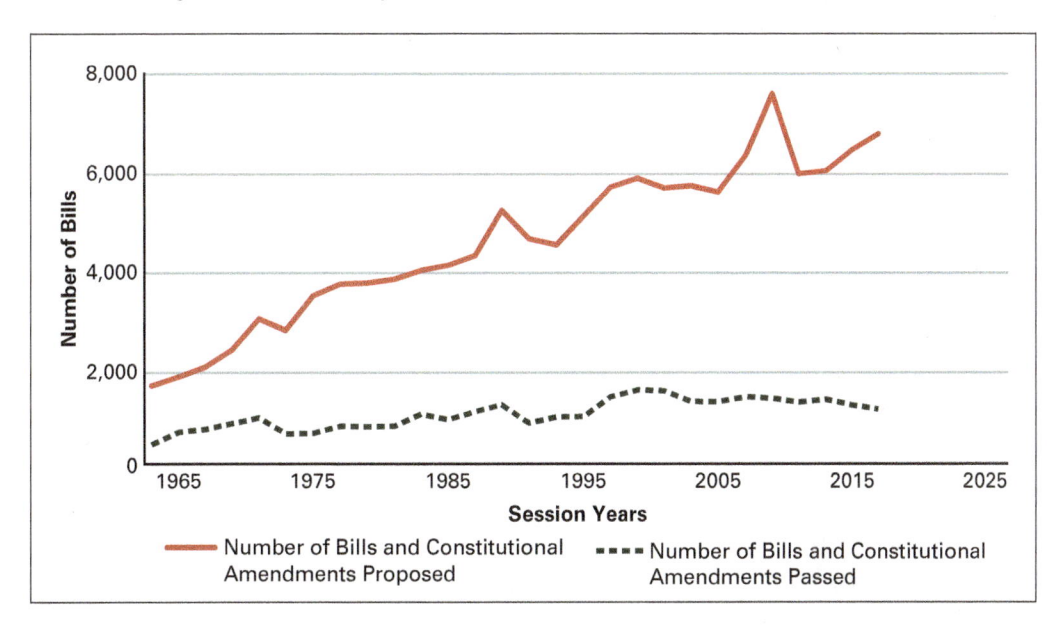

Committee chairs have considerable power over legislation assigned to their committees. They may kill bills by simply refusing to schedule them for a hearing. After a hearing, a chair may send a bill to a subcommittee that he or she stacks with members opposed to the legislation, thus allowing the bill to die slowly and quietly in a legislative deep freeze. Even if a majority of committee members want to approve a bill, the chair can simply refuse to recognize such a motion. Most chairs, however, are sensitive to the wishes of the presiding officers. If the speaker or the lieutenant governor wants a bill to win committee approval or another measure to die in committee, a chair usually will comply.

Referral to a subcommittee does not always mean the death of a bill. Subcommittees also help committees distribute the workload. They work out compromises, correct technical problems in bills, or draft substitute legislation to accommodate competing interests.

STANDING COMMITTEES The number and names of committees are periodically revised under House and Senate rules, but there have been relatively few major changes in the basic committee structure in recent years. During the 2019 regular session, the Senate had sixteen **standing committees**, varying in membership from five to fifteen. The House had thirty-four standing committees, with memberships ranging from five to twenty-seven (see Table 5–2). Each senator served on as many as four or five committees and each House member on two or three.

standing committee
A legislative committee that specializes in bills by subject matter or plays a procedural role in the lawmaking process. A bill has to win committee approval before the full House or Senate can consider it.

TABLE 5–2 SENATE AND HOUSE STANDING COMMITTEES, EIGHTY-SIXTH LEGISLATURE, REGULAR SESSION, 2019

Senate Committees	Number of Members	House Committees	Number of Members
Administration	7	Elections	9
Agriculture	5	Energy Resources	11
Business and Commerce	9	Environmental Regulation	9
Criminal Justice	7	General Investigating	5
Education	11	Higher Education	11
Finance	15	Homeland Security and Public Safety	9
Health and Human Services	9	House Administration	11
Higher Education	7	Human Services	9
Intergovernmental Relations	7	Insurance	9
Natural Resources and Economic Development	11	International Relations and Economic Development	9
Nominations	7	Judiciary and Civil Jurisprudence	9
Property Tax	5	Juvenile Justice and Family Issues	9
State Affairs	9	Land and Resource Management	9
Transportation	9	Licensing and Administrative Procedures	11
Veteran Affairs and Border Security	7	Local and Consent Calendars	11
Water and Rural Affairs	7	Natural Resources	11
House Committees	**Number of Members**	Pensions, Investments, and Financial Services	11
Agriculture and Livestock	9	Public Education	13
Appropriations	27	Public Health	11
Business and Industry	9	Redistricting	15
Calendars	11	Resolutions	11
Corrections	9	State Affairs	13
County Affairs	9	Transportation	13
Criminal Jurisprudence	9	Urban Affairs	9
Culture, Recreation, and Tourism	9	Ways and Means	11
Defense and Veterans' Affairs	9		

SOURCE: Texas Senate and House.

Most committees are substantive. They hold public hearings and study bills related to their particular subject areas, such as public education, public health, transportation, or insurance. A few committees are procedural, including the House Resolutions Committee, which handles many routine congratulatory resolutions, such as for a high school football team after a state championship or a prominent constituent on her 100th birthday, and the House Calendars Committee, which schedules bills for debate by the full House.

Some committees play more dominant roles than others in the lawmaking process, particularly in the House. The House State Affairs Committee, for example, handles many more major statewide bills than the Committee on Culture, Recreation, and Tourism or the Committee on Agriculture and Livestock. The House Urban Affairs and County Affairs committees handle several hundred bills of importance to local governments each session. The importance of a committee is determined by the area of public policy over which it has jurisdiction or by its role in the House's operating procedure.

The House **Calendars Committee** historically has had more life-and-death power over legislation than any other committee because it sets the order of debate on the House floor. During each regular session, it kills hundreds of bills that have been approved by substantive committees by refusing to schedule them for debate by the full House or scheduling them so late in the session that they do not have time to win Senate approval. This committee traditionally works closely with the speaker and is one means by which the speaker and the speaker's team control the House. Although legislators may complain about the committee killing their bills, some lawmakers appreciate the fact that the panel can keep controversial legislation—on which many members would rather not have to cast votes—from reaching the House floor.

Calendars Committee
A special procedural committee in the Texas House of Representatives that schedules bills that already have been approved by other committees for floor debate.

The state budget is the single most important bill—the only one that absolutely has to pass every other year—because, through it, lawmakers determine how much money is spent on the state's public programs and services. In the House, the Appropriations Committee takes the lead in drafting state budgets, and the House Ways and Means Committee normally is responsible for producing any tax or revenue measures necessary to balance the budget. The Ways and Means Committee also sometimes takes the lead in drafting legislation to reduce taxes. Two of the most important committees in the Senate are the Finance Committee, which handles the budget and, usually, tax bills, and the State Affairs Committee, which, like its House counterpart, handles a variety of major legislation.

CONFERENCE COMMITTEES To become law, legislation must be passed in exactly the same form by the House and the Senate. If one chamber refuses to accept the other's version of a bill, a **conference committee** can try to resolve the differences. The presiding officers appoint conference committees of five senators and five representatives. If at least three senators and three House members on a conference committee approve a compromise bill, it is sent back to the full House and the full Senate for approval or rejection. Neither chamber can amend the compromise bill. Over the years, some conference committees have drafted legislation dramatically different from earlier House or Senate versions, even though a conference panel is supposed to do no more than adjust the differences between the House and the Senate bills. Legislative rules now require both chambers to pass a concurrent resolution to allow a conference committee to add significant new language.

conference committee
A panel of House members and senators appointed to work out a compromise on a bill if the House and the Senate passed different versions of the legislation.

SELECT COMMITTEES Special **select committees** are sometimes appointed by the governor, the lieutenant governor, and the speaker to study major policy issues, usually during the interims between legislative sessions. These panels sometimes include private citizens as well as legislators, and they usually recommend legislation. Standing legislative committees also study issues in their assigned areas during the interims, and the presiding officers can ask them to conduct special investigations or inquiries pertaining to governmental matters.

select committee
A special committee—usually appointed by the governor, the lieutenant governor, and the speaker—that studies a specific issue and makes recommendations to the legislature. This panel usually includes private citizens as well as legislators.

5.4.4 Legislative Staff

A legislator's staff can help determine his or her success, and both the quality and quantity of legislative staffs have been significantly enhanced over the past forty years.[27] This change reflects the development of a professional approach to lawmaking. As Texas's population has grown, the state has become increasingly urban and its problems more complex. During recent regular sessions, the House and the Senate combined have had more than 2,000 employees. They include Capitol and district office staff for individual senators and representatives, committee staffs, assistants to the lieutenant governor and the speaker, and other support staff hired directly by the House and the Senate.

Other staff members are assigned to the Legislative Budget Board, the legislature's financial research arm; the Legislative Council, which researches issues and drafts bills and resolutions for introduction by legislators; and the Legislative Reference Library, which provides resource materials for lawmakers, their staffs, and the general public. Additional support staff members are assigned to the Sunset Advisory Commission, which assists the legislature in periodic reviews of state agencies, and to the state auditor, who is chosen by and reports to the legislative leadership.

A key support group in the House is the House Research Organization, which is supported by funds from the House budget and governed by a steering committee representing a cross-section of Democratic and Republican House members. During legislative sessions, its staff provides detailed analyses, including pro and con arguments, of many bills on the daily House calendar. During interims between sessions, it provides periodic analyses of proposed constitutional amendments and other issues. The Senate has a similar organization, the Senate Research Center.

The quality of other resources available to lawmakers also has improved in recent years. Legislators and their staffs can routinely check the status or texts of bills online, and so can the public. The Legislative Council maintains a website that includes committee schedules, bill texts and analyses, and other legislative information. Members of the public can use the website to identify their state representatives and senators and learn what bills their legislators are sponsoring. In addition, the public can view House and Senate floor debate and committee meetings online. Also, the House and the Senate each maintains its own website.

Rules and the Lawmaking Process

5.5 Outline how a bill becomes a law and the obstacles in the lawmaking process in Texas.

Laws are made in Texas according to the same basic process followed by the U.S. Congress and other state legislatures.[28] But, as the discussion of the committee system already has indicated, the rules that determine how and when legislation is considered are complex and loaded with traps whereby legislation can be killed. One often hears the remark around the Capitol that "there are a lot more ways to kill a bill than to pass one." Legislators and lobbyists with expertise in the rules can wield a tremendous amount of influence over the lawmaking process. The House and the Senate have detailed sets of rules governing the disposition of legislation, and each has a parliamentarian to help interpret them. Understanding how laws are made—or, at least, having a basic knowledge of the steps and potential traps involved in the process—is important to anyone wanting to navigate the policymaking arena.

5.5.1 The Lawmaking Process

In broad strokes, the process by which a bill becomes law starts with the introduction of a bill in the House or the Senate and its referral to a committee by the presiding officer, which constitutes the first **reading** (see Figure 5–5). That is the only reading most bills will ever get.

---

reading
Bills are required to go through three readings in both houses of the legislature. The first reading occurs with the introduction of a bill in the House or the Senate and its referral to a committee by the presiding officer. The second reading is the initial debate by the full House or Senate on a bill that has been approved by a committee. The third occurs with the final presentation of a bill before the full House or Senate.

FIGURE 5-5 HOW A BILL BECOMES A LAW

To become a law, a bill has to pass these basic steps in the legislative process and survive other procedural obstacles.

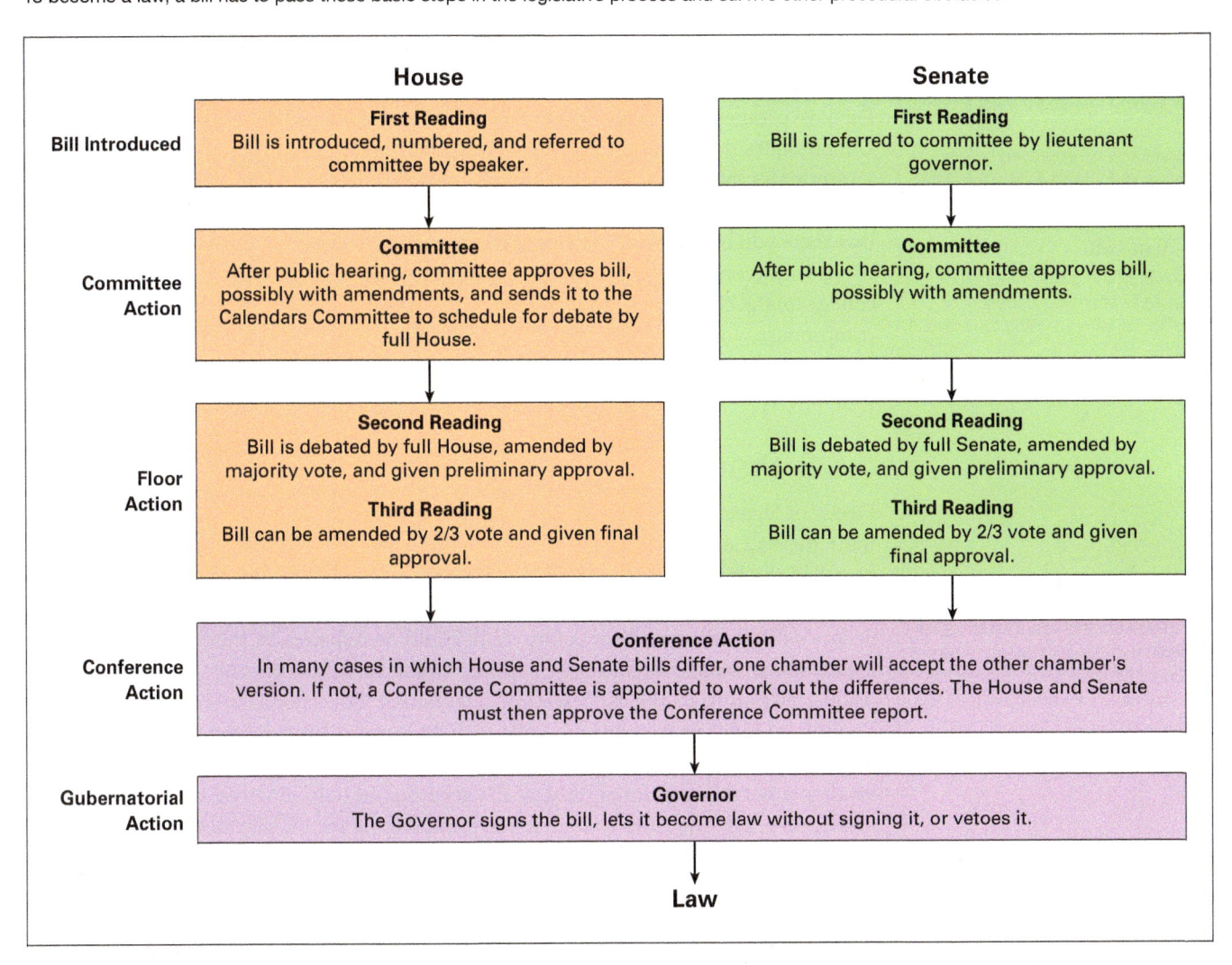

House

- **Bill Introduced — First Reading:** Bill is introduced, numbered, and referred to committee by speaker.
- **Committee Action — Committee:** After public hearing, committee approves bill, possibly with amendments, and sends it to the Calendars Committee to schedule for debate by full House.
- **Floor Action — Second Reading:** Bill is debated by full House, amended by majority vote, and given preliminary approval.
- **Third Reading:** Bill can be amended by 2/3 vote and given final approval.

Senate

- **Bill Introduced — First Reading:** Bill is referred to committee by lieutenant governor.
- **Committee Action — Committee:** After public hearing, committee approves bill, possibly with amendments.
- **Floor Action — Second Reading:** Bill is debated by full Senate, amended by majority vote, and given preliminary approval.
- **Third Reading:** Bill can be amended by 2/3 vote and given final approval.

Conference Action: In many cases in which House and Senate bills differ, one chamber will accept the other chamber's version. If not, a Conference Committee is appointed to work out the differences. The House and Senate must then approve the Conference Committee report.

Gubernatorial Action — Governor: The Governor signs the bill, lets it become law without signing it, or vetoes it.

Law

A bill that wins committee approval and clears procedural hurdles (the Calendars Committee in the House and a procedural vote, explained below, in the Senate) can be considered on second reading by the full House or Senate, where it is debated and often amended. Some amendments are designed to improve a bill or make it more acceptable to a political viewpoint; others are designed to kill it by loading it down with controversial or objectionable provisions that will prompt legislators to vote against it. Lawmakers may offer amendments that they know have little chance of being approved, merely to make favorable political points with constituents or interest groups.

If a bill is approved on second reading, it has to win one more vote on third reading before it goes to the other chamber for the same process, beginning with its referral to a committee. If the second chamber approves the bill without any changes or amendments, it then goes to the governor for signature into law or **veto**. The governor can allow a bill to become law without his or her signature. This procedure differs from the pocket veto power afforded the president of the United States. The presidential pocket veto varies, depending on whether Congress is in session or adjourned. If Congress is in session, the president has ten days (excluding Sundays) to either sign or veto the bill or the bill automatically becomes law. If Congress adjourns before the president acts, the bill does not become law unless signed by the president. If the governor of Texas does not sign or veto a bill by a certain deadline, it becomes law. A veto can be overridden and the bill allowed to become law by a two-thirds vote of both

veto
The power of the governor to reject, or kill, a bill passed by the legislature.

houses, but this process has rarely been attempted in Texas because in most cases the regular legislative session has ended before the governor has exercised his veto power.

The governor has to accept or reject a bill in its entirety, except for the general **appropriations bill**, or state budget, from which the governor can delete specific spending proposals while approving others. This power is called the **line-item veto**. Forty-two other state governors have the line-item veto, but the president of the United States does not. The budget or any other bill approved by the legislature that appropriates money has to be certified by the comptroller before it is sent to the governor. Texas has a pay-as-you-go state government, and the comptroller has to certify that there will be enough available revenue to fund the bill.

If the second chamber amends the bill, the originating house has to approve, or concur in, the changes or request that the bill be sent to a conference committee. Any compromise worked out by a conference committee has to be approved by both houses, without further changes, before it is sent to the governor. All bills except tax bills can originate in either the House or the Senate. Tax bills must originate in the House.

5.5.2 Procedural Obstacles to Legislation

Pieces of legislation encounter other significant procedural obstacles. In addition to the House's Calendars Committee (discussed earlier in this chapter), what used to be called the **two-thirds rule** for debating bills on the Senate floor was a high hurdle to controversial bills. The two-thirds rule required the approval of twenty-one of the Senate's thirty-one members before a bill could be debated on the Senate floor. That meant many bills with majority support could be killed by only eleven senators. At the beginning of the 2015 session, Lieutenant Governor Dan Patrick convinced Republican senators to change the rule to make it more difficult for a minority of senators to block the majority's legislative priorities. The rule was changed to require a smaller supermajority, three-fifths of the senators, or only nineteen votes, to approve debate on a bill. The rules change made it impossible for the eleven Democrats in the Senate that year to block any legislation without the support of at least one Republican because it now took at least twelve senators to block debate. Consequently, as noted earlier in this chapter, Patrick has won Senate approval of controversial Republican priorities, including gun rights bills, which were opposed by many Democrats.

The Senate rules also provide for **tags** and **filibusters**, both of which can be effective in killing bills near the end of a legislative session. A tag allows an individual senator to postpone a committee hearing on any bill for at least forty-eight hours, a delay that often is fatal in the crush of unfinished business during a session's closing days. The filibuster, a procedure that allows a senator to speak against a bill for as long as he or she can stand and talk, usually is little more than a nuisance to a bill's supporters early in a session, but it, too, can become a potent and ever-present threat against controversial legislation near the end of a session. Often, the mere likelihood of a senator speaking against a bill is sufficient to kill a measure. Late in a session, the lieutenant governor may refuse to recognize the sponsor of a controversial bill for fear a filibuster will fatally delay other major legislative proposals. State Senator Bill Meier of Euless spoke for forty-three hours in 1977 against a bill dealing with the public reporting of on-the-job accidents. In so doing, he captured the world's record for the longest filibuster, which he held for years.

The most well-known filibuster in recent years was Democratic state Senator Wendy Davis's eleven-hour filibuster that helped defeat an abortion regulation bill during the closing hours of a special session in 2013. Her victory was only temporary because the bill was passed during a subsequent special session. But the national publicity Davis received for her effort raised her political star power and fund-raising ability to the point that she easily won the Democratic nomination for governor in 2014, only to lose the general election to Republican Greg Abbott.

---

appropriations bill
A legislative action authorizing the expenditure of money for a public program or purpose. A general appropriations bill approved by the legislature every two years is the state budget.

line-item veto
The power of the governor to reject certain parts of an appropriation, or spending, bill without killing the entire measure.

two-thirds rule
A rule under which the Texas Senate used to operate that required approval of at least two-thirds of senators before a bill could be debated on the Senate floor. The rule was weakened in 2015 to require approval of three-fifths of senators instead of two-thirds.

tag
A rule that allows an individual senator to postpone a committee hearing on any bill for at least forty-eight hours, a delay that can be fatal to a bill during the closing days of a legislative session.

filibuster
A procedure that allows a senator to speak against a bill for as long as he or she can stand and talk. It can become a formidable obstacle or threat against controversial bills near the end of a legislative session.

SWARMING THE CAPITOL
Abortion-rights protesters crowded into the Capitol rotunda in July 2013 as the Texas legislature was completing work on a bill imposing new restrictions on abortion. The controversial law, which sparked repeated demonstrations by people on both sides of the issue and required two special sessions to pass, was struck down three years later by the U.S. Supreme Court.

5.5.3 Shortcuts and Confusion

Sponsors of legislation languishing in an unfriendly committee or subcommittee often try to resurrect their proposals by attaching them as amendments to related bills being debated on the House or Senate floor. Such maneuvers may be successful, particularly if opponents are absent or if the sponsor succeeds in "mumbling" an amendment through without challenge. Nevertheless, the speaker or the lieutenant governor must find that such amendments are relevant to the pending bill if an alert opponent raises a point of order against them.

To facilitate the passage of noncontroversial and local pieces of legislation, which affect one city or one county, the House and the Senate have periodic local and consent or local and uncontested **calendars**, which are conducted under special rules that enable scores of bills to be routinely and quickly approved by the full House or Senate without debate. Bills of major statewide significance sometimes get placed on these calendars, but it takes only one senator or three representatives to have any bill struck.

Compromises on controversial legislation often are worked out behind closed doors long before a bill is debated on the House or Senate floor or even afforded a public committee hearing. It can be argued that this approach to consensus building is an efficient, businesslike way to enact legislation, but it also serves to discourage the free and open debate that is so important to the democratic process.

Recent speakers also have discouraged the taking of **record votes** during House floor debate on most bills. A constitutional amendment approved by Texas voters in 2007 requires record votes on final House and Senate passage of all legislation, except local bills. But many important amendments in the House are decided with "division" votes, which, like record votes, are taken on the House's computerized voting machine. But division votes, unlike record votes, leave no formal record of how

calendar
Agenda or the list of bills to be considered by the House or the Senate on a given day.

record vote
A vote taken in the House or the Senate for which a permanent record is kept, listing how individual legislators voted.

individual legislators voted once the voting boards are cleared. This approach saves the taxpayers some printing costs and can give lawmakers some relief from lobby pressure. But it also serves to keep the public in the dark about significant decisions made by their elected representatives. The fewer record votes that legislators have to make, the more easily they can dodge accountability to their constituents. Sometimes, noncontroversial issues are decided with voice votes, in which legislators simply say "aye" or "no" with the presiding officer judging the outcome.

House rules restrict the practice of legislators punching the voting buttons on the desks of absent members when record votes are taken, but the practice occurs regularly. This phantom voting normally is challenged only in cases of close votes, when legislators on the losing side request a roll-call verification of the computerized vote, and the votes of members who do not answer the roll call are struck. The House was embarrassed in 1991 when a lawmaker, who had died several hours earlier, was recorded as answering the daily roll call and voting on several record votes. His body was discovered later at his Austin apartment. This voting practice is not a problem in the smaller Senate, where the secretary of the Senate orally calls the roll on record votes.

Legislators often have their minds made up on an issue before the matter is debated on the floor, but there are many bills that most lawmakers will have little or no interest in and will not bother to study. When legislators are not familiar with a bill, they often simply vote the way the sponsor votes. Despite what tourists in the gallery may think, legislators who raise their fingers above their heads when a vote is taken are not asking the presiding officer for a rest break. They are signaling their vote and encouraging other lawmakers to vote the same way. One finger means yes; two fingers mean no.

In part because of the rules under which the legislature operates, in part because of the heavy volume of legislation, and in part because of political maneuvering, the closing weeks of a regular session are hectic. Legislators in both houses are asked to vote on dozens of conference committee reports they do not have time to read. With hundreds of bills being rushed through the legislature to the governor's desk, mistakes occur. Deliberate attempts also are made—often successfully—to use the confusion to slip in major changes in law.

5.5.4 Legislative Norms

In addition to the formal rules of each legislative body, there are unwritten rules, or **norms**, that shape the behavior of legislators and other actors in the lawmaking process.[29] The legislature is like most other social institutions in that its members have perceptions of the institution and the process as well as the way they are expected to behave or carry out their responsibilities. Other participants also impose their views and expectations on lawmakers.

The legislative process is designed to institutionalize conflict, and the rules and norms of the legislature are designed to give this conflict an element of civility. Debate is often intense and vigorous, and it may be difficult for some lawmakers to separate attacks on their positions from attacks on their personalities. But most legislators have learned the necessity of decorum and courtesy. Even if lawmakers believe some of their opponents in the House and Senate are deceitful, personal attacks on other legislators are considered unacceptable. Such attacks, even to the point of fistfights, occasionally occur, but they are rare.

Women still are significantly outnumbered by men in both the House and the Senate, and sexist behavior and comments are not uncommon among some male legislators, staffers, and lobbyists. In 2011, one male legislator during debate on the House floor went so far as to ask a female lawmaker if her breasts were real or fake. He didn't use those words but inquired instead about real or man-made

norm
An unwritten rule of institutional behavior that is critical to the stability and effectiveness of the institution.

VOTING NO
These members of the Texas House are signaling "no" votes (two fingers held aloft) and encouraging colleagues to join them.

mountains when he addressed his female colleague during debate over a West Texas state park. His metaphor wasn't lost on anyone. State Senator Joan Huffman, a Republican from Houston, said the legislature was "probably the last of the good ol' boy clubs." Whatever anyone calls it, state Representative Senfronia Thompson, an African American Democrat from Houston and one of the most senior members of the House, has been fighting the problem since her first session in 1973, when a male lawmaker called her his "black mistress." In 2011, almost forty years later, she made a strong speech on the House floor, denouncing a well-known lobbying group for distributing an overtly sexist flier against one of her bills and lambasting sexist practices in the Capitol in general. In an interview with the *Texas Observer*, which published an article in 2013 about the legislature's "Sexist Little Secret," Democratic state Representative Donna Howard of Austin said some male legislators seemed to be "acting like middle-school boys." Several other women legislators of both parties also said they were offended by such practices. But Thompson said many other women didn't speak up because they feared that doing so would hurt their political careers.[30]

Complaints of sexism and sexual harassment at the Capitol surfaced anew in 2017 following national media reports of sexual misconduct by prominent men in the entertainment and political arenas and the birth of the #MeToo movement. After the *Daily Beast* and Texas media outlets began reporting complaints of women legislative staffers and former staffers against some lawmakers, the Texas House and Senate began taking initial steps to address the issue, but it was unknown how hard either body would eventually come down on elected offenders. The House Administration Committee adopted a policy defining actions that could amount to sexual harassment and a process for victims to pursue complaints. In 2019, the House strengthened that policy by giving the House General Investigating Committee the authority to investigate complaints of

STRONG ADVOCATE FOR WOMEN
State Representative Senfronia Thompson, a Democrat from Houston, delivered a forceful speech on the House floor against a sexist brochure distributed by a lobby group against an insurance bill she sponsored.

harassment and recommend sanctions. If a complaint involved a House member, the committee would be required to appoint an independent investigator. The Senate revised its sexual harassment policy in 2018 to provide examples of what constitutes sexual harassment and provide steps for reporting inappropriate behavior. But it didn't provide a penalty for harassment or establish a procedure for senators to investigate colleagues accused of harassment.[31]

The Emerging Party System

5.6 Outline the changes in partisanship in the Texas legislature.

Unlike the U.S. Congress, the Texas legislature is not organized along party lines, with rules automatically giving leadership positions to members of the majority party. The Texas arrangement is due primarily to the absence or near-absence of Republican legislators for almost a century and the more recent practice—before Republicans gained a House majority in 2003—of rural Democrats aligning with a Republican minority to produce an unofficial conservative coalition. As recently as 1971, the year before a federal court declared urban, countywide House districts unconstitutional, there were only ten Republicans in the House and two in the Senate. As Republicans increased their numbers, they aligned themselves with conservative Democrats to attempt to influence the lawmaking process. This ideological coalition became increasingly important as single-member districts boosted not only the number of Republican lawmakers but also the number of moderate and liberal Democratic legislators—including many Hispanics and African Americans—elected from urban areas. The coalition enabled conservative Democrats to maintain some control as the base of power shifted in their own party.

Republicans and conservative Democrats formally organized the Texas Conservative Coalition in the House in the 1980s. It remained a strong force through the 1990s, under the chairmanship of Representative Warren Chisum of Pampa, who switched from the Democratic to the Republican Party in 1995 and has since retired.

5.6.1 The Growth of Partisanship

With the growth of the Republican Party in Texas in the 1980s, Speaker Gib Lewis, a conservative urban Democrat, appointed Republicans to chair some of the major House committees. But partisan divisions increased in 1987 when Lewis, Democratic Lieutenant Governor Bill Hobby, and Republican Governor Bill Clements fought over a new state budget in the face of a large revenue shortfall. On one side of the debate were moderate and liberal Democratic legislators, including urban and South Texas minorities whose constituents had the most to gain from a tax increase and the most to lose from deep cuts in spending on education and human services. On the other side were a handful of conservative, primarily rural Democrats and a number of Republicans with middle- and upper-middle-class suburban constituents who insisted on fiscal restraint. Clements eventually gave in and supported a tax increase, but most of the House Republicans continued to fight the tax bill until it was approved in a summer special session.

In 1989, Republicans formed their first caucus in the House, and soon both parties had active caucuses in both the House and the Senate. These partisan organizations began to marshal legislative support on selected issues and become active in legislative races, as Republicans began to wage well-financed challenges of Democratic incumbents.

During the 1995 legislative session, when Democrats still held a majority of House and Senate seats, Lieutenant Governor Bob Bullock and Speaker Pete Laney, both Democrats, were strongly supportive of Republican Governor George W. Bush's legislative priorities. They were instrumental in helping Bush make major changes in public education and juvenile justice and set limits on civil liability lawsuits.

After many bitterly contested legislative races, Republicans won their first majority in the Senate in modern times during the 1996 elections and gained four seats in the House to narrow the Democratic majority in that body to 82 to 65. Bipartisanship still prevailed for the most part in the 1997 session, but legislative fights with strong partisan overtones increased that year and in subsequent sessions over such issues as abortion and gay rights and whether tax dollars should be spent to pay for private school tuition.

Another partisan-charged issue in 1999 and 2001 was an attempt by some Democrats to strengthen the state law against hate crimes after three white men in East Texas were accused—and later convicted—of dragging an African American man, James Byrd Jr., to death behind a pickup truck. Most of the Republican opposition to the bill stemmed from the fact that it increased penalties for crimes motivated by prejudice against homosexuals as well as prejudice related to race or religion. Social conservatives opposed that provision and, in 1999, Governor Bush—who did not want to anger conservatives on the eve of his race for the Republican presidential nomination—called the bill unnecessary. The measure, which sponsors named for Byrd, died in the Senate in 1999 but became law in 2001.

5.6.2 Republicans Take Control

Aided by the GOP-controlled 2001 redistricting process discussed earlier in this chapter, Republicans made major gains in the 2002 elections. They increased their majority in the state Senate to 19 to 12; captured an 88-to-62 majority in the Texas House, their first since Reconstruction; and elected Republican Tom Craddick as speaker. Those victories, along with Governor Rick Perry's and Lieutenant Governor David Dewhurst's elections, gave Republicans control of all the points of power in the statehouse. They made significant budgetary cuts to close a $10 billion revenue shortfall without raising state taxes, enacted significant new restrictions on civil lawsuits, and won the contentious fight over congressional redistricting. Partisanship was stronger that year than it had been since Republicans became competitive in Texas.

Craddick and Dewhurst appointed Democrats, as well as Republicans, to chair committees and serve in other leadership positions. Craddick also appointed a Democrat, state Representative Sylvester Turner of Houston, as speaker pro tempore. But Craddick stacked the chairs of key committees and the membership of the budget-writing House Appropriations Committee with Republicans who clearly reflected his conservative viewpoint. After winning a change in House rules that removed seniority as a factor in appropriations appointments, the new speaker bumped from the panel three outspoken Democrats who opposed budget cuts.

Democrats regained some of their lost House seats in subsequent elections and cut the Republican majority in the House to 76 to 74 in 2009. However, fueled by the rise of the ultraconservative Tea Party movement and midterm opposition to President Obama's policies, Republicans came roaring back in the 2010 elections, capturing a 101-to-49 House majority. After some subsequent losses, Republicans had an 83-to-67 majority in the House and a 19-to-12 majority in the Senate in 2019. Democrats are expected eventually to recapture majorities in both the House and the Senate, primarily because of the growing, Democratic-leaning Hispanic population. The legislature sooner or later even may organize itself along the same partisan lines as the U.S. Congress—with distinct party positions, such as floor leaders, caucus leaders, and whips. If this were to happen, the legislative rules and powers of the presiding officers discussed earlier in this chapter would change significantly. But this development will depend on how long Republicans continue to dominate the statehouse, on how Democrats react, and on the future leadership personalities that emerge in both parties. Another factor will be how well the factions in the Republican Party—the traditional, more-moderate Republicans and the social conservatives and ultraconservatives of the Religious Right and the Tea Party—accommodate each other. Their differences have become increasingly pronounced on some issues and in some legislative primary races in recent years.

5.6.3 Other Legislative Caucuses

caucus
A group of legislators who band together for common political or partisan goals or along ethnic or geographic lines.

In addition to Republican and Democratic **caucuses** in the Texas House and Senate, other groups, including Hispanic and African American House members, have formed caucuses as their numbers have increased. Their cohesive voting blocs have proved influential in speaker elections and the resolution of major statewide issues, such as health care for the poor, public school finance, and taxation. Their ability to broker votes has won them committee chairs and other concessions they may not otherwise have received.

Legislative Behavior

5.7 Assess the influences on the decision making of Texas lawmakers.

Although representative government is an essential component of American society, debates continue over how people elected to public office should identify the interests and preferences of the people they represent.[32] Political theorists as well as legislators struggle with the problem of translating the will of the people into public policy. Most legislators represent diverse groups and interests in their districts. During a normal legislative session, there are thousands of proposed laws to consider, and legislators must constantly make decisions that will benefit or harm specific constituents. Understanding legislative decision making is crucial toward understanding the policymaking process.

5.7.1 Legislators and Their Constituents

Except for an occasional emotional issue—such as abortion regulation or whether people should be allowed to carry guns on college campuses—most Texans pay little attention to what the legislature is doing. That is why they sometimes are surprised to discover they have to pay a few extra dollars to get their cars inspected or enter a state park. Few Texans—particularly in the large cities that are divided among numerous lawmakers—can identify their state representatives or senators by name, and far fewer can tell you what their legislators have voted for or against. This public inattention gives most legislators great latitude when voting on public policies. It also is a major reason most incumbent lawmakers who seek reelection are successful. But, of course, there are exceptions, such as the Republican surge in 2010, fueled, in part, by the conservative Tea Party movement and casualties of recent ideological warfare in the Republican primary.

Although legislators are aware of latent public opinion, they tend to be more responsive to interest groups or to attentive members of the public who operate in their individual districts or statewide.[33] People who pay attention to public policy issues are a relatively small portion of the total population, but they can be mobilized for or against an individual legislator. These include community opinion leaders, such as mayors and prominent businesspeople, who are able to communicate information to other individuals about a legislator's performance. Or they may belong to public interest, ideological, or special interest groups that compile legislative voting records on issues important to their memberships.

Tea Party groups and other ultraconservatives, who have had significant voting strength in the Republican primary in recent election cycles, are among the minority of voters who do pay attention to the legislature, and they have helped elect a significant bloc of House members who consistently vote to support the conservative ideology on selected issues. These legislators are antiabortion, anti–gay rights, anti-immigration, antitaxes, and pro–gun rights. Several in recent years have unseated more moderate Republicans, aided by grassroots campaigns, social media, and campaign contributions from wealthy, conservative Texans. Many have been elected with the support of Empower Texans, a conservative group that actively tried to unseat Speaker Joe Straus by targeting his House allies for defeat. After Straus's retirement, the group remained active, still supporting candidates who shared its conservative ideology.

Many special interest groups can contribute thousands of dollars to a legislator's reelection campaign or to the campaign of an opponent. Politically astute legislators take note of all the letters, phone calls, petitions, emails, social media comments, and visits by their constituents—plus media coverage—lest they lose touch with a significant number of voters.

A favorite voter-contact tool of many legislators is a newsletter they can mail to households in their districts at state expense. These mailings usually include photos of the lawmaker plus articles summarizing, in the best possible light, his or her accomplishments in Austin. Sometimes, legislators include a public opinion survey seeking constituent responses on a number of issues. In addition, lawmakers maintain their own websites, and nearly all are on social media. Even so, some legislators can become politically vulnerable if an ideological or interest group with significant resources is determined to unseat them.

5.7.2 Legislative Decision Making

With 7,500 pieces of legislation introduced during a regular session—the level reached in 2019—no legislator can possibly read and understand each bill, much less the hundreds of amendments offered during committee and floor debate. Despite moments of high drama when major statewide issues are being debated, much of the legislative workload is tedious and dull and produces little direct political benefit for most senators and representatives. But many of those bills contain hidden traps and potential controversies that can haunt a legislator later, often during a reelection campaign. So, legislators rely on numerous information sources and the norms of the process to assist them in decision making.

To make the process work, legislators must accommodate the competing interests they represent and achieve reciprocity with their fellow legislators. An individual legislator usually will have no direct political or personal interest in most bills because much legislation is local in nature and affects only a limited number of lawmakers and constituents. A legislator accumulates obligations as he or she supports other lawmakers' bills, with the full expectation that the action will be returned in kind (see Table 5–3).

A number of other factors, however, help shape lawmakers' decisions on major legislation.[34] The wishes of constituents are considered, particularly if there is a groundswell of dominant opinion coming from a legislator's district. This factor is strongly reflected in the voting patterns of conservative House members elected with Tea Party support in the Republican primary. As noted earlier, they consistently vote against abortion, gay rights, immigration, and taxes and vote for gun rights. If they don't, they may very well be replaced during the next election cycle. Legislators also exchange information with other lawmakers, particularly with members who share their political philosophy and colleagues from their counties or regions of the state. Lawmakers often take cues from the sponsors of a bill, the speaker's and lieutenant governor's leadership teams, or their party caucuses.

A legislator's staff also assists in decision making by evaluating the substantive merits and political implications of legislation. The Legislative Budget Board and the Legislative Council provide technical information and expertise.

TABLE 5-3 SOME INFLUENCES ON LEGISLATORS' VOTES

1. Personal political philosophies and policy interests
2. Personal and political friends
3. Other legislators
4. Committee chairs
5. Staff members
6. Interest groups and lobbyists
7. The governor
8. Other elected administrators and state agency heads
9. Legislative leaders
10. Party leaders
11. Local elected officials
12. The media
13. Court decisions
14. Regional blocs within the state
15. County delegations
16. Legislative caucuses
17. National and state trends
18. Programs that have worked in other states

Interest groups are major sources of information and influence. Although an individual legislator occasionally will rail against a specific group, most lawmakers consider interest groups essential to the legislative process. Through their lobbyists, interest groups provide a vast amount of technical information and can signal the level of constituency interest, support, or opposition to proposed laws. A senator or representative can use interest groups to establish coalitions of support for a bill, and some legislators become closely identified with powerful interest groups because they almost always support a particular lobby's position.

The governor also influences the legislature. He or she raises the public's consciousness of issues and promotes policies through speeches and the media. The governor communicates indirectly to individual lawmakers through the governor's staff, party leaders, and influential persons in a lawmaker's district. The governor also meets with legislators one-on-one or in groups. At the beginning of each regular session, the governor outlines his or her legislative priorities in a State of the State address to a joint session of the House and the Senate. Throughout the session, the governor usually has frequent meetings with the lieutenant governor and the speaker.

The governor also may visit the House or the Senate chamber in a personal show of support when legislation that he or she advocates is being debated. Unlike most recent governors, Governor Ann Richards personally testified before legislative committees on several of her priorities during her first year in office. A governor's arm-twisting can include appeals to a lawmaker's reason or conscience, threats of retaliation, appeals for party support, and promises of a quid pro quo. The greatest threat that a governor can hang over a legislator is the possible veto of legislation or a budget item of importance to the lawmaker. In special sessions, the governor can negotiate with a lawmaker over whether to add a bill that is important to the legislator to the special session's agenda, which is controlled by the governor.

Other sources of information and support for legislators are other elected officeholders, such as the attorney general, the comptroller, and the land commissioner. These officials and lawmakers can assist one another in achieving political agendas. Additionally, the news media provide information and perspective on issues in broader political terms.

The relative importance of any groups or actors on decision making is difficult to measure and varies from lawmaker to lawmaker and from issue to issue. Outside influences can be tempered by a legislator's own attitude and opinion. On many issues, legislators get competing advice and pressure. As much as lawmakers may like to be all things to all people, they cannot be. One cannot please both a chemical lobbyist—who is seeking a tax break for a new plant on the Gulf Coast and also happens to be a large campaign contributor—and environmentalists who fear the facility would spoil a nearby wildlife habitat. Nor can one please both the governor who is promoting casino gambling as a new state revenue source and most of the voters in the lawmaker's district who have consistently voted against gambling. The ultimate decision and its eventual political consequences are the legislator's.

Decision-making criteria reflect complex relationships between the legislator and the people represented. Because the overriding consideration for most lawmakers is to get reelected, the legislator must balance these relationships carefully.

5.7.3 Legislative Styles

Some legislators become known for their commitment to producing good legislation. These "workhorses" spend endless hours developing programs and are repeatedly turned to by the presiding officers to handle tough policy issues. Other lawmakers tend to look to their leadership for direction and cues.

Some legislators earn reputations as grandstanders. Almost every legislator has shown off for the media or spectators in the gallery at one time or another, but some develop reputations for this style of behavior. They appear to be more interested in scoring political points with their constituents or interest groups than with becoming proficient in the substance of legislation. Many of these lawmakers are lightweights who contribute little to the legislature's product. Although they may introduce many bills, they are not interested in the details of lawmaking and may have difficulty winning support for their legislation.

The legislature also has a number of opportunists, including members who may pursue policies to benefit their personal businesses or professions. Legislative rules prohibit legislators from voting on issues in which they have a personal monetary interest, but individual lawmakers can interpret that prohibition as they see fit. Many lawmakers will try to cash in on their legislative experience by becoming lobbyists after they leave office for considerably higher pay than they received as legislators.

Still other legislators appear to be little more than spectators. They enjoy the receptions and other perks of the office much more than the drudgery of committee hearings, research, and floor debate. Some quickly weary of the legislative process and, after a few sessions, decide against seeking reelection.[35]

5.7.4 Legislative Ethics and Reform

Most legislators are honest, hardworking individuals. But the weaknesses of a few and the millions of dollars spent by special interests to influence the lawmaking process can undermine Texans' confidence in their legislature and their entire state government. Although legislators cannot pass laws guaranteeing ethical behavior, they can set strong standards for themselves, other public officials, and lobbyists and provide stiff penalties for those who fail to comply. Such reform efforts are periodically attempted, but often they are the result of scandals and fall short of creating an ideal ethical climate.

THE SHARPSTOWN SCANDAL The **Sharpstown stock fraud scandal** rocked the Capitol in 1971 and 1972 and helped produce some far-reaching legislative and political changes.[36] It involved banking legislation sought by Houston banker-developer Frank Sharp that was approved by the legislature in a special session in 1969, only to be vetoed by Governor Preston Smith. A lawsuit filed in 1971 by the federal Securities and Exchange Commission broke the news that Smith, House Speaker Gus Mutscher,

Sharpstown stock fraud scandal

After rocking state government in 1971 and 1972, the scandal helped produce some far-reaching legislative and political changes. It involved the passage of banking legislation sought by Houston financier Frank Sharp and quick profits that some state officials made on stock purchased in an insurance company owned by Sharp with unsecured loans from Sharp's Sharpstown State Bank.

and Representative Tommy Shannon of Fort Worth who had sponsored the bills and others had profited from stock deals involving Sharp's National Bankers Life Insurance Company. Much of their stock was purchased with unsecured loans from Sharp's Sharpstown State Bank.

Mutscher, Shannon, and an aide to the speaker were convicted of conspiracy to accept bribes. Mutscher, who had consolidated power in the House and often was regarded as ironhanded and arbitrary, was forced to resign. Later, the House moved to limit the speaker's power through a modified seniority system for committee appointments. Subsequent speakers still exercised a great deal of power, but it was constrained by expectations that the speaker would be more responsive to the membership. The media also began giving more coverage to the speaker's activities. Fallout from the scandal helped Uvalde rancher Dolph Briscoe, a political outsider, win the 1972 gubernatorial race, and it also resulted in a large turnover in legislative elections that year, one of the rare examples in Texas political history of "kicking the rascals out."

In 1973, the legislature responded with a series of ethics reform laws, including requirements that lobbyists register with the secretary of state and report their total expenditures in their attempts to influence legislation. State officials were required to file public reports identifying their sources of income, although not specific amounts, and political action committees had to list their contributors.

SENATORS GET CHECKS; SPEAKER GETS INDICTED Weaknesses in the 1973 laws, however, were obvious in 1989, when wealthy East Texas poultry producer Lonnie "Bo" Pilgrim distributed $10,000 checks to several senators in the Capitol while lobbying them on workers' compensation reform. The Travis County district attorney could find no law under which to prosecute Pilgrim. Some senators had angrily rejected Pilgrim's checks on the spot; others returned them after the media pounced on the story. But the very next year, Pilgrim—a long-time political contributor—again contributed thousands of dollars to several state officeholders and candidates. This time, the checks were more traditionally sent through the mail, and they were gratefully accepted.

There also were published reports that lobbyists had spent nearly $2 million entertaining lawmakers during the 1989 regular session without having to specify which legislators received the "freebies," thanks to a large loophole in the lobby registration law. News stories about lobbyists treating lawmakers to golf tournaments, ski trips, a junket to Las Vegas for a boxing match, and limousine service to a concert sparked an uproar.

Despite all the headlines, legislative turnover was minimal in 1990. But in early December, about a month after the general election, a Travis County grand jury began investigating Speaker Gib Lewis's ties to a San Antonio law firm, Heard, Goggan, Blair, and Williams. The firm had made large profits collecting delinquent taxes for local governments throughout Texas under a law that allowed it to collect an extra 15 percent from the taxpayers as its fee. For several years, it had successfully lobbied to defeat legislation that would have hurt its business. The *Fort Worth Star-Telegram* reported that Heard Goggan had paid about half of a $10,000 tax bill owed to Tarrant County by a business that Lewis partly owned.[37] The *Houston Chronicle* reported that the grand jury also was looking into a trip that Lewis had taken to a Mexican resort during the 1987 legislative session with four Heard Goggan partners and a lobbyist (all males) and six unrelated women (including a waitress from a topless nightclub in Houston).[38] The trip occurred while a bill opposed by Heard Goggan was dying in a House committee.

On December 28, only twelve days before the 1991 regular legislative session was to convene and Lewis was to be reelected to a fifth term as the House's presiding officer, grand jurors indicted Lewis on two misdemeanor ethics charges. He was accused of soliciting, accepting, and failing to report an illegal gift from Heard Goggan—the partial payment of the tax bill. Insisting he was innocent, Lewis said the tax payment was the settlement of a legal dispute.[39] Lewis won a postponement of his trial under a law that automatically grants continuances to legislators when they are in session.

THE TEXAS ETHICS COMMISSION IS BORN During the 1991 session, with the speaker under indictment, Governor Ann Richards urged the legislature to pass a law imposing tougher ethical requirements on state officials and lobbyists. The Senate approved an ethics bill fairly early in the session, but the House did not act on its version until late in the session. The final bill was produced by a conference committee on the last night of the session in a private meeting and was approved by the House and the Senate only a few minutes before the legislature adjourned at midnight. There was no time to print and distribute copies, and very few legislators knew for sure what was in the bill.

Despite the secrecy and complaints that the bill was not strong enough, Richards signed it. The new law required more reporting of lobbyists' expenditures, prohibited special interests from treating legislators to pleasure trips, prohibited lawmakers from accepting honoraria—or fees—for speaking before special interest groups, and created the Texas Ethics Commission to review complaints about public officials.

But the new law did not put any limits on financial contributions to political campaigns, nor did it prohibit legislator-attorneys from representing clients before state agencies for pay. The new law also provided that complaints filed with the Ethics Commission would remain confidential unless the commission took action, a provision that would allow the commission to dismiss or sit on legitimate complaints without any public accounting.

In January 1992, Lewis announced that he would not seek reelection to another term in the House. In a plea bargain later the same month, prosecutors dropped the two ethics indictments against Lewis in return for the speaker's "no contest" plea to two minor, unrelated charges. Lewis paid a $2,000 fine for failing to publicly disclose a business holding in 1988 and 1989, for which he had already paid a minor civil penalty to the secretary of state.

ETHICS IN THE CONTEMPORARY ERA The legislature enacted other significant changes in ethics laws in 2003. The new provisions required officeholders and candidates to identify the occupations and employers of people who contribute more than $500; required financial reports to be filed with the Ethics Commission electronically; increased penalties for people who filed their reports late; and required—for the first time—officeholders and candidates for municipal offices in the large cities to file personal financial disclosure statements, similar to those already filed by state officeholders.

Also in 2003, Travis County District Attorney Ronnie Earle began a lengthy investigation of whether corporate contributions were used to affect several legislative elections in the Republican takeover of the Texas House in 2002. Republicans accused Earle, a Democrat, of playing politics, but Earle said that he was investigating the possibility that corporate funds had been spent illegally on political activity.

The investigation produced several criminal indictments, including charges against Tom DeLay of Sugar Land, the then-powerful Republican leader of the U.S. House of Representatives. DeLay and two associates were charged with money laundering and conspiracy relating to alleged improper campaign fund-raising for Republican legislative candidates. DeLay and the other defendants said they were innocent, but the politically charged controversy raged for months.

A state district judge dismissed the conspiracy indictment against DeLay and his two associates, but he let the money laundering charge stand. DeLay stepped down from his leadership position in January 2006 and resigned from Congress later that year. He finally went to trial on the money laundering charge in late 2010 and was convicted by a jury of illegally funneling $190,000 in corporate donations to seven Republican legislative candidates in Texas through a money swap with the Republican National Committee. The trial judge sentenced DeLay to three years in prison, but the former congressman remained free on appeal. In 2013, the Third Court of Appeals in Austin reversed DeLay's conviction, ruling that there had been "legally insufficient evidence" to convict him.[40] The reversal was upheld by the Texas Court of Criminal Appeals in 2014.

Governor Greg Abbott listed ethics reform among his priorities for the 2015 session, but lawmakers failed to accomplish his goal. Instead, they enacted a law to allow legislators and state employees accused of white-collar crimes to be prosecuted in their potentially friendlier home counties instead of in Austin by the Travis County district attorney. Senator Joan Huffman of Houston added amendments to two other ethics bills, attempting to create a loophole to allow state officials to avoid publicly disclosing information about their spouse's—including her nightclub-owner husband's—financial holdings. Abbott vetoed both bills that Huffman amended. But the overall result of the session left Texas Ethics Commission Chairman Paul Hobby unimpressed. "If there was any ethics reform, it was in reverse," he said.[41]

Abbott also listed ethics reform among his priorities for the 2017 regular session, but only modest ethics legislation was enacted. One proposal that failed was a bill that would have prohibited people who gave more than $2,500 in political contributions to a governor from serving as an appointee of the governor to a state board or commission. The bill was approved by the House but died in the Senate. Despite requests from some legislators, Abbott declined to include ethics legislation on the agenda for a summer special session in 2017.

CONCLUSION

As you have learned from this chapter, not all legislative issues and decisions are particularly dramatic. Much of the legislative process is tedious, and it is stocked with traps designed to kill more proposed laws than get enacted. As the old cliché suggests, many people consider the lawmaking process only slightly more exciting than

IT IS THE SAME CAPITOL

Congress Avenue and downtown Austin have undergone tremendous changes since this photo was taken in 1943, during World War II. But the Capitol, sitting at the head of the avenue, is clearly recognizable.

watching paint dry. But if you want to feel empowered to do more than complain about your state government, understanding how laws are made and other proposed policies are killed is an essential step. You also need to make a point of learning, if you don't already know, who your state representative and state senator are, and what their legislative records and priorities are. Holding your representative and senator accountable on Election Day is another important step in navigating state government, and one you can't take without knowing who they are and what they purport to stand for.

You also have learned something about the historical development, or institutionalization, of the Texas legislature and how it compares with legislatures in other states in terms of membership, legislative salaries, and length of sessions. The Texas legislature, for example, is one of only a handful of state legislatures that meet in regular session only every other year. And, in Texas, each regular session is only five months long. Is that enough time to meet the modern, complex challenges of a state with 29 million people in it? Most Texans either believe it is or just don't know, as there has been no viable attempt for many years to amend the state constitution to provide for annual sessions. And there won't be one for many more years unless people become convinced that the legislature should meet more often and start demanding change.

Most of you will never run for the legislature or become lobbyists. But each of you is affected every day by policies enacted by the legislature. Someday, you may come to consider a law so onerous or unfair that you want to see it changed or repealed, or you may encounter a situation that requires a new law to address it. If you remember what you learned in this chapter, you will know where to start.

REVIEW THE CHAPTER

Legislative Functions

5.1 List five functions of the Texas legislature, p. 137.

The Texas legislature enacts state laws; sets budgets for state programs and services and, if necessary, enacts new taxes to help pay for them; oversees how state agencies carry out their responsibilities; educates the public about what the legislature does; and represents the public. The representation function, which includes the election process, provides legitimacy to other legislative actions.

Organization of the Texas Legislature and Characteristics of Members

5.2 Explain the organizational structure of the Texas legislature and the characteristics of its members, p. 139.

Texas, the nation's second most populous state, has a part-time, low-paid legislature that operates under restrictions drafted by nineteenth-century Texans in the wake of the repressive Reconstruction era. This raises questions about the legislature's ability to respond readily to modern needs and crises. Because lawmakers meet in regular session every other year, emergencies sometimes require the governor to call special legislative sessions. On a continuum from a highly professional legislature to a citizen or amateur lawmaking body, the Texas legislature is somewhere in between, and turnover is moderate.

As recently as 1971, only a handful of African Americans, Hispanics, Republicans, and women served in the 150-member House of Representatives and the 31-member Senate. But political realignment and federal court intervention in redistricting, particularly the ordering of single-member House districts for urban counties, have significantly increased the number of women, ethnic minorities, and Republicans in the legislature. Republicans now have majorities in both the Texas House and the state Senate.

Representation and Redistricting

5.3 Explain redistricting and its impact on the composition of the Texas legislature, p. 144.

After every U.S. decennial census, the legislature or the Legislative Redistricting Board is required to redraw Texas House and state Senate districts to account for population growth and changing population patterns. Redistricting is governed by standards set by federal courts, including the one person, one vote principle that districts must be nearly equal in population. Redistricting, nevertheless, is often a contentious process. Minority groups continue to turn to the federal courts to challenge plans drawn by the legislature. Democrats and Republicans also continue to fight each other over redistricting with federal court lawsuits.

Legislative Leaders and Committees

5.4 Contrast the leadership and committee structure of the Texas House with that of the Texas Senate, p. 149.

Unlike the U.S. Congress, the Texas legislature is not organized along party lines and has only the tentative beginnings of an institutionalized leadership structure. The presiding officer of the House is the speaker, who is elected by the other House members. The presiding officer of the Senate is the lieutenant governor, who is elected by voters statewide. Leadership in both the House and the Senate traditionally has been highly personal, centering on the presiding officers and their legislative teams. The lieutenant governor is potentially more powerful than the speaker because of his or her statewide election, but in practical terms, differences depend on who holds the offices.

The most significant powers of the speaker and the lieutenant governor are the appointment of House and Senate members to committees that screen and draft legislation and the assignment of bills to committees. The fate of most pieces of legislation is decided at the committee level. The presiding officers also play key roles in the development of major legislative proposals and, to a great extent, depend on their handpicked committee chairs to sell their legislative programs to House and Senate colleagues.

Rules and the Lawmaking Process

5.5 Outline how a bill becomes a law and the obstacles in the lawmaking process in Texas, p. 160.

Any legislator can introduce a bill, but once it has been filed with the clerk of the House or the secretary of the Senate, it is subject to a potentially long, arduous process that requires a legislator's continuous attention. Tax bills must originate in the House. All other bills can originate in either chamber. To be sent to the governor for signature into law, a bill must be approved on three readings in both the House and the Senate. To become law, a bill has to be approved in exactly the same form by both chambers. A conference committee of House and Senate members often has to work out a compromise when the versions passed by the two chambers differ. The governor can sign a bill, veto it, or let it become law without his or her signature. The legislative rules and heavy volume of bills considered sometimes enable lawmakers to sneak major, controversial proposals into law by adding little-noticed amendments to other bills. Some other obstacles in the lawmaking process include the Calendars Committee, which schedules bills for debate by the full House; the filibuster, which allows a senator to speak at length against a bill; and a procedural rule that allows a minority of senators to block debate on controversial bills.

The Emerging Party System

5.6 Outline the changes in partisanship in the Texas legislature, p. 166.

From the post–Civil War period to the last quarter of the twentieth century, Texas was a one-party Democratic state in which few Republicans were elected to the Texas legislature. Conservative Democrats dominated the legislature, organizing both houses to ensure a conservative legislative agenda. Factions within the Democratic Party were evident, but there was no Democratic-Republican division of any consequence. As party realignment emerged in the last part of the twentieth century, increasing numbers of Republicans were elected to the legislature. The growth of Republican strength has increased partisan activity and fueled speculation that, sooner or later, attempts may be made to organize the legislature along the partisan lines of the U.S. Congress. Both major parties already have active legislative caucuses.

Legislative Behavior

5.7 Assess the influences on the decision making of Texas lawmakers, p. 168.

Legislators show considerable diversity in their style and work habits. Their decisions are influenced by a number of factors, including constituents, interest and ideological groups, colleagues, staff, and the governor. Legislators traditionally have been given a lot of latitude in their decision making because of widespread public inattention to the legislature's work. But activist groups, such as those aligned with the Tea Party movement, have been successful in recent years in helping ultraconservative challengers unseat more moderate Republican legislators in GOP primaries. Over the years, legislators have strengthened ethical standards for themselves and other state officials, but controversies periodically arise.

LEARN THE TERMS

institutionalization, p. 138
bicameral legislature, p. 140
regular legislative session, p. 140
special session, p. 140
redistricting, p. 144
gerrymandering, p. 146
speaker, p. 149
lieutenant governor, p. 151
standing committee, p. 158
Calendars Committee, p. 159
conference committee, p. 159
select committee, p. 159
reading, p. 160
veto, p. 161
appropriations bill, p. 162
line-item veto, p. 162
two-thirds rule, p. 162
tag, p. 162
filibuster, p. 162
calendar, p. 163
record vote, p. 163
norm, p. 164
caucus, p. 168
Sharpstown stock fraud scandal, p. 172

The Texas Executive

RESPONDING TO A HEALTH EMERGENCY
Governor Greg Abbott, joined by Lieutenant Governor Dan Patrick (left) and then-Speaker Dennis Bonnen, updated the news media and the public during the early months of the COVID-19 (coronavirus) pandemic. The governor's response to the crisis received mixed reviews from his Texas constituents.

LEARNING OBJECTIVES

6.1 Trace the evolution of the Texas governor from a strong unified executive to a plural executive, p. 180.

6.2 Assess what qualifies an individual to serve as governor, common career patterns that have led to the governorship, and select benefits of the office, p. 183.

6.3 Explain the legislative, budgetary, appointive, judicial, and military powers of the Texas governor, p. 186.

6.4 Evaluate the informal resources of the Texas governor for advancing public policy and political objectives, p. 192.

6.5 Differentiate the leadership styles of recent Texas governors, p. 196.

6.6 Describe the duties and responsibilities of the other offices of the executive branch in Texas, p. 205.

From a constitutional standpoint and in terms of formal powers, the governor of Texas is one of the weaker governors in the country, but during natural disasters, such as hurricanes and health-related emergencies, governors can assume emergency powers that allow them to temporarily override some regulations and the business-as-usual status quo in order to protect public health and public safety. This power comes from the Texas Disaster Act, initially enacted by the legislature in 1975 and updated several times since. When the coronavirus pandemic struck Texas and the rest of the world in 2020, Governor Greg Abbott declared a disaster in Texas and issued executive orders temporarily closing schools, most retail businesses, bars, gyms, and hair salons; limiting social gatherings; prohibiting dine-in service at restaurants; and stopping visitations to nursing homes and retirement facilities. He also activated the Texas National Guard to assist health-care providers and required state agencies to provide flexible and remote work options for employees.

Abbott's instructions reflected guidance from the federal government and were issued as many Texas workers in the private sector already were practicing "social distancing" and working from home at the request of their employers to try to slow the spread of the virus.

"Working together, we must defeat COVID-19 (the disease caused by the virus) with the only tool that we have available to us – we must strangle its expansion by reducing the ways that we are currently transmitting it," he said. "We are doing this now, today, so that we can get back to business as usual more quickly."[1] Abbott was the first Texas governor in more than a century to deal with a pandemic, and accomplishing his goal of resuming business as usual would be more difficult than the governor and most Texans had hoped.

Even during a health emergency, a governor's actions are not immune from criticism, and Abbott's detractors were quick to charge that his initial response to the crisis, issued in mid-March, was late, lagging behind similar orders already issued by other governors. They also noted that many of the state's 1,100 school districts already had closed their campuses before Abbott acted and that mayors in some Texas cities—including Dallas, Austin, and Houston—already had issued local orders closing restaurants and limiting public gatherings, while other communities had not. Letting local communities take emergency steps first, the governor's critics said, confused the public and slowed the state's response to the crisis.

Much of the criticism of the Republican governor came from Democrats, but not all of it. Some conservatives within Abbott's own party thought he had gone too far, infringing on personal freedoms and the ability of small business owners to provide a living for themselves and their employees. The business closures had helped to limit the virus's spread, but they also had created a large wave of unemployment and a drain on state and local tax revenue, as had occurred throughout the country. When a hair salon owner in Dallas defied both the governor and a local judge and refused to shut down, the judge ordered her jailed. Abbott then revised his executive order to exclude jail time for offenders, and the Texas Supreme Court ordered the woman released.

Governors, especially Republicans, also were feeling pressure from President Donald Trump, who was seeking reelection and anxious to try to restart the economy. So within only a month of his first emergency orders, Abbott became one of the first governors in the country to begin "reopening" his state. Although Texas at that time lagged behind most states in testing for the virus, Abbott issued new orders that, over the course of several weeks, phased in the reopening of restaurants, bars, hair salons, retail stores, gyms, amusement venues, and most other businesses that he had shut down. Abbott urged Texans to practice social distancing and wear masks in public, but he refused to order people to wear masks, and he overrode orders issued by local officials requiring mask use in their communities.

Many Texans were happy to see the restrictions on their jobs and daily lives lifted. But others, including some mayors and other local officials, said the action was premature. It also soon became clear that many Texans were ignoring the governor's pleas for social distancing and voluntary mask use. Over the Memorial Day holiday and other weekends, photos were taken of people flocking to beaches and parks and tubers crowding rivers. The state shut down some bars because they violated limitations on crowding. And COVID-19 cases in Texas started increasing rapidly, rising to more than 10,000 new reported cases a day in mid-July before temporarily receding. COVID deaths and the number of people hospitalized with the disease also increased.

Abbott responded by slowing the reopening process. He issued new orders for bars and river-rafting and tubing companies to close and restaurants to reduce their in-dining service to 50 percent of capacity. Retreating further, he also issued a statewide order requiring most Texans to wear masks in public. Abbott was hammered with angry reactions from two sides—from people who said the pandemic was spiking in Texas because the governor had tried to reopen the state too soon and from people, mainly in his own party, who complained that he was interfering with private businesses, taking away people's jobs, and encroaching on their freedoms.

By October, Texas still was reporting as many as 3,000 or more new COVID-19 cases a day, but the governor again began loosening restrictions on restaurants and many other businesses. He and his appointed education commissioner required schools to reopen, also to mixed reactions. School districts could provide virtual learning for students who preferred to stay home but also had to offer in-classroom instruction for students who chose that option, angering many teachers who feared exposure to the virus. As the November election approached, Abbott angered some of his fellow Republicans by expanding the period during which Texans could vote early in order to reduce, as a health precaution, lines at polling places. He also angered Democrats by enforcing the state's tight restrictions that prohibited most Texans from voting by mail, even during a pandemic. Soon, COVID-19 cases started rising again.

It doesn't require a public health emergency to provoke controversy for a Texas governor because controversy is part of the job, even for a governor who is a comparatively weak chief executive. The formal limitations on the office were sometimes easy to forget during much of the influential administration of Abbott's predecessor, Rick Perry. Abbott in his second term as governor seemed determined to follow in Perry's footsteps, and only time would tell how his response to the coronavirus emergency would affect that goal. Time also would tell if Perry's and Abbott's administrations signaled a changing, more powerful role for the office of Texas governor or were simply a reflection of the politics of an era.

Perry succeeded in building influence, partly because his conservative, business-oriented brand also matched the state's dominant conservatism, and he made strong use of the veto. His longevity also was a major factor. During more than fourteen years in the governor's office, a record, Perry made several thousand appointments to policy-setting state boards and commissions, and he demanded loyalty from his appointees. Many of those appointees, including a number of wealthy, influential business executives, helped keep Perry in office by donating millions of dollars to his political campaigns. Moreover, many of Perry's former staffers became influential administrators in state agencies or powerful lobbyists whose relationships with Perry remained strong. Abbott shared Perry's conservative, limited-government philosophy and his determination to enact conservative priorities.

The office of governor is the most visible office in state government, and most Texans probably associate it with power. But, as many people elected to the position have discovered, the term "chief executive" can be almost a misnomer, thanks to constitutional restrictions meant to ensure that no governor could recreate the type of near-authoritarian administration that Reconstruction Governor Edmund J. Davis practiced following the Civil War. Since 1876, a modest number of constitutional changes, such as a four-year term of office and very limited power to remove agency appointees, have been authorized by Texas voters, but these have not created a unified executive with the governor controlling the administrative branch of government.

Unlike the president of the United States and the governors of forty-four other states,[2] the governor of Texas has no formal appointive cabinet through which to impose policy on the governmental bureaucracy. Also, the governor shares the executive function with other elected officials. Independently elected officers who do not run with the governor on a party ticket, including such key players as the attorney general and the comptroller, head several other major state agencies. The governor appoints hundreds of individuals to boards and commissions that set policy for numerous other state agencies, but most of those boards are structured in such a way that a new governor has to wait until halfway through a first term to appoint a majority of panel members.

All of this is not to suggest that the governor is merely a figurehead. The governor can veto legislation and has the exclusive authority to schedule special sessions of the legislature and set their agendas. In addition, as Perry demonstrated, the appointments power offers the opportunity to make a strong mark on state government. The high visibility of the office also offers a governor a ready-made public forum. So, although the state constitution limits the formal powers of the office, a governor's personality, political adroitness, staff appointments, and ability to define and sell an agenda that addresses broad needs and interests all shape his or her influence.

Knowing what the governor and other elected officials of the executive branch can and cannot do—both formally and informally—is important to understanding state government and, if necessary, navigating state government as an active participant in the political process or simply as someone with a problem he or she would like state government to address.

A Historical Perspective on the Executive Function in Texas

6.1 Trace the evolution of the Texas governor from a strong unified executive to a plural executive.

governor
The state's top executive officeholder.

The **governor**, the top executive officeholder in Texas, has not always had such limited authority. In the 1836 Constitution of the Republic, the powers of the president of Texas "closely resembled the powers of the American president, except he was forbidden to lead armies without the consent of Congress."[3] The constitution adopted after Texas was annexed to the United States in 1845 continued the office of a strong single or unified executive and gave the governor significant powers, including the appointment of other executive officials.[4] The revised constitution Texas adopted upon joining the Confederacy in 1861 reflected only minor reductions in the powers of the governor. It included a constitutional amendment, approved by voters in 1850, providing for the popular election of the state treasurer and the comptroller of public accounts.[5]

The governor also retained extensive powers under the Constitution of 1866, written at the end of the Civil War. Although the treasurer and the comptroller continued to be elected, the line-item veto over budget bills (a power that still exists today) expanded the legislative power of the governor. The Constitution of 1866 was short lived, however, and was replaced by the Constitution of 1869 to bring the state into compliance with the Reconstruction policies of the Radical Republicans who had taken over the U.S. Congress. Jacksonian democracy influenced the Constitution of 1869, which led to the diffusion of the executive function among eight officeholders, six of whom were elected statewide.[6]

plural executive
A fragmented system of authority under which most statewide, executive officeholders are elected independently of the governor. This arrangement, which is used in Texas, places severe limitations on the governor's power.

Radical Reconstruction policies and the controversies of Governor Edmund Davis's administration prompted Texans to put strict limits on the power of the governor in the Constitution of 1876, which still forms the basic framework of state government. The new constitution retained the **plural executive** structure of independently elected officeholders. The only executive officer the governor appoints is the secretary of state. The constitution initially limited the terms of the governor and other elected members of the executive branch to two years. The constitution

IT COMES WITH THE JOB

The Texas Governor's Mansion, built in 1854 and located across the street from the Capitol in downtown Austin, was torched by an arsonist on June 8, 2008. Under renovation and unoccupied at the time, it suffered extensive damage. After a $24 million restoration, including security upgrades and some expanded space, it reopened in 2012, and then-Governor Rick Perry and his wife, Anita, moved back in.

also set their salaries and specified in great detail the duties of each office, thus limiting executive officeholders' discretionary powers. In addition, the constitution placed restrictions on outside employment and the holding of any other office or commission.[7]

Although constitutional amendments have loosened a few restrictions on the executive branch over the years, the changes have not significantly enhanced the governor's authority. In 1954, voters approved an amendment giving the legislature the authority to raise the governor's salary.[8] Another amendment, in 1972, expanded the term of office for the governor and most other statewide executive officeholders to four years. In 1980, the governor was given the power, with the approval of the state Senate, to remove persons from boards and commissions whom the governor had personally appointed.[9] But when Governor Ann Richards in 1991 tried to revive interest in giving the governor cabinet-style appointment powers over major state agencies, she met with only limited success.

6.1.1 The Constitutional Framework for the Plural Executive

Article 4, Section 1, of the 1876 Constitution created the executive branch, which "shall consist of a Governor, who shall be the Chief Executive Officer of the State, a **Lieutenant Governor**, Secretary of State, Comptroller of Public Accounts, Treasurer, Commissioner of the General Land Office, and Attorney General." Added later to the executive branch were the agriculture commissioner, the three-member Railroad Commission, and the fifteen-member State Board of Education. Only the secretary of state is appointed by the governor (see Figure 6–1). Members of the education board are elected from districts, and the other officeholders are elected statewide. The constitution requires most of these officials to be at least 30 years old and a resident of Texas for at least five years.[10] The office of the treasurer was eliminated through constitutional amendment in 1995. Other states elect as many members to the executive branch as Texas does (or more), but most states provide for a governor's council or cabinet and give their governors more appointive powers over individuals administering state agencies. In Texas, the governor appoints more than 200 policy-setting boards over state agencies and universities, but the boards appoint the individuals responsible for day-to-day agency administration.

lieutenant governor
The presiding officer of the Senate. This officeholder also becomes governor if the governor dies, resigns, becomes incapacitated, or is removed from office.

FIGURE 6-1 STRUCTURE OF THE EXECUTIVE BRANCH IN TEXAS

The governor shares powers and administrative responsibilities with other officials elected statewide under the constitutional provisions of the plural executive. There is no cabinet, but the governor appoints officials who serve in the governor's office and on some 200 boards, commissions, and state educational agencies. This schematic represents key components of the executive organization under Governor Greg Abbott.

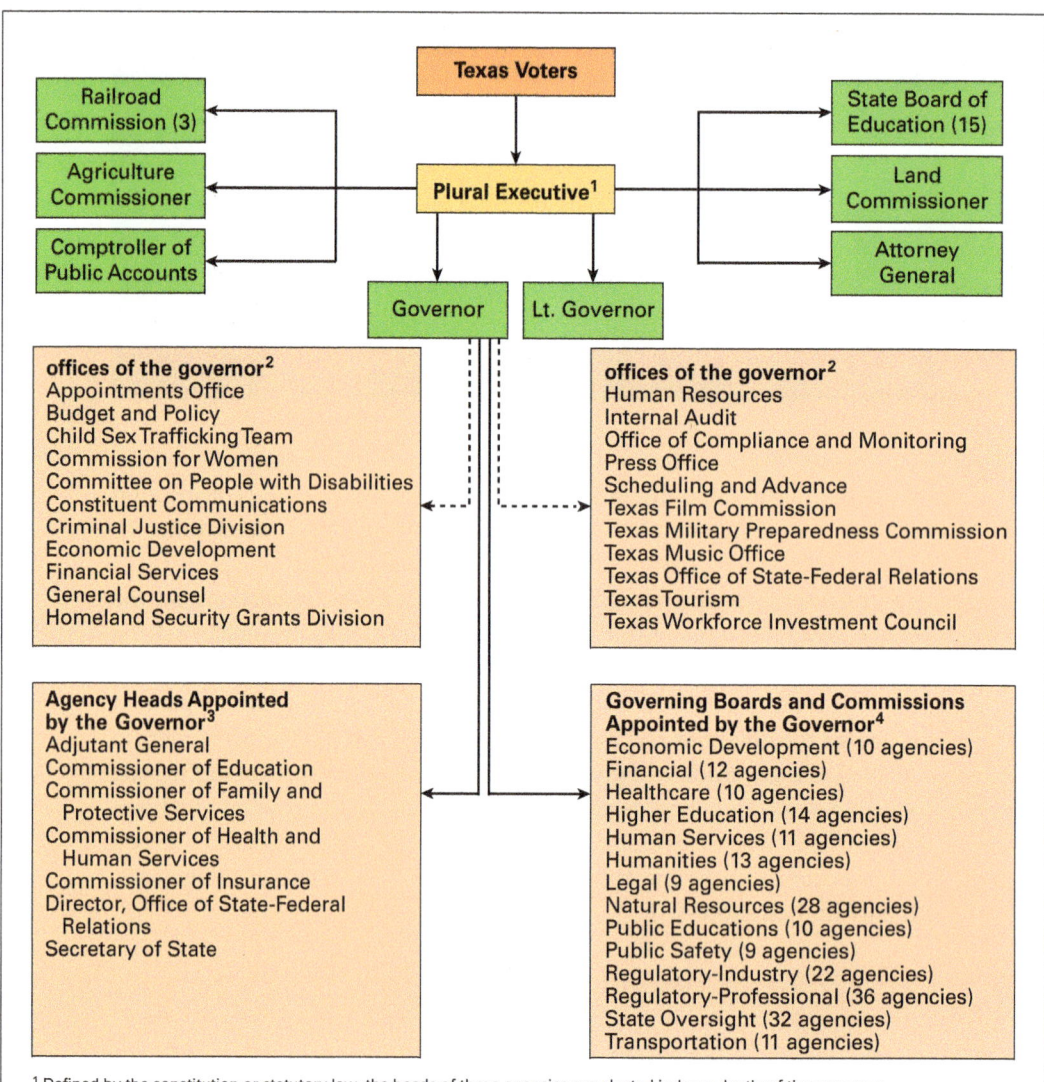

```
                           Texas Voters
                                │
    Railroad                    ▼                  State Board of
    Commission (3) ◄──────                  ──────► Education (15)
                         Plural Executive[1]
    Agriculture                                     Land
    Commissioner  ◄──────      │    │       ──────► Commissioner
                               │    │
    Comptroller of             ▼    ▼               Attorney
    Public Accounts ◄──────                 ──────► General
                          Governor  Lt. Governor
```

offices of the governor[2]
Appointments Office
Budget and Policy
Child Sex Trafficking Team
Commission for Women
Committee on People with Disabilities
Constituent Communications
Criminal Justice Division
Economic Development
Financial Services
General Counsel
Homeland Security Grants Division

offices of the governor[2]
Human Resources
Internal Audit
Office of Compliance and Monitoring
Press Office
Scheduling and Advance
Texas Film Commission
Texas Military Preparedness Commission
Texas Music Office
Texas Office of State-Federal Relations
Texas Tourism
Texas Workforce Investment Council

Agency Heads Appointed by the Governor[3]
Adjutant General
Commissioner of Education
Commissioner of Family and Protective Services
Commissioner of Health and Human Services
Commissioner of Insurance
Director, Office of State-Federal Relations
Secretary of State

Governing Boards and Commissions Appointed by the Governor[4]
Economic Development (10 agencies)
Financial (12 agencies)
Healthcare (10 agencies)
Higher Education (14 agencies)
Human Services (11 agencies)
Humanities (13 agencies)
Legal (9 agencies)
Natural Resources (28 agencies)
Public Educations (10 agencies)
Public Safety (9 agencies)
Regulatory-Industry (22 agencies)
Regulatory-Professional (36 agencies)
State Oversight (32 agencies)
Transportation (11 agencies)

[1] Defined by the constitution or statutory law, the heads of these agencies are elected independently of the governor.
[2] The offices of the governor are created under statutory authority and serve to assist the governor in policy development, budgeting and planning, and coordination of policy among agencies and governments. Some 200 persons serve in these offices and are appointed by the governor.
[3] With the exception of the Secretary of State, which is authorized under the Texas Constitution, these administrative positions were created under statutory law giving the appointment authority to the governor.
[4] Some 200 state agencies, including universities, are assigned by statutory law the responsibilities for the administration of public policy in these areas. The members of the governing bodies are appointed by the governor with the approval of the Senate. In turn, the agency executives are appointed by the governing boards.

6.1.2 The Potential for Conflict in the Plural Executive

Agencies headed by other officials are autonomous and—except for limited budgetary review—independent of the governor. In a confrontation with the governor over policy, agency heads can claim their own electoral mandates. For many years, there were only "scattered incidents of hostility within the executive branch," and elected officials generally "cooperated remarkably well with their chief executives."[11] This observation was based on the nineteenth- and twentieth-century periods during which Texas was a one-party Democratic state. Conservatives dominated party politics then, and statewide elected officials generally reflected those conservative interests and believed it was in their own best political interests to cooperate with one another.

The potential for conflict between the governor and other executive officials increased as Texas became a two-party state, and conflict is likely to become more common in the future, even among officials within the same party. During Republican Governor Bill Clements's first term (1979–1983), the other elected officers in the executive branch were Democrats, including Attorney General Mark White, who frequently feuded with the governor and jockeyed for the political advantage that allowed him to unseat Clements in 1982.

In 2003, budgetary differences erupted between Republican Comptroller Carole Keeton Strayhorn and other Republican officeholders, including Governor Perry. These differences resulted in the legislature's approval of a bill, signed by Perry, transferring two key programs from the comptroller's office to the Legislative Budget Board. The political animosity between Strayhorn and Perry intensified, and in 2006 the comptroller challenged the governor's reelection as an independent candidate. Perry ultimately won the election, but in the months leading up to it, official actions and pronouncements by both officeholders often had sharp political edges.

Conflict may also occur between other members of the executive branch. In 1994, for example, Perry, who at the time was agriculture commissioner, opposed a coastal management plan promoted by Democratic Land Commissioner Garry Mauro.

Some argue that the effect of the plural executive on state politics and the governor's control of the executive branch is minimal because, for the most part, rancorous conflict among these elected officials still appears to be infrequent. But others argue that the governor, in an effort to avoid conflict with officials over whom he or she has no control, often pursues policies that are not likely to be disruptive, innovative, or responsive to pressing contemporary issues. It is difficult to develop coordinated policies if those holding office in a plural executive system have sharply different or competing agendas. However, proponents of the plural executive contend that it does what it was intended to do: control and constrain the governor. Although collegial or collective decision making often is inefficient and potentially leads to deadlock, the advocates of the plural executive contend that democracy, in most instances, is to be preferred over efficiency.

Historical Overview of the Men and Women Who Have Served as Governor

6.2 Assess what qualifies an individual to serve as governor, common career patterns that have led to the governorship, and select benefits of the office.

For much of the state's history, the route to the governorship was largely through a career in law, service in the Texas legislature, or election to other offices of the plural executive. With the exceptions of governors Bill Clements and George W. Bush, whose occupations centered on business, these career patterns continue to be the route to the governor's office.

6.2.1 Qualifications and Backgrounds of Texas Governors

The Texas Constitution has few requirements, as do most states, for a person who desires to run for governor. A governor must be at least 30 years old, a U.S. citizen, and a resident of Texas for at least five years. There also is a requirement that no individual can be excluded from office for religious beliefs, "provided he acknowledges the existence of a Supreme Being."[12] The constitution, however, does not spell out all the roadblocks to winning the office.

Until the election of Bill Clements in 1978, every governor since 1874 had been a Democrat (see Table 6–1). Clements served two terms (1979–1983 and 1987–1991). With the increase of Republican strength in Texas, Republican George W. Bush was elected to the office in 1994 and again in 1998; Republican Rick Perry was elected in 2002, 2006, and 2010; and Republican Greg Abbott was elected in 2014 and 2018.

Most governors have been well-educated, middle-aged, and affluent white male Protestants. In many cases, their families were active in public life and helped shape their careers. Twenty-two of the governors elected since 1870 were trained in law, but a handful of these primarily pursued careers in business. Eleven others also can be identified with business interests, and four had newspaper interests or careers. No minorities and only two women have been elected to the office. Miriam A. "Ma" Ferguson—whose husband, James E. "Pa" Ferguson, earlier had served as governor—served for two terms (1925–1927 and 1933–1935), and Ann Richards served for one term (1991–1995). By the time Richards became governor, only three women had ever been elected to statewide executive office in Texas. Richards, a Democrat, served two terms as state treasurer before being elected governor, and Republican Kay Bailey Hutchison succeeded her as treasurer. From 1919 to 1923, Annie Webb Blanton served as the state superintendent of schools, an elective office that no longer exists.

With the high costs of statewide political campaigns, a candidate's personal wealth or ability to raise large sums of money has taken on increased importance. Otherwise-qualified prospects are dissuaded from running for governor and other offices because of the difficult burden of fund-raising. Bill Clements and fellow Republican Clayton Williams, a Midland businessman who lost the 1990 gubernatorial race to Ann Richards, spent millions of dollars out of their own pockets on gubernatorial races that were their first bids for elective office. Similarly, Democrat Tony Sanchez, a wealthy Laredo businessman, spent more than $50 million of his personal fortune on an unsuccessful race for governor against Perry in 2002. Their experiences raise the possibility that personal wealth and the willingness to spend it on one's own election campaign will continue to take on more importance in future races.

Previous public service often provides gubernatorial aspirants with public visibility and links to party leaders, interest groups, and public officials around the state. Such relationships help candidates develop broad electoral support. Eighty percent of the governors elected since 1870 served in a statewide or federal elected office. Six served as state attorney general, and six served as lieutenant governor. Only seven, including Republicans Bill Clements and George W. Bush, have been elected governor without any previous elected experience. Clements was a deputy U.S. secretary of defense prior to winning his first gubernatorial race, and Bush served as an unofficial adviser to his father, former President George H. W. Bush. Rick Perry had been a state representative, agriculture commissioner, and lieutenant governor before becoming governor, and Greg Abbott was a Texas Supreme Court justice and attorney general before winning election to the state's highest office.

TABLE 6-1 GOVERNORS OF TEXAS SINCE 1870

Texas Governor	Party Affiliation	Years Served	Public Office Held Prior to Election	Profession or Career	Public Office Held after Governorship
Edmund J. Davis	Republican	1870–1874	Officer in the U.S. Army/Reconstruction Governor	Lawyer	
Richard Coke	Democrat	1874–1876	Associate Justice, Texas Supreme Court	Lawyer	U.S. Senate
Richard B. Hubbard	Democrat	1876–1879	Lieutenant Governor	Lawyer	Minister to Japan
Oran M. Roberts	Democrat	1879–1883	Chief Justice, Texas Supreme Court	Lawyer	Professor of Law, UT
John Ireland	Democrat	1883–1887	Associate Justice, Texas Supreme Court	Lawyer	
Lawrence Sullivan Ross	Democrat	1887–1891	Texas Senate	Military, Farming	President, Texas A&M University
James Stephen Hogg	Democrat	1891–1895	Texas Attorney General	Publisher, Lawyer	
Charles A. Culberson	Democrat	1895–1899	Texas Attorney General	Lawyer	U.S. Senate
Joseph D. Sayers	Democrat	1899–1903	U.S. Congress	Lawyer	Regent, UT, Other State Agencies
Samuel W. T. Lanham	Democrat	1903–1907	U.S. Congress	Lawyer	Regent, UT
Thomas Mitchell Campbell	Democrat	1907–1911	Private Practice	Lawyer	Exemption Board
Oscar Branch Colquitt	Democrat	1911–1915	Texas Railroad Commission	Publisher, Lawyer	U.S. Board of Mediation
James E. Ferguson*	Democrat	1915–1917	Private Sector	Lawyer, Banker	
William Pettus Hobby	Democrat	1917–1921	Lieutenant Governor	Editor, Publisher	
Pat Morris Neff	Democrat	1921–1925	Private Sector	Lawyer	Texas Commission, President Baylor University
Miriam A. Ferguson**	Democrat	1925–1927	Private Sector	Housewife	
Dan Moody	Democrat	1927–1931	Texas Attorney General	Lawyer	
Ross S. Sterling	Democrat	1931–1933	Chairman, Texas Highway Commission	Oilman, Real Estate, Newspapers	
Miriam A. Ferguson	Democrat	1933–1935	Former Governor	Housewife	
James V. Allred	Democrat	1935–1939	Texas Attorney General	Lawyer	Federal Judgeship District
W. Lee O'Daniel	Democrat	1939–1941	None	Owner, Flour Mill	U.S. Senate
Coke Stevenson	Democrat	1941–1947	Lieutenant Governor	Lawyer, Businessman	
Beauford Jester***	Democrat	1947–1949	Texas Railroad Commission	Lawyer, Family Businesses	
Allan Shivers	Democrat	1949–1957	Lieutenant Governor	Lawyer, Businessman	UT Board of Regents
Price Daniel	Democrat	1957–1963	U.S. Senator	Lawyer	Justice, Supreme Court of Texas
John Connally	Democrat	1963–1969	U.S. Secretary of the Navy	Lawyer	U.S. Secretary of the Treasury
Preston Smith	Democrat	1969–1973	Lieutenant Governor	Businessman	
Dolph Briscoe****	Democrat	1973–1979	Texas House of Representatives	Rancher, Businessman	
Bill Clements	Republican	1979–1983	Private Sector	Oilman	
Mark White	Democrat	1983–1987	Texas Attorney General	Lawyer	
Bill Clements	Republican	1987–1991	Former Governor	Oilman	
Ann Richards	Democrat	1991–1995	Texas Treasurer	Educator	
George W. Bush	Republican	1995–2000	Private Sector	Partial Owner of Texas Rangers	President of the United States
Rick Perry	Republican	2000–2015	Lieutenant Governor	Farmer, Rancher	U.S. Secretary of Energy
Greg Abbott	Republican	2015–	Attorney General	Lawyer	

*Only Texas governor to be impeached and convicted.
**First woman elected governor.
***Died in office.
****Prior to 1974, governors were elected for two-year terms of office.
SOURCE: Texas State Library and Archives Commission, *Portraits of Texas Governors*, https://www.tsl.texas.gov/governors/modern/page3.html.

6.2.2 Impeachment and Incapacitation

A governor can be removed from office through impeachment proceedings initiated in the state House of Representatives and conviction by the state Senate in a trial of the impeachment charges. The constitutions of every state except Oregon have provisions for the impeachment of state executive officials, but only a few governors have been removed by impeachment. One Texas governor, James E. "Pa" Ferguson in 1917, has been removed from office through impeachment.

That year, a controversy erupted over Governor Ferguson's efforts to remove five University of Texas faculty members. The governor vetoed the university's appropriations, and when he called a special legislative session to consider other funding, he faced articles of impeachment based primarily on the misuse of public funds. He ultimately was convicted and removed from office, but for two more decades, the husband-and-wife team of Ma and Pa Ferguson, and the controversy that continued to surround them, dominated a great deal of Texas politics.[13]

Across the country, the most recent governor to be removed from office through the impeachment process was Rod Blagojevich of Illinois, who was impeached in early 2009 after being indicted on federal corruption charges.[14]

Nineteen states, including California, can remove a governor through recall as well as impeachment.[15] Through a process initiated by a petition of voters, a special election is held on the question of the removal of the governor. If the people vote to remove the governor, a new governor is then elected. This occurred in late 2003 in California, when Democrat Gray Davis was recalled as governor and voters, in the same election, selected actor Arnold Schwarzenegger, a Republican, to replace him. In 2012, Wisconsin voters forced a recall election against Republican Governor Scott Walker over legislation he promoted to eliminate most collective bargaining rights for public employee unions. Union members, teachers, and public employees from other states were mobilized by his opponents to join the fight against him. Walker survived the recall election in June 2012, garnering national attention and financial support from conservative groups. Texas does not have a recall process for statewide officeholders.

If a Texas governor dies, is incapacitated, is impeached and convicted, or voluntarily leaves office midterm, the lieutenant governor replaces the governor until the next general election. Whenever the governor leaves the state, the lieutenant governor serves as acting governor.

6.2.3 The Salary and "Perks" of the Governor's Office

In 2019, the governor of Texas was paid $153,750 a year. Governors' pay across the nation ranged from a low of $70,000 in Maine to a high of $201,680 in California.[16] Texas provides the governor with housing, a security detail, travel expenses, and access to state-owned planes and cars. For many years, governors and their families have lived in the Governor's Mansion in downtown Austin near the Capitol. That historic structure was severely damaged by an arsonist in 2008 while it was closed for renovations. Governor Rick Perry and his family already had relocated to a rental house elsewhere in Austin before the fire, and they remained there while the state rebuilt the mansion, a task that was completed in 2012.

The Powers of the Governor

6.3 Explain the legislative, budgetary, appointive, judicial, and military powers of the Texas governor.

Views of the chief executive's functions have changed over time. Early state constitutions in the period of the American Revolution limited gubernatorial powers, and governors in many states found themselves in a subordinate position to their legislatures. Throughout the nineteenth century, those relationships often were redefined. At times, the governors' powers were increased and those of the legislatures reduced. During other periods, such as the era of Jacksonian democracy, the powers of both institutions were subjected to strong restrictions to ensure greater responsiveness to the public.

Reform movements of the early twentieth century, responding to political corruption, focused on management and efficiency in the governors' offices. In some states, the office of governor was restructured around the organizational principles of an executive cabinet. Events such as the Great Depression contributed to a further redefinition of executive leadership, with an emphasis in some states on policy initiatives, administrative control and coordination, and expanded political leadership.[17] The Texas Constitution of 1845, adopted when the state was admitted to the Union, modeled the governor's authority on the strong executive principle found in the U.S. Constitution. Except for the Reconstruction constitution, however, later Texas constitutions, including the current document, reduced the powers of the office, reflecting apprehension of strong executive and political authority.

For many years, scholars have ranked state governors on their formal constitutional and legal powers, such as budgetary authority, appointment and veto powers, and term limitations.[18] From the earliest to the latest studies, the governor of Texas has ranked consistently with the weaker state governors (see Table 6–2).

Political scientist Thad Beyle's rankings are based on a six-point scale using the structure of the executive branch, tenure, appointment powers, budget powers, veto powers, and governor's party control. The data for party control was updated using the 2014 party composition of the state legislatures and the party affiliation of governors. The governor of Texas ranks thirty-seventh using this scale.

Texans, nonetheless, appear to have high expectations of their governor. They evaluate governors in terms of their policy agendas and the leadership they exercise in achieving those goals. But how does a governor meet such expectations when the formal powers of the office are limited? The sections that follow analyze both the formal powers and informal resources at the governor's disposal.

TABLE 6–2 COMPARISON OF THE FORMAL/INSTITUTIONAL POWERS OF GOVERNORS

Strong (4.0 and above)			
Alaska (4.1)	Maryland (4.1)	New York (4.3)	Utah (4.2)
Hawaii (4.1)	Massachusetts (4.3)	Pennsylvania (4.0)	West Virginia (4.1)
Moderately Strong (3.5–3.9)			
Arizona (3.8)	Idaho (3.5)	Minnesota (3.9)	Oregon (3.5)
California (3.5)	Illinois (3.8)	Nebraska (3.8)	Tennessee (3.9)
Colorado (3.9)	Iowa (3.7)	New Jersey (3.8)	Washington (3.6)
Connecticut (3.9)	Kansas (3.7)	North Dakota (3.9)	Wisconsin (3.7)
Delaware (3.7)	Kentucky (3.5)	Ohio (3.9)	Wyoming (3.8)
Florida (3.6)	Michigan (3.9)		
Moderate (3.0–3.4)			
Alabama (3.2)	Maine (3.1)	New Hampshire (3.0)	South Carolina (3.0)
Georgia (3.2)	Mississippi (3.3)	New Mexico (3.3)	South Dakota (3.0)
Indiana (3.1)	Missouri (3.1)	Oklahoma (3.0)	Texas (3.2)
Louisiana (3.4)	Montana (3.3)	Rhode Island (3.3)	Virginia (3.3)
Weak (2.9 and below)			
Arkansas (2.9)	Nevada (2.8)	North Carolina (2.9)	Vermont (2.8)

SOURCE: Based on Thad Beyle, "The Governors"; Multistate Associates Incorporated, "2014 Governors and Legislatures"; National Council of State Legislatures; and National Governors Association, "Governors Political Affiliations and Terms of Office."

6.3.1 Legislative Powers

The governor has the opportunity to outline his or her legislative priorities at the beginning of each regular biennial session through the traditional State of the State address to the legislature. The governor also can communicate with lawmakers—collectively or individually—throughout the session. In this fashion, the governor can establish a policy agenda, recommend specific legislation, and set the stage for negotiations with legislative leaders, other state officials, and interest groups. The media cover the governor's addresses and other formal messages to the legislature, giving the governor the opportunity to mobilize the public support that may be essential to the success of his or her initiatives.

The governor's effectiveness also may be enhanced by the office's two major constitutional powers over the legislature—the authority to call and set the agenda for special legislative sessions and the ability to veto proposed legislation. The governor may call any number of special sessions, each of which can last as long as thirty days, and designate the subjects to be considered during a session. Sometimes, the mere threat of a special session can be enough to convince reluctant lawmakers to approve a priority program of the governor or reach an acceptable compromise during a regular session. Most legislators, who are paid only part-time salaries by the state, dislike special sessions because they interfere with their personal livelihoods and disrupt their family lives. Governor Rick Perry called three special sessions in 2003 to overcome Democratic opposition—including a month-long walkout by Democratic senators—and win approval of a congressional redistricting bill that favored Republican candidates. The bill would not have passed without Perry's persistence. In 2013, Perry called back-to-back special sessions to win legislative passage of a controversial abortion-regulation bill.

It can be risky for the governor to call special sessions. The governor's influence and reputation are on the line, and further inaction by the legislature can become a political liability. In some instances, the legislative leadership has broadly interpreted the subject matter of a governor's special session proclamation and considered bills not sought by the governor. The speaker and the lieutenant governor make the parliamentary rulings that determine whether a specific piece of legislation falls within the governor's call; therefore, the governor has to be very careful in drafting a proclamation setting a special session's agenda. Once a special session is called, the governor can increase his or her bargaining power by adding

ADDRESSING THE LEGISLATURE
Governor Greg Abbott lays out his priorities to legislators during a recent session. This is only one way the governor promotes his agenda with lawmakers and the public.

Eric Gay/Associated Press

legislators' pet bills to the agenda in exchange for the lawmakers' support of the governor's program.

The governor of Texas has one of the strongest **veto** powers of any governor. When the legislature is in session, the governor has ten days (excluding Sundays) to veto a bill, sign it, or let it become law without his or her signature. A veto can be overridden by a two-thirds vote of both the House and the Senate. During the past fifty years, Governor Clements has been the only governor to have a veto overridden. It was a local game-management bill the legislature, then dominated by Democrats, voted to override during the Republican governor's first term. The governor has twenty days after the legislature adjourns to veto bills passed in the closing days of a session, which is when most legislation receives final passage. So, most gubernatorial vetoes are issued after the legislature has adjourned and no longer has the opportunity to attempt an override. The governor also has **line-item veto** authority over the state budget. This means the governor can delete specific spending items without vetoing the entire bill. All other bills have to be accepted or rejected in their entirety.

A governor may veto a bill for a number of reasons, including doubts about its constitutionality, objections to its wording, concerns that it duplicates existing law, or opposition to its policy. A governor's threat of a veto also can be effective because such threats can prompt legislators to make changes in their bills to meet a governor's objections.

Historic records on gubernatorial vetoes are not complete, but Governor Bill Clements issued 184 vetoes, and Governor Dan Moody (1927–1931) issued 117. Governor Ann Richards vetoed thirty-six bills and resolutions in one regular and two special sessions in 1991 and allowed 228 bills to become law without her signature that same year.

Governor Rick Perry, the longest-serving governor in Texas history, is believed to hold the record for vetoes at 301. He vetoed eighty-three bills, also believed to be a record, at the end of the 2001 legislative session alone. One of the 2001 vetoes, which struck down a bill that would have banned the execution of developmentally delayed convicts, received international attention. The veto was sharply criticized by death-penalty opponents but drew praise from crime victims' advocates. Soon afterward, however, the U.S. Supreme Court, ruling in a case from another state, imposed a national ban on the execution of developmentally delayed convicts. In 2011, Perry enraged many parents and other public safety advocates by vetoing a bill that would

veto
The power of the governor to reject, or kill, a bill passed by the legislature.

line-item veto
The power of the governor to reject certain parts of an appropriation, or spending, bill without killing the entire measure.

SIGNING CEREMONIES
Most bill-signing ceremonies are held in the Governor's Reception Room on the second floor of the Capitol. But Governor Greg Abbott chose a gun range in Pflugerville to sign laws permitting licensed Texans to carry concealed handguns on college campuses and openly carry handguns in many other locations.

have imposed a statewide ban on texting while driving. Governor Greg Abbott vetoed forty-three bills from his first legislative session in 2015, another fifty-one bills in 2017, and fifty-six bills in 2019.

6.3.2 Budgetary Powers

The governor of Texas has weaker budgetary authority than the governors of most states and the president of the United States. These budgetary constraints limit the governor's ability to develop a comprehensive legislative program. The legislature has the lead in budget setting, with a major role played by the Legislative Budget Board (LBB), a ten-member panel that includes the lieutenant governor, the speaker, and eight key lawmakers. Both the LBB and the governor make budgetary recommendations to the legislature, but lawmakers usually give greater attention to the LBB's proposals. To meet emergencies between legislative sessions, the governor and the LBB can transfer appropriated funds between programs or agencies. Either the governor or the LBB can initiate the proposal, but the other must agree to it.

6.3.3 Appointive Powers

One indication of a strong governor is the power to hire and fire the persons responsible for implementing public policy. As we discussed earlier in this chapter, the Texas governor's administrative authority is severely limited by the plural executive structure under which independently elected officeholders head several major state agencies.

Most of the remainder of the state bureaucracy falls under more than 200 boards and commissions that oversee various agencies created by state law. Most of these are part-time, unpaid positions whose occupants are heavily dependent on agency staffs and constituents for guidance. A governor normally appoints board members who share the governor's political philosophy and priorities, and appointees must be confirmed by the Senate. But the agency structure creates the potential for boards and commissions to become captives of the narrow constituencies they are serving or regulating and can reduce their accountability to both the governor and the legislature. Governors must effectively use their political relationships with appointees to assure their influence over board decisions and agency activities.

Most board members serve six-year **staggered terms**. That means it takes a new governor a few years to have a majority of appointees on most boards. Resignations or deaths of board members may speed up the process, but a governor cannot remove a predecessor's appointees. A governor, with the approval of two-thirds of the Senate, can fire only his or her own appointees. Governor Perry was in office long enough to have a lock on these board appointments and a strong influence on their policies.

The governor appoints individuals to boards and commissions with the approval of two-thirds of the Senate. **Senatorial courtesy**, an unwritten norm of the Senate, permits a senator to block the governor's nomination of a person who lives in that senator's district. The governor and staff members involved in appointments spend considerable time clearing potential nominees with senators because political considerations are as important in the confirmation process as a nominee's qualifications.

Individuals seek gubernatorial appointments for a variety of reasons, and the appointment process can be hectic, particularly at the beginning of a new governor's administration. The governor's staff screens potential nominees to determine their availability, competence, political acceptability, and support by key interest groups. Although most governors would deny it, campaign contributions also are a significant factor for governors of both parties. A number of Governor Clements's appointees made substantial contributions to his campaign.[19] Governors Richards, Bush, Perry, and Abbott also appointed major contributors to important posts. In 2003, less than

staggered terms
Terms that begin on different dates. The requirement that members of state boards and commissions appointed by the governor serve terms that begin on different dates ensures that a board maintains a level of experience by guarding against situations in which all board members leave office at the same time.

senatorial courtesy
An unwritten policy that permits a senator to block the confirmation of a gubernatorial appointee who lives in the senator's district.

one month after receiving a $100,000 contribution from homebuilder Bob Perry of Houston, Governor Perry appointed a top executive of the homebuilder's company to a new state commission charged with developing building performance standards. The legislature created the commission, the Texas Residential Construction Commission, to reduce consumer lawsuits against builders. A few years later, the legislature took the rare step of abolishing the agency, following numerous consumer complaints. Bob Perry, who was not related, remained a big contributor until his death in 2013. According to an analysis that a campaign finance watchdog group, Texans for Public Justice, conducted for the *Austin American-Statesman* a few months before Perry left office, nearly one-fourth of Perry's appointees were donors to his political campaigns. They contributed more than $20 million, about one-fifth of all the contributions Perry received during his fourteen years as governor.[20]

At least seventy-one of Abbott's 800 appointees during his first two years as governor each donated more than $2,500 to his campaign account for a total of at least $8.6 million, according to an analysis by *The Texas Tribune*. One appointee contributed more than $1 million. The *Tribune*'s analysis was conducted during the regular legislative session in 2017, after the House had passed a bill that would have prohibited a governor from appointing anyone to a state board or commission who had given more than $2,500 a year in political donations to the governor. The bill died in the Senate, and Abbott refused requests by the bill's sponsor, Representative Lyle Larson, a Republican from San Antonio, to add the measure to the agenda of a special session that the governor called for other issues a few months later. An Abbott spokesman said it was "absurd" to suggest that the governor's appointments were influenced by political contributions.[21] Not coincidentally, Larson was one of three incumbent Republican House members whom Abbott actively opposed in the 2018 GOP primaries, but the legislator won his primary race.

The governor appoints individuals to fill vacancies on all courts at the district level and above. If a U.S. senator dies or resigns, the governor appoints a replacement. When a vacancy occurs in another statewide office, except for that of the lieutenant governor, the governor also appoints a replacement. All of these appointees must later win election to keep their seats. If a vacancy occurs in the lieutenant governor's office, the state senators choose someone from among their membership to preside over the Senate as lieutenant governor until the next general election.

Governor Richards was particularly sensitive to constituencies that historically had been excluded from full participation in the governmental process and appointed a record number of women and minorities to state posts. About 41 percent of Richards's appointees during her four-year term were women, and about 33 percent were minorities. Governor Bush appointed the first African American, Michael Williams, to the Texas Railroad Commission, and, at different times during his administration, he appointed two Hispanics—Tony Garza and Alberto R. Gonzales—secretary of state. Bush later appointed Gonzales to fill a vacancy on the Texas Supreme Court. As president, Bush named Gonzales White House counsel and later U.S. attorney general and appointed Garza U.S. ambassador to Mexico. Among his several thousand appointments, Governor Perry named the first African American, Wallace Jefferson, to the Texas Supreme Court and appointed a large number of African Americans and Hispanics to other state posts. But overall, 77 percent of Perry's appointees were white, and 67 percent were men, according to an *Austin American-Statesman* report published about four months before he left office.[22]

In his first appointment, Governor Abbott named a Hispanic, Cameron County Judge Carlos Cascos, as Texas secretary of state. But after his first three years in office, nearly 72 percent of Abbott's appointees were white, and more than 63 percent were men. More than 45 percent were white men, according to an analysis published by the *Houston Chronicle*. About 16.4 percent were Hispanic, 6.6 percent were African American, and 3.3 percent were Asian American, although most Texans are people of color.[23]

6.3.4 Judicial Powers

Texas has a seven-member Board of Pardons and Paroles, appointed by the governor.[24] This panel decides when prisoners can be released early, and its decisions do not require action by the governor. The governor, however, can influence the board's overall approach to paroles, as Governor Ann Richards did when she convinced her appointees to sharply reduce the number of paroles, even though the state was struggling at the time with an overcrowding crisis in its prisons. Despite the crisis, Richards responded to citizen outrage over crimes committed by parolees.

The governor has the authority to grant executive clemency—acts of leniency or mercy—toward convicted criminals. One is a thirty-day stay of execution for a condemned murderer, which a governor can grant without a recommendation of the parole board. The governor, on the recommendation of the board, can grant a full pardon, a conditional pardon, or the commutation of a death sentence to life imprisonment.[25]

If a person flees a state to avoid prosecution or a prison term, under the extradition clause of the U.S. Constitution that person, upon arrest in another state, must be returned to the state from which he or she fled. The governor is legally responsible for ordering state officials to carry out such extradition requests.[26]

6.3.5 Military Powers

The Texas Constitution authorizes the governor to function as the "commander-in-chief of the military force of the state, except when they are called into actual service of the United States."[27] The governor appoints the adjutant general to carry out this duty. Texas cannot declare war on another country, and the president of the United States has the primary responsibility for national defense. When riots or natural disasters occur within the state, the governor can mobilize the Texas National Guard to protect lives and property and keep the peace. Should the United States go to war, the president can mobilize the National Guard as part of the national military forces. After the September 11, 2001, terrorist attacks on the World Trade Center and the Pentagon, some National Guard members from Texas were activated to temporarily bolster security at airports. Others went overseas to assist in the wars in Afghanistan and Iraq. In recent years, some have been assigned to support the U.S. Border Patrol along the U.S.–Mexico border amid an ongoing political debate about how the country should deal with illegal immigration. In 2020, Governor Greg Abbott activated the National Guard to help state and local officials respond to the coronavirus outbreak that created a health crisis in Texas and most of the world.

Informal Resources of the Governor

6.4 Evaluate the informal resources of the Texas governor for advancing public policy and political objectives.

Governors can compensate for constitutional limitations on their office with their articulation of problems and issues, leadership capabilities, personalities, work habits, and administrative styles (see Table 6–3). Some governors want to be involved in the minutiae of building policy coalitions and spend much of their time trying to develop agreements with legislators and other political players. Other governors find such hands-on involvement unpleasant, inefficient, and time consuming and leave such detailed work to subordinates. When things go well, the governor may receive credit that belongs to others, but during times of trouble, the governor may be blamed for problems beyond his or her control. If we give excessive weight to the formal or institutional powers of the governor, we are likely to miss those personal elements of the governor's personality and leadership style that explain gubernatorial successes or failures.

TABLE 6-3 THE GOVERNOR'S LEADERSHIP RESOURCES

Formal Constitutional Powers

1. Veto legislation
2. Exercise a line-item veto over the state budget
3. Call and set the agenda for special legislative sessions
4. Make recommendations on the budget
5. Propose emergency budgetary transfers when the legislature is not in session
6. Appoint hundreds of members of policymaking boards and commissions, subject to Senate confirmation
7. Remove his or her own appointees from boards, with Senate approval
8. Fill vacancies in U.S. Senate seats and certain elective state offices
9. Proclaim acts of executive clemency, including stays of execution, for convicted criminals
10. Mobilize the Texas National Guard to protect lives and property during natural disasters and other emergencies

Informal Resources

1. Governor's electoral mandate
2. A large staff to help develop and sell policy proposals
3. Ability to communicate to the public through the news media and social media
4. Public's perception and opinions about the governor's job performance
5. The governor's political party and relationships with legislative leaders
6. Support and mobilization of interest groups

6.4.1 The Governor's Staff

The earliest governors had only three or four people to help them, but staffs have grown as the growing state has increased demands on the governor's time. By 1963, under John Connally, the governor's staff had grown to sixty-eight full-time and twelve part-time employees.[28] Under Dolph Briscoe in the 1970s, the staff expanded to more than 300, but staffs have been smaller in most subsequent administrations. Governor Perry had about 200 employees.

The staff's organization reflects the governor's leadership style (see Figure 6–2). Some governors create a highly centralized office with a chief of staff who screens the governor's contacts and the information the chief executive receives. Other governors want greater personal contacts with numerous staff members. The critical question is whether the governor obtains enough information with which to produce good public policy and minimize the potential for controversy, conflict, or embarrassment. Under ideal circumstances, the staff enhances the governor's work. Some governors, however, have permitted their staffs to insulate them by denying access to people with significant information or recommendations.

Governors generally choose staffers who are loyal and share their basic political attitudes. Because communication with the governor's various constituencies is essential for success, some staffers are chosen for their skills in mass communications and public relations. Others are hired for their expertise in specific policy areas.[29] In many respects, staff members function as the governor's surrogates. If one makes a mistake, particularly a serious mistake, the public will perceive it as the governor's error.

The staff collects, organizes, and screens information; helps decide who sees the governor; and otherwise schedules the governor's time. Staffers also work to win support for the governor's proposals from legislators, agencies, interest groups, and the public. Key staff members often represent the governor in meetings and in lobbying lawmakers. Sometimes the governor will become personally involved, particularly if his or her participation is needed to break an impasse and produce a solution.[30]

FIGURE 6-2 THE GOVERNOR'S STAFF

Every governor organizes the agencies within the office of the governor to meet his or her leadership and management style. Seen here is the organizational structure of Governor Greg Abbott's office. Individuals who serve in these offices are appointed by the governor and perform a wide range of functions, including legal counsel, policy development, budgeting, legislative liaison, intra-agency communications, scheduling, and public communications.

SOURCE: Office of Governor Greg Abbott.

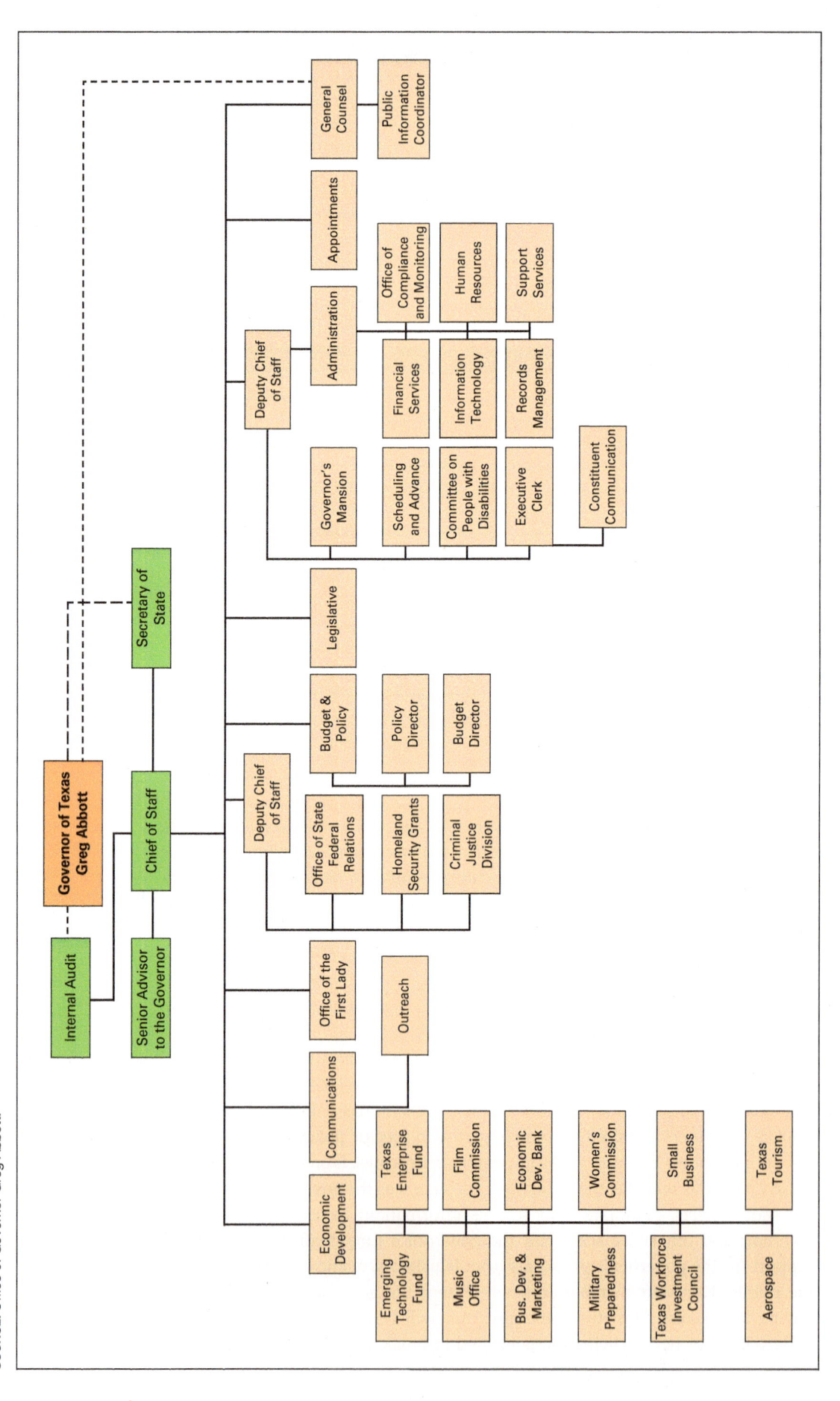

STAFF CAN REALLY MAKE A DIFFERENCE

A governor's success is dependent, in part, on a competent staff capable of assisting the governor in meeting expanded responsibilities and increased expectations from the general public, the legislature, administrative agencies, the media, and interest groups. Then-Governor-elect Greg Abbott, center left, is seen here in the Old Supreme Court Room in the Capitol introducing his key staff members prior to the 2015 legislative session.

6.4.2 The Governor and the Mass Media

The mass media help shape the governor's political and policy options. Governors who have failed to understand the media's influence often have courted disaster. A governor can develop a good working relationship with the media by being reasonably accessible to reporters and understanding the deadlines and other constraints under which they work. But success with the media requires more than being accessible and friendly. It also involves being honest—or, at least, avoiding being caught in a lie—as well as offering policies that are credible and demonstrating an ability to enact them.

Governors sometimes call press conferences to announce new policies or explain their positions on pending issues. They also stage "pseudo news events," such as visiting a classroom to discuss educational quality or a high-tech facility to talk about creating jobs. Their staffers sometimes leak information to selected reporters to embarrass the opposition, put an action of the administration in the best possible light, or float a trial balloon to gauge legislative or public reaction to a proposal. Some governors spend political funds to purchase radio or television time to try to mobilize public opinion in support of pet proposals before the legislature. In addition, the use of social media has become increasingly important. Governor Perry often sent Twitter alerts to supporters and members of the media, a practice that Governor Abbott also follows. Overall, the timely use of the media can contribute significantly to the power and influence of a governor.

Periodic statewide public opinion polls commissioned by media organizations often include questions about the governor's performance. Those ratings are widely monitored by players in the political arena.

GETTING THE MESSAGE OUT

The governor is not the only member of the plural executive who uses press conferences to communicate policy issues or publicize activities. Here, Texas Land Commissioner George P. Bush is touring the grounds of the Alamo following a news conference in San Antonio. Management and operation of the Alamo are now the responsibility of the General Land Office, which also manages the state's 22 million acres of public lands.

6.4.3 The Governor and the Political Party

The historic political factions within one-party Democratic Texas during much of the twentieth century were somewhat ill defined. There were liberal and conservative factions, as well as political differences between urban and rural Texans and between Texans who lived in different regions of the state. There also were differences between economic classes. Democratic governors built political coalitions around these various factions, but the coalitions usually were short lived, and most governors realized only limited power from their position as party leader.

Under the two-party system, however, the political party has become more important in providing support for the governor. During his second term in the late 1980s, Governor Bill Clements often had enough Republican votes in the House to thwart the will of the Democratic majority. After Republicans gained legislative control, Rick Perry received strong support from Republican lawmakers and party officials during the budgetary and redistricting battles of 2003 and for controversial policies, including deep budget cuts, enacted in 2011.

In 1995, during his first year as governor, Republican George W. Bush enjoyed the support of party leaders for his priorities—changes in education, civil and juvenile justice, and welfare. Initially, he kept his distance from much of the agenda advocated by the social conservatives who had taken control of the Texas Republican Party in 1994. But in 1999, while preparing for a presidential race and to appeal to conservative voters in Republican primaries across the country, Bush strengthened his antiabortion credentials by endorsing one of the social conservatives' major priorities at the time—a law requiring parents to be notified before their minor daughters could have abortions.

Bush's successor Governor Rick Perry courted social conservatives from the beginning of his administration. He solidified their support for his 2006 reelection race with the enactment of a state constitutional amendment banning same-sex marriages (a ban that has since been overturned by the U.S. Supreme Court) and a law that required parental approval, not just notification, for minors to obtain abortions. Perry, however, faced strong opposition from many conservatives in 2007 when he issued an order that schoolgirls be vaccinated against a virus linked to cervical cancer. Opponents, who convinced the legislature to overturn the order, said the governor was interfering with parental rights. Perry patched up those differences, in part, by heating up his rhetoric against President Obama and the federal government, in time to handily win reelection again in 2010. Governor Greg Abbott also has courted conservative Republicans, including members of the Tea Party movement.

6.4.4 The Governor and Interest Groups

Successful governors must be full-time political animals who continually nurture relationships throughout the political system. A gubernatorial candidate solicits the endorsements and contributions of various groups. These groups, in turn, develop stakes in gubernatorial elections and usually assume that the candidates they support will be responsive to their interests. A governor's policy initiatives often include legislation of benefit to key support groups, which maintain active roles throughout the policy process. Business groups, for example, were major political donors to Governor Perry, and the governor strongly supported business priorities throughout his record tenure.

Leadership Styles of Recent Texas Governors

6.5 Differentiate the leadership styles of recent Texas governors.

Gubernatorial leadership styles have been as varied as the personalities that molded the chief executives' approaches to their jobs. Some governors have come to the office with well-defined policy agendas and attempted to exploit every resource available to them. Other governors have taken a more limited view of the office. They adopted an administrative or managerial posture and left policy initiatives to other institutions or elected officials. New programs, especially those with far-reaching tax or social implications, were pursued with considerable caution.

Some governors have thrived on the constant attention and political and social interactions that go with the office. They have worked long hours and continually engaged in public relations and coalition building. Strange as it may seem, however, other governors were introverted and apparently found many aspects of the office distasteful. They often insulated themselves from the public and other political officials by communicating through their staffs and seemed detached from the activities necessary to influence public policy.[31]

6.5.1 Ann Richards (1991–1995)

Taking her oath in January 1991, Governor Ann Richards attempted to convince the public that her election marked the emergence of a "New Texas." She invited supporters to join her in a march up Congress Avenue to symbolically retake the Capitol for "the people." Hitting on the progressive Democratic themes of her campaign, she promised in her inaugural address a user-friendly, compassionate state government that would expand opportunities for everyone, particularly minorities and women. She promised to clean up the environment, improve education, attack crime, cut red tape, and boost ethical standards for public officeholders.

But the euphoria of the day was tempered by the reality of a $4-billion-plus potential deficit, a court order for school finance reform that could make the shortfall even greater, and a grand jury investigation into legislative behavior that had further eroded public confidence in state government.

The day after her inauguration, Richards marched over to a meeting of the State Board of Insurance to speak against a proposed increase in auto insurance premiums. Unlike her recent predecessors, she also testified before House and Senate committees, ensuring that her legislative priorities would receive maximum media coverage, and she used the media to attack the state bureaucracy.

Richards also quickly fulfilled a campaign promise to appoint more women and minorities to key positions in state government. She appointed the first African American to the University of Texas System Board of Regents, the first African American woman to the Texas A&M University governing board, and the first Hispanic to the Texas Court of Criminal Appeals. Twenty-five percent of the appointees during her first three months in office were Hispanic, 21 percent were African American, and 49 percent were women. Richards also named a disabled person to the Board of Human Services and a crime victim to the Board of Criminal Justice.[32]

With the state facing a revenue crunch, Richards took the lead in successfully lobbying legislators for a constitutional amendment to create a state lottery. Polls indicated the lottery had strong support among Texans as a new source of revenue for state government.

Most other major issues before the legislature during Richards's first year in office, however, were not so simple, and the new governor was less willing to take specific policy positions on them. She preferred to support the initiatives of Democratic legislative leaders or take the best bill they were willing to give her. Richards did outline strong provisions for a new ethics law for legislators and other public officials, but she ended up signing a much weaker bill rather than trying to force a showdown.

The progressive goals that Richards had outlined in her campaign also were tempered by the reality that Texas was a predominantly conservative state. Despite promoting a vision of a "New Texas" that offered more compassion for the poor, improved health care for the sick, and greater educational opportunity for all, Richards took pains to establish credentials for fiscal restraint. She opposed a proposal for a personal income tax, even though it could have provided a big boost in spending for health and human services programs and education.

Although Richards entered the 1993 legislative session with one of the highest public approval ratings of any governor in Texas history, she remained cautious, apparently to save political capital for a 1994 reelection race. She joined Democratic legislative leaders in insisting that a new state budget be written without an increase in state taxes. Without a tax bill, the new budget did not enable the legislature to give teachers a pay raise, which had been a Richards priority, and it did not keep up with growing caseloads in health and human services.

In one of the most emotional issues of the session, Richards sided with police chiefs, mayors, physicians, and members of the clergy—and against a majority of the legislature—in killing a proposal to allow private citizens to legally carry handguns. (It was revived and approved under Governor George W. Bush two years later.) She successfully advocated an immunization program for children and actively promoted the legislature's efforts to meet a Texas Supreme Court order for a constitutional school finance system but did not propose a plan of her own.

Richards was a national figure who was readily welcomed on Wall Street, at Hollywood parties, and in corporate boardrooms throughout the country. Many analysts believe her role as Texas's chief ambassador was her greatest contribution, along with the appointments that opened up the state policymaking process to a record number of women, Hispanics, and African Americans.

Richards, who had no legislative experience, did not seem to relish the often bloody give-and-take of the legislative process but obviously enjoyed her celebrity role as governor. During the 1993 session, Richards told reporters she wasn't the kind of leader who forced results. Instead, she said, she tried to contribute to "an atmosphere in which good things can happen."[33]

Although Republican George W. Bush unseated Richards in 1994, polls indicated she remained personally popular with her constituents. Most conservative, independent voters, however, had never been comfortable with Richards politically. Her defeat coincided with voter discontent with the Democratic Party that swept the country that year. A number of other Democratic governors also were defeated, and Republicans captured control of both houses of the U.S. Congress. Richards's opposition to the handgun bill during the 1993 legislative session was another factor, particularly among conservative voters. After leaving office, Richards was a lobbyist in Washington and remained in the public eye as a frequent television commentator. She died of cancer in 2006.

NEWSWORTHY STYLE

Governor Ann Richards (1991–1995), a progressive Democrat committed to increasing opportunities for women and minorities, had a keen sense of the national press's interest in her outspoken, flamboyant style.

6.5.2 George W. Bush (1995–2000)

George W. Bush, son of former President George H. W. Bush, had never held public office before being elected governor, but he had campaigned for and served as an unofficial adviser to his father. The younger Bush became Texas's second Republican governor in modern times by conducting an effective campaign for improvements in the public schools, tougher penalties for juvenile offenders, and changes in the welfare and civil justice systems. He succeeded in winning approval of all four programs during the 1995 legislative session, the first of his term.

Bush's public style was low key. He seemed to go out of his way to avoid controversy during his first year in office, but he remained focused on his four primary goals with the assistance of conservative, Democratic legislative leaders who shared his views and sensed that public sentiment was on the governor's side. Although Democrats had majorities in both the House and the Senate in 1995, conservatives of both major parties dominated the Texas legislature, and Democrats had already initiated work on some of the reforms the new governor wanted.

Bush actively worked with legislators behind the scenes, making minor compromises when necessary on his policy priorities. The governor had frequent private meetings with House and Senate members and would sometimes drop by their Capitol offices unannounced. He had weekly breakfast meetings with Lieutenant Governor Bob Bullock and Speaker Pete Laney, two Democrats whose work was crucial to the governor's program. "We disagree, but you'll never read about it," Bush said of his meetings with the two legislative leaders. "The way to forge good public policy amongst the leadership of the legislative branch and executive branch is to air our differences in private meetings that happen all the time."[34]

Unlike Governors White, Clements, and Richards before him, Bush did not face budgetary problems in state government that could have distracted lawmakers' attention from his priorities. Unlike Richards, Bush supported legislation that gave adult Texans the right to carry concealed handguns. The gun bill was not one of Bush's major priorities, but it had been an issue in his victory over Richards. He signed the gun bill approved by lawmakers in 1995.

Bush faced a tougher challenge during the 1997 legislative session, when he made school property tax reform a major goal. Bush said he wanted to lower property taxes because they had become so high that they were making home ownership difficult for many Texans. He proposed that the state government assume a larger share of the cost of funding the public schools by lowering local school taxes by about $3 billion a year. To replace the lost revenue, he proposed an increase in the state sales tax, the enactment of a new business tax, and the transfer of $1 billion in state budgetary savings to the public schools. The House rejected most of Bush's proposal and approved a controversial tax trade-off that would have increased numerous state taxes in exchange for major cuts in local school taxes. Bush lobbied Republican legislators for the House plan and helped convince about half of the sixty-eight Republicans in the House to vote for it. Assured that Bush was actively backing the plan, Speaker Laney helped persuade a large number of Democratic House members to vote for it. The bipartisan balancing act was necessary because many Republican legislators had campaigned against higher taxes of any kind, and Republicans had previously targeted many Democratic lawmakers over the tax issue.

TIME TO CELEBRATE

Then-Governor George W. Bush and his wife, Laura, are shown riding in the inaugural parade up Congress Avenue toward the state Capitol in Austin on January 19, 1999, after Bush had been sworn in for a second term as governor. A few months later, he would launch his first campaign for president.

Despite the success in the House, the Senate, which had a Republican majority, refused to approve a large increase in state taxes. In the end, Bush managed to salvage only a modest amount of property tax relief—about $150 a year for the average homeowner—by convincing the legislature to increase homestead exemptions, a form of tax break that homeowners get on their school taxes. The legislature used $1 billion in state budgetary savings to repay school districts for the revenue they lost from the higher exemptions.

Bush easily won reelection over Democratic challenger Garry Mauro in 1998 and entered the 1999 legislative session amidst widespread speculation that he was preparing for a presidential race. With his pending White House campaign obviously on his mind, he convinced the legislature to enact some additional tax cuts and increase education spending. He also accepted a priority of Democratic lawmakers to give schoolteachers a $3,000-a-year pay raise. Bush failed to win approval of a pilot program to allow students from low-performing public schools to use tax-backed vouchers to attend private schools. But, as noted earlier in this chapter, he won approval of a law to require parents to be notified before their minor daughters could receive abortions. At the time, it was the most significant piece of abortion-control legislation to be passed by Texas lawmakers since the U.S. Supreme Court had legalized abortion twenty-six years earlier.

Bush launched his successful 2000 presidential race in June 1999 and spent much of the next seventeen months campaigning outside the state. After his election to the White House, he resigned as governor in December 2000 and was succeeded by Rick Perry, the lieutenant governor.

6.5.3 Rick Perry (2000–2015)

Republican Rick Perry came to the governor's office with much more governmental experience than his immediate and more famous predecessor, George W. Bush. He had served six years as a state representative, eight years as state agriculture commissioner, and almost two years as lieutenant governor before succeeding Bush as governor in December 2000, after Bush resigned to become president. But Perry was not blessed with Bush's politically powerful name or his popularity, and he had not been elected governor. Moreover, the 2001 legislative session, with which Perry immediately had to deal, promised to be contentious because of political redistricting and a worrisome budgetary outlook.

Perry, nevertheless, survived his first session mostly unscarred, but he attracted a lot of attention by vetoing eighty-three bills, an early sign of what was to come. By the time his last term ended, Perry had vetoed 301 bills, more than any governor in Texas history and an important factor in what would become an influential administration.

Despite his rural, childhood roots in Paint Creek, a tiny town in West Texas, the governor was acutely aware of the clogged freeways that plagued the daily lives of urban and suburban Texans. Early on, he sought to make improved transportation a signature issue of his administration. In early 2002, he proposed a massive $175 billion transportation network for Texas, which would have included toll roads, railroads, and underground utility tunnels grouped in corridors stretching across the state. The plan, which Perry called the Trans Texas Corridor, generated controversy for years, in part because rural landowners viewed it as a "land grab" and as a way of enriching toll road operators. The legislature finally scuttled the proposal.

Perry defeated Democratic nominee Tony Sanchez, a multimillionaire Laredo businessman, in a bruising campaign to win a full term in the governor's office in 2002. Perry's victory and the first Republican takeover of the Texas House in modern times put the GOP in undisputed control of state government in 2003, and Perry acted accordingly. The governor joined Republican legislative leaders in demanding that a $10 billion revenue shortfall be bridged by cutting spending, not raising state taxes,

THE STATE'S LONGEST-SERVING GOVERNOR

Governor Rick Perry served in that capacity from 2000 to 2015, longer than any of his predecessors. His public career included a six-year stint as a state representative, eight years as the state's agriculture commissioner, and almost two years as lieutenant governor prior to assuming the governorship when George W. Bush won the presidency in 2000. He later served for more than two years as U.S. Secretary of Energy under President Donald Trump.

and Republicans prevailed. Advocates of health care programs and other services protested the spending reductions, and many of the state's daily newspapers editorialized for limited tax increases to help minimize the cuts in services. The legislature raised some state fees and enacted legislation to allow university governing boards to increase tuition, but Perry refused to budge on taxes, convinced that most middle-class Texans agreed with him. Perry also won from the legislature a special economic development fund that could be used to provide financial incentives for business recruitment, and he won significant new restrictions on medical malpractice claims and other civil lawsuits.

Perry also played a dominant role in a bitter, partisan fight over congressional redistricting in 2003. He supported an effort to increase the number of Republicans elected to the U.S. House from Texas, and he called three special sessions that summer to force the result, outlasting Democratic senators who had fled to New Mexico to break a Senate quorum.

Facing a Texas Supreme Court order for changes in the state's school finance system, Perry called the legislature into another special session in 2006. He endorsed a plan for cutting local school property taxes by about one-third and replacing most, but not all, of the lost revenue with an expanded business tax and an increase in the state cigarette tax. With Republicans still holding a legislative majority and a court deadline looming, Perry succeeded in getting the plan passed over the objections of Democrats and educator groups.

Perry already had taken other steps to strengthen his support among conservative Republican voters, including his advocacy in 2005 of a state constitutional amendment banning same-sex marriage, which Texans overwhelmingly approved and the U.S. Supreme Court, several years later, nullified. He also backed a new state law to require a minor to have her parents' permission before obtaining an abortion.

Perry attracted three high-profile reelection opponents, a Democrat and two independents, in 2006. He was reelected, but with only 39 percent of the vote. That low margin probably contributed to the rocky relationship the governor had with many lawmakers, including Republicans, during the 2007 and 2009 legislative sessions. In 2007, as noted earlier in this chapter, Perry infuriated many conservatives by issuing an executive order to require schoolgirls to be vaccinated against a virus linked to cervical cancer. With opponents protesting that the governor's order interfered with parental rights, Republicans took the lead in approving a law to rescind it. Many Republican lawmakers, particularly from rural areas, also fought the governor over the expanded use of toll roads, which Perry had supported instead of raising taxes for new highway construction.

In 2009, the Republican-led Senate rejected one of Perry's appointees to the Board of Pardons and Paroles as unqualified for the job and rejected his choice for chair of the State Board of Education, following complaints that the individual had tried to impose his religious beliefs on educational policies. But Perry could claim several political victories that year, including tax cuts for small business owners and shutting down legislative attempts to expand the Children's Health Insurance Program for low-income families, even though Texas had more children without health insurance than any other state.

Perry spent much of the 2009 session preparing for his next reelection campaign by launching repeated political criticisms at President Barack Obama and the federal government, a practice that would continue for the rest of Perry's administration. Attacking Obama helped Perry solidify his support among conservative voters in anticipation of a challenge from popular U.S. Senator Kay Bailey Hutchison in the 2010 Republican primary. Courting members of the emerging conservative Tea Party movement, one of the first prominent Texas political figures to do so, Perry attacked Hutchison as a "Washington insider" who did not know what was best for Texas. He easily won the GOP primary and the November general election against Democratic challenger Bill White, a former mayor of Houston.

Republicans also won an overwhelming majority of the Texas House in 2010, and Perry advocated for and won a strongly conservative agenda during the 2011 legislative session. At Perry's insistence, the legislative majority slashed billions of dollars from education and other public services to cover a $27 billion revenue shortfall without raising state taxes, as Texas was beginning to emerge from a national recession. With his advocacy, Republican lawmakers led a successful fight to enact new regulations for abortion and a law mandating that voters show photo identification in order to cast ballots.

A few months after the legislature adjourned, Perry launched a race for the 2012 Republican presidential nomination. His campaign had been highly anticipated by conservative Republicans but ended after only five months, following a series of highly publicized gaffes by the governor. It was the first political race Perry had ever lost. After cruising over the Texas political landscape for so long, he obviously was not prepared for the much greater scrutiny of a national campaign. He returned home unbowed but bruised.

With the economy improving, the legislature in 2013 restored many of the budget cuts that had been imposed two years earlier. But Perry and the legislative majority continued to shut the door on higher state taxes, despite worsening congestion on state highways, a state judge's ruling that the school funding system was inadequate, and Texas's dubious distinction of having the largest percentage of residents in the country without health insurance. Perry also rejected an option under the Affordable Care Act to expand Medicaid coverage to an estimated one million low-income Texans, even though the federal government would have picked up most of the cost. Perry said rising Medicaid costs eventually would cripple the state budget, and he again attacked the intrusion from Washington. Perry called back-to-back special legislative sessions in the summer of 2013 to win legislative enactment of additional restrictions on abortion, which later were overturned by the U.S. Supreme Court.

Perry announced later in 2013 that he wouldn't seek another term in 2014. In 2015, he began campaigning for the 2016 Republican nomination for president. He never gained much traction among a large group of contenders and, after consistently faring poorly in national polling, became the first Republican candidate to drop out of the race. President Donald Trump, the eventual winner, later appointed Perry to his Cabinet as secretary of energy. Ironically, the Department of Energy had been one of three federal agencies Perry had vowed to abolish during his first presidential campaign. During his U.S. Senate confirmation hearing for the Cabinet post in 2017, Perry said he had changed his mind about the agency's importance. "After being briefed on so many of the vital functions of the Department of Energy, I regret recommending its elimination," he said.[35]

Perry served in the Cabinet post for more than two years, presiding over a sharp increase in the production of fossil fuels, before he resigned in late 2019, shortly before the House of Representatives impeached President Trump for allegedly trying to pressure the president of Ukraine, in a telephone call, to investigate political rival Joe Biden. Trump, who later was acquitted of the charges by the Senate, said he called the Ukrainian president because Perry urged him to. Perry, who was a point person for the Trump administration with the Ukrainian government, said he wanted the two presidents to talk about strengthening energy business ties between their two countries, not to discuss Biden, whose son, Hunter, had done work with a Ukrainian company.[36]

Besides being the longest-serving governor in Texas history, Perry was one of the strongest. He had his political ups and downs, his admirers and his detractors, but he transformed a weak constitutional office into an influential one, due not only to his longevity, but also to thousands of appointments to policy-setting state agencies, record-setting use of the veto, and a conservative political philosophy that matched the majority sentiment in Texas during his administration.

6.5.4 Greg Abbott (2015–)

Greg Abbott compiled a lengthy conservative resume during six years on the Texas Supreme Court and a record twelve years as the state's attorney general. Although the office of attorney general is primarily a civil law agency, he established a cyber-crimes unit to arrest people using the Internet to prey upon children and a fugitive unit to arrest sex offenders who violated their parole. He also expanded the office's Medicaid fraud control unit, and he sued the federal government more than thirty times over a host of issues in which Abbott believed Washington had encroached upon state authority. Most were filed against the Democratic administration of President Barack Obama, a fact with which Abbott once summed up his typical workday: "I go into the office, I sue the federal government, and then I go home."[37]

After his lopsided victory over Democratic state Senator Wendy Davis in the 2014 governor's race, Abbott continued to promote his conservative principles. His pro-business, limited-government priorities differed little from those of his long-time

CRISIS MANAGEMENT

Texans expect their governor and other elected officials to be actively responsive when crises, such as natural disasters, occur. Governor Greg Abbott (left) and Vice President Mike Pence (right) participate in cleanup efforts and inspect damage caused by Hurricane Harvey, which left widespread devastation in the Houston area in August 2017.

predecessor, Rick Perry, but Abbott, at least initially, had a more-restrained style. "Stylistically, Perry was more a shoot-from-the-hip, gut-feel kind of guy, and [in Abbott] you've got a guy who's been a lawyer and a judge," Bill Miller, a veteran Austin lobbyist, told *The Texas Tribune*. Some politicians like political theater, but Abbott was "not an actor on that stage. He's more like a producer," Miller said.[38]

During his first legislative session in 2015, Abbott mostly avoided being drawn into controversies over hot-button conservative issues, such as an expansion of gun rights legislation, which was passed, and an effort to repeal a state law giving a tuition break to some undocumented immigrants, which failed. His priorities included improvements in pre-kindergarten and higher education, border security, transportation, ethics reform, and tax cuts. But he gave only as much public direction to legislators as he felt necessary. He declared early in the session, for instance, that he would veto any state budget that did not include reductions in business taxes, but he refused to publicly intervene in a debate between the House and the Senate over what other kinds of taxes should be cut. Eventually, the legislature approved cuts in business and local property taxes.[39]

Abbott actively lobbied for his pre-kindergarten legislation, even in the face of opposition from ultra-conservative Tea Party members aligned with Lieutenant Governor Dan Patrick. After a private, but well-publicized, confrontation between Abbott and Patrick over the issue, the Senate joined the House in passing the legislation. The only major priority Abbott lost that first session was ethics reform. Legislators failed to agree on comprehensive improvements in laws governing their own ethical behavior.

Despite the Tea Party's unhappiness with his pre-kindergarten program, Abbott seldom missed an opportunity to wave his conservative credentials. As did Perry before him, he refused to expand Medicaid under the Affordable Care Act. He also was active in a Republican effort to strip government funding from Planned Parenthood. After terrorist attacks in California and Paris, Abbott called for closing the Texas border to Syrian refugees. After the Obama administration began lifting economic sanctions against Iran following Iran's agreement to restrictions on its nuclear program, Abbott instructed Texas's pension systems to continue honoring a state ban on investments in companies doing business with Iran.

Abbott frequently criticized the Obama administration, serving notice that he wasn't going to give up his long-time fight against what he considered a federal government that meddled too much in the state's business. Early in 2016, he proposed a constitutional convention of the states to draft amendments to the U.S. Constitution to curtail federal power. The proposal, which would require the approval of two-thirds of the states, was a long shot that initially spurred discussion, both pro and con, although it never received any substantive attention from Texas lawmakers.

Abbott endorsed U.S. Senator Ted Cruz, a fellow Texan, for president a few days before the 2016 Texas Republican primary. But he later threw his support to eventual Republican nominee Donald Trump and remained supportive of Trump during the new president's controversial and sometimes-rocky administration, except for a dispute over the amount of federal aid allocated to Hurricane Harvey recovery efforts in Houston and much of southeast Texas.

Abbott joined forces with Lieutenant Governor Dan Patrick to back a conservative agenda during two legislative sessions in 2017, the regular session and a summer special session, the first special session called by Abbott. They secured additional restrictions on abortion and won enactment of a "sanctuary cities" law to require local law-enforcement officials to more actively enforce federal immigration laws. But they lost several other priorities, most notably a measure to put new limits on the ability of city and county governments to increase property taxes and a so-called "bathroom bill," which would have required transgender individuals to use the public restrooms that corresponded to the gender on their birth certificates. The governor and the lieutenant governor said the bathroom bill was necessary to protect women and children from potential assaults in public restrooms.

Both the property tax and bathroom bills were approved by the Senate, under Patrick's leadership, during both sessions. But they ran into trouble in the House, where Democrats and moderate Republicans, led by then-Speaker Joe Straus, shut the door on the bathroom bill and wouldn't agree to the strict limits on property taxes sought by Patrick and Abbott. Straus agreed with opponents of the bathroom bill, including many business leaders, that the measure was discriminatory and could hurt the state's economy by provoking boycotts of Texas by the sponsors of conventions and major athletic events.

Abbott had put twenty issues on the special session agenda, and before the session convened, he said he was going to keep a list of legislators who supported him and those who didn't. "No one gets to hide," he said.[40]

The legislature passed about half of the twenty pieces of legislation that Abbott had sought. After the session ended, the governor and Patrick blamed Straus for most of the failures, particularly the property tax limits and bathroom bill. Several weeks later, Straus announced that he would not seek reelection to the House. And in the weeks before the March 2018 Republican primary elections, Abbott took the unusual step of endorsing the opponents of three incumbent Republican House members with whom he had had conflicts over legislation. It was believed that Abbott was trying to help elect a more conservative House—and influence the election of a more conservative speaker—for the 2019 legislative session. When two of the three incumbents won their primary races anyway, Abbott called for Republican unity.

After Democrats gained twelve seats in the Texas House in the 2018 elections to narrow the Republican majority, Abbott joined Lieutenant Governor Patrick and new House Speaker Dennis Bonnen to advocate for a significant increase in public education funding, including teacher pay raises, a priority of Democrats and moderate Republicans. The education package was enacted during the 2019 legislative session. Abbott and Patrick made no effort to revive the bathroom bill during the 2019 session, but they won new limits on local property taxes, a conservative priority that had eluded them two years earlier, and they won legislative and voter approval of a constitutional amendment to make it more difficult for future legislatures to enact a state income tax.

During that same legislative session, Associated Press writer Paul J. Weber summarized Abbott's leadership style: "Unlike the swaggering figures who preceded him, Abbott has remade the job with a lower profile – a style that has stocked criticism of sometimes being too detached. He has likened himself to a CEO and wears the buttoned-down look. His politics are conventional hard-right, of late pushing immigration crackdowns and border security surges."[41]

In March 2020, as the coronavirus began to spread in Texas, creating a public health emergency, Abbott issued a disaster declaration, as other governors around the country did, and temporarily closed schools, restricted public gatherings and banned dine-in services in restaurants, among other directives, as discussed at the beginning of this chapter. Abbott's initial response to the emergency prompted Robert Garrett of *The Dallas Morning News* to write, "The feverish efforts come after five years in which Abbott has consolidated and built upon the clout that's been rapidly piling up in the office of governor – a key legacy of former GOP Gov. Rick Perry."[42] But also, as noted at the beginning of this chapter, Abbott's response to the coronavirus pandemic soon sparked controversy.

Other Offices of the Plural Executive

6.6 Describe the duties and responsibilities of the other offices of the executive branch in Texas.

Under the Texas Constitution of 1836, the executive branch of the Republic of Texas resembled the structure of the American presidency with an elected president and vice president. The Constitution of 1845 replaced the office of president with an elected governor and the office of vice president with an elected lieutenant governor.

This constitution also introduced the plural executive, giving the governor the power to appoint the attorney general and the secretary of state; however, the comptroller and treasurer were to be elected every two years by a joint session of the legislature. Subsequent constitutions created new offices to be elected statewide, producing the constitutional legacy of the plural executive. Many of the constitutional developments that occurred from the period of the Republic through the constitutional convention of 1875 paralleled developments in many other states, and the political movements that shaped the constitutions of other states were prevalent in Texas as well.

6.6.1 Lieutenant Governor

The lieutenant governor, the second highest-ranking official in Texas, has only limited executive powers. Were the governor to die, be incapacitated, removed from office, or voluntarily leave office mid-term, the lieutenant governor would become governor. That eventuality has occurred only four times. In 1917, William P. Hobby replaced James E. Ferguson, who was impeached. Governor W. Lee O'Daniel resigned in 1941 to enter the U.S. Senate and was succeeded by Coke Stevenson. Governor Beauford Jester died in office in 1949 and was replaced by Allan Shivers. Most recently, George W. Bush resigned in December 2000 after being elected president and was succeeded by Rick Perry.

As discussed in Chapter 5, the office of lieutenant governor is primarily legislative in Texas. Because of the lieutenant governor's key legislative role and statewide constituency, many experts over the years have considered this position to be the most powerful office in state government, although some people began to second-guess that notion during the Rick Perry and Greg Abbott administrations in the governor's office. The lieutenant governor is elected independently of the governor and does not have to belong to the same party as the governor. He or she is the presiding officer of the Senate, and Senate rules have traditionally given the lieutenant governor enormous power over that body. The lieutenant governor also chairs the Legislative Budget Board, which plays a key role in the state budgetary process. The office's legislative powers far exceed those of the vice president on the federal level.

Republican David Dewhurst was elected lieutenant governor in 2002 and reelected in 2006 and 2010. After losing a midterm race for the U.S. Senate to Republican underdog Ted Cruz in 2012, Dewhurst lost his 2014 reelection race to state Senator Dan Patrick. As discussed in Chapter 5, Patrick engineered a key rules change in the Senate that has helped him win Senate approval of several of his conservative priorities. Patrick won reelection in 2018 over Democrat Mike Collier, an accountant and former PriceWaterhouseCoopers partner.

6.6.2 Attorney General

attorney general
The state's chief legal officer. He or she represents the state in lawsuits; is responsible for enforcing the state's antitrust, consumer protection, and other civil laws; and issues advisory opinions on legal questions to state and local officeholders. This elected official has little responsibility for criminal law enforcement.

The **attorney general** is the state's chief legal officer and is called upon to defend state laws enacted by the legislature and orders adopted by regulatory agencies. The office also enforces the state's antitrust and consumer protection laws and helps collect child support payments from noncustodial parents in divorce cases. Recent attorneys general also have been called on to defend the state or negotiate settlements in federal and state court lawsuits challenging the constitutionality of state prisons, the school finance system, redistricting laws, and other major policies. In addition, the attorney general issues opinions on the legality of actions of other state and local officials.[43]

Unlike counterparts in the federal government and some other states, the Texas attorney general is primarily a civil lawyer. Except for representing the state in the appeals of death penalty cases and assisting local prosecutors, the position has relatively little responsibility for criminal law enforcement. Many candidates for the office like to campaign on tough law-and-order platforms, but most responsibilities for criminal prosecution are vested in locally elected county and district attorneys.

NO STRANGER TO CONTROVERSY
From almost the beginning of his tenure as the state's chief legal officer, Attorney General Ken Paxton has been under indictment for allegedly violating state securities laws while serving in the legislature. But he won reelection in 2018 and is a strong proponent of the conservative viewpoint.

Dan Morales, a former Democratic state representative from San Antonio, was elected attorney general in 1990, becoming the second Hispanic elected to statewide office in Texas. He won reelection in 1994 but chose not to run for a third term in 1998. In a major policy decision made independently of the governor, the legislature, and other state officials, Morales in 1996 filed a multibillion-dollar damage suit against tobacco companies, seeking reimbursement for public health care costs associated with smoking. Morales acted within his authority as the state's chief legal officer, and the lawsuit resulted in a $17.3 billion settlement for the state. The tobacco suit also sparked a controversy over legal fees. Several years after Morales left office, he was sentenced to federal prison for four years for mail fraud and for filing a false income tax return.

Morales was succeeded by former Texas Supreme Court Justice John Cornyn, Texas's first Republican attorney general in modern times. Cornyn was elected to the U.S. Senate in 2002 and was succeeded by Greg Abbott, a Republican and another former Texas Supreme Court justice. Abbott served a record twelve years in the office before running successfully for governor in 2014. He was succeeded by Republican Ken Paxton, a former state senator from McKinney.

Several months after taking office as attorney general in January 2015, Paxton was indicted in Collin County on felony charges that he had violated state securities laws several years earlier while still in the legislature. He was accused of offering to sell more than $100,000 worth of stock in a North Texas technology company to two people without telling the buyers—including a state representative—that he was being compensated by the company. Paxton also was charged with working as an investment adviser without a license. Paxton sent an email to supporters, saying he expected "to be fully vindicated."[44] But after years of legal maneuvers by his attorneys and special prosecutors in his case, he still had not come to trial by late 2020. He was reelected to a second term in 2018.

Paxton was hit with more allegations of wrongdoing in October 2020, when seven senior aides in the attorney general's office, including his first assistant, signed a letter accusing Paxton of several possible offenses, including abuse of office and bribery. The letter stemmed from Paxton's hiring of a private attorney as a special prosecutor to look into a federal criminal investigation of an Austin real estate investor who had contributed $25,000 to Paxton's 2018 reelection campaign. The whistleblowers suggested Paxton was trying to help his political donor impede the investigation. Paxton denied the allegations. At this book's deadline, it was unknown if or how the accusations would be investigated.

Among his major policy initiatives, Paxton created a unit in the attorney general's office to help local law-enforcement agencies crack down on cases of human trafficking, or forcing immigrants and other people into the sex trade and other jobs from which traffickers profited.

Paxton also has used his office to promote his religious and conservative political beliefs. In 2015, soon after the U.S. Supreme Court ruled that gay marriage was legal, Paxton issued an opinion advising county clerks in Texas that if they had religious objections to same-sex marriage, they could ignore the Supreme Court's decision and refuse to issue marriage licenses to same-sex couples. A group of lawyers filed a complaint against the attorney general, which the State Bar of Texas dismissed. Then, in 2020, Paxton said his office would not defend a state agency, the Commission on Judicial Conduct, which had sanctioned a justice of the peace for refusing to marry same-sex couples. The judge had responded to the sanction by suing the commission, which under most circumstances the attorney general would have defended in court as part of his office's routine responsibilities.

Paxton also sued the federal government, seeking to overturn the Affordable Care Act, or Obamacare, a frequent Republican target. In two previous lawsuits, the U.S. Supreme Court had upheld most of the law. But the high court agreed to hear Paxton's challenge in late 2020 with a ruling expected in 2021. Joined by other Republican states, Paxton argued that the individual mandate, which required people to have health insurance, was no longer valid since the penalty for failing to have insurance had been repealed in a subsequent tax bill enacted under the Trump administration. In an unusual move, the Trump administration refused to defend the health care law and sided with Paxton. So, the law was defended instead by a group of Democratic attorneys general from other states.

During the coronavirus pandemic in 2020, Paxton fought efforts by the Democratic Party to expand mail-in voting in Texas for people who feared exposure to the virus at polling places (see Chapter 11).

6.6.3 Comptroller of Public Accounts

comptroller of public accounts
The state's primary tax administrator and revenue estimator. It is an elective position.

pay-as-you-go
A constitutional prohibition against state government borrowing money for its operating budget.

The **comptroller of public accounts** is Texas's primary tax collector, accounting officer, and revenue estimator. Texas functions under a **pay-as-you-go** principle, which means that the legislature cannot adopt an operating budget that exceeds anticipated revenue. The comptroller is responsible for providing the revenue estimates on which the legislature drafts biennial state budgets. A budget cannot become law without the comptroller's certification that it falls within the official revenue projection, developed by using sophisticated models of the state's economy.[45] If the revenue estimate is below the legislature's budget proposals, appropriations must be reduced or taxes must be raised. In a volatile, changing economy, it is difficult to accurately project revenues two years in the future. In the mid-1980s, then-Comptroller Bob Bullock had to adjust his revenue estimate downward several times to account for plunging oil prices.

Republican Susan Combs, a former state representative and former agriculture commissioner, was elected comptroller in 2006 and reelected in 2010. Combs suffered a huge embarrassment when she discovered in 2011 that Social Security numbers and other personal information for 3.5 million people—including current and retired teachers and state employees—had accidentally been left exposed for a year or more on a publicly accessible computer server at her agency. She apologized and offered free credit monitoring and Internet surveillance to those affected. She also offered to spend her political funds for "identity restoration services" for anyone whose personal information was misused because of the breach.[46] After Combs chose not to seek another term in 2014, state Senator Glenn Hegar of Katy was elected comptroller from a crowded candidate field.

As Comptroller Bullock had discovered thirty years earlier, Hegar soon learned that it was extremely difficult to predict future state revenue when the price of oil, a major tax generator, starts plummeting, even in a diversified economy, as it did in 2015. Hegar, who was reelected in 2018, faced an even bigger challenge in 2020, when the coronavirus pandemic struck a huge blow to the state economy. Revenue from sales taxes and oil production taxes dropped, forcing the comptroller to lower the revenue estimate he had provided the legislature the previous year and forcing cuts in state spending (see Chapter 14).

6.6.4 Commissioner of the General Land Office

The state of Texas retains ownership, including mineral rights, to approximately 22 million acres of public lands, which are managed by the **commissioner of the General Land Office**. Revenues generated by mineral leases and other land uses are earmarked for education through the Permanent University Fund and the Permanent School Fund. This agency also is responsible for the Veterans Land Program, which provides low-interest loans to veterans for the purchase of land and houses.

During sixteen years in office, Land Commissioner Garry Mauro, a Democrat, developed several environmental initiatives, including beach cleanup efforts and a program for cleaning up oil spills off the Texas coast. After Mauro unsuccessfully ran for governor in 1998, the next land commissioner, Republican David Dewhurst, a businessman from Houston, continued the beach cleanup efforts. Dewhurst also administered a program to replenish beaches and protect them from erosion. Dewhurst was elected lieutenant governor in 2002 and was succeeded as land commissioner by Jerry Patterson, a former state senator from Harris County. Patterson's priorities also included beach protection as well as development of new nursing homes for veterans and new veterans' cemeteries. He was reelected in 2006 and 2010.

Patterson angered environmentalists by proposing to sell the remote, undeveloped Christmas Mountains in the Big Bend area of far west Texas to private interests, an issue that remained unresolved for several years. Finally, in 2011, the land commissioner agreed to give the mountains, some 9,000-plus acres, to the Texas State University System to use as a study site for archaeology, biology, geology, and wildlife management. The university agreed to provide public access to the site, and environmentalists endorsed the transfer.[47]

George P. Bush, a member of the prominent Bush political family, was elected state land commissioner in 2014 after Patterson ran unsuccessfully for lieutenant governor. Bush has spent much of his time at the land office working to preserve and enhance the Alamo, the historic Spanish mission and battle site in downtown San Antonio, whose management the General Land Office had taken over from the longtime custodians, the Daughters of the Republic of Texas. But considering his family's political legacy—former presidents George H. W. Bush (his grandfather) and George W. Bush (his uncle) and former Florida Governor Jeb Bush (his father)—and the fact that several recent land commissioners had used or tried to use the office as a stepping-stone to higher office, some observers believed Bush was looking ahead. That speculation increased after the younger Bush, in a video conference call with other supporters of Jeb Bush's unsuccessful 2016 presidential campaign, likened his land commissioner's job to being a "dog catcher."[48]

But Bush won reelection to the land office post in 2018, defeating Jerry Patterson, who tried to win his old office back, in the Republican primary.

commissioner of the General Land Office
An elected official who manages the state's public lands and administers the Veterans Land Program, which provides low-interest loans to veterans for the purchase of land and houses.

6.6.5 Commissioner of Agriculture

The office of **commissioner of agriculture**, created by statute rather than by the constitution, is responsible for carrying out laws regulating and benefiting Texas agriculture. The agency supports agricultural research and education and administers consumer protection laws in the areas of weights and measures, packaging and labeling, product quality, and marketing. Republican Rick Perry aggressively promoted

commissioner of agriculture
An elected state official responsible for administering laws and programs that benefit agriculture.

Texas agricultural products during two terms as commissioner. Republican Susan Combs, a former state representative from Austin who succeeded Perry, also urged Texans to buy more produce grown in the Lone Star State.

Republican Todd Staples, a former state senator from Palestine, was elected agriculture commissioner in 2006 and reelected in 2010. He promoted Texas produce and nutrition campaigns for children and, during the 2011 drought, publicized the devastating effects on farmers and ranchers. Staples ran unsuccessfully for lieutenant governor in 2014 and was succeeded by Republican Sid Miller, a former legislator from Stephenville.

As a legislator who prided himself on his conservatism, Miller had voted for deep budget cuts in state government. But, as agriculture commissioner, he complained that the legislature didn't appropriate enough money for his agency to do its job of ensuring the quality and safety of agricultural products sold to the public. After legislators in 2015 failed to approve as large an appropriation as Miller said was necessary to effectively carry out his duties, he angered some of his former colleagues by announcing that, over the next two years, he would raise fees on some of the industries that he regulated by more than $20 million. The fees would cover activities such as certifying pesticide applicators, inspecting grain warehouses, ensuring the quality of eggs and other agriculture products, and ensuring the accuracy of equipment used to weigh and measure agricultural products.

On several occasions, Miller—or his aides—have stirred controversy by posting inflammatory comments on social media. In one incident, Miller's political Facebook page shared a post that advocated dropping an atomic bomb on the "Muslim world." Miller, who was in China at the time, said he didn't post the item, and it later was deleted without an apology. A later posting on the Facebook page included separate photos of a rattlesnake pit and Syrian refugees with a caption that read: "Can you tell me which of these rattlers won't bite you? Sure some of them won't, but tell me which ones so we can bring them into the house." Then, a few days before the 2016 presidential election, a tweet from Miller's campaign Twitter account used an obscene term to refer to Democratic nominee Hillary Clinton. Miller initially claimed his Twitter account had been hacked and then said the tweet was posted by a staffer and apologized.

He was reelected in 2018.

6.6.6 Secretary of State

secretary of state
An officeholder appointed by the governor who administers state election laws, grants charters to corporations, and processes the extradition of prisoners to other states.

The **secretary of state**, the only constitutional official appointed by the governor, has a variety of duties, including granting charters to corporations and processing the extradition of prisoners to other states. The primary function of this office, however, is to administer state election laws. That responsibility includes reviewing county and local election procedures, developing statewide policies for voter registration, and receiving and tabulating election returns.

6.6.7 Elected Boards and Commissions

Only two—the Texas Railroad Commission and the State Board of Education—of the more than 200 boards and commissions that head most state agencies are elected.

Texas Railroad Commission
A three-member elected body that regulates oil and natural gas production and lignite mining in Texas.

TEXAS RAILROAD COMMISSION Originally created to regulate intrastate (within Texas) operations of railroads and trucking companies, the **Texas Railroad Commission** now regulates oil and natural gas production and lignite mining in Texas. The commission includes three elected members who serve six-year, staggered terms and rotate the position of chair among themselves. The oil and gas industry has historically focused much attention on this agency and made large campaign contributions to commission members. Many critics claim the commission is a prime example of a regulatory body that has been co-opted by those interests it was created to regulate.

In 2018, commission Chairwoman Christi Craddick, while running for reelection, drew some criticism after she was honored by an oil and gas industry group, the Texas Independent Producers and Royalty Owners Association, with its highest honor, the Hats Off Award. She was honored for "ensuring safe, responsible energy production in Texas, while reducing or removing unnecessary regulatory barriers that can restrict job growth and the energy industry's significant impact on the Texas economy." Craddick, who also received significant political contributions from members of the energy industry, defended the award and said the commission worked to "maintain a regulatory environment that ensures environmental protection and economic growth." But Adrian Shelley, director of the Texas office of Public Citizen, a consumer watchdog group, called the regulator's receipt of an industry award "unseemly." He said it was "in keeping with overly friendly, intertwined relationships our agencies have with the oil and gas industry."[49]

In 2015, the commission attracted public attention for refusing to endorse a scientific study that blamed an unusual series of earthquakes in North Texas on fracking, a form of oil and gas drilling, which had been conducted extensively in the area. Southern Methodist University, the University of Texas at Austin, and the U.S. Geological Survey had been involved in the peer-reviewed study, noted Rudolph Bush, an editorial writer for *The Dallas Morning News*. "So we know that drilling can be dangerous seismically. And we know that the regulatory agency over it will turn a blind eye," he wrote.[50]

The Texas Railroad Commission has been a staging area for opportunistic politicians who seek election to the commission primarily as a stepping-stone to higher office. A commissioner does not have to resign in the middle of his or her six-year term to seek another office and, as an incumbent regulator, has little trouble collecting large contributions from the oil and gas industry that can be used to further political ambitions. Both Democrat John Sharp and Republican Carole Keeton Strayhorn used seats on the commission to strengthen their political bases for successful races for state comptroller in 1990 and 1998, respectively. One commissioner, Tony Garza, resigned in midterm to accept President George W. Bush's appointment as ambassador to Mexico.

The closeness to the regulated industry and the commissioner turnover have prompted periodic calls for the commission to be abolished and its duties transferred

RENEWED IMPORTANCE?

The Texas Railroad Commission (shown here in the early 1900s) no longer regulates railroads. It regulates oil and natural gas production and lignite mining in Texas.

to other agencies appointed by the governor, including the Public Utility Commission, which already has oversight over electric utilities, and the Texas Commission on Environmental Quality, the state's main environmental protection agency. But efforts to rename or overhaul the commission have failed.

STATE BOARD OF EDUCATION Debate on public education in Texas has not been limited to educational quality and financing. It also has focused on state oversight of public education programs. The state has bounced back and forth between an elected state education board and an appointed one.

Prior to educational reforms enacted in 1984, the **State Board of Education** had twenty-seven members elected from then-existing congressional districts. At the urging of reformers dissatisfied with student performance, the legislature provided for a new education board of fifteen members to be appointed by the governor and confirmed by the Senate. The idea was to reduce the board's independence while education changes ordered by the legislature were being carried out. But the law also provided that the board would again become an elected body within a few years. The present board has fifteen members elected from districts established by the legislature. The State Board of Education sets some educational policies. But the daily administration of public education is conducted by the Texas Education Agency, which is directed by the commissioner of education, who is appointed by the governor.

State Board of Education districts are so large that most voters know little if anything about candidates for board seats, and, until recently, races for the board received little media attention. Social conservatives wanting to influence education policies started targeting the board and became successful in winning races for several board seats. Ideological and partisan bickering on the board then became so strident that the legislature reduced its powers. The panel's main remaining duties include investment of education dollars in the Permanent School Fund and some oversight over textbook selection and curriculum standards.

Political and ideological battles still erupted on the board. A major fight in 2010 over the history curriculum for Texas's public schools attracted national attention and ridicule. Several conservatives on the board succeeded in rewriting some of the curriculum standards to conform to their own religious or philosophical beliefs. The changes downplayed the role of Hispanics in Texas history and attempted to diminish Thomas Jefferson's historical standing because of his belief in the separation of church and state.[51]

The political and ideological bickering has abated in recent years. In 2018, the board approved a statewide elective course in Mexican American studies and two years later approved another statewide elective course in African American studies. But periodic controversy still threatened to erupt over issues such as sex education in the public schools.

State Board of Education
A fifteen-member body, composed of members who are elected from districts, which has responsibility over textbook selection, curriculum standards for public schools, and Permanent School Fund investments.

CONCLUSION

Considering the diffusion of responsibility and the politically ambitious officeholders eager to move to higher office if one of their colleagues steps down or stumbles, you may wonder how the executive branch of state government gets anything done. That has been a longtime criticism of the plural executive form of government by those who favor an appointed cabinet form with the governor clearly in charge. But things get done, and conflict among elected agency heads usually is minimal. Although some academicians and pundits may sharply criticize the plural executive and advocate for a unified executive, Texans seem content with the form of the executive that currently exists.

As we pointed out in this chapter, Governor Rick Perry didn't let the constitutional restrictions on the governor stand in his way, but even he, one of the strongest governors in Texas history, didn't always get what he wanted. Mainly the executive branch of state government works, however unpredictably sometimes, because elected and appointed officials are duty-bound to follow state law and the state constitution, and there can be legal and political consequences if they don't. Throughout much of the state's history, members of the executive branch have held similar ideological and partisan views. For much of the twentieth century, all statewide officeholders were Democrats. Now, all are Republicans. Whatever the officials' partisan affiliation, the people of Texas (the officials' constituents) expect their state government to work, just as residents of other states—with a strong governor or weak governor, cabinet style of government or plural executive—expect their governments to work.

Members of the executive branch are political leaders who pay a lot of attention to public opinion, the policy preferences of Texans, and partisan voting patterns. Although Texas has significant competing views of public policy, there is substantial evidence to indicate that members of the executive branch reflect the dominant values and views of most Texans.

GOVERNOR WILLIAM P. HOBBY (1917–1921)

Elected lieutenant governor in 1914, William P. Hobby became governor in 1917 when Governor James Ferguson was removed from office by impeachment. Hobby was part of the progressive movement that initiated policies to help modernize Texas. During his administration, changes were made in the party primary laws to permit women to vote; funding for schools and highways was increased; provisions were enacted for free textbooks; the first Highway Commission was organized; and the oil and gas division of the Railroad Commission was established.

REVIEW THE CHAPTER

A Historical Perspective on the Executive Function in Texas

6.1 Trace the evolution of the Texas governor from a strong unified executive to a plural executive, p. 180.

In Texas's formative period, the executive function was similar in structure to that of the president of the United States, but through the progression of the state's constitutions, the power of the governor was weakened by the creation of the plural executive and other constitutional constraints. The current structure of the executive branch was a reaction to the abuses of the Davis administration during the Reconstruction era. The governor shares administrative and policy authority with other officials, including the lieutenant governor, secretary of state, comptroller of public accounts, commissioner of the General Land Office, attorney general, agriculture commissioner, the three-member Texas Railroad Commission, and fifteen-member State Board of Education. Except for the secretary of state, who is appointed by the governor, all of these officials are elected. Candidates for these offices do not run with the governor on a partisan ticket, and sometimes these officeholders are from a different political party than the governor. Although more recent constitutional changes have been adopted, such as the extension of the governor's term from two to four years and legislative control over the governor's salary, the constitutional restrictions have created a weak "institutional governor." Reform advocates argue that the plural executive diminishes the ability of the executive branch to respond to modern-day problems.

Historical Overview of the Men and Women Who Have Served as Governor

6.2 Assess what qualifies an individual to serve as governor, common career patterns that have led to the governorship, and select benefits of the office, p. 183.

There are very few constitutional qualifications for the governor or other statewide elected officials. There are conditions for removal of the governor through impeachment, and Texas is among only a handful of states in which a governor has been impeached. From 1876 to 1979, when Republican Bill Clements assumed the governorship, only Democrats were elected to the office. With the exception of Ann Richards, Republicans have controlled the office since Clements's second election in 1986. Most governors came to the office after holding prior public offices, and this pattern is likely to continue. Texas governors are moderately well paid and receive other benefits, including the use of the Governor's Mansion and funds for state travel.

The Powers of the Governor

6.3 Explain the legislative, budgetary, appointive, judicial, and military powers of the Texas governor, p. 186.

Although it is the most visible office in state government and the public believes it has considerable power, the office of governor is weak in formal powers. As part of their legislative responsibilities, governors propose legislation, call special sessions when necessary, set the agenda for the special sessions, and exercise the veto, including the line-item veto over the budget. The governor has limited influence over the administrative responsibilities of the other elected state officials, but the governor appoints members of more than 200 policy-setting state boards and commissions authorized by statutory law. The governor's control over these agencies is diluted by board members' staggered terms, the need for senatorial approval of the governor's appointments, and legal requirements relating to the composition of these boards. The governor shares budget responsibilities with the state comptroller and the Legislative Budget Board. The governor activates the National Guard to help handle natural disasters and other emergencies but has limited administrative responsibilities for the state's military. The governor can help shape the philosophy of state courts through his or her appointments to vacancies on the bench.

Informal Resources of the Governor

6.4 Evaluate the informal resources of the Texas governor for advancing public policy and political objectives, p. 192.

Although the constitution potentially constrains a governor in his or her efforts to exercise leadership, governors compensate for these limitations with their ability to articulate problems and issues facing the state, their leadership skill in building coalitions in support of their policies, the appeal of their personalities, and their personal work habits and administrative styles. Governors have used their staffs, their access to the mass media, their party roles, and their relationships to key interest groups to influence the legislature and other elected officials. A governor can compensate for the institutional limitations with the effective use of the informal resources available to the office.

Leadership Styles of Recent Texas Governors

6.5 Differentiate the leadership styles of recent Texas governors, p. 196.

Some governors have relished tough policy negotiations and have used cajoling, intimidation, and intense bargaining to achieve their goals. By temperament or design, other governors have worked quietly behind the scenes, letting others do the heavy lifting. Some governors have been highly partisan, others, bipartisan. Some governors have come to the office with a rather extensive policy agenda; others have opposed expanding government. Some governors have exploited the mass media to achieve their objectives; others have had difficult relationships with the press. In recent years, though, governors of Texas have demonstrated that effective leadership can be exercised through a careful blending of both the formal powers and informal resources of the office.

Other Offices of the Plural Executive

6.6 Describe the duties and responsibilities of the other offices of the executive branch in Texas, p. 205.

The lieutenant governor serves as governor when the governor is out of state, but this officeholder serves primarily a legislative role as presiding officer of the Texas Senate. The attorney general is the state's chief legal officer and advises state and local agencies and represents the state in lawsuits in state and federal courts. The comptroller of public accounts is the state's chief budget officer, tax collector, and revenue estimator. The state land commissioner oversees millions of acres of public land and administers mineral leases on them. The agriculture commissioner has some regulatory and promotional authority over the agriculture industry. The three-member Texas Railroad Commission regulates intrastate oil and gas production, and the fifteen-member State Board of Education has limited responsibility over public education. The secretary of state is the state's chief elections officer.

LEARN THE TERMS

governor, p. 180
plural executive, p. 180
lieutenant governor, p. 181
veto, p. 189
line-item veto, p. 189
staggered terms, p. 190

senatorial courtesy, p. 190
attorney general, p. 206
comptroller of public accounts, p. 208
pay-as-you-go, p. 208
commissioner of the General Land Office, p. 209

commissioner of agriculture, p. 209
secretary of state, p. 210
Texas Railroad Commission, p. 210
State Board of Education, p. 212

The Texas Bureaucracy and Policy Implementation

7

ARE PRIVATE CONTRACTORS THE SOLUTION?
Billing for toll road charges is just one of many public services that state government has contracted out to private companies. Often, private contractors provide these services efficiently. Sometimes, though, private contracts create expensive headaches for both consumers and state officials.

LEARNING OBJECTIVES

7.1 Discuss the essential features of the bureaucratic systems in Texas, p. 218.

7.2 Assess the dynamics of policy implementation by state bureaucrats in Texas, p. 223.

7.3 Describe policies utilized by the Texas legislature to control the actions of state agencies and public employees, p. 227.

7.4 Summarize strategies available to citizens to impact or influence the actions of public employees, p. 231.

7.5 Differentiate among the personnel systems used by the state and local governments in Texas, p. 232.

Like many other people with low-paying public service jobs throughout the country, toll booth operators in Texas have been increasingly replaced by automation. Drivers on toll roads either pay for electronic toll tags, which they place on their vehicles, or they are billed by mail after automated cameras snap photos of their

216

license plates as they pass through tolling locations. As it has with a number of other public services, Texas has contracted the job of handling its toll billing operations to a private company. In 2014, the Texas Department of Transportation, or TxDOT, awarded corporate giant Xerox a five-year, $100 million contract for that responsibility. TxDOT had experienced some problems with a previous group of vendors, but Xerox would be more efficient and provide more customer satisfaction, transportation officials promised.

Several months later, however, TxDOT administrators were standing before an angry state Senate committee, trying to explain why the billing system was still entangled in problems. More than 3.5 million toll charges, some more than two years old, had not been processed in a timely manner, and another 30,000 drivers who had already paid to put TxTag electronic toll tags on their windshields had been mailed erroneous bills. Thousands of angry drivers had overwhelmed the single call center that Xerox had established in Austin. They faced long waits for calls to be answered or were placed on hold for long periods. Xerox added call centers in Houston and San Antonio, but they didn't stem the outrage. One senator told transportation officials that he had been charged about $30 in late fees for a 65-cent toll that had been delayed in the accounting quagmire. Another senator said that one of his constituents waited less than three minutes for a call to the call center in Austin to be answered but was then put on hold for 14 minutes. TxDOT blamed much of the problem on the previous vendors, but the agency also fined Xerox $177,000 for failing to meet deadlines and contractual requirements and said additional fines were likely.[1]

Several weeks later, TxDOT announced that it was continuing to find toll accounts that had been improperly billed and expected customer refunds to total about $1.7 million. "This is a very difficult transaction because the database that Xerox inherited was much more tainted than we originally anticipated," TxDOT Executive Director Joe Weber said.[2]

The toll billing contract is only one of a number of state contracts with private vendors that have sparked controversy in recent years, as we will discuss later in this chapter. All of them doubtlessly have played into the hands of the bureaucracy critics who contend that government services—whether conducted by employees directly on the public payroll or by private venders—are conduits for wasting tax dollars.

Attacking government bureaucracy has been a common theme in political campaigns in Texas and other states for decades, with candidates vowing that government agencies can be trimmed and the number of public employees reduced. Such campaign pledges play particularly well with many Texas voters and the state's dominant conservatism, derived, as it was, from a frontier legacy of self-help and individualism. Except for a handful of years, however, government employment in Texas has increased as the state population has grown and demands for public services have increased. The discussion in this chapter speaks, in part, to the public's demand for new government programs and services in the state, a pattern that can be found throughout the nation.

Undoubtedly, there is some waste in government, particularly in a state the size of Texas, where more than one million people work for state and local governments that perform services for 29 million people. But it is ironic that even those Texans who express hostility toward government and applaud political promises to reduce the public payroll take for granted a wide array of public services every day. Unless you are living in a tent in an isolated canyon in far West Texas, you interact daily with a public employee or contracted vendor or receive the benefits of a public employee's or vendor's work. Someone, for example, is responsible for making sure that traffic lights work properly. Someone else is responsible for responding when you request a camping permit for a state park. When you stop at your favorite eatery, you assume you won't contract food poisoning or find roaches or rats crawling across the table. You assume that the water flowing through your tap is clean. You also assume that your doctor is properly trained and licensed and that your barber or hair stylist works in a sanitary shop. You can make all these assumptions because government workers—members of the faceless and often maligned bureaucracy—are doing their jobs, providing public services and enforcing health and public safety laws and regulations. They don't make public policies. They carry them out, within the resources allocated by the policymakers.

You already have learned about how the legislature and the governor function as the chief policymakers for state government and enact policies that affect local governments as well. To learn how to successfully navigate government, however, you also need to learn something about the agencies and the people who carry out those policies and public services. This is the part of the policy process with which you will continue to have the most direct contact and for which, whether you realize it or not, you have the greatest expectations.

Bureaucratic Systems in Texas

7.1 Discuss the essential features of the bureaucratic systems in Texas.

With more than 5,100 different governments in Texas, people often are uncertain or confused about which government or agency has responsibility for what. We noted in the chapter on federalism that different governments have exclusive or primary functions, but some governments also share overlapping functions in some policy areas. The federal government, for example, imposes requirements and restrictions—often described as mandates or preemptions—on Texas and other state governments for health care services, environmental protection, and a host of other programs. The state also has enacted legislation and regulations applicable to these same policy issues. Procedures for cooperation and interaction among the different governments must be worked out within a formal framework. When functions or responsibilities are shared, funding issues must be addressed, accountability among governments must be established, and procedures for review must be put into place. Organizational structures can vary among different levels of government, but all governmental agencies share some common administrative characteristics, which we discuss in the section that follows.

7.1.1 The Characteristics of the Texas Bureaucracy

bureaucracies
The agencies of government and their employees responsible for carrying out policies and providing public services approved by elected officials.

Max Weber, a German sociologist writing in the early part of the twentieth century, regarded **bureaucracies** as efficient means of organizing large numbers of people to carry out the required tasks for accomplishing specific goals.[3] Bureaucratic structures are inevitable in large, complex societies that have a lot of individual and group interdependence. To a large extent, these complex organizations are "superior to other methods of organizing people to perform tasks."[4]

Scholars have identified a number of characteristics of bureaucracies, the first of which is size. Size in terms of cost alone can be staggering when you consider providing public services for Texas's 29 million residents. In one representative month in 2018, the payroll for 361,356 full- and part-time state employees was $1.59 billion. That same month, local governments in Texas spent $4.9 billion to pay another 1.3 million employees.[5] And these sums did not include taxpayer dollars paid to private companies to perform public services under government contracts.

Whether defined in terms of the number of employees, size of budgets, or number of programs administered, size also suggests complex relationships among the people working for an organization. Employees of some large state agencies are scattered among many cities, and both the size and geographic dispersion of these agencies contribute to their organizational hierarchy.[6]

Within governmental organizations, positions or jobs are assigned specific responsibilities or given specific authority in a hierarchical arrangement. Most agency staffs have one individual at the top, and the organization is divided into bureaus, divisions, field offices, or other units. The organization develops rules for supervision, management, and reporting of activities.

Bureaucracies require a division of labor among employees and encourage the development of expertise based on experience and education. State agencies break down the responsibilities given to them by the legislature into narrowly defined tasks for their employees. Thousands of workers become specialists in a limited number of activities.

The specialization and division of labor in large organizations require rules and procedures to coordinate the activities of many individuals. Rules reduce the need for continual supervision of employees and lay the foundation for standardized behavior.[7] They define how tasks are to be carried out, who is responsible for carrying them out, and who qualifies for the organization's or agency's services.

Contemporary bureaucracies also are characterized by impersonal relationships, which is why people often complain about having to deal with "faceless" bureaucrats. Responsibilities within an agency are assigned to positions, which can be held by several workers who are supposed to be able to provide the requested service. When you obtain a voter-registration card or have your driver's license renewed, the name of the person assisting you should make no difference. People come and go in large organizations, and the ongoing functions of organizations do not depend on specific individuals.[8]

WHERE SOME BUREAUCRATS WORK

Viewed from the Capitol looking north toward the campus of the University of Texas, these are office buildings housing a number of state agencies. Most state employees, however, work in other facilities scattered throughout Texas.

The sheer size of state government and the fragmented structure of the executive branch contribute to problems in the state bureaucracy. No single elected official is ultimately responsible for the overall quality of public services performed by every agency. A loosely connected and often confusing network of more than 200 state agencies and universities is responsible for carrying out programs and policies approved and funded by the legislature and the governor. Programs often are developed and agencies established with little thought for policy coordination between departments. The organization of many agencies is influenced by interest groups that believe agencies should serve their specific needs, not those of the general public.

The legislature and the governor enact the broad outlines of public policy, but hundreds of state agencies and local governments must transform those policies into specific programs, based on rules and procedures set by those agencies and local governments. The legislature meets in regular session only five months every other year. So systematic legislative review and oversight of every state agency is impossible. Moreover, the governor has only limited administrative control over most agencies in the executive branch. At the federal level, the president of the United States has the Office of Management and Budget to assist in reviewing federal agencies and their regulations, but the governor of Texas has no comparable resource.[9] The part-time boards and commissions that oversee most state agencies can exercise considerable independence in interpreting policies and determining the character and the quality of public services. Although the boards are independent, many depend heavily on the guidance of veteran administrators and career bureaucrats within the agencies they oversee.

As noted earlier, many people associate bureaucrats and bureaucracies with red tape, waste, inefficiency, indifference, or incompetence. Many candidates for elected office campaign on promises to reduce governmental waste and spending, streamline government, and reduce the number of people on public payrolls. Once elected, however, most public officials soon realize that governments run not on rhetoric but on the work of the same public employees, or bureaucrats, against whom they campaigned.

Most Texans know someone who works in government. Public employees are family members, friends, neighbors, members of our religious congregations, and people we see in the park every weekend. They are subject to the same laws and regulations and pay the same taxes as everyone else. We tend to have positive perceptions of individual public employees we know or interact with, but we also can be ambivalent about public employees as a group and the agencies for which they work.

Modern, interdependent societies require large bureaucracies to provide the range of services demanded by citizens. These bureaucracies, through the uniform application of rules and procedures designed to provide comparable treatment to everyone, contribute to the maintenance of a democratic society. Unlike people in other political systems in which bribery is widespread, we have come to expect routine public services without having to slip money under the table, in part because we have laws providing strong criminal penalties for bribery. Abuse and malfeasance can be found in some governmental agencies, but most agencies effectively carry out policy mandates, despite limited oversight from the legislature and the governor.

7.1.2 Replacing an Aging Workforce

State and local agencies have an aging workforce with many workers nearing retirement. Some students of public administration have written about the "silver tsunami," in which the number of employees retiring in the very near future will dramatically increase. Many governments are not prepared for the loss of these experienced workers and the potential difficulties of replacing them.

The Texas State Auditor's Office, the state agency responsible for managing state employment data, reported that the turnover rate for state employees was more than 20 percent in fiscal 2019, a ten-year high. Retirement accounted for some of the turnover, but the highest rate of voluntary separation from state agencies was among employees younger than 30, the group that will be needed to replace aging government workers. Almost 64 percent of the employees leaving had fewer than five years of state service, and dissatisfaction with pay and benefits was a primary reason for leaving government employment. Among the larger state agencies, the highest turnover rates were reported in the Juvenile Justice Department (35 percent), the Health and Human Services Commission (28 percent) and the Department of Criminal Justice (27 percent).[10]

National studies of public employment have indicated that millennials are turned off by the hierarchical structure of government agencies and prefer employment in organizations that emphasize individual development and creativity.[11]

Criticizing bureaucrats for political reasons doesn't help the employment picture for public agencies in Texas either. It has helped convince many young people that a career in public service is undesirable. Effective administration of public services requires competent employees, but some scholars argue that we have created an environment of "bureaucracy bashing" in which government at all levels will have a difficult time recruiting new employees who are among the best and the brightest of their generation.[12]

7.1.3 An Expanding Government Workforce

In 1972, there were approximately 2.1 million federal employees, a number that has changed very little since then.[13] By comparison, the number of state and local government employees in Texas has tripled during that time.

TABLE 7-1 EMPLOYMENT BY TYPE OF GOVERNMENT, 1972–2017

Unit of Government	Full-Time Equivalent Employees				
	1972	1982	1992	2002	2017
State	124,560	175,660	238,974	269,674	314,606
Total Local	380,038	557,082	744,325	979,164	1,201,730
Counties	37,302	67,228	94,145	120,885	159,567
Municipalities	93,107	127,794	147,812	172,846	191,967
School Districts	223,646	335,855	460,212	634,589	792,413
Special Districts	25,983	26,205	42,156	50,844	57,783
Total for Texas	504,598	732,742	983,299	1,248,838	1,516,336

SOURCE: U.S. Department of Commerce, Bureau of the Census, *Census of Governments, 1972*, vol. 3, no. 2, table 14; *Census of Governments, 1982*, vol. 3, no. 2, table 13; *Census of Governments, 1992*, vol. 3, no. 2, table 14; *Census of Governments, 2002*, vol. 3, table 9; *Census of Governments, 2007; Texas Government Employment and Payroll Data*, Build-a-Table, http://www.census.gov; and *Census of Governments, 2017*.

The number of full-time state and local employees in Texas increased from 504,598 in 1972 to more than 1.5 million in 2017 (the latest year for which comprehensive employment data were collected by the U.S. Bureau of the Census in its *Census of Governments*). More than 314,000 people (based on full-time equivalency) worked for the state government in 2017 and more than 1.2 million for cities, counties, school districts, and other local governments.[14] The growth in public employment would have been greater had not the recession in 2008–2011 forced governments to reduce employment and postpone hiring new workers (see Table 7–1). At the beginning of the summer of 2020, the state's economy was roiled by the coronavirus pandemic, and it was not clear what its impact on government employment would be.

Another way to measure public employment is the number of government workers compared to the state's total population. By 2017, the state had 543 full-time equivalent state and local government employees per 10,000 residents. State government alone had only 111 employees per 10,000 people. With more than 1.2 million employees working for local governments, there were 425 local government workers per 10,000 people.[15] Local governments have a larger number of public employees per capita because they are responsible for a wide range of services, including public schools.

Despite budget cuts in 2003 and 2011, state government spending in Texas has increased by some 75 percent since the 2002–2003 biennium, with the legislature appropriating $251 billion for the 2019–2021 budget period. Although the rate of spending growth outpaced growth in the state's population, Texas ranks among the lowest five states in per capita government expenditures. In 2018, the state spent approximately $4,024 per person.[16] When combined state and local spending are compared, Texas's ranking rises slightly, thanks in part to the large share of public school costs borne by local taxpayers. In such key areas as per capita state spending on public health, education, and welfare, Texas ranks below many other states.[17]

Except for budget crises in 2003 and 2011, efforts to curtail government growth and spending have met with only marginal success. Texas citizens have come to expect a wide range of public services, and these expectations increase as the population grows. The federal government has imposed mandates on state and local governments that require additional expenditures and personnel. The success of interest groups in winning approval of new programs adds to the growth of public employment. In 2003, though, the legislature reduced spending on many programs to help bridge a $10 billion revenue shortfall. That same year, it also ordered a major reorganization of health and human services agencies with the goal of privatizing some services.

In 2011, the legislature cut spending by several billion dollars to address another shortfall in revenue. The legislature reduced state aid to public school districts alone by $5.4 billion. Many state agencies trimmed employees, and school district payrolls statewide were reduced by about 25,000 employees, including almost 11,000 teachers, during the 2011–2012 school year, an overall school employment reduction of 3.8 percent.[18] Since the end of the recession, much of that funding has been restored.

According to the *2012* Census of Governments, the most recent data of this kind available, 85 percent of state government employees worked in higher education, public safety and corrections, or social services. Eighty-eight percent of county government employees worked in three areas: social services, public safety and corrections, and general governmental administration. About 39 percent of city employees were engaged in fire and police protection, and another 37 percent worked for city utilities, government administration, or in housing, sanitation, parks and recreation, or natural resources. Elementary and secondary school teachers are employees of local school districts. Close to 50 percent of the employees of other special districts worked in social services, including public hospitals, and approximately one-fourth worked in transportation. The remainder worked in utilities, housing, or environmental protection.[19]

7.1.4 Privatization of Public Services

The state and many local governments contract with private companies to carry out some public services. Contractors' employees are not public employees and are not counted in the public employment census data, although they are paid indirectly with tax dollars. Supporters of privatization say it can reduce governmental costs by promoting efficiency, and many privatization contracts are successfully carried out. Many local government contracts are for garbage collection services, and many state contracts are with private companies that build highways or pay doctors and other health care providers serving low-income Texans on Medicaid or the Children's Health Insurance Program. Most of these services are routinely carried out without controversy, but critics of privatization argue that some of the cost savings for some privatized services are realized by paying workers less than government workers or not providing benefits they would receive as government employees. Some vendors, such as the toll billing contractor discussed at the beginning of this chapter, have trouble delivering their promised services in an efficient manner or to consumers' satisfaction. The attorney general's office and the Health and Human Services Commission are among other state agencies dealing in recent years with private contracts that have resulted in cost overruns, allegations of insider influence, and other problems.

Some contractors are large companies, such as Xerox, Accenture, and IBM. Others are smaller, including consulting firms that, with little or no government oversight, specialize in finding contract technology workers for government agencies. The *Austin American-Statesman* reported in 2015 that these contract workers were some of the highest-paid government workers in the state. "Individual contractors' earnings aren't publicly reported as they are for the often lesser paid state employees who work beside them," the newspaper reported.[20]

State Representative Garnet Coleman of Houston said the legislature needed to provide state agencies enough resources to effectively monitor how well private vendors were carrying out their contracted responsibilities. "The only way to do outsourcing [privatization] properly is to have enough people working on the agency side to do appropriate oversight of the company that has the contract," Coleman said. "What we don't want is the tail wagging the dog, which is what usually happens."[21]

Bureaucrats and Public Policy

7.2 Assess the dynamics of policy implementation by state bureaucrats in Texas.

The bureaucracy does more than carry out the policies set by the legislature. It is involved in virtually every stage of the policymaking process. Legislators depend on numerous reports submitted to them by state agencies. Throughout a legislative session, personnel from these agencies are called to testify in legislative hearings. Legislators call on agencies for information or additional briefings on policy matters, and agency personnel visit privately with legislators.

In a large number of instances, the legislature broadly defines a program and gives the affected agency the responsibility for filling in the details.[22] The expansive responsibilities and authority delegated to agencies by the legislature have resulted in what is generally understood to be administrative law. Administrative agencies can sometimes interpret a vaguely worded law differently from its original legislative purpose. Although the legislature can use oversight committees and the budgetary process to exercise some control over the bureaucracy, agencies often have resources and political influence that protect their prerogatives. Many appointed agency heads have political ties to interest groups affected by the work of their agencies, and these officials help develop policy alternatives and laws because legislators depend on their technical expertise.

7.2.1 Policy Implementation

Implementation is the conversion of policy plans into reality.[23] Although one state agency may be primarily responsible for translating legislative intent into a specific program, other governmental bodies are involved. The courts, for example, shape the actions of the bureaucrats through their interpretation of statutes and administrative rules. Jurisdictional and political battles may occur between different agencies over program objectives. Such conflicts often result from Texas's plural executive system of government, in which the governor and several other statewide officials are elected independently and appointed boards and commissions head numerous other agencies.

In some cases, a new agency may have to be organized and staffed to carry out the goals of a new law. More often, however, new responsibilities are assigned by the legislature to an existing agency, which develops the necessary rules, procedures, and guidelines for operating the new program. Additional employees are hired if the legislature provides the necessary funding. If not, responsibilities are reassigned among existing personnel. Sometimes tasks are coordinated with other agencies. Ultimately, all this activity translates into hundreds of thousands of daily transactions between governmental employees—or an agency's private contractors—and the public.

Establishing rules and standards at the agency level for carrying out programs enacted by the legislature is a complex process that also involves the legislative sponsors, interest groups, sometimes specific businesses, and other interested parties. Rules and procedures are not hatched in a vacuum. The task is highly political and subject to intense negotiations; often contentious, it requires political adroitness by administrators to ensure a program's success.

Almost everyone has heard horror stories about persons who have suffered abuse or neglect at the hands of public employees and agencies. Whether they involve an indigent family that fell through the cracks of the welfare system or a county jail prisoner who was lost in the administrative processes of the judicial system, these stories tend to reinforce the suspicion and hostility that many people have toward bureaucracies and public employees. Unquestionably, such abuses deserve attention and demand correction, yet thousands of governmental programs are successfully carried out with little or no fanfare and are consistent with the purpose of the authorizing legislation.

7.2.2 Obstacles to Policy Implementation

When things go wrong in state government and problems go unresolved, the tendency is to blame the bureaucrats for excessive red tape, inefficiency, mismanagement, or incompetence. As noted earlier in this chapter, bureaucrat bashing plays well politically, and many candidates for public office run on such campaigns. But in many cases they unfairly blame government employees for complex problems that policymakers have been unable—or unwilling—to resolve. One high-profile issue is the perennial struggle to improve the quality of the public education system. Some of the criticism directed at educational bureaucrats has been justified, but ultimately the legislature and the governor are responsible for the enactment of sound educational policies and the development of a sufficient and equitable system of paying for them.

Some legislative policies may be misdirected, with little potential for producing the intended results. Or economic and social conditions may change, making programs inappropriate. Administrators also may find that approaches different from those outlined by the legislature would have worked better. In addition, the legislature frequently fails to fund programs adequately. In some cases, those charged with carrying out a new policy may not have the knowledge or the resources to make it work.[24] Finally, programs often produce unanticipated results.[25]

Well-designed policies that could potentially serve the needs of large numbers of citizens can be gutted or diluted by the efforts of interest groups or businesses that challenge an agency's actions. These efforts include litigation, appeals to members of the legislature, or any number of delaying tactics designed to wear out the public's interest in an issue or exhaust the resources of those individuals who were the original targeted beneficiaries of the policies. Thanks to the clout special interest lobbyists have with the legislature, the majority of members on the boards that oversee regulatory agencies are often from the professions or industries they are supposed to regulate. Taxpayers may think that this system is merely a legalized way of letting the foxes guard the henhouse. It is an extension of the "iron triangles" concept, whereby special interests seek to influence not only the legislators responsible for enacting laws but also the agencies responsible for enforcing them.

7.2.3 State Regulatory Functions

The legislature delegates much authority for carrying out state policy to regulatory agencies; regulation, in turn, takes various forms. Regulations, in pursuit of the public interest, are intended to control or constrain the activities of organizations or individuals.

One regulatory function involves economics. Economic regulation is one of the more significant regulatory functions of state government and affects the practices of some businesses, including the prices they can charge for their services. Not all economic regulations are perceived to be hostile to those businesses subject to regulations, and there are numerous instances in which businesses seek regulations to stabilize the markets in which they operate. Major state regulators in this area include the Department of Insurance, which oversees rates that can be charged for automobile and homeowners insurance, and the Public Utility Commission, which has authority over some practices of electric and water utilities and telecommunications companies.

A second regulatory function is the **licensing** of professions and franchising of corporations. Under state law, some occupations require formal training, testing, and subsequent licensing from a state agency. These include doctors, dentists, nurses, accountants, lawyers, barbers, and a host of other professions. Companies also must have state licenses to operate funeral homes or nursing homes, among other businesses. Licensing implies regulation, and the acceptance of a license implies a willingness to comply with state controls. On the local level, contractors are required to meet building codes established by city councils.

licensing
A key regulatory function of government that seeks to ensure that individuals and companies providing critical professional services to the public are properly trained or qualified.

ENVIRONMENTAL REGULATION

The Texas Commission on Environmental Quality is responsible for implementing state environmental laws, but its authority and actions can come into conflict with federal laws, which preempt state laws. Coal-burning plants, such as those constructed and maintained by San Antonio's City Public Service on Lake Calaveras, are subject to regulations of both the state and federal government.

State agencies regulate the allocation of natural resources and safeguard their quality. The Texas Commission on Environmental Quality is charged with enforcing state laws protecting air and water quality. Water districts throughout the state regulate the conservation of groundwater supplies, although their regulatory powers were curtailed by a major Texas Supreme Court decision in early 2012, holding that owners of property above an aquifer also own the groundwater. Two farmers successfully challenged governmental restrictions on how much water they could pump from a well on their own land.[26] In another crucial conservation area, the Texas Railroad Commission establishes the rate at which a well can pump oil from the ground.

Additionally, state and local governments are involved in regulation by providing operating subsidies to businesses, including tax breaks that are subject to limitations imposed by the legislature. These incentives are usually offered for specified periods to encourage businesses to locate or expand in a specific community. In return, the businesses may agree to conditions imposed on them by the participating government. Cities grant franchises to cable television systems, which agree to provide a specific level of service in return for the operating rights.

State agencies also regulate companies for fairness and competition. Although many federal laws deal with price fixing, monopolies, and unfair competition, state statutes also relate to the competitiveness of the state's economy. The Texas State Securities Board, for example, regulates the investment industry. Additionally, the state is involved in what some writers call social regulation.[27] Much broader than the economic regulation just described, social regulations affect "the conditions under which goods and services are produced and the physical characteristics of products that are manufactured."[28] Although the federal government has preempted many state policies in these areas, some state agencies are involved in regulating workplace safety and consumer protection.

7.2.4 Appointment to State Agencies

Business and professional groups argue that their professions can be effectively regulated only by individuals knowledgeable of the work they do. Although that argument has some validity, it also increases the potential for incestuous relationships that mock the regulatory process. The possibility—and often the likelihood—exists that industry representatives serving on boards or commissions will be inclined to protect

co-optation

Influence over state regulatory boards by the industries they are supposed to regulate, often to the detriment of the general public.

their industries against the best interests of consumers. This pattern of influence and control often is referred to as **co-optation**, underscoring the possibility that agencies may be captured by the industries they are supposed to regulate. Licensing agencies may seek to adopt unfair regulations designed to restrict new competitors from entering an industry.

Governor Ann Richards highlighted the "fox in the henhouse" approach to state regulation when she demanded that the Texas Department of Health crack down on deplorable conditions in some nursing homes. State inspectors had repeatedly found unsanitary conditions in three nursing homes partly owned by a member of the Texas Board of Health. The board member, an appointee of former Governor Bill Clements, denied any allegations of improper care but resigned after moving to another state.[29] Texas law then required that one member of the eighteen-member health board be involved in the nursing home industry and the remaining board members be appointed from other health care professions. The board has since been restructured.

Modest, short-lived efforts have been made since the early 1990s to reform the system of gubernatorial appointments to boards and agencies, but little has changed. The process serves the interests of governors as well as those of other participants in the state's political system. Prospects or promises of appointments cultivate political support within the electorate for the candidate as well as the candidate's political party. Whether motivated by personal ambition, self-interest, or a sense of public duty, many individuals aspire to serve in appointed offices. Thousands of appointed positions must be filled during a governor's tenure, and in order to effectively control and direct administrative agencies, the governor makes appointments on the basis of party loyalty, shared political and philosophical views and an appointee's skills, expertise, and links to key sectors of the state's economy.

Texas governors spend millions of dollars to get elected, and they historically have appointed political contributors to state boards and commissions. Nearly one-fourth of Governor Rick Perry's appointees were donors to his political campaigns.[30] Governor Greg Abbott continued the practice. Of the 889 appointments Abbott had made by the end of 2017, some 259—or their spouses—had contributed $14.2 million to his election campaigns since 2001.[31] Abbott, Perry, and their predecessors, Republicans and Democrats alike, denied that campaign donations affected their appointment choices, but many critics say it is a "pay-to-play" system.

THE GOVERNOR'S APPOINTMENTS

Governors historically have appointed many individuals to state boards who have contributed to their political campaigns or worked in some capacity for their election. John L. Nau, III, who heads a large distributing company in Houston, served as Governor Greg Abbott's campaign treasurer and contributed approximately one million dollars to Abbott's numerous campaigns over the years. Nau has a long-held interest in history, has served on numerous boards and commissions, and was appointed by Governor Rick Perry to chair the Texas Historical Commission (1995–2009). Governor Abbott appointed him to chair the commission a second time in 2015 for a six-year term.

Legislative Control of the Bureaucracy

7.3 Describe policies utilized by the Texas legislature to control the actions of state agencies and public employees.

The Texas legislature has taken several steps over the years to increase its control over state agencies, including limited budgetary oversight, performance reviews, sunset legislation, restrictions on the "revolving door" between government and industry employment, and provisions that protect whistle-blowers.

7.3.1 Legislative Budgetary Control

Every two years, the legislature sets the budgets for state agencies, but its review over spending between legislative sessions is limited. The Legislative Budget Board (LBB), which includes the lieutenant governor, the speaker of the House, and eight other legislators, has some oversight. The LBB can join with the governor to transfer appropriated funds between programs or agencies, if necessary, to meet emergencies when the legislature is not in session. Legislative committees also can hold hearings between sessions and question agency administrators about spending. When drafting state budgets, legislators include a number of line items that give agencies specific spending instructions or impose specific spending restrictions (see Table 7–2).

7.3.2 Performance Reviews

Facing a large revenue shortfall in 1991, the legislature directed Comptroller John Sharp to conduct performance reviews, or management audits, of all state agencies to determine ways to eliminate mismanagement and inefficiency and to save tax dollars. Sharp recommended $4 billion worth of spending cuts, agency and funds consolidations, accounting changes, some minor tax increases, and increases in various state fees to more accurately reflect the costs of providing services. Pressure from special interests killed many of the recommendations, but the legislature adopted about $2.4 billion of them. Sharp produced follow-up reports in 1993, 1995, and 1997, and his successor, Carole Keeton Strayhorn, continued the performance reviews after she took office. In 2003, the legislature transferred the responsibility for conducting performance reviews from the comptroller's office to the Legislative Budget Board, which also conducts performance reviews of school districts.

TABLE 7-2 HOW TO CONTROL BUREAUCRATS

Taking a cue from political scientist Robert Lineberry, Texas policymakers can use several strategies to control bureaucracies and help ensure that policies are carried out as intended:

1. Change the law or make legislation more detailed to reduce or eliminate the discretionary authority of an agency.
2. Overrule the bureaucracy and reverse or rescind an action of an agency. With the independence of many agencies, boards, and commissions at the state level, the governor can reverse few agency decisions, so this step often requires legislative action.
3. Transfer the responsibility for a program to another agency through administrative reorganization.
4. Replace an agency head who refuses to carry out or is incapable of carrying out program objectives. The governor can directly exercise such authority over only a few agencies in Texas.
5. Cut or threaten to reduce the budget of an agency to force compliance with policy objectives.
6. Abolish an agency or program through sunset legislation.
7. Pressure the bureaucracy to change, using legislative hearings and public disclosures of agency neglect or inadequacies.
8. Protect public employees who reveal their agencies' incompetence, mismanagement, or corruption by passing whistle-blower legislation.
9. Enact revolving-door restrictions to reduce or eliminate the movement of former state employees to industries over which they had regulatory authority.

SOURCE: Based on information found in Robert Lineberry, *American Public Policy* (New York: Harper & Row, 1977), pp. 84–85.

7.3.3 Sunset Legislation

Texas was one of the first states to require formal, exhaustive reviews of how effectively state agencies are doing their jobs. The sunset process, enacted in 1977, was so named because most agencies have to be periodically recreated by the legislature or automatically go out of business.[32] Relatively few agencies—except for a number of inactive ones such as the Pink Bollworm Commission and the Stonewall Jackson Memorial Board—have been abolished, but the review has produced some significant structural and policy changes in the state bureaucracy. It also has expanded employment opportunities for lobbyists because special interest groups have much at stake in the sunset process. Sometimes, special interests have succeeded in protecting the status quo.

Each agency is usually up for **sunset review** every twelve years under a rotating order set out in the sunset law. The review begins with the Sunset Advisory Commission, which includes five state representatives, five senators, and two members from the public, appointed by the speaker and the lieutenant governor. The commission employs a staff that studies each agency up for review during the next legislative session and reports its findings to the panel, which makes recommendations to the legislature.

In a few cases, the commission will propose that an agency—usually a minor one—be terminated or consolidated with another agency. In most cases, however, the commission recommends the continuation of an agency and proposes changes in its organization and operations. The agency's future is then decided by the full legislature. In recent years, the legislature has postponed controversial sunset decisions by passing special laws to allow some agencies to stay open past their review dates. The Texas Higher Education Coordinating Board is subject to sunset review, but individual universities are not. Also exempted from sunset review are the courts and state agencies created by the constitution, such as the governor's office, the attorney general, the comptroller, and the General Land Office.

The sunset process has not reduced the size of the state bureaucracy; in fact, government has continued to grow. When the sunset law was approved in 1977, there were 164,000 state employees. By 2017, there were more than 314,000. Although more than seventy agencies have been terminated or merged, others have been created (see Table 7–3). Supporters of the sunset process believe it has served to slow down the creation of new agencies.

The sunset review process has helped rid state government of some obsolete agencies, modernized state laws and bureaucratic procedures, and made some agencies more responsive to the public. For example, under sunset review provisions, members

> **sunset review**
> The process under which most state agencies have to be periodically reviewed and recreated by the legislature or be eliminated.

TABLE 7–3 SUNSET ADVISORY COMMISSION, 1979 TO 2019, SIXTY-SIXTH TO EIGHTY-SIXTH LEGISLATIVE SESSIONS

Agencies Reviewed by Commission*	Number of Agencies	
Total	546	
Agencies Not Subject to Abolishment**	46	
Agencies Subject to Abolishment	500	

Actions Taken by Commission	Number of Agencies	Percentage
Agencies Continued	410	82
Agencies Abolished Outright	38	8
Agencies Abolished and Functions Transferred	52	10

* Approximately 130 agencies are subject to sunset review on a periodic basis. Some agencies have been reviewed multiple times since the process was initiated.

**These agencies were subject to sunset review but not abolishment or were reviewed but their sunset dates were then removed from law.

SOURCE: Texas Sunset Advisory Commission, *Final Results of Sunset Reviews, 2018–2019*, June 2019.

of the public have been added to the boards of numerous small regulatory agencies that previously included only representatives of the professions or industries they regulated. The Sunset Advisory Commission concluded that boards consisting only of members of regulated professions may not respond adequately to public interests.[33]

The largest agencies and those with influential constituencies usually are the most difficult to change because special interests work hard and make large political contributions to protect their turf. In 1993, for example, the insurance lobby succeeded in weakening some pro-consumer provisions in the Department of Insurance sunset bill. In another case that year, there was such a high-stakes war involving telephone companies, newspaper publishers, electric utilities, and consumers over the Public Utility Commission (PUC) sunset bill that the legislature postponed action on PUC sunset for two years. The lobby's influence prompted Governor Ann Richards and some legislators to suggest that the sunset process should be changed or repealed because it was being abused by special interests. But consumer advocates, who value the sunset process, blamed the problem on legislators who had difficulty saying no to special interest lobbyists.

A major sunset battle erupted in 2009 over the Texas Residential Construction Commission, which had been created several years earlier with the strong support of homebuilders. The agency was intended to establish uniform building standards and crack down on shoddy construction in exchange for giving the homebuilding industry legal protections against lawsuits from unhappy customers. But consumer advocates complained that the agency functioned mainly to protect homebuilders. The Sunset Advisory Commission recommended that the agency be recreated with new consumer protections, but the legislature let the agency die.

7.3.4 The Revolving Door

Before the legislature started clamping down, many regulatory agencies had become taxpayer-financed training grounds for young attorneys and other professionals just out of college or law school. They would work for state agencies for a few years for relatively low pay but make influential contacts and gain valuable experience in a particular regulatory area. Then they would leave state employment for higher-paying jobs in the industries they had regulated and would represent their new employers before the state boards and commissions for which they had once worked. In other cases, they would become consultants or join law firms representing regulatory clients. Former gubernatorial appointees to boards and commissions, as well as hired staffers, participated in this **revolving-door** phenomenon, which raised ethical questions about possible insider influence over regulatory decisions.

An early step in slowing the revolving door was part of the 1975 law that created the Public Utility Commission. This law prohibited PUC commissioners and high-ranking staffers from going to work for regulated utilities immediately after leaving the agency. A 1991 ethics reform law expanded the restriction to other agencies.

revolving door
The practice of former members of state boards and commissions or key employees of agencies leaving state government for more lucrative jobs with the industries they used to regulate. It raises questions of undue industry influence over regulatory agencies.

7.3.5 Whistle-Blower Provisions

Governmental agencies can make mistakes that are costly in terms of financial waste or regulatory neglect and endanger the public's health or safety. Also, as agencies spend large sums of money for supplies, construction projects, and other services, the potential exists for public officials or employees to be offered kickbacks or bribes to influence decisions benefiting particular vendors or contractors.

To encourage public employees to report mistakes and intentional wrongdoing in their agencies, Texas has a **whistle-blower** protection law. If an employee is subjected to retaliation after having come forward, the law permits the worker to file a lawsuit against the offending agency. It is difficult to determine, though, how effective that law has been in weeding out governmental waste and corruption because many

whistle-blower
A government employee who publicly reports wrongdoing or unethical conduct within a government agency.

VINDICATED AFTER A LONG ORDEAL

Nurses Anne Mitchell, right, and Vickilyn Galle, left, who blew the whistle on questionable medical practices in a county hospital, are seen at the Andrews County Courthouse in February 2010, after winning their fight against retaliation from local officials.

Merissa Ferguson/Associated Press

public workers still may be intimidated by supervisors. As major tests of the law have shown, a whistle-blower's journey can be very rough, even with legal protections.

Anne Mitchell and Vickilyn Galle, two nurses in the tiny West Texas town of Kermit, were prosecuted in 2010 after they sent a letter to the Texas Medical Board questioning the standard of care provided by a physician working for the county hospital in which they were employed and the county's rural health clinic. They contacted the medical board after the hospital's administration had failed to act on their complaints about the doctor's practices, which included selling herbal supplements to patients in the county facilities.

When the doctor learned that he was being investigated by the state board, he complained of "harassment" to Winkler County Sheriff Robert Roberts, a friend and associate in his herbal supplement business. The sheriff began investigating hospital employees and found the letter to the medical board on a computer used by the two nurses. The evidence was presented to Winkler County Attorney Scott Tidwell, a political ally of the sheriff and, according to testimony in the case, the doctor's personal lawyer. The nurses lost their jobs and were charged with "misuse of official information," a third-degree felony that could have resulted in a ten-year prison sentence and a $10,000 fine for each woman.[34]

The case prompted charges of political cronyism and divided the residents of Kermit. It also attracted national attention and mobilized outside support for the nurses. The Texas Nursing Association and the American Nursing Association provided legal and financial assistance. The defendants also received small contributions from people around the state and country.[35]

Mitchell was acquitted by a jury, and the charges against Galle were dropped. The sheriff and the county attorney later were indicted for misuse of official information and retaliation and were forced out of office. The doctor about whom the nurses had complained eventually lost his medical license. Mitchell and Galle received $750,000 from Winkler County to settle a federal lawsuit they had filed over First Amendment rights violations and vindictive prosecution.[36]

The nurses eventually won because their attack on substandard care and the obvious unfairness of their prosecution resonated with nurses and other people throughout the country. But their case demonstrates that whistle-blowers, despite the protection of state law, can still face huge obstacles.

Several years earlier, under different circumstances, another whistle-blower underwent a similarly stressful ordeal. George Green, a state architect in Austin, was fired and threatened with prosecution on trumped-up charges after complaining of shoddy construction, kickbacks, and noncompliance with contracts at the Texas Department of Human Services. Green sued the state under the whistle-blower law and won a $13.6 million judgment from a Travis County jury in 1991. The amount included $3.6 million in actual damages that Green had suffered and $10 million in punitive damages to punish the state for the way he had been treated. Even after losing a lengthy appeal, the state initially refused to appropriate the money to pay Green's judgment. Finally, in 1995, Green negotiated a $13.8 million settlement, which included only a fraction of the interest he was owed on the four-year-old judgment, with legislative leaders.

Then-Lieutenant Governor Bob Bullock apologized to Green and called his ordeal a "black mark on the history of Texas."[37] The legislature also took steps to ensure that there never would be such a large whistle-blower judgment again. It changed the law to limit all whistle-blower–suit damages against the state to $250,000.

Texas Citizens and the Bureaucracy

7.4 Summarize strategies available to citizens to impact or influence the actions of public employees.

You probably have complained—or heard someone else complain—about the "red tape" or the "runaround" encountered in personal dealings with government agencies and employees. You may have encountered an arrogant or rude clerk in a government office, or you may have gone to the wrong agency for help. You also may have discovered that it was going to take longer to resolve your issue than you thought it should have, either because of an inefficient worker or legislative budget cutbacks that required an agency to lay off employees. Many routine, personal dealings with government agencies now can be accomplished online, although that also can be a frustrating experience. The more you deal with government bureaucracies and individual employees, however, the more you will learn about how to effectively navigate the public service or public information system.

Meanwhile, based on our many years of study and personal experience with government agencies, we will offer you some general guidelines. Our first suggestion

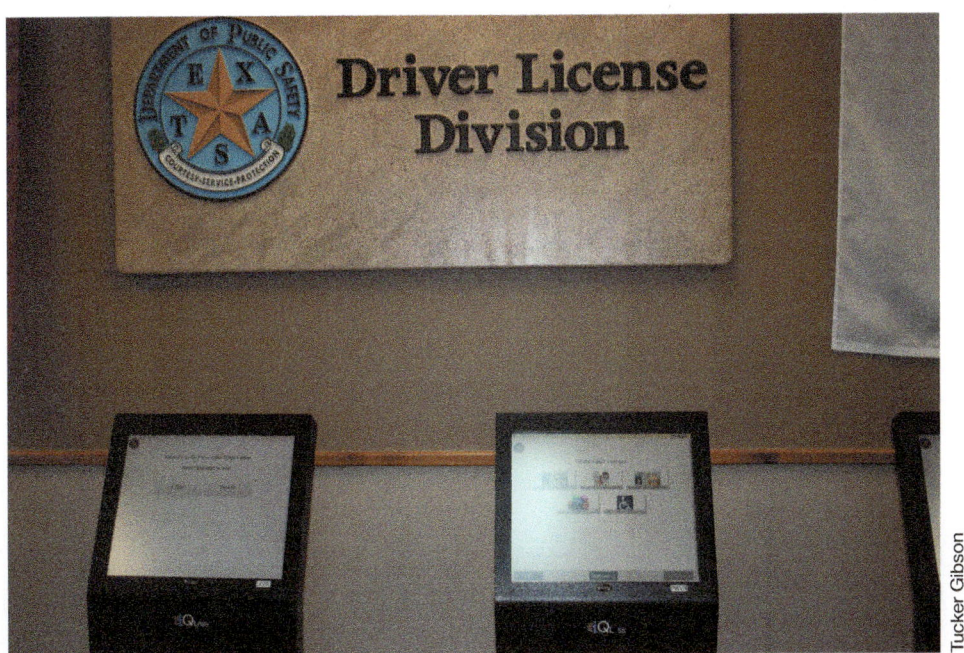

E-GOVERNMENT

Governments across the state are adapting new technologies to expedite the provision of services to Texas citizens. The days of delays and lines to transact business with a government employee are being replaced with e-government and an ever-expanding reliance on computers. The Texas Department of Public Safety introduced a queue management system in its Leon Valley–San Antonio driver's license center in 2013.

is to accomplish as much business as you can online or by phone. But if you have to visit a government office, follow these rules for "working the bureaucracy":

- *Remember that you are dealing with people.*

  Bureaucracies are composed of individuals. Many of them are overworked, but most want to be successful in carrying out their tasks. Approach them in a cooperative spirit, not as if you are looking for a fight.

- *Find the right agency and the right person or persons authorized to provide solutions.*

  Bureaucracies operate under organizational structures that divide responsibilities among employees. The first person you call or meet at an agency may not be the person who can deal with your issue. You may believe you are "getting the runaround" if you are transferred from person to person or agency to agency. But you can save yourself some time and frustration by making your needs or request clear in your first encounter with a governmental employee.

- *Be patient.*

  Employees of large organizations often do not know every service their agencies perform. Most public workers are specialists. They have specific areas of responsibility and specific tasks and often know little about other offices or divisions within their agency.

- *Be tenacious.*

  Dealing with bureaucracies can be frustrating, but persistence is imperative. The more questions you ask, the more you are going to understand the organization and the more quickly you are going to find someone who can help you.

- *Know your rights and act on them.*

  Governments exist for you. You do not exist for governments. The more you learn about governmental procedures, the more likely you are to be successful. If an employee of a state agency dismisses your inquiry or claim in a cavalier manner, go above that person's head to the next person in the chain of command. If the obstruction persists at the higher levels of the agency, call your legislator's office with a detailed summary of what occurred. (Here, it will help to know which state representative and state senator represent you.) Not all legislators will respond to your complaint, particularly if you have dealt with the agency erratically. But many will, and agencies normally respond to inquiries from legislators, who set their budgets and pass the laws under which the agencies operate.

- *Occasionally, you may have to be adversarial.*

  Sometimes, unfortunately, governmental agencies and their employees misinterpret the law or refuse to do what the law requires. In those cases, your only recourse may be to file a lawsuit against the agency. Corporations and well-organized interest groups usually have the financial resources for such a fight. Most citizens, however, do not. So keep the previous tactics in mind, and do everything you can to avoid getting to this one.

Merit Systems and Professional Management

7.5 Differentiate among the personnel systems used by the state and local governments in Texas.

Earlier in Texas history, public employees were hired on the basis of **political patronage**, or the personal relationships and friendships they had with elected or appointed public officials. Little consideration was given to their skills, competence,

---

political patronage
The hiring of government employees on the basis of personal friendships or favors rather than ability or merit.

or expertise. There were few rules concerning terms of employment, advancement, or the rights or conduct of public employees, and wide variations in pay existed from agency to agency. Employee turnover rates were high.

To better serve the public and state workers, some reform advocates pushed for a **merit employment system** based, in part, on the Civil Service Commission created by the federal government for its workers in 1883. Although other states have developed comprehensive, statewide employment or personnel systems administered by a single agency, the reform movement in Texas has not been as successful. Improvements have been made, but state government in Texas continues to function under a decentralized personnel system.[38]

Merit-based public employment was inconsistent with the individualistic views of government, politics, and public administration evolving from the dominant political subcultures of Texas. The plural executive system worked against efforts to centralize and coordinate personnel policies because the various elected executive officeholders jealously guarded their prerogatives to hire and fire the people who worked for them.

Governmental functions have expanded in modern times, and carrying out public policy has become more complex and technical.[39] Many programs require highly specialized skills, not political hacks who have no formal training or expertise for technical jobs. Furthermore, the public has gradually developed higher expectations of its government and reacts unfavorably to incompetent public workers. Additional pressure for merit employment has come from the federal government. Since the 1930s, numerous federal grants have required the state to enact a merit system for state employees administering them. In compliance with federal law, Texas created the Merit System Council in 1940 with limited jurisdiction and authority. The legislature eliminated the council in 1985 and assigned each agency the responsibility for developing its own merit system. While elements of merit-based employment have been adopted throughout most state agencies, employment practices are not developed or administered through a single civil service commission. The state's personnel system is highly decentralized and fragmented.

merit employment system
A personnel system under which public employees are selected for government jobs through competitive examinations and the systematic evaluation of job performance.

ORGANIZATIONAL EFFECTIVENESS DEPENDS ON A COMPETENT WORKFORCE

Seen here is a facility of the San Antonio Water System, which provides more than 450,000 customers with water services and 410,000 customers with waste management services in Bexar County and parts of Medina and Atascosa counties. A government service with this scope of responsibility requires a large, highly trained, well-managed, and well-funded workforce to carry out its mission.

In more recent years, federal laws prohibiting hiring discrimination on the basis of sex, age, disability, race, ethnicity, marital status, gender identity, or sexual orientation have been extended to state and local governments. These requirements, in turn, have forced the Texas government to pay more attention to employment practices.[40]

Ultimately, the legislature has the legal authority to define personnel practices, and the biennial budget is the major tool used by legislators to establish several hundred job classifications and corresponding salary schedules. The technical work on the state's classification schedule is assigned to the State Classification Office, a division of the State Auditor's Office. This is an agency of the legislature, not the executive branch, supervised by the Legislative Audit Committee, a standing joint committee of the legislature. The legislature also establishes policies on vacations, holidays, and retirement.

Within this highly decentralized personnel system, the primary responsibility for carrying out personnel policies is still delegated to the various state agencies. An administrator can develop specific policies for an agency as long as the agency works within the general framework defined by the legislature. Some agencies have developed modern personnel plans—including employee grievance procedures and competitive examinations for placement and advancement—whereas others have not.

All state job openings are required to be listed with the Texas Workforce Commission. Agencies also advertise for workers through the mass media and college placement centers. But many jobs still are filled as a result of friendships, personal contacts, and the influence of key political players.

In public education at all levels, employees are subject to various employment policies that are determined by each individual university governing board and local school district. Many cities and large counties across Texas, unlike state government, have adopted centrally administered merit systems organized around the accepted principles of modern personnel management. Their personnel departments include independent civil service commissions that have some rule-making authority and hear appeals of personnel matters. These changes, which resulted from the urban reform movement and were extended later to urban county governments, were designed to recruit quality employees and to insulate them from external political pressures. They have led to a high level of professionalism in some cities. Large metropolitan counties also have tried to structure their employment systems on the basis of merit, but the partisan election of county officials thwarts the full implementation of merit systems.

THE OLD LAND OFFICE BUILDING

Unlike most other states, Texas entered the Union in 1845 owning its public lands, which had been under the management of the General Land Office since 1836, when the Texas Congress created the agency. For many years, the agency was housed in this building, which was completed in 1857. Texas still owns large areas of land with extensive mineral reserves that have been used to finance state expenditures.

CONCLUSION

Even if you are not a public employee, you and those who work in government have a lot in common. Government workers are bound by the same laws and government regulations as you are. They also pay taxes, and they depend on the same people—their fellow bureaucrats—to enforce public health and public safety policies that are as important to them as they are to you. They, like you, need the services of fellow state and local workers who provide an array of public services. And sometimes they find the bureaucratic maze as confusing as you do. By keeping your shared interests in mind, you can appreciate what public employees do and not be intimidated by the system in which they work.

To effectively navigate the bureaucratic maze, you must first learn which level of government and which agency have jurisdiction over the problem or issue you need to have addressed. Remember that the authority of an agency and its employees is defined by state law enacted by the legislature or an ordinance, regulation, or policy enacted by a city council, school board, or other local government. Public employees are bound by those laws, regulations, and policies, so don't blame them for a law or a policy with which you may disagree. If you think a government worker may be misinterpreting a law or policy, you can challenge or appeal the decision through procedures provided by that agency. Patience may be required, but it is essential that you remain businesslike. Bureaucrats are people who respond to different types of behavior much like everybody else, and usually polite firmness works better than antagonism.

Texas's bureaucracy is larger than most state bureaucracies, but it shares a lot of the same characteristics with the bureaucracies of every state. Bureaucracies all over the country have grown with increased population. The state Capitol in Austin and city halls and courthouses throughout Texas have spawned annexes and related office buildings as the bureaucracy has outgrown its original confines.

Wherever you find them, public employees are there to serve you, either directly or indirectly. At some point, we all need their services. Our interests will be best served if we learn how to navigate the process they represent, rather than assuming that we "can't fight city hall."

REVIEW THE CHAPTER

Bureaucratic Systems in Texas

7.1 Discuss the essential features of the bureaucratic systems in Texas, p. 218.

Bureaucracies are administrative organizations created to carry out the policies of legislative bodies. They are complex, hierarchical organizations of varying sizes, with an emphasis on division of labor, specialization, and policy expertise. Bureaucracies develop comprehensive rules defining different jobs and establishing procedures for carrying out assigned responsibilities.

Despite their historical ambivalence toward government, Texans have come to expect a wide range of public services. With the growth of the state's population, government programs have been added or expanded, resulting in an increase of public employees at all levels of government. Of the more than 1.5 million Texans employed by state and local governments, most work for local governments. Although some reduction in public employment has occurred with recent recessions, the number of public employees is likely to continue to increase with future growth of the state's population.

Bureaucrats and Public Policy

7.2 Assess the dynamics of policy implementation by state bureaucrats in Texas, p. 223.

The bureaucracy has the primary responsibility of carrying out public policies adopted by the legislature and the local governing bodies. Administrative agencies are involved in virtually every stage of the policymaking process. Legislators depend on administrative agencies for counsel and advice when they draft public policies, and they rely on them to help assess the success or failure of policies. In addition to program implementation, agencies are assigned regulatory functions by the legislature, including the regulation of some public utilities, licensing of some professions and occupations, protection of natural resources, promotion of fairness and nondiscrimination in business and public practices, and social regulation.

When things go wrong and problems go unresolved, the tendency is to blame bureaucrats, but government employees often are unfairly blamed for complex problems that elected policymakers have been unwilling or unable to resolve. The fragmented structure of the executive branch of state government is, in itself, a major obstacle to the efficient, responsive delivery of public services. The potential also exists for agencies headed by appointed boards to become unaccountable to the voters and susceptible to the influence of special interest groups.

Legislative Control of the Bureaucracy

7.3 Describe policies utilized by the Texas legislature to control the actions of state agencies and public employees, p. 227.

The legislature has a number of ways to control administrative agencies. These include budgetary restrictions, performance reviews, sunset legislation, agency restructuring, the reassignment of program responsibilities, revolving-door restrictions on agency board members and key employees, and provisions to protect public employees who blow the whistle on corruption or mismanagement in public programs. Although candidates for the legislature and other state offices campaign on reducing the number of public employees, campaign rhetoric has not resulted in significant reductions in the government workforce.

Texas Citizens and the Bureaucracy

7.4 Summarize strategies available to citizens to impact or influence the actions of public employees, p. 231.

Attempting to navigate public agencies can be intimidating, but, to get started, know what service you want, know which agency is responsible for providing it, remember you are dealing with people, and be patient. If a government worker fails to provide satisfactory service, ask to speak to a supervisor. If a government agency refuses to respond or obey the law, contact your state representative or state senator for help. As a last resort, you can consider filing a lawsuit against the agency, but suing a government agency can be extremely expensive. Every day, state and local government agencies in Texas have hundreds of thousands of interactions with individuals, and most end satisfactorily.

Merit Systems and Professional Management

7.5 Differentiate among the personnel systems used by the state and local governments in Texas, p. 232.

Many cities and other local governments have adopted merit-based employment systems with rules for screening potential employees in order to hire competent workers without political interference. However, state government has not developed a centralized, comprehensive merit system for its employees, although some agencies use merit-based principles. The state's employment practices are fragmented, with each agency largely free to set its own personnel policies.

LEARN THE TERMS

bureaucracies, p. 218
licensing, p. 224
co-optation, p. 226
sunset review, p. 228
revolving door, p. 229
whistle-blower, p. 229
political patronage, p. 232
merit employment system, p. 233

The Judicial System in Texas

8

WHEN FUN BECOMES A LEGAL BATTLEGROUND

For generations, Texans have enjoyed free and open access to Gulf Coast beaches. But some environmentalists and legal experts believe a Texas Supreme Court decision weighing private property rights against beach access could lead to restricted access near some beach homes.

LEARNING OBJECTIVES

8.1 Describe the structure of the Texas court system and its position within the constitutional framework of federalism, p. 239.

8.2 Describe the roles of the participants in the Texas court system and the procedures used in trial and appellate courts, p. 246.

8.3 Trace the growth of minority and women judges in the Texas judiciary, p. 249.

8.4 Characterize the judicial controversies in Texas and their impact on public perception of the courts, p. 253.

8.5 Describe the legal and constitutional rights of suspects, the classes of crimes and punishments in the Texas Penal Code, and the administration of criminal justice in Texas, p. 259.

8.6 Illustrate the increased policy role of the state courts with examples, p. 264.

Sometimes, the courthouse is closer than you think. One beautiful day, you are driving toward the beach, enjoying a break from classes and your part-time job and looking forward to some sunshine and relaxation on your favorite stretch of Gulf Coast sand. You haven't been to the coast in more than a year, and a courtroom

237

full of high-priced lawyers shuffling stacks of paper is the last thing on your mind. Once you get to the beach, however, your mood is quickly shattered by a fence and a no-trespassing sign erected alongside a newly renovated beach house that sits much closer to the water than you remembered. Your initial response is that the property owner can't spoil your day because Texas historically has had one of the strongest open beaches laws in the country. You have always taken easy beach access for granted. But a storm that struck this portion of the coast since the last time you were here eroded your favorite beach, leaving behind that house sitting on what is now considered private property.

This scenario is more realistic than you may think, according to environmentalists and legal experts who have analyzed a Texas Supreme Court ruling that puts new restrictions on Texas's long history of open beaches. That decision will be discussed in more detail later in this chapter, but the point is that the long arm of the state judiciary can tap you on the shoulder when you least expect it.

Unless you are aspiring to be a judge or a lawyer, you probably would prefer to avoid courtrooms because the courtroom is often associated with conflict or something negative—a criminal conviction and prison sentence, a messy divorce, an expensive lawsuit, or even something as simple, yet annoying, as a traffic ticket. In reality, courtrooms and the judicial system they represent have widespread effects on people's lives, sometimes in a positive sense, sometimes not so positively, and sometimes when you do not realize it. Even law-abiding people can find themselves sued over alleged grievances by neighbors, customers, former business partners, creditors, or a stranger whose car they rear-ended on the way to work. Also, most people sooner or later will be summoned for jury duty, a sometimes unpopular interruption in work and personal lives, but an important part of our justice system. And if you should ever be accused of a crime, you will be at the mercy of the judicial system, so it would be in your best interests to know something about it. In a broader sense, courts determine the legitimacy and fairness of tax laws, voting procedures, and many other public policies affecting everyone's pocketbook and constitutional rights. But whether you are a civil litigant, a criminal defendant, or simply someone seeking fairness, the more you know about the judicial system—its history, the rules governing it, and the judges who operate it—the more easily you will be able to navigate the courthouse and make informed decisions about protecting your rights and interests.

One of the first things you need to learn is that justice in Texas isn't always blind, despite the ideal of everyone being treated equally under the law in the state's courts. Litigation is expensive, and many Texans do not have the money to pay for adequate legal assistance, much less the large fees that the best lawyers command and the huge expenses that some lawsuits can cost. Most judges try to be fair, but their decisions can be affected by their political and ideological views, life experiences, ethnicity, and gender. In recent years, moreover, Texas courts have been at the center of controversies that have severely strained the notion that the scales of justice are weighted in an atmosphere free of outside influences. Large campaign contributions to elected state judges—from lawyers who practice before them and from other special interests—have fueled an ongoing high-stakes war for philosophical and political control of the judiciary and have raised questions in the media and among many advocacy groups about whether some Texas courtrooms are "for sale."

Despite recent gains, minorities and women are underrepresented among the ranks of Texas judges. And the basic structure of the judicial system—an assortment of more than 2,700 courts of various, often overlapping, jurisdictions—is so outdated that many experts believe it should be overhauled.

State courts resolve civil disputes over property rights, personal injuries, and other issues. They determine guilt or innocence and set punishment in criminal cases involving offenses against people, property, and public institutions. To a more limited extent than the federal judiciary, they also help set policy by reviewing the actions of the executive and legislative branches of government.

This chapter will cover the historical development of the Texas court system, provide some comparisons to courts in the federal system and other states, and offer guidance on how to navigate an often-confusing array of state and local courts.

The Structure of the Texas Court System

8.1 Describe the structure of the Texas court system and its position within the constitutional framework of federalism.

To learn how to navigate the courts, you need to have some basic knowledge of court structure and the differences between the various courts and their jurisdictions. Texans, like people in every state, are subject to the jurisdiction of both state and federal courts. The primary focus of this chapter will be on state courts, but first we will briefly discuss the federal judiciary and its impact on Texas.

8.1.1 Texas in the Federal Court System

The federal judiciary has jurisdiction over violations of federal laws, including some criminal offenses, and over banking, securities, and other activities regulated by the federal government. Federal courts have had major effects on state government policies and Texas's criminal justice system through interpretations and applications of the U.S. Constitution and federal laws, including the Bill of Rights.

Although Texas has a bill of rights in its constitution, the federal courts have taken the lead in protecting many civil and political liberties. The U.S. Supreme Court's decision, for example, to declare the white primary election unconstitutional in the landmark *Smith v. Allwright* case (1944) was part of a long fight to end political discrimination against African American voters during the segregation era.[1] Federal court intervention continues in the redistricting of legislative and congressional district lines. The federal judiciary has ordered far-reaching improvements in the Texas prison system. When police officers read criminal suspects their rights, the officers comply with constitutional requirements determined by the U.S. Supreme Court in the *Miranda* case.[2] Nevertheless, estimates indicate that more than 95 percent of all litigation is based on state laws or local ordinances.[3] Thus, anyone involved in a lawsuit is likely to be found in a state rather than a federal court.

8.1.2 Criminal and Civil Procedure

The U.S. and Texas constitutions provide the basic legal framework for the Texas court system. Building on that framework, the Texas legislature has enacted codes of criminal and civil procedure to govern conduct in the courtroom and statutory laws for the courts to apply.

The Texas **Penal Code** defines most criminal activities and their punishments. In criminal cases, the state, often based on charges made by another individual, initiates action against a person accused of a crime. The most serious criminal offenses, for which prison sentences can be imposed, are called *felonies*. More minor offenses, punishable by fines or short sentences in county or city jails, are called *misdemeanors*.

Civil lawsuits, which can be initiated under numerous statutes, involve conflicts between two or more parties—individuals, corporations, governments, or other entities. Civil law governs contracts and property rights between private citizens, affords individuals an avenue for relief against corporate abuses, determines

Penal Code
A body of law that defines most criminal offenses and sets a range of punishments that can be assessed.

Civil lawsuit
A noncriminal/legal dispute between two or more individuals, businesses, governments, or other entities.

ON THE WITNESS STAND

A lawyer questions a witness giving testimony during the trial of a civil lawsuit. Many of these lawsuits are settled without going to trial. But trials of complex cases can take many weeks.

liability for personal injuries, and gives government regulatory enforcement powers over many aspects of the state's economy. The latter may include a lawsuit by the state against an oil company for violating a drilling permit or an environmental regulation.

An individual with a grievance has to take the initiative of going to court. A person can have problems with a landlord who refuses to return a deposit, a dry cleaner that lost a suit, or a friend who has borrowed and wrecked a car. But no legal issue can be resolved unless a lawsuit is filed. An injured person filing a lawsuit is a plaintiff, and the person or other entity being sued is a defendant. Both are considered litigants. Because even the most minor disputes in the lowest courts can require professional assistance from a lawyer, people involved in lawsuits soon discover that the pursuit of justice can be costly and time consuming.

8.1.3 Five Levels of Courts

Texas has five levels of courts, but some courts at different levels have overlapping authority and jurisdiction (see Figure 8–1). Some courts have only **original jurisdiction**; that is, they try to resolve only those cases being heard for the first time. They weigh the facts presented as evidence and apply the law in reaching a decision, or verdict. Other courts have only **appellate jurisdiction**; that is, they review the decisions of lower courts to determine if constitutional and statutory principles and procedures were correctly interpreted and followed. Appellate courts are empowered to reverse the judgments of the lower courts and to order cases to be retried if constitutional or procedural mistakes were made. Still other courts have both original and appellate jurisdiction.

At the highest appellate level, Texas has a **bifurcated court system** with the nine-member Texas Supreme Court serving as the court of last resort in civil and juvenile cases and the nine-member Texas Court of Criminal Appeals functioning as the court of last resort in criminal cases. Only one other state, Oklahoma, has a similar structure.[4]

Unlike federal judges, who are appointed by the president to lifetime terms, state judges, except for those on municipal courts, are elected to limited terms in partisan elections. Judges and judicial candidates are nominated in party primaries and listed on the general election ballot by their party affiliations. Midterm vacancies on courts,

original jurisdiction
The authority of a court to try to resolve a civil lawsuit or a criminal prosecution being heard for the first time.

appellate jurisdiction
The authority of a court to review the decisions of lower courts to determine if the law was correctly interpreted and legal procedures were correctly followed.

bifurcated court system
Existence of two courts at the highest level of the state judiciary. The Texas Supreme Court is the court of last resort in civil and juvenile cases, and the Court of Criminal Appeals has the final authority to review criminal cases. Texas and Oklahoma are the only two states that use this system.

The Judicial System in Texas 241

FIGURE 8-1 COURT STRUCTURE OF TEXAS, OCTOBER 1, 2019

The structure of the Texas court system, which is composed of five levels, is based on provisions of the Texas Constitution, state statutes, and city ordinances.

SOURCE: Texas Office of Court Administration. Available at https://www.txcourts.gov/media/1445794/court-structure-chart-october-2019.pdf.

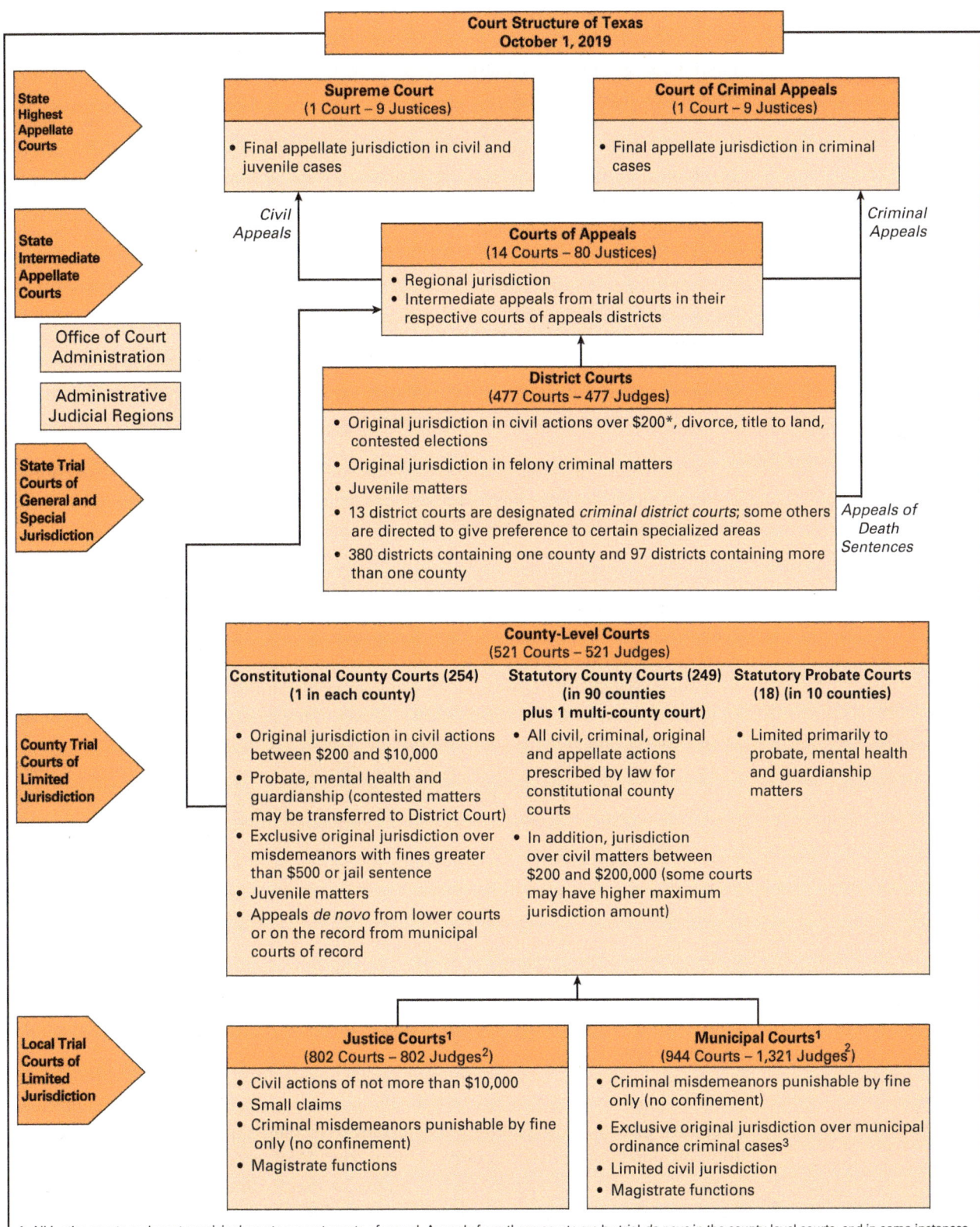

Court Structure of Texas — October 1, 2019

State Highest Appellate Courts

- **Supreme Court** (1 Court – 9 Justices)
  - Final appellate jurisdiction in civil and juvenile cases

- **Court of Criminal Appeals** (1 Court – 9 Justices)
  - Final appellate jurisdiction in criminal cases

Civil Appeals ↑ ... *Criminal Appeals* ↑

State Intermediate Appellate Courts

- **Courts of Appeals** (14 Courts – 80 Justices)
  - Regional jurisdiction
  - Intermediate appeals from trial courts in their respective courts of appeals districts

Office of Court Administration

Administrative Judicial Regions

State Trial Courts of General and Special Jurisdiction

- **District Courts** (477 Courts – 477 Judges)
  - Original jurisdiction in civil actions over $200*, divorce, title to land, contested elections
  - Original jurisdiction in felony criminal matters
  - Juvenile matters
  - 13 district courts are designated *criminal district courts*; some others are directed to give preference to certain specialized areas
  - 380 districts containing one county and 97 districts containing more than one county

Appeals of Death Sentences

County Trial Courts of Limited Jurisdiction

- **County-Level Courts** (521 Courts – 521 Judges)

  Constitutional County Courts (254) (1 in each county)
  - Original jurisdiction in civil actions between $200 and $10,000
  - Probate, mental health and guardianship (contested matters may be transferred to District Court)
  - Exclusive original jurisdiction over misdemeanors with fines greater than $500 or jail sentence
  - Juvenile matters
  - Appeals *de novo* from lower courts or on the record from municipal courts of record

  Statutory County Courts (249) (in 90 counties plus 1 multi-county court)
  - All civil, criminal, original and appellate actions prescribed by law for constitutional county courts
  - In addition, jurisdiction over civil matters between $200 and $200,000 (some courts may have higher maximum jurisdiction amount)

  Statutory Probate Courts (18) (in 10 counties)
  - Limited primarily to probate, mental health and guardianship matters

Local Trial Courts of Limited Jurisdiction

- **Justice Courts[1]** (802 Courts – 802 Judges[2])
  - Civil actions of not more than $10,000
  - Small claims
  - Criminal misdemeanors punishable by fine only (no confinement)
  - Magistrate functions

- **Municipal Courts[1]** (944 Courts – 1,321 Judges[2])
  - Criminal misdemeanors punishable by fine only (no confinement)
  - Exclusive original jurisdiction over municipal ordinance criminal cases[3]
  - Limited civil jurisdiction
  - Magistrate functions

1. All justice courts and most municipal courts are not courts of record. Appeals from these courts are by trial *de novo* in the county-level courts, and in some instances in the district courts.
2. Some municipal courts are courts of record—appeals from the courts are taken on the record to the county-level courts. As of April 2019, 179 courts indicated that they were a court of record; a list is posted at http://www.txcourts.gov/about-texas-courts.aspx.
3. An offense that arises under a municipal ordinance is punishable by a fine not to exceed: (1) $2,000 for ordinances that govern fire safety, zoning, and public health, (2) $4,000 for dumping of refuse or (3) $500 for all others.

however, are filled by appointment. County commissioners courts fill vacancies on justice of the peace and county courts, and the governor fills vacancies on district and appellate courts.

MUNICIPAL AND JUSTICE OF THE PEACE COURTS The lowest-ranking trial courts in Texas are **municipal courts** and **justice of the peace courts**. You or someone you know probably has appeared before a judge in one of these courts because both handle a large volume of traffic tickets. Some of these courts are big sources of revenue for local governments.

State law authorizes cities to create municipal courts, but some cities rely instead on justice of the peace courts. Some 944 cities, or about three-fourths of the incorporated cities in Texas, have municipal courts, and a number of those have multiple judges.[5] Individual cities determine the qualifications, terms of office, and method of selecting municipal judges, but they generally are appointed by the city council. Municipal courts have original and exclusive jurisdiction over city ordinances, but most of these courts are not courts of record, in which a word-for-word transcript is made of trial proceedings. Most of these courts record only very rudimentary information, and any appeal from them is heard *de novo* by a higher court. That is, the second court has to conduct a new trial and hear the same witnesses and evidence all over again because no official record of the original proceedings was kept.[6] Responding to this problem, the legislature in recent years has created municipal courts of record for some cities.

Each county in Texas must have one justice of the peace court, and each county government in the larger metropolitan areas may create sixteen. There are 802 of these courts in Texas. Justices of the peace are elected to four-year terms from precincts, or subdivisions of the county drawn by the commissioners court, which also sets their salaries. Justices of the peace are not required to be licensed attorneys.

Although their duties vary from county to county, justice of the peace courts, with certain restrictions, have original jurisdiction in civil cases when the amount in dispute is $10,000 or less, and they have original jurisdiction over criminal offenses that are punishable by fines only. In some areas of criminal law, they have overlapping jurisdiction with municipal courts. Justices of the peace also sit as judges of small claims courts, and in many rural counties they serve as coroners. They also function as state magistrates with the authority to hold preliminary hearings to determine if there is probable cause to hold a criminal defendant. Each justice of the peace court has an elected constable to serve warrants and perform other duties for the court.

COUNTY-LEVEL COURTS Any confusion about the authority and jurisdiction of municipal and justice of the peace courts is compounded by the county courts. The first county courts were created by the Texas Constitution to serve the needs of the sparsely populated, rural society that existed when the charter was approved in 1876. But population growth and urbanization have placed enormous demands on the judicial system, and rather than modernize the system, the state has added courts while making only modest changes in the structure and jurisdiction of the existing courts.

Each county has a **constitutional county court**. The holder of this office, the county judge, is elected countywide to a four-year term. This individual is the chief executive officer of the county and presides over the county commissioners court, the policymaking body of county government. Most urban county judges do not perform judicial duties, but county judges in many rural counties perform both executive and judicial functions, a dual responsibility that some experts believe is inconsistent with the Texas Constitution's separation-of-powers doctrine. Although many county judges are lawyers, they are not required to be. They are required only to be "well informed in the law" and to take appropriate courses in evidence and legal procedures.

---

municipal court
A court of limited jurisdiction that hears cases involving city ordinances and primarily handles traffic tickets.

justice of the peace court
A low-ranking court with jurisdiction over minor civil disputes and criminal cases.

constitutional county court
The Texas Constitution provides for 254 courts with limited jurisdiction. The county judge, who is also the presiding officer of a county's commissioners court, which is a policymaking body, performs some limited judicial functions in some counties.

THE LONG ARM OF THE LAW
You or someone you know may very well have had business before a municipal court or a justice of the peace court because these courts handle a lot of traffic violations.

The constitutional county court shares some original civil jurisdiction with both the justice of the peace and district courts. It has original criminal jurisdiction over misdemeanors punishable by fines of more than $500 and jail sentences of one year or less. These courts also probate wills and have appellate jurisdiction over cases tried originally in justice of the peace and municipal courts.

Over the years, the legislature also has created 267 **statutory county courts**, or county courts-at-law, in about 90 counties. Some specialize in probate cases and are called probate courts. These courts were designed to deal with specific local problems and, consequently, have inconsistent jurisdictions. Judges on these courts are elected countywide and have to be lawyers, but the authority of a particular court is defined by the legislation by which it was created. Some statutory county courts cannot hear civil disputes involving more than $2,500, whereas others can hear disputes involving as much as $200,000. Drunk driving cases are the primary criminal cases tried before these courts, but some also hear appeals *de novo* from lower courts.

statutory county court
A court created by the legislature that exercises limited jurisdiction over criminal and civil cases. Also known as county courts-at-law, the jurisdiction of these courts varies from county to county.

DISTRICT COURTS The primary trial court in Texas is the **district court**. Although there is some overlapping jurisdiction with county courts, district courts have original jurisdiction over civil cases involving $200 or more in damages, divorce cases, contested elections, suits over land titles and liens, suits for slander or defamation, all criminal felony cases, and misdemeanors involving official misconduct. In recent years, the legislature has created district courts with specialized jurisdiction over criminal or civil law or over such specialties as family law—divorces and child custody cases. In some large metropolitan counties that have numerous district courts, informal agreements among judges determine the jurisdictions of the respective courts. District court judges are elected to four-year terms, must be at least 25 years old, and must have practiced law or served as judges of other courts for four years prior to taking office.

district court
A court with general jurisdiction over criminal felony cases and civil disputes.

As the state's population has grown, the legislature has created new district courts: In 1981, there were 328; by 2019, the number had grown to 477. A single county may be allocated more than one district court with overlapping geographical jurisdiction. Harris County, the state's most populous county, has sixty district courts, each covering the entire county. By contrast, one rural district court may include several counties. As these courts evolved, the respective workloads of individual courts received little systematic consideration, and great disparities now exist in the number of people served by each district court.

plea bargain
A procedure that allows a person charged with a crime to negotiate a guilty plea with prosecutors in exchange for a lighter sentence than he or she would expect to receive if convicted in a trial.

Many urban counties suffer from a heavy backlog of cases that can delay a trial date in civil lawsuits and even some criminal cases for months or years. Delays in criminal cases have prompted a widespread use of **plea bargains**. In plea bargaining, a criminal defendant, through a lawyer, negotiates with prosecutors a guilty plea that will get a lesser sentence than he or she could expect to receive if convicted in a trial. The process saves the state the time-consuming expense of a full-blown trial and has become an essential tool in clearing urban court dockets.

Many civil lawsuits also are resolved through negotiations between the opposing parties, but those that are tried and appealed can take several years to be resolved.

Although the district courts are the state's primary trial courts and the state pays the district judges' base salaries, the counties pick up virtually all the other district court expenses. The counties provide courtrooms, pay the courts' operating expenses, and supplement the judges' state pay.

court of appeals
An intermediate-level court that reviews civil and criminal cases from the district courts.

COURTS OF APPEALS Texas has fourteen intermediate **courts of appeals** covering thirteen multicounty regions that hear appeals of both civil and criminal cases from the district courts (see Figure 8–2). Two courts, the First Court of Appeals and the Fourteenth Court of Appeals, are based in Houston and cover the same area. The Texas Constitution provides that each court shall have a chief justice and at least two other justices, but the legislature can add to that number and has done so for most courts. Each Houston court has nine judges, and the Fifth Court of Appeals in Dallas has thirteen judges. Five of these intermediate courts, however, have only three judges. Appellate judges are elected to six-year terms. They must be at least 35 years old and have at least ten years of experience as an attorney or a judge on a court of record.

To give you an idea of how clogged the state judicial system has become, all courts of appeals combined disposed of 10,294 cases—4,640 criminal cases and 5,654 civil lawsuits—during fiscal 2019 and left more than 6,500 cases pending on their dockets at the end of that year.[7] And these were only the appealed cases; these statistics didn't include the thousands of cases in the lower courts that weren't appealed. Disparities exist in the caseloads among individual appellate courts, with those in Houston and Dallas handling the lion's share. The Texas Supreme Court partially balances the load

FIGURE 8–2   MAP OF COURTS OF APPEALS

Texas has fourteen intermediate courts of appeals, each covering a number of counties. The First and Fourteenth Courts, based in Houston, cover the same area.

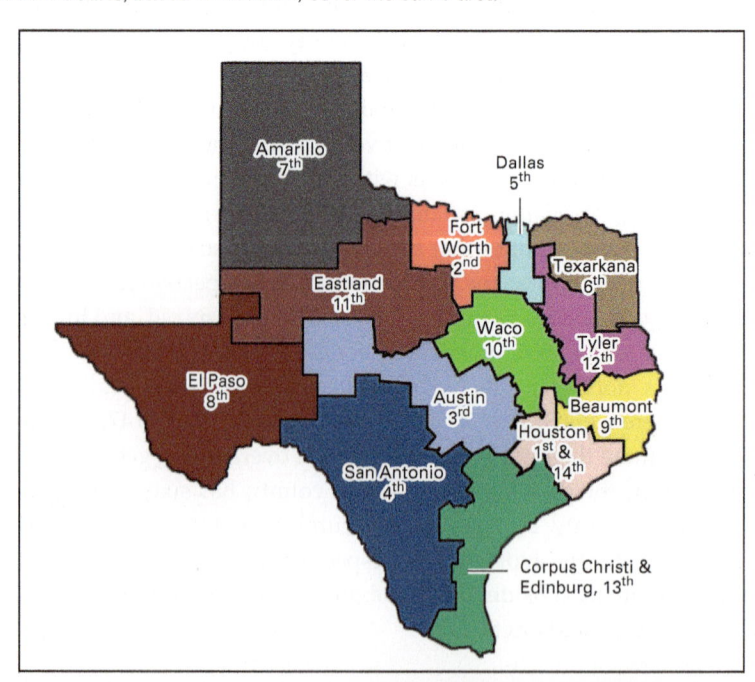

TEXAS SUPREME COURT

This nine-member court is the state court of last resort in civil lawsuits and cases involving juveniles. Criminal cases are handled by the Texas Court of Criminal Appeals.

by transferring cases among courts. The courts of appeals normally decide cases in panels of three judges, but an entire court can hear some appeals *en banc*—when all of the judges of an appellate court sit to hear a case.

SUPREME COURT AND COURT OF CRIMINAL APPEALS The creation of separate courts of last resort for civil and criminal cases was part of the effort by the constitutional framers of 1876 to fragment political power and decentralize the structure of state and local governments. It also was based on the rationale that criminal cases should be handled more expeditiously, and the way to accomplish this was through a separate appellate court.[8]

Although it decides only civil appeals and cases involving juveniles, the **Texas Supreme Court** is probably viewed by most Texans as the unofficial head of the state judiciary, and it has been given some authority to coordinate the state judicial system.[9] The Supreme Court is charged with developing administrative procedures for state courts and rules of civil procedure. It appoints the Board of Law Examiners, which is responsible for licensing attorneys, and has oversight of the State Bar, the professional organization to which lawyers in Texas belong. The Supreme Court also has disciplinary authority over state judges through recommendations of the State Commission on Judicial Conduct.

The Texas Supreme Court includes a chief justice and eight justices who serve staggered, six-year terms. Three members are up for election every two years on a statewide, partisan ballot. Members must be at least 35 years old and must have been practicing attorneys, judges of a court of record, or a combination of both for at least ten years.

The **Texas Court of Criminal Appeals**, which hears only criminal cases on appeal, includes a presiding judge and eight other judges elected statewide to staggered, six-year terms. The qualifications for members of this court are the same as those for the Supreme Court.

Under the federal system, some decisions of the Texas Supreme Court and the Texas Court of Criminal Appeals can be appealed to the U.S. Supreme Court. Those cases have to involve a federal question or a constitutional right assured under the U.S. Constitution.

Texas Supreme Court
A nine-member court with final appellate jurisdiction over civil lawsuits in Texas.

Texas Court of Criminal Appeals
A nine-member court with final appellate jurisdiction over criminal cases in Texas.

MAKING HISTORY ON THE COURT OF CRIMINAL APPEALS

Texas Court of Criminal Appeals Presiding Judge Sharon Keller, a former prosecutor, was the first woman elected to the court and, later, to be promoted to presiding judge.

Participants and Procedures in the Judicial System

8.2 Describe the roles of the participants in the Texas court system and the procedures used in trial and appellate courts.

Although judges and lawyers may be the first people we think of when discussing the courts, the judicial process in Texas includes thousands of law enforcement officers, administrative and support personnel who assist judges, and ordinary Texans who play critical roles in the administration of justice by serving on juries. The next step in navigating the court system is to learn more about these participants and what they do.

8.2.1 Texas Judges

Many judges on the intermediate and highest appellate courts previously served on lower courts. Most district judges came to their offices from private law practices or prosecutors' offices.

With the partisan realignment of Texas from Democratic to Republican control, which began in the late 1970s, Republicans saw election gains and more appointments to judicial vacancies. A number of judges also switched from the Democratic Party. By 2003, almost two-thirds of the judges at the district court level and higher were Republicans, but by 2006, Democrats were making a comeback. Democrats swept all judicial races on the ballot in Dallas County that year and made a strong showing in Harris County two years later. In a heavier-than-usual voter turnout in 2018, thanks in part to a highly contested U.S. Senate race at the top of the general election ballot, Democratic judicial candidates made additional huge gains. Democrats unseated 19 Republican justices from the courts of appeals and unseated 37 Republican district court judges in Harris County (Houston). After all the votes were counted, Democrats had flipped the four courts of appeals in Houston, Dallas, and Austin from Republican control and held all the district court seats in those cities.

But Republicans still held all nine seats on the Texas Supreme Court and all nine seats on the Texas Court of Criminal Appeals. In December 2013, Judge Lawrence Meyers, who had served on the Court of Criminal Appeals as a Republican for twenty-one years, switched to the Democratic Party in midterm, but he was unseated by a Republican challenger in 2016.

Most Texas judges are white males. More women, Hispanics, and African Americans are entering the legal profession and running for judicial offices, but they still are disproportionately underrepresented in the judiciary, as will be discussed in more detail later in this chapter.

Judicial elections have been diluted by a large number of appointments to judicial vacancies. The governor appoints judges to fill midterm vacancies on the district and appellate courts. County commissioners courts fill midterm vacancies on county courts-at-law and justice of the peace courts. Appointees are required to run for office in the next general election to keep their seats, but their incumbency can enhance their election chances. Six of the nine justices serving on the Texas Supreme Court at the beginning of 2020 had initially been appointed to the court, three by Governor Greg Abbott and three by former Governor Rick Perry.

8.2.2 Prosecuting Attorneys and Clerks

County attorneys and district attorneys prosecute criminal cases. Both positions are elected. Some counties do not have a county attorney. In those that do, the county attorney is the chief legal adviser to county commissioners, represents the county in civil lawsuits, and may prosecute misdemeanors, the more minor criminal offenses.

The district attorney prosecutes felonies and, in some counties, also handles misdemeanors. The district attorney exercises considerable power in the criminal justice process by deciding which cases to take to a grand jury for an indictment, whether to seek the maximum penalty for an offense, or whether to plea-bargain with a defendant for a reduced sentence. The office represents one county in metropolitan areas and several counties in less populated areas of the state.

County and district clerks, both elected officials, are custodians of court records. Bailiffs are peace officers assigned to the courts to help maintain order and protect judges and other parties. Other law enforcement officers play critical roles in the arrest, detention, and investigation of persons accused of crimes.

8.2.3 The Jury Systems

Other important players in the judicial process are the private citizens who serve on grand juries and trial, or petit, juries.

THE GRAND JURY The **grand jury** includes twelve persons who, until a change in state law in 2015, were selected by commissioners appointed by a district judge. This system led to complaints that many grand juries were stacked with judges' friends and other prominent people and overrepresented the interests of upper social and economic groups and underrepresented low-income people and minorities. In 2015, the legislature, in an effort to make grand juries more diverse, made the selection process for grand juries the same as that used to select petit, or trial, juries, which is described below. Now, the members of grand juries and trial juries are both chosen at random from the lists of people in each county who have driver's licenses or are registered to vote.

In theory, the grand jury functions to ensure that the government has sufficient reason to proceed with a criminal **prosecution** against an individual. A district attorney, however, can exercise great control over a grand jury through deciding which evidence and which witnesses jurors will hear. Grand jury meetings and deliberations are conducted in private, and the accused is not allowed to have an attorney present during grand jury questioning.

If at least nine grand jurors believe there is enough evidence to warrant a trial in a case under investigation, they will issue an **indictment**, or a "true bill," a written statement charging a person or persons with a crime. A grand jury investigation may result in no indictment, or a "no bill."

In some cases, grand juries will issue indictments alleging misdemeanors. That often happens after an investigation fails to produce a strong enough case for a felony indictment. Most misdemeanors, however, are not handled by grand juries; instead, they are handled by the district or county attorney, who prepares an information—a document formally charging an individual with a misdemeanor—on the basis of a complaint filed by a private citizen.

THE PETIT JURY The jury on which most people are likely to be called to serve is the trial or **petit jury**. Citizens who are at least 18 years old and meet other minimal requirements are eligible for jury duty, and anyone refusing to comply with a jury summons can be fined for contempt of court. Persons older than 70, individuals with legal custody of young children, and full-time students are exempted from jury duty.

8.2.4 Judicial Procedures and Decision Making

Different rules and procedures apply to criminal and civil trials, and procedures differ significantly between trial and appellate courts.

grand jury
Panel that reviews evidence submitted by prosecutors to determine whether to indict, or charge, an individual with a criminal offense. A grand jury can hear witnesses; all its meetings are held behind closed doors.

prosecution
The conduct of legal proceedings against an individual charged with a crime.

indictment
A written statement issued by a grand jury charging a person or persons with a crime or crimes.

information
A document formally charging an individual with a misdemeanor.

petit jury
A panel of citizens that hears evidence in a civil lawsuit or a criminal prosecution and decides the outcome by issuing a verdict.

COURTROOM DUTY
Bailiffs are law enforcement officers who provide security during trials and other judicial proceedings. This bailiff is helping swear in a witness.

REPORTING FOR JURY DUTY
Governor Greg Abbott waits with other prospective jurors at the Travis County courthouse after being summoned for jury duty. The governor, however, was not selected to serve on a jury.

Ralph Barrera/Austin American-Statesman/Associated Press

veniremen
Persons who have been called for a jury panel.

TRIAL COURTS Six persons make up a jury in a justice of the peace or county court and twelve in a district court. Attorneys for both sides in a criminal or civil case screen the prospective jurors, known as **veniremen**, before a jury is seated. In major felony cases, such as capital murder, prosecutors and defense attorneys may take several days to select a jury from hundreds of prospects.

Attorneys for each side in a criminal case are allowed a certain number of peremptory challenges, which allow them to dismiss a prospective juror without having to explain the reason, and an unlimited number of challenges for cause. In the latter case, a lawyer has to state why he or she believes a particular venireman would be unable to evaluate the evidence in the case impartially. The judge decides whether to grant each challenge for cause but can rule against a peremptory challenge only if he or she believes the prosecutor is trying to exclude prospective jurors because of their race. If that happens, the defendant is entitled to a new group, or panel, of prospective jurors.

In civil cases, attorneys for both sides determine whether any persons on the jury panel should be disqualified because they are related to one of the parties, have some other personal or business connection, or could otherwise be prejudiced. For example, a lawyer defending a doctor in a malpractice suit probably would not want to seat a prospective juror who had been dissatisfied with his or her own medical treatment. Attorneys' careful screening and questioning of veniremen discover such potential conflicts.

Unanimous jury verdicts are required to convict a defendant in a criminal case. Jurors have to be convinced "beyond a reasonable doubt" that a defendant is guilty before returning a guilty verdict. Agreement of only ten of the twelve members of a district court jury and five of the six on a county court jury, however, is necessary to reach a verdict in a civil suit. Civil litigants and criminal defendants (except those charged with capital murder) can waive their right to a jury trial if they believe it would be to their advantage to have their cases decided by a judge.

Following established procedures, which differ between civil and criminal cases and are enforced by the judge, the trial moves through the presentation of opening arguments by the opposing attorneys, examination and cross-examination of witnesses, presentation of evidence, rebuttal, and summation. Some trials can be completed in a few hours, but the trial of a complex civil lawsuit or a sensational criminal case can take weeks or months. Convicted criminal defendants or parties dissatisfied with a judge or jury's verdict in a civil lawsuit may then appeal their case to higher courts.

APPELLATE COURTS The procedure in the appellate courts is markedly different from that in the trial courts. There is no jury at the appellate level to rehear evidence. Instead, judges review the decision and the procedures of the lower court to determine if they meet constitutional and statutory requirements. The record of the trial court proceedings and legal briefs filed by attorneys are available for appellate judges to review.

Most civil and criminal appeals are initially made to one of the fourteen intermediate courts of appeals. Parties dissatisfied with decisions of the courts of appeals can appeal to the Texas Supreme Court or the Court of Criminal Appeals.

Cases reach the Texas Supreme Court primarily on **petitions for review**, usually filed by the losing parties, claiming that lower courts made legal or procedural mistakes. The petitions are divided among the nine justices for review. The justices and their briefing attorneys then prepare memoranda on their assigned cases for circulation among the other court members. Meeting in private conference, the court decides which petitions to reject outright—thus upholding the lower court decisions—and which to review and schedule for attorneys' oral arguments. A case will not be heard without the approval of at least four of the nine justices.

petition for review
Petition to the Texas Supreme Court stating that legal or procedural mistakes were made in the lower court, thus meriting a hearing before the court.

Lawyers present oral arguments in open court, relating their perspectives on the legal points at issue in their cases and answering questions from the justices. The responsibility for writing the majority opinions that state the court's decisions is determined by lot among the justices. It often takes several months after oral arguments for a decision to be issued. Justices debate legal points and their judicial philosophies behind the closed doors of their conference room, but differences sometimes spill out for public view through split decisions and strongly worded dissenting opinions.

Most cases taken to the Texas Supreme Court on appeal are from one of the courts of appeals, but occasionally the Supreme Court receives a direct appeal from a district court. In recent years, the court has been hearing about 12 to 15 percent of the petitions for review it receives.

The Texas Supreme Court also acts on petitions for **writs of mandamus**, or orders directing a lower court or another public official to take a certain action. Many involve disputes over procedure or evidence in cases still pending in trial courts. In some cases, the Supreme Court may issue writs of mandamus directing trial judges to consider certain legal factors in admitting evidence.

writ of mandamus
A court order directing a lower court or a public official to take a certain action.

The Texas Court of Criminal Appeals has appellate jurisdiction in criminal cases that originate in district and county courts. Death penalty cases are appealed directly to the Court of Criminal Appeals. Other criminal cases are appealed first to the intermediate courts of appeals. Either the defendant or the prosecution can appeal the courts of appeals' decisions to the Court of Criminal Appeals by filing **petitions for discretionary review**, which the high court may grant if a sufficient number of judges agree. The court schedules lawyers' oral arguments in the cases it agrees to review. The task of writing majority opinions is rotated among the nine judges.

petition for discretionary review
Petition to the Texas Court of Criminal Appeals stating that legal or procedural mistakes were made in the lower court, thus meriting a hearing before the court.

Changing the Face of the Judiciary

8.3 Trace the growth of minority and women judges in the Texas judiciary.

In relation to their share of the Texas population, minorities and women historically have been underrepresented among the ranks of Texas judges, and they still are (see Figure 8–3). Activists have failed to force changes in the judicial selection process to favor the election of more minority judges. But slowly the face of the Texas judiciary is changing, thanks in part to midterm appointments by recent governors.

FIGURE 8-3 DO TEXAS JUDGES REPRESENT THE STATE'S DIVERSITY?

Although minority Texans are increasing their presence in the judiciary, the number of Hispanics and African Americans who are judges is still disproportionately much smaller than their share of the state's population.

*Texas population represented by the three largest racial/ethnic groups in 2008, 2012, and 2017

**Based on the judges at the county court level or higher who reported their race/ethnicity

SOURCES: U.S. Census Bureau, Texas Office of Court Administration, "Profile of Appellate and Trial Judges," 2008, 2012, and 2017.

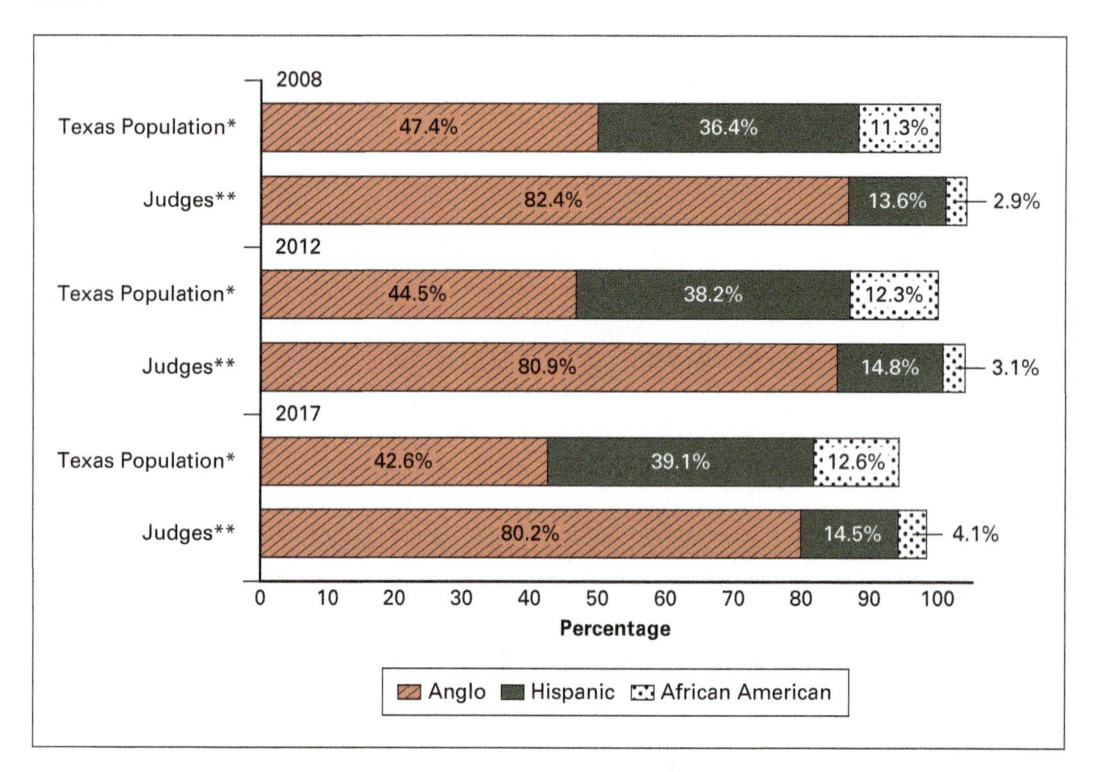

Year	Group	Anglo	Hispanic	African American
2008	Texas Population*	47.4%	36.4%	11.3%
2008	Judges**	82.4%	13.6%	2.9%
2012	Texas Population*	44.5%	38.2%	12.3%
2012	Judges**	80.9%	14.8%	3.1%
2017	Texas Population*	42.6%	39.1%	12.6%
2017	Judges**	80.2%	14.5%	4.1%

8.3.1 Minorities

In 2017, approximately 80 percent of Texas judges at the county court level and higher were white, although Anglos accounted for less than half of the state population.[10] Only five Hispanics have ever served on the Texas Supreme Court and three on the Texas Court of Criminal Appeals. Only two African Americans have ever been seated on the Texas Supreme Court and two on the Court of Criminal Appeals. Most of the minority judges on the high courts initially gained their seats by gubernatorial appointments to midterm vacancies, and some subsequently lost in elections.

Democratic Governor Mark White appointed the first Hispanic, Raul A. Gonzalez, the son of migrant workers, to the Texas Supreme Court in 1984 to fill a vacancy created by a resignation. Gonzalez made history a second time in 1986 by winning election to the seat and becoming the first Hispanic to win a statewide election in Texas. A native of Weslaco in the Rio Grande Valley, Gonzalez previously had served as a state district judge in Brownsville and a member of the Thirteenth Court of Appeals in Corpus Christi. Gonzalez, a Democrat, was one of the most conservative members of the Supreme Court during his tenure. Consequently, he came under frequent attack from trial lawyers and, ironically, from many of the constituent groups within his own party who advocated increasing the number of minority judges.

Raul Gonzalez resigned from the Supreme Court in midterm in late 1998 and was replaced by Alberto R. Gonzales, a Republican appointee of Governor George W. Bush and only the second Hispanic to serve on the high court. As had Raul Gonzalez, Alberto Gonzales came from a modest background. He had never been a judge before Governor Bush named him to the Supreme Court. However, he had been a partner in one of Houston's largest law firms. He also had been Bush's top staff lawyer and had served under Bush as Texas secretary of state.

Bush was actively trying to increase the Republican Party's appeal to Hispanics, and he acknowledged that it was important to him that Gonzales was Hispanic. "Of course, it mattered what his ethnicity is, but first and foremost what mattered is: I've got great confidence in Al," Bush said.[11] After Bush became president in 2001, he appointed Gonzales White House counsel and later U.S. attorney general.

On succeeding Bush, Republican Governor Rick Perry named the first African American, Wallace Jefferson, an appellate lawyer from San Antonio, to serve on the Texas Supreme Court. Jefferson succeeded Alberto Gonzales, who had resigned to take the White House job. Jefferson, a Republican and the great-great-great grandson of an enslaved person, was elected in 2002 to keep his seat on the high court, and he later was promoted to chief justice. Also in 2002, a second African American, Republican Dale Wainwright, a state district judge from Houston, was elected to an open Supreme Court seat.

Governor Perry later named two more Hispanics—Eva Guzman and David Medina—to the court to fill vacancies. Medina was elected to a new term in 2006 but was unseated in the 2012 Republican primary by John Devine, a white religious conservative and former state district judge from Houston. The two African American members of the court—Wallace Jefferson and Dale Wainwright—served several years before resigning to enter private law practice. Wainwright stepped down in 2012 and Jefferson in 2013. At the beginning of 2020, Eva Guzman, who was elected to a full term in 2010 and reelected in 2016, was the only minority member of the all-Republican court.

Governor Ann Richards appointed the first Hispanic, Fortunato P. Benavides, to the Texas Court of Criminal Appeals to fill a vacancy in 1991. Benavides had been a justice on the Thirteenth Court of Appeals and a district judge and a county court-at-law judge in Hidalgo County. Benavides was narrowly unseated in 1992 by Republican Lawrence Meyers of Fort Worth, an Anglo, who became the first Republican elected to the criminal court. President Bill Clinton later appointed Benavides to the Fifth U.S. Circuit Court of Appeals.

Governor Bill Clements appointed the first African American, Louis Sturns, a Republican state district judge from Fort Worth, to the Texas Court of Criminal Appeals on March 16, 1990. Sturns was unseated in the November general election that same year by another African American, Democrat Morris Overstreet, a county court-at-law judge from Amarillo, who became the first African American elected to a statewide office in Texas. Overstreet served on the court until 1998, when he lost a race for the Democratic nomination for Texas attorney general. Governor Rick Perry appointed the second Hispanic, Elsa Alcala, to the Court of Criminal Appeals to fill a vacancy in 2011, and Alcala was elected to the seat in 2012. Alcala didn't seek reelection in 2018, but another Hispanic, Michelle Slaughter, was elected to the court that year.

Obstacles to the election of minority judicial candidates have included the high cost of campaigns, polarized voting along ethnic lines in the statewide or countywide judicial races that are required for most judges, and low rates of minority participation in elections. Another factor has been a historical shortage of minority attorneys, from whose ranks judges are drawn.

In a lawsuit tried in September 1989 in federal district court in Midland, attorneys for the League of United Latin American Citizens (LULAC) and other minority plaintiffs argued that the countywide system of electing state district judges violated the federal Voting Rights Act by diluting the voting strength of minorities. They tried to force a change in state law to require district court judges in urban counties to be elected from geographic districts within the county, rather than countywide. This case, *League of United Latin American Citizens et al.* v. *Mattox et al.*, took almost five years and

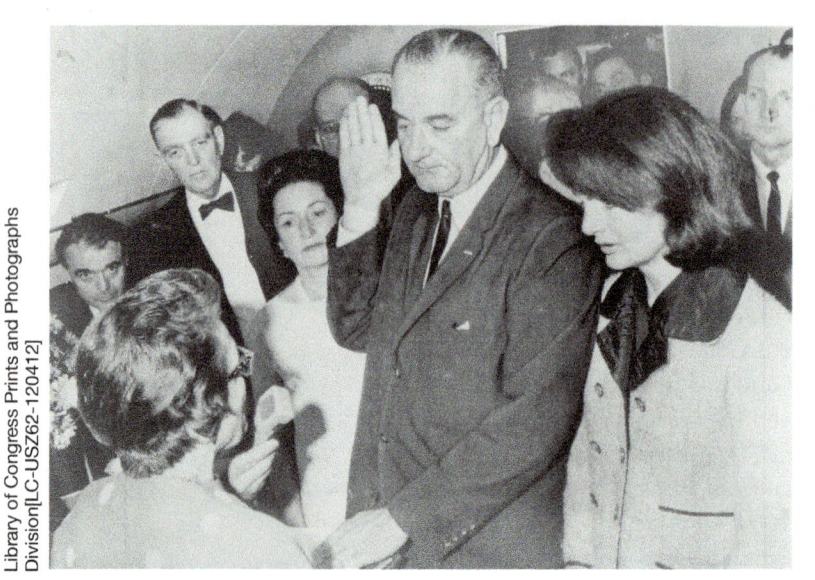

SARAH T. HUGHES

Judge Sarah T. Hughes (left foreground with back to camera) swears in President Lyndon B. Johnson aboard Air Force One on November 22, 1963, following President John F. Kennedy's assassination in Dallas. Hughes was a federal judge on this historic occasion. Years earlier, she had made history of a different sort when she became the first woman to be a state district judge in Texas.

two appeals to the U.S. Supreme Court before the high Court ultimately upheld the countywide election system in 1994.[12] Since then, the Texas legislature has left the countywide election system unchanged, ignoring pleas by advocates for change.

More recently, Hispanic plaintiffs went to federal court to sue the state over the statewide elections of members of the Texas Supreme Court and Court of Criminal Appeals. They argued that statewide elections for the high courts also diluted the voting strength of Hispanic voters, who were outnumbered by Anglo voters statewide but would have some electoral clout if justices were elected from smaller, geographic districts, some of which would be dominated by Hispanic voters. The plaintiffs cited the historically low numbers of Hispanics who have served on the two courts and argued that the statewide elections violated the Voting Rights Act. "The decisions that come out of these two courts directly impact the Latino community," said Jose Garza, one of the plaintiffs' attorneys. "And none of the people elected to these courts owe their election to the Latino community." But the state attorney general's office defended the statewide election system, arguing that election results for the two high courts were determined by political party preference, not racial polarization. Noting that Hispanic voters in Texas were more likely to vote for Democratic candidates, who had a recent history of losing statewide races in Texas, the state's lawyers argued, "There is no evidence that Hispanic candidates or voters in Texas suffer any additional disadvantages beyond that shared by their fellow party members."[13] U.S. District Judge Nelva Gonzales Ramos of Corpus Christi upheld the statewide election system for judges after a trial of the lawsuit in 2018.

In most states, minorities are underrepresented on state courts, according to a 2008 study by the American Judicature Society. Hawaii had the highest percentage of minorities on appellate and general-jurisdiction trial courts, but it was an outlier at 65.1 percent. The next highest percentages were in Louisiana, New York, and Texas, each at about 20 percent. When the data were collected, there were no minority judges on appellate and general-jurisdiction trial courts in six states—Maine, Montana, New Hampshire, South Dakota, Vermont, and Wyoming.[14]

8.3.2 Women

The first woman to serve as a state district judge in Texas was Sarah T. Hughes of Dallas, who was appointed to the bench in 1935 by Governor James V. Allred, nineteen years before she and other women were allowed to serve on juries in Texas. She served until 1961, when she resigned to accept an appointment by President John F. Kennedy to the federal district bench. Ironically, Hughes is best known for swearing a grim-faced Lyndon B. Johnson into office aboard Air Force One on November 22, 1963, following Kennedy's assassination in Dallas.

Ruby Sondock of Houston was the first woman to serve on the Texas Supreme Court. She had been a state district judge before Governor Bill Clements named her to the high court on June 25, 1982, to fill a temporary vacancy. Sondock chose not to seek election to the seat and served only a few months. She later returned to the district bench. Barbara Culver, a state district judge from Midland, became the second female Supreme Court justice when Clements appointed her in February 1988 to fill another vacancy. Culver also served less than a year before being unseated in the 1988 general election. Democrat Rose Spector, a state district judge from San Antonio, became the first woman elected to the Texas Supreme Court when she unseated a Republican justice in 1992. By 2020, nine women had served on the Texas Supreme Court, including three women—Justices Eva Guzman, Debra Lehrmann, and Jane Bland—who were still on the court that year.

In 1994, Republican Sharon Keller, a former Dallas County prosecutor, became the first woman elected to the Texas Court of Criminal Appeals, and she became the first female presiding judge of the court in 2001. Four women, including Keller, served on the nine-member court in 2019, and more than 300 women served as judges at the county court level or higher in Texas that same year.[15]

In what may have been a sign of changes to come, women candidates in the March 2020 Democratic primary in Texas won all the races for court seats, about 30 in all, in which a woman was running against a man. They included female challengers who unseated five incumbent district court judges in Houston. Their next step was the general election in November.[16]

Judicial Controversies and the Search for Solutions

8.4 Characterize the judicial controversies in Texas and their impact on public perception of the courts.

Ever since a historical, political earthquake began to rattle Texas in the 1970s, state courts have been beset with conflict and controversy. Large campaign contributions from lawyers and other special interests to elected judges and judicial candidates periodically raise allegations that Texas has the best justice that money can buy. With millions of dollars at stake in crucial legal decisions, the Texas Supreme Court is often at the center of a philosophical and political battleground. Meanwhile, lengthy ballots, particularly in urban areas, make it increasingly difficult for most voters to choose intelligently among judicial candidates. And, as we already have discussed, minorities, who hold a disproportionately small number of judicial offices, continue to press for greater influence in electing judges. Although these issues and concerns may seem unrelated, they all cast a cloud over the Texas judiciary. Each, in its own way, undermines public confidence in the state courts and makes many Texans question how just their system of justice really is.

8.4.1 Judicial Activism

Conservative Democrats still dominated Texas politics at the beginning of the 1970s, as they had for several decades, and they held all nine seats on the Texas Supreme Court. More often than not, the high court sided with insurance companies, banks, utilities, and other large corporate entities when they were sued by unhappy customers and other consumers claiming an assortment of damages or grievances. These outcomes reflected the historic domination of state politics by a conservative, business-oriented establishment, which is discussed in more detail in other chapters in this book.

Establishment-oriented justices, usually elected with the support of the state's largest law firms, tended to view their role as strict constructionists. They believed the legislature enacted public policy and that the courts narrowly interpreted and applied the law. Judges did not engage in setting policy but honored legal precedent and prior case law, which historically had favored the interests of corporations over those of consumers, laborers, and the lower social classes.

The establishment, however, began to feel the first tremors of a major philosophical shakeup in the mid-1970s. The Texas Trial Lawyers Association, whose members represent consumers in lawsuits against businesses, doctors, and insurance companies, increased its political activity. In 1973, the legislature, with increased minority and female membership from single-member House districts ordered by the federal courts, enacted the Deceptive Trade Practices–Consumer Protection Act, which encouraged injured parties to take their grievances to court. Among other things, the new law allowed consumers to sue for attorneys' fees as well as compensatory and punitive damages.

Trial, or plaintiffs', attorneys, who usually receive a healthy percentage of the monetary damages awarded their clients, began contributing millions of dollars to Texas Supreme Court candidates who unseated conservative justices and began to philosophically reshape the court. The new, consumer-oriented court issued significant decisions making it easier for consumers to win large monetary awards for medical malpractice, faulty products, and other complaints against businesses and their insurers. The new activist, liberal interpretation of the law contrasted sharply with the traditional record of the court.

The business community and defense lawyers accused the new court majority of exceeding its constitutional authority by trying to write its own laws. Some business leaders contended that the court's activism endangered the state's economy by discouraging new businesses from moving to Texas, a fear that was soon to be put to partisan advantage by leaders of an emerging Republican majority in the state.

The controversy escalated in 1987 when the Texas Supreme Court upheld a record $11 billion judgment awarded Pennzoil Company in a dispute with Texaco Inc. Several members of the Supreme Court were even featured on a network television program that questioned whether justice was "for sale" in Texas.

The record judgment awarded Pennzoil came after a state district court jury in Houston determined that Texaco had wrongfully interfered in Pennzoil's attempt to acquire Getty Oil Company in 1984. In a segment on CBS-TV's *60 Minutes*, correspondent Mike Wallace pointed out that plaintiff's attorney Joe Jamail of Houston, who represented Pennzoil, had contributed $10,000 to the original trial judge in the case and thousands of dollars more to Texas Supreme Court justices. In criticizing the elective system that allowed Texas judges to legally accept large campaign contributions from lawyers who practiced before them, the program presented what already had been widely reported in Texas. After national exposure, Republican Governor Bill Clements and other Republicans renewed attacks on the Democratic justices.

8.4.2 Campaign Contributions and Republican Gains

Supreme Court Chief Justice John L. Hill, a former attorney general who had narrowly lost a gubernatorial race to Clements in 1978, had been a strong supporter of electing state judges and had spent more than $1 million winning the chief justice's seat in 1984. As did his colleagues on the court, he accepted many campaign contributions from lawyers. But in 1986, Hill announced that the political contributions to judicial races had become so excessive that the partisan system of electing state judges needed to be changed. He began to advocate a so-called **merit selection** plan of gubernatorial appointments of judges with periodic retention elections. But the other eight Supreme Court justices—like Hill, all Democrats—still favored the elective system, and the legislature ignored pleas for change.

Hill resigned from the court on January 1, 1988, to return to private law practice and lobby as a private citizen for changing the judicial selection method. His resignation and the midterm resignations of two other Democratic justices before the 1988 elections gave Republicans a golden opportunity to make historic inroads on the high court. The resignations also helped the business community begin to regain control of the court from plaintiffs' attorneys.

merit selection
A proposal under which the governor would appoint state judges from lists of potential nominees recommended by committees of experts. Appointed judges would have to run later in retention elections in which voters would simply decide whether a judge should remain in office or be replaced by another gubernatorial appointee.

Party realignment and midterm judicial appointments by Clements already had increased the number of Republican judges across the state, particularly on district courts in urban areas. But only one Republican had ever served on the Texas Supreme Court in modern times and that was a very short tenure: Will Garwood was appointed by Clements in 1979 to fill a vacancy but was defeated by Democrat C. L. Ray in the 1980 election.

GOP leaders had already been planning to recruit a Republican slate of candidates for the three Supreme Court seats that normally would have been on the ballot in 1988. Now, six seats were contested, including those held by three new Republican justices appointed by Clements to fill the unexpected vacancies. Even though a full Supreme Court term is six years, the governor's judicial appointees are required to run in the next election to keep their seats. Clements appointed Thomas R. Phillips, a state district judge from Houston, to succeed Hill and become the first Republican chief justice since the Reconstruction era more than 100 years earlier. The competing legal and financial interests in Texas understood that the six Texas Supreme Court races on the 1988 ballot would help set the philosophy of the court for years to come. Consequently, these were the most expensive court races in Texas history, with the twelve Republican and Democratic nominees raising $10 million in direct campaign contributions. Much of the money was spent on television advertising.

Contributions to the winners averaged $836,347, and some individual donations to candidates were as large as $65,000.[17] Reformers argued that such large contributions created an appearance of impropriety and eroded public confidence in the judiciary's independence.

But the successes of Republicans and conservative Democrats in the 1988 races probably hindered, more than helped, the cause of reforming the judicial selection process. The business and medical communities, which had considerable success fighting the plaintiffs' lawyers under the existing rules with large campaign contributions of their own, were pleased with the election results. "I'm a happy camper today," said Kim Ross, lobbyist for the Texas Medical Association, whose political action committee had supported two conservative Democratic winners and the three Republican victors.[18] In several key cases over the next few years, the Supreme Court began to demonstrate a rediscovered philosophy favoring business defendants over plaintiffs.[19]

Republicans won a fourth seat on the Texas Supreme Court in 1990 and a fifth in 1994, to give the GOP a majority for the first time since Reconstruction. Benefited by straight-party voting, Republican challengers in 1994 also unseated nineteen incumbent Democratic district judges in Harris County. Republicans completed their sweep of the high court in 1998.

Phillips, who had been the chief justice since 1988, resigned in midterm in 2004 to eventually enter private law practice. He believed the court's reputation had been enhanced during his tenure, but, as his predecessor had done after stepping down sixteen years earlier, he criticized the money-driven, partisan election system for judges.[20] Wallace Jefferson, who succeeded Phillips as chief justice and would serve until late 2013, would come to the same conclusion.[21]

8.4.3 Legislative Reaction to Judicial Activism

The business community moved its war against the trial lawyers to the legislature, which in 1987 enacted a so-called **tort reform** package that attempted to put some limits on personal injury lawsuits and damage judgments entered by the courts. A *tort* is a wrongful act over which a lawsuit can be brought. Insurance companies, which had been lobbying nationwide for states to set limits on jury awards in personal injury cases, were major proponents of the legislation. The Texas Civil Justice League,

tort reform
Changes in state law to put limits on personal injury lawsuits and damage judgments entered by the courts.

an organization of trade and professional associations, cities, and businesses, joined them. Governor Bill Clements enthusiastically supported the high-stakes campaign for change, but consumer groups and plaintiffs' lawyers opposed it.

Among other things, the 1987 tort reform laws limited governmental liability, attempted to discourage frivolous lawsuits, and limited the ability of claimants to collect damages for injuries that were largely their own fault. The new laws also set limits on punitive damages, which are designed to punish whoever caused an accident or an injury and often were awarded in addition to an injured party's compensation for actual losses.

Later legislative sessions, including those in 1995, 2003, and 2011, enacted other limits on lawsuits. The 1995 changes, major priorities of then-Governor George W. Bush, imposed even stricter limits on punitive damages and limited the liability of a party who is only partially responsible for an injury. The 2003 legislation, actively sought by Governor Rick Perry and a new Republican majority in the Texas House, set new restrictions on class action lawsuits—which are brought on behalf of large groups of people—and imposed new limits on money that can be awarded for noneconomic damages—such as pain, suffering, or disfigurement—in medical malpractice cases. A leading proponent for civil justice restrictions in recent years has been Texans for Lawsuit Reform (TLR), a business group whose political action committee has given millions of campaign dollars to legislators and legislative candidates, as well as members of the Texas Supreme Court.

Another strong tort reform advocate has been the Austin-based Texas Public Policy Foundation, a conservative, free enterprise think tank that has been influential with Texas's Republican leadership on a number of issues. In an article published in 2017, Kathleen Hunker, a senior policy analyst with the foundation, said the limits on lawsuits and civil liability have been good for Texas and its economy. "The Texas model works because it strives to keep as much capital as possible in the hands of market participants. . . . Again and again, time has shown that excessive liability impedes economic activity. By instituting common-sense limits on that liability, Texas gave its current and prospective residents a reason to invest in their future and that of the state. The results speak for themselves." [22]

8.4.4 Winners and Losers—A New Era of Judicial Activism?

In a study released in 1999, Texas Watch, a consumer advocacy group, said that doctors, hospitals, and other business-related litigants had been big winners before the Texas Supreme Court during the previous four years and that consumers had fared poorly. This was a period during which most court members received substantial campaign funding from doctors, insurers, and other business interests. Most of the opinions were issued after the Texas legislature had enacted tort reform laws setting limits on civil lawsuits.

The study determined that physicians and hospitals had won 86 percent of their appeals, most of which involved medical malpractice claims brought by injured patients or their families. Other consistent winners were insurance companies (73 percent), manufacturers (72 percent), banks (67 percent), utilities (65 percent), and other businesses (68 percent). Insurance policyholders, injured workers, injured patients, and other individual litigants won only 36 percent of the time.[23] "Individuals are the lowest link in the legal food chain that ends in the Texas Supreme Court," said Walt Borges, who directed the study. "The study raises a question about the fairness of the Texas Supreme Court and state law," he added.[24]

CBS-TV's *60 Minutes*, which had turned the national spotlight on plaintiffs' lawyers and their political contributions to Texas judges in 1987, revisited the Texas judiciary in a follow-up program in 1998. Noting that the partisan system of electing judges had remained unchanged, the new *60 Minutes* segment suggested that justice may still be for sale in Texas, but with different people—the business community—now wielding the influence. The Texas legislature in 1995 imposed modest limits on campaign contributions to judges and judicial candidates and restricted the periods during which judges and their challengers could raise funds. A judge, however, still could receive as much as $30,000 from members of the same law firm and as much as $300,000 in total contributions from special interests through political action committees.

In 2012, Texas Watch, the consumer advocacy group, issued a follow-up report, analyzing the Texas Supreme Court's record from 2000 to 2010. During that period, the report said, consumer-plaintiffs lost 79 percent of the cases decided by the high court when the defendants were insurance companies, health care providers, corporations, or governmental entities. The report also found that the Supreme Court overturned 74 percent of decisions in which local juries had found in favor of consumers.[25] Texas Watch and other critics said Republican justices on this court were as much "judicial activists" for pressing their conservative, business-oriented viewpoint as the consumer-oriented Democratic justices had been for their opposing viewpoint in the 1970s.

In still another report, issued in 2008, Texas Watch analyzed campaign contributions to all incumbent Texas Supreme Court justices from 2000 to 2008 and the success rate of major contributors—many with strong ties to the business community—who had cases before the court. The average success rate was 54 percent for donors who gave less than $10,000 to court members and was 64 percent for those who gave more than $25,000, the consumer group reported. "There appears to be a strong correlation between the amount of money contributed and an entity's chance of success with the court," the study concluded.[26]

Texas Supreme Court justices rarely answer such allegations directly, at least in the media. Instead, they say they simply follow the law as they see it, and they see it from a decidedly different viewpoint than the plaintiff-oriented justices who were accused of judicial activism in the 1970s. Because of the tort reform changes in civil justice laws since the 1970s, they also are deciding cases under more legal restrictions than justices of the earlier era. Chief Justice Wallace Jefferson, like his two immediate predecessors, was troubled by the perception that money talks in the Texas judiciary. "I am concerned by the public's perception that money in judicial races influences outcomes. This is an area where perception itself destroys public confidence," he said in a State of the Judiciary address to the legislature in 2009.[27]

Shortly after leaving office in 2013, Jefferson discussed the issue in some detail in an interview with *The Atlantic*. "We shouldn't have partisan elections," he said. "I do not like the concept of a Republican or a Democratic judge. I think fundraising undermines the confidence in a fair and impartial judicial system. So I would change it completely if I were king." But the legislature, under both Democratic and Republican control, has repeatedly refused to scrap the partisan election system because both political parties have opposed change. Texas elects its judges supposedly to keep them accountable to the voters, Jefferson told *The Atlantic*. But most voters, particularly in urban counties with many judges on the election ballot, don't even know who the judges and judicial candidates are, much less their qualifications. All too often, the former chief justice said, they vote for a straight partisan ticket because they "have no clue about the experience or background of these candidates."[28]

Jefferson's successor, Chief Justice Nathan Hecht, also a Republican, echoed those concerns in an address to the legislature in 2019, following the losses in the 2018 election of many incumbent Republican judges at the appellate and district court levels to Democratic challengers, with straight-ticket voting a factor. Straight-ticket voting, which allows a voter to cast one ballot for all the Republican or all the Democratic candidates for all the offices in an election, has been banned in Texas, beginning with the 2020 election. Texas' district and appellate courts had "lost seven centuries of judicial experience at a single stroke," he said. "Qualifications did not drive their (challengers') election. Partisan politics did."

Hecht, whose own six elections to the Supreme Court over a long judicial career had been assisted by straight-ticket Republican voting, advocated a merit selection system in which the governor would appoint judges who later would run in retention elections (explained below) to keep their seats.[29]

8.4.5 Searching for Solutions

The composition of the courts makes a difference. Although some may argue that the role of a judge is simply to apply the law to the facts and issues of a specific case, judges bring to the courts their own values, philosophical views, and life experiences, and these factors serve to filter their interpretations of the law—and determine the shape of justice for millions of people.

Methods of selecting state judges vary widely among the states. Texas is one of only a few states with a formal, partisan election system for all of its judges (see Figure 8–4). A handful of other states have partisan elections for some lower court judges but require appointments by the governor for judges on the higher, appellate courts. Several states have nonpartisan judicial elections for some or all of their judges, while other states use some form of merit selection, in which judges are appointed by the governor from recommendations made by nominating commissions. Some of these alternatives could be improvements over Texas's current system, but no alternative would necessarily eliminate all undue political influences on the judiciary or make courts more representative of the whole population.[30]

FIGURE 8–4   HOW STATES SELECT THEIR JUDGES

There is no uniformity in the manner in which states select judges. In an effort to reduce the impact of politics and campaign contributions, many states have moved toward nonpartisan elections or gubernatorial appointments with retention elections. With the exception of municipal judges, Texas selects judges by partisan election. This map shows how states select their appellate judges.

SOURCE: Data from the American Judicature Society, "Judicial Selection in the States: Appellate and General Jurisdiction Courts." Updated 2017.

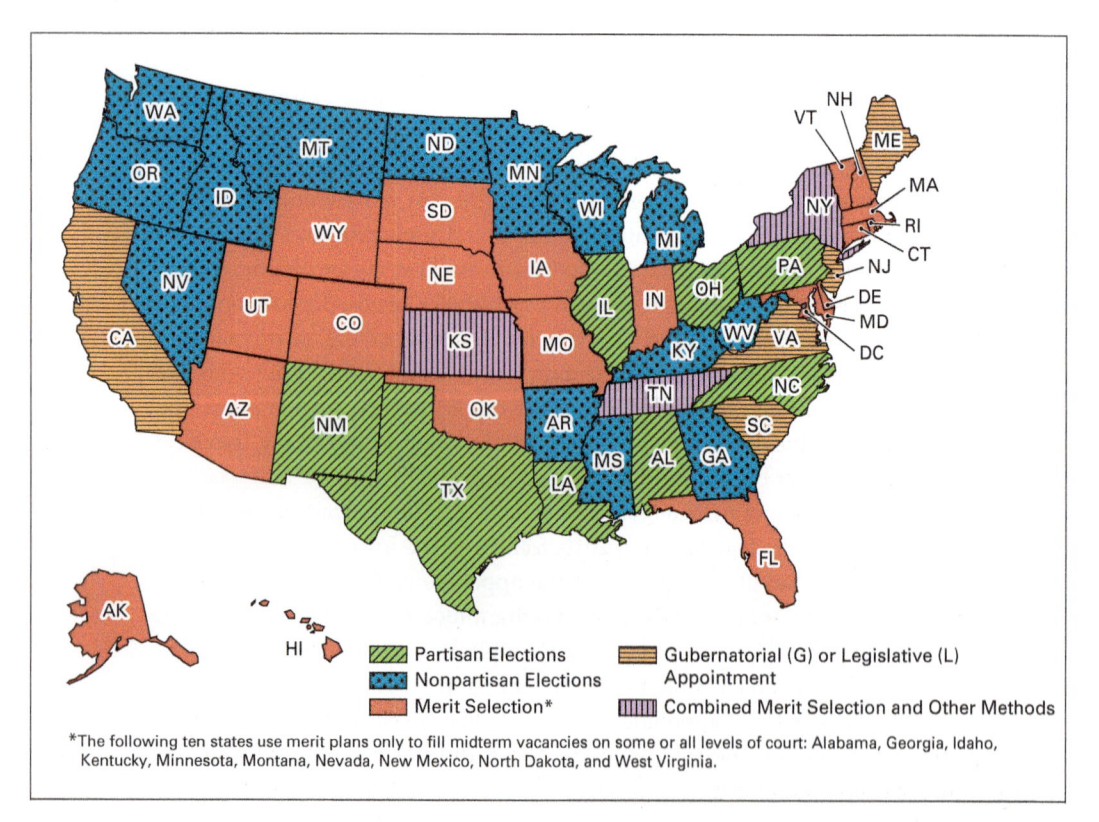

*The following ten states use merit plans only to fill midterm vacancies on some or all levels of court: Alabama, Georgia, Idaho, Kentucky, Minnesota, Montana, Nevada, New Mexico, North Dakota, and West Virginia.

Stricter limits on the amount of campaign funds that judges and judicial candidates can raise from lawyers and other special interests could reduce the appearance of influence peddling in the judiciary and temper the high-stakes war between the trial lawyers and the business community for philosophical control of the courts. Campaign finance reform also could help build or restore public confidence in the impartiality of the judiciary. Such reform, however, may not improve opportunities for minorities to win election to the bench. Nor would it shorten the long election ballots that discourage Texans from casting informed votes in judicial races.

Nonpartisan judicial elections may not help elect more minority judges or shorten long election ballots either, although they could eliminate partisan bickering on the multimember appellate courts and eliminate the possibility that a poorly qualified candidate is elected simply because of his or her party affiliation, which sometimes occurred when Texas allowed straight-ticket voting. Now that straight-ticket voting has been eliminated in Texas, it remains to be seen what effect that will have on voting for judicial offices, whose candidates are largely unknown to most voters. Candidates' party affiliations, however, will still be listed by their names on the ballot.

Under the merit selection plan (sometimes referred to as the "Missouri Plan"), the governor would appoint judges from lists of nominees recommended by nominating commissions. The appointed judges would have to run later in **retention elections** to keep their seats, but they would not have opponents on the ballot. Voters would simply decide whether a judge should remain in office or be removed—and replaced by another gubernatorial appointee.

retention election
Election in which judges run on their own records rather than against other candidates. Voters cast their ballots on the question of whether the incumbent judge should stay in office.

Under a merit selection system, interest groups still could apply pressure on the governor and members of the nominating commissions. The nominating panels could be required to make ethnically diverse recommendations to the governor, but minority appointees still could be at a disadvantage in retention elections if they had to run statewide or countywide, rather than in smaller geographic districts. Despite their popularity among minorities, district elections for judges still are viewed by many decision makers as a form of **ward politics** that may be appropriate or desirable for legislative seats but not for judges. Judges, they argue, do not represent a particular constituency.

ward politics
Term, often with negative connotations, that refers to partisan politics linked to political favoritism.

Crime and Punishment

8.5 Describe the legal and constitutional rights of suspects, the classes of crimes and punishments in the Texas Penal Code, and the administration of criminal justice in Texas.

Criminal justice is a multistep process designed not only to protect society from crime but also to reduce the risk of innocent people being punished for crimes they did not commit. Consequently, judges and other criminal justice officials operate under numerous constitutional restrictions; but, even so, mistakes sometimes occur. Even if you are never charged with a serious crime, you may very well find yourself involved in a criminal case as an attorney or a juror weighing evidence against a criminal defendant. So, the more you know about the rights of criminal suspects, the history of criminal justice in Texas, and political attitudes impacting the criminal justice process, the better prepared you will be to navigate the system, whatever your role.

8.5.1 Rights of Suspects

Under both the U.S. Constitution and the Texas Constitution, a person charged with a crime is presumed innocent until the state can prove guilt beyond a reasonable doubt to a judge or a jury. The state also has the burden to prosecute fairly and to follow principles of procedural due process outlined in constitutional and statutory law and interpreted by the courts. Even persons charged with the most heinous crimes retain these fundamental rights. This process is designed to protect an individual from governmental abuses and to lessen the chance that an innocent person is wrongly convicted of a crime.

In Texas, as well as in other states, these rights have sometimes been violated. Over the years, however, the courts, particularly the federal courts, have strengthened the enforcement of these rights. Through a case-by-case process, the U.S. Supreme Court has applied the Bill of Rights to the states by way of the "due process of law" and the "equal protection of law" clauses of the Fourteenth Amendment to the U.S. Constitution. The failure of police or prosecutors to comply with specific procedures for handling a person accused of a crime may result in charges against an individual being dropped or a conviction being reversed on appeal.

Arrested suspects must be taken before a magistrate—usually a justice of the peace or a municipal court judge—to be formally informed of the offense or offenses with which they are charged and told their legal rights. Depending on the charges, a bond (bail) may be set to allow them to get out of jail and remain free pending their trials. Suspects have the right to remain silent, to consult with an attorney, to have an attorney present during questioning by law enforcement officers or prosecutors, and to be warned that any statement they make can be used against them in a trial. Defendants who cannot afford a lawyer must be provided with court-appointed attorneys at taxpayer expense. The U.S. Supreme Court extended many of these protections to the states in the landmark **Miranda ruling** in 1966.

All criminal defendants have the right to a trial by jury but—except in capital murder cases—may waive a jury trial and have their cases decided by a judge. Defendants may plead guilty, not guilty, or *nolo contendere* (no contest). Prosecutors and defense attorneys settle many cases through plea bargaining, a process described earlier in this chapter. The trial judge does not have to accept the plea bargain but usually does. When defendants choose to have their guilt or innocence determined by a judge, the judge also determines the punishment if the defendant is convicted. A jury can return a guilty verdict only if all jurors agree that the defendant is guilty beyond a reasonable doubt. If the jury cannot reach a unanimous verdict—even after lengthy negotiations and prodding from the judge—the judge must declare a mistrial. In that case, the prosecution has to seek a new trial with another jury or drop the charges. In a jury trial, a defendant may choose to have the punishment set by the jury. If not, the judge determines the punishment.

8.5.2 Punishment of Criminals

Jury trials are required in **capital murder** cases, which are punishable by death or life in prison without parole. Executions in Texas used to be carried out by electrocution at the state prison unit in downtown Huntsville. In 1972, the U.S. Supreme Court halted executions in all states by striking down all the death penalty laws then on the books as unconstitutional. The high Court held that capital punishment, as then practiced, violated the constitutional prohibition against cruel and unusual punishment because it could be applied in a discriminatory fashion. Not only could virtually any act of murder be punished by death under the old Texas law, but so could rape and certain other crimes.

In 1973, the Texas legislature rewrote the death penalty statute to try to meet the Supreme Court's standards by defining capital crimes as murder committed under specific circumstances. The list was expanded later and now includes the murder of a law enforcement officer or firefighter who is on duty, murder committed during the course of certain other major crimes, murder for hire, murder of more than one person, murder of a prison guard or employee, murder committed while escaping or attempting to escape from a penal institution, and murder of a child younger than age 6.

Miranda ruling
A far-reaching decision of the U.S. Supreme Court that requires law enforcement officers to warn a criminal suspect of his or her right to remain silent and have an attorney present during questioning.

nolo contendere
A plea of no contest to a criminal charge.

capital murder
Murder committed under certain circumstances for which the death penalty or life in prison must be imposed.

A jury that has found a person guilty of capital murder must answer certain questions about the defendant before choosing between death or life imprisonment, the only punishments available. Jurors must consider whether a convicted murderer will be a continuing danger to society as well as whether there were mitigating circumstances, including evidence of intellectual disability, before deciding punishment.

The first execution under the 1973 Texas law was carried out in 1982. By then, the legislature, acting in 1977, had changed the method of execution from the electric chair to the intravenous injection of a lethal substance. Historically, the death penalty has enjoyed strong political popularity in Texas, which leads the nation in executions. But it also has been the focus of increasing controversy in recent years. The death penalty as a policy issue will be discussed in more detail in Chapter 14.

After capital murder, the most serious criminal offense is a first-degree **felony** (e.g., aggravated sexual assault, noncapital murder or theft of property valued at $200,000 or more), punishable by a prison sentence of five to ninety-nine years or life. Second-degree felonies, such as theft of property valued at $100,000 to $200,000 or reckless injury to a child, are punishable by two to twenty years in prison. Third-degree felonies, including theft of property valued at $20,000 to $100,000 or a drive-by shooting in which no one is injured, are punishable by two to ten years in prison. State jail felonies, which include many property crimes and drug offenses, are punishable by up to two years in a state-run jail or time in a community corrections program, each of which is supposed to emphasize rehabilitation as well as punishment.

felony
A criminal offense that can be punished by imprisonment and/or a fine. This is a more serious offense than a misdemeanor.

Less serious crimes are classified as Class A, B, or C **misdemeanors**. Crimes such as theft of cable service and some stalking offenses are examples of Class A misdemeanors and are punishable by a maximum $4,000 fine and one year in a county jail. Making terrorristic threats or possessing as much as four ounces of marijuana are examples of Class B misdemeanors and carry a maximum sentence of 180 days in a county jail and a $2,000 fine. Class C misdemeanors include theft of property valued at less than $20 and assault without bodily injury. They are punishable by a maximum $500 fine.

misdemeanor
A minor criminal offense punishable by a fine or a short sentence in the county jail. This is less serious than a felony.

People convicted of crimes can be sentenced to **probation** (also called community supervision). They are not sent to prison but must meet certain conditions, such as restrictions on where they travel and with whom they associate. Except for those under the death penalty and some capital murderers serving life sentences, convicted felons sentenced to prison can become eligible for **parole**—early release under supervisory restrictions—after serving a portion of their sentences. Capital murderers sentenced to life in prison before a significant change in state law in 2005 can be considered for parole after serving forty years. Those sentenced after the 2005 law, which imposed life without parole for capital murderers who are not sentenced to death, cannot be paroled. The Board of Pardons and Paroles, which is appointed by the governor, makes all parole decisions.

probation
A procedure under which a convicted criminal is not sent to prison if he or she meets certain conditions, such as restrictions on travel and with whom he or she associates.

parole
The early release of an inmate from prison, subject to certain conditions.

8.5.3 The Politics of Criminal Justice

The Texas Court of Criminal Appeals must try to balance the constitutional rights of convicts against the public welfare—a role that often puts the court at the center of major philosophical and political battles. The combatants on one side of the debate are the prosecutors—the elected district and county attorneys—who do not like to see the convictions they have won reversed. Judges of the trial courts also are sensitive to reversals, and so are the police and sheriff's departments that arrest the defendants and provide the evidence on which criminal convictions are based.

On the other side are defense attorneys, who have an obligation to protect the rights and interests of their clients and who in their appeals often attack procedures used by police, prosecutors, and trial judges. Also on this side are civil libertarians, who insist that a criminal defendant's every right—even the most technical—be protected, and minority groups, which have challenged the conduct of trials in which minorities have been excluded from juries weighing the fate of minority defendants.

The Texas Court of Criminal Appeals signaled a shift toward a strongly conservative philosophy after the 1994 elections of Judges Sharon Keller and Steve Mansfield increased the number of Republicans on the court to three. During the first thirteen months the new judges were in office, the court ordered the reinstatement of two death sentences it had reversed before the arrival of Keller and Mansfield.

The Republican takeover of the court was completed in 1998, and Keller, a former prosecutor, was elected presiding judge in 2000. The court then began compiling a strong, pro-prosecutorial record, particularly in death penalty cases. The court upheld a number of death sentences that later were overturned by federal courts. In one case, it affirmed a capital conviction even though the defendant's attorney had slept through part of his trial. In another case, it upheld a death sentence despite the fact that a prosecution witness had argued improperly that the defendant was a future danger to society, partly based on the defendant being Hispanic.

Some scholars and participants in the criminal justice system believe the Court of Criminal Appeals' strong prosecutorial stance, particularly in death penalty cases, can be attributed to the state's system of electing judges. The judges, who have to periodically face the voters, often with opponents on the ballot, know the death penalty is popular in Texas, and their decisions, at least in part, are believed to be politically guided. In this view, other Texas judges at the trial and appellate levels also consider that being tough on criminals, particularly those convicted of serious crimes, may be essential to reelection. "One of the few credible campaign promises judges can make is to be tough on crime. Crime seems easy to understand and resonates with voters," according to a webtext analysis by the Texas Politics Project. "Consequently, Texas judges may seem more committed to racking up convictions than to ensuring justice, especially during campaign season."[31]

The Reuters news agency reviewed 2,102 state high court rulings on death penalty appeals from thirty-seven states over a fifteen-year period and published its findings in September 2015. In the fifteen states where high court judges or justices are elected, including Texas, the courts rejected the death sentence in only 11 percent of appeals, Reuters reported. This was less than half of the 26 percent death penalty reversal rate in seven states where the judges are appointed. In fifteen states where justices are initially appointed but must face voters in retention elections, 15 percent of death penalty decisions were reversed. "The findings, several legal experts said, support the argument that the death penalty is arbitrary and unconstitutional because politics—in addition to the facts—influence the outcome of an appeal," the news agency wrote.[32]

In a separate, recent study of sentencing practices by Superior Court judges in Washington state, which selects its judges in nonpartisan elections, scholars Carlos Berdejo and Noam Yuchtman concluded that the prison sentences handed down for serious crimes were about 10 percent longer on average near the end of a judge's term, when he or she was facing reelection, than they were at the beginning of a term.[33]

8.5.4 Slamming the Courthouse Door on a Last-Gasp Appeal

Texas Court of Criminal Appeals Presiding Judge Sharon Keller, a former prosecutor, is a strong supporter of the death penalty. In the view of some lawyers, however, Keller went too far when she cut off a condemned inmate's attempt to file a last-gasp appeal only a few hours before he was executed.

Lawyers for Michael Richard, a convicted murderer and rapist, attempted to halt his execution on September 25, 2007, following the U.S. Supreme Court's decision earlier that day to accept for review two Kentucky cases challenging the constitutionality of chemicals used for lethal injection. Death penalty opponents had argued that the execution method might amount to cruel and unusual punishment, prohibited by the U.S. Constitution, because the condemned might feel intense pain as the mixture of drugs was administered. At that time, Texas used the same chemicals as Kentucky.

Richard's attorneys tried to get a stay of execution for their client until the nation's high Court decided the Kentucky cases, but computer problems at one lawyer's office slowed the preparation of their appeal. When they asked the Court of Criminal Appeals for more time, Keller refused, and Richard was executed later that evening.

Twenty lawyers from across Texas, including many who were prominent, later filed a formal complaint against Keller with the State Commission on Judicial Conduct. The complaint accused the judge of violating the constitutional due process of a condemned man. Keller blamed Richard's lawyers for being late. The State Commission on Judicial Conduct eventually issued a minor public sanction against the judge, but it was later vacated on a technicality.

Ultimately, after completing its review of the lethal chemicals used in executions, the U.S. Supreme Court upheld their constitutionality. Keller easily won reelection the next time she was on the ballot in 2012 and again in 2018.

8.5.5 Criminal Injustices

Although people accused of crimes are protected by constitutional and statutory rights, miscarriages of justice occur—either because of sloppy police work, overzealous prosecution, or tragic human mistakes—and innocent individuals are sent to prison and, sometimes, death row. Now, many of those miscarriages are being discovered, thanks largely to the development of DNA testing, but not before a good number of individuals have spent years in prison for crimes they didn't commit. The state offers monetary compensation to wrongly convicted people but obviously cannot restore the years lost from an individual's life. Through 2017, the state had paid $109 million to 109 men and women who had been wrongfully convicted. Combined, they had served 1,160 years in prison for crimes they didn't commit.[34] Some of the exonerated inmates were rescued from death row. The state has never admitted executing an innocent person, but some critics dispute that stance, an issue that will be discussed in more detail in Chapter 14.

Each miscarriage of justice is tragic in its own way, but two that received extensive media coverage in recent years were the convictions of Timothy Cole and Michael Morton. Timothy Cole was a student at Texas Tech University in Lubbock when he was wrongly accused of rape. He was convicted in 1986 and sentenced to prison. DNA testing later proved his innocence; he was exonerated by a judge in 2009 and pardoned by Governor Rick Perry in 2010. But his exoneration came years after Cole had died in prison in 1999 of a severe asthma attack.

Michael Morton served almost twenty-five years in prison for a crime—the murder of his wife, Christine—that he didn't commit, but he lived to witness his own exoneration. Christine Morton was bludgeoned to death in the couple's Georgetown home in Williamson County, near Austin, in 1986 while Michael Morton was away. He, nevertheless, was convicted of her murder and sentenced to life in prison. He was released in 2011 after attorneys, including members of the New York–based Innocence Project, won a protracted legal fight to obtain DNA testing on a blood-stained bandanna that had been found near the crime scene. DNA tests pointed to another man as the likely suspect, and that suspect was arrested, tried, and convicted after Morton's release.

Morton's attorneys also began an investigation to determine if prosecutors had deliberately withheld evidence from his defense lawyers that could have exonerated him at the time of his trial. Texas prosecutors are required to provide any evidence that could be used to support defendants' innocence. DNA testing was not available when Morton's wife was murdered; however, his attorneys said that other evidence, which was never disclosed to his defense team, was. The undisclosed evidence, they

MICHAEL MORTON

Michael Morton (center), who served almost twenty-five years in prison for a murder he didn't commit before being released on the basis of DNA evidence, is greeted by well-wishers.

said, included a transcript of a taped interview in which Christine Morton's mother told an investigator that the Morton's 3-year-old son apparently witnessed the attack on his mother and said that his father was not home when it happened. Also undisclosed was another police report that a stranger had been seen walking into a wooded area behind the Mortons' home on several occasions before the murder. The suspect eventually convicted of Christine Morton's death also was implicated in the murder of another woman, bludgeoned in her bed at her home about twelve miles away in Austin, while Michael Morton was in prison.

Ken Anderson, the district attorney who prosecuted Morton, had been well respected in his politically conservative community. While Morton was in prison, Governor Rick Perry promoted Anderson to fill a vacancy on a state district court bench, and Anderson was still a judge when Morton was released. He issued a public apology but denied any misconduct in prosecuting the case. A judge in a special court of inquiry determined that Anderson had intentionally withheld evidence that could have spared Morton from prison. The State Bar of Texas also filed a civil lawsuit accusing Anderson of professional misconduct. Anderson resigned his judgeship in 2013 as part of a settlement agreement with prosecutors and the State Bar. He also gave up his law license and was sentenced to ten days in jail after being found in contempt of court for telling Morton's trial judge, years earlier, that he had no evidence to turn over to defense lawyers.[35]

Increased Policy Role of the State Courts

8.6 Illustrate the increased policy role of the state courts with examples.

The federal judiciary has historically had more influence than the state courts in molding public policy and, over the years, has been at the center of political debate over the proper role of the judiciary in the policymaking process. This debate, often framed in terms of judicial activism versus judicial restraint, attempts to address the question of where judicial interpretation of the law and the Constitution ends and making laws in the courtroom begins. Similar debate, as discussed earlier in this chapter, has revolved around the Texas Supreme Court's rulings in business and consumer—or tort reform—cases. Much of the Texas Supreme Court's time historically has been spent refereeing often limited disputes among individuals and businesses, and it still is. In recent years, however, the Texas Supreme Court has increasingly played an active role in shaping broader public policies and addressing significant constitutional issues. Learning more about this role is key to navigating the state's policymaking process, which will be discussed in more detail in Chapter 14.

8.6.1 The Courts and Education

In one of its most significant and best-known rulings, the Texas Supreme Court, in the *Edgewood* v. *Kirby* school finance case in 1989, unanimously ordered major changes in the financing of public education to provide more equity between rich and poor school districts. Poor districts brought the lawsuit against the state after years of legislative inaction against a property tax–based finance system had produced huge disparities in local resources and the quality of local schools.

The unanimous opinion, written by then-Justice Oscar Mauzy, a Democrat, held that the school finance law on the books at the time violated a constitutional requirement for an efficient education system. The ruling was the product of considerable compromise among the nine justices, but compliance did not come easily. The first two plans the legislature enacted in response to the court's order were struck down by the high court. The legislature finally satisfied the court's majority in 1993 with the so-called Robin Hood law, which required wealthier school districts to share tax revenue with poor districts. The Texas Supreme Court upheld the law in a 5–4 decision in January 1995. By that time, a majority of the court's members were Republicans.

The Robin Hood law didn't completely close the funding gap between rich and poor school districts. It is still on the books, but there have been subsequent lawsuits over school funding and other changes to the school finance system. The most recent lawsuit, brought by several hundred school districts, resulted in a state district judge's ruling in 2013 that the school finance system was again unconstitutional because of inadequate and inequitable state funding of school districts. The Texas Supreme Court reversed that ruling in 2016, holding that the school finance system, although deficient, was constitutional. This issue will be discussed in more detail in Chapter 14.

In 1992, a state district judge in Brownsville ruled in *Richards* v. *LULAC* that the state's system of funding higher education also was unconstitutional because it shortchanged Hispanics in South Texas. However, the Texas Supreme Court reversed that decision and upheld the higher education system.[36]

In another education case with major implications, *Texas Education Agency* v. *Leeper*, the Texas Supreme Court in 1994 upheld the right of Texas parents to educate their own children. Ending a ten-year legal battle, the court overturned a Texas Education Agency ruling that home schools were illegal. The court held that a home school was legitimate if parents used books, workbooks, or other written materials and met "basic educational goals" by teaching basic subjects.[37] By 2015, an estimated 350,000 children were being home-schooled in Texas, and the issue was back before the Texas Supreme Court. In this case, *McIntyre* v. *El Paso Independent School District*, the court was asked to rule on what school districts could do to ensure that all the educational needs of home-schooled children were being met. Ruling in 2016, the court sided with a home-schooling family, which had been accused by a relative of not properly educating its children, but the court failed to address the larger constitutional issue of whether home-schooled children had to be properly educated. Although Texas requires home-schooling families to meet "basic educational goals," it doesn't require tests or another system of measuring how well home-schooled children are taught.[38]

8.6.2 The Courts and Environmental Policies

In recent years, the Texas Supreme Court has issued landmark rulings involving major environmental issues, including water rights and open beaches. In each case, the court said private property rights prevailed over historical traditions, prompting much political debate and likely setting the stage for more lawsuits on each issue.

WATER RIGHTS In February 2012, in a major water-rights case, *Edwards Aquifer Authority and the State of Texas* v. *Burrell Day and Joel McDaniel,* the Texas Supreme Court ruled in favor of two farmers who had challenged governmental restrictions on how much water they could pump from a well on their own land. In a significant change from previous regulatory practice, the court held that the owner of the property above the water source also owns that groundwater. The ruling was viewed as a substantial victory for landowners. But environmentalists greeted it with concern; they feared the ruling would curtail state water conservation efforts at a time when the state's water resources were rapidly being depleted in the face of a drought and continued population growth.[39]

The next year, the Fourth Court of Appeals in San Antonio issued a similar ruling when it held that Glenn and JoLynn Bragg had the right to pump as much water from the Edwards Aquifer as they needed for their 100-acre pecan orchard in Hondo. The Braggs owned the property over the aquifer, but the Edwards Aquifer Authority, as a conservation measure, had restricted how much water they could use. The authority imposed pumping restrictions to protect San Antonio's major water supply source and to protect endangered species of wildlife that lived in the aquifer. But the Fourth Court, in *Edwards Aquifer Authority* v. *Glenn and JoLynn Bragg,* held that the governmental restrictions on the Braggs' pumping rights amounted to a "taking" of their property rights in violation of the state constitution. Writing for the court, Justice Sandee Bryan Marion said the Braggs' property rights outweighed "the importance of protecting terrestrial and aquatic life, domestic and municipal water supplies, the operation of existing industries and the economic development of the state."[40] Some water rights specialists predicted more legal battles over this increasingly critical issue.

OPEN BEACHES Texas has had a long, historic tradition of public access to beaches, even the strips of beaches in front of privately owned property. The legislature codified public beach access in the Open Beaches Act of 1959, and Texas voters put it in the state constitution in 2009. But, in 2010, the Texas Supreme Court, ruling in *Severance* v. *Patterson,* struck another blow for private property rights that, in the view of many environmentalists and other beach-lovers, severely weakened the open beaches law.

In 2005, after Hurricane Rita had dramatically eroded Galveston's beaches, Carol Severance, a beachfront property owner on Galveston's West End, sued the Texas General Land Office to prevent the agency from initiating condemnation proceedings against her house, which now was much closer to the water and considered to be on a public beach. Beach erosion is a continual process on Gulf Coast barrier islands, such as Galveston. And for many years, the state had enforced a "rolling easement," meaning that when gradual erosion, rises in sea level, or storms pushed the beach landward, the strip of public beach also moved, sometimes onto what previously had been private property. But in this case, the Texas Supreme Court majority ruled that the "rolling easement" didn't apply after storms. What used to be public beach was now under water, and Severance's house was still on private property, the court held.

Then-state Land Commissioner Jerry Patterson, then-Attorney General Greg Abbott, the Galveston Chamber of Commerce, and numerous other parties sharply criticized the ruling and asked the court for a rehearing. But in March 2012 the high

Court upheld its earlier decision. "It seems that the Open Beaches Act—at least for Galveston's West End—is dead, thanks to the Supreme Court. This is truly a sad day," Patterson said.[41] But Patterson's successor as land commissioner, George P. Bush, supported the Supreme Court ruling.

PLASTIC BAGS In 2018, the Texas Supreme Court said cities could not prohibit the use of plastic bags for shopping because the local bans violated a state law governing waste containers. The case, *Laredo Merchants Association* v. *The City of Laredo,* originated in the border city but was expected to nullify bans in Austin and other cities as well. Laredo imposed its ban as an anti-pollution measure in 2015 and was sued by the Laredo Merchants Association, which contended the local prohibition was illegal. An attorney for the merchants said single-use plastic bags were defined as legal containers by the state. A state district court upheld the ban, but an appellate court ruled for the merchants and overturned it. The city then appealed to the Texas Supreme Court, where Texas Attorney General Ken Paxton joined the merchants in arguing that the Laredo ordinance should be struck down. Paxton said Laredo and other cities "flout the law" with bans against single-use bags.[42]

8.6.3 The Courts and Abortion Rights

In 1998, dealing with another controversial issue, the Texas Supreme Court upheld $1.2 million in damages against antiabortion protesters who had staged massive demonstrations at Houston abortion clinics during the 1992 Republican National Convention. Some clinics had been vandalized and patients harassed. In *Operation Rescue–National* v. *Planned Parenthood of Houston and Southeast Texas, Inc.*, the high Court upheld most of the restrictions a lower court had set on demonstrations near the clinics and the homes of several doctors who performed abortions. The court said it was trying to balance free speech rights with the rights of the clinics to conduct business, the rights of women to have access to pregnancy counseling and abortion services, and privacy rights of physicians.[43]

The Texas Supreme Court became embroiled in the abortion issue again in 2000 after a state law went into effect requiring parents to be notified by doctors before their minor daughters could have abortions. The law included a "judicial bypass" provision, giving a young woman who did not want her parents to be told an opportunity to convince a judge that she was mature and well informed enough to make an abortion decision by herself or that notifying her parents would be harmful. Acting on several early cases, the Texas Supreme Court set guidelines for district judges to follow in making bypass decisions.

In another abortion case, *Charles E. Bell* v. *Low-Income Women of Texas*, decided in 2002, the Texas Supreme Court held that the state's refusal to pay for medically necessary abortions for poor women did not violate the Texas Constitution. The court ruled that the restriction on funding abortions for women on Medicaid did not discriminate by gender and advanced a legitimate governmental interest of favoring childbirth over abortion.[44]

Lawsuits over recent laws enacted by the Texas legislature to restrict abortions, which will be discussed in Chapter 14, were filed and tried in federal, not state, courts.

8.6.4 The Courts and Voting

Mail-in voting is restricted in Texas. One exception is for voters who claim a disability or illness that prevents them from voting in person. During the coronavirus pandemic in 2020, the Texas Democratic Party and voting rights groups filed a lawsuit in state district court claiming that exception should be applied to people who feared contracting the potentially deadly virus at a polling place, and a state district judge agreed. But the effort was opposed by Attorney General Ken Paxton and other

Republicans, who argued that expanded mail-in voting would encourage voter fraud. An all-Republican Texas Supreme Court sided with Paxton and the Republicans, ruling that a lack of immunity to the coronavirus alone failed to meet the requirement for mail-in voting. But the court also noted that it was up to voters to evaluate their own physical conditions in determining whether they qualified for the mail-in exception. Applications for mail-in ballots didn't require voters to specify what their disability was or to provide documentation.[45] A federal lawsuit also was filed over the mail-in voting dispute, which will be discussed further in Chapter 11.

CONCLUSION

Although the purpose of this chapter was not to encourage you to become a lawyer or a judge, you may find that the legal profession is what you want, and if so, go for it. You have learned in this chapter how historical attitudes have helped shape Texas's sense of justice and how some aspects of the Texas judiciary compare to those of other states and the federal court system. You also have learned something about judicial responsibility and fairness: how those qualities can't be taken for granted, and how easy it is to cloud the all-important public perception that courtrooms are above reproach. Remember that the fair administration of justice is crucial in a democratic society; that jury duty is just that—a duty on which justice often depends; and that, despite our society's high ideals, justice is often tempered by political and personal beliefs and human prejudices and mistakes. The more you know about how Texas's judicial system has evolved—and continues to evolve—the better prepared you will be to navigate this system if you find yourself in it—as an attorney, plaintiff, defendant, witness, or juror.

FRONTIER JUSTICE

Justice of the Peace Roy Bean, the legendary "Law West of the Pecos," is shown presiding at the trial of an accused horse thief in a photo taken about 1900. He is on the porch of his Jersey Lilly Saloon, which doubled, on occasions such as this, as a courthouse. The location was a small, isolated, frontier town called Langtry on the Texas–Mexico border in southwestern Texas.

REVIEW THE CHAPTER

The Structure of the Texas Court System

8.1 Describe the structure of the Texas court system and its position within the constitutional framework of federalism, p. 239.

Federal courts play important roles in Texas, ruling on constitutional guarantees and making decisions affecting state policies. They also have jurisdiction over violations of federal laws, including many criminal laws dealing with fraud and drug offenses. But state courts handle the vast majority of criminal and civil litigation in Texas. State courts present a confusing array, with overlapping jurisdictions and varying qualifications for judges. Texas is one of only two states with a bifurcated court system at the highest appellate level. The Texas Supreme Court is the court of last resort in civil and juvenile cases, and the Texas Court of Criminal Appeals in criminal cases. There are fourteen intermediate courts of appeals that hear both civil and criminal appeals. The main trial courts are district courts, which have general jurisdiction over both civil and criminal cases. Lower-ranking courts include several hundred county, justice of the peace, and municipal courts with varying jurisdictions. All state judges, except those on municipal courts, are elected in partisan elections. In practice, however, Texas has a mixed judicial selection system because many judges quit or retire in midterm, allowing the governor or a county commissioners court to appoint their successors.

Participants and Procedures in the Judicial System

8.2 Describe the roles of the participants in the Texas court system and the procedures used in trial and appellate courts, p. 246.

The main participants in the court system are trial and appellate judges. Prosecutors (district and county attorneys), criminal defense lawyers, and lawyers representing plaintiffs and defendants in civil lawsuits also are major participants. Key support and security personnel include county and district clerks and bailiffs. Private citizens play critical roles in the judicial process by serving on juries. A grand jury determines if there is just cause for a criminal proceeding against a defendant. A petit (or trial) jury hears evidence in both civil and criminal trials and issues verdicts.

Trial procedures vary between civil and criminal cases. But, generally, they include jury selection, the presentation of opening arguments, examination and cross-examination of witnesses, presentation of evidence, rebuttal, and summation.

No juries are used in appellate courts. Appellate judges review the decisions and procedures of trial courts for compliance with constitutional and statutory requirements. Most civil and criminal cases are first appealed to an intermediate court of appeals. The final state level of appeal for civil cases is the Texas Supreme Court, and the final state level of appeal for criminal cases is the Texas Court of Criminal Appeals. Death penalty cases are automatically appealed directly from district court to the Court of Criminal Appeals. In all other cases, the two highest courts have discretion over whether to accept appeals.

Changing the Face of the Judiciary

8.3 Trace the growth of minority and women judges in the Texas judiciary, p. 249.

Most Texas judges are white males. Although they have made progress in recent years, in part through midterm gubernatorial appointments, women and minorities are still underrepresented on Texas courts, as they are in most other states. A Hispanic first joined the Texas Supreme Court in 1984 and the Texas Court of Criminal Appeals in 1991. An African American was first seated on the Texas Supreme Court in 2001 and the Texas Court of Criminal Appeals in 1990. A woman was first seated on the Texas Supreme Court in 1982. All were the result of gubernatorial appointments to midterm vacancies. The first woman on the Texas Court of Criminal Appeals was elected to the seat in 1994. Countywide election systems, polarized voting along ethnic lines, and the cost of judicial campaigns make it difficult for many minority candidates to win election to lower court judgeships. In the late 1980s, minority plaintiffs filed a federal lawsuit to try to force single-member district elections for local judges but lost before the U.S. Supreme Court.

Judicial Controversies and the Search for Solutions

8.4 Characterize the judicial controversies in Texas and their impact on public perception of the courts, p. 253.

Large campaign contributions to judges from lawyers and other parties with interests before the courts have helped create a cloud over the Texas judiciary. Much of the judicial controversy has been driven by a long-running war for control of the Texas Supreme Court between plaintiffs' attorneys, on one side, and businesses, doctors, and insurance companies on the other. The legislature has imposed limited restrictions on political contributions to judges, but it has refused to change the money-driven, partisan election system. Meanwhile, urban Texas counties have dozens of judicial offices, and most voters know little about their judges or judicial candidates. This has resulted in the election of some underqualified candidates, in part because of partisan voting. Possible alternatives to partisan judicial elections are nonpartisan elections or merit selection. The latter is a system in which judges are appointed by the governor, who chooses among recommendations from nominating commissions. Appointed judges would then run periodically in retention elections without opponents; those who were rejected by voters would be replaced by other appointees. Four chief justices of the Texas Supreme Court, one Democrat and three Republicans, have urged the legislature to change the partisan election system, but the legislature has refused their pleas.

Crime and Punishment

8.5 Describe the legal and constitutional rights of suspects, the classes of crimes and punishments in the Texas Penal Code, and the administration of criminal justice in Texas, p. 259.

The state's bill of rights and the federal Bill of Rights spell out the rights of those accused of crimes. Persons are entitled to be informed of their rights when arrested. They are entitled to be arraigned before a magistrate following well-defined rules. They are entitled to an attorney, even when they cannot afford one. They have the right to a jury trial, but many choose to waive this right. Many defendants negotiate lower sentences through plea bargains with prosecutors. A guilty jury verdict in a criminal case has to be unanimous. The state's schedule of criminal offenses ranges from misdemeanors—punishable by fines and short jail sentences—through felonies, for which long prison sentences can be imposed. The most serious offense is capital murder, punishable by death or life in prison without parole. Judges and other participants in the criminal justice system have to balance public safety with the rights of the accused, a process that sometimes puts the Texas Court of Criminal Appeals, in particular, at the center of political and philosophical disputes. Even with all the safeguards built into the judicial process, miscarriages of justice sometimes occur and innocent people are sentenced to prison.

Increased Policy Role of the State Courts

8.6 Illustrate the increased policy role of the state courts with examples, p. 264.

The federal judiciary traditionally has had more influence than the state courts in molding public policy. But in recent years, the Texas Supreme Court has increasingly played an active role in addressing significant constitutional and statutory issues, such as school funding, water policy, open beaches, abortion, and voting. The school funding issue has been a recurring legal controversy before the court. Decisions over water policy and other environmental concerns also may become more frequent in the future.

LEARN THE TERMS

Penal Code, p. 239
civil lawsuit, p. 239
original jurisdiction, p. 240
appellate jurisdiction, p. 240
bifurcated court system, p. 240
municipal court, p. 242
justice of the peace court, p. 242
constitutional county court, p. 242
statutory county court, p. 243
district court, p. 243
plea bargain, p. 244
court of appeals, p. 244

Texas Supreme Court, p. 245
Texas Court of Criminal Appeals, p. 245
grand jury, p. 247
prosecution, p. 247
indictment, p. 247
information, p. 247
petit jury, p. 247
veniremen, p. 248
petition for review, p. 249
writ of mandamus, p. 249
petition for discretionary review, p. 249

merit selection, p. 254
tort reform, p. 255
retention election, p. 259
ward politics, p. 259
Miranda ruling, p. 260
nolo contendere, p. 260
capital murder, p. 260
felony, p. 261
misdemeanor, p. 261
probation, p. 261
parole, p. 261

Political Socialization, Political Behavior, and Public Opinion

9

YOUNG PEOPLE MARCH FOR CHANGE
Parents teach children a variety of values that translate into opinions. One key political value that children learn from their parents is party affiliation. Pictured here is a group of people peacefully marching in downtown Austin to support the Black Lives Matter movement. Children often learn political activism at the sides of their parents.

LEARNING OBJECTIVES

9.1 Identify the role of public opinion in democracies and the stability of core values, p. 273.

9.2 Explain the process of acquiring views and attitudes and the dominant trends in political ideology in Texas, p. 276.

9.3 Describe how group membership impacts political values and opinions in Texas, p. 283.

9.4 Identify the manner in which opinion translates into political action, p. 290.

9.5 Explain how public opinion is measured and how to interpret public opinion poll results, p. 299.

Everyone decides whether to participate in politics and to what extent, but the choice may be easier for someone who represents the latest generation of America's best-known, contemporary political family. Then still in his 20s, George P. Bush, grandson of one U.S. president, nephew of another, and son of a former Florida governor, already was on a path toward a political career of his own when he worked in his Uncle George W. Bush's successful White House campaign in 2000. At the age of 12, he led the pledge of allegiance before the 1988 Republican National Convention on August 18, 1988; his grandfather, George H.W. Bush was nominated for president later that same day. George later earned a commission in the U.S. Navy Reserve; launched a successful career in his native Texas as a lawyer, investor, and business consultant; served as deputy finance chair of the Texas Republican Party; and cofounded the Hispanic Republicans of Texas. Then, in 2014, at age 38, George P. Bush was elected Texas land commissioner, a job sometimes viewed as a potential stepping-stone to higher office, earning 61 percent of the general election vote and an impressive 49 percent of the Latino vote. Some thought he might be vulnerable in the 2018 Republican primary, but he won with over 58 percent of the vote, followed-up with a decisive general election victory.

Few of us can trace our political roots, if we have any, to the White House. But we all are candidates for political socialization. This is the process through which we acquire our political values, our views of government, our party identification or nonidentification, and our attitudes toward participation in election campaigns and other political activities. This process affects our ability to navigate the political and government system, and it can be influenced by a number of factors, including our own beliefs and interests as well as those of families, friends, and other people with whom we come into contact. Some of these people may share our beliefs or interests, whereas others may introduce us to new and different goals or values.

The next time you go to your main campus eatery, look around and take note of where people sit and how they interact and communicate. What patterns do you see? Do international students sit with other international students, athletes with other athletes, commuter students with other commuter students, sorority or fraternity members with other Greeks? Or do people on your campus mix together?

Consider the implications of these patterns of social segregation or interaction in the development of civic and political values. Does participation in groups with diverse memberships produce more heterogeneous political values than participation in highly homogeneous groups? Is there pressure in some groups to develop a single view that might be described as "group think"?

Think about conversations with your classmates, friends, family, and other acquaintances. Do you ever talk about politics, or do you mostly ignore current political events and policymakers? If you do discuss politics, how receptive are you to opposing viewpoints?

Take a moment to think about your earliest memory of government or politics. Do you remember your parents placing a candidate's campaign sign in your yard? Do you recall watching a political debate on television with your family? How did your family respond to the controversies surrounding the 2020 presidential elections? Did your parents complain at the dinner table about Congress or the IRS? Where were you when you first heard about the killing of Osama bin Laden? Are your early political ideas similar to what you know or believe to be true today?

We all grow up in a social structure defined, in part, by those around us, including our families, neighbors, teachers, fellow students, and members of churches and other organizations to which we belong. Core values, learned early in life, help form our opinions and views of government and politics, and people with similar life experiences tend to share similar values. Collectively, our society and political system represent a diversity of viewpoints and levels of political participation because, of course, not everyone has the same experiences or influences or shares the same values.

In this chapter, we will discuss how groups and social networks contribute to individuals' acquisition and development of political values and opinions, with attention paid to changes over time so that you can better understand the context of contemporary policy differences. Next, we will examine how opinions translate into political action by looking at who votes and at some general patterns in how they vote. We will then briefly consider how public opinion is measured so that you can become an informed consumer of political information and a knowledgeable participant in the political system. We will pay close attention both to comparisons over time and to how Texas compares with national trends to see how citizens in Texas are both similar to and different from their peers in other areas of the country.

Opinion and Core Values

9.1 Identify the role of public opinion in democracies and the stability of core values.

Public opinion can be understood as the aggregation (the combination or collection) of individual and group preferences or views about an issue or set of issues. At first glance, *public opinion* seems like a straightforward term—the opinion of the public. However, in a society as large and diverse as ours, it is not an easy job to determine the opinion of "the public." Public opinion is grounded in political values and can impact how, when, and in what manner people participate in politics. In the United States there is a basic consensus of key political values as well as complex cleavages (divisions) based on diverse groups and their positions in American society.[1] The role of public opinion in democratic theory varies and has long been debated.

public opinion
The various opinions (views, perceptions, attitudes) about contemporary political issues, political leaders, and governmental institutions held by the population or by subgroups of the population. Public opinion tends to be grounded in political values and can impact political behavior.

9.1.1 Role of Public Opinion in Democratic Governments and Societies

The philosophical underpinnings of the American Revolution rested on social contract theory, which asserts that all legitimate governmental authority stems from the consent of "the people" and that government exists to preserve natural rights.[2] This theory assumes a rather pure or unified conception of "the public" in which "the people" would act in concert for the common good. "The people" would ratify the constitution, would select governmental leaders, and would "consent" to their rule. This view of government, based on collective opinion and consent, was articulated by Abraham Lincoln in his 1863 Gettysburg Address—our government is "of the people, by the people and for the people." Alexis de Tocqueville, a French aristocrat who wrote *Democracy in America* (1835, 1840), one of the most widely read commentaries on American democracy, stated that public opinion, in a generic sense, was the "predominant authority" in America, serving to make America a democracy.

Public opinion is often treated as though it has unified or homogeneous characteristics, but this conception of cohesiveness in public opinion may disguise the reality of politics, at the time of our founding as well as today. James Madison, often referred to as the "father of the American Constitution," argued in Federalist 10 that conflict and disagreement were inevitable in the American political system due to underlying differences regarding property. He warned that individuals and factions (or groups) pursuing their own self-interests had little concern for the common good. If efforts were made to eliminate the causes of diverse interests and opinions, liberty would be eliminated. His solution was to constrain and control the effects of diverse interests and opinions through institutional arrangements that balanced power with power.

Democracy is full of paradoxes or contradictions, and this relationship between unity and diversity is one of them. Americans have areas of broad consensus—property rights, individualism, and personal freedom—but in particular areas of public policy (such as abortion, capital punishment, and education policy), significant disagreement often exists.

In times of national crisis when the country's security appears to be threatened, such as the period immediately following the 2001 terrorist attacks, we are clearly "one people" united in the common good. During a crisis, we are bound by a common goal of preservation and an understanding of the need for common or collective action. Collective action is very much rooted in what de Tocqueville defined as "self-interest rightly understood." When the crisis or threat passes, individual needs reassert themselves, and divisions recur with individualism trumping the common good. De Tocqueville focused on the inherent paradox (the seemingly contradictory nature) of America's democracy and warned that individualism had the potential to undermine the public or common good and could be manipulated. John Stuart Mills expanded on de Tocqueville's warning, arguing that "moral coercion" in the form of manipulated collective opinion could be a key source of tyranny.[3]

Many theorists have debated the role of public opinion in policymaking. How central should the opinion of the public be in governing? How much attention should elected officials pay to the opinions of their constituents?

Some argue that since public opinion is often based on uninformed opinions and can easily be swayed, it is best to minimize the direct impact of public opinion on policymaking and allow citizens to indirectly influence policymaking primarily through elections.[4] In Federalist 71, Alexander Hamilton, a forceful proponent of the Constitution, warned against following the "sudden breeze of passion" or listening to every "transient impulse" of the public. Federalist 63 asserted that a "select and stable" Senate would serve as "an anchor against popular fluctuations," which would protect the people from their "temporary errors." The founders thought public opinion would impact governing only indirectly, through elections of public officials to offices with specified lengths of tenure. Proponents of this indirect relationship between public opinion and public policy are often referred to as elitist, since they subscribe to the theory of **elitism**. This view is less popular today, but nonetheless is held by some.

Elements of this disconnect between public opinion and public policy can be seen in Texas, where the state constitution does not allow citizens the right to petition statewide for policy changes through referendum, initiative, or recall. Some states give their citizens these rights, and even some cities in Texas allow these rights on a local level through individual city charters.

Far more common today—and in many ways in direct opposition to elitist theory—is a position based on **pluralism**. Pluralists argue that citizens need to be informed and active and that political leaders need to be responsive to public opinion to ensure a healthy and vital system, as no one group can then dominate governmental decisions. They argue that in a representative democracy, the will of the people ought to have great weight.[5] This line of reasoning goes back to the ancient Greek philosopher Aristotle, who believed that collective judgments based on diverse thought were more likely to be sound than the judgments of a few.

Elements of the pluralist view are found in Texas in the large number of amendments to the Texas Constitution. The heavy use of polling by political candidates, officeholders, interest groups, and think tanks also demonstrates a belief that public opinion is important and critical to the policymaking process.

The reality of contemporary Texas politics probably rests somewhere between the elitist and pluralist extremes. At times, public attention is focused on issues, and elected officials are under great pressure to heed public opinion. When a dominant opinion emerges, officials—elected and unelected—often are swayed and react accordingly. At other times, when the public is generally uninformed and inattentive, officials pay less attention to public opinion. Public opinion often is fragmented with no clear consensus. Knowing when to heed public opinion and when to resist it is one mark of great political leadership.

elitism
Theory holding the view that political power is primarily held by a few individuals who derive power from leadership positions in large business, civic, or governmental institutions.

pluralism
Theory holding that a diversity of groups and people is instrumental in the policymaking process and no one group should be able to dominate the decisions of government.

9.1.2 Stability of Key Values

The United States has been blessed with a long period of political stability. Granted, disagreements exist, but these disagreements—except for the Civil War—have tended to be more civil and less traumatic than those experienced in other countries. For the most part, we have been able to manage the times of disagreement peaceably and advance incremental change. Many other countries have been less successful and have had far more periods of volatility and internal conflict.

One key reason for stability is the fact that there is broad agreement on key values, and we are generally content. There is nearly unanimous agreement on our republican form of government, in which power rests with the people and is exercised by our elected officials. We see fair, free, and competitive elections as essential to democracy. We are proud to live in this country and, even when troubled by particular issues, would rather live in the United States than any other country. We believe in majority rule and the protection of minority rights. We have broad support for personal liberty and cherish our constitutionally guaranteed freedoms. We value individualism and individual rights. We also have near universal support for political equality. The notion of one person, one vote is deeply entrenched in our political culture. Generally, a wide level of support exists for equality of opportunity (the belief that everyone should have an equal chance of success). There is less agreement about other elements of equality, such as equality of outcomes or conditions (the belief that the government should institute policies to ensure people have equal access to resources, such as policies that redistribute wealth), but Americans by and large support equality as an ideal.

Most shifts in public opinion are gradual and can be explained by **cohort replacement**, or **generational changes**, which simply means that younger people replace older people; as each generation has different experiences, it is expected that they will have different worldviews. Common experiences that shape political attitudes are often used to explain the values of a specific generation such as the baby boomers or the millennials. A lot of people die, and a lot of people turn 18 in a twenty-year time span. In fact, it is estimated that 50 percent of the electorate is replaced every twenty years.[6] Broad political changes tend to follow cycles of approximately twenty years. In the chapter on political parties, we will address partisan realignment in Texas, a process that took more than two decades to complete.

cohort replacement (generational changes)
Natural occurrence of generational replacement due to death.

In addition to demographic shifts, changing technology is a factor in gradual changes in public opinion. As technology has changed, the world has become a smaller place, and it is logical that opinions would evolve differently. People are no longer as isolated as they were in the past. Modern transportation and communications have exposed people to diverse opinions, values, and lifestyles from other parts of the country and the world.

Geographic mobility also contributes to gradual change. Americans are moving constantly in pursuit of better employment, education, or living conditions. Texas's political culture was transformed, in part, because of large numbers of individuals moving to Texas from other states, beginning in the 1970s. Individuals bring different values and views with them, although people who move geographically tend to move into neighborhoods with individuals who have similar values and characteristics.

Even though most shifts in public opinion are gradual, there have been times of rapid change that have served to dramatically transform American politics. One such example occurred in the 1760s and 1770s, when colonists quickly transformed from overwhelmingly loyal British-American subjects into rebels against the monarchy. In the 1960s and 1970s, we saw dramatic changes on issues regarding race and gender, ushering in a period of far greater support of equality for all Americans. We have seen striking changes in support of LGBT rights (specifically same-sex marriage) and legalization of marijuana in the last few years.

Rapid changes in opinions are most likely to occur around foreign policy issues. Political scientists Benjamin Page and Robert Shapiro found that attitudes on foreign policy changed three times more quickly than opinions on domestic issues.[7] Opinions on wars, foreign aid, and the Middle East were the most likely to undergo abrupt changes.[8]

Formation of Political Values and Opinions

9.2 Explain the process of acquiring views and attitudes and the dominant trends in political ideology in Texas.

During the 2014 South by Southwest Festival, Governor Rick Perry appeared on the Jimmy Kimmel show (which was being filmed in Austin during the festivities). The governor was booed by so many audience members that Kimmel felt compelled to comment on the seeming lack of support voiced by members of the Austin audience. Governor Perry explained that Austin is like a blueberry in a bowl of tomato soup. Some were perplexed by the analogy, but those familiar with politics immediately got the reference. He was noting that Austin is a liberal city (a blue city) in a conservative state (a red state). Understanding contemporary issues of political ideology and the manner in which people acquire their political values is of fundamental importance to being an informed participant in politics today.

9.2.1 Political Ideology

Political ideology is a consistent set of values and beliefs about the proper purpose and scope of government. Our ideology structures our core values and serves as a filter through which we receive information about the external world and organize our responses. One's ideological perspective is shaped by the socialization process and life experiences, and it has a normative dimension that explains ideals or assumptions about how governmental institutions ought to address social problems.[9]

In some countries, there are widely divergent political ideologies. However, in Texas and the United States, we generally fall into two camps—liberals and conservatives. In general, **liberals** tend to support social and cultural change, especially pertaining to issues of equality, and believe government should be an important agent to promote that change. Liberals also tend to support governmental intervention in the economy, especially to protect the environment and rights of workers and to promote equality. **Conservatives** tend to favor traditional views on cultural, social, and economic issues and tend to demand a more limited role for government in promoting equality. Conservatives express confidence in markets and individual

---

political ideology
A consistent set of values and beliefs that form a general philosophy about the proper goals, purpose, and size of government. Ideology is grounded in political values.

liberal
A person who generally supports governmental action to promote equality, to alleviate social ills (like racism, bigotry, and poverty), and to protect civil rights and liberties. Liberals are said to be on the "left" of the political spectrum.

conservative
A person who generally believes that a large and powerful government is a threat to individual freedom and supports personal responsibility, limited governmental spending, traditional patterns of relationships, importance of religion in daily life, and free enterprise. Conservatives are said to be on the "right" of the political spectrum.

LOCAL DIVERSITY
Although Texas is generally a conservative state, the capital is known for being liberal and eclectic. In fact, the city's unofficial motto is "Keep Austin Weird." When considering public opinion, one needs to look not only at broad trends in the state, but also at local cultures, as significant differences exist within the same state.

JULIÁN CASTRO

Julián Castro, who was elected mayor of San Antonio in 2009 (at the age of 35) and served as Secretary of Housing and Urban Development under President Obama from 2014 to 2017, briefly ran for the Democratic nomination to be the president in 2020. While his candidacy for president only lasted a short while, he is still considered an important actor within the Democratic Party. He and his twin brother, Joaquin Castro (D-TX), a member of Congress since 2013, are the children of Mexican American political activists who epitomize an immigrant success story. Most analysts agree that both Castros are on track to become influential figures in Democratic politics.

behavior to address economic issues, but they tend to favor a more activist government in promoting order, including social order, and hence favor laws that promote the importance of religion in life, traditional gender roles, and severe punishment of criminals. Generally speaking, Texans and other Americans who are more liberal tend to be Democrats, while those who are more conservative tend to be Republicans. Often, popular media label liberal areas as "blue" and conservative areas as "red."

Texas is largely conservative. Even when it was a one-party Democratic state, conservative candidates typically won the Democratic nomination and controlled state government. Now most conservatives affiliate with the Republican Party. Across the state, Republicans expressed strong opposition to President Obama and many of his policies (notably the Affordable Care Act or "Obamacare"), and Republican candidates for federal, state, and county offices in Texas engage in extensive ideological debates within their party, usually trying to "out-conservative" each other. This same ideological debate is taking place throughout the United States as ultraconservatives and more moderate Republicans fight for control of their party.

There has been much talk about Texas growing more liberal, as well as efforts by Democratic organizations to turn the state more "purple" as demographics change. (We will discuss the impact of social groups on trends in political ideology shortly.) In 2020, for example, many thought the state might vote Democratic for president, but for the time-being it remains controlled by conservatives. However, public opinion polls have shown that support for President Trump was much lower than typical for Republican presidents. For example, in April 2020, a statewide poll conducted by the University of Texas and the *Texas Tribune* found that 42 percent of respondents stated they would definitely vote to reelect President Trump, and 42 percent would definitely vote for someone else; this was the highest percent for President Trump since February 2019 and the lowest percent for his hypothetical opponent. When presented with the question of the election being held today, however, the majority stated they would vote for President Trump over Vice President Biden.[10] Most believe these figures were more representative of concerns many had with President Trump and not with Republicans in Texas more generally, especially as other Republican leaders remained popular.

populist
A person who supports the rights and power of "common people" in their struggle against the privileged elite. Generally, populists believe that democracy should reflect and protect the will of the masses and that government can be a positive element in accomplishing that goal. Populists are frequently anti-establishment and offer unorthodox proposals to promote grassroots democracy often associated with the working class.

libertarian
A person who believes that individual well-being and prosperity are fostered by an extremely limited government and as much personal liberty in thought and action as possible. Generally, each person should be able to live his or her life as long as the rights of others are respected.

In addition to liberals and conservatives, a smaller number of Texans and other Americans identify themselves as populists or libertarians. **Populists** believe that government can be a positive element to protect "common people" against the "money elite" and can be used to both protect order and promote equality. Historically, populists came from a largely agrarian reform movement, but they are no longer limited to farmers and are growing in strength. They include others who challenge the great disparities in wealth in America and challenges to the status quo.

Libertarians support individual liberty in economic, personal, and social realms over governmental intervention and regulation. Libertarians argue that although governments are necessary, they must be severely limited. Libertarians are more common than populists today and have gained support in Texas, especially among conservative college students. College students seem to be attracted to the appeal of liberty and freedom—according to some, as a manifestation of youth that generally yields as individuals age. The passage of time will show whether current supporters of the philosophy maintain that viewpoint throughout their lifetimes. The Texas Libertarian Party has fielded hundreds of candidates for office and has grown in popularity in the past decade. It ran a full slate of candidates for statewide offices in 2016, but the party has never won a statewide election in Texas. The 2016 Libertarian Party presidential candidate, Gary Johnson, has gotten more attention than past nominees as some conservatives were frustrated with the Republican nominee, Donald Trump. The Texas Libertarian Party once again has a full slate of candidates for most congressional and state legislative races, as well as many statewide elections. Most national surveys do not ask if people are libertarians or populists, but a few do. A 2015 survey found that 20 percent of Americans self-identify as libertarians (with more young people holding this view than other age groups), while a 2017 study found that approximately 17 percent of Americans hold populist stances.[11] Readers should be cautious about these figures as they were found only in two surveys and, as we will see later in the chapter, more data is better when making generalizations.

Although the Libertarian Party is still small, its ideology has impacted Texas politics through the Tea Party. The Tea Party started with strong libertarian roots. It has since moved to include more social conservatives, but its libertarian slant has helped to strengthen the conservative hold on the Texas Republican Party.

9.2.2 Political Socialization

From the day a person is born, he or she is subject to socialization, or a learning process. The process is complex, lifelong, and structured by the interaction of the individual with the social environment in which he or she lives. As the person approaches adulthood, the process includes the shaping of political attitudes, beliefs, and behavior. **Political socialization** is the conscious and unconscious transmission of political culture and values from one generation to another. This socialization helps people process political information, categorize political knowledge, and develop political values.

Factors that influence the acquisition of political facts and the formation of values are called **agents of political socialization**. Research demonstrates that learning during childhood and adolescence can impact some elements of adult political behavior.[12] Material learned early in life conditions later learning, predisposing and shaping subsequent development, although this does not preclude the possibility of a dramatic change in core values during one's lifetime. We will first explore the agents of socialization, and then look at the society level implications, particularly the impact on political participation.

political socialization
The process that begins in early childhood whereby a person assimilates the beliefs, attitudes, and behaviors of society and acquires views toward the political system and government.

agents of political socialization
Entities such as families, schools, community, and the media that help integrate people into society and teach political values.

9.2.3 Agents of Socialization

Not all people experience socialization similarly, nor are they exposed to the same social institutions; hence, the variety in worldviews. However, common themes emerge. A number of your earliest political memories probably focused on your

CONTROVERSY SURROUNDING ABORTION

Since *Roe* v. *Wade* was decided in 1973, abortion has remained one of the most contentious issues in the United States. While a majority of people support some rights for women to terminate pregnancies, those in opposition feel very strongly and are very active in American politics. Pictured here are people in Austin at a Rally for Life event.

family, school, or church. Many people first learn of politics through the lens of the media; others can point to one key event (like a war or terrorist attack) that made a lasting impression. Regardless of the particular memories, most Americans learn about politics from similar agents of socialization, and these experiences significantly affect the development of political opinions and, subsequently, political engagement. Let's examine seven agents of socialization: family, schools, peers, community, the media, religion, and events.

FAMILY Children learn a wide range of economic, moral, political, and social values from their families. These values impact the way children see the world and their interaction with others. Families tend to be the first place children learn values that are often long lasting.

The impact of the family varies, largely dependent on the amount of time that is spent together and the level of political activity of the parents.[13] Politically active parents tend to have politically active children, predispositions that last throughout a lifetime.[14] Children typically try to copy the behavior of loved ones, so civic-minded parents tend to raise community-minded children.[15] Conversely, being raised in a poverty-stricken, crime-ridden community that fears the police can negatively impact civic engagement.[16]

Party identification is one of the most important political values transmitted through the social structure of family, especially when both parents are of the same political party. If children do not adopt their parents' political party, they are more likely to define themselves as independents than to align with the opposite party.[17] Racial attitudes learned in early life, largely through the lens of the family, shape views about race-related issues throughout life.[18] In fact, during our childhood, our families teach us much of our racial and ethnic identities, as well as the views we hold of other races.[19] Children can be taught bigotry by their families, and may remain bigots as adults, while those who are exposed to diverse racial environments and taught tolerance tend to grow into adults who value racial and cultural differences.[20] Children also tend to learn gender roles from their families. Children who are raised by mothers who work outside the home for wages, for example, often have more progressive views of gender roles.[21]

Pre-adult learning also impacts our political orientation as it pertains to ideology, party identification, and attitudes on social issues like abortion.[22] In essence, children absorb and reflect the values in the environments in which they are raised.[23] However,

SCHOOLS TEACH MORE THAN READING, WRITING, AND ARITHMETIC

Schools are important agents of socialization, as students are taught political facts that help to foster patriotism and promote shared political values. As such, presidential debates, both for the primaries and general elections, are held on college campuses and typically involve educational components for students and the community in the days leading up to the campus debate. Pictured here are presidential hopefuls at the third Democratic primary debate in the 2020 presidential campaign hosted by ABC News in partnership with Univision at Texas Southern University in Houston on September 12, 2019.

recent research regarding the relative role of families in influencing the values taught to children is mixed. As children spend less and less quality time with their families, other agents of socialization grow in importance.

SCHOOLS Primary and secondary schools teach political information, the value of political participation, the hierarchy of authority in society, and the importance of democratic principles. Children in Texas are taught the pledges of allegiance to the American and Texas flags, as well as the history and political traditions of the United States and Texas. Texas government, through public schools, attempts to train students to be good citizens and to accept social order.

As early as pre-kindergarten classes, children are taught collective decision-making and the rules of the majority when they are given choices by their teachers in class activities. In later grades, many schools allow students to conduct mock elections for president of the United States and elect their student body leaders; they even teach students the importance of registering, debating, and voting. Most students emerge from elementary school with a strong sense of patriotism and an idealized notion of American government, thus building a general sense of good will for the political system.[24]

High schools continue to help students understand their place in the political community and foster civic responsibility. Many schools build citizenship overtly through curricula and activities. An engaging high school civics class, for example, can result in students becoming more politically active as adults.[25] Individuals who attend schools that model positive democratic behavior (by promoting collaboration and shared decision-making as well as civic projects) tend to be more civically engaged as adults.[26] On the whole, however, high school seniors are not very interested in politics, have low levels of political knowledge, and demonstrate relatively low levels of support for democratic practices.[27]

A college education can dramatically impact political views in a number of ways.[28] During college, political orientations tend to crystallize, resulting in a lasting impact on an individual's value structure. On the whole, college graduates make more money over their lifetimes than nongraduates, and attitudes toward government policies and taxation are explained, in part, by the economic results of educational levels. In general, college graduates are more politically knowledgeable, more engaged in their communities, and more conservative on fiscal issues than nongraduates.

Consequently, college graduates are less supportive of increased taxation to provide social welfare than those who are less educated.

When it comes to noneconomic issues, research consistently demonstrates that a college education has a liberalizing effect. Adults with college experience tend to be more liberal on social issues like LGBTQ rights and free speech than adults with less education. College-educated adults see systematic racism as a widespread problem, are more likely to say that white people have advantages in society that black people do not have, and are more likely to support the Black Lives Matter movement than less educated Americans, regardless of other key features like race and religion.[29] A number of explanations exist for these patterns. College tends to expose students to a wide array of cultures and personal lifestyles, and to a diversity of thought, allowing individuals to see the complexity of issues. Exposure to differences teaches people to reject stereotypes and appreciate diversity, making individuals more supportive of First Amendment freedoms. Classes like the one you are now taking help students develop a greater appreciation for the controversies facing our society, thereby permitting them to see that intelligent people can and do disagree. Also, college faculty tend to be significantly more liberal than most people in society. Generally, those in the social sciences and humanities tend to be the most liberal, as are faculty in the Northeast, but variation does exist.[30] This trend leads some conservatives to hypothesize that liberal college faculty indoctrinate students, causing them to become more liberal. Whatever the explanation, people with college educations are generally more liberal on social issues than those who have not been to college.

One important way college impacts individuals is by providing a sense of **political efficacy**, an important predictor of being politically engaged. Political efficacy is multifaceted, reflecting views of the political system and of individual capacities. Internal political efficacy reflects a sense of personal abilities; people with high internal political efficacy tend to believe that they have the skills, knowledge, and abilities to impact politics. External efficacy, on the other hand, refers to confidence in the political system. Often, people have similar levels of both internal and external efficacy; however, it is not uncommon for people to have higher levels of one or the other. People who have attended college have a much stronger sense of internal political efficacy; in other words, they have more confidence in their personal ability to impact the world in which they live. Consequently, they tend to be more politically engaged. The more intense one's sense of efficacy, the more likely one is to become involved politically.

PEERS AND COMMUNITY Your community and peers are also agents of socialization. Your peers are friends, classmates, and coworkers who are generally your own age. Your community is the broader range of people of all ages that you come into contact with during daily life. These two groups tend to have less influence than family and school, but our friends and community do affect us. Peers tend to be reinforcing agents, as people often voluntarily associate with people like themselves (a fact evident in the cafeterias of most college campuses).

Research shows that in heterogeneous communities (communities marked by a lot of diversity), political participation tends to be higher, as there is more political debate and closer elections than in homogeneous environments.[31] Minorities living in politically and racially heterogeneous communities tend to have higher levels of political efficacy than minorities living in segregated environments. For example, researchers found that African Americans living in predominantly black communities generally are traditionally socialized in a manner that fails to encourage political participation.[32] Racial segregation tends to foster a sense of isolation and disinterest in the political system. Areas with high **voter turnout** and with racial diversity appear to be the best environments in which to raise politically aware and knowledgeable children who have a sense that their voice can count.

political efficacy
The belief that one can influence government. Internal political efficacy is the belief that one has the knowledge and ability to influence government. External political efficacy is the belief that the political system is responsive to citizens.

voter turnout
The percentage of citizens legally eligible to vote in an election who actually vote in the election.

MEDIA The media create an interesting agent of socialization as they promote values that both advance and complicate democracy. We will look more closely at the media in Chapter 12; here, it is important to note that the media are an important agent of socialization and that they have varied effects on public opinion.

Most observers believe the impact of the media is growing, given the fact that children consume more and more media—many children, for example, spend far more time watching television than interacting with their parents. It is hard to argue that the entertainment media, which seem to promote promiscuous sex, drug use, and materialism, are positive elements in developing an ideal democratic citizen. Most of these messages are in direct competition with the values promoted by families and religious organizations. Many analysts worry that the media's focus on violence and corruption can adversely affect political efficacy and trust in government.[33] During the early days of the COVID-19 pandemic, many commentators argued that the media's coverage exaggerated the dangers of the virus and led to unnecessary panic. Later, continued focus on rising death tolls complicated the White House messaging and efforts at economic stimulation. Many saw the coverage on a number of news outlets to be overly negative. Leading media commentators noted that they are responsible for sharing news, even if it is negative and depressing. Striking the correct balance is a difficult task.

However, as you will see in Chapter 12, people obtain most of their news about politics and government from the media, and the media can be a positive influence in promoting and highlighting democratic ideals. For example, most local news media, such as newspapers and television news programs, spotlight acts of heroism or celebrate national holidays and local triumphs.

A free press has long been considered paramount in maintaining a democratic society. This remains true in the digital age, even as people are routinely exposed to a variety of competing political viewpoints and a blurring of the line between fact and opinion. Individuals approach the media differently. Some people read or watch media sources with a desire to expose themselves to different philosophical and ideological perspectives, while others seek primarily information that will confirm or reinforce their preexisting values and views.

RELIGION Participation in religious institutions can have dramatic impact on an individual's sense of community, political philosophy, view of public policies, and level of civic engagement. People who are actively engaged in religious communities tend to contribute to society and get involved in their communities.[34] All denominations are engaged in education, hunger relief, agricultural initiatives, health care, and a host of other social activities. Americans gave $427.71 billion to charities in 2018 (a 4.1 percent increase from 2017), and 29 percent of this money went to religious institutions.[35]

Religious leaders can be very influential in the development of personal identity as it pertains to issues of morality and community engagement. Conservative denominations and religions (such as Southern Baptists, traditional Roman Catholics, and evangelical Protestants) tend to impart more conservative attitudes (especially regarding issues involving personal morality and sexuality) than more liberal churches do.[36] Individuals raised in religiously diverse communities are more likely to be engaged in politics and have higher levels of political participation.[37] Religion can act as a reinforcing mechanism of community and family values on a wide array of moral and political issues. People who are either less religious or atheists tend to have different policy preferences than do those who are actively engaged in the practice of their religion.

There also are connections between church membership or theological views and party affiliation. For example, Methodists, Presbyterians, Episcopalians, and Catholics are more likely to be involved in addressing economic and social problems, and many members of these denominations show a preference for the Democratic Party

VIGIL FOR GEORGE FLOYD
A candlelight vigil was held for George Floyd, the 46-year-old African American man whose killing highlighted calls for police reform, at Jack Yates High School in Houston on June 8, 2020. Mr. Floyd was laid to rest in Houston, where he grew up, on June 9, 2020.

(though many exceptions exist based on other factors). Evangelical fundamentalists, such as Southern Baptists and various Pentecostal groups, favor the Republican Party. Disproportionately, the Jewish population and African Americans of all religions support the Democratic Party.

EVENTS Events can have a lasting impact on political values and opinions. Sometimes events, such as the Great Depression and the Vietnam War, impact an entire cohort, or generation. At other times, events impact an entire society; examples would be the assassination of President Kennedy and the terrorist attacks of September 11th. Events may have different effects depending on one's age. They tend to have a lower impact on older adults, who process them through the lens of long-established attitudes, but they can have a significant impact on youth and young adults.[38] Some events, however, impact people of all ages. Research shows that the terrorist attacks of September 11th have had a lasting impact on many people's opinions regarding personal freedoms, government surveillance, foreign policy, and civil liberties.[39] We are in the midst of great societal change brought about by COVID-19 and the massive protests for racial justice first stemming from the killing of George Floyd. The pandemic is likely to impact our daily lives for a long time to come; the economic costs will last for years. The protests and call to action for racial justice are likely to have even longer-lasting impacts. Public opinion has shifted dramatically and quickly on these issues, indicating that prior viewpoints are unlikely to gain prominence. This time period is likely to mark a significant turning point in many people's lives in how they view race relations, police action, and the rights of protesters in the United States.

Group Membership and Public Opinion

9.3 Describe how group membership impacts political values and opinions in Texas.

People having similar experiences with agents of socialization tend to develop similar opinions, and these opinions influence political participation, including voting patterns. Although such trends are well documented in the academic literature, many exceptions to these general patterns exist. So, no one demographic factor can be used to explain political behavior. For example, on the whole, women tend to be more liberal than men (even when we control for race, religion, income, and educational attainment); however, there are many very conservative women. Younger people tend to support legalization of marijuana more than older people do, but there are still many younger people who are strongly opposed to the legalization of any drugs. Dividing people into demographic groups, however, helps social scientists determine general patterns in behavior, in spite of the exceptions that exist.

Moreover, individuals are often impacted by membership in multiple groups. For example, a Latina woman who is a highly educated, devout Catholic has many sources of influence on her behavior and opinions. Social scientists first used the term **intersectionality** to explain how two or more factors work to influence individuals.[40] Cleavages are social, economic, political, religions, racial, or cultural divisions within societies. The theory of cross-cutting cleavages refers to the idea that individuals are members of different social groups, so their membership in one group could come at odds with their membership in another group. Although crosscutting cleavages represent splits in the population that separate people into a variety of groups and often make it difficult to say which factors are the most important in shaping particular attitudes, they also can moderate opinions and lead to healthy discourse and incremental change. For example, someone's social class might predict opposing governmental spending on social welfare, but the same person's religious views may mitigate economic self-interest and lead to supporting higher expenditures on these types of programs. In 1989, Kimberlé Crenshaw coined the term intersectionality to indicate how race, gender, class, religion, sexuality, and other individual characteristics that are used to oppress intersect with one another.[41] For example, African American women have different experiences from white women and from African American men because of their race *and* sex. The intersection of these two identities creates a unique experience for these often-marginalized women. Rather than focus on different identities as though they are separate, Crenshaw and others argue we need to focus on how our identities reinforce and interact with one another. In essence, intersectionality focuses on how different types of discrimination interact with one another. Some do not support these definitions, often arguing that they create a culture of division and "victimhood."[42]

An examination of public opinion data drawn from statewide polls indicates a number of interesting patterns among social and demographic groups in Texas. In the sections that follow, we will illuminate many general trends, to show how social and demographic groups impose opinions and positions on public policy (and hence, voting). Note, however, that these trends are based on overall patterns; once individuals are examined, the findings become more complex and varied.

9.3.1 Political Party and Public Opinion

One important predictor of public opinion is political party affiliation. All things being equal, Democrats in a state are more likely to agree with other Democrats, and Republicans are far more likely to agree with each other than with Democrats. The manner in which people acquire their party identification is complex, and while political socialization is important, it does not fully explain party loyalties in the United States. As noted, many people learn their party loyalties from their families (especially when their parents have the same partisanship), but other factors are also significant.

One principal generalization that can be made about partisanship in the United States today is that partisan loyalties are often based on socioeconomic status. Historically, Democrats have been seen as the "party of the people" and Republicans as the "party of the rich" but this perception is largely no longer accurate. Class differences are less pronounced in the United States than in most other Western democracies, as both parties draw support from lower-, middle-, and upper-status groups. When one looks at economic issues pertaining primarily to taxation, the more affluent tend to be

---

intersectionality

A term coined to describe the combined effects of one's multiple identities (e.g., race, gender, sexual orientation, religion, and social class). The term was originally coined to describe the intersection of multiple forms of discrimination, such as racism, sexism, and classism, which often characterize the life experiences of marginalized individuals or groups.

more conservative while the less affluent tend to favor policies that redistribute wealth (making complete sense, as each group is acting out of its economic self-interest). However, when we add education to the mix, the relationship between partisanship and economics becomes far more complex. Recent discussions of income disparities (highlighted by the candidacy of Bernie Sanders as well as the debate surrounding the minimum wage) demonstrate that class remains salient and controversial.

Significant differences exist between self-identified partisans in Texas. Table 9–1 shows partisan differences in Texas in regard to evaluations of President Trump as well as differences in support of or opposition to particular public policies. The data on public opinion in this chapter were drawn from statewide surveys conducted by the University of Texas and *The Texas Tribune* of Texas citizens older than 18.[43] Republicans tend to be more likely to strongly approve of the job performance of President Trump, favor prohibiting health care providers from performing abortions, and believe that immigrants threaten traditional American customs and values. Democrats are more likely to view the coronavirus as a serious crisis, are more worried about climate change, believe the government is not doing enough to protect LGBTQ individuals, and believe that gun laws should be more strict. People who self-identify as independents tend to fall between the extremes of the two parties' positions.

9.3.2 Gender and Public Opinion

Differences between men and women in policy preferences, patterns of political engagement, and voting have existed for decades. Throughout much of our history, men participated in politics at higher rates than women. Texas women were not even allowed to vote until 1919. However, since 1980 the national turnout rate in every presidential election has been higher for women than for men. Numerically, far more women than men have voted in elections since 1964.[44] Turnout patterns for women in Texas follow similar patterns as national trends.

A statistically significant **gender gap** separates men and women in the country regarding their patterns of voting, partisan affiliations, and policy preferences.

gender gap
Differences in voting and policy preferences between men and women.

TABLE 9-1 PUBLIC OPINION OF TEXANS ON SELECT PUBLIC POLICIES BY PARTY

Texans who ...	Democrat %	Independent %	Republican %
Strongly approve of the job performance of President Trump***	2	21	60
Are very worried about climate change**	58	20	16
Believe gun laws should be stricter**	81	45	24
Believe that newcomers from other countries threaten traditional American customs and values**	21	40	67
Favor prohibiting health care workers from performing abortions***	21	40	74
Believe the Texas state government is not doing enough to protect LGBTQ Texans*	64	20	6
Believe the coronavirus is a serious crisis***	91	56	48
Strongly agree that undocumented immigrants should be deported immediately***	7	24	47
View the police very favorably*	11	21	48
Favor allowing Texans to vote by mail in response to the coronavirus***	86	51	29

*June 2019 (Conducted May 31 to June 9, 2019; 1,200 registered voters, margin of error +/−2.83 percentage points)
**October 2019 (Conducted October 18 to 27, 2019; 1,200 registered voters, margin of error +/−2.83 percentage points)
***April 2020 (Conducted April 10 to 19, 2020; 1,200 registered voters, margin of error +/−2.83 percentage points.)
SOURCE: Data from YouGov Texas Statewide Study, conducted at various intervals.

TABLE 9-2 PUBLIC OPINION OF TEXANS ON SELECT PUBLIC POLICIES BY SEX

Texans who ...	Men %	Women %
Strongly approve of the job performance of President Trump***	39	33
Are very worried about climate change**	36	41
Believe gun laws should be stricter**	43	57
Believe that newcomers from other countries threaten traditional American customs and values**	50	38
Favor prohibiting health care workers from performing abortions***	50	46
Believe the Texas state government is not doing enough to protect LGBTQ Texans*	27	35
Believe the coronavirus is a serious crisis***	61	71
Strongly agree that undocumented immigrants should be deported immediately***	32	25
View the police very favorably*	32	26
Favor allowing Texans to vote by mail in response to the coronavirus***	51	59

*June 2019 (Conducted May 31 to June 9, 2019; 1,200 registered voters, margin of error +/−2.83 percentage points)
**October 2019 (Conducted October 18 to 27, 2019; 1,200 registered voters, margin of error +/−2.83 percentage points)
***April 2020 (Conducted April 10 to 19, 2020; 1,200 registered voters, margin of error +/−2.83 percentage points.)
SOURCE: Data from YouGov Texas Statewide Study, conducted at various intervals.

Research demonstrates that consistent differences between men and women exist on a variety of public policy issues. Women are more liberal than their male counterparts (even when we control for other relevant factors like age, religion, education, and income) and are more likely to support the Democratic Party and to vote for Democratic candidates.[45] Policy differences exist in both domestic and foreign policy and have been statistically significant for decades. Women are more likely to favor social service programs that provide health care and protect basic human needs, to favor affirmative action, and to support governmental policies that promote equality based on race, gender, and sexual identity.[46] As you can see in Table 9–2, these national patterns exist in Texas as well. Compared to men, women are more likely to be concerned about climate change, favor stricter gun control laws, believe that the state is not doing enough to protect LGBTQ Texans, and believe that COVID-19 is a very serious crisis. Men are more supportive of the job that President Trump is doing, are more likely to believe that immigrants threaten traditional American values, and are more supportive of the immediate deportation of undocumented immigrants. Women are more supportive of allowing Texans to vote by mail in response to the coronavirus, while men tend to view the police more favorably; however, there are few differences between men and women regarding views on abortion rights.

9.3.3 Race, Ethnicity, and Public Opinion

For much of the twentieth century, the major ethnic minorities in the United States were from Europe, were incorporated into American politics as part of the New Deal Coalition, and were solidly supportive of the Democratic Party. As these groups became more and more assimilated into the American economic and political system, they became more diverse in their political views and party identification, making them less distinct as groups.

African Americans were enslaved and brought to this country beginning in 1619, and servitude placed them at the bottom of the socioeconomic system through the Civil War. The war ended slavery, but on most economic measures, the African American population in the United States, including Texas, fell into the lower economic stratum of the country. By nearly any measure available, African Americans, on the whole, have lower standards of living than white Americans. Following the Civil Rights movement in the 1960s, African Americans emerged as a cohesive and strong political force, largely because of their geographic settlement patterns. As a whole, African Americans strongly support the Democratic Party.[47]

Texas African Americans and Hispanics identify with the Democratic Party at much higher rates than Anglo Texans. As we saw in Chapter 1, African Americans are the second-smallest racial group in Texas, constituting around 12 percent of the population. Latinos constitute only 18 percent of the nation's population, but the group represents nearly 40 percent of Texans (and is growing at a fast rate both in the state and the country).

Non-Hispanic whites are supporting the Republican Party at higher rates than ever before. Currently over 60 percent of white Texans identify with or lean toward the Republican Party, which is substantially larger than the approximately 51 percent of non-Hispanic whites living in other states who lean Republican.[48] While the percentage of Asian Texans is growing rapidly, their numbers remain too small to be included in analyses such as is presented in Table 9–3. Generally, Asian American Texans tend to be more supportive of the Democratic Party.

On a number of policy issues, African Americans and Hispanics tend to display similar political attitudes, especially on voting rights, public education, health care, and other programs addressing income disparity. For some issues, there are marked differences in the positions often taken by Hispanics and African Americans. Although Hispanics as a whole are more likely to be Democratic, Texas Hispanics support the Republican Party at higher levels than do Hispanics nationally.[49]

As you can see in Table 9–3, substantial racial differences exist in Texas. Looking at each area of public policy presented, as well as evaluations of the president and perceptions of COVID-19, we can see interesting patterns among the major racial and ethnic groups in Texas. African Americans are generally (when compared to whites on the whole) more supportive of stricter gun laws, believe that the coronavirus is a serious crisis, are more concerned about climate change, are more supportive of allowing Texans to vote by mail in response to the coronavirus, and believe that the Texas government is not doing enough to protect LGBTQ Texans. On other issues, whites are more supportive of President Trump, believe that new immigrants threaten traditional American values, are more likely to believe that undocumented immigrants should be immediately deported, are more supportive of limiting abortion rights, and view

TABLE 9–3 PUBLIC OPINION OF TEXANS ON SELECT PUBLIC POLICIES BY MAJOR RACIAL AND ETHNIC GROUPS

Texans who ...	Anglo %	African American %	Hispanic %
Strongly approve of the job performance of President Trump***	45	10	26
Are very worried about climate change**	37	46	37
Believe gun laws should be stricter**	43	73	56
Believe that newcomers from other countries threaten traditional American customs and values**	51	28	36
Favor prohibiting health care workers from performing abortions***	51	40	45
Believe the Texas state government is not doing enough to protect LGBTQ Texans*	29	38	33
Believe the coronavirus is a serious crisis***	64	81	65
Strongly agree that undocumented immigrants should be deported immediately***	32	17	23
View the police very favorably*	36	9	24
Favor allowing Texans to vote by mail in response to the coronavirus***	51	71	60

*June 2019 (Conducted May 31 to June 9, 2019; 1,200 registered voters, margin of error +/−2.83 percentage points)
**October 2019 (Conducted October 18 to 27, 2019; 1,200 registered voters, margin of error +/−2.83 percentage points)
***April 2020 (Conducted April 10 to 19, 2020; 1,200 registered voters, margin of error +/−2.83 percentage points.)
SOURCE: Data from YouGov Texas Statewide Study, conducted at various intervals.

the police more favorably than black Americans tend to. Latino opinions tend to fall between these two groups. For example, only 10 percent of African Americans strongly approve of the performance of President Trump while 45 percent of white respondents and 26 percent of Latino respondents do. Race is an interesting variable, as it interacts with educational attainment, religion, and gender in noteworthy and complex ways.

9.3.4 Education and Public Opinion

Significant differences exist between the more and less educated across the country. Generally speaking, the more educated tend to be more supportive of First Amendment freedoms (like freedom of speech, press, and religion—including the right not to be religious) than those with lower educational attainment. More educated people tend to be more liberal on a variety of social and cultural issues and tend to have different foreign policy preferences. For example, the more educated favor policies that advocate a broader engagement in foreign affairs, while the less educated tend to support more isolationist foreign policies.[50] Table 9–4 shows distinct differences in opinions among Texans based on educational attainment regarding the job approval ratings of President Trump, views on climate change, gun control, abortion, LGBTQ rights, views of immigrants, the need for the immediate deportation of undocumented immigrants, and the seriousness of the coronavirus (when reading the table, it is often easiest to compare the two extreme groups to see the most marketed differences in opinions).

9.3.5 Religion and Public Opinion

Religion has always been extremely important in this state and country. Today, a substantial majority of Americans state that they belong to a religious body and that religious faith is an important component of their lives. In fact, 69 percent of Texans state that they have an absolute belief in the certainty of God (compared with 63 percent of people nationwide), with only 2 percent stating they do not believe in God. While this number is higher than the national average, it is down from 77 percent professing such a belief in 2007.[51] The United States remains a heavily Christian

TABLE 9–4 PUBLIC OPINION OF TEXANS ON SELECT PUBLIC POLICIES BY EDUCATIONAL ATTAINMENT

Texans who ...	Less than High School Diploma %	High School Diploma %	Some College %	Two-Year College Degree %	Four-Year College Degree %	Post-Graduate Degree %
Strongly approve of the job performance of President Trump***	43	31	40	37	36	32
Are very worried about climate change**	31	35	40	35	40	46
Believe gun laws should be stricter**	60	50	49	55	45	41
Believe that newcomers from other countries threaten traditional American customs and values**	30	50	39	54	38	40
Favor prohibiting health care workers from performing abortions***	40	48	40	48	34	33
Believe the Texas state government is not doing enough to protect LGBTQ Texans*	24	27	29	30	37	38
Believe the coronavirus is a serious crisis***	60	65	63	59	70	74
Strongly agree that undocumented immigrants should be deported immediately***	39	32	27	28	26	24
View the police very favorably*	11	31	30	32	29	28
Favor allowing Texans to vote by mail in response to the coronavirus***	44	51	56	50	59	60

*June 2019 (Conducted May 31 to June 9, 2019; 1,200 registered voters, margin of error +/−2.83 percentage points)
**October 2019 (Conducted October 18 to 27, 2019; 1,200 registered voters, margin of error +/−2.83 percentage points)
***April 2020 (Conducted April 10 to 19, 2020; 1,200 registered voters, margin of error +/−2.83 percentage points.)
SOURCE: Data from YouGov Texas Statewide Study, conducted at various intervals.

country, but the percentage affiliating with Christian faiths has been steadily declining while those professing no affiliation has been growing steadily since at least 2007.[52]

An examination of religious traditions in Texas shows that the largest faith is evangelical Protestants (substantially more Texans identify as evangelicals than do people nationally—31 percent in Texas versus 25 percent nationally). The next largest faith is Roman Catholic (23 percent), followed by mainline Protestant traditions (13 percent), and then historically African American religions (6 percent).[53] With growth in the Asian population, Texas has seen an increase in Muslims, especially in Houston and other major metropolitan areas, though statewide Muslims represent only 1 percent of the population.

Religious differences are evident in views on a variety of public policies. Even while controlling for other relevant factors, such as income, Catholics and Jewish people traditionally tend to be more liberal than Protestants. However, changes in political views have taken place, reflecting, in part, the effect of crosscutting pressures. We now see divisions in Catholics between those who are more traditional and those who are more liberal (differences motivated by issues of abortion, LGBTQ rights, and social justice). Consequently, the more conservative Catholics are increasingly voting Republican, while the more liberal Catholics are remaining Democratic. Across the nation and in Texas, mainline white Protestants (Episcopalians, Presbyterians, and some Methodists) have been engaged in divisive arguments about same-sex marriage, homosexuality, and the ordination of homosexuals to church leadership positions. These divisions have affected party identification and voting for some members of those denominations. White evangelicals tend to be very conservative, strongly opposed to abortion and same-sex marriage, and solid supporters of the Republican Party.[54]

A great variety of opinions exists within and between religions. Consequently, one good way to determine the impact of religion on public opinion is to look for differences by a common measure of religiosity (the self-reported importance of religion in daily life). Looking at religiosity is helpful in seeing the manifestations of patterns. Table 9–5 shows substantial differences among Texans based on the importance of religion regarding nearly every issue we have been examining. Notably, we see substantial differences in views of abortion, LGBTQ rights, the impact of immigrants on

TABLE 9-5 PUBLIC OPINION OF TEXANS ON SELECT PUBLIC POLICIES BY RELIGIOSITY

Texans who ...	Extremely Important %	Somewhat Important %	Not Very Important %	Not Important at All %
Strongly approve of the job performance of President Trump***	47	34	18	20
Are very worried about climate change**	46	35	34	45
Believe gun laws should be stricter**	46	50	51	64
Believe that newcomers from other countries threaten traditional American customs and values**	51	45	35	28
Favor prohibiting health care workers from performing abortions***	70	42	27	17
Believe the Texas state government is not doing enough to protect LGBTQ Texans*	19	25	44	63
Believe the coronavirus is a serious crisis***	63	59	80	75
Strongly agree that undocumented immigrants should be deported immediately***	34	28	14	23
View the police very favorably*	37	32	21	9
Favor allowing Texans to vote by mail in response to the coronavirus***	48	50	68	75

*June 2019 (Conducted May 31 to June 9, 2019; 1,200 registered voters, margin of error +/−2.83 percentage points)
**October 2019 (Conducted October 18 to 27, 2019; 1,200 registered voters, margin of error +/−2.83 percentage points)
***April 2020 (Conducted April 10 to 19, 2020; 1,200 registered voters, margin of error +/−2.83 percentage points.)
SOURCE: Data from YouGov Texas Statewide Study, conducted at various intervals.

TABLE 9–6 PUBLIC OPINION OF TEXANS ON SELECT PUBLIC POLICIES BY AGE

Texans who...	18–29 Years Old %	30–44 Years Old %	45–64 Years Old %	65+ Years Old %
Strongly approve of the job performance of President Trump***	13	27	44	48
Are very worried about climate change**	47	40	33	35
Believe gun laws should be stricter**	60	54	48	42
Believe that newcomers from other countries threaten traditional American customs and values**	40	28	50	53
Favor prohibiting health care workers from performing abortions***	36	43	53	55
Believe the Texas state government is not doing enough to protect LGBTQ Texans*	39	38	32	19
Believe the coronavirus is a serious crisis***	69	68	61	69
Strongly agree that undocumented immigrants should be deported immediately***	17	23	34	33
View the police very favorably*	22	20	30	43
Favor allowing Texans to vote by mail in response to the coronavirus***	69	68	48	42

*June 2019 (Conducted May 31 to June 9, 2019; 1,200 registered voters, margin of error +/–2.83 percentage points)
**October 2019 (Conducted October 18 to 27, 2019; 1,200 registered voters, margin of error +/–2.83 percentage points)
***April 2020 (Conducted April 10 to 19, 2020; 1,200 registered voters, margin of error +/–2.83 percentage points.)
SOURCE: Data from YouGov Texas Statewide Study, conducted at various intervals.

traditional American values, and gun laws. Moreover, we see significant differences regarding President Trump's job approval ratings based upon the importance individuals place upon their religious beliefs.

9.3.6 Age and Public Opinion

One of the best predictors of political engagement is age. Young people are far less likely than older people to engage in politics. The highest rates of participation are among middle-aged people. Younger adults tend to be in a transitory stage of their lives in which they do not identify with the issues or politics of the communities in which they live. They are less likely to be married, less likely to own homes, and more likely to move frequently (hence running into issues with voter registration and residency). Younger voters engage in a wide range of volunteer activities, but these tend not to be political.

Research shows that early adulthood is an important time for learning political values, and that once policy preferences become stable, they are likely to remain throughout a lifetime.[55] Consequently, differences in opinion by age that are present in Texas, some of which are displayed in Table 9–6, are likely to remain in the future. Job-approval ratings of President Trump, views of climate change, gun control, access to abortion, LGBTQ rights, and views of the police show distinct age-related patterns. Thirteen percent of younger Texans strongly approve of the job President Trump is doing versus 48 percent of older Texans.

Political Participation

9.4 Identify the manner in which opinion translates into political action.

Voting and running for office are the first two activities that may come to mind when we think of political participation. But they are just small parts of the ongoing process necessary to sustain a democratic political system, translate the interests and demands of the public into specific policies, and ensure governmental responsiveness. On any given day, Texas newspapers publish hundreds of letters to the editor addressing a wide range of state and local political issues. People contact public officials every day about stop signs, public facilities, garbage collection, and a multitude of governmental functions and responsibilities. Thousands of people are involved in politics as they attempt to shape the actions of public officials.

Most people who participate in politics engage in what scholars call conventional political behavior. This includes voting, running for office, contributing to and campaigning for candidates, writing letters, gathering petitions, participating in other grassroots activities, and lobbying. Fewer individuals participate in what is considered unconventional political behavior—acts that may offend some people. These acts can include boycotts, protest marches, and other nonviolent demonstrations, although many individuals consider any lawful, peaceful demonstration a conventional means of exercising their constitutional rights. To most people, however, destruction of property, personal injury, assassination, and other forms of violence are totally unacceptable forms of political behavior.[56]

Political behavior is complex and changes over time, and a number of factors can shape this behavior and produce different behaviors at different stages of a person's life. It is important to avoid drawing hard-and-fast conclusions. But, for purposes of comparing individuals, a number of scholars have developed classifications of political behavior that run from high levels of involvement in a wide range of activities to virtual passivity.

Sidney Verba and Norman H. Nie, well-known American political scientists specializing in political socialization, identified six categories of political participation, inactives, voting specialists, communalists, campaigners, parochial participants, and activists.[57] At one end of the spectrum are the **activists**, who engage in all types of political activity. These individuals are not only involved in political campaigns; they also participate in almost every other arena of community life. At the other end are the *inactives*, who participate rarely, if at all, in the political life of the community. Some scholars refer to the first group as *political gladiators* and the second group as *apathetics*.[58] This classification has been used regularly since Verba and Nie's seminal research in 1972 and is well established within the academic literature.

Also relatively inactive, and sharing many of the characteristics of the inactives, are the *voting specialists*. These individuals vote regularly in presidential and local elections but seldom engage in other organizational activities or attempt to contact policymakers personally. A small number of *parochial participants* do not vote or engage in collective activity or campaigns. Nevertheless, they do contact policymakers over specific issues that affect their personal lives. The *communalists* demonstrate a high rate of participation in community life but a low level of campaign activity. These people participate in community activities such as church, PTA, and neighborhood associations but rarely engage in the high-conflict game of political campaigns. The *campaigners* are just the opposite. They participate regularly in political campaigns but rarely in community activities. This group appears to be attracted to the conflict of campaigns.[59]

Why some people get actively involved in politics and public life and others seem totally uninterested in government, current events, or public policy is a question that has challenged scholars, candidates, journalists, and reform groups for years and has generated much research.

One area that has spawned a significant amount of academic research involves the individual calculation to vote. Why do some become habitual voters, while others never vote? Research on voting behavior generally focuses on two areas: voter turnout (the factors that lead a person to vote) and voter choice (the factors that lead a person to select one candidate or party over another).

When discussing the health of American democracy, many look at voter turnout (simply the percentage of eligible voters who cast a ballot in a given election) and declare that our political system is vulnerable, as participation levels in the United States are much lower than in other countries. Later in the chapter we examine the issue of nonvoting in greater

activists
A small segment of the population that is engaged in various political activities.

detail, as different perspectives on this topic exist. Some believe that since we have universal suffrage (meaning most adult citizens can vote), the fact that some choose not to vote indicates general satisfaction. In essence, we have the luxury of apathy. Others see nonparticipation as problematic, noting that surveys show increased distrust and heightened skepticism of governmental officials. As you continue to read this chapter, consider these two different positions to help you form your own opinion about this important matter.

First, we will look at the individual-level factors that influence turnout (the aggregate, or structural, factors impacting turnout are discussed in Chapter 11) and voter choice. Then we will look at the role of social group membership in explaining political participation. Once we see who participates and how, we will consider whether nonvoting is a problem, and then examine patterns in public opinion and the mechanisms in place to measure public opinion.

9.4.1 Voting Patterns

There is great variation in the levels of participation nationwide (see Figure 9–1). Oklahoma had the lowest percentage of the voting-age population participate in the 2020 presidential election with 55 percent turnout (compared with the national average of 66.7 percent, which was significantly higher than the 56 percent that voted nationally in 2016). In 2020, the highest level of participation was found in Minnesota, where 80 percent of eligible adults voted. The turnout rate for Texas was 60.4 percent, more than 6 percentage points below the national average (though this rate was higher than we saw in 2016 where less than 48 percent of the eligible population voted). Texas had the second lowest turnout rate in the country (behind only Hawaii). Texas has had one of the lowest turnout rates for adults in the entire country for the past four presidential elections. Turnout rates in midterm elections tend to be much lower but similar patterns of participation hold true. For example, in 2018 the turnout rate in Texas was 45.6 percent, 80 percent of the states had higher turnout rates though this was a much higher turnout than typical in the state. Maine had the highest turnout rate with 64.5 percent of its citizens participating in Congressional elections.[60] The turnout rate increased substantially in 2018 to 50 percent from a near-record low of 36.7 percent in

FIGURE 9–1 ESTIMATED TURNOUT AS A PERCENTAGE OF CITIZENS OF VOTING AGE FOR SELECTED STATES, 2020 GENERAL ELECTIONS

Voting participation rates vary dramatically throughout the country, from a high of 80 percent in Maine to a low of 55 percent in Oklahoma. The turnout rate in Texas ranks it in forty-fourth place in the country.

NOTE: The estimates presented here may not be directly comparable to some Census reports on voting and registration because the population considered is the voting-age population (which includes all adults, even those ineligible to vote like resident aliens and other immigrants), rather than the citizens of voting age (which includes only those eligible to vote) examined in most recent reports.

SOURCE: 2020 November General Election Turnout Rates, United States Elections Project, University of Florida, http://www.electproject.org/2020g.

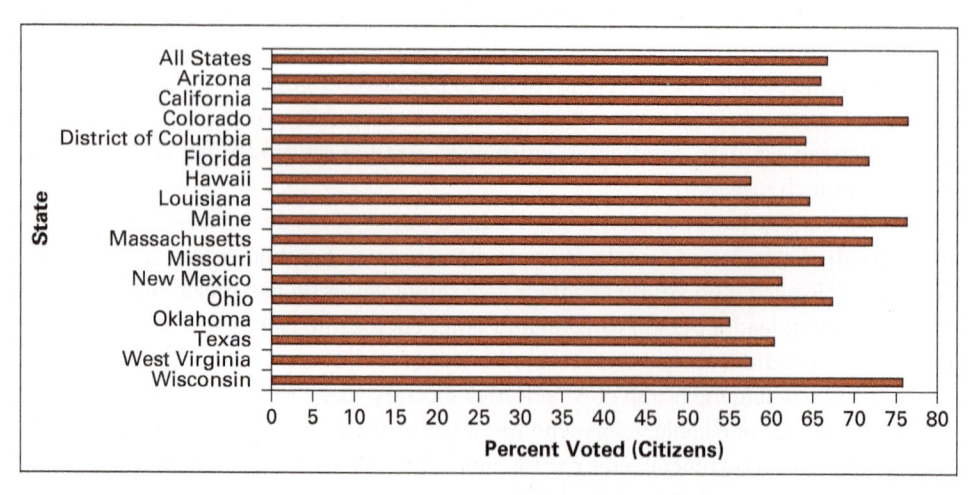

2014. Since 1972, turnout rates in midterm elections have hovered around 40 percent. Turnout in Texas increased to 45.6 percent in 2018 (up from 30.4 percent in 2014).

Habitual voters have markedly different characteristics than habitual nonvoters. Individuals with higher income levels are more likely to be active participants in a wider range of political activities than those with low incomes. Affluent people have more time and resources to engage in political activities. They have a better understanding of the process, and they are acquainted with other participants and public officials.

Participation also increases as the level of education increases. People with college degrees are more likely to participate in politics than those who are less educated. For example, in 2016, the turnout rate for those who did not complete high school was 34 percent, while the turnout rate for those with a bachelor's degree was 74 percent, and turnout for those with advanced degrees was 80 percent (at the time of publication, turnout rates for key demographic groups for 2020 were not yet available).[61] Turnout in the 2014 midterm election was significantly lower for all educational groups but similar patterns were observed.[62] Turnout in the 2018 midterm elections saw even more pronounced differentials in turnout rates based upon educational attainment. Only 20 percent of people without a high school diploma voted in 2018 versus 62 percent with a bachelor's degree and 68 percent with an advanced degree.[63] As noted earlier, education also is correlated with income, as well as race and ethnicity. Knowledge of political issues, public policies, the political process, and public officials makes a person aware of the importance and potential benefits of political participation.

Historically men had higher levels of participation, but women have been voting in higher rates nationally than men for decades. The only exception to this pattern is Asian women; their turnout rates did not exceed those of Asian men until 2002.[64] In 2016, the turnout rate for women in Texas was substantially higher than that of men (nearly 50 percent of women voted compared with only 46 percent of men). Even during the less visible midterm election of 2014, women's turnout rates in Texas exceeded that of men with nearly 33 percent of eligible women voting compared with 28 percent of men.[65] In 2018, nearly 45 percent of female Texans versus 40 percent of male Texans voted.[66]

Figure 9–2 depicts voting rates by key demographic groups. Note that the turnout in midterm elections (like 2010 and 2014) was historically much lower than evidenced in presidential election years (like 2008, 2012, and 2016). Moreover, since there are more women than men in Texas (as elsewhere), Texas women's higher turnout rates meant that women ended up constituting 53.6 percent of the electorate in 2016 and 54.2 percent in 2018.[67]

Rates of participation among Anglos have historically been highest among all ethnic groups. But African Americans, despite historical patterns of discrimination, now are participating at rates close to (and in some instances greater than) Anglos. In 2012, for the first time, the African American voter turnout rate in a presidential election exceeded that of whites (66.2 percent versus 64.1 percent nationally and 61.1 percent versus 59.8 percent in Texas).[68] Historical white participation rates have been substantially higher than other groups, in large part because of practices in Texas and other southern states in the pre–Civil Rights era of restricting minority voting. In 1992, the national turnout rate for white voters was about 10 percent higher than for African American voters. By 2004, the gap had narrowed to less than 8 points difference. In 2008, the turnout rate for African American and whites nationally was almost the same. In 2014, African American turnout rates were much lower than those for whites (with only 33.4 percent of eligible African Americans in Texas voting compared with nearly 41 percent of whites). In 2016, turnout rates for African Americans were also very low in comparison with recent presidential elections with only 55.9 percent turning out to vote (compared with nearly 64.1 percent of White non-Hispanic [this is the Census Bureau category] voters).[69] In 2018, significant differences in turnout rates were also evident among racial/ethnic groups in Texas. The turnout rate for

FIGURE 9-2 ESTIMATED TURNOUT AS A PERCENTAGE OF CITIZENS OF VOTING AGE BY KEY DEMOGRAPHICS, 2008, 2010, 2012, 2014, 2016, AND 2018 GENERAL ELECTIONS

Turnout levels in elections vary depending on a wide array of variables. For example, the type of election (midterm versus presidential), the presence of an incumbent, and key demographics impact turnout. Depicted here are turnout levels for men and women, Anglos, African Americans, Asians, and Hispanics for the 2008 through 2018 elections. As you can see, great variation exists based on race and gender.

NOTE: The estimates presented here may not be directly comparable to some reports on voting and registration because the population considered is the voting-age population (which includes all adults, even those ineligible to vote like resident aliens and other immigrants), rather than the citizens of voting-age (which includes only those eligible to vote) examined in most recent reports. Similar patterns emerge even if data were to depict eligible voters versus all adults.

SOURCE: Data from U.S. Census Bureau, *Voting and Registration in the Election of November 2018*, Table 4b accessed at https://www.census.gov/data/tables/time-series/demo/voting-and-registration/p20-583.html; *Voting and Registration in the Election of November 2016*, Table 4b accessed at https://www.census.gov/data/tables/time-series/demo/voting-and-registration/p20-580.html, U.S. Census Bureau, *Voting and Registration in the Election of November 2014*, Table 4b accessed at https://www.census.gov/data/tables/time-series/demo/voting-and-registration/p20-577.html, U.S. Census Bureau, *Voting and Registration in the Election of November 2012*, Table 4b accessed at https://www.census.gov/data/tables/2012/demo/voting-and-registration/p20-568.html, U.S. Census Bureau, *Voting and Registration in the Election of November 2010*, Table 4b accessed at https://www.census.gov/data/tables/2010/demo/voting-and-registration/voting-registration-2010-election.html, U.S. Census Bureau, *Voting and Registration in the Election of November 2008*, Table 4b accessed at https://www.census.gov/data/tables/2008/demo/voting-and-registration/p20-562-rv.html.

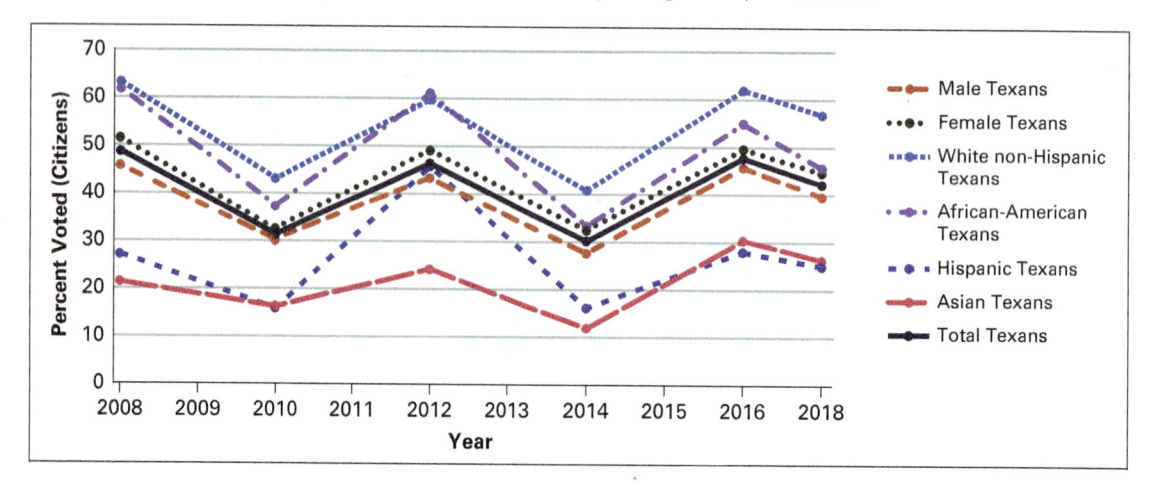

white non-Hispanic voters was 57.8 percent, while the turnout rates for blacks was 45.8 percent.

Hispanics tend to participate at much lower rates than either whites or African Americans. As we will see in Chapter 11, citizenship requirements constitute a significant factor in the ability of many Hispanics to participate in elections. Turnout rates can be calculated by examining the percentage of people who voted versus the entire adult population or the percent of people who voted versus the eligible adult population. The latter method controls for citizenship and other factors which prohibit some from participating (for example, some states have large ex-felon populations which are prohibited from voting). We report turnout using the more frequently used method of participation per eligible adult, but even if examining turnout per eligible citizen, Hispanic turnout rates would be consistently lower than those of whites and African Americans. Explanations for these variations include educational and income differences, alienation from and disappointment with both political parties, and the degree to which Hispanics have been assimilated into the political culture. Hispanic turnout rates were substantially below those of whites and African Americans in 2016 and 2018, with only 32.5 percent of eligible Hispanics voting in 2016 and 28.5 percent in 2018.[70] In 2014, only 16.2 percent of eligible Hispanics voted, a rate only slightly higher than that seen in 2010. Nationwide, the numbers of Latino people who voted in presidential elections increased by around 2.9 million between 2008 and 2016.[71] However, at the same time, the turnout rate did not increase as fast as one might think as the number of eligible Latino voters increased at a large rate. In 2016, the U.S. Census Bureau estimated that nearly 14 million Latinos across the nation chose not to vote even though they were eligible; that number increased to 17.2 million in 2018.[72] A 2019 study by the Pew Research Center estimates that for the first time, the percent of eligible Latino voters will exceed that of African American voters in 2020, with a projected 32 million Hispanics being eligible to vote nationwide. This same study found that the proportion of Asian Americans eligible to vote has doubled since 2000, from 5 million to more than an estimated 11 million voters. This figure represents nearly 5 percent of the expected electorate.[73] As is clear in Figure 9-2, these national turnout patterns are reflected in state patterns. The turnout rate for Asians has also been historically low, for many of the same reasons as for Latinos. However, nationally and in Texas, turnout rates for Asians exceeded those for Hispanics for the first time in 2016. This pattern continued in 2018.

In addition to changing demographic patterns in turnout, the racial composition of voters is changing as societal demographics change. Non-white voters were 26.7 percent of all voters nationwide in 2016, providing overwhelming support for Clinton (though to a lesser degree than they did for Obama in 2008 and 2012).[74] The percent of non-white voters increased to 27.2 in 2018.[75] It is estimated that in 2020, non-white voters will accounted for 33 percent of all voters, and by 2060 will account for nearly 55 percent of voters.[76] The recent turnout shows slight improvement, but certainly not the full potential for the state's Hispanic population. This is where the battle for Texas's political future will increasingly be fought.

Voter registration and turnout are not simply explained by racial or ethnic factors. Study after study of registration and turnout demonstrate a direct relationship between education and income.[77] Figure 9–3 depicts turnout rates over time by educational attainment. Although the figure contains national data, the trends are similar for Texans. Since 1964, turnout rates have declined for all groups, regardless of educational attainment; however, the differences between the groups remain steady and consistent over time. Across racial and ethnic groups, people with more education and higher incomes are more likely to vote than those at the lower end of the scales. Low income and educational levels serve to deter voter participation among all racial and ethnic groups.

FIGURE 9–3 TURNOUT RATES BY EDUCATIONAL ATTAINMENT

Depicted here are national turnout rates in presidential elections since 1964 by educational attainment. As you can see in the figure, overall levels of voting have declined regardless of educational attainment; however, there are great differences in patterns of participation between the more and less educated.

SOURCE: U.S. Census Bureau, *Voting and Registration in the Election of November 2018*, Table 5 accessed at https://www.census.gov/data/tables/time-series/demo/voting-and-registration/p20-583.html; U.S. Census Bureau, *Current Population Survey*, Historical Table A-2, https://www.census.gov/data/tables/time-series/demo/educational-attainment/cps-historical-time-series.html, U.S. Census Bureau, Current Population Survey, Historical Table A-2, https://www2.census.gov/programs-surveys/cps/tables/time-series/voting-historical-time-series/a2.xlsx.

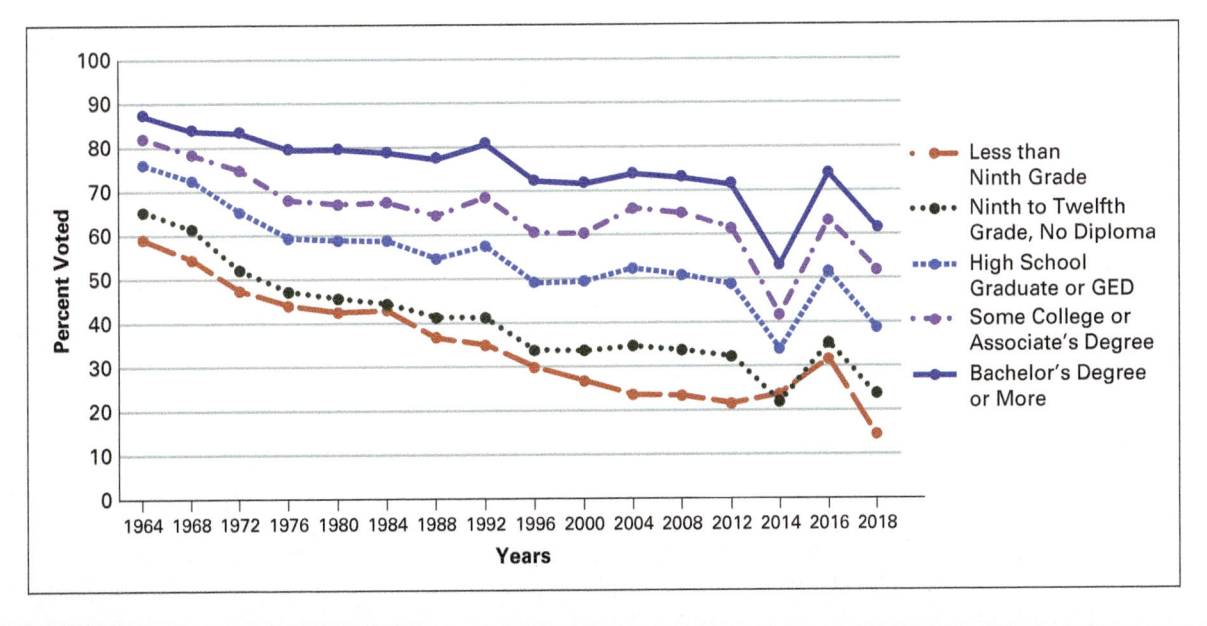

FIGURE 9–4 ESTIMATED TURNOUT AS A PERCENTAGE OF CITIZENS OF VOTING AGE FOR SELECTED AGE CATEGORIES, 2008, 2010, 2012, 2014, 2016 AND 2018 GENERAL ELECTIONS

Over time, American youth have tended to have lower turnout levels; however, as heightened levels in 2008 demonstrate, younger voters can be mobilized to participate at higher levels.

NOTE: Some researchers use the percent of the total population who voted, which would slightly alter the percentages, but the same general pattern would emerge.

SOURCE: U.S. Census Bureau, *Voting and Registration in the Election of November 2018*, Table 4c accessed at https://www.census.gov/data/tables/time-series/demo/voting-and-registration/p20-583.html; U.S. Census Bureau, *Voting and Registration in the Election of November 2016*, Table 4b accessed at https://www.census.gov/data/tables/time-series/demo/voting-and-registration/p20-580.html, U.S. Census Bureau, U.S. Census Bureau, *Voting and Registration in the Election of November 2014*, Table 4c accessed at https://www.census.gov/data/tables/time-series/demo/voting-and-registration/p20-577.html, U.S. Census Bureau, *Voting and Registration in the Election of November 2012*, Table 4c accessed at https://www.census.gov/data/tables/2012/demo/voting-and-registration/p20-568.html, U.S. Census Bureau, *Voting and Registration in the Election of November 2010*, Table 4c accessed at https://www.census.gov/data/tables/2010/demo/voting-and-registration/voting-registration-2010-election.html, and U.S. Census Bureau, *Voting and Registration in the Election of November 2008*, Table 4c accessed at https://www.census.gov/data/tables/2008/demo/voting-and-registration/p20-562-rv.html.

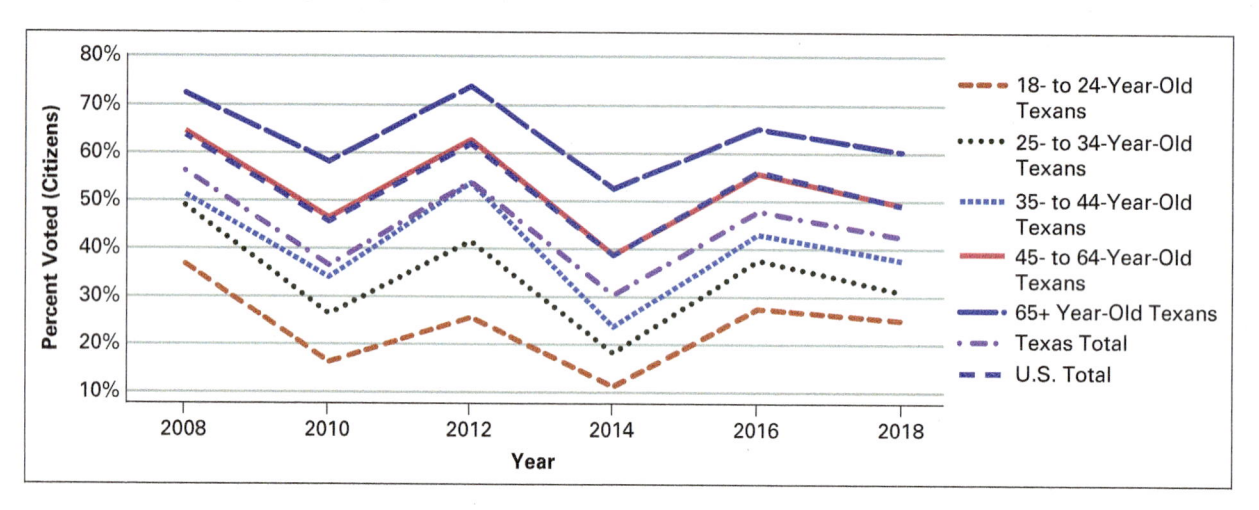

As noted earlier in the chapter, young people traditionally have the lowest turnout rates. Figure 9–4 depicts turnout rates for several elections by age. Since 2004, we have seen youth turnout rates vary considerably. In 2004 and 2008, they increased, but then returned to their prior low rates in 2012, 2014, and 2016. Turnout in 2018, while still very low, was higher than normal for a midterm election. Many expect turnout to be high for young voters in the 2020 presidential elections. The level of political engagement, notably through the Black Lives Matter and other protests for racial justice beginning in the summer of 2020, coupled with efforts by superstars like LeBron James and other athletes and celebrities to engage young and minority voters leads one to suspect this level of engagement will translate into higher voting rates and political activism in the future.

NONVOTING In Texas and elsewhere, there is a great deal of concern about decreased political participation. Election turnout has declined, and it often is difficult to get strong candidates to run for public office. Public discourse has lost its civility, and citizens do not seem to have learned the benefits and logic of collective action.[78] Surveys indicate much distrust of elected officials, and many people believe that government is for sale to the highest bidder. Moreover, some people just do not care. These findings lead many to conclude that an erosion of democratic practices has taken place in the state and the nation.

People in the higher socioeconomic groups are more likely to participate in a wider range of political activities, such as making political contributions, attending political conventions, or joining special interest groups. They have more influence on the policymaking process than people in the lower socioeconomic groups. One of the most disturbing aspects of the contemporary Texas political system is the low voter turnout in most elections, despite the elimination of discriminatory election laws, the creation of an extended voting period, and easy voter registration. Many people may be too uninformed about governmental actions to care to vote. Other people may be turned off by a belief that public officials put their own interests and moneyed special interests before the public interest. Increased levels of cynicism, distrust, and alienation may also be partly to blame. Negative attitudes about government and politicians continue to grow. Moreover, lifestyle changes have resulted in busier lives for most voters.

Other reasons for decreased turnout levels include high information costs. One reason some do not vote is that the costs of acquiring adequate information to feel sufficiently informed to be comfortable to vote is perceived to be higher than the benefit of voting. Even though registration is easier today than it was before, it can be confusing to many. In Texas, voters must register thirty days before the upcoming election, often before many become interested in the election. If a person moves, he or she needs to reregister. Moreover, unlike the vast majority of states, Texas does not allow citizens to register to vote online (in June 2018, 35 states and the District of Columbia allowed online registration). Since 2015, fifteen states and the District of Columbia have instituted automatic voter registration systems, whereby eligible citizens who interact with the governmental agencies are automatically registered to vote unless they decline.[79] Since we elect so many offices in Texas, the frequency of elections may confuse some potential voters. There are also *transition costs*—costs other than money associated with voting. Two of the largest transition costs are time and transportation. However, since 1987, Texas allows two kinds of early voting—in person and by mail. Mail-in ballots, as discussed in chapter 11, are only allowed under very narrow conditions. Many court challenges have arisen as attempts to expand the ability of Texans to vote by mail, especially during the coronavirus. Despite a majority of Texans supporting calls to expand the ability to vote by mail in response to the pandemic, Governor Abbott and Attorney General Paxton fought these efforts.

Some people say they do not vote because they fear that registering to vote may increase their chance of being summoned for jury duty, but Texas uses a combination list of registered voters, licensed drivers, and Department of Public Safety identification cards to identify potential jury members. Hence, fear of jury duty should not dissuade anyone from registering to vote.

Those who are willing to bear the costs, from learning how and where to register, to how and where to vote, tend to be those with higher levels of political efficacy. One way people gain efficacy is through formal education; another is through civic engagement. For these reasons, those with knowledge of the system have a responsibility to help others in their community learn how to exercise their political rights.

9.4.2 How Texans Voted in Recent Elections

In 2020, President Donald Trump carried 232 of Texas's 254 counties en route to his victory margin of 52.1 percent (he won 227 counties in 2016 with 52.6 percent of the vote, while Mitt Romney won 228 counties in 2012 with 57.2 percent of the vote). While Biden only won 22 counties, he won many of the highly populated counties, some by very large margins. For example, Biden won Bexar county (San Antonio) with 59 percent, Dallas county with 65 percent, Harris county (Houston) with 56 percent, and Travis county (Austin) with 72 percent of the vote. Most of Trump's strength came from heavily Republican and heavily conservative, rural and suburban Texas. Donald Trump won 162 counties—mostly rural—with more than 75 percent of the vote (which is more than Mitt Romney carried in 2012 and 70 more than he won this margin in 2016).[80] Biden did extremely well in the populated urban areas with large concentrations of minority and well-educated voters as well as some suburban counties but performed less well in the heavily Hispanic South Texas counties, especially as compared to Secretary Clinton in 2016 and President Obama in 2012. Both Clinton and Obama carried every major metropolitan county, except Tarrant County (Fort Worth), but lost nearly all the suburban counties around them.[81] Biden was able to perform as well, if not better, than Clinton in the urban areas, even winning Tarrant county; his performance in here was especially noteworthy since Tarrant county is considered perhaps the most conservative urban county nationwide. Obama was the first Democratic candidate since Lyndon Johnson to carry the state's largest urban areas. Biden did better than any Democrat in over twenty years, but it was insufficient for victory. In 2018, Democrats saw the closest race for the U.S. Senate in over a generation when Beto O'Rourke came within approximately 220,000 votes of defeating Senator Ted Cruz. O'Rourke won most of the same areas that Clinton and Obama carried, but he also won counties that had not voted for a Democrat in decades—such as Hays, Williamson, and Tarrant. While his victory in Tarrant was narrow, O'Rourke's victory was nevertheless notable as Democrats for statewide and national office had not been successful in Tarrant county for decades and may have helped Biden carry the county. Hays County is home to Texas State University, and many attribute O'Rourke's victory to his success in mobilizing college students; however, the county could be changing as Greg Abbott narrowly defeated his opponent despite beating Wendy Davis by nine points in 2014 and Biden beat Trump with over 54 percent of the vote in 2020. O'Rourke also did very well in what are seen as the more battleground counties of Farris and Fort Bend.[82] The popularity of his candidacy and general enthusiasm toward Democratic candidates in the state and nationwide, as well as higher-than-normal midterm turnout rates, propelled a number of Democratic candidates to Congress and the state legislature in 2018.

VOTING BY KEY DEMOGRAPHICS Limited exit polling was done in Texas in 2020, but that which was conducted indicated that Trump received 66 percent of the white vote, with 90 percent of African Americans, 58 percent of Latinos, and 63 percent of Asians voting for Biden.[83] Most suburban counties in Texas are heavily Anglo but this is changing. The metropolitan urban counties, which Biden carried in Texas, have large numbers of Hispanic and African American voters.

Although Anglos comprise some 45 percent of Texans, they accounted for 58 percent of the state's eligible voters and approximately 66 percent of the state's likely voters. Some were surprised with how well Trump did with Latinos, who constituted 23 percent of voters in 2020 (about the same as in 2016 and up from 22 percent in 2012), given his stance on immigration and the border wall. Latinos who voted for him seemed more concerned with economic issues and jobs than immigration. African Americans comprised 12 percent of the state's voting population, and evidence indicates that they turned out at high rates in many areas of the state.

Donald Trump won the vote of the majority of Texans, 55 percent, who are not college graduates and those earning more than $50,000 annually. Eighty-six percent of white evangelical Christians supported Trump, while those of other faiths or who are not religious were more likely to vote for Biden. Biden won 57 percent of voters younger than 29, those between 30 and 44 were equally split between Biden and Trump and Trump won with voters over 45. Those who voted for Trump did so because they cited concern over the economy, and crime and safety, while Biden voters were motivated by the coronavirus pandemic, health-care policy, and racial inequality.[84] Texans continued to liked Trump's promises of change and his outsider appeal.

Given the close Senate race in 2018, statewide polling of likely voters was conducted. Senator Cruz's supporters were more likely to be male (57 percent of men reported voting for Senator Cruz versus 44 percent of women—a larger-than-typical gender gap), older (62 percent of Texans over 65 voted for the Senator versus 29 percent of Texans under 30), white (68 percent of white voters supported Cruz while only 26 percent of voters of color did so), and rural (64 percent of rural voters reported voting for Cruz versus 51 percent of suburban and 36 percent of urban voters).[85] Similar patterns appeared in the successful reelection race of Governor Abbot as he defeated former Dallas Sheriff Lupe Valdez.

THE LOOMING HISPANIC VOTE Traditionally, Hispanics in Texas have voted heavily Democratic, leading to prolonged anticipation that Hispanic voters will turn the partisan tide and restore Democrats to political control in Texas. But that has not happened, at least not yet. Even though Texas has the second-largest Hispanic population in the country, the state went strongly for Republican Donald Trump in 2020 and 2016 (though to a lesser degree than it voted Republican in 2012), and Republicans remain firmly in control of state government and the congressional delegation from the Lone Star State.

Election results from heavily Hispanic counties in South Texas and along the Mexican border indicate the majority of Texas Hispanic voters cast their ballots for Biden in 2020, Clinton in 2016, Obama in 2012 and 2008, as well as O'Rourke and Valdez in 2018. In 2018, nearly 70 percent of Latinos voters preferred O'Rourke over Cruz, and 63 percent voted for Valdez over Abbott. O'Rourke won all of the Southern border counties except the rural counties of Hudspeth, Jeff Davis, Terrell, and Kenney. Biden performed worse than Clinton in the Southern border counties, for the most part, and worse with Hispanics in Texas than nationally demonstrating the complexity of attracting support from this rather diverse group.

Republicans already have made some inroads and suffered some setbacks among Hispanics. Strong Republican support for voter identification laws and tough laws cracking down on undocumented immigrants have hurt the party's cause with many Hispanics and may have contributed to President Obama's strong showing among Hispanics in the 2012 election. Interestingly, though, despite his inflammatory comments about Hispanics, Donald Trump won more of the Hispanic vote nationwide and within the state than did Mitt Romney. Despite his strong conservatism and support of the voter ID law, Governor Rick Perry, while he was in office, was among a growing number of Republicans trying to increase the party's appeal to Hispanics. He appointed several Hispanics to vacancies in statewide offices and signed a law giving the children of undocumented Hispanic immigrants a break through lower tuition at state universities. Only 16.4 percent of Governor Abbott's initial appointees have been Hispanic (less than 7 percent are African American and 3 percent Asian), the highest profile of which was the selection of former Cameron County Judge Carlos Cascos as his secretary of state.[86] Conservative Republicans believe that many Hispanics share their antiabortion viewpoint and concerns on other social issues. But Democrats counter that the Republican majority in the Texas legislature alienated most Hispanics with cuts in funding for education, health care, and other public programs important to low- and middle-income Hispanics.

Texas Republicans were encouraged by the 2012 election of Hispanic Ted Cruz—a Tea Party conservative Republican—to the U.S. Senate, despite his loss of most of the Hispanic vote, as well as George P. Bush's campaign for state land commissioner as a Republican in 2014 (and his victory after a tough primary battle in 2018). Bush is Hispanic—his mother is a native of Mexico—and he has a strong Republican pedigree. As noted at the beginning of the chapter, his father is former Florida governor Jeb Bush, his grandfather is former president George H. W. Bush, and his uncle is former president George W. Bush. The Democrats' list of candidates with the ability to wage an effective statewide campaign is short, but two Hispanics—the twin Castro brothers from San Antonio—have growing star power. Former San Antonio Mayor Julián Castro was appointed by President Obama to serve as the secretary of housing and urban development in 2014. His brother Joaquin was elected to the House of Representatives in 2012 to represent Texas district 20, which contains San Antonio and Bexar Counties. Veronica Escobar won O'Rourke's former seat in Congress, Texas district 16. As a former El Paso County Commissioner and then El Paso County Judge, many see her future as highly promising.

Public Opinion Polling

9.5 Explain how public opinion is measured and how to interpret public opinion poll results.

The origins of the polling industry usually are linked to George Gallup, who conducted a statewide poll in 1932 for his mother-in-law who was running for secretary of state in Iowa. Survey research or **public opinion polling** has a variety of applications, most of which are nonpolitical; market research is now a multibillion-dollar industry.[87]

Much of the public is unable to distinguish good public opinion polls from bad, making the public vulnerable to manipulation and misinformation. The purpose of this section is to provide you with basic information so you can become a good

public opinion polling
The scientific measurement of people's attitudes toward business products, public issues, public officeholders, or political candidates. It has become a key ingredient of statewide political campaigns and is usually conducted by telephone, using a representative sample of voters.

9.5.1 Survey Research

Polls represent an opportunity to present a snapshot of the opinion of the public on a variety of topics, from voting intentions, to opinions of Congress, to faith in the president. Polls are useful for politicians to gauge public concerns and create campaign strategies and for citizens to learn about the opinions of others.

All of these purposes have both positive and negative implications. For example, it is often helpful for isolated minorities to learn that others in the community, state, or nation have similar concerns, but polls tend to generate a "bandwagon effect" when undecided individuals agree with the positions that are getting the most media attention or those that seem more popular. Polls can create the **illusion of saliency** for issues (the false sense that issues are more important to voters than they actually are). They can simply capture fleeting opinions that are not deeply held, while other forms of political expression (like writing letters to the editor or volunteering for political candidates) are better measures of deeply held opinions and predispositions to be politically engaged. Moreover, some believe that politicians place too much reliance on poll numbers and fail to lead. One thing is certain: public opinion polling is widespread and unlikely to disappear.

Various types of polling methods exist, each with unique advantages and disadvantages. When a researcher wants in-depth and varied information, **personal interviews** are often desirable. Researchers can ask detailed questions with a good number of specifics, but personal interviews are time consuming and expensive. **Telephone surveys** are hugely popular today, as they produce reliable results quickly and far more cheaply than personal interviews. The media, for example, use telephone interviews almost exclusively to obtain quick information about public opinion, especially to gauge campaign activities. As you will see later in the chapter, however, increasing concern surrounds the use of telephone surveys, as technology (like caller identification) raises issues of accuracy.

Internet surveys are growing in popularity, some of which may produce reasonable results; however, consumers must be wary. Sometimes Internet research is reliable. For example, some universities use this method to evaluate faculty or to gauge student opinion regarding proposed changes in campus policies; but participation may or may not be even across campus, thereby offering the potential to skew results. Some universities make participation mandatory (for example, they will refuse to release transcripts or grades until faculty evaluations are complete), but many do not. Outside the university setting, use of Internet surveys is even more problematic. Although it may be hard for most who are reading this to appreciate, a large segment of the United States does not have easy access to the Internet, thereby potentially biasing the results toward those who are more affluent, more literate, and have higher educational attainment.

Besides different methods, there are different categories of polls. Early in the campaign cycle, **benchmark polls** are often conducted to provide campaigns with detailed information about perceived weaknesses or strengths of candidates to help develop campaign strategies. Benchmark polls are helpful in gauging the initial concerns of the public and determining areas of weakness that need to be addressed during the campaign. Campaigns and the media often use **tracking polls** to gauge the effectiveness of campaign strategies or to assess shifts in opinions or voting intentions. **Exit polls** are also commonly employed by the news media to see how and why people voted in a particular election. Some campaigns try to manipulate voters by using a marketing strategy called a **push poll**. A push poll is not a public opinion poll, but rather a telemarketing technique used to provide information (typically negative information) to

---

illusion of saliency
The misconception that an issue is more important to the public than it actually is.

personal interview
A technique of administering a public opinion poll in which researchers ask respondents for their opinions face to face. Personal interviews allow for more detailed questions but are far more expensive and time consuming than other techniques.

telephone survey
The most common method of administering public opinion polls by professionals. Telephone surveys produce reliable results in a less expensive and faster manner than personal interviews, though changes in technology are beginning to raise some questions about the reliability of such polls.

Internet survey
A survey done through the Internet. These are popular but can produce unreliable results, as not all residents have access to the Internet. Be leery of research conducted using Internet surveys.

benchmark poll
A poll conducted at the beginning of a campaign to provide in-depth information to help formulate campaign strategy.

tracking poll
A poll conducted repeatedly to check shifts in opinion or voting intentions.

exit poll
A survey, typically conducted by news media, of voters when they leave polling places.

push poll
A form of telemarketing disguised as a public opinion poll, often conducted to influence opinions.

voters to sway public opinion. Many observers consider these "polls" to be unethical, and the American Association of Political Consultants has condemned their use.

When measuring public opinion, one needs to be concerned not only with the mechanism for administering the survey, but also the method of selecting poll respondents. One of the major scientific breakthroughs in the twentieth century was the development of statistical sampling theory. This theory makes possible a whole array of scientific inquiry, from survey research to environmental science.

A **sample** (a subset) of a population (often called the universe), if drawn correctly, can represent the entire population under study, thereby negating (eliminating) the necessity of examining all the individual units of the population. For example, let's say you were concerned about the pollution levels of a local pond. You would not want to drain the entire pond to examine water quality; rather, you would draw samples from across the pond (from different locations, at different depths) to examine the water. The same concept is true for sampling the opinions of Texans. It would be prohibitively expensive and impossible to survey every adult residing in Texas. The good news is that we do not have to do that. The basic assumption of sampling theory is that individuals can represent others like them. Because people with similar life experiences are apt to hold similar opinions, we can study a subset of the population and still have accurate information. Researchers do not have to speak to all members of the population; they simply need to find a representative sample that contains sufficient numbers of key subgroups. In order to produce reliable information, samples must be representative of the key demographic groups that are likely to impact public opinion. Representativeness of a sample is highly dependent upon the sampling technique employed. More on this issue will be discussed in the section on controversies surrounding polls, as many are concerned that pollsters are unable to systematically create samples that are representative and hence question their findings.

The most common method used to select a sample is a probability technique in which all units in the population have an equal or known chance of being selected. Commercial polling agencies rely almost exclusively on **probability samples**, as they have known reliability rates and can be assessed for accuracy and error.[88]

Keep in mind that when employing a sample rather than examining the entire population, there is *always* a chance of error. Error is the cost of employing a sample. Thus, all reputable polling organizations provide readers information about error.

sample
A subset of the population under study.

probability sample
A sampling method in which every element in the target population has an equal chance of selection.

BERNIE SANDERS TEXAS RALLY
Bernie Sanders was especially popular with young people, invigorating them and creating excitement about politics. In the last several presidential elections, turnout by young voters has increased (though it is still very low). Candidates who draw strong support from young people help stimulate interest that can translate into higher rates of participation. Pictured here is a rally for Senator Sanders in Austin at a campaign rally.

margin of error
A measurement of how accurate a poll is in terms of reflecting the "true" sentiments of the population under study.

confidence level
The probability that the results found in the sample reflect the true opinion of the entire population under study.

Two important considerations when interpreting polling numbers are the **margin of error** and the **confidence level**. Let's say, for example, we are curious about how popular the governor is with likely voters in Texas. We hire a polling agency to survey likely Texas voters, which is the target universe to be studied. The agency does so and reports that 58 percent of likely voters believe the governor is doing a good job, with a margin of error of ±3 and a 95 percent confidence level. The margin of error constitutes a range in which we would expect the real approval rating to fall if we were able to interview every single likely voter (rather than the approximately 1,200 voters the company interviewed). The confidence level is the percentage of confidence that we have that the poll truly represents the feelings of everyone in the population. Turning back to the 58 percent figure, the best interpretation of this number is that we are 95 percent confident that between 55 percent and 61 percent (58 percent − 3 and 58 percent + 3) of likely voters in Texas actually approve of the job the governor is doing.

To be an informed consumer, you must understand how to interpret and apply both the margin of error and the confidence level. In many competitive elections, the numbers fall within the margin of error. When this happens, the media often declare that the election is "too close to call."

9.5.2 Controversies Surrounding Polls

A variety of concerns surround public opinion polling. First, there is concern with how public opinion polls are used by politicians, campaign managers, and the media. Some observers assert that politicians are too dependent on public opinion polls in crafting their messages and fail to provide much-needed vision. These people argue that politicians need to lead the public, charting a path forward to fulfill a vision, rather than relying on the often-fickle perceptions of the public. Others are concerned with how the media use polls and the impact polls might have on opinions and behavior. Research raises the concern that media coverage of polls may impact opinions rather than opinions being reflected in polls.[89]

Poll coverage in elections is also troubling. The media often take the easy road and report who is ahead in the polls, who is gaining, and who is losing. This so-called "horse-race" coverage is superficial and, many assert, damaging, as it limits more substantive coverage of issues. For example, *The Texas Tribune*, in partnership with the University of Texas, published its first horse-race poll on the 2018 Senate race between Republican Ted Cruz and Democrat Beto O'Rourke in October 2017, a full year before the 2018 general election.[90]

Technology has raised significant concerns about the representativeness of samples today. Caller ID and do-not-call lists have made it increasingly difficult for pollsters to reach many people and to select a random sample of the population. Additionally, more and more people refuse to participate in surveys, with refusal rates at remarkably high levels. Research conducted by several professional polling organizations found that bias associated with low response rates is important to note but not insurmountable.[91] Historically, telephone surveys have been conducted on landlines only, as federal regulations prohibit computers from randomly dialing cell phones (random digit dialing is the most common mechanism for selecting telephone samples). As cell phone–only households have increased in number, the accuracy of telephone surveys that rely on landlines has been called into question. Research conducted in 2018 by the National Center for Health Statistics (the most recent comprehensive study conducted by the government) found that 57.1 percent of U.S. homes have no landlines and rely exclusively upon cell phones.[92] During severe economic crises, like the economic crisis brought on by the COVID-19 pandemic, the percent without a telephone grow. Research shows that surveys that include landlines only miss key—and distinct—subgroups of the population (most notably younger and minority individuals).[93] Because of these concerns, many pollsters are including cell phones in their research, though they must dial the numbers manually. Manually dialing numbers drives up the costs of the polls but often produces superior results.

In order to address concerns associated with the representativeness of the sample (because of low response rates or reliance on landline-only surveys), pollsters often weight results to account for the lack of respondents of certain demographics. Many pollsters who use statistical techniques to account for such trends argue that the results are reliable.[94] However, in the 2020 and 2016 presidential elections (as well as other key races and the Brexit vote), pollsters were inaccurate. In 2020, pollsters suggested that a number of states would be closer than they were (Texas for example was discussed as being more competitive than it proved to be) while they underestimated how competitive other states ultimately were (like Wisconsin and Florida). Early analysis of the 2020 polls showed they were more inaccurate than those in 2016 (which were not as inaccurate as many in the public think). In 2016 polls were shown to have a slight, though not statistically significant, Democratic bias. In 2020, there continued to be a slight Democratic bias in the polls, with nearly all overestimating the support for Biden. Looking at the accuracy in a more historical context, the 2020 polls were the most inaccurate since 1996.[95] In 2020, most polls predicted a larger victory for Biden than occurred and in 2016 most polls predicted that Hillary Clinton would have an easy electoral victory. Each election cycle, the polls significantly underestimated support and enthusiasm for Donald Trump. Problems relating to response rates and technology will continue to raise issues for pollsters as they grapple with the best way to ensure representative samples.

In 2016, most pollsters overestimated the support and enthusiasm Hillary Clinton had (especially among young people, Hispanics, and African Americans) and underestimated the support Donald Trump had across key battleground states (especially with white working-class voters). Pollsters were highly criticized for failing to predict Donald Trump's victory (even his own internal polling had him losing). Some of the derision may be too harsh (though some criticism is reasonable to encourage more accurate results in the future).[96] National polls were fairly accurate with the national vote total. Immediately preceding the election, the average of national polls (which is the best gauge of support rather than using a single poll) had Secretary Clinton winning by 3.2 percent; she won the popular vote by 2 percent (within the margin of error for many key polls). FiveThirtyEight (founded by Nate Silver and historically very accurate) had Secretary Clinton leading in its average of polls by 3.5 percent, and RealClearPolitics (another very good source of polling data) had her leading in its average of polls by 2.3 percent. In 2020, the polls, as noted above, were less accurate. While they correctly predicted the Biden victory, and only incorrectly predicted the overall outcome in two states (North Carolina and Florida), they tended to overestimate the margin by which Biden would win his states and underestimated the margin by which Trump would win Republican states.[97]

Nevertheless, several key lessons need to be learned from the polling failures of 2016 and 2020. First, we need to be very careful to ensure that samples are representative, notably paying closer attention to nonresponse bias. This bias occurs when people systematically refuse to participate in polls. The two groups most likely to refuse to participate are younger adults and those less educated. Pollsters account for low response rates from these groups by weighting responses of sample participants who fall into the underrepresented groups. They estimate how much to weight the responses by what they think will be the likely turnout for each group based upon past turnout patterns in similar elections. These models underestimated the appeal Donald Trump had with the less-educated voters and failed to accurately weight their responses.[98] Since this group was a key demographic in Mr. Trump's victory, this error could have been partly to blame for the inaccuracy of most polls. Another key lesson to be learned is the importance of accurate state polling data. Given that candidates win the presidency by winning states in the Electoral College, we need reliable state-by-state polling. Several states that experts thought were "safe" for Secretary Clinton (like Pennsylvania and Michigan) did not receive adequate polling and were pivotal in Donald Trump's victory. Even during the primaries, state-level polls were less accurate than desired. For example, one week prior to the Texas primary, the *UT-Texas Tribune* poll had Ted Cruz leading the Republican primary by 37 percentage points; he won the primary with nearly 44 percent of the vote.[99] The poll more accurately predicted Donald Trump's performance, with the poll estimating he'd receive 29 percent of the vote when he received 27 percentage points. National polls are interesting, make good news stories, and are good for fundraising, but winning the presidency is a state-by-state endeavor, so accurate data at the state level is imperative for correct predictions.

Also important for consumers to remember is that polls provide only a snapshot of opinions at a set point in time. They provide useful information and, through advanced statistical analysis, help provide explanations for complex political phenomena. That said, it is unwise to put too much stock in one piece of research or in one public opinion poll. Social scientific inquiry is predicated on the commitment to build a body of knowledge, ascertain patterns, and build on prior research. Hence, one needs to look for broad and consistent patterns in data over time before statistical generalizations can be made. This is one reason, for example, that social scientists increasingly use multiple sources of data for political forecasts (most notably election forecasts); single data points are less reliable sources of information.[100] One such forecaster who has gotten a significant amount of attention in recent years is Nate Silver, who publishes FiveThirtyEight.com (a web page designed to provide the public with more reliable statistical predictions on politics as well as other matters of eclectic interest).

As you become more and more politically active, remember that there is a wide variety of ways to express your opinions beyond simply responding to public opinion polls and voting on Election Day. For example, you could call or write your political leaders or participate in an online petition or a march to express your opinions. The key is to become involved in your community.

CONCLUSION

In this chapter we learned how people acquire their political values and how values translate into opinions and serve to structure voting behavior. Political socialization occurs throughout a lifetime, but early learning is particularly important, as it influences later experiences. The manner in which people learn about political information, acquire political values, and develop their political ideology is fundamentally important to understanding how and why people participate in their communities and in the political arena as they do. Although no two people experience agents of socialization exactly the same way (even within the same family), generally speaking, people who have similar life experiences tend to develop similar viewpoints. Political ideology helps us understand and navigate a complex political world, allowing us to make generalizations and behave in a rational and informed manner.

Since the beginning of our republic, different viewpoints have existed regarding what importance political actors should place on public opinion. Although this quandary has never been solved, political leaders do heed and try to manipulate the opinion of the public. To be an informed participant in politics, you must understand

FAMILY TIME IN YESTERYEAR

Pictured here is a family listening to the radio circa 1945. Political leaders began communicating regularly with the masses in the 1930s. Franklin D. Roosevelt held a series of thirty evening radio addresses in 1933, continuing the practice throughout World War II until 1944. Since that time, communication has changed dramatically, but individuals still rely on the media to inform them about the world and to help shape their opinions and values.

how political values are formed, how they evolve over time, and how they impact participation and voting. Moreover, comprehending the impact of subgroups on opinions and voting is helpful in learning to appreciate how and why opinions change and why people act as they do. As the demographic composition of our country continues to change in the future, understanding the foundation of political opinions will become increasingly important. Finally, understanding the sources of information on politics and public opinion is vitally important if you are to become a political participant who can knowledgeably evaluate such information and formulate your own conclusions based on both your own beliefs and interests and what you perceive as society's best "self-interest rightly understood."

REVIEW THE CHAPTER

Public Opinion and Core Values

9.1 Identify the role of public opinion in democracies and the stability of core values, p. 273.

Since the earliest days of our founding, the role of public opinion in governing has been debated. Of central importance are questions regarding how influential the opinion of "the public" ought to be to our elected officials and on the development of public policy. On the whole, we have a very stable country, partly because we successfully transmit core values from one generation to another. Most change in our society comes slowly and incrementally.

Formation of Political Values and Opinions

9.2 Explain the process of acquiring views and attitudes and the dominant trends in political ideology in Texas, p. 276.

Many political opinions are based on political ideology, which is grounded in political values. Once established, ideology tends to remain rather stable throughout one's lifetime. The key ideological groups in the United States are liberals and conservatives, although libertarians and populists are popular in some areas of our country and at times throughout our history. Political socialization is the process by which people learn political facts and develop political values. Most people experience the socialization process through common entities, called agents of socialization. The most important agents of socialization include the family, school, media, community and peers, religious institutions, and events.

Group Membership and Public Opinion

9.3 Describe how group membership impacts political values and opinions in Texas, p. 283.

Generally speaking, people with similar life experiences tend to develop similar opinions. Although many exceptions exist, people whose experiences with agents of socialization are alike tend to develop political values and opinions that are alike. Consequently, patterns within social groups help explain public opinion and, hence, political participation.

Political Participation

9.4 Identify the manner in which opinion translates into political action, p. 290.

Certain demographic groups are more likely to be involved in politics than others. One key factor separating people who vote, for example, from those who do not vote is political efficacy. Moreover, social groups tend to behave in predictable patterns, although there are many exceptions.

Public Opinion Polling

9.5 Explain how public opinion is measured and how to interpret public opinion poll results, p. 299.

To become informed consumers, individuals need to understand how public opinion data are collected and interpreted. To conduct public opinion polls, pollsters use a sample of individuals who can represent others like themselves, rather than interviewing the entire population. One drawback is the always-present potential for error, but if the research is done well and within professionally established parameters, error is predictable and easy to comprehend. Many controversies surround how the media report on poll data, how politicians use poll data, and whether technology may render such data unreliable. As a consumer, it is important to know the advantages and liabilities of public opinion data so you can assess for yourself how much sway such information will have on your behavior.

LEARN THE TERMS

public opinion, p. 273
elitism, p. 274
pluralism, p. 274
cohort replacement (generational changes), p. 275
political ideology, p. 276
liberal, p. 276
conservative, p. 276
populist, p. 278
libertarian, p. 278

political socialization, p. 278
agents of political socialization, p. 278
political efficacy, p. 281
voter turnout, p. 281
intersectionality, p. 284
gender gap, p. 285
activists, p. 291
public opinion polling, p. 299
illusion of saliency, p. 300
personal interview, p. 300

telephone survey, p. 300
Internet survey, p. 300
benchmark poll, p. 300
tracking poll, p. 300
exit poll, p. 300
push poll, p. 300
sample, p. 301
probability sample, p. 301
margin of error, p. 302
confidence level, p. 302

The Party System in Texas

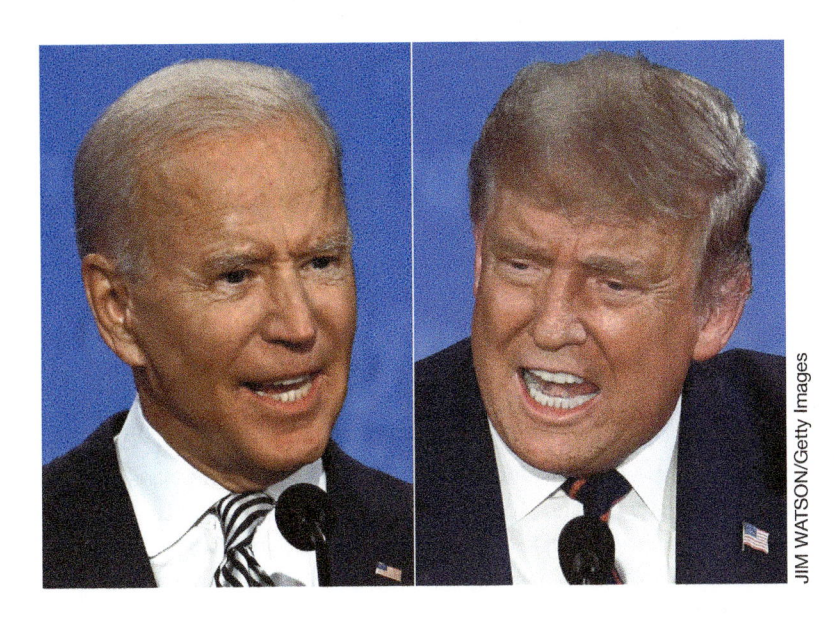

10

TRUMP LOST THE WHITE HOUSE BUT WON TEXAS AGAIN

Although he was unseated by Democrat Joe Biden in 2020, Donald Trump carried Texas as Republicans continued their long-time domination of statewide races in the Lone Star State.

LEARNING OBJECTIVES

10.1 Explain what political parties are and why Texas has a two-party system, p. 308.

10.2 Explain the primary functions of political parties in Texas, p. 313.

10.3 Summarize the partisan history of Texas, p. 317.

10.4 Explain the structure of the party organization in Texas, p. 330.

10.5 Summarize the challenges of producing cohesive policy-oriented coalitions in Texas government, p. 334.

Before President Donald Trump and his Democratic opponent, Joe Biden, squared off in the 2020 presidential election, no Democratic nominee for the White House had carried Texas since Jimmy Carter in 1976, more than a generation earlier. Democrat Hillary Clinton had lost to Trump by nine percentage points in 2016, and a Democrat had not won any statewide office in Texas since 1994. But Democrats believed they had reasons to be optimistic about Biden's chances in 2020.

The demographics of Texas were changing. The Hispanic population, which leans heavily Democratic, continued to grow and was becoming a greater factor in elections. This included many citizen children of immigrants who were coming of age and beginning to vote, fighting back against anti-immigration policies of the Trump administration. Their influence already had been felt in Democratic victories in major urban areas, where much of the state's population was centered.

Beto O'Rourke, a Democratic congressman from El Paso, had tapped into those changes and generated enough enthusiasm and voter turnout in 2018 to narrowly miss unseating Republican U.S. Senator Ted Cruz by 2.6 percentage points. For the first time since 2008, more people voted in the 2020 Texas Democratic primary than in the Republican primary. Unlike the Republicans, the Democrats had a contested primary race for president, which Biden won to help secure the party's nomination over Senator Bernie Sanders of Vermont.

The Texas economy, like much of the country's, had been battered by the COVID-19 pandemic, and many Texans had lost their jobs. It was unknown how many people would avoid voting for fear of being exposed to the disease at a polling place. Mail-in voting options in Texas were limited, and Texas Republican officials fought efforts by Democrats and voting rights groups to expand them. In the end, voting in Texas was heavy, but Democrats fell short again. Biden was elected president, but Trump carried Texas, and Republicans maintained their grip on state government.

Texas hasn't always been a Republican state, but historically it has been predominantly conservative, even during the 100 years, including most of the twentieth century, that it was a one-party, Democratic state. During the Democratic era, conservative and liberal factions competed for control of the Democratic Party. But white conservatives rarely lost control until court orders and new election laws of the civil rights era in the 1960s and 1970s opened up the political process to growing numbers of Hispanics and African Americans, most of whom gravitated to the Democratic Party. Members of these minority groups also began to take over Democratic leadership positions. Eventually, the Democratic Party became more progressive, or liberal, with leaders and candidates supporting civil rights initiatives and policies, such as public assistance and health care, benefiting lower-income Texans. Conservative white voters soon began to migrate to Texas's growing Republican Party, and after a realignment period that took a number of years, the GOP took control of state government in Texas. As Republican influence and power in the state grew, the new dominant party developed factions of its own. Now, the hard-right conservative faction, including followers of the Tea Party movement and social conservatives, is more influential within the party than more moderate Republicans.

Some political experts, including Republican leaders, are predicting that the Republican Party's growing conservatism combined with a growing Hispanic population in Texas will produce another partisan realignment in the state in the not-too-distant future. Hispanics were on the verge of becoming Texas's largest population group, surpassing white residents, and Hispanics traditionally have voted overwhelmingly for Democrats. Despite some Republican overtures to the Hispanic community and limited inroads among Hispanic voters—Senator Ted Cruz, for example, is Hispanic—many Hispanics have been alienated by the anti-immigration rhetoric of conservative Republicans. And many are wary of Republican policies that have produced significant funding cuts in education and health care, services valued by many Hispanic families.

While party systems may persist for extended periods of time, as occurred during the long period when the Democratic Party dominated state politics, political systems are not static, and more changes will occur. It is our intent to help you anticipate these changes, understand how they could affect your own interests, and assist you in deciding where you fit into the new political configurations of the state. The current party system is rooted, in part, in earlier historical events, including the Civil War and its aftermath. The state's transition from a one-party Democratic state to a Republican-dominated state is a story repeated in large measure in most of the former Confederate states. Overall, there are many historical similarities in the realignments that have occurred in these states, but there also are state-by-state differences in responses that have been made to issues of economic development, race, ethnicity, and class and to more general demographic changes.

Political Parties and a Democratic Society

10.1 Explain what political parties are and why Texas has a two-party system.

As long as a few individuals rule a society and the interests or concerns of the general population have no political significance or influence, leaders have little reason to be concerned with what the masses think or want. But democratic societies are based on the principle that those who rule have a fundamental obligation to consider the preferences, interests, and opinions of those who are governed. Because it is impossible for every individual to participate in every public policy decision, we have chosen to construct representative governments in the United States. We choose individuals to act on our behalf, which makes it necessary for us to find mechanisms to ensure that these individuals are selected fairly and are responsive and responsible. We try to accomplish this objective through several means, including elections, interest groups, and political parties.[1]

10.1.1 What Are Political Parties?

Although political parties share their representative roles with other institutions, scholars tend to agree that parties perform critical functions that other institutions cannot. There is considerable debate about formal definitions of parties, their characteristics, organizational and membership criteria, and the relationship of the parties to the governing institutions and the social system.[2] Our purpose is to focus on that part of the debate that will help us understand the political parties in Texas.

We find the party definition given by political scientist Leon D. Epstein to be best suited to Texas. A **political party** is "any group, however loosely organized, seeking to elect governmental officeholders under a given label."[3] Although we tend to think only in terms of Democratic and Republican, other political parties that meet this definition have emerged at both state and local levels in Texas history. Although political parties share some characteristics with other groups that function in the political arena, they are distinguished by their primary preoccupation with contesting elections and the fact that parties alone can "run candidates on their own labels."[4]

Political parties are complex structures that relate to most other facets of government and politics. V. O. Key suggested that parties are social structures that are best understood from three perspectives: the party in the electorate, the party as an organization, and the party in government. The party in the electorate involves the party's relationship to voters and election activities. The party organization includes a wide range of activities, officials, and workers from the precinct to the state level that are necessary to support the party's structure. The party in government covers the activities of those elected individuals who take office at the national, state, and local levels and carry out the functions of government (see Figure 10–1).

political party
A group that seeks to elect public officeholders under its own name.

10.1.2 Parties versus Interest Groups

At first glance, political parties and interest groups often appear indistinguishable, but there are differences. Interest groups are concerned with shaping public policy by influencing the actions and decisions of public officials, regardless of party affiliation. Political parties are structured under a "common label to recruit, nominate, and elect candidates for public office" under specific partisan labels.[5] An interest group usually focuses on a narrow range of policy issues. It can attempt to influence the outcome of elections, but it does not nominate candidates or take responsibility for the day-to-day management of government.[6] These are functions of the political parties and officials elected under their banners. Weak political parties, however, can be subject to excessive influence by interest groups that attempt to manipulate the parties' activities.

Studies conducted during the years of one-party Democratic domination in Texas concluded that the interest groups were especially powerful.[7] Some expected the relative power balance between interest groups and parties to change in a two-party Texas, but that remains to be seen.

FIGURE 10-1 THE THREE-PART POLITICAL PARTY

V. O. Key put forward the view that parties are social structures best understood from three perspectives: the party in the electorate, the party as an organization, and the party in government. These three functions can be found at the federal, state, and local levels.

SOURCE: Based on V. O. Key, *Politics, Parties, and Pressure Groups* (New York: Cromwell, 1958); and Paul Allen Beck, *Party and Politics in America* (New York: Longman, 1997).

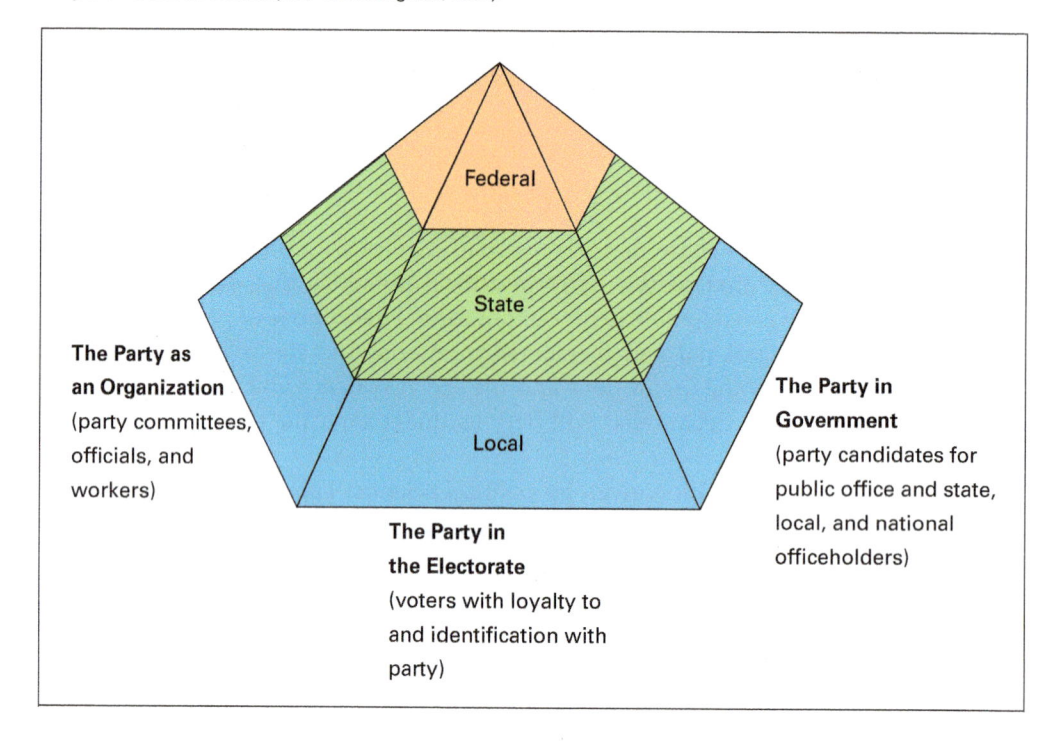

The Party as an Organization (party committees, officials, and workers)

The Party in Government (party candidates for public office and state, local, and national officeholders)

The Party in the Electorate (voters with loyalty to and identification with party)

Federal / State / Local

10.1.3 Two-Party System

Why are there only two major political parties in Texas and the United States? Many other democratic countries have multiparty systems that function quite well. Given the economic, regional, and social diversification of this nation and this state, one might conclude that multiple parties would be better able to translate the interests of their members and supporters into public policy. Yet, the United States has a 200-year history of two-party politics.

By historical accident and certainly not by design, the first national party system in this country was configured around two identifiable coalitions of interests that articulated two alternative views of American government. Some have suggested that there was a natural dualism in American politics and parties aligned along these fundamental differences. By itself, that is not a very convincing argument in that it glosses over complex social and economic divisions among the electorate, but subsequent generations have been politically socialized or educated to think that two parties are inevitable and preferred over any alternatives. Democrats and Republicans can fight over a wide variety of issues, but one will hear spokespersons of both parties extolling the virtues of two-party politics. Democrats and Republicans just do not talk about multiparty politics.

State election laws, which are written by Democratic and Republican legislators, also contribute to the persistence of a two-party system. Unlike the party primaries, where runoffs are held, if necessary, to select a nominee by majority vote, general elections are won by a simple plurality. The candidate who gets more votes than any other candidate, regardless of how many are in the race, is elected. There are no runoffs. Governor Rick Perry was reelected in 2006 with less than a majority over three major opponents—a Democrat and two independents. Governor Dolph Briscoe also won election with less than a majority in 1972, when La Raza Unida candidate

Ramsey Muniz siphoned off traditional Democratic votes. Without a runoff, third-party candidates have little chance of winning office over major party nominees. Election laws also impose specific requirements that make it difficult for third parties to get their candidates listed on the ballot.

Most Texans do not have the intense ideological positions that could prompt the formation of a third party. Winning elections takes precedence over ideological purity, and only a relatively few individuals are "true believers" with a highly cohesive, systematic set of beliefs shaping their political behavior.[8] A conservative Republican may support marketplace economics and deregulation but oppose a ban on abortion. A liberal Democrat who is a Catholic may favor greater economic regulation and expanded social services but oppose government programs subsidizing family planning or sex education.

Over the long history of political parties, pragmatic considerations usually have won out over ideology. Party activists are motivated primarily to win public offices for their respective parties, but there have been periods when evidence indicated that ideology triumphed over pragmatism. Some believe that John Tower, a Republican, won the U.S. Senate seat in 1961 due, in part, to liberal Democrats voting for Tower out of their anger at conservative Democrats who were alleged to be obstructing changes supported by the liberals. Since 2010, Tea Party Republicans have attempted to push the party farther to the right and have expressed outrage at conservative and moderate Republicans who are more disposed to find common ground on public policy issues with Democrats. Many of these more traditional and pragmatic Republican officeholders, sometimes called RINOs (Republicans in Name Only) by their more conservative critics, have been challenged in recent years by conservatives aligned with the Religious Right or the Tea Party movement. Many of these challenges have occurred, some successfully, in races for the Texas legislature, as noted in Chapter 5. Making a strong appeal to the Tea Party and to social conservative priorities against abortion, undocumented immigration, and gun control, conservative Dan Patrick unseated a more-moderate Republican incumbent, David Dewhurst, to win the Republican nomination and then election as lieutenant governor in 2014.

Party politics have been described as a verbal blood sport, and verbal attacks on individuals, their integrity, actions, and policies are considered fair game, but most political participants recognize unwritten limits. Two staff members of Empower Texans, a group closely aligned with the ultra-conservative wing of the Texas Republican Party, were widely criticized, and so was the group they represented, after they ridiculed Governor Greg Abbott's disability and use of a wheelchair during the COVID-19 pandemic. The group had a history of attacking moderate Republicans, but in this case the two staffers, in attacking some of the governor's emergency policies, made the mistake of becoming too personal.

Although class and race shape politics and public policy debates, other issues and concerns cut across these groupings. There is a tendency for one party to attract more of one group of citizens than the other party, but no party has a monopoly on key segments of the electorate. There are Hispanics, Anglos, and African Americans in both major parties. Labor divides its support between the two parties, as do religious, economic, and educational groups. The multiclass and heterogeneous base of support for the two major parties minimizes the potential for third parties.[9]

10.1.4 Third Parties in Texas

Over the years, Texas has had a number of **third parties**, including Grangers, Populists, Progressives, Socialists, Dixiecrats, the American Independent Party, La Raza Unida, the Natural Law Party, the Green Party, and Libertarians. None has had statewide electoral success. But both the Populists in the 1890s and La Raza Unida in the early 1970s were perceived to be significant threats to the established state party structure and those who controlled political and economic power.

third party
A minor political party. There have been many in Texas over the years, but none has had significant success on a statewide level.

LA RAZA UNIDA

Young Hispanic activists organized a political party, La Raza Unida, and recruited Ramsey Muniz in 1972 to run for governor of Texas. His candidacy threatened the dominance of the Democratic Party with the possibility of a Republican victory. Dolph Briscoe, the Democratic candidate, won the election, but the political organization of Hispanics anticipated future changes in the state's political system.

Ferd Kaufman/Associated Press

Major third-party movements surfaced when Texas was still a one-party Democratic state, and, in some respects, they suggested an alternative to the then-weak Republican Party. But from both state and national perspectives, they were movements of crisis or discontent.[10] The Democratic Party, particularly its conservative wing, either co-opted these movements by making minor public policy concessions or enacted restrictive legislation, such as the poll tax, to reduce the third party's electoral base. In some instances, economic recriminations were the price individuals paid for participating in these third-party movements.[11]

La Raza Unida (People United) raised the particularly interesting prospect of a political party built upon an ethnic group. In the 1960s, young Hispanic leaders began to develop student organizations across the state that became the organizational framework on which this party developed.[12] Low-income Hispanics historically had been excluded from any major role in the Democratic Party by restrictive voter-registration laws, at-large elections, and racial gerrymandering of political districts designed to minimize Hispanic voting strength. An even more fundamental problem was that state public policy in those days was not responsive to the educational and economic needs of Hispanics because conservative Democrats refused to enact legislation that would benefit that major part of the population.

La Raza Unida, led by Jose Angel Gutierrez and Mario Compean, began in 1969 to organize in Crystal City in Zavala County and then extended its efforts to Dimmit, La Salle, and Hidalgo Counties.[13] Overwhelmingly Hispanic and poor, these were characteristic of many South Texas counties, in which the Anglo minority controlled both the political and economic institutions and showed little sensitivity to the needs of low-income residents.

The struggle for access to the ballot box and fair elections in Zavala County parallels the experience of African Americans throughout the South. The Anglo minority used manipulation of the election laws, economic reprisals, and intimidation by the police and Texas Rangers to try to retain control. La Raza Unida, however, won control of local and county offices in Crystal City and Zavala County in 1972, the same year that Ramsey Muniz ran as the party's gubernatorial candidate. During the general election campaign, there was considerable speculation in the press and apprehension among conservative Democrats that La Raza would drain a sufficient number of votes from Dolph Briscoe, the Democratic nominee, to give Henry (Hank) Grover, a right-wing Republican, the governorship. Briscoe won the election, but without a majority of the votes. The subsequent growth of liberal and minority influence within the Democratic Party, internal dissension within La Raza Unida, and legal problems encountered by Muniz contributed to the demise of this third party after 1978.

The most successful third party in Texas in recent years has been the Libertarian Party. Libertarians have qualified for a place on the ballot in every Texas general election since 1986 because the party has won at least 5 percent of the vote in at least one statewide race during each election year, the former requirement for automatic ballot access for a third party in Texas. Legislation enacted recently by the Texas Legislature reduced the 5 percent requirement to 2 percent, thus assuring the Green Party, in addition to Libertarians, a place on the ballot in 2020. By reducing the ballot eligibility percentage for third parties, some Democrats believed, Republicans in the legislative majority hoped third-party candidates would siphon more votes from Democrats. The Libertarian and Green Parties have won a handful of local elections, but neither has ever won a statewide office in Texas. In addition to statewide third parties, local political organizations connected to neither major party have been influential in some cities. Elections for city offices are nonpartisan, and many are held during odd-numbered years when there are no state offices on the ballot. Cities such as San Antonio and Dallas developed citizens' associations, which had all of the characteristics of political parties. Many of these local organizations controlled city governments for decades and maintained a virtual monopoly over city elections, but these groups have disappeared in recent years due to the changing economic and population characteristics of the cities they dominated.

The Functions of Political Parties

10.2 Explain the primary functions of political parties in Texas.

The 29 million people who live in Texas have a wide range of interests and needs that they expect their governments to fulfill. Samuel Huntington, an influential American political scientist, noted that political parties, although they share some characteristics with other social and political institutions, have a unique function in modern societies "to organize participation, to aggregate interests, and to serve as the link between social forces and the government."[14] Simply stated, the political parties link diverse segments of the population to government and thus contribute to the stability and legitimacy of the government.

10.2.1 Recruit and Nominate Candidates

There are thousands of partisan officeholders in Texas, ranging from constable to governor. Except for city, school board, and special district elections, which are nonpartisan, the parties have a virtual monopoly on nominating candidates. Under Texas law, an individual who receives the majority vote in the primary election (or its runoff) of one of the two major parties wins that party's nomination and a place on the general election ballot. It is possible, through a petition process, for an independent candidate to win a place on the general election ballot with no party affiliation, but an independent is not likely to be elected, as Carole Keeton Strayhorn and Kinky Friedman, two highly publicized independents, discovered in the 2006 gubernatorial election.

Many local elected positions do not pay well and are not politically attractive; in some areas of the state, it is difficult to convince people to run for them. In some counties, the parties aggressively recruit candidates. In other counties, they do not. In some counties, one party may be nothing more than a shell or paper organization. In other counties, the parties are competitive, with sophisticated organizations and paid professional staffs capable of providing prospective candidates with

MOBILIZING THE CAMPAIGN TROOPS

Most political pundits gave President Barack Obama little chance of carrying Texas in the 2012 presidential race, and he didn't. But his quick trip to Texas in mid-July raised significant campaign funds from Democratic loyalists and mobilized campaign volunteers who helped with his campaign in other states where he was competitive. In this photo, he was speaking to some 1,100 supporters in Austin.

considerable campaign resources. Most candidates, though, are self-recruited, raise their own funds, and hire their own campaign managers.

Parties have not always used the primary to nominate candidates. Prior to reforms enacted in the Terrell Election Laws of 1903 and 1905, the party faithful nominated candidates at conventions. Although the primary is now the most prevalent method for nominating party candidates for state offices, the convention process is still part of the nomination process for third parties in a number of states, including Texas, Virginia, Minnesota, and New York. Based on their respective party rules, Libertarians nominate their candidates in Texas through a party convention, and the Green Party uses the primary and convention process.

10.2.2 Contest Elections and Mobilize Voters

Throughout Texas, candidates nominated by political parties for federal, state, and county offices run in November general elections with the support of their respective parties. Although candidate-centered campaigns have reduced the role of political parties in some elections, many voters still take cues about whom to support from candidates' partisan affiliations. Parties also support their nominees' campaigns and still are the most important institutions for mobilizing voters for specific candidates.

Most Texans are not active in party affairs, but approximately 70 percent of Texas voters identify with either the Republican or the Democratic Party. These two parties have a near monopoly on the votes cast. Political parties recruit a significant number of volunteers to assist candidates in contacting and mobilizing voters in the election cycle, provide technical support to candidates, and funnel money into campaigns of the party's candidates.

10.2.3 Organize and Manage the Government

Once elected, officeholders use their party affiliations in carrying out their public responsibilities, and with the development of a competitive party system in Texas, the parties have taken on a more significant role in the organization and management of government. Governor Ann Richards, a Democrat, appointed primarily Democrats to hundreds of positions on policymaking state boards and commissions and to vacancies on state courts. Her successors, Republicans George W. Bush, Rick Perry, and Greg Abbott, appointed primarily Republicans.

After taking office in 1979 as Texas's first Republican governor in more than 100 years, Bill Clements appointed many Republicans to state boards, but he also named some Democrats, in part to encourage conservative Democrats to switch parties. His successful strategy was instrumental in adding to the strength and influence of the Republicans (often referred to as the Grand Old Party [GOP]) in Texas.

Despite the growth of the Republican Party and increased GOP representation in the legislature, the organizational structure of the legislature remains bipartisan. In the last quarter of the twentieth century, Democratic legislative leaders built coalitions by appointing Republicans as well as Democrats as chairs of major committees. Republican leaders in the House of Representatives have generally continued this practice, but in the Senate, fewer Democrats are now appointed to chair standing committees. Republican Lieutenant Governor Dan Patrick appointed only two Democrats and seventeen Republicans to chair Senate committees in 2019.

POLITICAL PARTIES AND INSTITUTIONAL COOPERATION

Policy differences and conflict are inherent in a constitutional system of separation of powers, but political parties serve, in part, to promote policy cooperation and coordination. Lieutenant Governor Dan Patrick, Governor Greg Abbott and Speaker Dennis Bonnen, left to right, were all Republicans and united on their goals, including increased education funding, during the 2019 legislative session.

Although the bipartisan tradition, shaped by political philosophy and local interests cutting across party lines, mostly continues, party caucuses now appear to be more influential in defining policy positions and legislative strategies. Voting along party lines has increased in both the House and the Senate in recent legislative sessions, due in large part to the strengthened influence of social and limited-government conservatives in Republican primary elections. The ideological positions dividing the two parties in the legislature have been sharper, and there has been less willingness to compromise on selected major issues. In 2011, for example, most Republicans voted for deep budget cuts, and most Democrats voted against them. In recent years, there also have been sharp partisan divisions on politically charged issues such as abortion regulation.

If partisanship continues to increase, the majority party in the legislature may begin to use its organizational powers to further reduce the influence of the minority party. Despite growing partisanship, however, the Texas legislature usually functions more effectively than the U.S. Congress, which often has been paralyzed by extreme partisanship in Washington in recent years.

10.2.4 Mediate the Effects of Separation of Powers

Political parties help bridge the inherent conflicts between the executive and legislative branches of government. The governor needs legislative support for key programs, and, in turn, legislators often need the governor's support and assistance to enact their bills. The chances of such cooperation are enhanced if the governor and a majority of the legislature are of the same party. Republican Governor George W. Bush usually worked well with Democratic lawmakers and shared many of their priorities. But his Republican successor, Governor Rick Perry, had a stormier relationship with most Democratic legislators. Bush had a more accommodating style than Perry, he was less ideological, and he had to seek Democratic support because key legislative leaders were Democrats, who still held a majority in the Texas House. With Republican majorities in both the House and the Senate during most of his administration, Perry used partisanship and ideology to marginalize Democratic influence in the legislative process. Perry's successor, Republican Governor Greg Abbott, also had the political advantage of working with Republican legislative majorities, but he encouraged bipartisanship to win enactment of a major school finance law in 2019.

10.2.5 Provide Accountability

One of the fundamental problems of a democratic government is keeping public officeholders responsive and accountable to the people. Elected officials can abuse power. They can engage in graft and corruption. They can pursue policies that conflict with the interests of most of their constituents or pursue foolish or shortsighted policies that produce adverse results. The political parties, in their criticisms of each other and their electoral competitiveness, serve to inform the voters of the shortcomings and failures of elected officials. This process provides alternatives for the voters and gives them an opportunity to "turn the rascals out."

10.2.6 Manage Conflict and Find Common Interests

For most of its history, the United States has had a stable political system for managing conflict among competing groups and interests, and political parties have played a major role in that process. In recent years, particularly following the election of Barack Obama as president, the national party system has been marked by intense conflict that has blocked a great deal of policy. The Democratic-led impeachment of President Donald Trump, which ended in acquittal by the Senate, mostly along partisan lines, was one manifestation of a dysfunctional party system that continued through the election of 2020. A few bipartisan agreements on policy were mostly obscured by news reports focusing on what was not being accomplished. There generally appeared to be greater collaboration and cooperation between Texas Democrats and Texas Republicans than between the national parties during this era, but sharp policy differences also existed at the state level. For effective governance political parties often have to reach out to find areas of shared interest.

Under normal circumstances, a party tries to find common ground among the varied interests of the electorate so that successful coalitions of voters can combine to support the party's candidates on Election Day. The Texas Democratic Party, for example, is built on a diverse coalition of African Americans, Hispanics, lower socioeconomic groups, labor, and some professionals, to name a few. The Republican Party's base is markedly different from that of the Democrats, but party leaders and candidates also work to build stable coalitions of voters. To build durable support for its candidates, the party must find common interests, reach compromises, and develop accommodations among groups of voters. As competing interests within the party agree to support a variety of programs and common principles, the party succeeds in resolving conflict.[15] But sometimes highly ideological segments embrace ideology over electoral victory and refuse to accommodate or compromise with other factions within the party.

10.2.7 Set the Policy Agenda

Public policy does not just happen. It is the result of groups organizing around issues and keeping pressure on elected officials to respond. Some issues are longstanding problems that have produced sharp differences of opinion and will take years to resolve. Others emerge rapidly, perhaps as a result of a catastrophic event. Groups seeking change often try to build support for their programs through the political parties.

The parties also play a role in establishing policy priorities. Candidates running for public office under a party's banner announce their support or opposition to specific policies and, once elected, are expected to use the resources of their offices to try to achieve those objectives. In anticipation of future elections, officeholders spend much time and energy trying to carry out policies that will solidify their support among the voters.

The Party in the Electorate

10.3 Summarize the partisan history of Texas.

The Texas party system has been restructured by the social and economic changes that the state has experienced since the 1970s. Texas now has a strong Republican Party, and although Democrats still hold many local and district offices, Republicans dominate statewide politics. From the 1870s through the 1970s, however, Texas was a one-party Democratic state.

10.3.1 One-Party Democratic Politics

Texas's long domination by the Democratic Party can be traced to the period immediately after the Civil War, when the Republican Party was able to capture control of Texas government for a short period. The Reconstruction administration of Radical Republican Governor Edmund J. Davis generated strong anti-Republican feelings, and the Republican Party was perceived by most Texans of that era to be the party of conquest and occupation. By the time the Constitution of 1876 was approved, the Republican Party's influence in state politics was negligible. From 1874 to 1961, no Republican won a statewide office in Texas, and in only a few scattered areas were Republicans elected to local offices.

In the early part of the twentieth century, Texas usually voted for the Democratic candidate in presidential elections. The state voted for Herbert Hoover, the Republican presidential candidate, in 1928. For many Texans, the key issue in that election was that Al Smith, the Democratic nominee from New York, was a Catholic and favored the repeal of Prohibition. Anti-Catholicism and support for Prohibition had deep roots among many fundamentalist religious groups in Texas during that period.

The anti-Republicanism that evolved from the Civil War and Reconstruction, however, is only a partial explanation for the Democratic Party's longtime domination of Texas politics. V. O. Key, in his classic study *Southern Politics*, presents the provocative thesis that Texas politics might be better understood in terms of "modified class politics."[16] As Texas's conservative agricultural leaders attempted to regain control over the state's political system after Reconstruction, the postwar economic devastation divided Texas along class lines. Small farmers, African Americans, and an emerging urban labor class suffered disproportionately from the depression of this period. They turned their discontent into support for agrarian third parties, particularly the Populist Party, which began to threaten the monopoly of the traditional Texas power structure.

To protect their political power, the established agricultural leaders moved to divide the lower-class social groups by directing the discontent of the lower-income whites against the African Americans. The rural elites manifested traditionalistic political values and wanted to consolidate power in the hands of the privileged few. They created alliances with the mercantile, banking, and emerging industrial leaders, who reflected the individualistic view of a limited government that served to protect their interests. These two dominant forces consolidated political power and merged the politics of race with the politics of economics. Then, for more than eighty years, the conservative Democratic Texas establishment pursued policies that best served its interests rather than those of the general population.

The elites were able to institutionalize their control through the adoption of constitutional restrictions and the enactment of legislation designed to reduce

Jim Crow laws
Legislation enacted by many states after the Civil War to limit the rights and power of African Americans.

the number of voters. The effect of these actions was to reduce the potential of a popular challenge to the establishment's political monopoly.[17] Segregation legislation, called **Jim Crow laws**, stripped African Americans of many economic, social, and political rights and eliminated most of this group from the political process. Restrictive voter-registration laws, including a poll tax, which also were designed to exclude African Americans, reduced the participation of low-income whites in the political process as well. In addition, the costs of statewide political campaigns boosted the electoral prospects of candidates financed by the establishment.[18] The result of all this was a one-party Democratic system dominated by influential conservatives.

10.3.2 Factionalism in the Democratic Party

The Texas Democratic Party was not homogeneous: Factions, regional differences, and personal political rivalries caused splits. Initially, there were no sustained, identifiable factions, as voting coalitions changed from election to election through much of the first third of the twentieth century. The onset of the Great Depression in 1929, the election of President Franklin Roosevelt in 1932, and the policies of the New Deal reshaped Texas politics in the 1930s.

State party systems are linked to the national party system, and developments in the Texas party system must be understood as part of this relationship. During the period from the Civil War to Franklin Roosevelt's election, the Republican Party dominated the national party system. The elections from 1928 to 1936, however, produced a major national party realignment, and the Democratic Party, capitalizing on the devastation of the Great Depression, replaced the Republicans as the dominant national party.

Roosevelt's administrations articulated and developed a policy agenda that was radically different from that of the Republican Party. Government was to become a buffer against economic downturns as well as a positive force for change. Under Roosevelt, the regulatory function of the federal government was expanded to exercise control and authority over much of the nation's economy. The federal government also enacted programs such as Social Security, public housing, and labor legislation to benefit lower socioeconomic groups.

PRELUDE TO THE VOTING RIGHTS ACT

For decades, states including Texas enacted laws to exclude African Americans and other minorities from voting. As the U.S. Congress debated the Voting Rights Act proposed by President Lyndon Johnson, marches were held across the country in support of the act. On March 14, 1965, this group marched through downtown Dallas in support of Johnson's proposals. Some five months later, the Voting Rights Act became law.

These national policies had a direct impact on many Texans and produced an active philosophical split within the Texas Democratic Party that was to characterize Texas politics for the next two generations. A majority of Texas voters supported Roosevelt in his four elections, and the Democratic Party maintained its monopoly over Texas politics. But competing economic interests clearly—and often bitterly—divided Texas Democrats along liberal and conservative lines.

A strong Republican Party did not emerge at this time in Texas or any other southern state because "southern conservative Democratic politicians, who would have been expected to lead such a realignment, or any politicians for that matter, did not relish jumping from a majority-status party to one in the minority."[19] Furthermore, the restrictive voter-registration laws designed to reduce participation by minorities and poor whites continued to limit the electoral prospects of liberal Democrats and allowed conservatives to remain largely in control of the state party: "As long as the conservative Democrats remained dominant, they served as a check on the potential growth of the Republican Party."[20] There also were residual feelings from the Civil War and an antipathy toward the Republican Party that required generations to die off before new voters were willing to change party allegiances.

Despite some liberal successes under Governor James Allred, who was elected in 1934 and again in 1936, the conservative wing of the party prevailed in state elections from the 1940s to the late 1970s. Democratic presidential candidates carried Texas in 1944, 1948, 1960, 1964, 1968, and 1976, even though some candidates were too liberal to suit the tastes of the state's conservative Democratic establishment.

By 1941, the conservative Democrats began to lay the groundwork for an all-out attack on the New Deal, or liberal, Democrats in the 1944 presidential election. Roosevelt won the nomination and election for a fourth term, but in Texas there was a bitter intraparty battle between conservative and liberal (loyal to Roosevelt) Democrats for control of the party organization and delegates to the Democratic National Convention. This election was followed by three successive presidential elections in which conservative Democrats fled the party to support either third-party candidates or the Republican nominee.[21]

10.3.3 Modified One-Party Democratic Politics

At first glance, it might appear that the **bifactionalism** in the Democratic Party partially compensated for the lack of a competitive two-party system in Texas. In his study of southern politics, however, V. O. Key argued against that perception. He concluded that factionalism resulted in "no-party politics." Factionalism produces discontinuity in leadership and group support, so that the voter has no permanent reference point from which to judge the performance of the party or selected candidates. Because there are no clear distinctions between who holds power and who does not, the influence of pressure groups increases.[22] In one-party Democratic Texas, state government and public policy were vulnerable to control by wealthy and corporate interests. If the factionalism that has emerged in recent years within the ranks of the Republican Party increases, Key's earlier observation about intense internal divisions in the Democratic Party may be applicable to the Republican Party as well.

A number of factors tested this bifactional pattern of state Democratic politics, including the national party's increased commitment after 1948 to civil rights and social welfare legislation. These liberal developments alienated segments of the white population and eventually prompted many voters to leave the Democratic Party and align with the Republicans.

Efforts by Texas oil interests to reestablish state control over the oil-rich tidelands off the Texas coast also played a key role in the demise of **one-party politics** and the development of a two-party system. President Harry Truman, concerned about national security and federal access to these offshore oil resources, refused

bifactionalism
The presence of two dominant factions organized around regional, economic, or ideological differences within a single political party. For much of the twentieth century, Texas functioned as a one-party system with two dominant factions—liberal and conservative.

one-party politics
The domination of elections and governmental processes by a single party, which may be split into different ideological, economic, or regional factions. In Texas, the phrase is used to describe the period from the late 1870s to the late 1970s, when the Democratic Party claimed virtually all elected, partisan offices.

to accede to state demands and vetoed legislation favorable to Texas oil interests in 1952. That veto prompted a series of maneuvers orchestrated by Democratic Governor Allan Shivers to move the support of conservative Democrats to the Republican Party.

Promising to support the Democratic Party, Shivers and his allies captured control of the Texas delegation to the 1952 Democratic National Convention. The Democrats nominated Adlai Stevenson for president, and the Republicans nominated Dwight Eisenhower. When the Texas Democratic Party convened its fall convention, Shivers succeeded in winning the party's endorsement of Eisenhower. The "Shivercrats," as they were called, were successful in carrying Texas for the Republican nominee. This election helped establish a pattern of Texas retaining its Democratic leanings at the state and local levels but voting for Republicans for president.[23]

For years, the Republican Party's limited presence in Texas basically had been a patronage base for leaders who were more interested in an occasional appointment than in winning elections.[24] The 1952 election marked a change in the party's state leadership and led to efforts to create a party capable of winning local and statewide elections.[25] It took years to develop the necessary organization, but the process would accelerate after the 1964 presidential election.

In 1960, Democrat Lyndon B. Johnson ran both for vice president and for reelection to the U.S. Senate from Texas—a dual candidacy permitted under state law—and won both offices. His Republican opponent in the Senate race was John Tower, a relatively unknown college professor from Wichita Falls, who received 41 percent of the vote. After Johnson won the vice presidency and resigned from the Senate, a special election to fill the Senate seat was called in 1961. It attracted seventy-one candidates, including Tower, who defeated conservative Democrat William Blakely with 50.6 percent of the vote in a runoff.[26]

There is some evidence that liberal Democrats, in retaliation for having been locked out of the power centers of their party and in anticipation of an ideological realignment of the party system, supported Tower in this election.[27] The *Texas Observer*, an influential liberal publication, endorsed Tower with an argument for a two-party system. "How many liberals voted for Tower will never be known, nor will it be known how many 'went fishing' (and didn't vote)," wrote Republican campaign consultant and author John R. Knaggs, who was a volunteer worker

LEADER OF THE SHIVERCRATS

Texas Governor Allan Shivers, right, a leader of conservative Democrats in the 1950s, stands with General Douglas MacArthur, center, in a ceremony greeting the World War II leader in Austin in June 1951.

HIS ELECTION MARKED THE BEGINNING OF THE MODERN REPUBLICAN ERA

John Tower's surprise election to the U.S. Senate seat vacated by Lyndon Johnson, after Johnson was elected vice president in 1961, was the first statewide victory by a Republican following Reconstruction. His election marked the beginning of the gradual expansion of the Republican Party in Texas, culminating in the party's domination of the state's party system. Senator Tower is seen here in conversation with President Johnson in the early part of 1967.

for Tower during the 1961 race. He added, "But in reviewing Tower's razor-thin 10,343-vote margin out of 886,091 cast, it must be concluded that the liberal element was pivotal in electing the first Republican United States senator to represent Texas during the twentieth century."[28] Texas Republicans, incidentally, had not even held a primary in 1960.

Tower was reelected in 1966, 1972, and 1978, but no other Texas Republican won a statewide office until 1978, when Bill Clements was elected governor. Nevertheless, many students of Texas politics regard Tower's election in 1961 as a key factor in the development of the state's **two-party system**.[29]

Although Republicans made some gains in suburban congressional districts and local elections in the 1960s, including the election to Congress of a Houston Republican named George Herbert Walker Bush, the numbers were inconsequential. Most significant election battles continued to take place for a while longer within the Democratic Party.

The only liberal Democratic candidate who was successful on a statewide basis during this period was Ralph Yarborough. After several losing campaigns, he was elected to the U.S. Senate in a special election in 1957 and held that office until his defeat in 1970 by conservative Democrat Lloyd Bentsen. Yarborough, who had a distinguished legislative career, was "the mainstay of the liberal wing until his primary defeat in 1970 and comeback failure in 1972."[30]

Despite some indications of an energized Republican Party and the increased mobilization of minorities in support of the liberal wing of the Democratic Party, conservative Democrats controlled state politics until 1978. Conservatives dominated the nominating process in the Democratic primaries through well-financed and well-executed campaigns. In the general elections, liberal Democrats had little choice but to vote for a conservative Democrat against a candidate who was usually perceived to be an even more conservative Republican.[31] During this period of Democratic factionalism, Texas Democrats played major roles in the U.S. Congress and national politics. Sam Rayburn, the longtime speaker of the U.S. House of Representatives (regarded as one of a handful of great speakers in U.S. history) came from a rural congressional district in northeastern Texas. Before moving on to the vice presidency and then the White House, Lyndon B. Johnson was majority leader in the U.S. Senate. Other members of Congress from Texas, as a result of the seniority system used in the selection of committee chairs, had influential committee posts and used their positions to funnel large sums of federal dollars to the state.

two-party system
A political system in which each of the two dominant parties has the possibility of winning national, statewide, or county elections.

realignment

A major shift in political party support or identification, which usually occurs around a critical election. In Texas, this was a gradual transformation from a one-party system dominated by Democrats to a two-party system in which Republicans became the dominant party statewide.

10.3.4 Two-Party Politics in Texas

On the national level, **realignment** of political parties often is associated with a critical election in which economic or social issues cut across existing party allegiances and produce a dramatic, permanent shift in party support and identification.[32] Realignment did not occur in one single election in Texas, but over several decades. The early stages of this transformation often are hard to identify, but by the mid-1990s, it was clear that one-party politics had given way to a two-party system.

The civil rights movement was a major factor contributing to the transformation of the state's party system. African Americans and Hispanics went to federal court to attack state laws promoting segregation and restricting minority voting rights. Successful lawsuits were brought against the white primary, the preprimary endorsement, the poll tax, and racial gerrymandering of political districts. Then minorities turned to the U.S. Congress for civil rights legislation, a process that produced the 1965 Voting Rights Act, which Congress extended to Texas after 1975. African Americans and Hispanics challenged electoral systems throughout the state using federal law and a growing body of U.S. Supreme Court decisions prohibiting the dilution of minority voting power in the drawing of congressional, legislative, and other political districts. Minorities made significant progress in their long, tortuous effort to increase electoral equity, although the fight continues today. But the creation of more political districts from which African Americans and Hispanics could win election also resulted in the creation of more districts from which Republicans could win public office. As the number of minority elected officials increased, the number of Republican elected officials also increased.

Economic factors also contributed to two-party development. African Americans and Hispanics are disproportionately low-income populations and generally support such governmental services as public housing, public health care, day care, and income support. Many people associate these policies with the liberal wing of the Democratic Party. Minority organizations made concerted efforts to register, educate, and mobilize the people in their communities. Approximately 90 percent of the African American vote in Texas is Democratic, and although there is less cohesion among Hispanic voters, approximately 75 percent of the Hispanic vote goes to Democrats. As the numerical strength of minorities increased, conservative Anglo Democrats found their position within the party threatened and began to look to the Republican Party as an alternative.

LANDMARK LEGISLATION THAT CHANGED THE POLITICAL LANDSCAPE

President Lyndon Johnson signed the Voting Rights Act on August 6, 1965. The law's purpose was to protect the voting rights of minorities, which had been denied by many states. The long-term results of this law were to increase political participation by Texas minorities and to produce a significant increase in the number of elected minority officials.

Large numbers of people migrated to Texas from other states, particularly during the 1970s and early 1980s when the economy of the Sun Belt—the southern region of the country from Virginia to California—was booming and many northern industrial states struggled. This migration also contributed to the two-party system because many of these new arrivals were Republicans from states with strong Republican parties, and many of them settled in high-income, suburban, Anglo areas in Texas.[33] Other significant factors included President Ronald Reagan's popularity in the 1980s and the 1978 election of Republican Governor Bill Clements, who encouraged many conservative Democratic officeholders to switch parties. Some scholars see an earlier outline of these changes in the so-called southern strategy of Richard Nixon in 1968. Simply stated, the national Republican Party made calculated efforts to peel off whites using wedge issues that were likely to resonate within the southern political culture.[34]

During the 1970s, the Texas Republican Party had an organizational edge on the Democrats. As the minority party, the only way the GOP could successfully challenge the Democrats' numerical strength was to develop local party organizations capable of mobilizing membership, providing continuity between elections, and providing candidates with campaign resources.

Other events of the 1970s and the 1980s demonstrated that the transformation of the Texas party system was well on its way. After the Sharpstown stock fraud scandal rocked state government in 1971, the Texas House elected a liberal Democrat, Price Daniel, Jr., as speaker in 1973. Three other moderate-to-liberal Democrats were elected to statewide office in the early 1970s: Bob Armstrong as land commissioner in 1970, John Hill as attorney general in 1972, and Bob Bullock as comptroller in 1974. These men initiated and carried out policies that were more equitable in the treatment of lower socioeconomic Texans.[35]

In 1978, John Hill defeated Governor Dolph Briscoe, a conservative, in the Democratic primary, and Bill Clements, then a political unknown, defeated Ray Hutchison, a former state legislator who had the endorsement of most Republican state leaders, in the Republican primary. Hill neglected to mend fences with conservative Democrats, and Clements, a multimillionaire, used much of his own money on an effective media campaign to defeat Hill for governor by 17,000 votes in the general election. Four years later, Clements lost to Democratic Attorney General Mark White, but in 1986 he returned to defeat White in an expensive, bitter campaign.

In the 1982 election, Democratic candidates who were considered liberal won additional statewide offices. Ann Richards was elected state treasurer; Jim Mattox, attorney general; Jim Hightower, agriculture commissioner; and Garry Mauro, land commissioner.

The 1990 election further demonstrated how far the realignment process had gone. Democratic gubernatorial nominee Ann Richards defeated conservative businessman Clayton Williams, who had spent $6 million of his own money to win the Republican primary. But Republican Kay Bailey Hutchison was elected state treasurer, and Republican Rick Perry unseated Hightower to become agriculture commissioner. Republicans also retained one of the U.S. Senate seats from Texas when Phil Gramm easily won reelection to the seat once held by John Tower, and the GOP claimed eight of the twenty-seven congressional seats that Texas then had in Congress.

In a special election in 1993 to fill the U.S. Senate seat vacated by Democrat Lloyd Bentsen when President Bill Clinton appointed him secretary of the treasury, Kay Bailey Hutchison defeated Democrat Bob Krueger to give the Republicans both U.S. Senate seats from Texas. Hutchison easily won reelection in 1994.

Also in 1994, Republican nominee George W. Bush, the son of former President George H. W. Bush and a future president himself, unseated Governor Ann Richards. In addition, Republicans that year captured four other statewide offices that had been held by Democrats, marking the most statewide gains by Texas Republicans in any single election since Reconstruction. Meanwhile, Republicans also were increasing their share of seats in the Texas legislature. In the same election, Republicans posted sweeping victories across the country, cashing in on anger over President Bill Clinton's policies and gaining control of both houses of Congress and a majority of the nation's governorships.

10.3.5 Republican Dominance

The political transformation of Texas accelerated even more in 1996, when Republicans swept all statewide offices on the general election ballot and captured a majority of the state Senate for the first time since Reconstruction. Republican presidential nominee Bob Dole even carried the Lone Star State, despite a poor national showing against President Clinton. Republicans also increased their numbers in the Texas House and in the Texas congressional delegation. When the electoral dust had cleared, Republicans held twenty of Texas's twenty-nine statewide elected offices, including the top three. That number increased to twenty-one in 1997, when Presiding Judge Michael McCormick of the Texas Court of Criminal Appeals switched from the Democratic to the Republican Party.

Lieutenant Governor Bob Bullock and Attorney General Dan Morales, both Democrats, chose not to seek reelection or any other office in 1998, and Republicans cashed in on the opportunity. With Governor Bush winning reelection in a landslide, Republicans again swept all statewide offices. A few weeks after the 1998 election, the GOP secured all statewide offices in Texas for the first time since Reconstruction when Texas Supreme Court Justice Raul A. Gonzalez, a Democrat, retired in midterm and was replaced by Bush's Republican appointee. Republicans did not capture control of the Texas House, but they picked up four seats to narrow the Democratic margin to six seats. In the governor's race, Bush won 69 percent of the vote against Democratic challenger Garry Mauro, the longtime land commissioner.

Democrats fielded candidates for only three of the nine statewide offices up for election in 2000. They lost all three but held their ground in state legislative races. Republicans also swept all statewide races in 2002, including Governor Rick Perry's victory over Democratic nominee Tony Sanchez and former Texas Attorney General John Cornyn's victory over former Dallas Mayor Ron Kirk in a race to succeed retiring U.S. Senator Phil Gramm. Republicans finally gained control of the Texas House of Representatives in 2002, capturing 88 of the 150 seats after the Legislative Redistricting Board in 2001 had drawn new districts that favored Republicans. In addition, the GOP increased its margin in the state Senate by winning nineteen of the thirty-one seats. All statewide elected officials remained Republican.

Republicans achieved still another long-sought goal in 2004 when they gained a majority of Texas's congressional delegation. This majority was achieved after the legislature, in a bitter partisan fight in 2003, redrew congressional district boundaries to favor GOP candidates.

Republican Governor Rick Perry was reelected in 2006 over three major opponents, including Democratic nominee Chris Bell, a former congressman and former city councilman from Houston. Republican Comptroller Carole Keeton Strayhorn and musician-author Kinky Friedman challenged Perry as independents. Republicans also won all other statewide offices against a Democratic ticket that was less experienced and more poorly financed than the party's slate of candidates in 2002. Texas Republicans in 2006 kept their majorities in the legislature and in the congressional delegation.

Republicans also won all statewide races from 2008 through 2020, including Rick Perry's reelection to a third full term as governor in 2010, Governor Greg Abbott's two elections in 2014 and 2018 and Ted Cruz's elections to the U.S. Senate in 2012 and 2018. After the 2020 elections, Republicans held all statewide offices and 23 of the 36 U.S. House seats from Texas and had majorities of 18 to 13 in the state Senate and 83 to

TABLE 10-1 GROWTH OF REPUBLICAN OFFICEHOLDERS IN TEXAS, 1974–2015

Year	U.S. Senate	Other Statewide	U.S. Congress	Texas Senate	Texas House	County Offices*	District Offices**	Total
1974	1	0	2	3	16	53		75
1976	1	0	2	3	19	67		92
1978	1	1	4	4	22	87		119
1980	1	1	5	7	35	166		215
1982	1	0	5	5	36	191	79	317
1984	1	0	10	6	52	287	90	446
1986	1	1	10	6	56	410	94	578
1988	1	5	8	8	57	485	123	687
1990	1	6	8	8	57	547	170	797
1992	1	8	9	13	58	634	183	906
1994	2	13	11	14	61	734	216	1051
1996	2	18	13	17	68	938	287	1343
1998	2	27	13	16	72	1,108	289	1,527
2000	2	27	13	16	72	1,233	346	1,709
2002	2	27	15	19	88	1,443	372	1,966
2004	2	27	21	19	87	1,608	402	2,166
2006	2	27	19	20	82	1,814	389	2,353
2008	2	27	20	19	76	1,862	389	2,395
2010	2	27	23	19	102	2,365	432	2,970
2012	2	27	24	19	95	2,583	460	3,210
2013	2	26	24	19	95	2,668	463	3,297
2015***	2	26	25	20	98	2,992	497	3,660

*County offices include: county judge, commissioners, constables, county attorneys, county clerks, district clerks, county judicial positions, treasurers, surveyors, justices of the peace, sheriffs, tax assessor/collectors, and other local offices.
**District offices include: State Board of Education, court of appeals, district judges, and district attorneys.
***The 2015 data were compiled to the end of the calendar year.
SOURCE: Courtesy of Cassie Daniel, Senior Director of Party Organization & Training, Republican Party of Texas.

67 in the Texas House. The GOP has made significant gains across Texas at the county level as well. In 1974 Republicans held 53 county offices but claimed 2,992 by the end of 2015, paralleling the dramatic statewide realignment (see Table 10–1).

10.3.6 Changing Party Identification

The changes in party affiliations over the past forty years illustrate Texas's political realignment. Belden Associates of Dallas reported in a 1952 survey that 66 percent of Texans called themselves Democrats, and only 6 percent claimed to be Republicans, a pattern that changed little from 1952 to 1964.[36] During this period of Democratic dominance, it was quite common to refer to Democrats as "yellow dog Democrats," Texans who would vote for a yellow dog if it were a Democrat.

A modest change occurred after 1964, the year President Lyndon Johnson defeated Senator Barry Goldwater in an election in which ideology played a significant role. During the next decade, Republican Party identification increased to 16 percent, and Democratic Party identification declined to 59 percent (see Figure 10–2). Between 1975 and 1984, a dramatic decline in voter identification with the Democratic Party and a significant increase in Republican Party identification took place.

Since the first decade of this century, more Texas voters have called themselves Republicans than Democrats. In 2020, some 33 percent of voters said they were Republicans, and 31 percent identified as Democrats. About one-third of voters indicated they were "independents," but when their party orientation was probed in follow-up questions, most of this group indicated that they leaned toward one of the

FIGURE 10-2 CHANGING PARTY AFFILIATION IN TEXAS, 1964–2020

Republicans held all statewide offices and controlled both houses of the Texas Legislature in 2020, and this figure shows part of the reason why. After years of near-parity or equality among Texas voters who identified with one or the other major political party, Republicans had a distinct advantage that year. Additionally, surveys have indicated, more "independent voters" (41 percent in 2020) "lean" toward the Republican Party than lean toward the Democratic Party (31 percent in 2020).

SOURCE: The Texas Polls, 1993–2004; Pew Research Center, "Fewer Voters Identify as Republicans," March 20, 2008; and University of Texas/*The Texas Tribune* Polls, February 2012 through April 2020.

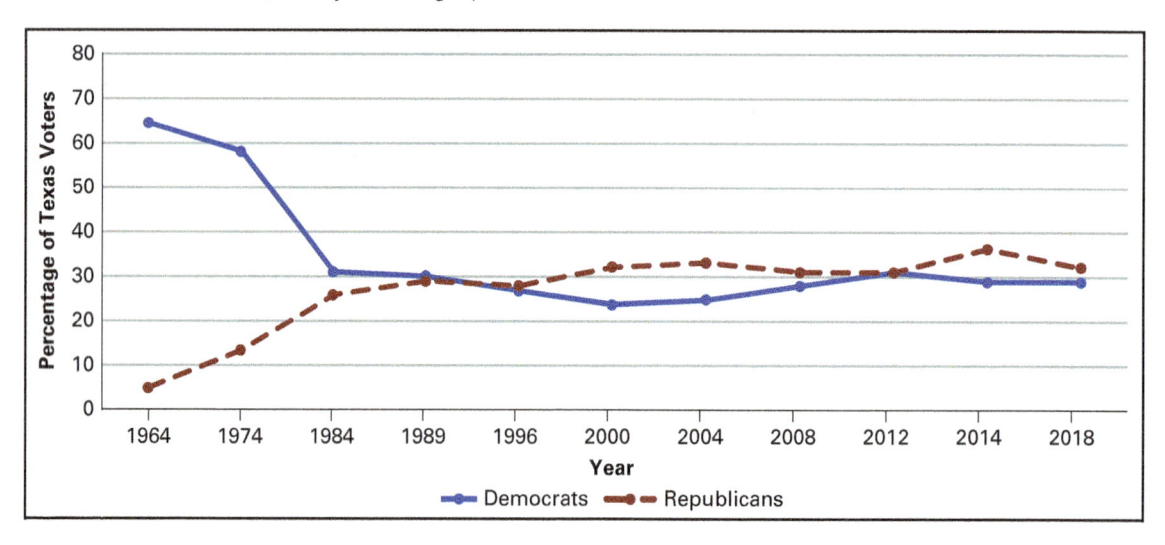

ticket splitting
The decisions of voters to divide their votes among candidates of more than one political party in the same election.

two major parties. The combined tabulations resulted in 48 percent of Texas voters calling themselves Republican or Republican-leaners and 42 percent identifying as Democrats or Democratic-leaners.[37]

This shift in party identification is further proof that Texas, at least on a statewide basis, is now Republican dominant, but party identification does not always translate into winning elected offices at the county level. Nationally in 2020, some 34 percent of registered voters identified as Democrats, 29 percent as Republicans, and 34 percent as independents.[38]

Many Texas voters identify as independents. Independents do not have their own party, and their choices in most elections are limited to candidates from the two major parties. As noted earlier, however, more self-proclaimed independents in Texas tend to vote for Republican candidates.[39]

Through 2018, Texans could vote a straight-party ticket, and many did. That is, they pulled one lever or marked one box or icon on their ballots that automatically cast all their votes for all the candidates of one party. But this practice was ended after the 2018 elections under a law enacted by the legislature in 2017. Even before the change in law, many Texans had chosen to split their votes between the two parties, going down the ballot and voting on candidates for each office individually, regardless of party affiliation. **Ticket splitting**, as this practice was called, was associated with the realignment process, and it was common during the years in which Republicans were beginning to loosen the one-party Democratic grip on the state. Ticket splitting began to decline with Republican growth and increased ideological polarization in Texas. But it helped to explain how, even in the days of straight-ticket voting, Democrats were able to win election to many legislative and county offices despite Republican sweeps of statewide offices. Many Texans cast their votes selectively as they went down the general election ballot. Now, the law requires them to do that.

Voting differences and party identification sometimes are based on gender. Nationally, differences in the voting patterns of men and women have been significant. These differences usually are not as pronounced in Texas politics, but on occasion they have been. The gubernatorial election of 1990 produced one of the largest gaps between women and men in recent Texas political history. According to surveys of voters leaving the polls, Democrat Ann Richards enjoyed a lead of as much as 20 percent among women voters in some precincts in her defeat of Republican Clayton Williams. Part of that difference was believed to have been attributable to Williams's clumsy outspokenness, including a rape joke gaffe, which prompted a negative reaction among women across the state. Voter polls in the 1994 gubernatorial race indicated that Richards held a more modest lead among women over Republican George W. Bush, who unseated her.[40]

As reported in the previous chapter, there also is evidence that older and younger voters in Texas view the world in markedly different ways, a difference reflected in how they vote. According to survey data, younger voters, for example, are more tolerant of candidates who have experienced problems with alcohol or drug abuse. Many younger voters also are more tolerant of various lifestyles, which can create problems for conservatives who campaign against homosexuality and gay rights. Unlike older voters, fewer 18- to 29-year-olds express any party identification. Moreover, younger people vote at much lower rates than older citizens.[41]

In 1992, Republican President George H. W. Bush carried Texas while losing his reelection bid to Democrat Bill Clinton. That election marked the first time a Democratic candidate won the White House without winning Texas's electoral votes, a feat that Clinton repeated in 1996 and Barack Obama accomplished in 2008 and 2012. The 1992 and 1996 elections also included the independent candidacy of Ross Perot, a billionaire computer magnate from Dallas, who attracted a lot of attention but finished third in Texas each time, as he did nationwide.

10.3.7 Differences between traditional Republicans, Tea Party Republicans, and Democrats

Political parties are not homogenous demographically or ideologically, but survey data point to rather significant differences between the two major parties in Texas in terms of demographics. The Texas Republican Party is composed disproportionately of people who are college educated, Anglo, newcomers to Texas, rural or suburban residents, and have higher incomes. More men identify with the Republican Party than do women, and support for the Republican Party is higher among older Texans. Republicans tend to classify themselves as very conservative, conservative, right of center, or moderate, with significant numbers reporting high levels of religiosity with frequent church attendance. Anglo evangelical Protestants disproportionately identify with the Texas Republican Party.

Texas Democrats are more likely to have lower incomes and to be younger, African American or Hispanic, and less educated (although a large percentage of highly educated professionals are Democrats). More women identify themselves as Democrats than do men. Democrats tend to classify themselves as moderate to liberal, attend church less regularly, and live in more urban environments and counties on the Texas-Mexico border.[42]

Democrats and Republicans have markedly different positions on federal spending, immigration, income inequality, the national economy, and border security.

In twenty surveys conducted by the University of Texas/*The Texas Tribune* Poll, respondents were asked questions about the Texas Tea Party. This is not a formal party but a movement almost exclusively linked to the Republican Party. Tea Party identifiers share the same conservative orientation as do Republicans in general but are more conservative than many of their party colleagues. They also share similar characteristics with other Republicans as to race, education, and religion. More males identify with the Tea Party than females. Tea Party identifiers are more intensely interested in politics than Republicans in general, which explains, in part, the significant influence of this movement in the party's primary elections. The emergence of the Tea Party initially was believed to have been based on disenchantment with the established party leaders or elites, but much study remains to be done on the motivations of those who identify with this movement.[43] This group has pushed the Republican Party farther to the right, and its electoral choices in Republican primaries have frequently spawned sharp internal party rivalries.

10.3.8 Party Realignment, Dealignment, or Revitalization?

Although the party system has been transformed in Texas, there is considerable disagreement about what these changes will mean in the long run. V. O. Key, writing in the 1940s, concluded that race was becoming less important and the electorate was dividing along liberal and conservative lines. He concluded that a "modified class politics seems to be evolving."[44] More than a half-century later, the parties appear, in part, to be aligning around economic issues that are manifested in liberal and conservative philosophies, but issues involving race and ethnicity continue to shape attitudes.

Chandler Davidson has argued that "the Republican Party's hardline racial policy" attracted large numbers of conservative Democrats as well as supporters of George Wallace, the conservative American Independent Party's 1968 presidential nominee, and "strengthened the commitment of African Americans and Mexican Americans to the Democratic Party."[45] Some Texas African Americans and Hispanics, primarily well-educated, well-to-do individuals, have become Republicans. But the vast majority remain Democrats, and Sunday morning visits to African American churches in Houston and Dallas and appearances at South Texas *pachangas* (cookouts) are practically mandatory for Democratic candidates serious about winning statewide office.

Seeking to expand the Republican Party's base, Governor George W. Bush made a strong appeal to Hispanics during his 1998 reelection campaign and, according to some estimates, was rewarded with about 40 percent of the Hispanic vote. Some Republican strategists have been arguing for years that the GOP must strengthen its appeal to the growing Hispanic population—and chip away at Hispanics' traditional support for the Democratic Party—if the GOP is to continue to maintain its control over state politics. Anglo Protestants, who form the core of the Republican Party, are declining in proportion to the increasing number of Hispanics in Texas. To maintain dominance, it has been argued, Republicans must embrace issues that are central to Hispanic voting interests, such as improved health care and educational opportunities. Texas spends billions of dollars on health care and education, but advocates complain that the Republican-led legislature doesn't provide enough resources to keep up with the state's growing needs. Immigration and changes in election law are other polarizing issues. Many Hispanics were angered by the Republican-led enactment of a photo ID requirement for voting in Texas. The opposition of many Republicans to immigration reform also has pushed many Hispanics away from the party. And President Donald Trump's proposal for a wall along the border with Mexico and his crackdown on undocumented immigrants have added to the controversy. Republicans also have spoken about the need to appeal to African American Texans who share their core values, but the GOP has had little success attracting African Americans from the Democratic Party.

The transformation of Texas from a one-party Democratic state to Republican dominance was the key realignment story of the last part of the twentieth century, but political systems are subject to change. Recent predictions that Texas will once again become a competitive two-party state are based on a number of factors, the most prominent of which is the fact that Hispanics will soon become Texas's biggest population group. It has been argued that Hispanics will continue to vote in large numbers for Democratic candidates and will become a greater factor in statewide elections. They already have been influential in Democratic gains in Houston, Dallas, and other major urban areas, and there has been a resurgence of grassroots, voter-mobilization organizations that identify with the Democratic Party. Another major factor was the outcome of the 2020 races for the Texas Legislature, which determined party control of the legislature when new political boundaries were drawn in 2021 for the next ten years of legislative and congressional races, and which party those new district lines favored.

If Republicans continue to campaign against immigration, some political experts believe, they will undermine their own attempts to attract Hispanics from the Democratic Party. Also unknown are the potential effects of the COVID-19 pandemic and the economic downturn that it caused and the widespread demonstrations against police brutality that broke out in the late spring of 2020.

An alternative view to realignment is that the party system is undergoing disintegration or **dealignment**.[46] This view is supported by the decline of the parties' electoral functions, their general organizational weaknesses, and voter indifference toward partisan labels, as manifested in ticket splitting and the increasing numbers of people calling themselves independents. According to the dealignment arguments, political parties no longer perform their traditional functions because other institutions—including special interest and ideological groups, the media, political action committees with large campaign coffers, and the candidates themselves—have more resources and are more effective in achieving electoral objectives.

A well-financed candidate, for example, can ignore party leaders and still win a party's nomination by using effective campaign and media tactics in the primary. Interest groups, which offer sophisticated organizations to shape public policy, may provide more access to policymakers through campaign contributions than do the parties, and the media play a much greater role in screening candidates, exposing candidates to the electorate, and shaping public opinion. Huge amounts of campaign funds, sometimes referred to as dark money, are now raised and contributed to candidates, not to the political parties. Money provides access to elected officials, and it can be argued that it shapes or influences positions that candidates take on policy issues.

The dealignment arguments, however, were more prominent in the last two decades of the twentieth century than they have been in recent years. Although the arguments still may have some validity, newer evidence suggests that the party doomsayers were somewhat premature in their predictions. The argument of dealignment moves in a different direction with a more-recent assertion that the national Republicans are a party that has "quit governing but has seized American politics."[47]

A contrary view in Texas is that the parties are undergoing a process of revitalization, attempting to reclaim basic party functions, especially in the areas of elections and campaigns.[48] **Party activists** are attempting to adapt modern campaign technology to the party organization. If the parties are able to provide strong support in fundraising, campaign advertising, phone banks, and other campaign functions, some candidates likely will become more dependent on the party organization. What used to be a large infusion of money from corporations, labor unions, and other interest groups—so-called soft money—into state and local party organizations has been one factor in this new vitality of state political parties, but those funds have been slowed by federal limits in national elections.[49] There also has been considerable collaboration between the state parties and the national parties in voter identification, voter mobilization, funding of campaigns, and organizational development. Increasingly, money is coming from various sources to support the parties' efforts to provide increased campaign services, but candidates also raise significant amounts of campaign money independently of the parties.

dealignment
A view that the party system is breaking up and the electoral influence of political parties is being replaced by interest groups, the media, and well-financed candidates who use their own media campaigns to dominate the nomination and election process.

party activist
Member of a political party involved in organizational and electoral activities.

The Party Organization

10.4 Explain the structure of the party organization in Texas.

To carry out their functions, the two major parties in Texas have developed permanent and temporary organizations, structured by general provisions of state law, state and national party rules, and a series of court decisions protecting voters' rights. Party organizations are built around geographic election districts.[50] Party organization, however, has no hierarchical arrangement. V. O. Key described the party structure as a "system of layers of organization," with each level—county, state, and federal—concentrating on the elections within its jurisdiction.[51] Each party level has a great deal of autonomy, based on the limited sanctions that one level can impose on another, and the fact that each level of the party needs the others to carry out electoral functions.[52]

There are no membership requirements for either the Democratic or the Republican Party. Party members do not have to pay dues, attend meetings, campaign for candidates, or make contributions. When people register to vote in Texas, they are not required to state their party preference as they are in many other states. The right to participate in a party's electoral activities is based on voting in that party's primary election. When a person votes in one of the major party primaries, his or her voter-registration card is stamped "Democrat" or "Republican."

10.4.1 The Permanent Organizations

Election **precincts**—some 9,174 in Texas in early 2020—are created by the county commissioners of each of Texas's 254 counties. Population, political boundaries, and available voting sites help determine the number of precincts within a county. But across the state, many counties have reduced their number of election precincts.

PRECINCT CHAIR Voters in each precinct elect a **precinct chair** in the party primary. Any eligible voter within the precinct can file for this position, and the names of write-in candidates can be added to the ballot. Although there are many contested precinct chair elections, often no one runs for the office, leaving many precinct vacancies throughout the state. In turn, these vacancies can be filled by the county party organization, but this problem has contributed to the parties' organizational decline. The chair calls the precinct convention or caucus (discussed later) to order and serves as a member of the county executive committee. Precinct chairs also can mobilize party supporters to vote. Some people have done nothing with the position; others have contributed much time and energy and have successfully delivered the precinct for their party's candidates in the general election. In some counties, the precinct chair is responsible for staffing the polling places with election judges and clerks on Election Day, but increasingly the county election administrator does this.

COUNTY EXECUTIVE COMMITTEE AND COUNTY CHAIR The second level of the party organization is the **county executive committee**, which includes each precinct chair and the **county chair**, who is elected to a two-year term by primary voters countywide. A major responsibility of the county chair and the executive committee is the organization and management of the primary election in their county. The county executive committee accepts filings by candidates for local offices and also is responsible for planning the county or district conventions. Funds for the management of primary elections are provided to the county party by the state through the secretary of state's office.

County committees may be well organized and actively work to carry out a wide range of organizational and electoral activities, or they may meet irregularly and have difficulty getting a quorum of members to attend. The county chair is an unpaid position. Party organizations in some counties have successful fund-raising operations,

---

precinct
A specific, local voting area created by a county commissioners court. The state election code outlines detailed requirements for drawing up these election units.

precinct chair
A local officer in a political party who presides over the precinct convention and serves on the party's county executive committee. Voters in each precinct elect a chair in the party's primary election.

county executive committee
A panel responsible on the local level for the organization and management of a political party's primary election. It includes the party's county chair and each precinct chair.

county chair
The presiding officer of a political party's county executive committee. Voters in the party primary elect him or her by countywide election.

and they support a party headquarters, retain professional staff, and are engaged in various party activities between elections.

The Texas Election Code provides for other district committees that correspond to a state senatorial, state representative, judicial, or congressional district. District committees that are solely within a county include precinct chairs, whereas multicounty district committees include representatives of all affected counties. These committees select candidates for vacancies in local and district offices if the vacancies occur between the primary and general election.

STATE EXECUTIVE COMMITTEE, CHAIR, AND VICE CHAIR At the state level, a party's permanent organization, prescribed by statutory law, is the **state executive committee**, which includes sixty-four members. When the parties meet in their biennial state conventions, delegates from each of the thirty-one state senatorial districts select two committee members—a man and a woman. The **state chair and the vice chair**, one of whom must be a woman, also are selected by the convention delegates to serve on the executive committee. The executive committee can be expanded, which both parties have done to include party officials or to represent the interests of auxiliary party groups, but these additional committee members are limited to voting on nonstatutory matters. The chair and vice chair of the Democratic Party serve four-year terms, while the Republican chair and vice chair serve for two years.

Statewide candidates file for office with the executive committee, which also is responsible for planning and organizing the party's state convention and helps raise funds for the ongoing operations of the party. The committee serves to establish party policy, but day-to-day party operations are entrusted to the party's executive director and professional staff. The Texas Democratic Party and the Texas Republican Party have permanent staffs and headquarters in Austin.

Sometimes, the state committees have been highly effective with strong, energetic leadership that has carried over into the development and retention of a competent professional staff. At other times, however, the state committees have been divided along ideological, factional, or personal lines, producing conflict that sometimes has become open warfare. In such instances, a party finds it difficult to raise funds, maintain a highly qualified staff, and carry out its electoral functions.

10.4.2 The Temporary Organizations: The Party Conventions

The temporary organizations of the political parties are the series of conventions that are held every two years, beginning sometime after the party primaries. They are particularly significant in presidential election years because they—together with the presidential preference primary—help select the state's delegates to the national party conventions, which nominate the presidential candidates. The convention system also helps organize the permanent party structure and brings party activists together to share common political concerns and shape party policies. Most Texans, however, have little knowledge of the convention system, and few participate in it.

THE PRECINCT, COUNTY, AND SENATORIAL CONVENTIONS Conventions are about politics, selection of candidates, and control of the party apparatus. There have been intermittent periods of lackluster conventions, but during Texas's one-party, Democratic era, frequent, bitter convention fights took place between conservatives and liberals for control of the Democratic Party. Although those fights were most evident at the state convention, they also permeated the precinct, county, and district conventions. As Texas Republicans have increased in number and developed more diversified interests, similar intraparty struggles have surfaced.

Historically, precinct conventions—the lowest level of conventions—were held after the polls closed on primary Election Day. These conventions normally were held

state executive committee
The statewide governing body of a political party. It includes the state chair and vice chair, a committee man and a committee woman elected by party convention delegates from each of the thirty-one state senatorial districts, and other officers or members designated by the political parties.

state chair and vice chair
The two top state leaders of a political party, one of whom must be a woman. Delegates to the party's state convention select these officers. The Republican chair and vice chair serve for two years, while the Democratic chair and vice chair serve for four years.

in the same locations where the voting was conducted, and anyone who had voted in that party's primary was eligible to attend, but as noted below, the precinct conventions have been integrated into the county or senatorial conventions.

Each precinct is assigned a specific number of delegates, based on the party's voting strength in that precinct. These delegates are then eligible to participate in the county or senatorial district conventions. Since 1972, Democrats have used complex procedures designed to ensure broad-based delegate representation by ethnicity, gender, and age.

Precinct conventions held in nonpresidential election years often are poorly attended; sometimes no one shows up. The precinct meeting may last fifteen minutes, and those attending may not be able to get enough people to volunteer to be delegates to the county or senatorial convention. Among scholars who debate the status of political parties, those who conclude that the parties are in decline cite such low participation rates.

In the past, highly motivated political and ideological movements have been able to capture precinct conventions and advance candidates who had little in common with mainstream party voters. Supporters of Barry Goldwater used this strategy in 1964 to help win the Republican presidential nomination for their candidate, as did supporters of Democrat George McGovern in 1972. Both men were soundly defeated in the general election.

Religious Right
An ultraconservative political faction that draws considerable support from fundamentalist religious groups and economic conservatives.

The **Religious Right** used a similar strategy to extend its influence in the Republican Party and was successful for the first time in Texas in 1994. Republican candidates nominated with the support of the Religious Right and other social conservatives were highly successful in general elections in Texas. In 2008, the presidential primary campaigns of Democrats Barack Obama and Hillary Clinton went to great lengths to organize their support in the precinct conventions during their fight for the presidential nomination. The Tea Party movement became a major force in Republican primary races in Texas in 2010 and continued to be a significant factor in subsequent Republican primaries and party conventions.

Under recent changes in its party rules, the Texas Democratic Party now holds its precinct conventions on the same day as its next level of conventions—the county and state senatorial district conventions—a few weeks after the primary. Attendees include those who voted in the primary as well as those who affirm support for the Democratic Party, a significant change in the procedures for selecting delegates from the precinct conventions to the county or senatorial district conventions. County conventions are held in those counties not divided by state senatorial districts. Senatorial district conventions are held in the counties that include more than one state senatorial district.

Under its current rules, the Democratic county or state senatorial district conventions first convene, elect officers, and appoint committees. Upon completion of these organizational activities, attendees then caucus by precinct for the purpose of electing delegates and alternates to the county or senatorial district conventions.

Under its rules, Texas Republicans continue to hold many of their precinct conventions on primary Election Day but permit the county parties to hold conventions at other times, including the morning of the county or senatorial district conventions.

Even with the procedural changes that have occurred in recent years, these series of conventions remain key steps in the process of electing delegates to the parties' state conventions and, in presidential election years, to the national conventions that nominate the major parties' presidential candidates. Convention participants also may adopt resolutions for possible inclusion in the party's **platform**.

platform
A set of principles or positions on various issues adopted by a political party at its state or national convention.

STATE CONVENTIONS Although there have been a few exceptions, historically, the two major parties hold their state conventions in June of even-numbered years.

Convention delegates certify to the secretary of state the names of those individuals who were nominated to statewide offices in the March primaries and May runoff primaries; adopt a party platform; and elect the state party chair, the vice chair, the state executive committee, and other officers designated by party rules.

In presidential election years, the state conventions also select delegates to their respective parties' national nominating conventions, elect members to their parties' national committees, and choose presidential electors. Electors from the party that carries Texas in the presidential race will formally cast the state's electoral votes for that party's candidate in December after the general election.

The presidential primary determines how many delegates each candidate is entitled to at the Republican National Convention, but the actual delegates who attend the convention are selected at the state convention. Texas delegates to the Democratic National Convention are determined through a more complicated process, based both on the primary vote and on candidate support from attendees at the series of party conventions, beginning at the precinct level.

The COVID-19 pandemic created havoc for the party conventions in 2020. The district conventions were canceled, and the Texas Democratic Party, rather than risk infections among convention attendees and service staff, called off its scheduled in-person state convention and held a virtual convention online. Texas Republicans were planning to hold their state convention in Houston in mid-July with as many as 6,000 attendees. But a week before the event was scheduled to begin, Houston First Corp, which operated the convention venue, the George R. Brown Convention Center, canceled the in-person event at the urging of Mayor Sylvester Turner, citing the pandemic and health concerns. The party then held an online state convention. The Democratic National Convention and most of the Republican National Convention also were held virtually. Republicans conducted part of their national convention business in a pared-down, in-person event in Charlotte, N.C.

10.4.3 The Party Activists

Texans participate in party politics for a variety of reasons, including some that are similar to reasons people join and participate in interest groups. Some see their participation in party organizational and campaign activities as a way to help shape or influence public policy.[53] Some are brought into party activities through issues or specific candidates running for office. Others, influenced by politically active families, have absorbed party loyalty and interest in the political process. Some hope that party activism will serve as a stepping-stone to public office or political appointments. Political campaigns have a social component to them, and many activists enjoy the social contacts and friendships that come with actively working for the party or a candidate.

Texans who participate in the organizational activities of the political parties have characteristics that vary, to some extent, from other voters who support their respective political parties. In general terms, party activists tend to be more ideological than the voters who regularly support their party. Republican activists tend to be more conservative than most Republicans, and Democratic activists tend to be more liberal than most Democrats in the electorate. Activists tend to be better informed about candidates and issues than the general electorate, and they have "the time and financial resources to afford political activity, the information and knowledge to understand it, and the skills to be useful in it."[54]

Demographic and social characteristics of activists also differ between the two major parties. Democratic activists include more Hispanics, African Americans, union members, and Catholics. But despite differences in backgrounds and political views, activists of both parties tend to be better educated, to have higher incomes, and to hold higher-status occupations than the general population.[55]

When David Broder published *The Party's Over* four decades ago, there was a growing sense that the campaign and organizational functions of the political parties dependent on the party activists were on a trajectory of sharp decline. Fewer people appeared to be involved in party and campaign activities as the political parties lost organizational, material, and symbolic incentives to recruit and sustain their involvement. Self-recruited candidates now communicated directly with voters utilizing the tools of the electronic media and mass marketing. Candidates, campaign consultants, and party leaders tended to view the party activists as largely irrelevant to successful campaigns, and if campaign volunteers were to be used, they were frequently recruited by the candidates and motivated by their relationships with the candidates, not the political party.

With the decline of party activism, some scholars focused on the decline in voting and its relationship to personal contacts by party workers or campaign volunteers. Study after study concluded that voter turnout increased with personal contacts, with numerous examples of voter turnout increasing by 5 to 10 percent because of organized grassroots efforts.[56] Obviously, party activists did not disappear, but it has taken a series of elections at all levels to reestablish an emphasis on the importance of grassroots or local campaign and party activity. The 2008 presidential campaign demonstrated how technology and new media could be used to mobilize large numbers of volunteers to contact voters effectively. In subsequent election years, the technology has become more sophisticated. Parties at all levels are adapting some aspects of these tools to their organizational and campaign efforts, and the political parties and their consultants continue to integrate large numbers of volunteers in the technology-driven campaigns.

The Party in Government

10.5 Summarize the challenges of producing cohesive policy-oriented coalitions in Texas government.

As part of V. O. Key's three-part perspective on political parties, we have begun our discussion of the political party in the electorate. In other chapters, we expand on this analysis by looking more closely at voting behavior, partisan attitudes, and the party activists. We also have presented a brief summary of the party organization. We discussed the party in government in the earlier chapters on the legislature, the executive branch, the bureaucracy, and the judiciary.

Political parties in Texas have historically been unable to produce cohesive, policy-oriented coalitions and have been unable to hold their elected officials accountable or responsive to those supporting the party. Under ideal circumstances, some students of government believe, the two major parties would lay out clearly defined political philosophies and policies they would pursue if their candidates were elected. Once elected, persons supported by the party would be committed to these programs, giving the voters a clear standard by which to evaluate their performance in office. This perspective is often referred to as the "responsible party model."

Texas parties have been incapable of functioning in this manner for several reasons. First, the political parties in Texas are decentralized and rarely able to discipline members who pursue goals that conflict with the parties' stated objectives. The large number of elected officials at state and local levels serves to diffuse party leadership. A recent, but largely symbolic, exception to this observation occurred in 2018, when a two-thirds majority of the State Republican Executive Committee, the party's governing body, voted to censure then-Speaker Joe Straus for impeding some conservative GOP priorities. During the regular and special legislative sessions the previous year, Straus, who was a moderate Republican leader, and a majority of House members had blocked conservative goals such as legislation to spend state tax dollars on vouchers for private school tuition and a bill to regulate the use of public restrooms by transgender persons. The conservative faction had strong influence on the party's executive committee, but the censure was more symbolic than anything else because Straus already had announced, a few months earlier, that he wasn't seeking reelection to the legislature.

Additionally, the coalitions that parties form with groups harboring different objectives, interests, and agendas have traditionally made it difficult to develop clearly stated positions that would always differentiate one party from another. The more ideologically different the parties become, however, on abortion, gun rights, taxes, education, and other major issues, the more likely some of these cross-party coalitions may dissolve.

Another explanation for the lack of partisan accountability is the long-standing antiparty tradition of American politics. Many voters are ambivalent, even outright hostile, toward political parties and make little, if any, effort to become informed on political and public issues. In addition, the parties make only limited efforts to include a large number of individuals in their organizational activities.

CONCLUSION

The roles and relative dominance of political parties have changed over the years, and their long-term futures, in Texas as well as other states, are uncertain. But, for now at least, they remain an integral part of our political system, and being able to navigate the party organizations, rules, and primaries is essential for anyone planning to seek elective office and important for anyone who simply wants to be an informed voter. Many Texans consider themselves political independents, perhaps reflecting the state's individualistic tradition, perhaps reflecting an antagonism toward partisanship. But the partisan label remains an important factor in elections, as reflected until recently in significant levels of one-party, straight-ticket voting, a practice that has been ended by the legislature. Barring dramatic change in the political landscape, almost everyone elected to a significant state or federal government office in Texas for the foreseeable future will continue to be either a Republican or a Democrat, and they will continue to write the rules for elections. Even candidates in city elections, which officially are nonpartisan, are becoming increasingly identified by their party affiliations.

A NATIONAL CONVENTION RETURNS TO THE SOUTH
The Democratic National Convention was held in Houston in late June of 1928. This was the first time a southern state hosted a Democratic convention since the Civil War. Al Smith of New York, a Catholic and proponent of the repeal of Prohibition, was nominated with little opposition. Subsequently, Texas Democrats defected to Herbert Hoover, giving him the state's electoral votes.

REVIEW THE CHAPTER

Political Parties and a Democratic Society

10.1 Explain what political parties are and why Texas has a two-party system, p. 308.

A political party is a group of individuals who organize to elect candidates to office under their banner for purposes of enacting a broad array of public policies. Although it was not always the case, Texas now has a two-party system. Third parties have developed from time to time, but their impact on the outcome of elections has been negligible. The pattern of two-party politics has been shaped by a long tradition that developed early in the nation's history. Other factors that have helped preserve a two-party system include plurality elections in which the candidate with the largest number of votes wins, state election laws that restrict third parties, the absence of intense ideological differences among most Texans, and issues that cut across race and economic class.

The Functions of Political Parties

10.2 Explain the primary functions of political parties in Texas, p. 313.

Political parties build broad electoral coalitions and serve as intermediaries between the voters and the government. Parties recruit and nominate candidates, contest elections, attempt to mobilize voters, organize and manage governments, mediate the effects of separation of powers, provide accountability, resolve conflicts among diverse groups, and set the policy agenda.

The Party in the Electorate

10.3 Summarize the partisan history of Texas, p. 317.

Significant changes in the state's party structure have occurred over the past four decades, transforming Texas from a one-party Democratic state into a two-party state dominated by the Republican Party. Party realignment in the state reflects patterns that have occurred in most other southern states. Realignment has occurred for a number of reasons, including in-migration of residents from states with strong Republican parties, changes in the ethnic and racial composition of the state, the impact of the Voting Rights Act, and policy shifts of the national political parties. Republicans have won all statewide races in Texas since 1996. They captured a majority of the Texas Senate in 1997 and a majority of the Texas House in 2002. Democrats, however, still hold many county offices throughout Texas. Historically, politics in Texas were configured around class and race, and despite the partisan changes, these two factors still are significant in party alliances.

The Party Organization

10.4 Explain the structure of the party organization in Texas, p. 330.

State laws outline the formal party structure, but the vitality and strength of local party organizations vary widely from one area of the state to another. The permanent organization of the parties begins with the voting precinct and moves from the county party organization to the state organization. All of these levels elect party officials who serve to carry out party functions. There are no membership requirements, and any voter can opt to participate in the organizational activities of one or the other party.

Every two years, the parties hold conventions. A succession of conventions begins with the precinct convention, followed by a county or senatorial district convention and then the state convention. In presidential election years, the focus of the state convention is on the selection of delegates to the national nominating convention. Conventions, which are described as the temporary organizations of the parties, also serve other functions, including the mobilization of party activists and the development of party platforms.

The Party in Government

10.5 Summarize the challenges of producing cohesive policy-oriented coalitions in Texas government, p. 334.

Political parties in Texas do not produce cohesive, policy-oriented coalitions in government because they have few resources with which to hold elected officials accountable. Elected officials are self-recruited and usually raise funds for their campaigns with minimal party assistance. With candidate-centered campaigns, the parties have lost much of their control over those elected under party labels. Legislators and other elected officials are somewhat like free agents, taking sides on issues with little concern of recrimination from their political parties.

The parties are highly decentralized, and party leadership is diffused across the state. Legislative alliances have cut across party labels with leaders from both parties appointing members of the opposite party to be chairs of committees. Voting in the legislature tends to follow philosophical rather than partisan lines. Persistent antiparty attitudes on the part of many Texans also have weakened the parties' efforts at disciplining their elected officials.

LEARN THE TERMS

political party, p. 309
third party, p. 311
Jim Crow laws, p. 318
bifactionalism, p. 319
one-party politics, p. 319
two-party system, p. 321

realignment, p. 322
ticket splitting, p. 326
dealignment, p. 329
party activist, p. 329
precinct, p. 330
precinct chair, p. 330

county executive committee, p. 330
county chair, p. 330
state executive committee, p. 331
state chair and vice chair, p. 331
Religious Right, p. 332
platform, p. 332

Elections, Campaigns, and Voting in Texas

11

Pictured here is Anthony "Tony" Gonzales II, the man who should always remind you of the importance of your vote. Mr. Gonzales narrowly won the primary election against Paul Reyes in 2020 by seven votes. He subsequently won the general election and currently represents Texas's 23rd congressional district in Congress.

LEARNING OBJECTIVES

11.1 Describe the functions of elections in a democratic society, p. 340.

11.2 Compare and contrast the types of state and local elections held in Texas, p. 341.

11.3 Explain the measures taken to keep some Texans from voting and the countermeasures employed to curtail these discriminatory practices, p. 350.

11.4 Describe the use of marketing technology in political campaigns, p. 360.

11.5 Describe the role of controlled and uncontrolled media in the advertising strategy of campaigns, p. 366.

11.6 Evaluate the impact of money on campaigns and the effectiveness of campaign finance reforms, p. 369.

The next time you decide to skip voting in an election because you are convinced your vote will not count, think about Tony Gonzales and Paul Reyes. The two men were in a fierce battle to win the Republican nomination to replace Representative Will Hurd, R-Helotes, in Texas Congressional District 23 in the Republican run-off primary on July 14, 2020. Mr. Gonzales was backed by President Donald Trump and the national Republican leadership to be the nominee to face Democrat Gina Ortiz Jones in the November general election. Ms. Jones represents a great hope for Democrats to turn the Republican district in their quest to turn the state blue. Mr. Gonzales was also supported by outgoing Representative Hurd. Senator Cruz stunned many when he endorsed conservative candidate Ryes just two weeks before early voting began. After all ballots were counted, Gonzales won by seven votes out of more than 24,600 votes cast. Imagine, if only four people voted differently, Reyes would have won the election instead of Gonzales. Gonzales, meanwhile, was grateful that seven of his voters—any seven—did not skip the election. This is not the first close election in the state's history, nor was it the closest. After tying in the general election and again in the runoff election, Sean Skipworth became mayor of Dickinson, TX on January 7, 2021 when a ping pong ball with his name on it was pulled from a top hat. According to state law, when no one wins following the runoff, the election is resolved by casting lots. This is not the first time this was done, but it still seems like an odd way to select our leaders.[1] Each of these elections demonstrate the importance of political engagement.

Voting matters. That is why millions of people around the world have spilled blood and made other great sacrifices to eliminate authoritarian political systems and win free and open elections. Yet, Texans traditionally do not exercise this cherished right. During the hotly contested presidential election of 2020, only 45.5 percent of eligible voters in Texas cast ballots (up from 51.4 percent in 2016). In 2018, a highly competitive midterm election, the percentage of eligible voters who participated was only 45.6 percent (up substantially from the last midterm election of 2014 when only 28.3 percent voted). In 2012 presidential election turnout was only 49.6 percent.[3] The 2016 presidential primary turnout numbers were the highest in the state's history, with nearly 4.3 million Texans voting (in 2020, less than 3.9 million or 21 percent of eligible voters participated in the primaries of both major political parties).[4] Approximately 2.375 million more people in Texas voted in the 2020 presidential election than voted in the 2016 presidential election (which is an impressive increase though our turnout rates are still below the national average, hence other states saw larger proportionate increases in participation) Turnout rates in the 2018 midterm elections were remarkably high for a nonpresidential election with turnout nearly 20 percent higher than a typical midterm election. However, even with this surge, over 54 percent of eligible voters did not vote. Such poor turnout trends cannot be blamed on a lack of opportunity, as during most of these elections Texans did not face more stringent voter-registration laws than other states, though the turnout in recent elections might have been higher if new voter identification laws had not been enacted (more on this issue later in the chapter). Contemporary political campaigns, especially those for national and statewide offices, have high media visibility. People are bombarded by television and Internet advertising, direct mail, email, Twitter feeds, social networking messages, phone bank solicitations for candidates, and daily news coverage. But something fundamental is turning off Texas voters, as well as voters across the nation. Statewide election turnout rates in Texas are consistently low, and turnout rates in many local elections are downright appalling.

Some suggest that Texans do not care about what happens in government as long as their own self-interests are being met. Others argue that there is a sense of disenchantment, disillusionment, or alienation among Texas voters. Voters, they believe, feel disconnected from government and elected officeholders. They do not trust public officials to do what they say they are going to do in their election bids, and they believe politicians are using their offices to line their own pockets. In this view, Texans care about politics, government, and public policy but believe that a single vote will make no difference.

Elected officials, moreover, are perceived to be increasingly insulated from the popular will, especially in Washington in recent years, where, more and more, partisanship is crippling government. Although they articulate a commitment to elections and political participation, some officeholders ignore their constituents' wishes as they make policy decisions. Some observers also have argued that different elections scheduled throughout the year, as they are in Texas and other states, are designed to reduce voter participation. The real brokers of politics and public policy, they believe, are the interest groups, lobbyists, political action committees (PACs), and the "fat cats" who contribute large sums of money to candidates and parties. With the decline of political parties, many candidates seem to become free agents ready to sell their services to the highest bidders—the biggest campaign contributors. When voters read or hear that candidates are raising hundreds of thousands of dollars for their campaigns from PACs or individual donors, it is difficult to convince them that politicians are not on the take or that they really care about the average citizen.

Much has been written indicting contemporary elections in Texas and the United States. Elections were designed to give the people the opportunity to direct public policy through chosen officials who would then be held accountable at the next election, but the system will not work properly if people do not vote. Elections are clearly imperfect instruments, but they are one of the most successful in peacefully translating the needs, interests, and expectations of the public into public policy.

Consequently, in your journey to become more active participants in your community and in politics, an understanding of how to be more informed voters and participants will help you navigate the complex electoral system in Texas. Moreover, having a deeper appreciation for the struggles faced by many, both in Texas and in the nation, to receive full voting rights will make it less likely that you will take this important right of citizenship for granted.

The Functions of Elections

11.1 Describe the functions of elections in a democratic society.

For more than 230 years, we in the United States have been debating electoral issues. Who should participate? Should individuals who cannot read at a certain level be permitted to vote? When should elections be held? What percentage of the popular vote should be required to win an election—a majority or a plurality? What are the policy consequences of elections? Does it really make any difference who gets elected? Although these questions are significant, the most important issue is the relationship of elections to our definition of a democratic society. In the most fundamental terms, "elections are used to assure popular support and legitimacy for those who make governmental decisions."[5] A stable political system depends on popular support, and people freely participating in the process of choosing those who make public policy are more likely to accept and support policy without coercion or force.

Although elections provide broad statements of the voters' expectations for future public policy and a prospective judgment on the performance of elected officials, they seldom articulate or direct precise programs. Successful political parties and candidates build broad-based campaign coalitions, and the competing demands of the diverse groups courted by candidates make it difficult for candidates to specify in detail the policies they plan to pursue once elected. Most people seeking public office, therefore, prefer to speak in general concepts and try to avoid answering hypothetical "what if" questions posed by reporters, such as "What if there isn't enough money in the budget to raise teachers' pay or improve health care? Will you support a tax increase or cut back on other programs?"

Nevertheless, after an election, a successful candidate is likely to indicate that the people have spoken and claim a mandate to pursue specific public policies of his or her choosing. If there is a mandate, it is often for the person elected, not for a specific program.[6] Even in the absence of a specific mandate, elections allow the masses to express their will and are critical components of representative democracy.

Elections enable voters to replace public officials or force officeholders to change their policies.[7] They are, in effect, the one institution that a democratic society can use to control its leaders and provide a retrospective judgment of the past actions of elected officials. Elections offer safe mechanisms (or "safety valves") by which disgruntled individuals can peacefully petition their elected officials to express political discontent. In 1964, for example, Malcolm X gave an impassioned speech entitled the "Ballot or the Bullet" in which he urged African Americans to exercise their right to vote to bring about change, but warned that if the government continued to ignore their needs, they might have to take up arms to force change. Elections are considered important linkage mechanisms between the people and their elected officials, offering the potential for citizens to hold officials accountable. But this role is based on the assumptions that (1) there is universal **suffrage**, (2) voters are offered clear alternatives, (3) large segments of the population are informed about those aspiring to hold public office and determine public policy, and (4) voter participation is significant. Throughout Texas's history, elections often have been manipulated for the advantage and interests of the few.

Texas's political culture has unwritten rules about how elections should be conducted and what candidates should and should not do. For example, we expect a candidate to shake the hand of his or her opponent even after a bitter defeat or attack. That is why Republican Clayton Williams's snub of the handshake offered by Democrat Ann Richards during one joint appearance in the 1990 gubernatorial campaign received much media attention. Candidates can attack, counterattack, and make charges and countercharges against each other and still be considered politically acceptable and civilized. Such election rituals are manifestations of the way in which we have institutionalized conflict.

Some would argue that elections and election rituals have only a symbolic function that serves to "quiet resentments and doubts about particular political acts, reaffirm belief in the fundamental rationality and democratic character of the system, and thus fix conforming habits of future behavior."[8] Although this position may be extreme, the trivialization of elections may ultimately result in even more disenchantment, disdain, and disgust with politics and government.[9]

CAMPAIGN ETIQUETTE
Pictured here is one event that helped solidify the 1990 victory of Democratic candidate for governor, Ann Richards. Mr. Williams offended the propriety of a number of Texans when he refused to shake Richards's hand. Learning the rules and expectations—including the informal norms—is good advice for anyone looking for a new job.

suffrage
The right to vote.

State and Local Elections

11.2 Compare and contrast the types of state and local elections held in Texas.

Texans have numerous opportunities to vote, often as many as three or four times a year, in a variety of elections. Voters in Texas and other states, in fact, vote on more candidates and issues than citizens of any other democracy.[10] Turnout and interest are highest in the general election in presidential election years, but both can be abysmally low in elections for constitutional amendments, school boards, and the governing bodies of single-purpose districts, such as hospital and water districts. As you strive to become a more educated voter, know that the system, though complicated and complex, offers many opportunities for you to become involved and to influence political actors.

11.2.1 Election Cycles

Except for some constitutional amendment elections, which are set by the legislature, and emergency elections set by the governor to fill vacancies in specific offices, elections are held at regular, predictable intervals mandated by state law. There has been a systematic effort to separate elections and thereby minimize the convergence of issues in state and local races.[11] Most city and school board elections are held in May of odd-numbered years to separate them from party primaries held in March of even-numbered years and general elections held in November. Some city and school board elections, however, are held in November, but on separate ballots from state and federal races. Many constitutional amendment elections are scheduled for the same day as the general election, but they can be held separately. Although all kinds of explanations and justifications are provided for this election scheduling, there is evidence to suggest that it contributes to "voter fatigue," reduced voter turnout, and the disproportionate influence of a few individuals in many of the local and special elections for which voter turnout usually is the lowest. Some experts believe that many voters have tired of elections and tuned them out, but others challenge this view.[12]

These election cycles also shape the policymaking process. A tax increase, for example, is likely to take place soon after an election, not immediately prior to one. Voter dissatisfaction, officeholders hope, would be dissipated by the time the next election takes place. This is a double-edged sword. It insulates public officials from immediate voter retaliation when hard and unpopular decisions must be made. It also makes it difficult to punish elected officials for pursuing questionable or highly unpopular programs.

11.2.2 Primary Elections

primary election
An election in which the Democratic or Republican Party chooses its nominees for public offices. In presidential election years, the primary also plays a key role in selecting Texas delegates to the parties' national nominating conventions.

Texas and most other states use the direct **primary election** to nominate major party candidates for public office. Prior to the adoption of the primary in 1903, political parties nominated their candidates in party conventions, but changes were made for two basic reasons. Throughout the country during that era, a Progressive reform movement criticized the conventions as undemocratic, corrupt, and dominated by a few of the party elites. That movement advocated the party primary as an alternative. Second, the personal rivalries and factional disputes that erupted at nominating conventions threatened the monopoly that the Democratic Party had over Texas politics during that era, and the primary elections were a solution to excessive intraparty conflict. Under current law, any party that received 20 percent of the vote in the previous gubernatorial election is required to nominate candidates by the primary method. Other parties can continue to use the nominating convention.

Primaries are now held on the second Tuesday in March in even-numbered years, a change that was made in 1988 as part of the strategy of southern states to increase the region's influence in the presidential nominating process. The 2012 Texas primaries, however, were delayed until May 29 and the May runoffs until July 31 because of lawsuits over the redistricting of legislative and congressional districts. Since 2014, the primaries have been back on schedule, held in March as usual. Primary runoff elections in 2020 were delayed from May 26 to July 14 in response to the coronavirus outbreak. As we will see later in the chapter, these runoff elections have sparked debate, and legal challenges, regarding who should be eligible to vote by mail in elections in Texas. In a proclamation on May 11, 2020, Governor Abbott ordered that early voting begin on June 29 instead of July 6, doubling the length of time to allow voters more flexibility and to lessen crowding at the polls in response to COVID-19.

For practical purposes, the primaries in Texas are open because no party membership is designated on an individual's voter-registration card. A voter does not register as a Republican or a Democrat. Only after a person has voted in a party's primary is the party's name stamped on the card or otherwise noted, which restricts a person to voting only in that party's runoff, if there is one.

Some students of Texas politics suggest that the structure of the state's primary delayed the development of the two-party system and contributed to the conservative establishment's long domination of state politics.[13] Comparisons between earlier primary elections and general elections suggest that many Republicans voted for the most conservative candidates in the Democratic primaries and then voted for Republicans in the general elections. This practice helped ensure that conservative candidates usually were nominated by both parties and that conservatives were elected in the general election.[14] During the period of one-party Democratic politics, the person who won the Democratic primary usually won the general election. One student of the early Texas primaries noted, "The only campaigning, therefore, to which the state is usually subjected comes in connection with the Democratic primaries, and it is largely taken up with personalities."[15] State law requires that a candidate must receive an absolute majority of votes (meaning over one half of those cast) for a specific state or local office in a primary to receive a party's nomination. If no candidate receives a majority in multi-candidate races, the two top vote-getters must face each other in a **runoff election**. Voter turnout rates for runoffs are consistently lower than those for the first primary.

Minority groups have argued that the absolute majority requirement discriminates against African American and Hispanic candidates.[16] Although there has been no successful challenge to the requirement in the party primaries, runoff elections have been successfully challenged under the **Voting Rights Act** in many elections for local governments, in which candidates usually are elected on a nonpartisan ballot. When challenges have been successful, candidates who received a plurality of votes (more votes than any other candidate) were elected.

Voter turnout in contemporary primary elections is significantly lower than in the general election, but this has not always been the case. From 1904, when the primary was first used for nominations, through 1950, turnout in the primary matched or exceeded that of the general election, except for the elections of 1924 and 1944. Still, turnout for primary elections was nothing to write home about. From the 1920s through 1970, the rate of turnout for the Democratic primary never exceeded 35 percent of the voting-age population.

Participation in party primaries has eroded since the 1970s, as a result, in part, of partisan realignment, weak party organization, and candidate-centered campaigns. About 28 percent of the voting-age population (persons 18 or older) voted in a hotly contested Democratic gubernatorial primary in 1972 (see Figure 11–1). After that year, turnout in Democratic primaries fell below 20 percent, with a low point of 3.1 percent of the voting-age population in the 2006 gubernatorial primary. Prior to 1980, participation in the Republican primaries never exceeded 5 percent of the voting-age population or more than 7 percent of registered voters.[17] That rate has increased somewhat since then, but the percentage of Texans voting in a Republican primary has never reached the levels of participation that the Democratic Party experienced when it dominated state politics.

The battle between Barack Obama and Hillary Clinton for the 2008 Democratic presidential nomination sparked a record turnout of nearly 2.9 million voters in the Democratic primary that year. Almost 1.4 million voters cast ballots in the Republican primary for a total primary turnout of slightly more than 4.2 million. Approximately 8 percent of the state's 18.3-million-plus residents over 18 participated in the 2012 Republican primary, prompted in part by interest in the selection of the delegates to the Republican National Convention as well as a heated U.S. Senate race.[18] The 2012 Republican primary was noteworthy as nine candidates vied to replace retiring Senator Kay Bailey Hutchison. Lieutenant Governor David Dewhurst, favored by the GOP establishment, received 44.6 percent of the votes, and Ted Cruz, favored by Tea Party supporters, won 34.2 percent, forcing a runoff. Despite a record amount of

DONALD TRUMP IN TEXAS

Donald Trump did not perform as well in Texas as he did in other Super Tuesday states. His presence, however, may have helped explain why turnout was higher in the 2016 primaries than it was in the 2012 race, though so could the presidential campaign of Senator Cruz. While he is not on the ballot in 2018, his presence is certainly felt as Republican candidates are campaigning to support his agenda while Democratic candidates are campaigning against him (and trying to tie their Republican opponents to his agenda in districts where he is less popular).

runoff election
A required election if no candidate receives an absolute majority of the votes cast in a primary race or in many nonpartisan elections. The runoff is between the top two vote-getters.

Voting Rights Act
A federal law designed to protect the voting rights of minorities with the inclusion of several provisions that regulate elections. The act, as amended, has eliminated most of the more restrictive state laws that limited minority political participation.

FIGURE 11-1 TURNOUT SINCE 1970

Voter turnout levels can be calculated in three ways: by figuring the percentage of registered voters who voted, the percentage of eligible citizens (over 18) who voted, or the percentage of the voting-age population that voted. The figures presented here (consistent with those released by the state) are the percentage of the voting-age population (VAP) that voted. Although it is not common in the United States, some countries present turnout rates as the percentage of registered voters who voted, so be cautious when examining turnout data, as each will paint a slightly different perception of the same event. Some sources release data based upon the percent of the eligible population (VEP) that voted. VAP figures are lower because they include noncitizens, ineligible convicted felons, and prisoners. The difference between the VEP and VAP for all elections has increased over time. It has grown steadily from 1.6 percent in 1980 to 4.7 percent in 2020, though in Texas the figure is much higher.[19] As you can see here, voter participation rates change depending on the type of election, and they have varied over time. Even so, the numbers are still low, rarely exceeding 60 percent since 1970.

SOURCE: Texas Politics, http://www.laits.utexas.edu/txp_media/html/vce/features/0302_01/turnout.html (citing Federal Election Commission, Texas Secretary of State, and U.S. Elections Project, George Mason University); the United States Election Project, http://www.electproject.org/; and Texas Secretary of State, http://www.sos.state.tx.us/elections/historical/70-92.shtml.

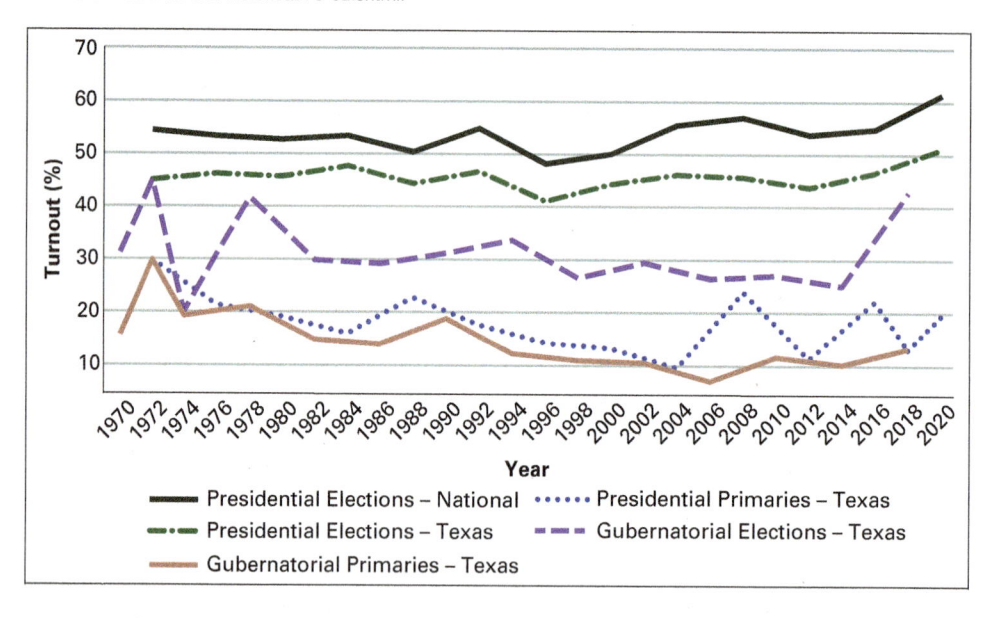

spending (one of the most expensive nonpresidential races in the country, with more than $60 million spent), turnout for the primary dropped to 6 percent, and then to only 1.3 percent for the July runoff.[20] Turnout in the Democratic primary was even lower, with only 3.2 percent of voters participating in the May primary. Turnout in the 2014 Democratic gubernatorial primaries was 3 percent of eligible voters.[21] Far more Republicans, 7.2 percent, participated in the primaries in 2014 than did Democrats. Turnout for both parties increased in 2016 over 2012. Nearly 15 percent participated in the Republican presidential primary while 7.4 percent participated in the Democratic primary in 2016. Turnout in the 2018 primaries was similar to what we have seen in the last decade, with 7.8 percent participating in the Republican primary and 5.4 percent participating in the Democratic primary.[22] As noted above, participation in the 2018 midterm elections was much higher than typical, as it was nationwide.

A number of generalizations can be drawn from these historical data. Only a small percentage of the population normally participates in the selection of the political parties' nominees, and primary voters are not similar to nonvoters. Those who do participate in party primaries tend to be more ideological than the general population. This often prompts candidates to take more extreme positions on issues during their primary campaigns, only to try to move to the center in the general election campaign to appeal to more moderate voters.[23]

Although the primary has helped make the nominating process more democratic than when the party conventions determined the nominees, some scholars and party advocates argue that the primary has contributed to the decline of the political parties.[24] The parties no longer control the nomination process because any eligible individual can be listed on a primary ballot by paying the required filing fee or submitting the required petitions. Also, potential officeholders, organizing and funding their own campaigns, have little allegiance to the parties. Even a person who is hostile toward the party's leadership, the party's platform, or its traditional public policy positions can win the party's nomination. In addition, primary contests can be vicious, with personal attacks between candidates that can weaken the eventual winner and lead to a loss in the general election. The 2016 Republican Party presidential nominating contests vividly depicted this tension between rank-and-file party voters and the party elite. Both Donald Trump and Ted Cruz tapped into the anti-establishment sentiment to distinguish themselves from the crowded field of seventeen. Despite several victories and strong popularity in his home state, Senator Cruz suspended his campaign for president on May 3, 2016. Donald Trump was able to successfully translate his anti-establishment campaign message to a surprise victory and become the 45th President of the United States. Increasingly, Republicans are having to demonstrate their conservative credentials in order to secure the party nomination. For example, in a hotly contested state senate election, Angela Paxton beat Phillip Huffines in her 2018 nomination, despite attacks that she was not conservative enough (even though her conservative credentials were well established). The two spent over $9 million in their bitter primary to win the nomination for this open state senate seat.[25] Parties function primarily to win elections, but the primaries may result in an unbalanced ticket that for ideological or other reasons has limited appeal to voters in the general election. This imbalance can impact a party's electoral strength. Bitter primary challenges between conservative Tea Party candidates challenging establishment Republican Party candidates are becoming increasingly common. Even the threat of serious intraparty contenders in the primaries (most notably Tea Party candidates challenging more moderate Republicans) can impact politics, resulting in a more conservative slant in state and national politics. In other states, the Tea Party's success in nominating ultraconservative candidates in the primary election has resulted in unelectable general election candidates. However, Senator Cruz's defeat of the GOP establishment candidate David Dewhurst in the 2012 primary demonstrates that ideologically extreme candidates can win the general election and have significant impact on national politics. When unsuccessful, however, bitter primaries can leave the party's eventual candidate weakened and underfunded for the general election.[26]

Despite trailing in the polls and early contests, Joe Biden handily won the Texas primary in what amounted to a stunning reversal of what then appeared to be a candidacy on the brink of extinction. Early primary voters favored Senator Bernie Sanders, however election day voters propelled Biden to victory by a lead that was unpredictable even a week or two earlier. In a large disappointment, especially given the large amount of hype and phenomenal amounts of money spent, former New York mayor and billionaire Michael Bloomberg placed a distant third. Former Vice President Biden ultimately won ten of the fourteen states holding nominating contests on Super Tuesday, sweeping all southern contests propelling him into front runner status. These victories proved pivotal in ultimately securing him the Democratic nomination in this unusual year. Primaries for state and federal offices in 2020 were less contentious than in previous years, but still had a number of interesting races. Republican Representative Kay Granger (Fort Worth) and Democratic Representative Henry Cuellar (Laredo) were both successful in beating more ideologically extreme primary challengers. Incumbent Republican Railroad Commissioner Ryan Sitton had a surprising primary loss. No other statewide incumbents lost primaries, nor did any incumbent members of the state legislature; however, Republican representatives Dan Flynn (Canton) and J.D. Sheffield (Gatesville) and Democrat representative Harold Dutton (Houston) all had runoff elections (Flynn and Sheffield both lost, Dutton won). The most watched runoff primary was between Mary "MJ" Hegar and Royce West. Hegar, a decorated retired Air Force pilot, and Royce, a state Senator, were forced to conduct virtual campaigns given the coronavirus, both relying heavily upon endorsements. Hegar had significant fund-raising advantages over Royce, largely due to her support from the Democratic Senatorial Campaign Committee, DSCC, and other national organizations such as EMILY's List, Planned Parenthood, NARAL Pro-Choice American and the Brady PAC (a powerful gun-control group), but Royce's strong ties to the state Democratic party and leaders across the state through his work in state politics, as well as support from the national liberal group Democracy for America, made for a close election.[27] Hegar ultimately lost the general election to Senator John Cornyn.

11.2.3 General Elections

general election
An election for state, federal, and county offices held in November of even-numbered years. The ballot includes nominees of the two major political parties plus other candidates who meet certain legal requirements.

General elections for state and federal offices are held on the first Tuesday after the first Monday in November in even-numbered years. Unlike with the primaries, the administration and costs of the general election are the responsibility of the county. The names of the candidates nominated in the primaries by the two major parties are placed on the ballot, along with the names of any third-party candidates who have submitted petitions bearing enough names of registered voters to equal at least 1 percent of the vote in the previous gubernatorial election.

In the election of 1896, the turnout rate was more than 80 percent of the eligible voting-age population, but only twelve years later in 1908, turnout had fallen to approximately 35 percent. During much of the period from 1910 to 1958, turnout rates in nonpresidential-year general elections were less than 20 percent, mainly because the outcome already had been determined in the Democratic primaries. Presidential elections generated a higher turnout, but in very few instances did the turnout rate exceed 40 percent of eligible voters.[28]

In more recent years, turnout rates in presidential elections have been considerably higher than in years when the governor and other statewide officials were elected. Since 1970, the average turnout in gubernatorial elections in Texas has been 29 percent of the voting-age population and approximately 42 percent of registered voters. By contrast, average turnout in presidential elections has been 45 percent of the voting-age population and 62 percent of registered voters. These turnout rates are significantly higher than turnout rates in the primaries, but it still is evident, if not distressing, that many Texans do not participate in the selection of their leaders.

State officials quoted in the news media often refer to the voter turnout in terms of a percentage of registered voters. Referring to the turnout of registered voters produces a higher rate and sounds better than citing the percentage of the voting-age population, but it omits critical information about voter participation. If we compare voter-registration figures with census data identifying the population eligible to vote, it is clear that a large part of the population does not even register to vote. Rates of participation are important in our efforts to maintain the vitality of democratic values or norms.

11.2.4 City, School Board, and Single-Purpose Districts

Most local elections, which are nonpartisan, are held in May in odd-numbered years to minimize the convergence of issues in national, state, and local races, although increasingly some of these local elections are being moved to November to save administrative costs. Across the state, wide variations exist in the competitiveness of these elections, campaign costs, and turnout.

local election
An election for city council, the school board, and certain other local offices. Most of these are nonpartisan.

Although turnout rates in **local elections** rarely match those in the general elections, competition for control of local governments became more intense in the 1970s and 1980s, in part because of the increased political mobilization of minority voters. Even now, contested local campaigns in large urban areas can be as expensive as state legislative and congressional races. Nevertheless, in recent years voter participation in local government elections seems to have declined.

Most elections for school boards or single-purpose districts, such as hospital or water districts, have abysmally low rates of voter participation. It is not uncommon for many seats to go uncontested, and turnout rates, even in large urban districts, can be as low as 2 to 5 percent. Candidates often spend little, if any, money on these elections, and their campaigns usually are informal. Recent state legislation permits local governments to cancel an election if no offices are contested, and numerous communities in recent years have canceled elections for this reason. For example, local elections for city council seats in Garland, University Park, and Hillsboro were canceled in 2016 because of a lack of competition.[29] The cities and school districts of Tomball and Magnolia, outside of Houston, have canceled twenty elections between 2008 and 2018 because of lack of competition.[30]

11.2.5 Special Elections

Most constitutional amendments are placed on the general election ballot in November of odd-numbered years, a few months after a regular legislative session ends, or they are scheduled for a **special election**. In either case, voter turnout normally is low, which results in most amendments being approved.

In constitutional amendment elections since 1970, the average turnout of registered voters has been 11.3 percent, but only 8.2 percent of the voting-age population. A few of those were special elections. Most, however, were held on the general election date in November of odd-numbered years, when the only other significant races on the ballot were in Houston for mayor and city council. Unlike most Texas cities, Houston holds its municipal elections in November. Consequently, the turnout in Houston is heavier than in the rest of the state for constitutional amendment elections and usually is a major factor in determining the outcome. It is somewhat disturbing that in 86 percent of these constitutional amendment elections since 1970, fewer than 10 percent of Texas citizens cared enough to vote. The low turnout also means that special interest groups can mount well-organized campaigns to place provisions favoring them into the constitution with little public scrutiny or interest.

One example of this phenomenon occurred in Houston in 2015. In May, 2014, the Houston city council voted to enact the Houston Equal Rights Ordinance (HERO), which banned discrimination based upon sexual orientation, gender identity, sex, race, color, ethnicity, national origin, age, religion, pregnancy, genetic information, disability, and family, marital, or military status in city employment, city services, housing, public accommodations, and private employment (religious organizations were exempt). Opponents went through a long battle to get the ordinance put before city voters. After a number of legal battles and heated public debates, the measure was voted upon in November 2015. The proposition was defeated despite more than $1.9 million spent to lobby on behalf of the measure (with "only" $400,000 spent to defeat the motion). Even with these remarkable amounts of money and national attention, only 13 percent of Houstonians voted in the election.[31]

Local governments also conduct special elections for bond issues, local initiatives and referenda, and the recall of local officials. Although occasional high-interest, emotionally charged elections are held, turnout rates in these elections still are extremely low. People who do vote tend to have higher incomes and educational levels. The governor also can call special elections to fill vacancies in certain offices, including legislative and congressional seats.

special election
An election set by the legislature or called by the governor for a specific purpose, such as voting on constitutional amendments or filling a vacancy in a legislative office. Local governments also can call special elections.

11.2.6 Extended Absentee Balloting

In 1988, Texas made a major change in the requirements for absentee voting. Prior to 1988, voters who were not going to be in the county on Election Day or were incapacitated could vote absentee at a designated polling place or by mail before Election Day. Now, anyone can vote early, without having to state an excuse, during

absentee (or early) voting

A period before the regularly scheduled election date during which voters are allowed to cast ballots. With recent changes in election law, a person does not have to offer a reason for voting absentee.

an extended period for **absentee (or early) voting**. Urban counties, in particular, now maintain multiple voting places, including stations conveniently located in shopping malls, during the extended voting period, which runs from the twentieth day to the fourth day before the scheduled Election Day. The result has been a notable increase in the number of votes cast early. In 2014, over 40 percent of ballots in the general election in Texas were cast with early voting. Early voting continued to increase in popularity in 2016, with 43.5 percent all ballots cast early.[32] Early voting turnout rates dipped to 39.9 percent in 2018, which is similar to the last midterm election.[33] In 2020, more people voted by early voting than voted in the 2016 presidential election. Over 9.7 million Texans (57.3 percent of registered voters) voted before election day in 2020, either in person or by mail (only less than 6 percent were cast by mail, the rest of the ballots were cast early in person). Only 13 percent of votes were cast on election day in 2020 (down from 25 percent in 2016).[34]

Extended early voting, now used in thirty-two states and the District of Columbia, has radically changed campaign strategies and tactics.[35] A candidate now has to communicate earlier to that part of the population that has a high likelihood of voting prior to Election Day. With a large portion of votes cast early, a candidate might well carry the Election Day totals but lose the early vote and lose the election. A candidate also has to mobilize those voters who cast their votes on Election Day. Thus, a campaign must "peak" twice. The importance of early voting was made clear in the 2020 Democratic presidential primary. The campaign of former Vice President Joe Biden seemed doomed until he had a surprising, come-from-behind victory in South Carolina on February 29, 2020, which ultimately proved to be the beginning of the resurgence of his ultimately successful campaign. This key victory dramatically shifted his momentum going into Super Tuesday just three days later, when he was the night's big winner by carrying ten of the fourteen states. Senator Sanders won the most votes cast by early voters, but Vice President Biden won the most votes for people voting on Election Day.[36]

Texas, like all other states, allows voters to vote by mail, but unlike most states strictly limits who can vote by mail. According to state law, Texas only allows people with disabilities, people over 65, and voters (such as college students and those in jail awaiting trial) to request ballots by mail. Most states allow far greater flexibility for its voters to select this voting method. For example, five states send all registered voters mail-in ballots. Twenty-eight states and the District of Columbia allow voters to request mail-in ballots without any reasons required. The remaining states require voters meet requirements for requests for these ballots; however, several are easing these rules in response to the coronavirus. For example, Connecticut sent absentee ballots to all registered voters, with return postage, while Delaware allowed voters concerned about the coronavirus to qualify as "sick" or "physically disabled" to allow them to receive a mail-in ballot. Massachusetts, New Hampshire, New York, South Carolina, Tennessee, and West Virginia all eased their restrictions.[37] Texas did not followed suit, resulting in a number of lawsuits. The state was already being sued by voters who had their mail-in ballots rejected by local officials in 2019. The officials determined that the signatures were not valid. The Texas Civil Rights Project helped bring the legal challenge asserting that giving untrained local officials this power, without providing voters notice or recourse, violates the Fourteenth Amendment, The Americans with Disabilities Act, and the Rehabilitation Act of 1973. The case has been supported by groups representing individuals with disabilities, veterans, and young voters.[38] On September 9, 2020, a U.S. district court judge ruled that the state's procedure for verifying signatures on mail-in ballots was unconstitutional as it was "inherently fraught with error with no recourse for voters."[39] The judge ordered the secretary of state to notify voters their ballots were being rejected so they could challenge the decisions or have the state not reject ballots for this reason. On October 19, 2020, the U.S. Courts of Appeal issued an injuction stopping this order (in other words allowing the state to use their original plan to verify signatures, potentially rejecting a large number). The appellate court ruled that the state had a vested interest in protecting the integrity of its elections against fraud.[40] New lawsuits allege that the normal strict rules are unconstitutional during a pandemic. A federal lawsuit filed in San Antonio argued that the rules place an undue burden on the right to vote during the pandemic. The Texas Democratic Party argued that the state's current rules are discriminatory, only affording certain people protections against the public health crisis posed by COVID-19. They argued that fear of contracting coronavirus should be a legitimate reason to vote by mail. After unsuccessfully suing in state court, state Democrats turned to the federal courts. The U.S. Court of Appeals for the 5th Circuit ruled the state, not the courts, were able to determine voting rules during the pandemic. The Democratic party appealed to the Supreme Court but the case was not heard. Even though a majority of people believed voters should be given this option, being afraid of the coronavirus was not to be considered a legitimate reason to request a mail-in ballot in Texas. However, the Texas Supreme Court noted that it is up to voters to assess their own health to determine for themselves if they meet the election code's definition for having a disability. Voters are not required to indicate the nature of a disability when requesting a mail-in ballot.[41] Several lawsuits were filed in both state and federal courts to challenge Governor Abbott's October 1, 2020 order limiting each county to one absentee ballot drop-off location. The governor asserted that limiting each county to one drop-off location would reduce voter fraud and limit the possibility of ballot harvesting (an illegal practice where an individual or group collects ballots from others to turn in). Those opposed to the practice, which would disproportionately impact citizens in more populated counties and counties that are geographically large, state that the order could unduly expose citizens to COVID-19, would harm voters with disabilities or no transportation, and amounts to a form of voter suppression. The order was initially held to be illegal in federal court but upheld by appeal. A state district court judge issued an injunction against the order, allowing counties to have multiple drop-off locations to hand deliver absentee ballots. The decision was upheld by a state appeals court on October 23, 2020. The governor and secretary of state immediately appealed to the state supreme court which ruled in their favor on October 27, 2020.[42] With the competitive presidential election being conducted during a pandemic, it is not surprising that a good deal of litigation has arisen. By the end of October 2020, over 415 pandemic-related cases were filed nationally, 34 in Texas.[43] The number of lawsuits nationally increased dramatically following President Trump's loss. Many lawsuits stemmed from the use of mail-in ballots in some battleground states, though their use was not disputed in all states nor for all elections.

11.2.7 Straight-Ticket Voting

The election ballot historically was styled in such a way as to permit straight-party voting by pulling one lever, marking one block, punching one hole, or selecting the straight-party ticket option.[44] In campaigns, candidates and political leaders often urge voters to "pull one lever" in support of one party's entire slate of candidates. Many voters claim to be independent—to vote for the individual, not the party—and yet, evidence suggests that many Texas voters do not split their tickets.[45] For example, the practice of straight-ticket voting has been significant in recent elections. In the 2016 general election, 63 percent of voters in Texas cast straight-ticket ballots.[46] As of 2020, Texans will no longer have the option to vote a straight-ticket ballot under a bill signed into law on June 1, 2017, by Governor Abbott. Some criticize the law, saying it is motivated by partisanship.[47] In many of the state's largest metropolitan counties more straight-ticket ballots are cast for Democrats than for Republicans. In fact, in the state's largest ten counties over the past four presidential elections, more straight-ticket ballots have been cast for the Democratic party than for the Republican party.[48] However, Republicans carried most of the other major counties, and there was a pattern of straight-party voting in those counties as well.[49] Data collected by state and county election offices showed that, statewide, more Republicans voted a straight ticket than Democrats did. This pattern greatly contributes to the Republican dominance of Texas elections.

WAITING TO VOTE

Voters in Austin wait in long lines to cast their votes. Many feel that more voting locations need to be provided so voters do not have to wait in such long lines.

11.2.8 Ballot Security

Although some governments in Texas still use paper ballots and mechanical voting machines, many other governments use punch cards, mark-sense ballots, or touch-screen voting machines that permit the election returns to be counted by computer.[50] In the aftermath of the ballot problems in Florida in the 2000 presidential election, ballot security and the accurate tabulation of votes received more attention in Texas as well as in other states. Allegations of voter fraud include "stuffing" ballot boxes, votes from people who were dead or nonexistent, persons voting more than once, lost ballots, and failure to count ballots. Relatively little voting fraud has been proven in recent years, but electronic voting does not eliminate such potential problems, and there are legitimate concerns that tabulation software can be hacked or electronic voting devices manipulated. Concern over ballot security has increased nationwide in recent years, especially over increased fear of foreign meddling in domestic elections, the belief that noncitizens are voting illegally, and that more people are casting fraudulent votes. These concerns partly motivate opposition to increased use, even during COVID-19, of mail-in ballots. Concern over ballot security and alleged voter fraud fueled much of the controversy over the 2020 presidential election results. While the lawsuits brought by President Trump to demonstrate voter fraud were unsuccessful and little or no legally admissible evidence was provided, many in the electorate have continued concerns about what they see as significant improprieties, if not outright allegations of fraud. These concerns are consequential as public faith in our electoral institutions appears be be eroding.

Political Suffrage in Texas: A Struggle for Mass Suffrage

11.3 Explain the measures taken to keep some Texans from voting and the countermeasures employed to curtail these discriminatory practices.

Despite the rhetoric of democratic theory in the state's constitution and the somewhat venerable view that people have of elections and voting, Texas has a dark history of voter disfranchisement. For many years, African Americans, Hispanics, and low-income whites were systematically excluded from the political process. Texas had a political system in which the interests of a few could prevail over the interests of the majority. Many people paid a high price for this early legacy of discrimination.

After the Civil War, the state initiated efforts to organize a civilian government that would reestablish Texas's full statehood in the Union. The Constitutional Convention of 1866 accepted the supremacy of the national government and eliminated slavery, but it refused to adopt the Thirteenth Amendment, which gave African Americans the right to vote and hold public office.[51] This constitution was rejected by the Radical Reconstructionists in the U.S. Congress in 1867, and subsequent Texas constitutions extended full voting rights to African Americans. Forty-one African Americans served in the Texas legislature from 1868 to 1894.[52] Even though the Texas Constitution extended political rights to African Americans, many were threatened with physical violence and economic recriminations, such as loss of their jobs, that reduced their political participation well into the twentieth century. In addition, several state laws were enacted to block African American access to the ballot.

11.3.1 The Poll Tax

The conservative Texas establishment's reaction to the Populist movement and its potential for building a coalition between African Americans and low-income whites resulted in the legislature's adoption of a **poll tax**, which went into effect in 1904.[53] It was a tax of $1.50 to $1.75 that had to be paid each year before a person could vote. In the early 1900s, that was a large sum of money for low-income people. It was to be paid between October 1 and January 31, three months before the primaries were then held and nine months before the general elections, long before most people even began to think about voting. Consequently, the tax eliminated large numbers of voters who were likely to support the Populist Party and undermine the political establishment.[54]

The poll tax was in effect for more than sixty years in Texas. It was outlawed for federal elections by the Twenty-Fourth Amendment to the U.S. Constitution, adopted in 1964, but Texas retained the poll tax for state and local elections, thus requiring two sets of registered voters and separate ballots when a federal election was held at the same time. In November 1966, Texas voters approved an amendment to the state constitution eliminating the poll tax for state elections and implementing annual voter registration. By that time, the U.S. Supreme Court had already ruled that the state poll tax was unconstitutional.[55]

poll tax

A tax that Texas and some other states used to require people to pay before allowing them to vote. The purpose was to discourage minorities and poor whites from participating in the political process. The tax was declared unconstitutional in the 1960s.

ANTI-POPULIST MOVEMENT TACTIC

The poll tax was a requirement for voting until it was eliminated by a constitutional amendment in 1966. The voter would register to vote by paying the tax of $1.50 to $1.75 yearly at the courthouse. Given the value of a dollar in 1904, the tax was hefty.

white primary

A series of state laws and party rules that denied African Americans the right to vote in the Democratic primary in Texas in the first half of the twentieth century.

11.3.2 The White Primary

Texas, along with several other southern states, also created the **white primary**, which was designed to eliminate African American participation in the elections that counted most during the years of one-party, Democratic control.[56] In 1923, the Texas legislature enacted a law that denied African Americans the right to vote in the Democratic primary. The U.S. Supreme Court declared that law unconstitutional in 1927 on the basis of the Fourteenth Amendment.[57] Almost immediately, the legislature authorized the state party executive committee to establish the qualifications for voting in the primaries, and the Democratic Party adopted a resolution that only whites could vote. This was challenged in the federal courts, and again, in 1932, the Supreme Court declared the white primary unconstitutional.[58]

Acting through its state convention and without legislative authorization, the Democratic Party then proceeded in May 1932 to exclude African Americans from the primary again. The issue was taken a third time to the Supreme Court, which this time ruled that the party, as a voluntary organization and not a government entity, had the authority to determine membership and the right of participation.[59] But African Americans continued to use the courts to attack the white primary. Finally, in the case of *Smith* v. *Allwright* in 1944, the Supreme Court reversed its earlier decision and declared the white primary unconstitutional.[60]

Those who persisted in excluding African Americans from participation were extremely imaginative in their efforts to circumvent the Court's decisions. They substituted a restrictive, preprimary selection process through the private Jaybird Democratic Association—open only to whites—to choose candidates who then were formally nominated in the Democratic primary and subsequently elected in the general election. In 1953, the U.S. Supreme Court also declared this arrangement unconstitutional.[61]

11.3.3 Restrictive Registration Law

Until 1971, Texas had one of the most restrictive voter-registration systems in the nation. Voters had to register annually between October 1 and January 31. If voters did not register in person at the county courthouse, they could register with deputy registrars. However, these officials were allowed to deliver or mail in only one registration form at a time, thus minimizing the possibilities of coordinated voter-registration drives. These restrictions discouraged voter registration across the state, especially among African American, Hispanic, and low-income populations.[62]

More court intervention forced major changes in the voter-registration law in 1971.[63] The highly restrictive system was transformed, in a relatively short time, into one of the most progressive systems in the country. Annual registration was replaced with permanent registration. An individual now can register by mail or in person as near as thirty days prior to an election. Persons working individually or with a political campaign can be deputized to register voters, and large voter-registration drives are encouraged. County voter-registration officials now must send out cards to voters, automatically renewing their registrations, every two years. Officials also are restricted in how soon they can remove from registration lists the names of voters who have moved.

11.3.4 Property Ownership and the Right to Vote

From colonial times, one requirement for the right to vote was property ownership, a practice that continued in modified form through the 1970s in many states, including Texas. Property ownership was not required to vote in primaries and most other elections, but it was required in bond elections that were used by local governments to win financing of new buildings, roads, sewer systems, and other infrastructure needs. The exclusion of non–property owners from these elections was based on the argument that revenue from property taxes was used to repay these bonds, and if a person did not own property on which to pay a tax, he or she should not have the right to vote for the bonds.

Landlords, however, passed on their property taxes to renters, and many renters, therefore, had a direct interest in the outcome of bond elections. In urban areas, moreover, large numbers of rental properties meant that there were many residents who were barred from participating in those elections. Eventually, the federal courts declared property ownership as a requirement for voting in bond elections unconstitutional.

11.3.5 Women and the Right to Vote

The national movement for women's suffrage, or the right to vote, was a long struggle fought in state capitals as well as in Washington. In 1915, the Texas legislature considered a constitutional amendment extending the right to vote to women but rejected it. In 1918, women were given the right to vote in primary elections and party conventions. Then, in 1919, Texas became the first southern state to approve the Nineteenth Amendment to the U.S. Constitution, which, by late 1920, was approved by the required number of states to grant women's suffrage in all elections.[64]

11.3.6 Extension of the Vote to Those 18 Years of Age and Older

A long-standing debate over the age at which a person should be permitted to vote became more intense during the Vietnam War. Many people believed that individuals who were required to comply with the draft and risk death in battle should no longer be denied the right to vote. The Twenty-Sixth Amendment, which lowered the voting age from 21 to 18, was adopted in 1971, and the first election in which 18-year-olds could vote was in 1972. Perhaps because of the political activism of many college students during the Vietnam era, young people were expected to vote at higher rates than older adults, but this never has happened. The lowest voter turnout rates, in fact, are among voters 18 to 29 years old.

11.3.7 Other Discriminatory Aspects of Election Systems

Even after the most obvious discriminatory practices against minorities were eliminated, there have been more subtle, but just as pervasive, techniques for reducing the political power and influence of these groups. One technique is racial **gerrymandering** of political boundaries. State legislators and many city council members are elected from **single-member districts**, each of which represents a specific number of people in a designated area. After the 2010 Census, for example, each member of the Texas House ideally represented 167,637 people, and each member of the state Senate represented 811,147 people (these numbers are due to increase significantly after the next census in 2020). Currently, the state uses the total population to apportion districts; however, some argue that this can be unfair and that states ought to base the calculations upon the number of eligible voters, not total residents (that is, total population, which includes legal as well as undocumented immigrants, people under age 18, and people in prison). In *Evenwel* v. *Abbott* (2016), the Supreme Court ruled that states can use total population when drawing district lines (rather than the voting-eligible population). In efforts to minimize the possibility of minority candidates being elected, it was now possible for policymakers to divide minority communities and attach them to predominantly nonminority communities—a tactic called *cracking*. It was also possible for minority communities to be consolidated into one district, a tactic called *packing*, with an 80- to 90-percent minority population, which would reduce the number of districts

gerrymandering
Drawing of political district lines in such a way that they favor a particular political party or racial group.

single-member district
A system in which a legislator, city council member, or other public official is elected from a specific geographic area.

in which minorities might have a chance of winning office. The federal Voting Rights Act forbids such practices, but minority groups continue to go to court to challenge redistricting plans. In 2017, a panel of federal judges invalidated two congressional districts (congressional districts 27 and 25, by Corpus Christi and Austin, respectively) and nine state house districts in four counties, stating that the districts were illegally gerrymandered based upon race (the case originally began shortly after the state redistricted following the 2010 Census). The judges ruled that minority voters were illegally disenfranchised; however, the state quickly appealed the decision. In January 2018, the United States Supreme Court agreed to consider the case (*Abbott v. Perez*). In a 5-4 decision issued on June 25, 2018, the majority of the Court ruled that the lower court "erred" in stating that several districts were illegally gerrymandered to disenfranchise Latino voters and left the district lines in place for the 2018 midterm elections. The majority did not believe that the lines were drawn in a discriminatory manner (either with regard to intent or result); the minority vehemently opposed in a strongly worded dissent. The Supreme Court declined to hear a case on partisan gerrymandering in Texas, and ruled that partisan gerrymandering claims were nonjusticiable (meaning that they were outside the purview of the court and needed to be resolved by the legislative branch) in cases from North Carolina and Maryland in July 2019.

At-large election

A system under which city council members or other officeholders are elected by voters in the entire city, school district, or single-purpose district. Many of these election systems have been struck down by the federal courts or by the U.S. Justice Department under the Voting Rights Act as discriminatory against minorities.

At-large elections also have been used to reduce minority representation. At one time, members of the Texas House who came from urban counties were elected in multimember districts, which required candidates to win election in countywide races, a difficult prospect for many minority candidates. The practice was eliminated in legislative races in the 1970s as a result of federal lawsuits. But many cities, school districts, and special districts across Texas continue to use at-large elections, requiring candidates to run for office citywide or district-wide. This system dilutes minority representation in most communities in which it is used.[65] In addition to the increased costs of running in at-large elections, which discourage minority candidates, a minority group that may account for 60 percent of a city's total population and 52 percent of the voting-age population may account for only 45 percent of registered voters. With the possibility of polarized voting, whereby minorities vote for the minority candidates and nonminorities vote for white candidates, there is a high likelihood that no minority could get elected in many at-large systems. At-large elections have come under increasing attack under the Voting Rights Act, and many local governments have adopted some form of single-member districting.

11.3.8 The Voting Rights Act

In 1965, the U.S. Congress enacted the Voting Rights Act, which was extended to Texas in 1975. This law has been central to efforts by minorities in challenging discriminatory election systems and practices. Under the Voting Rights Act, minority groups can challenge state and local election systems in the federal courts. The burden of proof in such challenges is on the government. An election system that dilutes minority voting strength is illegal, even without a clear intent to discriminate against minorities. Furthermore, any changes in the election systems of state or local governments, including redistricting plans, must be precleared (or approved) by the U.S. Department of Justice or must be approved by the U.S. District Court in Washington, D.C. This legislation has produced changes in election systems across the state and has helped increase minority representation in the Texas legislature and on local governing bodies.

By the mid-1990s, however, the Voting Rights Act was under attack by conservatives. The U.S. Supreme Court, in "reverse discrimination" cases from Texas and Georgia, ruled that some congressional districts had been illegally gerrymandered to elect minority candidates. In the Texas case, three federal judges held that the Texas legislature had violated the U.S. Constitution by designing two districts in Houston and one in the Dallas area to favor the election of African American or Hispanic candidates. The court redrew thirteen congressional districts in Texas—the three minority districts and ten districts adjoining them—and ordered special elections to fill the seats. Despite the redrawn boundaries, two incumbent female, African American members of Congress in the affected districts were reelected.

In effect, recent court cases have held that race or ethnicity can be considered in drawing legislative boundaries but cannot be the predominant factor. Representatives of minority groups fear that these recent cases will reduce the number of potentially winnable legislative districts for African American and Hispanic candidates.

In a 2013 case, *Shelby County* v. *Holder*, the Supreme Court ruled that the formulas used to determine which states were subject to preclearance were unconstitutional, as they used data that were more than forty years old. In doing so, the Supreme Court effectively ended the requirement of Section 5 of the Voting Rights Act for preclearance until Congress passes legislation to create a new formula to determine the existence of race-based electoral discrimination. Given the current balance of power in Congress, it appears unlikely that such legislation will be passed. Consequently, for the time being, no state or jurisdiction will be subject to the preclearance rules of Section 5 (largely considered the most significant component of the Voting Rights Act). As you will see later in the chapter, this decision paved the way for voter identification laws in a number of states, including Texas.

11.3.9 Motor Voter Registration

The **motor voter registration** law was passed by the U.S. Congress in 1993 and signed by President Bill Clinton, despite the opposition of Republicans, who apparently feared it would benefit the Democratic Party. The first President Bush had vetoed an earlier version of the bill in 1992. The federal law, similar to a 1991 Texas law, requires states to provide eligible citizens the opportunity to register to vote when they apply for or renew a driver's license. The law also requires states to make voter-registration forms available at certain agencies that provide welfare benefits or assist the disabled.[66] In 2018, more than 3.1 million voter registration forms were submitted from motor vehicle offices (representing 47.3 percent of applications that year), nearly 197,000 (3 percent) from public assistance offices, and about 10,000 applications from disability services offices (accounting for 0.2 percent of applications).[67] The law has expedited the voter-registration process for many Texans; however, controversy has arisen from the process followed for online renewals. Since most states allow voters to register to vote online, when they renew their driver's licenses online, they can easily be directed to register to vote online as well. However, in Texas, when renewing driver's licenses online, anyone wishing to register to vote is directed to the Texas Secretary of State's web page, which requires them to print out a voter registration form that must then be signed and mailed to their county registrar. The state was sued, with plaintiffs alleging this process violated federal law; however, thus far, the process has been allowed to stand.[68]

motor voter registration
Term referring to federal and state laws that allow people to register to vote at offices where they receive their drivers' licenses.

11.3.10 Facilitating Voter Participation

Since the 1980s, efforts have been made across the nation to reduce administrative barriers to political participation. Several states have adopted procedures for online registration. Other states have adopted "same-day" registration, allowing people to register to vote on Election Day. Others have provided for online voting. Following the lead of Texas and a handful of other states, extended early voting has been allowed. Some people advocate longer hours for voting, and others push for making Election Day a holiday, among other recommendations. Some of these proposals eventually may be adopted. Various means of eliminating barriers can increase voter registration and increase turnout, but they will not resolve voter indifference, problems of getting transportation to the polls, and health issues that deter voting.

11.3.11 Contemporary Restrictions on Voting

Despite a number of efforts in the last thirty years to facilitate voting, restrictions still exist. One of the most significant voting restrictions upon adult Texans is the citizenship requirement. For example, according to data from the U.S. Census Bureau, over 3 million adults in Texas are prohibited from voting because they are not citizens.[69] Texas also restricts convicted felons from voting while they are incarcerated and under state supervision. However, unlike some states that restrict felon voting indefinitely, felons in Texas regain their right to vote if they are not incarcerated and are no longer on probation or parole. Ex-offenders who have lost their right to vote must reregister to ensure eligibility. In 2018, there were approximately 480,000 ineligible felons in Texas, and over 3.2 million nationwide.[70] Nationwide, there is a growing movement to restore felon voting rights, with states like Florida and Nevada changing these laws in the last few years. Florida, following a citizen-initiated constitutional amendment in 2018, moved to restore voting rights to felons after completing their sentences. In 2019, Colorado gave voting rights to all individuals on parole, only disenfranchising individuals who are in prison. Nevada, Illinois, and Washington all passed laws in 2019 regarding felon voting rights.

After several years of trying, Republicans in the Texas legislature enacted a voter identification law in 2011, which required voters to present photo identification in order to cast a ballot. Republican legislators insisted the step would reduce voter fraud and should be allowed as the Texas Department of Public Safety (DPS) would issue free election identifications. But Democrats argued that the requirement would intimidate many minority and elderly voters who were likely to vote for Democratic candidates. Recently married women could also be impacted if they changed their last names and did not change their voter identification in sufficient time. In March 2012, the U.S. Department of Justice refused to "preclear," or approve, the identification law under the Voting Rights Act. The department said Texas had not proved that the requirement would not discriminate against minority voters. It said Hispanic voters were much more likely than non-Hispanic voters to lack a driver's license or a personal identification card. About 5.6 million of Texas's 18 million registered voters are Hispanic.[71] However, when the Supreme Court invalidated the preclearance requirement of the Voting Rights Act in *Shelby* v. *Holder* in 2013, the law was allowed to take effect. Voters were required to show photo identification issued by the DPS or the U.S. government (military identification cards, citizen certificates, and passports are all accepted). The identification was required to be current or to have expired no more than sixty days before the election to qualify.

The law was in effect between 2013 and 2016 (notably for the 2014 gubernatorial, state, and federal midterm elections and the 2016 primary elections). However, on July 20, 2016, the U.S. Court of Appeals for the Fifth Circuit ruled that the law violated the 1965 Voting Rights Act. The Court ruled that the law had a discriminatory impact on black and Hispanic voters and required that the district court had to approve of remedies before the November 2016 elections. Evidence submitted in the lawsuit demonstrated that as many as 600,000 eligible Texas voters did not have one of the seven approved forms of identification, a disproportionate number of whom were African American and Hispanic.[72] Other voter identification laws in North Carolina and Wisconsin were also ruled unconstitutional while North Dakota had to provide more options for acceptable identification.

On August 3, 2016, the state, civil rights groups, and the Justice Department reached an agreement to weaken the identification restrictions. Under the agreement, residents with valid identifications are still required to show them, but those without valid identifications can show a voter registration certificate, a birth certificate, a utility bill or bank statement, a government check, or any other government document with their name and address. If individuals do not have any of these, they can be allowed to sign an affidavit stating they were not able to obtain one of these documents and be allowed to vote. If it is determined that they have lied (meaning they have one of the identification forms required), they can be convicted of a felony and sentenced to up to two years in jail. The state is also required to spend $2.5 million on education drives to inform voters of the new rules. Research indicates that education campaigns can be useful in promoting participation and minimizing confusion.[73] The state had been unsuccessfully trying to defend the law since its enactment, and Governor Abbott and other elected officials pledge to continue the fight. On April 10, 2017, a federal judge once again ruled that the 2011 law intentionally discriminated against minority voters. The state appealed the ruling and in a major win for the state, the U.S. Fifth Circuit Court of Appeals reversed the lower court's ruling that the law was discriminatory. In a 2–1 ruling issued on April 27, 2018, the appeals court upheld the law. The central issue was whether lawmakers intentionally discriminated against voters of color when they passed the photo ID legislation and the subsequent revision. Demonstrating intention is of fundamental importance in either maintaining the law or overturning it. Lower courts have ruled that the law puts an undue burden on voters of color who are less likely to have the required photo identification, but the appeals court ruled that the state made sufficient changes in the law so that the photo identification requirement was not discriminatory.[74] As it stands, voters need to be diligent to ensure they have the proper and valid identification to ensure they have the ability to vote on Election Day. A historic number of gay, lesbian, bisexual, and transgender candidates ran for office in Texas in 2018, with records winning. Fourteen LGBTQ candidates, of thirty-five, won office in Texas in what some called a "rainbow wave." More than 400 LGBTQ individuals ran nationwide in 2018. Some assert they were mobilized by controversial "bathroom bills" and Trump administration challenges to transgender rights (for example, trying to ban transgender individuals from serving in the military). Others cited concerns voiced by all candidates. Following the election, there will be more than double the number of LGBTQ members (five) in the Texas House and several more judges serving. In Harris county, five Democratic LGBTQ judicial candidates defeated Republican incumbents, joining three gay judges in Houston. While not successful, the candidacy of Lupe Valdez, the first openly gay and first Latina to be nominated by a major party for governor, was a large step forward for others seeking to break down barriers for all who want to be of service to their state and their communities.[75] An additional LGTBQ member of the House, Ann Johnson from district 134, was elected in 2020. Nationally, a number of milestones were achieved for the LGBTQ community when the first openly gay Black men were elected to congress (two Democrats from New York). They join seven openly LGBTQ members of the House of Representatives. In Delaware, the first transgender woman was elected to serve as a state senator and all but three states (Alaska, Louisiana, and Mississippi) have now elected openly LGBTQ individuals to serve as state legislators.

11.3.12 Political Gains by Minorities and Women

Since the mid-1970s, African Americans and Hispanics have made substantial gains in the electoral process. Elimination of restrictive voting laws, the adoption of a more liberal state voter-registration system, and changes mandated by the National Voter Registration Act of 1993 have contributed to an increase in minority voters across the state. Voter-registration and mobilization drives coordinated by groups such as the National Association for the Advancement of Colored People (NAACP) and the Southwest Voter Registration Education Project have contributed to increased participation, as has an increase in the number of minority candidates and elected officials. Minority candidates who have a good chance of winning often encourage minority voters to vote. Yet, it would be premature to conclude that the state's election system is now "color blind." The contentious debate over the 2011 voter identification law is a case in point. The elections of 2018 brought about significant changes for historically underrepresented groups in Texas; some of these changes mark years of steady progress (see the section on Women), but for others, 2018 was a groundbreaking year. Despite the fact that the legislature was more diverse following the 2018 elections, the Republican delegation in the state senate was all white. All governors, lieutenant governors, and attorney generals in the state have been white. Senator Cruz, Republican, is the only non-Anglo Senator elected from the state.

FIGURE 11–2 RACIAL AND ETHNIC DIFFERENCES IN THE TOTAL POPULATION OF TEXAS, THE VOTING AGE OF ALL TEXANS, AND CITIZENS OF VOTING AGE

Demographics help explain voter participation rates in Texas and across the nation. Although we have mass suffrage, the numbers of people who choose not to vote vary dramatically by social group. As you can see, depending upon the definition of "population," different groups will have different levels of relative influence. For example, if we look at the entire population, the percentage that is Anglo is smaller than if we examine the percentage of voting-age population that is Anglo, helping to partly explain the political influence of Anglos in Texas relative to population size.

SOURCE: U.S. Census Bureau, *2014–2018 Five-Year American Community Survey* (ACS).

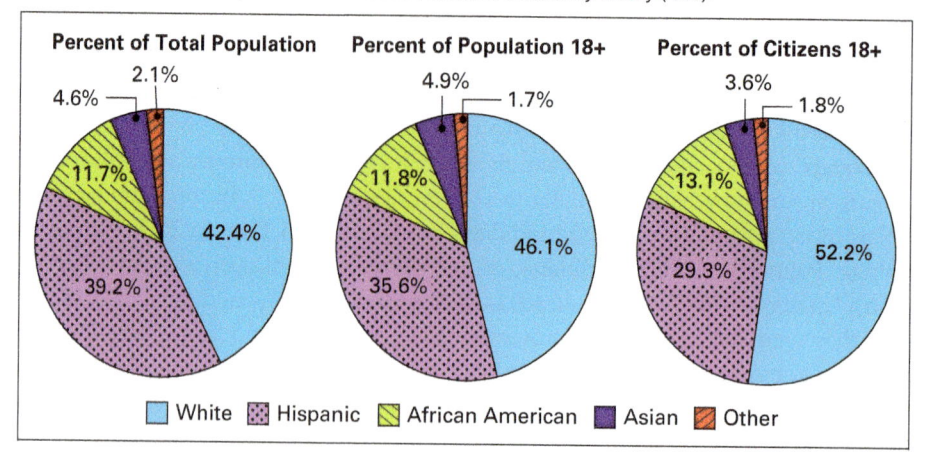

Percent of Total Population
- White: 42.4%
- Hispanic: 39.2%
- African American: 11.7%
- Asian: 4.6%
- Other: 2.1%

Percent of Population 18+
- White: 46.1%
- Hispanic: 35.6%
- African American: 11.8%
- Asian: 4.9%
- Other: 1.7%

Percent of Citizens 18+
- White: 52.2%
- Hispanic: 29.3%
- African American: 13.1%
- Asian: 3.6%
- Other: 1.8%

Legend: ■ White ▨ Hispanic ▨ African American ■ Asian ▨ Other

HISPANICS According to data from the 2018 U.S. Census Bureau's American Community Survey, Hispanics made up 39.6 percent of Texas's population. However, the Hispanic population is younger than the Anglo and African American populations, so Hispanics account for only 35.5 percent of Texans of voting age (see Figure 11–2). The Hispanic population also includes many immigrants who are not citizens, thus reducing to approximately 29 percent the Hispanic portion of adults eligible to register and vote. Although, as we saw in Chapter 9, Hispanics are getting increasing attention as a key voting group that typically has voted for the Democratic Party, the percentage of Hispanics who vote is lower than one would expect. Hence, voter-registration and mobilization drives are often conducted to increase participation of this quickly growing group.

The increased electoral strength of the Hispanic population is borne out in Table 11–1, which compares the change in the number of elected Hispanic officials in Texas from 1974 to 2020 some 540 Hispanics held elected office in 1974. By 2020, there were 2,739 Hispanic elected officials, the highest in any state. The marked increase can be attributed to a more equitable apportionment of city, county, and school district political boundaries; the growth of the Hispanic population; and increased organizational efforts among Hispanics.

By 2020, only ten Hispanics had been elected to statewide office in Texas. Four were Texas Supreme Court Justices Raul A. Gonzalez, Alberto R. Gonzales, David M. Medina, and Eva Guzman. Elsa Alcala is a judge on the Court of Criminal Appeals. The others were Senator Ted Cruz, Attorney General Dan Morales, Land Commissioner George P. Bush, and Texas Railroad Commissioners Tony Garza and Victor Carrillo. In 2020, 24.3 percent of the state legislature was Hispanic. With changing demographics and the increased political sophistication of the Hispanic population, Hispanics will win additional statewide and local offices in the future.

AFRICAN AMERICANS African Americans constitute approximately 11.7 percent of the state's population and 13 percent of the eligible voting-age population. In 2020, they constituted approximately 10 percent of the state legislature. When voting cohesively as a group, African Americans, who overwhelmingly consider themselves

TABLE 11-1 LATINO ELECTED OFFICIALS IN TEXAS, 1974–2020

	1974	1996	2001	2011	2020
Federal	2	5	6	6	7
State	13	35	36	38	45
County	102	203	213	298	288
Municipal	251	536	555	632	799
Judicial/Law Enforcement	172	323	280	472	447
School Board	–	536	701	1,025	1,096
Special District	–	51	37	49	56
Total	540	1,689	1,828	2,520	2,739

SOURCE: Juan A. Sepulveda Jr., *The Question of Representative Responsiveness for Hispanics*, Harvard College, Honors Thesis, March 1985; National Association of Latino Elected and Appointed Officials, *National Roster of Hispanic Elected Officials*, 1996, 2001; NALEO Educational Fund, *2011 National Directory of Latino Elected Officials*; and NALEO Educational Fund, *National Directory of Latino Elected Officials 2019*. Data presented in table is the most current at the time of publication.

Democrats, have considerable potential to influence the outcome of both primaries and general elections.

The increased political clout of the African American population is manifested in the number of African American elected officials (Table 11–2). In 1970, there were only twenty-nine African Americans elected to public office in Texas. The number increased to 175 in 1980 and 419 in 2002. The total number of African Americans elected in Texas decreased from 2002 to 2007. Data at the local level has not been collected since this time so we do not know if this trend has continued. Only four African Americans have been elected to statewide office in Texas: former Railroad Commissioner Michael Williams, Texas Supreme Court Chief Justice Wallace Jefferson, and Texas Supreme Court Justice Dale Wainwright, all Republicans, and former Texas Court of Criminal Appeals Judge Morris Overstreet, a Democrat. In 2020, three cities with populations of over 40,000 were led by African American mayors, Dallas, DeSoto, and Plano.[76]

WOMEN Historically, the world of Texas politics has been dominated by men, but that is changing. Ann Richards was elected state treasurer in 1982 and then governor in 1990, and Kay Bailey Hutchison, who succeeded Richards as state treasurer, was elected to the U.S. Senate in 1993. As governor, Richards appointed more women than her predecessors to key positions on state boards and commissions. Prior to Richards's election as state treasurer in 1982, only two women had been elected to statewide office. The first was Annie Webb Blanton, elected to state superintendent of public instruction in 1928. Miriam (Ma) Ferguson was elected to serve as governor for two terms—from

TABLE 11-2 AFRICAN AMERICAN ELECTED OFFICIALS IN TEXAS, 1970, 1980, 2002, 2007, AND SELECTED OFFICES FOR 2020*

	1970	1980	2002	2007	2020
Federal	–	1	2	3	6
State	3	14	17	15	18
County	–	5	21	14	NA
Municipal	16	75	285	211	NA
School Board	10	78	94	69	NA
Special District	–	2	–	–	NA
Total	29	175	419	312	NA

*****NOTE:** All public data on African American local officials has not been updated since 2007. Data presented in table is the most current at the time of publication.

SOURCE: Metropolitan Applied Research Center and Voter Regional Council, *National Roster of Black Elected Officials*; Joint Center for Political and Economic Studies, *National Roster of Black Elected Officials*, 1980, 1998, and 2002; and The Gender and Multi-Cultural Leadership Project, http://www.gmcl.org/maps/texas/state.htm; https://www.texastribune.org/2015/01/14/demographics-2015-texas-legislature/.

1925 to 1927 and 1932 to 1935—becoming the second woman to serve as a governor in the country. No woman has ever served as Texas lieutenant governor, attorney general, or land commissioner (three important offices for candidates seeking to be governor).

By 2020, nine women had held twelve statewide elective executive offices (some women held more than one office) in Texas: four railroad commissioners, three state treasurers, two state comptrollers, two governors, and one agriculture commissioner. Since 2016, Christi Craddick has been the only woman to hold a statewide elected executive position (railroad commissioner). In 2020, nine women served in the state Senate and thirty-three in the Texas House (23.6 percent of the total legislature compared with approximately 29.2 percent nationally). After gaining 4 seats in the 2020 elections, there will be 38 women, 25.3 percent, in the legislature in 2021. Women serving in the state legislature are more diverse than the men, with over 56 percent of them being women of color.[77] Twenty years ago, only 9.4 percent of the legislature was female (three women in the Senate and fourteen in the House), however, in 2009 a record 43 women served. There has been only one female U.S. Senator (Kay Bailey Hutchison) from Texas. In 2021, only 19.4 percent of Texas's congressional delegation is female, which lagged behind the national average of 26.9 percent. In 2018, there were several new women elected to the state's congressional delegation, which was notable as very few new women had been elected to Congress from the state since 1996. Following the 2018 midterm election, Texas sent its first Hispanic women to Congress with the successful election of Democrats Fletcher and Escobar. Another new woman, Republican Beth Van Duyne, was elected in 2020 joining the other six female incumbents.

Women play an increasing role in local government as well, and this pattern can be expected to continue. In 2020, 13 cities with populations over 30,000 had female mayors (Amarillo, Beaumont, Coppell, Copperas Cove, DeSoto, Euless, Fort Worth, Missouri City, Nacogdoches, Rowlett, San Angelo, San Marcos, and Socorro).[78] A 2013 survey by the Texas Municipal League counted 210 women mayors (17 percent) in the state's 1,214 cities. The 6,090 council members in the cities included 1,702 women, or 28 percent of the total.[79] Of the 254 county judges in 2014, 24 (9.5 percent) were women. Women constituted nearly 34 percent (1,064 out of 3,151) of all judges across the state.[80] In a 2006 survey of county commissioners conducted by the V.G. Young Institute of County Government, women held 65 (6.4 percent) of 1,016 county commissioner posts. There was little change in the number of women commissioners in 2016.[81] Women also held a large number of other county offices. Of the 7,167 elected school board trustees in 2014, some 1,996 (28 percent) were women, and 166 (or 16 percent) of the 1,036 school superintendents in 2008 were women.[82]

Campaign Technology

11.4 Describe the use of marketing technology in political campaigns.

When Texas was a one-party Democratic state during much of the twentieth century, the only state elections that counted were the Democratic primaries, and they often would include five or six candidates for a single office. In statewide or local campaigns, candidates seldom ran as a ticket or coalition. Each candidate developed his or her own campaign organization, thus precluding the development of party organizations. Individuals who became involved in a campaign were primarily motivated by their personal loyalties to a candidate and not to the political party.

With low rates of voter participation in the primaries and the absence of viable Republican challengers in the general elections, Democratic candidates stumbled through the election process with loose coalitions that often disintegrated after Election Day. Although there was competition in the Democratic primaries, conservative candidates, tied to the establishment, generally prevailed. Despite differences in personality and style, these conservative candidates were fundamentally committed to the policy agendas of the economic elites of the state.

By today's standards, political campaigns through the 1950s were amateurish and unsophisticated. A number of factors have reshaped modern political campaigns, including an expanded and highly mobile electorate, the growing dominance of the Republican Party, the organizational weaknesses of both political parties, the continuation of the candidate-centered campaign, the increased reliance on the electronic media for news and political information, and the emergence of the Internet and social networking sites.[83] Today's successful campaigns rely on sophisticated public opinion polling, slick campaign ads, analyses of demographics, and targeting of selected populations through direct mail, phone banks, and online resources—all orchestrated by professional **campaign consultants**.

Such consultants have been in Texas in some form or another for a long time. W. Lee "Pappy" O'Daniel, the owner of a flour mill that produced Hillbilly Flour and expert of ceremonies of a daily radio talk show, ran for governor in 1938, exploiting a rustic image couched in religious, evangelical language that had a wide appeal in the rural areas of the state. His speeches were designed to create identification with the "common folks," but he was a wealthy businessman who had ties to Texas's corporate leaders. His homespun style was contrived, and O'Daniel relied heavily throughout his campaign on public relations expert Phil Fox of Dallas.[84]

Contemporary campaign consulting is an identifiable industry with diversified expertise. More significantly, few candidates for statewide office or major local offices now run without using the services of campaign consultants. Nowadays statewide campaigns are often evaluated by the quality and reputation of the consultants hired, as high-quality and well-known consultants can generate media coverage and assist with fund-raising. In 2014, the Republican primary season had so many competitive candidates running for office across the state that it became hard to find quality consultants to fill vacancies. The last several election cycles have seen an increasing number of professionals hired from out of state, causing some to become concerned that the character of the state will be lost.

campaign consultant
A professional expert who helps political candidates plan, organize, and run their campaigns.

11.4.1 Social Media and Public Opinion Polling

In a society based on mass consumption, it is no wonder that techniques were developed to measure public attitudes and opinions. As we saw in Chapter 9, political uses of public opinion polling continue to grow as new techniques and applications are perfected. Public opinion polling is used in political campaigns for a number of purposes. As would-be candidates consider running for office, they often hire pollsters to conduct benchmark polls of people who are likely to vote in the upcoming election. The length and type of survey usually are determined by available funds and the information desired by the candidate and those developing the campaign. Surveys are expensive and can consume a significant chunk of a campaign budget.

Surveys also are used to develop campaign strategy, monitor or track the progress of the campaign, and modify the campaign as changes take place in the attitudes, perceptions, or mood of the electorate. The benchmark poll, often taken some time before the official campaign gets under way, is wide ranging and attempts to assess public opinion relating to the office a candidate seeks. Issues are identified, perceptions of candidates are probed, and trial races against potential opponents are tested. A large number of specific demographic questions permits the segmentation of the electorate into small groups whose specific interests or concerns can be identified and targeted.

As the campaign proceeds, tracking surveys are used to determine shifts in attitudes, perceptions, and support for the candidate. Does the candidate now have greater name identification? Do more people perceive the candidate positively and express their support with greater intensity? Is there a particular event or emerging campaign issue that might spell defeat? This information is used to adjust the campaign to changing conditions. Toward the end of the campaign, surveys often are taken nightly to permit further fine-tuning of the campaign in the final days.

A variation on the survey is the focus group. As television advertisements are developed, the campaign staff may choose to test them before they are aired. A series of focus groups, each including eight to twelve persons recruited for specific demographic characteristics, will be asked to review these ads and provide their impressions and reactions. An experienced staff will watch these proceedings to identify subtle responses to the ads, the theme, or the message. On the basis of these qualitative assessments, the media consultants will decide which ads to use or discard.

Some campaigns have resorted to "push polls," a practice that most scholars and reputable pollsters consider a violation of research ethics. The survey is presented to the voter as an effort to solicit perceptions and attitudes toward candidates, but as the interviewer moves through the questions, a controversial or negative position or attribute of a potential candidate is introduced. Finally, this attribute is linked to a specific candidate, and the voter is then asked if this fact would change his or her vote.

In addition to the growing dependence upon polling, we have seen an explosive growth of online communication, which has dramatically altered the execution of contemporary campaigns. Gone are the days when a campaign recruited a college student to create a web page. While online marketing is not new, its use in the 2008 presidential campaign was unprecedented. Unlike in the past when candidates largely duplicated offline activities, Barack Obama's 2008 campaign used sophisticated websites and listservs to reach new voters, often instructing them how to register to vote in their locality and how to request absentee ballots. The online campaign gave information on options for early voting and conducted massively successful mobilization campaigns. The Democrats used blogs, social media, and search engine optimization to revolutionize data collecting and targeting (see more on this below). The Obama campaign not only effectively raised money (often in small increments, which also helps to build support) from its web page, but also used the web page and social media in a well-organized and highly effective voter mobilization drive that many assert was the key in Obama's 2008 victory. These strategies were especially successful in mobilizing young voters, many of whom were reminded to vote with well-timed text messages.

Impressive gains in successful online marketing have continued through today. Candidates in the 2016 presidential election used Instagram (which is now larger than Twitter), Facebook, Snapchat, and Twitter (a popular communication tool of Donald Trump) to directly connect with voters. Just following the two presidential nominating

SMART PHONE POLITICS

The dramatic growth in the use of smart phones and tablets has changed the way that people consume news and discuss politics. Some argue that people are better informed, while others argue that the lack of professional standards and ethics present on some web pages result in the dissemination of less reliable information that may be untrustworthy and biased.

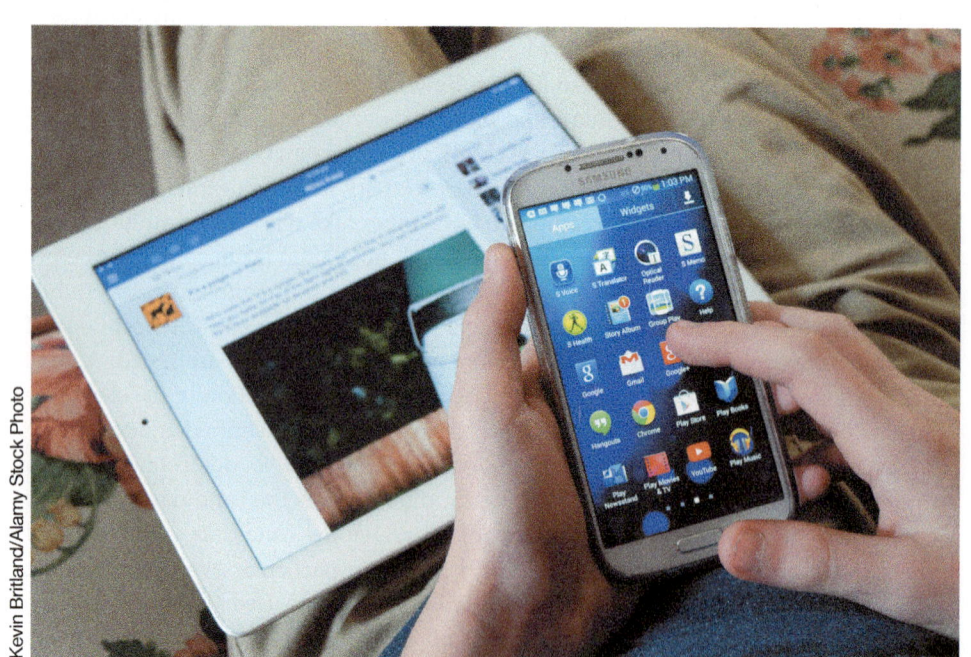

Kevin Britland/Alamy Stock Photo

conventions in 2016, Donald Trump had over 10.8 million Twitter followers (up from slightly more than 4 million followers in early October 2015 and 6.7 million in March 2016). Hillary Clinton had 8.2 million Twitter followers in August. During this same time period, Trump had 2.2 million followers on Instagram (compared with 1.8 for Clinton). Spending on social media was more than $500 million dollars (more than one half of the estimated $1 billion budget for digital media).[85] Bernie Sanders mobilized supporters to attend rallies with the effective use of #feeltheBern. Candidates at all levels have been able to extend political debates by engaging in Twitter "discussions." Increasingly, candidates are doing live Facebook events to reach supporters and becoming more and more creative in voter outreach. Campaigning in 2020 was upended with the challenges posed by COVID-19 and the inability to have large events. Candidates were forced to rely more heavily than ever upon social media (including ample use of Facebook Live events), virtual candidate forums, and tele-town halls. TikTok and Instagram videos were employed to garner voter attention. Many did not explicitly focus on campaigning but rather highlighted how they can help voters. For example, some candidates helped people find food banks or provided guidance on securing a small business loan. Dr. Pritesh Gandhi, a Democratic candidate running in the 10th congressional district, for example, had weekly Facebook Live events and posted videos on social media about the challenges in treating patients and obtaining personal protective equipment during the pandemic. These events were the most heavily trafficked and most watched videos of his campaign.[86] Candidates also used some "tried and true" methods of voter contact, direct mail, telephone calls, and text messages. In campaigns garnering national attention, some virtual phone banks include activists calling voters and donors from out of state. The National Democratic Training Committee, which provides free campaign training to Democrats seeking offices at all levels, has seen a large surge in individuals seeking training in new techniques.[87]

Social media allows candidates to directly engage with voters and successfully serves to humanize the candidates. According to a Pew Research Center survey, social media is by far the most common way millennials (especially Democrats) learned about the 2016 presidential election.[88] Following revelations about false news on social media sites (especially Facebook) and concern that foreign governments or nationals might be trying to influence our elections by placing fake stories online, Facebook, Twitter, and other social media sites (and even traditional media sites) implemented indicators (often symbols) to denote the trustworthiness of the sources of stories shared on the platforms. Many are concerned they are not doing enough to combat the sharing of fake news on their sites. Concern seems warranted given the widespread use of social media to become politically informed. In 2017, Pew Research found that two-thirds of adults in the United States get some news from social media sites (with 20 percent saying they get news "often" from social media). Television remains the preferred platform for news; however, more than a third of Americans say they prefer to read or watch their news on news websites, and 20 percent say they prefer to get their news from social media.[89] More people prefer to get their news from social media than from print newspapers. While Facebook remains the most popular social media platform for reading political news, Twitter has seen the largest growth from 2016 to 2017 (certainly due in large part to our former president).[90] President Trump preferred to use Twitter to engage in all sorts of communication, seeing it as a successful device to bypass the traditional media (which he believes is largely biased) to communicate directly with the public. Twitter (soon followed by other social media companies) took the remarkable step of banning Trump from its platform on January 8, 2021 "due to the risk of further incitement of violence" following the criminal acts in the Capital on January 6th. At the time, he had 88 million followers. Some support this form of direct communication with the people; others see it as corroding many American ideals given the nature of some of his more controversial tweets.

Prior to 2008, the Internet was seen largely as a way to generate support from political "junkies"; now it is seen as an effective way to mobilize supporters, raise money, and target independents. As a result of the changes noted here, nearly all candidates for national, state, and many local offices are trying to use social media and the Internet to connect with potential supporters, contributors, and voters.

11.4.2 Segmentation and Targeting of the Electorate

A political campaign is fundamentally an organized effort to communicate with the electorate with the goal of convincing a majority of those who participate to vote for a specific candidate or political party. But effective communication is difficult for a number of reasons. One is the low voter turnout in most elections indicating that most people are not interested in any candidate's message. Another reason is that voter turnout rates vary among different ethnic, income, and education-level groups, and some of these voters will not support a particular candidate no matter what he or she says or does. In a partisan election, many people will vote for or against a candidate strictly on the basis of party identification. Obviously, not every voter will be receptive to a particular candidate's concerns and priorities.

For decades, candidates have used census data, surveys, and previous election returns with turnout and party voting patterns to divide voters into segments. In recent years, significant progress has been made in micro targeting, based upon direct market data-mining techniques. Both political parties and some well-funded candidates use cluster analysis to target potential supporters and craft tailored messages to narrow subgroups of the electorate. Additionally, psycho-demographics, a technique used by some opinion specialists, combines survey and census data to divide populations by lifestyles rather than party identification. Whether direct mail, social networking, television, radio, newspapers, phone banks, or block walking is used to reach its audience, the modern campaign directs a specific, relevant message to these segmented populations based on sophisticated market research. Additionally, location-focused (known as "geofencing") targeting allows candidates, political parties, and groups to target individuals by location based on location data from cellphones and third-party apps. Many raise ethical concerns about the use of such applications and little research has been conducted regarding the use of "geofencing" for political campaigns, but the use of the technique is likely to grow in the future.

Campaign specialists help candidates target their message based upon sophisticated data collected about potential voters. For example, survey data may suggest that a disproportionate number of men between the ages of 45 and 54 have not heard of the candidate but are concerned about the cost of medical insurance. Based on demographic data and television program ratings, the media specialist knows that a large number of these men watch local sports programs. To get a specific message to these voters, television spots with a message on health care costs oriented to the specific concerns of men ages 45 to 54 will be developed and aired during these programs. Most populations can be identified and targeted in this manner, increasing the likelihood that a desired message gets to the specific voters whose perceptions and attitudes the consultant wants to influence. The use of the Internet for political communications has made many aspects of segmentation and targeting even more sophisticated as large amounts of data on users can be captured via consumption and search patterns and analyzed to determine the messages that should be sent to specific populations. Consequently, well-funded campaigns create many variations of a message to deliver to a narrowly defined subgroup. This segmentation of the electorate has gotten increasingly more sophisticated, especially with the use of larger amounts of highly specific data available about voters. In 2018, it was revealed via reporting from several media outlets (notably *The Guardian* and *The New York Times*) that personal information from as many as 87 million Facebook users was harvested without permission and sold to a variety of companies by Cambridge Analytica.[91] Many of the companies who used the data worked for or supported political candidates (including Ted Cruz and Donald Trump). They used the data to better tailor messages to individuals and groups.[92] Facebook executives knew the data was stolen in 2015 and began implementing safeguards to prevent other data breaches, but the public was not told about the scandal until 2018.[93] In April 2018, Mark Zuckerberg testified before Congress, pledging to do better with the data people entrust with Facebook. There is no evidence that the candidates who hired Cambridge Analytica had any knowledge that the information was obtained inappropriately.[94]

Although it is an effective campaign tool, segmentation of the electorate may lead to a fracturing of the political debate, and many argue it has been a factor in increasing the polarization so evident in American politics today. Various segments of voters are exposed to narrow slices of the candidate's image, personality, and concerns. The campaign hopes that each group of voters will respond favorably to its own limited knowledge of the candidate, but some critics argue that this segmentation "further diminishes the importance of language, logic, and reason in the articulation of campaign issues."[95] All too often, people consume information on social (and even traditional) media that reinforces their viewpoints, rather than challenges them to look at issues from a critical perspective, objectively evaluating the arguments and evidence.

11.4.3 Grassroots

Over the past few decades, many political candidates and consultants often have neglected **grassroots** campaigning in favor of mass media. They believed the mass media were more efficient because large numbers of voters could be contacted in a short period. If attacked by an opponent, a quick response could be aired. Repeated contacts also could be used to mobilize voters. Messages could be targeted to specific segments of the electorate. The campaign did not have to engage in the time-consuming process of recruiting and managing volunteers. Although grassroots campaigns never went away, they often were conducted on a shoestring budget with little careful thought as to how volunteers could be effectively integrated into the overall campaign.

As noted earlier, however, effective, well-organized grassroots activities can make a difference, especially in closely contested elections, as we saw in the successful 2012 Senate campaign of Ted Cruz. Interestingly, Cruz faced a challenger in his bid for reelection in 2018—Beto O'Rourke, who also has relied heavily upon grassroots support (much of which was energized by live streaming most campaign events on Facebook). When initially considering a run, O'Rourke traveled the state and spoke to small groups of people. He continued this grassroots approach even after winning the Democratic nomination and out fund-raising Senator Cruz (by approximately $33 million). By mid-April 2018, for example, he had traveled to 234 of the 254 counties in Texas (he traveled to all of them before the election) and had raised $6.7 million from 141,000 people from January to March 2018. He pledged not to accept money from PACs (corporate or progressive) even if he believed in their causes. He placed his fund-raising in the hands of a large base of individual donors, targeted with the help of Revolution Messaging (the company that helped Bernie Sanders with his digital campaign in 2016). While his campaign to defeat Senator Cruz was unsuccessful, he received national attention in his remarkable attempt (making the

THE ALLURE OF CELEBRITY ENDORSEMENTS
Politicians can often be "star-struck" and find celebrity endorsements to be attractive. In some cases, however, the celebrities can bring negative press, as they often make unfiltered and controversial remarks. Pictured here is Ted Nugent, who campaigned for Greg Abbott. Nugent made the news a number of times in recent years for his inflammatory comments about President Obama, which some felt were racist.

grassroots
A term used to describe a wide range of political activities designed to organize and mobilize the electorate at the local level. Modern campaigns are increasingly dominated by the campaign consultants, but such support can prove crucial for political candidates, particularly for those with limited financial resources.

election closer than any Democrat has been able to do in decades) and helped give his candidacy for the 2020 Democratic presidential nomination some good initial support. Traditional grassroots activities include door-to-door campaigning (block walking), neighborhood gatherings, recruiting other volunteers, addressing and stuffing envelopes, making signs, staffing phone banks, staffing the polls on Election Day, live streaming on social media, TikTok and Instagram videos, and a host of other tasks. Whether the grassroots organization staff is paid or unpaid, a telephone call, text message, letter, postcard, personal email, or visit from a campaign worker who demonstrates an intense commitment to a candidate still can have a strong impact on voters. But it takes a great deal of planning and resources to successfully coordinate these activities.

Media and Advertising

11.5 Describe the role of controlled and uncontrolled media in the advertising strategy of campaigns.

It is easy to assume that a campaign can market a candidate much like a six-pack of beer or a box of cereal, and our increasing cynicism often leads to this facile conclusion. But voter response to candidates, the progress of the campaign, and the various ads and messages that voters receive form an extremely complex decision-making process. Scholars in various disciplines have attempted to unravel the effects of news reports, campaign advertising, and campaign strategies and tactics on voter behavior. But the conclusions are only tentative because it is difficult to demonstrate that a specific event, news story, or campaign ad results in the final decision of a voter. To be an informed participant, you need to pay attention to the changing role of the media in marketing candidates and programs and in organizing individuals and groups for collective action. The more you learn, the less likely you are to be manipulated and the more active and involved you can become.

11.5.1 Controlled Media

Candidates can communicate their messages to the voters through numerous media. For those media that can be purchased commercially, the only limitations are availability and finances. Candidate-purchased media often are referred to as the **controlled media**. The candidate controls decisions concerning which media to use, when to purchase advertisements, and what message to convey. Some technical and legal questions pertain to campaign advertising, but the candidate has a wide range of options.

Billboards, bench signs, advertisements on buses and cabs, and electronic signs can be purchased to establish voter awareness and name identification. Although such ads are not likely to convert or mobilize voters, they help increase the candidate's visibility.

Candidates talk about "pressing the flesh" and making direct contact with the voters, but it is simply impossible to talk personally to the number of people necessary to win an election, particularly in a statewide or urban race. Candidates stage block walks and rallies in which they personally participate and meet with supporters, but many of these are **media events** they hope the press will cover. Campaigns also shoot their own videos of these events for posting on candidates' websites, for distribution through social media, and for coordinating with the paid media campaign, direct mail, and other tactics.

In many local elections across Texas, radio and television advertising is too costly or inefficient. But it is almost impossible to run a viable statewide campaign without the use of the electronic media. Texas is large and diverse and has about twenty-three

controlled media
Paid advertising in the media where content and presentation are determined by a political candidate's campaign or by a candidate and his/her staff.

media event
An event staged by an officeholder or political candidate that is designed to attract media, especially television, coverage.

separate media markets. Candidates often spend half of the campaign budget for television and radio advertising, and media specialists—ranging from creative staff to time buyers—have taken on increased importance. Candidates also increasingly use Internet advertising, either to save money or to supplement the more expensive TV advertising.

The thirty-second spot is the standard for television advertising, and the candidate's consultants attempt to carefully craft advertisements that address concerns, perceptions, and expectations of varied segments of the electorate.[96] The media blitz usually picks up steam as the campaign moves closer to Election Day because it is assumed that it takes several exposures to a given ad for a voter to respond, and, in many cases, allegations raised in an opponent's advertisements must be addressed.

Campaign advertising in the 1990 and 2002 gubernatorial races is still considered some of the ugliest, most negative in Texas history. In 1990, "gay-bashing" advertisements were used against Democratic nominee Ann Richards after she received the endorsement of groups alleged to be linked to lesbian rights, and a fund-raising letter from the national Democratic chair attempted to link Republican nominee Clayton Williams with neo-Nazism and racism.[97] Most observers agreed that advertisements in the 1990 gubernatorial race were more vitriolic, aired with more frequency, and seemingly more irrelevant to the issues facing the state than most ads had been in the past. As the advertisements continued, newspapers began to analyze their themes and veracity, and voters indicated that they were displeased with them. But consultants continued to convince their clients that negative attacks worked and that people, although objecting to negative ads, had higher recall of them than of many other television spots. Research has demonstrated that consultants are correct in that people are more apt to recall negative advertisements; however, evidence is mixed regarding the effect of negative advertisements on voter turnout and vote choice.[98]

Computers and smart phones also are major vehicles for campaign communications. Officeholders and candidates communicate with volunteers, supporters, the news media, and the general public through email, Twitter feeds, Facebook pages, Instagram, Snapchat, and updates on campaign websites. This, in part, is a further extension of the controlled media, although a candidate cannot control how a message may be used—or misused—after it hits cyberspace.

A PURPLE TEXAS?

Many believe that Texas can become more supportive of the Democratic Party and perhaps become a Democratic state once again. However, in what started as a hopeful opportunity for a statewide Democratic victory, Wendy Davis lost to Greg Abbott by 20 percentage points in the 2014 gubernatorial election. More recently, Beto O'Rourke unsuccessfully tried to turn the tide in the Democratic favor with an intense campaign against Senator Ted Cruz. Pictured here is a group dedicated to promoting Democrats throughout the state. Others assert that demographic changes that may make the state more competitive will take years to reach practical fruition.

11.5.2 Uncontrolled Media

Positive news stories and blog posts about a candidate are potentially more valuable than paid advertising (since the public often sees them as being more objective) and do not cost the campaign money. Candidates and their handlers thus attempt to exploit the press (the old media as well as the new) by getting positive coverage and reducing as much as possible any negative slants in campaign stories. But the relationship between political candidates and the press, as well as much of the blogosphere, is often adversarial. The news media, ever alert for weaknesses in a candidate and tips spread by political opponents, can make or break a candidate by the coverage and slant given to the candidate's personality, reputation, view of the issues, and campaign activities. A candidate's mistakes or "oops" moments spread instantaneously on the Internet, and often a candidate is unable to recover from them.

Many campaigns hire press secretaries who specialize in media relations. One author has suggested that a successful media strategy entails the following: "Keeping the candidate away from the press; feeding the press a simple, telegenic political line of the day; and making sure the daily news line echoes [*magnifies* may be the better word] the images from the campaign ads, thus blurring the distinction between commercials and 'reality.'"[99] It is common to hear consultants speak of "staying on message" as they attempt to influence media coverage.

Members of the press are keenly aware of these efforts to manipulate them, and the best reporters usually are able to resist. But the hectic, irrational nature of statewide campaigns, the online pressure of constant news deadlines, the propensity for pack journalism (a group of reporters chasing the same news source), and the fear of being beaten on a major story by a competitor often work against a reporter's sincere efforts to get the "straight skinny" on the candidate's abilities, leadership potential, and stand on the issues.

Increasingly, outside groups are running independent advertisements for or against political candidates. The growth in this area is the direct result of the Bipartisan Campaign Reform Act of 2002 (more on this later in the chapter) and the Supreme Court's interpretation of the law in *Citizens United* v. *FEC* (2010), which asserted that the First Amendment prohibits the government from restricting independent expenditures by corporations, associations, and labor unions. As a result of this ruling, the number of independent groups—often called 501(c) organizations or 527 committees—has grown dramatically, as have their independent advertisements and expenditures. These advertisements are best seen as uncontrolled media, as these groups are not allowed to coordinate with campaigns. Since the ads are run independently, the advertisements (even those designed to be helpful) may not be appreciated by the candidate. For example, in 2012, one conservative group, Club for Growth Action, spent nearly $5 million during the Republican Senate primary election attacking Lt. Governor David Dewhurst for not being conservative enough (they spent $630,000 for Ted Cruz). To counter the influence of these attack ads, the Texas Conservatives Fund spent nearly $5.9 million opposing the campaign of attorney Ted Cruz. The Center for Responsive Politics notes that twenty-six independent organizations (PACs, SuperPACs, or 501c organizations) were involved in this one Senate election.[100] In addition to all the money spent by independent organizations, Ted Cruz's own campaign spent over $14 million. In 2020, Senator Cruz spent nearly $45.6 million, while outside organizations spent a total of over $1.2 million to support his candidacy and $8 million against his opponent, O'Rourke. Conversely, O'Rourke, in his unsuccessful bid to unseat Cruz, spent nearly $79 million, with outside groups spending $1.7 million to support his efforts. Over $3 million was spent against Cruz by outside groups in 2018.[101] This was a remarkably expensive, though highly competitive, election.

11.5.3 Direct Mail and Online Fund-Raising

People like to receive mail. Some people even like to receive junk mail, experts say, and direct mail has become a highly sophisticated component of modern campaigns. Direct-mail specialists provide campaigns with a technique for "persuasion and fund-raising."[102] As a further refinement of the segmentation and targeting of voters, this technique permits the campaign to craft a specific message for a narrowly defined population and ensure, with high probability, that households with the specified demographic or psychographic characteristics will receive the campaign message. In a sense, it is "narrow casting" a specific message to an identifiable audience rather than "broadcasting" to a broader audience. Increasingly, direct mail is also sent via email, though many campaigns for state and local election still rely upon "snail" mail.

Direct mail is big business in the United States, and it has been easily adapted to political campaigns. As new innovations are developed with direct Internet communications, we are seeing its increased use for communicating with voters and fund-raising. In many instances, the campaign messages and appeals are emotional, designed to push the voters' "hot buttons" on specific issues. They are crafted by specialists who have studied the emotional appeals of such communications, and the attention to detail often astonishes the uninitiated. The length of a letter, the color of the paper on which it is printed, the underlining and highlighting of specific words or phrases, and teasers on the envelope to convince the recipient to open the letter receive the specialist's critical attention. Evidence indicates that people respond to direct-mail appeals, and if the technique is integrated with phone banks, block walks, the media campaign, and data available from online activity it becomes an extremely valuable campaign tool.[103]

Direct mail, either through the United States Postal Service or electronic mail, also has become a major tool in campaign fund-raising. Massive lists targeting virtually every population group in the state have been developed and refined as more information about voters is made available, and computers can easily extract names of persons with probable political attitudes and beliefs from these files. Successive outreach to probable supporters have a high likelihood of producing campaign dollars. Although campaigns still rely on large contributions, the more modest contributions received from direct-mail solicitation have taken on increased importance.

Large amounts of money also can be raised using the Internet, and both of the state's major political parties encourage online contributions.[104] A campaign that merges modern technology, the knowledge of segmentation and targeting, and well-developed appeals that speak to the interests or "hot buttons" of groups of voters can raise money from a vast number of small contributors giving less than $200 apiece. In addition to traditional direct mail and email, candidates are increasingly relying upon text message solicitations for fund-raising.

Many campaigns for minor, down-ballot offices often cannot afford the technologies just discussed. Nor do they have the technical staff available to develop and implement these new tools. However, campaigning in 2020 has forced candidates, even those on tighter budgets, to be creative in both their mobilization and fund-raising efforts. The Internet has offered some modestly funded candidates for lesser-known offices less expensive alternatives to communicate with voters.

Money and Campaigns

11.6 Evaluate the impact of money on campaigns and the effectiveness of campaign finance reforms.

No one knows precisely how much is spent on political campaigns in Texas because there is no single place where all this information is collected. Candidates for state office file campaign finance reports with the Texas Ethics Commission, but candidates for city councils, county offices, and school boards file reports with the jurisdictions in which they run. Campaign costs vary widely among the different contested offices, but it is evident that costs, even at the local level, continue to increase. You might think that money only serves to corrupt, but you will see that historically money has been used as a means to advance informed participation and is a vehicle of expression and a mechanism to mobilize voters.

11.6.1 Campaign Costs and Fund-Raising

City council races in major cities such as San Antonio, Houston, Fort Worth, and Dallas can easily cost $50,000 to $100,000, and they can go higher. Multimillion-dollar races for mayor in the big cities are rather common. Bob Lanier spent $3 million to be elected mayor of Houston in 1991, and eight candidates spent more than $6.6 million in the 1997 race to succeed him. The 1997 winner, Lee Brown, spent more than $2.1 million alone, and the second-place finisher, businessman Rob Mosbacher, spent more than $3.5 million.[105] These figures, however, pale in comparison to the nearly $9 million that businessman Bill White spent to win the 2003 Houston mayor's race.[106] However, most races, even for mayors of large cities, are not nearly this expensive. For example, according to city records, Fort Worth Mayor Betsy Price spent approximately $800,000 in her first election (an open seat election to replace Mayor Mike Moncrief in 2011).[107] She had over $400,000 in her campaign fund after her unopposed reelection campaign in 2015 (an amount that grew to over $425,000 in July of 2017, immediately preceding her successful election that November, but decreased to $345,000 in January 2018). She spent nearly $100,000 in her last bid for reelection, 2019, ending the year with over $307,000 in unspent contributions for future elections.[108] Reports have indicated that candidates for county commissioner have spent $100,000 or more, and district judges in metropolitan counties have spent more than $150,000; however, much less is typically spent. Historically, school board elections have been low budget, but it is not uncommon for slates of candidates in large urban school districts to spend $10,000 to $15,000 in low-turnout elections.

In the 2018 election cycle, 483 candidates for governor, lieutenant governor, and legislative offices reported raising nearly $264 million. Candidates for governor, including unsuccessful primary candidates, raised almost $82.2 million. Republican Greg Abbott, the winner for governor, raised over $78.1 million of that total (Table 11–3). Some $90.3 million was raised in races for the Texas House, in which all 150 seats were on the ballot. State Senate incumbents and challengers reported $58.6 million in contributions.[109] According to an analysis of early donations in the 2020 election, donors contributed $49.5 million to campaigns for the state legislature (from the beginning of 2019 through January 2020) with 50 percent coming from contributions less than $1,000 each.[110]

Campaigning is big business. However, despite what many think, the person spending the most amount of money does not always win. Heading the list of biggest-spending but losing candidates in a Texas gubernatorial race is Democrat Tony Sanchez, who spent more than $50 million from his own pocket in losing to Rick Perry in 2002.[111]

TABLE 11–3 CAMPAIGN CONTRIBUTIONS TO CANDIDATES SEEKING STATE OFFICES, 2018 ELECTION CYCLE

	Winner	Loser	Primary Losers	Total Democratic/ Republican Candidates
Governor	78,143,014	2,043,080	2,005,632	9
Lt. Governor	31,023,592	1,519,711	299,598	4
Comptroller	4,623,450	71,104	24,058	3
Railroad Commissioner	6,138,045	39,738	47,133	5
Attorney General	12,164,809	6,576,343	—	2

SOURCE: National Institute on Money in State Politics—Follow the Money. Accessed at http://www.followthemoney.org/election-overview.

There are a number of explanations for such high campaign finance figures. The population has increased, requiring more money to be spent to reach more voters. Candidates increasingly rely on electronic media, which are very costly, as is the increased use of consultants to organize and run political campaigns. Meanwhile, the growing number of interest groups and PACs has made more money available to candidates.

Unspent funds raised for a campaign can be carried over as a "war chest" for the successful candidate's next election. Even unopposed officeholders will attempt to raise large amounts of money to discourage potential opponents in the future. A significant question about House and Senate fund-raising is why a person would go to such lengths to raise huge sums of money to win an office that pays only $7,200 a year. In the 2018 election season, spending reports indicated that great variations in spending patterns existed for state legislative races. In most districts, more is spent in primaries than in general elections as primaries tend to be more hotly contested (this occurs for a number of reasons from partisan gerrymandering making the districts safe for one political party to the demographics of the district or region). By far, the most, $4.79 million, was raised by Speaker of the Texas House, Dennis Bonnen; followed by $3.8 million by David Middleton, II; Sarah Davis and Charlie Geren each raised over $1.5 million. Thomas McNutt and Paul Workman each spend $1.1 million in primary losses. Thirteen candidates total (twelve Republicans and one Democrat) spent over one million dollars. However, thirty-eight Democratic and Republican candidates for the state legislature spent less than $1,000 each.[112] As you can see in Figure 11–3, the amount of money spent in state legislative races has increased a good deal since the 1990s.

FIGURE 11-3 MONEY SPENT IN RACES FOR THE STATE LEGISLATURE, 1998–2020

The amount of money spent in races for the state legislature has increased substantially in the last twenty years, especially for House races since 2004. These trends are troubling for many as escalating costs make fund-raising increasingly important. It is also becoming increasingly difficult for average citizens to win races to elective office as they often do not have the resources needed to be competitive.

SOURCE: National Institute on Money in State Politics—Follow the Money. Accessed at http://www.followthemoney.org/election-overview; https://www.followthemoney.org/tools/election-overview?s=TX&y=2018; https://www.followthemoney.org/at-a-glance?y=2020&s=TX.

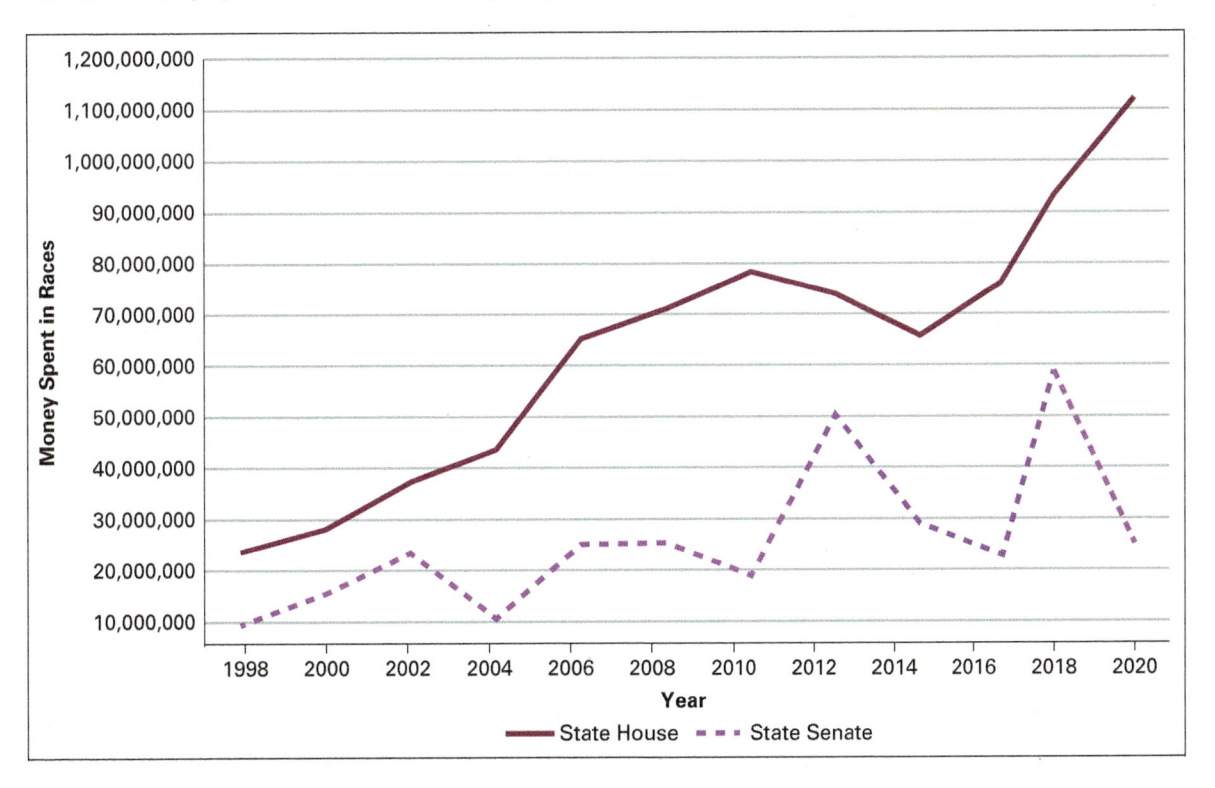

11.6.2 PACs, Fat Cats, and the Really Big Money

political action committee (PAC)
Often referred to as a PAC, a committee representing a specific interest group or including employees of a specific company that raises money from its members for distribution to selected officeholders and political candidates.

Political action committees (PACs) are often an extension of interest groups (though they can be independent entities). These committees, that collect money from their members for redistribution to candidates, have increased their importance at the state and local levels, just as they have nationally, by bringing sophisticated fund-raising skills to political campaigns. Representing special interest groups, individual companies, or political leaders, PACs collect money from their members and are a ready source of campaign dollars. They are in the business of influencing elections. During the two-year 2020 election cycle, 1,886 Texas PACs spent a record high $323.4 million, a 18 percent increase over the 2018 cycle and a 59 percent increase over 2016. While it used to be common for less money to be spent in nongubernatorial elections (e.g., spending decreased in 2012 as compared with 2010) that did not occur in 2016 or 2020. Texas PAC spending increased by 307 percent, and the number of active PACs grew by 370 percent, between 2004 and 2020, according to Texans for Public Justice and Transparency USA, both of which track money in Texas politics (Table 11–4).[113]

PACs are big business in Texas, and they continue to get bigger. Many PACs are organized by corporations and are a major source of business funding to political candidates. Corporations also can influence elections by spending money on issue advertising, provided they do not endorse a specific candidate. In addition, many company executives make individual contributions to candidates. According to Texans for Public Justice, the two largest categories of PAC spending came from business and ideological groups. In recent years, a few of the top spending ideological groups are ActBlue Texas, Forward Majority Action, Powered by People, Annie's List, Texas Leads PAC, and the Republican State Leadership Committee, and the Associated Republicans of Texas. The first four are dedicated to electing more Democrats to office; Annie's list specifically targets progressive, pro-choice Democratic women. The others are working to elect conservative Republicans. ActBlue Texas spent over $25.6 million in 2020, a substantial increase from the less than $1.6 million spent in 2016 and $10 million in 2018. Annie's list spent over $3.8 million in 2018 but only $2.7 million in 2020. Powered by People, a PAC organized by Beto O'Rourke, spent over $3.2 million and the Forward Majority Action PAC spent over $6.7 million in 2020. The Republican State Leadership Committee (RSLC) was founded in 2002 to help elect Republican candidates at all levels of state politics. The organization spent nearly $12.5 million in 2020. Associated Republicans of Texas, dedicated to helping Republican candidates across Texas, spent over $2.5 million in 2016, $5 million in 2018 and over $7.3 million

TABLE 11–4 PAC SPENDING IN STATE ELECTIONS

Election Cycle	Number of Active PACs	Total PAC Spending	Spending Increase (%)
2004	850	$68,904,524	−19
2006*	1,132	99,167,646	44
2008	1,209	119,561,861	21
2010*	1,302	133,466,187	12
2012	1,364	126,367,460	−5
2014*	1,421	159,314,633	26
2016	1,944	203,988,381	+28
2018*	2,224	280,710,390	+38
2020	1,886	323,371,729	+18

*Gubernatorial election

SOURCE: Data for 2014 through 2014 from the Texas Ethics Commission, Political Committee Lists, https://www.ethics.state.tx.us/dfs/paclists.htm; data for 2014 is from "Texas PACs: 2014 Election Cycle Spending," Texans for Public Justice, February 2016, http://info.tpj.org/reports/pdf/PACs2014.pdf; Data for 2016 and 2018 from Transparency USA, https://www.transparencyusa.org/tx/pacs?cycle=2016-election-cycle&page=78; https://www.transparencyusa.org/tx/pacs?cycle=2018-election-cycle; data for 2020 is from https://www.transparencyusa.org/tx/pacs.

in 2020. Another ideological group is the Pro-life America PAC, which spent over $2.6 million in 2020. The business-related PAC that consistently spends the most is Texas Association of Realtors PAC. In 2020, the group reported spending over $45.6 million, which was substantially less than the $60.5 million they spent in 2018 but significantly more than the $26.8 million spent in 2016. The Texas Medical Association PAC spent nearly $1.5 million in 2016, $1.2 million in 2018, and $1.1 million in 2020.[114]

One key business-related PAC is Texans for Lawsuit Reform (TLR). TLR has played a leading role in recent years in a successful lobbying effort that has produced significant restrictions on damage lawsuits filed against doctors and businesses. This one PAC spent nearly $7.8 million in 2012 and over $7 million in 2014. In 2016, they had over $8.3 million in contributions but spent only $4.8 million. 2018 saw a large increase in expenditures for the group, up to $8.6 million from their $9.8 million in contributions. In 2020, the group saw record spending with over $18.8 million in total expenditures.[115] TLR is business oriented, but because its goal is winning additional limits on civil lawsuits and damage judgments, it is classified as a single-issue PAC. TLR spent $1.3 million to help Senator Konni Burton win her election and $682,000 on Dan Patrick's campaign in 2016. In 2020, Republican State Senator Pete Flores received $580,000 from the group, Republican Representative Drew Springer, Jr. received $342,500, Republican Representative Jeff Leach received $95,000 in 2020. In 2018, Republican Attorney General Ken Paxton received $345,000 from the group. In the last twenty-five years, TLR has donated over $45 million, 87 percent of which has gone to Republican candidates.[116] Other major PACs include those for the Texas Association of Realtors (spending over $16.4 million in 2016, nearly $60 million in 2018, and $45.6 million in 2020), and Exelon Corporation (a nuclear power corporation spending $1.3 million in 2016 and nearly $2.2 million in 2018, and over $1.7 million in 2020).[117]

Unlike the federal government, Texas places no limits on the amount of money an individual or PAC can contribute to most political candidates, and there are no limits on how much a candidate can contribute to his or her own campaign. The only exceptions are limits to campaign contributions in judicial races, which were imposed by the Texas legislature in 1995. Large contributions have long played a role in Texas politics, and, over the years, most large contributions have gone to the conservative candidates, both Democratic and Republican. The role of large money may be mitigated in the future through the use of direct mail and the Internet to solicit small campaign donations. From the available data, however, it is still too early to discern such a pattern. For now, large donors—including PACs and a relatively small number of super-wealthy individuals, sometimes called **fat cats**—still dominate the contributions to Texas political campaigns.

fat cat
An individual who contributes a large amount of money to political candidates.

In addition to PACs and "fat cats," a major source of money in elections today is the less-regulated and often hard-to-track independent organization. As noted earlier in the chapter, spending by 501(c) organizations and 527 committees (both named after their IRS tax-exempt codes) has increased dramatically since 2010 (as a direct result of *Citizens United*). These groups, along with other nonconnected political party organizations, spent a record amount of money, nearly $1.67 billion, in 2016 and $1.32 billion in 2018 nationally (note the final, more accurate, figures for 2020 were not available at the time of publication).[118] Between 2010 and 2018, far more money was spent to benefit conservative candidates than liberal candidates but, for the first time since 2008, liberals had an advantage in 2018.[119] While these figures are national, there is no doubt that these groups are impacting the dynamic of Texas politics—both directly (as in the case of Senator Cruz's first election and reelection, and the elections of Governor Abbott) and indirectly (impacting voter cynicism and perhaps turnout). An example of a group active in state politics is Empower Texans, a conservative advocacy 501c(4) nonprofit organization. Empower Texas was the fastest-growing PAC in Texas with more than 5,000 percent growth between 2012 and 2014. In 2012, the group spent $107,257 to elect conservative Texans. That amount exploded two short years later to nearly $5.5 million.[120] In 2018, they had nearly $5.9 million dollars in contributions and spent nearly $5.8 million on the 2018 elections.[121] Although groups like these are legally allowed to spend money to influence elections, many people are concerned about their influence, as they frequently do not have to disclose expenditures in a timely fashion and often do not disclose the sources of their funds. This lack of transparency is the source of concern for those who believe democracy thrives when secrets are minimized.[122]

11.6.3 Why People Contribute to Campaigns

Soaring campaign costs have raised considerable concern about campaign fund-raising and contributions in Texas, as they have nationally. There is concern that elections are being bought and that major campaign contributors are purchasing influence in the policymaking process. Some critics of contemporary campaigns have argued that current practices are a form of legalized bribery, implying that public officials are available to the highest bidder. Other critics have asserted that some officeholders engage in "shaking down" organizations for campaign contributions with implied threats.

Money is critical to most successful campaigns for public office because it permits the candidate to purchase advertising and other resources for communicating with the voters. But money is not the only factor affecting an election. Incumbency, existing party loyalties, the availability of party or campaign activists, the public's perceptions of a candidate, and a candidate's campaign skills or expertise also help determine electoral success. In numerous elections, well-financed candidates have been defeated by opponents with far fewer dollars. This may suggest that there are genuine limits on what money can accomplish in a campaign.[123]

Contributions are made to influence the outcome of an election and, subsequently, to shape public policy by electing persons who share similar political views with or who will be sympathetic or accessible to those making the contributions. Reports of large campaign contributions often prompt remarks that Texas has the "best Supreme Court that money can buy" or the "best legislature that money can buy." These remarks are given credence if key policy votes seem to be influenced by an officeholder's relationship to his or her political contributors.

Some people undoubtedly make contributions to candidates out of a sense of civic duty, general concern for good public policy, partisan loyalty, or personal friendship. But contributions of hundreds of thousands of dollars, either from individuals or PACs, raise different questions about intent and purpose. For example, James Leininger, a wealthy businessman from San Antonio, is known for his support of conservative causes, particularly a proposal to spend tax dollars on private school vouchers. When a voucher proposal was defeated in the 2005 session of the legislature with the support of five Republicans, he then gave more than $2 million to their opponents in the 2006 Republican primaries.

Rarely will anyone admit publicly that he or she is attempting to buy a candidate. Individuals and PACs making large political contributions usually say they are doing so for the purpose of "gaining access" to elected officials.[124] Since officeholders have limited time to consider and assess competing interests, lobbyists representing interest groups and their PACs contend that campaign contributions are necessary to give them an opportunity to present their cases on specific legislation.

Political scientists and others have attempted to prove that a relationship exists between campaign contributions and public policy, but so far the research is inconclusive. Multiple factors shape the decisions of public policymakers, including an officeholder's personal views, the views of his or her constituents, legal and technical issues, and the merits of the requests made by specific individuals or groups.[125] Nevertheless, the strong appearance of a relationship between money and public policy exists, and advocates of campaign finance reform can make strong arguments for change.

11.6.4 Attempts at Reform

On the heels of the Sharpstown scandal, in which high-ranking state officials were given preferential treatment in the purchase of stock in an insurance company, the legislature enacted a major campaign finance disclosure law in 1973. The Texas Ethics

Commission now administers this law, with some changes. Although the law did not limit the size of political contributions, for the first time it required candidates to list the addresses as well as the names of donors and the amounts and dates of contributions. It also required PACs contributing to candidates or officeholders to report the sources of their donations, which in the past usually had been hidden. Also for the first time, officeholders were required to file annual reports of their political contributions and expenditures—even during years when they were not seeking reelection— and candidates were required to report contributions and other financial activity that occurred after an election. In addition, a candidate had to formally designate a campaign treasurer before he or she could legally accept political contributions. Campaign finance reform, however, remains a difficult and seemingly endless struggle as officeholders, individuals, and organizations resist efforts to reduce the influence of money and require the fund-raising process to be more transparent.

CONCLUSION

Americans profess a love for elections and the right to vote. We believe in representative democracy and are deeply committed to peacefully petitioning our government through campaigns and elections. In fact, Americans elect far more officials than any other country.

Elections, however, are messy and less than ideal. At times, people feel overwhelmed by the number of elections and the various complex rules. Low turnout rates in Texas elections (especially as compared to other states) pose a true quandary, and the fact that elections are called off when there are no challengers should raise some significant questions. Perhaps having so many elections during the course of a year contributes to "voter fatigue." It might also be argued that Texans are "happy as clams" with the status quo, and nonvoting is an endorsement for these conditions.

Regardless of whether Texans think their vote won't count (and feel it doesn't matter if they vote), don't care about elections, or just don't want to be bothered, campaigns and elections are important linkages between public officials and the populace. During the campaign, potential leaders inform the public of their vision, their preferred policy agenda, and their goals for the future. When voting, we the people have the opportunity to hold our officials accountable and to help shape the future of our locality, state, and nation. In the absence of elections, people are forced to use violent means to effect change. In the United States, we have been largely, though not entirely, spared from the far too common violent disagreements that have plagued other nations.

Becoming informed about the types of elections, the schedule of elections, and the historical evolution of mass suffrage in Texas can be highly valuable to those who strive to become politically active and influential. The struggle of mass suffrage (a right that so many take for granted) has been difficult and turbulent. Examining the history of suffrage in Texas is crucial to understanding the importance of political participation in a contemporary light.

CAMPAIGNS THROUGH TIME

Much about campaigns today is different from those of the past because of the changes in communication media brought about by technology. One thing, however, remains the same: Candidates today still try to persuade voters that their vision for Texas is the best one for building a better future.

Campaigns are undergoing significant changes as more and more candidates employ new and costly technology to persuade voters. Successful candidates, however, understand that some older methods, like meeting and greeting people to build grassroots support, are still important. As we move forward, we need to continue to be concerned over the role of money in elections, because even if no evidence exists to definitively demonstrate that money corrupts politics, the perception that it does is widespread and dangerous. We also need to be concerned about the increased polarization and growing cynicism of voters, as neither of these traits is useful in our democracy, with its emphasis on minority rights, incremental change, and consensus building.

REVIEW THE CHAPTER

The Functions of Elections

11.1 Describe the functions of elections in a democratic society, p. 340.

In a democratic society, elections link citizens to their political leaders and institutions. Elections provide the general population with an opportunity to shape public policy indirectly through the selection of leaders. They serve to keep public officials accountable, and they provide the electorate with opportunities for replacing one set of leaders with another. For elections to achieve their ideal purpose under democratic theory, voters must be well informed and attentive to the actions of their leaders and must care about the outcome of elections.

State and Local Elections

11.2 Compare and contrast the types of state and local elections held in Texas, p. 341.

Texans have ample opportunities to exercise their right to vote; with frequent elections, it often appears that the election cycle is endless. Candidates for partisan state and county offices are nominated in the party primaries and runoff elections, normally held in March and April of even-numbered years. Statewide general elections are held in November of even-numbered years, and candidates nominated in the primaries and runoffs compete in these elections. Vacancies in some offices require special elections to fill unexpired terms. Partisan elections include high levels of straight-ticket voting.

Each regular session of the Texas legislature proposes several constitutional amendments, which normally are on the general election ballot in odd-numbered years. Constitutional amendment elections can be held at other times, if the legislature chooses. Candidates for city, school board, and special district offices run for election on nonpartisan ballots. Most local governments hold their elections in May of odd-numbered years, although some cities and school boards have elections in May of even-numbered years or November in either odd- or even-numbered years. In addition, local governments hold special elections at various times to seek voter approval of charter changes or bond issues.

Political Suffrage in Texas: A Struggle for Mass Suffrage

11.3 Explain the measures taken to keep some Texans from voting and the countermeasures employed to curtail these discriminatory practices, p. 350.

Constitutional amendments following the Civil War extended full citizenship to African Americans, but Texas, along with some other states (mostly southern) engaged in many years of denying full voting rights to minority and poor residents. Texas used a variety of discriminatory legislation, including the poll tax, white primary, restrictive registration laws, and property ownership, as a way to prevent some residents from voting. Eventually, U.S. Supreme Court decisions and constitutional amendments eliminated all of these restrictions. In 1971, Texas replaced a highly restrictive voter-registration law with a system, still in place, making it much easier for large numbers of voters to be registered by minority-rights groups and political campaigns. The fight over the 2011 voter identification law demonstrates how controversies arise from altering laws and the manner in which laws that may seem to be "neutral" can actually have a disparate impact on various groups.

The federal Voting Rights Act, extended to Texas in 1975, has helped Hispanics and African Americans fight discriminatory redistricting of congressional, legislative, and local political districts and replace discriminatory county- or district-wide election requirements with single-member districts. That struggle, however, continues.

Women won the right to vote in Texas party primaries in 1918, and the ratification of the Nineteenth Amendment to the U.S. Constitution in 1920 gave women the right to vote in all elections throughout the country. The Twenty-Sixth Amendment lowered the voting age from 21 to 18 in 1971, and 18-year-olds voted for the first time in 1972. Since the 1970s, Hispanics and African Americans have realized substantial gains in the electoral process with an increased number of elected officials at the state and local levels of government.

Campaign Technology

11.4 Describe the use of marketing technology in political campaigns, p. 360.

Political parties once played a major role in elections, but now candidates increasingly rely on paid campaign consultants, who have taken over many of the traditional party functions. Candidates contract with campaign specialists for a wide variety of campaign-related functions, including public opinion polling, demographic studies, digital campaigns, and segmentation of the electorate into identifiable groups of people with shared interests or concerns. The consultants then target tailored advertising and other communications efforts to specific groups. The consultants' primary objective is to win campaigns, and they appear to give little consideration to the subsequent effects of campaigns on governance and policymaking.

Media and Advertising

11.5 Describe the role of controlled and uncontrolled media in the advertising strategy of campaigns, p. 366.

Candidates must communicate an array of messages to win support and mobilize voters to turn out and vote for them on Election Day. Candidates use controlled and uncontrolled media. Controlled media include messages that are paid for by the candidate: on television, radio, the Internet, and other paid media. Candidates also maintain their own websites and pay for direct mail, door-to-door canvassing, telephone banks, and a variety of grassroots activities. Increasingly, candidates are aggressively using digital media to reach voters, include live streaming on Facebook and being active on Twitter and Instagram. In addition, candidates attempt to manipulate and use uncontrolled media. They try to garner free, positive coverage by issuing news releases, holding press conferences, and staging pseudo-news events.

Money and Campaigns

11.6 Evaluate the impact of money on campaigns and the effectiveness of campaign finance reforms, p. 369.

The costs of statewide campaigns, as well as of many regional and local campaigns, have escalated since the late 1970s. Candidates receive much of their money in large campaign contributions from political action committees (PACs) and wealthy individuals. Although money may not buy public officials, it certainly buys access to them, and it creates the impression that well-organized interests, corporations, and wealthy individuals have a disproportionate influence on policymakers. Texas law prohibits corporations and labor unions from making contributions directly to political candidates; however, except for modest limits on judicial campaigns, Texas law puts no limits on the amount of money that can be contributed to political races by individuals and PACs. Nevertheless, Texas law does require fairly thorough and timely reporting of campaign contributions and expenditures.

LEARN THE TERMS

suffrage, p. 341
primary election, p. 342
runoff election, p. 343
Voting Rights Act, p. 343
general election, p. 346
local election, p. 346
special election, p. 347
absentee (or early) voting, p. 348
poll tax, p. 351
white primary, p. 352
gerrymandering, p. 353
single-member district, p. 353
at-large election, p. 354
motor voter registration, p. 355
campaign consultant, p. 361
grassroots, p. 365
controlled media, p. 366
media event, p. 366
political action committee (PAC), p. 372
fat cat, p. 373

The Mass Media in Texas Politics

12

ADDRESSING THE MEDIA
Some members of the Texas House participate in a news conference in the Speaker's Committee Room at the state Capitol. This is a popular place for legislators and advocacy groups to schedule news events, especially during legislative sessions.

LEARNING OBJECTIVES

12.1 Describe the influence of the mass media on the policy agenda in Texas, p. 380.

12.2 Describe the media coverage of campaigns and elections in Texas, p. 384.

12.3 Trace the early development of the news media in Texas, p. 390.

12.4 Describe the impact of the Internet and other digital information sources on traditional media outlets and news consumers, and how newspapers and television news departments have adjusted to the changes, p. 393.

12.5 Assess the effort of Texans and other Americans to stay informed and how their views of the media affect that effort, p. 405.

Before a recent legislative session convened to begin its normal work of deciding which new laws to enact and how much money to spend on state programs, members of the House Administration Committee had another chore to handle. They had to define *news reporter* for purposes of issuing media credentials that would allow reporters access to the floor of the House chamber while lawmakers were in session. In the not-too-distant but rapidly disappearing past, media accreditation was an easy job. Reporters for newspapers, wire services, and television or radio stations presented letters from their employers and were issued media passes. But with the spread of blogs, social media sites, and online publications that regularly blur the line between simply reporting the news and advocating for a political or ideological viewpoint, the media credentialing task had become more difficult. News reporters traditionally have been granted access to the House and Senate chambers while the lawmaking bodies are in session, but lobbyists and other advocates have to wait outside or watch from the gallery or online. Legislators regularly listen to—and are influenced by—lobbyists on a wide variety of interests. But traditionally they have drawn the line at having lobbyists present to bend their ears or tug on their sleeves while they are in session, debating proposed laws and casting votes.

The House Administration Committee resolved the issue, at least for the time being, by adopting a new credentialing procedure that required reporters to affirm that they did not lobby or advocate for another person, group, or political party. They also had to affirm that they worked for publications that were "editorially independent of any institution, foundation, or interest group that lobbies the government, or that is not principally a general news organization."[1]

The group primarily responsible for forcing the House to update its media credentialing policy was Empower Texans, an ultraconservative group with a political action committee that has spent millions of dollars during recent election cycles promoting hardline conservative Republicans to the legislature, often at the expense of more moderate Republicans. Empower Texans also includes a right-wing publication, *Texas Scorecard*, which tracks how lawmakers vote on conservative priorities and was seeking media credentials for its reporters. Although *Texas Scorecard* was denied media credentials for the House floor, its reporters were granted credentials in 2019 to sit at the press table in the Senate chamber. The difference, Capitol insiders believed, was Lieutenant Governor Dan Patrick, the Senate's presiding officer, who had received more than $850,000 from Empower Texans's political action committee during the previous five years and supported the credentialing.[2]

Thousands of mainstream newspaper reporters and editors and television and radio journalists have lost their jobs in the United States during the past three decades as newspapers have closed, merged, or shrunk and broadcast stations have reduced newsroom budgets to compensate for hundreds of millions of advertising dollars lost because of the Internet's dominant role in what people read and hear. Thousands more journalists, from both traditional and digital media, were laid off or furloughed during the coronavirus pandemic in 2020 when a slumping economy wiped out additional advertising revenue. Why, you may ask, should anyone care? Anyone with a laptop, smart phone, or other electronic device can instantaneously gain access to online feeds, emails, Tweets, and videos from hundreds of surviving news outlets, aggregators, bloggers, social media gurus, and political, cultural, and corporate news and opinion disseminators. Some of these sources, to one degree or another, can keep you informed about what's happening in government, how a law being considered by the legislature could raise your tuition next year, or how a new policy being considered by the city council could affect your electric bill. This information can help you decide whether to contact your state representative to object to the proposed tuition law and help you decide how to vote in the next election.

However, not all the information you have literally at your fingertips should be considered equally reliable. Many electronic publications, blogs, and other online information sources are opinion-based and fail to fulfill the crucial fact-finding and fact-checking roles of traditional media. The writers at these sites may call themselves "reporters," but many make no effort to filter truth from unsubstantiated rumor, political opinion, outright lies, or pure fiction as they advocate for a particular viewpoint or ideology. Some sources, such as political parties or political candidates, are unabashedly partisan and opinionated and make no effort to hide that fact. Others, including many elected officials and government or corporate public relations operatives, may be more subtle, skillfully weaving their viewpoints in such a way that their "news" can seem factual.

In adopting First Amendment guarantees of press freedom more than 200 years ago, the framers of the U.S. Constitution recognized that a free press was an independent provider of information essential to making a representative democracy work. By providing a public forum for the exchange of ideas and a means of scrutinizing the actions of public officials, the press established accountability. The Internet and an influx of online sources have turned up the volume on that public discourse. Both the traditional media and the new, digital media play important roles in helping people like you navigate the political and policymaking process.

It is important, however, that you—the information consumer—learn how to filter out noise well enough to differentiate among news, opinion, and unsubstantiated rumor if you are going to make the best use of your information sources. In this chapter, we will discuss this challenge as we trace the historical development of the media in Texas, its continuing transformation, and its impact on policymakers and voters.

The Mass Media and the Policy Agenda

12.1 Describe the influence of the mass media on the policy agenda in Texas.

Throughout our country's history, a free and vigorous press has been widely considered fundamental to democracy as an important link between the people and the government. Traditional, objective journalism has long been seen as essential in disseminating reliable and accurate information, allowing citizens to make informed political decisions, thereby enhancing collective accountability. Most people experience the world not directly but rather through the lens of the news media. The media allow people to learn about events in their own communities and across the globe. Historically, news agencies have been considered "watchdogs" of government and governmental officials, continually monitoring and assessing actions and outcomes. Thomas Jefferson remarked in 1787, "If it were left to me to decide whether we should have a government without newspapers or newspapers without a government, I should not hesitate for a moment to prefer the latter."[3] But times have changed, and the role of mainstream media is increasingly being challenged by an increase in political polarization, the rise of ideologically oriented media outlets, and political attacks that intensified during the Trump administration, as the president regularly labeled news reports that he disliked as "fake news."

On February 17, 2017, about a month after taking office, President Trump wrote on Twitter that the nation's news media "is an enemy of the American people," a claim he subsequently repeated.[4] While relationships between presidents and the press are often marked by tension, this unprecedented attack is notable and troubling to nearly all scholars. A poll by Hill-Harris in June 2019 found that one-third of Americans believe that the press is the enemy of the people, while 67 percent think the media is important for democracy. However, if we control for partisanship, most of the people who think the media is an enemy of the state are Republicans (51 percent, while only 14 percent of Democrats and 35 percent of Independents feel that way).[5]

A national survey conducted by Pew Research Center in October 2019 showed that 73 percent of the public believe that it is important for journalists to serve as watchdogs over elected officials. But it showed a significant gap between Democrats and Republicans on this question. Some 83 percent of Democrats responding to the poll agreed that the media serving as watchdogs was important, while only 61 percent of Republicans agreed.[6] Interestingly, views on how well journalists are performing their jobs as watchdogs of elected officials vary not only by political party but also by news diet. Three years earlier, during the 2016 presidential election campaign, Democrats (74 percent) and Republicans (77 percent) expressed comparable support for the media's watchdog responsibility.[7]

More recently, a Texas Lyceum Poll conducted in 2019 found that 19 percent of all Texans believe the news media is the greatest internal threat to American democracy, second only to money in politics (28 percent). Almost one-third of Texas Republicans (29 percent) believe the news media is the greatest internal threat, compared to 10 percent of Texas Democrats.[8]

The news media have undergone significant changes in the past twenty years, causing many to be alarmed. As newspapers, which play particularly important roles in covering state and local politics, have fallen upon hard economic times, for example, many have come to worry that vertical accountability (between elected officials and the public) has been harmed, especially as papers increasingly lose their ability to initiate investigations and scrutinize behavior due to budget cuts.[9]

Changing trends in consumption and production of news have resulted in audiences that are far more involved in production (think about the number of stories that begin with cell-phone videos, blogs, and viral rants) and have significantly more choices in consumption sources. These trends are potentially both positive for and challenging to democracy. On the one hand, individuals have unprecedented access to information that can be used to empower accountability and governmental scrutiny. Some assert that the increased variety of sources of information can enhance public discourse by providing a level playing field for the expression of more diverse thought.[10] According to this line of thought, the power of the "old media gatekeepers" has diminished, with more and more information flowing into the hands of consumers. Others disagree, asserting that traditional news outlets are still influential in this changing environment, playing a role in filtering information (though less pronounced with today's technology, where search engines filter far more information than many imagine).[11]

Many assert that these changes in consumption and production of news also complicate democracy, as people can become increasingly isolated, relying more and more upon sources of information that reinforce their world views and are narrowly and often divisively framed in ways that make collective decision making, incremental change, and consensus building difficult, if not impossible. The psychological tendency for individuals to seek out information that reinforces their preconceived notions is called confirmation bias and has been made easier with the current consumption patterns of news.[12] While many researchers point to confirmation bias as a significant concern, others have found the idea of an "echo chamber," where people only consume information that reinforces their world view, is overstated and that availability of diverse media and political interests moderates this effect.[13]

Opportunistic, affluent, and well-organized groups can seize upon new sources of information to make rumors seem like fact and to manipulate and mobilize a narrow segment of the public to influence the policy agenda and political leaders. New technology has made it much easier for these groups to bypass traditional media and take their own messages—and threats—on policy priorities directly to voters and policymakers.

During a Texas budgetary crisis in 2011, for example, many newspaper articles and editorials expressed people's desire for the legislature to spend a significant part of the state's emergency Rainy Day Fund to minimize spending cuts to important state programs. Late in the legislative session, a majority of the Texas House, including many Republican members, approved an amendment to make a contingent Rainy Day appropriation of $2 billion for the public schools, if economic conditions improved. Overnight, well-organized conservatives, who were intent on seeing the legislature make deep cuts in government spending, barraged the offices and constituents of Republican House members with calls and emails protesting the vote. The next day, the House took another vote on the same amendment and it was defeated, with many Republican legislators—fearful of retaliation by conservative voters back home—switching their votes.

12.1.1 Media Influence on Public Opinion and Policy

agenda setting
A theory that the media's choice of which news events and issues to cover helps define what is important for the public to know and which issues should be addressed.

Some scholars and experts who study the traditional media—newspapers, television, and radio—believe one of the major contributions of the media to politics is **agenda setting**. By choosing which events and issues to cover and how extensively to cover them, they say, the media help define what is important for the public and, by omission, what is not important. Maxwell McCombs and Donald Shaw, recognized authorities on the traditional mass media, argued some years ago that "the idea of agenda setting asserts that the priorities of the press to some degree become the priorities of the public. What the press emphasizes is in turn emphasized privately and publicly by the audiences of the press."[14] As we will see later in the chapter, agenda setting is still an important function of the media, but it is evolving in this era of instant communications. The audience increasingly plays a role in framing the stories as they share on social media and gather raw footage with cell-phone cameras in real time. And just as interest groups use social networks to bypass the traditional media, elected officials increasingly use social media to communicate their priorities and political agendas directly to the public.

The media use some or all of five basic criteria to select which events and subjects to cover. First, a story must have a significant impact on their audience, such as a legislative proposal to increase taxes or, as in the 2011 legislative debate, making deep cuts to public education and other state programs. Second, it can be something that generates considerable interest. That may be an act of violence or conflict, a natural disaster, a political scandal, or legislation to regulate abortion or ban assault rifles. A third component is familiarity—the public identifies with well-known individuals or familiar situations. A fourth consideration is that an event occurs in some proximity to readers and viewers, and, finally, a news story should be timely.[15] Some stories on governmental policy and politics, of course, include more than one of these elements, and some stories are going to attract and sustain more public interest than others.

agenda building
The process of groups or individuals identifying problems or issues that affect them and keeping pressure on policymakers to develop and implement public policy solutions.

When the public interest is aroused, some experts extend the agenda-setting role of the media to **agenda building**. The media's coverage of specific issues creates a climate for political action by shaping the atmosphere in which these issues will be debated and their solutions developed.[16] By helping to make an issue relevant, the media give people reasons for taking sides and converting the problem into a serious political issue. From this perspective, "the public agenda is not so much set by the media as built up through a cycle of media activity that transforms an elite issue into a public controversy."[17] Issues and concerns of a few individuals now become the concerns of many, and the dynamics of the policymaking process change.[18]

issue-attention cycle
A pattern in which public interest in an issue or problem is heightened by intensive media coverage. Media attention and public interest will wane after government takes steps to address their concerns, but most issues or problems are never permanently resolved. Another crisis, perhaps years later, will restart the cycle.

The media's attention to public problems and officialdom's response form something of a never-ending cycle, what scholar Anthony Downs once described as an **issue-attention cycle**.[19] There is a pre-public phase in which a problem, such as poor nursing home conditions, quietly affects numerous individuals. Someone, perhaps a relative of a nursing home resident, then attempts to transform the issue into a public concern through social or traditional media. A newspaper or television station may get interested and start carrying stories about the problem. This coverage may intensify with additional media coverage, prompting more and more outraged citizens to discuss the problem, posting their opinions and links to media articles on social media. But initial enthusiasm for solutions gives way to the realization that significant progress will be costly in terms of not only money but also political conflict, and many people begin to lose interest. Government may enact policies, such as more inspections of nursing homes, to address some of the problems, and media interest in the issue will then begin to wane. Sooner or later, new issues with nursing homes may arise, perhaps because budgetary issues force reductions in the number of inspections. Although press coverage may continue intermittently, it has limited effect in renewing

PART OF THE GOVERNOR'S JOB
Governor Greg Abbott meets with reporters around a conference table at the state Capitol. Communicating effectively with the public through the media can be crucial to the governor's policy agenda.

public opinion or prompting further governmental action—until someone, usually several years later, restarts the cycle.

The media's degree of influence over specific governmental actions can vary considerably, and sometimes the media fail in their efforts at agenda building, as occurred in 2011 during the legislative debate over the budget. Governor Rick Perry and the Republican legislative majority ignored viewpoints expressed in the traditional media for a balanced approach to bridging a $27 billion revenue shortfall that would have included spending several billion dollars from the state's Rainy Day Fund and, perhaps, some modest tax increases in addition to spending reductions. Instead, the governor and the legislative majority followed the demands of conservative activists and made deep cuts in public services. As noted earlier, those demands in some cases bypassed the news media and were delivered directly to legislators. Similarly, prominent Texas newspapers in recent years have urged the governor and the legislature to begin overhauling an outdated school finance system. But the governor and most legislators turned a deaf ear until the election of additional pro-public education advocates to the Texas House in 2018 prompted the approval of several billion dollars in additional school funding in 2019.

In 2017, Lieutenant Governor Dan Patrick used his own social networks, conservative radio shows, and conservative ideological groups to help rally support for a key piece of his legislative agenda, the so-called "bathroom bill," legislation that would have regulated the use of public restrooms by transgender Texans. The traditional media covered the issue extensively as a major news item but also carried many editorials and other opinion articles attacking the bill as discriminatory, and the measure failed during the regular session and a special session that year.

12.1.2 Guardians of Open Government

Because the soundness of any governmental policy or program is affected by the motives and capabilities of those officials who design and administer it, most reporters who cover the state Capitol take very seriously their role as watchdogs over the behavior and performance of elected officials and bureaucrats. As a result, newspeople are persistent guardians of the public's access to governmental business through the state's **Open Meetings and Public Information Acts**. These laws, which apply to state and local governments, basically require the public's business be conducted in public and that most records produced in the conduct of the public's business made available to the public on demand. Each law provides for certain exceptions.

Open Meetings and Public Information Acts
Laws that require state and local governmental bodies to conduct most of their actions in public and maintain records for public inspection.

Governmental bodies, for example, are allowed to hold closed-door meetings to consider personnel matters, to discuss lawsuits in which they are involved, to consider real estate purchases, and for certain other actions. Media representatives are engaged in a constant struggle against abuses and outright violations of the laws and attempts by school boards, city councils, and other governments to expand the list of exceptions that allow them to discuss business in private.

Media organizations are obviously in the business of disseminating information, but it is important to remember that they are not the only ones with a stake in strong open government laws. Every Texan has a right to know what his or her government is doing, to find open doors to city council chambers and school board meeting rooms, and to have ready access to public documents.

News Media and the Electoral Process

12.2 Describe the media coverage of campaigns and elections in Texas.

Candidates for public office in Texas still attend rallies in the park, make speeches at conventions, and salute the flag at Fourth of July parades. Some legislative and local candidates, particularly those with more shoe leather than money, still rely heavily on door-to-door campaigning. But in most races for statewide offices, and many local and district offices as well, the campaign stump of old has long since been replaced in importance by the **sound bite**; the press conference; the contrived pseudo-news event developed by the campaign consultant; and, increasingly, Twitter feeds, emails, YouTube videos, social networking, and other online overtures. Campaigning is constructed around the media, and all these voices—including paid television and Internet advertising, traditional news media, blogs, and social media—are major information links between voters and candidates. But the roles and relative influences of each media source are changing as instant communications technology continues to evolve. For many weeks during the coronavirus pandemic in 2020, which was an election year, candidates were largely limited to Zoom meetings and other forms of virtual campaigning and fund-raising.

Traditional reporters for newspapers and television and radio stations still believe their job is to be as objective as possible in outlining the issues and reporting and evaluating the backgrounds, philosophies, activities, and policy proposals of candidates. As they have done for many years, they double-check the accuracy of their information before reporting it and try to avoid even the perception of taking sides. At the same time, they also try to determine which issues are of the greatest potential public importance and should be emphasized in their campaign reporting. But they are increasingly challenged in these roles by sources such as paid advertising, in which candidates or special interest groups seek to dictate what the electorate should consider important; opinionated cable television commentators; and political bloggers and social media specialists, who use the Internet to spread their own points of view and may openly take sides in political campaigns. Some of these bloggers and social media gurus may even be employed by candidates or political parties and may use online social networks to cloud campaign facts with political or partisan opinions.

Despite all these information and opinion sources, studies have indicated that party identification helps determine many voters' choices in general elections because there historically was a lot of straight-ticket, one-party voting, a practice that was disallowed in Texas beginning with the 2020 election.[20] Nevertheless, long ballots in primaries and general elections prompt voters to seek other sources of information to help them navigate political campaigns, and this is where the media has traditionally played an influential role.[21] The ability to win favorable exposure on news and

sound bite
A short, quotable phrase by a public official or political candidate that may sound good on television or radio but lacks depth and often is meaningless.

editorial pages, television screens, and the Internet's communications network can be crucial to a candidate's electoral success. But increasingly, this requires a candidate to be able to out-shout an opponent amid the din. And it requires that independent-minded voters have a keen ability to distinguish fact and objective analysis from opinion and candidate spin.

12.2.1 Covering the "Horse Race"

The media have long been criticized for covering campaigns much as they would a horse race (i.e., who is ahead and who is behind). Some critics argue that reporters often neglect candidates' positions on substantive policy issues in favor of stories about how much money candidates are raising, their stable of consultants, campaign strategies, tactics, and personalities. The criticism is not entirely fair because many media outlets devote a lot of political coverage to substantive issues as well. But the "horse race" is never far from view.

Political polls of candidate matchups at different stages of a campaign have become a staple of media coverage and may be increasing in frequency. The results of an internal campaign poll sometimes are released to reporters if the poll makes a candidate look strong or an opponent appear weak. The media, partisan organizations, and independent groups regularly conduct other polls as well. Although some of these surveys also attempt to measure public opinion on selected issues, their primary focus is on who is winning and who is losing.

12.2.2 Television and Digital Advertising

Most candidates for major offices plan their daily campaign appearances with television newscasts in mind. They participate in activities, such as visits to schools or high-tech plants, which look good in a thirty-second news segment as the candidate discusses an education or jobs-creation proposal. Unfortunately for the viewers, such superficial coverage does not even begin to shed light on the complex issues in a race or the candidate's positions on them. Neither does a candidate's paid television advertising.

The tone of a candidate's advertising can change significantly during a campaign. Initially, he or she likely will run a positive, "feel-good" spot with positive biographical information, attempting to introduce the candidate to the voters in the best possible light. It may portray the candidate playing with children, visiting a hospital, or shaking hands with the president of the United States, if the president is a member of the same political party. Later in the campaign, particularly if a candidate is behind in the polls, he or she may air negative, "attack" advertisements, charging an opponent with weaknesses or indiscretions unworthy of the public trust or deliberately misrepresenting the opponent's record or position on an issue. News organizations often review the ads, rating them for accuracy or fairness.

There is little government regulation of the accuracy of political advertising. Texas law puts some limited restrictions on political ads, but neither state nor federal regulations are strong enough to protect voters from flagrantly false information in political ads, either on television or online, which also has become a major political advertising platform. Facebook was widely criticized for allowing disinformation in political ads that it carried during the 2016 presidential campaign, and early in 2020 it announced that it would not ban political ads during that year's presidential race either, wouldn't check them for falsehoods or limit how the ads could be targeted to specific groups. Twitter said it would ban political ads, and Google said it would limit how the ads were targeted. Facebook did remove from its platform in 2020 the Trump campaign ads that suggested that antifa, a loose anti-fascist coalition, was behind violence that broke out during some of the demonstrations against racial injustice that spring.

Although there was little evidence that antifa was involved in any coordinated actions during the protests, questions about truthfulness were not behind Facebook's removal of the ads. Facebook removed the ads because they violated a company policy against posting hateful symbols. The ads prominently featured a large red triangle, a symbol used by Nazis to mark political prisoners during World War II.[22]

Over the past forty years or so, television has allowed wealthy or well-financed candidates, to try, in effect, to "buy" elections in Texas. Multimillionaire Bill Clements, who had never held elective office and was a stranger to most Texans, spent millions of dollars of his own fortune on television advertisements in 1978 to become the first Republican to capture the governor's office in modern times. In 1990, Clayton Williams, another wealthy businessman and political neophyte, spent more than $21 million, including $8.4 million from his own pocket, to create an attractive public image that won him the Republican nomination for governor before he lost a close race to Democrat Ann Richards. Laredo businessman Tony Sanchez, a Democrat making his first statewide race, spent $56.7 million of his own fortune on a 2002 gubernatorial campaign, only to lose to Republican Rick Perry.

Nationwide, objective television coverage of political campaigns has given way more and more to paid commercials, soft news, and "talking-head" commentary with distinct political viewpoints, particularly on some cable TV channels. Many opinion leaders fear the trend is further destroying Americans' interest in politics and have urged the major television networks to voluntarily give free airtime to presidential candidates. "Politics isn't going very well on television these days. . . . Campaigns unfold on all commercial television as a bread-and-circus blur of thirty-second attack ads and eight-second sound bites. Citizens feel cheated. They grow cynical," wrote the late *CBS News* anchor Walter Cronkite.[23] Cronkite wrote this two decades ago, but the problem he addressed is still with us, and it has been compounded by candidate Tweets, campaign posts, and other online chatter.

Slightly more than $1.82 billion was spent on paid television advertising in the presidential and other federal races in the 2015–2016 election cycle, according to research by the Wesleyan Media Project, which was less than that spent in 2012 (which is odd). The $1.82 billion covered more than a million broadcast and national cable ads for the presidential candidates concentrated in a relatively small number of so-called "battleground" states, where the results of the presidential race weren't a foregone conclusion. Few, if any, presidential ads aired in Texas because Republican nominee Donald Trump was expected to easily carry the Lone Star State, which he did.[24] Normally, spending on advertising increases each election cycle, so having less spent in 2016 than 2012 was odd. More than $891 million had been spent on television advertising in all races for federal offices in the 2019-2020 election cycle by early April 2020, but spending slowed considerably when the coronavirus pandemic struck in the early spring, about the same time that Joe Biden all but clinched the Democratic nomination for president. More than $751 million of the federal-race spending was on the presidential race, in which more than a dozen candidates initially contended for the Democratic nomination, including billionaire Michael Bloomberg, who alone spent more than $500 million, much of it on TV advertising. Bloomberg dropped out after badly losing in Texas and other Super Tuesday states. According to the Wesleyan Media Project, an additional $185 million was spent on Facebook ads and $132 million on Google ads in the presidential race between January 2019 and early April 2020.[25]

12.2.3 Media Coverage of Recent Statewide Races in Texas

Each gubernatorial campaign, at least in recent memory, has been marked by controversy. Each has had its highs and lows—for the media as well as for the candidates and the voters. A few recent elections strongly illustrated the role of independent news media as well as paid advertising in the process of influencing voters in an often-confusing array of candidate claims and counterclaims.

2014: STRONG DIFFERENCES Early on, the 2014 gubernatorial race between Republican Greg Abbott and Democrat Wendy Davis promised to be extremely contentious. The two candidates offered widely different stands on major policy issues and presented sharply contrasting styles. Davis, a state senator from Fort Worth, had launched her campaign for governor after receiving national publicity for filibustering against a controversial abortion regulation law. Abbott, wheelchair-bound since an accident as a young man, was the long-time state attorney general and a conservative stalwart. The blogosphere was hyperactive, but arguably the first significant story of the race was broken by one of the Capitol's most veteran newspaper reporters, Wayne Slater, for one of the state's most established newspapers, *The Dallas Morning News*.

In January, more than nine months before the November election, Slater broke a story pointing out that Davis had been misstating some facts in a compelling life story narrative that had become an important piece of her early campaign. Emphasizing hard work and determination, Davis had often touted her successful rise from being a teen-aged, divorced mother living in a trailer to becoming a successful graduate of Harvard Law School. Her campaign hoped to use the story to inspire more women, minorities, and young people to help Davis break the long Republican hold on the governor's office. Through careful reporting, Slater discovered that Davis had misstated her age when she was divorced and neglected to mention that much of her higher education was paid for by her former husband. Much of the basic rags-to-riches narrative remained intact, but the story brought Davis's credibility into question. Davis acknowledged that she needed to be more careful with details. "My language should be tighter," she told Slater. "I'm learning about using broader, looser language. I need to be more focused on the detail."[26]

Slater's story had an impact, both in Texas and nationally, at least during the early stage of the gubernatorial race. The story noted that during part of the time that Davis was attending Harvard Law School, her two daughters lived in Fort Worth with her husband. It also reported that after the couple divorced several years later, the younger daughter lived with her father and Davis was ordered to pay child support. All this led to an email and social media campaign, which seemed to have been at least partially organized, in which detractors repeatedly accused Davis of "abandoning" her children. The Davis campaign responded by publicly releasing personal letters in which both daughters detailed their mother's active involvement in their lives and strongly denied the abandonment allegations. Wendy Davis said both parents had been awarded joint custody, and she accused Republicans of distorting her life story.

The dispute also raised the issue of whether political figures' family relationships are treated differently by the media based on a candidate's gender and whether Davis was singled out because she was a woman. Anna Greenberg, a Democratic pollster who had once worked for Davis, pointed out to *The New York Times* that former White House Chief of Staff Rahm Emanuel had left his family behind in Washington so his children could finish school when he moved to Chicago to campaign successfully for mayor. "And nobody ever said a thing about it," Greenberg said. "Think about the number of women who put their husbands through school, and the wife is the self-sacrificing role model."[27]

In a blog post defending Slater's story, George Rodrigue, managing editor of *The Dallas Morning News*, acknowledged that sometimes journalists, readers, or voters may apply a double standard to the biographies of male and female politicians.[28] "But, not, I think, as pertains to our pursuit of this story," he wrote. "Austin correspondent Wayne Slater was applying the same standard we often use for politicians: How do their claims compare with reality?"[29]

About two months after the controversy over Davis's background erupted, Abbott was asked in an interview on WFAA-TV in Dallas if he, like Governor Perry, would have vetoed a bill that Davis had sponsored in 2013 to make it easier for women to file lawsuits over pay discrimination. Abbott said he supported equal pay for women but declined to say whether he would have vetoed the bill. Davis seized on Abbott's failure to clarify his position on Perry's veto by attacking him over the equal pay issue in a state where women are paid on average about 80 cents for every $1 that men earn. Perry said he vetoed the bill because a federal law on equal pay made a state law unnecessary, but Davis and supporters of her bill said a state law would give women quicker access to justice through state courts. The debate intensified a couple of weeks later when reporter Peggy Fikac wrote in the *San Antonio Express-News* that female assistant attorneys general in Abbott's state office were paid less on average than men in the same job classifications.[30] Davis traveled around the state, continuing to challenge Abbott on the issue, and Democratic supporters sent hundreds of emails to the news media in a well-orchestrated campaign.

2010: PERRY IS UNTOUCHABLE One reason Governor Rick Perry stumbled so badly during his brief campaign for the 2012 Republican presidential nomination was that he was unprepared for the tough, high-stakes competition of a national campaign and the intense media spotlight. Texas reporters had aggressively covered the governor. But Perry had lived a mostly charmed life in Texas politics. He was a Republican governor in a state where Republicans had won all statewide elections since 1996; his conservative ideology appealed to the conservative voters who dominated Texas's Republican primary; he was a strong fund-raiser; he was an aggressive campaigner (at least in Texas); and his reelection opposition had mostly wilted.

In Perry's last reelection race in 2010, U.S. Senator Kay Bailey Hutchison challenged him in the Republican primary, but Perry never gave her a chance. Perry repeatedly attacked the senator for being a Washington "insider"—a bad word in the Republican primary—and Hutchison never recovered. Throughout the campaign year, Texas reporters wrote about Texas's lackluster record on such critical issues as education and health care funding during Perry's administration and questioned whether some of Perry's major financial backers were getting special treatment from the governor's office. But Perry barged ahead, sending Twitter feeds to supporters; bragging about Texas's job creation record under his watch; and blaming Washington, particularly President Obama, for most of the country's problems. Either out of disdain for the Texas media or simply because he felt the exercise would be a waste of time, he took the unusual step of boycotting all meetings with newspaper editorial boards. Breaking with another political tradition, he refused to debate his Democratic opponent, former Houston Mayor Bill White. Perhaps it was no accident that Perry, a year later, found himself stumbling through Republican presidential debates. He was out of practice.

All of the state's major newspapers endorsed White in the general election, but Perry defeated White by more than 12 percentage points.

2002: CAMPAIGNING IN THE MUD Perry's toughest election campaign as governor was in 2002, and it included some of the worst aspects of contemporary political campaigning. The race between Perry and Democratic challenger Tony Sanchez, a multimillionaire businessman from Laredo who spent about $56.7 million of his own money on his unsuccessful race, was characterized by **negative television ads** and personal attacks by the candidates on each other's integrity.

The news media's performance in covering the 2002 campaign was thorough. Voters who followed the campaign through the state's major daily newspapers were given more than enough information to compare the candidates' qualifications and personalities and evaluate their proposed solutions, or lack thereof, to the state's major problems. But many voters never got past the paid TV commercials, and Perry's became vicious.

In one series of commercials the Perry campaign attacked Sanchez over his previous ownership of Tesoro Savings & Loan, a financial institution in Laredo that had failed during the recession of the 1980s. In his advertising and campaign statements,

negative television ad
A television commercial in which a political candidate attacks an opponent, sometimes over a legitimate issue, but more often over an alleged flaw in the opponent's character or ability to hold office. Many such ads are deliberately misleading or outright false.

Perry repeatedly attacked Sanchez over $25 million in drug money that had been laundered through Tesoro, though no one was charged with a crime. Sanchez and other former Tesoro officials said they had not known the money belonged to drug dealers. One particularly brutal commercial featured two former Drug Enforcement Agency (DEA) agents blaming the drug lords who had laundered the money through Tesoro for the torture and slaying of a DEA agent. Sanchez called the attack sleazy, and some of his supporters said it was racist.

Perry's Tesoro ads ensured the Republican governor's election, said University of Houston political scientist Richard Murray. He said the ads were influential because Sanchez had never held elective office and many voters already were uncertain of his abilities.[31]

12.2.4 The 2012 and 2018 U.S. Senate Races: Grass Roots and "Betomania"

Republican U.S. Senator Kay Bailey Hutchison's decision not to seek reelection in 2012, after twenty years in the office, set off a scramble among Republicans eager to climb the political ladder. Nine candidates filed for the office in the Republican primary, but only three were perceived to be viable candidates—David Dewhurst, the state's lieutenant governor; Ted Cruz, a former state solicitor general who had never run for elective office; and Tom Leppert, a former mayor of Dallas. Dewhurst, a multi-millionaire who had won the lieutenant governor's office three times and, before that, a statewide race for land commissioner, was the strong, early favorite. He had deep pockets, strong fund-raising ability, was well known among Republican primary voters, and had helped push conservative Republican priorities through the legislature. Dewhurst ran a strong media campaign, counting on his advertising, name identification, and endorsements from other establishment Republicans to carry him to the GOP nomination and, effectively, the Senate seat in a state where Republicans dominated statewide elections.

Unable to match Dewhurst's financial firepower, Cruz waged an aggressive grassroots campaign, appealing to members of the Tea Party movement and other conservative groups as an "outsider" who would shake up a government that they disliked. A fiery speaker, Cruz was much more comfortable than the more reserved Dewhurst in meeting with neighborhood groups, participating in candidate forums, and building relationships among conservative activists. And he did so tirelessly, earning support, building name identification, and mobilizing an effective ground campaign among conservative voters. Cruz also relied heavily on social media, organizing a "virtual campaign" through the Internet. In addition, he eagerly took combative stances, attacking President Obama and the federal government over health care, immigration, and other issues that were lightning rods for conservative Texas Republicans. His fiery rhetoric and campaign energy attracted significant coverage from newspaper and television reporters. Dewhurst led all candidates in the Republican primary with 44.6 percent of the votes, but Cruz won 34.2 percent, enough for second place and a runoff spot.

Cruz continued his grassroots strategy during the runoff campaign, although he began to receive significant financial contributions from Tea Party and other conservative organizations. Dewhurst received funding from outside, independent groups as well. Cruz beat Dewhurst, 56.8 percent to 43.2 percent, in a low-turnout Republican runoff and then easily beat Democratic nominee Paul Sadler, a former state legislator, in the general election to become the first Hispanic elected to the U.S. Senate from Texas.

According to the Federal Election Commission, the race for the Republican nomination for the Senate seat—including spending by outside, independent groups—cost more than $60 million, making it the most expensive nonpresidential race in the country that year. The Cruz and Dewhurst campaigns combined spent more than

$32 million, with more than $24 million coming from Dewhurst, who dug deeply into his own personal wealth.[32]

Cruz benefited from the outside contributions and television advertising during the runoff campaign. But without his effective grassroots campaigning during the early months of the race, he likely would never have won enough votes to force a runoff, and Dewhurst might have won the nomination outright in the first primary. It wasn't known at the time, but it was revealed a few years later, during Cruz's 2016 presidential campaign, that his grassroots Senate campaign had been financed initially with about $1 million in loans from two major financial institutions, Goldman Sachs and Citibank.[33]

Cruz was challenged for reelection in 2018 by Beto O'Rourke, a Democratic congressman who wasn't well known outside his home city of El Paso, but who waged a tireless grassroots campaign, much like Cruz six years earlier. This time, Cruz was much better known because of his incumbency and his unsuccessful 2016 presidential race, and O'Rourke was a Democrat running for statewide office in a state that had not elected a Democrat to statewide office in more than twenty years. O'Rourke was the underdog, and he campaigned like an underdog. He visited all 254 Texas counties, including some that may never have been visited by a candidate for statewide office, and he was an effective fund-raiser, raising $80 million to Cruz's $37 million. O'Rourke rejected donations from political action committees and raised all his campaign money from individual donors, many of whom contributed via ActBlue, an online portal used by Democratic donors across the country. O'Rourke also was an early leader in political advertising on social media, spending about $8 million on Facebook and another $2 million on Google.[34]

Cruz was very unpopular among Democratic voters but remained very popular among Republicans, including the conservatives who had helped sweep him into office in 2012. President Trump came to Texas to campaign for Cruz, his former political opponent, in the nationally watched race, and Cruz was reelected by a 2.6 percent margin. But O'Rourke's enthusiasm and fund-raising helped inspire a larger-than-normal turnout—a so-called "Betomania"—among Democratic voters, who unseated twelve incumbent Republican members of the Texas House of Representatives and two incumbent Republican state senators. A few months later, O'Rourke tried to ride the enthusiasm into a national campaign and entered the race for the 2020 Democratic presidential nomination, but he made little headway in a large field of candidates before leaving the race.

The Early Development of the Media in Texas

12.3 Trace the early development of the news media in Texas.

The dissemination of news and information in Texas has come a long way from the days of the frontier, and the journey has not always been easy. To see how far we have come, let us first look at where Texas political journalism began. The basic purposes have always been the same—to inform people, help them navigate the politics of their era, and influence the way they think about government.

12.3.1 Frontier Newspapers

Frontier Texans, isolated in their farmhouses and small settlements, lacked many creature comforts, but most had the opportunity to keep informed about the political sentiment of the day. The short-lived *Graceta de Tejas*, or *Texas Gazette*, was established in Nacogdoches in 1812, long before Texas won its independence in 1836.[35] By 1860, according to historian T. R. Fehrenbach, there were seventy-one daily and weekly newspapers in Texas, with a total circulation of about 100,000: "Ninety-five percent of the white population could read and write and some publication reached virtually every family."[36] Like other early American newspapers, these publications often were highly partisan and primarily devoted to commentary on public issues—the local, state, and national political events of that turbulent period. Social calendars and stories about floods, fires, murders, and other everyday disasters were not yet standard journalistic fare. Editorial writing, however, had already developed into a backwoods art form: "This writing was often irate, biased, and misinformed—but much of it was clear and sound. It kept the freeholders of Texas fully aware of events; many farmers could quote Senator Stephen Douglas or Sam Houston at length. Texans were already keen political animals."[37]

12.3.2 Newspapers and "The Establishment"

Throughout much of the twentieth century, Texas's major newspapers were active members of the conservative, big-business, big-oil establishment that ran the state Capitol and the state. During the pre-television years of the 1940s and 1950s, in particular, some newspaper publishers, such as Amon Carter in Fort Worth and Jesse Jones in Houston, were oilmen and financiers who helped control local and state politics for the dominant conservative wing of the Texas Democratic Party. Another strong voice for the establishment was *The Dallas Morning News*, a tireless anticommunist, antilabor, antiliberal crusader. At various times, the *Morning News* editorialized that "the presidency of Franklin Roosevelt was actually destructive of the Republic, the Senate's censure of Joe McCarthy [was] 'a happy day for Communists,' and the Supreme Court [was] 'a threat to state sovereignty second only to Communism itself.'"[38] There was little pretense of detached, neutral reporting, as the newspapers actively participated in the political process.

12.3.3 The Evolution of Texas Newspapers

News coverage began to change significantly in the 1970s and 1980s, which were turning points for many Texas newspapers. Many changed owners during this period, and the overall quality of Texas journalism began to improve noticeably. The most dramatic and influential change occurred in Dallas, and it was brought about by the brief entry of the Times Mirror Company, then one of the nation's media giants, into the Dallas newspaper market.

Times Mirror, then publisher of the *Los Angeles Times*, one of the country's most respected newspapers, purchased the *Dallas Times Herald* from local owners in 1970. Within a few years, it precipitated a major newspaper war with its dominant competitor, *The Dallas Morning News*. Times Mirror brought in new editors, recruited reporters from all over the country, improved the quality and aggressiveness of its news coverage, and awakened the *Morning News* from what many media watchers had considered a long, provincial slumber. At one point, the *Times Herald* briefly passed the *Morning News* in Sunday circulation. But the *Morning News* responded by bringing in new editors, expanding its news staff, and vastly improving its product. During this period, both newspapers became major national award winners.

During a serious decline in the Texas economy in the 1980s, however, the *Times Herald* began to lose money and was still second in advertising and circulation. The paper was sold in 1986 to a Texan, who was unable to reverse its financial position. It changed hands one more time before the *Morning News* purchased the

A HISTORIC NEWSMAKER
Houston financier Frank Sharp, shown here at left in 1971, was a major figure in the Sharpstown stock fraud scandal that rocked state government and was a major news story in the 1970s.

struggling property and closed it in 1991. Nevertheless, the higher journalistic standards that emerged in Dallas during that period had positive effects on some of the state's other newspapers, which soon began undergoing transformations of their own.

The traditional media of today—newspapers and most broadcast television stations—are much more disposed to covering issues that affect lower-income people, minorities, and others struggling against the power structure. Still, Texas is largely a conservative state, and a resurging business community remains influential in setting state policy. But traditional media outlets are much more eager to challenge the political and business establishment today than they were in the mid-twentieth century.

For one reason, there is a high level of distrust of government now. A turning point in Texas was the Sharpstown stock fraud scandal that broke in 1971 (see Chapter 5). It revealed that the legislature had given quick passage in 1969 to two banking regulation bills sought by Houston financier Frank Sharp and that high-ranking state officials had profited from insurance stock purchases financed with loans from Sharp's bank. That was soon to be followed by the Watergate scandal, which would force the resignation of President Richard Nixon and shake public confidence in government throughout the country, much as the bitter experience of the Vietnam War already had begun to do. More recently, the economic devastation caused by questionable, high-risk practices in the financial industry—and what many people considered a weak response from government—further heightened public distrust of those in power.

The ethical behavior of officeholders and their relationships to the special interests that spend millions of dollars trying to influence government came under closer scrutiny after the Sharpstown and Watergate scandals. Today's news reporters more readily question the motives of the governor, legislators, and other public officeholders and political candidates. The media also have reexamined their own ethics. Most traditional news organizations have adopted policies prohibiting their reporters from accepting free airplane rides, junkets, and other "freebies" from state officials or candidates, practices that had been fairly common in Texas in the past.

Another significant factor in the evolution of the Texas press was the change in management that occurred due to the passing of the high-profile publishers who had been part of the conservative establishment. Many of their newspapers were subsequently sold to large national conglomerates with newspapers and broadcast holdings in many cities. Purchases of major, once independently owned newspapers such as the *Houston Chronicle*, the *Fort Worth Star-Telegram*, and the *Austin American-Statesman* were part of a consolidation of media ownership across the country, a development regarded as unhealthy by many within and outside of the industry.

This consolidation of media ownership raised concerns that national owners, who had no personal ties to the local communities, would be more concerned about profits and losses than the quality of news coverage or diversity of editorial viewpoints in their local outlets. Such concerns have been renewed, and in some cases validated, in the wake of more-recent corporate mergers, downsizing of newspaper staffs, and newspaper closures.

Perhaps paradoxically, national ownership can offer newspapers a greater degree of independence than that available in the past. Absentee corporate owners do not have sacred cows to protect in the Texas Capitol, local courthouse, or city hall, and do not feel compelled to defend old provincial prejudices. Texas newspapers, for the most part, have maintained considerable **editorial autonomy** under national owners. But the potential value of more editorial autonomy is compromised when faraway corporate owners lay off reporters and editors in order to please investors who are less interested in journalism than they are profits.

The Dallas Morning News is the only major metropolitan newspaper in the state still owned by a Texas-based corporation. It still aggressively covers governmental and political institutions on its news pages and its website. Nevertheless, the

editorial autonomy
The freedom of a local newspaper or television station to set its own news policies independently of absentee owners who may run a chain of media outlets throughout the country.

journalistic improvements that have taken place in Texas since the 1970s and 1980s have been significantly affected by the financial decline in the newspaper industry and cutbacks in reporting and editing staffs.

Current News Media Trends

12.4 Describe the impact of the Internet and other digital information sources on traditional media outlets and news consumers, and how newspapers and television news departments have adjusted to the changes.

The newspaper was the primary source of information for Texans and other Americans for many years preceding the television and Internet eras. The newspaper industry has made many changes throughout its history to meet a never-ending stream of societal, readership, and technological changes. But today, with an explosion of information sources, the traditional print newspaper is fighting for its very survival, in Texas as well as in other states. Television and radio news outlets also are making significant changes, and more are likely on the way. Increasingly, Americans, especially young people, are relying on digital sources, including cell phones, tablets, and other mobile devices, for their news. The percentage of Americans relying on traditional media—newspapers, television, and radio—continues to decline. Prior to the 1990s, television was the dominant mechanism by which people learned about news. That began to change in the mid-1990s, when people became less reliant on television for political information. The most dramatic change, though, is the decline in the number of people who relied on traditional newspapers for news. In 1991, 56 percent of people stated they read a newspaper for news; however, by 2013, that number dropped to 28 percent. In 2018, the share of adults who said they often got news from social media (20 percent) surpassed the share who chose print newspapers (16 percent) for the first time, according to the Pew Research Center. The changes in consumption patterns are likely to continue, as more sources of information become available (see Figure 12–1).[39]

FIGURE 12-1 CHANGES IN NEWS CONSUMPTION FROM 2016 TO 2018

An ongoing trend in news consumption is to rely more heavily upon news website and social media stories (many of which come from traditional news outlets like *The New York Times* and *The Washington Post*, Fox News, or CNN) and less heavily upon traditional news sources like network news, local papers, and the radio. Pictured here are the percentages of Americans who *often* got news from each news platform in 2016 versus 2018.

SOURCE: Data from A.W. Geiger, "Key Findings About the Online News Landscape in America," Pew Research Center, September 11, 2019, https://www.pewresearch.org/fact-tank/2019/09/11/key-findings-about-the-online-news-landscape-in-america/.

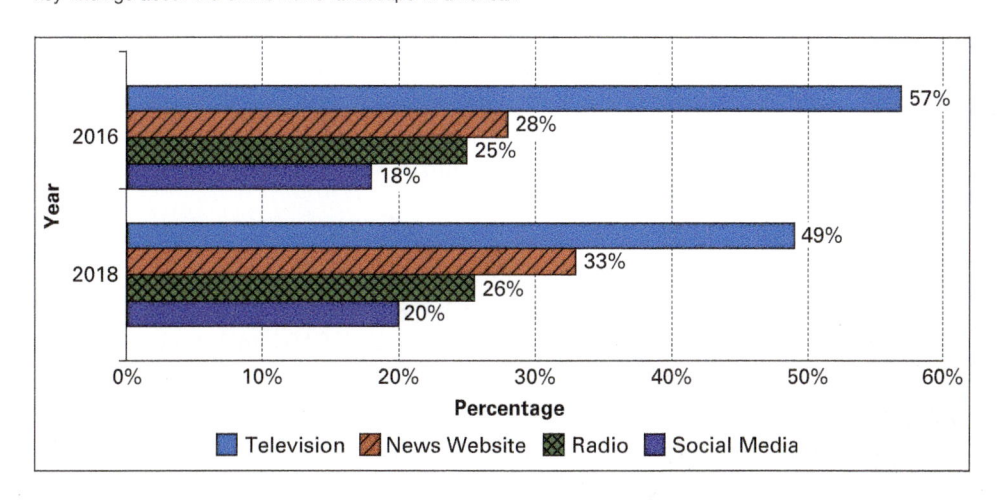

Year	Television	News Website	Radio	Social Media
2016	57%	28%	25%	18%
2018	49%	33%	26%	20%

The digital world of instantaneous communications has not come without a price. As the number of traditional news reporters dwindles, the media screen that filters fact from opinion and objectivity from subjectivity is increasingly compromised, and the media's watchdog role is weakened. Consequently, some news consumers may find their journey through government and politics more difficult to maneuver with confidence. We provide some suggestions about how to become more media literate later in Section 12.5.

12.4.1 Modern Newspapers, Modern Problems

Hundreds of newspapers in the United States have ceased publication since 1900, a reflection of declining circulation and advertising, corporate consolidations, the emergence of television, the proliferation of radio stations with targeted audiences, the development of specialized magazines, and, most recently, the development of the Internet as a major information and advertising source. The folding of the *Dallas Times Herald* was followed by the closing of the *San Antonio Light* in 1993, the *Houston Post* in 1995, and the *El Paso Herald-Post* in 1997, leaving all of the large cities in Texas with only one traditional daily newspaper each.

As of 2014, according to the Texas Press Association, Texas had 76 daily newspapers and 399 paid-circulation weeklies and semi-weeklies.[40] The surviving newspapers continue to take cost-cutting steps, including staff reductions, to stay afloat in the face of declining circulation and advertising revenue for their print editions. In 2015, the *Austin American-Statesman* stopped using its own presses for print editions to save production costs. The paper signed a seven-year contract with Hearst Newspapers to print the *American-Statesman* at Hearst's newspaper plants in San Antonio and Houston. The change trimmed 100 jobs at the *American-Statesman*, and the remote printing required earlier news deadlines, which meant many sports events and other late-breaking news stories were left out of the print paper and reported only on the paper's website, much to the unhappiness of many subscribers.[41] In 2018, Atlanta-based Cox Enterprises, which had owned the *American-Statesman* for more than forty years, announced it was selling the paper to New York-based GateHouse Media for $47.5 million. GateHouse owned 130 newspapers across the country, including the *Amarillo Globe-News*, the *Lubbock Avalanche-Journal*, and *Sherman Herald Democrat* in Texas. In 2019, New Media Investment Group, a holding company that controls GateHouse Media, announced it was purchasing the Gannett newspaper chain, which owns *USA Today* and many local newspapers throughout the country, including the *Corpus Christi Caller-Times*, *El Paso Times*, and *San Angelo Standard-Times* in Texas. The $1.4 billion transaction would create a mega-newspaper chain, to be called Gannett, owning more than 260 daily newspapers and more than 300 weekly publications in the United States and Guam with a combined circulation of more than 8 million. The companies, which have histories of laying off journalists, said the merger could save them as much as $300 million a year. New Media, the holding company announcing the merger, is managed by an affiliate of Fortress Investment Group of New York. Fortress is owned by a Japanese conglomerate, SoftBank.[42]

Many small-town weekly newspapers are oriented primarily to their local communities and carry little news of state government or politics, but many of the small towns served by weeklies also are in the circulation areas of daily newspapers. There are also a number of African American–oriented and Spanish-language papers in Texas, but they have limited circulations. The demise of major daily newspapers has raised the profiles of aggressive, alternative weeklies in some Texas cities. Two of the better known are the *Houston Press* and the *Dallas Observer*. Statewide, the *Texas Observer*, a favorite of Texas liberals for more than fifty years, continues to publish.

THE DALLAS MORNING NEWS

The Dallas Morning News remains a major source of news about Texas government and political institutions, despite financial setbacks that have beset the industry and prompted reductions in staff.

Newspapers now have their own websites, which are updated with breaking news stories throughout the day. Some newspapers also post staff-produced audio reports, or podcasts, as well as video reports on their websites. They post blogs by staff reporters on politics, sports, and a variety of other subjects. The Internet makes a newspaper's stories easily accessible to a national, or even international, audience well beyond its local or regional print circulation.[43] Most newspapers initially made their online content available to readers free of charge, but most newspapers now charge for access. Newspapers sell advertising on their websites, but that revenue has not replaced the once-lucrative print advertising the papers have lost to online competitors.

The Texas Tribune, a nonpartisan, nonprofit, online news source, opened a new chapter in Texas journalism when it made its debut on November 3, 2009. Whether it represents the future of daily journalism remains to be seen, but eleven years later, it was still in business. Cofounded by Austin venture capitalist John Thornton and journalists Evan Smith and Ross Ramsey, *The Tribune* announced an ambitious goal—"to serve the journalism community as a source of innovation and to build the next great public media brand in the United States."

Devoting itself primarily to coverage of Texas government and politics, it publishes news articles online and supplements those with explanatory features and interactive databases, which readers can peruse for information about political contributions, government employee salaries, public expenditures for their local school districts, and a variety of other facts and figures. It also posts video stories and podcast discussions of political news and views and streams interviews with government and political figures and news events live. *The Tribune* provides its content free to newspapers and television and radio stations throughout Texas and nationally in partnership with *The Washington Post*.

The Tribune's reporting staff includes several former reporters from other Texas news organizations. Smith, the CEO, is a former editor of *Texas Monthly* magazine, and Ramsey, the executive editor, is a longtime Austin-based reporter. As a nonprofit organization, *The Tribune* supports itself through tax-exempt donations from individuals, foundations, and corporations; ticket sales to sponsored events; and income from advertising sales.

To try to answer critics who may suspect *The Tribune's* coverage of being affected by sponsors or donors, each *Tribune* story includes an explanatory paragraph at the end, listing any major contributors who are featured or quoted in the article and a link to the paper's full list of contributors. "Those who contribute to *The Tribune* do so with the understanding that we are only beholden to great journalism," the newspaper's code of ethics reads, in part. "Our fundraisers inform all potential donors—individuals, foundations, corporate sponsors, underwriters—that their contributions to *The Tribune* do not entitle them to preferential treatment or to relationships with newsroom staff, and in no way protect them from investigations or scrutiny."

Another nonprofit and nonpartisan online news source, specializing in news about San Antonio, is the *San Antonio Report,* formerly known as the *Rivard Report*. It was founded by Robert Rivard, former editor of the *San Antonio Express-News*, and his wife, Monika Maeckle, a publishing executive, as a community blog in February 2012; it was reorganized as a nonprofit in 2015. Calling itself "San Antonio's leading online local news service," it publishes content from a staff of journalists as well as news and opinion contributions from freelancers, elected officials, and other community members. Access to its content is free. The *San Antonio Report* is supported by individual and business memberships, paid advertising, and philanthropic and foundation funding.

12.4.2 Electronic Media

Television and the emergence of the Internet have had major impacts on the role of the media in government and politics. An estimated 98 percent of American homes have at least one television set, most are linked to cable television systems, and broadband

MEDIA COVERING A TRUMP RALLY

A Trump supporter is stopped after entering the news media area at a rally held by President Trump in El Paso.

connection to the Internet is widely accessible across most of the country (and most areas of the globe). Television long ago replaced the newspaper as the public's primary source of news, but, as noted earlier, it now has to fight with online sources for the public's attention.

Texas has about 150 television stations in about twenty-three markets, ranging in size from Dallas–Fort Worth and Houston, which rank among the largest markets in the country, to numerous small cities. Not every TV station provides news, but some cable stations now are offering full-time news coverage. The first was established in Austin in 1999 by Time Warner Cable, renamed Spectrum after an ownership change. Political news coverage by Texas TV stations is not dominated by the partisan and political bickering and hyperbole that mark the talking-head lineups on some national cable networks, but television coverage of state government and politics in Texas has become less robust in recent years, even in the larger cities. Austin TV stations regularly cover events at the state Capitol, but no TV station from outside Austin has a full-time Capitol bureau. Stations sometimes send news crews to Austin for special events, such as a gubernatorial inauguration or the opening day of a legislative session, but their overall coverage is inconsistent.

On a national scale, the spoofing of political figures and journalists by television comedians, which former TV host Jon Stewart helped pioneer, entertains millions of Americans, but viewers are mainly political liberals, and the satire results in little, if any, political change, some observers believe. Writing in *The Atlantic*, Adam Felder explained that an audience's attention to an issue raised by John Oliver or another comedian in one show usually dies down quickly after that show airs, and attention is soon focused, briefly, on another show and another issue. This tendency, he wrote, "Explains why late-night comedy rarely causes policy change—it undoes its own work the moment the next segment airs." And he added, "Interest isn't the same thing as action, which itself is a far cry from political change."[44]

12.4.3 Growing Media Conglomerates

Several newspapers and broadcast outlets in Texas are owned by large corporate conglomerates, as are major media properties elsewhere. The New York–based Hearst Corporation owns six daily newspapers in Texas, including the *Houston Chronicle* and the *San Antonio Express-News*, as well as other newspapers and television stations throughout the country. Hearst also publishes more than 300 magazines in the United States and around the world, including *Cosmopolitan, ELLE, Men's Health*, and *Car and Driver*. It has a 20 percent ownership interest in ESPN, the sports network, whose major owner is ABC, Inc., an indirect subsidiary of The Walt Disney Company, owner of theme parks and other entertainment ventures. Hearst's newspapers in Texas have separate staffs and facilities, but in recent years they have reduced their staffs and begun sharing stories and editing functions to save money. As noted earlier in this chapter, the *Austin American-Statesman* and several other daily Texas newspapers are now part of a new and enlarged Gannett newspaper chain.

The only major Texas newspaper still owned by a Texas-based company is *The Dallas Morning News*, which is owned by the A. H. Belo Corporation. This company should not be confused with Belo Corporation, a separate company that owned television stations in Dallas, Houston, San Antonio, Austin, and several cities in other states and was itself purchased by media giant Gannett in 2013. San Antonio–based iHeartMedia (formerly Clear Channel Communications) owns several hundred radio stations around the country.

The large conglomerates that own major television networks, which provide national political news to millions of Texas households, also own newspapers, movie distribution companies, theme parks, and other ventures. In addition to ABC's ownership by The Walt Disney Company, the NBC television network is part of NBCUniversal, which is owned by cable giant Comcast. The company also includes, among other entities, Universal Pictures, Universal theme parks, and Fandango, the online source of movie reviews and tickets. Two media giants, CBS Corporation and Viacom, merged in 2019 to form ViacomCBS, which includes, among many companies, the CBS television empire, the Paramount movie studio, the Showtime cable channel, Nickelodeon, and Simon & Schuster, the publishing company. Another large media conglomerate, Rupert Murdoch's News Corporation, owns several newspapers in Great Britain and Australia as well as *The Wall Street Journal* and the *New York Post* in the United States. A sister company, Fox Corporation, owns Fox News and the Fox broadcasting network.

These are only some of the mega-companies that link, at least indirectly, major newspapers and television news divisions to entertainment and other nonjournalistic pursuits. As a result, there has been debate over how much independence news outlets may be losing with these consolidations. "The worry is not that there are fewer media outlets—the opposite is true—but that few people have ultimate control over them," Felicity Barringer wrote in *The New York Times*. "Critics wonder if news judgments will be bent, with executives suppressing news deemed harmful to corporate interests. They wonder if companies will use their journalists to promote their other interests, be they movies, television shows, or sports teams." Media experts interviewed by the newspaper, however, offered different opinions about those potential problems. "Defenders of the news divisions point out that plenty of media outlets would be eager to pick up on a story suppressed by a competitor. Top media executives also know and have argued to their corporate bosses that cheap or compromised journalism costs the enterprise both trust and profits," the newspaper story noted.[45]

The Federal Communications Commission believes that concentration of ownership does not hinder a diversity of voices and thoughts from being aired. But political scientist C. Edwin Baker argued that concentration is harmful to an effective flow of diverse thought. Consequently, he asserted that, at a minimum, mergers should undergo strict governmental scrutiny, and editorial independence post-merger should be protected and assured.[46]

A related issue, which has become a growing concern of some media watchers, is an effort by one company, the Sinclair Broadcast Group, to expand its ownership of

WHERE NEWS MEETS FANTASY

Although best known for Disneyworld and its other entertainment ventures, The Walt Disney Company owns the ABC television network and its news division. This is only one example of corporate ownership that includes both news outlets and a variety of other business interests.

Ian Dagnall/Alamy Stock Photo

local television stations throughout the country. The company received national attention in 2018 when, over one weekend, videos on social media showed a large number of local newscasters across the country reading from the same script to criticize the news industry and express concern about the "troubling trend of irresponsible, one-sided news stories plaguing our country." All of those newscasters worked for TV stations owned by Sinclair and had been instructed to deliver the message. At the time, Sinclair, whose stations often ran commentary favorable to the Trump administration, was trying to purchase Tribune Media for $3.9 billion. If successful, Sinclair could become the owner of more than 200 TV stations across the country, reaching 70 percent of American households. At the time, Federal Communications Commission regulations prohibited companies from owning stations that reached more than 39 percent of households. But the Trump administration had been relaxing restrictions on broadcasters. Critics of Sinclair's attempted expansion feared it would limit the diversity of local news and the diversity of political commentary offered on local newscasts.[47]

In 2018, the Federal Communications Commission refused to approve the merger, and Sinclair and Tribune Media dropped their merger plans. Two years later, the FCC fined Sinclair a record $48 million and closed three separate investigations of the company, including an investigation into whether Sinclair had misrepresented its intentions to divest itself of TV stations in order to comply with the ownership limit.[48]

In addition to concerns over concentration of ownership, some media watchers are concerned that super-wealthy individuals with political and/or business agendas will take advantage of the declining newspaper industry to purchase papers at fire-sale prices and then convert the properties into promotional organs for their own causes, rather than continuing to practice traditional journalism. Two recent high-profile newspaper purchases offer contrasting examples in this area.

Amazon.com founder Jeffrey P. Bezos purchased *The Washington Post*, one of America's premier newspapers, for $250 million in 2013 from the Graham family, which had locally owned the paper for four generations. Signaling that he intended to leave traditional journalists in control, he kept the publisher, Katharine Weymouth, and executive editor, Martin Baron, whom he had inherited from the Graham family, in place, at least initially. Bezos replaced Weymouth with a new publisher about a year later. But, according to *The Post*, he "vowed to continue the newspaper's long history of independent journalism," while he planned to spend most of his time attending to Amazon, headquartered across the country in Seattle.[49]

It was a different story, at least initially, in San Diego, where wealthy developer and hotelier Douglas F. Manchester purchased *The San Diego Union-Tribune* from the Copley family in 2011. Manchester changed the name of the paper to *U-T San Diego* and, according to *The New York Times'* media critic David Carr, changed the paper into "what often seems like a brochure for his various interests," including promotion of his political allies and a new downtown sports stadium and arena.[50] In 2015, Manchester sold the newspaper to the Tribune Publishing Co., owner of the *Los Angeles Times*, which planned to operate both newspapers as separate entities in southern California. Tribune Publishing later spun off its newspaper division into a company that became known as Tronc. Tronc sold the *Los Angeles Times*, the *San Diego Union-Tribune*, and smaller publications to a Los Angeles billionaire health care magnate and former surgeon, Patrick Soon-Shiong, for $500 million in 2018.[51]

12.4.4 The Capitol Press Corps

Most of the state's major newspapers, the Associated Press, and a few other news services and online publications are represented at the Texas State Capitol by reporters who cover state government and politics full time. These full-time reporters, known as the **Capitol press corps**, numbered fifty-three in 2014, the highest number of full-time news people assigned to any statehouse in the country, according to a study by the Pew Research Center (this is the most current data available as this data is not often collected). The lowest number was two in South Dakota, a much less-populous state.[52] The study indicated statehouse bureaus in some states may be making a comeback after major reductions in Capitol staffs, including in Texas, a decade or so earlier, but shortages of experienced reporters were still an issue. The earlier cutbacks were part of the more-general down-sizing by the newspaper and broadcast industries following their financial losses when the Internet emerged as a major competitor for information and advertising. The 2008-2009 recession also was a factor.

The *Fort Worth Star-Telegram* closed its Austin bureau in 2012, and other major Texas newspapers reduced their staffs of Austin reporters about that time, although some staffing has since been restored. The muckraking *Texas Observer* also still publishes in Austin. It devotes a lot of coverage to state government and has a faithful following among Texas liberals. The slick magazine *Texas Monthly* offers Capitol coverage, including an online blog and its ranking of what it considers to be the ten best and ten worst legislators after each regular session. Harvey Kronberg's *Quorum Report*, available to subscribers online, offers a daily compilation of newspaper headlines and alerts of breaking news throughout the day. It also has a small staff of reporters who post stories online about statehouse and political events. As discussed earlier in this chapter, the online *Texas Tribune* devotes much of its coverage to state government and politics.

Nationally, according to the 2014 Pew study, the number of full-time newspaper reporters covering statehouses across the country decreased by 164 between 2003 and 2014, a decline of 35 percent. Some of those newspaper jobs have been replaced at state capitols with digital news organizations, subscriber newsletters targeted to insiders and ideologically based information sources, Pew reported, but the general public may still be underserved. "I think you're seeing fewer stories. The public is not being kept aware of important policy decisions that are

Capitol press corps
Representatives of Texas newspapers, wire services, and other media outlets who are assigned to Austin full time to report on state government and politics.

KEEPING TABS ON THE LEGISLATURE

Members of the Capitol press corps are shown working at the press table (foreground) in the state Senate chamber during a recent session.

spin
The presentation of information in the best possible light for a public official or political candidate. It usually is provided by a press secretary, campaign consultant, or another individual representing the officeholder or candidate.

being made that will affect their daily lives," said Gene Rose, former communications director for the National Conference of State Legislatures.[53]

"The decline of the media's statehouse presence increases the risk of complacency [on the part of public officials]. Without reporters walking the halls, the question of whether something would pass the front-page [or smell] test begins to lose its meaning," Paul W. Taylor observed several years ago in *Governing*.[54] Professor Paul Starr saw another problem. "The concern about statehouse coverage—indeed, about newspaper retrenchment in general—is not just the declining number of reporters, but deterioration in the quality of journalism," he wrote in the *New Republic*. "As the editorial ranks are thinned, internal checks on accuracy are being sacrificed. As reporters with years of experience are laid off, newspapers are losing the local knowledge and relationships with trusted sources that those reporters had built up, which enabled them to break important stories."[55]

Blurring the lines between objective news reporting and political advocacy has increased. During the 2015 legislative session, activists calling themselves "journalists" began secretly recording with hidden cameras the social activities of many legislators and lobbyists away from the Capitol. Then the camera crews started showing up at the Capitol, confronting legislators in hallways and asking questions about their after-hours activities. The group behind the effort, the American Phoenix Foundation, claimed the 800 hours of video it amassed included evidence of illicit or illegal activity on the part of some lawmakers.

The group said its goal was to "transcend traditional media," but legitimate Capitol reporters soon learned that the group's leaders had a history of activist involvement in undercover sting operations against political liberals in other states. That group has since disappeared or moved on, but other publications with political agendas still report on legislative proceedings. As noted at the beginning of this chapter, the *Texas Scorecard*, a publication of the conservative Empower Texans political advocacy group, was granted Senate media credentials for the 2019 session, but its reporters' coverage offered no pretense of objectivity, which is the basic goal of mainstream journalists.

12.4.5 Governmental Public Relations

Most of the state's top elected officials, administrators of major agencies, and legislators spend thousands of tax dollars each year on press secretaries and public relations operations to help disseminate public information and promote themselves, their agencies, their agendas, and their accomplishments. In policy or political disputes, public officials' media specialists often try to put a **spin** on stories to present information in the best possible light for their bosses. Websites and social media accounts, in particular, give governors and other officeholders an excellent opportunity—unfiltered by the media's critical eye—to promote their proposals directly to the public and tout what they claim as their accomplishments.

Most of the Austin-based trade associations and other special interest groups have public relations specialists to promote their causes and keep their members informed of developments at the Capitol. Interest groups are at the center of the policymaking process, and their proposals and efforts to get those proposals enacted are inherently newsworthy. Lobbyists also provide a wealth of insider information to reporters, but journalists must carefully evaluate it because of the large stakes that special interests have in the workings of state government.

On a national scale, which may be reflected in Texas, the number of public relations practitioners has been growing as the number of news reporters has been decreasing, according to at least one study.[56] This development and the growth of digital communications are giving government officials and the corporations and other special interests attempting to influence them more opportunities to bypass the news media's filter and communicate directly with the public, sometimes in campaigns that resemble traditional media reporting. Some television stations have aired video news releases prepared by government or corporate public relations offices with no disclaimers and little or no editing. Viewers who don't know better—and many don't—assume they are watching balanced story packages produced by the TV stations' own reporters, when, in fact, they are seeing advocacy videos.

Additionally, some advocacy groups financed by corporate or other special interests—but disguised with vague or misleading names as citizen grassroots organizations—attempt to influence public opinion with paid advertising, news conferences, websites, social media campaigns, and opinion articles offered to newspapers. They sometimes use these tactics to try to generate so-called citizen campaigns as fronts to promote their own interests, and they attempt to influence legislators with conferences and other lobbying tactics. Charles Koch and the late David Koch, who died in 2019, were wealthy brothers who financed a number of groups to promote their conservative, limited-government goals.

Some see these trends as dangerous. "What we are seeing now is the demise of journalism at the same time we have an increasing level of public relations and propaganda. We are entering a zone that has never been seen before in this country," said Robert McChesney, a communications professor at the University of Illinois and coauthor of *The Death and Life of American Journalism*, which tracked the recent increase in public relations specialists as the number of journalists fell. *ProPublica*, the independent, nonprofit news organization, published a lengthy analysis of the problem in 2011. "The dangers are clear," the article noted. "As PR [public relations] becomes ascendant, private and government interests become more able to generate, filter, distort, and dominate the public debate, and to do so without the public knowing it."[57]

12.4.6 Twitter Nation: The Role of Social Media and "Citizen Journalism"

Beginning in the late 1990s, online news sources (like *Slate* and the *Drudge Report*) first began to become popular. The online news and social media websites, with which we are so familiar today, are relatively new. *The Huffington Post* (a partisan online news aggregator and blog) was founded in 2005, Facebook was created in 2004, and Twitter in 2006. These websites, and others like them, have significantly changed the news environment. Old news sources (like network news programs and newspapers) are struggling to adapt. Most have developed a hybrid combination with both traditional and online delivery, much of which is cross-genre. For example, newspapers are posting "video stories," and television stations are posting longer, written stories. Reporters are increasingly engaged with social media.

Technological developments have sparked significant social changes in the ways people communicate and relate to one another. These changes are profoundly important in the manner in which people consume, process, and use political information and also in how they form social connections. These developments are causing a social revolution, as the planet has become a much smaller place and the changing interpersonal dynamics significantly impact political values, political engagement, and political activism. To demonstrate the potential power of technology, most totalitarian governments limit access to social media (or strictly monitor accounts and postings). When there are any suggestions that discontent is on the rise, governments often crack down on Internet, especially social media, access.

In the United States, we increasingly see groups use social media to organize marches and protests and demand social change. For example, the 2017 Women's March on January 21 (the day after President Trump's inauguration) was primarily organized online, largely through social media. The main march occurred in Washington, D.C., but sister marches were held throughout the nation (and worldwide on every continent) in what is thought to be the largest single-day protest in our history. The Parkland student activists organized March for Our Lives (on March 24, 2018) and started the #NeverAgain movement to protest gun violence. Thousands of students participated in the National School Walkout on April 20, 2018, another event largely organized on social media. The #MeToo movement (created over a decade ago by Tarana Burke to raise awareness of sexual assault and harassment and bring together survivors, especially women of color) gained prominence because of social media and has resulted in many powerful men in Hollywood, politics, academics, and corporate America losing their positions because of abusing women. The TIMES'S UP Legal Defense Fund was created to help survivors bring their harassers to justice. The Black Lives Matter movement has relied heavily upon social media to organize events. From May 26 to July 1, 2020, there were more than 4,700 demonstrations, marches, and protests demanding racial justice in the United States.[58] While not all of these were directly organized by Black Lives Matter, many were and nearly all relied on social media to organize and mobilize participants. Citizens have captured police brutality on video, bringing to light abuse of power and excessive use of force. To the horror of most, videos have shown unarmed people (especially young men of color) being killed by police officers, leading many to call for changes in our criminal justice system. Citizens have also captured police officers going above and beyond the call of duty in demonstrating kindness and commitment to their communities.

However, not all of the uses of social media are positive. Many people who rely on blogs, Twitter, YouTube, or other digital sources for their political news often are not getting complete and unbiased reports. Many disseminators of information on social media are interested primarily in publicizing their own viewpoints, which gives them a different agenda from that of the mainstream media. Even so, they rely heavily on traditional media for their information. Unless they work for a traditional media organization, most bloggers do little, if any, original reporting. At the same time, many of them seldom discuss news events without including their own personal or partisan spin.

When we combine the reduced number of traditional reporters with the increased variety of new information sources (only some of which are reliable and objective), we can see that we are facing an environment in which consumers can increasingly tailor their news consumption to reinforce preconceived notions and narrow perspectives. Today, skilled professionals (trained in the ethics and responsibilities of good journalism) are often placed on the same plane with less knowledgeable partisans (purporting to be experts), making the marketplace of ideas more and more complex to navigate. Consequently, it is more important today than ever before to become informed consumers of information.

Amateur news providers, sometimes referred to as "citizen journalists," enter the world of reporting without professional training and are perhaps best thought of as distributors and commentators, rather than gatherers, of news. Professionals with training and resources traditionally gathered the news through investigative journalism and even-handed reporting. However, in this current period of flux when traditional news organizations are under increasing pressure to cut costs, less professional commentators are unprepared to fill the void with credible and objective news. Social networking websites are relied on more and more by younger consumers, but much of the information posted there by citizen journalists is far from trustworthy.

Although new technologies have opened up the dissemination of news, research has yet to demonstrate that individual consumers are becoming more politically informed. In fact, with personalized web pages and search engines, consumers are now able to control the content brought to their attention in ways unimagined fifteen years ago. Remember, however, that most of these sites do link to traditional news organizations. So while consumption patterns are no doubt being changed by new media, claims that technology is transforming individual empowerment may be exaggerated.[59]

12.4.7 Fake News and the Abuse of Social Media

Much of the misinformation found on social media and other Internet sites goes beyond simple political opinion or spin. It is patently false, spread by ideological manipulators or by conspiracy theorists promoting beyond-the-fringe ideas to an audience that is highly skeptical of government and eager to spread the latest off-the-wall rumor.

During his 2016 presidential campaign, Donald Trump was widely accused by the mainstream media of playing fast and loose with the facts, an issue that continued to plague the new president after he took office. The debate over Trump's truthfulness became so intense that at least one major news organization, *The Washington Post*, published a running total of the president's alleged misstatements, exaggerations, and falsehoods. "Facts may be undervalued or losing their value in today's world," said Robert Mason, a University of Washington professor who has studied the spread of false information. "If you say it loud enough or long enough, people will believe it. That's okay in theory, but when people act on it, that's a problem."[60]

The extent to which fake news, or fabricated stories posted on Facebook and other social media sites, was a factor in the 2016 presidential campaign was still being debated long after Trump took office. American intelligence agencies concluded that some of the "fake news" was generated by Russian agents attempting to interfere in the election. In an example involving Texas, Russians created a "Heart of Texas" Facebook page, which promoted an anti-Islamic protest in Houston, attempted to stir up racial unrest, and promoted conspiracy theories, among other things.[61] Michael Hayden, a former head of the U.S. National Security Agency, said in a 2018 interview that a Russian disinformation campaign helped promote fears among some Texans that Jade Helm, a legitimate American military training exercise staged in Texas in 2015, was an Obama administration plan to round up political dissidents. Hayden said the Russians' success with stirring up fears over Jade Helm was a template for later interference in the presidential election.[62]

One academic study published about a year after President Trump took office concluded that about one-fourth of Americans saw at least one fake story during the 2016 campaign, but the study didn't settle the controversy over what effect, if any, fake news may have had on election returns. Researchers analyzed web traffic data from a representative sample of 2,525 Americans. About 80 percent of the bogus stories on the fake news sites they monitored supported Trump. The most conservative 10 percent of the monitored sample of participants accounted for about 65 percent of visits to bogus sites. And Trump supporters were about three times more likely to visit bogus sites backing their candidate than supporters of Hillary Clinton, the Democratic nominee, were to visit fake sites promoting her. But fake stories were only a small fraction of the news articles that either group of partisans viewed—1 percent for Clinton backers and 6 percent for Trump supporters. The study found that Facebook was the main platform through which people most often reached a fake news site.[63]

President Trump and other politicians soon began misusing the term fake news to push back against news stories they didn't like, including, in Trump's case, stories questioning his priorities and reporting the political and personal controversies he encountered as president. He has co-opted the term fake news to include news that he feels is biased or not flattering.[64] However, there is a difference between "fake news"—which is fabricated news designed to manipulate and mislead others—and biased news—which is news that shows prejudice in the stories covered, the tone of the coverage, or in nonobjective or unfair commentary that is interjected within the story.

When Facebook founder Mark Zuckerberg announced in 2015 that he wanted to give away $45 billion, *The Washington Post* columnist Anne Applebaum had some advice. "He should use it to undo the terrible damage done by Facebook and other forms of social media to democratic debate and civilized discussion all over the world."

"Just follow the right Twitter accounts, and you'll get links to the fake websites and dubious organizations that produce invented statistics," she added. "You'll find friends who believe in the invented statistics, too. If you so desire, you can then go on to live in a bubble entirely divorced from reality except one created by far-right bloggers, left-wing anarchists, or Kremlin spin doctors, all of whom excel at developing this kind of alternate reality."

Applebaum said that many people who invent fake statistics and "facts" have specific goals, such as the election of certain political candidates or even the recruitment of terrorists. But the longer-term impact of such disinformation, she said, is even more profound because it creates cynicism and apathy. "Eventually it means that nobody believes anything," she said. People aren't bothered by political leaders' lies "because they don't believe anything they read anyway. There's so much garbage information out there, it's impossible to know what is true."[65]

Half (50 percent) of the respondents to a Pew Research Center national survey in 2019 said made-up news or information was a "very big problem" in the country today, bigger than climate change, racism, illegal immigration, terrorism or sexism. Fifty-two percent said they had shared made-up news themselves, although the vast majority said they didn't know the information was made up when they shared it. There were some partisan differences among respondents, but most put the blame for such fake information on political leaders and staffs (57 percent) and activist groups (53 percent).[66]

In the White House, President Trump used Twitter as his primary means of directly communicating with the American public, and he continued to be called out by mainstream news media for inaccuracies, exaggerations, and untruthful statements. Twitter let him go unchallenged until May 2020, when, during the coronavirus pandemic, an economic meltdown, and his reelection campaign, Trump tweeted that mail-in ballots, which he opposed but many Democrats and voting rights advocates were promoting as a safe way to vote during the health crisis, would cause the November presidential election to be "rigged." Twitter did not remove the tweet, but it attached a notice urging readers to "get the facts," with a link to news sources. A few days later, Twitter added a warning to another Trump tweet that the company said violated the platform's rules by "glorifying violence." In that tweet, Trump suggested that demonstrators violently protesting the death of an African American man, George Floyd, in police custody in Minneapolis could be shot. Floyd had pleaded for air as a white police officer kneeled on his neck in an incident shown on bystanders' videos, setting off weeks of protests around the country against racial injustice. Most of the protests were peaceful. Twitter soon added a warning to a third Trump post, this one of a "racist baby" video that the social media platform said had been manipulated to mislead people. The video tweet, shared by Trump, featured two toddlers running down a sidewalk. It had been altered to appear as if it had been broadcast by CNN and included a fake caption reading, "Racist baby probably a Trump supporter." The video then accused "fake news" of providing misinformation.[67]

Trump retaliated against Twitter by issuing an executive order challenging a law that protected social media companies from legal liability over material that users post on their platforms. But experts noted that only Congress had the authority to change the law.

How Well Informed Are Texas Citizens?

12.5 Assess the effort of Texans and other Americans to stay informed and how their views of the media affect that effort.

Despite the media's efforts, most Texans—if national news surveys are any indication—have only minimal knowledge of what their elected officials in Austin are doing and are at risk of becoming lost in what to them is a confusing political and governmental maze. A few high-profile issues, such as taxes, abortion, and firearms regulation, attract a lot of attention. But many taxpayers, particularly those who live in metropolitan areas that have numerous legislators, do not even know who their state representatives or state senators are, much less how they have voted on significant issues.

This may be partly the media's fault. Many small newspapers carry only brief wire service stories about news events in Austin, and others give an incomplete picture by concentrating primarily on issues of local interest. The major newspapers provide more complete coverage, although it is shrinking, but they seldom publish recorded votes of legislators within their readership areas.

Even so, ample information sources, expanded by the Internet and mobile communications devices, allow anyone, with minimal effort, to stay informed of major developments in government. It is up to the individual to take the time and effort to become informed and to take care to differentiate fact and straight reporting from opinion, lies, and fabrications. Each person should learn how to be engaged in government and how to navigate the political process, or at least vote regularly and be able to make informed choices when he or she casts a ballot.

Ignorance among the general electorate plays into the hands of special interests that not only stay abreast of developments in Austin but also spend millions of dollars on political donations and legislative lobbying to influence those developments to their advantage, not necessarily to the benefit of the general public. Most governmental actions, whether taken by the legislature or a state regulatory board, eventually will affect the pocketbooks or quality of life of millions of Texans, many of whom will be caught by surprise. If recent patterns of news consumption continue, the influence of special interests over the public's business will become even greater in the future, and increasing numbers of everyday citizens will wonder what happened.[68]

12.5.1 Media Literacy: Becoming an Informed Consumer

For more than three decades, Americans have reported in national surveys that they are reading or viewing less news than in the past, a disturbing pattern for those concerned with the information literacy citizens require in order to make informed judgments about politics and public policy. Significant declines have been reported in the consumption of print, network, and local television news, while online consumption of news and information has increased. Given the increased variety of sources of news compared to a few decades ago, Americans today have more ways to be informed than ever before. However, there is little evidence that they are better informed. First, many choose not to consume any news at all. Researchers at the Pew Research Center found that 31 percent of young people were "newsless" the previous day. They had not read or viewed news even on digital devices. This was the highest percentage of any age group.[69] Another survey in 2012 reported similar results. That year, 29 percent of the 18-to-24 age group said they had read or viewed no news the previous day, either on cell phones or other digital sources or on traditional news platforms.[70]

According to a more recent survey, younger Americans were keeping up with the news far less than were older people (see Figure 12–2). Newspaper readership and

FIGURE 12-2 NEWS CONSUMPTION BY AGE

News consumption patterns vary significantly by age. On the whole, younger people consume less news than older individuals, but they also receive their news from different sources. Young people are most likely to consume news online, especially on social media, while other age groups are more likely to consume news from more traditional sources such as television, print newspapers, and radio.

NOTE: Survey conducted July 30-August 12, 2018.

SOURCE: Elisa Shearer, "Social Media Outpaces Print Newspapers in the U.S. as a News Source," Pew Research Center, December 10, 2018, https://www.pewresearch.org/fact-tank/2018/12/10/social-media-outpaces-print-newspapers-in-the-u-s-as-a-news-source/.

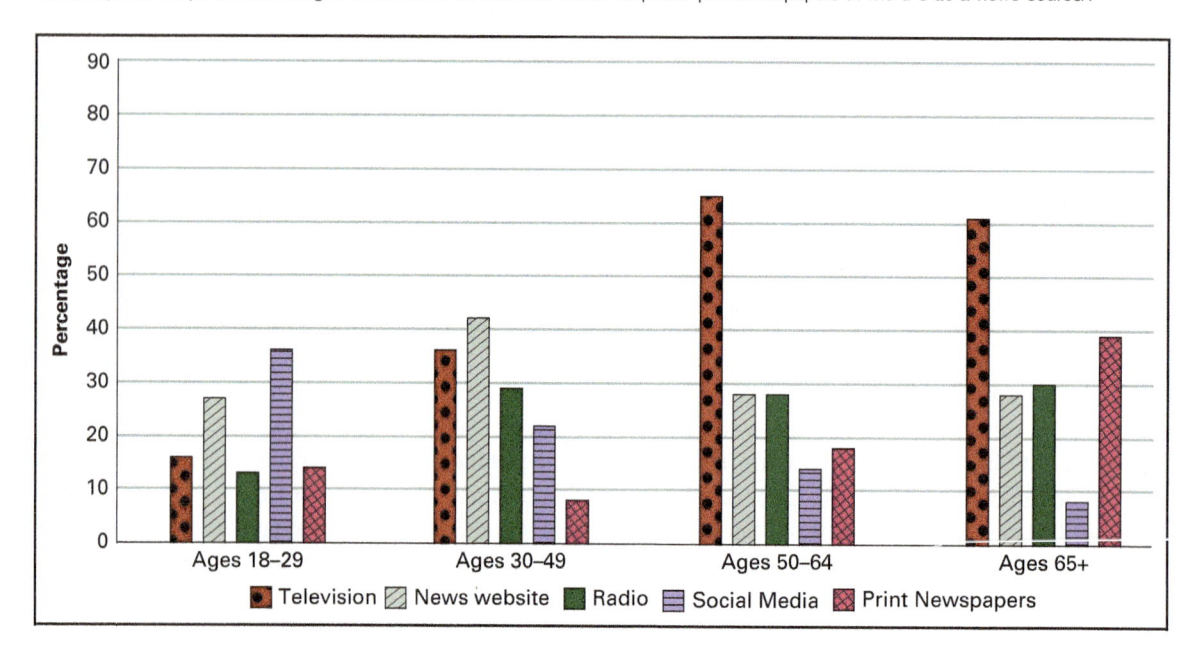

fake news
The publication of material which is known to be false or deliberately misleading for political or economic purposes.

news consumption from television were highest among older Americans and much lower among younger Americans. Conversely, younger people are far more likely to get news from Facebook than are older generations. Given the fact that much of the "news" on Facebook is often opinions rather than actual facts, these consumption patterns concern many.

Judging the reliability of "news" stories one reads online has become increasingly difficult, especially with the common claims of "fake news." **Fake news** entails intentionally publishing material that is known to be false or misleading to influence opinions or to make a profit (fake news sites earn revenue from advertisers when people click on their web pages). During the 2016 election, a large amount of fake news was posted on Facebook. In April 2017, Facebook CEO Mark Zuckerberg announced that Facebook was expanding security protocols to root out these fake news stories and was going to be more aggressive in deleting fake accounts. Beginning in April 2018, Facebook added new features to help users discern the quality of news information being shared. There is now an "about this article" bubble that can be clicked on for information about the publisher, including other articles it has published. If the publisher lacks a Wikipedia entry, that is an indication that the article is from a fake source. Zuckerberg has stated that he is committed to ensuring users are being provided with trustworthy news, and he has pledged to continue to work to improve these sorts of features. But as noted earlier in this chapter, Facebook didn't plan to fact check political advertising or limit how it was targeted during the 2020 presidential campaign.

To determine if news is "fake," look carefully at the URL (as the web page often mimics that of the real news source). Many fake news stories are published on web pages with domain names that end with ".com.co" or "lo." Another way to detect if a story is fake news is to do a reverse image search. Often the propagandists reuse photos from other stories as they may be on the other side of the globe. You can also see if other news sources are publishing the information in the story; if not, be highly suspect. Also

TABLE 12-1 POLITICAL INTEREST AND AWARENESS BY GENERATION

	Percent who say politics and government is a top-three interest	Percent who talked about politics at least a few times a week
Millennials (born 1981 or later)	26	35
Generation X (born 1965–1980)	34	40
Baby Boomers (born 1946–1964)	45	49

Every day, people have a wide variety of activity choices. As this table shows, younger people are less interested in politics and consequently discuss politics less than older generations. This is not a new trend as younger people have historically been less interested in politics than older Americans. As people age, their priorities tend to shift, with politics gaining in importance.

SOURCE: Pew Research Center, Millennials and Political News: http://www.journalism.org/2015/06/01/political-interest-and-awareness-lower-among-millennials/.

use fact-checking sites like FactCheck.org. Lastly, note that some sites like The Onion and ClickHole are satirical, existing to be humorous and should not be taken literally.

Young people are far less interested in politics than are older generations (see Table 12–1). Historically, as people age, they become more concerned with political matters and discuss these concerns with others at higher rates. These findings supplemented earlier studies showing that young people were less likely than their parents to be able to identify major newsmakers or be knowledgeable, or literate, about news events, especially local news. Researchers have attributed part of the blame to deficiencies in public education.[71] In addition, it has been suggested that many young people believe they cannot make a difference, do not link the actions of governments to their lives, and have tuned out the political process. As they grow older, get married, have families, obtain mortgages, and have higher tax obligations, their views start to change, and they become more engaged. Or so one theory holds.

Interest in the 2016 presidential race was widespread—even among young people—during the contentious and highly publicized campaigns for the Republican and Democratic nominations. With the surprising candidacies of Donald Trump and Bernie Sanders likely contributing to the high level of public attention, 91 percent of U.S. adults had heard or read some recent news about the election, according to a survey conducted by the Pew Research Center in January, shortly before the first-in-the-nation Iowa nominating caucuses. This group included 83 percent of 18- to 29-year-olds. The news source cited as most helpful by the 3,760 people surveyed was cable TV (24 percent). Social media and local TV stations (each at 14 percent) were the next most popular sources, followed by news websites or apps (13 percent), radio (11 percent), and network nightly news programs (10 percent). Bringing up the rear were late night comedy shows (3 percent), print editions of local newspapers (3 percent), print editions of national newspapers (2 percent), issue-based groups (2 percent), and direct communications from candidates or their campaigns (1 percent). The findings not only reinforced earlier surveys showing the continued decline of print newspapers as news sources, but also highlighted age differences in news source preferences. Cable TV was the most popular among respondents 65 and older, and social media was the strong favorite among the youngest age group, 18 to 29.[72] The 2020 presidential election competed with COVID-19 throughout the summer, a time when most Americans begin to pay attention to the presidential campaign. Attention begins to focus with each party's nominating conventions. The 2020 election was atypical given the pandemic; however, attention became more focused closer to the election.

12.5.2 Public Confidence and Media Bias

Public confidence in the media and the public's perception of **media bias** in the reporting of news events affect the level of media literacy among Texans and other Americans, and these obstacles remain a problem—for the public, members of the media, and political and governmental newsmakers.

media bias

A perception—sometimes real, sometimes imagined—that reporters and news organizations slant their news coverage to favor one side or the other in particular issues or disputes.

Public esteem for journalists, as a group, has been falling, according to periodic national surveys rating public regard for major occupational or professional groups. Only 28 percent of Americans believed journalists contributed "a lot" to society's well-being, according to a Pew Research Center survey conducted in 2013. This was a drop of 10 percentage points from a similar survey in 2009, with almost equal drops among Democrats and Republicans, and it was the largest drop of any of ten groups that were rated.[73] In a national Pew survey in 2017, only 5 percent of respondents said they had a "great deal" of confidence in the news media, ranking journalists behind the military (33 percent), medical scientists (24 percent), scientists (21 percent), school principals and superintendents (13 percent), and religious leaders (13 percent). Only business leaders (4 percent) and elected officials (3 percent) were ranked lower. In the same survey, 21 percent of respondents said they had "no confidence" in the news media at all, the highest measure of no confidence of any of the rated groups.[74] A number of surveys in 2019 and 2020 find similar patterns.[75]

It is difficult to say how much of the public attitude toward journalists reflects a willingness to "shoot the messenger." People are tired of "negative" news—political and civil turmoil, natural and human-made disasters—and tend to blame the reporters along with the perpetrators. Maybe some Americans also associate all journalists with the dueling talking heads on cable TV and are weary of shouting matches.

A perception of media bias is another likely factor in the change in attitude toward journalists. The percentage of Americans who believe there is a great deal of political bias in news coverage is increasing, another Pew Research Center survey has indicated. According to that survey, the percentage increased from 31 percent in 2008 to 37 percent in 2012. This perception of bias was significantly higher among all Republicans (49 percent)—and especially the most conservative Republicans (57 percent)—than among Democrats (32 percent) and independents (35 percent). But it had increased among all political affiliations. Men (41 percent) were more likely to suspect media bias than women (33 percent). And people 50 and older (44 percent) were more likely to perceive bias than people younger than 50 (31 percent).[76]

In a related, follow-up survey in 2017, Pew found that public belief that the media are biased had grown significantly. Some 72 percent of all Americans believed that news organizations tended to favor one side in presenting news on political and social issues. Republicans (87 percent) were much more likely to believe this than Democrats (53 percent).[77]

Bias, or at least the perception of it, also affects many people's choice of which news outlets to use, as illustrated in a Pew survey conducted after the 2016 election. In this survey, 40 percent of people who voted for Republican Donald Trump for president said Fox News was their main source for news about the campaign, followed by CNN, 8 percent; Facebook, 7 percent; NBC, 6 percent; and local TV, 5 percent. Only 3 percent of people who voted for Democrat Hillary Clinton identified Fox News as their main source for campaign news. Clinton voters had a wider array of top news sources. CNN was first at 18 percent, followed by MSNBC, 9 percent; Facebook, 8 percent; local TV, 8 percent; and National Public Radio, 7 percent. "These findings are consistent with past research revealing that those on the right and left have significantly different media diets, with Fox News in particular standing out among conservatives," the researchers wrote. Although Facebook as a source of campaign news shared a similar percentage among Trump and Clinton voters, researchers noted the likelihood "that the specific news outlets that filled their Facebook feeds differed substantially."[78]

News' consumers media preferences—and perhaps their own political biases—affected their views of a deadly health crisis as the coronavirus, or COVID-19, outbreak was beginning to spread in the United States. A Pew Research Center survey conducted in March 2020 showed that people who identified the liberal-leaning MSNBC as their main source of political news had sharply different opinions of the coronavirus and the media's coverage of it than did people who got most of their political news from the conservative Fox News. Sixty-six percent of MSNBC viewers but only 37 percent of the Fox News group believed that the coronavirus originated in nature rather than in a laboratory. Similarly, 78 percent of MSNBC viewers believed it would be a year or more before a vaccine became available, compared to 51 percent of Fox News viewers. A third group, people who identified CNN as their main source of political news, fell between the other two groups. Seventy-nine percent of Fox viewers believed the media had exaggerated the risk of the coronavirus, compared to 35 percent of the MSNBC group and 54 percent of CNN viewers.[79]

Few people who regularly watch news and commentary on cable television would deny that Fox News' approach to political coverage is more conservative than MSNBC's. Nevertheless, some national studies have indicated that most mainstream media reporters as a whole are more liberal than the general population in personal ideology and on many public policy issues, and conservatives have exploited these findings to support their contention of a liberal media bias.[80]

Meanwhile, other people, including many liberals, have pointed to corporate media ownership and concluded that those who make the final decisions as to what news is covered and how it is covered reflect more conservative biases. Subjective decisions, such as a reporter's or editor's strong interest in an issue, may determine which news events are covered on a particular day or which angle is emphasized in a particular story. More often than not, however, news organizations eagerly provide a forum for the viewpoints of consumer advocates, environmentalists, and other individuals purporting to promote the public interest. One reason for this is that spokespersons for these groups are readily accessible, hold news conferences, send emails and Tweets, and actively cultivate media contacts. They depend on free media exposure to compensate for limited budgets in their battles against the business lobby for the tougher regulations and higher taxes that progressive programs often require. Another reason is that stories about the age-old struggle between the powerful and the powerless, the rich and the poor, attract considerable reader and viewer interest, centering as they do on controversy and conflict.

Stories about governmental scandals and political corruption often are displayed on the front pages of newspapers, at the top of evening television newscasts, or prominently on newspaper or television websites. Attempting to follow in the footsteps of the early muckrakers of American journalism, some Texas newspeople view themselves as crusaders and are determined to "clean up" government. In their eagerness, however, they can become susceptible to charges of unfair, personal bias against the public officials they are targeting. This is particularly true when haste to be the first with the latest development in an ongoing scandal produces reporting or editing mistakes.

The newspaper, television, and radio reporters who cover events and personalities at the state Capitol in Austin normally attempt to present all sides of an issue. Most believe they are objective, dedicated to principles of fairness and balance, and report events as they happen. This view of the press as a mirror was summarized years ago, well before the digital age, by Frank Stanton, former president of CBS, when he testified before a congressional committee that "what the media do is to hold a mirror up to society and try to report it as faithfully as possible." But newspeople and the organizations they represent sometimes have strong personal or corporate opinions about the issues or individuals they cover, and bias and the perception of bias are problems the media constantly have to fight.[81]

Media bias—both real and perceived—is likely to grow with the continued expansion of online information sources, including bloggers and other so-called "citizen journalists" who are not bound by traditional journalistic ethics and make no pretense of objectivity. The digital environment is "more open to bias and to journalism for hire," warned Paul Starr, a professor of communications and public affairs at the

Woodrow Wilson School at Princeton University. "Online there are few clear markers to distinguish blogs and other sites that are being financed to promote a viewpoint from news sites operated independently on the basis of professional rules of reporting," he wrote in the *New Republic*. He added, "So the danger is not just more corruption of government and business—it is also more corruption of journalism itself."[82]

CONCLUSION

AN EARLIER INFORMATION AGE
A linotype operator in San Augustine, Texas, punches out lines of type for the next issue of that city's newspaper in 1939.

Media technology has been transformed in Texas and throughout the country in a comparatively short period. But the media's purpose remains the same as it has been since the frontier era—to inform. And never has information been more readily available than it is now, in the digital age. But for many people, never has it been more confusing. With opinionated bloggers and social media pontificators competing for attention with legitimate news reporters on your smart phone, tablet, or laptop screens and talking heads of various political stripes trying to out-scream each other on television, you may feel the din isn't worth the effort to try to comprehend. Like countless other people, you may simply tune it all out.

Granted, the idea of developing media literacy and becoming an informed news consumer can seem intimidating, especially when you have many other interests and obligations competing for your time and attention. But if you want to become more than a bystander or, worse, a victim when governmental decisions are made, you need to learn about the people who make those decisions and the ideas they are seeking to advance—and who and what in the political arena reflect or don't reflect your own priorities. And the media, for all its controversies, challenges, and changes, still offer the best road map.

First, though, you need to know how to navigate the media—differentiate fact from opinion, credible information sources from rumor mills. We hope this chapter has helped you figure out how to do that. By reading, listening, watching, and then evaluating your news sources and your political choices, you will be able to truly make informed decisions when you vote and effectively begin to navigate the political process.

REVIEW THE CHAPTER

The Mass Media and the Policy Agenda

12.1 Describe the influence of the mass media on the policy agenda in Texas, p. 380.

The news media are the primary information link between those who govern and those who are governed. The news media affect the development of public policy by influencing the election of policymakers and informing and educating the public on policy alternatives. They can make the causes of a few individuals the concerns of many. This role has remained basically unchanged in this country since the adoption of the First Amendment to the U.S. Constitution more than 200 years ago, but vast changes in technology have transformed the dissemination of information and challenged the media's traditional role.

News Media and the Electoral Process

12.2 Describe the media coverage of campaigns and elections in Texas, p. 384.

Candidates for public office depend on the mass media to develop name identification and convey information about their policy positions to the public. Although the media cover substantive policy issues and candidates' positions on them, much media coverage is on the "horse-race" aspects of campaigns—who is running ahead in the polls and who has raised the most money. Most voters get their news about political campaigns from television, but increasingly the Internet is emerging as a major source of political news. Much of the online political information is highly partisan and opinionated. Candidates cannot control what is reported in the mainstream media, but they try to influence coverage through news releases and staged news or pseudo-news events. Candidates also have Twitter accounts, Facebook pages, and websites through which they can communicate directly with voters, bypassing the traditional media. Most serious candidates for statewide office and many local and district offices in metropolitan areas spend large amounts of money on advertising, which also allows candidates to control the message. The use of negative or attack ads against opponents is common in political campaigns.

The Early Development of the Media in Texas

12.3 Trace the early development of the news media in Texas, p. 390.

Texans have seen many changes in how they obtain their news since the frontier era, when many settlers had access only to published political opinions in primitive newspapers. For much of the twentieth century, influential newspaper publishers in Texas were part of the state's business-oriented political establishment and had close ties to elected officials. In the 1970s, Texas newspapers began to more eagerly challenge public officials and governmental decisions, in part because out-of-state corporate owners, who had only limited interest in local Texas politics, replaced establishment-oriented publishers. The expanded coverage also reflected a changing state political system, and newspapers began covering issues of particular concern to minority groups and low-income Texans. In the late twentieth century, many Texans started to get more of their news from television, rather than newspapers. Today, both newspapers and TV stations are losing news consumers to the Internet and a variety of digital information sources.

Current News Media Trends

12.4 Describe the impact of the Internet and other digital information sources on traditional media outlets and news consumers, and how newspapers and television news departments have adjusted to the changes, p. 393.

Several major Texas daily newspapers folded during the 1990s, leaving each major Texas city with only one daily. Many of the surviving newspapers have since reduced staffs and coverage because of the Internet and the growth of digital information sources. The Internet also has forced changes in television and radio news departments. Many newspapers and TV and radio stations in Texas and throughout the country now are owned by large corporate conglomerates that include a variety of communications and entertainment properties, including movie companies and theme parks. *The Dallas Morning News* is the only major Texas newspaper still owned by a Texas-based corporation. Like newspapers in other states, Texas newspapers have reduced the number of reporters assigned to cover the state Capitol. This has created greater opportunities for government public relations specialists, who have subjective interests in the information they disseminate. There also has been an expansion of social media and other digital information sources, many of which are partisan or opinionated. *The Texas Tribune*, a nonprofit online news source, made its debut in 2009 and covers state government and politics from a multimedia platform. It remains to be seen if the *Tribune* is the wave of the future for daily news coverage of government and politics, but its first several years of operation have been promising.

How Well Informed Are Texas Citizens?

12.5 Assess the effort of Texans and other Americans to stay informed and how their views of the media affect that effort, p. 405.

Even with an explosion of digital devices, young Americans continue to lag, as they have for a number of years, behind their parents in news consumption. Among older Americans who read about or view news regularly, however, media literacy—the ability to identify newsmakers or significant news events—is uneven. Surveys indicate differences in quality and depth among the information sources from which people get news. They suggest that newspapers, despite their declining readership, may still offer the most thorough coverage of political events. Meanwhile, public esteem for news reporters is declining as perceptions of media bias increase. Media bias, both real and perceived, is likely to grow as bloggers and contributors to social media networks continue to post their opinions and report information with little regard for its accuracy. Confusion and ignorance among the general public play into the hands of special interests that make it their business to know what government is doing and to influence public policy.

LEARN THE TERMS

agenda setting, p. 382
agenda building, p. 382
issue-attention cycle, p. 382
Open Meetings and Public Information Acts, p. 383

sound bite, p. 384
negative television ad, p. 388
editorial autonomy, p. 392
Capitol press corps, p. 399
spin, p. 400

fake news, p. 406
media bias, p. 407

Interest Groups and Political Power in Texas

13

FIGHT FOR RACIAL JUSTICE
Thousands gather to mourn the death of George Floyd and others killed by police during a march across downtown Houston on June 2, 2020. Anti-racism protests swept across the country in the summer of 2020 with significant calls for criminal justice reform.

LEARNING OBJECTIVES

13.1 Differentiate interest groups from other types of organizations and describe the role of interest groups in democracies, p. 414.

13.2 Apply the pluralist and elitist theories of political behavior to Texas, p. 418.

13.3 Describe the tactics involved in direct and indirect lobbying, p. 423.

13.4 Describe the characteristics of interest groups active in Texas, p. 430.

13.5 Describe sources of interest group power and the contemporary challenges facing interest groups in Texas, p. 435.

People in the United States have a long tradition of coming together to work toward change. In the early 1830s, Alexis de Tocqueville wrote that "in no country of the world has the principal of association been more successfully used, or more unsparingly applied to a multitude of different objects, than in America."[1] He went on to characterize the United States as a "nation of joiners" because of our affinity toward and support of political associations. The right to work together to impact our government, either through direct action or through organized groups, is protected by a number of liberties in our federal and state constitutions. The First Amendment guarantees the freedoms of speech and press as well as the right to peaceably assemble to petition our government. These are also included in the Texas Constitution to protect individuals from any infringement of these cherished rights by state officials (the First Amendment specifically protected citizens from Congressional action). These rights are no less important today than when they were first enshrined in these beloved political documents.

Support for these rights was put to the test in the late spring and early summer of 2020 when we saw what might prove to be the largest political movement of our time. Following the killings of unarmed black Americans cumulating in the slaying of George Floyd on May 23, 2020, record numbers of people took to the street to call for racial justice in the United States. Quickly, the protests included others besides Mr. Floyd: Breonna Taylor (killed on March 13, 2020) in Louisville, Atatiana Jefferson (killed on October 12, 2019 in Fort Worth), Mike Ramos (killed on April 24, 2020 in Austin), Rayshard Brooks (killed on June 12, 2020 in Atlanta) and many others across the country. Polling organizations estimate between 15 million and 26 million people in the United States participated in a demonstration or march in the six weeks after the killing of Mr. Floyd.[2] The protests were across the country, often in towns that had never seen such protests, and were sustained for weeks. On the peak day, June 6, 2020, approximately 550 events were held nationwide, with at least twenty in Texas.

While many of the protests were initially spontaneous, with people taking to the streets to protest Mr. Floyd's death, some quickly became more organized under the organization of the Black Lives Matter movement. The Black Lives Matter protests represent a scale of protesting that, given their longevity and breadth of participation and organic nature, are remarkably rare. Initially focused specifically on police brutality, the protests have come to include a more broad focus on criminal justice reform as well as proposals to "defund" the police (most proposals do not literally mean to defund the police, but to rather have more accountability in police funding, transferring funding and responsibility for tasks that are better suited to other professionals like mental health and substance abuse specialists). The protesters have forced the country to face many of the direct legacies of slavery and have pushed us to examine how we may have glorified the institution. Also, unlike past Black Lives Matter protests, these involved far more diverse protesters and supporters in areas with a much larger percentage of white residents. Many of the protesters were new to protesting, being compelled to literally take to the streets to right what they consider to be unacceptable wrongs.

Public opinion on the Black Lives Matter movement, race relations, and systematic racism has been slowly changing. For example, in 2009, 36 percent of white Americans indicated that the country needed to do more to promote equal rights for black Americans; that number increased to 54 percent just four years later after the start of the Black Lives Matter movement. During this time period, research by social psychologists also found that people's implicit attitudes toward race had begun to shift.[3] In 2015, only one-third of the country thought that the police were more likely to use excessive force with a black person than with a white person in similar situations; that percentage increased to 57% in late May 2020.[4] From the time it started in 2013 until early in 2018, more Americans opposed the Black Lives Matter movement than supported it (meaning there was a net negative evaluation). In 2018, there was the beginning of a net positive evaluation, with more people favoring than opposing the movement. Throughout 2018 and most of 2019, overall evaluations of the movement remained largely stable, with slightly more people being favorable than unfavorable. The overall net approval began to increase in late 2019 and continued to slowly increase in early 2020. However, net approval surged with the mass protests following the killing of George Floyd. In just a little over two weeks, the net approval increased by 17 points, phenomenal in public opinion, which is typically slow to change.[5] Public opinion in support of the Black Lives Matter movement decreased from the record highs in June (when 67 percent of the entire nation strongly or somewhat supported the movement) to September 2020 (when 55 percent of Americans felt similarly), but the movement remained very popular with people of color in the country and was more popular with White Americans than it was before the summer protests.[6]

Significant generational, racial, and partisan differences exist in views of the Black Lives Matter movement, police brutality, and racism. For example, Millennials and members of Generation Z are far more likely to say they believe that the police act in racist ways, are more supportive of Black Lives Matter and are more supportive of NFL player protests.[7] Not all think that the protests and the Black Lives Matter movement are advancing race relations. Notably, Republicans and independents who lean Republican are less likely than others to believe that the movement will improve race relations and are substantially less likely to say that discrimination is a significant problem. Republicans are also less likely than others to see the underlying anger motivating the protesters as justified. The support among Republicans diminished during the summer of 2020.[8] Historically, it is not uncommon for initial support for social movements to wane as time passes.

These substantial changes in public opinion, brought on what may prove to be unprecedented levels of collective action, have already resulted in a wide array of change. The city council in Minneapolis, Minnesota, pledged to dismantle their police department. Lawmakers in New York voted to repeal a law to keep police disciplinary records private. Cities and states across the country banned chokeholds. The Mississippi state legislature voted to retire their state flag, which prominently displayed the Confederate battle emblem. NASCAR announced that fans will no longer be able to fly Confederate flags at races. The Pentagon announced they were open to examining the renaming of military bases bearing the name of Confederate soldiers. Confederate monuments and statues have been removed across the country in states such as Virginia, Kentucky, North Carolina, South Carolina, Florida, Alabama, Tennessee, and Georgia. Several statues have been removed in Texas as well. For example, the "Spirit of the Confederacy" statue was removed ahead of schedule in Sam Houston Park on June 16, 2020. The statue stood in the park near downtown Houston for more than 100 years. Three confederate monuments in North Texas were also removed: one outside the courthouse in downtown Fort Worth and another in Denton County. The largest confederate monument in Dallas was removed on June 26, 2020, after a court battle. Many oppose the removal of the statues and memorials, arguing they are important historical tributes, while others believe they serve as vivid reminders of slavery and glorify racism. Students across the country are demanding their universities examine ways to better address what is seen as systematic racism on their college campuses and to face their racist pasts to better move forward toward a better future. The effects are also being felt internationally. For example, Black Lives Matter protesters in Bristol, United Kingdom, tore down a statue of a person involved in the trading of enslaved people in the 17th century. The mayor of London, Sadiq Khan, announced a commission to examine landmarks (including street names, art, and statues) across the city on June 9, 2020. Protesters in France are forcing the country to examine race relations as well.

In this chapter, you will see that interest groups serve as important linkages between the public and their governmental officials. Interest groups play both positive and negative roles in politics today. Understanding how and why interest groups form, the keys to their success, concerns over their influence, and their changing role in state and national politics will give you a far better appreciation of the nature of collective action and how groups can augment and exert their influence to effect change. Since interest groups are fundamentally important in both American and Texas politics, a comprehensive understanding of their changing dynamics will help you navigate local, state, and national politics.

What Are Interest Groups?

13.1 Differentiate interest groups from other types of organizations and describe the role of interest groups in democracies.

Americans have a long tradition of and belief in collective action. One of the earliest systematic studies of America occurred in the 1830s (interestingly by a young Frenchman in his 20s). In *Democracy in America* (originally published in 1835 but still widely read today), Alexis de Tocqueville noted that compared to Europeans, Americans had a much stronger belief in collective action. He stated that freedom of association allowed "partisans of an opinion" to unite to preserve liberty. He asserted that the liberty of association was necessary to fight the tyranny of the majority. In a participatory democracy, like that in the United States, the right to petition government and the right to full association to freely express opinions are fundamentally important to the exercise of democratic citizenship. Activism is essential in our "do something" political culture that is predicated upon excellence and innovation. Forming groups to promote collective interests is essential in navigating our complex and potentially overwhelming government. When like-minded individuals come together to influence government, as they have since the earliest days of our republic, they are preserving and protecting democracy by empowering people to influence the world in which they live.

The U.S. and Texas Constitutions both provide substantial protections and guarantees to allow citizens to petition their government to institute change. The First Amendment, for example, protects the freedoms of speech, press, and assembly and the right to petition government for a redress of grievances. Although this amendment initially applied only to Congress, the nationalization of the Bill of Rights through the incorporation of the Fourteenth Amendment applied these protections to state governments as well. Moreover, the state constitution guarantees people the unalienable right to "alter, reform, or abolish their government." Consequently, we are among the freest people in the world and able to exercise these freedoms in the form of collective action to influence our fellow citizens. In this chapter, we will see how groups can be used to both advance and complicate democracy as well as how interest group mobilization has changed over time.

13.1.1 Roles and Functions of Interest Groups

An **interest group** may be defined as "an organized collection of individuals who are bound together by shared attitudes or concerns and who make demands on political institutions in order to realize goals which they are unable to achieve on their own."[9] Members of an interest group share common interests or goals, organize to pursue those goals collectively because they cannot achieve them individually, and focus some of their efforts on influencing governmental decisions.[10] These characteristics,

interest group
A group of people with common goals who are organized to seek political or policy objectives they are unable to achieve by themselves.

THE COVID RESTRICTIONS
Many people thought that restrictions implemented to curb the spread of COVID-19 infringed upon their freedoms and were excessive use of governmental authority. Pictured here are protesters who peacefully came together to show their disapproval of Governor Abbott's mask mandate and business restrictions which they saw as unduly infringing upon their personal liberties.

particularly the political and policy objectives, distinguish these groups, also known as pressure groups, from other organizations.

We do not know exactly how many groups or organizations there are in the United States or even in Texas. The *Encyclopedia of Associations* has identified more than 24,000 associations of national scope. Across the country at the regional, state, and local levels, approximately 100,000 associations have been documented.[11] Comparing these totals with earlier estimates, it is clear that there has been an "explosion" of group formation since the 1950s.[12] One scholar suggests that only 10 percent of people participated in interest groups in the 1970s. Contemporary scholars state that approximately 65 percent of Americans over the age of 18 belong to at least one politically active organization (though many organizations are not overtly political).[13] Thousands of groups exist in Texas. Some have long histories; others are formed to address a specific need, interest, or problem and disappear after a relatively short period of time. Although most organizations have the potential to participate in the policymaking process, many will not. In our attempt to define the pressure-group system in Texas, we focus on those groups that can be identified as continuous active players.

We also should distinguish between categorical groups and interest or pressure groups. Women collectively constitute a categorical grouping of the female population; senior citizens, African Americans, and Hispanics are also categorical groups. Although these often are spoken of as groups of people with similar political objectives, individuals within each group hold widely diverse interests, concerns, and goals. By contrast, an interest group is a segment of the population that organizes for specific purposes and objectives in the policymaking process.

13.1.2 Role in Democracies

When most people think of interest groups, negative connotations typically are attached. However, it is important to note that interest groups play significant and helpful roles in democracies. First, interest groups represent their members before the government, helping members' voices be heard in what can be a complex and overwhelming process. Interest groups are also vehicles for political participation. People who volunteer their time, energy, and money to interest groups typically also engage in other forms of political participation and are more involved in their communities. In addition, interest groups educate the public. Groups often sponsor research, hire experts to testify before legislative hearings, and conduct public relations campaigns serving to inform the public (and public officials) about a variety of issues that otherwise might go unnoticed. Lastly, interest groups can serve as government watchdogs, monitoring programs and officials, thereby promoting accountability.

13.1.3 Who Joins Political Groups?

Americans join a wide array of civic, sports, service, fraternal, hobby, economic, religious, and professional organizations. Surveys of American adults in the mid-1970s indicated that approximately 74 percent belonged to some type of organization, while 28 percent reported that they belonged to three or more organizations. Thirty years later, surveys conducted from 2000 to 2004 indicated that an estimated 62 percent of American adults belonged to some type of organization, while 25 percent indicated that they belonged to three or more organizations. The nature of political engagement has changed dramatically, with much activism moving online. For example, nearly 40 percent of American adults have participated in political activities through social network sites—activities that include following political candidates, sharing political thoughts, "liking" political groups, and promoting political issues.[14] Moreover, substantial generational differences exist between definitions of "membership" in organizations, with young people asserting that people "join" by "liking" or "following" groups online or "retweeting" posts, while older people define joining as becoming a

PROTEST FOR CHANGE

Raising awareness through protests is one effective technique that groups can employ to advance their agenda. Pictured is a candlelight vigil to remember the five slain police officers in Dallas in 2016. Balancing demands for criminal justice reform and respecting police efforts can be difficult. Protesting for change does not mean that one does not respect the police or supports violence against the police. Rather, protesting is often done to raise consciousness and to promote change.

formal member of an organization. Groups must balance the need to mobilize online support with engaging members in more traditional, overt activities, as the latter sorts of political engagement are typically more positive for individuals, groups, and society. While there are some benefits to "armchair" activism, nothing replaces traditional involvement for affecting change or reaping personal rewards from working to advance a cause. However, online activities can often lead to activism as we saw with youth organizing school walkouts and marches.

Regardless of how we define "membership," it would appear that the overwhelming majority of Americans have potential access to the policymaking process through their group associations. Closer inspection, however, raises serious questions about the distribution of political power and resources. The argument that the policy playing field is tilted to benefit some groups or interests to the exclusion of others has some validity.[15] If part of the population has limited potential to affect the decisions of government, that raises serious questions about the very nature of a democratic society and the role of groups within this political structure.

Those who study organizations generally agree that persons with higher incomes, better educations, higher-status occupations, and higher standards of living are more likely than other people to belong to groups.[16] Historically, men have joined at a higher rate than have women; older people join at higher rates than do younger people; whites are more likely to be members than are Hispanics or African Americans; and people with established community ties are more likely to participate. Not only do these people join more groups, but they also are more likely to be active participants. These findings suggest that there is a class bias in the interest group system in Texas. People from higher socioeconomic classes are more easily organized and are more likely to maintain their support for these organizations.[17] Lower socioeconomic groups, minorities, and diffused constituencies, such as consumers, find it very difficult to compete on an equal footing with business, industrial, and professional groups, which also can better afford lobbying expenses and the financial contributions to political campaigns that usually guarantee access to officeholders.

13.1.4 Why Do People Join Interest Groups?

Individuals join groups for a variety of reasons, which may change over time. One is the personal and material benefits that can be derived from interest groups.[18] A teacher, for example, may join the Texas State Teachers Association (TSTA) because it lobbies for higher teacher salaries, better fringe benefits and working conditions, and general educational issues. But TSTA also offers its members publications, insurance programs, potential legal assistance, discounts for travel, and valuable professional information.

People also realize social benefits from joining groups. Membership and participation provide them with a sense of personal identification with larger organizations and institutions that are likely to be more visible and potentially effective in the policymaking process than an individual would be if acting alone.[19] They may believe group membership enhances their personal status and prestige.[20]

Finally, a person can receive personal satisfaction or a sense of purpose from belonging to a group that he or she believes has a worthwhile cause or objective. Some people join groups to try to make the world a better place.[21] One motivation for joining such groups as Common Cause or the League of Women Voters, for example, may be a commitment to improving the election system in Texas. For many people, reform of the election system provides broad, but intangible, benefits that go well beyond the group or organization.

Interest Group Theory

13.2 Apply the pluralist and elitist theories of political behavior to Texas.

The issue of interest groups and political power in American politics has been debated since the Constitutional Convention of 1787. Writing in *The Federalist Papers* at a time when there were no political parties or interest groups as we know them today, James Madison argued that it was inevitable that people would organize into groups, or "factions," and attempt to impose their will on others and use governments for their specific purposes. Madison recognized two basic problems with these groups: There was a potential for the majority to tyrannize or impose its will on others, and a potential for the minority, in its pursuit of narrow self-interests, to harm the long-term interests of society as a whole. Most of his argument centered on the problem of majorities, since small groups (the minority) could be outvoted.[22]

mischief of factions
Term coined by James Madison to describe the complex relationships among groups and interests within the American political system and the institutional arrangements that potentially balance the power of groups.

The cure for this **mischief of factions** was both institutional and socioeconomic. If the number of factions or groups increased, there would be greater competition and less likelihood that any one group could dominate the policymaking process. Competitors would have to find compromises. Also, institutional power would be fragmented among three branches of government and a federal system, in which powers would be further divided between the national government and the states. Elections for different offices would be staggered in different years, and there would be significant variations in electoral constituencies. The effect of the variations in national, state, and local elections would be to make it even more difficult to construct large, permanent coalitions that could exercise absolute control over all institutions and subsequently dominate all policies.

13.2.1 Pluralism and Democratic Theory

Drawing in part on this tradition established by Madison, David Truman, an American political scientist, argued in his classic study, *The Governmental Process*, that American politics can be understood primarily in terms of the way groups interact with one another.[23] Expanding on Truman's theories, other scholars have attempted to develop a general understanding of politics organized around groups. These scholars, often referred to as pluralists and their philosophy as **pluralism**, believe that significant numbers of diverse and competing interest groups share political influence in a way that limits the power of any single group.

pluralism
Theory holding that a diversity of groups and people is instrumental in the policymaking process and no one group should be able to dominate the decisions of government.

Although there are differences in emphasis among pluralists, they have established the following general characteristics of a pluralistic society:

- Groups are the primary actors in the policymaking process. They provide the individual with political resources and a link to governmental institutions.
- Politics is basically group interaction, in which groups come into conflict with one another over the limited resources of society, and public policy is ultimately the resolution of group conflict and differences.
- Because there are so many groups, no one group can dominate the political process. Although some groups have more resources than others, a group always has the potential to influence policy. If there is no group to address a particular concern or problem, one can be organized.
- Although most people do not actively participate in the policymaking process, they have access to the process through the leaders of the groups to which they belong. There are numerous leadership opportunities within groups for individuals who want active roles.
- Most group leaders are committed to democratic values, and competition makes them responsive to other members and serves to check or constrain their actions.[24]

Pluralism is appealing because it gives credence to our general views of a democratic society and offers potential solutions, or at least hope, for those people who are excluded from full political participation or benefits. One can find evidence in Texas to support the pluralist view. Thousands of groups are organized on a statewide or community level. Hundreds of lobbyists are registered in Austin to represent a wide variety of economic, social, civic, and cultural organizations. A growing state population and a diversifying economy have significantly increased the number of interest groups over the past three decades.

David Truman suggests that there are periods, or "waves," in American political history in which groups proliferate rapidly in response to economic, social, or political change.[25] To compensate for imbalances (or disturbances) in the political system, additional groups organize in an attempt to reestablish equilibrium. Truman's disturbance theory asserts that groups form and grow during times of societal change and in response to threats. In contrast to Truman's theory, Robert Salisbury argued that interest groups form to compete for scarce resources and that leaders serve as entrepreneurs (hence his theory is called the entrepreneur theory).[26]

Groups form for any number of reasons. Concerns over economic changes, public school funding, environmental protection, medical care for low-income Texans, and other pressing issues have generated additional interest groups in Texas in recent years. Movements focusing on the interests of Hispanics, African Americans, women, and the LGBTQ community have led to the creation of interest groups lobbying to advance their concerns. Still other organizations have emerged to protect existing interests, or the status quo, and some groups have formed in response to new governmental policies and regulations.[27]

With the elimination of the most obvious historical discriminatory practices, Texans from historically marginalized groups have made significant economic, social, and political gains. In addition to having increased access to mainstream groups, minorities have formed their own professional and economic organizations. It is not uncommon to find Hispanic chambers of commerce or African American bar associations in many Texas cities.

Advocates of pluralism use the foregoing arguments and examples to support their views. They argue that, in spite of earlier periods in Texas history when large segments of the population were excluded from the political and policymaking processes, the political system is now open and accessible to new groups. They believe that those holding public office are responsive to the needs and interests of a greater diversity of Texans than ever before.

13.2.2 The Elitist Alternative

Other political scientists insist that pluralist theories simply do not describe the realities of power and policymaking in Texas or the United States. They say the pluralists have not given enough attention to the fact that a few individuals still control enormous resources. Although there are thousands of groups, they are not equal in political resources, nor can they equally translate their interests or demands into public policy. These scholars believe the political system in Texas can be more accurately described in terms of **elitism**.

elitism
Theory holding the view that political power is primarily held by a few individuals who derive power from leadership positions in large business, civic, or governmental institutions.

According to this view, a few individuals who derive power from their leadership positions in large organizations or institutions, particularly those with great financial resources, monopolize the influence on most important policy decisions. From the elitist perspective, power is not an individual commodity or resource but an attribute of social organizations.[28]

People who subscribe to this theory also believe that the existence of elites within any society is inevitable. Robert Michels, a European social scientist writing during the first part of the twentieth century, argued that any organization, no matter how it is structured, will eventually produce an "oligarchy," or rule by a few individuals. Michels's **iron rule of oligarchy** was not only applicable to organizations but was also a universal law that applied to all social systems.[29]

iron rule of oligarchy
A theory developed by Robert Michels, a European sociologist, that all organizations inevitably are dominated by a few individuals.

Beginning with C. Wright Mills and his book *The Power Elite*, many American scholars have been proponents of the elitist theory.[30] A number of generalizations can be derived from the elitist school of thought:

- Power is held by a few individuals and is derived from their positions in large institutions. In addition to economic institutions, these include the government, the mass media, and civic organizations.
- Historically, political elites constituted a homogeneous group drawn primarily from the upper and upper-middle classes. They were older, well-educated, primarily white, Anglo-Saxon males.
- Although there is competition among elites and the institutions they represent, there is considerable consensus and cohesion among elites on primary values, interests, and the rules of the game.
- Elites are linked by a complex network of interlocking memberships on the governing bodies of corporations, financial institutions, foundations, and civic and cultural organizations.
- Policy decisions are made by a few individuals and primarily reflect the interests of the dominant institutions. The interests of the dominant elites are not necessarily opposed to those of other classes of society.
- The vast majority of people are passive spectators to the policymaking process. Voting has been the primary means by which the general population can participate in governmental decisions, but other than selecting governmental officials, elections have limited effects on policy decisions.[31]

A number of students of Texas government and politics have argued from the elitist perspective. George Norris Green, writing about the period from 1938 to 1957, concluded that Texas was "governed by conservatives, collectively dubbed the Establishment."[32] **The Establishment** was a "loosely knit plutocracy comprised mostly of White businessmen, oilmen, bankers and lawyers" that emerged in the late 1930s, in part as a response to the liberal policies of the New Deal.[33] They were extremely conservative, producing a "virulent" strain of conservatism marked by "Texanism" and "super-Americanism."[34]

the Establishment
A loosely knit coalition of white businessmen, oilmen, bankers, and lawyers who assert control of state policymaking.

Texas's "traditionalistic-individualistic" political culture was especially conducive to the dominance of the conservative establishment, which had little interest in the needs of the lower socioeconomic groups within the state. The exclusion of minorities from participation in elections and the low rates of voter turnout resulted in the election of public officials who were sympathetic to the views of the conservative elites. In addition, "unprincipled public relations men" and "the rise of reactionary newspapers" manipulated public opinion.[35]

In a more recent study of Texas politics, Chandler Davidson argued that a group of Texans who are extraordinarily wealthy or linked to large corporations constitute "an upper class in the precise meaning of the term: a social group whose common background and effective control of wealth bring them together politically."[36] Although warning against a hasty conclusion that an upper class is a ruling class, Davidson describes their shared values, group cohesiveness, and interlocking relationships.[37] The upper class has enormous political power. When united on specific policy objectives, its members usually have prevailed against "their liberal enemies concentrated in the working class."[38] Moreover, the institutional arrangements of the state's economic and political structures work to produce an upper-class unity that contributes to its successes in public policy.[39]

In a longitudinal study of criminal justice policymaking in Texas, Michael Campbell found that law enforcement elites exhibited a significant amount of influence in shaping public policy, largely because public attention toward specific policy development was low and the traditional political culture supported the development of a move toward mass incarceration.[40] In a state with a part-time legislature that only meets for 140 days every two years (unless special sessions are called), there is great potential for a small group of committed and well-placed elites to dominate institutional decision making, especially when the public is focused upon more salient issues. In these circumstances, behind-the-scenes negotiations that exclude less-powerful groups are often commonplace. However, balance can be achieved when policies are in place to increase transparency, encourage groups to compete for resources, and involve more groups with greater diversity in the political process.

The sharply contrasting views of political power in Texas have produced an ongoing debate. To a large extent, the issue of who controls Texas politics has not been resolved because of insufficient data to support one position over the other. There also is evidence suggesting that power relationships have changed over time. Historically, an upper class or a conservative establishment based on oil, gas, finance, and agriculture dominated Texas government and public policy, but economic diversification has created additional economic sectors that are not all of a like mind when it comes to the actions of governments and public policy. In addition to potential competition among increased and more diversified economic sectors, cities in Texas have their respective interests, which can potentially lead to policy differences and conflicts. If we add to this mix the cultural, educational, and entertainment interests of different regions, it is hard to argue that the influential groups in the state comprise a cohesive elite structure that dominates consistently all of the major policy decisions. Moreover, the growing influence of and attention to minority groups (and their corresponding interest groups) indicate that this debate is far from over.

13.2.3 Hyperpluralism, Policy Subsystems, and Single-Issue Interest Groups

Some scholars believe that the rapid increase in the number of interest groups in Texas and the nation has produced a system of hyperpluralism. In effect, **hyperpluralism** is the interest group system out of control.[41] Historically, competition and bargaining among interest groups achieved political stability. Public policy had some degree of coherence and reflected shared views of the general interest. But as groups proliferate,

hyperpluralism
The rapid increase in the number of interest groups that serve to disrupt and potentially deadlock the policymaking process.

TEXANS GO TO WASHINGTON

The Texas abortion debate turned to the national stage when the Supreme Court heard oral arguments over HB2 (in the case *Whole Women's Health* v. *John Hellerstedt*). Pictured here are protesters from both sides of the issue on March 2, 2016. The case involved a challenge to the provision in the bill signed into law by then-Governor Rick Perry on July 18, 2013, that would have severely restricted access to legal abortion in the state. The U.S. Supreme Court ruled the law to be unconstitutional on June 27, 2016. On June 29, 2020, the Supreme Court ruled similarly in a very similar case from Louisiana. The Louisiana case was expected to reverse this decision as the ideological makeup of the Court had changed, but Chief Justice John G. Roberts Jr. sided with the Court's four liberal justices to uphold the precedent set in the Texas case.

iron triangles of government
A term used to describe how permanent relationships eventually evolve from the interactions among interest groups, administrative agencies, and legislative committees as they respond to the demands of various groups by enacting laws and regulations and appropriating funds to address their priorities.

single-issue group
A highly ideological group that promotes a single issue or cause with only limited regard for the views or interests of other groups. Such groups often are reluctant to compromise.

multi-issue group
A group that is interested in pursuing a broad range of public policy issues around a central theme.

there is a potential for the policy process to degenerate into a series of subsystems. The problem is compounded by the notion that the demands of all interest groups are legitimate and governments should attempt to respond to as many groups as possible. This theory of interest group liberalism is developed at length by Theodore Lowi in *The End of Liberalism* and has generated a good degree of academic debate.[42]

Governments respond to the demands of various groups by enacting laws and regulations or appropriating funds to address their priorities. In many cases, additional governmental agencies may be created to carry out the new laws. Legislative committees also may be given control over new programs. Eventually, the interactions among interest groups, administrative agencies, and legislative committees produce permanent relationships that have been described as the **iron triangles of government**.

Lowi's concerns about the excesses of pluralism may be valid. Some state agencies are closely tied to the industries they regulate. Sometimes, interest groups even lobby for dedicated sources of funding for their programs, thus ensuring they will benefit from specific taxes year after year, regardless of other state needs.

Hyperpluralism also can lead to deadlock. Lobbying, described in the next section, has become increasingly sophisticated. Often, lobbyists representing a single influential group can block policy initiatives that have widespread support but threaten the group's priorities. Considering the lack of progress in addressing the pressing problems facing state and local governments in recent years, one can conclude that it is easier to block solutions than to enact policies that will bring about needed change.

In recent years, a number of scholars have identified another threat to the stability of the political system—**single-issue groups**. These highly ideological groups attempt to push on the public agenda a single issue or cause without regard for the views or attitudes of other groups. **Multi-issue groups**, in contrast, pursue a broader range of issues centered around a central theme or issue. For example, the National Organization for Women works to advance the rights and status of women with regard to educational equality, sexual harassment, reproductive freedom, and pay issues. Single-issue groups, such as the National Rifle Association and NARAL Pro-Choice Texas, are often far more reluctant to compromise than multi-issue groups. Their position on an issue leaves little grounds for accommodation or compromise. In addition, these groups base their support for or opposition to a political candidate on a single issue with little regard for the candidate's other policy positions.

Interest Groups and the Policymaking Process

13.3 Describe the tactics involved in direct and indirect lobbying.

For many people, the term **lobbying** may suggest shady characters lurking in the halls of the state Capitol, attempting to bribe legislators with money, sex, or booze. That perception was reinforced, especially before a new ethics law in 1991, by published reports of lobbyists treating legislators to trips, golf tournaments, concerts, and other diversions. Lobbyists still spend money to entertain legislators, but wining and dining now are limited by state law and are only one aspect of the complex relationships between interest groups and policymakers. Lobbying is central to a pluralistic society, and, as we saw earlier in the chapter, the legal foundations of lobbying activity are found in the U.S. and Texas Constitutions, which provide for the right to petition "the governments for a redress of grievances."[43]

In the broadest sense, lobbying is "simply the practice of attempting to influence the decisions of government."[44] Most scholars take this view. Lobbying may be indirect or direct and includes, but is not limited to, electoral activities, public relations campaigns, protests and demonstrations, and direct contact with policymakers (see Table 13–1). According to political scientist Carol Greenwald, "Lobbying may thus be defined as any form of communication, made on another's behalf, and intended to influence a governmental decision."[45]

lobbying
An effort, usually organized and using a variety of strategies and techniques, to influence the making of laws or public policy.

TABLE 13-1 TECHNIQUES USED BY LOBBYISTS TO INFLUENCE POLICYMAKERS

Interest groups or their representatives will not be engaged in all of these activities concurrently.

1. Conduct and maintain relevant research and information pertaining to policy issues.
2. Provide reliable research results or technical information supporting a group's policy interests to decision makers, the press, and other audiences.
3. Contact government officials or their key staff members directly to present the organization's point of view on policy.
4. Testify at hearings of committees and subcommittees.
5. Engage and maintain informal contacts with legislators and other policymakers at conventions, over lunch, on the golf course, and so on.
6. Communicate by email or newsletter with members of the organization to inform them about organizational activities on public policy issues.
7. Enter into coalitions with other organizations to support or block policy initiatives.
8. Establish and cultivate media contacts to advance a group's policy position.
9. Consult with government officials to plan and execute legislative strategies.
10. Help draft legislation.
11. Work with group's members, allies, or the general public in letter-writing, email, or telephone campaigns to influence policymakers' decisions.
12. Mount grassroots lobbying efforts to encourage members and the general public to contact public officials.
13. Mobilize influential constituents to contact their representatives' offices.
14. Help formulate and draft administrative regulations, rules, or guidelines.
15. Serve on advisory commissions and boards.
16. Inform legislators of the effects of a bill on their districts.
17. Make campaign contributions to political candidates, campaign committees, or political action committees.
18. Endorse and/or recruit candidates running for office.
19. File lawsuits or *amicus curiae*, or otherwise engage in litigation to impact policy.

SOURCES: From Kay Lehman Scholzman and John T. Tierney, *Organized Interests and American Democracy* (New York: Harper and Row, 1986); Rogan Kersh, "The Well-Informed Lobbyist: Information and Interest Groups Lobbying," in Allan J. Cigler and Burdett A. Loomis, eds., *Interest Group Politics*, 8th ed. (Washington, D.C.: CQ Press, 2011), pp. 389–411.

GATHERING IN THE LOBBY
Effective lobbying depends on developing good relationships. Pictured here are lobbyists, visitors, and lawmakers conversing in the central rotunda of the Capitol.

direct lobbying
The communication of information and policy preferences directly to policymakers or their staffs.

13.3.1 Direct Lobbying

Although interest groups may spend much time and money electing "friendly" candidates and building public support for their objectives, at that point their work has only begun. The next crucial step is **direct lobbying**, or the communication of information and policy preferences directly to policymakers. Lobbying often is associated with legislatures, but it is directed to other governmental institutions as well. Public officials depend on the information provided by interest groups, and many policy initiatives, including proposed legislation, come from lobbyists. Interest groups also attempt to use the courts to advance their policy goals. They file lawsuits to challenge and force changes to existing laws or regulations, or file briefs supporting or opposing other groups' positions in pending litigation.[46] Win-or-lose litigation can bring about change by drawing attention to issues, garnering additional support, and even influencing public opinion.

Lobbyists engage in a wide range of activities, from drafting legislation to personally contacting legislators and other groups to testifying at hearings. Most groups understand the necessity of pursuing their legislative agendas at every conceivable opportunity and, as noted earlier, also realize it usually is easier to block policy initiatives than to enact new policies.

DRAFTING LEGISLATION Interest groups often draft proposed laws for formal introduction by legislators. In any given legislative session, hundreds of bills are drafted by the legal or technical staffs of interest groups. The groups usually work closely with legislative sponsors or their staffs in the drafting process, and they may consult staffers from the agencies that would be affected by the legislation.[47]

PLANNING AND IMPLEMENTING A LEGISLATIVE STRATEGY Interest groups supporting a bill usually work closely with the bill's sponsor, committee chairs, and other legislative leaders at every stage of the process. Strategy is planned to cover each step from introduction of the legislation in committee hearings through final action by the House and Senate. Potential opposition is assessed, and ways of diffusing that opposition and building support for the bill are mapped out.

PERSONAL CONTACTS AND COMMUNICATIONS If one were to ask most interest groups what they expect in return for their contributions to political candidates, the overwhelming response would be "access." The interest group system revolves around communication and the exchange of ideas and information with policymakers. To have some prospects of success, a group must have access to lawmakers, which often is no small task.

With thousands of bills considered during each regular legislative session, interest groups have to compete for the opportunity to discuss their programs with lawmakers. Lobbyists are denied direct access to legislators on the floor of the House and the Senate while legislators are in session, but there are numerous other opportunities for direct or indirect contact.

During House and Senate sessions, many lobbyists wait outside the chambers to stop legislators who pass by. Or they have the doorkeepers send messages to individual lawmakers, asking them to step outside the chambers for brief meetings in the lobby—hence, the term "lobbyists." It is not unusual for several dozen lobbyists to be gathered at one time outside the House or the Senate chamber on the second floor of the Capitol, particularly on days when major bills are being debated. Lobbyists also sit in the House and Senate galleries. In some instances, a lobbyist's presence in the gallery is simply a matter of minor interest or a way to kill some time before a committee meeting, but sometimes special interest groups pack the gallery in a show of force to threaten recrimination against lawmakers who do not vote their way.

Effective lobbyists, however, do most of their work long before a bill reaches the House or the Senate floor for a vote. They stop by legislators' offices to present information and solicit support for or against specific legislation. If they cannot meet personally with a legislator, they meet with his or her staff. In many cases, lobbyists provide lawmakers with written reports, summarizing the highlights of an issue and their position on it. Many interest groups back up the personal efforts of their lobbyists with letter-writing, email, or telephone campaigns directed at legislators by the groups' members.

Much personal lobbying is done away from the Capitol, sometimes far away—over lunch and dinner tables, at cocktail parties, and on golf courses. Although these occasions involve a great deal of socializing, they also provide lobbyists with golden opportunities to solidify friendships with lawmakers and make pitches for or against specific legislative proposals. A five- or ten-minute business conversation reinforced with a few hours of social camaraderie can work wonders, as many interest groups and their lobbyists very well know. Such entertainment, however, is expensive, and it can be used to abuse the policymaking process. Repeated news accounts of extravagant and questionable lobby spending finally convinced the legislature in 1991 to ban many interest group-paid trips for lawmakers and to limit lobbyist expenditures on entertaining legislators. Many lobbyists and legislators were concerned that the 1991 ethics law also might have outlawed that most sacred and basic of lobby handouts—the free lunch. Their uncertainty prompted the legislature to pass a bill in 1993 to make sure that it remained legal for lawmakers to dine at lobbyists' expense. State law requires lobbyists to disclose on whom they spend money if the amount exceeds 60 percent of the legislative per diem per legislator. For example, the per diem in 2020 is $221, so lobbyists can spend up to $132 per legislator and not report the money. Hence, a lobbyist could take four representatives to dinner, spending over $500 and not be required to report the meal or any expenditure at all.[48] Several attempts to make the reporting more stringent have been unsuccessfully proposed in recent legislative sessions.

TESTIFYING AT HEARINGS During each regular legislative session, House and Senate committees and subcommittees hold hundreds of hearings on bills that have to win committee approval before they can be considered by the full House and Senate. Interest groups can use committee hearings to present information formally to legislators or to help mobilize public support for or against a bill. Frequently, testifying at public hearings is symbolic and secondary to the personal communications with legislators and their staffs.

PUBLIC OPINION OF LOBBYING Political candidates often claim to be running against "the special interests" and promise to be responsive to all the people rather than to a few well-financed business, trade, or union groups. But most successful candidates freely accept campaign contributions from interest groups, and many Texans, along with other Americans, believe that a few big interests looking out for themselves dominate governments. National election surveys conducted by the University of Michigan for many years indicate a clear pattern of increased public distrust of government. In 1964, only 29 percent of those surveyed thought that a few big interests ran government, but during most of the years since 1974, more than 60 percent of Americans expressed this sentiment. By 2016, 82 percent thought the federal government was run by a few big interests, while only 17 percent said the government is run for the benefit of all people.[49] These views correlate with trust in government. In 1964, 77 percent of Americans trusted officials in Washington to do the right thing most or all the time; in 2019, only 17 percent did (you should note that people tend to trust the government more when their party is in control, but the overall percentages have been at remarkably low levels for decades).[50] Americans do have more confidence in their state and local governments; 72 percent trusted their local governments and 63 percent trusted their state governments in 2018 (figures that have been rather consistent for decades).[51]

Texans tend to have more confidence in their state and local governments than in the national government, but there are also elements of distrust or dissatisfaction. For example, a UT-Austin Texas Politics Poll in 2019 reported that only 25 percent of those surveyed stated that they had a very or somewhat favorable view of the federal government, while 50 percent had a similarly favorable view of the state government and 49 percent had favorable views of their local governments.[52] In a 2017 survey, people had similar views about state and local government stewardship of tax dollars. Forty-four percent of people thought the state government was careful with people's tax dollars and 42 percent thought local governments were careful with their tax dollars. Forty-nine percent of people thought the state mostly addressed the needs of Texans (47 percent thought their local government was responsive).[53]

Even though people feel more confidence and trust in their state and local governments than federal government, the concerns many have about the influence of special interests may be warranted. Two studies, conducted more than forty years apart, placed Texas among states with strong pressure group systems.[54] Powerful pressure groups usually evolve in states with weak political parties, which always has been the case in Texas.[55] During the many years that Texas was a one-party Democratic state, the Republican Party posed no serious challenge to the Democratic monopoly, and intense factionalism marked the Democratic Party. Although the conservative Democratic wing dominated state politics through the 1970s, interest groups often played a greater role in the policymaking process. Subsequent Republican growth has changed Texas's party system, but interest groups remain strong in the state and spend millions of dollars trying to elect favored candidates and influence governmental decisions. For example, in the 2020 election cycle, one political action committee representing realtors (the Texas REALTORS Political Action Committee) spent $45.6 million dollars.[56] Research by Texans for Public Justice, Public Citizen, and the Sierra Club's Lone Star Chapter found that oil and gas interests provided 60 percent of the political funds to commissioners on the Texas Railroad Commission (the entity responsible for regulating the industry). For example, Wayne Christian, elected to the Commission in 2016, got 65 percent of his campaign funds from the industries he is charged with regulating.[57] We are not saying that elected individuals will necessarily be beholden to the interests that helped finance their elections, but it is little wonder that the public is skeptical of the ability of the government to do the right thing most of the time.

13.3.2 Indirect Lobbying

Effective lobbying starts with the election of officeholders supportive of a group's viewpoint on key issues and the building of general public support for a group and its objectives. **Indirect lobbying** takes different forms and is used in tandem with direct communications with public officials. It is designed to mobilize public support for a policy position and bring pressure to bear on public officials through electoral activities, public relations campaigns, and sometimes protests or marches. Creating a favorable climate and mobilizing citizen action in support of or opposition to policy proposals often are central to the success of a group in the policy process.

indirect lobbying
Activities designed to mobilize public support for a policy position and bring pressure to bear on public officials through electoral activities, public relations campaigns, and sometimes protests or marches.

ELECTORAL ACTIVITIES Although the electoral activities of interest groups are similar to those of political parties, there are some significant differences. Political parties are broad coalitions of voters concerned with a wide range of issues, whereas most interest groups are focused on only a limited set of issues. Parties function not only to contest elections but also to govern once elected. Interest groups primarily are concerned with influencing and shaping only those policies that directly affect them. Most interest groups also cross party lines in supporting candidates.

Interest groups must decide which candidates they will back through campaign contributions, organizational support, and public endorsements. Most groups are not interested in political ideology or philosophy but primarily are concerned with electing their "friends" and defeating their "enemies." They spend their money selectively, contributing to those legislators who serve on the committees that have jurisdiction over their industry or areas of concern. The Texas legislature's highly centralized leadership encourages groups to concentrate their resources on a small number of key lawmakers.

In some cases, interest groups use promises of financial campaign support to recruit opponents for incumbent legislators who consistently vote against them. In other instances, incumbents and potential challengers approach interest groups for support. Although this process has become a permanent fixture of contemporary elections, it still can present an unsavory image of a mutual shakedown. During legislative sessions, legislators are prohibited by state law from accepting campaign contributions. The law is intended to diminish the possibility of contributions impacting legislative voting. A candidate cannot legally promise a specific vote in return for financial or other campaign support, but interest groups make every effort to ensure that potential recipients of campaign contributions are "sympathetic" and will be "accessible" to them.

Under state and federal laws, interest groups and many corporations may form political action committees (PACs) for raising and distributing campaign funds. Money is contributed to a PAC by individual members of a group or employees of a corporation and then distributed among selected candidates. In most instances, the professional staff of the interest group manages the PAC, and the campaign contributions are a key part of the organization's overall lobbying strategy.

Federal campaign finance restrictions and reporting requirements are stricter than the state's. Federal law limits individual contributions to $2,700 per candidate for each election. PAC contributions by corporations, labor unions, trade associations, and other organizations are limited to $5,000 per candidate per election.[58] But the U.S. Supreme Court, ruling in *Citizens United* v. *Federal Election Commission* (2010), opened up a major loophole by allowing independent super-PACS (also known as independent expenditure-only committees, or IEOCs) to make unlimited contributions to federal races, provided there is no coordination between the PAC and the candidate.[59] These super-PACs have become major players since 2010. For example, according to the Center for Responsive Politics based upon data compiled from the Federal Election Commission, in the 2020 presidential election cycle, nearly 2,258 super-PACs spent more than $2 billion dollars to influence federal elections, nearly doubling the $1.07 billion spend by 2,393 super-PACs in 2016.[60] In 2018, 2,395 super PACs spent over $822 million dollars compared with the midterm election of 2014 where 1,282 super PACs spent more than $345 million.[61] In April 2014, the Supreme Court (in *McCutcheon v. Federal Election Commission*) further eroded federal campaign finance rules when it decided that aggregate limits on individual donations were no longer permissible.

Many believe that influence of well-financed individuals will only continue to grow as these individuals can play larger roles in funding elections. Examining data on money spent for Texas legislative campaigns is telling. PACs spent record amounts in the 2014 elections, with 1,421 PACs spending over $159 million (based upon data submitted to the Texas Ethics Commission and reported by Texans for Public Justice). Business groups spent over $81 million, and ideological groups spent over $65 million. One PAC, Texans for Lawsuit Reform, spent more than $7 million to influence the 2014 state legislative races (they spent over $17.4 million in 2020), while the Texas Association of Realtors spent nearly $6.9 million.[62] In 2016, 185 individuals and groups collectively spent $131 million (representing 67 percent of all money raised by candidates for Texas public office in that election cycle). In total, over $200 million was spent by over 1,700 PACs in Texas; over $275.4 million was spent in 2018 and preliminary figures indicate over $323.4 million was spent by PACs in Texas in 2020.[63] Approximately 650 registered PACs spent $5,000 or less, while approximately 84 spent over $500,000 in 2020. Those with the top expenditures in 2020 were Texas Realtors PAC (which spent over $45.6 million), ActBlue Texas (which spent approximately $24.6 million), and Texans for Lawsuit Reform (which spent over $18.9 million).[64] In 2018, 2,220 registered PACs in Texas spent over $275.4 million. The top spenders in this election cycle were the Texas Realtors PAC ($60.5 million), ActBlue Texas ($10.2 million), Texans for Lawsuit Reform ($8.6 million) and the Republican Party of Texas ($5.9 million).[65]

Texas law prohibits corporations and labor unions from making direct contributions to state and local political candidates, but it sets no limits on the amount of money a PAC or an individual can give to candidates for races other than those for judicial offices. In many cases, PACs and wealthy individuals have given several hundred thousand dollars to a single candidate.

Interest groups sometimes provide in-kind support for political candidates. A group may make its phone banks available to a candidate, conduct a poll, and give the candidate the results, or provide office space and equipment to a candidate's campaign. Some organizations even "loan" the services of their staffers to a campaign or provide postage, cars for travel, printing services, and other types of assistance. State law requires such in-kind contributions to be publicly reported to the Texas Ethics Commission, just as financial donations are. Some groups, depending on how they are organized under federal tax laws, cannot make in-kind contributions directly but can do so through their political action committees.

Groups also publicize their endorsements of candidates on their websites; in emails and newsletters; and through social media, news releases, press conferences, and conventions. Some groups maintain phone banks during election campaigns to inform their members of their endorsements and encourage them to get out and vote for their chosen candidates. Candidates often seek public endorsements when a group's size, prestige, and influence are considered valuable; candidates use these endorsements in their advertising campaigns.

PUBLIC OPINION Interest groups may try to cultivate favorable public opinion through media campaigns. One objective is to "develop a reservoir of good will in the minds of the citizenry that can be drawn upon when political battles over specific issues occur."[66] Although this practice is more pronounced at the national level, state organizations in Texas that are associated with national interest groups often participate in national campaigns.

Public relations campaigns also are used to mobilize public support for a group's position on a specific issue being debated in Austin.[67] Voters may be encouraged to write, call, fax, or send email messages to their legislators. Groups are increasingly

COURTING SUPPORT

Governor Abbott speaks at a reception at the annual Houston Hispanic Chamber of Commerce Business Expo and Luncheon in Houston.

using social media to alert supporters to upcoming legislative action and to mobilize support. The Texas Medical Association, for example, has sought public support for restrictions on medical malpractice awards by distributing cards to doctors' waiting rooms that attempt to explain how the high cost of malpractice insurance can affect the costs and quality of health care.

Organized efforts of interest groups can intentionally distort the perception of public support and make it seem greater than it is. For example, Podgorski and Kockelman found that vocal members of interest groups often obscure true public opinion at Texas Department of Transportation public hearings.[68] Consequently, interest groups often encourage their members, who might be small in number, to become involved in local politics, resulting in disproportionate influence. The lesson to be learned here is that anyone with strong feelings about a zoning, road development, or other matter to be considered at a public hearing should attend the hearing or council meeting; involvement at this level is often key in achieving success.

Interest groups may sponsor advertising campaigns featuring emotional language and imagery. They may use press conferences and informal media contacts to encourage favorable editorials or put their "spin," or viewpoint, on news coverage. For years, Texas legislators resisted pari-mutuel horse race betting and the lottery. But groups supporting those proposals continued to wage strong media campaigns, insisting that gambling would boost state revenue. Eventually, during economic downturns when the legislature was struggling to find new sources of revenue, they won the fight.

Public interest advocates, in their efforts to protect consumers and the environment, cannot match the financial firepower that utilities, insurance companies, and other big industries can muster. Their success depends on their ability to stir up public concern—or outrage—over pocketbook issues and the relationships between moneyed special interests and government. Quality research that focuses on political issues, such as campaign contributions or policy options, is one of the more effective resources available to public interest groups. Using this research, these groups arduously work the traditional news media and social networking sites, which are crucial to their ability to spread their message. They seldom can afford paid advertising campaigns, but they hold frequent news conferences, issue a stream of press releases and emails, and readily return reporters' phone calls. They also recognize strength and efficiency in numbers and sometimes issue joint statements or hold joint news conferences on issues of mutual concern.

PROTESTS AND MARCHES Staged demonstrations against governmental decisions or inaction have long been used by individuals and groups attempting to influence public policy. Although many people have mixed feelings about such tactics, protests and marches can be effective in capturing public attention. Television coverage of such events, in particular, can convey powerful and intense images. The civil rights movement capitalized on this resource, and that movement's success, in large measure, turned on the ability of minority leaders to show the nation that discriminatory policies were incompatible with the values of a democratic society.

In recent years, both antiabortion groups and abortion rights activists in Texas have marched in support of their positions. LGBTQ groups have held vigils to protest incidents of violence and discrimination, and many groups have marched and protested instances of suspected police brutality or excessive use of force. As we saw at the beginning of the chapter, following the killings of George Floyd and Breonna Taylor (and others), a wave of protests and marches for racial justice swept across the country. Researchers have estimated between 15 and 26 million people participated in demonstrations between May 26 and July 1, 2020. The peak day appears to have been June 6, 2020, when nearly 550 demonstrations occurred across the nation.[69] In addition to these examples, a large variety of groups have used public demonstrations to dramatize their particular issues or concerns. As restrictions were enacted to fight COVID-19, many Americans came together to protest what they saw as infringements of their liberties. On July 4, 2020, for example, protestors came together outside the governor's mansion for a "Shed the Mask" rally to protest infringements of personal liberties being mandated by Governor Abbott. A number of anti-gun advocates have successfully organized marches and protests recently. These marches have been largely organized online by students (with the help of established gun control advocacy groups). The effects of these tactics are not clear, but many groups that use them have limited resources and recognize their value in gaining free media attention.

Dominant Interest Groups in Texas

13.4 Describe the characteristics of interest groups active in Texas.

Throughout much of Texas's history, large corporations and banks, oil companies, and agricultural interests that backed conservative Democratic officeholders (who had a stranglehold on the legislature, the courts, and the executive branch) dominated state government.[70] Big business still carries a lot of weight in Austin and can purchase a lot of influence with major political contributions and the sophisticated skills of public affairs strategists. State officials who want to build public support for new policy proposals usually solicit the support of the business community first.

Beginning in the 1970s, however, influence began to be more diffused. The number of minorities, Republicans, and liberal Democrats elected to the legislature from single-member districts increased. Consumer, environmental, and other public advocacy groups emerged. Organized labor, which had been shut out by the corporate establishment, found some common interests with the trial lawyers who earned fees by suing businesses on behalf of consumers and other plaintiffs claiming damages or injuries caused by various companies or products. The decline of oil and gas production and the emergence of high-tech service industries also helped diffuse the business lobby into more competitive factions.

The following is a brief synopsis of the dominant interest groups in Texas. Although the list is not exhaustive, it provides a general overview of the variety of influential groups currently active in Texas politics.

13.4.1 Business

The diverse business interests in Texas organize in several ways to influence the policymaking process. First, broad-based associations, including the Texas Association of Business (TAB) and the Texas Taxpayers and Research Association (TTRA), represent business and industry in general. Their overall goal is to maintain and improve upon a favorable business climate by seeking favorable tax and regulatory policies.

The business community also organizes through trade associations that represent and seek to advance the interests of specific industries. Some of the more active associations include the Texas Bankers Association, the Texas Association of Realtors, the Wholesale Beer Distributors of Texas, the Texas Independent Producers & Royalty Owners Association, the Texas Chemical Council, the Texas Automobile Dealers Association, and the Texas Restaurant Association. In addition, many individual companies retain their own lobbyists to represent them before the legislature and administrative agencies. Finally, a group representing a broad range of business members can be organized to pursue a single issue. Perhaps the best-known example is Texans for Lawsuit Reform, which for years has doggedly lobbied for a series of limitations on civil lawsuits and damage awards against businesses and their insurance companies. The Texas Public Policy Foundation, a conservative think tank based in Austin, has in recent years developed a strong influence over a state government dominated by conservative legislators and other officials. Although not limited to business issues, it shares many of the priorities—low taxes and a relaxed regulatory climate—of most other business groups. It also advocates for changes in education, criminal justice, and other state policies.

Although the business lobby has much in common, it is far from monolithic. Various companies and trade associations differ on numerous issues, including tax policy and utility regulation.

13.4.2 Professional Groups

A number of professional groups have played dominant roles in Texas politics and the policymaking process. One of the better known is the Texas Medical Association (TMA), which in recent years has joined forces with business against trial lawyers to push for laws putting limits on malpractice suits and other damage claims against physicians and the business community. The TMA's political action committee (TEXPAC) is a major contributor of campaign dollars to candidates for the legislature, the Texas Supreme Court, and other state offices. It won a major victory in 2003, with legislative and voter approval of a constitutional amendment imposing new limits on monetary damages in medical malpractice cases.

13.4.3 Labor

Organized labor has traditionally taken a back seat to business in Texas, a strong "right-to-work" state in which union membership cannot be required as a condition of employment. Antilabor sentiment ran particularly high in the 1940s and 1950s, at the height of the conservative Democratic establishment's control of Texas politics. Labor-baiting campaigns in which unions were portrayed as evil communist sympathizers were not uncommon then.[71]

In 2019, about 497,000 Texans, or 4 percent of the workforce, are members of labor unions (compared to 4.1 percent in 2009). This percentage, already low compared to other states, has been decreasing in the last several years (the national average is 10.3 percent).[72] The largest unions in the state include the Communications Workers of America (CWA) and the American Federation of State, County, and Municipal Employees (AFSCME). Unions can provide grassroots support for political candidates through endorsement cards, phone banks, and other get-out-the-vote efforts, and this support historically has gone to Democratic candidates. With Republican and conservative gains in recent years, however, many labor-backed candidates have not fared well in Texas, especially in statewide elections.

13.4.4 Public Interest Groups

Most of the **public interest groups** represented in Austin are concerned primarily with protecting consumers and the environment from big business; promoting stronger ethical standards for public officials; and increasing funding for health and human services programs for the poor, the elderly, the young, and the disabled. Many have full-time lobbyists and some staff, but nowhere near the financial resources of the business and professional groups. Grassroots volunteer efforts and the effective use of the mass media are crucial to their success. The most active include the Center for Public Policy Priorities, the Sierra Club, Texas Watch, the Gray Panthers, Americans Disabled for Attendant Programs Today (ADAPT), and Public Citizen. Although public interest lobbyists concentrate most of their attention on the legislature, some consumer groups also are active before state regulatory agencies, particularly the Public Utility Commission, the Department of Insurance, and the Texas Commission on Environmental Quality.

public interest group
A group that is primarily concerned with consumer or environmental protection, the promotion of strong ethical standards for public officials, or increased funding for health and human services programs. Grassroots, volunteer efforts are crucial to the success of these groups, since they often are poorly funded.

13.4.5 Education

A variety of educational interests are visible in the policymaking process in Austin. The changing global economy and increased technology have enhanced the importance of education in developing the state's future, and there is widespread public support for improving the public schools and expanding access to colleges and universities.

Most university regents, chancellors, and presidents are well connected politically. Universities also are capable—through the use of donations and other non-tax funds—of hiring a well-paid cadre of legislative liaisons, or lobbyists. Another effective lobbying source for universities, particularly the larger ones, is the armies of alumni, many of them politically influential, ready to make phone calls, send emails, or write letters on behalf of their alma maters when the need arises. In addition, the business community is a strong supporter of higher education.

The struggle for equity and quality in public elementary and secondary education involves a number of groups representing various, and sometimes conflicting, interests within the educational community. Four associations or unions represent teachers and other school employees, one represents school boards, and a separate lobby group represents school administrators. Still another group, the Equity Center, which represents school districts with low property wealth, has been a major player in lawsuits over school finance. All of these groups lobby the legislature, and they all seek to improve public education. But, individually, they also seek to protect the specific interests of their members, which means they can line up against one another on some issues.

13.4.6 Minorities

The advent of single-member, urban legislative districts in the 1970s significantly increased the number of African American and Hispanic lawmakers and strengthened the influence of minority interest groups. Although groups often have found that the courthouse is a shorter route to success than the statehouse, the legislature has become increasingly attentive to their voices.

A variety of groups exist to represent people of color in Texas. The League of United Latin American Citizens (LULAC) and the Mexican American Legal Defense and Educational Fund (MALDEF) are two of the better-known Hispanic organizations. LULAC, founded in 1929, is the oldest and largest Hispanic organization in the

LULAC SPEAKS UP

LULAC provides a voice for many Hispanics across Texas. Pictured here are former-Democratic presidential candidate Hilary Clinton, LULAC President Roger C. Rocha, Jr., and Lizeth Urdiales, a University of Texas student who fought for the DREAM Act (which would allow undocumented residents who received a GED or graduated from a Texas high school to pay in-state tuition to attend a public university or college within the state).

United States and continues to be particularly influential in causes such as education and election reform in Texas. MALDEF, formed in San Antonio in 1968, fights in the courtroom for the civil rights of Hispanics. It has been successful in numerous battles over the drawing of political boundaries for governmental bodies in Texas and in lengthy litigation over public school finance. The National Association for the Advancement of Colored People (NAACP) is a leader in promoting and protecting the interests of African Americans. The NAACP initiated many of the early court attacks on educational inequality and has fought for voting rights for minority citizens. More recently, Asian American groups have begun to organize, including the Asian American Democrats of Texas (AADT), Asian Pacific American Heritage Association (APAHA, a Houston-based group), the Greater Austin Asian Chamber of Commerce, and the Organization of Chinese Americans.

In recent years, the Industrial Areas Foundation (IAF), a collection of well-organized, church-supported community groups, has been a strong and effective voice for low-income minorities. Member groups include Valley Interfaith in South Texas, Communities Organized for Public Service (COPS) in San Antonio, The Metropolitan Organization (TMO) and the Fort Bend Interfaith Council in the Houston area, and the El Paso Interreligious Sponsoring Organization (EPISO). At the state level, the IAF has lobbied for health care for the poor; more equity in school funding; and water and sewer service for the *colonias*, or unincorporated slums, along the Texas–Mexico border.

13.4.7 Agricultural Groups

Although Texas is now predominantly urban, agriculture still is an important part of the state's economy, and a number of agricultural groups are represented in Austin. Their influence is obviously strongest among rural legislators. But the Texas Farm Bureau, the largest such group, was instrumental in Rick Perry's 1990 election defeat of liberal Democratic Agriculture Commissioner Jim Hightower, who had angered many agricultural producers and the chemical industry with tough stands on farm worker rights and pesticide regulation. Other producer groups include the Texas and Southwestern Cattle Raisers Association (TSCRA), the Texas Nursery & Landscape Association (TNLA), and the Texas Corn Producers Board (TCPB). The United Farm Workers Union (UFW) has been a strong advocate of better conditions for workers and frequently has been at odds with agricultural producers.

13.4.8 Religious Groups

Influenced in part by their views of separation of church and state, many people think religious groups have little or no legitimate role in the political process. Nevertheless, religious groups have helped influence policy in Texas, and the abortion issue and other social and economic issues have increased the presence of religious groups in Austin.

A number of religious groups began emerging on the political scene in the 1940s, with an identifiable conservative orientation. These groups, predecessors of what now is known as the "Religious Right," combined Christian rhetoric and symbols with anticommunism, antilabor, anti–civil rights, antiliberal, or anti–New Deal themes. Although these groups often were small, they were linked to the extreme right wing of the Texas establishment, and they were the precursors to many of the conservative ideological groups that have emerged in American politics since the 1970s.[73]

The Texas Freedom Network, founded in 1995, provides an alternative voice to the Christian right. It now claims a membership of more than 130,000 religious and community leaders supporting religious freedom and individual liberties. The organization claims success in "defeating initiatives backed by the religious right in Texas, including private school vouchers, textbook censorship, and faith-based deregulation."[74]

Many religious denominations have boards or commissions responsible for monitoring governmental action. One well-known religious interest group is the Christian Life Commission of the Baptist General Convention of Texas, a strong advocate of human services programs and an outspoken opponent of gambling. Churches across the state, particularly the Catholic Church, have established links to community-based organizations that address the social and economic needs of the poor. The Texas Catholic Conference serves as the "public policy voice of the Catholic Bishops of Texas."

13.4.9 Local Governments

State laws and budgetary decisions significantly affect local governments. The stakes are particularly high now because governments are finding revenue harder to raise, especially with the federal government passing the cost of numerous programs on to the states, and the states issuing similar mandates to local governments. As a result, lobbyists represent counties, cities, prosecutors, metropolitan transit authorities, and various special districts in Austin.

Many local governments belong to umbrella organizations, such as the Texas Municipal League, the Texas Association of Counties, and the Texas District and County Attorneys Association, which have full-time lobbyists. Several larger cities and counties retain their own lobbyists, and while they are not lobbyists, mayors, city council members, and county judges frequently travel to Austin to visit with legislators and testify for or against bills. When we say that these local governments hire lobbyists, it is important to note that they are using tax dollars to hire lobbyists. Taxpayer-funded lobbying can rightfully raise concerns about the responsiveness of governments. For example, a city council can use tax dollars to hire lobbyists to try to oppose a law that would reduce property taxes. Many taxpayers in the locality might appreciate having their property taxes reduced and are unaware that their local taxes are being used to hire lobbyists to oppose their preferences and interests. Transparency USA, a nonprofit interested in transparency in campaign finance, tracks money spent in politics. They estimate that over $108 million dollars was spent in taxpayer-funded lobbying in 2020 in Texas (compared with over $545 million in private lobbying).[75] Taxpayer-funded lobbying can be useful to try to counter privately funded lobbying, but the practice can make some feel that their government is not as responsive and trustworthy as possible.

Resources and Power of Interest Groups

13.5 Describe sources of interest group power and the contemporary challenges facing interest groups in Texas.

Interest groups are likely to be a permanent fixture in Texas politics for the foreseeable future; consequently, anyone interested in being involved in shaping the political arena needs to be well versed in the elements of interest group action. Interest groups have both positive and negative elements, serving to both advance and complicate democratic decision making.

Perhaps among the most troubling aspects of interest groups is that not all interests are equally represented, nor do all interest groups have the same likelihood of exerting influence in politics today. As you have seen, interest groups are not all created alike; some have significant resources and hence greater political power. Money is one key factor in determining influence, but it is not the only factor. From time to time, poorly financed groups can be influential if they have dynamic leadership and politically active and committed members.

Moreover, interest groups are often seen as too powerful, with growing percentages of Americans believing they have too much influence, potentially negating the influence of everyday people.[76] One of the most important challenges facing the state is the role of special interest money in politics. For example, when Texas Attorney General Ken Paxton issued an opinion in January 2016 that fantasy sport leagues constituted illegal gambling, lobbyists sprang into action. Before this opinion, the gambling industry had one registered lobbyist in Texas; by the end of 2016, there were fifteen lobbying contracts worth up to $270,000. Lobbying increased by 80 percent in 2017 with twenty-five lobbying contracts worth up to $485,000 (the state releases lobbying data in ranges, so it is hard to determine exactly how much is being spent).[77] Speaker of the House Dennis Bonnen, was hired to serve as new Texas lobbyist for the Las Vegas Sands Corporation (primarily owned by the Adelsons) following the 2020 election. Complicating the issue is the need to represent the interests of indigenous people and the gaming industry. One federally recognized tribe, the Alabama-Coushatta Tribe, spent between $350,000 and $550,000 in lobbying in 2019.[78] Given that the interests of indigenous people have rarely been adequately represented, these lobbyists can be very helpful in advocating the interests of the group.

Balancing the influence of the affluent versus that of the general public will continue to be a crucial challenge as government struggles to address growing concerns over public trust. Moreover, while some interest groups are extremely powerful and exercise considerable influence over the formation of public policy, others are ineffectual and weak. The differences can be explained by a number of factors. One is the size of a group and the number of members and voters it can potentially influence. Numerous teachers' and educational groups within the state, for example, represent a significant number of people. The promise of support or the threat of retaliation by such groups will be assessed by a legislator as he or she decides to support or oppose the groups' policy proposals. Individual educational groups do not always agree on legislation, but their numbers are difficult to ignore. Teachers who were instrumental in the 1982 election of Governor Mark White withdrew that support in 1986 in a dispute over some of White's educational reforms; the loss of that support contributed to his defeat.

The size of a group alone, however, does not guarantee power or influence. A large group internally divided, with no clear policy focus, is less likely to be successful than a smaller, highly cohesive group with a fixed goal. Other major factors in a group's success are its cohesiveness and the ability of its leaders to mobilize its membership in support of policy objectives.

Another key factor in how much power a group has is the distribution of the group's membership across the state. A group concentrated in one geographic area has less potential impact on the election of a large number of legislators than does a group with members distributed across the state. Organized labor, for example, has its greatest membership strength in the Houston and Beaumont areas in southeastern Texas. On the other hand, teachers and small business owners are plentiful throughout the state and have the potential to affect more local and district elections.

A group's financial resources also determine its power. Groups that represent low-income people have difficulty raising the dollars necessary to mount effective lobbying or public relations campaigns. By contrast, organizations representing large corporations or high-income professional groups are in a much better position to raise funds for campaign contributions and lobbying expenditures necessary to ensure access to policymakers.

In addition, a group's reputation, both within the legislature and among the general public, affects a group's influence. A major function of interest groups is to provide information to policymakers, and the reliability and accuracy of this information are critical. If a group lies, unduly distorts information, or is less than forthright in its dealings with other actors in the policymaking process, its reputation can be irreparably damaged.[79]

The leadership of a group and its hired staff contributes to the group's success as well. As policy issues develop, a competent staff will conduct research, provide position papers, draft specific proposals, contact key decision makers and the press, maintain communication with the membership, and develop public relations strategies to mobilize the membership to bring pressure on policymakers.

13.5.1 Who Are the Lobbyists?

During each regular session of the Texas legislature, hundreds of individuals representing businesses, trade associations, and other interests register as lobbyists with the Texas Ethics Commission. Some 1,886 lobbyists represented approximately 4,000 clients in 2019.[80] Lobbyists run the gamut from well-dressed corporate types with generous expense accounts to volunteer consumer and environmental advocates in blue jeans and sneakers. Most are male, although the number of female lobbyists has increased in recent years, and many women now hold major lobbying positions. Most lobbyists came to their careers by way of other occupations and jobs, but they have, on the whole, an acute understanding of the policymaking process and the points of access and influence in that process.

Many lobbyists are former legislators. Across the country, it is very common for former legislators to become lobbyists (as is true for legislative staff members). According to the Center for Public Integrity, Texas has among the highest number of former state legislators serving as registered lobbyists. Former legislators bring to the process their legislative skills, personal relationships with former legislative colleagues, and expertise in substantive policy areas. A number of other lobbyists are former legislative staffers, like we saw with Massingill lobbying for the Las Vegas Sands Corporation. Some are former gubernatorial assistants. In recent years, a number of bills have been introduced, though not passed, to curb the practice of individuals leaving the legislature and immediately becoming lobbyists. This practice, known as "revolving door lobbyists," can undermine the integrity of the legislature as it appears that former public servants are "cashing in" to the detriments of the public.

Many of the trade and professional associations, labor unions, and public interest groups have full-time staffs in Austin who function as their lobbyists. Many corporations also use their own employees to lobby. Some companies have governmental affairs departments or offices staffed by employees with experience in government or public affairs. In large corporations that do business across the country, the governmental affairs staffs may be rather large because such companies will attempt to follow the actions of numerous state legislatures, city councils, and the U.S. Congress.

A number of lawyers have developed highly successful lobbying practices. Some of these professional freelancers specialize in specific policy areas, whereas others represent a wide array of clients. Some may be identified as "super lobbyists" because

BIG BUSINESS—GOOD FOR ALL?
Many Americans fear that interest group money corrupts American politics. As this chapter has demonstrated, interest groups play a complicated role, both advancing and challenging the democratic process. Pictured here are ships transporting oil from refineries. While the oil industry is important in the Texas economy, many are concerned about the potential environmental impact of these refineries.

of their ability to exercise considerable influence in the policymaking process. Many work for the state's largest law firms, which have established permanent offices in Austin. Some top-notch freelancers are not attorneys, but they have a strong knowledge of the governmental process.

Some public relations firms also offer their services to interest groups. These companies specialize in "image creation" or "image modification."[81] Although they may not handle direct lobbying efforts, they often are retained to assist in indirect lobbying campaigns. They are responsible for developing relationships with the press, developing media campaigns, and assisting in political campaigns.

CONCLUSION

Americans have a love/hate relationship with interest groups. On the one hand, we are leery of the disproportionate influence interest groups exert in state and national politics. On the other hand, we have a long and firm tradition of supporting and engaging in collective action. Consider, for example, what you would do to mobilize support for a situation that caused you concern. Imagine that a zoning request has been made for land immediately adjacent to your neighborhood that would allow a strip club to be built. You fear that your property value would decrease and children would be at risk, and so you want to thwart the club's ability to build on the land. What would you do? Would you simply call your city hall, hoping they would listen to your concerns? Or would you try to mobilize your neighbors, believing that the voices of many are likely to be more powerful than the voice of one? You might organize a group of your neighbors and perhaps church members to oppose the proposed zoning ordinance change.

From the nation's formative period, Americans, and subsequently Texans, learned the value and effectiveness of collective action. Throughout this chapter we learned how interest groups differ from other groups and how interest groups both advance and complicate democracy. As we saw with the example of the NRA, interest groups employ a variety of strategies to exert power and advance the position of their members. Money, supporters, and dynamic leadership all influence the power of interest groups. Although not all people are equally likely to be members of interest groups, all have the constitutionally protected right to become involved, allowing individuals

STUDENTS UNITED

Students have a long tradition of activism, collective action, and interest group involvement in Texas. Pictured here are African American and white students from six schools marching for equal rights in Austin on April 27, 1949.

ample opportunities to get involved in politics to advance their individual interests. Interest groups are important vehicles of political participation; hence, understanding them is crucially important for students of politics and for those interested in influencing the world in which they live.

REVIEW THE CHAPTER

What Are Interest Groups?

13.1 Differentiate interest groups from other types of organizations and describe the role of interest groups in democracies, p. 414.

There are literally thousands of groups and organizations of all sizes and purposes in Texas. Only some, however, are interest groups in the political sense. Social scientists use the term "interest group" to define an organization of people who have shared attitudes or concerns and make demands on political or governmental institutions. In effect, interest groups want governments to do something for them. Although most people are familiar with the negative component of interest groups (largely that moneyed interests have a disproportionate amount of influence and power), the positive components of these groups are often overlooked. Interest groups are the vehicles that allow for collective action of like-minded individuals, providing an important link between individuals and their elected officials and promoting political participation and civic engagement. The interaction and conflict among these groups in the policymaking process help policymakers decide who gets what, when, and how.

Interest Group Theory

13.2 Apply the pluralist and elitist theories of political behavior to Texas, p. 418.

For years, political scientists have debated whether politics and public policy in Texas are controlled or dominated by a small handful of people (the elitist theory) or based on a complex system of many groups or sectors of society (the pluralist theory). Pluralists recognize the inequities in political resources but argue that individual interests are adequately represented through membership in interest groups. With thousands of groups competing, no one group can dominate the policy process. New groups are constantly formed to provide new leadership opportunities and greater access to the decision-making process for people who have been historically denied influence. Elitists, on the other hand, emphasize the marked differences in the resources and consequent political influence of groups and contend that relatively few corporations and other institutions with great financial resources dominate the policy process in Texas. Evidence suggests that the source of political power and influence lies somewhere between the elitist and pluralist positions. The narrow, limited interests of a few groups sometimes prevail, but public policy at other times is responsive to the needs and interests of broad segments of the population.

Interest Groups and the Policymaking Process

13.3 Describe the tactics involved in direct and indirect lobbying, p. 423.

Interest groups and other organizations engage in indirect lobbying (campaign financing and other efforts to elect candidates who share a group's views, as well as efforts to shape and mobilize public opinion in favor of the group's objectives) and direct lobbying (a variety of strategies and techniques, including direct one-on-one conversations with legislators and other policymakers, testifying at legislative hearings, providing information about pending legislation, communicating with legislative staff, and building coalitions in support of legislative goals). Although lobbying has a negative connotation for many Texans, elected and appointed policymakers depend on the information, coalition building, and public support of groups for their decisions and actions.

Dominant Interest Groups in Texas

13.4 Describe the characteristics of interest groups active in Texas, p. 430.

Groups are classified according to their place within the state's economic and social structure. Some economic or social sectors are dominated by a small number of groups, whereas other sectors have multiple groups. Although people join groups for diverse reasons, there are common political interests among groups. Some single-issue groups are concerned with only one policy, while other groups have a range of interests. Professional groups and corporations have significant financial resources, and they wield political power in Texas. Public interest groups rarely have the funds to match those of corporations or professional groups and usually rely on the mass media to mobilize support for their issues.

Resources and Power of Interest Groups

13.5 Describe sources of interest group power and the contemporary challenges facing interest groups in Texas, p. 435.

Not all groups are equal players in the state's interest group system. The effectiveness of an interest group in the policymaking process is determined by its size, the geographical distribution of its membership, its economic resources, its reputation, and its leadership and staff. Generally speaking, better-financed and better-organized interest groups tend to have more influence (as they can hire specialists to lobby policymakers, sponsor research, testify before legislative hearings, and conduct public opinion campaigns); however, groups with energetic leaders and committed members also can be influential in affecting change. Historically, lobbying was a "man's world," but this is beginning to change. A large number of lobbyists are ex-legislators and former legislative staff, but association officials, lawyers, and public relations or media specialists also have gravitated toward lobbying.

LEARN THE TERMS

interest group, p. 415
mischief of factions, p. 418
pluralism, p. 418
elitism, p. 420
iron rule of oligarchy, p. 420

the Establishment, p. 420
hyperpluralism, p. 421
iron triangles of government, p. 422
single-issue group, p. 422
multi-issue group, p. 422

lobbying, p. 423
direct lobbying, p. 424
indirect lobbying, p. 427
public interest group, p. 432

Contemporary Public Policy Issues in Texas

14

A POPULAR UNIVERSITY DESTINATION
Bill Heinsohn/Alamy Stock Photo

During football season, Darrell K. Royal Memorial Stadium is a popular venue at the University of Texas at Austin. Academically, the university is a popular choice for young people seeking higher education degrees. Paying for the degree can be a politically charged issue, as the cost of higher education continues to increase.

LEARNING OBJECTIVES

14.1 Apply the stages of the policymaking process to the framework of issue networks, p. 441.

14.2 Describe recent developments in the formation of the Texas budget and the constraints on those responsible for it, p. 446.

14.3 Identify four types of taxes in Texas and the regressive aspects of the Texas tax system, p. 449.

14.4 Relate the factors affecting education policy in Texas to questions of equity and quality, p. 453.

14.5 Explain the implications of court-ordered prison reforms on the criminal justice system in Texas and the state's large number of executions, p. 465.

14.6 Evaluate patterns of support for health and human services in Texas, p. 468.

14.7 Assess the response of Texas to environmental issues, p. 472.

14.8 Trace the development of Texas's transportation issues, p. 476.

It may not sound sexy, and you may not always realize it, but your life is largely governed by a series of encounters with public policy. Think about it. The quality of the water you drink and the air you breathe, how fast you can drive without risking a ticket, and even the amount you paid for a new shirt at the mall are all important parts of your daily life that are affected by governmental decisions on public health, public safety, and tax policies. If you are a student at a state-supported university in Texas, what about those tuition payments that you or your parents have to pay every semester to keep you in school? Tuition is the product of a government policy, and it may have gone up this year at your university.

Let us assume for a moment that the threat from the coronavirus has largely passed, your life is beginning to return to normal, and you recently saw a news item on television indicating tuition may go up again before you graduate. You don't want to take out another student loan, and you don't have time for a second part-time job. Rising tuition clearly is a government policy you don't like, but what can you do about it? You could call the TV station or local newspaper and complain, or you could go on Facebook and Twitter and do the same thing. But would that keep some unknown (to you) government policymaker or policymakers from raising your tuition again?

You assume the university's president is responsible for setting tuition. But before you approach the president, you want to enlist some help. As you have read in earlier chapters, people who want to change public policies are more effective if they band together. You know that many of your fellow students don't want to pay more for tuition, either. Your next step is to start a social media campaign against a tuition increase. By identifying a problem and assuming the role of a leader in seeking to address it, you have taken some important first steps. But as you will learn in this chapter, the policy process is complex and often difficult, and you are likely to encounter a series of obstacles in trying to navigate it.

The policy process also is never-ending. State policies are always being reviewed and changed: tuition and other educational issues, pollution control, health care, transportation, criminal justice, water management, and outdated tax structures. Sometimes, policies are revised because of a growing population, changing needs, or changing technology; other times they are revised because of public outrage or changing political viewpoints.

We will discuss some of the enduring issues and the political controversies surrounding them in this chapter. But first we will take a detailed look at the steps involved in making and changing policy and how you can participate.

The Policy Process

14.1 Apply the stages of the policymaking process to the framework of issue networks.

Political scientists and policy analysts spend a lot of time defining public policy and all of its critical elements. We will use the definition developed by Thomas Dye, who defined public policy as "whatever governments choose to do or not to do."[1] Except for an occasional federal judge, individuals acting alone have not forced many changes in public policy. The political power necessary to shape policy is exercised through the influence of like-minded people coming together as groups, and, as we have pointed out throughout this book, some groups or interests have been more influential than others.

14.1.1 The Elements of Public Policy

Setting public policy usually involves the determination of costs and benefits. The ultimate political questions to resolve are who will benefit from specific policy decisions and who will pay the bill.[2] Certain groups, businesses, or individuals receive direct benefits from governmental decisions—benefits that are paid for by other individuals through taxes. In this process, money, perhaps in the form of higher health care payments for low-income people or a tax break for certain businesses, is transferred from one segment of the population to another. Critical decisions must be made on the allocation of the remaining tax burden—how the benefits will be paid for—a process that can produce intense political conflict. In the case of higher college tuition, you and other students stand to benefit because the additional revenue can be used to improve facilities, offer more academic programs, and increase faculty pay to encourage highly qualified professors and instructors to remain at your university. But a highly educated work force also benefits the state's society and economy as a whole, and all Texans, even those who don't attend college or have children in state-supported universities, also support higher education through their state taxes. The key is finding a politically acceptable balance between tuition and taxes in university budgets.

Public policies also provide indirect benefits. Low-income Texans receive the direct benefits of welfare assistance, job training programs, and subsidized housing and health care. But the entire population can benefit indirectly if the poverty cycle is interrupted and low-income people use government assistance to become more productive citizens. Similar arguments can be made for funding equity between poor and rich school districts. The state's economic growth and future prosperity will be adversely affected, and its crime rate will rise, if serious problems of illiteracy and school dropout rates are not successfully addressed now.

Public policy also includes regulation of the private sector. Indiscriminate use of land, water, and other natural resources has been curtailed by environmental policies seeking to protect the best interests of the state as a whole. But those policies often conflict with private property rights and spark angry responses from some businesses and other property owners, who threaten political retaliation against public officeholders or file lawsuits against government regulators.

Additionally, public policy affects the governmental process itself. Decisions on political redistricting, revisions in election laws, and changes in the structure and organization of state and local governments ultimately address the issue of how power is distributed. They help determine how many people will be able to achieve their personal and collective objectives and improve their lives.

Another dimension of public policy is rooted in the notion of the general good of the community. Related to the concept of indirect benefits, it reflects the values upon which a political culture is based. Whether defined in terms of "it's the right thing to do" or a more systematic theory of the bonds that create the political community, elements of public policy reflect the common needs or interests of those who live in the state.

14.1.2 The Stages of the Policy Process

Many activities in the private sector have an effect on public policy, such as a decision by a large corporation to close its operations in a city. But the following discussion focuses on the governmental institutions that make binding and enforceable decisions affecting all those who live in the state.[3] A number of scholars have approached policymaking as a sequential process (Table 14–1). Although this approach may suggest artificial start and stop points, the process is dynamic and continuous.

TABLE 14–1 STAGES OF THE POLICY PROCESS

Stages of the Process	Actions Taken
Identification and formation of an issue	Defining a common problem and building coalitions to force the issue on the public agenda
Access and representation	Gaining access to elected or administrative officials and getting them to see the problem
Formulation	Convincing those in government to initiate action on the problem by sifting through alternative solutions
Adoption or legitimation	The government's specific solution to the problem, including the authorization of programs and allocation of funds
Implementation	The application of the government's policy to the problem
Evaluation	Assessing the effects of the policy and determining if its objectives were achieved

SOURCES: Charles O. Jones, *An Introduction to the Study of Public Policy*, 2nd ed. (North Scituate, MA: Duxbury, 1977); and James E. Anderson, David W. Brady, Charles S. Bullock III, and Joseph Stewart Jr., *Public Policy and Politics in America*, 2nd ed. (Monterey, CA: Brooks/Cole, 1984).

IDENTIFICATION AND FORMATION OF AN ISSUE People have to identify a problem before they can expect the government's help in resolving it.[4] Subsequent steps in the policymaking process include gaining access to public officials, getting a solution drawn up and adopted, seeing it carried out, and evaluating its effectiveness.

Let us take another look at that hypothetical problem, mentioned at the beginning of this chapter, about your interest in trying to prevent another increase in tuition at your university. You have identified the issue. You believe tuition already is too high and shouldn't be increased. You launch a Twitter campaign, inviting other students to join you in signing an online petition to the university president, demanding that tuition remain unchanged. You believe a large number of signatures is more likely to get the president's attention than a letter from you alone. Groups are central to the policymaking process. By banding together, people increase their leadership capabilities, political strength, and financial resources and are better prepared to navigate the policy process.

ACCESS AND REPRESENTATION Your next step is to find the governmental body or agency that can address the tuition problem and then convince it to do so. When you take your petition to the president's office, you learn that she doesn't set tuition. That responsibility rests with the board of regents that governs the university system that includes your campus. So, you and a few classmates take your petition to the regents at their next meeting. Several members of the board seem sympathetic to your concerns, but the chairman says the board has little choice but to consider raising tuition because the legislature's appropriation of tax dollars for higher education has not kept pace with enrollment growth and inflation. He says that has been a recurring problem ever since the legislature, during a state budgetary crisis several years earlier, changed state law to deregulate tuition. That law gave regents the authority to raise tuition, without legislative approval, whenever they felt it was necessary to cover budgetary needs. Previously, the legislature had set tuition. The chairman encourages you, your fellow students, and your parents to help the regents convince the legislature to increase the amount of tax revenue it appropriates to universities.

FORMULATION Identifying a problem and convincing other people to share your concerns are a good start. But solutions must be developed and enacted through specific laws, regulations, or other policy changes. In the final analysis, "successful policy formulations must deal with the question of selecting courses of action that can actually be adopted."[5] As you are beginning to discover in your campaign against higher tuition, that process can be littered with obstacles.

You and your friends are ready to ask the legislature, which is in session, to crack down on high tuition, but where do you start? You are still collecting petition signatures online and now have several hundred signatures from students at your university and other colleges where similar tuition increases are being considered. You decide to ask for higher appropriations of state revenue for your campuses and for the legislature to repeal the tuition deregulation law. You think your state representatives and senators, not unelected regents, should set tuition. You start with your local state representative, who happens to be a member of the House Higher Education Committee. You deliver your petitions to his office and ask him to sponsor a bill to restore the legislature's control over tuition. You also deliver your petitions to the House Appropriations Committee and testify for more funding when it has a public hearing on the higher education budget.

Your state representative on the Higher Education Committee agrees to sponsor the bill you want. The chairman of your board of regents joins you during the appropriations hearing to ask for more funding, and several members of the committee seem receptive to your testimony. You are encouraged, but the chairwoman of the Appropriations Committee says the budget will be tight. Universities are competing with hundreds of other public programs for tax dollars, and the governor has warned lawmakers that he will not approve any budget that requires higher taxes. The committee also hears testimony from a conservative taxpayer watchdog group, demanding that the legislature hold the line on higher education funding. This group insists there is administrative waste in university budgets and that university officials should "tighten their belts." Another group, advocating for limited government, testifies that any shortfalls in university budgets should be covered with higher tuition, not by state taxpayers. Soon, to your dismay, you learn that your regents chairman and most higher education regents throughout the state oppose your effort to repeal the tuition deregulation law. They want to keep the ability to raise tuition as a budget option. Furthermore, regents say, state-supported universities in Texas charge lower tuition than universities in many other states.

You and your fellow students can use your social media networks to mobilize large groups of students and parents from around the state to come to the Capitol to rally and lobby their legislators to put a halt to tuition increases. You can do interviews with your campus newspapers and local media organizations. You also may enlist the help of organized consumer protection groups. But, win or lose, your task will be anything but simple and easy. It will be time-consuming and potentially expensive, two huge barriers for everyday people fighting against well-organized and influential interests, including higher education leaders. As a full-time student, you simply may not have the time.

Not every policy issue is as complex or divisive as the hypothetical one we just described. But the policy process always includes many steps and players, and often involves conflicting points of view.

ADOPTION OR LEGITIMATION The legislature is primarily responsible for sifting through proposed alternatives and setting policy at the state level. But the separation of powers doctrine under which our government operates gives the governor the authority to veto proposed laws to which he or she objects. And it gives the judiciary important scrutiny over legislative action—or inaction. In recent years, several major federal and state court decisions have forced the legislature to make far-reaching changes in education, criminal justice, and mental health and disability programs. Those court orders have prompted some lawmakers and other critics to complain that the judiciary overstepped its authority and was attempting to preempt the legislature. Others believe, however, that the legislature had neglected its responsibilities and needed some prodding.

Virtually every public policy has a cost. It is not enough for the legislature to create a program. Programs have to be funded, or they are meaningless. Sometimes the legislature requires local governments to pick up the tab, but most programs have to compete with hundreds of other programs for a limited number of state tax dollars. Thus, the state's complex budgetary process is at the heart of policymaking and is closely monitored by individuals and organizations interested in policy development. Conflicts over the budgetary process can be intense.

IMPLEMENTATION Once legislation has been enacted and funded, its specific provisions must be implemented, or carried out. Much of this activity is the responsibility of state and local agencies that have been created to carry "a program to the problem."[6] Political scientists once referred to this stage of the policy process as public administration, and much of it falls within the domain of administrative agencies and departments. But government bureaucrats are not alone in carrying out policy; they are joined by legislators, judges, interest groups, and nonprofit organizations. There are three main activities in this implementation phase:

- *Interpretation*—the translation of program language into acceptable and feasible directives

- *Organization*—the establishment of organizational units and standard operating procedures for putting a program into effect
- *Application*—the routine provision of services, payments, or other agreed-upon program objectives or instruments[7]

EVALUATION Governments spend a lot of time evaluating the effects of public policy. In Texas, this is called performance review. Information is gathered to determine if programs have met stated goals and, if not, what changes or adjustments are required. Legislative committees, in their oversight function, demand information from agencies to help determine whether to continue to fund programs, expand them, or change them. With an eye on future funding, agencies spend considerable resources assessing the impact of their own activities and performance. Program evaluation is part of the broader issue of accountability of public officials and their responsiveness to the needs, demands, and expectations of their constituents. Interest groups, think tanks, scholars, and the news media actively participate in this phase of the policy process.

Program assessment and evaluation become the basis for future policy and funding decisions. We have found some comprehensive solutions to a limited number of problems, including some diseases, but most governmental policy produces only limited or partial solutions. Problems and issues are ongoing, and policymakers often have to adjust or redirect their efforts to solve them. A solution enacted today can produce additional problems requiring further attention tomorrow.

14.1.3 Iron Triangles and Issue Networks

Thousands of players interact in the policy arenas of state and local governments, including bureaucrats, the courts, interest groups, businesses, the news media, and policy specialists. Although some of these have a broad perspective on state policy and a wide range of policy interests, most have narrow and highly specialized interests. One way to think about the relationships among policy participants is to "identify the clusters of individuals that effectively make most of the routine decisions in a given substantive area of policy."[8]

At the state level, these clusters, sometimes referred to as "iron triangles" of government, include members of the House and the Senate and their staffs, high-level bureaucrats, and representatives of interest groups. Both houses of the legislature are divided into standing committees that have jurisdiction over specific policy areas, and key committee members usually form one leg of each triangle. Hundreds of these subsystems exist in state government, although the use of this concept to explain policy development does not always identify all the critical players or explain the complexity of the process.

Political scientist Hugh Heclo argues that "the iron triangle concept is not so much wrong as it is disastrously incomplete," and he offers a more complex model—**issue networks**—for mapping out the relationships inherent in the policy process.[9] This concept acknowledges the key roles of the iron triangle players but also takes into account other factors, including the increased interdependence between state and local governments and the federal government. Specialists from all three levels of government frequently are involved in developing specific policies. Groups such as the National Governors' Association, the Council of State Governments, and the U.S. Conference of Mayors actively seek to influence federal policies that affect state and local governments.

The policy process is increasingly dominated by specialists who may be identified with interest groups, corporations, legislative committees, or administrative agencies. These experts, or "technopols," understand the technical nature of a problem and, more

issue networks
Term coined by Hugh Heclo to describe the complex institutional and political relationships in the policymaking process.

importantly, the institutional, political, and personal relationships of those involved in trying to solve it.[10]

The number of actual participants in policy development will vary from issue to issue. Sometimes only a few individuals are involved in shaping a specific policy; on other occasions, when changes are being considered in tax law, health care, or public education, for example, a "kaleidoscopic interaction of changing issue networks" takes place, involving hundreds of people.[11] You will see some practical applications of these concepts in the discussion of contemporary state policies that follows.

The State Budget

14.2 Describe recent developments in the formation of the Texas budget and the constraints on those responsible for it.

The state budget is a major reflection of the policy priorities of the governor and the legislature because it determines which policies and public programs are funded and at what level. So, anyone who hopes to influence policy decisions needs to learn the basics of the budget-setting process first. As recent budgetary decisions have demonstrated, it makes a difference who has the most influence over drafting this essential government document.

In a major Texas budgetary crisis in 2011, the legislature faced a $27 billion revenue shortfall, and it dominated that year's legislative session to an extraordinary degree. State government had suffered a sharp decline in tax revenue because of the Great Recession. Governor Rick Perry was reelected the previous year with the support of conservative Tea Party voters, and he courted their continued support. Perry was the longest-serving governor in Texas history partly because his conservative fiscal approach appealed to many Texans. He insisted that the budget gap be closed with spending cuts alone, without raising taxes. This approach appealed to conservatives and many moderate Texans who also opposed higher taxes. Schoolteachers, health care advocates, and many other Texans rallied against the cuts, but with a 101 to 49 Republican supermajority in the Texas House and a Republican majority in the state Senate, the governor got his way. Lawmakers cut billions of dollars from state services over the next two years, including $5.4 billion from public schools alone. At Perry's insistence, the legislature also left more than $7 billion unspent in the state's emergency Rainy Day Fund to please conservative Republican activists intent on shrinking state government.

As a result, the two-year 2012–2013 state budget, which totaled $173.5 billion, was about $14 billion, or 7.5 percent, smaller than the previous budget. The spending reductions cost thousands of schoolteachers and state workers their jobs and reduced health care benefits for thousands of low-income Texans. The action had a historical basis; in 2003, the year the Republicans first took control of the Texas House, smaller spending reductions were imposed to bridge a $10 billion revenue shortfall, also without raising state taxes.

After the Texas economy started to recover, the legislature in subsequent sessions began restoring much of the money cut in 2011, but with Republicans still in charge and conservatives still influential, lawmakers continued to refuse to raise state taxes.

The Republican approach to the budgetary emergencies of 2011 and 2003 differed from how the legislature had resolved a budgetary crisis in 1991, when Democrats still held the governor's office and a majority of both legislative houses. The legislature balanced the 1991 budget with some cuts and other cost-savings steps plus a $2.7 billion package of tax and fee increases. The legislature, with voter approval, also created the Texas lottery that year as a future revenue source.

Nevertheless, under Republicans and Democrats alike, Texas historically has taken a more conservative approach to spending and taxation than many other states. In recent years, Texas's budgetary and tax system has become increasingly strained,

FIGURE 14-1 STATE APPROPRIATIONS FOR 2018–2019 BIENNIUM (ALL FUNDS)

What is in the state budget? As this figure illustrates, education and health and human services are the biggest expenditures.

NOTE: Figures exclude interagency contracts. Biennial change and percentage change are calculated on actual amounts before rounding; therefore, figure total may not add up due to rounding.

SOURCE: Legislative Budget Board, "Summary of Conference Committee Report for House Bill 1, Appropriations for the 2020–21 Biennium," May 2019. See "Funding by Article, Figure 1, Funding by Article, All Funds," page 3. Available at: https://www.lbb.state.tx.us/Documents/Appropriations_Bills/86/Conference_Bills/5872_S12_Bill_Summary.pdf.

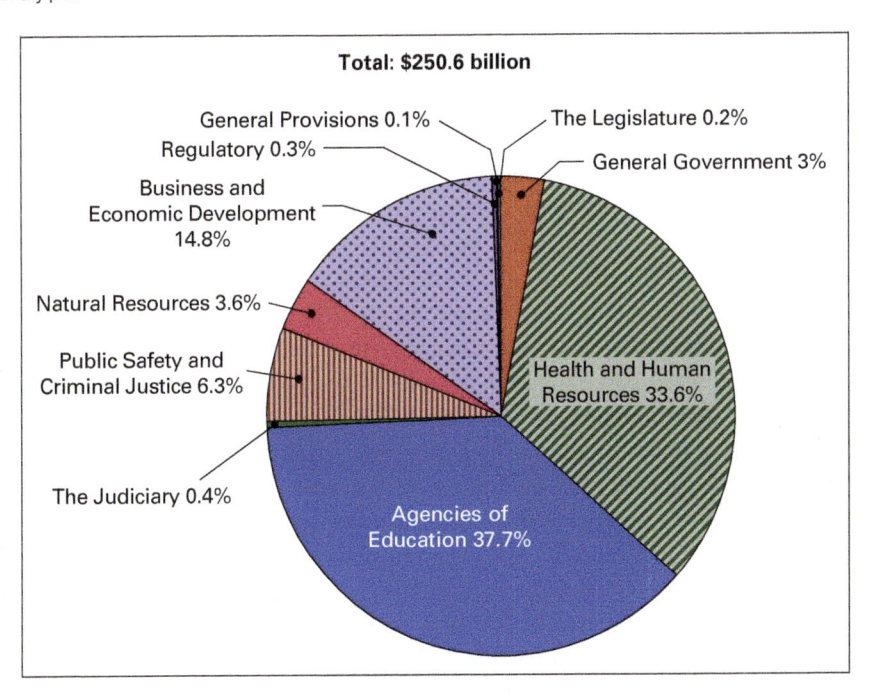

Total: $250.6 billion
- General Provisions 0.1%
- The Legislature 0.2%
- Regulatory 0.3%
- General Government 3%
- Business and Economic Development 14.8%
- Natural Resources 3.6%
- Public Safety and Criminal Justice 6.3%
- Health and Human Resources 33.6%
- The Judiciary 0.4%
- Agencies of Education 37.7%

in part because of growing public needs and in part because of historical budgetary restrictions, including the use of a two-year budgetary period.

Like most other states and unlike the federal government, Texas operates on a pay-as-you-go basis that prohibits **deficit financing**. The comptroller must certify that each budget can be paid for with anticipated revenue from taxes, fees, and other sources. Also like other states, Texas increased its spending on state government programs in the 1970s, 1980s, and 1990s. Population growth and inflation were major factors, in addition to federal mandates and court orders for prison and education reforms.

The biggest share of state expenditures (including federal funds appropriated by the legislature) traditionally has been for education, with health and human services running second, although Texas spends less per person in both areas than do most other states.

The total 2020–2021 budget was about $248.3 billion, a 6.3 percent increase over the budget for 2018–2019. The biggest share of the budget, almost 38 percent or $94.5 billion, was for education. The second largest share was for health and human services, almost 34 percent or $84.3 billion. The next biggest slice of the budget pie went to business and economic development programs, which received $37 billion, or about 15 percent of the total. Public safety and criminal justice programs received $16 billion, or about 6 percent (see Figure 14–1).

deficit financing
Borrowing money to meet operating expenses. It is prohibited by the Texas Constitution, which provides that the state government must operate on a pay-as-you-go basis.

14.2.1 Two-Year Budgets

Even in normal times, the legislature's budget-writing task is compounded by the length of the budget period and the structure of the budget itself. Since the Texas Constitution provides that the legislature shall meet in regular session only every other year, lawmakers must write two-year, or biennial, budgets for state government.

That means state agencies, which begin preparing their budget requests several months before a session convenes, have to anticipate some of their spending needs three years in advance. Critics, including many legislators and agency directors, say two-year budgets require too much guesswork and cause inadequate funding of some programs and wasteful spending in other areas. They believe that Texas, which is the nation's second most populous state and has a wide diversity of needs in a changing economy, should have annual budgetary sessions of the legislature, a change that would require a constitutional amendment.

The governor and legislative leaders have the authority between legislative sessions to transfer appropriated funds between programs and agencies to meet some emergencies. The governor proposes such transfers to the Legislative Budget Board (LBB), a ten-member panel that includes the lieutenant governor, the speaker, and eight key legislators. The LBB can accept, reject, or modify the governor's proposal and can propose budgetary changes to the governor.

Agencies submit their biennial appropriations, or spending, requests to the Legislative Budget Board (LBB). After its staff reviews the requests, the LBB normally recommends a budget that the full legislature uses as a starting point in its budgetary deliberations.

The difficulty of two-year revenue-estimating and budgeting was highlighted when the coronavirus pandemic struck Texas in the spring of 2020, less than a year after the legislature had enacted the 2020–2021 budget. The pandemic prompted Governor Greg Abbott and local elected officials, as noted in earlier chapters, to order the temporary closures or limit operations of thousands of businesses throughout the state to help slow the spread of the virus. The closures resulted in a huge loss of tax revenue for state and local governments and required Comptroller Glenn Hegar to slash one billion dollars from the revenue estimate on which the 2020–2021 state budget had been based. Hegar's action, in turn, prompted emergency cuts in many public programs and services, including some of those discussed later in this chapter.

14.2.2 Dedicated Funds

dedicated funds
Constitutional or statutory requirements that restrict some state tax or fee revenues to spending on specific programs.

The legislature's control over the budget-setting process is further restricted by legal requirements that dedicate or set aside a major portion of state revenue for specific purposes, leaving legislators with discretion over only about one-half of total appropriations. Restrictions involving **dedicated funds** include federal funds earmarked by the federal government for specific programs such as Medicaid or the Children's Health Insurance Program, and monies dedicated to specific uses by the state constitution or state law. The state treasury has numerous separate funds, including many that are dedicated to highways, education, parks, teacher retirement, and dozens of other specific purposes. These restrictions hamper the legislature, particularly during lean periods. The dedicated funds are jealously guarded by the interest groups that benefit from them, and many funds have become "sacred cows" that most legislators do not dare try to change.

One of the major dedicated funds is the Highway Trust Fund, which automatically gets three-fourths of the revenue from the motor fuels tax. Under the Texas Constitution, revenue in that fund can be spent only to purchase rights-of-way for highways or to construct, maintain, and police highways. The remainder of the motor fuels tax revenue goes to public education. In recent years, revenue in the Highway Trust Fund hasn't kept up with Texas's growing needs for highway construction and maintenance. To help address that problem, the legislature and Texas voters in 2015 approved an amendment to the state constitution to also dedicate a portion of sales tax revenues to the highway fund. Other major dedicated funds include the Permanent School Fund and the Permanent University Fund, land and mineral-rich endowments that help support the public schools and boost funding for the University of Texas and Texas A&M University systems.

State Taxes

14.3 Identify four types of taxes in Texas and the regressive aspects of the Texas tax system.

As of 2020, Texas was one of only seven states without a personal income tax of any kind. The other six states were Alaska, Florida, Nevada, South Dakota, Washington, and Wyoming. Two other states, New Hampshire and Tennessee, taxed only interest and dividends, not salaries or wages. Tennessee was phasing out its tax and would eliminate it in 2022.[12] Opposition to an income tax remained high in Texas, and in 2019 Texas voters, as noted in Chapter 2, approved a constitutional amendment to make it more difficult for the legislature to ever enact one.

Each budgetary crisis has seemingly stretched the existing tax structure to the breaking point, but each time the legislature has come up with another patch or, in recent years, has cut spending. Critics compare the tax structure to an ugly patchwork quilt stitched together over the years to accommodate various special interest groups and cover an assortment of emergencies. But Texas remains a fast-growing state, attractive to many outsiders who choose to move here; and undoubtedly many individuals and business owners are attracted to Texas, at least in part, because of its overall tax structure, especially the absence of a personal income tax.

14.3.1 A Regressive Tax System

According to the Tax Policy Center, taxes collected by state and local governments in Texas in 2017 averaged 8.8 percent of personal income, lower than the national average of 9.8 percent, ranking Texas thirty-sixth among the states and the District of Columbia. Texas's state and local tax load was ranked significantly lower than those of several other populous states, including New York (13.9 percent), California (10.3 percent), and Illinois (10.6 percent). A major reason was the lack of a personal income tax in Texas. Largely for the same reason, however, taxes in Texas are not distributed equally.[13]

In another study, in 2018, the Institute on Taxation and Economic Policy ranked Texas's tax system the second most regressive in the country, behind only Washington state, which doesn't have a personal income tax either. The Texas system is based largely on the sales tax, the local property tax, and fees that are considered regressive because they consume a larger portion of the incomes of the poor and the middle classes than of the upper class. Based on this study's calculations, state and local governments in Texas taxed the poorest 20 percent of families, earning less than $20,900 a year, at an average of 13 percent of their incomes. The middle 20 percent of income-earners, between $35,800 and $56,000 a year, paid an average of 9.7 percent of their incomes in state and local taxes, while the wealthiest Texans (the richest 1 percent with incomes of $617,900 or more a year) were taxed an average of 3.1 percent. Political leaders have long touted Texas as a low-tax state, but, according to this study, that is mainly from the perspective of wealthy Texans.[14] Nevertheless, public opposition to a personal income tax is not limited to the wealthiest Texans.

SALES TAX The legislature enacted the state's first **sales tax** in 1961, with an initial rate of 2 percent of the cost of purchased goods. The rate has since been increased several times (the last time in 1991), and now this tax is the single biggest generator of state revenue. At 6.25 percent, the statewide rate is among the highest sales tax rates in the country. An 8.25 percent rate is charged in many Texas metropolitan areas, where city and mass transportation authority taxes of 1 percent each are added to the state tax, a practice that many other states follow.[15] The general sales tax generated $34 billion for state government alone in fiscal 2019. The sales tax on motor vehicle sales and rentals generated another $5 billion.[16]

sales tax
A tax charged as a set percentage of most retail purchases and many services. It is the main source of tax revenue for state government and an important source of revenue for many cities and metropolitan transit authorities.

Even though groceries and medicine are tax exempt, critics charge that the sales tax is regressive because it affects low-income Texans disproportionately more than wealthier citizens. Moreover, the sales tax is heavily weighted toward products and leaves many services, including legal and medical fees and advertising, untaxed. Thus, sales tax revenue does not automatically grow with the state's economy because the Texas economy is becoming more and more service oriented.

FRANCHISE, OR MARGINS, TAX The franchise tax, which was overhauled in 1991, was for many years the state's major business tax. It applied only to corporations, which were taxed on their income or assets, whichever was greater. The tax did not cover partnerships or sole proprietorships and was paid by fewer than 200,000 of the state's 2.5 million businesses. At the urging of Governor Rick Perry, the legislature in a special session in 2006 replaced the franchise tax with a broader-based business tax, also called a **margins tax**, which applied to corporations and additional forms of businesses, including professional partnerships, such as law firms. Most sole proprietorships were still exempt.

The new tax was part of a partial trade-off for lower school property taxes. It was enacted in response to a Texas Supreme Court order for changes in the public school finance system. Although the smallest businesses were exempted from the tax, the new levy still raised taxes for many companies that had been paying little, if any, taxes under the franchise tax. And the fact that the tax was based on gross receipts rather than income meant that some companies had to pay it even if they didn't earn a profit during the tax year. To defuse business opposition, the legislature has excluded additional businesses and lowered the tax rate since the margins tax was enacted. The margins tax raised about $4.2 billion in fiscal 2019.[17]

PROPERTY TAX The biggest source of taxpayer dissatisfaction and anger in Texas in recent years has been the local **property or ad valorem tax**, a major source of revenue for cities, counties, and special districts, and the only source of local revenue for school districts. It is levied on homes, businesses, and certain other forms of property, based on their assessed values. State government doesn't levy a property tax, but state policies affect the tax bills that school districts and other local governments levy.

Property tax revenue more than tripled between 1998 and 2017, according to the state comptroller's office.[18] Much of the increase was in local school taxes, which have been significantly raised to pay for state-ordered education programs and school finance requirements, including a law, to be discussed later in this chapter, ordering the transfer of millions of dollars from wealthy to poor school districts. School districts accounted for $32.1 billion of the $59.4 billion in property taxes raised in 2017.

As discussed in Chapter 4, the legislature in 2019 enacted stricter limits on property tax growth. The new restrictions prohibit cities and counties from increasing property tax revenue by more than 3.5 percent a year without voter approval and impose a 2.5 percent annual limit on school districts. Tax revenue from new construction is excluded from the limits. The previous cap was 8 percent a year for all local governments.

SEVERANCE TAX Oil and gas severance, or production, taxes rise and fall with production in the state's energy sector. They helped the legislature balance the budget with relative ease when oil prices were high in the 1970s, but energy-tax revenue slowed considerably after the energy industry crashed in the 1980s and the state economy began to diversify. Oil and gas production has subsequently recovered, but revenue from the energy-related taxes continues to rise and fall with the industry's fortunes. These taxes raised more than $5.5 billion in fiscal 2019.[19]

OTHER TAXES AND FEES State government has several volume-based taxes on such items as cigarettes, alcoholic beverages, and motor fuels. These tax rates are set per pack or per gallon and do not bring in more revenue when inflation raises the

---

margins tax

The state's main business tax, enacted in 2006 to replace the franchise tax. This tax, which applies to corporations and professional partnerships such as law firms, is based on a company's annual revenue. Companies can deduct some of their costs, such as employees' salaries, from the tax base. Many of the smaller companies in the state do not have to pay the tax.

property or ad valorem tax

A tax on homes, businesses, and certain other forms of property that is the main source of revenue for local governments. The tax is based on the assessed value of the property.

price of the product. The so-called **sin taxes** on cigarettes and alcohol have been raised frequently over the years and produced about $2.8 billion in fiscal 2019.[20] The legislature raised the cigarette tax from 41 cents per pack to $1.41 per pack in 2006, as part of the trade-off for lower school property taxes. Three-fourths of the revenue from motor fuels taxes, including 20-cents-per-gallon taxes on gasoline and diesel, is dedicated by the state constitution to highways, and one-fourth is dedicated to the public schools.

State government also assesses dozens of fees—to register your car, to obtain a hunting or fishing license, and to obtain a license to practice as a doctor, dentist, or lawyer, to name but a few. Some of the fee revenue is dedicated to designated programs.

14.3.2 Gambling on New Revenue

For years, Texas government maintained a strong moralistic opposition to gambling. Charitable bingo games were tolerated and eventually legalized. But the state constitution prohibited lotteries, and horse race betting was outlawed in the 1930s. After the oil bust in the 1980s, however, many legislators began to view gambling as a financial opportunity rather than a moral evil, and in key elections most Texas voters indicated they agreed.

In a special session in 1986, when spending was cut and taxes were raised to compensate for lost revenue from plummeting oil prices, the legislature legalized local option, pari-mutuel betting on horse and dog races. This is a form of betting in which bettors determine the size of the winning pool of money and the greater the number of people who bet on the winner in a race, the lower the payoff to each winning bettor. Voters approved the measure the next year. In 1991, under strong pressure from Governor Ann Richards, the legislature approved a constitutional amendment to legalize a state **lottery**, which voters also endorsed that year. Limited casino gambling on cruise ships operating off the Texas coast also has been legalized by the legislature. Gambling, however, has not cured the state's financial needs. Years after pari-mutuel betting had been approved, the horse and dog racing tracks still had not produced any significant revenue for the state.

Texas's lottery became the first in the United States to sell more than $4 billion worth of tickets in its first two years of operation, and it reached that milestone in twenty-two months. By late 1997, however, lottery sales had begun to lag behind projections, and even supporters of the game warned that the lottery could not

sin tax
A common nickname for a tax on tobacco or alcoholic beverages.

lottery
A form of gambling, conducted by many states, in which participants purchase tickets that offer an opportunity to cash in on a winning number or set of winning numbers. Voters legalized a state lottery in Texas in 1991.

HOPING TO CASH IN
A man purchases a lottery ticket at a convenience store. Proceeds from the Texas lottery are dedicated to education but pay for only a small part of the total public education budget.

necessarily be depended upon as a reliable, long-term revenue source. Lawmakers in 1997 dedicated lottery revenue to public education but also ordered that shortfalls in school funding from the lottery be made up with tax dollars.[21] Each year the lottery normally raises 5 percent or less of the total funds spent on public education in Texas. It raised $2.5 billion in 2019.[22]

Despite its popularity in many other states, full-blown casino gambling remains a contentious issue in Texas. There are no commercial casinos in the state, and efforts of the state's three Native American tribes to run casinos on their reservations have been challenged by state officials.

14.3.3 Bonds: Build Now, Pay More Later

Although the Texas Constitution has a general prohibition against the state government going into debt, the state had $56.8 billion in total debt outstanding at the end of fiscal 2018. All of it had been approved by voters in the form of constitutional amendments for a variety of purposes, and 87 percent of it, about $50 billion, was self-supporting.[23] That is, the debt was in the form of bonds for self-supporting programs, such as water reservoirs or veterans' assistance programs. These programs use the state's credit to borrow money at favorable interest rates. The state lends that money to a local government to help construct a water treatment plant or to a veteran to help purchase a house, and the loan recipients, not the state's taxpayers, repay the debt.

Non-self-supporting debt, which totaled almost $7 billion for state government at the end of fiscal 2018, is paid off by state tax dollars and is issued in the form of **general obligation bonds**, which are used to finance expensive construction, or capital improvement, projects that the legislature wants to pay for over an extended period. Some people call this the "credit card" approach to state financing, and it was used extensively in the 1980s to pay for a massive prison expansion program. More recently, these bonds, which have to be authorized by the legislature and approved by voters in the form of constitutional amendments, also have been issued for highway construction.

Bond issues traditionally have been widely supported by Democrats and Republicans alike. But the state's total debt more than doubled between 2003 and 2012, and some legislators have become increasingly uneasy about loading up the extra tax liability for non-self-sustaining debt on future taxpayers. Interest on bonds can double the cost of a construction project, experts say. The 2020–2021 state budget included $4.2 billion for debt service payments.[24]

Local governments also issue bonds for construction projects and also have debt. Outstanding debt for all cities, counties, school districts, and other local governments in Texas totaled about $240 billion at the end of fiscal year 2019, an increase of about $37 billion (18.6 percent) over the previous five years. About $157 billion (65.7 percent) was general obligation debt, which would have to be paid off with future property tax revenue, while the remainder was secured by fees generated by various public projects, such as water, sewer, and electric utility facilities. All the tax-secured debt was authorized by local voters in the form of bonds for new schools, roads, water distribution systems, and numerous other capital improvement projects. Based on 2016 census data, the most recent available, the local tax-secured debt averaged $8,013 per Texas resident, second highest among the 10 most populous states. Only New York, at $11,209 per resident, was higher.[25]

14.3.4 The Income Tax: An Unpopular Alternative to a Regressive Tax System

Lieutenant Governor Bob Bullock shocked much of the Texas political establishment by announcing in March 1991, less than two months after taking office, that he would actively campaign for a state **income tax**, a revenue alternative that had long been

---

general obligation bond
A method of borrowing money to pay for new construction projects, such as prisons, hospitals, streets, or drainage systems. Interest on such bonds, which require voter approval, is paid with tax revenue.

income tax
A tax based on a corporation's or an individual's income. Texas is one of only a few states without a personal income tax.

politically taboo in Texas among Democrats and Republicans alike. Bullock, a former state comptroller, said it was the only way to meet the state's needs fairly and adequately while also providing relief from existing unpopular taxes. Bullock proposed making local school property taxes deductible from the income tax, and he recommended the repeal of the franchise tax.[26]

Bullock did not receive much support. Eventually, the legislature that year changed the corporate franchise tax to include a hybrid corporate income tax, which has since been replaced by the margins tax described earlier in this chapter. But lawmakers held the line against a personal income tax.

Pulling another surprise during the 1993 legislative session, Bullock proposed a constitutional amendment, which won easy legislative approval, to ban a personal income tax unless the voters approved one. Bullock's 1994 reelection date was approaching, and maybe he felt the need to defuse any political problems caused by his endorsement of an income tax two years earlier. Whatever Bullock's motivations, the amendment was overwhelmingly approved by Texas voters in November 1993, leaving many people convinced that a major revenue option had been removed from the state's budget picture for years to come.

Bullock's amendment would have allowed the legislature to propose an income tax to voters on simple majority votes of the House and the Senate, which the legislature never made any attempt to do for the next 25 years. But, in 2019, Governor Greg Abbott and some Republican legislators, wishing to make a strong statement against an income tax, proposed another constitutional amendment to erect an even higher barrier. That amendment, which will require a two-thirds vote of the House and the Senate, instead of simple majorities, to put an income tax on the ballot, was approved by the legislature and by Texas voters that year, as discussed in Chapter 2. The new amendment repealed the Bullock amendment, including a provision that would have dedicated much of the revenue from an income tax to public education funding.

Educational Policies and Politics

14.4 Relate the factors affecting education policy in Texas to questions of equity and quality.

As noted earlier in this chapter, education is one of Texas's biggest public expenditures. And funding is one of many major policy issues swirling around education, from pre-kindergarten to universities. Understanding these policies, how they evolved, and how Texas compares to other states is important for anyone who plans to begin a career or start a business in Texas because the educational system is a major part of the state's economic foundation. As readers know from first-hand experience, education—from elementary school to college—has been widely disrupted by the coronavirus, or COVID-19, pandemic. School districts and universities in Texas and across the country were shut down and classes were converted to online instruction for much of the 2020 spring semester. Universities lost millions of dollars during the first few months of the emergency alone; many college students and their families suffered financially as well. Education officials were unsure how their institutions would deliver instruction—on campus, online, or a combination of the two—in the immediate and perhaps longer-term future. When public schools reopened for the fall semester, with the pandemic remaining a critical health issue, many districts offered virtual classes for students. But Governor Greg Abbott and the Texas Education Agency required all districts to also offer in-classroom instruction for students who wanted to return to campuses. The Texas Education Agency recommended schools follow health and safety precautions, such as social distancing, mask use, and strict sanitation, but many teachers returned to schools reluctantly and fearfully.

14.4.1 Public Education: A Struggle for Equity and Quality

In 1949, the legislature enacted the Gilmer-Aikin law, which made major improvements in the administration of public elementary and secondary education and significantly increased school funding, but it soon became outdated. By the 1970s, it was obvious that quality and equity were lacking in many classrooms. Many high school graduates were unprepared for college or the workplace, and they included thousands of children in poor school districts with substandard facilities and insufficient educational aids.

Public education in Texas—pre-kindergarten through twelfth grade—is financed primarily by a combination of state and local taxes, a system that has produced wide disparities in education spending among the state's approximately 1,100 local school districts. The only local source of operating revenue for school districts is the property tax, and the money it raises is determined by the value of the property that is taxed and the tax rate that is imposed on that property. Districts with a lot of oil production, expensive commercial property, or subdivisions with large, luxurious houses have wealthy tax bases that enable them to raise large amounts of money with relatively low tax rates. Poor districts with low tax bases, on the other hand, have to impose higher tax rates to raise only a fraction of the money that the wealthy districts can spend on education.

Before the state began addressing this issue, many poor districts struggled to maintain minimal educational programs, whereas rich districts could attract the best teachers with higher pay; build more classrooms; purchase more books and computers; and, in some cases, have enough money left over to put AstroTurf in their football stadiums. Educational resources varied greatly between different regions of the state and sometimes between districts within the same county. Many of the poorest districts were, and still are, in heavily Hispanic South Texas. Ethnicity became a significant factor in a protracted struggle between the haves and the have-nots. Hispanic leaders played major roles in the fight to improve their children's educational opportunities, and over the years they have had some success, thanks to a series of lawsuits. But inequities and litigation still persist.

The first major lawsuit (*Rodriguez* v. *San Antonio Independent School District*) was filed in 1968, when a group of parents led by Demetrio P. Rodriquez, a San Antonio sheet metal worker and high school dropout, went to federal court to challenge the school finance system. The plaintiffs had children in the Edgewood Independent School District, one of the state's poorest. A three-judge federal court agreed with the parents and ruled in 1971 that the school finance system was unconstitutional. But the state appealed, and the U.S. Supreme Court in 1973 reversed the lower court decision. The Court said that the Texas system of financing public education was unfair but held that it did not violate the U.S. Constitution.

By the early 1980s, Texas leaders were expressing a growing concern over not just the financing of public education but also the quality of that education. In 1983, Governor Mark White joined Lieutenant Governor Bill Hobby and House Speaker Gib Lewis in appointing the Select Committee on Public Education. Billionaire computer magnate Ross Perot of Dallas, who several years later would be an independent candidate for president, was selected to chair the panel. In an exhaustive study, the committee found that high schools were graduating many students who could barely read and write and concluded that major reforms were necessary if the state's young people were to be able to compete for jobs in a changing and highly competitive state and international economy.

With Perot spending some of his personal wealth on a strong lobbying campaign, the legislature in a special session in 1984 enacted many educational changes in a landmark piece of legislation known as **House Bill 72** and raised taxes to boost education spending. The bill raised teacher pay, limited class sizes, required pre-kindergarten

House Bill 72
A landmark school reform law enacted in 1984 that reduced class sizes; imposed the no pass, no play rule; and made other educational improvements.

classes for disadvantaged 4-year-olds, required students to pass a basic skills test before graduating from high school, and required school districts to provide tutorials for failing students.

House Bill 72 also imposed the so-called **no pass, no play rule**, which prohibited students who failed any course from participating in athletics and other extracurricular activities for six weeks. The rule infuriated many coaches, students, parents, and school administrators, particularly in the hundreds of small Texas towns where Friday night football was a major social activity and an important source of community pride. Education reformers, however, viewed the restriction as an important statement that the first emphasis of education should be on the classroom, not on the football field or the band hall.

The 1984 law, however, did not change the basic, inequitable finance system, and the state was soon back in court. This lawsuit, *Edgewood v. Kirby*, was filed in state district court in Austin, and it contended that the inequities violated the Texas Constitution. It was initially filed in 1984, shortly before the enactment of House Bill 72, by the Edgewood Independent School District, twelve other low-income districts, and a number of families represented by the Mexican American Legal Defense and Educational Fund (MALDEF). Dozens of other districts and individuals joined the case, and in 1987, state District Judge Harley Clark of Austin ruled that the school finance system violated the state constitution.

The state appealed the ruling, but the Texas Supreme Court, in a unanimous, landmark decision in October 1989, struck down the finance system and ordered lawmakers to replace it with a new law that gave public school children an equal opportunity at a quality education. The bipartisan opinion, written by Democratic Justice Oscar Mauzy, a former chair of the Senate Education Committee, did not outline a specific solution. But the court said the existing finance system violated a state constitutional requirement for an efficient system of public education. It warned the legislature that merely increasing the amount of state education aid was not enough. The decision concluded that "a Band-Aid will not suffice; the system itself must be changed."[27]

no pass, no play rule
A law stating that a student failing a course is restricted from participating in extracurricular activities for a specified period.

Edgewood* v. *Kirby
A lawsuit in which the Texas Supreme Court in 1989 declared the Texas school finance system unconstitutional because of wide disparities in property wealth and educational opportunities among school districts.

14.4.2 Persistence of Funding Problems

The issue was so divisive that it took three more school finance plans and more than three years before the legislature enacted a school funding plan that met the Supreme Court's approval. It was a 1993 law, signed by Governor Ann Richards, requiring wealthy school districts to share their property tax revenue with poor districts. The "Robin Hood" law, as it was dubbed, was upheld by the high court in 1995. Robin Hood was still largely in effect in 2020, although subsequent lawsuits and legislation have produced additional school finance changes.

A number of school districts went to court again only a few years later because an increasingly greater share of school funding, approaching 60 percent, was being borne by local school taxes, while the state's share was decreasing. Ruling in the new lawsuit in 2005, the Texas Supreme Court held that the heavy reliance on local property taxes for school funding amounted to an unconstitutional statewide property tax and gave the state until June 1, 2006, to correct the problem. Governor Rick Perry called the legislature into special session and won approval of a proposal to cut school property tax rates by one-third. To replace the lost revenue, legislators enacted the new, broad-based business tax described earlier in this chapter and raised the state cigarette tax by $1 per pack. The legislature, however, did not increase overall state funding for public schools, and the local tax savings soon were eroded by rising property values. As property values increased, tax bills increased without any change in local tax rates.

The 2006 law also put strict limits on how much school districts could raise their local property tax rates in the future. These restrictions soon created additional budgetary problems for many districts. Moreover, the new business tax failed to generate

DISTRIBUTING SCHOOL LUNCHES DURING A HEALTH CRISIS

School nutrition services workers provide meals at a Houston high school for students and their families to pick up and take home, while students were taking remote lessons during the COVID-19 pandemic.

enough state revenue for schools to make up for the local revenue lost to the 2006 property tax cuts. That deficit accounted for part of a $27 billion revenue shortfall that state lawmakers faced in 2011. To help bridge the funding gap, the legislature imposed $5.4 billion in school budget cuts, spread over two years, at a time when public school enrollment was growing by 80,000 to 85,000 students a year, statewide.

Because of the budget cuts, school districts eliminated 25,000 jobs, including almost 11,000 teaching positions, during the 2011–2012 school year; increased class sizes; delayed the opening of some new schools; and, in at least one district in North Texas, charged children to ride school buses. Over the next several years, the legislature restored much of the cut funding, but as enrollment continued to increase, Texas consistently lagged behind most states in the amount of money it spent on each child's education. By the 2018–2019 school year, Texas was spending $10,712 per student, or $2,946 less per student than the national average, the National Education Association (NEA) reported, drawing on Texas budgetary data. Texas ranked thirty-ninth among the states and the District of Columbia in per-student funding.[28]

Within a few months after the 2011 school budget cuts were imposed, several hundred school districts were back in court, suing the state yet again over the school finance system. In a decision in early 2013, state District Judge John Dietz of Austin ruled that the school funding system was once again unconstitutional because it was inadequate and treated poor districts unfairly. After the legislature failed to overhaul the school funding system during the 2013 session, Dietz reinforced his first order with a second, similar ruling in 2014. But the state appealed, and in 2016, the Texas Supreme Court brought this lawsuit to an end by overturning Dietz's order. The high court ruled that the school finance system, although seriously flawed, met "minimum constitutional requirements."

After teachers and other public school advocates made education funding a major issue in the 2018 state elections, Governor Greg Abbott and the legislature made school funding a priority in the 2019 legislative session. Lawmakers enacted a major school finance law, House Bill 3, which increased state funding for public schools by $6.5 billion, including money for teacher pay raises. Legislators also appropriated about $5 billion to buy down local school property taxes and limited annual increases in property tax revenue for school districts to 2.5 percent a year. The legislation also reduced the payments that some wealthy districts had to make to subsidize poorer districts under the Robin Hood school finance law.

Meanwhile, Texas's public school enrollment, now about 5.4 million, is becoming more racially and ethnically diverse—and poorer. During the 2018–2019 school year, about 53 percent of Texas's public school students were Hispanic and about 27 percent were Anglo, with smaller percentages of African Americans, Asian Americans, and multi-ethnic groups. Some 60 percent of students were economically disadvantaged, meaning they were eligible for free or reduced-price lunches or other public assistance.

14.4.3 Other Issues Affecting the Public Schools

The legislature also confronts a number of other issues affecting public schools, including teacher morale, student testing, and the quality and availability of special education programs. Some new proposals, such as charter schools, have been adopted; others, including private school vouchers, have been rejected but may be revived in the future.

TEACHER PAY, WORKING CONDITIONS, AND MORALE In a 2018 survey of its members commissioned by the Texas State Teachers Association (TSTA), 39 percent of the respondents said they took extra jobs during the school year to make ends meet, spending an average of about 14 hours a week moonlighting. Some 79 percent of the moonlighting teachers believed the time spent on the extra jobs affected their teaching but said they could not afford to lose the extra income. Some 53 percent of respondents said they were seriously considering leaving the teaching profession.

Conducted for TSTA by Dr. Robert Maninger and Dr. Casey Creghan of Sam Houston State University, the survey also found that teachers spent an average $738 a year from their own pockets on school supplies. The average teacher pay in Texas during the 2017–2018 school year was $53,167. It had been increased since the 2011 school budget cuts but was still about $7,300 less than the national average.[29]

Controversies over inadequate pay and education funding prompted teachers in several states to walk off their jobs in protest in 2018. Texas teachers, who are prohibited by state law from striking, stayed on the job, although many Texas teachers applauded the teachers who walked out. And as noted above, teachers and other education advocates made school funding a major issue in Texas's 2018 elections, prompting legislators during their 2019 session to approve a significant boost in school funding, including money for teacher pay raises.

STUDENT TESTING AND "ACCOUNTABILITY" For years, students in public schools have been required to take standardized tests to be promoted to higher grades, graduate from high school, and help measure a school's effectiveness. Much of this emphasis was developed while George W. Bush was governor, and it helped inspire the No Child Left Behind Act, the federal education law that Bush promoted as president. But the tests and the so-called school "accountability" system to which the test results contribute have been controversial. Critics have leveled accusations that teachers are pressured to concentrate on teaching students how to pass the tests in order to attain favorable ratings for their schools rather than presenting a more enriching educational curriculum. A major cheating scandal in the El Paso Independent School District, where the superintendent's bonus was tied to test scores, resulted in the superintendent being sentenced to federal prison and the school district being placed under state supervision for a few years.

The testing and accountability systems have been revised several times, as legislators and educators have struggled to balance political and educational concerns. The most recent version—the State of Texas Assessments of Academic Readiness (STAAR)—debuted in the 2011–2012 school year. The new system, including end-of-course exams in core subject areas for high school students, was designed to be more difficult than the standardized testing system it had replaced. Some STAAR requirements quickly prompted strong vocal opposition from many parents. One was the large number (fifteen) of end-of-course exams that high school students had to pass. Many parents also disliked the fact that scores on the end-of-course exams could count toward course grades and high school class rankings, which helped determine university admissions. The legislature in 2013 reduced the number of end-of-course exams to five and repealed the provisions that the exams count toward course grades and class rankings, but many parents and educators believed the standardized testing regimen was still excessive.

In late 2015, Congress replaced No Child Left Behind with a new federal education law, the Every Student Succeeds Act, which allowed states to develop new ways to measure student accomplishment and school accountability. But standardized testing and the debate over it continued in Texas. In the spring of 2020, with many schools closed and educators teaching online because of the coronavirus outbreak, Governor Greg Abbott suspended STAAR testing for that school year.

SPECIAL EDUCATION In 2004, the Texas Education Agency set a "target" of 8.5 percent of enrollment for the maximum number of students who should receive special education services in a school district, and districts that violated the target—which critics would later call a cap—were subject to penalties. The target was significantly lower than the 12 percent enrollment that long had been the average for special education students in Texas and throughout the country. The Texas target was imposed after the legislature in 2003 had imposed reductions in state spending to close a revenue shortfall. Federal regulators later determined that during the twelve years the target was in place, the portion of students receiving special education services in the state dropped from 11.6 percent in 2004 to 8.6 percent in 2016, the year the *Houston Chronicle* reported the existence of the policy, which had been carried out with little, if any, public attention.

The *Chronicle*'s reporting created an immediate political firestorm, which carried over into the 2017 legislative session. Teachers and other special education advocates said the policy had deprived tens of thousands of children with autism, speech impairments, mental illness, blindness, deafness, and other disabilities of the special education services to which they were entitled under federal law, and parents were furious. The enrollment limit was lifted, and the U.S. Department of Education concluded in early 2018, after conducting an investigation, that the policy had violated federal law. Federal regulators ordered state officials to take corrective actions, including finding a way to help eligible children who had been deprived of special education services to get the assistance they needed.[30]

CHARTER SCHOOLS Upon taking office in 1995, Governor George W. Bush advocated more innovation for local schools and less red tape for teachers and administrators. The legislature responded with a major rewrite of the education law to allow school districts, universities, and independent groups or organizations to create charter schools that would be free of some state regulations. The charter school movement got off to a mixed start. Some of these schools had financial problems or were mismanaged and had to shut down after brief periods of operation. Others flourished, strongly supported by parents and students who believed their innovative techniques enhanced the learning experience. In the 2018–2019 school year, almost 317,000 students, or almost 6 percent of the state's public school enrollment, attended about 750 open-enrollment charter campuses, which operate independently of school districts but still are considered public schools. They are regulated by the Texas Education Agency and receive state funding based on their enrollment.[31]

PRIVATE SCHOOL VOUCHERS For several years, a number of legislators, primarily Republicans, have advocated a voucher program that would allow some public school children to attend private schools at state expense. The idea, supporters say, is to allow disadvantaged children from struggling public schools to have a chance at a quality education. Opponents, including public education groups, say such a program would unfairly divert money from the public schools at a time when public classrooms need more funding. Voucher bills have failed during several recent legislative sessions, but proponents were expected to keep trying.

14.4.4 Higher Education: Another Quest for Excellence and Equity

Texas has about 100 state-supported, general-academic universities, medical, dental, law, and other professional schools plus 50 community college districts with multiple campuses. Additionally, the state is home to about 40 private, or independent, universities. The public and private general-academic universities and community colleges alone serve more than 1.5 million students a year. The state-supported institutions are governed by boards appointed by the governor or, in the case of community colleges, elected by local voters. The Texas Higher Education Coordinating Board, which is appointed by the governor, oversees university construction and degree programs and works to align higher education outcomes with workforce needs and increase university accessibility and graduations.

In 2019, according to the Texas Higher Education Coordinating Board, only 31 percent (less than one-third) of Texans aged 25 to 34 had bachelor's degrees or higher. This ranked Texas 34th among the states, below the national average of 35.7 percent and well below the leader, Massachusetts, 52.4 percent.[32]

Thousands of new students, including growing numbers of Hispanics and African Americans, have enrolled in Texas colleges and universities since 2000, the Coordinating Board has reported, but many of those students don't graduate. The board has warned that Texas needs to pick up the pace to remain competitive with other states for the best jobs for its people in an increasingly complex world. "Texas is getting better, but not fast enough to be a leader in the global economy."[33]

Higher education funding is often an issue, including periodic cuts in funding to financial aid programs of critical importance to middle- and low-income students already struggling with recent tuition increases. These students include many young people who are the first generation of their families either attending or planning to attend college.

Heeding its own warning, the Coordinating Board in 2015 adopted a new goal: to have 60 percent of Texans between ages 25 and 34 earn a postsecondary degree or certificate by the year 2030. To meet the goal, about 550,000 students would have to earn a certificate or associate, bachelor's, or master's degree in Texas by that time. That would be more than double the 256,000 people who received a bachelor's or master's degree in Texas in 2014. Much of the attention, the Coordinating Board indicated, would be focused on helping more Hispanic and African American young people get into college and graduate.[34]

That goal and the short-term future of higher education in Texas and throughout the country were thrown into turmoil by the arrival of the COVID-19 pandemic in 2020. Most universities finished the spring semester that year with online classes and offered only online instruction during the summer. Some universities reopened their campuses for the fall semester, and others offered only online instruction. Sports seasons were canceled or shortened in the spring. Many university teams participated in football in the fall, although some limited attendance at their games, some universities shortened their schedules and some games were canceled because of COVID-19 outbreaks. Universities cut spending—eliminating some programs and laying off faculty and staff—to compensate for millions of dollars in pandemic-related revenue losses. Despite the crisis, though, Texas Higher Education Commissoner Harrison Keller said higher education will be critical for people seeking new skills and credentials to recover from the layoffs and economic downturn caused by the pandemic. Education officials also predicted future enrollment growth in health care courses and online offerings.[35]

The University of Texas at Austin and Texas A&M University at College Station are the state's largest universities; they have higher entrance requirements than many other schools and, thanks to a constitutional endowment, some of the state's best educational

EQUALITY IN EDUCATIONAL OPPORTUNITY

The student body at the University of Texas at Austin is diverse, but debate continues over the role of affirmative action in university admissions as the state works to increase minority enrollment in higher education.

Permanent University Fund (PUF)

A land- and mineral-rich endowment that benefits the University of Texas and Texas A&M University systems, particularly the flagship universities in Austin and College Station.

facilities. They receive revenue generated by the land- and mineral-rich **Permanent University Fund (PUF)**, in which other university systems in the state do not share. For many years, UT-Austin and the A&M College Station campus also were set apart by their research programs, but more recently several other state-supported universities have increased their research capabilities, boosted by a 2009 state law that created a matching fund to use tax dollars to encourage private donations for university research.

In 2001, the legislature overwhelmingly approved, and Governor Rick Perry signed, a law allowing some children of undocumented immigrants to qualify for lower, in-state tuition rates at Texas colleges and universities. Years later, some conservatives heavily criticized Perry for that law. But Perry and other supporters of the law believed it was important to encourage young, longtime residents of Texas, including immigrants, to obtain college educations and better prepare themselves for productive futures.

14.4.5 A Struggle over Affirmative Action in Higher Education

Texas's efforts to increase minority enrollments in its universities suffered a setback in 1996 when the Fifth U.S. Circuit Court of Appeals in New Orleans ruled that a race-based admissions policy previously used by the University of Texas School of Law was unconstitutional. The U.S. Supreme Court in *Hopwood* v. *State of Texas* refused to grant the state's appeal and let the appellate court's decision stand. Lead plaintiff Cheryl Hopwood was one of four white students who sued after not being admitted into the law school.[36]

Texas Attorney General Dan Morales held in 1997 that the *Hopwood* ruling went beyond the law school and prohibited all universities in Texas from using race or ethnicity as a preferential factor in admissions, scholarships, and other student programs. Morales's opinion was attacked as overly broad by many civil rights leaders and minority legislators, but it had the force of law.[37] The Texas legislature, meeting in 1997, attempted to soften the blow to affirmative action by enacting a new law that guaranteed automatic admissions to state universities for high school graduates who finished in the top 10 percent of their classes, regardless of their scores on college entrance examinations. The law was designed to give the best students from poor and predominantly minority school districts an equal footing in university admissions with graduates of wealthier school districts. The new law also allowed university officials to consider other admissions criteria, including a student's family income and parents' education levels.

The drop-off in minority enrollment was significant at the UT Law School the first year after the *Hopwood* restrictions went into effect. The first-year law class of almost 500 students in the fall of 1997 included only four African Americans or Hispanics. Thirty-one African Americans or Hispanics had entered the previous year. The more flexible admissions standards set by the legislature applied only to entering undergraduate students, not to those seeking admission to law school and other professional schools.[38]

In 2003, the U.S. Supreme Court, ruling in *Grutter* v. *Bollinger*, from the University of Michigan, effectively repealed *Hopwood* by holding that universities could use affirmative action programs to give minority students help in admissions, provided that racial quotas were not used. The University of Texas then began developing new admissions criteria that could include race, among other factors, to apply to applicants who didn't automatically qualify for admission under the top 10 percent law.

In 2008, two white students, Abigail Fisher and Rachel Michalewicz, who were denied admission as undergraduates to the University of Texas at Austin, filed another lawsuit challenging UT's consideration of race and ethnicity in admissions. They were recruited by Edward Blum, an activist opponent of race-based laws, who organized the lawsuit and arranged financing. The plaintiffs lost in federal district court in Austin and before the Fifth U.S. Circuit Court of Appeals in New Orleans. Michalewicz dropped out of the case, but Fisher appealed to the U.S. Supreme Court. In *Fisher* v. *University of Texas*, the high Court, in a 7–1 decision in June 2013, did not overturn *Grutter*, but did order the Fifth Circuit Court to take another look at the University of Texas's admissions policy to ensure that the university's use of race complied with a strict standard. Racial preferences in college admissions were constitutional if "no workable-race-neutral alternatives would produce the educational benefits of diversity," the high Court ruled.[39] Fisher already had graduated from Louisiana State University in 2012, but her legal fight against UT continued until 2016, when the U.S. Supreme Court upheld a subsequent finding by the Fifth Circuit Court that the university's admissions policy complied with the high Court's strict standard. But the war over affirmative action didn't end. In 2017, Edward Blum, the activist who had recruited Fisher, filed another lawsuit challenging UT's admissions policy, but this suit was filed in state district court in Austin, not federal court. Blum and his nonprofit group, Students for Fair Admissions, contended that UT's policy of giving slight admissions preferences to some minorities discriminated against white and Asian students and violated the Texas Constitution. A state district judge dismissed that lawsuit over a technicality, but the group came back to file a virtually identical lawsuit against the university two years later.[40]

Blum and his group also represented more than a dozen Asian American students who sued Harvard University, alleging discrimination, after their applications for admission were rejected. In this case, the Asian Americans argued that Harvard penalized them for their high academic achievements while giving admission preferences to other racial and ethnic minorities. They alleged that Harvard's admissions process amounted to an illegal racial quota system. In the nationally watched case, a federal district judge ruled against the plaintiffs in 2019, upholding Harvard's admissions system as constitutional. But the group appealed to the First U.S. Circuit of Appeals in Massachusetts. Regardless of how that court ruled, the case was expected to be ultimately decided by the U.S. Supreme Court, which had become more conservative with the appointment of three justices by President Donald Trump since the high court's last ruling in 2016 in Blum's unsuccessful lawsuit against the University of Texas.[41]

While the legal challenge against Harvard was still pending, the Trump administration rescinded Obama administration policies that had encouraged universities to consider race as a factor in admissions in order to diversity their campuses. The action did not have the force of law, but it was a strong signal that the Trump administration favored race-blind admissions standards.[42]

Meanwhile, the vast majority of freshman admissions to UT-Austin each year, including African Americans and Hispanics, were under the top 10 percent law, which limited the school's options for admitting other students. At the university's urging, the legislature in 2009 modified the law as it applied to the Austin campus. High school graduates in Texas had to be in the top 8 percent of their classes to be guaranteed automatic admission to UT-Austin by 2013, in the top 7 percent of their classes by 2017, and in the top 6 percent by the fall of 2019.

For the first time in UT-Austin's history, fewer than half (47.6 percent) of entering freshmen in the fall of 2010 identified themselves as "white." The total UT-Austin enrollment that fall, including those who enrolled in undergraduate school, graduate schools, and the law school, was 52.1 percent white. Some 17 percent were Hispanic; 4.5 percent were African American; 15.2 percent were Asian American; and 0.4 percent were Native American. The remainder were foreign-born students or those who declined to report their race or ethnicity.[43]

14.4.6 Tuition Issues

With tax dollars becoming increasingly tight, University of Texas officials successfully lobbied the legislature in 2003 for a new law that gave university governing boards the freedom to set tuition rates independent of legislative action. Subsequently, regents raised tuition several times for public universities over the next twelve years to compensate for what they considered inadequate appropriations of tax dollars by the legislature. By the 2015–2016 academic year, student costs had increased on average by 65 percent, while state funding per college student had dropped by 27 percent, with both figures adjusted for inflation, Texas Higher Education Commissioner Raymund Paredes reported. Universities approved additional tuition increases in subsequent years, as the percentage of state funding continued to lag. University of Texas regents approved a 2-percent increase in tuition and fees for the fall of 2018 and another 2-percent increase for the fall of 2019 for students at UT-Austin. By the end of the two-step increase, full-time undergraduate students who were Texas residents would be paying an average $10,818 for an academic year. Full-time undergraduates from out of state would be paying an average $38,228. UT-Austin President Gregory L. Fenves said the university also would continue to increase student financial assistance. Regents raised the tuition at other UT campuses, but at varying amounts.[44]

Even with the higher tuition, some university officials said Texas college costs were still a bargain compared to many other states, where public universities also were increasing tuition and, in some cases, suffering from state budget cuts. The University of Texas at Austin, in a posting on its website, noted that it was "annually recognized as one of the best values in higher education by national publications that evaluate academic quality and cost." For the 2018–2019 academic year (two semesters), UT-Austin said its average academic cost for a Texas resident undergraduate student taking thirty credit hours was $10,610 (see Figure 14–2). It listed eleven other major public universities in other states that charged their residents more, including $18,454 for two semesters at Pennsylvania State University–University Park, $15,262 at the University of Michigan–Ann Arbor, and $15,094 at the University of Illinois–Urbana/Champaign.[45]

Some universities have started giving free tuition to students from low-income and some middle-income families. Texas A&M has provided free tuition to students with annual family incomes of $60,000 or less since 2011. More than 6,700 students benefited from that program in the 2018–2019 school year. The University of Texas at Austin started waiving tuition and fees for students whose families earned $30,000 or less a year in 2018. Beginning in the fall of 2020, UT-Austin raised the standard to $65,000 a year. The expansion was expected to eliminate tuition and fees for about 8,600 students, or 24 percent of the undergraduate student body. Graduate students and students from out of state are not eligible for the program, but transfer students are. UT regents approved using $160 million from the Permanent University Fund to create a separate endowment to cover the tuition waiver program.[46]

FIGURE 14-2   IS TEXAS TUITION A BARGAIN?

Compared to charges at other major, state-supported universities, resident tuition at the University of Texas at Austin is relatively low.

NOTE: Average academic costs for resident undergraduate students taking thirty credit hours during the fall and spring semesters, 2018–2019 academic year.

SOURCE: https://onestop.utexas.edu/managing-costs/cost-tuition-rates/compare-ut-tuition.

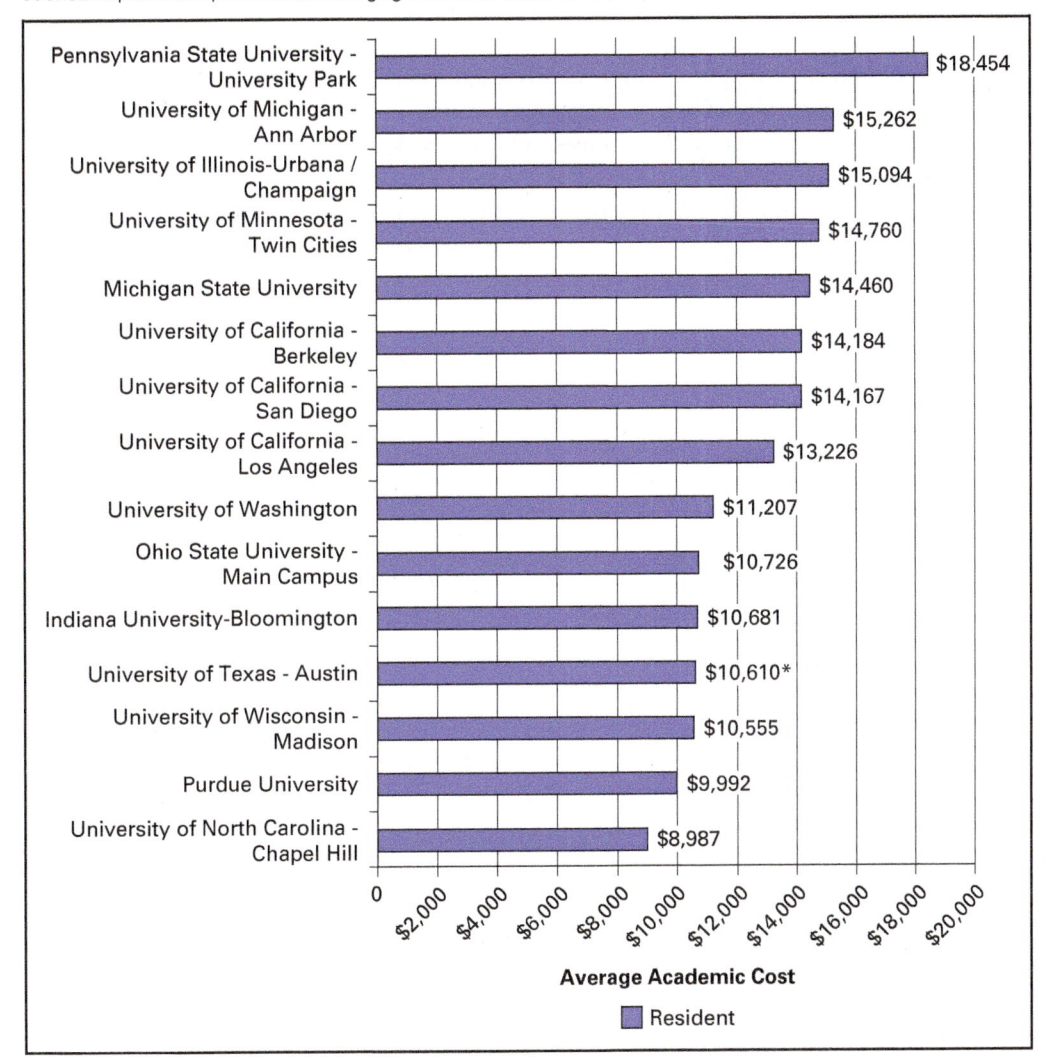

University	Average Academic Cost (Resident)
Pennsylvania State University - University Park	$18,454
University of Michigan - Ann Arbor	$15,262
University of Illinois-Urbana / Champaign	$15,094
University of Minnesota - Twin Cities	$14,760
Michigan State University	$14,460
University of California - Berkeley	$14,184
University of California - San Diego	$14,167
University of California - Los Angeles	$13,226
University of Washington	$11,207
Ohio State University - Main Campus	$10,726
Indiana University-Bloomington	$10,681
University of Texas - Austin	$10,610*
University of Wisconsin - Madison	$10,555
Purdue University	$9,992
University of North Carolina - Chapel Hill	$8,987

In another move to reduce college costs for some low-income and working-adult students, the Texas Higher Education Coordinating Board administers the Texas Affordable Baccalaureate Grant Program, which supports alternative degree programs that can reduce the time and money required to obtain a bachelor's degree.

14.4.7 Guns on Campus

The legislature in 2015 enacted a law allowing adults, including students, with handgun licenses to bring their weapons on campus, provided the guns were concealed from public view. The law went into effect at four-year state-supported universities in 2016 and at community colleges in 2017. Although many university officials opposed the law, some didn't. Notably, the chancellors of the two largest university systems took opposite sides. Then-University of Texas System Chancellor William McRaven opposed the law, arguing it would make campuses less safe, while Texas A&M University System Chancellor John Sharp supported the measure. Even after the law had been signed by the governor and universities prepared to carry it out, controversy continued. The law allowed university officials to declare limited gun-free zones on their campuses, but sponsors of the statute made it clear they intended for handguns to be allowed in classrooms.

Campus leaders considered rules allowing guns in classrooms but banning them from most dormitories and certain other locations, such as laboratories and sports venues. Many faculty members were outraged, fearing that the presence—or possible presence—of weapons could dampen classroom discussion about sensitive, controversial issues. Three University of Texas at Austin professors raised that fear as a First Amendment issue in a lawsuit they filed in federal court seeking to overturn the law. But a federal district judge dismissed their suit, ruling that they didn't have standing to sue and couldn't present any "concrete evidence" to substantiate their claims.[47]

The University of Texas at Austin's longtime architecture dean, Fritz Steiner, said the new gun law was the main reason he decided to leave UT to become dean of the University of Pennsylvania School of Design in 2016. "I would never have applied for another job if not for campus carry. I felt that I was going to be responsible for managing a law I didn't believe in," he said in an interview with *The Texas Tribune*. The new law also had its supporters on campuses. A group at UT-Austin called Students for Concealed Carry said opponents were stirring up unreasonable concerns. "Campus carry is not to blame for the current atmosphere of fear on Texas college campuses," the group said in a statement.[48]

The law allowed private universities to continue to ban guns from their campuses, and most did.

14.4.8 Keeping Campuses Safe

Over a two-year span, between 2011 and 2013, colleges and universities in Texas reported that assaults on or near their campuses had almost doubled, from 100 to 198. Some officials doubted the actual number of crimes had increased that much. They suspected the higher number in 2013 was instead the result of increased awareness and better reporting. Nevertheless, the Texas legislature responded in 2015 by enacting a law requiring higher education institutions to increase their efforts to prevent and respond to sexual assaults and heighten student awareness of the issue. The new law required, among other things, colleges and universities to inform students during freshman orientation of their policies for dealing with sexual assaults and to update those policies every two years. About the same time, the University of Texas System began conducting what it called its largest-ever review of sexual assault on its campuses. Federal law, including Title IX, also imposes requirements on universities for dealing with sexual assault and other violent crimes, but victims' advocates had accused some schools of being lax in meeting federal requirements.[49] In an effort to strengthen reporting, the legislature in 2019 enacted still another law that some experts believed would be one of the toughest reporting laws in the country. Under the new law, university employees who failed to report incidents of sexual harassment, assault, or stalking could lose their jobs and face criminal charges.[50]

Baylor University, one of Texas's most prominent private universities, had been accused of mishandling campus investigations of rape allegations brought by female students, in separate incidents, against two Baylor football players. The players were convicted of sexual assault in 2014 and 2015. In 2016, an investigation ordered by the university concluded that Baylor officials had "failed to consistently support" students who reported sexual assault and "failed to take action to identify and eliminate a potential hostile environment, prevent its recurrence, or address its effects." As a result, Baylor's board of regents fired the head football coach, Art Briles, and demoted the university's president, Ken Starr, who later left the university.[51] But the controversy continued. Baylor regents said that nineteen football players had been accused of assault or rape since 2011, and a number of lawsuits were filed against the school. As it worked to move past the scandal and improve campus safety, Baylor in 2017 hired its first female president, Linda Livingstone, a former faculty member and administrator at the university who promised to address each assault case. Despite the problems, Baylor continued to rise in national academic ratings.[52]

Criminal Justice

14.5 Explain the implications of court-ordered prison reforms on the criminal justice system in Texas and the state's large number of executions.

Texas did away with public hangings on the courthouse square years ago but retained a frontier attitude toward crime and criminals, an attitude that produced a criminal justice system based more on retribution than rehabilitation. Candidates were elected to the legislature on tough, anticrime promises to "lock 'em up and throw away the key." Once in office, they passed laws providing long sentences for more and more offenses. Eventually, the system was overwhelmed by sheer numbers, and crime, for a while, became a bigger problem than ever.

State policymakers ignored deteriorating prison conditions until U.S. District Judge William Wayne Justice of Tyler declared the prison system unconstitutional in 1980 in a landmark lawsuit brought by inmates (*Ruiz v. Estelle*). He cited numerous problems, including overcrowded conditions, poor staffing levels, inadequate medical and psychiatric care for prisoners, and the use of "building tenders"—inmates who were given positions of authority over other prisoners, whom they frequently abused. Judge Justice ordered extensive reforms with which the state agreed to comply, and he appointed a monitor to help him supervise what was then known as the Texas Department of Corrections and now is the institutional division of the Texas Department of Criminal Justice.[53] This court intervention led to extensive changes in Texas's criminal justice system, but state government still retains a tough attitude toward crime and Texas continues to lead the nation in prisoners and executions.

Ruiz v. Estelle
A 1980 landmark federal court order that declared the state prison system unconstitutional and resulted in significant changes in state lockups.

THE EXECUTION GURNEY
More than 560 persons convicted of capital murder have been executed in Texas since 1982. Texas leads the country in this criminal justice statistic.

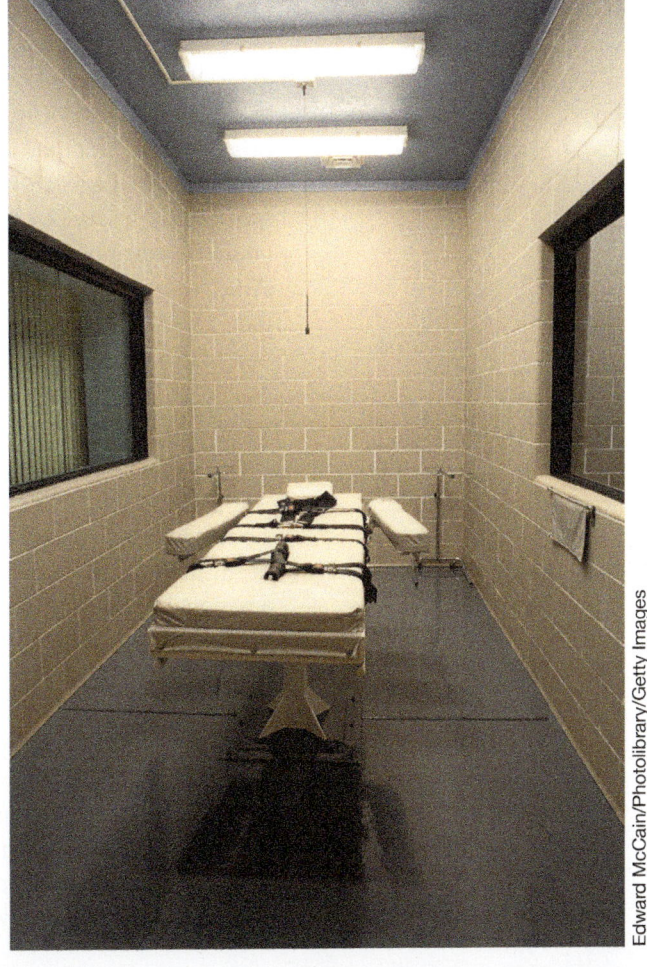

14.5.1 Reforms Prompted by Crowded Prisons

One of Judge Justice's key orders limited the population of prison units to 95 percent of capacity. This was implemented to guard against a recurrence of overcrowding and to allow for the housing of inmates according to classifications, which separated youthful, first-time offenders from more hardened criminals and those with special needs from the general prison population. But the prison population limit and an increase in violent crimes in the 1980s helped produce a criminal justice crisis that lasted for several years. Thousands of convicted felons were backlogged in overcrowded county jails because there wasn't enough room in the state prisons. This resulted in hundreds of criminals being paroled early, which outraged law-abiding Texans who felt endangered by the freed convicts.

Many of the convicts overloading the system were nonviolent, repeat offenders, including alcoholics and drug addicts who continued to get in trouble because they were unable to function on their own in the free world. Experts believed that alcoholism, drug addiction, or drug-related crimes were responsible for about 85 percent of the prison population.[54] At the urging of Governor Ann Richards in 1991, the legislature created a new alcoholism and drug abuse treatment program within the prison system, with the goal of reducing that recidivism.

In settling the *Ruiz* lawsuit in 1992, the state agreed to maintain safe prisons, and the federal court's active supervision of the prison system ended. Then, in 1993, the

TABLE 14-2 COMPARISONS OF STATE PRISON POPULATIONS, 2016–2017

State	Prison Population 2016	Prison Population 2017	Percentage of Change, 2016–2017
Texas	163,703	162,523	−0.7
California	130,084	131,039	+0.7
Florida	99,974	98,504	−1.5
Georgia	53,627	53,667	+0.1
New York	50,716	49,461	−2.5
Pennsylvania	49,244	48,333	−1.8
Ohio	52,175	51,478	−1.3
All states	1,318,937	1,306,305	−1.0

SOURCE: U.S Department of Justice, Bureau of Justice Statistics, "Prisoners in 2017—Table 2: Prisoners under jurisdiction of state or federal correctional authorities, by jurisdiction and sex, 2016 and 2017," April 2019.

legislature enacted a major package of criminal justice reforms, including the first overhaul of the penal code in twenty years. The plan doubled the minimum time that violent felons would have to serve in prison—from one-fourth to one-half of their sentences—before becoming eligible for parole. To reserve more prison space for the most dangerous criminals, however, the legislature lowered the penalties for most property crimes and drug offenses. Many of these nonviolent offenders were diverted to community corrections programs or a new system of state-run jails, to which they could be sentenced for a maximum of two years and offered rehabilitation opportunities. The legislature also authorized doubling the size of the prison system during the mid-1990s, creating a construction boom financed by voter-approved bonds. Although prisons traditionally had been located in East Texas, new prisons were built throughout the state.

By 2011, Texas's 100-plus prisons, state jails, and substance-abuse facilities held more than 170,000 inmates, more than any other state. But the Texas crime rate began to decline, and so, slowly, did the prison population. This allowed the legislature, seeking relief from a huge revenue shortfall in 2011, to order the closure of a state prison for the first time in Texas history. Over the next nine years, the state closed nine more prisons. Legislators also invested more resources in diversion programs, such as mental health services, to keep minor offenders out of prison. The Texas prison population had dropped to 162,523 by the end of 2017, but Texas still operated the largest state prison system in the country, surpassing the more-populous California by more than 31,000 inmates. Prison populations for all states combined dropped about 1 percent between 2016 and 2017 (see Table 14–2).[55]

14.5.2 The Death Penalty in Texas: Popular and Controversial

Texas continues to lead the nation in executions. More than 560 persons were put to death in Texas by lethal injection between 1982, after the U.S. Supreme Court ended a national moratorium on the death penalty, through the end of 2019. This was more than one-third of the executions carried out in the United States during that period. Virginia and Oklahoma, each with more than 100, had the next highest numbers of executions, followed by Florida with 99. The number of executions has been decreasing in recent years, nationally and in Texas. There were no executions in 29 states, including Virginia and Oklahoma, in 2019, and some of those states have abolished the death penalty. Texas executed nine convicts in 2019, down from a high of 40 in 2000.[56]

Texas's execution record reflects the fact that most Texans support the death penalty. Some 65 percent of respondents to a University of Texas/*Texas Tribune* poll in 2018 said they supported it.[57] And a *Houston Chronicle* survey in 2002 found that 69 percent of respondents supported the death penalty, even though 55 percent believed that innocent people probably had been executed.[58]

As previously noted in Chapter 8, the death penalty can be given only to people convicted of capital murder, or acts of murder committed under specific circumstances, including the murder of a law enforcement officer or a firefighter who is on duty, murder committed during the course of certain other major crimes, murder for hire, murder of more than one person, murder of a prison employee, murder committed while attempting to escape from a penal institution, and murder of a child younger than 6. The only alternative punishment for someone convicted of capital murder is life in prison without parole.

RISK OF EXECUTING THE INNOCENT Even in Texas, the death penalty is not without controversy, and the loudest controversy rages around the question of whether innocent people have been executed. Former Governor Rick Perry, who presided over more executions than any governor in U.S. history, has said that they have not, but others, including the American Bar Association, aren't so sure. "In many areas, Texas appears out of step with better practices implemented in other capital [punishment] jurisdictions," the organization said in a study released in 2013. The bar association recommended several steps to help ensure that Texans aren't wrongfully convicted and sentenced to death. One included the indefinite preservation of biological evidence in violent crimes.[59] Several people have been released from death row in Texas after post-conviction evidence, mainly the result of DNA testing, proved them innocent. As forensic and DNA testing have become more sophisticated, challenges to murder convictions have become more commonplace.

In a nationally watched case, a state commission considered the possibility that at least one executed inmate, Cameron Todd Willingham, was innocent. Willingham, who was convicted of capital murder for setting a house fire in which his three young daughters died in 1991 in Corsicana, was executed in 2004. He always insisted he was innocent. Shortly before the execution, an internationally known arson scientist retained by Willingham's attorneys reviewed the evidence used to determine arson and concluded that it was flawed. If the fire was accidental, there was no arson and no crime. But the Texas Board of Pardons and Paroles and then-Governor Rick Perry refused to stay the execution.

The Texas Forensic Science Commission, which did not exist when Willingham was executed, decided in 2008 to review his case. The commission hired another arson expert, who also concluded that the arson science used to convict Willingham was seriously flawed. But Perry replaced four of the nine commissioners, including the chair, and the panel's investigation was put on hold. Then-Attorney General Greg Abbott eventually ended the investigation by ruling in 2011 that the panel could not consider evidence in cases that predated 2005, the year in which the legislature created the commission. The commission issued a report agreeing that the arson science used to secure Willingham's conviction was faulty, but it did not say whether it believed the executed convict was innocent or guilty. "There were other issues," said Dr. Nizam Peerwani, the commission's new chair. "There were eyewitness accounts; there were hospital and doctor testimony given and investigative findings."[60]

INTELLECTUALLY DISABLED CONVICTS After considerable controversy in Texas and other states, the U.S. Supreme Court in *Atkins v. Virginia* (2002) banned the execution of intellectually disabled convicts. Death penalty opponents argued that before the court ruling, Texas had executed at least six inmates who were demonstrably disabled. After the ruling, questions lingered about what standards to use to determine a convict's intellectual ability and, thus, eligibility for being put to death.

The Texas Court of Criminal Appeals established standards for determining intellectual disability, but those standards were struck down by the U.S. Supreme Court in a 5–3 ruling in 2017. In the majority opinion by Justice Ruth Bader Ginsburg, the court said Texas's use of outdated medical standards as well as nonclinical factors in determining whether an inmate was intellectually eligible for execution violated the Eighth Amendment's ban on cruel and unusual punishment. The decision came in the case of Bobby Moore, a 57-year-old man who had been on death row for more than thirty-six years for fatally shooting a supermarket clerk in Houston in 1980. In a subsequent ruling, the Texas Court of Criminal Appeals upheld the death penalty for Moore a second time, ruling that he was eligible for execution under current medical standards as well. But in 2019, the U.S. Supreme Court overruled the Texas court again, holding that Moore was disabled and ineligible for execution.[61]

Health and Human Services

14.6 Evaluate patterns of support for health and human services in Texas.

Health and human services are areas in which state government weighs compassion against the cold realities of its budget, and, compared to many states, Texas—under both Democratic and now Republican control—historically has been tight-fisted. To be sure, state government spends billions of state and federal dollars each year on health care and other welfare programs for the poor. But traditionally it has spent less money per resident on these programs than many other states have. In 2017, the most recent data available, state and local governments in Texas spent an average of $1,355 per resident on public welfare, including direct cash assistance through the Temporary Assistance for Needy Families (TANF) program, Supplemental Security Income, and other payments made directly to individuals plus payments to physicians and other service providers under programs such as Medicaid. This ranked Texas in the lowest tier of states in the public welfare category and well below the national average of $2,070 and per capita expenditures in other populous states such as New York, $3,624, and California, $2,840.[62]

Texas's austere approach to spending springs, historically, from the legacy of frontier colonists standing on their own two feet to fight adversity and win a better life. Countless politicians claiming that Texans can prevail in hard times by pulling themselves up by their bootstraps and hanging tough have perpetuated this view, but this perception ignores the reality that many people in modern Texas cannot pull themselves up by their bootstraps because they cannot afford boots, symbolically or otherwise. More than 4.2 million Texans—14.9 percent of the state's population—lived in poverty in 2018, with the state well above the national poverty rate of 11.8 percent. The poverty stricken included more than 1.5 million children, one of every five living in the state. Hispanic and African American children were three times more likely to live in poverty in Texas than white children.[63] To give you a better idea of what this means, a family of four is considered poor under government guidelines if its combined annual income is $25,750 or less.

14.6.1 The Struggle of Many Texans for Health Care

Along with its high incidence of poverty, Texas for a number of years has had the dubious distinction of being a national leader in the number of residents without health insurance. About five million Texas residents, or 17.7 percent of the state's population, had no health coverage in 2018. This included 11.2 percent of Texas children younger than 19 and marked the second year in a row that coverage had declined following two years of improvements. Even worse, the number of uninsured threatened to swell by an additional one million or more during the coronavirus pandemic in 2020, as many Texans lost their jobs and their employer-sponsored coverage.

Many Texans who can't afford health insurance or don't get coverage through an employer's insurance plan can purchase subsidized coverage through the Affordable

Care Act, or Obamacare, although that law remains under attack by opponents in federal court. Many other people have to rely on Medicaid or the Children's Health Insurance Program (CHIP), provided they meet Texas's strict eligibility requirements.

The number varied from month-to-month, but more than 4.7 million Texans were covered at any given time in 2017 by Medicaid or CHIP. Medicaid is for low-income people—mainly children, the elderly, and the disabled—and CHIP is for the children of working parents who earn too much to qualify for Medicaid but do not have insurance through their jobs or cannot afford private coverage, even under Obamacare. Between December 2017 and April 2019, the number of Texas children enrolled in those two programs decreased by more than 200,000. Health care advocates blamed the drop on excessive red tape and difficult enrollment processes imposed by Texas, state government's failure to effectively market the programs, and anti-immigrant rhetoric and proposed immigration policies of the Trump administration in Washington. Many children who receive health care services in Texas are from immigrant families, and many immigrant parents reportedly were unenrolling their children from Medicaid and CHIP for fear of being deported or suffering other retaliations, such as being denied a green card for employment, even though the children had been born in the United States and were American citizens.[64]

Under the Affordable Care Act, Texas could expand Medicaid coverage by easing eligibility restrictions to allow more low-income people to quality for coverage and the federal government would pick up most of the additional cost. By 2020, Texas was one of 14 states refusing to expand their Medicaid programs, even though health care advocates have estimated that as many as one million additional Texans could become eligible for Medicaid if Texas were to ease its restrictions. Former Governor Rick Perry said Medicaid expansion was a "misguided" idea that soon would crumble the state budget and raise taxes "under the weight of oppressive Medicaid costs." He warned that it would "cost tens of billions in combined state and federal funds over the next 10 years."[65] His successor, Governor Greg Abbott, also opposed expansion.

Texas also refused to establish an online health insurance exchange under the Affordable Care Act to assist Texans in shopping for their own insurance policies in the private marketplace. Texas residents had to rely instead on the federal government's online exchange, healthcare.gov, which—after a 2013 launch marred by technical glitches—helped many Americans obtain coverage, often at rates lowered by

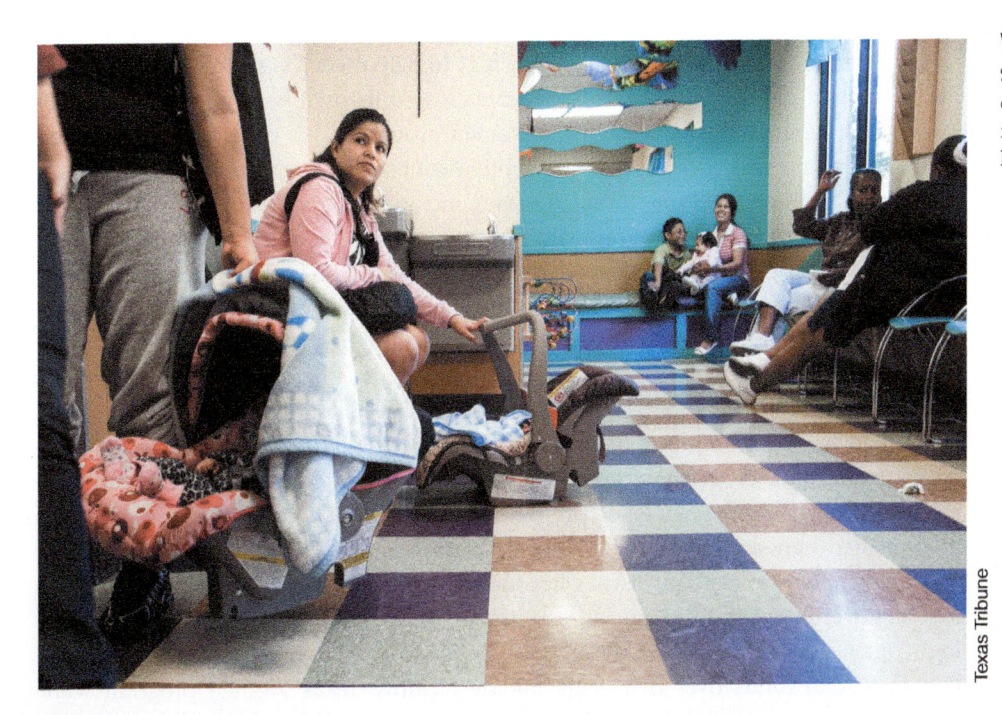

WAITING TO SEE THE DOCTOR

State budget cutbacks and controversy over abortion have made it difficult for many Texas women to obtain some health services.

federal tax credits. Many low-income Texans who remained excluded from Medicaid, however, were too poor to qualify for the tax credits. Although some provisions of the Affordable Care Act, including the provision that insurance companies cannot deny coverage to someone because of a pre-existing medical condition, are popular with many Texans, the state's Republican leadership and many Republicans throughout the country remain opposed to the law. As discussed in Chapter 6, Texas Attorney General Ken Paxton filed a federal lawsuit in 2018 seeking to overturn the law. The U.S. Supreme Court, which had upheld the law on two previous occasions, agreed to hear attorneys' arguments in Paxton's suit in late 2020 with a decision expected in 2021.

Frequently, low-income people who do not receive preventive care through Medicaid or CHIP end up in public hospital emergency rooms when they become sick. Emergency room care, paid for by taxpayers in the communities where the hospitals are located, is much more expensive than preventive care under Medicaid or CHIP.

14.6.2 Controversy over Abortion and Women's Health Care

Even though it has been more than forty years since the U.S. Supreme Court upheld abortion rights, the issue remains a major policy and political controversy in Texas and throughout much of the country. The debate, which is part of a larger debate over women's health care, began to heat up in Texas after conservative Republicans tightened their grip on state government and began taking steps to restrict the procedure.

CONTROVERSY OVER PLANNED PARENTHOOD State government in 2012 approved a rule banning Planned Parenthood clinics and other "affiliates of abortion providers" in Texas from participating in the Medicaid Women's Health Program. This program, largely federally funded, helped low-income women obtain birth control pills, family planning help, and cancer screenings. The Obama administration refused to renew the program because Planned Parenthood had been responsible for serving about 40 percent of the women who participated, and the federal government's policy was to deny Medicaid funding to states that restricted patients' provider choices. Planned Parenthood did not provide abortions at the clinics participating in the program because clinics that provide abortions were prohibited from receiving money from the Women's Health Program. Even so, then-Governor Rick Perry and Republican legislative leaders did not want Planned Parenthood to perform cancer screenings or dispense birth control pills either. The legislature also made deep cuts in other family planning programs in 2011 to help meet a state revenue shortfall.

To replace the federal program, the state created its own health care program for low-income women, the Healthy Texas Women program. This program provided services such as pregnancy testing, contraceptive counseling, breast and cervical cancer screenings, and treatment for chronic diseases, including diabetes, high blood pressure, and high cholesterol. The program did not offer abortion services. By 2016, the new program had added about 3,700 health care providers. But in 2017, the Center for Public Policy Priorities, a politically left-leaning advocacy and research group, issued a report that concluded the new state program was serving about 45,000 fewer low-income women than the federal program had served. The report said that was because Planned Parenthood had been the biggest service provider by far under the federal program, which had been discontinued in Texas after Planned Parenthood was removed from participation. But Joe Pojman, executive director of Texas Alliance for Life, an anti-abortion group, said the new state program was successful because the new providers the state had signed up to replace Planned Parenthood provided "more comprehensive and preventive primary care." After Republican Donald Trump became president, the federal government and the state agreed in 2020 on a five-year Medicaid waiver covering women's health services in Texas. The waiver would provide Texas with $350 million in federal funds over five years for the Healthy Texas Women program while continuing to exclude Planned Parenthood from participating. Governor Greg Abbott praised Trump's "commitment to protecting the unborn while providing much-needed health resources to Texas women." The state said the federal funds would enable the program to serve more than 200,000 women a year. But the Center for Public Policy Priorities said the federal money would simply replace money the state already was spending without providing more or better health care for women.[66]

Texas Republican leaders increased their attacks on Planned Parenthood in 2015, following the release of undercover videos, made by antiabortion activists, purporting to show that the organization had improperly harvested fetal tissue from abortions for use by researchers. Planned Parenthood denied any wrongdoing and insisted the videos, including one shot at a Planned Parenthood facility in Houston, were edited to mislead viewers.

NEW ABORTION RESTRICTIONS In 2011, the Texas legislature enacted a law requiring a woman to have a sonogram of her fetus before receiving an abortion, and similar laws have been passed in more than twenty other states. Abortion opponents hoped these laws would discourage some women from having the procedure, but it isn't clear what effect they have had. During a contentious, special legislative session in 2013, abortion opponents won a more far-reaching Texas law imposing restrictions on abortion providers. This law banned most abortions after the twentieth week of pregnancy, restricted the protocol that doctors could use in performing so-called medication abortions, required all abortion clinics to meet the expensive design and staffing standards of ambulatory surgical centers, and required any doctor who performed abortions at an abortion clinic to have formal admitting privileges at a hospital within 30 miles of the clinic.

Abortion providers sued the state in federal court to try to overturn the last two requirements—that abortion clinics upgrade their standards and that abortion clinic doctors have admitting privileges at nearby hospitals. Abortion opponents said the requirements were essential to protecting the health and safety of women receiving abortions. But clinic operators said they rarely encountered emergencies and, if they did, a patient still could be treated at a nearby hospital. More than forty abortion clinics were operating in Texas when the law went into effect in 2013. By the time the case *Whole Woman's Health* v. *Hellerstedt* reached the U.S. Supreme Court almost three years later, only nineteen clinics were still open, and abortion rights advocates blamed the law's restrictions for the closures of the other clinics.

Abortion rights supporters believed the Texas restrictions, similar to abortion laws enacted in several other states, were part of a coordinated national effort to chip away at the landmark *Roe* v. *Wade* decision, in which the U.S. Supreme Court in 1973 established a constitutional right to an abortion, until a more conservative Supreme Court outlawed abortion altogether or, at least, imposed more restrictions on the procedure. Governor Rick Perry, who signed the 2011 and 2013 abortion laws, said he hoped to make abortion "a thing of the past."[67]

Since *Roe* v. *Wade* was handed down, the U.S. Supreme Court has allowed some abortion restrictions. In *Casey* v. *Planned Parenthood* in 1992, the Court allowed "reasonable" regulations of abortions provided they didn't impose an "undue burden" on a woman's right to end a pregnancy. And in 2007, the Supreme Court upheld the federal partial-birth abortion ban. The Supreme Court heard attorneys' arguments over the new Texas restrictions on abortion clinics in March 2016, only a few weeks after the death of conservative Justice Antonin Scalia. The remaining conservative justices questioned whether abortion providers could prove that the law was responsible for the closure of clinics. Liberal justices asked the state to prove that the new restrictions were necessary to protect the health of abortion patients. In June 2016, the Supreme Court struck down the two controversial provisions. The justices ruled, 5–3, that the restrictions placed an undue burden on a woman's constitutional right to an abortion. The majority said the restrictions provided "few, if any, health benefits for women."[68]

Four years later, the issue was back before the Supreme Court, with an almost identical antiabortion law from Louisiana under consideration and a court lineup with two conservative justices, Neil M. Gorsuch and Brett M. Kavanaugh, appointees of President Trump, who weren't on the court when the Texas law was struck down. Gone was the retired former Justice Anthony M. Kennedy, who had sided with the liberal wing of the court to form the majority against the Texas law. In a hearing of the Louisiana case in March 2020, the arguments were similar to the 2016 arguments in the Texas case. Justice Stephen G. Breyer, who wrote the majority opinion against the Texas law, noted the divisiveness of the debate over abortion. "In the country, people have very strong feelings, and a lot of people morally think it's wrong and a lot of people morally think the opposite is wrong," he said. "The court is struggling with the problem of what kind of rule of law do you have in a country that contains both sorts of people." He added, "Why depart from what was pretty clear precedent?"[69] Three months later, with Breyer again writing the majority opinion, the court struck down the Louisiana law, 5–4. Chief Justice John Roberts was the deciding vote. In 2016, he had dissented when the court invalidated the Texas law. This time, he sided with the majority because of the precedent the court had set in the Texas case.

Environmental Problems and Policies

14.7 Assess the response of Texas to environmental issues.

Texas is blessed with an abundance of fragile natural resources that can no longer be taken for granted, but efforts to impose environmental regulations are difficult for a number of reasons. For starters, Texas has the largest concentration of petrochemical plants and refineries in the country, and it has coal-burning power plants and a large amount of oil and natural gas production. Although efforts have been made to reduce environmental risks from these industries, state policymakers are influenced by economic considerations because these same industries employ thousands of people and pump billions of dollars into the economy and the state treasury. Compounding the problem are a state legacy emphasizing individual property rights and Texans' love for their automobiles, pickups, and sport utility vehicles.

14.7.1 Dirty Air

Texas received some national notoriety in 1999 when Houston beat out Los Angeles for the dubious distinction of being the U.S. city with the "dirtiest air." The Houston metropolitan area led the nation that year in the number of days (fifty-two) in which the city's air violated the national health standard for ozone, the main ingredient in smog. Los Angeles regained its first-place standing in 2002, and overall air quality in Texas continues to improve, thanks largely to federal environmental requirements for automobiles and industrial plants. But air pollution remains a problem in Texas, as it does in many other states.[70]

Unlike large cities in some states, Texas cities have been slow to develop local rail transportation systems. Dallas and Houston built the state's first two and Austin followed with a third limited rail system. But none is comparable to the more extensive rail systems in major cities along the East Coast. So, automobiles continue to clog streets and freeways in urban and suburban Texas, spewing tons of pollutants into the air. State officials responded with antipollution restrictions after being forced to do so by the federal government. To meet federal Clean Air Act standards for smog reduction, for example, the state now requires motorists in the Houston, Dallas–Fort Worth, and certain other metropolitan areas to have special emissions inspections of their cars.

Many state political leaders, including recent governors, have preferred to encourage industries to voluntarily reduce pollution, rather than impose strict cleanup requirements. In 2010, the Obama administration attempted to crack down on Texas's regulatory system as too lax, sparking one in a series of legal and political battles over pollution regulation between Texas and the federal government.

In its national study of air pollution updated in 2019, the American Lung Association placed three Texas locations on its list of the twenty-five metropolitan areas most polluted by ozone in the United States. The rankings were based on data collected at official monitoring sites across the United States in 2015, 2016, and 2017. The Houston area was ninth, Dallas-Fort Worth was seventeenth and the El Paso area, which included nearby Las Cruces, New Mexico, was twenty-second. Ten of the twenty-five most ozone-polluted areas were in California, with Los Angeles–Long Beach leading the list. California and Pennsylvania each had several cities that were the most polluted in terms of their year-round average for particle pollution, a mix of very tiny solid and liquid particles in the air. Houston was ranked seventeenth and the McAllen-Edinburg area in the heavily agricultural Rio Grande Valley in South Texas was tied for twenty-second on that list.

Two Texas metropolitan areas—McAllen–Edinburg and Brownsville-Harlingen-Raymondville, also in the Rio Grande Valley—made the "cleanest" cities list for ozone. Four Texas metropolitan areas were rated among the "cleanest" cities for short-term particle pollution. They were Dallas-Fort Worth, Longview, McAllen-Edinburg, and the Corpus Christi-Kingsville-Alice area. Thanks to the federal Clean Air Act, the American Lung Association said, some areas of the country have made significant long-term progress in reducing air pollution. But, the report noted, about 141 million Americans, 43.3 percent of the U.S. population, a higher number than in the previous two reports, lived in counties that had unhealthy levels of ozone and/or particle pollution. "More must be done to address climate change and to protect communities from the growing risk to public health," the report said. "This year's report covered the three warmest years in modern history and demonstrates the increased risk of harm from air pollution that comes despite other protective measures being in place."[71]

Dr. Arch Carson, an air quality researcher at the University of Texas Health Science Center at Houston, said Texas is fortunate because much of it is flat and doesn't suffer from pollution being trapped by mountains, as does California. "But I still don't think we can go to sleep at night thinking that our job is done. There's much more to do in terms of cleaning up the air," he said.[72]

14.7.2 Global Warming

Texas dumped 653.8 million metric tons of energy-related carbon dioxide emissions into the atmosphere in 2016, more than the next two highest emitters, California and Florida, combined—12.7 percent of all the carbon dioxide produced in the country that year.[73] Most scientists believe that carbon dioxide emissions are a major contributor to global warming. Scientists at Texas A&M University issued a report in 2009 warning that global warming, in the not-too-distant future, would pose a potentially devastating threat to the Texas coast. The scientists predicted that global warming would cause sea levels to rise, spawn more intense hurricanes, and increase coastal flooding. Damage to coastal communities from hurricanes would more than triple by the 2080s, they said.[74] More recent reports also have warned of similar consequences, as well as predicting an increase in temperatures and heat-related deaths. After Hurricane Harvey dumped torrential rains over Houston and much of southeast Texas in August 2017, studies produced by two scientific research groups concluded that the rainfall, totaling more than 50 inches in some areas, was as much as 38 percent higher than it would have been without global warming. The studies considered only the impact of climate change on rainfall—warmer air holds more moisture, scientists

RUNNING ON EMPTY
Aquatic biologists survey what is left of the Double Mountain Fork of the Brazos River near Sagerton, Texas, during the 2011 drought.

pointed out—not whether global warming affected Harvey's formation or made it a stronger storm. The effect of climate change on hurricane formation remained an issue of scientific debate, researchers said.[75]

Scientists' findings on climate change, particularly relating to how human activities affect the earth's warming, have been questioned and disputed by many in the political arena, including former Texas Governor Rick Perry, who was appointed U.S. secretary of energy by President Donald Trump in 2017. While he was still governor, Perry made national headlines by publicly disputing the science on global warming, and his doubts have been shared by other—although not all—policymakers and regulators in Texas. At his confirmation hearing for energy secretary before a U.S. Senate committee in 2017, though, Perry indicated that his views on global warming had changed. He said he would pursue "sound science" on the issue of climate change, while also considering the economic impact. "I believe the climate is changing. I believe some of it is naturally occurring, but some of it is caused by manmade activity," Perry said. "The question is how we address it in a thoughtful way, that doesn't compromise economic growth,... the affordability of energy or American jobs."[76]

A University of Texas/*Texas Tribune* poll taken in 2019 showed that about two-thirds of Texans (66 percent) believed that climate change was happening and that 63 percent believed government should be doing something to address it. But there were sharp differences of opinion between Democrats and Republicans. An overwhelming majority of Democratic respondents (88 percent) believed both that climate change was occurring and that government should do something about it. Republican respondents were divided on the existence of climate change—44 percent said it was happening, and 42 percent said it wasn't—and only 38 percent wanted government to do something about it.[77]

The Obama administration issued a Clean Power Plan that would have required states to significantly reduce carbon dioxide emissions from power plants. The goal was to encourage states to replace coal with cleaner natural gas and renewable energy sources for electricity generation. Texas joined many other states in filing a federal court lawsuit to block the plan, and the U.S. Supreme Court in early 2016 blocked the plan until the lawsuit was resolved by the courts. Then in 2017, President Donald Trump, who had promised during his election campaign to revitalize a slumping coal industry, issued an executive order directing the Environmental Protection Agency to withdraw and rewrite Obama's plan. Trump's directive was applauded by fossil fuel advocates in Texas, who said Obama's order would have increased the costs of electricity and eliminated jobs. But environmentalists warned Trump's decision to rescind Obama's plan could worsen the consequences of climate change.[78]

Utility companies announced plans to close at least four coal-fired electricity-generating plants in Texas in 2018, yielding to the economic realities of less-expensive and cleaner natural gas and an emerging renewable energy market. Wind created 22 percent of the energy used in Texas in the first half of 2019, surpassing coal for the first time by 1 percent, according to the Electric Reliability Council of Texas. Natural gas, at 38 percent, produced more electricity than any other source.[79]

Even as coal-fired power plants decline, though, scientists warn that increased oil and gas production and petrochemical plants will continue to spew huge amounts of carbon dioxide and other greenhouse gases into the atmosphere. A report by University of Texas researchers, published in early 2020, predicted those additional emissions could total more than 178 million tons per year by 2030. The researchers estimated that in Texas and Louisiana combined, new oil, gas, and petrochemical plant emissions will equal the greenhouse gas output of 131 coal-fired power plants by that year.[80]

14.7.3 An Endangered Water Supply

Population growth has led to an increasing concern about the adequacy of Texas's water supply. That concern was heightened in 2011, when Texas was struck by the worst one-year drought on record, and again in 2012, when a Texas Supreme Court decision threatened to dismantle the state's regulatory plan for conserving groundwater (see Chapter 8). Also in 2011, the Texas Water Development Board published a draft report, warning that in serious drought conditions, "Texas does not and will not have enough water to meet the needs of its people, and its businesses, and its agricultural enterprises." As the Texas population grew to an anticipated 46 million by 2060, the report said, existing water supplies would decrease by 10 percent as the Ogallala (in West Texas) and other aquifers were depleted.[81] Drought conditions in some parts of the state were even more severe in 2013 than they had been in 2011, but by 2015 the drought had ended in most of Texas.

WATER DEVELOPMENT AND CONSERVATION   In 2013, the legislature and Texas voters approved Proposition 6, a constitutional amendment promoted as a long-term solution to the state's water problems. The plan took $2 billion from the state's Rainy Day Fund savings account to provide seed money for a special water development fund to help finance future water supply and conservation projects, including the construction of new reservoirs and the improvement of existing water facilities. The plan had strong support from the business community, most legislators, top state leaders, and some environmental groups, including the Sierra Club. But it was opposed by other environmentalists, who feared much of the money would be used to benefit major industrial plants and other special interests at the expense of conservation.

SUBSIDENCE   A different problem is posed by subsidence, or the sinking of land after water has been pumped from the ground. Near the coast, in the Houston area of southeastern Texas, removal of groundwater over the past century to serve the growing Houston metropolitan area has caused layers of the Gulf Coast Aquifer to collapse and the land above to sink, as much as 10 feet over the past 100 years in some places. This has increased the danger of flooding and caused cracked pavement, and it threatens more serious infrastructure damage. Most of the problem so far has been in Harris and Galveston counties, but experts believe it also is becoming a greater threat in fast-growing, suburban Fort Bend County as well. All three counties have special subsidence districts to restrict groundwater pumping and help develop alternative water sources.[82]

14.7.4 Oil Field Pollution Risks

The Rainy Day Fund, which provided the seed money for the new water development plan, has been flush with money (several billion dollars in 2020) because it receives a share of severance taxes from the production of oil and natural gas, an important contributor to the Texas economy. But the industry also has been implicated in air and water pollution.

A major factor in a recent oil and gas boom was the industry's widespread use of hydraulic fracturing, or fracking, a process of injecting millions of gallons of water, sand, and chemicals under high pressure to release natural gas and oil from rock formations that older drilling methods often were unable to penetrate. The process unlocked large amounts of previously untapped energy reserves. But fracking also has been linked to water pollution and earthquakes. Much of the problem has been blamed on disposal wells in which used and contaminated drilling fluids are injected for permanent storage. Industry officials say the disposal wells are carefully constructed and encased in concrete to prevent pollution. But with thousands of such wells scattered around Texas, environmentalists and some scientists believe the drilling fluids pose a contamination danger to groundwater.

Disposal wells also have been suspected as the cause of numerous minor earthquakes that have struck Texas in recent years, including in the Barnett Shale area around heavily populated Dallas–Fort Worth. Scientists say that injecting fluids into disposal wells located over faults can cause the faults to slip, producing earthquakes. Other earthquakes have occurred in another area of heavy drilling during the boom, the Eagle Ford Shale formation in South Texas. After a study, University of Texas at Austin scientists concluded that the act of drilling—the removal of large amounts of oil and water byproduct—was responsible for most of the Eagle Ford earthquakes.[83] In a later study, a Southern Methodist University research team concluded that some earthquakes in North Texas were most likely caused by high volumes of wastewater injection combined with the extraction of saltwater from natural gas wells. But the scientists had difficulty convincing the Texas Railroad Commission, which regulates oil and gas production, to accept their findings.[84]

The number of earthquakes in Texas has dropped in recent years, perhaps because a slowdown in oil and gas production means energy companies have been injecting less oilfield waste into the ground. The Texas Railroad Commission also has approved new regulations for disposal well operators, which may have had an effect, and it has hired a staff seismologist.[85]

Transportation in Texas

14.8 Trace the development of Texas's transportation issues.

In 1916, the first year that Texans were required to register their automobiles, state government recorded 194,720 of the still relatively new driving machines owned by its residents. Texas was largely rural, its population was about 4.5 million, and much of the state was still emerging from the horse-and-buggy era. Roads and highways were built and maintained by county governments, and many were primitive by today's standards. That soon began to change. The legislature in 1923 enacted a new state gasoline tax of 1 cent per gallon and dedicated three-fourths of its revenue to highways. A newly created Texas Highway Department (since renamed the Texas Department of Transportation) was given authority in 1925 to construct a state highway system and, armed with revenue from the gasoline tax and the federal government, it oversaw construction of a highway network that became the envy of many other states, and it mostly remained that way through the 1960s and 1970s.[86]

But Texas has since undergone dramatic growth and change, and it faces vastly different transportation challenges today. Texas now has more than 28 million residents and, as of 2017, more than 24.5 million motor vehicles crowding roads and highways.

THE LONG CRAWL HOME
Congestion such as this is a daily sight in urban and suburban areas around Texas. Highway construction has fallen behind population growth as legislators struggle to come up with an acceptable and adequate means of transportation funding.

Most are in the Texas Urban Triangle, an area including and bounded by Houston, San Antonio, Austin, and Dallas–Fort Worth, where the vast majority of Texans live.[87] In 2014, average auto commuters in Houston spent sixty-one hours a year in congested traffic, more than double the peak "rush-hour" commute time in 1982 (see Figure 14–3). Drivers in the Dallas–Fort Worth Metroplex averaged fifty-three hours in congestion, more than six times what Metroplex commuters had experienced in 1982. Long commutes also were common in Austin and several other Texas cities, and in most urban areas they continued to worsen.[88] Texas had exceeded its highway capacity, its highway funding structure was outdated and inadequate, and there was a lot of political reluctance to drafting a funding system that would keep Texas moving.

FIGURE 14-3 COMPARING "RUSH-HOUR" PARKING LOTS

It now takes longer to get from here to there. As this graph of the congestion-induced, extra hours spent by auto commuters in traffic each year shows, congestion during peak driving periods has grown significantly in metropolitan areas in Texas and around the country since 1982.

SOURCES: Texas A&M Transportation Institute, 2012 Annual Urban Mobility Report; Texas A&M Transportation Institute and INRIX, 2015 Urban Mobility Scorecard.

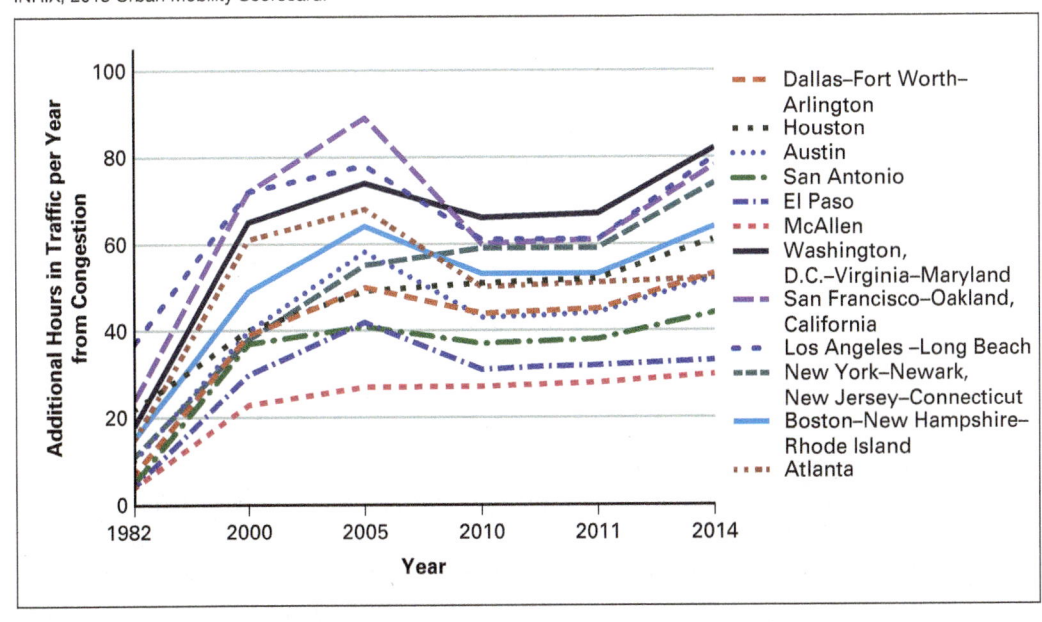

14.8.1 Texas Traffic Exhausting Tax Revenue

Because Texas is second only to Alaska in land mass, and much of Alaska is inaccessible by automobile, it is no surprise that Texas has the largest highway system in the United States. Texas has more than 79,000 miles of paved highway, and in 2006, according to the most recent data available, spent $1.8 billion on pavement maintenance alone. Although this total was more than any other state, Texas ranked twenty-second in the dollars spent per mile and spent significantly less per mile than California, Florida, New York, and other highly populous states. Texas also has been falling behind in new highway construction. The 2030 Committee, a study panel of business, government, and academic leaders, concluded in a 2009 report that Texas needed to spend an additional $315 billion (in 2008 dollars) on highway construction and maintenance between 2009 and 2030 to catch up with its growing population.[89]

An improved highway and transportation system is considered vital to Texas's future economic growth and job creation. It also is key to accommodating the state's growing role in trade with Mexico, fueled in large part by the North American Free Trade Agreement (NAFTA) and its successor, the United States–Mexico–Canada Agreement (USMCA), which were discussed in Chapter 3. Interstate 35, which runs north from Laredo on the Mexican border through San Antonio, Austin, and Dallas–Fort Worth before continuing on through the Midwest, was dubbed the "NAFTA Highway," and it is a major congestion headache. In 2019, a segment of Interstate 35 from south Austin to the University of Texas area in central Austin was rated the sixth worst traffic corridor in the United States by INRIX, the traffic data firm. Only two corridors in Los Angeles, two corridors in New York City, and one in Atlanta were considered worse.[90]

Three-fourths of the revenue from the state motor fuels tax and motor vehicle registration fees are dedicated by the state constitution to highway construction, maintenance, and policing, but that doesn't generate enough money to meet the growing need. The tax has been raised periodically over the years and now is set at 20 cents per gallon for gasoline and diesel. That flat rate, however, hasn't allowed the state to benefit from increases in fuel prices as a percentage of fuel costs would, and the legislature has refused to raise the rate since 1991. The tax as a revenue source peaked in 2008 and may decline as motorists drive an increasing number of fuel-efficient cars.[91] The highway construction cost index, meanwhile, increased by 62 percent between 2002 and 2007 alone, the Legislative Budget Board reported, while the number of vehicles on roads continued to increase.[92]

14.8.2 Building Highways and Toll Roads with Plastic

With a public and political antipathy to higher taxes, in 2001 the legislature began to rely heavily on the highway construction version of the credit card. The legislature scuttled Governor Rick Perry's proposed Trans Texas Corridor, a massive transportation network that would have included toll roads, railroads, and underground utility tunnels grouped in corridors stretching across the state. Lawmakers reacted to opposition primarily from rural landowners, who believed the plan was an attempt to take their land in order to enrich toll road operators. But, with voter approval, legislators authorized the Texas Department of Transportation to issue bonds to build a mix of highways, including toll roads. The agency entered comprehensive development agreements with private companies to build and operate some toll roads and help pay off the bonds with toll revenue.

One of the more ambitious public-private partnerships was involved in the construction of State Highway 130, a 90-mile bypass to ease congestion on Interstate 35 through San Antonio and Austin. The bypass opened in 2012, after the state had

NO TRAFFIC JAM HERE

Despite the potential appeal of an 85-mile-per-hour speed limit, the State Highway 130 toll road in central Texas didn't appeal to many motorists, at least not initially. That would gradually change.

built the northern portion and a private consortium—including Cintra, a Spanish company—had spent $1.3 billion to build the southern 41 miles. The consortium had a fifty-year contract with the state to operate and maintain the southern portion of the road in exchange for a share of toll revenue. To help attract motorists, the state set the speed limit on the road at 85 miles per hour, the highest in the country at the time, and lowered tolls for large trucks. During its first years of operation, the highway struggled financially because most drivers stayed on Interstate 35 to avoid tolls. In 2016, the private consortium filed for bankruptcy, although the road remained open as the operator went through bankruptcy proceedings. A spokesman for the Texas Department of Transportation said the state was not liable for any of the consortium's outstanding debt.[93] Meanwhile, traffic on the highway began to increase in subsequent years.

By 2013, the Texas Department of Transportation had issued $13 billion in bonds and had authorization for another $4.9 billion, all of which would be paid off with tax dollars, creating a much higher cost than traditional, pay-as-you-go highway financing. Repaying that debt was beginning to erode the highway budget.

The legislature in 2013 appropriated $17.9 billion for the 2014–2015 budget period for highway planning, rights-of-way purchases, construction, and maintenance. That was a 9.3 percent increase over 2012–2013. The legislature appropriated $2.4 billion for debt service on highway bonds for 2014–2015. That was a 49 percent increase over the previous budget period.[94]

Despite their party's traditional opposition to higher taxes, key Republican legislators in recent years have proposed limited tax increases for highway projects, but to no avail, largely (but not totally) because of opposition from other Republican legislators. "Their voters want roads (and education, water, and many other things) and don't want the prices to go up," *The Texas Tribune*'s Ross Ramsey wrote in *The New York Times*. "Politicians who promised to solve the road problem and promised not to raise taxes find themselves in a pickle. They were listening. They were responsive. Now they're stuck." But Ramsey also noted that some of the state's most Republican communities are in suburban counties, where residents endure long, slow commutes to work on crowded roads and highways. "Not everybody on that interstate parking lot is a Republican, but there are enough Republicans on the road to have a political impact," he wrote.[95]

Governor Greg Abbott and the legislative leadership agreed in 2015 on a plan to supplement the motor fuels tax revenue in the highway fund without raising additional taxes. It involved a constitutional amendment, which lawmakers and voters approved, to dedicate a portion of existing motor vehicle sales and rental taxes and a portion of general tax revenue to highways. The new funding plan was projected to raise an extra $3 billion a year for highway projects within a few years with additional billions soon after that. The plan did not raise taxes, but it diverted revenue that could have been spent on other state programs, including education and health care, to pay for more road construction and maintenance.

14.8.3 Mass Transit Offers Limited Relief

Unlike some major cities in the Northeast and the Midwest, Texas cities have been slow to embrace any form of mass transportation besides buses. Dallas, Houston, and Austin have constructed light rail systems in recent years. Dallas Area Rapid Transit (DART) now has lines linking downtown to several suburban communities. It also has connections to the Trinity Railway Express, which takes passengers from downtown Dallas to Dallas–Fort Worth International Airport and downtown Fort Worth. Passenger rail systems in Houston and Austin are more limited. Austin has only one rail line. Even in Dallas, the trains, plus buses, make only a minor dent in daily commuter traffic.

Except for Amtrak, the national rail line, Texas has no regular passenger rail service between cities, although periodic studies have been conducted and proposals made to link by rail the metropolitan areas in the Texas Urban Triangle—Houston, San Antonio, Austin, and Dallas–Fort Worth. The most recent plan was being developed by a private company, Texas Central Partners, which proposed to offer bullet train service between Houston and Dallas. Backed by private investors, the company said it wouldn't need public money to subsidize its operations but could need help building its track and other infrastructure. It also was likely to seek eminent domain authority to secure private land for part of its track right-of-way, a prospect that was attracting opposition from some rural property owners and elected officials. Opposition from rural landowners was a big reason the legislature had killed Governor Rick Perry's proposed Trans Texas Corridor transportation network only a few years earlier.[96]

CONCLUSION

Hopefully you have observed, while reading this chapter, that the most constant thing about Texas—except, perhaps, for the Lone Star in the state flag—is change. The state's population is changing, and so are its needs and the public policies designed to address those needs. No one has carved these policies in stone because they will keep changing as Texas, which has reinvented itself several times since the legendary days of the frontier, continues its transformation in the twenty-first century. Today's public school system of more than 5 million students is as far removed from the one-room schoolhouse as the laptop is from the slate tablet and today's curriculum and educational policies are from the "three Rs" and the hickory stick. A similar contrast can be drawn between the congested, urban freeway system and the country lanes on which traveled horse-drawn buggies and farm wagons of old.

But even more change is in store for education, transportation, health care, criminal justice, and a host of other policies because the policymaking process never stops. The players in the policy process will change, but the basic policy process itself—identifying a problem, banding together to develop and propose a solution, convincing policymakers to adopt the solution, seeing it carried out, and then evaluating the result—will remain essentially unchanged. Learning how to navigate that

Contemporary Public Policy Issues in Texas **481**

POLLUTION ISN'T NEW
This locomotive of old clouds the air as it chugs westward toward Amarillo in the days before the Clean Air Act.

process is essential for anyone seeking to influence how the Texas of the future educates its children, unclogs its highways, protects the purity of its drinking water, and deals with many other challenges.

We hope this book has helped you learn something about the history, the people, the culture, and the politics of Texas, as well as the governmental institutions through which the policymaking process works. All of that information is crucial to you and your peers because the future of Texas soon will be in your hands.

REVIEW THE CHAPTER

The Policy Process

14.1 Apply the stages of the policymaking process to the framework of issue networks, p. 441.

In the broadest sense, public policy is what governments do or choose not to do. Policymaking can be broken down into a series of stages: identification of a problem, enactment of a solution into law, implementing—or carrying out—the solution, and evaluating the solution's effectiveness. This process plays out within a framework of issue networks. Each network includes interactions among participants with interests in a specific policy. These participants include legislators, issue specialists, special interest lobbyists, and the courts.

The State Budget

14.2 Describe recent developments in the formation of the Texas budget and the constraints on those responsible for it, p. 446.

The Texas Constitution prohibits deficit financing for state government programs and operations. That means the legislature must pass a balanced budget that can be financed from anticipated revenue. Because the legislature meets in regular session only every other year, state government operates under two-year budgets. Agencies and legislators must anticipate spending needs months in advance, a prospect that can be difficult during recessions and other periods of economic uncertainty. The legislature's budget-setting prerogatives are constrained further by provisions in the state constitution and laws dedicating, or restricting, some sources of revenue to specific programs or purposes. Strong population growth and a healthy economy resulted in regular increases in state budgets until the recession began in 2008. The legislature, meeting in 2011, reduced state spending to bridge a $27 billion revenue shortfall without raising state taxes. Much of the funding has since been restored, after the economy started recovering. But the eruption of the coronavirus pandemic in 2020 threatened to plunge the state's economy into another tailspin.

State Taxes

14.3 Identify four types of taxes in Texas and the regressive aspects of the Texas tax system, p. 449.

Governments in Texas rely on a large number of taxes and fees. Unlike most states, Texas has no personal income tax but relies on regressive taxes that include the sales tax and the property tax. A regressive tax requires lower-income people to pay a disproportionately larger share of their income in taxes than wealthier people. The sales tax is the primary revenue raiser for state government. Other state taxes include a business tax, motor fuels taxes, severance taxes on oil and natural gas production, and taxes on alcoholic beverages and tobacco products. Property taxes and sales taxes are the main revenue sources for local governments. Proponents of a personal income tax argue that it would be fairer and a more dependable revenue source, but historically there has been strong political opposition to an income tax in Texas.

Educational Policies and Politics

14.4 Relate the factors affecting education policy in Texas to questions of equity and quality, p. 453.

For years, Texas's system of funding public schools has been attacked as inequitable and, in many respects, inadequate. Texas's 1,100-plus school districts are funded by a combination of state aid and local revenue raised through property taxes. Districts with wealthier property tax bases, including those with oil production or expensive commercial property, are able to raise more money for their schools than districts with less wealth. Prodded by a series of court orders, the legislature in recent years has taken steps to try to reduce disparities, including a law requiring rich districts to share some of their tax revenue with poor districts. But the struggle continues, with many school officials contending that the legislature also should increase state aid to the schools.

The state has established an accountability system for public schools, based largely on students' scores on standardized tests. Students have to pass these tests to be promoted from some grades and graduate from high school. Texas also has approved charter schools, which have more flexibility in operations than traditional public schools.

State-supported universities and junior colleges, like public schools, struggle with tightened budgets amid growing enrollments. An increasing share of college education costs has been transferred to students and their families in the form of higher tuition, following the legislature's deregulation of university tuition in 2003, which has allowed appointed university governing boards to raise tuition without legislative approval. Universities also continue to deal with affirmative action issues as the Hispanic population, in particular, continues to rapidly increase in Texas.

Criminal Justice

14.5 Explain the implications of court-ordered prison reforms on the criminal justice system in Texas and the state's large number of executions, p. 465.

Texas spent millions of dollars expanding and improving its prison system following a landmark federal court order for prison reform in 1980. The ruling stemmed from a lawsuit brought by an inmate concerning overcrowded and inhumane prison conditions. Texas has more prison inmates than any other state and enforces criminal justice policies reflecting a strong law-and-order tradition. Some state leaders also recognize that many convicts require treatment for drug and alcohol problems and believe that improvements in the public education system may be more crucial than more prisons in the long-term fight against crime. Texas leads the nation in executions because the death penalty has strong political support in the state, but it also is a source of controversy among many Texans.

Health and Human Services

14.6 Evaluate patterns of support for health and human services in Texas, p. 468.

Texas has a high incidence of poverty and is a national leader in the percentage and number of people without health insurance. Texas also has ranked lower than many states in per capita spending on health and human services programs for the poor and the elderly. One reason, some believe, is the state's conservative political culture, which is based on individualism and self-help and has a strong resistance to new or higher taxes. Since the enactment of the federal Affordable Care Act, thousands of middle- and low-income Texans have received health insurance through the subsidized marketplace, but state leaders have refused to expand the Medicaid health care program to additional low-income people, even though the federal government would pick up most of the cost. In recent years, the legislative majority also has imposed restrictions on abortion, resulting in nationally watched political controversy.

Environmental Problems and Policies

14.7 Assess the response of Texas to environmental issues, p. 472.

Texas has some of the highest pollution levels in the country, resulting from oil and natural gas production, petrochemical and other industrial plants, and heavy traffic on streets and highways. The oil and gas and petrochemical industries provide thousands of jobs, and Texans love their automobiles, pickup trucks, and SUVs. Because of these factors and a conservative political climate, Texas's environmental regulatory attitude is often criticized as lax. Much of the regulation that Texas imposes is required by the federal government, which state officials have frequently challenged. Many state leaders also dispute the scientific conclusions of global warming, even though scientists say Texas is a major contributor to the problem. Recent, severe drought conditions in Texas prompted the legislature and voters in 2013 to approve a new fund for future water development projects.

Transportation in Texas

14.8 Trace the development of Texas's transportation issues, p. 476.

With more than 79,000 miles of roadways crisscrossing the state, Texas has the largest highway system in the country, and it used to be the envy of other states. Now, the Texas Department of Transportation is struggling to provide necessary maintenance and keep traffic moving in urban and suburban areas, where population growth has transformed many freeways and other highways into parking lots during peak traffic periods. Despite the growing need, the legislature for many years has refused to raise the gasoline tax, the major source of highway funding, and that revenue source has peaked. In recent years, state leaders instead have turned to toll roads and voter-approved plans to borrow money for highway construction. After payment of that debt began to eat into the state's transportation budget, the legislature and voters in 2015 approved a plan to divert some existing sales tax revenue into highway funding. Although a few Texas cities have built light rail lines, highways are still the primary means of transportation in the state.

LEARN THE TERMS

issue networks, p. 445
deficit financing, p. 447
dedicated funds, p. 448
sales tax, p. 449
margins tax, p. 450
property or ad valorem tax, p. 450

sin tax, p. 451
lottery, p. 451
general obligation bonds, p. 452
income tax, p. 452
House Bill 72, p. 454
no pass, no play rule, p. 455

Edgewood v. *Kirby*, p. 455
Permanent University Fund (PUF), p. 460
Ruiz v. *Estelle*, p. 465

Appendix

The Constitution of the United States of America 484
Federalist #10, James Madison 490
Excerpts from the Texas Constitution 493

The Constitution of the United States of America

We, the People of the United States, in order to form a more perfect union, establish justice, ensure domestic tranquility, provide for the common defence, promote the general welfare, and secure the blessings of liberty to ourselves and our posterity, do ordain and establish this Constitution for the United States of America.

Article I

Sect. 1. ALL legislative powers, herein granted, shall be vested in a Congress of the United States, which shall consist of a Senate and House of Representatives.

Sect. 2. The House of Representatives shall be composed of Members chosen every second year by all the people of the several States, and the Electors in each State shall have the qualifications requisite for Electors of the most numerous branch of the State Legislature.

No person shall be a Representative who shall not have attained to the age of twenty-five years, and been seven years a citizen of the United States, and who shall not, when elected, be an inhabitant of that State in which he shall be chosen.

Representatives and direct taxes shall be apportioned among the several States which may be included within this Union, according to the respective numbers, which shall be determined by adding to the whole number of free persons, including those bound to service for a term of years, and excluding Indians not taxed, three fifths of all other persons. The actual enumeration shall be made within three years after the first meeting of the Congress of the United States, and within every subsequent term of ten years, in such manner as they shall by law direct. The number of Representatives shall not exceed one for every thirty thousand, but each State shall have at least one Representative; and until such enumeration shall be made, the State of New-Hampshire shall be entitled to choose three, Massachusetts eight, Rhode-Island and Providence Plantation one, Connecticut five, New-York six, New-Jersey four, Pennsylvania eight, Delaware one, Maryland six, Virginia ten, North-Carolina five, South-Carolina five, and Georgia three.

When vacancies happen in the Representation from any State, the Executive authority thereof shall issue writs of election to fill such vacancies.

The House of Representatives shall choose their Speaker and other officers, and shall have the sole power of impeachment.

Sect. 3. The Senate of the United States shall be composed of two Senators from each State, chosen by the Legislature thereof, for six years; and each Senator shall have one vote.

Immediately after they shall be assembled in consequence of the first election, they shall be divided as equally as may be into three classes. The seats of the Senators of the first class shall be vacated at the expiration of the second year, of the second class at the expiration of the fourth year, and of the third class at the expiration of the sixth year; so that one third may be chosen every second year; and if vacancies happen, by resignation or otherwise, during the recess of the Legislature of any State, the Executive thereof may make temporary appointments until the next meeting of the Legislature, which shall then fill such vacancies.

No person shall be a Senator who shall not have attained to the age of thirty years, and been nine years a citizen of the United States, and who shall not, when elected, be an inhabitant of that State for which he shall be chosen.

The Vice-President of the United States shall be President of the Senate, but shall have no vote, unless they be equally divided.

The Senate shall choose their other officers, and also a President pro tempore, in the absence of the Vice-President, or when he shall exercise the office of President of the United States.

The Senate shall have the sole power to try all impeachments. When sitting for that purpose, they shall be on oath or affirmation. When the President of the United States is tried, the Chief Justice shall preside; and no person shall be convicted without the concurrence of two thirds of the members present.

Judgment, in cases of impeachment, shall not extend further than to removal from office, and disqualification to hold and enjoy any office of honour, trust or profit, under the United States; but the party convicted shall nevertheless be liable and subject to indictment, trial, judgment and punishment, according to law.

Sect. 4. The times, places and manner, of holding elections for Senators and Representatives, shall be prescribed in each State by the Legislature thereof; but the Congress may at any time, by law, make or alter such regulations, except as to the place of choosing Senators.

The Congress shall assemble at least once in every year, and such meeting shall be on the first Monday in December, unless they shall by law appoint a different day.

Sect. 5. Each House shall be the judge of the elections, returns and qualification, of its own members, and a majority of each shall constitute a quorum to do business; but a smaller number may adjourn from day to day, and may be authorized to compel the attendance of absent members, in such manner, and under such penalties, as each House may provide.

Each House may determine the rules of its proceedings, punish its members for disorderly behavior, and, with the concurrence of two thirds, expel a member.

Each House shall keep a journal of its proceedings, and from time to time publish the same, excepting such parts as may in their judgment require secrecy; and the yeas and nays of the members of either House on any question shall, at the desire of one fifth of those present, be entered on the journal.

Neither House, during the session of Congress, shall, without the consent of the other, adjourn for more than three days, nor to any other place than that in which the two Houses shall be sitting.

Sect. 6. The Senators and Representatives shall receive a compensation for their services, to be ascertained by law, and paid out of the treasury of the United States. They shall in all cases, except treason, felony and breach of peace, be privileged from arrest during their attendance at the session of their respective Houses, and in going to and returning from the same; and for any speech or debate in either House, they shall not be questioned in any other place.

No Senator or Representative shall, during the time for which he was elected, be appointed to any civil office under the authority of the United States, which shall have been created, or the emoluments whereof shall have been encreased, during such time; and no person holding any officer under the United States shall be a member of either House, during his continuance in office.

Sect. 7. All bills for raising revenue shall originate in the House of Representatives; but the Senate may propose or concur with amendments, as on other bills.

Every bill which shall have passed the House of Representatives and the Senates shall, before it become a law, be presented to the President of the United States; if he approve; he shall sign it; but if not, he shall return it, with his objections, to that House in which it shall have originated, who shall enter the objections at large on their journal, and proceed to reconsider it. If after such reconsideration two thirds of that House shall agree to pass the bill, it shall be sent, together with the objections, to the other House, by which it shall likewise be reconsidered, and if approved by two thirds of that House, it shall become a law. But in all such cases the votes of both Houses shall be determined by yeas and nays, and the names of the persons voting for and against the bill shall be entered on the journal of each House respectively. If any bill shall not be returned by the President within ten days (Sundays excepted) after it shall have been presented to him, the same shall be a law in like manner as if he had signed it, unless the Congress by their adjournment prevent its return, in which case it shall not be a law.

Every order, resolution or vote, to which the concurrence of the Senate and House of Representatives may be necessary (except on a question of adjournment) shall be presented to the President of the United States; and before the same shall take effect, shall be approved by him, or being disapproved by him, shall be re-passed by two thirds of the Senate and House of Representatives, according to the rules and limitations prescribed in the case of a bill.

Sect. 8. The Congress shall have power To lay and collect taxes, duties, imposts and excises, to pay the debts and provide for the common defence and general welfare of the United States; but all duties; imposts and excises, shall be uniform throughout the United States;

To borrow money on the credit of the United States;

To regulate commerce with foreign nations, and among the several States, and with the Indian tribes;

To establish an uniform rule of naturalization, and uniform laws on the subject of bankruptcies, throughout the United States;

To coin money, regulate the value thereof, and of foreign coin, and fix the standard of weights and measures;

To provide for the punishment of counterfeiting the securities and current coin of the United States;

To establish post-offices and post-roads;

To promote the progress of science and useful arts, by securing for limited times to authors and inventors the exclusive right to their respective writings and discoveries;

To constitute tribunals inferior to the Supreme Court;

To define and punish piracies and felonies committed on the high seas and offences against the law of nations;

To declare war, grant letters of marque and reprisal, and make rules concerning captures on land and water;

To raise and support armies, but no appropriation of money to that use shall be for a longer term than two years;

To provide and maintain a navy;

To make rules for the government and regulation of the land and naval forces;

To provide for calling forth the militia to execute the laws of the Union, suppress insurrections, and repel invasions;

To provide for organizing, arming and disciplining the militia, and for governing such part of them as may be employed in the service of the United States, reserving to the States respectively the appointment of the officers, and the authority of training the militia according to the discipline prescribed by Congress;

To exercise exclusive legislation, in all cases whatsoever, over such district (not exceeding ten miles square) as may, by cession of particular States, and the acceptance of Congress, become the seat of the government of the United States, and to exercise like authority over all places purchased by the consent of the Legislature of the State in which the same shall be, for the erection of forts, magazines, arsenals, dock-yards, and other needful buildings;—and,

To make all laws which shall be necessary and proper for carrying into execution the foregoing powers, and all other powers vested by this Constitution in the government of the United States, or in any department or officer thereof.

Sect. 9. The migration or importation of such persons as any of the States now existing shall think proper to admit, shall not be prohibited by the Congress prior to the year one thousand eight hundred and eight; but a tax or duty may be imposed on such importation, not exceeding ten dollars for each person.

The privilege of the writ of habeas corpus shall not be suspended, unless when in cases of rebellion or invasion the public safety may require it.

No bill of attainder, or ex post facto law, shall be passed.

No capitation or other direct tax shall be laid, unless in proportion to the sensus or enumeration herein before directed to be taken.

No tax or duty shall be laid on articles exported from any State. No preference shall be given by any regulation of commerce or revenue to the ports of one State over those of another: Nor shall vessels bound to or from one State, be obliged to enter, clear, or pay duties, in another.

No money shall be drawn from the treasury, but in consequence of appropriations made by law; and a regular statement and account of the receipts and expenditures of all public money shall be published from time to time.

No title of nobility shall be granted by the United States: And no person holding any office of profit or trust under them shall, without the consent of the Congress, accept of any present, emolument, office or title, or any kind whatever from any King, Prince, or foreign State.

Sect. 10. No State shall enter into any treaty, alliance or confederation; grant letters of marque and reprisal; coin money; emit bills of credit; make any thing but gold and silver coin a tender in payment of debts; pass any bill of attainder, ex post facto law, or law impairing the obligation of contracts, or grant any title of nobility.

No State shall, without the consent of Congress, lay any imposts or duties on imports or exports, except what may be absolutely necessary for executing its inspection laws; and the new produce of all duties and imposts, laid by any State, on imports or exports, shall be for the use of the treasury of the United States; and all such laws shall be subject to the revision and controul of the Congress. No State shall, without the consent of Congress, lay any duty of tonnage, keep troops or ships of war in time of peace, enter into any agreement or compact with another State, or with a foreign power, or engage in war, unless actually invaded, or in such imminent danger as will not admit of delay.

Article II

Sect. 1. The executive power shall be vested in a President of the United States of America. He shall hold his office during the term of four years, and, together with the Vice-President, chosen for the same term, be elected as follows.

Each State shall appoint, in such manner as the Legislature thereof may direct, a number of Electors, equal to the whole number of Senators and Representatives to which the State may be entitled in the Congress; but no Senator or Representative, or person holding an office of trust or profit under the United States, shall be appointed an Elector.

The Electors shall meet in their respective States, and vote by ballot for two persons, of whom one at least shall not be an inhabitant of the same state with themselves. And they shall make a list of all the persons voted for, and of the number of votes for each; which list they shall sign and certify, and transmit sealed to the seat of the government of the United States, directed to the President of the Senate. The President of the Senate shall, in the presence of the Senate and House of Representatives, open all the certificates, and the votes shall then be counted. The person having the greatest number of votes shall be the President, if such number be a majority of the whole number of Electors appointed; and if there be more than one who have such majority, and have an equal number of votes, then the House of Representatives shall immediately choose by ballot one of them for President; and if no person have a majority, then from the five highest on the list the said House shall in like manner choose a President. But in choosing the President the votes shall be taken by States, the representation from each State having one vote; a quorum for this purpose shall consist of a member or members from two thirds of the States, and a majority of all the States shall be necessary to a choice. In every case, after the choice of the President, the person having the greatest number of votes of the Electors, shall be the Vice-President. But if there should remain two or more who have equal votes, the Senate shall choose from them by ballot the Vice-President.

The Congress may determine the time of choosing the Electors, and the day on which they shall give their votes; which day shall be the same throughout the United States.

No person, except a natural born citizen, or a citizen of the United States at the time of the adoption of this Constitution, shall be eligible to the office of President; neither shall any person be eligible to that office, who shall not have attained to the age of thirty-five years, and been fourteen years a resident within the United States.

In case of the removal of the President from office, or of his death, resignation, or inability to discharge the powers and duties of the said office, the same shall devolve on the Vice-President; and the Congress may by law provide for the case of removal, death, resignation, or inability, both of the President and Vice-President, declaring what officer shall then act as President, and such officer shall act accordingly, until the disability be removed, or a President shall be elected.

The President shall, at stated times, receive for his services a compensation, which shall neither be increased nor diminished during the period for which he shall have been elected, and he shall not receive within that period any other emolument from the United States, or any of them.

Before he enter on the execution of his office, he shall take the following oath or affirmation:

"I do solemnly swear (or affirm) that I will faithfully execute the office of President of the United States; and will, to the best of my ability, preserve, protect and defend, the Constitution of the United States."

Sect. 2. The President shall be Commander in Chief of the army and navy of the United States, and of the militia of the several states, when called into the actual service of the United States; he may require the opinion, in writing, of the principal officer in each of the executive departments, upon any subject relating to the duties of their respective offices, and he shall have power to grant reprieves and pardons for offences against the United States, except in cases of impeachment.

He shall have power, by and with the advice and consent of the Senate, to make treaties, provided two thirds of the Senators present concur; and he shall nominate, and by and with the advice and consent of the Senate shall appoint Ambassadors, other public Ministers, and Consuls, Judges of the Supreme Court, and all other offices of the United States, whose appointments are not herein otherwise provided for, and which shall be established by law. But the Congress may by law vest the appointment of such inferior officers as they think proper in the President alone, in the courts of law, or in the heads of departments.

The President shall have power to fill up all vacancies that may happen during the recess of the Senate, by granting commissions, which shall expire at the end of their next session.

Sect. 3. He shall from time to time give to the Congress information of the state of the Union, and recommend to their consideration such measures as he shall judge necessary and expedient; he may, on extraordinary occasions, convene both Houses, or either of them, and in case of disagreement between them, with respect to the time of adjournment, he may adjourn them to such time as he shall think proper; he shall receive Ambassadors and other public Ministers; he shall take care that the laws be faithfully executed, and shall commission all the officers of the United States.

Sect. 4. The President, Vice-President, and all civil officers of the United States, shall be removed from office, on impeachment for and conviction of treason, bribery, or other high crimes and misdemeanors.

Article III

Sect. 1. The judicial power of the United States shall be vested in one Supreme Court, and in such Inferior Courts as the Congress may from time to time ordain and establish. The Judges, both of the supreme and Inferior Courts, shall hold their offices during good behaviour; and shall, at stated times, receive for their services a compensation, which shall not be diminished during their continuance in office.

Sect. 2. The judicial power shall extend to all cases in law and equity, arising under this Constitution, the laws of the United States, and treaties made, or which shall be made, under their authority; to all cases affecting Ambassadors, other public Ministers, and Consuls; to all cases of admiralty and maritime jurisdiction; to controversies to which the United States shall be a party; to controversies between two or more States, between a State and citizen of another State, between citizens of different States, between citizens of the same State claiming lands under grants of different States, and between a State, or the citizens thereof, and foreign States, citizens or subjects.

In all cases affecting Ambassadors, other public Ministers and consuls, and those in which a State shall be party, the Supreme Court shall have original jurisdiction. In all the other cases before mentioned, the Supreme Court shall have appellate jurisdiction, both as to law and fact, with such exceptions and under such regulations as the Congress shall make.

The trial of all crimes, except in cases of impeachment, shall be by jury; and such trial shall be held in the State where the said crimes shall have been committed; but when not committed within any State, the trial shall be at such place or places as the Congress may by law have directed.

Sect. 3. Treason, against the United States, shall consist only in levying war against them, or in adhering to their enemies, giving them aid and comfort. No person shall be convicted of treason, unless on the testimony of two witnesses to the same overt act, or on consession in open court.

The Congress shall have power to declare the punishment of treason, but no attainder of treason shall work corruption of blood, or forfeiture, except during the life of the person attainted.

Article IV

Sect. 1. Full faith and credit shall be given in each State to the public acts, records and judicial proceedings, of every other State. And the Congress may by general laws prescribe the manner in which such acts, records and proceedings, shall be proved, and the effect thereof.

Sect. 2. The citizens of each State shall be entitled to all privileges and immunities of citizens in the several states.

A person, charged in any State with treason, felony, or other crime, who shall flee from justice, and be found in another State, shall, on demand of the executive authority of the State form which he fled, be delivered up, to be removed to the State having jurisdiction of the crime.

No person, held to service or labour in one State, under the laws thereof, escaping into another, shall, in consequence of any law or regulation therein, be discharged from such service or labour; but shall be delivered up, on claim of the party to whom such service or labour may be due.

Sect. 3. New States may be admitted by the Congress into this Union; but no new State shall be formed to erected within the jurisdiction of any other State; nor any State be formed by the junction of two or more States, or parts of States, without the consent of the Legislatures of the States concerned, as well as of the Congress.

The Congress shall have power to dispose of an make all needful rules and regulations, respecting the territory or other property belonging to the United States; and nothing in this Constitution shall be so construed, as to prejudice any claims of the United States, or of any particular State.

Sect. 4. The United States shall guarantee, to every State in this Union, a republican form of government, and shall protect each of them against invasion; and, on application of the Legislature, or of the Executive, (when the Legislature cannot be convened) against domestic violence.

Article V

The Congress, whenever two thirds of both Houses shall deem it necessary, shall propose amendments to this Constitution; or, on the application of the Legislatures of two thirds of the several States, shall call a Convention, for proposing amendments; which, in either case, shall be valid, to all intents and purposes, as part of this Constitution, when ratified by the Legislature of three fourths of the several States, or by conventions in three fourths thereof, as the one or the other mode of ratification may be proposed by the Congress: Provided, that no amendment which may be made prior to the year one thousand eight hundred and eight shall in any manner affect the first and fourth clauses, in the ninth section of the first article; and that no State, without its consent, shall be deprived of its equal suffrage in the Senate.

Article VI

All debts contracted, and engagements entered into, before the adoption of this Constitution, shall be as valid against the United States under this Constitution, as under the Confederation.

This Constitution, and the laws of the United States which shall be made in pursuance thereof, and all treaties made, or which shall be made, under the authority of the United States, shall be the supreme law of the land; and the Judges in every State, shall be bound thereby; any thing in the constitution or laws of any State to the contrary notwithstanding.

The Senators and Representatives before mentioned, and the members of the several State Legislatures, and all executive and judicial officers, both of the United States and of the several States, shall be bound by oath or affirmation to support this Constitution; but no religious test shall ever be required as a qualification to any office, or public trust, under the United States.

Article VII

The ratification of the Conventions of Nine States shall be sufficient for the establishment of this constitution, between the States so ratifying the same.

Done in Convention, by the unanimous consent of the States present, the seventeenth day of September, in the year of our Lord one thousand seven hundred and eighty-seven, and of the Independence of the United States of America the twelfth. In witness whereof, we have hereunto subscribed our names.

GEORGE WASHINGTON
President and Deputy from Virginia.

NEW-HAMPSHIRE
John Langdon,
Nicholas Gilman.

MASSACHUSETTS
Nathaniel Gorham,
Rufus King.

CONNECTICUT
William Samuel Johnson,
Roger Sherman.

NEW-YORK
Alexander Hamilton.

NEW-JERSEY
William Livingston,
David Brearley,
William Paterson,
Jonathan Dayton.

PENNSYLVANIA
Benjamin Franklin,
Thomas Mifflin,
Robert Morris,
George Clymer,
Thomas Fitzsimons,
Jared Ingersoll,
James Wilson,
Gouverneur Morris.

DELAWARE
George Read,
Gunning Bedford, jun.
John Dickenson,
Richard Bassett,
Jacob Broom.

MARYLAND
James McHenry,
Daniel of St. Tho. Jenifer,
Daniel Carrol.

VIRGINIA
John Blair,
James Madison, jun.

NORTH-CAROLINA
William Blount,
Richard Dobbs Spaight,
Hugh Williamson.

SOUTH-CAROLINA
John Rutledge,
Charles Cotesworth Pinckney,
Charles Pinckney,
Pierce Butler.

GEORGIA
William Few,
Abraham Baldwin.

ATTEST,.........
William Jackson,
Secretary.

Bill of Rights and the Fourteenth Amendment [which guarantees individuals the protections of the Bill of Rights against state intrusion and provides for equality under the law]

Amendment I—Religion, Speech, Assembly, Petition

Congress shall make no law respecting an establishment of religion, or prohibiting the free exercise thereof; or abridging the freedom of speech, or of the press; or the right of the people peaceably to assemble, and to petition the Government for a redress of grievances.

Amendment II—Right to Bear Arms

A well regulated Militia, being necessary to the security of a free State, the right of the people to keep and bear Arms, shall not be infringed.

Amendment III—Quartering of Soldiers

No Soldier shall, in time of peace be quartered in any house, without the consent of the Owner, nor in time of war, but in a manner to be prescribed by law.

Amendment IV—Searches and Seizures

The right of the people to be secure in their persons, houses, papers, and effects, against unreasonable searches and seizures, shall not be violated, and no warrants shall issue, but upon probable cause, supported by Oath or affirmation, and particularly describing the place to be searched, and the persons or things to be seized.

Amendment V—Grand Juries, Double Jeopardy, Self-incrimination, Due Process, Eminent Domain

No person shall be held to answer for a capital, or otherwise infamous crime, unless on a presentment or indictment of a Grand Jury, except in cases arising in the land or naval forces, or in the Militia, when in actual service in time of War or public danger; nor shall any person be subject for the same offence to be twice put in jeopardy of life or limb; nor shall be compelled in any criminal case to be a witness against himself, nor be deprived of life, liberty, or property, without due process of law; nor shall private property be taken for public use, without just compensation.

Amendment VI—Criminal Court Procedures

In all criminal prosecutions, the accused shall enjoy the right to a speedy and public trial, by an impartial jury of the State and district wherein the crime shall have been committed, which district shall have been previously ascertained by law, and to be informed of the nature and cause of the accusation; to be confronted with the witnesses against him; to have compulsory process for obtaining witnesses in his favor, and to have the assistance of counsel for his defence.

Amendment VII—Trial by Jury in Common-law Cases

In Suits at common law, where the value in controversy shall exceed twenty dollars, the right of trial by jury shall be preserved, and no fact tried by a jury, shall be otherwise re-examined in any Court of the United States, than according to the rules of the common law.

Amendment VIII—Bails, Fines, and Punishment

Excessive bail shall not be required, nor excessive fines imposed, nor cruel and unusual punishments inflicted.

Amendment IX—Rights Retained by the People

The enumeration in the Constitution, of certain rights, shall not be construed to deny or disparage others retained by the people.

Amendment X—Rights Reserved to the States

The powers not delegated to the United States by the Constitution, nor prohibited by it to the States, are reserved to the States respectively, or to the people.

Amendment XIV—Citizenship, Due Process, and Equal Protection of the Laws (Ratified on July 9, 1868)

Section 1. All persons born or naturalized in the United States, and subject to the jurisdiction thereof, are citizens of the United States and of the State wherein they reside. No State shall make or enforce any law which shall abridge the privileges or immunities of citizens of the United States; nor shall any State deprive any person of life, liberty, or property, without due process of law; nor deny to any person within its jurisdiction the equal protection of the laws.

Section 2. Representatives shall be apportioned among the several States according to their respective numbers, counting the whole number of persons in each State, excluding Indians not taxed. But when the right to vote at any election for the choice of electors for President and Vice President of the United States, Representatives in Congress, the Executive and Judicial officers of a State, or the members of the Legislature thereof, is denied to any of the male inhabitants of such State, being twenty-one years of age, and citizens of the United States, or in any way abridged, except for participation in rebellion, or other crime, the basis of representation therein shall be reduced in the proportion which the number of such male citizens shall bear to the whole number of male citizens twenty-one years of age in such State.

Section 3. No person shall be a Senator or Representative in Congress, or elector of President and Vice President, or hold any office, civil or military, under the United States, or under any State, who, having previously taken an oath, as a member of Congress, or as an officer of the United States, or as a member of any State legislature, or as an executive or judicial officer of any State, to support the Constitution of the United States, shall have engaged in insurrection or rebellion against the same, or given aid or comfort to the enemies thereof. But Congress may by a vote of two-thirds of each House, remove such disability.

Section 4. The validity of the public debt of the United States, authorized by law, including debts incurred for payment of pensions and bounties for services in suppressing insurrection or rebellion, shall not be questioned. But neither the United States nor any State shall assume or pay any debt or obligation incurred in aid of insurrection or rebellion against the United States, or any claim for the loss or emancipation of any slave, but all such debts, obligations and claims shall be held illegal and void.

Section 5. The Congress shall have power to enforce, by appropriate legislation, the provisions of this article.

(The first ten amendments were passed by Congress on September 25, 1789 and were ratified on December 15, 1791.)

Federalist #10, James Madison

November 22, 1787

To the People of the State of New York.
Among the numerous advantages promised by a well constructed Union, none deserves to be more accurately developed than its tendency to break and control the violence of faction. The friend of popular governments, never finds himself so much alarmed for their character and fate, as when he contemplates their propensity to this dangerous vice. He will not fail therefore to set a due value on any plan which, without violating the principles to which he is attached, provides a proper cure for it. The instability, injustice and confusion introduced into the public councils, have in truth been the mortal diseases under which popular governments have every where perished; as they continue to be the favorite and fruitful topics from which the adversaries to liberty derive their most specious declamations. The valuable improvements made by the American Constitutions on the popular models, both ancient and modern, cannot certainly be too much admired; but it would be an unwarrantable partiality, to contend that they have as effectually obviated the danger on this side as was wished and expected. Complaints are every where heard from our most considerate and virtuous citizens, equally the friends of public and private faith, and of public and personal liberty; that our governments are too unstable; that the public good is disregarded in the conflicts of rival parties; and that measures are too often decided, not according to the rules of justice, and the rights of the minor party; but by the superior force of an interested and over-bearing majority. However anxiously we may wish that these complaints had no foundation, the evidence of known facts will not permit us to deny that they are in some degree true. It will be found indeed, on a candid review of our situation, that some of the distresses under which we labor, have been erroneously charged on the operation of our governments; but it will be found, at the same time, that other causes will not alone account for many of our heaviest misfortunes; and particularly, for that prevailing and increasing distrust of public engagements, and alarm for private rights, which are echoed from one end of the continent to the other. These must be chiefly, if not wholly, effects of the unsteadiness and injustice, with which a factious spirit has tainted our public administrations.

By a faction I understand a number of citizens, whether amounting to a majority or minority of the whole, who are united and actuated by some common impulse of passion, or of interest, adverse to the rights of other citizens, or to the permanent and aggregate interests of the community.

There are two methods of curing the mischiefs of faction: the one, by removing its causes; the other, by controlling its effects.

There are again two methods of removing the causes of faction: the one by destroying the liberty which is essential to its existence; the other, by giving to every citizen the same opinions, the same passions, and the same interests.

It could never be more truly said than of the first remedy, that it is worse than the disease. Liberty is to faction, what air is to fire, an aliment without which it instantly expires. But it could not be a less folly to abolish liberty, which is essential to political life, because it nourishes faction, than it would be to wish the annihilation of air, which is essential to animal life, because it imparts to fire its destructive agency.

The second expedient is as impracticable, as the first would be unwise. As long as the reason of man continues fallible, and he is at liberty to exercise it, different opinions will be formed. As long as the connection subsists between his reason and his self-love, his opinions and his passions will have a reciprocal influence on each other; and the former will be objects to which the latter will attach themselves. The diversity in the faculties of men from which the rights of property originate, is not less an insuperable obstacle to a uniformity of interests. The protection of these faculties is the first object of Government. From the protection of different and unequal faculties of acquiring property, the possession of different degrees and kinds of property immediately results: and from the influence of these on the sentiments and views of the respective proprietors, ensues a division of the society into different interests and parties.

The latent causes of faction are thus sown in the nature of man; and we see them every where brought into different degrees of activity, according to the different circumstances of civil society. A zeal for different opinions concerning religion, concerning Government and many other points, as well of speculation as of practice; an attachment to different leaders ambitiously contending for pre-eminence and power; or to persons of other descriptions whose fortunes have been interesting to the human passions, have in turn divided mankind into parties, inflamed them with mutual animosity, and rendered them much more disposed to vex and oppress each other, than to co-operate for their common good. So strong is this propensity of mankind to fall into mutual animosities, that where no substantial occasion presents itself, the most frivolous and fanciful distinctions have been sufficient to kindle their unfriendly passions, and excite their most violent conflicts. But the most common and durable source of factions, has been the various and unequal distribution of property. Those who hold, and those who are without property, have ever formed distinct interests in society. Those who are creditors, and those who are debtors, fall under a like discrimination. A landed interest, a manufacturing interest, a mercantile interest, a monied interest, with many lesser interests, grow up of necessity in civilized nations, and divide them into different classes, actuated by different sentiments and views. The regulation of these various and interfering interests forms the principal task of modern Legislation, and involves the spirit of party and faction in the necessary and ordinary operations of Government.

No man is allowed to be a judge in his own cause; because his interest would certainly bias his judgment, and, not improbably, corrupt his integrity. With equal, nay with greater reason, a body of men, are unfit to be both judges and parties, at the same time; yet, what are many of the most important acts of legislation, but so many judicial determinations, not indeed concerning the rights of single persons, but concerning the rights of large bodies of citizens, and what are the different classes of legislators, but advocates and parties to the causes which they determine? Is a law proposed concerning private debts? It is a question to which the creditors are parties on one side, and the debtors on the other. Justice ought to hold the balance between them. Yet the parties are and must be themselves the judges; and the most numerous party, or, in other words, the most powerful faction must be expected to prevail. Shall domestic manufactures be encouraged, and in what degree, by restrictions on foreign manufactures? are questions which would be differently decided by the landed and the manufacturing classes; and probably by neither, with a sole regard to justice and the public good. The apportionment of taxes on the various descriptions of property, is an act which seems to require the most exact impartiality; yet, there is perhaps no legislative act in which greater opportunity and temptation are given to a predominant party, to trample on the rules of justice. Every shilling with which they over-burden the inferior number, is a shilling saved to their own pockets.

It is in vain to say, that enlightened statesmen will be able to adjust these clashing interests, and render them all subservient to the public good. Enlightened statesmen will not always be at the helm: Nor, in many cases, can such an adjustment be made at all, without taking into view indirect and remote considerations, which will rarely prevail over the immediate interest which one party may find in disregarding the rights of another, or the good of the whole.

The inference to which we are brought, is, that the causes of faction cannot be removed; and that relief is only to be sought in the means of controlling its effects.

If a faction consists of less than a majority, relief is supplied by the republican principle, which enables the majority to defeat its sinister views by regular vote: It may clog the administration, it may convulse the society; but it will be unable to execute and mask its violence under the forms of the Constitution. When a majority is included in a faction, the form of popular government on the other hand enables it to sacrifice to its ruling passion or interest, both the public good and the rights of other citizens. To secure the public good, and private rights, against the danger of such a faction, and at the same time to preserve the spirit and the form of popular government, is then the great object to which our enquiries are directed: Let me add that it is the great desideratum, by which alone this form of government can be rescued from the opprobrium under which it has so long labored, and be recommended to the esteem and adoption of mankind.

By what means is this object attainable? Evidently by one of two only. Either the existence of the same passion or interest in a majority at the same time, must be prevented; or the majority, having such co-existent passion or interest, must be rendered, by their number and local situation, unable to concert and carry into effect schemes of oppression. If the impulse and the opportunity be suffered to coincide, we well know that neither moral nor religious motives can be relied on as an adequate control. They are not found to be such on the injustice and violence of individuals, and lose their efficacy in proportion to the number combined together; that is, in proportion as their efficacy becomes needful.

From this view of the subject, it may be concluded, that a pure Democracy, by which I mean, a Society, consisting of a small number of citizens, who assemble and administer the Government in person, can admit of no cure for the mischiefs of faction. A common passion or interest will, in almost every case, be felt by a majority of the whole; a communication and concert results from the form of Government itself; and there is nothing to check the inducements to sacrifice the weaker party, or an obnoxious individual. Hence it is, that such Democracies have ever been spectacles of turbulence and contention; have ever been found incompatible with personal security, or the rights of property; and have in general been as short in their lives, as they have been violent in their deaths. Theoretic politicians, who have patronized this species of Government, have erroneously supposed, that by reducing mankind to a perfect equality in their political rights, they would, at the same time, be perfectly equalized and assimilated in their possessions, their opinions, and their passions.

A republic, by which I mean a government in which the scheme of representation takes place, opens a different prospect, and promises the cure for which we are seeking. Let us examine the points in which it varies from pure democracy, and we shall comprehend both the nature of the cure and the efficacy which it must derive from the union.

The two great points of difference, between a democracy and a republic, are, first, the delegation of the government, in the latter, to a small number of citizens, elected by the rest; secondly, the greater number of citizens, and greater sphere of country, over which the latter may be extended.

The effect of the first difference is, on the one hand, to refine and enlarge the public views, by passing them through the medium of a chosen body of citizens, whose wisdom may best discern the true interest of their country, and whose patriotism and love of justice, will be least likely to sacrifice it to temporary or partial considerations. Under such a regulation, it may well happen, that the public voice, pronounced by the representatives of the people, will be more consonant to the public good, than if pronounced by the people themselves, convened for the purpose. On the other hand the effect may be inverted. Men of factious tempers, of local prejudices, or of sinister designs, may by intrigue, by corruption, or by other means, first obtain the suffrages, and then betray the interest of the people. The question resulting is, whether small or extensive republics are most favorable to the election of proper guardians of the public weal, and it is clearly decided in favor of the latter by two obvious considerations.

In the first place, it is to be remarked that, however small the republic may be, the representatives must be raised to a certain number, in order to guard against the cabals of a few; and that however large it may be, they must be limited to a certain number, in order to guard against the confusion of a multitude. Hence, the number of representatives in the two cases not being in proportion to that of the constituents, and being proportionally greatest in the small republic, it follows, that if the proportion of fit characters be not less in the large than in the small republic, the former will present a greater option, and consequently a greater probability of a fit choice.

In the next place, as each Representative will be chosen by a greater number of citizens in the large than in the small Republic, it will be more difficult for unworthy candidates to practise with success the vicious arts, by which elections are too often carried; and the suffrages of the people being more free, will be more likely to center on men who possess the most attractive merit, and the most diffusive and established characters.

It must be confessed, that in this, as in most other cases, there is a mean, on both sides of which inconveniences will be found to lie. By enlarging too much the number of electors, you render the representative too little acquainted with all their local circumstances and lesser interests; as by reducing it too much, you render him unduly attached to these, and too little fit to comprehend and pursue great and national objects. The Federal Constitution forms a happy combination in this respect; the great and aggregate interests being referred to the national, the local and particular, to the state legislatures.

The other point of difference is, the greater number of citizens and extent of territory which may be brought within the compass of Republican, than of Democratic Government; and it is this circumstance principally which renders factious combinations less to be dreaded in the former, than in the latter. The smaller the society, the fewer probably will be the distinct parties and interests composing it; the fewer the distinct parties and interests, the more frequently will a majority be found of the same party; and the smaller the number of individuals composing a majority, and the smaller the compass within which they are placed, the more easily will they concert and execute their plans of oppression. Extend the sphere, and you take in a greater variety of parties and interests; you make it less probable that a majority of the whole will have a common motive to invade the rights of other citizens; or if such a common motive exists, it will be more difficult for all who feel it to discover their own strength, and to act in unison with each other. Besides other impediments, it may be remarked, that where there is a consciousness of unjust or dishonorable purposes, communication is always checked by distrust, in proportion to the number whose concurrence is necessary.

Hence it clearly appears, that the same advantage, which a Republic has over a Democracy, in controlling the effects of faction, is enjoyed by a large over a small Republic—is enjoyed by the Union over the States composing it. Does this advantage consist in the substitution of Representatives, whose enlightened views and virtuous sentiments render them superior to local prejudices, and to schemes of injustice? It will not be denied, that the Representation of the Union will be most likely to possess these requisite endowments. Does it consist in the greater security afforded by a greater variety of parties, against the event of any one party being able to outnumber and oppress the rest? In an equal degree does the increased variety of parties, comprised within the Union, increase this security? Does it, in fine, consist in the greater obstacles opposed to the concert and accomplishment of the secret wishes of an unjust and interested majority? Here, again, the extent of the Union gives it the most palpable advantage.

The influence of factious leaders may kindle a flame within their particular States, but will be unable to spread a general conflagration through the other States: a religious sect may degenerate into a political faction in a part of the Confederacy but the variety of sects dispersed over the entire face of it, must secure the national Councils against any danger from that source: a rage for paper money, for an abolition of debts, for an equal division of property, or for any other improper or wicked project, will be less apt to pervade the whole body of the Union, than a particular member of it; in the same proportion as such a malady is more likely to taint a particular county or district, than an entire State.

In the extent and proper structure of the Union, therefore, we behold a Republican remedy for the diseases most incident to Republican Government. And according to the degree of pleasure and pride, we feel in being Republicans, ought to be our zeal in cherishing the spirit, and supporting the character of Federalists.

Excerpts from the Texas Constitution

Article 3

Legislative Department

Sec. 1. SENATE AND HOUSE OF REPRESENTATIVES. The Legislative power of this State shall be vested in a Senate and House of Representatives, which together shall be styled "The Legislature of the State of Texas."

Sec. 2. MEMBERSHIP OF SENATE AND HOUSE OF REPRESENTATIVES. The Senate shall consist of thirty-one members. The House of Representatives shall consist of 150 members.

(Amended Nov. 2, 1999.) (TEMPORARY TRANSITION PROVISIONS for Sec. 2: See Appendix, Note 1.)

Sec. 3. ELECTION AND TERM OF OFFICE OF SENATORS. The Senators shall be chosen by the qualified voters for the term of four years; but a new Senate shall be chosen after every apportionment, and the Senators elected after each apportionment shall be divided by lot into two classes. The seats of the Senators of the first class shall be vacated at the expiration of the first two years, and those of the second class at the expiration of four years, so that one half of the Senators shall be chosen biennially thereafter. Senators shall take office following their election, on the day set by law for the convening of the Regular Session of the Legislature, and shall serve thereafter for the full term of years to which elected.

(Amended Nov. 8, 1966, and Nov. 2, 1999.) (TEMPORARY TRANSITION PROVISIONS for Sec. 3: See Appendix, Note 1.)

Sec. 4. ELECTION AND TERM OF MEMBERS OF HOUSE OF REPRESENTATIVES. The Members of the House of Representatives shall be chosen by the qualified voters for the term of two years. Representatives shall take office following their election, on the day set by law for the convening of the Regular Session of the Legislature, and shall serve thereafter for the full term of years to which elected.

(Amended Nov. 8, 1966, and Nov. 2, 1999.) (TEMPORARY TRANSITION PROVISIONS for Sec. 4: See Appendix, Note 1.)

Article 4

Executive Department

Sec. 1. OFFICERS CONSTITUTING THE EXECUTIVE DEPARTMENT. The Executive Department of the State shall consist of a Governor, who shall be the Chief Executive Officer of the State, a Lieutenant Governor, Secretary of State, Comptroller of Public Accounts, Commissioner of the General Land Office, and Attorney General.

(Amended Nov. 7, 1995.)

Sec. 7. COMMANDER-IN-CHIEF OF MILITARY FORCES; CALLING FORTH MILITIA. He shall be Commander-in-Chief of the military forces of the State, except when they are called into actual service of the United States. He shall have power to call forth the militia to execute the laws of the State, to suppress insurrections, and to repel invasions.

(Amended Nov. 2, 1999.) (TEMPORARY TRANSITION PROVISIONS for Sec. 7: See Appendix, Note 1.)

Sec. 8. CONVENING LEGISLATURE ON EXTRAORDINARY OCCASIONS. (a) The Governor may, on extraordinary occasions, convene the Legislature at the seat of Government, or at a different place, in case that should be in possession of the public enemy or in case of the prevalence of disease threat. His proclamation therefor shall state specifically the purpose for which the Legislature is convened.

Sec. 9. GOVERNOR'S MESSAGE AND RECOMMENDATIONS; ACCOUNTING FOR PUBLIC MONEY; ESTIMATES OF MONEY REQUIRED. The Governor shall, at the commencement of each session of the Legislature, and at the close of his term of office, give to the Legislature information, by message, of the condition of the State; and he shall recommend to the Legislature such measures as he may deem expedient. He shall account to the Legislature for all public moneys received and paid out by him, from any funds subject to his order, with vouchers; and shall accompany his message with a statement of the same. And at the commencement of each regular session, he shall present estimates of the amount of money required to be raised by taxation for all purposes.

Sec. 10. EXECUTION OF LAWS; CONDUCT OF BUSINESS WITH OTHER STATES AND UNITED STATES. He shall cause the laws to be faithfully executed and shall conduct, in person, or in such manner as shall be prescribed by law, all intercourse and business of the State with other States and with the United States.

Sec. 14. APPROVAL OR DISAPPROVAL OF BILLS; RETURN AND RECONSIDERATION; FAILURE TO RETURN; DISAPPROVAL OF ITEMS OF APPROPRIATION. Every bill which shall have passed both houses of the Legislature shall be presented to the Governor for his approval. If he approve he shall sign it; but if he disapprove it, he shall return it, with his objections, to the House in which it originated, which House shall enter the objections at large upon its journal, and proceed to reconsider it. If after such reconsideration, two-thirds of the members present agree to pass the bill, it shall be sent, with the objections, to the other House, by which likewise it shall be reconsidered; and, if approved by two-thirds of the members of that House, it shall become a law; but in such cases the votes of both Houses shall be determined by yeas and nays, and the names of the members voting for and against the bill shall be entered on the journal of each House respectively. If any bill shall not be returned by the Governor with his objections within ten days (Sundays excepted) after it shall have been presented to him, the same shall be a law, in like manner as if he had signed it, unless the Legislature, by its adjournment, prevent its return, in which case it shall be a law, unless he shall file the same, with his objections, in the office of the Secretary of State and give notice thereof by public proclamation within twenty days after such adjournment. If any bill presented to the Governor contains several items of appropriation he may object to one or more of such items, and approve the other portion of the bill. In such case he shall append to the bill, at the time of signing it, a statement of the items to which he objects, and no item so objected to shall take effect. If the Legislature be in session, he shall transmit to the House in which the bill originated a copy of such statement and the items objected to shall be separately considered. If, on reconsideration, one or more of such items be approved by two-thirds of the members present of each House, the same shall be part of the law, notwithstanding the objections of the Governor. If any such bill, containing several items of appropriation, not having been presented to the Governor ten days (Sundays excepted) prior to adjournment, be in the hands of the Governor at the time of adjournment, he shall have twenty days from such adjournment within which to file objections to any items thereof and make proclamation of the same, and such item or items shall not take effect.

Sec. 16. LIEUTENANT GOVERNOR. (a) There shall also be a Lieutenant Governor, who shall be chosen at every election for Governor by the same voters, in the same manner, continue in office for the same time, and possess the same qualifications. The voters shall distinguish for whom they vote as Governor and for whom as Lieutenant Governor.

(b) The Lieutenant Governor shall by virtue of his office be President of the Senate, and shall have, when in Committee of the Whole, a right to debate and vote on all questions; and when the Senate is equally divided to give the casting vote.

(c) In the case of the temporary inability or temporary disqualification of the Governor to serve, the impeachment of the Governor, or the absence of the Governor from the State, the Lieutenant Governor shall exercise the powers and authority appertaining to the office of Governor until the Governor becomes able or qualified to resume serving, is acquitted, or returns to the State.

Sec. 21. SECRETARY OF STATE. There shall be a Secretary of State, who shall be appointed by the Governor, by and with the advice and consent of the Senate, and who shall continue in office during the term of service of the Governor. He shall authenticate the publication of the laws, and keep a fair register of all official acts and proceedings of the Governor, and shall, when required, lay the same and all papers, minutes and vouchers relative thereto, before the Legislature, or either House thereof, and shall perform such other duties as may be required of him by law. He shall receive for his services an annual salary in an amount to be fixed by the Legislature.

(Amended Nov. 3, 1936, and Nov. 2, 1954.)

Sec. 22. ATTORNEY GENERAL. The Attorney General shall represent the State in all suits and pleas in the Supreme Court of the State in which the State may be a party, and shall especially inquire into the charter rights of all private corporations, and from time to time, in the name of the State, take such action in the courts as may be proper and necessary to prevent any private corporation from exercising any power or demanding or collecting any species of taxes, tolls, freight or wharfage not authorized by law. He shall, whenever sufficient cause exists, seek a judicial forfeiture of such charters, unless otherwise expressly directed by law, and give legal advice in writing to the Governor and other executive officers, when requested by them, and perform such other duties as may be required by law.

(Amended Nov. 3, 1936, Nov. 2, 1954, Nov. 7, 1972, and Nov. 2, 1999.) (TEMPORARY TRANSITION PROVISIONS for Sec. 22: See Appendix, Note 1.)

Sec. 23. COMPTROLLER OF PUBLIC ACCOUNTS; COMMISSIONER OF GENERAL LAND OFFICE; ELECTED STATUTORY STATE OFFICERS; TERM; SALARY; FEES, COSTS AND PERQUISITES. The Comptroller of Public Accounts, the Commissioner of the General Land Office, the Attorney General, and any statutory State officer who is elected by the electorate of Texas at large, unless a term of office is otherwise specifically provided in this Constitution, shall each hold office for the term of four years. Each shall receive an annual salary in an amount to be fixed by the Legislature; reside at the Capital of the State during his continuance in office, and perform such duties as are or may be required by law. They and the Secretary of State shall not receive to their own use any fees, costs or perquisites of office. All fees that may be payable by law for any service performed by any officer specified in this section or in his office, shall be paid, when received, into the State Treasury.

(Amended Nov. 3, 1936, Nov. 2, 1954, Nov. 7, 1972, Nov. 7, 1995, and Nov. 2, 1999.) (TEMPORARY TRANSITION PROVISIONS for Sec. 23: See Appendix, Note 1.)

Article 5
Judicial Department

Sec. 1. JUDICIAL POWER; COURTS IN WHICH VESTED. The judicial power of this State shall be vested in one Supreme Court, in one Court of Criminal Appeals, in Courts of Appeals, in District Courts, in County Courts, in Commissioners Courts, in Courts of Justices of the Peace, and in such other courts as may be provided by law.

The Legislature may establish such other courts as it may deem necessary and prescribe the jurisdiction and organization thereof, and may conform the jurisdiction of the district and other inferior courts thereto.

(Amended Aug. 11, 1891, Nov. 8, 1977, and Nov. 4, 1980.)

Sec. 2. SUPREME COURT; JUSTICES; SECTIONS; ELIGIBILITY; ELECTION; VACANCIES. (a) The Supreme Court shall consist of the Chief Justice and eight Justices, any five of whom shall constitute a quorum, and the concurrence of five shall be necessary to a decision of a case; provided, that when the business of the court may require, the court may sit in sections as designated by the court to hear argument of causes and to consider applications for writs of error or other preliminary matters.

(c) Said Justices shall be elected (three of them each two years) by the qualified voters of the state at a general election; shall hold their offices six years; and shall each receive such compensation as shall be provided by law.

(Amended Aug. 11, 1891, Aug. 25, 1945, Nov. 4, 1980, and Nov. 6, 2001.) (TEMPORARY TRANSITION PROVISION for Sec. 2: See Appendix, Note 3.)

Sec. 4. COURT OF CRIMINAL APPEALS; JUDGES. (a) The Court of Criminal Appeals shall consist of eight Judges and one Presiding Judge. The Judges shall have the same qualifications and receive the same salaries as the Associate Justices of the Supreme Court, and the Presiding Judge shall have the same qualifications and receive the same salary as the Chief Justice of the Supreme Court. The Presiding Judge and the Judges shall be elected by the qualified voters of the state at a general election and shall hold their offices for a term of six years.

(b) For the purpose of hearing cases, the Court of Criminal Appeals may sit in panels of three Judges, the designation thereof to be under rules established by the court. In a panel of three Judges, two Judges shall constitute a quorum and the concurrence of two Judges shall be necessary for a decision. The Presiding Judge, under rules established by the court, shall convene the court en banc for the transaction of all other business and may convene the court en banc for the purpose of hearing cases. The court must sit en banc during proceedings involving capital punishment and other cases as required by law. When convened en banc, five Judges shall constitute a quorum and the concurrence of five Judges shall be necessary for a decision. The Court of Criminal Appeals may appoint Commissioners in aid of the Court of Criminal Appeals as provided by law. (Amended Aug. 11, 1891, Nov. 8, 1966, Nov. 8, 1977, and Nov. 6, 2001.)

(TEMPORARY TRANSITION PROVISION for Sec. 4: See Appendix, Note 3.)

Sec. 5. JURISDICTION OF COURT OF CRIMINAL APPEALS; TERMS OF COURT; CLERK. (a) The Court of Criminal Appeals shall have final appellate jurisdiction coextensive with the limits of the state, and its determinations shall be final, in all criminal cases of whatever grade, with such exceptions and under such regulations as may be provided in this Constitution or as prescribed by law.

(b) The appeal of all cases in which the death penalty has been assessed shall be to the Court of Criminal Appeals. The appeal of all other criminal cases shall be to the Courts of Appeal as prescribed by law. In addition, the Court of Criminal Appeals may, on its own motion, review a decision of a Court of Appeals in a criminal case as provided by law. Discretionary review by the Court of Criminal Appeals is not a matter of right, but of sound judicial discretion.

Sec. 6. COURTS OF APPEALS; TERMS OF JUSTICES; CLERKS. (a) The state shall be divided into courts of appeals districts, with each district having a Chief Justice, two or more other Justices, and such other officials as may be provided by law. The Justices shall have the qualifications prescribed for Justices of the Supreme Court. The Court of Appeals may sit in sections as authorized by law. The concurrence of a majority of the judges sitting in a section is necessary to decide a case. Said Court of Appeals shall have appellate jurisdiction co-extensive with the limits of their respective districts, which shall extend to all cases of which the District Courts or County Courts have original or appellate jurisdiction, under such restrictions and regulations as may be prescribed by law. Provided, that the decision of said courts shall be conclusive on all questions of fact brought before them on appeal or error. Said courts shall have such other jurisdiction, original and appellate, as may be prescribed by law.

Sec. 8. JURISDICTION OF DISTRICT COURT. District Court jurisdiction consists of exclusive, appellate, and original jurisdiction of all actions, proceedings, and remedies, except in cases where exclusive, appellate, or original jurisdiction may be conferred by this Constitution or other law on some other court, tribunal, or administrative body. District Court judges shall have the power to issue writs necessary to enforce their jurisdiction.

The District Court shall have appellate jurisdiction and general supervisory control over the County Commissioners Court, with such exceptions and under such regulations as may be prescribed by law.

(Amended Aug. 11, 1891, Nov. 6, 1973, and Nov. 5, 1985.)

Sec. 13. NUMBER OF GRAND AND PETIT JURORS; NUMBER CONCURRING. Grand and petit juries in the District Courts shall be composed of twelve persons, except that petit juries in a criminal case below the grade of felony shall be composed of six persons; but nine members of a grand jury shall be a quorum to transact business and present bills. In trials of civil cases in the District Courts, nine members of the jury, concurring, may render a verdict, but when the verdict shall be rendered by less than the whole number, it shall be signed by every member of the jury concurring in it. When, pending the trial of any case, one or more jurors not exceeding three, may die, or be disabled from sitting, the remainder of the jury shall have the power to render the verdict; provided, that the Legislature may change or modify the rule authorizing less than the whole number of the jury to render a verdict.

(Amended Nov. 6, 2001, and Sept. 13, 2003.) (TEMPORARY TRANSITION PROVISION for Sec. 13: See Appendix, Note 3.)

Article 9
Counties

Sec. 1. CREATION OF COUNTIES. The Legislature shall have power to create counties for the convenience of the people subject to the following provisions:

(1) Within the territory of any county or counties, no new county shall be created with a less area than seven hundred square miles, nor shall any such county now existing be reduced to a less area than seven hundred square miles. No new counties shall be created so as to approach nearer than twelve miles of the county seat of any county from which it may in whole or in part be taken. Counties of a less area than nine hundred, but of seven hundred or more square miles, within counties now existing, may be created by a two-thirds vote of each House of the Legislature, taken by yeas and nays and entered on the journals. Any county now existing may be reduced to an area of not less than seven hundred square miles by a like two-thirds vote. When any part of a county is stricken off and attached to,

or created into another county, the part stricken off shall be holden for and obliged to pay its proportion of all the liabilities then existing, of the county from which it was taken, in such manner as may be prescribed by law.

(2) No part of any existing county shall be detached from it and attached to another existing county until the proposition for such change shall have been submitted, in such manner as may be provided by law, to a vote of the voters of both counties, and shall have received a majority of those voting on the question in each.

(Amended Nov. 2, 1999.) (TEMPORARY TRANSITION PROVISIONS for Sec. 1: See Appendix, Note 1.)

Article 11
Municipal Corporations

Sec. 1. COUNTIES AS LEGAL SUBDIVISIONS. The several counties of this State are hereby recognized as legal subdivisions of the State.

Sec. 4. CITIES AND TOWNS WITH POPULATION OF 5,000 OR LESS; CHARTERED BY GENERAL LAW; TAXES; FINES, FORFEITURES, AND PENALTIES. Cities and towns having a population of five thousand or less may be chartered alone by general law. They may levy, assess and collect such taxes as may be authorized by law, but no tax for any purpose shall ever be lawful for any one year which shall exceed one and one-half per cent of the taxable property of such city; and all taxes shall be collectible only in current money, and all licenses and occupation taxes levied, and all fines, forfeitures and penalties accruing to said cities and towns shall be collectible only in current money.

(Amended Aug. 3, 1909, and Nov. 2, 1920.)

Sec. 5. CITIES OF MORE THAN 5,000 POPULATION; ADOPTION OR AMENDMENT OF CHARTERS; TAXES; DEBT RESTRICTIONS. (a) Cities having more than five thousand (5000) inhabitants may, by a majority vote of the qualified voters of said city, at an election held for that purpose, adopt or amend their charters. If the number of inhabitants of cities that have adopted or amended their charters under this section is reduced to five thousand (5000) or fewer, the cities still may amend their charters by a majority vote of the qualified voters of said city at an election held for that purpose. The adoption or amendment of charters is subject to such limitations as may be prescribed by the Legislature, and no charter or any ordinance passed under said charter shall contain any provision inconsistent with the Constitution of the State, or of the general laws enacted by the Legislature of this State. Said cities may levy, assess and collect such taxes as may be authorized by law or by their charters; but no tax for any purpose shall ever be lawful for any one year, which shall exceed two and one-half per cent. of the taxable property of such city, and no debt shall ever be created by any city, unless at the same time provision be made to assess and collect annually a sufficient sum to pay the interest thereon and creating a sinking fund of at least two per cent. thereon, except as provided by Subsection (b). Furthermore, no city charter shall be altered, amended or repealed oftener than every two years.

(b) To increase efficiency and effectiveness to the greatest extent possible, the legislature may by general law authorize cities to enter into interlocal contracts with other cities or counties without meeting the assessment and sinking fund requirements under Subsection (a).

(Amended Aug. 3, 1909, Nov. 5, 1912, Nov. 5, 1991, and Nov. 8, 2011.)

Glossary

absentee (or early) voting A period before the regularly scheduled election date during which voters are allowed to cast ballots. With recent changes in election law, a person does not have to offer a reason for voting absentee.

activists A small segment of the population that is engaged in various political activities.

agenda building The process of groups or individuals identifying problems or issues that affect them and keeping pressure on policymakers to develop and implement public policy solutions.

agenda setting A theory that the media's choice of which news events and issues to cover helps define what is important for the public to know and which issues should be addressed.

agents of political socialization Entities such as families, schools, community, and the media that help integrate people into society and teach political values.

annexation The authority of cities to add territory, subject to restrictions set by state law.

appellate jurisdiction The authority of a court to review the decisions of lower courts to determine if the law was correctly interpreted and legal procedures were correctly followed.

appraisal district Countywide tax office that appraises the value of property and certifies the tax rolls used by every taxing authority in the county.

appropriations bill A legislative action authorizing the expenditure of money for a public program or purpose. A general appropriations bill approved by the legislature every two years is the state budget.

at-large election A system under which city council members or other officeholders are elected by voters in the entire city, school district, or single-purpose district. Many of these election systems have been struck down by the federal courts or by the U.S. Justice Department under the Voting Rights Act as discriminatory against minorities.

attorney general The state's chief legal officer. He or she represents the state in lawsuits; is responsible for enforcing the state's antitrust, consumer protection, and other civil laws; and issues advisory opinions on legal questions to state and local officeholders. This elected official has little responsibility for criminal law enforcement.

benchmark poll A poll conducted at the beginning of a campaign to provide in-depth information to help formulate campaign strategy.

bicameral A lawmaking body, such as the Texas legislature, that includes two chambers.

bifactionalism The presence of two dominant factions organized around regional, economic, or ideological differences within a single political party. For much of the twentieth century, Texas functioned as a one-party system with two dominant factions—liberal and conservative.

bifurcated court system Existence of two courts at the highest level of the state judiciary. The Texas Supreme Court is the court of last resort in civil and juvenile cases, and the Court of Criminal Appeals has the final authority to review criminal cases. Texas and Oklahoma are the only two states that use this system.

block grant A federal grant of money to states and local governments for broad programs or services rather than narrowly defined programs. A block grant gives state and local governments more discretion over the use of the funds than other types of grants do.

bureaucracies The agencies of government and their employees responsible for carrying out policies and providing public services approved by elected officials.

calendar Agenda or the list of bills to be considered by the House or the Senate on a given day.

Calendars Committee A special procedural committee in the Texas House of Representatives that schedules bills that already have been approved by other committees for floor debate.

campaign consultant A professional expert who helps political candidates plan, organize, and run their campaigns.

capital murder Murder committed under certain circumstances for which the death penalty or life in prison must be imposed.

Capitol press corps Representatives of Texas newspapers, wire services, and other media services who are assigned to Austin full time to report on state government and politics.

categorical grant-in-aid A grant of federal money that can be spent only for specific programs or purposes. This is the source of most federal assistance to state and local governments.

caucus A group of legislators who band together for common political or partisan goals or along ethnic or geographic lines.

city charter A document, defined or authorized by state law, under which a city operates. In Texas home rule cities, local voters may choose among several forms of city government.

city commission A form of city government in which elected commissioners collectively serve as a city's policymaking body and individually serve as administrative heads of different city departments. Often referred to as the Galveston Plan, this form of government, which was part of the city reform movement, does not appear to be used in any Texas city today. Although some cities still refer to their legislative bodies as commissions, these cities function much like council–manager cities.

civil lawsuit A noncriminal legal dispute between two or more individuals, businesses, governments, or other entities.

civil service system A personnel system under which public employees are selected for government jobs through competitive examinations and the systematic evaluation of job performance.

cohort replacement (generational changes) Natural occurrence of generational replacement due to death.

commissioner of agriculture An elected state official responsible for administering laws and programs that benefit agriculture.

commissioner of the General Land Office An elected official who manages the state's public lands and administers the Veterans Land Program, which provides low-interest loans to veterans for the purchase of land and houses.

commissioners court The principal policymaking body for county government. It includes four commissioners and the county judge, all elected offices. It sets the county tax rate and supervises expenditures.

comptroller of public accounts The state's primary tax administrator and revenue estimator. It is an elective position.

concurrent powers Powers shared by both the national and state governments.

confederacy A view of the national government taken by eleven southern states, including Texas, that a state could withdraw, or secede, from the Union. Upon secession that began in 1860, the Confederate States of America was formed, leading to the Civil War.

confederation A system in which each member government is considered sovereign, and the national government is limited to powers delegated to it by its member governments.

conference committee A panel of House members and senators appointed to work out a compromise on a bill if the House and the Senate passed different versions of the legislation.

confidence level The probability that the results found in the sample reflect the true opinion of the entire population under study.

conservative A person who generally believes that a large and powerful government is a threat to individual freedom and supports personal responsibility, limited governmental spending, traditional patterns of relationships, importance of religion in daily life, and free enterprise. Conservatives are said to be on the "right" of the political spectrum.

constable An elected law enforcement officer assigned as an administrative officer in a justice of the peace precinct. He or she is responsible primarily for executing court judgments, serving subpoenas, and delivering other legal documents. Constables also are authorized to patrol their precincts, make arrests, and conduct criminal investigations.

constitution A document that provides for the legal and institutional structure of a political system. It establishes government bodies and defines their powers.

Constitutional Convention of 1974 The last major attempt to write a new Texas Constitution. Members of the legislature served as delegates and failed to overcome political differences and the influence of special interests.

constitutional county court The Texas Constitution provides for 254 courts with limited jurisdiction. The county judge, who is also the presiding officer of a county's commissioners court, which is a policymaking body, performs some limited judicial functions in some counties.

controlled media Paid advertising in the media where content and presentation are determined by a political candidate's campaign or by a candidate and his/her staff.

cooperative federalism Policies emphasizing cooperative efforts among the federal, state, and local governments to address common problems and provide public services to citizens.

co-optation Influence over state regulatory boards by the industries they are supposed to regulate, often to the detriment of the general public.

council-manager government A form of city government in which policy is set by an elected city council, which hires a professional city manager to head the daily administration of city government. With the exception of Houston, larger cities in Texas are organized under this form of government.

county attorney An elected official who is the chief legal officer of some counties. He or she also prosecutes lesser criminal offenses, primarily misdemeanors, in county courts.

county auditor An officer appointed by the district judges of the county. This person is primarily responsible for reviewing every bill and expenditure of a county to ensure that it is correct and legal. In counties with more than 225,000 people, the auditor also is the budget officer who prepares the county budget for consideration by the commissioners court.

county chair The presiding officer of a political party's county executive committee. Voters in the party primary elect him or her by countywide election.

county clerk The chief record-keeping officer of a county.

county executive committee A panel responsible on the local level for the organization and management of a political party's primary election. It includes the party's county chair and each precinct chair.

county judge The presiding officer of a county commissioners court. This office also has some judicial authority, which is assumed by separate county courts-at-law in most urban counties.

county tax assessor–collector An elected official who determines how much property tax is owed on the different pieces of property within a county and then collects the tax. This officeholder acts on the basis of property values determined by the county appraisal district and a tax rate set by the county commissioners court.

county treasurer An elected officer who is responsible for receiving and disbursing county funds. The office's primary functions are now carried out by the county auditor, and the office has been eliminated in a number of counties.

court of appeals An intermediate-level court that reviews civil and criminal cases from the district courts.

dealignment A view that the party system is breaking up and the electoral influence of political parties is being replaced by interest groups, the media, and well-financed candidates who use their own media campaigns to dominate the nomination and election process.

dedicated funds Constitutional or statutory requirements that restrict some state tax or fee revenues to spending on specific programs.

deficit financing Borrowing money to meet operating expenses. It is prohibited by the Texas Constitution, which provides that the state government must operate on a pay-as-you-go basis.

delegated powers Powers specifically assigned to the national, or federal, government by the U.S. Constitution, including powers to tax, borrow and coin money, declare war, and regulate interstate and foreign commerce.

denied powers Powers that are denied to both the states and national government. The best-known restrictions are listed in the Bill of Rights.

devolution Return of powers assumed by the federal government to the states.

Dillon rule A principle holding that local governments are creations of state government and their powers and responsibilities are defined by the state.

direct lobbying The communication of information and policy preferences directly to policymakers or their staffs.

district attorney An elected official who prosecutes the more serious criminal offenses, usually felonies, in state district courts.

district court A court with general jurisdiction over criminal felony cases and civil disputes.

dual federalism Nineteenth-century concept of federalism in which the powers or functions of the national and state governments were sharply differentiated with limited overlapping responsibilities.

economic diversification The development of new and varied business activities. New businesses were encouraged to relocate to or expand in Texas after the oil and gas industry, which had been the base of the state's economy, suffered a major recession in the 1980s.

Edgewood v. *Kirby* A lawsuit in which the Texas Supreme Court in 1989 declared the Texas school finance system unconstitutional because of wide disparities in property wealth and educational opportunities among school districts.

editorial autonomy The freedom of a local newspaper or television station to set its own news policies independently of absentee owners who may run a chain of media outlets throughout the country.

elitism Theory holding the view that political power is primarily held by a few individuals who derive power from leadership positions in large business, civic, or governmental institutions.

the Establishment A loosely knit coalition of white businessmen, oilmen, bankers, and lawyers who asserted control of state policymaking during much of the 20th century.

exit poll A survey, typically conducted by news media, of voters when they leave polling places.

extradition A process by which a person in one state can be returned to another state to face criminal charges.

extraterritorial jurisdiction The power of an incorporated city to control development within nearby unincorporated areas.

fake news The publication of material that is known to be false or deliberately misleading for political or economic purposes.

fat cat An individual who contributes a large amount of money to political candidates.

federalism A system that balances the power and sovereignty of state governments with those of the national government. Both the states and the national government derive their authority directly from the people, and the states have considerable autonomy within their areas of responsibility.

felony A criminal offense that can be punished by imprisonment and/or a fine. This is a more serious offense than a misdemeanor.

filibuster A procedure that allows a senator to speak against a bill for as long as he or she can stand and talk. It can become a formidable obstacle or threat against controversial bills near the end of a legislative session.

formula grant A federal grant based on specific criteria, such as income levels or population.

full faith and credit clause A provision in the U.S. Constitution (Article IV, Section 1) that requires states to recognize civil judgments and official documents rendered by the courts of other states.

gender gap Differences in voting and policy preferences between men and women.

general election An election for state, federal, and county offices held in November of even-numbered years. The ballot includes nominees of the two major political parties plus other candidates who meet certain legal requirements.

general law city A Texas city with fewer than 5,000 residents. Such cities are allowed to exercise only those powers specifically granted to them by the legislature. Most cities in Texas are classified as general law cities.

general obligation bond A method of borrowing money to pay for new construction projects, such as prisons, hospitals, streets or drainage systems. Interest on these bonds, which require voter approval, is paid with tax revenue.

gerrymandering Drawing of political district lines in such a way that they favor a particular political party or racial group.

globalization of the economy Increased interdependence in trade, manufacturing, and commerce between the United States and other countries.

governor The state's top executive officeholder.

grand jury Panel that reviews evidence submitted by prosecutors to determine whether to indict, or charge, an individual with a criminal offense. A grand jury can hear witnesses; all its meetings are held behind closed doors.

Grange An organization formed in the late nineteenth century to improve the lot of farmers. Its influence in Texas after Reconstruction was felt in constitutional provisions limiting taxes and government spending and restricting banks, railroads, and other big businesses.

grassroots A term used to describe a wide range of political activities designed to organize and mobilize the electorate at the local level. Modern campaigns are increasingly dominated by the campaign consultants, but such support can prove crucial for political candidates, particularly for those with limited financial resources.

home rule city A Texas city with more than 5,000 residents. Such cities can adopt any form of government residents choose, provided it does not conflict with the state constitution or statutes. Home rule powers are formalized through local voters' adoption of a city charter spelling out how the city is to be governed.

homestead exemption Legal provision that permits a person who owns a home and is living in it to obtain a reduction in property taxes on the house.

House Bill 72 A landmark school reform law enacted in 1984 that reduced class sizes; imposed the no pass, no play rule; and made other educational improvements.

hyperpluralism The rapid increase in the number of interest groups that serve to disrupt and potentially deadlock the policy-making process.

illusion of saliency The misconception that an issue is more important to the public than it actually is.

implied powers Although not specifically defined by the U.S. Constitution, these are powers assumed by the national government as necessary in carrying out its responsibilities.

income tax A tax based on a corporation's or an individual's income. Texas is one of only a few states without a personal income tax.

independent school district A specific form of special district that administers the public schools in a designated area. It is governed by an elected board of trustees empowered to levy local property taxes, establish local school policies, and employ a school superintendent as its chief administrator.

indictment A written statement issued by a grand jury charging a person or persons with a crime or crimes.

indirect lobbying Activities designed to mobilize public support for a policy position and bring pressure to bear on public officials through electoral activities, public relations campaigns, and sometimes protests or marches.

individualism An attitude, rooted in classical liberal theory and reinforced by the frontier tradition, that citizens are capable of taking care of themselves with minimal governmental assistance.

individualistic subculture A view that government should interfere as little as possible in the private activities of its citizens while ensuring that adequate public facilities and a favorable business climate are available to permit individuals to pursue their self-interests.

information A document formally charging an individual with a misdemeanor.

initiative A petition and election process whereby voters propose laws or constitutional amendments for adoption by a popular vote.

institutionalization The complex process of institutional change and adaptation in the organization and operations of the legislature.

interest group A group of people with common goals who are organized to seek political or policy objectives they are unable to achieve by themselves.

intersectionality A term coined to describe the combined effects of one's multiple identities (e.g., race, gender, sexual orientation, religion, and social class). The term was originally coined to describe the intersection of multiple forms of discrimination, such as racism, sexism, and classism, which often characterize the life experiences of marginalized individuals or groups.

Internet survey A survey done through the Internet. These are popular but can produce unreliable results, as not all residents have access to the Internet. Be leery of research conducted using Internet surveys.

interstate compact A formal, long-term cooperative agreement among the states dealing with common problems or issues and subject to approval of the U.S. Congress.

iron rule of oligarchy A theory developed by Robert Michels, a European sociologist, that all organizations inevitably are dominated by a few individuals.

iron triangles of government A term used to describe how permanent relationships eventually evolve from the interactions among interest groups, administrative agencies, and legislative committees as they respond to the demands of various groups by enacting laws and regulations and appropriating funds to address their priorities.

issue-attention cycle A pattern in which public interest in an issue or problem is heightened by intensive media coverage. Media attention and public interest will wane after government takes steps to address their concerns, but most issues or problems are never permanently resolved. Another crisis, perhaps years later, will restart the cycle.

issue networks Term coined by Hugh Heclo to describe the complex institutional and political relationships in the policymaking process.

Jim Crow laws Legislation enacted by many states after the Civil War to limit the rights and power of African Americans.

justice of the peace court A low-ranking court with jurisdiction over minor civil disputes and criminal cases.

liberal A person who generally supports governmental action to promote equality, to alleviate social ills (like racism, bigotry, and poverty), and to protect civil rights and liberties. Liberals are said to be on the "left" of the political spectrum.

libertarian A person who believes that individual well-being and prosperity are fostered by an extremely limited government and as much personal liberty in thought and action as possible. Generally, each person should be able to live his or her life as long as the rights of others are respected.

licensing A key regulatory function of government that seeks to ensure that individuals and companies providing critical professional services to the public are properly trained or qualified.

lieutenant governor The presiding officer of the Senate. This officeholder also becomes governor if the governor dies, resigns, becomes incapacitated, or is removed from office.

limited government The constitutional principle restricting governmental authority and spelling out personal rights.

line-item veto The power of the governor to reject certain parts of an appropriation, or spending, bill without killing the entire measure.

lobbying An effort, usually organized and using a variety of strategies and techniques, to influence the making of laws or public policy.

local election An election for city council, the school board, and certain other local offices. Most of these are nonpartisan.

lottery A form of gambling, conducted by many states, in which participants purchase tickets that offer an opportunity to cash in on a winning number or set of winning numbers. Voters legalized a state lottery in Texas in 1991.

mandate A federal law or regulation that requires state or local governments to take certain actions, often at costs that the federal government does not reimburse. The state government also imposes mandates on local governments.

maquiladora program Economic program initiated by Mexico to increase manufacturing and the assembly of goods.

margin of error A measurement of how accurate a poll is in terms of reflecting the "true" sentiments of the population under study.

margins tax The state's main business tax, enacted in 2006 to replace the franchise tax. This tax, which applies to corporations and professional partnerships such as law firms, is based on a company's annual revenue. Companies can deduct some of their costs, such as employees' salaries, from the tax base. Many of the smaller companies in the state do not have to pay the tax.

matching funds Money that states or local governments have to provide to qualify for certain federal grants.

media bias A perception—sometimes real, sometimes imagined—that reporters and news organizations slant their news coverage to favor one side or the other in particular issues or disputes.

media event An event staged by an officeholder or political candidate that is designed to attract media, especially television, coverage.

merit employment system A personnel system under which public employees are selected for government jobs through competitive examinations and the systematic evaluation of job performance.

merit selection A proposal under which the governor would appoint state judges from lists of potential nominees recommended by committees of experts. Appointed judges would have to run later in retention elections in which voters would simply decide whether a judge should remain in office or be replaced by another gubernatorial appointee.

metro government Consolidation of city and county governments to avoid duplication of public services. This approach has been tried in several other parts of the country but so far has attracted little interest in Texas.

Miranda ruling A far-reaching decision of the U.S. Supreme Court that requires law enforcement officers to warn a criminal suspect of his or her right to remain silent and have an attorney present during questioning.

mischief of factions Term coined by James Madison to describe the complex relationships among groups and interests within the American political system and the institutional arrangements that potentially balance the power of groups.

misdemeanor A minor criminal offense punishable by a fine or a short sentence in the county jail. This is less serious than a felony.

moralistic subculture A view that government's primary responsibility is to promote the public welfare and that government should actively use its authority and power to improve the social and economic well-being of its citizens.

motor voter registration Term referring to federal and state laws that allow people to register to vote at offices where they receive their driver's licenses.

multi-issue group A group that is interested in pursuing a broad range of public policy issues around a central theme.

municipal court A court of limited jurisdiction that hears cases involving city ordinances and primarily handles traffic tickets.

negative television ad A television commercial in which a political candidate attacks an opponent, sometimes over a legitimate issue, but more often over an alleged flaw in the opponent's character or ability to hold office. Many such ads are deliberately misleading or outright false.

new federalism A term used to describe recent changes in federal–state relationships. Used primarily by conservative presidents, it suggests a devolution or return of power to the states and a decreased role of the federal government in domestic policy.

nolo contendere A plea of no contest to a criminal charge.

nonpartisan election A local election in which candidates file for place, position, or district with no political party label attached to their names.

no pass, no play rule A law stating that a student failing a course is restricted from participating in extracurricular activities for a specified period.

norm An unwritten rule of institutional behavior that is critical to the stability and effectiveness of the institution.

one-party politics The domination of elections and governmental processes by a single party, which may be split into different ideological, economic, or regional factions. In Texas, the phrase is used to describe the period from the late 1870s to the late 1970s, when the Democratic Party claimed virtually all elected, partisan offices.

Open Meetings and Public Information Acts Laws that require state and local governmental bodies to conduct most of their actions in public and maintain records for public inspection.

original jurisdiction The authority of a court to try to resolve a civil lawsuit or a criminal prosecution being heard for the first time.

parole The early release of an inmate from prison, subject to certain conditions.

party activist Member of a political party involved in organizational and electoral activities.

pay-as-you-go A constitutional prohibition against state government borrowing money for its operating budget.

Penal Code A body of law that defines most criminal offenses and sets a range of punishments that can be assessed.

Permanent University Fund (PUF) A land- and mineral-rich endowment that benefits the University of Texas and Texas A&M University systems, particularly the flagship universities in Austin and College Station.

personal interview A technique of administering a public opinion poll in which researchers ask respondents for their opinions face to face. Personal interviews allow for more detailed questions but are far more expensive and time consuming than other techniques.

petition for discretionary review Petition to the Texas Court of Criminal Appeals stating that legal or procedural mistakes were made in the lower court, thus meriting a hearing before the court.

petition for review Petition to the Texas Supreme Court stating that legal or procedural mistakes were made in the lower court, thus meriting a hearing before the court.

petit jury A panel of citizens that hears evidence in a civil lawsuit or a criminal prosecution and decides the outcome by issuing a verdict.

platform A set of principles or positions on various issues adopted by a political party at its state or national convention.

plea bargain A procedure that allows a person charged with a crime to negotiate a guilty plea with prosecutors in exchange for a lighter sentence than he or she would expect to receive if convicted in a trial.

plural executive A fragmented system of authority under which most statewide, executive officeholders are elected independently of the governor. This arrangement, which is used in Texas, places severe limitations on the governor's power.

pluralism Theory holding that a diversity of groups and people is instrumental in the policymaking process and no one group should be able to dominate the decisions of government.

political action committee (PAC) Often referred to as a PAC, a committee representing a specific interest group or including employees of a specific company that raises money from its members for distribution to selected officeholders and political candidates.

political culture A widely shared set of views, attitudes, beliefs, and customs of a people as to how their government should be organized and run.

political efficacy The belief that one can influence government. Internal political efficacy is the belief that one has the knowledge and ability to influence government. External political efficacy is the belief that the political system is responsive to citizens.

political ideology A consistent set of values and beliefs that form a general philosophy about the proper goals, purpose, and size of government. Ideology is grounded in political values.

political myths Generally held views rooted in the political culture that are used to explain common historical and cultural experiences.

political party A group that seeks to elect public officeholders under its own name.

political patronage The hiring of government employees on the basis of personal friendships or favors rather than ability or merit.

political socialization The process that begins in early childhood whereby a person assimilates the beliefs, attitudes, and behaviors of society and acquires views toward the political system and government.

poll tax A tax that Texas and some other states used to require people to pay before allowing them to vote. The purpose was to discourage minorities and poor whites from participating in the political process. The tax was declared unconstitutional in the 1960s.

popular sovereignty The constitutional principle of self-government; the belief that the people control their government and governments are subject to limitations and constraints.

population density Number of persons residing within a square mile.

populist A person who supports the rights and power of "common people" in their struggle against the privileged elite. Generally, populists believe that democracy should reflect and protect the will of the masses and that government can be a positive element in accomplishing that goal. Populists are frequently antiestablishment and offer unorthodox proposals to promote grassroots democracy often associated with the working class.

precinct A specific, local voting area created by a county commissioners court. The state election code outlines detailed requirements for drawing up these election units.

precinct chair A local officer in a political party who presides over the precinct convention and serves on the party's county executive committee. Voters in each precinct elect a chair in the party's primary election.

preemption A federal law that limits the authority or powers of state and local governments.

primary election An election in which the Democratic or Republican Party chooses its nominees for public offices. In presidential election years, the primary also plays a key role in selecting Texas delegates to the parties' national nominating conventions.

privatization Government contracting with private companies to provide some public services.

privileges and immunities The right of a resident of one state to be protected by the laws and afforded the legal opportunities in any other state he or she visits. Certain exceptions, however, have been allowed by the courts, including the right of states to charge nonresidents higher college tuition or higher hunting and fishing license fees.

probability sample A sampling method in which every element in the target population has an equal chance of selection.

probation A procedure under which a convicted criminal is not sent to prison if he or she meets certain conditions, such as restrictions on travel and with whom he or she associates.

project grant A federal grant for a defined project.

property or ad valorem tax A tax on homes, businesses, and certain other forms of property that is the main source of revenue for local governments. The tax is based on the assessed value of the property.

prosecution The conduct of legal proceedings against an individual charged with a crime.

public improvement district (PID) Specific area of a city in which property owners pay special taxes in return for improvements to streets and other public facilities in their neighborhood.

public interest group A group that is primarily concerned with consumer or environmental protection, the promotion of strong ethical standards for public officials, or increased funding for health and human services programs. Grassroots, volunteer efforts are crucial to the success of these groups, since they often are poorly funded.

public opinion The various opinions (views, perceptions, attitudes) about contemporary political issues, political leaders, and governmental institutions held by the population or by subgroups of the population. Public opinion tends to be grounded in political values and can impact political behavior.

public opinion polling The scientific measurement of people's attitudes toward business products, public issues, public officeholders, or political candidates. It has become a key ingredient of statewide political campaigns and is usually conducted by telephone, using a representative sample of voters.

push poll A form of telemarketing disguised as a public opinion poll, often conducted to influence opinions.

Radical Reconstructionists The group of Republicans who took control of Congress in 1866 and imposed military governments on the former Confederate states after the Civil War.

reading Bills are required to go through three readings in both houses of the legislature. The first reading occurs with the introduction of a bill in the House or the Senate and its referral to a committee by the presiding officer. The second reading is the initial debate by the full House or Senate on a bill that has been approved by a committee. The third occurs with the final presentation of a bill before the full House or Senate.

realignment A major shift in political party support or identification, which usually occurs around a critical election. In Texas, this was a gradual transformation from a one-party system dominated by Democrats to a two-party system in which Republicans became the dominant party statewide.

record vote A vote taken in the House or the Senate for which a permanent record is kept, listing how individual legislators voted.

redistricting The process of redrawing legislative and other political district boundaries to reflect changing population patterns. Districts for the Texas House, state Senate, State Board of Education, and U.S. Congress are redrawn every ten years by the legislature.

referendum An election, usually initiated by a petition of voters, whereby an action of a legislative body is submitted for approval or rejection by the voters.

regressive tax A tax that imposes a disproportionately heavier burden on low-income people than on the more affluent.

regular legislative session The 140-day period in odd-numbered years in which the legislature meets and can consider laws on any issue or subject.

Religious Right An ultraconservative political faction that draws considerable support from fundamentalist religious groups and economic conservatives.

representative government The constitutional principle that people elect representatives to make laws and other governmental decisions on their behalf.

republic A political system in which sovereign power resides in the citizenry and is exercised by representatives elected by and responsible to them.

reserved powers Powers given to state governments by the Tenth Amendment. These are powers not delegated to the national government nor otherwise prohibited to the states by the Constitution.

retention election Election in which judges run on their own records rather than against other candidates. Voters cast their ballots on the question of whether the incumbent judge should stay in office.

revenue bond A bond sold by a government that is repaid from the revenues generated from income-producing facilities.

revenue sharing A program begun under President Nixon and later repealed in which state and local governments received federal aid that could be used for virtually any purpose the recipient government wanted.

revolving door The practice of former members of state boards and commissions or key employees of agencies leaving state government for more lucrative jobs with the industries they used to regulate. It raises questions of undue industry influence over regulatory agencies.

right-to-work law Law prohibiting the requirement of union membership in order to get or hold a job.

rollback election An election in which local voters can nullify a property tax increase that exceeds 3.5 percent for most local governments or 2.5 percent for school districts in a given year.

Ruiz v. Estelle A 1980 landmark federal court order that declared the state prison system unconstitutional and resulted in significant changes in state lockups.

runoff election A required election if no candidate receives an absolute majority of the votes cast in a primary race or in many nonpartisan elections. The runoff is between the top two vote-getters.

sales tax A tax charged as a set percentage of most retail purchases and many services. It is the main source of tax revenue for state government and an important source of revenue for many cities and metropolitan transit authorities.

sample A subset of the population under study.

school board The governing body of a public school district.

school superintendent Chief administrator of a school district who is hired by the school board.

secretary of state An officeholder appointed by the governor who administers state election laws, grants charters to corporations, and processes the extradition of prisoners to other states.

select committee A special committee—usually appointed by the governor, the lieutenant governor, and the speaker—that studies a specific issue and makes recommendations to the legislature. This panel usually includes private citizens as well as legislators.

senatorial courtesy An unwritten policy that permits a senator to block the confirmation of a gubernatorial appointee who lives in the senator's district.

separation of powers The division of authority among three distinct branches of government—the legislative, the executive, and the judicial—that allows the branches to serve as checks and balances on one another's power.

Sharpstown stock fraud scandal After rocking state government in 1971 and 1972, the scandal helped produce some far-reaching legislative and political changes. It involved the passage of banking legislation sought by Houston financier Frank Sharp and quick profits that some state officials made on stock purchased in an insurance company owned by Sharp with unsecured loans from Sharp's Sharpstown State Bank.

sheriff An elected official who is the chief law enforcement officer of a county. In urban areas, his or her jurisdiction usually is limited to the unincorporated areas of a county, while local police departments have jurisdiction over incorporated cities.

sin tax A common nickname for a tax on tobacco or alcoholic beverages.

single-issue group A highly ideological group that promotes a single issue or cause with only limited regard for the views or interests of other groups. Such groups often are reluctant to compromise.

single-member district A system in which a legislator, city council member, or other public official is elected from a specific geographic area.

social contract The view that governments originate from the general agreement among and consent of members of the public to address common interests and needs.

sound bite A short, quotable phrase by a public official or political candidate that may sound good on television or radio but lacks depth and often is meaningless.

speaker The presiding officer of the House of Representatives.

special district A unit of local government created by the state to perform a specific function or functions not met by cities or counties, including the provision of public services to unincorporated areas.

special election An election set by the legislature or called by the governor for a specific purpose, such as voting on constitutional amendments or filling a vacancy in a legislative office. Local governments also can call special elections.

special session A legislative session called by the governor at any time other than the regular legislative session. Special sessions are limited to thirty days and can consider only subjects or issues designated by the governor.

spin The presentation of information in the best possible light for a public official or political candidate. It usually is provided by a press secretary, campaign consultant, or another individual representing the officeholder or candidate.

spoils system Practice, usually identified with machine politics, of awarding public jobs to one's political friends or supporters with little regard to abilities or skills.

staggered terms Terms that begin on different dates. The requirement that members of state boards and commissions appointed by the governor serve terms that begin on different dates ensures that a board maintains a level of experience by guarding against situations in which all board members leave office at the same time.

standing committee A legislative committee that specializes in bills by subject matter or plays a procedural role in the lawmaking process. A bill has to win committee approval before the full House or Senate can consider it.

State Board of Education A fifteen-member body, composed of members who are elected from districts, which has responsibility over textbook selection, curriculum standards for public schools, and Permanent School Fund investments.

state chair and vice chair The two top state leaders of a political party, one of whom must be a woman. Delegates to the party's state convention select these officers. The Republican chair and vice chair serve for two years, while the Democratic chair and vice chair serve for four years.

state executive committee The statewide governing body of a political party. It includes the state chair and vice chair, committee chair elected by party convention delegates from each of the thirty-one state senatorial districts, and other officers or members designated by the political parties.

statutory county court A court created by the legislature that exercises limited jurisdiction over criminal and civil cases. Also known as county courts-at-law, the jurisdiction of these courts varies from county to county.

statutory law A law enacted by a legislative body. Unlike constitutional law, it does not require voter approval.

strong mayor A form of city government that gives the mayor considerable power, including budgetary control and appointment and removal authority over city department heads.

suffrage The right to vote.

sunset review The process under which most state agencies have to be periodically reviewed and recreated by the legislature or be eliminated.

supremacy clause A provision of the U.S. Constitution that says federal law prevails in conflicts between the powers of the states and the national government.

tag A rule that allows an individual senator to postpone a committee hearing on any bill for at least forty-eight hours, a delay that can be fatal to a bill during the closing days of a legislative session.

tax abatement A device used by governments to attract new businesses through the reduction or elimination of property taxes for a specific period of time.

telephone survey The most common method of administering public opinion polls by professionals. Telephone surveys produce reliable results in a less expensive and faster manner than personal interviews, though changes in technology are beginning to raise some questions about the reliability of such polls.

Texas Court of Criminal Appeals A nine-member court with final appellate jurisdiction over criminal cases in Texas.

Texas Railroad Commission A three-member, elected body that regulates oil and natural gas production and lignite mining in Texas.

Texas Supreme Court A nine-member court with final appellate jurisdiction over civil lawsuits in Texas.

third party A minor political party. There have been many in Texas over the years, but none has had significant success on a statewide level.

ticket splitting The decisions of voters to divide their votes among candidates of more than one political party in the same election.

tort reform Changes in state law to put limits on personal injury lawsuits and damage judgments entered by the courts.

tracking poll A poll conducted repeatedly to check shifts in opinion or voting intentions.

traditionalistic subculture A view that political power should be concentrated in the hands of a few elite citizens who belong to established families or influential social groups. Public policy basically serves the interests of this small group.

transnational regionalism The expanding economic and social interdependence of South Texas and Mexico.

two-party system A political system in which each of the two dominant parties has the possibility of winning national, statewide, or county elections.

two-thirds rule A rule under which the Texas Senate used to operate that required approval of at least two-thirds of senators before a bill could be debated on the Senate floor. The rule was weakened in 2015 to require approval of three-fifths of senators instead of two-thirds. But the rule will continue to allow a minority of senators to block controversial legislation.

unicameral A single-body legislature.

United States–Mexico–Canada Agreement (USMCA) Treaty signed in 2018 to lower trade barriers among the United States, Mexico, and Canada and to continue the common economic market created by the North American Free Trade Agreement (NAFTA), which it replaced.

unitary system A system in which ultimate power is vested in a central or national government and local governments have only those powers granted to them by the central government. This principle also describes the relationship between the state and local governments in Texas.

urbanization The process by which a predominantly rural society or area becomes urban.

veniremen Persons who have been called for a jury panel.

veto The power of the governor to reject, or kill, a bill passed by the legislature.

voter turnout The percentage of citizens legally eligible to vote in an election who actually vote in the election.

Voting Rights Act A federal law designed to protect the voting rights of minorities with the inclusion of several provisions that regulate elections. The act, as amended, has eliminated most of the more restrictive state laws that limited minority political participation.

ward politics Term, often with negative connotations, that refers to partisan politics linked to political favoritism.

weak mayor A form of city government in which the mayor shares authority with the city council and other elected officials but has little independent control over city policy or city administration.

whistle-blower A government employee who publicly reports wrongdoing or unethical conduct within a government agency.

white primary A series of state laws and party rules that denied African Americans the right to vote in the Democratic primary in Texas in the first half of the twentieth century.

writ of mandamus A court order directing a lower court or a public official to take a certain action.

Notes

Chapter 1

1. Tom Orsborn, "With San Antonio Food Bank in nationalspotlight, lawmakers to pressure state for help," *San Antonio Express-News*, April 11, 2020.
2. U.S. Census Bureau, "Census Bureau Reports at Least 350 Languages Spoken in U.S. Homes," November 3, 2015, Release Number CB15-185, http://www.census.gov/newsroom/press-releases/2015/cb15-185.html, accessed January 2, 2016; and U.S. Census Bureau, American FactFinder, "Annual Estimates of the Resident Population: April 1, 2010 to July 1, 2014, United States Metropolitan Statistical Area and Puerto Rico," https://factfinder.census.gov/faces/tableservices/jsf/pages/productview.xhtml?src=bkmk, accessed June 15, 2018.
3. U.S. Census Bureau, 2018 American Community Survey, "Selected Characteristics of the Native and Foreign-Born Populations," https://data.census.gov/cedsci/table?q=S0501%20texas&g=0400000US48&tid=ACSST1Y2018.S0501; Zong, Jeanne Batalova, and Jeffrey Hallock, "Frequently Requested Statistics on Immigrants and Immigration in the United States," February 18, 2018, https://www.migrationpolicy.org/article/frequently-requested-statistics-immigrants-and-immigration-united-states.; and Pew Research Center, "Estimated Unauthorized Immigrant Population, by state, 2019," February 5, 2019, http://www.pewhispanic.org/interactives/u-s-unauthorized-immigrants-by state/.
4. See Alexis de Tocqueville, "The Americans Combat Individualism by the Principle of Interest Rightly Understood," in *Democracy in America* (1835), edited by Issac Kramnick, Book 2, Chapter VIII (New York: W.W. Norton, 2007).
5. Harold Lasswell, *Who Gets What, When, and How* (New York: Meridian, 1958).
6. Institute on Taxation and Economic Policy, "Texas Is a 'Low Tax State' Overall, But Not for Families Living in Poverty," September 19, 2013, http://itep.org/itep_reports/2013/09/texas-is-a-low-tax-state-overall-but-not-for-families-living-in-poverty.php; David S. Knight, Elena Izquierdo, and David E. DeMatthews, "Implementation, Cost, and Funding of Bilingual Education in Texas: Lessons for Local and State Policymakers," Center for Education Research and Policy Studies, College of Education, University of Texas at El Paso, Policy Brief #2, February 2017, https://www.utep.edu/education/cerps/_Files/docs/briefs/CERPS_Policy_Brief_2_Bilingual_Education.pdf; and Kaiser Family Foundation, *State Health Facts*, "Total State Expenditures Per Capita - 2018," https://www.kff.org/other/state-indicator/per-capita-state-spending/?currentTimeframe=0&sortModel=%7B%22colId%22:%22Per%20Capita%20State%20Spending%22,%22sort%22:%22desc%22%7D.
7. David Easton, *A Framework for Political Analysis* (Englewood Cliffs, NJ: Prentice Hall, 1965), Chapter 5.
8. Louise Cowan, "Myth in the Modern World," in *Texas Myths*, edited by Robert F. O'Conner (College Station: Texas A&M University Press, 1986), p. 4.
9. Joseph Campbell, *Thou Art That* (Novato, CA: New World Library, 2001), pp. 1–9.
10. Christopher G. Flood, *Political Myth* (New York: Garland, 1996), Chapter 2. The author also links political myths to political ideology.
11. Cowan, "Myth in the Modern World," p. 14. For an excellent analysis of the concept of the "myth of origin" as integrated into the American mythology, see Robert N. Bellah, *The Broken Covenant: American Civil Religion in Time of Trial* (New York: Seabury, 1975).
12. Texas functioned as a sovereign nation from 1836 to 1845, maintaining diplomatic and trading relationships with other sovereign nations. Some students of state government argue that California and Vermont were sovereign republics prior to joining the union; however, the California "republic" lasted for only 26 days, and Vermont, although in 1771 it declared independence from other British colonies and later American states, never functioned as a sovereign nation and joined the union in 1791.
13. T. R. Fehrenbach, "Texas Mythology: Now and Forever," in *Texas Myths*, pp. 210–17.
14. Robin Doughty, "From Wilderness to Garden: Conquering the Texas Landscape," in *Texas Myths*, p. 105.
15. Michael Granberry, "The Texas Rangers didn't invent police brutality," says the author of a new book, "they perfected it." *The Dallas Morning News*, June 3, 2020.
16. See James E. Crisp, *Sleuthing the Alamo* (New York: Oxford University Press, 2005); and William C. Davis, *Three Roads to the Alamo: The Lives and Fortunes of David Crockett, James Bowie, and William Barret Travis* (New York: HarperCollins, 1998).
17. Lucian W. Pye, "Political Culture," in *International Encyclopedia of the Social Sciences, 12* (New York: Crowell, Collier and Macmillan, 1968), p. 218.
18. Ellen M. Dran, Robert B. Albritton, and Mikel Wyckoff, "Surrogate Versus Direct Measures of Political Culture: Explaining Participation and Policy Attitudes in Illinois," *Publius: The Journal of Federalism, 21* (Spring 1991), p. 17.
19. Daniel Elazar, *American Federalism: A View from the States* (New York: Thomas Y. Crowell, 1966), p. 86. Elazar's three subcultures closely parallel observations made in 1835 by Alexis de Tocqueville in *Democracy in America*, with an introduction by Joseph Epstein (New York: Bantam Dell, 2004).
20. Ibid., pp. 97, 102, 108.
21. Kim Quaile Hill, *Democracy in the Fifty States* (Lincoln: University of Nebraska Press, 1994), Chapter 5.
22. Elazar, *American Federalism*, p. 86.
23. Ibid., pp. 86–89.
24. Ibid., p. 90.
25. Ibid., p. 90.
26. Ibid., p. 91.
27. Ibid., p. 92.
28. Ibid., pp. 92–94.
29. Ellen N. Murray, "Sorrow Whispers in the Winds," *Texas Journal, 14* (Spring–Summer 1992), p. 16.

30. Terry G. Jordan, with John L. Bean Jr. and William M. Holmes, *Texas: A Geography* (Boulder, CO: Westview, 1984), pp. 79–86.
31. David Montejano, *Anglos and Mexicans in the Making of Texas, 1836–1986* (Austin: University of Texas Press, 1987), p. 38.
32. U.S. Census Bureau, *2018 American Community Survey*, "Hispanic or Latino Origin by Race." Hispanics can be of any race.
33. Texas State Data Center, "Texas Population Projections Program, 2018," http://demographics.texas.gov/Data/TPEPP/Projections/.
34. National Association of Latino Elected Officials, *2019 National Directory of Latino Elected Officials* (Los Angeles, CA: NALEO Educational Fund, 2019), https://naleo.org/wp-content/uploads/2019/12/2019.
35. Jordan et al., *Texas: A Geography*, p. 71.
36. Ibid., pp. 71–77.
37. Naomi Andu, Clare Proctor and Miguel Gutierrez Jr., "Conspiracy Theories and Rracist Memes: How a Dozen Texas GOP County Chairs Caused Tturmoil Within the Party," The Texas Tribune, June 5, 2020 updated: June 6, 2020, https://www.texastribune.org/2020/06/05/texas-gop-chairs-racist-george-floyd/
38. V. O. Key, *Southern Politics in State and Nation* (New York: Vintage, 1949), p. 261.
39. For an excellent analysis of Key's projections for political change in Texas, see Chandler Davidson, *Race and Class in Texas Politics* (Princeton, NJ: Princeton University Press, 1990).
40. U.S. Census Bureau, *2010 American Community Survey*, "Selected Social Characteristics in the U.S.," Five Year Estimates, http://www.census.gov.
41. U.S. Census Bureau, "Annual Estimates of the Resident Population for the U.S., Regions, States and Puerto Rico: April 1, 2010 to July 1, 2019," National and State Population Estimates, December, 2019," https://www.census.gov/newsroom/press-kits/2019/national-state-estimates.html.
42. Office of the Governor, Texas 2000 Commission, *Texas Trends*, pp. 5–6; and Office of the Governor, Texas 2000 Commission, *Texas Past and Future: A Survey*, p. 6.
43. U.S. Census Bureau, *2018 American Community Survey*, "Place of Birth by Nativity and Citizenship Status, Total Population" (B05002), http://www.census.gov.
44. U.S. Census Bureau, 2000 Census, "Profile of the Foreign-Born Population in the U.S.: 2000 Tables," https://www.census.gov/data/tables/2000/demo/foreign-born/ppl-145.htm.
45. U.S. Census Bureau, *2018 American Community Survey*, Selected Characteristics of the Native and Foreign-Born Population" (S0501), https://data.census.gov/cedsci/table?q=Characteristics%20of%20Native%20and%20Foreign%20Born%20populations%20in%20texas&g=0400000US48&hidePreview=false&tid=ACSST1Y2018.S0501&t=Native%20and%20Foreign%20Born&vintage=2018&layer=VT_2018_040_00_PY_D1&cid=DP02_0001Ehttps.
46. Ibid.
47. Texas Transportation Institute, Texas A&M University, *2015 Urban Mobility Study*, August 2015, http://mobility.tamu.edu/ums/report/.
48. Texas Transportation Institute, Texas A&M University, *2012 Urban Mobility Study*, December 2012.
49. Texas Transportation Institute, Texas A&M University, *2007 Urban Mobility Study*, September 2007.
50. U.S. Census Bureau, *American Community Survey 2018*, Table S0101:Texas, https://data.census.gov/cedsci/table?q=S0101%20texas&g=0400000US48&tid=ACSST1Y2018.S0101.
51. Texas State Data Center, "Texas Population Projections Program, 2014." This projection is based on Scenario 0.5, which projects "rates of population growth that are slower than 2000–2010 changes, but with steady growth." http://txsdc.utsa.edu/Data/TPEPP/Projections/. The state's population is projected to increase to 37.3 million, and the population of 65-plus to 6.97 million or approximately 18.7 percent of the state's population.
52. U.S. Department of Agriculture, Economic Research Service, *State Fact Sheets: Texas*. Data updated May 23, 2020, https://data.ers.usda.gov/reports.aspx?StateFIPS=48&StateName=Texas&ID=17854.
53. U.S. Census Bureau, "Southern and Western Regions Experience Rapid Growth This Decade," May 21, 2020, https://www.census.gov/newsroom/press-releases/2020/south-west-fastest-growing.html.
54. U.S. Census Bureau, *2018 American Community Survey*, "State and County Quickfacts, Loving and Harris Counties," https://www.census.gov/quickfacts/fact/table/harriscountytexas,US/PST045219., https://factfinder.census.gov/faces/tableservices/jsf/pages/productview.xhtml?src=CF.
55. U.S. Census Bureau, *2018 American Community Survey*, "Income in the Past 12 Months," S1901, https://data.census.gov/cedsci/table?q=income%20data%20for%20texas&g=0400000US48&hidePreview=false&tid=ACSST1Y2018.S1901&t=Income%20%28Households,%20Families,%20Individuals%29&vintage=2018&layer=VT_2018_040_00_PY_D1&cid=S1901_C01_001E.
56. Ibid.
57. U.S. Census Bureau, *2016 American Community Survey*," HOUSEHOLD INCOME IN THE PAST 12 MONTHS (IN 2016 INFLATION-ADJUSTED DOLLARS," (B19001D), https://factfinder.census.gov/faces/tableservices/jsf/pages/productview.xhtml?pid=ACS_16_1YR_B19001D&prodType=table.
58. U.S. Department of Labor, Bureau of Labor Statistics, "Local Area Unemployment Statistics Map," November 2015, http://data.bls.gov/map/MapToolServlet.
59. U.S. Census Bureau, *Income and Poverty in the United States: 2018*, "Poverty Thresholds for 2018 by Size of Family and Number of Related Children Under 18 Years," https://www.census.gov/content/dam/Census/library/publications/2019/demo/p60-266.pdf.
60. U.S. Census Bureau, 2018 *American Community Survey*.
61. Ibid.
62. Alex Arriaga, "Fewer Texans Were Uninsured in 2016, but State Still Has Largest Health Coverage Gap," The Texas Tribune, September 12, 2017, https://www.texastribune.org/2017/09/12/census-report-finds-45-million-texans-are-still-uninsured/; *2018 American Community Survey*.
63. "The Forbes 400," Forbes, October 2, 2019, https://www.forbes.com/forbes-400/#382bfe6f7e2f.
64. Steve H. Murdock, Md. Nazrul Hoque, Martha Michael, Steve White, and Beverly Pecotte, *The Texas Challenge: Population Change and the Future of Texas* (College Station: Texas A&M University Press, 1997), pp. 64–65.

65. U.S. Census Bureau, 2000 Census of the Population; and U.S. Census Bureau, *2018 American Community Survey.*
66. Rupert N. Richardson, Ernest Wallace, and Adrian Anderson, Texas: *The Lone Star State*, 5th ed. (Englewood Cliffs, NJ: Prentice Hall, 1988), p. 2; and U.S. Census Bureau, *2010 Quick Facts.*
67. Key, *Southern Politics in State and Nation*, p. 260.
68. Jordan et al., Texas: *A Geography*, p. 7.
69. Ibid., pp. 18–21.
70. For an expanded analysis of the Texas economy and the dominant role played by corporations, see James W. Lamare, *Texas Politics: Economics, Power and Policy*, 7th ed. (St. Paul, MN: West, 2001), Chapter 2.
71. Texas Comptroller of Public Accounts, "Texas Economic Outlook," *Texas Economic Quarterly* (December 1996), p. 2; Texas Comptroller of Public Accounts, "Fall 2019 Economic Forecasts," https://comptroller.texas.gov/transparency/reports/forecasts/fall2019/rgsp-calendar.php; Statista, "Real Value Added to Gross Domestic Product of Texas in 2019, by Industry," https://www.statista.com/statistics/304890/texas-real-gdp-by-industry/.
72. "Boom, Bust and Back Again: Bullock Tenure Covers Tumultuous Years," *Fiscal Notes* (December 1990), pp. 6–7.
73. "Road to Recovery Long and Bumpy, but Positive Signs Begin to Appear," Fiscal Notes (March 1989), p. 4.
74. Ibid.
75. "Boom, Bust and Back Again," p. 7.
76. Harry Hurt, "Birth of a New Frontier," *Texas Monthly* (April 1984): pp. 130–35.
77. See monthly reports generated by the Texas Railroad Commission, http://www.rrc.state.tx.us.
78. Ali Anari and Mark G. Dotzour, "Monthly Review of the Texas Economy—May 2009," Real Estate Center at Texas A&M University, Technical Report 1862.
79. Susan Combs, Texas Comptroller of Public Accounts, Window on State Government, "American Recovery and Reinvestment Act: Stimulus Tracking," http://www.window.state.tx.us/recovery/transparency/tracking.php.
80. Collin Eaton, "Oil, Manufacturing Will Energize Texas Economy in 2018, Dallas Fed Says," *Houston Chronicle*, January 10, 2018, https://www.houstonchronicle.com/business/economy/article/Texas-economy-to-pick-up-speed-in-18-forecast-12486035.php.
81. U.S. Department of Commerce, Bureau of Economic Analysis, *Regional Economic Accounts*, Table 3, April 7, 2020, https://bea.gov/regional/index.htm.
82. Center for Continuing Study of the California Economy, "California Remains the World's 6th Largest Economy; Could Pass the U.K. in 2017," July 2017, http://www.ccsce.com/PDF/Numbers-July-2017-CA-Economy-Rankings-2016.pdf. World Bank, GDP Growth (Annual %), https://data.worldbank.org/indicator/NY.GDP.MKTP.KD.ZG.
83. Jeffrey Hall "Jobs Supported by State Exports, 2016," Office of Trade and Economic Analysis, International Trade Administration, Department of Commerce, December 2017, https://www.trade.gov/mas/ian/build/groups/public/@tg_ian/documents/webcontent/tg_ian_005558.pdf.
84. International Trade Administration, U.S. Department of Commerce, "Texas Exports, Jobs, and Foreign Investment," February 2018, https://www.trade.gov/mas/ian/statereports/states/tx.pdf.
85. U.S. Census Bureau, "State Exports from Texas," https://www.census.gov/foreign-trade/statistics/state/data/tx.html.
86. Patrick Gillespie "Trump Hammers American's 'Worst Trade Deal,' *CNNMoney*, September 27, 2016: https://money.cnn.com/2016/09/27/news/economy/donald-trump-nafta-hillary-clinton-debate/index.html.
87. Katie Lobosco, Brian Fung and Tami Luhby, 6 key differences between NAFTA and the USMCA deal that replaces it *CNN*, December 17, 2019, https://www.cnn.com/2019/12/10/politics/nafta-us-mexico-canada-trade-deal-differences/index.html.
88. The following discussion of the economic regions is based on a series of reports produced by the Texas Comptroller of Public Accounts. The reports are part of a series initially entitled "Texas in Focus," which began with a statewide summary published in 2008. Detailed reports for the twelve regions were available in 2018 and now are entitled *2018 Regional Reports.*
89. Texas Comptroller of Public Accounts, *Texas in Focus*: The High Plains, April 2008; Texas Comptroller of Public Accounts, "Regional Snapshots: High Plain Region," http://texasahead.org/regionalrpts/img/region_1.pdf; Lubbock Economic Development Alliance, "Health Care," http://lubbockeda.org/why-lubbock/health-care/; and Carey Gillam, "Ogallala Aquifer: Could Critical Water Sources Run dry"; and Texas Comptroller of Public Accounts, "Economy: The High Plains Region: 2018 Regional Report," https://comptroller.texas.gov/economy/economic-data/regions/high-plains.php.
90. John MacCormack, "Shale Play Turns Karnes County Around, but Not Without Trouble," *Houston Chronicle*, February 23, 2013, http://www.chron/news/Houston-texas/Houston/article/Shale-play-turns-Karnes-County-around-but-not-4303201.php; and Center for Community and Business Research, The University of Texas at San Antonio, "Eagle Ford Shale Economic Impact for Counties with Active Drilling," October 2012, http://utsa.edu/today/2013/03/efsstudy.html.
91. "Texas Oil Production Leads Recovery in 2017, Record Output Predicted in 2018," *World Oil*, January 24, 2018, https://www.google.com/search?source=hp&ei=aOKzWuC-KOzPjwTWtYqwCw&q=Texas+Oil+production+leads+recovery+in+2017&oq=Texas+Oil+production+leads+recovery+in+2017&gs_l=psy-ab.3...2082.44296.0.50087.49.48.1.0.0.0.256.6432.1j44j3.48.0....0...1.1.64.psy-ab..0.42.5694...0j46j0i131k1j0i46k1j0i10k1j0i13k1j0i22i30k1j33i22i29i30k1j33i21k1j33i160k1.0.wUi7pWUGNjU.
92. Texas Comptroller of Public Accounts, *Texas in Focus: South Texas*, August 2008; and Texas Comptroller of Public Accounts, "Economy: South Texas Region:2018," https://comptroller.texas.gov/economy/economic-data/regions/south.php.
93. Texas Comptroller of Public Accounts, "Economy: Upper East Region: 2018," https://comptroller.texas.gov/economy/economic-data/regions/upper-east.php.
94. Texas Comptroller of Public Accounts, *Texas in Focus: Upper East Texas*, October 2008.

Chapter 2

1. G. Allan Tarr, *Understanding State Constitutions* (Princeton, NJ: Princeton University Press, 1998), p. 3.
2. Daniel Elazar, "The Principles and Traditions Underlying American State Constitutions," *Publius: The Journal of Federalism*, 12 (Winter 1982), p. 23.
3. Donald S. Lutz, "The Purposes of American State Constitutions," *Publius: The Journal of Federalism*, 12 (Winter 1982), pp. 31–36.

4. Tarr, *Understanding State Constitutions*, pp. 4–5.
5. David Saffell, *State Politics* (Reading, MA: Addison-Wesley, 1984), pp. 23–24.
6. Tarr, *Understanding State Constitutions*, pp. 6–11.
7. Elazar, "Principles and Traditions," pp. 20–21.
8. T. R. Fehrenbach, *Lone Star: A History of Texas and the Texans* (New York: Macmillan, 1968), pp. 152–73.
9. Richard Gambitta, Robert A. Milne, and Carol R. Davis, "The Politics of Unequal Educational Opportunity," in *The Politics of San Antonio*, edited by David R. Johnson, John A. Booth, and Richard J. Harris (Lincoln: University of Nebraska Press, 1983), p. 135.
10. Joe B. Frantz, *Texas: A Bicentennial History* (New York: W.W. Norton, 1976), p. 73.
11. Ibid., p. 76.
12. Fehrenbach, *Lone Star*, p. 265.
13. Frantz, *Texas*, p. 92.
14. Fehrenbach, *Lone Star*, p. 396.
15. Ibid., pp. 398–99.
16. Ibid., p. 401.
17. Ibid., p. 429.
18. J. E. Ericson, "The Delegates to the Convention of 1875: A Reappraisal," *Southwestern Historical Quarterly*, 67 (July 1963), p. 22.
19. Ibid., p. 23.
20. Ibid.
21. Ibid., pp. 25–26.
22. Fehrenbach, *Lone Star*, pp. 374, 431, 434.
23. Ericson, "The Delegates to the Convention of 1875," pp. 24–25.
24. Fehrenbach, *Lone Star*, p. 435.
25. *Texas Constitution*, Art. 1, Sec. 2 and 3.
26. See James Madison, "Federalist 10," in *The Federalist Papers*, by Alexander Hamilton, James Madison, and John Jay with an introduction by Clinton Rossiter (New York: New American Library, 1962), p. 77.
27. Janice May, "Constitutional Revision in Texas," in *The Texas Constitution: Problems and Prospects for Revision* (Arlington, TX: Texas Urban Development Commission, 1971), p. 82.
28. Ibid.
29. David Berman, *State and Local Politics*, 6th ed. (Dubuque, IA: Wm. C. Brown, 1991), p. 61.
30. May, "Constitutional Revision in Texas," p. 76.
31. John E. Bebout, "The Problem of the Texas Constitution," in *The Texas Constitution*, p. 9.
32. Ibid., p. 11.
33. *Houston Chronicle*, January 8, 1974.
34. Nelson Wolff, *Challenge of Change* (San Antonio, TX: Naylor, 1975), pp. 45–46.
35. Bebout, "The Problem of the Texas Constitution," pp. 45–46.
36. *Houston Chronicle*, October 15, 1975.
37. Lewis A. Froman, Jr., "Some Effects of Interest Group Strength in State Politics," *American Political Science Review*, 60 (December 1966), pp. 952–63.

Chapter 3

1. "The Nation's Medical Countermeasure Stockpile: Opportunities to Improve the Efficiency, Effectiveness, and Sustainability of the CDC Strategic National Stockpile: Workshop Summary," https://www.ncbi.nlm.nih.gov/books/NBK396378/#:~:text=It%20began%20in%201998%20with,vaccine%20stockpiling%20activities%20at%20CDC.
2. Most Americans Say Federal Government Has Primary Responsibility for COVID-19 Testing", https://www.people-press.org/2020/05/12/most-americans-say-federal-government-has-primary-responsibility-for-covid-19-testing/
3. Patrick Svitek and Cassandra Pollock, "County Republican Parties in Texas' GOP Strongholds Say Gov. Greg Abbot Going Too Far in Coronavirus Response," *Texas Tribune*, July 9, 2020, https://www.texastribune.org/2020/07/09/greg-abbott-republican-criticism-coronavirus-response/.
4. See Alexis de Tocqueville's highly informative assessment of the American experience with centralized authority. Alexis de Tocqueville, *Democracy in America*, with an introduction by Joseph Epstein (New York: Bantam Dell, 2004).
5. David C. Nice, "The Intergovernmental Setting of State-Local Relations," in *Governing Partners: State-Local Relations in the United States*, edited by Russell L. Hanson (Boulder, CO: Westview, 1998), p. 17.
6. James Madison, "The Federalist No. 10: The Utility of the Union as a Safeguard Against Domestic Faction and Insurrection," *Daily Advertiser*, November 22, 1787.
7. For a discussion of the Dillon rule, see Anwar Syed, *The Political Theory of American Local Government* (New York: Random House, 1966), Chapter 3.
8. Thomas J. Anton, *American Federalism and Public Policy* (New York: Random House, 1989), p. 3.
9. See William H. Stewart, "Metaphors, Models, and the Development of Federal Theory," *Publius: The Journal of Federalism*, 12 (Winter 1982), pp. 5–24; and William H. Stewart, *Concepts of Federalism* (Lanham, MD: Center for the Study of Federalism and University Press of America, 1984).
10. William T. Gormley Jr., "Money and Mandates: The Politics of Intergovernmental Conflict," *Publius: The Journal of Federalism*, 36 (May 2006), pp. 523–40. This is an excellent article that provides a method for disaggregating broad trends in federal–state relationships.
11. Anton, *American Federalism and Public Policy*, p. 19.
12. U.S. Constitution, Article I, Section 8, paragraph 18.
13. U.S. Constitution, Article VI.
14. For an excellent summary of the guarantees to and limitations on state governments defined by the U.S. Constitution, see Thomas Dye, *American Federalism* (Lexington, KY: D. C. Heath, 1990), pp. 9–11.
15. U.S. Constitution, Article IV, Section 1.
16. *Commonwealth of Kentucky v. Denison, Governor*, 65 U.S. (24 How.) 66 (1861).
17. *Puerto Rico v. Branstad*, 483 U.S. 219 (1987).
18. Kenyon Bunch and Richard J. Hardy, "Continuity or Change in Interstate Extradition? Assessing *Puerto Rico v. Branstad*," *Publius: The Journal of Federalism*, 21 (Winter 1991), p. 59.
19. National Center for Interstate Compacts, The Council of State Governments, "10 Frequently Asked Questions," http://www.csg.org/knowledgecenter/docs/ncic/CompactFAQ.pdf; National Center for Interstate Compacts, The Council of State Governments, "Texas Compacts," http://apps.csg.org/ncic/State.aspx?search=1&id=43.
20. U.S. Constitution, Article III, Section 2.
21. Morton Grodzins and Daniel Elazar, "Centralization and Decentralization in the American Federal System," in

A Nation of States, 2nd ed., edited by Robert A. Goldwin (Chicago: Rand McNally, 1974), p. 4.
22. Deil S. Wright, *Understanding Intergovernmental Relations*, 2nd ed. (Monterey, CA: Brooks/Cole, 1982), pp. 60–68.
23. Ibid., p. 46.
24. *McCulloch v. Maryland*, 4 Wheaton 316 (1819).
25. Thomas R. Dye, *Politics in States and Communities*, 8th ed. (Englewood Cliffs, NJ: Prentice Hall, 1994), p. 67.
26. Timothy Conlan, with an introduction by Samuel H. Beer, *New Federalism* (Washington, D.C.: The Brookings Institution, 1988), p. 5.
27. V. O. Key, *The Responsible Electorate* (Cambridge, MA: Harvard University Press, 1966), p. 31.
28. Daniel J. Elazar, *American Federalism: A View from the States*, 2nd ed. (New York: Harper & Row, 1972), p. 47.
29. Office of Management and Budget, Historical Tables, Table 21.1, "Summary Comparison of Total Outlays for Grants to State and Local Governments: 1940–2023 (in Current Dollars, as Percentages of Total Outlays, as Percentages of GDP, and in Constant [FY 2009] Dollars)," https://www.whitehouse.gov/omb/budget/Historicals; and Natalie Keegan, "Federal Grants-in-Aid Administration: A Primer," *Congressional Research Service*, October 3, 2012, https://www.fas.org/sgp/crs/misc/R42769.pdf.
30. Note that all figures are presented in FY 2012 dollars to make comparisons over time while accounting for inflation. Office of Management and Budget, Historical Tables, Table 12. 1, "Summary Comparison of Total Outlays for Grants to State and Local Governments: 1940–2025," https://www.whitehouse.gov/omb/historical-tables/.
31. "Percentage of State Revenue from Federal Funds, FY 2000-2017," Fiscal 50: State Trends and Analysis, Pew Charitable Trust, https://www.pewtrusts.org/en/research-and-analysis/data-visualizations/2014/fiscal-50#ind1. Accessed on June 8, 2020.
32. Ibid.
33. Conlan, *New Federalism*, p. 6 ; Glenn Hegar, "Revenue by Source for Fiscal Year 2018," Texas Comptroller of Public Accounts, https://comptroller.texas.gov/transparency/reports/revenue-by-source/.
34. Dye, *Politics in States and Communities*, p. 83.
35. Conlan, *New Federalism*, p. 3.
36. Ibid., pp. 3, 19–30, 77–81.
37. Ibid., p. 90.
38. Joseph F. Zimmerman, "Federal Preemption under Reagan's New Federalism," *Publius: The Journal of Federalism, 21* (Winter 1991), p. 11.
39. Ibid., p. 26.
40. Ibid.
41. Ibid., p. 27.
42. Timothy J. Conlan, "And the Beat Goes On: Intergovernmental Mandates and Preemption in an Era of Deregulation," *Publius: The Journal of Federalism, 21* (Summer 1991), p. 52.
43. Joseph F. Zimmerman, "Preemption in the U.S. Federal System," *Publius: The Journal of Federalism, 23* (Fall 1993), p. 9.
44. Timothy J. Conlan and David R. Beam, "Federal Mandates: The Record of Reform and Future Prospects," *Intergovernmental Perspective, 18* (Fall 1992), p. 9.
45. State of Texas, Legislative Budget Board, *Analysis of Federal Initiatives and State Expenditures*, June 15, 1994.
46. G. Ross Stephens and Nelson Wikstrom, *American Intergovernmental Relations: A Fragmented Federal Polity* (New York: Oxford University Press, 2007), pp. 40–41.
47. Paul L. Posner, "Unfunded Mandates Reform Act: 1996 and Beyond," *Publius: The Journal of Federalism, 27* (Spring 1997), p. 53; and "Unfunded Mandates Reform Act: History, Impact, and Issues," *Congressional Research Service*, January 2, 2020, https://fas.org/sgp/crs/misc/R40957.pdf/
48. Sanford F. Schram and Carol S. Weissert, "The State of American Federalism, 1996–1997," *Publius: The Journal of Federalism, 27* (Spring 1997), pp. 5–8.
49. Alan K. Ota, "Highway Law Benefits Those Who Held Purse Strings," *Congressional Quarterly Weekly, 56* (June 13, 1998), pp. 1595–96.
50. Schram and Weissert, "The State of American Federalism, 1996–1997," p. 8.
51. Ibid., p. 1.
52. John Kincaid, "The Devolution Tortoise and the Centralization Hare," *New England Economic Review* (May–June 1998), pp. 36, 38.
53. Richard L. Cole, Rodney V. Hissong, and Enid Arvidson, "Devolution: Where's the Revolution?" *Publius: The Journal of Federalism, 29* (Fall 1999), pp. 99–112.
54. George W. Bush, "Memorandum on the Interagency Working Group on Federalism," February 26, 2001; and Joseph Francis Zimmerman, *Contemporary American Federalism*, 2nd ed. (Albany: State University of New York Press, 2008), p. 127.
55. Daniel Henniger, "Homeland Security Will Reshape the Homeland," *Wall Street Journal*, November 22, 2002, p. 16.
56. John Dinan, "The State of American Federalism 2007–2008: Resurgent State Influence in the National Policy Process and Continued State Policy Innovation," *Publius: The Journal of Federalism, 38* (May 2008), p. 383.
57. Ibid.
58. Deil S. Wright, "Federalism and Intergovernmental Relations: Traumas, Tensions, and Trends," in *The Book of the States, 2003* (Lexington, KY: The Council of State Governments, 2003), p. 23.
59. Sidney M. Milkis and Jesse H. Rhodes, "George W. Bush, the Party System, and American Federalism," *Publius: The Journal of Federalism, 37* (May 2007), p. 483.
60. Tim Conlan and John Dinan, "Federalism, the Bush Administration, and the Transformation of American Conservatism," *Publius: The Journal of Federalism, 37* (April 2007), pp. 283–88.
61. Milkis and Rhodes, "George W. Bush, the Party System, and American Federalism," p. 478.
62. John Dinan, "The State of American Federalism 2007–2008," p. 381.
63. Ibid., pp. 382–401.
64. "Economic Stimulus—Jobs Bills," *New York Times*, updated March 15, 2012.
65. For detailed information about the stimulus funds in Texas, see the Texas Comptroller of Public Accounts website at http://www.window.state.tx.us/recovery/, accessed April 12, 2016.
66. U.S. General Accounting Office, "Recovery Act: As Initial Implementation Unfolds in States and Localities, Continued Attention to Accountability Issues Is Essential," GAO-09-580, April 23, 2009; and Texas Comptroller of Public Accounts, "American Recovery and Reinvestment Act: A Texas Eye on the Dollars," *Window on State Government*, http://window.state.tx.us/recovery/, accessed April 12, 2016.

67. Kate Nocera, "Perry's Texas Awash in Federal Money," *Politico*, December 25, 2011.
68. Barack Obama, "Memorandum for the Heads of Executive Departments and Agencies," May 20, 2009.
69. Lauren McGaughy, "With Trump in Charge, Why Is Texas Still Suing the Federal Government? Because Now It Can Win." *Dallas Morning News*, February 8, 2019, https://www.dallasnews.com/news/politics/2018/02/08/with-trump-in-charge-why-is-texas-still-suing-the-federal-government-because-now-it-can-win/, accessed on June 1, 2020.
70. Daniel C. Vock, "How Obama Changed the Relationship Between Washington, the States and the Cities," *Governing: The States and Localities*, June 2016, http://www.governing.com/topics/politics/gov-obama-federalism.html (accessed on April 2, 2018); and Noah Feldman, "Sanctuary Cities Are Safe, Thanks to Conservatives," *Bloomberg View*, November 29, 2016, http://www.bloomberg.com/view/articles/2016-11-29/sanctuary-cities-are-safe-thanks-to-conservatives, accessed April 2, 2018.
71. Hanna Nordhaus, "What Trump's Shrinking of National Monuments Actually Means," *National Geographic*, February 2, 2018, http://news.nationalgeographic.com/2017/12/trump-shrinks-bears-ears-grand-staircase-escalante-national-monuments/, accessed April 2, 2018.
72. Nadja Popovich, Livia Labeck-Ripka and Kendra Pierre-Louis, "The Trump Administration is Reversing 100 Environmental Rules. Here's the Full List," *The New York Times*, May 20, 2020, https://www.nytimes.com/interactive/2020/climate/trump-environment-rollbacks.html.
73. Juliet Eilperin and Seung Min Kim, "Trump Defends Environmental Record That Critics Call Disastrous," *The Washington Post*, July 8, 2019, https://www.washingtonpost.com/climate-environment/trump-defends-environmental-record-that-critics-call-disastrous/2019/07/08/e46d390e-a193-11e9-bd56-eac6bb02d01d_story.html, accessed October 1, 2020; Juliet Eilperin and Jeff Stein, "Trump Signs Order to Waive Environmental Reviews for Key Projects," *The Washington Post*, June 4, 2020, https://www.washingtonpost.com/climate-environment/2020/06/04/trump-sign-order-waive-environmental-reviews-key-projects/, accessed October 1, 2020.
74. Katie Benner and Jennifer Medina, "Trump Administration Sues California Over Immigration Laws," *The New York Times*, March 6, 2018, http://www.nytimes.com/2018/03/06/us/politics/justice-department-california-sanctuary-cities.html, accessed April 2, 2018.
75. Kathleen Ronayne, "California Governor Finds New Friend in Washington: Trump," *NBC Bay Area*, April 24, 2020, https://www.nbcbayarea.com/news/california/california-governor-finds-new-friend-in-washington-trump/2278723/, accessed October 1, 2020.
76. Laurel Rosenhall, "Trump and Newsom: Political Frenemies Make Nice Amid California's Mounting Disasters," *Cal Matters*, September 14, 2020, https://calmatters.org/politics/2020/09/newsom-trump-california-meeting/, accessed October 1, 2020.
77. Ilya Somin, "Federalism, the Constitution, and Sanctuary Cities," *The Washington Post*, November 26, 2016, https://www.washingtonpost.com/news/volokh-conspiracy/wp/2016/11/26/federalism-the-constitution-and-sanctuary-cities/?utm_term=.62e6a22f784d, accessed April 2, 2018.
78. "Federalism Under President Trump," National Constitution Center, https://constitutioncenter.org/debate/podcasts/federalism-under-president-trump, accessed April 1, 2018; and Scott Bomboy, "Federal Marijuana Policy ChTange Raises Significant Questions," National Constitution Center, https://constitutioncenter.org/blog/federal-marijuana-policy-change-raises-significant-questions.
79. See for instance, Sachariah Sippy, "Trump and Biden Debate Over 'Law and Order' Highlighted a Secret to Biden's Success," *NBC News*, September 30, 2020, https://www.nbcnews.com/think/opinion/trump-biden-s-debate-over-law-order-highlighted-secret-biden-ncna1241367, accessed on October 1, 2020; Tim Alberta, "Is This the Last Stand of the 'Law and Order' Repubicans?" *Politico*, June 8, 2020, https://www.politico.com/news/magazine/2020/06/08/last-stand-law-and-order-republicans-306333, accessed on October 1, 2020.
80. Population Statistics, Federal Bureau of Prisons, https://www.bop.gov/mobile/about/population_statistics.jsp.
81. *Garcia* v. *San Antonio Metropolitan Transit Authority*, 105 S. Ct. 1005 (1985).
82. Anton, *American Federalism and Public Policy*, pp. 14–16.
83. Dye, *American Federalism*, pp. 8–12.
84. *United States* v. *Lopez*, 115 S. Ct. 1624 (1995); and Schram and Weissert, "The State of American Federalism, 1996–1997," p. 10.
85. *Bush* v. *Vera*, 116 S. Ct. 1941 (1996); *Easley* v. *Cromartie*, 121 S. Ct. 2239 (2001); and *The New York Times*, April 19, 2001, p. 1.
86. Weissert and Schram, "The State of American Federalism, 1995–1996," p. 12; and *Medtronic, Inc.* v. *Lohr et vir.*, 116 S. Ct. 2240 (1996).
87. *City of Boerne, Texas* v. *Flores*, 117 S. Ct. 2157 (1997).
88. Schram and Weissert, "The State of American Federalism, 1996–1997," p. 26.
89. *Printz* v. *United States*, 117 S. Ct. 2365 (1997).
90. Weissert and Schram, "The State of American Federalism, 1995–1996," p. 13.
91. Ibid., p. 10; *Romer et al.* v. *Evans et al.*, 116 S. Ct. 1620 (1996); and *United States* v. *Virginia et al.*, 116 S. Ct. 2264 (1996).
92. Weissert and Schram, "The State of American Federalism, 1995–1996," p. 13; and *Seminole Tribe* v. *Florida*, 116 S. Ct. 1941 (1996).
93. Shama Gamkhar and J. Mitchell Pickerill, "The State of American Federalism 2010–2011: The Economy, Healthcare Reform, and Midterm Elections Shape the Intergovernmental Agenda," *Publius: The Journal of Federalism*, 41 (Summer 2011), p. 379.
94. Ibid.
95. Ibid., p. 380.
96. Ibid., pp. 382–84.
97. John Dinan, "The U.S. Supreme Court and Federalism in the Twenty-First Century," *State and Local Government Review* 49 (September 2017), pp. 215–28.
98. Laura Schultz and Michelle Cummings, "Giving or Getting? New York's Balance of Payments with the Federal Government," Rockefeller Institute of Government, January 8, 2019, https://rockinst.org/issue-area/new-yorks-balance-of-payments-with-the-federal-government/.
99. Rockefeller Institute of Government, "Giving or Getting? New York's Balance of Payments with the Federal Government," September 2017, https://rockinst.org/issue-area/giving-getting-new-yorks-balance-payments-federal-government-2/.

100. Hillary Hoffower, "11 States Pay More in Federal Taxes Than They Get Back – Here's How Every State Fares," January 14, 2019, *Business Insider*, https://www.businessinsider.com/federal-taxes-federal-services-difference-by-state-2019-1#connecticut-7
101. Texas Legislative Budget Board, Legislative Budget Board Fiscal Size-Up: 2018–2019 Biennium, Austin, TX: Legislative Budget Board, May 2016, Figure 28, p. 31–35, http://www.lbb.state.tx.us/Documents/Publications/Fiscal_SizeUp/Fiscal_SizeUp.pdf. 100.5: Ibid., Figure 139, pp. 178
102. Ibid., Figure 148, pp. 199.
103. Office of the Governor, State Grants Team, https://egrants.gov.texas.gov/Default.aspx.
104. Robert B. Hawkins, "Pre-emption: The Dramatic Rise of Federal Supremacy," *Journal of State Government*, 63 (January–March 1990), p. 12.
105. M. Delal Baer, "North American Free Trade," *Foreign Affairs*, 70 (Fall 1991), p. 138.
106. Office of the United States Trade Representative, "USTR Robert Lighthizer Issues Statement on Status of NAFTA Renegotiation." Accessed on June 26, 2018 at https://ustr.gov/about-us/policy-offices/press-office/press-releases/2018/may/ustr-robert-lighthizer-issues-statement.
107. Joan B. Anderson, "Maquiladoras and Border Industrialization: Impact on Economic Development in Mexico," *Journal of Borderland Studies*, 5 (Spring 1990), p. 5.
108. Michael Patrick, "Maquiladoras and South Texas Border Economic Development," *Journal of Borderland Studies*, 4 (Spring 1989), p. 90.
109. Martin E. Rosenfeldt, "Mexico's in Bond Export Industries and U.S. Legislation: Conflictive Issues," *Journal of Borderland Studies*, 5 (Spring 1990), p. 57.
110. Patrick, "Maquiladoras and South Texas Border Economic Development," p. 90.
111. Steven Downer, "Proposal Would Boost Taxes on Maquiladora Plants," *Plastics News*, October 8, 2013, accessed December 1, 2013, at http://www.plasticsnews.com/article/20131008/NEWS/131009932/proposal-would-boost-taxes-on-maquiladora-plants#; and Dr. Francisco Lara-Valencia, "Report of the 108th Arizona Town Hall 'Arizona & Mexico,'" April, 2016, p.42, https://eller.arizona.edu/sites/default/files/Arizona-and-Mexico-Final-Report-108th-Arizona-Town-Hall-April-2016.pdf.
112. Corinne Chin and Erika Schultz, "Disappearing Daughters," *Seattle Times*, March 8, 2020, https://projects.seattletimes.com/2020/femicide-juarez-mexico-border/.
113. Baer, "North American Free Trade," pp. 132–49.
114. https://data.worldbank.org/indicator/NY.GDP.MKTP.CD.
115. https://www.census.gov/foreign-trade/balance/c2010.html; and https://www.census.gov/foreign-trade/balance/c1220.html.
116. https://data.worldbank.org/indicator/NY.GDP.MKTP.CD?locations=EU-US-CN.
117. Villarreal and Fergusson, "NAFTA at 20," *Congressional Research Service*, February 21, 2013, http://www.fas.org/sgp/crs/row/R42965.pdf.
118. Binyamin Appelbaum, "U.S. and Mexico Sign Trucking Deal," *The New York Times*, July 6, 2011.
119. Emily Cochrane, "Senate Passes Revised NAFTA, Sending Pact to Trump's Desk," *The New York Times*, January 16, 2020.
120. Villarreal and Fergusson, "NAFTA at 20," *Congressional Research Service*, February 21, 2013, http://www.fas.org/sgp/crs/row/R42965.pdf; "U.S. Trade in Goods by Country," United States Census Bureau, https://www.census.gov/foreign-trade/balance/index.html; "Trade in Goods with Mexico," United States Census Bureau, https://www.census.gov/foreign-trade/balance/c2010.html; and "Top Trading Partners," United States Census Bureau, https://www.census.gov/foreign-trade/statistics/highlights/top/top1712yr.html.
121. http://www.census.gov/foreign-trade/statistics/state/data/tx.html; http://www.thetexaseconomy.org/business-industry/trade-logistics/border-trade/index.php; and "State Exports from Texas," United States Census Bureau, https://www.census.gov/foreign-trade/statistics/state/data/tx.html.
122. Villarreal and Fergusson, "NAFTA at 20," *Congressional Research Service*, February 21, 2013, http://www.fas.org/sgp/crs/row/R42965.pdf; see also International Trade Administration, *TradeStats Express*, http://tse.export.gov/TSE/TSEhome.aspx; and "Top Trading Partners," United States Census Bureau, https://www.census.gov/foreign-trade/statistics/highlights/top/top1712yr.html.
123. United States Department of Transportation, Border Crossing/Entry Data, Annual Data, https://data.transportation.gov/Research-and-Statistics/Border-Crossing-Entry-Data/keg4-3bc2/data. Accessed on June 9, 2020.
124. This discussion of the history of immigration laws is based on Clarke E. Cochran, Lawrence C. Mayer, T. R. Carr, and N. Joseph Cayer, *American Public Policy*, 9th ed. (Boston: Wadsworth, 2009), pp. 400–406; Federation for American Immigration Reform, "History of U.S. Immigration Laws," January 2008; and Cornell University Law School, "Immigration Law: An Overview," http://www.law.cornell.edu/wex/Immigration.
125. Robert W. Gardner and Leon F. Bouvier, "The United States," in *Handbook on International Migration*, edited by William J. Serow, Charles B. Nam, David F. Sly, and Robert H. Weller (New York: Greenwood Press, 1990), p. 342.
126. James F. Pearce and Jeffery W. Gunther, "Illegal Immigration from Mexico: Effects on the Texas Economy," *Federal Reserve Bank of Dallas Economic Review* (September 1985), p. 4.
127. "Congress Clears Overhaul of Immigration Law," *Congressional Quarterly Almanac*, 1986 (Washington, D.C.: Congressional Quarterly Press, 1987), pp. 61–67.
128. Dan Carney, "Law Restricts Illegal Immigration," *Congressional Quarterly Weekly Report*, 54 (November 16, 1996), p. 3287.
129. Steven A. Camarota, "Immigrants in the United States, 2007: A Profile of America's Foreign-Born Population," Center for Immigration Studies, November 2007.
130. Jeffrey L. Katz, "Welfare Overhaul Law," *Congressional Quarterly Weekly Report*, 54 (September 21, 1996), pp. 2696–2705; and Stephen A. Camarota, "Back Where We Started: An Examination of Trends in Immigrant Welfare Use since Welfare Reform," Center for Immigration Studies, March 2003.

131. U.S. Customs and Border Protection, Secure Border Initiative, "Pedestrian Fence 225," November 2008.
132. Josh Gerstein and Jonathan Allen, "Barack Obama Orders Guard to Mexican Border," *Politico*, May 25, 2010.
133. Scott Wong and Shira Toeplitz, "DREAM Act Dies in Senate," *Politico*, December 20, 2010.
134. Emma Platoff, "Texas and 6 Other States Sue to End DACA," The Texas Tribune, May 1, 2018, https://www.texastribune.org/2018/05/01/texas-and-six-other-states-sue-end-daca/.
135. Adam Liptak, "'Dreamers' Tell Supreme Court Ending DACA During Pandemic Would Be 'Catastrophic,'" *The New York Times,* March 27, 2020.
136. Mike Guo, "Immigration Enforcement Action: 2019," Table 6, Office of Immigration Statistics, Homeland Security, September 2020, Table 7, https://www.dhs.gov/sites/default/files/publications/immigration-statistics/yearbook/2019/
137. Ibid.
138. Bryan Baker, "Estimates of the Unauthorized Immigrant Population Residing in the United States: January 2014," Department of Homeland Security, Population Estimates, July 2017, https://www.dhs.gov/sites/default/files/publications/Unauthorized%20Immigrant%20Population%20Estimates%20in%20the%20US%20January%202014_1.pdf; Office of Immigration Statistics, "Population Estimates: Illegal Alien Population Residing in the United States: January 2015," Department of Homeland Security, December 2018, https://www.dhs.gov/sites/default/files/publications/18_1214_PLCY_pops-est-report.pdf
139. Jens Manuel Krogstad, Jeffrey S. Passel, and D'Vera Cohn "5 Facts About Illegal Immigration in the U.S.," Pew Research Center, July 12, 2019, http://www.pewresearch.org/fact-tank/2019/06/12/5-facts-about-illegal-immigration-in-the-u-s/.
140. Ibid.
141. "Fact Sheet: Immigrants in Texas," American Immigration Council, June 4, 2020, https://www.americanimmigrationcouncil.org/research/immigrants-in-texas.
142. Ibid.
143. Ibid.
144. Ibid.
145. Jenny Jarvie, "Number of Immigrants Caught at Mexican Border Plunges 40% under Trump," *Los Angeles Times*, March 9, 2017, http://www.latimes.com/nation/la-na-border-apprehensions-20170309-story.html.
146. U.S. Border Control, https://www.cbp.gov/sites/default/files/assets/documents/2017-Dec/BP%20Total%20Monthly%20Apps%20by%20Sector%20and%20Area%2C%20FY2000-FY2017.pdf.
147. Christopher Sherman, Martha Mendoza and Garance Burke, "U.S. held record number of migrant children in custody in 2019," The Associated Press, November 12, 2019.)
148. Julia Ainsley and Jacob Soboroff, "Lawyers Say They Can't Find the Parents of 545 Migrant Children Separated by Trump Administration," NBC News, October 20,2020, https://www.nbcnews.com/politics/immigration/lawyers-say-they-can-t-find-parents-545-migrant-children-n1244066.
149. Rose L. Thayer, "Additional 540 Troops Heading to the US-Mexico Border To Back Up Border Agents During Coronavirus Outbreak," *Stars and Stripes*, April 1, 2020, https://www.stripes.com/news/us/additional-540-troops-heading-to-us-mexico-border-to-back-up-border-agents-during-coronavirus-outbreak-1.624512.
150. National Conference of State Legislators, Immigration Policy Project, "2009 Immigration-Related Bills and Resolutions in the States," April 2009.
151. Adam Liptak, "Court to Weigh Arizona Statute on Immigration," *The New York Times*, December 12, 2011.
152. Julián Aguilar, "Federal Appeals Court's Ruling Upholds Most of Texas' 'Sanctuary Cities' Law," *Texas Tribune*, March 13, 2018. https://www.texastribune.org/2018/03/13/texas-immigration-sanctuary-cities-law-court/.
153. Vanessa Romo, "Gov. Greg Abbott Says New Refugees Won't Be Allowed to Settle in Texas," January 10, 2020, https://www.npr.org/2020/01/10/795414116/gov-greg-abbott-says-new-refugees-wont-be-allowed-to-settle-in-texas.
154. David Agren, "Mexico Maelstrom: How the Drug Violence Got So Bad," The Guardian, December 26, 2017, https://www.theguardian.com/world/2017/dec/26/mexico-maelstrom-how-the-drug-violence-got-so-bad; and Vanessa Romo, "Mexico Reports Highest Ever Homicide Rate in 2018, Tops 33,000 Investigations," NPR, January 23, 2019, https://www.npr.org/2019/01/23/687579971/mexico-reports-highest-ever-homicide-rate-in-2018-tops-33-000-investigations
155. "Drug Violence Blamed for Mexico's Record 29,168 Murders in 2017," *The Guardian*, January 21, 2018, https://www.theguardian.com/world/2018/jan/21/drug-violence-blamed-mexico-record-murders-2017; and "Mexico Records Most Violent Year in Decades," *DW*, December 15, 2017, http://www.dw.com/en/mexico-records-most-violent-year-in-decades/a-41924460.
156. "Julián Aguilar, "In Texas and Beyond, Some Watch Mexican Presidential Campaign with Free Trade Concerns," The Texas Tribune, January 11, 2018, https://www.texastribune.org/2018/01/11/will-free-trade-be-chopping-block-after-mexicos-elections-some-fear-s-/; and "2019 was the 4th Deadliest Year in Juarez; Nearly 1,500 Slain," *KVIA ABC-7*, https://kvia.com/news/border/2020/01/02/2019-was-4th-deadliest-year-in-juarez-nearly-1500-slain/.
157. *CQ Researcher*, 2014, CQ Press, http://os.cqpress.com/citycrime/2013/2014_CityCrimeRankingsbyPopulation.pdf; and "How Safe Is El Paso, TX?", *U.S. News & World Report*, https://realestate.usnews.com/places/texas/el-paso/crime, accessed June 3, 2020.
158. Joan Anderson and Martin de la Rosa, "Economic Survival Strategies of Poor Families on the Mexican Border," *Journal of Borderland Studies,* 6 (Spring 1991), p. 51.
159. Howard G. Applegate, C. Richard Bath, and Jeffery T. Trannon, "Binational Emissions Trading in an International Air Shed: The Case of El Paso, Texas, and Ciudad Juarez," *Journal of Borderland Studies*, 4 (Fall 1989), pp. 1–25.
160. "Military Active-Duty Personnel, Civilians by State," *Governing the State and Localities,* https://www.governing.com/gov-data/public-workforce-salaries/military-civilian-active-duty-employee-workforce-numbers-by-state.html

Chapter 4

1. Ross Ramsey, "Analysis: When Local Control Is Remote," *The Texas Tribune*, March 12, 2015, http://www.texastribune.org/2015/03/12/analysis-local-control-sometimes/.
2. Brandon Formby, "City Leaders, Advocates Criticize Abbott for Special Session Agenda," *The Texas Tribune*, June 6, 2017, https://www.texastribune.org/2017/06/06/city-leaders-advocates-criticize-abbott-special-session-agenda/.
3. Shaila Dewan, "States Are Blocking Local Regulations, Often at Industry's Behest," *The New York Times*, February 23, 2015.
4. U.S. Bureau of the Census, "Population of the 100 Largest Urban Places: 1880," https://www.census.gov/population/www/documentation/twps0027/tab11.txt.
5. For an excellent overview of urban development in Texas, see Char Miller and David R. Johnson, "The Rise of Urban Texas," in *Urban Texas: Politics and Development*, edited by Char Miller and Heywood T. Sanders (College Station: Texas A&M University Press, 1990).
6. U.S. Bureau of the Census, "Population of the 100 Largest Urban Places: 1880, http://www.census.gov/population/www/censusdata/files/urpop0090.txt.
7. U.S. Census Bureau, *2018 American Community Survey*, https://www.census.gov/acs/www/data/data-tables-and-tools/data-profiles/2018/.
8. Texas Municipal League, "TML City Officials Directory," https://directory.tml.org/search/government; and Texas State Historical Association, *Texas Almanac*, "Facts," http://texasalmanac.com/topics/facts-profile.
9. Anwar Hussain Syed, *The Political Theory of American Local Government* (New York: Random House, 1966), p. 27.
10. Ibid., pp. 38–52. Syed presents a summary of Jefferson's theory of local government.
11. Roscoe C. Martin, *Grass Roots* (Tuscaloosa: University of Alabama Press, 1957), p. 5; and Robert C. Wood, *Suburbia* (Boston: Houghton Mifflin, 1958), p. 18.
12. Texas Conference of Urban Counties, http://www.cuc.org.
13. Advisory Commission on Intergovernmental Relations, *State and Local Roles in the Federal System* (Washington, D.C.: ACIR, 1982), pp. 32–33.
14. *City of Clinton* v. *The Cedar Rapids and Missouri River Railroad Co.*, 24 Iowa 455 (1868).
15. Roscoe C. Martin, *The Cities in the Federal System* (New York: Atherton, 1965), pp. 28–35.
16. Texas Municipal League, "TML City Officials Directory: Search by Government Type," https://directory.tml.org/search/government.
17. Ibid.
18. Zeke MacCormack, "Boerne Rejects Charter Changes," *San Antonio Express-News*, May 7, 2002, p. 58.
19. Bexar County Elections, "Official Results," Joint City and School Election, May 9, 2015, http://home.bexar.org/elections/reports/PDF/20150509_EL45A.HTM.
20. Texas Municipal League, "TML City Officials Directory: Search by Government Type," https://directory.tml.org/search/government.
21. Rachael Pitts, Texas Municipal League, phone and e-mail conversations, December 17, 2013, and January 6, 2014.
22. Murray S. Stedman, *Urban Politics*, 2nd ed. (Cambridge, MA: Winthrop. 1975), p. 51.
23. Beryl E. Pettus and Randall W. Bland, *Texas Government Today*, 3rd ed. (Homewood, IL: Dorsey, 1984), p. 347.
24. "Government Salaries Explorer," *The Texas Tribune*, updated July 17, 2019.
25. National League of Cities, *Forms of Municipal Government*, http://nlc.org/build-skills-and-networks/resources/cities-101/city-structures/forms-of-municipal-government; and Auditor's Office, City of Portland, *City Government Structure*, http://www.portlandonline.com/auditor/index.cfm?a=9178&c=27481.
26. Texas Municipal League, *Local Government in Texas*, www.tml.org/Handbook-M&C/Chapter1.pdf; Rachael Pitts, Texas Municipal League, phone and e-mail conversations, December 17, 2013, and January 6, 2014.
27. "Mayor and Council Salaries at Austin," *Texas Tribune*, https://salaries.texastribune.org/austin/departments/mayor-council/.
28. *Dallas City Charter*, Chapter 3, Section 4.
29. Tom Benning, "Dallas Voters Approve Pay Raise for City Council, Mayor," *Dallas Morning News*, November 5, 2014, http://www.dallasnews.com/news/politics/headlines/20141105-dallas-voters-approve-pay-raise-for-city-council-mayor.ece.
30. See the city charter of San Antonio, Article 2, Sections 6 and 9.
31. Drew Joseph, "Voters Pass Rail, Council-pay Amendments," *mySA*, Updated 10:21 am, Sunday, May 10, 2015, http://www.mysanantonio.com/news/local/article/Early-voters-favor-rail-council-pay-amendments-6253597.php.
32. Wilbourn E. Benton, *Texas Politics*, 5th ed. (Chicago: Nelson-Hall, 1984), p. 260.
33. Dennis Foley, "How Does San Antonio's City Manager Salary Compare to Other Cities?" KTSA, January 26, 2018, http://www.ktsa.com/san-antonios-city-manager-salary-compare-cities/.
34. Audrey McGlinchy, "Here's What the New City Manager's Salary and Benefits Could Look Like," Austin Monitor, January 24, 2018, https://www.austinmonitor.com/stories/2018/01/heres-new-city-managers-salary-benefits-look-like/; U.S. Census Bureau, 2016 American Community Survey, "State and County Quickfacts: Seguin," https://www.census.gov/quickfacts/fact/table/seguincitytexas,US/PST045216#viewtop; and "City Manager Talks Growth, Role in Seguin," *Seguin Gazette*, March 16, 2018, http://seguingazette.com/news/article_3baa9b06-28b1-11e8-ad29-3b223ffc2af3.html.
35. "City Funds–Where Do They Come from, Where Do They Go (and What About Debt)," *Texas Town and City*, 102 (January 2015), pp. 16–17.
36. John Bender, "Fiscal Conditions Survey Reflects Improving Economy," *Texas Town and City*, 100 (May 2013), pp. 20–21; and Texas Municipal League, "2018 Fiscal Conditions Survey Results," https://www.tml.org/p/2018FiscalConditionsSurveyResults.pdf.
37. Juan Pablo Garnham, "Local Governments, Already Hard Hit by the Coronavirus, Are Facing a Fresh Budget Threat: Economic Recession," *The Texas Tribune*, April 2, 2020.
38. Texas Bond Review Commission, "2017 Local Government Annual Report: Fiscal Year Ended August 31, 2017," p. 2, http://www.brb.state.tx.us/publications_local.aspx#LC.
39. "Where Do Texas Cities Get Their Money," *Texas Town and City*, 100 (January 2013), pp. 16–17.
40. Miller and Sanders, *Urban Texas: Politics and Development*, p. xiv.
41. Tyler Cowen, "The United States of Texas: Why the Lone Star State Is America's Future," *Time*, October 28, 2013, pp. 32–36.

42. U.S. Census Bureau, *2016 American Community Survey*, https://factfinder.census.gov/faces/tableservices/jsf/pages/productview.xhtml?pid=ACS_16_1YR_S0101&prodType=table, and Texas State Data Center, *Texas Population Projections Program*, "Population Projections for the State of Texas," http://osd.texas.gov/Data/TPEPP/Projections/.
43. *Texas Almanac*, 1992–1993 (Dallas, TX: A.H. Belo, 1991), pp. 137–38; and U.S. Census, 2000.
44. William H. Frey, "Population Growth in Metro America Since 1980: Putting the Volatile 2000s in Perspective," Metropolitan Policy Program at Brookings, https://www.brookings.edu/wp-content/uploads/2016/06/0320_population_frey.pdf.
45. Kyle Shelton, "Should Minority Houstonians be Moving to Newer Suburbs?" March 31, 2015, Rice Kinder Institute for Urban Research, https://kinder.rice.edu/2015/03/31/36/.
46. American Society of Civil Engineers, "2017 Report Card for America's Infrastructure: Texas," https://www.infrastructurereportcard.org/state-item/texas/.
47. Ibid.
48. Jennifer Stowe, "The Emerging Need for Water and Wastewater Affordability Programs," *Texas Town and City*, 96 (May 2009), pp. 10–11.
49. Ali Anari and Mark G. Dotzour, *The Texas Economy*, August 2014, https://assets.recenter.tamu.edu/Documents/Articles/1862-201408.pdf.
50. The Disaster Center.Com, "Texas Population and Rate of Crime per 100,000 People, 1960–2018." Data is taken from the annual *Uniform Crime Reports* published by the Federal Bureau of Investigation.
51. Frank Sturzl, "The Tyranny of Environmental Mandates," *Texas Town and City*, 79 (September 1991), pp. 14–15, 32, 65–66.
52. Scott Houston, "Legal Q&A," Texas Town & City, CV (January 2018), p. 22.
53. David B. Brooks, *Texas Practice: County and Special District Law*, vol. 35 (St. Paul: West Publishing Company, 1989), p. 2.
54. Ibid., p. 14.
55. For a sample of Texas court decisions that affirm the general principle of the Dillon rule, that the county can perform only those functions allocated to it by law, see Robert E. Norwood and Sabrina Strawn, *Texas County Government: Let the People Choose*, 2nd ed. (Austin: Texas Research League, 1984), pp. 11–14.
56. Ibid., p. 9.
57. U.S. Census Bureau, *2018 American Community Survey*.
58. Texas Association of Counties, *2018 Salary Survey* (Austin: Texas Association of Counties, 2018), https://www.county.org/about-texas-counties/county-data/Documents/SalarySurvey2018.pdf. Data for nine counties were not included in this report.
59. Ibid.
60. *Avery* v. *Midland County*, 88 S. Ct. 1114 (1968).
61. David B. Brooks, *2018 Guide to Texas Laws for County Officials*, Texas Association of Counties, https://www.county.org/member-services/legal-resources/publications/Documents/Guide%20to%20Laws%202018.pdf.
62. Norwood and Strawn, *Texas County Government*, p. 22.
63. Brooks, *Texas Practice: County and Special District Law*, vol. 35, p. 331.
64. Texas Commission on Intergovernmental Relations, *An Introduction to Texas County Government* (Austin, TX: Author, 1980), p. 10.
65. Brooks, *Texas Practice: County and Special District Law*, vol. 35, pp. 392–93.
66. Ibid., vol. 36, pp. 104–105.
67. Texas Association of Counties, *2018 Salary Survey*.
68. Brooks, *Texas Practice: County and Special District Law*, vol. 36, pp. 4–8.
69. Ibid., pp. 49–50.
70. Ibid., pp. 18–49.
71. Texas Association of Counties, *2018 Salary Survey*, https://www.county.org/TAC/media/TACMedia/Legislative/2018-Salary-Survey-Complete.pdf.
72. Norwood and Strawn, *Texas County Government*, p. 24.
73. Brooks, *Texas Practice: County and Special District Law*, vol. 35, p. 495.
74. Ibid., vol. 36, pp. 122–23.
75. Texas Commission on Intergovernmental Relations, *An Introduction to County Government*, p. 22.
76. Norwood and Strawn, *Texas County Government*, p. 27.
77. Brooks, *Texas Practice: County and Special District Law*, vol. 35, pp. 273–74.
78. Virginia Marion Perrenod, *Special Districts, Special Purposes: Fringe Governments and Urban Problems in the Houston Area* (College Station: Texas A&M University Press, 1984), p. 4.
79. Texas Public Policy Foundation, "Local Government: Legislator's Guide to the Issues, 2017-18," https://www.texaspolicy.com/2017-18-legislators-guide-to-the-issues-special-session-edition/
80. Perrenod, *Special Districts, Special Purposes*, p. 4.
81. Woodworth G. Thrombley, *Special Districts and Authorities in Texas* (Austin: Institute of Public Affairs, University of Texas, 1959), pp. 17–18.
82. Benton, *Texas Politics: Constraints and Opportunities*, p. 282.
83. Perrenod, *Special Districts, Special Purposes*, p. 18.
84. Shelley Kofler, "The $97 Million Vote: One Voter with Personal Ties Decides a Huge Project in Dallas," KERANews, November 15, 2013, http://keranews.org/post/97-million-vote-one-voter-personal-ties-decides-huge-project-dallas.
85. Thrombley, *Special Districts and Authorities in Texas*, p. 13.
86. Robert S. Lorch, *State and Local Politics*, 3rd ed. (Englewood Cliffs, NJ: Prentice Hall, 1989), p. 246.
87. Ibid., p. 247.
88. Texas Education Agency, *Snapshot 2017–2018: School District Profiles*, https://rptsvr1.tea.texas.gov/perfreport/snapshot/2018/index.html.
89. Texas Comptroller of Public Account, "Biennial Property Tax Report: 2016-2017," https://comptroller.texas.gov/taxes/property-tax/reports/.
90. Texas Bond Review Board, "Local Government Annual Report, 2019," http://www.brb.state.tx.us/publications_state.aspx#AR.
91. Texas Association of School Boards, Membership Services, telephone conversation and e-mail, May 1, 2018; summary documents of board electoral systems provided by the TASB.
92. "Houston: City/Community Information," http://www.texasbest.com/houston/houston.html; and U.S. Census, *Census 2010*, "Texas Quick Facts."
93. City of San Marcos, Texas, City's Annexation Strategy "Annexation Planning," http://www.sanmarcostx.gov/DocumentCenter/View/3208/Citys-Annexation-Strategy-PDF?bidId=.

94. For a more detailed discussion of earlier annexation authority, see Benton, *Texas Politics*, pp. 264–66.
95. Scott N. Houston, "Municipal Annexation in Texas," *Texas APA-Southmost Section*, McAllen, Texas, November 2004, p. 10.
96. "Texas Legislature Adjourns," *Texas Town and City*, 86 (July 1999), p. 10.
97. "Texas Legislature Adjourns," *Texas Town and City*, 89 (July 2001), p. 11.
98. Texas Municipal League, "Home Rule Cities Take Heed: Annexation Reform Effective December 1," *TML Legislative Update*, August 25, 2017, p. 33, https://www.tml.org/legis_updates/home-rule-cities-take-heed-annexation-reform-effective-december-1.
99. Norwood and Strawn, *Texas County Government*, pp. 75–81.
100. Joel B. Goldsteen and Russell Fricano, *Municipal Finance Practices and Preferences for New Development: Survey of Texas Cities* (Arlington: Institute of Urban Studies, University of Texas at Arlington, 1988), pp. 3–11.
101. Bill R. Shelton, Bob Bolen, and Ray Perryman, "Passing a Sales Tax Referendum for Economic Development," *Texas Town and City*, 79 (September 1991), p. 10.
102. Brooks, *Texas Practice: County and Special District Law*, vol. 36, pp. 229–42.
103. Tom Adams, "Introduction and Recent Experience with the Interlocal Contract," in *Interlocal Contract in Texas*, edited by Richard W. Tees, Richard L. Cole, and Jay G. Stanford (Arlington: Institute of Urban Studies, University of Texas at Arlington, 1990), p. 1.
104. Tees et al., *Interlocal Contract in Texas*, pp. B1–B7.
105. Vincent Ostrom, *The Meaning of American Federalism* (San Francisco: Institute for Contemporary Studies, 1991), p. 161. Ostrom suggests that advocates of metropolitan government often overlook the "rich and intricate framework for negotiating, adjudicating, and deciding questions" that is now in place in many urbanized areas with multiple governmental units.
106. Ann Long Diveley and Dwight A. Shupe, "Public Improvement Districts: An Alternative for Financing Public Improvements and Services," *Texas Town and City*, 79 (September 1991).
107. City of Fort Worth, "Public Improvement Districts," http://fortworthtexas.gov/pid/.

Chapter 5

1. On the general concept of legislative institutionalization, see Nelson W. Polsby, "The Institutionalization of the U.S. House of Representatives," *American Political Science Review*, 62 (March 1968), pp. 144–65. For a discussion of the emergence of the modern Congress, see Randall B. Ripley, *Congress: Process and Policy*, 4th ed. (New York: W. W. Norton, 1988), pp. 48–67.
2. Thomas R. Dye and Susan MacManus, *Politics in States and Communities*, 12th ed. (Upper Saddle River, NJ: Pearson Prentice Hall, 2007), pp. 209–12.
3. For an extended discussion of legislative functions, see William J. Keefe and Morris S. Ogul, *The American Legislative Process*, 10th ed. (Upper Saddle River, NJ: Prentice Hall, 2001), pp. 21–44.
4. Council of State Governments, *Book of the States, 2015 Edition*, vol. 47 (Lexington, KY: Council of State Governments, 2015), Table 3.4.
5. National Conference of State Legislatures, "Annual Versus Biennial Legislative Sessions," http://www.ncsl.org/research/about-state-legislatures/annual-versus-biennial-legislative-sessions.aspx.
6. See Article 3 of the Texas Constitution for the constitutional provisions pertaining to the structure, membership, and selection of the Texas legislature.
7. National Conference of State Legislatures, "2019 Legislator Compensation," June 18, 2019.
8. Alexa Ura and Darla Cameron, "In Increasingly Diverse Texas, the Legislature Remains Mostly White and Male," *The Texas Tribune*, January 10, 2019.
9. For a comprehensive analysis of the literature on legislative recruitment and careers, see Donald R. Matthews, "Legislative Recruitment and Legislative Careers," *Legislative Studies Quarterly*, 9 (November 1984), pp. 547–85.
10. Gary F. Moncrief, Richard G. Niemi, and Lynda W. Powell, "Time, Term Limits, and Turnover: Trends in Membership Stability in U.S. State Legislatures," *Legislative Studies Quarterly*, 29 (August 2004), p. 364.
11. Texas Senate and House rosters, 2019.
12. Calculations for the tenure of House members are based on Texas House of Representatives, "Biographical Data, 82nd Legislature." Data for the members of the Senate are taken from Texas State Senate, "Facts About the Senate of the 82nd Legislature."
13. Paul T. David and Ralph Eisenberg, *Devaluation of the Urban and Suburban Vote* (Charlottesville: Bureau of Public Administration, University of Virginia, 1961).
14. Stephen Ansolabehere and James M. Snyder Jr., *The End of Inequality: One Person, One Vote and the Transformation of American Politics* (New York: W. W. Norton, 2008), pp. 50–51.
15. *Baker* v. *Carr*, 369 U.S. 186 (1962); *Reynolds* v. *Sims*, 337 U.S. 533 (1964); and *Kilgarlin* v. *Martin*, 252 F. Supp. 404 (S.D. Tex 1966).
16. Ross Ramsey, "Court Delivers Election Maps for Texas House, Congress," *The Texas Tribune*, February 28, 2012.
17. Ross Ramsey, "Judges: 2014 Primaries Can Use Lege-Approved Maps," *The Texas Tribune*, September 6, 2013.
18. Jordan Rudner, "High Stakes for Democrats in Redistricting Case," *The Texas Tribune*, December 6, 2015.
19. Robert T. Garrett, "Hands-off Speaker Gets Mixed Reviews—Straus Ends First Session with Republicans Split on His Style," *Dallas Morning News*, June 1, 2009, p. 1A.
20. Ibid.
21. Fred Gantt, *The Chief Executive in Texas: A Study of Gubernatorial Leadership* (Austin: University of Texas Press, 1964), p. 235.
22. Ross Ramsey and Cindy Rugeley, "Leaders of the Pack—Bullock, Laney Carry a Big Stick in Legislature," *Houston Chronicle*, June 6, 1993, p. 1A.
23. Jim Vertuno, The Associated Press, "Texas Senate Blowup Threatens Lt. Gov.'s Future," *Austin American-Statesman*, June 28, 2013.
24. Chuck Lindell, "Dan Patrick Snaps Selfies, Vows 'Next Level' Conservatism," *Austin American-Statesman*, January 20, 2015.
25. R.G. Ratcliffe, "The Big Three Breakfast Blows Up," Burkablog, *Texas Monthly*, April 22, 2015.
26. For a summary of the earlier scholarly work on legislative committees, see Heinz Eulau and Vera McCluggage, "Standing Committees in Legislatures: Three Decades of Research," *Legislative Studies Quarterly*, 9 (May 1984), pp. 195–270.
27. For a general discussion of staff in state legislatures, see Alan Rosenthal, *Engines of Democracy: Politics and Policymaking in State Legislatures* (Washington, D.C.: CQ Press, 2007), pp. 185–89.

28. See Malcolm E. Jewell and Samuel C. Patterson, *The Legislative Process in the United States*, Chapter 11 (New York: Random House, 1966), for a summary of the function of legislative rules and procedures. See Barbara Sinclair's *Unorthodox Lawmaking*, 3rd ed. (Washington, D.C.: CQ Press, 2007) for an expanded discussion of rule changes in the U.S. Congress and their impact on policy formulation.
29. There have been a number of studies of these informal norms within the legislative process. One is Donald R. Matthews's, *U.S. Senators and Their World* (New York: Vintage, 1960). For the adaptation of this concept to state legislatures, see Alan Rosenthal, *Legislative Life: People, Process, and Performance of the States* (New York: Harper & Row, 1981).
30. Olivia Messer, "The Texas Legislature's Sexist Little Secret," *The Texas Observer*, July 31, 2013.
31. Alexa Ura and Jolie McCullough, "Texas House Votes to Strengthen Sexual Harassment Investigations," *The Texas Tribune*, January 9, 2019.
32. For a brief overview of the representative problem, see Neal Riemer, ed., *The Representative: Trustee? Delegate? Partisan? Politico?* (Boston: D. C. Heath, 1967). For a more comprehensive treatment of the subject, see Hanna F. Pitkin, *The Concept of Representation* (Berkeley: University of California Press, 1967).
33. For an excellent treatment of the relationship of U.S. legislators to their districts and constituencies, see Richard F. Fenno Jr., *Home Style: House Members in Their Districts* (Boston: Little Brown, 1978).
34. The general concepts for this discussion are based on John W. Kingdon, *Congressmen's Voting Decisions*, 2nd ed. (New York: Harper & Row, 1981).
35. These legislative styles are similar to those developed by James David Barber, *The Lawmakers*, Chapters 2–5. (New Haven, CT: Yale University Press, 1965).
36. Richard Morehead, *50 Years in Texas Politics* (Burnet, TX: Eakin, 1982), pp. 236–37.
37. *Fort Worth Star-Telegram*, December 4, 1990.
38. Bob Sablatura and Robert Cullick, "Lewis' Luxury Vacation at Mexico Resort Probed," *Houston Chronicle*, December 12, 1990, p. 1A.
39. R. G. Ratcliffe, "Speaker Turns Himself in to Sheriff—Lewis Rips Indictment, Press," *Houston Chronicle*, January 1, 1991, p. 1A.
40. Laylan Copelin, "DeLay Appellate Lawyer: 'We Won the Super Bowl,'" *Austin American-Statesman*, September 19, 2013.
41. Jim Malewitz, "Ethics Commissioners: Lawmakers Went Backward in 2015," *The Texas Tribune*, June 11, 2015.

Chapter 6

1. Patrick Svitek, "Gov. Greg Abbott closes bars, restaurants and schools as he anticipates tens of thousands could test positive for coronavirus," *The Texas Tribune*, March 19, 2020.
2. National Governors' Association, "Governors' Powers and Authority," https://www.nga.org/cms/management/powers-and-authority; and Council of State Governments, *Book of the States 2017*, Chapter 4: State Executive Branch, Table 4-6, State Cabinet Systems, http://knowledgecenter.csg.org/kc/system/files/4.6.2017.pdf.
3. Fred Gantt, Jr. *The Chief Executive in Texas* (Austin: University of Texas Press, 1964), p. 24.
4. Ibid., pp. 24–25.
5. Ibid., p. 27.
6. Ibid., pp. 27–32.
7. Ibid., pp. 32–36.
8. Ibid., p. 37.
9. Charles F. Cnudde and Robert E. Crew, *Constitutional Democracy in Texas* (St. Paul, MN: West, 1989), p. 90.
10. *Texas Constitution*, Art. 4, Sec. 4.
11. Gantt, *The Chief Executive in Texas*, p. 116.
12. Texas Constitution, Art. 1, Sec. 4.
13. Gantt, *The Chief Executive in Texas*, pp. 229–30.
14. Ray Long and Rick Pearson, "Impeached Illinois Gov. Rod Blagojevich Has Been Removed from Office," *Chicago Tribune*, January 20, 2006.
15. National Conference of State Legislatures, "Recall of State Officials," September 11, 2013, http://www.ncsl.org/research/elections-and-campaigns/recall-of-state-officials.aspx.
16. Heather Perkins, "The Governors: Compensation, Staff, Travel and Residence," Table 4.3, *Book of the States 2019*, The Council of State Governments.
17. For an excellent treatment of the American governor through the Great Depression years, see Leslie Lipson, *The American Governor from Figurehead to Leader* (Chicago: University of Chicago Press, 1939).
18. Joseph A. Schlesinger, "The Politics of the Executive," in *Politics in the American States*, 2nd ed., edited by Herbert Jacob and Kenneth N. Vines (Boston: Little, Brown, 1971), Chapter 6; and Thad L. Beyle, "The Governors, 1988–89," in *The Book of the States, 1990–1991* (Lexington, KY: Council of State Governments, 1990), p. 54.
19. Wayne Slater, "Clements Puts Stamp on Panels, Minorities, Women Neglected, Critics Say," *Dallas Morning News*, April 27, 1987, p. 1A.
20. Christian McDonald and Asher Price, "The Rick Perry Legacy: Government Overseers Who Think Like He Does," *Austin American-Statesman*, September 22, 2014.
21. Jolie McCullough, "Dozens of Abbott Appointees Surpass Donor Threshold Targeted by Stalled 'Pay for Play' Bill," *The Texas Tribune*, May 23, 2017, https://www.texastribune.org/2017/05/23/texas-pay-play-bill-abbott-donors-appointees/.
22. McDonald and Price, "The Rick Perry Legacy."
23. Peggy Fikac, "Analysis: Abbott Favors Donors, White Men for Appointments," *Houston Chronicle*, January 7, 2018.
24. Texas Constitution, Art. 4, Sec. 11.
25. Wilbourn E. Benton, *Texas Politics: Constraints and Opportunities*, 5th ed. (Chicago: Nelson-Hall, 1984), pp. 164–66.
26. Ibid., pp. 166–67.
27. Texas Constitution, Art. 4, Sec. 7.
28. Gantt, *The Chief Executive in Texas*, pp. 90–107.
29. Robert S. Lorch, *State and Local Politics*, 3rd ed. (Englewood Cliffs, NJ: Prentice Hall, 1989), pp. 115–16.
30. Ibid., pp. 116–19.
31. See James E. Anderson, Richard W. Murray, and Edward L. Farley, *Texas Politics*, 6th ed. (New York: HarperCollins, 1991), for an excellent analysis of the leadership styles of Governors Shivers, Daniel, Connally, Smith, and Briscoe.
32. *Texas Government Newsletter*, 19 (February 25, 1991), p. 1.
33. Clay Robison, "Richard's Caution Saves Precious Political Capital," *Houston Chronicle*, June 2, 1993, p. 1A.
34. R. G. Ratcliffe, "Away from the Spotlight, Governor Makes His Mark," *Houston Chronicle*, April 15, 1995, p. 1A.

35. Abby Livingston, "At Confirmation Hearing, Rick Perry Vows to Pursue 'Sound Science' on Climate Change," *The Texas Tribune*, January 19, 2017, https://www.texastribune.org/2017/01/19/rick-perry-testifies-senate/.
36. Jeff Brady, "Energy Secretary Rick Perry to Resign," National Public Radio, October 17, 2019.]
37. Peggy Fikac, "Taxpayers' Tab for Abbott vs. Obama Continues to Grow," *Houston Chronicle*, August 20, 2013. http://www.houstonchronicle.com/news/houston-texas/houston/article/Taxpayers-tab-for-Abbott-vs-Obama-continues-to-4744781.php.
38. Patrick Svitek, "In First Session, Abbott Keeps Drama at Bay," *The Texas Tribune*, June 23, 2015. http://www.texastribune.org/2015/06/23/first-session-abbott-keeps-drama-minimum/.
39. Ibid.
40. Morgan Smith, "Gov. Abbott: I'm Keeping a List of Lawmakers Who Oppose Me During Special Session," *The Texas Tribune*, July 17, 2017, https://www.texastribune.org/2017/07/17/abbott-property-taxes-are-top-issue-special-session/.
41. Paul J. Weber, "Texas Governor Stockpiles Cash but not for the Usual Reason," Associated Press, February 24, 2019.
42. Robert T. Garrett, "Greg Abbott Confronts Coronavirus as Stronger Governor than Texas had 50 Years Ago," *The Dallas Morning News*, March 22, 2020.
43. Daniel Elazar, "The Principles and Traditions Underlying State Constitutions," *Publius: The Journal of Federalism*, 12 (Winter 1982), p. 17.
44. Matthew Watkins, "Paxton to Supporters: 'I Expect to Be Fully Vindicated,'" *The Texas Tribune*, August 4, 2015, https://www.texastribune.org/2015/08/04/paxton-supporters-i-expect-be-fully-vindicated/.
45. Texas Comptroller of Public Accounts, Fiscal Notes (December 1990), p. 6.
46. Kelley Shannon, "Texas Comptroller Susan Combs Apologizes for Data Breach, Offers Credit Monitoring to Millions Affected," *The Dallas Morning News*, April 28, 2011.
47. Gary Scharrer, "Gift of Christmas Mountains to Texas State Earns Praise," *Houston Chronicle*, September 15, 2011.
48. Brian M. Rosenthal, "George P. Bush Names 4 Contenders to Be His Dad's Running Mate," *Houston Chronicle*, December 2, 2015, https://www.chron.com/news/politics/us/article/George-P-Bush-names-4-contenders-to-be-his-dad-s-6670821.php.
49. Asher Price, "Texas' Chief Oil-and-Gas Regulator Honored by Oil-and-Gas Industry," *Austin American-Statesman*, March 29, 2018, December 2, 2015, https://www.mystatesman.com/news/state-regional-govt-politics/texas-chief-oil-and-gas-regulator-honored-oil-and-gas-industry/MhimY3DkCSU4eAo7QYsddM/.
50. Rudolph Bush, "Opinion Blog: Earthquakes and the Ever-dissolving Credibility of the Texas Railroad Commission," *The Dallas Morning News*, April 21, 2015, http://dallasmorningviewsblog.dallasnews.com/2015/04/earthquakes-and-the-ever-dissolving-credibility-of-the-texas-railroad-commission.html/.
51. James C. McKinley, Jr., "Texas Conservatives Win Curriculum Change," *The New York Times*, March 12, 2010, http://www.nytimes.com/2010/03/13/education/13texas.html.

Chapter 7

1. Ben Wear, "TxDOT Taken to Legislative Woodshed over Toll Tag Billing Debacle," *Austin American-Statesman*, February 11, 2015, http://www.mystatesman.com/news/news/state-regional-govt-politics/txdot-taken-to-legislative-woodshed-over-toll-tag-/nj843/.
2. Aman Batheja, "Botched Toll Bills Prompt $1.7 Million in Refunds," *The Texas Tribune*, March 17, 2015. http://www.texastribune.org/2015/03/17/txdot-refunding-17-million-erroneous-toll-bills/.
3. See Max Weber, "Bureaucracy," in *Max Weber Essays in Sociology*, edited by H. H. Gerth and C. Wright Mills (New York: Oxford University Press, 1971), pp. 196–244.
4. Jeffrey D. Straussman, *Public Administration* (New York: Longman, 1990), p. 65.
5. U.S. Census Bureau, "2018 Annual Survey of Public Employment and Payroll," March 2018. https://www.census.gov/data/datasets/2018/econ/apes/annual-apes.html.
6. The following discussion is based on Dennis Palumbo and Steven Maynard-Moody, *Contemporary Public Administration* (New York: Longman, 1991), pp. 26–31; and Straussman, *Public Administration*, pp. 63–64.
7. Melvin J. Dubnick and Barbara S. Romzek, *American Public Administration* (New York: Macmillan, 1991), p. 248.
8. Ibid., pp. 248–49.
9. Donald F. Kettl and James W. Fesler, *The Politics of the Administrative Process*, 3rd ed. (Washington, D.C.: Congressional Quarterly Press, 2005), pp. 127–28.
10. Texas State Auditor's Office, "An Annual Report on Classified Employee Turnover for Fiscal Year 2019," March 2020.
11. Pew Charitable Trusts, "Recruiting and Retaining Public Sector Workers," September 15, 2014, http://www.pewtrusts.org/en/research-and-analysis/issue-briefs/2014/09/recruiting-and-retaining-public-sector-workers.
12. R. Sam Garrett, James A. Thurber, A. Lee Fritschler, and David H. Rosenbloom, "Assessing the Impact of Bureaucracy Bashing by Electoral Campaigns," *Public Administration Review*, 66 (March/April 2006), pp. 228–40; and Marissa Martino Golden, *What Motivates Bureaucrats? Politics and Administration During the Reagan Years* (New York: Columbia University Press, 2000).
13. Congressional Research Service, *Federal Workforce Statistics, Sources: OPM and OMB*, October 2019, https://fas.org/Sqp/crs/misc/R43590.pdf/. Some federal agencies, such as the Post Office, are not included in this figure of 2.1 million employees.
14. U.S. Census Bureau, 2017 Census of Governments, "Employment Methodology," https://www2.census.gov/programs-surveys/apes/technical-documentation/methodology/2017_methodology.pdf. The U.S. Census Bureau conducts a census of all U.S. governments every five years. In compiling employment data, part-time and full-time employees are counted. Using payroll data from the states, this total is recalculated as "full-time equivalent" employees.
15. U.S. Census Bureau, 2017 Census of Governments Organizations, https://www.census.gov/data/tables/2017/econ/gus/2017-governments.html; United States Census Bureau, American Factfinder https://factfinder.census.gov/faces/tableservices/jsf/pages/productview.xhtml?pid=ACS_16_1YR_S0101&prodType=table2012.

16. KFF, "State Health Facts: Total State Expenditures Per Capita," https://kff.org/other/state-indicator/per-capita-state-spending.
17. Ibid and Tax Policy Center, "State and Local General Expenditures Per Capita, 2004–2017," June 2020, https://www.taxpolicycenter.org/statistics/state-and-local-general-expenditures-capita.
18. Ryan Murphy and Morgan Smith, "25,000 Fewer School Employees," *The Texas Tribune,* March 8, 2012, http://www.texastribune.org/library/data/school-district-fte-totals.
19. U.S. Department of Commerce, Bureau of the Census, *Census of Governments, 2012,* Government Employment and Payroll Tables, https://www.census.gov/data/tables/2012/econ/apes/annual-apes.html.
20. Andrea Ball, Andrew Chavez, and J. David McSwane, "With No Oversight, Texas IT Contractors Made Millions," *Austin American-Statesman,* March 7, 2015, http://www.mystatesman.com/news/news/state-regional-govt-politics/with-no-oversight-texas-it-contractors-made-millio/nkQpq/.
21. Aman Batheja, "In State Contracting, Failure Is an Option," *The Texas Tribune,* February 1, 2015, http://www.texastribune.org/2015/02/01/cost-overruns-and-bungles-state-contracting/.
22. Theodore J. Lowi, *The End of Liberalism,* 2nd ed. (New York: W.W. Norton, 1979), p. 274.
23. Larry N. Gerston, *Making Public Policy* (Glenview, IL: Scott, Foresman, 1983), p. 95.
24. Palumbo and Maynard-Moody, *Contemporary Public Administration,* p. 304.
25. Straussman, *Public Administration,* p. 246.
26. Jim Malewitz, "State Supreme Court Punts on Major Water Case," *The Texas Tribune,* May 1, 2015, http://www.texastribune.org/2015/05/01/supreme-court-punts-major-water-case/.
27. Straussman, *Public Administration,* p. 286.
28. William Lilley III and James C. Miller III, "The New Social Regulation," *Public Interest,* 47 (Spring 1977), p. 53.
29. Lee Hancock, "Nursing Homes Under Fire—Ex Official Defends His Facilities," *Dallas Morning News,* October 24, 1991, p. 1A.
30. Christian McDonald and Asher Price, "The Rick Perry Legacy: Government Overseers Who Think Like He Does," *Austin American-Statesman,* September 22, 2014, http://www.mystatesman.com/news/news/the-rick-perry-legacy-government-overseers-who-thi/nhRK7/.
31. Peggy Fikac and Annie Millerbernd, "Gov. Abbott's Appointees Have Given Him More Than $14 Million," *San Antonio Express News,* January 5, 2018, https://www.expressnews.com/news/local/article/Gov-Abbott-s-appointees-have-given-him-more-12477690.php.
32. Colorado was the first state to adopt sunset legislation in 1976. See Straussman, *Public Administration,* p. 39.
33. Sunset Advisory Commission, Final Report, March 1991, p. 5, https://www.sunset.texas.gov/public/uploads/files/reports/Report%20to%20the%2072%20Leg%201991.pdf.
34. Jim Mustian, "Kermit Nurse Not Guilty," *Odessa American Online,* March 27, 2010.
35. Texas Nursing Association, "Winkler County Nurses Update," *Advocacy,* March 27, 2010.
36. Jim Mustian, "Winkler Approves Nurses Settlement," *Odessa American Online,* January 6, 2012.
37. Clay Robison, "Long Wait for Justice Pays Off/$13.8 Million Goes to Whistle Blower," *Houston Chronicle,* November 16, 1995, p. 1A.
38. Council of State Governments, *The Book of the States,* 1990–1991, vol. 28 (Lexington, KY: Council of State Governments, 1990), p. 346.
39. For a summary of the merit system movement, see Palumbo and Maynard-Moody, *Contemporary Public Administration,* pp. 165–74.
40. The Division of Planning Coordination of the Office of the Governor published a report in 1972 entitled the Quality of Texas Government anticipated reforms in the state's employment practices.

Chapter 8

1. *Smith* v. *Allwright,* 321 U.S. 649 (1944).
2. *Miranda* v. *Arizona,* 384 U.S. 436 (1966).
3. American Bar Association, "State and Federal Courts," in *ABA Family Legal Guide,* http://www.americanbar.org/groups/public_education/resources/law_issues_for_consumers/books_family_home.html.
4. Texas Research League, *The Texas Judiciary: A Structural-Functional Overview,* Report 1 (Austin, TX: Texas Research League, 1990).
5. The number of courts may change from year to year as a result of legislative action or actions of local governments.
6. Allen E. Smith, *The Impact of the Texas Constitution on the Judiciary* (Houston: University of Houston, Institute for Urban Studies, 1973), p. 45.
7. Office of Court Administration, "FY2019 Annual Statistical Report."
8. Smith, *The Impact of the Texas Constitution on the Judiciary,* p. 28.
9. Ibid., p. 31.
10. Texas Office of Court Administration, "Profile of Appellate and Trial Judges as of September 1, 2017."
11. Clay Robison, "Bush Names Gonzales for High Court," *Houston Chronicle,* November 13, 1998, p. 1A.
12. *League of United Latin American Citizens* v. *Mattoxs,* 999 F.2d 831 (1993).
13. Chuck Lindell, "Federal Trial to Begin on Ending Statewide Election of Texas Judges," *Austin American-Statesman,* February 8, 2018.
14. Malia Reddick, Michael J. Nelson, and Rachel Paine Caufield, "Racial and Gender Diversity on State Courts: An AJS Study," *The Judges' Journal,* 48(3) (Summer 2009), American Bar Association.
15. Texas Office of Court Administration, "Profile of Appellate and Trial Judges as of September 1, 2019."
16. Emma Platoff, "Democratic Male Judges May Be Headed for Extinction in Texas. The Cause? Voters," *The Texas Tribune,* March 9, 2020.
17. Anthony Champagne, "Campaign Contributions in Texas Supreme Court Races," *Crime, Law and Social Change,* 17 (1992), pp. 91–106.
18. *Houston Post,* November 10, 1988.
19. Bruce Hight, "Texas Supreme Court Sides with Business," *Austin American-Statesman,* December 9, 1993, p. E1.

20. Clay Robison, "Texas' Chief Justice Resigning—Longtime Foe of State's System of Electing Judges to Teach Law," *Houston Chronicle*, April 30, 2004, p. 1A.
21. Wallace Jefferson, "The State of the Judiciary in Texas." Presented to the 81st Legislature, February 11, 2009, Austin, Texas.
22. Kathleen Hunker, "Limited Liability, Unlimited Growth: How Tort Reform Helped Ignite the Texas Boom," *City Journal*, January 11, 2017.
23. Texas Watch, *The Food Chain: Winners and Losers in the Texas Supreme Court, 1995–1999* (Austin: Texas Watch Foundation, 1999).
24. Texas Watch press release, May 3, 1999.
25. Texas Watch Foundation, "Thumbs on the Scale: A Retrospective of the Texas Supreme Court, 2000–2010," in *Court Watch*, January 26, 2012.
26. Texas Watch, "Show Us the Money: An Analysis of Political Donations to the Texas Supreme Court," October 2008, Austin, TX.
27. Wallace Jefferson, "The State of the Judiciary in Texas." Presented to the 81st Legislature, February 11, 2009, Austin, Texas.
28. Andrew Cohen, "'A Broken System': Texas's Former Chief Justice Condemns Judicial Elections," *The Atlantic*, October 18, 2013.
29. Emma Platoff and Jolie McCullough, "Texas Supreme Court Chief Justice Nathan Hecht Calls for Nonpartisan Judicial Elections, Bail Reform," *The Texas Tribune*, February 6, 2019.
30. American Judicature Society at Vanderbilt Law School, "Judicial Selection Methods in the States: Appellate and General Jurisdiction Courts," updated 2013, http://www.judicialselection.us/uploads/documents/Judicial_Selection_Charts_1196376173077.pdf.
31. Texas Politics Project, University of Texas at Austin, "The Justice System. The Impact of Judicial Selection in Texas," *Texas Politics*.
32. Dan Levine and Kristina Cooke, "Uneven Justice: In States with Elected High Court Judges, a Harder Line on Capital Punishment," Reuters.com, September 22, 2015.
33. Carlos Berdejo, Loyola Law School, and Noam Yuchtman, Haas School of Business, University of California-Berkeley, "Crime, Punishment, and Politics: An Analysis of Political Cycles in Criminal Sentencing," April 2012.
34. Brandi Grissom, "Rebuilding after Prison: Texas Has Spent $109 Million on the Wrongfully Convicted," *The Dallas Morning News*, October 23, 2017.
35. Chuck Lindell, "Ken Anderson to Serve 10 Days in Jail," *Austin American-Statesman*, November 8, 2013.
36. *Richards* v. *LULAC*, 868 S.W.2d 306 (1993).
37. *Texas Education Agency* v. *Leeper*, 893 S.W.2d 432 (1994).
38. Will Weissert, "Texas Supreme Court Sidesteps Key Home Schooling Issue," Associated Press, June 24, 2016.
39. Kate Galbraith, "Texas Supreme Court Rules for Landowners in Water Case," *The Texas Tribune*, February 24, 2012.
40. Neena Satija, "In Texas, Fight over Water Spills Underground," *The Texas Tribune*, September 16, 2013.
41. Forrest Wilder, "Beach Bummer: The Texas Supreme Court Guts the Open Beaches Act," *Texas Observer*, March 30, 2012.
42. Paul Cobler, "Texas Supreme Court Hears Oral Arguments in Plastic Bag Ban Case," *The Texas Tribune*, January 11, 2018.
43. *Operation Rescue–National* v. *Planned Parenthood of Houston and Southeast Texas, Inc.*, 975 S.W.2d 546 (1998). See also Clay Robison, "Anti-Abortion Protesters Lose '92 Case Ruling," *Houston Chronicle*, July 4, 1998, p. 1A.
44. *Charles E. Bell* v. *Low Income Women of Texas*, 95 S.W.3d 253 (2002).
45. Alexa Ura, "Plaintiffs Fold Hand in Texas State Court Lawsuit Seeking Expansion of Voting by Mail During Coronavirus," *The Texas Tribune*, June 10, 2020.

Chapter 9

1. There is a long and complex history of discussion on these concepts, which are far too detailed to cover in this introductory material. For more discussion, see, for instance, David Truman, *The Governmental Process* (New York: Knopf, 1951); Earl Latham, *The Group Basis of Politics* (Ithaca, NY: Cornell University Press, 1952); and Robert Dahl and Charles Lindblom, *Politics, Economics and Welfare* (New York: Harper, 1953).
2. A number of theorists contributed to the development of social contract theory; one of the most cited as influencing our founders was John Locke (*Second Treatise of Government*, 1689). However, other notable contributors to the development of social contract theory were Thomas Hobbes (*Leviathan*, 1651) and Jean-Jacques Rousseau (*Du Contrat Social*, 1762).
3. Alexis de Tocqueville, *Democracy in America*, I, trans. H. Reeve (Boston: J. Allyn. First published 1835, 1976), p. 156; and John Stuart Mill, *On Liberty* (London: Longmans, Roberts and Green, 1859).
4. Robert Weissberg, *Polling, Policy, and Public Opinion: The Case Against Heeding the "Voice of the People"* (New York: Palgrave-Macmillan, 2002).
5. Walter Lippmann, *Public Opinion* (New York: Macmillan, 1922).
6. Paul Abramson, *Political Attitudes in America* (San Francisco: Freeman, 1983).
7. Benjamin I. Page and Robert Y. Shapiro, *The Rational Public* (Chicago: University of Chicago Press, 1992), p. 178.
8. Ibid., p. 179.
9. See, for instance, Anthony Downs, *An Economic Theory of Democracy* (New York: Harper & Row, 1957); and William Jacoby, "Is a Liberal-Conservative Identification an Ideology?" in *Understanding Public Opinion*, edited by Barbara Norrander and Clyde Wilcox, 3rd ed. (Washington, D.C.: CQ Press, 2009).
10. University of Texas/Texas Tribune Poll, April 10-19, 2020, questions 15 and 16A, https://texaspolitics.utexas.edu/sites/texaspolitics.utexas.edu/files/202004_poll_topline.pdf.
11. Brian Rathbun, Evgeniia Iakhnis, and Kathleen E. Powers, "This New Poll Shows that Populism Doesn't Stem from People's Economic Distress," October 19, 2017, *Washington Post*, Monkey Cage, accessed May 8, 2018, https://www.washingtonpost.com/news/monkey-cage/wp/2017/10/19/this-new-poll-shows-that-populism-doesnt-stem-from-economic-distress/?utm_term=.f39902ce426d; and Mike Corones, "Not That Kind of Libertarian: Poll Shows Fondness for Government Programs," April 30, 2015, Reuters, accessed May 8, 2018, https://www.reuters.com/article/idUS237986176120150430.
12. See, for instance, David J. Jackson, *Entertainment and Politics: The Influence of Pop Culture on Young Adult Political Socialization*, 2nd ed. (New York: Lang, 2009), p. 9; and M. Kent Jennings, Laura Stroker, and Jake Bowers, "Politics

13. Jennings, Stroker, and Bowers, "Politics Across Generations: Family Transmission Reconsidered," *Journal of Politics*, 71:3 (2009) pp. 782–99.
14. Sidney Verba, Kay Schlozman, and Nancy Burns, "Family Ties: Understanding the Intergenerational Transmission of Political Participation," in *The Social Logic of Politics*, edited by Alan S. Zuckerman (Philadelphia: Temple University Press, 2005).
15. M. Kent Jennings and Richard G. Niemi, *Generations and Politics: A Panel Study of Young Adults and Their Parents* (Princeton, NJ: Princeton University Press, 1981).
16. Julianna Sandell Pacheco and Eric Plutzer, "Political Participation and Cumulative Disadvantage: The Impact of Economic and Social Hardship on Young Citizens," *Journal of Social Issues*, 64 (2008), pp. 571–93.
17. Stuart Oskamp, *Attitudes and Opinions*, 2nd ed. (Englewood Cliffs, NJ: Prentice Hall, 1991), p. 160.
18. David O. Sears and Carolyn L. Funk, "Evidence of the Long-Term Persistence of Adults' Political Predispositions," *Journal of Politics*, 61 (1999), pp. 1–28.
19. David O. Sears and Jack S. Levy, "Childhood and Adult Political Development," in *Oxford Handbook of Political Psychology*, edited by Leonie Huddy, David O. Sears, and Jack S. Levy (Oxford: Oxford University Press, 2003).
20. David Easton, *A Systems Analysis of Political Life* (New York: Wiley, 1965).
21. Ibid., Chapter 15.
22. Jennings, Stoker, and Bowers, "Politics Across Generations: Family Transmission Reconsidered."
23. See, for instance, Richard G. Niemi and Jane Junn, *Civic Education: What Makes Students Learn* (New Haven, CT: Yale University Press, 1998); Daniel Hart, Thomas M. Donnelly, James Youniss, and Robert Atkins, "High School Community Service as a Predictor of Adult Voting and Volunteering," *American Education Research*, 44 (2007), pp. 197–219; and Jonathan F. Zaff, Oksana Malanchuk, and Jacquelynne S. Eccles, "Predicting Positive Citizenship from Adolescence to Young Adulthood: The Effects of Civic Context," *Applied Development Science*, 12 (2008), pp. 38–53.
24. James G. Gimpel, J. Celeste Lay, and Jason E. Schuknecht, *Cultivating Democracy: Civic Environments and Political Socialization in America* (Washington, D.C.: Brookings Institution Press, 2003), p. 147.
25. Niemi and Junn, *Civic Education*, p. 791.
26. Daniel A. McFarland and Ruben J. Thomas "Bowling Young: How Young Voluntary Associations Influence Adult Political Participations," *American Sociological Review*, 71 (2006), pp. 401–25.
27. U.S. Census Bureau, *Educational Attainment in the United States, 2003* (Washington, D.C.: Government Printing Office, 2003).
28. See, for instance, Duane F. Alwin, Ronald L. Cohen, and Theodore Newcomb, *Political Attitudes over the Life Span* (Madison: University of Wisconsin Press, 1991); and David Sears and Carolyn Funk, "Evidence of the Long-Term Persistence of Adults' Political Predispositions," *Journal of Politics*, 61 (1999), pp. 1–28.
29. Nate Cohn and Kevin Quealy, "How Public Opinion has Moved on Black Lives Matter," *The New York Times*, June 10, 2020, https://www.nytimes.com/interactive/2020/06/10/upshot/black-lives-matter-attitudes.html; "In a Politically Polarized Era, Sharp Divides in Both Partisan Coalitions," Pew Research Center, December 17, 2019, https://www.people-press.org/2019/12/17/in-a-politically-polarized-era-sharp-divides-in-both-partisan-coalitions/.
30. Ernest Boyer and Mary Jean Whitelaw, *The Condition of the Professorate* (New York: Harper and Row, 1989); Scott Jaschik, "Professors and Politics: What the Research Says," *Inside Higher Education*, February 27, 2017, https://www.insidehighered.com/news/2017/02/27/research-confirms-professors-lean-left-questions-assumptions-about-what-means.
31. Gimpel, Lay, and Schuknecht, *Cultivating Democracy*, p. 63.
32. Ibid., p. 92.
33. See, for instance, Gimpel, Lay, and Schuknecht, *Cultivating Democracy*, p. 35.
34. See, for instance, Penny Edgell Becker and Pawan H. Dhingra, "Religious Involvement and Volunteering: Implications for Civil Society," *Sociology of Religion*, 62 (2001), pp. 315–35; and Corwin Smidt, "Religion and Civic Engagement: A Comparative Analysis," *Annals of the American Academy of Political and Social Sciences*, 565 (1999), pp. 176–92.
35. National Philanthropic Trust, Charitable Giving Statistics, https://www.nptrust.org/philanthropic-resources/charitable-giving-statistics/.
36. Gimpel, Lay, and Schuknecht, *Cultivating Democracy*, p. 142.
37. Ibid., p. 143.
38. Howard Schuman and Willard L. Rogers, "Cohorts, Chronology and Collective Memories," *Public Opinion Quarterly*, 17 (2004), pp. 217–54.
39. See, for instance, Ole R. Holsti, *Public Opinion and American Foreign Policy* (Ann Arbor: University of Michigan Press, 2007); Dietram A. Scheufele, Matthew C. Nisbet, and Ronald E. Ostman, "September 11 News Coverage, Public Opinion and Support for Civil Liberties," *Mass Communication and Society*, 8 (2005), pp. 197–218; Stephanie Craft, "U.S. Public Concerns in the Aftermath of 9-11: A Test of Second Level Agenda-Setting," *International Journal of Public Opinion Research*, 16 (2004), pp. 456–63; and Amy Gershkoff and Shana Kushner, "Shaping Public Opinion: The 9/11–Iraq Connection in the Bush Administration's Rhetoric," *Perspectives on Politics* (2005), pp. 525–37.
40. Paul Lazarfeld, Bernard Berelson, and Hazel Gaudet, *The People's Choice* (New York: Columbia University Press, 1944).
41. Kimberlé Crenshaw, "Mapping the Margins: Intersectionality, Identity Politics, and Violence Against Women of Color," *Stanford Law Review*, 43 (July, 1991), pp. 1241-1299.
42. Eleanor Robertson, "Intersectional-what? Feminism's Problem with Jargon Is that Any Idiot Can Pick It Up and Have A Go," *The Guardian*, September 30, 2017, https://www.theguardian.com/world/2017/sep/30/intersectional-feminism-jargon; Karen Lehrman Bloch, "Intersectionality: The New Caste System," *Jewish Journal*, February 27, 2019, https://jewishjournal.com/commentary/columnist/294500/intersectionality-the-new-caste-system/; Omayma Mohamed, "How Intersectionalism Betrays the World's Muslim Women," *Quillette*, April 28, 2019, https://quillette.com/2019/04/28/how-intersectionalism-betrays-the-worlds-muslim-women/.
43. Most surveys have a margin of error of ± 3 with 95 percent confidence.

44. Center for American Women and Politics, *Gender Differences in Voter Turnout* (New Brunswick, NJ: Eagleton Institute of Politics, Rutgers University, 2011).
45. Bella Abzug, *Gender Gap*, (Boston: Houghton Mifflin, 1984); Kelly Dittmar, Center for American Women and Politics, *The Gender Gap: Gender Differences in Vote Choice and Political Orientations* (New Brunswick, NJ: Eagleton Institute of Politics, Rutgers University, 2014); Karen M. Kaufmann and John R. Petrocik, "The Changing Politics of American Men: Understanding the Sources of the Gender Gap," *American Journal of Political Science*, 43 (July, 1999), pp. 864-87; Daniel Wirls, "Reinterpreting the Gender Gap," *The Public Opinion Quarterly*, 50 (Autumn, 1986), pp. 316-30.
46. Center for American Women and Politics, *The Gender Gap: Attitudes on Public Policy Issues* (New Brunswick, NJ: Eagleton Institute of Politics, Rutgers University, 1997); and Susan J. Carroll and Richard F. Fox, eds., *Gender and Elections*, 4th Edition, (New York: Cambridge University Press, 2016).
47. For more information about the role of race in American politics, see Paula D. McClain, Jessica D. Johnson Carew, Eugene Walton, Jr., and Candis S. Watts, "Group Membership, Group Identity and Group Consciousness: Measures of Racial Identity in American Politics?" *Annual Review of Political Science*, 12 (2009), pp. 471–85; Evelyn M. Simien, *Black Feminist Voices in Politics* (Albany, NY: State University of New York Press, 2006); Melanye T. Price, *Dreaming Blackness: Black Nationalism and African-American Public Opinion* (New York: New York University Press, 2009); Natalie Masuoka, "Together They Become One: Examining the Predictors of Panethnic Group Consciousness among Asian Americans and Latinos," *Social Science Quarterly*, 7 (2006), pp. 993–1011; and Deborah J. Schildkraut, "Which Birds of a Feather Flock Together? Assessing Attitudes About Descriptive Representation Among Latinos and Asian Americans," *American Politics Research*, 41 (2013), pp. 699–729.
48. Andrew Dugan, "Texan Hispanics Tilt Democratic, but State Likely to Stay Red: Hispanics Statewide Are Less Likely to Be Democratic than Other U.S. Hispanics," Gallup, February 7, 2014, accessed at http://www.gallup.com/poll/167339/texan-hispanics-tilt-democratic-state-likely-stay-red.aspx; Pew Research Center for the People and the Press, "Trends in Party Affiliation Among Demographic Groups," March 20, 2018, https://www.people-press.org/2018/03/20/1-trends-in-party-affiliation-among-demographic-groups/.
49. Ibid.
50. See, for instance, Edward D. Mansfield and Diana C. Mutz, "Support for Free Trade: Self-Interest, Sociotropic Politics, and Out-Group Anxiety," *International Organization*, 63 (2009), pp. 425–57; and Benjamin I. Page and Robert Y. Shapiro, *The Rational Public* (Chicago: University of Chicago Press, 1992), p. 178.
51. Pew Research Center for the People and the Press, "U.S. Religious Landscape Survey, 2015," accessed at http://www.pewforum.org/religious-landscape-study/.
52. "In U.S., Decline of Christianity Continues at Rapid Pace," Pew Research Center, Religion & Public Life, October 17, 2019, https://www.pewforum.org/2019/10/17/in-u-s-decline-of-christianity-continues-at-rapid-pace/.
53. Ibid.
54. See, for instance, Darren E. Sherkat, Melissa Powell-Williams, Gregory Maddox, and Kylan Mattias de Vries, "Religion, Politics and Support for Same-Sex Marriage in the United States, 1988–2008," *Social Science Research*, 40 (2011), pp. 167–80; Amy Becker, "Determinants of Public Support for Same-Sex Marriage: Generational Cohorts, Social Contact and Shifting Attitudes," *International Journal of Public Opinion Research*, 24 (2012), pp. 524–33; and Christopher G. Ellison, Gabriel A. Acevedo, and Aida I. Ramos-Wada, "Religion and Attitudes Toward Same-Sex Marriage among U.S. Latinos," *Social Science Quarterly*, 92 (2011), pp. 35–56.
55. See, for instance, Eric Plutzer, "Becoming a Habitual Voter: Inertia, Resources and Growth in Young Adulthood," *American Political Science Review*, 96 (2002), pp. 41–56; Duane F. Alwin and Jon A. Krosnick, "Aging, Cohorts and the Stability of Sociopolitical Orientations over the Life Span," *American Journal of Sociology*, 97 (1991), pp. 169–95; and Duane F. Alwin, Ronald J. Cohen, and Theodore M. Newcomb, *Political Attitudes over the Life Span* (Madison: University of Wisconsin Press, 1991).
56. Samuel H. Barnes and Max Kaase, *Political Action*, Chapter 2 (Beverly Hills, CA: Sage, 1979).
57. Sidney Verba and Norman H. Nie, *Participation in America* (New York: Harper & Row, 1972), pp. 79–80, 118–19.
58. See Lester Milbrath, *Political Participation: How and Why Do People Get Involved in Politics?* (Chicago: Rand McNally, 1965).
59. Verba and Nie, *Participation in America*, pp. 79–80, 118–19.
60. 2018 November General Election Turnout Rates, United States Elections Project, University of Florida, http://www.electproject.org/2018g.
61. U.S. Census Bureau, *Voting and Registration: Percent Voted in 2016*, http://thedataweb.rm.census.gov/TheDataWeb_HotReport2/voting/voting.hrml
62. U.S. Census Bureau, *Voting and Registration in the Election of November 2014*, Detailed Tables, Table 5, accessed at http://www.census.gov/hhes/www/socdemo/voting/publications/p20/2014/tables.html.
63. U.S. Census Bureau, *Voting and Registration in the Election of November 2018*, Detailed Tables, Table 5, accessed at https://www.census.gov/data/tables/time-series/demo/voting-and-registration/p20-583.html.
64. According to the U.S. Census Bureau's *Current Population Survey* for various years since the 1980s.
65. U.S. Census Bureau, *Voting and Registration in the Election of November 2014*, Table 4b, accessed at https://www.census.gov/data/tables/time-series/demo/voting-and-registration/p20-577.html; and U.S. Census Bureau, Voting and Registration in the Election of November 2016, Table 4b accessed at https://www.census.gov/data/tables/time-series/demo/voting-and-registration/p20-580.html.
66. U.S. Census Bureau, *Voting and Registration in the Election of November 2018*, Detailed Tables, Table 4b, accessed at https://www.census.gov/data/tables/time-series/demo/voting-and-registration/p20-583.html.
67. U.S. Census Bureau, *Voting and Registration in the Election of November 2016*, Table 4b accessed at https://www.census.gov/data/tables/time-series/demo/voting-and-registration/p20-580.html; U.S. Census Bureau, *Voting and Registration in the Election of November 2018*, Detailed Tables, Table 4b, accessed at https://www.census.gov/data/tables/time-series/demo/voting-and-registration/p20-583.html.

68. U.S. Census Bureau, *Voting and Registration in the Election of November 2016*, Table 4b accessed at https://www.census.gov/data/tables/2012/demo/voting-and-registration/p20-568.html.
69. U.S. Census Bureau, *Historical Time Series Tables*, Table A-3, accessed at https://www.census.gov/data/tables/time-series/demo/voting-and-registration/voting-historical-time-series.html.
70. U.S. Census Bureau, *Voting and Registration in the Election of November 2016*, Table 4b accessed at https://www.census.gov/data/tables/time-series/demo/voting-and-registration/p20-580.html; U.S. Census Bureau, *Voting and Registration in the Election of November 2018*, Detailed Tables, Table 4b, accessed at https://www.census.gov/data/tables/time-series/demo/voting-and-registration/p20-583.html.
71. U.S. Census Bureau, *Voting and Registration in the Election of November 2008*, Table 2 accessed at https://www.census.gov/data/tables/2008/demo/voting-and-registration/p20-562-rv.html.
72. U.S. Census Bureau, *Voting and Registration in the Election of November 2016*, Table 4b accessed at https://www.census.gov/data/tables/time-series/demo/voting-and-registration/p20-580.html.
73. Anthony Cilluffo and Richard Fry, "An Early Look at the 2020 Electorate," Pew Research Center, January 30, 2019, https://www.pewsocialtrends.org/essay/an-early-look-at-the-2020-electorate/.
74. Alec Tyson and Shiva Maniam, "Behind Trump's Victory: Divisions by Race, Gender, Education," Pew Research Center, November 9, 2016, http://www.pewresearch.org/fact-tank/2016/11/09/behind-trumps-victory-divisions-by-race-gender-education/; and U.S. Census Bureau, Voting and Registration in the Election of November 2016, Table 4b https://www.census.gov/data/tables/time-series/demo/voting-and-registration/p20-580.html.
75. U.S. Census Bureau, *Voting and Registration in the Election of November 2018*, Detailed Tables, Table 4b, accessed at https://www.census.gov/data/tables/time-series/demo/voting-and-registration/p20-583.html.
76. Anthony Cilluffo and Richard Fry, "An Early Look at the 2020 Electorate," Pew Research Center, January 30, 2019, https://www.pewsocialtrends.org/essay/an-early-look-at-the-2020-electorate/. Paul Taylor and Mark Hugo Lopez, "Six Take-Aways from the Census Bureau's Voting Report," accessed at http://www.pewresearch.org/fact-tank/2013/05/08/six-take-aways-from-the-census-bureaus-voting-report/, on September 16, 2014.
77. See William H. Flanigan and Nancy H. Zingale, *Political Behavior of the American Electorate* (Boston: Allyn and Bacon, 1987), p. 18; Steven J. Rosenstone and John Mark Hanson, *Mobilization, Participation, and Democracy in America* (New York: Macmillan, 1993); and Warren E. Miller and J. Merrill Shanks, *The New American Voter* (Cambridge, MA: Harvard University Press, 1996).
78. This term is the title of a book by Mancur Olson, *The Logic of Collective Action: Public Goods and the Theory of Groups* (Cambridge MA: Harvard University Press, 1965).
79. "Automatic Voter Registration and Modernization in the States," March 29, 2019, The Brennan Center for Justice, accessed at https://www.brennancenter.org/analysis/voter-registration-modernization-states.
80. "Donald Trump Won in Texas," *Politico*, December 16, 2020, https://www.politico.com/2020-election/results/texas/; Texas Secretary of State, Elections Division, "1992—Current Election History," https://www.sos.state.tx.us/elections/historical/index.shtml; "2016 Texas Presidential Election Results," Politico, accessed at https://www.politico.com/2016-election/results/map/president/texas/.
81. Ibid.
82. Alexa Ura, Chris Essig, and Darla Cameron, "Are Texas Suburbs Slipping Away from Republicans?" *Texas Tribune*, November 7, 2018, texastribune.org/2018/11/07/are-texas-suburbs-slipping-away-republicans/.
83. "Exit Poll Results and Analysis from Texas," November 9, 2020, The Washington Post, https://www.washingtonpost.com/elections/interactive/2020/exit-polls/texas-exit-polls/.
84. Ibid.
85. "2018 Voter Poll Results: Texas," *The Washington Post*, November 30, 2018, https://www.washingtonpost.com/graphics/2018/politics/voter-polls/texas.html#methodology.
86. Jamie Knodel, "Gov. Greg Abbott Gives Most of His Appointments to Whites," *The Dallas Morning News*, April 17, 2016, http://trailblazersblog.dallasnews.com/2016/04/gov-greg-abbot-gives-most-of-his-appointments-to-whites.html/; Peggy Fikac, "Analysis: Abbott Favors Donors, White Men for Appointments," *The Houston Chronicle*, January 7, 2018, https://www.houstonchronicle.com/news/houston-texas/houston/article/Analysis-Abbott-favors-donors-white-men-for-12480587.php.
87. For a general introduction to polls and polling techniques, see Herbert Asher, *Polling and the Public: What Every Citizen Should Know*, 8th ed. (Washington, D.C.: CQ Press, 2010).
88. For more information about the value in probability versus nonprobability surveys, see David S. Yeager, Jon A. Krosnick, LinChiat Chang, Harold S. Javitz, Matthew S. Levendusky, Alberto Simpser, and Rui Wang, "Comparing the Accuracy of RDD Telephone Surveys and Internet Surveys Conducted with Probability and Non-Probability Samples," *Public Opinion Quarterly, 75* (2011), pp. 709–47.
89. See, for example, Vicki G. Morwitsz and Carol Pluzinski, "Do Polls Reflect Opinions or Do Opinions Reflect Polls?" *Journal of Consumer Research, 23* (1996), pp. 53–67; Barbara A. Bardes and Robert W. Oldendick, *Public Opinion: Measuring the American Mind*, 4th ed. (Lanham, MD: Rowman & Littlefield, 2012); Wolfgang Donsbackh and Michael W. Traugott, eds., *The SAGE Handbook of Public Opinion Research* (Thousand Oaks, CA: Sage, 2008); and Yue Tan, "Local Media, Public Opinion, and State Legislative Policies: Agenda Setting at the State Level," *International Journal of Press/Politics, 14* (2009), pp. 454–76.
90. Ross Ramsey, "UT/TT Poll: Texas voters familiar with Cruz but not Democratic rival O'Rourke," *The Texas Tribune*, October 19, 2017.
91. See for instance, Drew Desliver and Scott Keeter, "The Challenges of Polling When Fewer People Are Available to Be Polled," July 21, 2015, accessed March 7, 2016, http://www.pewresearch.org/fact-tank/2015/07/21/the-challenges-of-polling-when-fewer-people-are-available-to-be-polled/.
92. Scott Keeter, "Research Roundup: Latest Findings on Cell Phones and Polling," Pew Research Center, May 22, 2009, accessed January 2, 2010, http://pewresearch.org/pubs/848/cell-only-methodology; Stephen J. Blumberg et al., "Wireless Substitution: State-level Estimates From the National Health

Interview Survey, January 2007-June 2010," National Health Statistics Reports, no 39 (Hyattsville, MD: National Center for Health Statistics, 2011); and Stephen J. Blumberg and Julian V. Luke, "Wireless Substitution: Early Release of Estimates From the National Health Interview Survey, July–December 2018," June 2019, accessed May 26, 2020, https://www.cdc.gov/nchs/data/nhis/earlyrelease/wireless201906.pdf.

93. Scott Keeter, Courtney Kennedy, April Clark, Trevor Tompson, and Mike Mokrzycki, "What's Missing from National Landline RDD Surveys?" *Public Opinion Quarterly*, 71 (2007), pp. 772–92; see also Michael Mokrzycki, Scott Keeter, and Courtney Kennedy, "Cell-Phone-Only Voters in the 2008 Exit Poll and Implications for Future Noncoverage Bias," *Public Opinion Quarterly*, 73 (2009), pp. 845–65.

94. J. Michael Brick, Sarah Dipko, Stanley Presser, Clyde Tucker, and Yangyang Yuan, "Nonrepsonse Bias in a Dual Frame Sample of Cell and Landline Numbers," *Public Opinion Quarterly*, 70 (2006), pp. 780–93.

95. Costas Panagopoulos and Kyle Endres, "Which 2020 Election Polls Were Most- and Least - Accurate? Some Were on the Nose. Overall, Though, They Did Worst Than in 2016." The Washington Post, November 25, 2020, https://www.washingtonpost.com/politics/2020/11/25/which-2020-election-polls-were-most-least-accurate/.

96. Nicole Narea, "After 2016, Can We Ever Trust the Polls Again?" December 14, 2016, *The New Republic*, accessed May 8, 2018, https://newrepublic.com/article/139158/2016-can-ever-trust-polls-again.

97. Gloria Dickie, "Why Polls Were Mostly Wrong," Scientific American, November 13, 2020, https://www.scientificamerican.com/article/why-polls-were-mostly-wrong/.

98. Ibid.

99. Ross Ramsey, "UT/TT Poll: Cruz Holds Lead Over Trump in Texas," *The Texas Tribune*, February 23, 2016, https://www.texastribune.org/2016/02/23/uttt-poll-cruz-leads-trump-texas-rubio-lags-behind/.

100. See, for instance, Nate Silver, *The Signal and the Noise: Why So Many Predictions Fail—But Some Don't* (New York: Penguin Group, 2012).

Chapter 10

1. Dennis S. Ippolito and Thomas G. Walker, *Political Parties, Interest Groups, and Public Policy: Group Influence in American Politics* (Englewood Cliffs, NJ: Prentice Hall, 1980), p. 2.
2. John F. Bibby, *Politics, Parties, and Elections in America* (Chicago: Nelson-Hall, 1987), pp. 3–4.
3. Leon Epstein, *Political Parties in Western Democracies* (New York: Praeger, 1967), p. 9.
4. Bibby, *Politics, Parties, and Elections in America*, p. 15.
5. Sarah McCally Morehouse, *State Politics, Parties, and Policy* (New York: Holt, Rinehart and Winston, 1981), p. 118.
6. Ibid., pp. 118–19.
7. Ibid., p. 117.
8. John Crittenden, *Parties and Elections in the United States* (Englewood Cliffs, NJ: Prentice Hall, 1982), p. 11.
9. Robert J. Huckshorn, *Political Parties in America*, 2nd ed. (Monterey, CA: Brooks/Cole Publishing Company, 1981), p. 11.
10. Daniel Mazmanian, *Third Parties in Presidential Elections* (Washington, D.C.: Brookings Institution Press, 1974), p. 5.
11. George Rivera, "Building a Chicano Party in South Texas," *New South, 26* (Spring 1971), pp. 75–78.
12. Ibid.
13. Juan Gomez Quinones, *Chicano Politics* (Albuquerque, NM: University of New Mexico Press, 1990), pp. 128–31.
14. Samuel Huntington, *Political Order in Changing Societies* (New Haven, CT: Yale University Press, 1980), p. 91.
15. Bibby, *Politics, Parties, and Elections in America*, p. 12.
16. V. O. Key, *Southern Politics* (New York: Vintage, 1949), p. 225.
17. Chandler Davidson, *Race and Class in Texas Politics* (Princeton, NJ: Princeton University Press, 1990), p. 21.
18. Ibid., p. 6.
19. Alexander P. Lamis, *The Two-Party South*, exp. ed. (New York: Oxford University Press, 1988), p. 23.
20. Ibid., p. 194.
21. George Norris Green, *The Establishment in Texas Politics, 1938–1957* (Westport, CT: Greenwood, 1979), p. 57.
22. Key, *Southern Politics*, pp. 302–310.
23. Green, *The Establishment in Texas Politics*, pp. 142–48.
24. Key, *Southern Politics*, pp. 294–97.
25. Green, *The Establishment in Texas Politics*, p. 148.
26. Lamis, *The Two-Party South*, p. 195.
27. Ibid., p. 195; and Davidson, *Race and Class in Texas Politics*, p. 201.
28. John R. Knaggs, *Two-Party Texas: The John Tower Era, 1961–1984* (Austin, TX: Eakin, 1986), p. 15.
29. Davidson, *Race and Class in Texas Politics*, p. 199.
30. Lamis, *The Two-Party South*, p. 194.
31. Ibid., pp. 196–97.
32. For an excellent summary of realignment theory and conditions under which realignment is likely to take place, see James L. Sundquist, *Dynamics of the Party System*, rev. ed. (Washington, D.C.: Brookings Institution Press, 1983).
33. James A. Dyer, Arnold Vedlitz, and David B. Hill, "New Voters, Switchers, and Political Party Realignment in Texas," *Western Political Quarterly*, 41 (March 1988), p. 164.
34. See Kevin P. Phillips, *The Emerging Republican Majority* (New Rochelle, NY: Arlington House, 1969); and Richard M. Scammon and Ben J. Wattenberg, *The Real Majority* (New York: Coward-McCann, 1970).
35. Green, *The Establishment in Texas Politics*, p. 208.
36. Dyer, Vedlitz, and Hill, "New Voters, Switchers, and Political Party Realignment in Texas," p. 156.
37. University of Texas/*The Texas Tribune Poll*, Texas Statewide Survey, Field Dates: April 10 to 19, 2020, https://texaspolitics.utexas.edu/latest-poll.
38. "In Changing U. S. Electorate, Race and Education Remain Stark Dividing Lines," Pew Research Center, U.S. Politics & Policy, June 2, 2020, http://www.people-press.org/2020/06/02/in-changing-u-s-electorate-race-and-education-remain-stark-dividing-lines/.
39. See surveys conducted by the University of Texas and *The Texas Tribune* from 2008 through 2017 for questions pertaining to party identification and voting for specific candidates, available at http://texaspolitics.laits.utexas.edu.
40. *Dallas Morning News*, November 9, 1994.

41. See surveys conducted by the University of Texas and *The Texas Tribune* in which positions on public policy issues are assessed by different age groups. These surveys are now available at http://texaspolitics.laits.utexas.edu.
42. Dyer, Vedlitz, and Hill, "New Voters, Switchers, and Political Party Realignment in Texas," pp. 165–66; Scripps Howard, *Texas Poll*, Summer 2003, Fall 2003, Winter 2004, and Spring 2004; and *Rasmussen Reports*, "Election 2008: Texas Presidential Election," October 23, 2008.
43. Jim Henson and Joshua Blank, "Conservatives by Another Name: Change and Continuity in Texas Tea Party Identification," Texas Politics Project at the University of Texas at Austin, https://drive.google.com/file/d/1lo1VVhPN6PSAh2y4q-kKqvDua5HZfEg_/view.
44. Key, *Southern Politics*, p. 255.
45. Davidson, *Race and Class in Texas Politics*, p. 238.
46. Walter Dean Burnham, *Critical Elections and the Mainsprings of American Politics*, Chapter 5 (New York: W. W. Norton, 1970); and Walter Dean Burnham, *The Current Crisis in American Politics* (Oxford: Oxford University Press, 1982).
47. Steve Benen, "The Imposters: How Republicans Quit Governing and Seized American Politics," 2020
48. See Huckshorn, *Political Parties in America*, pp. 358–60.
49. Allan Greenblatt, "The Waning Power of State Political Parties," Governing, December 2015, http://www.governing.com/topics/politics/gov-waning-power-state-parties.html.
50. John F. Bibby, "State Party Organizations: Coping and Adapting to Candidate-Centered Politics and Nationalization," in *The Parties Respond: Changes in American Parties and Campaigns*, 3rd ed., edited by L. Sandy Maisel (Boulder, CO: Westview, 1998), pp. 23–49.
51. V. O. Key, Jr., *Parties, Politics and Pressure Groups*, 4th ed. (New York: Thomas Y. Crowell Company, 1958), p. 347.
52. Bibby, *Politics, Parties, and Elections in America*, p. 82.
53. This discussion of party activists draws from Marjorie Randon Hershey and Paul Allen Beck, *Party Politics in America*, 10th ed., Chapter 5 (New York: Longman, 2003); and Samuel J. Eldersveld and Hanes Walton, Jr., *Political Parties in American Society*, 2nd ed., Chapter 8 (Boston: Bedford/St. Martin's, 2000).
54. Hershey and Beck, *Party Politics in America*, p. 97.
55. Ibid.
56. Eldersveld and Walton, *Political Parties in American Society*, pp. 166–68.

Chapter 11

1. "Gillespie is Nominated," *The San Angelo Press*. September 10, 1902. https://chroniclingamerica.loc.gov/data/batches/txdn_belgium_ver01/data/sn86090049/00206535969/1902091001/0353.pdf
2. There are several ways in which turnout can be calculated. The two most commonly employed are the percent of voting eligible population (VEP) that voted and the percent of the voting age population (VAP) that voted. The VAP is lower than the VEP because it includes noncitizens, prisoners, and ineligible convicted felons.
3. United States Election Project, http://www.electproject.org/2016g.
4. Ibid.
5. L. Sandy Maisel, *Parties and Elections in America* (New York: Random House, 1987), p. 1.
6. Gerald Pomper, *Elections in America* (New York: Dodd, Mead, and Company, 1968), p. 12.
7. Herman Finer, *The Theory and Practice of Modern Government* (New York: Holt, 1949), p. 219.
8. Murray Edelman, *The Symbolic Uses of Politics* (Urbana: University of Illinois Press, 1964), p. 111.
9. V. O. Key, Jr., with the assistance of Milton C. Cummings, Jr., *The Responsible Electorate* (Cambridge, MA: Harvard University Press, 1965), p. 11.
10. Maisel, *Parties and Elections in America*, p. 1.
11. Ibid., p. 3.
12. See Caroline J. Tolbert, John A. Grummel, and Daniel A. Smith, "The Effects of Ballot Initiatives on Voter Turnout in the American States," *American Politics Research*, 29 (November 2001), pp. 625–48, for a bibliography on turnout rates in elections.
13. V. O. Key, Jr., *Southern Politics*, Chapter 12 (New York: Vintage Books, 1949); and James E. Anderson, Richard W. Murray, and Edward L. Farley, *Texas Politics: An Introduction*, 4th ed. (New York: Harper & Row, 1984), pp. 40–42, 605–11.
14. Frank J. Sorauf, *Party Politics in America*, 5th ed. (Boston: Little, Brown, 1984), p. 213; and George Norris Green, *The Establishment in Texas Politics* (Westport, CT: Greenwood, 1979), p. 164.
15. Douglas O. Weeks, "The Texas Direct Primary System," *Southwestern Social Science Quarterly*, 12 (September 1932), p. 99.
16. See, for instance, Frederick Hess, *School Boards at the Dawn of the 21st Century* (Alexandria, VA: National School Board Association, 2002); and Zoltan Hajnal, *Changing White Attitudes toward Black Political Leadership* (New York: Cambridge University Press, 2007). Note that research on Latinos is less clear—see, for instance, Rodolfo Espino, David L. Leal, and Kenneth J. Meier, eds., *Latino Politics: Identity, Mobilization and Representation* (Charlottesville: University of Virginia Press, 2007).
17. Chandler Davidson, *Race and Class in Texas Politics* (Princeton, NJ: Princeton University Press, 1990), p. 24.
18. United States Election Project, http://www.electproject.org/2018g.
19. Texas Office of Secretary of State, Elections Division, https://www.sos.state.tx.us/elections/historical/70-92.shtml.
20. Federal Election Commission, 2012 House and Senate Campaign Finance for Texas, https://classic.fec.gov/disclosurehs/HSState.do.
21. http://sos.state.tx.us/elections/historical/70-92.shtml.
22. Ibid.
23. James Adams and Samuel Merrill, III, "Candidate and Party Strategies in Two-Stage Elections Beginning with a Primary," *American Journal of Political Science*, 52 (2008), pp. 344–59.
24. Majorie Randon Hershey, *Party Politics in America*, 12th ed. (New York: Pearson Longman, 2007), pp. 158–59.
25. Valerie Wigglesworth, "Paxton Beats Huffines in Bitter Republican Primary Race for Texas Senate District 8," *The Dallas Morning News*, March 6, 2018, https://www.dallasnews.com/news/2018-elections/2018/03/06/paxton-ahead-huffines-bitter-republican-primary-race-texas-senate-district-8.
26. See, for instance, Paul A. Djupe and David A. M. Peterson, "The Impact of Negative Campaigning," *Political Research Quarterly*, 55 (2002), pp. 845–60; and David W. Romero, "Divisive Primaries and the House District Vote," *American*

Politics Research, 31 (2003), pp. 178–90. Robert E. Hogan, "The Effects of Primary Divisiveness on General Election Outcomes in State Legislative Elections," *American Politics Research, 31* (2003), pp. 27–47, finds that divisive primaries can result in higher general election vote totals.

27. Patrick Svitek, "Cascade of Endorsements Animates Texas' Democratic U.S. Senate Runoff, which Coronavirus Has Upended," *The Texas Tribune*, May 13, 2020, https://www.texastribune.org/2020/05/13/texas-democrat-senate-runoff/.
28. Davidson, *Race and Class in Texas Politics*, p. 24.
29. City Council Officers Election May 7, 2016 Cancelled, http://www.hillsborotx.org/news-updates/city-council-officers-election-may-7-2016-2016-04-6768; Julie Fancher, "With all candidates unopposed, University Park officials vote to cancel May election," *Dallas Morning News*, March 2, 2016, https://www.dallasnews.com/news/news/2016/03/02/with-all-candidates-unopposed-university-park-votes-unanimously-to-cancel-upcoming-election; and Municipal Elections in Garland, Texas, https://ballotpedia.org/Municipal_elections_in_Garland,_Texas_(2016).
30. Tierra Smith, "Tomball and Magnolia School Districts, Cities Cancel 20 Local Elections in 10 Years," *Community Impact Newspaper*, April 4, 2018, https://communityimpact.com/houston/tomball-magnolia/at-the-capitol/2018/04/04/school-districts-cities-cancel-20-local-elections-in-10-years/.
31. "City of Houston Anti-Discrimination HERO Veto Referendum, Proposition 1 (November 2015)," Ballotpedia. Accessed at https://ballotpedia.org/City_of_Houston_Anti-Discrimination_HERO_Veto_Referendum,_Proposition_1_(November_2015).
32. Texas Secretary of State, Ruth R. Hughs, Early Voting, available at https://www.sos.texas.gov/elections/earlyvoting/archive.shtml.
33. "Early Voting," Texas Secretary of State, https://www.sos.texas.gov/elections/earlyvoting/2018/nov2.shtml.
34. Mandi Cai, "At Least 9.7 Million Texans - 57% of Registered Voters - Voted Early," The Texas Tribune, November 17, 2020, https://apps.texastribune.org/features/2020/texas-early-voting-numbers/.
35. National Association of State Legislatures, "Absentee and Early Voting," http://www.ncsl.org/research/elections-and-campaigns/absentee-and-early-voting.aspx.
36. Alex Samuels, "Joe Biden Wins Texas Primary in a Stunning Turnaround," *The Texas Tribune*, March 3, 2020, https://www.texastribune.org/2020/03/03/texas-2020-presidential-results-bernie-sanders-joe-biden/.
37. J. Edward Moreno, "Here's Where Your State Stands On Mail-In Voting," *The Hill*, June 9, 2020, https://thehill.com/homenews/state-watch/501577-heres-where-your-state-stands-on-mail-in-voting.
38. Alexa Ura, "Federal Lawsuit Claims Texas' Mail-In Ballot Procedures are Unconstitutional," *The Texas Tribune*, August 7, 2019, https://www.texastribune.org/2019/08/07/two-texas-voters-sue-state-after-their-mail-ballots-were-rejected/.
39. Sydney Ember, "Texas' System for Verifying Signatures on Mail-In Ballots is Unconstitutional, a Judge Ruled," *The New York Times*, September 9, 2020, https://www.nytimes.com/2020/09/09/us/elections/texas-system-for-verifying-signatures-on-mail-in-ballots-is-unconstitutional-a-judge-ruled.html.
40. Guy-Uriel E. Charles, "Texas Legal Battles Highlight How the 2020 Election Is Being Fought in the Courts," *NBC News*, October 22, 2020, https://www.nbcnews.com/think/opinion/texas-legal-battles-highlight-how-2020-election-being-fought-courts-ncna1244306.
41. Alexa Ura, "Plantiffs Fold Hand in Texas State Court Lawsuit Seeking Expansion of Voting by Mail During Coronavirus," *The Texas Tribune*, June 10, 2020, https://www.texastribune.org/2019/08/07/two-texas-voters-sue-state-after-their-mail-ballots-were-rejected/.
42. Jolie McCullough, "Texas Counties Will Be Allowed Only One Drop-Off Location for Mail-In Ballots, State Supreme Court Rules," *Texas Tribune*, October 27, 2020, https://www.texastribune.org/2020/10/27/texas-voting-elections-mail-in-drop-off/.
43. "COVID-Related Election Litigation Tracker," Stanford-MIT Healthy Elections Project, accessed on October 25, 2020, https://healthyelections-case-tracker.stanford.edu/.
44. Robert S. Lorch, *State and Local Politics*, 3rd ed. (Upper Saddle River, NJ: Prentice Hall, 1989), p. 63; and Bexar County Elections Administration, telephone conversation, November 26, 2003.
45. Office of the Secretary of State, "1992–Current Election History," https://elections.sos.state.tx.us/index.htm.
46. Elena Mejia Lutz, "Although Texas Leads the Nation in Straight-Ticket Voting, Bill to Eliminate It Gains Traction," San Antonio Express-News, May 11, 2017, https://www.expressnews.com/news/local/article/Although-Texas-leads-nation-in-straight-ticket-11140532.php.
47. Jolie McCullough, "Gov. Abbott Signs Bill to Eliminate Straight-Ticket Voting Beginning in 2020," *The Texas Tribune*, June 1, 2017, https://www.texastribune.org/2017/06/01/texas-gov-greg-abbott-signs-bill-eliminate-straight-ticket-voting/.
48. Ibid.
49. Counties report election results and several calculate straight-party voting.
50. Office of the Secretary of State, Elections Division, telephone conversation, July 30, 2009.
51. Rupert Richardson, Ernest Wallace, and Adrian Anderson, *Texas: The Lone Star State*, 5th ed. (Englewood Cliffs, NJ: Prentice Hall, 1988), p. 231.
52. See Merline Pitre, *Through Many Dangers, Toils and Snares: Black Leadership in Texas, 1868–1890* (Austin, TX: Eakin, 1985).
53. Richardson, et al., *Texas*, p. 312.
54. Wilbourn E. Benton, *Texas Politics: Constraints and Opportunities*, 5th ed. (Chicago: Nelson Hall, 1984), pp. 72–73.
55. *Harper* v. *Virginia State Board of Elections*, 86 S. Ct. 1079 (1966).
56. Benton, *Texas Politics*, pp. 67–72.
57. *Nixon* v. *Herndon, et al.*, 273 U.S. 536 (1927).
58. *Nixon* v. *Condon*, 286 U.S. 73 (1932).
59. *Grovey* v. *Townsend*, 295 U.S. 45 (1935).
60. *Smith* v. *Allwright*, 321 U.S. 649 (1944).
61. *John Terry, et al., Petitioners* v. *A. J. Adams, et al.*, 345 U.S. 461 (1953); and National Voting Rights Institute, "'Wealth Primary'—Legal Theory," NVRI.org, http://www.nvri.net/about/wealth1.shtml.
62. Beryl E. Pettus and Randall W. Bland, *Texas Government Today: Structures, Functions, Political Processes*, 3rd ed. (Homewood, IL: Dorsey, 1984), pp. 85–86.

63. *Beare, et al. v. Preston Smith, Governor of Texas*, 321 F. Supp. 1100 (1971).
64. Benton, *Texas Politics*, p. 65.
65. See, for instance, Susan Welch, "The Impact of At-Large Elections on the Representation of Blacks and Hispanics," *Journal of Politics*, 52(4) (1990), pp. 1050–76; and David L. Leal, Valerie Martinez-Ebers, and Kenneth J. Meier, "The Politics of Latino Education: The Biases of At-Large Elections," *Journal of Politics*, 66(4) (2004), pp. 1224–44. However, others find the differences between at-large and single-member districts to be insignificant; see, for instance, Luis Ricardo Fraga, Kenneth J. Meier, and Robert E. England, "Hispanic Americans and Educational Policy: Limits to Equal Access," *Journal of Politics*, 48 (1986), pp. 850–76; and Rene R. Rocha, "Black-Brown Coalitions in Local School Board Elections," *Political Research Quarterly*, 60(2) (2007), pp. 315–27.
66. *Congressional Quarterly Weekly Report*, 51 (September 1993), p. 2318.
67. "Election Administration and Voting Survey, 2018 Comprehensive Report: A Report to the 116th Congress," U.S. Election Assistance Commission. Report accessed at https://www.eac.gov/sites/default/files/eac_assets/1/6/2018_EAVS_Report.pdf
68. "League of Women Voters of Texas Files Lawsuit Demanding Online Motor Voter Registration," January 15, 2020, https://www.lwv.org/newsroom/press-releases/league-women-voters-texas-files-lawsuit-demanding-online-motor-voter.
69. 2014 American Community Survey, https://www.census.gov/acs/www/data/data-tables-and-tools/index.php; see also http://www.electproject.org/.
70. According to the U.S. Elections Project. Data available at http://www.electproject.org/2016g.
71. Luis Noe-Bustamante, Abby Budiman, and Mark Hugo Lopez, "Where Latinos have the most eligible voters in the 2020 election," Pew Research Center, January 31, 2020. Accessed at https://www.pewresearch.org/fact-tank/2020/01/31/where-latinos-have-the-most-eligible-voters-in-the-2020-election/.
72. Michael Wines, "Texas Agrees to Soften Voter ID Law after Court Order," *The New York Times*, August 3, 2016, http://www.nytimes.com/2016/08/04/us/texas-agrees-to-soften-voter-id-law-after-court-order.html?_r=0.
73. Bill Hobby, Mark P. Jones, Jim Granato, Renee Cross, "The Texas Voter ID Law and the 2014 Election: A Study of Texas's 23rd Congressional District," August 2015. Accessed at http://bakerinstitute.org/media/files/files/e0029eb8/Politics-VoterID-Jones-080615.pdf.
74. Jim Malewitz, "Texas Voter ID Law Violates Voting Rights Act, Court Rules," *The Texas Tribune*, July 20, 2016, https://www.texastribune.org/2016/07/20/appeals-court-rules-texas-voter-id/; and Alexa Ura, "Federal Appeals Judges Question Challenge to Revised Texas Voter ID Law," *The Texas Tribune*, December 5, 2017. Accessed at https://www.texastribune.org/2017/12/05/texas-heads-back-5th-circuit-long-winding-voter-id-fight/.
75. Hannah Wiley, "In Texas, the 'Rainbow Wave' Outpaces the Blue One,' *The Texas Tribune*, November 8, 2018, https://www.texastribune.org/2018/11/07/texas-midterm-election-rainbow-wave-lgbtq-candidates/.
76. "Black Mayors," https://blackdemographics.com/culture/black-politics/black-mayors/.
77. "Women Elected Officials by Race/Ethnicity," Center for American Women and Politics, Eagleton Institute of Politics, Rutgers University, https://cawpdata.rutgers.edu/women-elected-officials/race-ethnicity?current=1&yearend_filter=All&level%5B%5D=State+Legislative&state%5B%5D=Texas&items_per_page=50.
78. Data provided by the Center for the American Women and Politics, Rutgers University, https://cawp.rutgers.edu/levels_of_office/women-mayors-us-cities-2019.
79. This is the most current fully comprehensive study of women in elected office in Texas. Texas Municipal League, *Texas Municipal League Directory of City Officials*, 2013 (Austin, TX: 2013). Courtesy of Ms. Rachael Pitts and League staff.
80. http://www.txcourts.gov/news/texas-female-judges-celebrated.aspx.
81. Data for 2016 taken from the websites of the state's 254 counties; data for 2006 courtesy of Richard O. Avery, director of the V. G. Young Institute of County Government, Texas A&M University. Survey completed in 2006.
82. Texas Association of School Boards, data provided courtesy of the Association, February 20, 2014.
83. For an excellent analysis of the early development of campaign professionals, see Larry J. Sabato, *The Rise of the Political Consultants* (New York: Basic Books, 1981).
84. Norris, *The Establishment in Texas Politics*, pp. 24–25.
85. R. Kay Green, "The Game Changer: Social Media and the 2016 Presidential Election," November 16, 2015, *Huffpost Politics*, http://www.huffingtonpost.com/r-kay-green/the-game-changer-social-m_b_8568432.html.
86. Christopher Adams, "COVID-19 is Changing Political Campaigning in 2020," Reform Austin, June 26, 2020, https://www.reformaustin.org/coronavirus/covid-19-is-changing-political-campaigning-in-2020/.
87. Sarah Ewall-Wice, Aaron Navarro and Elanor Watson, "Campaigning Amid Coronavirus: Candidates Look for New Ways to Connect," CBS News, April 4, 2020, https://www.cbsnews.com/news/campaigning-during-coronavirus-candidates-look-for-new-ways-to-connect/.
88. Jeffrey Gottfried and Michael Barthel, "Among Millennials Engaged in Primaries, Dems More Likely to Learn about the Election from Social Media," Pew Research Center, February 9, 2016. Accessed at http://www.pewresearch.org/fact-tank/2016/02/09/among-millennials-engaged-in-primaries-dems-more-likely-to-learn-about-the-election-from-social-media/.
89. Elisa Shearer, "Social Media Outpaces Print Newspapers in the U.S. as a News Source," Pew Research Center, December 10, 2018, https://www.pewresearch.org/fact-tank/2018/12/10/social-media-outpaces-print-newspapers-in-the-u-s-as-a-news-source/.
90. Elisa Shearer and Jeffrey Gottfried, "News Use across Social Media Platforms 2017," Pew Research Center, September 7, 2017. Accessed at http://www.journalism.org/2017/09/07/news-use-across-social-media-platforms-2017/.
91. Harry Davies, "Ted Cruz Using Firm That Harvested Data on Millions of Unwitting Facebook Users," *The Guardian*, December 11, 2015, https://www.theguardian.com/us-news/2015/dec/11/senator-ted-cruz-president-campaign-facebook-user-data; Matthew Rosenberg, Nicholas Confessore and Carol Cadwalladr, "How Trump Consultants Exploited the Facebook Data of Millions,"

91. *The New York Times*, March 17, 2018, https://www.nytimes.com/2018/03/17/us/politics/cambridge-analytica-trump-campaign.html.
92. Matthew Rosenberg, Nicholas Confessore, and Carole Cadwalladr, "How Trump Consultants Exploited the Facebook Data of Millions," *The New York Times*, March 17, 2018, https://www.nytimes.com/2018/03/17/us/politics/cambridge-analytica-trump-campaign.html.
93. Sam Meredith, "Facebook-Cambridge Analytica: A Timeline of the Data Hijacking Scandal," CNBC, April 10, 2018, https://www.cnbc.com/2018/04/10/facebook-cambridge-analytica-a-timeline-of-the-data-hijacking-scandal.html.
94. Patrick Svitek and Haley Samsel, "Ted Cruz Says Cambridge Analytica Told His Presidential Campaign Its Data Use Was Legal," *Texas Tribune*, March 20, 2018, https://www.texastribune.org/2018/03/20/ted-cruz-campaign-cambridge-analytica/.
95. W. Lance Bennett, *The Governing Crisis: Media, Money and Marketing in American Elections* (New York: St. Martin's Press, 1992), p. 32.
96. See Edwin Diamond and Stephen Bates, *The Spot: The Rise of Political Advertising on Television*, rev. ed. (Cambridge, MA: MIT Press, 1988).
97. *Texas Observer*, September 28, 1990, p. 8.
98. See, for example, Stephen D. Ansolabehere, Shanto Iyengar, and Adam Simon, "Replicating Experiments Using Aggregate and Survey Data: The Case of Negative Advertising and Turnout," *American Political Science Review*, 93(4) (1999), pp. 901–909; and Richard R. Lau, Lee Sigelman, and Ivy Brown Rovner, "The Effects of Negative Political Campaigns: A Meta-Analytic Reassessment," *Journal of Politics*, 69(4) (2007), pp. 1176–1209.
99. Bennett, *The Governing Crisis*, pp. 33–34.
100. Adam Wollner, "Texas Senate Duel Is Off the Charts for Outside Spending," *OpenSecretsblog*, July 31, 2012, https://www.opensecrets.org/news/2012/07/outside-spending-tops-14m-in-texas.html.
101. "Texas Senate 2018 Race," Open Secrets, The Center for Responsive Politics, https://www.opensecrets.org/races/summary?cycle=2018&id=TXS2.
102. Sabato, *The Rise of the Political Consultants*, p. 220.
103. S. J. Guzzeta, *The Campaign Manual: A Definitive Study of the Modern Political Campaign Process*, 6th ed. (Flat Rock, NC: AmeriCan GOTV Enterprises, 2002), Chapter 9.
104. Moveon.org—Democracy in Action and the campaign of President Obama are two cases that merit further attention for their fund-raising strategies.
105. Alan Bernstein, "Election '97—The Race for City Hall—Record Spent on Mayoral Election Despite Limits," *Houston Chronicle*, December 2, 1997, p. 1A.
106. John Williams, Salatheia Bryant, and Rachel Graves, "Election 2003—It's White in a Rout—Parker Wins Controller Post," *Houston Chronicle*, December 7, 2003, p. 1A.
107. Data available at http://fortworthtexas.gov/elections/campaign-finance/.
108. Data available at http://fortworthtexas.gov/files/071515_Betsy_Price_Campaign_Finance_Report.pdf; http://fortworthtexas.gov/files/c68ddf44-0ad4-43b6-a57c-5c83bf0738e5.pdf; http://fortworthtexas.gov/files/d7ad91c3-fc68-4e9c-9bc7-836e869b9cb0.pdf; and http://fortworthtexas.gov/files/c1d71e29-ef54-4a83-a71d-5e180c894094.pdf.
109. National Institute on Money in State Politics—Follow the Money. Accessed at http://www.followthemoney.org/election-overview.
110. Ryan Murphy and Jay Root, "Texas Republicans Getting Almost 90 percent of Money Flowing into State Elections," *The Texas Tribune*, February 19, 2018. Accessed at https://www.texastribune.org/2018/02/19/texas-republicans-getting-almost-90-percent-money-flowing-state-electi/.
111. Texans for Public Justice, "Money in PoliTex: A Guide to Money in the 2002 Texas Elections," November 2003.
112. Becca Aaronson, "How Much Texas Politicians Spent per Vote in 2016," *The Texas Tribune*, March 3, 2016. Accessed at http://www.texastribune.org/2016/03/03/how-much-texas-politicians-spent-per-vote-in-2016/.
113. Texans for Public Justice, "Texas PACs: 2014 Election Cycle Spending," February 2016. Accessed at http://info.tpj.org/reports/pdf/PACs2014.pdf "Texas Finance Summary," Transparency USA, https://www.transparencyusa.org/tx/.
114. All data for this paragraph comes from "Political Action Committees," Texas, Transparency USA, https://www.transparencyusa.org/tx/pacs.
115. All data from Transparency USA, https://www.transparencyusa.org/tx/pac/texans-for-lawsuit-reform-pac-28135-gpac?cycle=2016-election-cycle; https://www.transparencyusa.org/tx/pac/texans-for-lawsuit-reform-pac-28135-gpac?cycle=2018-election-cycle.
116. "Texans for Lawsuit Reform," Follow the Money, https://www.followthemoney.org/entity-details?eid=4675&default=contributor.
117. Transparency Texas, "Top Ten PACs of the 2018 Texas Election Cycle," September 6, 2017. Accessed at https://www.transparencytexas.org/top-ten-pacs-of-the-2018-texas-election-cycle/on April 19, 2018.
118. "Outside Spending," Center for Responsive Secrets, https://www.opensecrets.org/outsidespending/fes_summ.php?cycle=2016 and https://www.opensecrets.org/outsidespending/fes_summ.php?cycle=2018.
119. Robert Maguire, "$1.4 Billion and Counting in Spending by Super PACs, Dark Money," Center for Responsive Politics, November 9, 2016. Accessed at https://finance.transparencytexas.org/filers?e=2016-election-cycle; Center for Responsive Politics, "2016 Outside Spending by Group." Accessed at Center for Responsive Politics, "Outside Spending by Cycle through March 10th of Election Year, Excluding Party Committees," http://www.opensecrets.org/outsidespending/on April 19, 2018.
120. Texans for Public Justice, "Texas PACs: 2014 Election Cycle Spending," February 2016, http://info.tpj.org/reports/pdf/PACs2014.pdf.
121. Transparency Texas, "PACs." Accessed at https://finance.transparencytexas.org/filers on April 19, 2018 and "Empower Texans PAC," Transparency USA, https://www.transparencyusa.org/tx/pac/empower-texans-pac-61927-gpac/?cycle=2018-election-cycle.
122. Texans for Public Justice, "Texas PACs: 2012 Election Cycle Spending," October 2013, available at http://info.tpj.org/reports/pdf/PACs2012.pdf.
123. Frank J. Sorauf, *Money in American Elections* (Glenview, IL: Scott, Foresman, 1988), pp. 298–301.
124. Larry Sabato, *PAC Power* (New York: W. W. Norton, 1985), pp. 126–28.
125. Sorauf, *Money in American Elections*, pp. 306–311.

Chapter 12

1. John Reynolds, "New Texas House Rules: Press Must Affirm They Do Not Lobby," *The Texas Tribune*, December 4, 2014.
2. Emma Platoff, "In the Texas House, They're Seen as Lobbyists. In the Senate, They Sit at the Press Table," *The Texas Tribune*, January 29, 2019.
3. Thomas Jefferson. 1903–1904. *The Writings of Thomas Jefferson*, Memorial Edition, XX, eds., A. A. Lipscomb and A. E. Bergh. (Washington, D.C.: Thomas Jefferson Memorial Association of the United States).
4. Brett Samuels, "Trump Ramps Up Rhetoric on Media, Calls Press 'The Enemy of the People," *The Hill*, April 5, 2019, https://thehill.com/homenews/administration/437610-trump-calls-press-the-enemy-of-the-people.
5. "Poll: One-Third of Americans Say News Media Is the 'Enemy of the People,'" *The Hill*, July 2, 2019, https://thehill.com/hilltv/what-americas-thinking/451311-poll-a-third-of-americans-say-news-media-is-the-enemy-of-the-people.
6. Mark Jurkowitz and Amy Mitchell, "Most Journalists Should Be Watchdogs, But Views of How Well They Fill This Role Vary by Party, Media Diet," Pew Research Center, February 26, 2020, https://www.journalism.org/2020/02/26/most-say-journalists-should-be-watchdogs-but-views-of-how-well-they-fill-this-role-vary-by-party-media-diet/.
7. Michael Barthel and Amy Mitchell, "Americans' Attitudes about the News Media Deeply Divided along Partisan Lines," Pew Research Center, May 10, 2017, accessed May 11, 2017, http://www.journalism.org/2017/05/10/americans-attitudes-about-the-news-media-deeply-divided-along-partisan-lines/.
8. "Democracy, Approval Ratings and the 2020 Presidential Election," Texas Lyceum Poll, 2019.
9. Michael Schudson, *Why Democracies Need an Unlovable Press* (Cambridge: Polity Press, 2008).
10. Benjamin I. Page, *Who Deliberates? Mass Media in Modern Democracy* (Chicago: University of Chicago Press, 1996); and Lawrence R. Jacobs, Fay Lomax Cook, and Michael X. Delli Carpini, *Talking Together: Public Deliberation and Political Participation in America* (Chicago: University of Chicago Press, 2009).
11. Matthew Hindman, *The Myth of Digital Democracy* (Princeton: Princeton University Press, 2009).
12. See, for example, Silvia Knobloch-Westerwick, Cornelia Mothes, and Nick Polavin, "Confirmation Bias, Ingroup Bias, and Negativity Bias in Selective Exposure to Political Information," *Communication Research* (2017), pp. 1–21.
13. Elizabeth Dubois, "The Echo Chamber Is Overstated: The Moderating Effect of Political Interest and Diverse Media," *Information, Communication & Society*, 21(2018): pp. 729–45.
14. Maxwell E. McCombs and Donald L. Shaw, "The Agenda-Setting Function of the Press," in *Media Power in Politics*, 2nd ed., edited by Doris A. Graber (Washington, D.C.: Congressional Quarterly Press, 1990), p. 712.
15. Doris A. Graber, *Mass Media and American Politics*, 2nd ed. (Washington, D.C.: Congressional Quarterly Press, 1984), pp. 78–79.
16. Ibid., pp. 268–69.
17. Gladys Engel Lang and Kurt Lang, *The Battle for Public Opinion: The President, the Press, and the Polls during Watergate* (New York: Columbia University Press, 1983), p. 58.
18. Larry N. Gerston, *Making Public Policy: From Conflict to Resolution* (Glenview, IL: Scott, Foresman and Company, 1983), pp. 55–56.
19. The following discussion of the attention cycle is drawn from Anthony Downs, "Up and Down with Ecology—The Issue Attention Cycle," *Public Interest*, 32 (Summer 1972), pp. 38–50.
20. See, for example, Angus Campbell, Philip Converse, Warren Miller, and Donald Stokes, *The American Voter* (New York: Wiley, 1960); Marc J. Hetherington, "Resurgent Mass Partisanship," *American Political Science Review*, 95 (2001), pp. 619–32; and Michael S. Lewis-Beck, Helmut Norpoth, William G. Jacoby, and Herbert F. Weisberg, *The American Voter Revisited* (Ann Arbor: University of Michigan Press, 2008).
21. See Marjorie Randon Hershey, *Party Politics in America*, 12th ed., Chapter 8 (New York: Pearson Longman, 2007); and Richard R. Lau and David P. Redlawsk, *How Voters Decide: Information Processing during Election Campaigns* (New York: Cambridge University Press, 2006).
22. Annie Karni, "Facebook Removes Trump Ads Displaying Symbol Used by Nazis," *The New York Times*, June 18, 2020.
23. Walter Cronkite and Paul Taylor, "To Lift Politics Out of TV Swamp," *Houston Chronicle*, March 10, 1996, p. 1E.
24. Erika Franklin Fowler, Travis N. Ridout, and Michael M. Franz, "Political Advertising in 2016: The Presidential Election as Outlier?" *The Forum: A Journal of Applied Research in Contemporary Politics*, 14 (2016): pp. 445–69.
25. "President, House Ads Slow to Trickle," Wesleyan Media Project, April 9, 2020.
26. Wayne Slater, "As Wendy Davis Touts Life Story in Race for Governor, Key Facts Blurred," *The Dallas Morning News*, January 19, 2014.
27. Manny Fernandez and Laurie Goodstein, "Life Story of Wendy Davis Swings from Strength to Flash Point in Texas Campaign," *The New York Times*, January 29, 2014.
28. Assessing the role of gender in American politics is complex. For more information see, for instance, Nancy Burns, "Gender in the Aggregate, Gender in the Individual, Gender in Political Action," *Politics & Gender*, 3 (2007), pp. 104–24; Susan J. Carroll and Kira Sanbonmatsu, *More Women Can Run: Gender and Pathways to the State Legislatures* (New York: Oxford University Press, 2013); and Deborah Jordan Brooks, *He Runs, She Runs: Why Gender Stereotypes Do Not Harm Women Candidates* (Princeton: Princeton University Press, 2013).
29. George Rodrigue, "Ask the Editor," *The Dallas Morning News*, January 21, 2014.
30. Peggy Fikac, "Equal Pay Debate Shifts to Attorney General's Office," *San Antonio Express-News*, March 18, 2014.
31. John Williams, R. G. Ratcliffe, and Rachael Graves, "Poll Puts Perry in Double-Digit Lead; Cornyn Maintains Slim Advantage over Kirk for Senate," *Houston Chronicle*, November 3, 2002, p. 1A.
32. Federal Election Commission, 2012 House and Senate Campaign Finance for Texas.
33. Mike McIntire, "Ted Cruz Didn't Report Goldman Sachs Loan in a Senate Race," *The New York Times*, January 13, 2016.
34. Tom Benning, "How much of the record $80 million Beto O'Rourke raised to beat Ted Cruz is left for another run?" *The Dallas Morning News*, December 7, 2018.

35. Archie P. McDonald, "Anglo-American Arrival in Texas," in *The Texas Heritage*, 2nd ed., edited by Ben Proctor and Archie McDonald (Arlington Heights, IL: Harlan Davidson, 1992), p. 28.
36. T. R. Fehrenbach, *Lone Star: A History of Texas and the Texans* (New York: Macmillan, 1968), p. 302.
37. Ibid., p. 303.
38. George Norris Green, *The Establishment in Texas Politics, 1938–1957* (Westport, CT: Greenwood, 1979), p. 10.
39. Pew Research Center for the People and the Press, "In Changing News Landscape, Even Television Is Vulnerable, Trends in News Consumption: 1991–2012," September 27, 2012, accessed May 10, 2018, http://www.people-press.org/2012/09/27/in-changing-news-landscape-even-television-is-vulnerable/; Pew Research Center, "Social Media Outpaces Print Newspapers in the U.S. as a News Source," December 10, 2018.
40. Texas Press Association, texaspress.com.
41. Dan Zehr, "*American-Statesman* to Outsource Production of Its Print Edition," *Austin American-Statesman*, April 30, 2015.
42. Marc Tracy, "Gannett, the Owner of *USA Today*, Is About to Get a Whole Lot Bigger," *The New York Times*, August 5, 2019.
43. Erin Mulvaney, "Capitol Press Corps Adapts to Technology's Impact on Journalism," *Daily Texan*, March 2, 2009.
44. Adam Felder, "The Limits of the Late-Night Comedy Takedown," *The Atlantic*, April 17, 2016.
45. Felicity Barringer, "Does Deal Signal Lessening of Media Independence?" *The New York Times*, January 11, 2000, p. C12.
46. C. Edwin Baker, *Media Concentration and Democracy: Why Ownership Matters* (New York: Cambridge University Press, 2007).
47. Zach Wichter, "Sinclair Videos Renew Debate over Media Ownership," *The New York Times*, April 2, 2018.
48. Ted Johnson, "Sinclair Broadcast Group to Pay $48 Million Penalty to Close FCC Investigations," *Deadline*, May 6, 2020.
49. Paul Farhi, "*The Washington Post* Closes Sale to Amazon Founder Jeff Bezos," *The Washington Post*, October 1, 2013.
50. David Carr, "The Media Equation: Newspaper as Business Pulpit," *The New York Times*, June 10, 2012.
51. Sydney Ember, "Tronc Sells the Los Angeles Times to Local Billionaire for $500 Million," *The New York Times*, February 7, 2018.
52. Jodi Enda, Katrina Eva Matsa and Jan Lauren Boyles, "America's Shifting Statehouse Press. Can New Players Compensate for Lost Legacy Reporters?" Pew Research Center, Journalism & Media, July 10, 2014, accessed May 9, 2018, http://www.journalism.org/2014/07/10/americas-shifting-statehouse-press/.
53. Ibid.
54. Paul W. Taylor, "Statehouse Reporting Loses Its Bite," *Governing* (October 2013).
55. Paul Starr, "Goodbye to the Age of Newspapers (Hello to a New Era of Corruption)," *New Republic*, March 4, 2009, http://www.newrepublic.com/article/goodbye-the-age-newspapers-hello-new-era-corruption.
56. Robert W. McChesney and John Nichols, *The Death and Life of American Journalism: The Media Revolution That Will Begin the World Again* (New York: Nation Books, 2010).
57. John Sullivan, "PR Industry Fills Vacuum Left by Shrinking Newsrooms," *ProPublica*, May 1, 2011.
58. Lary Buchanan, Quoctrung Bui and Jugal K. Patel, "Black Lives Matter May Be the Largest Movement in U.S. History," *The New York Times*, July 3, 2020, https://www.nytimes.com/interactive/2020/07/03/us/george-floyd-protests-crowd-size.html.
59. Lorrie Faith Cranor and Shane M. Greenstein, eds., *Communications Policy and Information Technology: Promises, Problems, Prospects* (Cambridge, MA: MIT Press, 2002).
60. Paul Farhi, "Thanks to Trump, Fringe News Enters the Mainstream," *The Washington Post*, December 11, 2015.
61. Casey Michel, "How the Russians Pretended to Be Texans and Texans Believed Them," *The Dallas Morning News*, October 18, 2017, accessed May 9, 2018, https://www.dallasnews.com/opinion/commentary/2017/10/18/russians-pretended-texansand-texans-believed.
62. Asher Price, "Jade Helm Controversy Part of Russian Interference, ex-NSA Head Says," *Austin American-Statesman*, May 3, 2018.
63. Benedict Carey, "'Fake News': Wide Reach but Little Impact, Study Suggests," *The New York Times*, January 2, 2018.
64. See for instance, Dara Lind, "President Donald Trump Finally Admits That 'Fake News' Just Means News He Doesn't Like," *Vox*, May 9, 2018, https://www.vox.com/policy-and-politics/2018/5/9/17335306/trump-tweet-twitter-latest-fake-news-credentials; Margaret Sullivan, "What It Really Means When Trump Calls a Story 'Fake News,'" *The Washington Post*, April 13, 2020, https://www.washingtonpost.com/lifestyle/media/what-it-really-means-when-trump-calls-a-story-fake-news/2020/04/13/56fbe2c0-7d8c-11ea-9040-68981f488eed_story.html.
65. Anne Applebaum, "Mark Zuckerberg Should Spend $45 Billion on Undoing Facebook's Damage to Democracies," *The Washington Post*, December 10, 2015.
66. "Many Americans Say Made-Up News Is a Critical Problem That Needs To Be Fixed," Pew Research Center, June 5, 2019.
67. Kate Conger, "Twitter Labels Trump Tweet About 'Racist Baby' as Manipulated Media," *The New York Times*, June 18, 2020.
68. See Jeffrey M. Berry and Clyde Wilcox, *The Interest Group Society*, 5th ed. (New York: Pearson Longman, 2009); and Allan J. Cigler and Burdett A. Loomis, eds., *Interest Group Politics*, 8th ed. (Washington: CQ Press, 2012).
69. Pew Research Center for the People and the Press, "Americans Spending More Time Following the News," September 12, 2010.
70. Pew Research Center for the People and the Press, "In Changing News Landscape, Even Television Is Vulnerable," September 27, 2012.
71. Sara Lipka, "Freshmen Increasingly Discuss Politics, Worry About Money, Survey Finds," *Chronicle of Higher Education* (January 19, 2007), p. 21.
72. Jeffrey Gottfried, Michael Barthel, Elisa Shearer, and Amy Mitchell, "The 2016 Presidential Campaign—a News Event That's Hard to Miss," Pew Research Center: Journalism & Media, February 4, 2016.
73. Katie Reilly, "Respect for Journalists' Contributions Has Fallen Significantly in Recent Years," Pew Research Center, July 25, 2013.
74. Cary Funk and Brian Kennedy, "Public Confidence in Scientists Has Remained Stable for Decades," Pew Research Center, April 6, 2017, accessed May 9, 2018, http://

www.pewresearch.org/fact-tank/2017/04/06/public-confidence-in-scientists-has-remained-stable-for-decades/.

75. Jeffrey Gottfried, Galen Stocking, Elizabeth Grieco, Mason Walker, Maya Khuzam and Amy Mitchell, "Trusting the News Media in the Trump Era," Pew Research Center, December 12, 2019, https://www.journalism.org/2019/12/12/within-both-parties-approval-of-trump-is-closely-linked-to-trust-in-the-news-media/; Mark Jurkowitz, Amy Mitchell, Elisa Shearer and Mason Walker, "U.S. Media Polarization and the 2020 Election: A Nation Divided," Pew Research Center, January 24, 2020, https://www.journalism.org/2020/01/24/u-s-media-polarization-and-the-2020-election-a-nation-divided/.

76. Pew Research Center for the People and the Press, "Cable Leads the Pack as Campaign News Source," February 7, 2012.

77. Michael Barthel and Amy Mitchell, "Democrats, Republicans Now Split on Support for Watchdog Role," Pew Research Center, Journalism & Media, May 10, 2017, accessed May 9, 2018, http://www.journalism.org/2017/05/10/democrats-republicans-now-split-on-support-for-watchdog-role/.

78. Jeffrey Gottfried, Michael Barthel and Amy Mitchell, "Trump, Clinton Voters Divided in Their Main Source for Election News," Pew Research Center, Journalism & Media, January 18, 2017.

79. "Cable TV and COVID-19: How Americans perceive the outbreak and view media coverage differ by main news source," Pew Research Center, April 1, 2020.

80. William Schneider and I. A. Lewis, "Views on the News," *Public Opinion* (August–September 1985), p. 7; and Pew Research Center for the People and the Press, "Press Widely Criticized, but Trusted More than Other Information Sources," September 22, 2011.

81. Edward Jay Epstein, *News from Nowhere* (New York: Random House, 2000), pp. 13–14.

82. Starr, "Goodbye to the Age of Newspapers (Hello to a New Era of Corruption)."

Chapter 13

1. Alexis de Tocqueville, *Democracy in America*, Chapter XII (New York: Dearborn & Co.,1938).

2. Larry Buchanan, Quoctrung Bui, and Jugal K. Patel, "Black Lives Matter May Be the Largest Movement in U.S. History," *The New York Times*, July 3, 2020, https://www.nytimes.com/interactive/2020/07/03/us/george-floyd-protests-crowd-size.html.

3. Giovanni Russonello, "Why Most Americans Support the Protests," *The New York Times*, June 5, 2020, https://www.nytimes.com/2020/06/05/us/politics/polling-george-floyd-protests-racism.html.

4. "Protestors' Anger Justified Even If Actions May Not Be," Monmouth University Polling Institute, June 2, 2020, https://www.monmouth.edu/polling-institute/reports/monmouthpoll_us_060220/.

5. Nate Cohn and Kevin Quealy, "How Public Opinion Has Moved on Black Lives Matter," *The New York Times*, June 10, 2020, https://www.nytimes.com/interactive/2020/06/10/upshot/black-lives-matter-attitudes.html.

6. Deja Thomas and Juliana Menasce Horowitz, "Support for Black Lives Matter Has Decreased Since June But Remains Strong Among Black Americans," Pew Research Center, September 16, 2020, https://www.pewresearch.org/fact-tank/2020/09/16/support-for-black-lives-matter-has-decreased-since-june-but-remains-strong-among-black-americans/.

7. Giovanni Russonello, "Why Most Americans Support the Protests," *The New York Times*, June 5, 2020, https://www.nytimes.com/2020/06/05/us/politics/polling-george-floyd-protests-racism.html.

8. "National: Partisanship Drives Latest Shift in Race Relations Attitudes," Monmouth University Poll, July 8, 2020, https://www.monmouth.edu/polling-institute/documents/monmouthpoll_us_070820.pdf/.

9. Dennis S. Ippolito and Thomas G. Walker, *Political Parties, Interest Groups, and Public Policy* (Englewood Cliffs, NJ: Prentice Hall, 1990), p. 271.

10. Ibid., pp. 270–71.

11. Alan Hedblad, ed., *Encyclopedia of Associations: National Organizations of the U.S.*, 55th ed. (Detroit: Gale/Cengage Learning, 2015), and Alan Hedblad, ed., *Encyclopedia of Associations: Regional, State and Local Organizations*, 26th ed. (Detroit: Gale/Cengage Learning, 2015).

12. Kay Lehman Schlozman and John T. Tierney, *Organized Interests and American Democracy* (New York: Harper & Row, 1986), p. 75.

13. See E. E. Schattschneider, *The Semi-Sovereign People* (Hinsdale, IL: Dryden Press, 1975); Sidney Verba, Kay Lehman Schlozman, and Henry E. Brady, *Voice of Equality: Civic Volunteerism in American Politics* (Cambridge, MA: Harvard University Press, 1995), pp. 81–82; and Aaron Smith, Kay Lehman Schlozman, Sidney Verba, and Henry Brady, *The Internet and Civic Engagement*, Pew Internet and American Life Project, September 1, 2009, accessed January 9, 2014, at http://www.pewinternet.org/Reports/2009/15-The-Internet-and-Civic-Engagement/2-The-Current-State-of-Civic-Engagement-in-America/2-Participation.aspx.

14. See, for instance, Lee Rainie and Aarron Smith, "Politics on Social Networking Sites," Pew Internet and American Life Project, September 4, 2012, accessed January 8, 2014, at http://pewinternet.org/Reports/2012/Politics-on-SNS.aspx; as well as James Allan Davis and Tom W. Smith, *General Social Surveys, 1972–2006* [machine-readable data file]/Principal Investigator, James A. Davis; Director and Co-Principal Investigator, Tom W. Smith; Co-Principal Investigator, Peter V. Marsden; Sponsored by National Science Foundation.—NORC ed.—Chicago: National Opinion Research Center [producer]; Storrs, CT: The Roper Center for Public Opinion Research, University of Connecticut [distributor], 2007. Courtesy of Dr. Michael Kearl, Department of Sociology and Anthropology, Trinity University, San Antonio, Texas.

15. Schlozman and Tierney, *Organized Interests and American Democracy*, pp. 73–74.

16. Ronald J. Hrebenar and Ruth K. Scott, *Interest Group Politics in America*, 2nd ed. (Englewood Cliffs, NJ: Prentice Hall, 1990), p. 29.

17. Ippolito and Walker, *Political Parties, Interest Groups, and Public Policy*, p. 278.

18. For an extended discussion of these incentives, see Jeffrey M. Berry and Clyde Wilcox, *The Interest Group Society*, 5th ed. (New York: Pearson Longman, 2009), pp. 36–46. See also Robert H. Salisbury, "An Exchange Theory of Interest Groups," *Midwest Journal of Political Science*, 13 (February 1969), pp. 1–32.

19. Greenwald, *Group Power*, pp. 32–35.

20. Ippolito and Walker, *Political Parties, Interest Groups, and Public Policy*, pp. 279–80.
21. Berry and Wilcox, *The Interest Group Society*, p. 42.
22. Lawrence J. R. Herson, *The Politics of Ideas* (Prospect Heights, IL: Waveland, 1990), p. 68.
23. David B. Truman, *The Governmental Process*, 2nd ed. (New York: Alfred A. Knopf, 1971).
24. For a succinct summary of the elitist-pluralist debate, see Thomas R. Dye and Harmon Zeigler, *The Irony of Democracy*, 7th ed. (Monterey, CA: Brooks/Cole, 1987), Chapter 1.
25. Truman, *The Governmental Process*, Chapter 4.
26. For more information about these competing theories, see Truman, *The Governmental Process*; and Robert H. Salisbury, "An Exchange Theory of Interest Groups," *Midwest Journal of Political Science*, 13 (February 1969), pp. 1–32.
27. Ippolito and Walker, *Political Parties, Interest Groups, and Public Policy*, pp. 275–76.
28. Thomas R. Dye, *Who's Running America: The Bush Era*, 5th ed. (Englewood Cliffs, NJ: Prentice Hall, 1990), p. 4.
29. Robert Michels, *Political Parties: A Sociological Study of the Oligarchical Tendencies of Modern Democracy*, translated by Eden Paul (1915, reprint, New York: Free Press, 1962), p. 70.
30. C. Wright Mills, *The Power Elite* (New York: Oxford University Press, 1956).
31. See Dye and Zeigler, *The Irony of Democracy*, Chapter 1.
32. George Norris Green, *The Establishment in Texas Politics: 1938–1957* (Westport, CT: Greenwood, 1979), p. 1.
33. Ibid., p. 17.
34. Ibid., p. 1.
35. Ibid., p. 10.
36. Chandler Davidson, *Race and Class in Texas Politics* (Princeton, NJ: Princeton University Press, 1990), p. 513.
37. Ibid., Chapters 4 and 5.
38. Ibid., p. 83.
39. Ibid., p. 108.
40. Michael Campbell, "Politics, Prisons, and Law Enforcement: An Examination of the Emergence of 'Law and Order' Politics in Texas," *Law & Society Review*, 45(3) (2011), pp. 631–65.
41. Robert L. Lineberry, George C. Edwards III, and Martin P. Wattenberg, *Government in America*, 5th ed (New York: HarperCollins, 1991), p. 342.
42. See Theodore J. Lowi, *The End of Liberalism*, 2nd ed. (New York: W. W. Norton, 1979); Robert Grady, "Juridical Democracy and Democratic Values: An Evaluation of Lowi's Alernative to Interest Group Liberalism," *Polity* 16(3), pp. 404–22; and Elizabeth Sanders, "The Contributions of Theodore Lowi to Political Analysis and Democratic Theory," *Political Science and Politics* 23(4), pp. 574–76.
43. *U.S. Constitution*, First Amendment; *Texas Constitution*, Art. 1, Sec. 27.
44. Alan Rosenthal, *Third House: Lobbyists and Lobbying in the States* (Washington, D.C.: Congressional Quarterly Press, 1993), p. 1.
45. Greenwald, *Group Power*, pp. 61–62.
46. Ippolito and Walker, *Political Parties, Interest Groups, and Public Policy*, pp. 364–65.
47. This and the following sections draw from the research of Scholzman and Tierney, *Organized Interests and American Democracy*, Chapter 7.
48. "Wining and Dining Elected Officials," February 15, 2017, Transparency USA, https://www.transparencyusa.org/article/wining-and-dining-elected-officials?state=tx.
49. Pew Research Center, "Beyond Distrust: How Americans View Their Government," November 23, 2015, http://www.people-press.org/2015/11/23/beyond-distrust-how-americans-view-their-government/; "Is the Government Run for the Benefit of All 1964-2016," The ANES Guide to Public Opinion and Electoral Behavior, Univerity of Michigan, https://electionstudies.org/resources/anes-guide/top-tables/?id=59.
50. See Robert S. Erikson, Norman R. Luttbeg, and Kent L. Tedin, *American Public Opinion*, 3rd ed. (New York: Macmillan, 1988), p. 118; Lineberry et al., *Government in America*, p. 341; and Pew Research Center, "Public Trust in Government: 1958–2017," December 14, 2017, http://www.people-press.org/2017/12/14/public-trust-in-government-1958-2017/; see also Gallup, "In-depth Topics: Trust in Government" https://news.gallup.com/poll/5392/trust-government.aspx.
51. Justin McCarthy, "Americans Still More Trusting of Local Than State Governments," Gallup, October 8, 2018, https://news.gallup.com/poll/243563/americans-trusting-local-state-government.aspx.
52. The University of Texas/Texas Tribune Poll Cross Tabulations, The Texas Project at The University of Texas at Austin, June 11, 2019, https://texaspolitics.utexas.edu/sites/texaspolitics.utexas.edu/files/201906_poll_crosstabs.pdf.
53. UT/TT Statewide Survey, October 2017, https://texaspolitics.utexas.edu/sites/texaspolitics.utexas.edu/files/201710_poll_toplines_final.pdf.
54. Belle Zeller, *American State Legislatures* (New York: Thomas Y. Crowell, 1954); and Clive S. Thomas and Ronald J. Hrebenar, "Interest Groups in the States," in *Politics in the American States*, 6th ed., edited by Virginia Gray and Herbert Jacob (Washington, D.C.: Congressional Quarterly Press, 1996), p. 152.
55. Harmon L. Zeigler and Hendrik van Dalen, "Interest Groups in State Politics," in *Politics in the American States*, 3rd ed., edited by Herbert Jacob and Kenneth N. Vines (Boston: Little, Brown, 1976).
56. Political Action Committees, Texas, 2020, Transparency USA, https://www.transparencyusa.org/tx/pacs. "Lobbying Watch," Texans for Public Justice, December 21, 2020.
57. "Rigged: How the Texas Oil and Gas Industry Bankrolls Its Own Regulators," Texans for Public Justice, Sierra Club Lone Star Chapter, Public Citizen's Texas Office, November 2016, http://info.tpj.org/reports/RRC$Report.Nov2016.pdf.
58. Federal Election Commission, *Citizen's Guide*, February 2011.
59. *Citizens United v. Federal Election Commission*, 130 S. Ct. 876 (2010).
60. OpenSecrets.org, Center for Responsive Politics, "2020 Outside Spending, by Super PAC," https://www.opensecrets.org/outsidespending/summ.php?chrt=V&type=S; OpenSecrets.org, Center for Responsive Politics, "2016 Outside Spending, by Super PAC," https://www.opensecrets.org/outsidespending/summ.php?cycle=2016&chrt=V&disp=O&type=S
61. OpenSecrets.org, Center for Responsive Government, "2014 Outside Spending, by Super PAC," https://www.opensecrets.org/outsidespending/summ.php?cycle=2014&chrt=V&disp=O&type=S; OpenSecrets.org, Center for Responsive Government, "2018 Outside Spending, Super PAC," https://www.opensecrets.org/outsidespending/

62. Texans for Public Justice, "Texas PACs: 2014 Election Cycle Spending," http://info.tpj.org/reports/pdf/PACs2014.pdf.
63. "Texas PACs 2020," Transparency USA, https://www.transparencyusa.org/tx/pacs.
64. Political Action Committees, Texas, 2020, Transparency USA, https://www.transparencyusa.org/tx/pacs.
65. Political Action Committees, Texas, 2018, Transparency USA, https://www.transparencyusa.org/tx/pacs?cycle=2018-election-cycle____.
66. Ippolito and Walker, *Political Parties, Interest Groups, and Public Policy*, p. 323.
67. Hrebenar and Scott, *Interest Group Politics in America*, pp. 114–15.
68. Kaethe V. Podgorski and Kara M. Kockelman, "Public Perceptions of Toll Roads: A Survey of the Texas Perspective," *Transportation Research Part A: Policy and Practice*, 40(10) (2006), pp. 888–902.
69. Larry Buchanan, Quoctrung Bui and Jugal K. Patel, "Black Lives Matter May Be the Largest Movement in U.S. History," *The New York Times*, July 3, 2020, https://www.nytimes.com/interactive/2020/07/03/us/george-floyd-protests-crowd-size.html.
70. See Green, *The Establishment in Texas Politics*, Chapter 1.
71. See Green, *The Establishment in Texas Politics*, for an excellent analysis of the labor-bashing techniques used by the Texas business community in the 1940s and 1950s.
72. U.S. Department of Labor, Bureau of Labor Statistics, "Union Membership in Texas – 2019," https://www.bls.gov/regions/southwest/news-release/2020/unionmembership_texas_20200130.htm#:~:text=PDF%20version-,Union%20Members%20in%20Texas%20%E2%80%93%202019,of%20Labor%20Statistics%20reported%20today.&text=Texas%20had%20497%2C000%20union%20members%20in%202019.
73. Green, *The Establishment in Texas Politics*, Chapter 5.
74. Texas Freedom Network, "About Us," TFN.org, http://www.tfn.org/site/PageServer?pagename=about_mission.
75. "Lobbyists, 2020 Texas," Transparency USA, https://www.transparencyusa.org/tx/lobbying/lobbyists.
76. See, for instance, Brian Montopoli, "Alienated Nation: Americans Complain of Government Disconnect," *CBS News*, June 28, 2011, accessed January 12, 2014, at http://www.cbsnews.com/news/alienated-nation-americans-complain-of-government-disconnect/.
77. "Fantasy Sports Bookies Recruit Deep Lobby Bench," Lobbying Watch, Texans for Public Justice, April 3, 2017, http://info.tpj.org/Lobby_Watch/pdf/FantasySports2017.pdf.
78. See both "Alabama Coushatta Tribe of Texas," Transparency USA, https://www.transparencyusa.org/tx/lobbying/client/alabama-coushatta-tribe-of-texas/?cycle=2018-election-cycle and "Client Profile: Alabama-Coushatta Tribe of Texas, 2019," Center for Responsive Politics, https://www.opensecrets.org/federal-lobbying/clients/summary?id=D000046571&cycle=2019.
79. Schlozman and Tierney, *Organized Interests and American Democracy*, p. 103.
80. Data calculated from Texas Ethics Commission, https://www.ethics.state.tx.us/search/lobby/loblistsREG2016-2020.php.
81. Hrebenar and Scott, *Interest Group Politics in America*, p. 83.

Chapter 14

1. Thomas R. Dye, *Understanding Public Policy*, 12th ed. (Upper Saddle River, NJ: Prentice Hall, 2008), p. 1.
2. This section draws primarily from L. L. Wade and R. L. Curry Jr., *A Logic of Public Policy: Aspects of Political Economy* (Belmont, CA: Wadsworth, 1970), Chapter 1.
3. Ibid. This same chapter is an excellent introduction to the definitional issues and approaches to public policy analysis.
4. The following discussion is organized around the general stages presented by James E. Anderson, David W. Brady, Charles S. Bullock III, and Joseph Stewart Jr., *Public Policy and Politics in America*, 2nd ed. (Monterey, CA: Brooks/Cole, 1984); and Charles O. Jones, *An Introduction to the Study of Public Policy*, 2nd ed. (North Scituate, MA: Duxbury Press, 1977).
5. Anderson et al., *Public Policy and Politics in America*, p. 8.
6. Jones, *An Introduction to the Study of Public Policy*, pp. 138–39.
7. Ibid., p. 139.
8. Randall B. Ripley and Grace A. Franklin, *Congress, the Bureaucracy, and Public Policy*, 3rd ed. (Homewood, IL: Dorsey, 1984), p. 10.
9. Hugh Heclo, "Issue Networks and the Executive Establishment," in *The New American Political System*, edited by Anthony King (Washington, D.C.: American Enterprise Institute, 1978), p. 88. Much of this section is based on this article.
10. Ibid., p. 107.
11. Ibid., p. 104.
12. "The State of State (and Local) Tax Policy," *Briefing Book*, Tax Policy Center, a joint project of the Urban Institute & Brookings Institution, 2020.
13. "Rankings of State and Local General Revenue as a Percentage of Personal Income, 2017" Tax Policy Center, a joint project of the Urban Institute & Brookings Institution.
14. *Who Pays: A Distributional Analysis of the Tax Systems in All Fifty States*, 6th ed. (Washington, D.C.: Institute on Taxation and Economic Policy, 2018).
15. Federation of Tax Administrators, "State Sales Tax Rates and Food & Drug Exemptions," January 2020.
16. Comptroller of Public Accounts, *State of Texas Annual Cash Report 2019*, p. 13.
17. Ibid.
18. Texas Comptroller of Public Accounts, *Biennial Property Tax Report: Tax Years 2016 and 2017*, December 2018, Appendix 5: "Property Tax Levy Growth by Taxing Unit Type, 1998–2017," p. 13.
19. Comptroller of Public Accounts, *State of Texas Annual Cash Report 2019*, p. 13.
20. Ibid.
21. R. G. Ratcliffe, "Lottery Names Latest Director—$248 Million Expected Shortfall to Schools Seen," *Houston Chronicle*, December 17, 1997, p. 37A.
22. Comptroller of Public Accounts, *State of Texas Annual Cash Report 2019*, p. 13.
23. Texas Bond Review Board, *Debt Affordability Study*, February 2019.
24. Legislative Budget Board, "Summary of Conference Committee Report for House Bill 1, 2020–21 Biennium," May 2019, p. 17.
25. Texas Bond Review Board, *Local Government Annual Report 2019*, January 2020, pages 2, 4.

26. Clay Robison, "Bullock Backs State Income Tax—Richards, Lewis Dubious," *Houston Chronicle,* March 7, 1991, p. 1A.
27. *Edgewood Independent School District, et al. v. William Kirby, et al.,* 777 S.W. 2d 391 (1989).
28. Texas State Teachers Association news release, "Texas per-student funding dropped during the current school year," April 29, 2019.
29. Texas State Teachers Association news release, "Teachers taking extra jobs and subsidizing under-funded education budget," August 6, 2018. (Based on "Texas Teachers, Moonlighting and Morale," survey conducted for TSTA by faculty at Sam Houston State University, Spring 2018, and National Education Association research on teacher salaries, 2017-18.)
30. Brian M. Rosenthal, "Texas Illegally Excluded Thousands from Special Education, Federal Officials Say," *The New York Times,* January 11, 2018.
31. Texas Education Agency, "Enrollment in Texas Public Schools, 2018-19."
32. "How Does Texas Compare to the Rest of the Country?" *Texas Public Higher Education Almanac 2019,* p. 5, Texas Higher Education Coordinating Board.
33. "60x30TX," Texas Higher Education Coordinating Board website (accessed March 6, 2016).
34. Matthew Watkins, "New State Goal: 60 Percent of Adults with a Degree By 2030," *The Texas Tribune,* July 23, 2015.
35. Brittany Britto, "Texas Colleges Flexible on Fall Admissions While Navigating Through Coronavirus Pandemic," *Houston Chronicle,* April 10, 2020.
36. *Hopwood, et al. v. State of Texas, et al.,* 78 F.3d 932 (1996).
37. Lydia Lum, "UH Won't Award Scholarship Pending Review of AG Ruling," *Houston Chronicle,* February 7, 1997, p. 20A.
38. Lydia Lum, "The Hopwood Effect/Minorities Heading Out of State for Professional Schools," *Houston Chronicle,* August 25, 1997, p. 1A.
39. *Fisher v. University of Texas,* U.S. Supreme Court, June 2013.
40. Ralph K.M. Haurwitz, "Group keeps vow to sue UT again over race in admissions," *Austin American-Statesman,* May 16, 2019.
41. Anemona Hartocollis, "The Affirmative Action Battle at Harvard Is Not Over," *The New York Times,* February 18, 2020.
42. Erica L. Green, Matt Apuzzo and Katie Benner, "Trump Officials Reverse Obama's Policy on Affirmative Action in Schools," *The New York Times,* July 3, 2018.
43. UT-Austin News Release, "Class of First-time Freshmen Not a White Majority This Fall Semester at the University of Texas at Austin," September 14, 2010.
44. Ralph K.M. Haurwitz, "Regents Raise UT Tuition 2 Percent in Fall and Again in Fall '19," *Austin American-Statesman,* March 19, 2018.
45. The University of Texas at Austin: UT Tuition, "How We Stack Up Nationally."
46. Rebekah Allen, "UT-Austin Promises Free Tuition to Students with Family Incomes Less than $65,000 in 2020," *The Dallas Morning News,* July 9, 2019.
47. Matthew Watkins, "Federal Judge Throws Out Effort by UT Professors to Overturn Campus Carry," *The Texas Tribune,* July 7, 2017.
48. Matthew Watkins, "UT Architecture Dean Cites Campus Carry as a Reason for Departure," *The Texas Tribune,* February 25, 2016.
49. Matthew Watkins, "Colleges Heighten Focus on Campus Sexual Assaults," *The Texas Tribune,* July 9, 2015.
50. Maria Mendez, "Under New Texas Law, College Employees Could Be Fired and Charged for Not Reporting Sexual Misconduct," *The Dallas Morning News,* Dec. 30, 2019.
51. Matthew Watkins and Madlin Mekelburg, "Briles Fired, Starr Reassigned in Baylor Shakeup," *The Texas Tribune,* May 26, 2016.
52. Matthew Watkins, "In Aftermath of Rape Scandal, Baylor Hires Its First Female President," *The Texas Tribune,* April 18, 2017.
53. *Ruiz v. Estelle,* 503 F. Supp. 1265 (1980).
54. Clay Robison, Julie Mason, and Jim Zook, "Building of Prisons Under Gun—2 Legislators Say It's up to County," *Houston Chronicle,* September 8, 1991, p. 25A.
55. U.S. Department of Justice, Bureau of Justice Statistics, "Prisoners in 2017—Table 2: Prisoners under Jurisdiction of State or Federal Correctional Authorities, by Jurisdiction and Sex, 2016 and 2017," April 2019.
56. "Execution by State and Year," Death Penalty Information Center.
57. University of Texas/*Texas Tribune* Poll, June 2018.
58. *Houston Chronicle,* December 31, 2002. Poll was conducted by the University of Houston's Center for Public Policy Survey Research Institute, which conducted random telephone interviews with 1,773 adults from November 29 to December 21, 2002.
59. Brandi Grissom, "Bar Association: Texas Death Penalty System Falls Short," *The Texas Tribune,* September 18, 2013.
60. Brandi Grissom, "New Head of Forensic Science Panel Takes on Arson Case," *The Texas Tribune,* July 22, 2011.
61. Jolie McCullough, "For the Second Time, U.S. Supreme Court Reverses Death Sentence Decision for Texas Inmate Bobby Moore," *The Texas Tribune,* February 19, 2019.
62. "State and Local General Expenditures, Per Capita, FY2017," compiled by the Urban-Brookings Tax Policy Center, March 10, 2020.
63. "Our Top Takeaways from the New Census Data," CPPP Blog, Center for Public Policy Priorities, September 26, 2019.
64. "Backsliding on Texas Children's Health: More Uninsured, Fewer Enrolled in Medicaid and CHIP," CPPP Blog, Center for Public Policy Priorities, September 6, 2019.
65. "Gov. Perry, Sen. Cornyn, Sen. Cruz: Texas Stands Firm against Medicaid Expansion," Press Release, Office of the Governor, April 1, 2013.
66. Maria Mendez, "Trump Renews Medicaid Funding Texas Lost for Excluding Planned Parenthood from Women's Health Program," *The Dallas Morning News,* January 22, 2020.
67. "Erik Eckholm, "Rights Groups and Clinics Sue Texas over Provisions in Its New Abortion Law," *The New York Times,* September 27, 2013.
68. Alexa Ura, "U.S. Supreme Court Overturns Texas Abortion Restrictions," *The Texas Tribune,* June 27, 2016.

69. Adam Liptak, "Justices Give Few Hints on How They Will Rule on Louisiana Abortion Law, *The New York Times*, March 4, 2020.
70. Dina Cappiello, "Houston Avoids Title of Smoggiest U.S. City," *Houston Chronicle*, September 24, 2003, p. 23A.
71. "State of the Air 2019," American Lung Association.
72. Dave Fehling, "Researching Dirty Air's Effect on Health: Are Some Texans Immune?" StateImpact Texas, National Public Radio, August 22, 2013.
73. "How Much Carbon Dioxide Does Your State Produce?" ChooseEnergy.com, analysis of data from the U.S. Energy Information Administration.
74. Matthew Tresaugue, "Global Warming: Warning for Texas Coastal Damage Could Triple by 2080s," *Houston Chronicle*, June 2, 2009, p. 3B.
75. Henry Fountain, "Scientists Link Hurricane Harvey's Record Rainfall to Climate Change," *The New York Times*, December 13, 2017.
76. Abby Livingston, "At Confirmation Hearing, Rick Perry Vows to Pursue 'Sound Science' On Climate Change," *The Texas Tribune*, January 19, 2017.
77. University of Texas/*Texas Tribune* Poll, October 2019.
78. Kiah Collier, "Texas GOP Welcomes Trump Order Repealing Climate Regulations," *The Texas Tribune*, March 28, 2017.
79. Emily Martin, "Texas Has Generated More Electricity from Wind than Coal So Far This Year," KUT Radio, Austin, July 24, 2019.
80. Erin Douglas, "Reporter's Notebook: A Little Math Shows How Texas Will Suffer from Climate Change," *Houston Chronicle*, January 17, 2020.
81. Kate Galbraith, "Draft Water Plan Says Texas 'Will Not Have Enough,'" *The Texas Tribune*, September 27, 2011.
82. Neena Satija, "Groundwater Pumping on Gulf Coast Leads to Subsidence," *The Texas Tribune*, December 20, 2013.
83. Terrence Henry, "New Study Finds Another Link between Drilling and Earthquakes," StateImpact Texas, National Public Radio, August 27, 2013.
84. Asher Price, "Texas Policymakers Unconvinced as Scientists Link Quakes to Drilling," *Austin American-Statesman*, April 23, 2015.
85. Kiah Collier, "Expect Fewer Man-Made Earthquakes in Texas, Federal Agency Says," *The Texas Tribune*, March 1, 2017.
86. Kirk Kite, "Highway Development," *Handbook of Texas Online*.
87. Texas Department of Motor Vehicles, Number of Vehicles Registered, FY2017.
88. Texas A&M Transportation Institute, Annual Urban Mobility Report, 2012; Texas A&M Transportation Institute and INRIX, 2015 Urban Mobility Scorecard.
89. The 2030 Committee, "Texas Transportation Needs Summary," February 2009.
90. "INRIX 2019 Global Traffic Scorecard," March 2020, INRIX, Kirkland, WA.
91. Gary Scharrer, "Texas on Road to Highway Crisis," *San Antonio Express-News*, January 29, 2011.
92. Legislative Budget Board, "Texas Highway Funding Legislative Primer," April 2016.
93. Jamie Lovegrove, "SH 130 Toll Road Operator Files for Bankruptcy," *The Texas Tribune*, March 2, 2016.
94. Legislative Budget Board, "Transportation Funding Overview, 83rd Legislature, 2013," a presentation for the Senate Select Committee on Transportation Funding, October 9, 2013.
95. Ross Ramsey, "On Matters of Transportation, Some Dare to Bring Up Taxes, Tolls and Debt," *The New York Times*, April 6, 2013.
96. Aman Batheja, "The Politics of High-Speed Rail in Texas," *Texas Weekly*, October 9, 2013.

Index

Note: Page numbers followed by "f" and "t" indicate figure and table respectively.

60 Minutes, on Texas judicial system, 254, 256–257
Abbott, Greg, 2, 16, 33, 34, 46, 60, 66, 93, 99–100, 119, 148, 151, 155, 156, 157, 162, 174, 177–179, 184, 188, 189–190, 191, 195, 196, 203–205, 207, 226, 246, 248, 266, 297, 298, 299, 311, 314, 315–316, 324, 342, 349, 357, 365, 370, 383, 387–388, 429, 430, 448, 453, 456, 458, 467, 469, 471
Abbott v. Perez (2018), 354
Abortion rights and laws, 80, 154, 162, 163, 200, 267, 279, 299, 422, 430, 470–472
Absentee (or early) voting, 347–349
Accenture, 222
ActBlue, 390
ActBlue Texas PAC, 372, 428
Activists, 291, 329, 333–334
Advertising in political campaigns, 366–369, 385–386
Affirmative action, 460–462
Affordable Care Act. *see* Patient Protection and Affordable Care Act (2010)
AFL-CIO, endorsed USMCA, 84, 86
African Americans. *see also* Racial segregation
 as city council members, 112
 at Constitutional Convention of 1875, 42, 43
 early history of, 13
 educational attainment, 23t, 24
 electoral gains, 357–359, 358f, 359t
 as gubernatorial appointees, 197
 history of in public education, 8
 history of voting rights limitations, 42
 income comparisons, 22, 22t
 Jim Crow laws, 318
 as judges, 250, 250f, 251
 living at poverty level, 468
 party identification, 286–287, 322
 political socialization and, 281
 public opinion on select policies, 287t
 state holidays and, 8
 state population of, 13, 29, 102
 in Texas legislature, 143, 143t, 151, 153, 165, 351
 in urban areas, 19
 voter turnout and, 293–294, 294f
Age
 public opinion and, 290, 290t
 voter turnout and, 296, 296f
 voting patterns and, 327
 voting rights and, 353
Agenda building, 382
Agenda setting, 382
Agents of political socialization, 278–283
Aging population, 19, 114, 220
Agriculture industry, 28, 29
A. H. Belo Corporation, 397
Aid to Families with Dependent Children, 73
Air pollution, 472–473
Alabama-Coushatta Tribe, 10–11, 435

Alamo, battle of, 6, 8, 39, 209
Alamodome, 125
Alcala, Elsa, 358
Allred, James V., 252, 319
American Association of Political Consultants, 301
American Bar Association, 467
American Community Survey (2018), 3, 19, 23, 101, 102, 117, 358
American Federation of State, County, and Municipal Employees (AFSCME), 431
American Immigration Council, 91
American Independent Party, 328
American Judicature Society, 252
American Lung Association, 473
American Nursing Association, 230
American Phoenix Foundation, 400
American Red Cross, 59
Americans Disabled for Attendant Programs Today (ADAPT), 432
American Society of Civil Engineers, Report Card for America's Infrastructure (2017), 115
Americans with Disabilities Act (1990), 348
American Trucking Associations, 86
Amtrak, 480
Anderson, Ken, 264
Anglos
 early history of, 13–15
 educational attainment, 23t, 24
 gentrification by, 21
 income comparisons, 22, 22t
 as judges, 250–251, 250f
 as majority of appointees, 191
 public opinion on select policies, 287–288, 287t
 state population of, 12f, 14, 29
 in Texas legislature, 143t
 voter turnout and, 293–294, 294f
Annexation, 129–130
Annie's List, 372
Anti-commandeering doctrine, 78
Antifa, 385–386
Anti-Federalists, 82
Appellate courts, 249
Appellate jurisdiction, 240
Applebaum, Anne, 404
Appointive powers, of governor, 190–191
Appraisal districts, 121
Appropriations bills, 162
Arizona, immigration laws, 92–93
Armstrong, Bob, 323
Asian Americans
 early history of, 15
 educational attainment, 23t, 24
 income comparisons, 22, 22t
 party identification, 287
 state population of, 15, 102
 in Texas legislature, 143t
 in urban areas, 19
 voter turnout and, 295

536

Asian Pacific American Heritage Association (APAHA), 433
Associated Republicans of Texas, 372–373
Association, freedom of, 414–415
Atkins v. *Virginia* (2002), 467
At-large elections, 111, 112, 354
Attorney General, 206–208
Austin, 174
   "Keep Austin Weird," 276
   population growth, 19, 101
   State Capitol, 140, 142, 142f
Austin, Stephen F., 38, 39
Available School Fund, 126
Avery v. *Midland County* (1968), 118

Bailiffs, 247
Baker, C. Edwin, 397
Baker v. *Carr* (1962), 146
"Ballot or the Bullet" (Malcolm X), 340–341
Ballot security, 350
Bandwagon effect, 300
Banking system, 26
Baron, Martin, 399
Barringer, Felicity, 397
Baylor University, 464
Beach access, 237–238, 266–267
Bean, Roy, 268
Belden Associates, 325
Bell, Chris, 324
Belo Corporation, 397
Benavides, Fortunato P., 251
Benchmark polls, 300, 361
Bendy, Edgar, 13
Bendy, Minerva, 13
Bentsen, Lloyd, 321, 323
Berdejo, Carlos, 262
Beyle, Thad, 187
Bezos, Jeffrey P., 398–399
Bicameral legislature, 140
Biden, Joseph
   election campaigns, 277, 303, 307–308, 345, 348, 386
   immigration policies, 91
   public opinion of Texans on, 297–298
Bifactionalism, 319
Bifurcated court systems, 240
Bill of Rights, 65, 260
Bipartisan Campaign Reform Act (2002), 368
Black Lives Matter movement, 7–8, 16, 17, 281, 283, 296, 402, 413–414
Blagojevich, Rod, 186
Blakely, William, 320
Blanco, Kathleen, 74
Bland, Jane, 253
Bland, Sandra, 15–16
Blanton, Annie Webb, 184, 359
Block grants, 72
Bloomberg, Michael, 345, 386
Blum, Edward, 461
Board of Law Examiners, 245
Bond issues, 452, 478
Bonnen, Dennis, 137, 150, 151, 156, 177, 205, 315, 371, 435
Border drug violence, 89, 93–94
Border wall, 89
Borges, Walt, 256
Bracero program, 88

Brady Handgun Violence Prevention Act (1993), 79
Bragg, Glenn, 266
Bragg, JoLynn, 266
Breyer, Stephen G., 472
Briscoe, Dolph, 50, 52, 143, 172, 193, 310–311, 312–313, 323
Broder, David, 334
Brooks, Rayshard, 413
Brown, Lee, 370
Budgeting and finances
   balanced budget requirement, 47
   state budget, 446–448, 447f
Bullock, Bob, 34, 152, 153, 166, 199, 208, 231, 323, 324, 452–453
Bureaucracies, 218
Bureaucracy and policy, 4, 216–236
   appointments to state agencies, 225–226
   characteristics of bureaucratic system, 218–220
   citizen interface with, 231–232
   government employees, 218, 220–222, 221t, 228, 232–234
   legislative control of bureaucracy, 227–231, 227t
   merit systems and professional management, 232–234
   policy implementation, 223–224
   privatization of public services, 129, 216–217, 222
   regulatory functions, 224–225
Burger, Warren E., 37
Burrows, Dustin, 137
Burton, Konni, 373
Bush, George H. W., 72–73, 272, 321, 327, 355
Bush, George P., 195, 209, 271–272, 299, 358
Bush, George W.
   absence of climate policies, 116
   immigration policies, 88, 89
   new federalism under, 74–75
   as Texas governor, 150, 152, 153, 166, 183, 184, 190, 191, 196, 198–200, 250–251, 256, 314, 315, 323, 324, 327, 328, 457, 458
Bush, Jeb, 209, 299
Bush v. *Vera* (1996), 79
Business interests
   coffee bean imports, 49, 50
   influence over public policy, 54
Button, Angie Chen, 15
Byrd, James, Jr., 15–16, 167

Cable television systems, 225, 407
Calendars, 163
Calendars Committee, 159
California
   California Values Act (2018), 77
   cooperation over wildfires, 77–78
   immigration laws, 77
   lawsuits against Trump administration, 77
   oil and gas leases on public lands, 77
Cambridge Analytica, 364–365
Campaign consultants, 361
Campaigners, 291
Campaign finance, 190–191, 253–254, 257
Campaign finance reform, 191, 374–375
Campbell, Michael, 421
Capital murder, 260–261
Capitol press corps, 399
Carr, David, 399
Carrillo, Victor, 358
Carson, Arch, 473
Carter, Amon, 391

Carter, Jimmy, 307
Cascos, Carlos, 191, 299
Casey v. *Planned Parenthood* (1992), 471
Casinos, 11
Castro, Joaquin, 277, 299
Castro, Julián, 277, 299
Castroville, 106f
Categorical grant-in-aid, 70
Catholic Church, 434
Cato Institute, 148
Caucuses, 168
Celebrity endorsements, 365
Center for Disease Control (CDC), 59
Center for Public Integrity, Texas, 436
Center for Public Policy Priorities, 432, 470, 471
Center for Responsive Politics, 368, 427
Challenge of Change (Wolff), 52
Charles E. Bell v. *Low-Income Women of Texas* (2002), 267
Charter schools, 458
Cheney, Dick, 74
Children's Health Insurance Program (CHIP), 202, 222, 448, 469
Chinese Exclusion Act (1882), 88
Chisum, Warren, 166
Christian, Wayne, 426
Christian Life Commission of the Baptist General Convention of Texas, 434
Cinco de Mayo, 8
Cintra, 479
Cities. *see* Local government; *specific cities*
Citizen journalism, 401–403
Citizens United v. *Federal Election Commission* (2010), 368, 373, 427
City charters, 104–105
City commission, 106–107, 108f, 347. *see also* Local government
City managers, 110
City of Boerne, Texas v. *Flores* (1997), 79
Ciudad Juarez, Mexico, 94
Civil lawsuits, 239–240, 244, 264
Civil rights movement, 322, 430, 438
Civil service system, 123
Civil unions, 65–66
Clark, Edward, 41
Clark, Harley, 455
Clayton, Bill, 151
Clean Air Act (1963), 472–473
Cleavages, in societies, 284
Clements, Bill, 46, 166, 183, 184, 189, 190, 196, 251, 252, 254, 255, 256, 314, 321, 323, 386
Climate change, 77, 116, 473–475
Clinton, Bill, 73–74, 251, 323, 324, 327, 355
Clinton, Hillary, 295, 297, 299, 303–304, 307, 332, 343, 363, 403, 433
Club for Growth Action, 368
Coal industry, 474–475
Coherent replacement, 275
Coke, Richard, 43
Cole, Timothy, 263
Coleman, Garnet, 222
Collier, Mike, 155, 206
Colonias (slums), 94
Colorado, unconstitutional laws in, 79
Combs, Susan, 208, 210
Comcast, 397

Commissioners courts, 117–120, 120t, 124
Commissions. *see* Elected Boards and Commissions
Common Cause, 418
Communalists, 291
Communications Workers of America (CWA), 431
Communities Organized for Public Service (COPS), 433
Community schools, 126
Compassionate Use Program, 66
Compean, Mario, 312
Comptroller of public accounts, 208–209, 226
Concurrent powers, 65
Confederacy, 41
Confederate symbols, 414
Confederation, 63
Conference committees, 159
Confidence level, in polling, 302
Confirmation bias, 381
Connally, John, 50, 193
Conservatives, 276–277, 281
Consolidated Appropriations Act (1998), 59
Constables, 121–122
Constitution (1876)
  amendments to, 33–34, 46, 48–49t, 48–50, 52, 141, 144, 181, 197, 448, 451, 453, 475
  branches of government, 45–47, 181
  comparison to other state constitutions, 36, 38, 48f
  comparison to U.S. Constitution, 36–37, 37t, 45
  Constitutional Convention of 1974, 50–52
  criticisms of, 34, 46, 47–49
  First Amendment rights, 412–413
  principles of, 45
  prohibition on state debt, 452
  provisions, interest groups, and elites, 52–54
  public education, 126
  reform efforts (1971-1975), 50–52
  reform efforts (1976-2019), 52
  scope of, 33–34, 35, 35t, 36, 43–44
  structure of legislature, 141, 144
  tax system, 448
Constitution, defined, 35
Constitution, early history of, 33–43, 35t
  1827, Constitution of *Coahuila y Tejas*, 38
  1836, Constitution of the Republic of Texas, 39–40, 117, 180, 205
  1845, Constitution, 40–41, 180, 187, 205–206
  1861, Civil War Constitution, 41, 180
  1866, Constitution, 41–42, 180
  1869, Constitution of Reconstruction, 42–43, 180
  constitutionalism, 35–38
Constitutional Convention of 1875, 42, 43–44, 139–140
Constitutional Convention of 1974, 50–52
Constitutional county courts, 242–243
Contract workers. *see* Privatization
Controlled media, 366–367
Conventional political behavior, 291
Conventions, 331–332
Cooper, Eric, 2
Cooperative federalism, 68, 69–71
Co-optation, 226
Cornyn, John, 207, 324, 346
Coronavirus pandemic. *see* COVID-19 pandemic
Council-Manager city government, 107–110, 109f
Council of State Governments, 445
County attorneys, 121

County auditors, 122
County chairs, 330
County clerks, 120–121
County executive committees, 330–331
County government, 117–123, 222. see also Local government
County jails, 122
County judges, 117–118, 126
County tax assessor-collectors, 121
County treasurers, 122
Courts of appeals, 244, 244f. see also specific courts
Court structure, 238–245, 241f, 244f
COVID-19 pandemic
   cancellation of conventions due to, 333
   early voting due to, 342
   economic impacts, 27, 29, 99–100, 113, 448
   election campaigns during, 363, 384
   federal response, 59, 78
   food bank distribution, 1–2
   long-term impacts of, 283
   mail-in voting expansion during, 208, 267–268, 297, 348–349
   mask orders, 60
   media coverage of, 282
   protests over personal liberties, 430
   public health response in Texas, 60, 119, 177–179
   school shutdowns due to, 453, 459
   state responses, 59–60
Cowboy mythology, 6–7
Cox Enterprises, 394
Cracking, 353–354
Craddick, Christi, 360
Craddick, Tom, 147, 150, 156, 167
Creghan, Casey, 457
Crenshaw, Kimberlé, 284
Criminal justice, 259–264
   appeals, 262–263
   death penalty, 260–263, 466–468
   miscarriage of justice, 263–264
   politics of, 261–262
   punishment of criminals, 260–261
   reform efforts, 465–468
   rights of suspects, 259–260
Criminal justice reform, 413
Cronkite, Walter, 386
Cruz, Ted, 154, 204, 206, 297–299, 302, 304, 307, 308, 324, 339, 343–344, 357, 358, 365, 368, 389–390
Cuellar, Henry, 345
Cult of Glory: The Bold and Brutal History of the Texas Rangers (Swanson), 7
Culver, Barbara, 252–253

DACA (Deferred Action for Childhood Arrivals), 90–91
Dallas
   citizens' association, 313
   council-manager form of government, 109f
   population growth, 19, 21f, 101
Dallas Area Rapid Transit (DART), 480
Dallas-Fort Worth, multilingualism of, 3
Dallas–Fort Worth International Airport, 480
Daniel, Price, Jr., 50, 51, 322
DAPA (Deferred Action for Parents of Americans and Lawful Permanent Residents), 76, 90
Davidson, Chandler, 328, 421
Davis, Edmund J., 42–43, 44, 139, 179, 180, 317

Davis, Gray, 186
Davis, Sarah, 371
Davis, Wendy, 154, 162, 203, 298, 387–388
Dealignment, 329
The Death and Life of American Journalism (McChesney and Nichols), 401
Death penalty, 260–263, 466–468
Dedicated funds, 448
Defense of Marriage Act (1996), 65–66
Deficit financing, 447
DeLay, Tom, 173–174
Delco, Wilhelmina, 151
Delegated powers, 64
Democracy in America (Tocqueville), 273, 414–415
Democratic Party
   beliefs about the press, 380–381, 408
   elected governors from, 185t
   impact of in-migration on, 18
   judicial elections, 246, 253–255
   members in Texas legislature, 143t, 147–148, 155, 166–167
   partisan history in Texas, 308, 312, 314, 317–322, 325–329, 325t, 326f
   party organization, 330–334
   public opinion on select policies, 285t
   religious affiliation and, 282–283
   self-identified partisans, 285
   support for federal grant programs, 71
   views on federal vs. state response to COVID-19, 60
Demographics of Texas, 17–29. see also specific ethnic groups
   aging population, 19, 114
   economic regions, 27–29, 28f
   economy, 25–27
   education and literacy, 23–24, 23t
   population growth, 17–18, 21f, 147–148
   size and geographic diversity, 24–25
   urbanization, 19–21, 20f, 21f
   wealth and income distribution, 22–23, 22t
Denied powers, 65
Development, Relief and Education for Alien Minors (DREAM) Act, proposed, 89
Devolution, 64, 73–74
Dewhurst, David, 153–154, 167, 206, 209, 311, 343, 345, 368, 389–390
Dietz, John, 456
Diez y Seis, 8
Dillon rule, 63, 104
Dinan, John, 80
Direct lobbying, 424–426
Direct mail fund-raising, 369
Disaster Relief Council, 59
District attorneys, 121, 123
District clerks, 121
District courts, 243–244
DNA testing, 263–234, 467
Doggett, Lloyd, 146
Dole, Bob, 324
Downs, Anthony, 382
Drinking age laws, 83
Drought, 475
Drug cartels, Mexican, 93–94
Drug trafficking, 29, 93–94
Dual federalism, 67, 68
Due process, 259–260, 263
Dutton, Harold, 345

Earle, Ronnie, 173
Earthquakes, 476
Easton, David, 5
Economic development, 130–131
Economic diversification, 5
Economic regulation, 224
Economy, 25–27
  diversification of, 5, 25–26
  downturn in 1980s, 25–26
  economic regions, 27–29, 28f
  global exports, 27
  during Great Recession, 26
  gross product, 27
  impact of COVID-19 pandemic on, 27, 29, 99–100, 113, 448
  links to Mexican economy, 27, 29
Edgewood v. *Kirby* (1989), 264, 455
Editorial autonomy, 392
Education levels, 23t. *see also* Public education
  political opinion and, 288, 288t
  voter turnout and, 293, 295, 295f
Edwards, Edwin, 50
Edwards Aquifer Authority, 266
Edwards Aquifer Authority and the State of Texas v. *Burrell Day and Joel McDaniel* (2012), 266
Edwards Aquifer Authority v. *Glenn and JoLynn Bragg* (2013), 266
Eighth Amendment, 467–468
Eiland, Craig, 151
Eisenhower, Dwight, 320
Elazar, Daniel, 8
Elected and Appointed Boards and Commissions
  Board of Pardons and Paroles, 192, 261, 467
  Commissioner of Agriculture, 209–210
  Commissioner of the General Land Office, 209, 228
  Constitutional Revision Commission, 50
  Ethics Commission, 141, 173, 369, 374–375, 428, 436
  Forensic Science Commission, 467
  General Education Board, 126
  Health and Human Services Commission, 59, 81
  Higher Education Coordinating Board, 228, 459
  Public Utility Commission, 229
  Railroad Commission, 210–212, 426, 476
  Residential Construction Commission, 191, 229
  State Board of Education, 126, 212
  State Commission on Judicial Conduct, 245, 262
  State Securities Board, 225
  Sunset Advisory Commission, 228–229, 228t
  Water Development Board, 475
  Workforce Commission, 234
Elections, 338–348. *see also* Political campaigns; Voting rights; *specific candidates*
  election cycles, 341–342
  functions of, 340–341
  general elections, 346
  local elections, 346–347
  primary elections, 342–346, 344f
  special elections, 347
Electric Reliability Council of Texas, 475
Elites
  constitutional provisions and, 52–54
  influence over public policy, 54
  post-Reconstruction, 317–318
  in traditionalistic subculture, 10, 14
Elitism, 274, 420–421
Ellis, Rodney, 148–149, 153

El Paso, 94, 129
El Paso Interreligious Sponsoring Organization (EPISO), 433
Emanuel, Rahm, 387
Emergency Management Assistance Compact (EMAC) (1996), 59, 60, 67
Employees, of Texas government, 218, 220–222, 221t, 228, 232–234
Empower Texans, 137, 169, 311, 373, 379, 400
Encyclopedia of Associations, 416
The End of Liberalism (Lowi), 422
Enterprise zones, 131
Environmental policies
  air pollution, 472–473
  court cases on, 266–267
  global warming, 473–475
  oil field pollution risks, 476
  regulation, 225
  water supply, 475
Epstein, Leon D., 309
Equity Center, 432
Escobar, Veronica, 299, 360
Esper, Mark, 92
The Establishment, 420
European Union, GDP of, 85
Evenwel v. *Abbott* (2016), 148, 353–354
Every Student Succeeds Act (2015), 458
Executive branch, 46–47, 182f. *see also* Governorship
Exelon Corporation, 373
Exit polls, 298, 300
Extended early voting, 347–349
External political efficacy, 281
Extradition, 66–67
Extraterritorial jurisdiction, 129

Facebook
  advertising in political campaigns, 385–386, 390
  fake news and, 403, 406
Facebook hacks, 364–365
Facebook Live, 363, 365
FactCheck.org, 407
Fair Labor Standards Act (1938), 79
Fake news, 403–404, 406
Family, in political socialization, 279–280
Family separation practice, 92
Farenthold, Frances, 143
Farm Bill (2018), 66
Fat cats, 339–340, 373
Federal Communications Commission (FCC), 397–398
Federal Election Commission (FEC), 389–390
Federal Emergency Management Agency (FEMA), 59
Federal grant programs, 70–71, 83
Federal income taxes, 80–81
Federalism, defined, 39, 63–64
Federalism and federal-state relations, 58–97
  centralized federalism, 71
  comparative context of, 62–63
  constitutional perspective of, 64–65
  cooperative federalism, 68, 69–71
  federalism in U.S., 63–64
  impact on state finances, 80–83
  interstate relations, 65–67
  metaphors for federalism, 67–68
  phases of new federalism, 71–80
  scope of U.S. governmental units, 61–62, 61f

state-centered and dual federalism, 67, 68
structures of federal-state relations, 61
transnational regionalism, 83–95
U.S. Supreme Court role and, 78–80
The Federalist Papers, 418
Federal Register, 82
Fehrenbach, T. R., 43, 390–391
Felder, Adam, 396
Felonies, 239
Felon voting, 356
Fenves, Gregory L., 462
Ferguson, James E. "Pa," 184, 186, 206
Ferguson, Miriam A. "Ma," 184, 186, 359–360
Fifth U.S. Circuit Court of Appeals, 90, 244, 251, 349, 356, 357, 460, 461
Fikac, Peggy, 388
Filibusters, 162
First Amendment, 230, 281, 288, 368, 380, 412–413, 415
First Court of Appeals, 244
First Step Act (2018), 78
Fisher, Abigail, 461
Fisher v. University of Texas (2013), 461
501(c) organizations, 368, 373–374
527 committees, 368, 373–374
FiveThirtyEight, 303, 304
Fletcher, Lizzie, 360
Flores, Pete, 373
Floyd, George, 16, 17, 283, 404, 413, 430
Flynn, Dan, 345
Focus groups, 362
Food banks, 1–2
Forbes 400, Texans on list (2019), 23
Ford, John S. "Rip," 44
Formula grants, 70, 82
Fortress Investment Group of New York, 394
Fort Worth, population growth, 19, 21f, 101
Forward Majority Action, 372
Fourteenth Amendment, 65–66, 79, 260, 348, 352, 415
Fourteenth Court of Appeals, 244
Fourth U.S. Court of Appeals, 266
Fox, Phil, 361
Fox, Vincente, 84
Fracking. *see* Hydraulic fracking
Franchise taxes, 450, 453
Friedman, Kinky, 313, 324
Full faith and credit clause, 65–66
Fund-raising, direct mail and online, 369

Galle, Vickilyn, 230
Gallup, George, 299
Galveston, 106
   city commission form of government, 108f
   population growth, 101
Gambling industry, 435, 451–452
Gandhi, Pritesh, 363
Gannett, 394, 397
Garcia, Sylvia, 93
Garcia v. San Antonio Metropolitan Transit Authority (1985), 79
Garrett, Robert, 205
Garwood, Will, 255
Garza, Jose, 252
Garza, Tony, 191, 358
Gas industry, 25, 26, 29, 450, 475
GateHouse Media, 394

Gender. *see also* Women
   public opinion and, 285–286, 286t
   voter turnout and, 294f
   voting patterns and, 326–327
Gender gap, 285–286
General elections, 346
General law cities, 104
General Motors, 59
General obligation bonds, 113–114, 452, 478
Generational changes, 275
Gentrification, 21, 115
Geofencing, 364
George R. Brown Convention Center, 333
Geren, Charlie, 371
Gerrymandering, 146, 353–355
Getty Oil Company, 254
Gettysburg Address (1863), 273
G.I. Forum, 112
Gillespie, Oscar W., 339
Ginsburg, Ruth Bader, 467–468
Globalization of the economy, 27
Global warming, 473–475
Goals 2000: Educate America Act (1994), 73
Goldwater, Barry, 325, 332
Gonzales, Alberto R., 191, 250–251, 358
Gonzales, Tony, 338–339
Gonzalez, Raul A., 250, 324, 358
Google, advertising in political campaigns, 385, 386, 390
Gore, Al, 73
Gorsuch, Neil M., 472
Governing (P. Taylor), 400
The Governmental Process (D. Truman), 418–419
Governor, defined, 180
Governorship, 170, 177–215. *see also specific governors*
   history of elected governors, 185t
   history of governors, 183, 185t
   history of plural executive, 180–183
   impeachment and incapacitation, 186
   informal resources of, 192–196, 193t
   leadership styles of recent governors, 196–205
   mass media and, 195
   other offices of plural executive, 205–212
   powers of, 177–180, 186–192, 187t
   staff of, 193, 194f
   structure of executive branch, 182f
Governor's Mansion, 181, 186
Gramm, Phil, 323, 324
Grand juries, 247
Grange, 44
Granger, Kay, 345
Grant, Ulysses S., 42, 43
Grassroots, 365–366
Gray Panthers, 432
Great Depression (1930s), 69
Greater Austin Asian Chamber of Commerce, 433
Great Recession (2008), 26, 71, 75
Great Society programs, 71
Green, George, 230–231
Green, George Norris, 420
Greenberg, Anna, 387
Green Party, 313, 314
Greenwald, Carol, 423
Grodzins, Morton, 67–68
Gross product, 27

Group think, 272
Grover, Henry "Hank," 312–313
Grutter v. *Bollinger* (2003), 461
Gulf Coast Aquifer, 475
Gun-Free School Zones Act (1990), 79
Gun rights and laws, 155, 198
Gutierrez, Jose Angel, 312
Guzman, Eva, 251, 253, 358

Hamilton, A. J., 41, 42
Hamilton, Alexander, 274
Handguns, 463–464
Hatch, Orrin, 89
Hate crimes, 167
Hayden, Michael, 403
Health and human services, 468–472
Health care, 468–472
Health insurance, 23, 468–469
Healthy Texas Women program, 470–471
Heard, Goggan, Blair, and Williams, 172–173
Hearst Corporation, 394, 396–397
Hecht, Nathan, 257–258
Heclo, Hugh, 445
Hegar, Glenn, 46, 208–209, 448
Hegar, Mary "MJ," 345–346
Hidalgo, Lina, 119, 120
Higher education, 459–464. *see also specific universities*
    affirmative action, 460–462
    equity and quality in, 459–460
    guns on campus, 463–464
    safety on campus, 464
    tuition, 462–463, 463f
High Plains Region, 28–29, 28f
High-tech industry, 26
Hightower, Jim, 323, 433
Highway Trust Fund, 448
Hill, John L., 254, 323
Hill-Harris polls, 380
Hispanics. *see also specific advocacy organizations*
    on city councils, 112
    early history of, 11–12
    educational attainment, 23t, 24
    electoral gains, 357–358, 358f, 359t
    as gubernatorial appointees, 197
    history of in public education, 8
    income comparisons, 22, 22t
    influence on Texas party system, 328–329
    interest groups, 432–433
    as judges, 250–252, 250f
    living at poverty level, 468
    as majority of Texas's residents, 3
    noncitizen, 18
    party identification, 287, 298, 322
    public opinion on select policies, 287t, 288
    state population of, 11, 12, 12f, 29, 102
    support for Trump, 298, 299
    in Texas legislature, 143, 143t
    in urban areas, 19
    voter turnout and, 294–295, 294f
Hobby, William P. "Bill," 50, 152, 166, 206, 213, 454
Home rule cities, 104, 108
Home-schooling, 265
Homestead exemption, 114
Hoover, Herbert, 317, 335

Hopwood v. *State of Texas* (1996), 460–461
House Bill 72, 454–455
Household income, 22, 22t
House of Representatives. *see also* Texas legislature
    Administration Committee, 378–379
    House Research Organization, 160
    leadership roles, 136–137, 149–151
    Rainy Day Fund, 381, 383, 475, 476
    state districts, 147
    Texas Conservative Coalition, 166
    within legislative branch, 45–46, 140
Houston
    extraterritorial jurisdiction of, 129
    Harris County Courthouse, 102
    Houston Equal Rights Ordinance (HERO), 347
    multilingualism of, 3
    population growth, 19, 21f, 101
    strong mayor form of government, 107f
Houston, Sam, 10–11, 39, 41
Houston First Corp, 333
Howard, Donna, 165, 338–339
Huffines, Phillip, 345
Huffman, Joan, 165, 174
Hughes, Sarah T., 252
Hunker, Kathleen, 256
Huntington, Samuel, 313
Hurd, Will, 338–339
Hurricane Harvey, 473–474
Hutchison, Kay Bailey, 154, 184, 202, 323, 343, 359, 360, 388, 389
Hydraulic fracking, 26, 99, 116, 476
Hyperpluralism, 421–422

IBM, 222
Illusion of saliency, 300
Immigration and immigrants, 87–93
    CHIP program, 469
    family separation practice, 92
    federal laws and policies, 87–92
    state actions, 92–93
Immigration and Nationality Act (1952), 88
Immigration and Nationality Act (1965), 88
Immigration Reform and Control Act (1986), 88
Impeachment, 186
Implied powers, 64
Inactives, 291
Income taxes, 33–34, 449, 452–453
Independent Party, public opinion on select policies, 285t
Independent school districts, 124, 125–128
Indictment, 247
Indirect lobbying, 427–430
Individualism, 6
Individualistic subculture, 9, 13–14
Individual rights, 47
Industrial Areas Foundation (IAF), 433
Industrial development corporations, 131
Information (document), 247
Initiatives, 49
In-kind election support, 428
In-migration, 18
Innocence Project, 263
INRIX, 478
Instagram, 363, 366
Institute of Texan Cultures, 14
Institute on Taxation and Economic Policy, 449

Institutionalization, 138
Insurrection Act (1807), 78
Intellectual disability, and death penalty, 467–468
Interest groups, 170. *see also* Political action committees (PACs)
    constitutional amendments and, 52–53
    defined, 415
    governors and, 196
    lawsuits by, 54
    news media and, 400–401
    political parties vs., 309
Interest groups and political power, 412–439
    characteristics of dominant groups, 430–343
    influence on policy, 329
    interest group theory, 418–422
    membership of, 416–418
    policymaking process, 423–430, 423t
    resources and power of, 435–437
    roles and functions of groups, 415–416
Interest group theory
    elitist alternative, 420–421
    hyperpluralism and, 421–422
    pluralism and democratic theory, 418–420
    single-issue groups, 422
Interlocal contracting, 131
Internal political efficacy, 281
Internet surveys, 300
Intersectionality, 284
Interstate Compact on Adoption and Medical Assistance, 67
Interstate compacts, 67
Interstate Compact to Conserve Oil and Gas, 67
Iron rule of oligarchy, 420
Iron triangles of government, 422, 445–446
Issue-attention cycle, 382–383
Issue networks, 445–446

Jamail, Joe, 254
Jaybird Democratic Association, 352
Jefferson, Atatiana, 413
Jefferson, Thomas, 103, 380
Jefferson, Wallace, 191, 251, 255, 257, 359
Jenkins, Clay, 60, 119
Jester, Beauford, 206
Jim Crow laws, 318
Johnson, Andrew, 42
Johnson, Ann, 357
Johnson, Gary, 278
Johnson, Lyndon B., 71, 252, 320, 321, 322, 325, 339
Jones, Gina Ortiz, 338–339
Jones, Jesse, 391
Jordan, Barbara, 143
Judge selection, state comparisons, 258–259, 258f
Judicial activism, 253–254, 255–258
Judicial branch, 47
Judicial powers, of governor, 192
Judicial system, 237–270. *see also* Texas Supreme Court
    campaign contributions and Republican gains, 254–255
    court structure, 238–245, 241f, 244f
    criminal and civil procedure, 239–240
    criminal justice, 259–264
    federal court system and, 239
    judges, 238, 240–241, 244–245, 246, 249–253, 250f
    judicial activism, 253–254, 255–258
    jury systems, 247
    policy role in state courts, 264–268

    procedures and decision making, 247–249
    prosecuting attorneys and clerks, 246–247
    state judge selection, 258–259, 258f
Juneteenth holiday, 8
Jury duty, 297
Justice, William Wayne, 465
Justices of the peace courts, 242, 268

Kavanaugh, Brett M., 472
Keller, Sharon, 245, 253, 262–263
Kennedy, John F., 71, 252, 283
Key, V. O., 17, 69, 309, 317, 319, 328, 330, 334
Kickapoo tribe, 10–11
Kimmel, Jimmy, 276
Kincaid, John, 73–74
King, Martin Luther, Jr., 16
Kirk, Ron, 324
Knaggs, John R., 320–321
Koch, Charles, 401
Koch, David, 401
Kronberg, Harvey, 399
Krueger, Bob, 323

Labor unions, 50, 86, 431–432, 436
Lamar, Mirabeau B., 11
Laney, James E. "Pete," 149–150, 166, 199
Lanier, Bob, 370
La Raza Unida (People United), 311–313
Laredo Merchants Association, 267
Laredo Merchants Association v. *The City of Laredo* (2018), 267
Larson, Lyle, 191
Las Vegas Sands Corporation, 435, 436
Leach, Jeff, 373
League of United Latin American Citizens (LULAC), 251–252, 432–433
League of United Latin American Citizens et al. v. *Mattox et al.* (1989), 251–252
League of Women Voters, 418
Lee, Tom, 15
Legislative branch, 45–46. *see also* House of Representatives; Senate; Texas legislature
Lehrmann, Debra, 253
Leininger, James, 374
Lewis, Gib, 149, 151, 166, 172–173, 454
LGBTQ candidates, 357
Liberals, 276–277, 281
Libertarian Party, 313, 314
Libertarians, 278
Licensing, 224
Lieutenant Governor, 151–152, 156, 163, 181, 186, 188, 206
Limited government
    defined, 45
    origins of, 13–14, 44
Lincoln, Abraham, 41, 273
Line-item vetoes, 162, 189
Literacy. *see* Public education
Livingstone, Linda, 464
Lobbying, 422
    characteristics of lobbyists, 436–437
    defined, 423
    direct, 424–426
    indirect, 427–430
    of local governments, 434
    techniques used, 423t

Local elections, 346–347
Local government, 98–135, 132t
  bond issues, 452
  cities and urban areas, 100–102, 102t, 129–130
  city revenue and expenditures, 112–114, 113f, 225
  county government, 103, 117–123, 118t, 119f, 130–131
  government employees, 222
  independent school districts, 124, 125–128
  interest groups and, 434
  legal and constitutional framework for, 103–112
  municipal election systems, 110–112
  plastic bag ordinances, 267
  property taxes, 450
  solutions to challenges of, 128–132
  special districts, 123–125
  urban problems, 114–116
Lone Star State, use of nickname, 6
Lottery, 197, 451–452
Lowi, Theodore, 422

MacArthur, Douglas, 320
Madison, James, 63, 273, 418
Mail-in voting, 208, 267–268, 297, 348–349
Malcolm X, 340–341
Manchester, Douglas F., 399
Mandates, 72, 74–76, 82–83, 116
Maninger, Robert, 457
Mansfield, Steve, 262
Manufacturing, 29
Maps
  of 1846, 55
  Energy Map of Texas, 14
Maquiladora program, 27, 84–85, 95
March for Our Lives (2018), 402
Margin of error, in polling, 302
Margins taxes, 450, 453
Marijuana laws, 66
Marion, Sandee Bryan, 266
Marketing technology, in political campaigns, 360–366
Marshall, John, 68
Martin Luther King, Jr. holiday, 8
Mason, Robert, 403
Mass media, in political socialization, 282
Mass media in Texas politics, 195, 378–411
  advertising in political campaigns, 366–369, 385–386
  coverage of polls, 302, 385
  current trends, 393–404, 393f
  early history of, 390–392
  electoral process and, 384–390
  governors and, 195
  as guardians of open government, 383–384
  history of newspapers, 390–395
  informed citizens, 405–410, 406f, 407t
  policy agenda, 380–384
  television conglomerates, 396–397
Matching funds, 70
Mauro, Garry, 183, 200, 209, 323, 324
Mauzy, Oscar, 265, 455
Mayor-Council city government, 105–106, 106f
McChesney, Robert, 401
McCombs, Maxwell, 382
McCormick, Michael, 324
McCulloch v. *Maryland* (1819), 68
McCutcheon v. *Federal Election Commission* (2014), 428

McGovern, George, 332
McIntyre v. *El Paso Independent School District* (2015), 265
McNutt, Thomas, 371
McRaven, William, 463
Media bias, 407–410
Media events, 366
Medicaid program, 19, 76, 202, 203, 204, 222, 448, 468, 470–471
Medical examiners, 122
Medical malpractice, 53
Medical marijuana, 66
Medina, David M., 251, 358
Meier, Bill, 162
Merit employment system, 232–234
Merit selection, 254, 259
#MeToo movement, 165, 402
Metro government, 131
The Metropolitan Organization (TMO), 433
Mexican American Legal Defense and Educational Fund (MALDEF), 112, 432–433, 455
Mexican American Legislative Caucus (MALC), 90
Mexico. *see also* U.S.-Mexico interdependency
  Border Industrialization Program, 84
  bracero program, 88
  drug cartels, 93–94
  gender-based violence in, 85
  independence of Texas from, 39
  links to Texan economy, 27, 29, 478
  Texas as state of, 38–39
Meyers, Lawrence, 251
Michalewicz, Rachel, 461
Michels, Robert, 420
Middleton, David, II, 371
Military powers, of governor, 192
Miller, Bill, 204
Miller, Sid, 16, 210
Mills, C. Wright, 420
Mills, John Stuart, 274
Mineral leases, 209
Minority-focused interest groups, 432–433
Miranda ruling, 260
Mischief of factions, 418
Misdemeanors, 239
Missouri Plan. *see* Merit selection
Mitchell, Anne, 230
Moncrief, Mike, 370
Moody, Dan, 189
Moody, Joe, 151
Moore, Bobby, 468
Morales, Dan, 207, 324, 358, 460
Moralistic subculture, 10
Morton, Michael, 263–234
Mosbacher, Rob, 370
Motor fuels taxes, 448, 450–451, 478, 480
Motor voter registration, 355
Multi-issue groups, 422
Multilingualism, 3, 18
Municipal courts, 242
Municipal utility districts (MUDs), 124
Muniz, Ramsey, 310–311, 312–313
Murdoch, Rupert, 397
Murphy v. *National Collegiate Athletic Association* (2018), 78, 80
Murray, Richard, 389
Mutscher, Gus, 143, 171–172

NARAL Pro-Choice Texas, 422
National Association for the Advancement of Colored People (NAACP), 112, 357, 433
National Center for Health Statistics, 302
National Defense Production Act (1950), 59
National Democratic Training Committee, 363
National Domestic Preparedness Office, 59
National Education Association (NEA), 456
National Governors' Association, 445
National Guard, 74, 89, 92, 94. *see also* Texas National Guard
National Institute for Statistics and Geography (INEGI), 84
Nationalization Act (1790), 88
National Organization for Women, 422
National Rifle Association, 422
National School Walkout (2018), 402
National Voter Registration Act (1993), 73, 74
Native Americans
  early history of, 10–11
  proposed casinos, 452
  state population of, 10, 12f
Nau, John L, III, 226
Navarro, Jose Antonio, 11–12
Negative television ads, 388
#NeverAgain movement, 402
New Deal, 69, 286, 318
New federalism, 71–80
  Bush II years (2001–2009), 74–75
  Clinton years (1993–2001), 73–74
  defined, 72
  Obama years (2009–2017), 75–76
  Republican opposition (1969–1974), 72–73
  Trump years (2017), 76–78
New Jersey, legalized sports betting, 80
New Media Investment Group, 394
News Corporation, 397
News media, 378–379, 380, 400–401, 408–409
Newsom, Gavin, 77
Newspapers, history of, 390–395
New Texas vision (Richards), 197–198
New York (state), Green Light Law and Global Entry program, 77
New York v. *U.S.* (1992), 78
Nie, Norman H., 291
Nieto, Enrique Peña, 84
Nineteenth Amendment, 353
Nixon, Richard, 51, 72, 322, 392
No Child Left Behind (NCLB) Act (2002), 74–75, 457–458
Nolo contendere, 260
Non-Hispanic white. *see* Anglos
Nonpartisan elections, 111, 124
Nonresponse bias, in polls, 303–304
No pass, no play rule, 455
Norms, 164–166
North American Free Trade Agreement (NAFTA), 27, 29, 84, 85–86, 478
Nugent, Ted, 365
Nurse Licensure Compact, 67
Nursing homes, 226

Obama, Barack, 313
  Clean Power Plan, 474–475
  election campaigns, 297, 299, 327, 332, 343, 362
  executive orders, 76, 90
  failed to renew Women's Health Program, 470
  immigration policies, 89–90, 91, 92–93, 94
  new federalism under, 75–76
  on same-sex marriage laws, 65–66
  Texas pollution regulation reform, 473
Obamacare. *see* Patient Protection and Affordable Care Act (2010)
Obergefell v. *Hodges* (2015), 66
O'Daniel, W. Lee "Pappy," 206, 361
Ogallala Aquifer, 28–29
One-party politics, 18, 47, 182–183, 195, 277, 308, 309, 317–320, 343
Operation Rescue–National v. *Planned Parenthood of Houston and Southeast Texas, Inc.* (1998), 267
Organization of Chinese Americans, 433
Original jurisdiction, 240
O'Rourke, Beto, 297–298, 299, 302, 307, 365–366, 368, 372, 390
Overstreet, Morris, 251, 359

Packing, 353–354
PACs. *see* Political action committees (PACs)
Page, Benjamin, 275
Paredes, Raymund, 462
Paris Climate Agreement, 77
Parochial participants, 291
Parole, 261
Parr machine, 24
Partisanship, growth of, 166–167
Party activists, 291, 329, 333–334
Party conventions, 331–333
Party identification, 279, 284–285, 314, 325–327, 326f
The Party's Over (Broder), 334
Party system, 307–337
  challenges for policy-oriented coalitions, 334–335
  functions of political parties, 313–317
  interest groups, 309
  partisan history in Texas, 317–329, 325t, 326f
  political parties, 309–313, 310f
  structure of party organizations, 330–334
Patient Protection and Affordable Care Act (2010), 23, 76, 80, 208, 468–470
Patrick, Dan, 33, 46, 99, 151, 154–156, 162, 177, 204–205, 206, 311, 314, 315, 373, 379, 383
Patterson, Jerry, 209, 266
Paxton, Angela, 345
Paxton, Ken, 90, 207–208, 267–268, 297, 373, 435, 470
Pay-as-you-go, 26, 208, 447
Pay-to-play system, 226
Peabody, George, 126
Peabody Education Fund, 126
Peers and community, in political socialization, 281
Peerwani, Nizam, 467
Penal Code, 239
Pence, Mike, 203
Pennzoil Company, 254
Permanent School Fund, 209, 448
Permanent University Fund (PUF), 209, 448, 460
Perot, Ross, 327, 454–455
Perry, Bob, 191
Perry, Rick, 46, 75, 140, 147, 152–153, 154, 167, 179, 183, 184, 186, 188, 189–191, 193, 196, 200–203, 206, 209–210, 226, 246, 251, 256, 263, 264, 276, 299, 310–311, 314, 315, 323, 324, 370, 383, 386, 387–389, 433, 450, 455, 460, 467, 469, 470, 471, 474, 478, 480
Personal interviews, in polling, 300
Petitions for discretionary review, 249
Petitions for review, 249

Petit juries, 247
Petroleum industry, 25, 26–27, 29, 426, 450, 476
Pew Research Center, 91, 294–295, 363, 380, 393, 399–400, 404, 405, 407, 408–409
Phelan, Dade, 137, 151
Phillips, Thomas R., 255
Picket fence theory of federalism, 68
Pilgrim, Lonnie "Bo," 172–173
Planned Parenthood, 470–471
Plastic bag ordinances, 267
Platforms, 332
Plea bargain, 244
Plural executive, 40, 180–181. *see also* Governorship
Pluralism, 274, 418–420
Pojman, Joe, 470
Policy implementation. *see* Bureaucracy and policy
Political action committees (PACs), 339–340, 365, 372–374, 372t, 427–428. *see also specific PACs*
Political campaigns, 360–375. *see also* Elections
    campaign finance, 369–375, 370t, 371f, 372t
    controlled media and, 366–367
    costs and fund-raising, 370, 370t, 371f
    direct mail and online fund-raising, 369
    finance reform attempts, 374–375
    grassroots efforts, 365–366
    marketing technology in, 360–366
    PACs and fat cats, 339–340, 365, 372–374, 372t
    rationale for contributions, 374
    segmentation and targeting of electorate, 364–365
    size of state and, 24
    social media and public opinion polling, 361–364
    uncontrolled media and, 368
Political culture, 8
Political efficacy, 281
Political gladiators, 291
Political ideology, 276–278
Political myths, 6–8
Political participation, 290–299
    categories of, 291
    nonvoting, 296–297
    recent voting patterns in Texas, 293, 297–299
    transitions costs in voting, 297
    voting patterns, 292–297, 292f, 294f
Political parties, 309. *see also* Democratic Party; Green Party; Independent Party; Republican Party
Political patronage, 232–233
Political socialization, 278–283
Polk, James K., 40
Poll taxes, 351
Pollution, 95, 116
Popular sovereignty, 45
Population density, 21, 101
Population growth, 17–18, 21f
Populist Party, 351
Populists, 278, 311
Port of Corpus Christi, 29
Port of Houston, 5, 49
Poverty
    future trends, 23
    income guidelines, 22
    minorities living in, 468
    percentage of population in, 22–23
    school funding and, 16–17
Powered by People, 372

The Power Elite (C. Mills), 420
Powers of governors, state comparisons, 187t
Precinct chairs, 330
Precincts, 330, 331–332
Preemptions, 72, 75–76, 79, 100
Press, freedom of, 380. *see also* Mass media in Texas politics
Press secretaries, 368
Price, Betsy, 370
Primary elections, 342–346, 344f
Printz v. *United States* (1997), 78, 79
Prison reform, 78, 465, 466t
Private school vouchers, 458
Privatization, 129, 216–217, 222
Privileges and immunities, 66
Probability samples, 301
Probation, 261
Professional and Amateur Sports Protection Act (PASPA) (1992), 80
Project grants, 70
Pro-life America PAC, 373
Property or ad valorem taxes, 450
Proposition 12, 53
ProPublica, 401
Prosecution, 247
Protests and marches, 430. *see also specific events and movements*
Psycho-demographics, 364
Public Citizen, 426, 432
Public education, 23t
    charter schools, 458
    court cases on, 265
    decentralization of, 47, 103
    equity and quality in, 126, 454–455
    funding of, 5, 23, 255–257, 450, 459–460
    higher education, 459–464
    independent school districts, 124, 125–128
    interest groups and, 432
    political socialization and, 280–281
    private school vouchers, 458
    school boards, 128
    segregation in, 126
    special education, 458
    student testing, 457
    teacher pay and morale, 457
Public employment, 116
Public Health Security and Bioterrorism Preparedness Response Act (2002), 59
Public improvement districts (PID), 132
Public interest groups, 432
Public opinion, defined, 273
Public opinion and political ideology, 271–306
    democracy and, 273–274
    group membership and, 283–290, 285–290t
    political ideology and, 276–278
    political participation, 290–299
    political socialization, 278–283
    polling and, 299–304
    stability of key values, 274–275
Public opinion polling, 274, 298–304, 360–364
Public policy issues, present day, 440–483
    criminal justice, 465–468
    educational policies, 453–464
    elements of public policy, 441
    environmental policies, 472–476
    health and human services, 468–472

iron triangles and issue networks, 445–446
regressive tax system, 449–453
stages of policy process, 442–445, 442t
state budget, 446–448, 447f
transportation, 476–480
Public relations firms, 437
Push polls, 300–301, 362

Race, ethnicity and school funding, 16–17
Racial segregation, 7–8, 126, 281
Racism, public opinion on, 413–414
Radical Reconstructionists, 42
Ramos, Mike, 413
Ramos, Nelva Gonzales, 252
Ramsey, Ross, 395, 479
Ratliff, Bill, 153
Ray, C. L., 255
Rayburn, Sam, 321
Readings, 160
Reagan, John H., 44
Reagan, Ronald, 72–73, 322
RealClearPolitics, 303
REAL ID Act (2005), 89
Realignment, 322
Record votes, 163–164
Redistricting, 144–149, 354–355
Red River Compact, 67
Referendums, 49
Regressive tax, 112
Regular legislative session, 140
Regulatory functions, 224–225
Rehabilitation Act (1973), 348
Rehnquist, William, 37, 79
Religion
  in political socialization, 282–283
  public opinion on select policies and, 288–290, 289t
  Religious Right, 311, 332, 434
Religious Freedom Restoration Act (1993), 79
Religious Land Use and Institutionalized Persons Act (RLUIPA) (2000), 79–80
Representative government, 45
Republican Party
  beliefs about the press, 380–381, 408
  decentralization and devolution platform of, 71
  elected governors from, 185t
  impact of in-migration on, 18
  judicial elections, 246, 253–255
  members in Texas legislature, 143t, 147–148, 153, 155, 166–168
  partisan history in Texas, 308, 314, 317–329, 325t, 326f
  party organization, 330–334
  public opinion on select policies, 285t
  religious affiliation and, 283
  self-identified partisans, 285
  traditional vs. Tea Party Republicans, 327–328
  views on federal vs. state response to COVID-19, 60
Republican Party of Texas PAC, 428
Republican State Leadership Committee (RSLC), 372
Republics, 6
Reserved powers, 65
Responsible party model, 334
Retention elections, 259
Reuters, study on death penalty, 262
Revenue bonds, 113–114

Revenue sharing, 72
Reverse discrimination, 354–355
Revolving door, 229
Reyes, Paul, 338–339
Reynolds v. *Sims* (1964), 146
Richard, Michael, 262–263
Richards, Ann, 170, 173, 181, 184, 189, 190, 191, 192, 197–198, 226, 251, 314, 323, 327, 341, 359, 367, 386, 451, 455, 465
Right-to-work law, 50, 51, 431–432
RINOs (Republicans in Name Only), 311
Rivard, Robert, 395
Roberts, John, 79–80, 90, 472
Roberts, Robert, 230
Rocha, Roger C., Jr., 433
Rockefeller, John D., 126
Rockefeller Institute of Government, 80
Rodrigue, George, 387
Rodriquez, Demetrio P., 454
Roe v. *Wade* (1973), 471
Rollback elections, 113
Rolling easements, 266
Romney, Mitt, 299
Roosevelt, Franklin, 318–319
Rose, Gene, 399–400
Ross, Kim, 255
Ruiz v. *Estelle* (1980), 465–466
Runoff elections, 111, 343–344
Rural population decline, 20f
Rural-urban divide, 21
Russia, infiltration of US elections, 403, 404

Sadler, Paul, 389
Sales taxes, 449–450
Salinas de Gortari, Carlos, 85
Same-sex marriage, 37, 53, 65–66, 201, 208
Samples, 301, 302
San Antonio
  citizens' association, 313
  City Hall (1891), 101
  population growth, 19, 21f, 101
  Toyota plant, 131
  zoning and land use, 21
San Antonio Report, 395
Sanchez, Tony, 184, 200, 324, 370, 386, 388–389
Sanders, Bernie, 301, 345, 363, 407
Sandlin, Bennett, 113
San Jacinto, battle of, 39
San Jacinto Monument, 30
Santa Anna, general, 39
School boards, 128, 347
Schools, in political socialization, 280–281
School superintendents, 128
Schumer, Chuck, 86
Schwarzenegger, Arnold, 186
Secession Ordinance of 1861, 41
Secretary of State, 210
Seguin, Juan, 11
Select committees, 159
Seminole Tribe v. *Florida* (1996), 79
Senate. *see also* Texas legislature
  leadership roles, 151–156
  Senate Research Center, 160
  state districts, 145f, 146, 147
  within legislative branch, 45, 46, 140

Senatorial courtesy, 190
Separation of powers, 45
September 11, 2001 terrorist attacks, 283
Severance, Carol, 266
Severance taxes, 450
Severance v. Patterson (2010), 266–267
Sexism, 164–165
Sexual assault, on campus, 464
Sexual harassment policies, 165–166
Shannon, Tommy, 172
Shapiro, Robert, 275
Sharp, Frank, 171–172, 391, 392
Sharp, John, 152, 153, 226, 463
Sharpstown stock fraud scandal, 171–172, 322, 374–375, 392
Shaw, Donald, 382
Sheffield, J.D., 345
Shelby County v. Holder (2013), 148, 355, 356
Sheriffs, 121–122
Shivers, Allan, 8, 206, 320
Sierra Club, 426, 432, 475
Silver, Nate, 304
Sinclair Broadcast Group, 397–398
Single-issue groups, 422
Single-member districts, 111, 112, 353
Single-purpose districts, 347
Sin taxes, 450–451
Sitton, Ryan, 345
Slater, Wayne, 387
Slaughter, Michelle, 251
Slavery system, 13, 40, 42
Smith, Al, 317, 335
Smith, Evan, 395
Smith, Preston, 171
Smith v. Allwright (1944), 352
Social and economic environment of Texas politics, 1–32
    growth and changing demographics, 17–29
    myths of political culture, 6–8
    population groups, 10–17
    subcultures of, 8–10, 12, 13–14
    twenty-first century challenges, 4–5
Social contract, 45
Social media. *see also specific platforms*
    citizen journalism, 401–403
    fake news and abuse of, 403–404
    public opinion polling, 361–364
    social protest and, 402
Society of the Patrons of Husbandry, 44
SoftBank, 394
Sondock, Ruby, 252
Soon-Shiong, Patrick, 399
Soros, George, 16
Sossamon v. Texas (2011), 79–80
Sound bites, 384
Southern Politics (Key), 317
South Texas Border Region, 28f, 29
Southwest Voter Registration and Education Project, 112
Speaker, 149–150, 156, 163, 188
Special districts, 123–125, 222
Special education, 458
Special elections, 347
Special sessions, 140, 154, 180, 188–189, 201, 202, 205
Spector, Rose, 253
Spectrum, 396
Spin, 400, 429

Spoils system, 123
Springer, Drew, Jr., 373
Staggered terms, 190
Standing committees, 158–159, 158t
Stanton, Frank, 409
Staples, Todd, 210
Starr, Paul, 400, 409–410
State Bar of Texas, 208, 245, 264
State chairs, 331
State conventions, 332–333
State executive committees, 331
State holidays, 8
State lawmaking bodies, comparisons, 138f, 140, 141
State of Texas Assessments of Academic Readiness (STAAR), 457–458
Statutory county courts, 243
Statutory law, 36
Steiner, Fritz, 464
Stevenson, Adlai, 320
Stevenson, Coke, 206
Stewart, Jon, 396
Straight-ticket voting, 257–258, 349, 384
Strategic National Stockpile, 59
Straus, Joe, 99, 149, 150–151, 155, 156, 169, 205, 334–335
Strayhorn, Carole Keeton, 46, 183, 226, 313, 324
Strong mayor, 105–106, 107f
Students for Concealed Carry, 464
Students for Fair Admissions, 461
Student testing, 457
Sturns, Louis, 251
Subsidence, 475
Suburban population, 21
Suffrage, 341
Sullivan, Michael Quinn, 137
Sunbelt in-migration, 18
Sunset review, 228–229, 228t
Supplemental Nutrition Assistance Program (SNAP), 22–23
Supplemental Security Income, 468
Supremacy clause, 64, 69
Survey research, 300–302, 361
Swanson, Doug J., 7

Tags, 162
Tax abatement, 131
Tax Policy Center, 449
Tax system, 449–453
    bonds, 452
    gambling and lottery, 451–452
    income tax, 33–34, 449, 452–453
    margins tax, 450, 453
    motor fuel tax, 448, 450–451, 478, 480
    property or ad valorem tax, 450
    regressive system, 449–451
    sales tax, 449–450
    severance tax, 450
    sin tax, 450–451
Taylor, Breonna, 413, 430
Taylor, Paul W., 400
Teacher pay, 457
Tea Party movement, 151, 154, 155, 167, 168–169, 202, 204, 278, 311, 327–328, 345, 389
Technopols, 445–446
Telephone surveys, in polling, 300, 302–303

Temporary Assistance for Needy Families (TANF) program, 73, 468
Tenth Amendment, 65, 78, 80
Texaco Inc., 254
Texans for Lawsuit Reform (TLR), 256, 373, 428, 431
Texans for Public Justice, 191, 372, 426
Texas A&M University, 448, 459–460, 462, 473
Texas Alliance for Life, 470
Texas and Southwestern Cattle Raisers Association (TSCRA), 433
Texas Association of Business (TAB), 431
Texas Association of Counties, 434
Texas Association of Realtors PAC, 373, 428, 431
Texas Automobile Dealers Association, 431
Texas Bankers Association, 431
Texas Catholic Conference, 434
Texas Central Partners, 480
Texas Chemical Council, 431
Texas Civil Justice League, 255–256
Texas Civil Rights Project, 348–349
Texas Conference of Urban Counties, 103
Texas Conservatives Fund, 368
Texas Corn Producers Board (TCPB), 433
Texas Court of Criminal Appeals, 47, 245, 249, 251, 252, 253, 261–263, 467–468
Texas District and County Attorneys Association, 434
Texas Education Agency v. *Leeper* (1994), 265
Texas Election Code, 331
Texas Farm Bureau, 433
Texas Freedom Network, 434
Texas government. *see also* Elected Boards and Commissions
　Agencies of Education–Higher Education, 81
　Agencies of Education–Public Education, 81
　appointments to state agencies, 225–226
　Board of Pardons and Paroles, 192, 261
　Civil Service Commission, 233
　Commission on Environmental Quality, 225
　Commission on Judicial Conduct, 208
　Division of Emergency Management, 59
　General Land Office, 209, 228, 234, 266
　Health Department, 226
　Health Services, 59
　Human Services, 230–231
　Legislative Budget Board, 73, 190, 226, 448, 478
　Legislative Redistricting Board, 144, 146, 147, 324
　Medical Board, 230
　Office of State–Federal Relations, 81
　Public Safety Department, 59, 356
　sources of revenue, 81f
　Texas Education Agency, 126, 128, 453, 458
　Transportation Department, 217, 476–480
Texas Independent Producers & Royalty Owners Association, 431
Texas Leads PAC, 372
Texas legislation
　annexation authority, 130
　bathroom bill, proposed, 99, 156, 204–205, 383
　campaign finance reform, proposed, 191, 374–375
　Deceptive Trade Practices–Consumer Protection Act (1973), 254
　hate crime law, 167
　House Bill 72, 454–455
　Interlocal Cooperation Act (1971), 131
　marijuana laws, 66
　Municipal Annexation Act (1963), 129
　Open Beaches Act (1959), 266–267
　Open Meetings and Public Information Acts, 383–384
　Optional Road Law (1947), 120
　property tax revenue, 99–100, 112–113
　ride-sharing law, 99
　Robin Hood law, 265, 455
　sales tax, 130
　Senate Bill 4, sanctuary cities law (2017), 93, 99, 155, 204–205
　Terrell Election Laws (1903/1905), 314
　Texas Civil Protection Act (1951), 59
　Texas Disaster Act (1975), 59, 177
　Trans Texas Corridor, proposed, 200
　unconstitutional white primary law, 352
Texas legislature, 136–176. *see also* House of Representatives; Senate
　Auditor's Office, 234
　career patterns, 144
　control of bureaucracy, 227–231, 227t
　ethics and reform, 171–174
　functions of, 138–139
　influences on voting decisions, 168–171, 170t
　lawmaking process, 139, 157f, 160–164, 161f, 169–171
　leaders and committees, 149–160, 158t
　Legislative Audit Committee, 234
　meeting facilities, 142
　members of, 143, 143t
　member styles and reputations, 171
　norms of, 164–166
　partisanship in, 166–168
　pay and compensation, 141–142
　regular sessions of, 140
　representation and redistricting, 144–149, 145f
　terms of office and qualifications, 141
　turnover, 144
Texas Libertarian Party, 278
Texas Lyceum Polls, 381
Texas Medical Association PAC, 255, 373, 429, 431
Texas Municipal League (TML), 99, 103, 105, 113, 360, 434
Texas National Guard, 178
Texas Nursery & Landscape Association (TNLA), 433
Texas Nursing Association, 230
Texas Politics Project, 262
Texas Press Association, 394
Texas Public Policy Foundation, 256, 431
Texas Ranger mythology, 6–8, 312
Texas Restaurant Association, 431
Texas Rural Legal Aid, 112
Texas Scorecard, 379, 400
Texas State Teachers Association (TSTA), 34, 417–418, 457
Texas Supreme Court
　access to beaches, 237–238, 266–267
　appeals jurisdiction, 244–245, 249
　jurisdiction of, 47
　justices, 250, 252–253
　lawsuit against regarding court elections, 252
　on school finance, 140, 264, 450, 455, 456
　Texas Watch study on, 256–257
　on water regulation, 225
Texas Taxpayers and Research Association (TTRA), 431
Texas Trial Lawyers Association, 253–254
The Texas Tribune, 395
Texas Urban Triangle, 19, 20f
Texas Watch, 256–257, 432
Third parties, 311–313

Thirteenth Amendment, 351
Thompson, Senfronia, 165
Thornton, John, 395
3M, 59
Ticket splitting, 326
Tidwell, Scott, 230
Tigua tribe, 10–11
TikTok, 363, 366
Times Mirror Company, 391
TIMES'S UP Legal Defense Fund, 402
Title IX, 464
Tocqueville, Alexis de, 273–274, 412, 414–415
Toll roads, 216–217
Tort reform, 255–256
Tower, John, 311, 320–321
Toyota plant, 131
Tracking polls, 300
Traditionalistic subculture, 10, 12, 13–14
Transnational regionalism, defined, 83. *see also* U.S.-Mexico interdependency
Transparency USA, 372
Transportation system, 476–480
  border crossings, 28
  funding of, 24
  highway and toll road construction, 478–480
  mass transit, 480
  population growth and, 18
  rush-hour traffic, 477, 477f
  tax and fee revenue, 478
Trans Texas Corridor, proposed, 480
Trial courts, 248–249
Tribune Media, 398
Tribune Publishing Co., 399
Trinity Railway Express, 480
Tronc, 399
Truman, David, 418–419
Truman, Harry, 319–320
Trump, Donald, 85
  attacked news media, 380
  Cabinet appointees, 202–203, 474
  campaign ads violations on Facebook, 385–386
  election campaigns, 156, 204, 277, 288, 303–304, 307, 343, 345, 365, 385–386, 390, 407
  executive orders, 76, 90, 91, 93
  falsehoods by, 403–404
  handling of COVID-19 pandemic, 59, 60, 78, 178
  immigration policies, 87, 90, 91–92, 93, 94
  impeachments of, 316
  on marijuana laws, 66
  new federalism under, 76–78
  public opinion of Texans on, 285–290, 285–290t, 297–299
  race-blind college admissions, 461
  use of Twitter, 363
  U.S.-Mexico relations, 83–84
  withdrawal of Clean Power Plan, 474–475
Tuition rates, 462–463, 463f
Turner, Sylvester, 167, 333
2030 Committee, 478
Twenty-Fourth Amendment, 351
Twenty-Sixth Amendment, 353
Twitter, 363, 385, 404
2012 Census of Governments, 222
Two-party systems, 310–311, 321–323, 342–343
Two-thirds rule, 162

Unconstitutional laws, in Texas, 16, 65–66, 352, 422
Uncontrolled media, 368
Unconventional political behavior, 291
Unfunded Mandates Reform Act (1995), 73
Unicameral, 38
Unitary system, 39, 63
United Farm Workers Union (UFW), 433
United States v. Comstock (2010), 79
United States v. Lopez (1995), 79
University of Texas, 285, 440, 448, 459–462
University of Texas/*The Texas Tribune* Poll, 327–328
Upper East Texas Region, 28f, 29
Urbanization, 19–21, 20f
Urdiales, Lizeth, 433
U.S. Armed Forces, deployed to Mexican border, 92
U.S. Bureau of Land Management, 77
U.S. Bureau of the Census, 22
U.S. Census Bureau, 294
U.S. Conference of Mayors, 445
U.S. Constitution. *see also specific amendments*
  commerce clause, 69
  comparison to Texas Constitution, 36–37, 37t, 45
  delegated powers, 64
  denied powers, 65
  extradition, 66–67
  full faith and credit clause, 65–66
  guarantees to the states, 65
  interstate compacts, 67
  privileges and immunities, 66
  supremacy clause, 64, 69
U.S. Constitutional Convention of 1787, 63
U.S. Constitutional Convention of 1866, 351
U.S. Homeland Security Department, 74, 89, 90, 91
U.S. House of Representatives, Texas members of, 65
U.S. Immigration and Customs Enforcement (ICE), 91
U.S. Justice Department, 356
U.S.-Mexico-Canada Agreement (USMCA), 27, 84, 86, 95, 478
U.S.-Mexico interdependency, 83–95
  border drug violence, 89, 93–94
  common issues, 94–95
  immigration, 87–93
  maquiladoras, 27, 84–85, 95
  NAFTA, 84, 85–86
  trade patterns between Texas and Mexico, 86–87, 87f
  USMCA, 27, 84, 86, 95, 478
U.S. Senate, Texas members of, 65
U.S. Supreme Court. *see also specific cases*
  on abortion, 471–472
  on affirmative action, 460–461
  on apportionment, 118
  on Arizona immigration law, 92–93
  ban on execution of developmentally delayed persons, 189–190
  on campaign finance, 427–428
  on capital punishment, 260, 262
  on DACA, 90
  on extradition as mandatory, 67
  on intellectual disability and death penalty, 467–468
  Miranda ruling, 260
  on poll taxes, 47
  on public education for immigrant children, 89
  on redistricting, 146, 148–149, 354–355
  role and federalism, 67, 78–80
  on same-sex marriage, 37, 66

state courts in reaction to decisions of, 37
on state–federal relationships, 68
on Texas school funding, 454
on unconstitutionality of Texas HB2 abortion law, 422
on unconstitutionality of white primaries, 352
UT-Austin Texas Politics Polls, 426

Valdez, Lupe, 298, 299, 357
Valley Interfaith, 433
Van de Putte, Leticia, 154
Van Duyne, Beth, 360
Veniremen, 248
Verba, Sidney, 291
Vetoes, by governors, 46, 161–162, 171, 174, 180, 189, 200
V.G. Young Institute of County Government, 360
ViacomCBS, 397
Vice chairs, 331
Virginia Military Institute, 79
Vo, Hubert, 15
Voter identification laws, 299, 328, 356–357
Voter turnout, 281
   in early elections, 346
   by election type, 52, 53f, 54, 341, 343–344, 347
   in recent elections, 339
   since 1970, 344f, 346, 347
   state comparisons, 292–293, 292f
Voting rights. *see also* Political participation
   automatic registration, 297
   ballot security, 350
   citizenship requirement, 356
   contemporary restrictions on, 356–357
   extended absentee balloting, 347–348
   facilitation of participation, 355
   for felons, 356
   gains by minorities and women, 357–360, 358f, 359t
   history of, 9
   history of limitations on, 42, 45, 47, 208, 350–354
   mail-in voting, 208, 267–268, 297, 348–349
   motor voter registration, 355
   online registration, 297
   property ownership requirement, 352–353
   same-day registration, 355
   straight-ticket voting, 257–258, 349, 384
   unconstitutional laws in Texas, 16
   voter suppression, 312–313
   for women, 353
Voting Rights Act (1965/1975), 16, 112, 118, 128, 146, 148, 252, 318, 322, 343, 354–355, 356
Voting specialists, 291

Wainwright, Dale, 251, 359
Walker, Scott, 186

Wallace, George, 328
Wallace, Mike, 254
The Walt Disney Company, 397
Ward politics, 259
Washington, Craig, 151
The Washington Post, 398–399, 403
Watergate scandal, 392
Water resources
   court cases on, 266
   state funding of, 4
   supply policies, 475
Weak mayor, 105, 106f
Wealth and income distribution, 22–23, 22t
Weber, Joe, 217
Weber, Max, 218
Weber, Paul J., 205
Wesleyan Media Project, 386
West, Royce, 345–346
Weymouth, Katharine, 399
Whistle-blowers, 229–231
White, Bill, 202, 370, 388
White, Mark, 183, 250, 323, 435, 454
White flight, 19, 114–115
White primaries, 352
Wholesale Beer Distributors of Texas, 431
Whole Woman's Health v. *Hellerstedt* (2016), 80, 471
Williams, Clayton, 184, 323, 327, 341, 367, 386
Williams, Michael, 191, 359
Willingham, Cameron Todd, 467
Wolf, Chad, 77
Wolff, Nelson, 50, 52
Women. *see also* Abortion rights and laws
   electoral gains, 357, 359–360
   as gubernatorial appointees, 197
   as judges, 245, 252–253
   in Texas legislature, 164
   voting rights for, 353
Women's Health Program, 470–471
Women's March (2017), 402
Wong, Martha, 15
Workforce, in government. *see* Employees, of Texas government
Workman, Paul, 371
Writs of mandamus, 249
Wu, Gene, 15

Xerox, 217, 222

Yarborough, Ralph, 321
Yuchtman, Noam, 262

Zuckerberg, Mark, 365, 404, 406